2

American Silent Horror, Science Fiction and Fantasy Feature Films, 1913–1929

American Silent Horror, Science Fiction and Fantasy Feature Films, 1913–1929

JOHN T. SOISTER *and* HENRY NICOLELLA
with STEVE JOYCE *and* HARRY H LONG
Researcher/Archivist BILL CHASE

Volume 2

(*Neptune's Bride – The Zero Hour*;
Appendix; Bibliography; Index)

McFarland & Company, Inc., Publishers
Jefferson, North Carolina, and London

Volume 2

LIBRARY OF CONGRESS CATALOGUING-IN-PUBLICATION DATA

Soister, John T., 1950–
American silent horror, science fiction and fantasy feature films, 1913–1929 /
John T. Soister and Henry Nicolella ; with Steve Joyce and Harry H Long ; researcher/archivist Bill Chase.
p.   cm.
Includes bibliographical references and index.

2 volume set—
ISBN 978-0-7864-3581-4
softcover : acid free paper ∞

1. Horror films—United States—Catalogs.   2. Science fiction films—United States—Catalogs.
3. Fantasy films—United States—Catalogs.   4. Silent films—United States—Catalogs.
I. Nicolella, Henry.   II. Joyce, Steve, 1952– .   III. Long, Harry.   IV. Title.
PN1995.9.H6S6185 2012   791.43'6164—dc23   2011048184

BRITISH LIBRARY CATALOGUING DATA ARE AVAILABLE

On the cover: Conrad Veidt in the 1928 film *The Man Who Laughs*
(Universal Pictures/Photofest)

Manufactured in the United States of America

McFarland & Company, Inc., Publishers
Box 611, Jefferson, North Carolina 28640
www.mcfarlandpub.com

Table of Contents

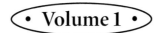

· Volume 1 ·

Acknowledgments   v
Authors' Notes   x
Preface   1

THE FILMS

After His Own Heart	5	
Aladdin's Other Lamp	7	
All Souls' Eve	9	
The Ancient Mariner	10	
The Ape	12	
At the Sign of the Jack O'Lantern	14	
The Avenging Conscience	16	
The Bat	21	
The Battle Cry of Peace	24	
Behind the Curtain	28	
The Bells (1918)	30	
The Bells (1926)	32	
Between Friends	34	
Beyond	36	
The Bishop of the Ozarks	38	
The Black Crook	39	
Black Fear	42	
Black Magic	43	
Black Orchids	46	
Black Oxen	48	
The Black Pearl	52	
Black Shadows	54	
A Blind Bargain	55	
Body and Soul	58	
Borderland	61	
The Bottle Imp	63	
The Brand of Satan	66	
The Brass Bottle	68	
Buried Treasure	71	

The Call of the Soul	72	
The Careless Woman	73	
The Case of Becky (1915)	74	
The Case of Becky (1921)	77	
The Cat and the Canary	79	
The Charlatan	84	
Chinatown Charlie	87	
The Circular Staircase	89	
Civilization	92	
Code of the Air	95	
(The) Conjure Woman	97	
A Connecticut Yankee in King Arthur's Court	99	
Conscience	104	
The Cowardly Way	105	
The Craving	107	
The Crystal Gazer	108	
The Curious Conduct of Judge Legarde	111	
Dante's Inferno	112	
The Dark Mirror	116	
Dark Secrets	119	
The Dark Star	121	
The Darling of Paris	123	
A Daughter of the Gods	126	
The Dawn of Freedom	129	
De Luxe Annie	130	
The Devil (1915)	131	
The Devil (1921)	135	

The Devil to Pay	137	
The Devil Within	139	
The Devil's Claim	141	
The Devil's Toy	143	
The Devil-Stone	146	
Do the Dead Talk?	148	
Dr. Jekyll and Mr. Hyde (Barrymore)	149	
Dr. Jekyll and Mr. Hyde (Lewis)	155	
Double Trouble	158	
The Dream Cheater	160	
The Dream Doll	162	
The Dream Woman	163	
Dusk to Dawn	165	
The Dust of Egypt	167	
Earthbound	170	
Easy Pickings	174	
Eleven PM	176	
The Eleventh Hour	178	
Elusive Isabel	180	
The Enchanted Cottage	182	
Even as You and I	184	
The Evolution of Man	186	
Eyes of Youth (1919)	187	
Eyes of Youth (1920)	191	
The Faker	192	
The Fall of a Nation	194	
Fantasma	196	
Feet of Clay	198	

The Fighter	200	Her Temptation	267	The Love Doctor	345
The Firing Line	202	The Hidden Code	268	The Love of Sunya	347
A Florida Enchantment	204	The Hidden Menace	269	Love Without Question	350
The Flying Dutchman	205	His Brother's Keeper	271	Love's Whirlpool	353
The Flying Torpedo	207	The Hole in the Wall	273	Luring Shadows	355
The Folly of Vanity	210	The House of a Thousand Candles	275	Made for Love	356
For the Defense	212	The House of Horror	277	The Magic Skin	359
Forever	214	The House of the Lost Court	280	The Magic Toy Maker	362
The Fox Woman	217	The House of the Tolling Bell	282	The Magician	363
The Germ	219	The Hunchback of Notre Dame	284	The Man from Beyond	370
The Ghost Breaker (1914)	219	The Image Maker	292	The Man of Mystery	372
The Ghost Breaker (1922)	222	In Judgment Of	294	The Man Who Laughs	374
The Ghost House	225	The Intrigue	296	The Man Who Saw Tomorrow	379
The Ghost of Old Morro	227	The Invisible Power	297	The Marriage Chance	379
The Ghost of Tolston's Manor	228	The Isle of Lost Ships	298	M.A.R.S./Radio-Mania	383
Go and Get It	229	King Tut-Ankh-Amen's Eighth		A Message from Mars	386
God's Witness	233	Wife	301	A Midnight Bell	389
A Good Little Devil	234	The Last Man on Earth	301	Midnight Faces	390
The Gorilla	237	The Last Moment	304	Midstream	392
The Greater Will	241	The Last Performance	306	The Miracle Man	394
The Greatest Power	244	The Last Warning	310	The Missing Link	399
The Greatest Question	245	Laughing at Danger	315	The Monkey Talks	400
The Green-Eyed Monster	248	Legally Dead	316	The Monster	404
The Haunted Bedroom	249	The Leopard Lady	319	The Moonstone	409
The Haunted House	252	Life Without Soul	322	Mortmain	411
The Haunted Pajamas	256	The Light	327	The Mysterious Island	414
Haunting Shadows	259	Lola	329	The Mystery of Edwin Drood	418
The Headless Horseman	260	London After Midnight	332	The Mystic	420
The Heart Line	263	Lorraine of the Lions	337		
Her Surrender	265	The Lost World	339		

• Volume 2 •

Neptune's Bride	425	Public Opinion	469	The Silent Command	519
Neptune's Daughter	427	Puritan Passions	470	Singed Wings	520
Niobe	431	Queen of the Sea	474	Sinners in Silk	522
On Time	432	The Quest of the Sacred Jewel	476	The Sins of Rosanne	525
One Exciting Night	434	Rasputin the Black Monk	478	Slave of Desire	527
One Glorious Day	437	The Raven	481	The Sleep of Cyma Roget	528
One Hour Before Dawn	439	Red Lights	484	A Sleeping Memory	531
One Million Dollars	441	The Return of Peter Grimm	488	Something Always Happens	532
One Way Street	442	The Reward of the Faithless	491	A Son of Satan	535
The Outsider	444	The Right to Be Happy	494	The Sorrows of Satan	536
Peer Gynt	445	The Road to Yesterday	496	Spellbound	540
Peter Pan	447	The Romantic Journey	500	The Star Rover	542
The Phantom Honeymoon	451	Saint, Devil and Woman	502	The Stolen Play	545
The Phantom Melody	453	The Savage	503	The Stolen Voice	546
The Phantom of the Opera	455	A Scream in the Night	505	The Story Without a Name	549
The Phantom Violin	461	Seven Footprints to Satan	507	(The Strange Story of) Sylvia Gray	551
The Poison Pen	464	The Shadow of the East	511	The Stranglers of Paris	552
The Price of Silence	465	She	514	Tarzan and the Golden Lion	553
Princess of the Dark	467	The Show	516	The Temptations of Satan	555

Terror Island   557
The Thief of Bagdad   559
The Thirteenth Chair   566
The Thirteenth Hour   568
Tin Hats   570
The Tip Off   572
Trifling Women   573
Trilby (1915)   577
Trilby (1923)   581
A Trip to Paradise   584
The Triumph of Venus   586
20,0000 Leagues Under the Sea   587
Twisted Souls   592
The Two Natures Within Him   594
The Two-Soul Woman   594
Unconquered   597
Undine   599
The Undying Flame   602

The Unfaithful Wife   603
The Unknown   605
The Unknown Purple   610
Unknown Treasures   613
Unseen Forces   615
The Untameable   618
Up the Ladder   620
Vanity's Price   622
Voices   624
Waking Up the Town   625
West of Zanzibar   627
When Dr. Quackel Did Hide   631
Where Is My Father?   632
While London Sleeps   634
While Paris Sleeps   636
Whispering Shadows   640
Whispering Wires   642
The White Flower   644

The White Rosette   646
Why I Would Not Marry   648
Wild Oranges   650
The Willow Tree   653
The Witch   655
Witchcraft   657
The Witching Hour (1916)   659
The Witching Hour (1921)   662
The Wizard   665
Wolf Blood   668
The Woman of Mystery   670
Womanhood, the Glory of a
  Nation   672
The Young Diana   674
The Young Rajah   676
The Zero Hour   681

APPENDIX OF TANGENTIAL FILMS

Blow Your Own Horn   685
Brace Up   686
Brain Cinema   686
Castles for Two   687
Circe the Enchantress   688
The Crimson Cross   689
Curlytop   690
Darkened Rooms   691
The Dead Alive   693
Destiny; or, the Soul of a Woman   694
The Devil's Bondwoman   696
The Devil's Confession   697
The Empire of Diamonds   697
The Eternal Mother   698
Feathertop   699
Fig Leaves   700
Finger Prints   701
The Fool and the Dancer   702
Fools in the Dark   703
The Ghost in the Garret   704
The Girl on the Stairs   706
The Gray Mask   707
The Hands of Nara   708
The Heart of the Hills   709
Hell's 400   710
An Hour Before Dawn   711
The House of Mystery   712
The House of Whispers   714
Infidelity   715

The Inspirations of Harry Larrabee   717
The Isle of Lost Ships (1929)   718
The Jungle Child   719
The Jungle Trail   720
The Kaiser's Shadow   721
Keep Moving   721
The Kid's Clever   722
The Land of the Lost   723
Life or Honor?   724
Little Lady Eileen   724
The Little Red Schoolhouse   725
Lord John in New York   726
The Lost Zeppelin   727
Lotus Blossom   729
The Love Girl   730
The Lust of the Ages   730
Madonnas and Men   732
The Magic Eye   733
The Man Who Couldn't Beat God   733
The Marble Heart   735
The Market of Souls   736
The Miracle of Life   736
My Friend, the Devil   738
The Mysterious Dr. Fu Manchu   739
The Mystery of the Yellow Room   741
The Mystic Hour   742
The Nation's Peril   743
Ransom   745
Restitution   746

The Ruling Passion   747
The Satin Girl   747
The Sky Skidder   749
Smilin' Through   750
The Soul of Bronze   751
The Soul's Cycle   752
The Speed Spook   753
The Star of India   754
Stark Mad   755
The Tame Cat   757
The Temple of Venus   758
The Terror   760
A Thief in the Dark   761
The Thirteenth Chair   763
Those Who Dare   764
Three Ages   766
To Hell with the Kaiser   767
Unseen Hands   767
Vamping Venus   768
War and the Woman   770
The Warning   771
Wasted Lives   771
Wee Lady Betty   773
When the Clouds Roll By   774
The Whispering Chorus   775
Whispering Palms   776
The Witching Eyes   777
Woman   777

Bibliography   779
Index   785

Neptune's Bride

Neptune's Bride. Ormsby Film Corp./Western Pictures Exploitation Co. & States Rights, 19 July 1920, 6/7 reels [LOST]

CAST: Roxy Armstrong (*Pluvia*); Richard Melfield (*Neptune*); with Jack Daugherty, Thornton Edwards, Al McKinnon, Joseph Havel, Howard SCott, Lucille Best, Anita Meredith, Carolyne Wood, Elsa Erlicher, Maude Howe, Pearl West, Lucille Breter, Mary Dodge, Dadie Rarvey

CREDITS: *Producer* Albert H. Ormsby; *Director* Leslie T. Peacocke; *Scenario* Leslie T. Peacocke; based on the scenarist's original story (England; publication date undertermined); *Cinematographer* Frank Cotner (?)

Do not read this essay! That is, don't read this until you've read our coverage of *Neptune's Daughter. Daughter*, made a half-dozen years prior to *Bride*, marked our introduction to one Captain Leslie T. Peacock(e), and you ought not to plunge in here, cold, until you've wet your tootsies over there.

Neptune's Daughter (1914) — a big moneymaker regardless of whether it was the brainchild of Leslie T. Peacock, Annette Kellerman(n), or Otis B. Driftwood — was the first feature-length movie in which Annette — the Awesome Aussie — played a mermaid. (Fun fact: back in 1911, Miss Kellerman *had* played the title character in *The Mermaid* and the title character in *Siren of the Sea*, but those were shorts.) Depending upon what you read and whom you choose to believe, either Peacock was Colonel Parker to Miss Kellerman's Elvis (or, at least, to Miss Kellerman's *body's* Elvis), or the shapely swimmer had herself decided to exploit the curves that nature (and diet and exercise) had given her, and Peacock merely went along for the ride. While a natural reaction might be "What difference does it make?" the fact that *Bride* was made at all and that it was publicized the way it was seems to indicate that *something* had stuck in the Captain's craw for years.

Needed here is a quick look at the 31 October 1914 issue of *Moving Picture World*:

> Working quietly on a seven reel feature which bids fair to surpass his *Neptune's Daughter*.... Captain Leslie T. Peacocke, one of the best known scenario writers, has been too busy to inform his friends that he had joined the staff of the World Film Corporation, and had been at work for weeks before they learned of his change of position.... One may be sure that the man who has written several hundred successful photoplays and who has been a standby of every organization that he has been associated with, may be expected to deliver the goods when he announces that there will be 100 beautiful women in this feature.

So much for 1914; fast forward to 1920...

Some five and a half years after that hymn to him (apologies to Lerner and Loewe), we can envision the tireless scribe stewing over having been left behind at Universal when Miss Kellerman and the whole mermaid franchise defected to Fox. Job security had not been the problem: the intervening years had seen miles of Laemmle film stock (whether run through a camera at Nestor, or Victor, or any of the other subsidiary companies that fed into Universal's distributing arm) transformed into middling comedy shorts or forgettable programmers based on Peacock's paycheck-driven inspiration. The sticky bit was that the whole pseudo-fantasy-oriented, soft-core formula that he had helped create had slipped from his grasp and had been generat-

ing much bigger bucks for Fox and Miss Kellerman (see *A Daughter of the Gods*) than stuff like his scenario for 1917's *Putting One Over on Ignatz* (which he also directed) was doing for him. More galling must have been the fact that Universal (in its Bluebird Photoplay guise) had, in 1916, hired an improbably-curved Austrian swimmer named Ida Schnall, hyped her as "The Girl with the 100% Figure" (Son of a bitch!), and — instead of bringing him back to write the mermaid screenplay to end *all* mermaid screenplays — had based the whole shebang on some royalty-free, Germanic fairy tale that had probably tickled Uncle Carl's fancy when he was a toddler, a hundred or so years earlier. (See *Undine.*)

Thus, from the moment Annette Kellerman wrested away from him the claim to authorship of exhibitionist fantasy during the filming of *Neptune's Daughter*, Captain Leslie T. Peacocke (the "e" came and went, as did the final "n" in Kellerman) watched helplessly as the self-centered swimmer — and her doppelganger from Austria — paraded their pulchritude in tales modeled on the formula he claimed he had sired, but which had since been screwed with by other, talentless hacks.

Then dawned the new decade: the Great War ended, thousands upon thousands of males returned from overseas, thousands upon thousands of wives and girlfriends enjoyed ... *ummm* ... newfound attention, and the Captain saw that the time was ripe for the Return of the Mermaid. Annette Kellerman's ongoing contempt and Ida Schnall's "retirement" from the screen were but minor speed bumps on the road to raunch and riches; in 1920, as now, there was no shortage of sweet young things willing to disrobe to get into the pictures. Peacocke already had a story — essentially the same one that had allowed Annette Kellerman to take it all off in 1914 — and needed only for one piece to fall into place: a studio.

But, despite the optimism of the *MPW* puff piece from 1914, the Captain's celebrated association with the World Film Corporation had gone nowhere; in fact, we could find not even an intimation that he wrote so much as a postcard for the company.

Other than those Universal (or independent) two-reelers he scripted (and, at times, directed), the Captain's verifiable, pre-*Bride* industry credits pretty much centered on his acting chops; he was to be found on the cast lists of such unforgettable features as *Betty Be Good* (1917, for the Horkheimer brothers), Plaza Pictures' *Angel Child* (1918), and *Shadows of Suspicion* (Yorke Film Corporation, 1919). These turns most likely did not make critics or casting directors sit up and take notice, and — given the outcome we're about to discuss — they did zip in terms of getting those same production companies to green-light *Neptune's Bride* (now on the back-burner since mid–1914).

Having witnessed Miss Kellerman's last fantasy-on-the-foam (1918's *Queen of the Sea*) sink beneath the waves, none of the majors was interested and — without an established name on which to at least mount a go-for-broke publicity campaign — the independents likewise opted to pass. Fumbling about for seed money in a manner that would have done Ed Wood proud, Peacock chanced upon Albert B. Ormsby, a Canadian looking to get into the movie business. We've no eye-witness account to verify the whys and wherefores of the deal, but — when the smoke cleared — Peacocke's generic story was reworked to include choice exterior locations (lots of beaches and neat rock formations out there in Southern California), and the newly-minted Ormsby Film Corporation gave the financial go-ahead for *Neptune's Bride*.

With Ormsby's checkbook buoying him up, the Captain set about casting his picture and — once again — comparisons with Ed Wood are in order. Not a one of the gals who received screen credit in *Bride* had been in a film beforehand or were in a film ever again. Sketchy data available on the picture suggests that Peacocke cast the females in his project based on a) their being able to walk and/or swim, b) their physical charms and, c) their willingness to share their physical charms with the all-seeing lens. The titular bride — yclept Pluvia (the Latin word for *rain*) in the screenplay — was impersonated by Roxy Armstrong, a 19-year-old who, like every other female in the cast, had zero going for her in terms of experience. In place of our speculation on the process by which young Roxy was tapped for the assignment, we offer one of the *only* extant pieces of publicity on *Neptune's Bride* we could find anywhere:

> Miss Roxie Armstrong, who portrays the character of Pluvia in *Neptune's Bride*, the wonderful sea fantasy that was written and directed by Captain Leslie T. Peacocke, was selected for this role from a long list of contestants. Eminent artists claim that there is no bathing girl beauty who can compare with her in pulchritude of face or figure…. All her bodily measurements are absolutely perfect, in addition to which she has the charm of youth. It can safely be said that there is no bathing beauty that can compare with her. Miss Armstrong is a natural born actress and Captain Peacocke, author director of *Neptune's Bride*, says that he has never found an actress of her age with so much natural dramatic ability. She is also an accomplished pianist and has a voice of peculiar sweetness. Dancing is not foreign to Miss Armstrong. Her Wood Nymph Dance in *Neptune's Bride* is one of the strongest features of the photoplay production. The fish tail worn by Roxie Armstrong in the opening reels of the production cost the producers many thousands of dollars and is considered the most perfect piscatorial appendage ever devised. Its scales are entirely covered with pure gold leaf, which glistens in the sun and absolutely answers every movement of her graceful body.

(In all honesty, we're a mite skeptical 'bout the "pure gold leaf," although the rest of the paragraph has the unmistakable ring of Gospel.) Printed under the headline "World's Most Perfectly Formed Girl Advocates Good Apple Pie," this publicity puff appeared in its entirety on the front page of the 23 May 1922 edition of *The Mexia* [Texas] *Evening News*. A moment spent considering the date reveals that the item was printed almost *two years* after the picture's premiere in Los Angeles. A moment spent perusing some of the other headlines that graced *The Mexia Evening News*' front page that day…

Georgia Mob Lynches Another Negro
Mexia Ku Klux Klan sends $30 to Little Girl in Hospital Here
Man and Woman Sell Soul of Young Girl Who Falls Victim
    to Their Snares
Body of Marlin Mayor Recovered from Watery Grave Yesterday

… puts the picture's rather outdated publicity blather in context. Still, as late in the day as May 1922 was for *Neptune's Bride*, the "review" printed (by the critic for *The Mexia Evening News*) promised that there was still titillation to be had for any of the readership that could make it over to the Grand Theatre for the picture's limited engagement:

One of the most beautiful locations depicted in the picture is a long shot of a mountain forest, in which the immaculately-formed Pluvia is shown wending her way, garmented solely with her sheen of golden, long flowing hair — before she has been discovered by the Queen of the Wood Nymphs and her shapely attendants and clothed by them with leaves and flowers. To attain to the great height necessary to show the full beauty of this mountain fastness, Pluvia was forced to make a truly perilous climb; a daring feat indeed for so young and tenderly fashioned a maiden garbed absolutely as was Mother Eve. On viewing her shapely white form standing with arms outstretched evoking aid from the gods to guide her safely through all earthly perils a sunlit perfection of female loveliness standing forth amidst the sombre [*sic*] forest like a chaste pearl in a black velvet casket, a gasp of genuine admiration is drawn from even the most hardened film audience.

Nothing like mermaid fantasies to keep the kiddies amused, is there?

To present a more balanced view of what might otherwise be considered risqué goings-on, we offer an alternate take on the Lady Pluvia. (Please note: the newspaper hit the Lethbridge streets scarcely a month after the picture's actual release date. Please ignore: the paper's interesting variation on the picture's title.)

> Lethbridge Girl Is a Movie Star
> Miss Roxy Armstrong Wins Out
> Plays Lead in "Neptune's Queen"

Lethbridge has been slowly winning its place on the map as a prominent centre for many activities; in the sporting world the city has won its place and now comes a conquest of the film world. Miss Roxy Armstrong is the star who is putting Lethbridge on the map.

Miss Roxy is a rival to Annette Kellerman and her star is glowing brightly in the firmament of the film world. She is truly a Lethbridge girl, having been a member of the public school staff after graduating from high school here and before she left her home to play a part in film production in California, she had the honor of dancing with H.R.H. the Prince of Wales on his recent tour of the Dominion.

Mrs. Fred G. Norton of Coaldale is loud in her praise of Lethbridge's movie star…. Mrs. Norton says the picture was pronounced as wonderful and Roxy's acting made it. The film was produced by the Ormsby Film Corporation [*Lethbridge* (Alberta, Canada) *Daily Herald*, 17 July 1920].

And we thought Roxy Armstrong was her stage name…

Anyhow, some of the men (yes, Virginia; there were men in *Neptune's Bride*) in the picture had a modicum of screen experience even before the camera(s) rolled. Joseph Havel and Richard Melfield (signed on to play the titular Neptune) may have come to the party empty-handed, experience-wise, but Howard Scott showed up with a grand total of three (3) titles under his belt: an uncredited bit in D.W. Griffith's *Intolerance* and honest-to-God roles in a couple of 1920 Fox potboilers. Now, we're not getting into any *post hoc, propter hoc* argument, but — following the release of *Neptune's Bride* — Howard Scott was never heard from again. Coincidentally(?), *Neptune's Bride* was Al McKinnon's last picture but one, and nearly half of his film credits (including *Putting One Over on Ignatz*) involved Captain Peacocke. Hence, other than the jaw-dropping beautiness of the afore-paean'd Miss Armstrong, only the acting chops of Thornton Edwards and Jack Daughtery — with about a dozen or so titles between them at the time — lent weight and stability to the project. (To give the devil his due, we concede that one of Edwards' pre–*Neptune* gigs was in 1917's *Wee Lady Betty*, see appendix).

The long and the short and the tall of it saw *Neptune's Bride* shot mainly in the Great Outdoors (possibly by Frank Cotner, although we could find no corroboration to this claim made by … *ummm* … *The Mexia Evening News*), with interiors and post-production done at the for-hire Bernstein Studios (on South Boyle Street, in Boyle Heights), and released on the 19 July 1920. The *Los Angeles Times* (in its 4 July 1920 edition) revealed that "in all, some 700 people were in the cast" of *Neptune's Bride*, that the "Ormsby company" planned on handling the seven-reel picture as a road show, and that the producer "will shortly leave for New York with Captain Peacocke to supervise exploitation in that city." It may be that the Western Pictures Exploitation Company was not a'hankerin' to do business back East and *that's* when the States' Rights folks were brought in to deal with the "road show." We don't know. But we've almost nothing — not even in terms of local press coverage (the Texan and Canadian puff pieces apart) — from which we can garner production information, film reviews, or even plot details. Synopsis-wise, we can only quote *The AFI Catalog*: "The film is set in an undersea kingdom and at a summer resort, and the characters include Neptune's new bride, mermaids and wood nymphs."

The picture premiered at the Philharmonic Auditorium in Los Angeles, and the 25 July issue of the *Los Angeles Times* not only reported that the picture was held over a second week, but also that "the musical part of the program is supplied by the full piece Philharmonic Orchestra and the auditorium organ." Initially, Peacocke negotiated that the Ormsby Film Corp. production be distributed by the Western Pictures Exploitation Company, a concern that would not only prove much more adept at exploiting Western Pictures than sea sagas, but also would prove to be notoriously short-lived. The contractual details of this agreement are nonexistent, but it can't have been terribly long afterwards that the picture was offered to anyone who'd take it, courtesy of the States Rights system.

Neptune's Bride may have convinced Albert Ormsby that investing in the movies was just not in the cards for an honest guy from Toronto, but it didn't deter Peacocke. Scarcely allowing the grass to even *think* about growing under his feet, the captain — a scriptwriting/direction gig in hand — was off to work on *Reformation*, the first production of the Loyalty Film Company. The Peacocke magic proved to be as potent as ever: *Reformation* was also the *last* production of the Loyalty Film Company.

Two pictures later, in 1923, Captain Leslie T. Peacock(e) left the movie business to dabble briefly in the world of legitimate theater. At the end of the decade, he dropped from sight and went on to become the Stuff of Legend.

You go, Cap!   — *JTS*

Neptune's Daughter

Neptune's Daughter. Universal Film Manufacturing Co./Universal, A Universal Special Feature, 25 April 1914, 7 reels/8000 feet, fragments at Soundscreen Australia

CAST: Annette Kellerman (*Annette*); Leah Baird (*Princess Olga*); Herbert Brenon (*Roador the Wolf*); Edmund Mortimer (*Duke Boris*); William E. Shay (*King William*); William Welch (*King Neptune*); Edward Boring (*The Old Man of the Sea*); Mrs. Allen Walker (*The Sea Witch*); Lewis Hooper (*Count Rudolph*); Francis Smith (*The Jailer*); Millie Listen (*Jailer's Mother*); Katherine Lee (*Angela*)

CREDITS: *Producer and Director* Herbert Brenon; *Assistant Director* Otis Turner; *Scenario* Capt. Leslie T. Peacock; *Cinematographer* André Barlatier; *Electrical Work* Joseph O'Donnell

Film buffs who have been around a while will probably slip into a default setting on this title and recall immediately the 1949 MGM musical comedy (in Technicolor) starring Ricardo Montalban, Red Skelton, and (Who else?) Esther Williams as Annette Kellerman(n). We duffers now ask those film buffs to backstroke to our current offering, which crested the waves some 35 years earlier. "Our" *Neptune's Daughter* was a fantasy (a rather *violent* fantasy, if surviving documentation is to be believed) rather than a musical comedy, and it marked the feature-film debut of the real, no-holds-barred Annette Kellerman, a beauteous young Aussie swim champion whose cinematic career was spent, for the most part, in similar aquatic daydreams.

Annette's *Neptune's Daughter* wasn't the first rendering of the tale for the big screen (or the last: see 2010's *Ondine*); in 1912, Essanay had cast Harry Cashman (as Neptune) and Martha Russell (as daughter) for that studio's own short take on the mythic meld. (Prior to Essanay's turn, several other studios cranked out their own mini-epics; none are germane to our discussion.) Whereas Ms. Kellerman cavorted in the waters surrounding Bermuda, though, Ms. Russell — who was, for several months only, Essanay's *leading* leading lady — had been forced to keep herself afloat in the chill of Michigan's Lake Superior. Sadly, any and all empirical evidence of her water-treading capabilities has disappeared, as has most of the 1914 Universal feature; however, some 19½ minutes of Ms. Kellerman's fury-in-the-foam have survived and — thanks to Screensound Australia, one of the few film archives in the world that will sell and mail a video to researchers, rather than demand that they show up at the front door, with cake — we have screened them. Demurring from attempting to fabricate the storyline around the fragments we have, we will share the plot synopsis filed by Universal with the Library of Congress and save opinion on the surviving footage until later.

> King William grants his people fishing rights, but through the machinations of Olga, his fiancée, and her lover, Duke Boris, his throne is in jeopardy. Annette, the mermaid daughter of Neptune, seeks revenge against the mortal responsible for the death of her five-year-old sister when the child is caught in a fishing net. [An incredibly lengthy summary from the 6 June 1914 *Moving Picture World* differs, claiming that "Little Angela, unable to extricate herself *from the seaweed*, dies." Emphasis ours.] After assuming human form through means of a magic shell, she meets and falls in love with William, disguised as a forester. When Annette learns that it is the king who granted fishing rights, she determines to slay him, but when she goes to the palace, she recognizes her lover and desists. William then tells Annette that he is rescinding fishing rights in exchange for hunting privileges because of the suffering which he has caused her. After she returns to the sea, however, Olga and Boris delete the permission to hunt from the royal decree, thus causing a rebellion. Annette returns in human form to aid the jailed William, but she is surprised by Boris who orders Roador the Wolf to execute her. After many struggles, Annette

slays William's adversaries, and upbraids the people for their injustice to him. Olga then wanders to the shore where she uses the shell to turn herself into a mermaid. Annette can no longer go back to the sea after the shell breaks and thus becomes William's queen.

The great Fishing Net vs. Seaweed controversy aside, if this synopsis is any way an accurate reflection of the picture as released, *Neptune's Daughter* was by no means a jolly fantasy concocted primarily to allow the men in the audience to ogle the figure of "The Perfect Woman." The image of a mermaid's cadaver in a fishing net (or wherever) is, even now, rather unsettling (but she couldn't have drowned, could she?), and that, plus Annette's impulsive resolve to slay King William —followed by her successfully slaying "William's adversaries" (note the plural)— helped the picture wriggle away from being dismissed as the naughty (1914-speak for "soft-core") adventures of a scantily-clad knockout ... but just barely. (*Ouch!*) The minuscule wriggle-room that separated picture from picaresque is apparent in this one-sentence snapshot of *Neptune's Daughter*, penned by Kellerman biographer, Emily Gibson*: "As a delightful water sprite, Annette dances about freely and nearly naked in a tiny piece of diaphanous fabric, is then captured and bound [!], and pushed over a cliff; yet she emerges, Houdini-like, to fight like a man and save the prince."

She saved the *king's* bacon, actually, and proper respect must be shown, if only because the cinematic DNA of this semi-nude, ass-kicking hottie is shared by virtually every Millennium-Age female movie star worth her salt who hasn't narrowed her professional focus to adaptations of the works of Oliver Goldsmith, William Congreve, or Richard Brinsley Sheridan. Jolly fantasy or no, the picture's revenue-haul (reputedly $1,000,000+ on a $35,000 investment†) suggests that lots of folks got their jollies watching the nubile Kellerman doing what would — time and again — become "her thing."

"Her thing" was the pivot around which the screenplay was writ, and credit for said screenplay was given to Captain Leslie T. Peacock(e), as fascinating a character as any mermaid could ever hope to be. Albeit scarce is the silent-film buff who can provide off the top of his/her head salient facts about the captain nowadays, this was not always the case. Per the 31 October 1914 *Moving Picture World*, the old darling was apparently at one time as near a household word as Coca Cola, or Coke, or even ... *ummmmm* ... coke:

> So much has been written about the Captain that he is as well known as many of the players who have appeared in his photoplays, but it's not amiss at this time to mention the fact that the Captain is of English birth. He served in India as an officer of the 88th regiment. He became interested in literature when he worked as a correspondent for the *Irish Times*, while in his native land. There is hardly a successful magazine published in either America, England, Canada, or the Orient [sic], that has not published one of the captain's stories. For several years Captain Peacocke was the

feature writer for the *Los Angeles Times*, which has a reputation second to none in this country, as a unique newspaper.

Some three months earlier (in its 11 July 1914 issue, to be exact), the same magazine reported that — to that date — Peacocke had written 338 scenarios. Inasmuch as *The AFI Catalog* lists the film under discussion (released the 25 April 1914) as the captain's first feature-length movie and names his second as *Salvation Nell* (released October 1915), we must assume the other 337 screenplays were for shorts. Even allowing for the wildly spectacular number of films that have disappeared since the birth of the industry, it's tough to reconcile those supposed 337 scenarios with the IMDb's listing only some *nine* pictures bearing the Peacock signature prior to *Neptune's Daughter*.

Research into Peacock's credentials has produced scant results, as his motion-picture writing credits extend back only to 1911, and there are fewer than 50 of those. And while the man also acted in a dozen or so films (and directed half-again as many), following the release of *The Midnight Flower* by Aywon Pictures (see *The Evolution of Man, When Dr. Quackel Did Hide*) in 1923, he seems to have abjured the movies. The 1931 *Catalog of Copyright Entries* does include his filing (as author) the three-act legitimate comedy, *An American Bride*, and the Captain's name may be found in the cast list of Leo De Valery's play, *A Comedy of Women*, which illuminated the marquee of New York's Ambassador Theatre for a couple of dozen performances in September-October 1929.

We don't know what became of the Captain, and we're not completely satisfied that the possibly-prolific scenarist was born in England, the *MPW* notwithstanding; there is evidence that he had debuted this life in Bangalore. Such biographical details aren't really germane to the present situation, though; suffice it to say that — no matter whence he came or whither he went — the vintage–1914 Leslie T. Peacock(e) sought credit as the creative sire of *Neptune's Daughter*.

However, per biographer Gibson, the idea for *Neptune's Daughter* did not evolve from Captain Peacock's mind, but had sprung, full-grown, from the head of Ms. Kellerman. (Ms. Gibson also writes that not only was Ms. Kellerman more than casually involved in the direction of the film, as well, but also that director Herbert Brenon "immediately fell out with Peacock because he took over the script and claimed it as his own.") Perhaps simultaneously inspired and threatened by dint of the Kellerman persona, the captain's subsequent return to the lair of the Sea God (1920's *Neptune's Bride*; see entry) was effected without either the onscreen or behind-the-camera presence of "The Perfect Woman." *Sic* transit gloria mundi. The good captain resurfaces in our coverage on *Neptune's Bride*, and more skinny on the anything-but Miss Kellerman is to be found in our essay on *A Daughter of the Gods*.

Other than that of the Million Dollar Mermaid, the most enduring name to appear onscreen in *Neptune's Daughter* was that

---

***The Original Million Dollar Mermaid: The Annette Kellerman Story* (Sydney: Allen and Unwin, 2005).

†Many of Ms. Gibson's facts and figures that we quoted here and elsewhere are taken from the information provided by the various studios' publicity departments to the readership of then-contemporary fan magazines, newspapers, and such, and thus cannot be taken at face value. For example, the movie herald issued by Universal to announce/accompany screenings of the film claimed that the production costs were $50,000 — not $35,000 — a more probable estimate of a project that supposedly employed 1000 extras and was crafted on a scope that would demand a suggested running time of 2½ hours. Of course, Universal itself was responsible for planting that "$35,000" seed in the first place.

of the aforementioned Herbert Brenon. Brenon, a Dubliner, was a five-tool movie-man: acting up a storm (albeit sporadically) from 1912; writing scenarios upon demand (1916's *The Marble Heart* was, in essence, his idea); producing pictures when the occasion presented itself (as it did with the splendid *Peter Pan* [1924] and Lon Chaney's striking *Laugh, Clown, Laugh* [1928]); supervising a brace of genre features (see 1916's *The Ruling Passion*, appendix); and directing well over 125 shorts and full-length films, with Universal's 1913 *Dr. Jekyll and Mr. Hyde* an example of the former, and *The Passing of the Third Floor Back* (UK, 1918), an instance of the latter. For his directing skills in non-genre efforts, Brenon was nominated once for the Oscar (1926's *Sorrell and Son*; he lost out) and once for the Photoplay Medal of Honor (1926's *Beau Geste*; he copped it). For his involvement in his decidedly genre-friendly projects, he won a place in our hearts.

The 19-plus minutes of extant footage seems to consist of a handful of outtakes and/or alternate shots interspersed with one, fairly smooth, continuous stretch of action from the middle the of the picture. While there are a number of quick cuts, these were probably purposeful on Brenon's part, although a handful of abrupt jumps indicate missing bits even here. Following immediately is our annotated recapitulation of the fragment:

Annette [hereafter, "AK"], covered in some sort of serape, is hanging about a rocky coastline, with the surf banging up around her legs. She takes her magic shell from its hiding place in a nearby crevice, kisses it, and puts it right back.

TITLE: "Farewell."

We cut to a long shot of AK — now seemingly naked — tiptoeing along a heavily-vegetated cliff that overlooks what appears to be a pond. For the next minute or so, she dives off the cliff into the still waters of the pond *four times*. [The fourth is a pip; in essence, she jumps in the air and falls squarely on her derriere, whence she *bounces* off the cliff into the water. "Bounces" is the only word.]

A cut reveals AK, now clad in a gossamer dress, dancing about gracelessly.

Another cut, and we've some extended footage of her — still in the gossamer thing — swimming underwater, hither and thither, occasionally surfacing to push a second scrap of gossamer around with her hand.

Cut — now we get to the story proper. AK is back on that stretch of rocky coastline. She rubs the magic shell and, via a quick dissolve, transforms into a mermaid.

TITLE: "Homeward."

Now burdened by a bulky and not-altogether-convincing fish-tail, AK wriggles off the rock and into the shallows. Cut: she's back in that vegetation-heavy pool, where she's greeted by her old dad [Neptune], who is wearing a long, white beard and wig — topped with a crown — a short-sleeved shirt, and what looks like a diaper. And sandals. [Another still exists of Neptune holding his trident; in this shot, he is — as is more appropriate — shirtless.] They embrace (awkwardly), AK drags herself half onto the shore, and dad begins to stroke her hair and pat her head as if she were Neptune's dog.

Cut to a council-chamber of some sort. King William, Boris, and Boris's lackey [name unknown — he's not wearing a sign, you know] are reading the royal proclamation that brings a halt to local fishing, but opens up the forest to local hunting. The proclamation boasts some marvelous calligraphy, while the men are accoutered a la the late Tudor period, with ruffs, doublets, hose, etc. The king looks splendid in black; Boris and the lackey appear to be in matching, striped outfits. Neither of these lads is happy with the proclamation, so they take it into the next room, where Princess

Olga cheers them up by neatly crossing out the paragraph that green-lights the hunting.

Cut: AK is lying on her side on a rock in the water, obviously bored; this is reinforced by several cuts between her and a bevy of nearby mermaids looking to have her swim over and join in the fun. She repeatedly declines.

Cut: a group of people — some of whom are lugging nets, suggesting that they are fishermen — are walking down a hill when a second group of people — possibly soldiers— approaches. Following an insert of the blatantly-edited proclamation, the first group starts muttering, shaking fists and what-have-you, and then runs off.

TITLE: "She determines to see the King once more."

AK rolls off the rock and into the water.

Cut: The irate fishermen, who have obviously stopped off at an armory to grab the swords they are now waving about, approach the palace. A man motions for them to stay right there for a moment and goes in to alert the King.

Cut: Boris is inciting the mob, which responds to his every gesture by shaking their fists, waving their swords, and jumping up and down.

A series of quick cuts follows immediately:

AK, rubbing the magic shell, is once again transformed into a biped, and is, evidently, starkers; fully incited, the fishermen begin climbing up the walls of the palace; AK, still naked, slinks among the rocks; the fishermen are climbing; AK, now somehow wearing a dress, is at the palace gates; fishermen climbing; the palace guards confront the fishermen; the King looks out the window; AK is coming up through the shrubbery; the fishermen have won over the palace guard; the king steps outside and is mobbed by the fishermen.

TITLE: "They refuse to hear the King."

The king is marched into jail, followed [surreptitiously] by AK.

TITLE: "Knowing her foster-brother is keeper of the jail [!], she plans to save the King."

While the king is seated languidly in his cell, AK makes her way into a room somewhere, changes from her dress into the local garb [everyone other than the Mer-people and the Tudors is dressed like a member of the chorus of *The Gondoliers*], and then — seated at a mirrored vanity — scissors off her long, long hair.

TITLE: "A noble sacrifice."

More quick cuts: the king has a drink of water; Boris and Olga are swanning about; AK is first in the room, then back in the shrubbery; Boris and Olga appear to notice something off-screen and head in that direction; then...

Cut: the jailer, seated right in front of the camera, is on the verge of napping. Sneaking in behind him is AK, who throws a rag over his face, pulls him backwards off his stool, and — following a brief struggle — leaves him there, unconscious.

Abrupt cut to inside of king's cell, where AK bows to king and then pantomimes the latest news.

Cut: Boris and Olga show up at the jail and enter the king's cell.

TITLE: "Resenting the insult, the king challenges his cousin to a duel for he throne."

Rather refreshingly — rather than have this force the sort of climactic swordplay that convention would lead one to expect — Boris and Olga think this is hilarious, walk out, and leave the king still locked the hell up. In the corridor, the jailer — who has come to in the interim — seizes AK, and she is tossed into an adjoining cell.

Cut to an inn. A bunch of locals is standing around when in walks a guy with a bear on a leash. The bear climbs onto a seat. Cut to the king, sitting in his cell. Cut to the bear, which has stood up, thus astounding the locals; all applaud. Cut to AK, in her cell. Cut back to the bear, who is now shuffling about on the floor. A Boris-lackey enters and informs another, identically-attired Boris-lackey:

TITLE: "The Wolf is hired to do away with Annette."

The lackey then yanks Herbert Brenon [named, on that title card, as "Olaf, the Wolf"] out of the crowd that is gaping at the bear and hands him [the Wolf, not the bear] a purse.

Viewing odd clips of a 90-plus-year-old fantasy with eyes grown accustomed to cyber-age technology is, if anything, the diametric opposite of looking at a plain gal through beer-goggles; either way, though, the reality has been colored by the perception. Sitting thorough the entire film back in 1914, the audience's curiosity as to how a mermaid could have a jailer as a foster-brother, why she would manhandle him into oblivion, and just when "Olaf, the Wolf" ended up rechristened "Roeder, the Wolf" might have been well and truly satisfied. Even now, the transformative dissolves betwixt tush and tail remain impressive, although not nearly so much as Annette's knack (Thank you, Magic Shell!) for coming upon urgently-needed clothing (to say nothing of unlikely shrubbery, private changing areas, and tonsorial tools) at the damnedest times. If the rest of the picture has the Sea King's daughter changing her raiment at anything near the pace she exhibits in these surviving reels, 'tis little wonder that Neptune is reduced to sashaying about in diaper and sandals. Speaking of clothing, a couple of stills that have survived the years depict William Welch's King Neptune standing in the surf and wielding his hefty trident, while clad in nothing save for some swaddling about his nether-regions. It is difficult to fathom why, then, in the extant film clips, the Sea God wanders onscreen dressed like a rather hirsute old gentleman who is just back from taking out the trash.

So much for us; the reviewers who covered the picture's premiere were of a different mind altogether. George Blaisdell's opened his coverage in the 9 May 1914 *Moving Picture World* with an almost poetic exuberance:

> There is something new on the screen. It is a marine fantasy, an interweaving of the real and the mythical, a craftsmanlike blending of the spectacular, of the sensational, of the dramatic, and above all of the pictorial…. It was photographed under the brilliant sun and in the clear atmosphere of Bermuda — in gardens framed by the hand of man and in primitive wood, on beach and on cliff, in ocean waters above the earth and in stalactite-mirroring caved pools beneath it.

The New York Times' "Sime" was also enthusiastic about the picture, if a tad less eloquent: *"Neptune's Daughter* is healthy, clean, full of life and action, the life and action that come from athletics and outdoor scenes, and, as far as may be recollected, this is the first picture almost entirely set in a mountain of water" (10 April 1914).

The 29 April 1914 *New York Dramatic Mirror* jumped in with both feet:

> What the Hippodrome is to the patron of the speaking stage, this class of photoplays is to the motion picture, and to *Neptune's Daughter* must be given the credit for bringing the type from the experimental period to that of achievement. The producer takes us from the rush and roar of Broadway to the peaceful picturesqueness of the Land of Make-Believe, and for two hours we wander from one beautiful scene to another, while the creatures of this mystic land unfold a tale that might well have come from the pages of Hans Christian Andersen.

The rest of the trade and important general press continued in this same vein, with credit being given — here, there, and virtually everywhere — for the lighting, the locations, the sets, the acting, the direction, the special effects, the photography, the acting, and the esthetics of Annette's physique. The 2 May 1914 *Motography* went these one better and awarded extra letters to scenarist, Peacock(e); producer-director-Olaf/Roeder, the Wolf, Bren(n)on; and to nubile Amazon, Kellerman(n). Due to the novelty of the theme; the length of the exposition, the expense evident on the screen, and (we always get back to) the presence of Annette Kellerman, *Neptune's Daughter* was a resounding success, and the box-office take may well have approached (or even exceeded) the for-the-time astonishing $1 million figure reported by the studio publicity mills and repeated by Ms. Gibson.

The picture's special effects were not limited solely to shuffling Miss Kellerman's stems in and out of a lower-end body stocking, and a few of the visuals — as related in the *New York Times* review — must have had the audiences (especially the children) spellbound: "'The Cave of the Wind' and 'The Witch of the Sea,' all in one scene, with the Witch employing her supernatural powers of transformation to make a mermaid mortal and immortal at will, or change, as she did, Leah Baird from a handsome young woman of a kingly court into an octopus as punishment, are sufficient for the youthful to ask their elders to please take them again 'to see that picture.'"

If nothing else, it's cathartic to see that the evil Princess Olga got hers at the end. Boris, as we all well know, went on to associate with a certain Natasha.

Just a couple of quick notes: *Neptune's Daughter* was the only film on which Otis Turner served as assistant director; it was he who manned the megaphone whenever Herbert Brenon stepped in front of the camera to emote. Per the afore-cited *Motography* piece, Turner was in command when some real-life dramatics threatened the reel-life narrative:

> One of the scenes calls for a struggle by Miss Kellermann and Brenon, who is playing the part of a fisherman, on the top of a high cliff overlooking the sea, and a plunge headlong into the water by the two clasped in each other's arms. As both fell, Mr. Brenon's head struck Miss Kellermann's temple. To the astonishment of hundreds of spectators she arose to the surface quite unconscious. It took but a few seconds to realize that she was seriously hurt; a boat near by, manned by Mr. Sullivan, Miss Kellermann's husband, and Hooper, Mr. Brenon's assistant, quickly came to the spot and the plucky little woman was pulled into the boat. She recovered shortly, but was unable to continue with the picture until the following day.

The fact that no stunt-persons were called into play for this scene is astounding, especially (no disrespect intended) in the case of Herbert Brenon, whose career bona fides do not point to a single (other) example of the man's physical prowess or aquatic ability.

Turner was chief — or only — director for nearly 150 shorts and features from c. 1908 to 1918, when he died from angina. Among those many films were several titles of particular interest here, including a trio of Frank. L. Baum–inspired *Oz* shorts from 1910; 1913's *The Evil Power*; Universal's 1915 chapterplay, *The Black Box*; and the 1908 Selig-Polyscope *Dr. Jekyll and Mr. Hyde*, purportedly the earliest cinematic adaptation of Stevenson's story. Turner penned the screenplay for a good number of the films he also directed, and produced several, as well. As did Herbert Brenon, he appeared as himself in 1914's *The Great Universal Mystery*.

William Welch (aka Welsh), the non-traditionally dapper King Neptune herein, also cameo'd as himself in *The Great Universal Mystery*, so we've yet another personality whose renown has slipped somewhat during the passage of some 90 years. Welch, once and always an actor, likewise numbered around 150 films among his credits, with his biggest genre titles remain 1916's *20,000 Leagues Under the Sea* and *Elusive Isabel* (see entries). William E. Shay (the hapless King William) didn't have a healthy fantasy file in his résumé, either, with just a brace of 1916 epics—*The Ruling Passion* and *A Daughter of the Gods*—complementing his turn here.

To the end of her life, Annette Kellerman told anyone who was interested that *Neptune's Daughter* featured the best work she ever did.   — *JTS*

Niobe

Niobe. Famous Players Film Co./Paramount Pictures Corp., 4 April 1915, 5 reels [LOST]

CAST: Hazel Dawn (*Niobe*); Charles S. Abbe (*Peter Amos Dunn*); Maude Odell (*Caroline Dunn*); Marie Leonard (*Helen*); Leigh Denny (*Cornelius Griffin*); Irene Haisman (*Beatrice Sillocks*); Wilmuth Merkyl (*Tompkins*)

CREDITS: *Presented by* Daniel Frohman; *Directors* Hugh Ford, Edwin S. Porter; based on the eponymous play by Harry Paulton and Edward A. Paulton (London, April 1982).

Another of those statues-that-come-to-life flicks, *Niobe* melded Greek mythology with drawing-room comedy and, according to the critical literature, came up aces. (The mythos had Niobe cheesing off the gods by bragging that she had 14 children to Leto's two, but Leto's two were Apollo and Artemis, who then proceeded to slay all of Niobe's brood. Grief-stricken, Niobe fled the scene, but was caught and transformed into a stone crag/waterfall because she was weeping incessantly.) Sophocles and Aeschylus both made pin money writing their own versions of Niobe's tragic turn of events.

The picture was derived from the eponymous Harry and Edward Paulton comedy, which was wildly popular in Britain c. 1892, but which never illuminated any of those million lights on Broadway. The Paultons, who together or separately *did* have more than a dozen-and-a-half plays (other than this one) winning audiences and making money on The Great White Way, were approached by the Famous Players organization in 1914, and the entity was transferred from the floor to the wall by the first week of April of the following year. The principal cast members all had more than their fair share of stage experience, and the direction of the picture was split between Hugh Ford — also possessed of a theatrical background — and Edwin S. Porter, whose bread was famously buttered only with celluloid.

The story that follows may be found — to a greater or lesser extent, with variations, much smoke, and many mirrors — elsewhere in these pages. The plot outline is taken from the 1 May 1915 *Motography*:

> Peter Amos Dunn, president of an insurance company, takes home a statue of Niobe, and, falling asleep before the fire, is

aroused by sounds from behind the screen back of which the statue has been placed. On investigating, he finds the statue has come to life, and when the vision flings her arms around his neck and hails him as her master, he is petrified with horror, since there is a Mrs. Dunn and a sister, both of whom are at the theater. Dunne succeeds in getting Niobe upstairs and dresses her in some clothes which have recently arrived for the new governess, but later when she descends, clad in various parts of the governess's wardrobe, and meets Mrs. Dunn and the sister, there is a scene.

> Niobe escapes in the night to dance upon the greensward. Dunn follows and finally succeeds in getting her back into the house, though the situation between Niobe and Mrs. Dunn becomes more strained when Niobe flings her arms around Dunn's neck. He will have nothing to do with her, and she plunges a knife into her heart, expiring in his arms. Just then the family really returns from the theater and find Dunn fast asleep before the fire. Upon being awakened, he goes tremblingly over to the screen, finds the statue just as he had left it, and nearly collapses with joy.

Variety (9 April 1915) provides a bit more detail, adding a vegetable or two to the stone soup: "A chase through a park wherein Niobe playfully gamboled with the statues of her former colleagues, including Hercules, closing with the arrival of a thunderstorm in which Niobe and her pursuer were drenched and intercepted in their night clothing by a park policeman, reached the comedy climax."

We assume that the word "gamboled" implies that the other statues were somehow animated as well, a detail that not only enhances Dunn's dream, but augments the fantasy element of the picture. Also, a science-fiction slant is raised by the mention — made in the 17 April 1915 *Moving Picture World*— that "charged electric wires, draped around the figure by careless electricians, are responsible for the restoration of life."

The big name for us may well be that of Reginald Denny, although neither the plot summary printed above nor any of the other story-related bits and pieces we could find so much as mentioned Denny's character, one Cornelius Griffin. (FYI: Denny, for whom this may well have been his first screen appearance, was billed in on the cast crawl as *Leigh* Denny, that being his real middle name.) The actor went on to make a slew of movies ("slew" meaning over 150), and definitely occupies a place in the detective-film fan's heart for his turns as Algy Longworth in the late–1930s Bulldog Drummond feature series. That having been said, we've no idea what he did here in *Niobe*.

Niobe was impersonated by Hazel Dawn, a pretty and personable, young (24), Utah-born Mormon who had at least three legitimate musical-comedy hits under her belt by the time she assumed Greek statuary attitudes for the camera. Dawn didn't make many films (although she did return, late in life, to taking direction for a few early–1950s television theater-anthologies), and *Niobe* was as close to a genre feature as she ever came. (Still, those detective buffs we wrote of earlier may have misty memories of Miss Dawn's playing the skirt in the 1917 *The Lone Wolf*, which starred Bert Lytell.) The lady returned to her musical comedy roots in the latter half of the Roaring Twenties, when she toured with Florenz Ziegfeld and his renowned extravaganza.

Maude Odell — who had just appeared onstage at Broadway's Knickerbocker Theater alongside Hazel Dawn in Victor Herbert's *The Debutante* — was cast as Caroline Dunn, the Missus who returned from the theater only to find her husband pursued by the shapely Golem from ancient Athens. Odell made even fewer films than did her *Debutante* colleague, much preferring the intimacy of the proscenium arch to the anonymity of the lens: her non–Broadway venues and touring company appearances apart, the South Carolina–born thespian was seen here and there in the midtown theater district in no fewer than 22 legitimate offerings, from 1898 through 1941. (Her last triumph was as Sister Bessie Rice in the renowned *Tobacco Road*, a part she played over 3100 times in the course of some seven and a half years.)

The much set-upon Peter Amos Dunn was played by Charles S. Abbe, yet another stage veteran whose Broadway résumé was more extensive and impressive than his film credentials. Abbe haled from Connecticut, making him very much more of a local, theatrically speaking, than either Miss Dawn or Miss Odell. Onstage since 1895, the actor numbered among his credits the role of Asa Ashling in the original run of Max Marcin and Charles Guernon's supernatural melodrama, *Eyes of Youth* (1917; see our entry on both film versions).

The critics seem to have liked *Niobe*, as this spattering of opinion shows. Per *Variety*, cited above: "The Famous Players has constructed a very promising comedy feature around the ancient Greek yarn of Niobe, wife of Amphion, King of the Thebes…. It makes a good feature for those who prefer the better grade of pictures both in subject and photography."

The 17 April 1915 *Moving Picture World* found it "a dream picture based on a whimsical idea…. There is humor in the picture, some of it rather obvious farce, come of it more finely pointed comedy, and there is the interest born of a story whose culmination is in doubt."

And the *Motion Picture News*, published on that same date, enthused thusly:

It is some time since Hazel Dawn made her initial appearance on the screen in the Famous Players feature, *One of Our Girls*, but the interim between that picture and *Niobe* is not so long that she has been forgotten by the many who admired her in that pleasing comedy-drama. Her return to the screen is most assuredly an even to remember with the greatest pleasure, for in *Niobe* her performance is delightful….

The situations … are extremely funny, and are made the most of by Miss Dawn, as the dazed, animated statue and Charles Abbe, who appears as the fearsome Peter Amos Dunn…. Photographically the picture is fine. The light effects are most pleasing, and the scenes, both interiors and exteriors, are very beautiful.

The rest of the body of criticism pretty much follows suit, and it's a pity that the the cinematographer whose work was praised more than once went unnamed.

— *JTS*

On Time

On Time. Carlos Productions/Truart Film Corp., 1 March 1924, 6 reels/6030 feet [LOST]
CAST: Richard Talmadge (*Harry Willis*); Billie Dove (*Helen Hendon*); Stuart Holmes (*Richard Drake*); George Siegmann (*Wang Wu*); Tom Wilson (*Casanova Clay*); Charles Clary (*Horace Hendon*); Douglas Gerard (*Mr. Black*); Fred Kirby (*Dr. Spinks*); Frankie Mann (*Mrs. Spinks*)
CREDITS: *Director* Henry Lehrman; *Scenario* Garrett Fort; based on a story by Al Cohn; *Titles* Ralph Spence; *Cinematographer* William Marshall; *Film Editor* Ralph Spence

This six-reel indie feature *must* have had a following back in 1924, as it seems to have been the precursor of later, fun, nutty, horror catch-alls like *Seven Footprints to Satan*, that had their audiences leaving the theaters appreciatively shaking their heads while chuckling under their breath. Then again—considering that not only did *On Time* up and vanish, but commentary on it also seems to have gone extinct close in—maybe not. If there *was* any popular groundswell about the film, it escaped the notice of the contemporary media, and the sparsity of prose that's out and about nowadays on the picture makes us think that the film must have flown under the radar due a) to poor publicity and distribution, or b) the fact that the picture didn't play as well as the AFI plot summary reads.

Cueing AFI plot summary!

Harry Willis returns to Helen Hendon discouraged by his failure to make a fortune in 6 months as he promised. Accepting a job that will pay him $10,000 for following instructions for a day, Harry soon finds himself in a series of adventures that include an imbroglio at a costume ball, a doctor's attempts to transplant a gorilla's brains into his head, and a brawl in a temple with some Chinese who want a small idol belonging to him. When he applies for a

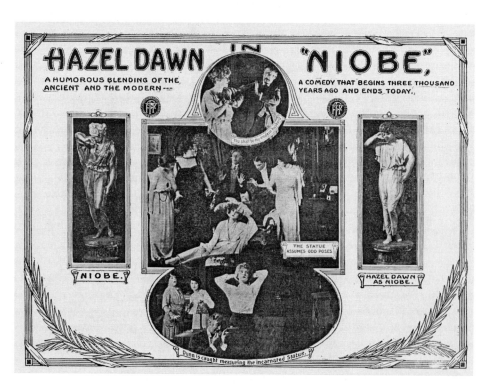

Multiple Hazel Dawns grace this herald from the picture's original release.

marriage license, Harry discovers that these incidents were created to test his capacity to become a movie star. He wins both Helen and a movie contract.

Now, if those sundry plot elements don't make you all warm and fuzzy, you're smack dab in the wrong book.

(A film that shared the same bent as *Time and Satan* was FP-L's *Wild, Wild Susan* [1925], a Bebe Daniels' adventure-spoof about a rich young woman from New York who—in her quest to abjure ennui and embrace frissons—joins a private detective agency. She has a few adventures in the course of falling for her guy, and the pair end up in one of those crook-filled, old, dark houses that were once as ubiquitous in American cinema as were the fleets of convenient [and empty] cabs in which hero told hackie to "follow that car!" Had *Susan* mined *Time* and *Satan*'s gorilla/Chinaman vein rather than merely skimming the surface of those pictures' *joie de vivre*, it, too, would be profiled herein.)

The original story (with the operative terms being "original" and "story") of *On Time* was penned by Al Cohn, a fascinating personality and talented writer who had already done the titles for *The Unknown Purple* and who would work on the screenplays for *The Cat and the Canary*, *The Gorilla*, and Paul Leni's *The Last Warning* (see entries). Likewise, one might argue that Cohn was the spiritual sire of the similar (albeit qualitatively and quantitatively more bizarre) scenario of *Seven Footprints to Satan*—written, in fact, by director Benjamin Christensen under the *non de plume* Richard Bee; God only knows, *Footprints*' producer Wid Gunning saw to it that author Abraham Merritt's source novel was virtually ignored.

Working in conjunction with Cohn was Garrett Fort, a Big Apple–born scribe whose most renowned genre contributions—Universal's *Dracula* and *Frankenstein*—would come at the outset of the 1930s, and Ralph Spence, whose name may be found all throughout these pages, but nowhere in such depth as within our essay on *The Gorilla*. Early on Spence was regarded as the master of witty title cards, and it was to play to that strength that he was hired for *On Time*; (actually, considering that he also did the final edit on the footage, the man ought to have taken two bows). With a trio of genre-friendly talents like that working together, it's a mortal sin that this film is still among the missing while nondescript programmers—featuring casts composed of the ancestors of Ed Wood's troupe and cranked out by one-shot production companies that subsequently disappeared—seem to turn up under the floorboards or behind the wainscoting in some goddamned place or another every third day.

The footage that Ralph Spence cut had been shot by Henry Lehrman, a cinematic multi-tasker who started out in the industry on a wing and a prayer and a tall tale. The story has it that, in hopes of getting a job in the pitchers, Lehrman introduced himself at Biograph as an employee of the Pathé Film Company. It was supposedly only after the Austrian-born resume-padder proved to be worth his salt that Biograph caught on to the fabrication, so Lehrman's versatility not only saved him his job for him, but also gained him the nickname, Pathé. Prior to helming *On Time*, Lehrman worked with D. W. Griffith (at Biograph), Mack Sennett (at Biograph and Keystone), and

Charlie Chaplin (at Keystone), plus started his own, comedy-oriented production company, L-KO (Lehrman-KnockOut), and then signed on at Fox. For a couple of years there, early in the 1920s, Pathé went missing from the Hollywood scene, and the story there concerns his extended mourning over the death of his girlfriend, Virginia Rappe. (Yes, *that* Virginia Rappe.) He eased back in the saddle with a couple of so-what features for independent studios and the occasional "Sunshine Comedy" for Fox, and that's where we find him in early 1924.

On Time starred Richard Talmadge, who—like Pathé Lehrman—was a European expatriate and a cinematic Jack of All Trades. Talmadge, born Sylvester Metzetti in Switzerland, had been an acrobat as a child, and it was as a member of the family troupe that he sailed past the Statue of Liberty in the early 1900s. Come 1914, the newly-adult "Richard Talmadge" was doing stunt work for James Cruze, et al., in Thanhouser's excruciatingly long serial, *The Million Dollar Mystery*. Thence to 1920, when the erstwhile acrobat began choreographing stunts for Douglas Fairbanks; films such as *The Mark of Zorro* (1920), *Robin Hood* (1922), *Laughing at Danger* (1924; see entry), and *The Black Pirate* (1926) earned Talmadge bucks but no screen credit. He started earning the latter as an actor—also c. 1920—starring as the action hero (usually named Dick or Richard or some such) in stuff like *The Unknown* (1921, playing "Dick Talmadge"), *Watch Him Step* (1922, playing "Dick Underwood"), and, of course, *On Time* (playing "Harry Willis" and making a liar of us). He was still acting in 1967 (playing a Keystone Kop in Charles Feldman's *Casino Royale*, wherein he also directed second-unit scenes).

Between the 1910s and the late 1960s, Talmadge also earned his money as a director of *first*-unit scenes (like 1953's *Project Moon Base*), as an onscreen stuntman (in, for example, Universal's loopy 1934 serial, *The Vanishing Shadow*), and as a producer (of nothing in which we've any interest). For the record, he also turned in a couple of screenplays, acted as production manager on an early 1950s' Spade Cooley oater, and actually lent whatever expertise he had to the sound department on 1938's immortal *The Duke of West Point*. The wildly versatile former acrobat died in 1981.

Talmadge's romantic interest in *On Time* was played by New York City's Billie Dove. Miss Dove, one heck of a looker if not much of a thespian, was born around the turn of the century and ran the gamut from modeling to the movies in no time, with an extended stint of sashaying about onstage during Florenz Ziegfeld's *Follies* and *Frolics* and Whatever somewhere in between. From the early 1920s through the early 1930s, the lady added her comeliness to over four dozen films (including Douglas Fairbanks' *The Black Pirate*, 1926). Following her taking the title role in First National's *The American Beauty* (1927), Miss Dove was publicized by that soubriquet, much as Mary Pickford had been crowned "America's Sweetheart" years before. For a while there, the blonde bombshell was married to director Irvin Willat (*The Story Without a Name*, 1929's *The Isle of Lost Ships*), but, other than Fox's fantasy, *The Folly of Vanity* (1924; see entry), *On Time* was Miss Dove's only picture that was On Topic.

Playing Richard Drake—one of the many characters involved

somehow in Cohn/Fort/Spence's mishegas — was Stuart Holmes, the Sound Era's King of Uncredited Bits (with some 350+ to his uncredit). During the Silent Era, Holmes was seen in over 150 shorts and features (commencing in 1909), and that he was seen in stuff like *Dr. Rameau* (1915), *The Green-Eyed Monster, A Daughter of the Gods* (1916, the pair), *The Unknown Purple* (1923), *Between Friends* (1924), and *The Man Who Laughs* (1928) is an especial mitzvah to us. On the Awkward Scale, our not knowing what his character did in *On Time* is really no worse than our not knowing which character he played in 1916's *The Witch*. It's the Grateful Scale that counts, and Holmes is a heavyweight on that one.

We're also grateful for George Siegmann, another character man with a good number of genre credits to his name. Like Holmes, Siegmann entered films in 1909 and, like Holmes', his name will be found in our discussion of *The Man Who Laughs*. Sadly, though, Siegmann died of pernicious anemia (at 40 years of age) several months before Paul Leni's American masterpiece — which had completed shooting over a year earlier, but was held back to be outfitted with a music/effects track — went into general release in November 1928. The New York–born actor — who definitely participated in that "brawl in a temple" over the "small idol" — also racked up points for appearing in *The Avenging Conscience* (1914), *A Connecticut Yankee* (1921), and *The Cat and the Canary* (1927).

Other genre-friendly thesps in *Our Time* included Douglas Gerrard (acted in *Undine* [1916], *Conscience* [1917], and *Wolf's Clothing* [1927]; directed *The Phantom Melody* [1920]); and Charles Clary (*A Connecticut Yankee* [1921], *Behind the Curtain* [1924], *Whispering Wires* [1926]). Also throwing in his lot with ours was cinematographer William Marshall, who will come back to haunt anyone reading our coverage on *A Daughter of the Gods, Terror Island* (1920), *The Ghost Breaker* (1922), and *Laughing at Danger* (1924). Fans of mainstream silents may recall Marshall's having photographed a little programmer yclept *The Sheik* (1921).

Well, despite all *our* enthusiasm for the film, the folks who actually viewed same (and lived to publish about it) were less than thrilled. "This is 'way past being merely bad,'" opined the 22 June 1927 *Variety*. All that stuff we liked so much, the Bible of Show Business didn't: "There are crazy Chinamen, a wildeyed, bushy-haired guy with an operating room where the bathroom should be, a fantastic dwarf, a symbolic devil given to leering and trap-door exits, and a miscellaneous assortment of Desperate Desmonds in silk hats."

Even the normally dependable Ralph Spence "botched his job." Sheesh! (Making things even worse, *Variety* didn't get around to covering the picture until some *three years* after its initial appearance. Talmadge had nothing to offer moviegoers throughout 1927 — his only contribution to the Bastard Art was an *uncredit* for stunts in Fairbanks' *The Gaucho* — and *On Time* was apparently reissued as the lower half of a double-bill by Tiffany Pictures. Still, why *that* would merit *Variety*'s attention when the picture's initial release came up empty is anyone's guess.)

Back in 1924 (on the 8 March, to be precise), *Harrison's* had reported on the film, and while not crazy about it, either, at least the trade was more polite than *Variety* would be: "This comedy-melodrama does not measure up to the standard set by previous Richard Talmadge productions." *MPW* was also less than enthusiastic, calling it "a film tale that starts out with promise but soon develops into such a bewildering maze of nonsense that there is one hope left in the mind of the observer — that the end may soon arrive."

What the Hey! They didn't much like *Seven Footprints to Satan*, either.

— *JTS*

One Exciting Night

One Exciting Night. D.W. Griffith, Inc./United Artists, 24 December, 1922, 11 reels/11,500 feet [available]

CAST: Carol Dempster (*Agnes Harrington*); Henry Hull (*John Fairfax*); Porter Strong (*Romeo Washington*); Morgan Wallace (*J. Wilson Rockmaine*); C.H. Crocker-King (*The Neighbor*); Margaret Dale (*Mrs. Harrington*); Frank Sheridan (*The Detective*); Frank Wunderlee (*Samuel Jones*); Grace Griswold (*Auntie Fairfax*); Irma Harrison (*The Maid*); Herbert Sutch (*Clary Johnson*); Percy Carr (*Porter, the Butler*); Charles E. Mack (*A Guest*)

CREDITS: *Director* D.W. Griffith; *Story* Irene Sinclair (pseudonym for D.W. Griffith); *Cinematographer* Hendrik Sartov; *Additional Photography* Irving B. Ruby; *Music Score Arranged and Synchronized by* Albert Pesce

In 1922 D.W. Griffith was desperately trying to keep his studio at Mamaroneck, Long Island, from going under. His epic *Orphans of the Storm* had cost a fortune to make and hadn't done as well as hoped at the box office. Griffith needed to produce a number of inexpensive, quickly-made films that would turn a profit and keep his studio solvent as well as provide financing for his special projects. He noticed that *The Bat* and other comedy thrillers were packing them in on Broadway and thought that a film along similar lines would do equally well. True, the idea had been tried before, notably in the 1914 film adaptation of *The Ghost Breaker* (see entry), but the public appetite for a combination of scares and laughs had grown considerably since then. Griffith made inquiries about doing a movie version of *The Bat*, but the producers wanted $150,000 for the film rights as well as a delay in shooting while the play was running. Griffith balked and — using the name Irene Sinclair ("a young Kentucky authoress") — came up with his own variation and titled the script *The Haunted Grange*.

Unfortunately, as his later comments about the film indicate, Griffith was incapable of doing a quickie: "You can bet I will not attempt another play like that again. I started out to do this in six weeks and at a low cost. It has taken me six months and cost me four times what I expected … I have made one, that is enough. My next picture will be far different. Life is too short to work as hard as I did on this one" (*Lincoln* [Nebraska] *State Journal*, 17 September 1922).

The film was previewed in Derby, Connecticut, under the title *The Haunted House* and ran a whooping 13 reels. Footage kept getting cut after each preview and, by the time of its Boston showing on 10 October 1922, the film was down to 11 reels and the title had been changed to *One Exciting Night*. We can be grateful that Griffith passed on *The Bat* because *One Exciting Night* is one of the Master's worst films. The main problem is that Griffith simply has no feel for this type of story. It doesn't help that the plot is much too convoluted and while throwing out two reels of footage no doubt helped pick up the pace, it left audiences confused.

Our synopsis comes from a viewing of the film:

The film opens with a series of title cards describing the film as a "comedy drama of mystery" and asking the audience not to give away the ending and to also pay close attention to the early scenes.

In "somber Africa," Stuart Bruce-Douglas is on a treasure hunt with his brother. Stuart's sister-in-law is with them and has recently given birth to a baby girl and then fallen ill. The brother is at another campsite when word reaches his loyal kaffir that he has died. The news kills the young mother. Stuart laments the fact that his brother's great wealth will go the infant. He bribes his haughty female travelling companion to take the child and raise her as her own.

Sixteen years later, Stuart dies and in his will recounts his misdeed and leaves his fortune to his niece if she can be found. The lawyers handling the estate make note of the fact that they have only a short time to find the girl before the fortune legally passes to the other heirs.

The scene shifts to Louisville, Kentucky, and the home of the socialite, Mrs. Harrington, and her teenage daughter Agnes. Mrs. Harrington is a cold, unfeeling woman and Agnes is starved for maternal affection. Mrs. Harrington wants Agnes to marry the wealthy J. Wilson Rockmaine, but the young girl has no interest in the middle-aged man. Mrs. Harrington tells her daughter that they have fallen on hard times and — even worse — that Rockmaine has observed Mrs. Harrington stealing a bracelet at a party and has threatened to expose her unless Agnes marries him. After her mother finally shows her a little warmth, Agnes reluctantly agrees.

Nearby, John Fairfax is returning to the family estate after a year's absence. During that time, the great house has been closed up and there are rumors that it is haunted, as a spectral scarecrow has been seen skulking about. Actually, this is all the work of a gang of bootleggers who have been using the empty house to hide both liquor and their profits. The gang is led by Clary Johnson and his mysterious partner — whom none of the other bootleggers has ever seen.

Since the house is about to be re-opened, the gang quickly removes all the hooch. That night Johnson returns to the house to get some receipts and has with him a satchel containing a half-million dollars with which he intends to abscond. Servants for the house are being hired that very night and — startled by some commotion — Johnson hides the satchel in a trunk under some old papers. He is interrupted by his partner who shoots him dead but who has to flee before he can search for the money. The other bootleggers and the detective investigating the case know about the satchel. John Fairfax had earlier quarreled with Johnson so he is a prime suspect in the shooting, but the detective is much more interested in finding the loot.

Parker, John's butler, has completed hiring the servants, among them the cowardly Romeo Washington and Sam Jones — who is actually "Black Sam," the most feared of the gang of bootleggers. Romeo is ready to quit when he learns of the murder, but the sight of a sexy housemaid changes his mind. Parker discovers the trunk and, not knowing the satchel is concealed within, brings it downstairs and puts it in a hidden cabinet.

At a hotel lawn party, John and Agnes meet and immediately take to each other, much to the annoyance of both Mrs. Harrington and Rockmaine. John invites everyone over to his house. At the Fairfax mansion, the detective and his cronies keep a close eye on the guests, suspicious that one or more of them is there looking for the money. A mysterious and sinister stranger crashes the party, telling Fairfax that he was a friend of his late father's.

Later, John accompanies some of the guests back to the hotel, but Agnes and her mother spend the night. The detective has in-sisted that all the servants but the maid leave for the night. The maid later opens the door for Romeo and, shortly afterwards, a masked, black-cloaked figure takes advantage of the unlocked door and enters. He embarks on a fruitless search for the money, but succeeds in terrifying the houseguests. As he finally heads for the door, he runs into a returning guest who unmasks him. He fatally stabs the guest and flees.

John comes back to the house and Rockmaine and the mysterious stranger have found excuses to return. The detective insists that no one leave for the remainder of the night. Later, Black Sam prowls around the bedroom where Agnes and her mother are sleeping. He leaves as the startled women wake up and scream.

The cloaked figure is seen stalking about the house. Parker suddenly realizes what's really in the trunk and shows the satchel to Agnes and Fairfax. They hide it in a flour barrel. Shortly afterwards, a clutching hand pulls the butler behind a secret panel. Agnes nearly suffers the same fate. The killer removes the satchel from the flour barrel.

The detective confronts John and accuses him of both murders. John brings him to the kitchen to show him the loot, but it's gone. The enraged detective tries to arrest Fairfax and struggles with him and Agnes. Just as a fierce storm arises, Agnes sees the killer flee with the satchel into the night. She follows him and is trapped by a fallen tree branch and, as a tree is about to fall on her, Fairfax — still in handcuffs — rescues her. They seize the killer and bring him back into the house where he is unmasked and revealed as Rockmaine. Parker reappears and tells everyone the masked man forced him to tell the location of the satchel.

The mysterious stranger turns out to be a Scotland Yard investigator in search of the heiress to the Stuart Burt-Douglas estate. He tells Agnes of her true identity and reveals that Mrs. Harrington is not really her mother. Black Sam is actually the kaffir faithful to her father, and he had come to the house searching for evidence. John and Agnes wed while Romeo returns to his old neighborhood with the maid.

Even for a thriller, the story is overburdened with improbabilities. What is a woman who is about to give birth doing on a treasure hunt in the jungle? Why does everyone assume the money is still in the house when it's more logical to think it was taken by Johnson's murderer after he shot him? How did the "ignorant kaffir" from South Africa make his way to America and end up as Black Sam the bootlegger? Why does Parker hide the trunk and what inspired him to finally realize what's in it? What's Scotland Yard doing in Kentucky anyway? These, of course, are the questions you ask only when a thriller fails to thrill.

The first half of the film is so disjointed and dull that Griffith is obliged to remind the audience that there are scares ahead by showing the silhouette of a clutching hand double-exposed over the exterior of the Fairfax mansion. To make sure no one misses the message, we also get titles like the following: "Around this house a terrible mystery, that one might say rules the world: the mystery of *fear*. *Fear* that is nothing and yet every man trembles at this invisible thing from the cradle to the grave. Even as you read, are you not *afraid* of *something*?"

At that point in the story, audiences were probably afraid that all they were going to get for their money was standard melodrama and florid title cards. Was there ever a *hoarier* cliché in the Silent Era than the young girl who must sell herself to a rich man to save her family? To make matters worse, the girl is played by Carol Dempster at her most cloying (though Griffith can probably be blamed for this), and Morgan Wallace practically twirls his moustache as her would-be seducer. There is, however, one interesting title regarding his character: "His own youth squandered, he imagines in some mysterious way its joy will return to him in a young girl's love." This could almost be an ironic comment on Griffith's infatuation with Carol Dempster.

After heavy doses of cornball humor and romantic treacle, and the parading of a bewildering succession of red herrings, the film finally settles down to a few chills as the Bat-like killer stalks the mansion. Still, he creeps about the place in such a stagey and melodramatic manner that his posturing is funnier than the intentional comedy. To make matters worse, the lighting and camerawork of these scenes are too bland to create a sinister atmosphere. Griffith seems more interested in the humor, and there are endless bits of business involving the terrified Romeo (Porter Strong in blackface) reacting in bug-eyed horror to the masked villain. Such scenes pleased contemporary audiences, but are cringe-inducing today.

While few would agree with *The New York Times* critic that the climatic storm surpasses the finale on the ice floes of *Way Down East,* the gale is certainly the highlight of the film and contains actual footage of a hurricane that swept through Westchester County in June of 1922. Carol Dempster, a bit frustrated that her movies for Griffith had been small-scale to that point, suggested going all out for the climax, and Griffith obliged by spending a small fortune on the sequence. He hired the local fire department to use their hoses in the woods while propellers mounted on trees blew the resulting torrents around furiously. Other firemen threw branches into the maelstrom while some trees were pulled around on wires (this effect is pretty obvious). Dempster and Henry Hull (John Fairfax) run back and forth in the middle of the chaos, but the end result is strangely uninvolving. One admires the effects, but cares little for the safety of this uninteresting couple. Perhaps the highlight of the storm sequence is when Romeo flees to his small house which is then picked up and tossed by the wind. Alas, he's not blown away to Oz.

Publicity for the film made a point of stressing that it was not another Griffith costume spectacle. As per the 8 September 1922 *Oakland* [California] *Tribune,* "The main action takes place in one afternoon and evening, with the principal scenes all laid in one house. The settings are modern in every sense. The players appear in the latest of present day fashions. For this picture, Griffith has stepped entirely away from costumes, mob scenes and vast sets."

An ad in *The Denton* [Texas] *Record Chronicle* (23 January 1923) went further still and promised: "No ponderous sets. No annoying mobs. No queer costumes." Whether this was an effective come-on is arguable, given the fact that Doug Fairbanks' *Robin Hood* and Rex Ingram's *Prisoner of Zenda*, both contemporary with *One Exciting Night*, were big hits and demonstrated that the public appetite for spectacles was far from diminishing.

Naturally, ads for *One Exciting Night* were not shy about comparing the film to *The Bat* and *The Cat and the Canary*, while promising a "blithe romance of exhilarating mystery" that would provide "the laughing thrill." An exhibitor in San Antonio had a special midnight showing of the film complete with a prelude of spooky music and ushers dressed as ghosts. The promotion worked a bit too well and drew such a large crowd that those who couldn't get in nearly broke down the theater doors.

Most reviewers agreed with the favorable audience response, though there were the usual complaints about Griffith's pretentious title cards and the film being overlong. While there was some grousing that Griffith was slumming, few argued with his right to make a buck by doing something different that focused more on sheer entertainment than on moralizing. *The New York Times* called it a "hilarious thriller" that delivered its scares and laughs unashamedly. An ad for the film in the *Reno Evening Gazette* (23 March 1923) displayed a number of glowing comments from the critics. A sampling:

> A masterpiece — women screamed, everybody gasped — and then the audience went into hysterics of laughter [*Chicago Herald and Examiner*].
>
> Stupendous is the word. You will rise up on the edge of your seat and scream [*The Boston Traveller*].
>
> The audience as one man shivers at *One Exciting Night*. The action is terrific [*The New York Herald*].

And so on. One dissenting voice came from Frederick James Smith of the *Los Angeles Times*, who called the film "exciting, but mostly in name" and dismissed it as a "mere potboiler — a fair average program picture." Unlike virtually every other critic, Smith was skeptical of the film's box office appeal and predicted it would share the fate of an earlier Griffith misfire, *Dream Street*.

The picture's only so-so, but that's one exciting lobby card for *One Exciting Night.*

Variety (13 October 1923) opined the film would be a hit and while calling the mystery "admirably sustained" was not terribly impressed with the plot:

> It is a melodramatic hodge-podge of every mystery thriller from serial, dime novel, ten-twent-thirt, etc. right up to the modern *Bat* and *Cat and the Canary*. If the truth be told however it is probably more reminiscent of Griffith's old Biograph curdlers of a dozen years ago, particularly *The Lonely Villa*, than a lift from any of the present day mystery tinglers.

Disregarding Griffith's admonition not to give away the ending, *Variety* had no qualms about revealing the identity of the killer.

Henry Hull was finishing up his run as the star of *The Cat and the Canary* when *One Exciting Night* began shooting. Hull's lean, angular features give him a furtive, slightly haughty look. One ad for the film depicts him at the climax, wild-eyed and disheveled and raising the handcuffs over his head; he looks rather scary and one would assume he was the villain rather than the leading man. Indeed, the film presents him as a rather ineffectual hero who gets punched out or overpowered more than once and doesn't swing into action until the heroine has tackled the villain. Hull would play a somewhat similar role later that same year in *The Last Moment* (see entry for further info on his career). Carol Dempster is game enough at the film's finale, but it's not enough to make up for her annoying simpering in the rest of the film (though what can you do with a character who gets all misty-eyed playing with a doll?) For a brief career sketch of Dempster, see *The Sorrows of Satan* (which features her best performance).

C.H. Crocker-King, looking a bit like Lucien Littlefield in *The Cat and the Canary*, strikes the right creepy note as the strange neighbor who turns out to be a detective. Crocker-King, an import from Yorkshire, had just finished a decent run at Broadway's Knickerbocker Theatre as an honest-to-goodness villain in "Sapper's" *Bulldog Drummond*, another play that was sometimes mentioned in connection with publicity for *One Exciting Night*.

The best notices of the film went to Porter Strong as Romeo Washington. Strong had started his career as a cabaret singer and it was there that he was noticed by Al Jolson, who called him "a natural comedian" and who later lauded his performance in *One Exciting Night*. Griffith, who reportedly had once told Jolson that "he has more in his one eye than the Gish sisters have in their whole bodies," had tried to get Jolson to do a movie for him in the early 1920s; certainly some sort of film history would have been made had Jolie ended up in *One Exciting Night* playing Romeo Washington. In 1923 Jolson did agree to do a mystery film for Griffith — the working title was to have been *Mammy's Boy* — but the singer took one look at the rushes and skipped to England. Griffith and company sued for $250,000; the suit was not settled (in Griffith's favor) until 1927, the year of Jolson's triumph in *The Jazz Singer*.

As for Porter Strong, he didn't have long to capitalize on his good reviews; just a few months after the release of *One Exciting Night*, the 44-year-old actor was found dead in his hotel room, apparently of natural causes.

One Exciting Night is not in the same league as *The Bat* or *The Cat and the Canary*, nor even as much fun as many a Poverty Row "old dark house" film. Nonetheless, Griffith's movie is significant in that it generated enough money and hoopla to inspire a whole slew of comedy/thrillers, many of them (like *The Gorilla*, *The Monster*, and a redone *The Ghost Breaker*) adaptations of Broadway plays. How much money it *did* make for Griffith isn't certain, though the film certainly showed at least some profit. Perhaps the Master might just as well have handed the whole thing over to his onetime assistant, Christy Cabanne, to shoot in a couple of weeks. After all, in *One Frightened Night* (1935), Cabanne demonstrated that he had a better feel for this kind of hokum than had his mentor.

— HN

One Glorious Day

One Glorious Day. Famous Players–Lasky/Paramount Pictures, 5 February 1922, 5 reels/5100 feet [LOST]
CAST: Will Rogers (*Ezra Botts*); Lila Lee (*Molly McIntyre*); Alan Hale (*Ben Wadley*); John Fox (*Ek*); George Nichols (*Pat Curran*); Emily Rait (*Mrs. McIntyre*); Clarence Burton (*Burt Snead*)
CREDITS: *Presented by* Jesse Lasky; *Director* James Cruze; *Scenario* Walter Woods; from a Story by Walter Woods and A.B. Baringer; *Cinematographer* Karl Brown

"Where do we come from? Why are we here, in a world full of reformers, landlords and other pests? And, as dear old hamlet asked, where do we go from here?"

"Some experts have it doped that before we put on our first safety-pin we were spirits, romping around without earthly bodies to bother us, and with the whole doggone firmament for a playground."

"Go through the Pleiades, down the Milky Way, turn to the right and there you are — in the Kingdom of the Not-Yet-Born."
                    —first three inter-titles from *One Glorious Day*

In a volume literally riddled with films centered on the concept of spiritualism — with their fictional accounts of reincarnation, out-of-body experiences, souls with unfinished business, and a multitude of mediums, both genuine and fraudulent — *One Glorious Day* stands unique; it deals with a spirit who hasn't even been born yet! Our detailed synopsis comes courtesy of Scott O'Dell's *Representative Photoplays Analyzed*:

> The flesh and blood part of this play deals with a quite ordinary human story. Ezra Botts, an odd, good-natured, and very shy professor, is shown in a mildly conducted love affair with Molly McIntyre, the landlady's daughter. Ben Wedley [*sic*], rich and idle, also desires Mollie, and is quite villainous in his direct methods of love-making. Professor Botts is a candidate for mayor. In this, he is the unsuspecting instrument of one Pat Curran, a grafting politician, who plans to put the Professor in office, and then constitute himself as "the power behind the throne."
>
> As the story opens, the Professor's most evident interest is in spiritualism. Here, and here only, does he show daring. He announces to a spiritualistic society that on the occasion of a certain meeting he will separate his soul from his body and travel in spirit, to appear apparitionally before the assembled spiritualists.
>
> Now enters the hero in the "form" of a gay little spirit called Ek, who is first introduced as the soul of an unincarnated being, exceedingly anxious to be born into the mortal experience.
>
> Off on the edge of the Universe, this impatient little spirit, Ek, dives into space and down among the whirling spheres toward Earth. He arrives just too late to make connections with the stork, and goes about disconsolately until he is so fortunate as to find the

body of Professor Botts, which is temporarily unoccupied, the Professor having gone upon his spirit visit to the Society.

Ek enters his new role with enthusiasm and sprightly vim. Immediately, things begin to happen which are contrary to the obvious; both from Ek's viewpoint, and that of the characters so long accustomed to the shy, unobtrusive temperament of the professor. To begin with, Ek finds that incarnation interferes with his free passage through doors. His accustomed aerial acrobatics require adaptation to the sluggishness of the human body. But in this adaptation he is swift of accomplishment.

As for Professor Botts himself, or rather in his spiritual essence, he fails in the crucial test of making the Society members see him at the meeting. In despair, he decides to return and re-enter his own body. But we know that the body has acquired a new tenant; and, during this "glorious day" the Professor is constrained to the inglorious part of waiting.

Meanwhile, thought and deed are one and the same to Ek. He espouses the Professor's interests, both as regards Molly and the mayoralty campaign. He takes Botts' body to the Club, where Ben Wedley, Pat Curran and others are drinking. With fine abandon, he enters into the spirit of dissipation; and the amazed members of this convivial group see the quiet Professor Botts drinking. Moreover, immediately afterwards, Ek knocks several men down, and leaves the place with a big cigar and a mug of beer. Thereupon, he encounters the spiritualists leaving their hall. They are quite convinced that the Professor failed utterly in his attempt at spiritual detachment. Now, they receive an added shock when they encounter the form of the Professor possessed by Ek; and from their viewpoint, possessed of a devil.

Ek repairs to a gilded café and goes in for a good time. This naturally upsets all of Pat Curran's plans for boosting the candidacy of Professor Botts on the strength of his well-known respectability. Also, he finds in this new Professor a less manageable instrument to his ends. He remonstrates, and Ek promptly gives him a beating. The effect upon the onlookers is quite favorable to the Professor's candidacy. They are pleased with this assertiveness. Ek has proven himself a better campaign manager than Pat.

As for Molly, she is quite delighted with the sudden, radical change in the Professor and his present ardent disposition. While her mother is absent at a picture show, she is deceived into making a call at the home of Ben Wadley. Ben is intoxicated and becomes exceedingly offensive. Ek upon his return home with the Professor's body finds a note from Molly, telling of her whereabouts. He goes thither, and is just in time to save Molly from the violence of Ben. He treats Ben roughly, and promptly tells Molly of his love before taking her home to her mother.

But the body of Professor Botts, compelled by its new spirit tenant to perform such antics, is speedily worn out. The result is a swoon. Ek, himself, has found incarnation under such circumstances more of a job than he anticipated, so this fainting spell becomes his liberation. He departs into the free, untrammeled spirit realm, to await the regular course of his incarnation by birth.

Now, the true spirit of Professor Botts finds opportunity to re-enter his body. He comes back into his "normal" existence, only to find that it is a necessarily new existence by reason of Ek's brief occupancy. He is never able to explain the events of this day; but, as the play ends, there is indication that his future life has been projected for him along the lines instituted by Ek.

The movie is still among the missing, notwithstanding Internet rumors that place the film elements in an "unknown European archive." At least we have the paper holdings of the Academy of Motion Picture Arts and Sciences: a scenario, a continuity (whence comes our introduction), and 17 stills.

One Glorious Day was the first "imagi-movie" viewed by the five-year-old Forrest J Ackerman, and the experience started him on his way to becoming the foremost collector of sci-fi,

fantasy, and horror movie memorabilia. Over 80 years later, he still mentioned the picture as one of the forgotten, unsung genre features of the Silent Era, and our research reveals that he was right on the money. The National Board of Review listed it among the best films of the year. Syndicated columnist James W. Dean, in his end-of-year rundown of 1922's cinematic achievements declared, "I consider *One Glorious Day* the most distinctive picture yet filmed" and, in another piece written well into 1923, was still hurling superlatives: "No other picture before or since has been so well presented in the native terms of the cinema." The same sentiments were expressed in *The New York Times* summary entitled "Screen Pictures of 1922": "The American screen has achieved something distinctive in this, an imaginative and spirited work." Earlier reviews following the movie's debut were equally the stuff of a press agent's dreams.

Variety offered on 3 February 1922: "Here is a distinct screen achievement, a story of whimsical humor and fanciful design, translated by the picture medium with a delicacy of treatment that would be possible in no other way.... The picture art can claim *One Glorious Day* as its own.... The photoplay is a distinct novelty."

Moving Picture World said on 11 February 1922: "Exhibitors who supply entertainment to a clientele that has been heard to grumble mildly about the sameness of the fare it might have been getting will do well to counteract the criticism with *One Glorious Day*. The film is a distinct novelty, written with imagination, which no one will contradict is an all too rare quality."

Alan Dale wrote in *The American* (date unknown): "Here is a picture that is a triumph of imagination—a scintillant [*sic*] example of adroit intelligence.... It would make a movie fan of the screen's bitterest foes. You must see it. It is so well done, it is such good fun, it is so clever. Don't miss it. Take my tip. It is an achievement. It is a colossal surprise."

The only critiques showing the slightest negativity seemed to focus on the fantastic nature of the story, as did the 11 February 1922 *Exhibitor's Herald*, which held that "*One Glorious Day* is long on novelty and short on story." Rebutting this claim was the 13 March 1922 entry in "Miss Wagner's Up-to-Date Theatrical News and Gossip" in *The Lima* [Ohio] *News*: "It has been heard, hither and yon, that the story is so highly improbable. Mebbe so, but how many stories of this nature could be probable? It's a question for those spiritually inclined to answer, and in the meantime, it doesn't make a whole lot of difference, because the film as it now stands is a winner."

Sharing Miss Wagner's home-spun manner, Will Rogers—the picture's star—offered his irrefutable analysis of film criticism: "The average life of the movie is till it reaches the critic."

Soon after the picture's premiere at the Rivoli Theater, *The New York Times* offered two illuminating columns (30 January 22 and 5 February 1922) that expertly dissected *One Glorious Day* by meticulously evaluating its cast and crew. The verdict was that *all* concerned contributed to the outcome of a "skillful and ingenious piece of work," with leading-man Rogers considered ... a revelation. See him first when the Professor's spirit is at home, and then when Ek occupies his body, and you'll say again that Will Rogers can be a good deal more on the screen than just himself.

And while the paper acknowledged that the entire cast had turned in good performances, singular praise was given to John Fox, who portrayed the disembodied Ek: "[Fox] is a delight [and] brings to the part all the sprightliness and spice it needs." The film's special effects were lauded, as was the camerawork, original story, and scenario. For director James Cruze were reserved the greatest accolades: "Mr. Cruze has given evidence of just such humor and cinematographic skill as make *One Glorious Day* truly glorious." (Mr. Cruze's bona fides are to be found in our essay on *Terror Island*.)

Sadly, not a word in either commentary was devoted to Roscoe "Fatty" Arbuckle. In 1921, Arbuckle comedies like *Crazy to Marry*, *The Dollar-a-Year Man*, *Gasoline Gus*, *Fast Freight* and *Leap Year* were being released to profit and acclaim just as quickly as James Cruze could direct them. Roscoe had begun work on yet another venture with Cruze and frequent co-star, Lila "Cuddles" Lee—*The Melancholy Spirit*—when the notorious Virginia Rappe scandal broke. Even as the rotund comic was actively maintaining his innocence, those of his films currently enjoying their run were withdrawn from theaters, and the actor was barred from the set of *The Melancholy Spirit* after receiving a telegram from Paramount mogul, Adolph Zukor, terminating his services. Arbuckle was cleared of any wrongdoing in Rappe's death following three, drawn-out trials, but his career was in shambles. As for *The Melancholy Spirit*, it was shot under its working title—*Ek*—and was eventually released as *One Glorious Day*. Cruze and Lee had been retained, but Will Rogers was brought in (for far less money) to replace Arbuckle. Of three other projects that originally had been designated for Arbuckle, two were likewise handed to other stars, and the third was shelved entirely.

The film success of Will Rogers, American icon, was just another of his many accomplishments. Born on the 4 November 1879 to part–Cherokee parents, Rogers grew up in what would later become the state of Oklahoma. His expert roping abilities may have led to his appearing in wild-west shows, circuses, Vaudeville, two World's Fairs and the Ziegfeld Follies, but it was his homespun wit that made him unique. Rogers made his first film — a Western, of course — in 1918, and dozens more were to follow. While many of those, too, were Westerns, the laconic actor demonstrated enough versatility to star in such genre fare as 1922's *The Headless Horseman* (see entry) and 1931's *A Connecticut Yankee*. Before perishing in a 1935 Alaskan plane crash, Rogers added "successful author," "syndicated newspaper columnist," "Broadway performer," and "radio personality" to his resume.

Rogers' co-star, Lila Lee — of whom *Moving Picture World* commented, "for what she is called upon she performs charmingly"— was born in Union Hill, New Jersey, on the 25 July 1905. A Vaudeville star as a child, Lee moved on to pictures with Famous Players–Lasky when she was but 13 years of age. During the Silent Era, she toiled with everyone from De Mille (*Male and Female*, 1919) and Valentino (*Blood and Sand*, 1922) to Houdini (*Terror Island*, 1920) and Lugosi (*The Midnight Girl*, 1925). Her work in the talkies consisted mainly of 1930's thrillers like *The Gorilla*, *The Unholy Three* (both 1930), *Radio Patrol*, and *War Correspondent* (both 1932). Lila Lee passed away on the 13

November 1979 in — of all places— Will Rogers Memorial Hospital.

Tall (6' 2"), burly Alan Hale was used to playing heavies. A Washington, D.C. native, the actor would have a film career that spanned some 40 years and featured over 225 credits while also finding work as a writer, director, singer, inventor, Broadway performer, and newspaperman. He got the chance to play the benevolent outlaw, Little John, when both Douglas Fairbanks and Errol Flynn took their respective turns as *Robin Hood*, and reprised the role again in 1950, when John Derek assumed the leadership of *The Rogues of Sherwood Forest* for Columbia Pictures. The actor did not live to see *Sherwood* released, having passed away from liver problems in late January of that year, Besides *One Glorious Day*, Hale's pertinent genre pictures include *The Eleventh Hour* (1923) and *Black Oxen* (1924)— see essays on both — but fans of silent Westerns will regard as iconic his Sam Woodhull in James Cruze's famed *The Covered Wagon* (1923) Hale's son, Alan Jr., achieved his own media immortality as the Skipper on the popular 1960s television comedy series, *Gilligan's Island*.

For John Fox — aka Johnnie Fox, Jr.— the blithe "Ek" was probably his first role of … errrr … substance, and he came *this close* to being the picture's title character: the film was shot under the working title, *Ek*. He would go on to become a popular child actor of the 1920s, appearing (like Alan Hale) in *The Covered Wagon* (starring as young Jed Wingate). Like another of the era's child stars, Wesley Barry, Fox possessed a highly freckled face, and this was apparently enough to land him the title role as the one-armed orphan boy in the cinematic adaptation of Gene Stratton Porter's 1904 eponymous novel, *Freckles* (1928). An interesting cast, good writing and directing, solid camera work — all that's missing so far as *One Glorious Day* is concerned is the film itself.

— *SJ*

One Hour Before Dawn

One Hour Before Dawn. Jesse D. Hampton Productions/Pathé Exchange, Inc., 1 August 1920, 5–6 reels/4696 feet [LOST]

CAST: H.B. Warner (*George Clayton*); Anna Q. Nilsson (*Ellen Aldrich*); Augustus Phillips (*Bob Manning*); Frank Leigh (*Norman Osgood*); Howard Davies (*Harrison Kirke*); Adele Farrington (*Mrs. Montague*); Lillian Rich (*Dorothy*); Dorothy Hagan (*Mrs. Copeland*); Thomas Guise (*Judge Copeland*); Ralph McCullough (*Fred Aldrich*); Edward Burns (*Arthur*); Wilton Taylor (*Inspector Steele*)

CREDITS: *Director* Henry King; *Scenario* Fred Myton; *based on the novel* Behind Red Curtains *by* Mansfield Scott (Boston, 1919); *Cinematographer* Victor Milner

There is a house party in the home of the Copelands. Norman Osgood, one of the guests, is a hypnotist and, to prove his powers, he brings Harrison Kirke, a boastful, too-talkative member of the party, under his influence and succeeds in making a fool of him. Out of his trance, Kirke is furious at Osgood and in a mad moment threatens to kill the hypnotist. George Clayton, a novelist, also a guest of the Copelands, disapproves of Osgood's trick but submits to his hypnotic powers himself. While under the domination of Osgood's mind, he is told to kill Kirke one hour before dawn.

During the night Clayton has a particularly vivid nightmare in which he sees himself kill Kirke. He awakes in a cold sweat and the next morning is more than nervous when Kirke fails to appear. Then when the butler rushes downstairs to announce that Kirke has been found dead in his bed, Clayton believes that the nightmare was reality itself. A detective is called in to investigate and Clayton's fears, of course, cause suspicion to fall upon him. After several false leads, the detective finally unmasks the real killer as Bob Manning, an old enemy of Kirke's.

     — Courtesy of *Wid's Daily* (18 July 1920) and *The AFI Catalog*

Well, we came upon a copy of *Behind Red Curtains* in an old bookstore and we give you our word that the above précis of the screenplay is a pretty decent recap of Mansfield Scott's source novel. The film was shot as *Behind Red Curtains*, with the title change effected during post-production for reason or reasons unknown. Because of that close similarity between print (as in press) and print (as in projector), the switch can't have been due to discomfort with Mr. Scott's scribblings, although the book does contain more than its fair share of baloney. Like…

> "Dr. Manning," cried Steele, "do you mean to say that you unlatched that door, threw that pencil, and then got to the table and back again, with five men in the room?"
> "It was easy," said Bob. "When I was hunting in Africa, I learned a trick of moving noiselessly. When necessary, I can move quickly, too. Not everyone can do it."

Among other joys, there's a fairly lengthy conversation on how "the man under hypnotic influence, no matter what else he may do, will not commit a crime," a hypothesis which is raised only so that it might be debunked both by scientific hypnotists and spry ex–Big Game Hunters. The narrative is told in the first person by Mr. Clayton, who is "a chemist, in New York," a phrase that establishes pithily that neither the narrator's particular branch of science nor his native intelligence lends itself kindly toward hypnotic tomfoolery. It is chiefly the hypnotic tomfoolery, though, that enrages the protagonist, who threatens the mesmerist, who then does his worst, which enslaves yet another mind, which furthers the plot that grants the movie mention in these pages, and all in the house that George Clayton built.

With the movie's being lost, though, and the surviving body of commentary giving the hypnosis business rather short shrift, there's not much else of relevance that can be said about the plot and/or its unfolding. While we're sure that the above-cited outrage was enacted in full compliance with the performance standards of 1920-vintage silent melodrama, we've little indication whether the actual act of hypnotizing anyone was effected with whirling discs or low key lighting or what-not, or whether the whole thing was treated "scientifically," i.e., sterilely. In other words, we're clueless as to whether Mandrake's gesturing hypnotically was a snoozer or a lollapalooza. The extant screeds aver that the picture itself delivered the goods ("An exciting and thrilling murder melodrama, every inch of which is gripping"— *Harrison's Reports*, 17 July 1920), without focusing on the deed, itself.

The New York Times (12 July 1920) devoted its allotted space to more than a sketchy rundown on the principals, but the opening paragraphs didn't augur well:

> Mystery stories, especially those involving murder, almost invariably follow the same formula. There is nearly always an obvious effort to mislead spectators, readers or audiences into suspecting the hero or heroine, although no one ever suspects either for a moment, and at the end the foregone conclusion that the crime was committed by some one who has been carefully denied popular sympathy is revealed by clever detective work or an accommodating trick of fate — and the mystery is solved.
> *One Hour Before Dawn*, a screen adaptation of Mansfield Scott's novel *Behind Red Curtains*, at the Capitol this week, is a mystery story, and as mechanical as most of its kind. There is never any mystery about it, except, perhaps, in the question of which of two equally unattractive men the author will arbitrarily select as the murderer when the time comes to acquit the hero.

Had the parties concerned with the production read further, though, they would have breathed a bit easier: "Its photography in general is excellent. Also a number of scenes meant to be 'creepy' are made so by the cinematographic skill of Henry King, presumably, who directed the production. And the acting is good."

As for *our* scenes, the scenes "showing the hypnotist at work, the hero's hypnotically suggested dream of murder and the actions of the hero and the hypnotist after the crime," the reviewer opined (rather awkwardly) that "the motion pictures are able to stir up considerable interest." You betcha. He then summed up neatly, "If the spectator will not be too exacting in the demand for logic and honesty in the plot and will forget the formula for a while, he can be pleasantly interested in much of *One Hour Before Dawn*."

Wid's Daily (cited above) acknowledged the hypnosis pivot in its plot recap, but declined to elaborate. Admitting that *One Hour* was "a splendid picture," the critic went on to praise director, Henry King:

> The action isn't underway very long before you sense the fact that there is a murder coming. And it is this note of impending tragedy that Director King has sounded in a very subtle fashion again and again before the actual deed takes place…. It is another tribute to his skill that he has kept up the fine pace of the beginning right through until the detective cleverly brings in the solution of the mystery.

Anyone interested in another example of Henry King's skill (and his curriculum vitae) should flip back to our discussion of *Haunting Shadows*.

Henry B. Warner — more familiarly known as H.B. — was born in London in late October 1875. For silent film buffs, he was most famously the Christ in Cecil B. De Mille's *The King of Kings* (1927); for most of the common cinematic clay, he is best remembered as Mr. Gower in Frank Capra's *It's a Wonderful Life* (1946); for genre aficionados, his 40+-year career includes such notable product as *The Ghost Breaker* (1914), *Haunting Shadows* (1920) (see entries), *Stark Mad* (1929; see appendix), and the quirky *Supernatural* (1933), among others. Most quirkily, he played himself — as one of Norma Desmond's Hollywood "waxworks" bridge partners — in Billy Wilder's sensational *Sunset Blvd.* (1950).

Coincidentally, so did Anna Q. Nilsson, the female juvenile of *One Hour before Dawn*. Born in Sweden in 1888, in the USA by 1910 (she was one of the more famous models for illustrator-turned-director, Penrhyn Stanlaws — see *Singed Wings*) and in films by the following year, Miss Nilsson went on to make well over 150 pictures before sound worked its perverse magic on her career. Among her genre credits is the 1923 version of *The Isle of Lost Ships* and two more "rejuvenation" pictures—

Vanity's Price (1924) and *One Way Street* (1925; see essays on all three). There's a bit more on the statuesque Swedish import in our write-up on *Between Friends*.

Augustus Phillips— the heavy of the piece — was home-grown (Rensselaer, Indiana), but died in London in 1944, some 20-odd years after he called it quits, industry-wise. *One Hour Before Dawn*, the actor's antepenultimate appearance, sat some 120 or so credits after his debut in Edison's *Frankenstein* (1910), and more on Mr. Phillips may be found in the entry on *Aladdin's Other Lamp* (1917).

It seems, then, that *One Hour Before Dawn* would have made for an intriguing 50–69 minutes for the right sort of audiences back then, and the adjectives that the picture earned might tend to put it somewhere on the more comprehensive "lost films that merit rediscovery" lists.

— *JTS*

One Million Dollars

One Million Dollars. Rolfe Photoplays, Inc./Metro Pictures Corp., 22 November 1915, 5 reels [LOST]

CAST: William Faversham (*Richard Duvall*); Henry Bergman (*Count Raoul D'Estes*); George Le Guere (*Emile*); Mayme Kelso (*Countess D'Estes*); Carlotta De Felice (*Grace Ellicott*); Arthur Morrison (*Purtab Gar*); Charles Graham (*Chief of Police*); Camilla Dalberg (*Mrs. Cooke*)

CREDITS: *Director* John W. Noble; *Scenario* George D. Proctor; based on the novel *One Million Francs* by Arnold Fredericks (pseudonym of Frederic Arnold Kummer) (New York, 1912); *Cinematographer* Herbert O. Carlton

From the 6 November 1915 issue of *The Moving Picture World*:

Richard Duvall, a noted English criminologist, while touring in India, saves the life of a Buddhist priest who rewards him with the presentation of a wonderful crystal globe. By gazing in it the priest demonstrates that Duvall can fall into a cataleptic state and his astral body is released and free to roam at will. Leaving the temple, Duvall collides with grace Ellicott, who is touring the Far East with her aunt, the Countess D'Estes and the Count. A mutual admiration between Grace and Duvall results from the accidental meeting.

Later, in England, the mistress of Count D'Estes makes financial demands which he cannot keep. With his housekeeper, Mrs. Cooke, he plans to put his wife out of the way and thus obtain her fortune. Poison is put in candy which the countess eats. Her sudden death arouses the suspicion of her niece. On his return to England, Duvall experiments with the magic globe. He is surprised and pleased to see the face of the girl he met in India. Further experiments, while in the cataleptic state, disclose part of the plot that resulted in the death of Grace's aunt, which has cheated her out of the fortune.

Duvall seeks out Grace to explain his strange experiments. She tells him that previous to the death of the countess she had seen her will and that the entire fortune, which included one million dollars in cash, was to be left to her. Grace is puzzled when the count produces a new will in which he is named as sole beneficiary. Duvall succeeds in having his East Indian servant, Purtab Gar, secure a position in the count's home. Then he proceeds to unravel the mystery and at the same time recover the one million dollars for Grace. Count D'Estes is driven to distraction by finding, everywhere he turns in his home, cards that read; "I want One Million Dollars. Victor Gerard."

Disguised as Victor Gerard, Duvall pays a visit to the count. He insists that one million dollars be ready for him at midnight, when he will call again. D'Estes notifies the police and the chief calls in Duvall to assist in solving the mystery and in apprehending Gerard. Duvall outlines a plan in which the count is directed to have the money as demanded. He assures that the premises will be well protected and that Gerard cannot escape. Gerard arrives at the appointed time and mysteriously disappears, together with the money, as the police close in. Duvall walks out of a room where they think they have Gerard trapped. Count D'Estes accuses Grace of stealing the money and attempts to strangle her when Purtab Gar saves her. Duvall succeeds in obtaining a confession of the murder from the housekeeper, when he traps her as she is about to poison Grace. Duvall explains everything to the mystified police. D'Estes is carried off under arrest and Grace and Duvall are left happily together.

For the most part a straightforward mystery, *One Million Dollars* would never have found shelter in these pages were it not for that bloody crystal ball, or for those cataleptic states and astral projections, none of which seems to figure in the unfolding of Duvall's grand scheme. Inasmuch as the crystal came from a Buddhist monk — Who has ever known a saffron-robed holy man to go protesting or begging without one? — there can be no question of fraud or mechanical trickery. Somehow, though, the supernatural has intruded into what otherwise seems like a rather predictable social melodrama, and that's why this title is here.

None of the contemporary critiques dwells on these supernatural elements, nor does anyone wonder at the density of the Machiavellian count, who never once marvels at how the arrival of the mansion's newest lackey coincides with the sudden plethora of extortion notes. And as for that plethora of pithy extortion demands: Writer's cramp acquired in the process of producing a flurry of criminally-oriented stationery would figure into more than one other cinematic "classic" of detective-oriented ratiocination. Just ask Charlie Chan.

This Rolfe Photoplay was based on Arnold Fredericks' *One Million Francs*, a piddling novel that we read on a rainy Sunday afternoon. ("Not bad. Not *good*, but not bad.") The novel contains no mention of crystal-carrying Buddhists, but it does turn on that highly improbable escape (involving crepe hair and cleverly-stowed raiment) from a locked-and-surrounded room. Fredericks was a pseudonym of Frederic Arnold Kummer, whose one, true, performance-art claim to fame was his having written the book and lyrics to fit Victor Herbert's music for the 1920 musical *My Golden Girl*. It ran for a while (about 100 performances) on Broadway and featured such notable singing actors as Ned Sparks and Edna Mae Oliver (and we're not kidding, either). Other than his stage and screen credits (in 1914, under his own name, Kummer dashed off some stories that served as the basis for some comedy/mystery shorts that featured "Octavius, the Amateur Detective"), the author/playwright penned any number of monographs and articles for contemporary magazines. Born in Maryland in 1873, he died in Maryland seven decades later; the reason why he chose to set *One Million Dollars'* source novel in France rather than, say, Baltimore, was buried with him.

The logic behind scenarist George D. Proctor's decision to abandon all that was French (save for that flock of patronymics) and instead to begin in India, repair to London, and settle (finally) in New York, was likewise interred with his bones. It was he, we guess, who injected all the supernatural blather into the story, so he beareth the blame for having it all peter out so flaccidly. Come on! That business about astral bodies and whatnot would naturally lead one to believe that Duvall's escape from the room was accomplished by other means than false beards and baggy overcoats.

Briton William Faversham won more (and better) notices for his stage work than ever he did for his screen stuff, even though his Q-factor (back in 1918) was staunch enough to permit his being celebrated in/by the doubtless-inspiring short, *William Faversham in a Liberty Loan Appeal*. We're out on a not-terribly strong limb when we claim that the Londoner's name *might* strike a chord with fans of 1934's troubled marriage of French bibliophilism and Universal Pictures, *Secret of the Chateau*, in which the actor portrayed a false-beard-wearing heavy that almost no one could keep track of (or interest in) in the course of the movie's 66-minute running time. 20 years earlier — when *One Million Dollars* was on the cusp of its release — the 16 October 1915 edition of *The Moving Picture World* lauded Faversham (and director John W. Noble) for being fleet of foot (or is that "fleet of footage"?) by managing to polish off the picture in under three weeks; said rush was due to the British actor feeling the heat caused by prior contractual obligations. The 20 November 1915 number of the same journal opined that "Mr. Faversham gives a good impersonation of the international, cold-blooded crime detector," without hypothesizing whether a few more weeks in front of the camera would have warmed either the actor's performance or the *MPW*'s assessment of it.

As for director John W. Noble, please see our remarks on *Black Fear* (also 1915).

Henry Bergman's name is forever associated with Charlie Chaplin's and not that of William Faversham. Before his involvement with the Little Tramp, though, he was a constant presence at the Yonkers studios of Rolfe Photoplays, Inc., and his most notable pre–*One Million Dollars* title there might well have been *Destiny; Or, the Soul of a Woman* (earlier in 1915), wherein he foreshadowed his *Million* role as the greedy count by playing "Avarice." Those interested in further details on Mr. Bergman might wish to consult almost any of the published or on-line works concerning Mr. Chaplin.

Carlotta De Felice (aka *Charlotte* De Felice and Carlotta De *Felico*) didn't receive much press (that we could find), and the items we could locate don't have her participating in many more than a dozen pictures in the course of four or five years. This may indicate either that Ms. De Felice was rather pretty without being particularly capable, or that she was fairly capable without necessarily being pretty. Or any combination thereof, sans that *je ne sais quoi* that others in that same boat had, which kept their boats afloat longer than hers. This appears to have been the actress's only genre credit, and the only commentary on her Grace Ellicott that merits mention was from that selfsame 20 November *MPW* piece that did William Faversham no favors: "Carlotta De Felice has the role of the niece of the Count D'Este [*sic*]."

Considering that the splendidly appreciative Buddhist monk in the first reel set up all the supernatural stuff that followed

(but, alas, did not follow far enough), one might think his impersonator would have earned the right to see his name in print somewhere. Anywhere. Alas! (Part II), even had he been portrayed by a doubling Arthur Morrison — who *did* get screen credit for the colorfully monickered Purtab Gar — neither monk nor Morrison was acknowledged for the feat. Mr. Morrison, at home more with the Old West than the Far East, saw his movie career wane at the end of the 1920s and vanish when the decade turned over. (And how many silent movie folk were on *that* boat?) His genre appearances — other than the picture at hand — were limited to *The Curious Conduct of Judge Legarde* (see entry), which was later released as *The Valley of Night*. Inasmuch as the actor's role in *Legarde* seems to have been one of only a very few that survived the transition to *Valley* without a similar change in nomenclature, for Morrison we can count those two releases as only one picture.

— *JTS*

One Way Street

One Way Street. First National Pictures/First National, 12 April 1925, 6 reels/5600 feet [LOST]
CAST: Ben Lyon (*Bobby Austin*); Anna Q. Nilsson (*Lady Sylvia Hutton*); Marjorie Daw (*Elizabeth Stuart*); Dorothy Cumming (*Lady Frances Thompson*); Lumsden Hare (*Sir Edward Hutton*); Mona Kingsley (*Kathleen Lawrence*); Thomas Holding (*John Stuart*)
CREDITS: *Producer* Earl Hudson; *Director* John Francis Dillon; *Scenario* Arthur Statter, Mary Alice Scully; based on the eponymous novel by Beale Davis (New York, c. 1924); *Adaptation* Earl Hudson; *Cinematographer* Arthur Edeson

Our synopsis is cobbled together from material in *Exhibitor's Herald* (4 April 1925) and the Library of Congress copyright summary, dated 20 March 1925:

> Bobby Austin is sent to Madrid on a diplomatic mission. He is followed by Lady Sylvia Hutton, a society adventuress who is infatuated with him. She takes him on a yachting trip to Monte Carlo where he meets Kathleen Lawrence, a notorious "kept" woman, who tries to save him from the ruin that Lady Sylvia bears in her wake. Sylvia takes up with another man and Bobby turns to Kathleen. He loses his post, returns to London, and makes his living by his card winnings. Refusing to return to Lady Sylvia when she wants him back, she is revenged by slipping an ace into his hands. He is branded a cheat. In the meantime, Kathleen meets Elizabeth Stuart, a sweet young girl whom she knows is a good match and will save Bobby from the fate that threatens him.
> Elizabeth finds proof of Lady Sylvia's duplicity and confronts her with the evidence. Lady Sylvia goes into a violent rage. She suddenly changes — her great beauty fades and leaves her a bent, wrinkled old hag. The she confesses that a famous surgeon had restored her youth so that she could return to claim the admiration of a society which had thrown her aside. Lady Sylvia confesses that Bobby had not cheated. His honor restored, Bobby is free to tell Elizabeth of his love, while Lady Sylvia, now a bent, haggard old woman, finds solace in her husband's arms.

Given the fairly large number of rejuvenation films of the 1920's, it had to fall to one of them to repose at the bottom of the barrel, and *One Way Street* seems to have claimed squatter's rights. Regardless of the literary merits of Gertrude Atherton's 1923 *Black Oxen* or Marie Corelli's 1918 *The Young Diana* (we cover the film versions of both elsewhere herein), at least those works dealt head-on with the theme. Not so Beale Davis' 1924 prose from which the plot summarized above was derived. *That* consisted of little more than pure romance/soap opera, and, in the denouement—when ingénue Elizabeth bears proof that the infamous stacked deck belonged to cougar Sylvia—there's not so much as a hint of an Ayesha moment:

> Sylvia made her decision quickly. She was beaten, and knew it. Elizabeth had said that she could prove the facts about the pack of cards and she was convinced that she could make good her claim. And that interview with Bobby! Did she know all of that too? That she had begged him—almost on her knees—for his love,—and he had refused it. Better to retire with such tatters of her old supremacy as remained, than to have them completely torn from her back by this girl, against whom she had no weapon. That interview with Bobby! Every humiliating detail of it was as clear as if it had occurred that afternoon. Let them guess what they pleased. Anything rather than to sit and listen to it repeated.

> Slowly, almost lazily, she rose from her chair. Deliberately, she closed the big feather fan which she held in her hand. The eyes of everyone in the room were fastened on her. Look for look, she returned their glances. "You are quite right. I did do it—and if the occasion arose, would do the same thing again."

Even given the chaos at First National—with the company's crews rapidly and simultaneously grinding out three other pictures—it's hard to fathom how studio honcho Earl Hudson could okay tripe like this as source material for a fourth ... and for a souped-up rejuvenation flick, no less. One can only hope that Lady Sylvia's thick skin rubbed off on all concerned, the better to digest the critical drubbing that *One Way Street* took. First whacks went to the 4 April 1925 *Harrison's Reports*:

> The most sensible thing for First National to do with this picture is to take their medicine manfully and lay the picture on the shelf, charging up the expense to experience. If the dialogue subtitles were omitted, there would be no picture. There is no plot, no human interest, and none of the characters arouses any interest in what he or she does.... Not worth showing even on a stormy night.

The *Exhibitor's Trade Review* of the same day was just as unrelenting:

> It is extremely doubtful whether *One Way Street* will prove a successful box-office attraction, for it appears to be sadly lacking in what is known as audience appeal. ... The machinery in this production not only creaks but groans laboriously.

From *Motion Picture News*, 11 April 1925:

> So much stress is laid upon painting the central figure's character that one naturally expects some dramatic fireworks will develop. But when the explosion comes it presents little reason making such a fuss over it. Pathological stories are not well suited for screen expression. They invariably defy logic. And this particular story is faulty and inconsistent all the way. It depends upon a surprise ending for its punch, but the scene is so unconvincing that one wonders how it ever appeared to its sponsors as picture material.... The picture seems to us, pointless and weak.

MPN went on to dash the hopes of those looking the thrill of a good ol' gruesome transformation scene: "Now monkey glands that refuse to function might bring on a sagging of facial muscles, but they wouldn't take the curl out of her hair nor the make-up off her face. It's a ridiculous transformation."

Consensus had it that Anna Q. Nilsson (bio found in *Between Friends*, 1924) failed to turn in much of performance, and this strikes us as being a bit odd considering that only a year earlier—for a similar part in *Vanity's Price* (see entry)—she had received generally top marks. With respect to *Street*, *ETR* assessed, "The role is not one well suited for her talents, and in her endeavor to bring out the note of tragedy, she overacts her part." (The vox populi, though, may have been quite different. An Anna fan wrote into the *Chicago Daily Tribune*, "What a wonderful actress is Anna Q. Nilsson! I have just returned from seeing her in *One Way Street*, and if I had missed that picture I think I would have cried *real salt tears*." Anyone know what they called groupies back in 1925?)

Ben Lyon, whose performance was also viewed askance by *ETR* ("not of the best quality"), would go on to bigger and better things. A veteran of the stage before his Hollywood years—and arguably more successful in talkies than he was in silent films—

Anna Q. Nilsson and Ben Lyon exchange soulful glances, which are cheaper than gifts, in *One Way Street.*

Lyon's most heralded screen performance came in Howard Hughes' *Hell's Angels* (1930). Away from the cinema — and together with his wife, actress Bebe Daniels — Ben regularly entertained World War II–era Londoners on a radio show entitled "Hi Gang." Ever the showman, Ben Lyons died while in the capacity of entertainment director aboard the steamship, Queen Elizabeth II, at the age of 71.

— SJ

The Outsider

The Outsider. Fox Film Corp./Fox Film Corp, 17 January 1926, 6 reels/5424 feet [LOST]

CAST: Jacqueline Logan (*Leontine Sturdee*); Lou Tellegen (*Anton Ragatzky*); Walter Pidgeon (*Basil Owen*); Roy Atwell (*Jerry Sidon*); Charles Lane (*Sir Jasper Sturdee*); Joan Standing (*Pritchard*); Gibson Glowland (*Shadow*); Bertram Marburgh (*Dr. Talley*); Crauford Kent (*Dr. Ladd*); Louis Payne (*Dr. Helmore*)

CREDITS: *Presented by* William Fox; *Director* Rowland V. Lee; *Adaptation* Robert N. Lee; based on the eponymous play by Dorothy Brandon (London, 1926); *Cinematographer* O.G. Post; *Assistant Director* Daniel Keefe

Elsewhere in this volume we have railed against melodramas featuring generic mystical types whose preternatural powers led them either to hurt or heal, depending upon their particular personality-proclivity and/or sexual intensity, the alignment of the stars, and/or the bent of the scenario. Whatever we said there, we would say here, too, if only we could remember it. One might think that, by January 1926, the notion of faith-healing, or love-healing, or anything-other-than-recognized-medical/surgical-healing would have been passé. The Twenties were Roaring, the bathtub gin was flowing, the Als were Capone-ing, and all was— if not well in the world — at least safely predictable within these United States. Enough already with the turban'd swamis who were in tune with The Other Side; God (the real One!) was in His Heaven, "Silent Cal" Coolidge — patron saint of the American cinema — was in the White House, and Ethel Barrymore, Edith Barrett and Walter Hampden were on Broadway in *The Merchant of Venice*.

This was probably not lost on Rowland V. Lee, just as the bona fides associated with Mr. Lee's name are not lost on genre lovers worth their salt. (For genre lovers still working on their salt, Mr. Lee was the guiding force behind the first two Warner Oland Fu Manchu films and the last two Universal horror films [*Son of Frankenstein* and *Tower of London*] of the 1930s. Plus a batch of gems from other genres which you will have to examine elsewhere.) Anyhow, Rowland hired his brother, Robert (as he would for *Tower of London*), to adapt Dorothy Brandon's eponymous stage play (that had starred Lionel Atwill and Katharine Cornell a couple of years earlier), which was fortuitously set in a clime other than the United States. Like England. What with the sun never setting (at that point) on the British Empire, turban'd swamis were as likely to be encountered in London's manor houses as were Cockney flower girls in Covent Garden. *But* ... playwright Brandon had done the formula one better and had made her pivotal mystic not just another Sensitive from the Sub-Continent, but, rather, a gypsy miracle-worker fresh

from the campfires that ringed Budapest. And if *that* didn't get 'em to fork over the price of admission, nothing would.

It didn't, actually, and that might go a ways in explaining why *The Outsider* doesn't immediately jump to mind when one brings up Jacqueline Logan or Walter Pidgeon or Lou Tellegen or Rowland V. Lee.

Das plot, courtesy of les copyright registration documents:

> Leontine Sturdee, an aristocratic English dancer, goes to a Gypsy camp in Hungary to learn some native dances and there meets Anton Ragatzy, a mystic who has effected many impressive cures. Leontine sustains an injury so serious that she is unable to walk, but she refuses the help of Ragatzy, whom she considers a fraud. Leontine returns to England, and leading British surgeons pronounce her a hopeless cripple. Ragatzy comes to England and begs Leontine (whom he has come to love) for a chance to cure her. She consents, but at first he can do nothing for her. As he is about to leave her, however, Leontine realizes that she loves Ragatzy and walks to him.

Well, much like the Lady or the Tiger, we are left to our own devices to choose whether Anton did, in fact, do the mystic deed, or whether love (as the plot précis would have us believe) was the true cause of Leontine's hopping out of bed, doing the kazatsky, and then falling for Ragatzy. It does make (something of) a difference, because — if Leontine was right all along and Ragatzky was a fraud — we're left with faith/love healing and, Jeebus only knows, we're up to *here* with that. On the other kéz (that's *hand* in Hungarian), if Anton had pronounced the words, performed the ritual, waved the wand (or whatever), and it just *took a while* for the magic to sink in (what with Leontine being a skeptic and all), he was the Real Deal, and we've got a body-of-the-book entry, rather than still more appendix-fodder. We're not sure which was the better take, as the critiques the picture received had a tendency to lump it with the batch of post–*Miracle Man* pictures that went looking to cash in on the public's hopes, fears, dreams, and, *well* ... cash.

The 24 January 1926 *Moving Picture World* leaned toward the love business, claiming the film "offers no particular argument for faith-healing, but by mixing romance with idea, developes [*sic*] appeal." *Variety* (24 February 1926), in elaborating on the plotline, also seems to indicate that love trumps faith. After having severely injured herself while trying to learn the Gypsy moves, she returns to London, where her ol' dad tells her that she's about had it, walking-wise. Then, "the faith healer returns, forces his way into her home, and takes her away for almost a year, in which time he cures her of her affliction. She, in turn, falls in love with him. Finally it is her love that gives her the faith to walk, and the cure is complete."

If we had stopped there, the faith-forceful entry-abduction-some cure-love-faith-total cure progression would have cleared things up quite nicely. But *nooooo!* We had to come upon the 23 January 1926 *Harrison's Reports*:

> Its one drawback ... is the fact that the would-be hero, a healer or a hypnotist, does not awaken any sympathy, because he allows his primitive nature to control him; he uses his mystic power to charm the heroine, making her fall in love with him. Had he been shown as a good fellow, using his power unselfishly at all times, he would have awakened warm sympathy. The picture, then, would have appealed to everybody.

Well, if the "hero" is a rotter — using his healing powers or his hypnotic powers or his sexy moves or whatever to force our poor girl into demonstrating feelings of affection for him — then he is no better than a dancing Svengali. And rather than awakening the kind of warm sympathy that would have led to universal appeal, he stirred merely (we assume) *tepid* sympathy, and the film was thus doomed to be found unappealing by that segment of the movie-going population who wanted the Boy to win the Girl fair and square.

All three of the above-cited trade journals were effusive with faint praise for the picture. *Harrison's*, for example, thought it had "moments of real interest," while *Variety* opined that "the picture measure[s] up fairly well with the regular run of program stuff." We still don't know whether Ragatsky and Leontine danced their way to wholeness, or whether the healing process involved pentagrams and the light of the full moon, or whether full recovery incorporated telling one's fortune while picking one's pocket. All we can say for sure is that, were there not the added wrinkle of much of this baloney taking place in a Gypsy camp where the extras doubtless were all accoutered in shmatas and handlebar moustaches, this title would have been an also-ran in our essay on *The Miracle Man*.

The skeptical Leontine was played by the lovely Jacqueline Logan (see *A Blind Bargain* and *The Leopard Lady*), while Lou Tellegen (*Between Friends*) and Walter Pidgeon (*The Gorilla*) provided the male histrionics. Enacting the impotent force of medical science — Leontine's father, surgeon Sir Jasper Sturdee — was Charles Lane, who was a bit more useful to the plot development of the 1920 *Dr. Jekyll and Mr. Hyde*, wherein he was Dr. Richard Lanyon to the Great Profile's schizophrenic lead. Lane, not to be confused with the identically-monikered character actor (*Twentieth Century*, *You Can't Take It with You*) who lived into his 103rd year, basically wrapped his career in 1929, a year highlighted for him by *The Canary Murder Case*, first of the onscreen adventures of Philo Vance.

As for the faith vs. love Cage Match fought in *The Outsider*, we can do no better than to cap this discussion with the words of *MPW*'s George T. Purdy: "In the final analysis you discover that the gypsy-gent healer's power over the girl was due to the fact that she reciprocated his affections, which doesn't say much for his chances with ordinary patients who couldn't all be expected to love him."

Yeah! What *he* said… — *JTS*

Peer Gynt

Peer Gynt. The Oliver Morosco Photoplay Company/Paramount Pictures, 16 September 1915, 5 reels, reels one, three, four and five at Library of Congress
CAST: Cyril Maude (*Peer Gynt*). Myrtle Stedman (*Solveig*); Fanny Stockbridge (*Ase*); Mary Reubens (*Anitra*); Mary Ruby (*Ingrid*); Winifred Bryson (*Annabel Lee*); Evelyn Duncan (*Virginia Thorne*); Kitty Stevens (*Notanah*); Herbert Standing (*St. Peter*); Charles Ruggles (*The Button Moulder*); William Desmond (*The Parson*); Juan de la Cruz (*Robert*); Alma Rubens.
CREDITS: *Director* Oscar Apfel; *Scenario* Oscar Apfel; based on the eponymous play by Henrik Ibsen (Copenhagen, 1867); *Music* George W. Beynon

NOTE: Modern sources say Raoul Walsh was assistant director.
"The devil has no more stauncher ally than the Want of Perception."

— Henrik Ibsen

Some literary works were simply beyond the power of silent cinema to handle effectively. The best way to do silent Shakespeare was not to do it at all; Asta Nielsen proved that with her version of *Hamlet*, which was based not on the Bard but rather on earlier versions of the tragic Prince's tale that Shakespeare had incorporated into his play. Nielsen's film thus gave a new and unconventional perspective on some very familiar characters while other silents taken from Shakespeare's plays could do little more than recap the plots and take a select few verses to use for the title cards. This was hardly a good substitute for actually *hearing* Shakespeare's poetry. Still, at least Shakespeare's plays did have plots; Henrik Ibsen's *Peer Gynt* is a dramatic poem and, as such, is far from traditional storytelling. Ibsen incorporated folk tales and legends into his account of the real and imagined adventures of a lazy braggart who doesn't realize until the very end of his existence that he's lived without commitment and has understood nothing; Meant as a satire of Norway's self-satisfied bourgeoisie, the poem had not been written for the stage, but, in 1876 — nine years after the book was published to more criticism than acclaim — Ibsen did a five-act version with Edvard Grieg writing the incidental music. The play was later translated into English and provided one of the last roles for stage legend, Richard Mansfield, best known in these pages for *Dr. Jekyll and Mr. Hyde*.

In the summer of 1915, famous British actor/stage manager, Cyril Maude, was just wrapping up a tour of the United States when he was approached by the Oliver Morosco Photoplay Company about appearing in a film version of *Peer Gynt*. Like many other stage actors, Maude did not have a high opinion of the silent drama, but as he was offered a "record sum" to go slumming, he consented. (Some say, though, that the real incentive was not the quick cash but the opportunity to act as front-man for some British investors trying to buy a pumice mine.) No doubt Morosco, anticipating considerable skepticism about the project from the intelligentsia, wanted a renowned stage actor to lend it an air of legitimacy. Nevertheless, the publicity department was a bit less interested in selling the film as an adaptation of a classic than in promoting it as a romance by stressing the "five beautiful women" who are part of Peer Gynt's adventures. Based on the Library of Congress synopsis that follows, they were perhaps just being honest:

When a capricious Gubrandsdal bride refuses to come out to be married, the rollicking Peer Gynt pretends to lend a hand but once he has coaxed the girl out of the cabin he claps the bridegroom in and, locking the door on the howling swain, spirits the not unwilling girl to a cave in the woods in the mountains. Banished for "bride theft," Peer begins a worldwide wandering and his susceptibility to beautiful women plunges him into thrilling experiences with beauties typical of any land and clime. But one after another they reveal selfish ends and work to his undoing. He loses his sailing ship and narrowly escapes irons when his beautiful Annabel Lee turns out to be an agent from the secret service on his trail for slaving. By mere luck he emerges unscathed from a duel he is dragged into by an aristocratic little flirt of old Virginia. An Indian girl in the North woods inveigles him out of his precious pelt of silver fox and then deserts him and his escape from lurking red-skins is by such a hair that a rifle bullet knocks the very paddle out of his hands. Years pass but do not bring him any better women and he falls victim to the voluptuous charms of Anitra, a soulless dancing girl of the desert, only to have her strip him of the very gems in his turban and the rings upon his fingers. Age finds him an embittered, cynical old man and Peer Gynt drifts back to Gubrandsdal to die but he finds there waiting the faithful sweetheart of his wild youth, the pure gentle Solveig, as lovely a character as man ever left weeping behind him. So when the Button Moulder, personifying the Saver of Souls, comes to cast Peter back into the melting pot to be moulded over because his wasted life proves him without design, it is Solveig's devotion which saves him. The good in him has lived after all in her faith, in her hope and in her love.

The synopsis omits Peer's stay in the land of the trolls, but reviews indicate the sequence was very brief. Other macabre elements in the film include an appearance to Solveig of a sinister preacher (William Taylor) who turns out to have cloven hooves. He returns near the end of the film, when Peer begs him for a place in hell since he's already been rejected by St. Peter because of his sinful life; however, the devil — who carries a butterfly net — tells Peer that his sins are trivial and that he's not bad enough for hell, but should simply submit to getting melted down by the Button Moulder. There is also an eerie moment during a shipwreck sequence wherein a decidedly creepy character approaches Peer and asks, "If you flounder, may I have your body? I'm a great collector of corpses." This incident is right out of the play and has always puzzled Ibsen interpreters, but the Great Man himself said it was only "a caprice."

Walter Pritcher Easton (in the 29 September 1915 *Boston Evening Transcript*) wrote that Cyril Maude had debased his standing and had sold his soul for silver by appearing in such a travesty of Ibsen. Easton, who admitted he was bored by movies, found the film "ludicrous" and "pathetic" and expressed dismay that people who had never read the book or seen the Mansfield play would get a totally wrong impression of what the Ibsen masterpiece was all about.

The New York Times critic was able to keep his composure, but still felt the film was a good illustration of the limitations of the movies:

> The thread of the story, plus some of the exuberance of the invention — these are used but that it is all. The poetry is almost completely missing as if it had never been conceived. All the implications of this song of a self wasted soul are gone. Of course its finer subtleties and all of its social satire are left untouched but most of the poem's conspicuous beauties also escaped the camera.... *Peer Gynt* is a great adventure always but *Peer Gynt* on the screen is as subtle and significant as the story of "Sinbad the Sailor" ... to call it "Peer Gynt" is in the nature of an impertinence [20 September 1916].

In the 11 October 1915 edition of *The* [New York] *Independent*, the film critic took the opposite tack and proclaimed that Ibsen's original was perfect for the movies:

> The peculiar blending of the symbolic and the supernatural with the directest realism which was Ibsen's specialty is exactly the sort of thing that can be much better done with the resources of the camera than actors on stage. It was only because the invention of the cinematograph was so delayed that Ibsen was compelled to turn from his poetic allegories to realistic social dramas with five or so actors and no cost worth mentioning for scenery.

The reviewer had high praise for Cyril Maude's interpretation of Peer as "half Peter Pan, half Kipling's Tomlinson." He did feel, though, that the film would have been better served by sticking to Peer's encounters with the supernatural rather than inventing adventures for him in America.

The trade papers, not overawed by great literature, were very positive about the film, with Harvey F. Thew of *Motion Picture News* (18 September 1915) lauding writer/director Oscar Apfel for making "almost a continuous, coherent story out of Peer Gynt's allegorical vagaries":

> The director has not attempted to make much more than a series of "romantic episodes" out of the tale. In some cases allegory is dragged in so unexpectedly that the spectators wonder what has become of the story, and a little trimming in other places would let the public more into the actors' confidence, but the locations have been so carefully selected, the lighting and time arranged with such expert knowledge of photography, that every foot of the film is enjoyable.

Still, Thew was annoyed by the dueling scene which is supposed to take place at dawn but, judging from the shadows, was actually filmed at noon. He was even more irritated that "Peer Gynt is abandoned on a desert shore where he wanders alone 'for months.' But at the end of all his wandering, his flannel trousers are still carefully creased. They tell us there is a way of pressing pants like this under a mattress, but no mattress is introduced on the desert shore."

"Jolo" of *Variety* (24 September 1915) also noticed the pressed trousers, but felt that *Peer Gynt* was such a great film that it would be nitpicking to point out the mistake (though *Variety* could usually be expected to pounce on just such minor lapses of realism). "Jolo" had nothing but glowing words for the film, especially Cyril Maude's performance: "Throughout he literally 'exudes' the spirit of romance. His 'swashbuckling' recalls the younger Salvini's performance of D'Artagnan which has again gone down into history as a classic. Then again when, as an old man, he has an encounter with an allegorical Mephisto, he suggests the best character work of Albert Chevalier."

A good deal was made of the music that accompanied the film on its premiere:

> This photoplay for the first time in history of regular program releases is to be set entirely to specially prepared music. George W. Beynon, who is known to the music world as an orchestration writer of wide repute, has arranged with the Oliver Morosco Photoplay Co. to arrange a specially written introductory overture and following music to fit each foot of the film with Grieg's immortal melodies representing the different characters Peer meets in his wanderings so interwoven as not only to bring out the thought of Ibsen and Grieg but to positively identify the characters themselves.... By reason of this ... the producers have been able to eliminate sub-titles which otherwise would have been absolutely necessary [*Logansport* (Indiana) *Pharo Reporter*, 11 September 1915].

MPN's Harvey Thaw found the score "admirably adapted to the spirit of the film" and described it as ranging "from the heavy harmony of Grieg to Southern plantation melodies. It seems to us a gross mistake however, to introduce a vocal solo just as the picture approaches one of its most dramatic situations."

We have seen the Library of Congress print of *Peer Gynt* which, unfortunately, lacks the second reel wherein Peer encounters the trolls. Also, many scenes in the third and fourth reels are out of order (Maestro Beynon's musical clues might have been helpful), but we were able to figure most of it out, nonetheless. It may not be Ibsen, but it's highly entertaining: a well produced, fast-moving, tongue-in-cheek adventure with a likeable scoundrel as the central character. There are also some nice touches of humor: at one point, when his crew him leaves him stranded, Peer curses the departing ship and, moments later, it sinks. His temporary satisfaction fades when he realizes that his own dire situation is not in the least bit alleviated. Later, trudging across the desert, he cries out, "My kingdom for a horse" and then, thinking better of such a rash offer, says, "Half my kingdom for a horse." Maude's zestful performance lives up to the critical acclaim it received in 1915, and his transformation from amoral youth to grasping, middle-aged adventurer to pathetic and desperate old man is helped greatly by his splendid makeup (which Maude did himself).

Maude found making *Peer Gynt* strenuous and exhausting and kept a very droll diary about the week he spent shooting the film; the diary was printed in the December 1915 issue of *Sunset* (and elsewhere), and Maude later incorporated it into his autobiography. The veddy, *veddy* British (and quite proper) stage actor was nonplussed by the way the movie was shot out of continuity and, while he was certainly familiar enough with Ibsen, he was sometimes baffled by the Hollywood version. Maude was rushed back and forth from forest to desert to mountains and was obliged to keep changing from young to old Peer a couple of times a day. He was also rather disconcerted by the scene in which he has to flee angry Indians by canoe and then engage in a knife fight in the water with one of his pursuers (this after having had his paddle shot out of his hand with real bullets):

But the first Indian was short of breath and, I hear, was funky of my knife, having once before done this sort of thing and having been stabbed by his excited enemy. So I had to do it all over again with another Indian who looked like Sir Henry Irving when young and he came after me quite ferociously and we had an awful ducking together and I sputtered to his side and was dragged out more dead than alive.

He found the shipwreck sequence equally trying:

Five or six men stood at the corners of the platform [of the mock-up of the ship] and tilted it this way and that while men overhead sprayed heavy rain on us from above and others showered buckets of water all over us; meanwhile bombs of lightning powder kept exploding, everybody shouted and cursed and the Devil or Death or something horrible came out of the cabin and glared at me and then came an awful scene with any amount of terribly realistic waves coming over me — and at last home to bed by one o'clock.

It's perhaps not surprising that, when later asked how he felt about acting in the movies, Maude replied that "next to being a stoker in the hold of a retreating battleship, it's the best job in the world." Maude was persuaded — again by a huge fee — to do one other Hollywood silent, *The Greater Will* (see entry), but there he was obliged to do nothing more taxing than to register a hypnotic stare.

Of the "five beautiful women" around and about Peer Gynt only one, Myrtle Stedman, had a notable film career. Stedman had trained as a singer and did become prima donna of the

Chicago Grand Opera; in addition, she toured with the Whitney Opera Company. Chicago was also the home of Selig Polyscope and, in 1911, Stedman — along with her actor/director husband Marshall Stedman — signed with them and went, apparently without skipping a beat, from light opera to horse opera; (it helped that she was an expert rider). She subsequently moved to Hobart Bosworth Productions where she appeared in a number of adaptations of Jack London stories, as well as in Lois Weber's controversial *Hypocrites*. After a brief time at Morosco, she became leading lady at Pallas Pictures (whose moves were distributed by Paramount) and scored a big success with *The American Beauty* (1916), wherein she played two parts. (Inasmuch as the klieg lights used for some interior shots in that film burned Stedman's eyes, it wasn't just the audience that was seeing double. Stedman, popularly known as the "girl with the search-light eyes" came close to needing an operation to clear her vision but in the end she fully recovered.)

The actress/singer also tried her hand at penning scenarios and wrote a couple of two-reelers (directed by husband Marshall) for Universal. She continued to sing as well, but, more often than not, it was for charity; (she frequently went to prisons to perform). Top-flight stardom eluded her and in the 1920s she played mostly supporting roles; by the 1930s, she was doing uncredited bit parts. In 1936 she was put under contract to Warner Bros, but this reflected a practice of the time in which a number of former stars were given studio contracts more in an effort to keep them off the dole than to make good use of their talents. In any case, Stedman died of heart trouble two years later.

The sinister Button Moulder was played by *Charles Ruggles*, of all people. Ruggles, whose comic antics in *Murders in the Zoo* and *Terror Aboard* can still cause horror fans to grind their dentures, is merely bland (rather than annoying) here. Conrad Veidt doubtless brought far more to the role when he played it in Richard Oswald's version of *Peer Gynt* in 1918.

In 1934 there was a second German version of *Peer Gynt*, this one tailored to the talents of Hans Albers; the fantastic elements of the poem were totally omitted. Seven years later, a film student at Northwestern University shot a silent version with Charlton Heston in the title role; the film was reissued years later with Francis X. Bushman providing a narration. Ibsen's story was also done for television numerous times.

A few words about Oscar Apfel can be found in the entry on *The Ghost Breaker* (1914).

While Ibsen cannot be said to have contributed much to the horror genre, Eduard Grieg's "In the Hall of the Mountain King," written for *Peer Gynt*, became the tune to commit murder by for movie psychos like Peter Lorre in *M* and Basil Rathbone in *Love From a Stranger*.

— *HN*

Peter Pan

Peter Pan. Famous Players–Lasky/Paramount Pictures, 29 December 1924, 10 reels/9593 feet, Eastman House
CAST: Betty Bronson (*Peter Pan*); Ernest Torrence (*Captain Hook*);

Cyril Chadwick (*Mr. Darling*); Virginia Brown Faire (*Tinker Bell*); Anna May Wong (*Tiger Lily*); Esther Ralston (*Mrs. Darling*); George Ali (*Nana, the Dog*); Mary Brian (*Wendy*); Philippe De Lacey (*Michael*); Jack Murphy (*John*)

CREDITS: *Presented by* Adolph Zukor, Jesse L. Lasky; *Director* Herbert Brenon; *Adaptation/Screenplay* Willis Goldbeck: Based on *Peter Pan, or the Boy Who Wouldn't Grow Up* (London, 1904), by James Matthew Barrie; *Cinematographer* James Wong Howe; *Special Effects* Roy Pomeroy

The story of the boy who won't grow up has appeared time and again in so many cinematic, theatrical and small-screen adaptations — and has been fodder for so many cartoons — that there may be kids out there who may never realize that some of the best Peter Pans ever over the years were gals. This wonderful 1924 version — the first to work its magic on the beaded screen — may have started that fashion, but who can be sure? Surviving records of earlier dramatic adaptations are just so: *surviving* records; only el buen Dios knows how many times, in how many burgs, how many distaff Peter Pans leapt (or were yanked) onto the stage to cross swords without subsequent press coverage.

The very first time Pan came onto the scene, he was constructed purely of ink and the alphabet, and wasn't even the center of attention. Rather, his debut was in J.M. Barrie's *The Little White Bird* (1902), an episodic novel that some literary critics came to regard as being slightly skewed toward a seamier side of life. Anyhow, in *Bird*, Peter Pan is scarcely a week old when he eschews life's mundane mores to hang with fairies and the like; thus, this was *not* the Peter Pan that would take Britain by storm. Still, the idea that a tyke could somehow forever put at arm's length his awkward teenage years, acne, and the stultifying pressures of the British Public School system — yet still arrive at the point when a winsome young wench named Wendy could give him pause — caught the public's fancy, and the character was brought back to the shop, tinkered with, and pushed out onstage in 1904.

Nobody's fool, Barrie did the tinkering himself, and *Peter Pan; or, the Boy Who Wouldn't Grow Up* opened to acclaim and cash, and even if the young protagonist's feet seldom hit the ground, the play had legs. The play also had an assemblage of what would prove to be timeless characters from the very beginning: Pan (of course), Tinker Bell, Wendy Darling (et frères), Captain Hook, Tiger Lily, the Lost Boys, and so on and so forth. Opening in London a couple of days after Christmas in 1904, *Peter Pan* was played by Nina Boucicault, daughter of Irish playwright, Dion Boucicault, whom we choose to remember for his 1852 play, *The Vampire* [!], which starred Dion Boucicault as the titular horror. Unlike her ol' dad — who'd made his name playwrighting over a dozen years prior to playacting — daughter Nina's celebrity came only after (and because of) playing Peter Pan. With or without her, the play became a British perennial, returning to the legitimate stage time and again throughout the 20th century, and appearing with greater frequency as a staple of English Christmas Pantomime.

If it was good enough for the West End, it was good enough for The Great White Way, and a production that starred the veteran actress, Maude Adams — still beauteous and limber enough for the requisite acrobatics at the advanced age of 33 — premiered at the Empire Theatre on the 6 November 1905. Adams reprised the role in three subsequent revivals — all staged at the Empire — in the course of the ensuing decade; she was 43 years of age the last time she foiled Hook's plans for domination. When it was next revived — during the mid–1920s — Peter was impersonated by Marilyn Miller and the role of Captain James' Hook was on the capable hand of Leslie [*The Most Dangerous Game, Transatlantic Tunnel*] Banks. Not long thereafter, Eve Le Gallienne did the cross-dressing (and shared the director's credit) for yet another (albeit brief) revival. Her Captain Hook was Egon Brecher — years before he creeped us out in 1934's *The Black Cat* — Smee was John (*Sh! The Octopus*) Eldridge, Wendy was Josephine (*Arsenic and Old Lace*) Hutchinson, and *Son of Dracula*'s canny (if somewhat corpulent) vampire-fighter, J. Edward Bromberg, was onstage, on all fours, as Nana.

In late April 1950, the play was revived yet again, albeit this time complemented by Leonard Bernstein's words and music. Running for well over 300 performances — and necessitating a change of theater, due to prior commitments — this first "Baby Boomer" version of *Peter Pan* starred Jean Arthur (in her 40s!) as the boy who won't grow up, and Boris Karloff as Captain Hook. Arthur had put up $25,000 of her own money into the production, but — in his article on Arthur in the June-July 1966 issue of *Films in Review* — Jerry Vermilye revealed that while the actress *was* following in Maude Adams' footsteps, "she was not doing so with ease." Arthur claimed vocal problems and took to writing to her colleagues offstage to conserve her voice. Per Vermilye: "Finally, claiming to have laryngitis, she notified the management, only two hours before curtain time, that not only was she not able to play that performance but she needed three weeks' rest." Actors' Equity arranged to have Arthur's contract cancelled, but — following concerns about Betty Field's assuming the role — Arthur was reinstated, her contract rewritten (Vermilye confessed that "few members of the cast were said to have been on Miss Arthur's side during the dispute"), and *Peter Pan* ran (or flew) for 321 performances. A set of 78rpm records of the score as performed by Arthur, Karloff, et al., was transferred to the more durable (and less ponderous) long-playing (LP) format the moment that technology settled in comfortably, and the association of Barrie's story with music and dance was pretty much set for good at that point.

Still, the Arthur/Karloff hit hadn't been absent from Broadway for much more than three seasons when the property was dusted off, new music and lyrics (Mark Charlap and Carolyn Leigh, respectively) were added, and — headed by a cast that would impress itself on the collective consciousness of a generation of Panatics — the limit was pushed above and beyond the sky: Mary Martin and Cyril Ritchard assumes iconic status both beneath the proscenium arch and on the small screen. The time was such that Television had seemingly found *The* Peter Pan and *The* Captain Hook.

Flashback to 1906. Happily surprised by the revenue-generating popularity of his flying boychik, Barrie reworked the chapter on the infant Pan from *The Little White Bird* and had same published — as a no-nonsense kiddies' book — as *Peter Pan in Kensington Gardens*. Money-wise, this scored barely a blip on the Pound-o-meter, so the diminutive scribe turned to his next Neverland spin-off, 1908's *When Wendy Grew Up — An After-*

thought. Researching this title has led us on a merry chase, with disparate information claiming it to be everything from a novel-length screed to an epilogue to the 1904 play, added by the playwright on the night the first London run ended so as to address the innumerable questions Barrie supposedly received about Wendy's future.

Following said *Afterthought*, the only Pan-path left for Barrie to traverse was an all-out novel recapping the action and featuring all the dramatis personae of the play that had packed them in at the Duke of York's Theatre. Thus, in 1911, *Peter and Wendy* made a collective appearance, and the work included as its final chapter the full text of *When Wendy Grew Up — An Afterthought*, the aforementioned curiosity that had made its debut (somehow) three years earlier. It was from this end-product that the scenario for the 1924 feature-length fantasy was crafted. And here, solely for the record, is the surely superfluous synopsis of *Peter Pan*.

> Peter Pan, the boy who never grew up, is looking for his shadow in the Darling nursery when he awakens the Darling children — Wendy, John, and Michael. Peter tells the children of the Never-Never Land, teaches them to fly, and guides them to his forest home, where he is the king of the Little Lost Boys. Tinker Bell, a fairy, becomes jealous of Wendy and persuades one of the boys to shoot her with an arrow. Wendy recovers and is adopted by the boys as their mother. Captain Hook, a notorious pirate whose hand Peter once cut off, kidnaps the children after a fierce fight with Indians who are the children's friends and guardians. Peter, discovering that the children are missing, goes to the pirate ship and frees them. The children fight the pirates and subdue them. Captain Hook is forced to walk the plank. Peter then returns with the Darling children to their nursery. Wendy asks him to stay, but Peter refuses and returns to his home in the woods.

The barely-18-year-old Betty Bronson donned the tights and feathered cap for this Famous Players–Lasky ten-reeler, and, and based on the film's success and the affection that audiences felt for the lovely lass from Trenton, New Jersey, she was then tapped to play the title role in *A Kiss for Cinderella*, a follow-up fairy-tale. In comparison with *Pan*, *Cinderella* tanked, and the momentum that had been building with respect to deluxe retellings of children's literature slowed to a standstill. Before all that happened, though, the papers were publicity rich for the Boy Who Wouldn't, etc. PR had it that J.M. Barrie had hand-picked Bronson for the role due to her terpsichoreal talent, while *sub rosa* bitchy gossip averred that he did so solely because the young actress— 5'0" in longitude — was the only Pan possibility over whom Barrie (at 5'2") could tower. Some sources reported that Mary Pickford (5½" [!], but 32 years old) was up for the part, while other scribes revealed that Gloria Swanson (5'1") was a shoe-in (if she wore flats). BS hasn't changed much in 90 years, has it?

(To get all the silliness out of the way right now, we address the conundrum that was J[ames] M[atthew] Barrie. Scots-born in May 1860, the author/playwright grew large in fame [he also penned *The Admirable Crichton* and *The Little Minister*] if not in frame, and there are online/in-print cinema blowhards who maintain that the persona of Peter Pan was the alter ego of this diminutive person who was a man in appearance only. Screeds positing that Barrie was a homosexual dismiss outright his marriage to actress Mary Ansell, arguing that the lady was a beard and that the union went unconsummated anyhow. Other writings focus [albeit with cocked eyebrow] on Barrie's closeness to the five sons of barrister Arthur Llewelyn Davies, preferring the suggestion that something untoward may very well have marked the boys' relationship with their "Uncle Jim" rather than the more widely held theory that the children served as inspiration for Peter, the Darling brothers, and the Lost Boys. Such speculation matters not at all at this late date [and should likewise have mattered not at all during the schizophrenic manifestations of the Victorian Era], but the silliness lies not in the man's being a homosexual or not: one's philosophy, disposition, and lifestyle do impact one's creativity, after all. Rather, it lies first in the effort to portray homosexuality as being intrinsically dirty and repulsive, and then in the subsequent suggestion that this tale of childhood and fantasy might legitimately be interpreted as being deviant and morally unhealthy. While it may have done nothing to silence his more salacious critics, Barrie's willing all profits and royalties from his sundry Peter Pan materials to London's Great Ormand Street Hospital for Children must surely be taken as a gesture of the man's concern for all those younger folk who might otherwise never, never have the chance to refuse to grow up.)

Captain Hook was ably played by Ernest Torrence (see *The Brass Bottle*), and Tiger Lily's exuberance was captured perfectly by the exotically beautiful Anna May Wong (see *Chinatown Charlie*). Calling the shots was Herbert Brenon (*A Daughter of the Gods*) and making sure those shots were in the frame was James Wong Howe — born Wong Tung Jim in what used to be called Canton, China — for whom *Peter Pan* would be the only Silent Era fantastic excursion. Howe had immigrated to the USA in 1905 and by 1917 was working as a clapper man (the guy who held the slate marking the scene for the cinematographer prior to the camera rolling) for Cecil B. De Mille. Canniness and a knack for being in the right place at the right time helped the young man up the ladder, photography-wise, and, by 1923, Howe was Director of Photography for Mary Miles Minter's *Drums of Fate*. Horror/mystery fans are indebted to Howe for the look of such Sound Era goodies as *The Spider*, *Chandu the Magician*, *The Thin Man*, and *Mark of the Vampire*, although the volume of his big-name, mainstream titles dwarfs his genre work. Between 1939 and 1976 — the year of his death — Howe was nominated for the Academy Award nine times, taking the Oscar home with him for 1955's *The Rose Tattoo* and 1963's *Hud*.

Howe's camerawork in *Peter Pan* is magical, and the scene wherein Peter flits about the Darling bedroom sans shadow is wonderfully effected, even if St. Peter on the lights couldn't have prevented Peter's flailing arms from casting shadows across his body. And Bronson's background in dance allowed her to prance hither, thither and yon with grace, if with a bit more of a feminine lilt than some young kid named Peter ought to be displaying. Despite the picture's not having been shot in sequence, the flying sequences seem to grow more accomplished as the picture progresses, although in the bedroom scene only Peter Pan appears to be actually flying; while the wires are not visible in the dim light, the Darlings seem to be hanging by their armpits as they are spun about by an industrial-strength ceiling fan. As for the balance of the film, special effects accomplished via forced perspective; actors made to cavort in animal costumes; lovely close-ups afforded Virginia Brown Faire's gorgeous Tinker Bell; take-offs, landings and short spurts of zipping through the ether: all are totally acceptable without ever being completely credible. Equally incredible is the complete lack of logic to be found in this (or any fairy tale)—Hook (backed by at least eight burly, armed pirates) opts to feed the crocodile the alarm clock rather than skewer its reptilian behind—but that sort of thing goes with the territory. And we hasten to add that there's nary a shred of complaint to be found in any of this assessment, either.

Barrie's story crossed the Atlantic way back then without losing too much in its translation into American. The greatest speed-bump in the path to acceptance by readers/listeners in the Colonies probably came in the need to comprehend fairies, a species as deeply engrained in the sitz-im-leben of pre-pubescent Brits as were Indians (and cowboys) in the minds of American boys. (Pirates and reptiles, on the other hand, have always been in the consciousness of the youth of just every Western nation.) Still, the story won big in an era in which childhood was celebrated as *the* forum for flights of fancy because it melded the least threatening denizens of the supernatural dimension, the most romantic and picturesque elements of real life, and

Striking artwork from one of the original window cards.

the anthropomorphosis of the animal world into one, enormously clever mix while a diapered Walt Disney was still toddling about his family's living room on North Tripp Avenue in Chicago.

Watching *Peter Pan* nowadays (we managed to view a German Arte television screening), one is struck by the simplicity of the picture's emotional palette: the sort of charming naiveté upon which fairy tales rely is here in spades, and the Millennium-Age viewer will probably have to strain to relate to or to recall the extent of innocence as displayed by the Darling children. As so often happens with the passage of time/the onset of sexual maturation, the manner in which the ideal parental/filial relationship is expressed in the film has become outdated and terms that once were commonplace are regarded now as being hopelessly corny. Can one even begin to imagine the following exchange taking place anywhere in the contemporary United States?

> "Can anything harm us, Mummy dear, after the night lights are lit?"
>
> "Nothing, precious. They are the eyes a mother leaves behind to guard her children."

And Mum's using her taper to rev up three nightlights when her children lie supine mere feet from a fireplace that's blazing away must be seen as being equally quaint.

But this is now, and that was then...

Critic Laurence Reid was taken by the whole thing, writing:

> Anyone, who having seen the play feels that the screen could not do it justice, must admit that it is a faithful reproduction—one that even goes so far as reproducing scene by scene and title after title from the spoken version.... There is delicate whimsy and fancifulness in the screen conception of the spirit of eternal youth—the note that the eminent Scot searched for and found in his creation [11 January 1925].

And we might as well take Reid's assessment and that of the 3 January 1925 *Harrison's Reports* as typical of the response the film received from the Usual Suspects:

> A wonderful picture, for its kind; it is a credit to the motion picture art.... Miss Betty Bronson seems to have been created for the part of Peter Pan.... Mr. Herbert Brenon deserves a great deal of credit for the piece; he has created his fantastic world with realism; one is made to feel as if the things one sees are possible; he has interpreted Mr. J.M. Barrie's book with a masterful touch.

Nonetheless, Harrison signed off by opining that *Peter Pan* might not do so well with male audiences, on whom fairy tales and costume plays usually made little impact.

During the 1910s—when feature-length pictures with genuine genre credentials were as scarce as facts at a political rally—there was produced and released a passel of cinematic fairy tales whose *raison d'être* was a) to expand the revenue base by insuring a second (or third, or fourth, or...) paid admission at the box office, and b) to provide entertainment for those citizens who couldn't reach high enough to push the money in through the ticket-booth window (or afford a ticket) themselves, which quandary thus led to a). We're talking titles like Daniel Frohman's *Cinderella* (1914), Thomas H. Ince's *Rumplestiltskin*, (1915), J. Searle Dawley's *Snow White* (1916), and Maurice Tourneur's *The Blue Bird* (1918). Also in the running were *semi*–fairy tales (emphasis ours) such as Mary Pickford's *Fanchon, the*

Cricket or Marguerite Clark's *The Goose Girl* (1917): syrupy moral lessons served up in only slightly less preposterous fashion. These offerings opened, made their way through their engagements, and then closed, in many cases having ended up in the black without much help at all from legions of male ticket-buyers. The seats were filled mainly with moms and squirts; dads, apparently, were up for flickers only when loose women were … ummm … running loose, or the photoplay turned on boxing, shooting, or some other act of virile violence.

Occasionally, these sorts of tales—by cynical definition, genre material for those with allowances, not on salaries—were supplanted/complemented by stories that were either set in mythical kingdoms or were chock-a-block with lower-shelf monstrosities that did *not* have their provenance in the imaginations of Aesop, Hans Christian Andersen, or the Brothers Grimm (see *Fantasma*). These items—perhaps best represented by 1914's autumn cloudburst of L. Frank Baum material (*The Magic Cloak of Oz, The Patchwork Girl of Oz,* and *His Majesty, the Scarecrow of Oz* put zillions of family-oriented bottoms in seats between the end of September and the Christmas holidays of that year)—had their (usually) kindhearted-if-misunderstood grotesques interacting with protagonists who were scarcely older than the audience members. Thus, the ratio of the "scare quotient" to the average age of the viewers was in direct proportion to the attendant indifference on the part of the male segment of the movie-going population and that all adds up to our mentioning only briefly the above titles, Betty Bronson's *A Kiss for Cinderella,* and so forth and so on. In this light, 1925's *The Wizard of Oz*—played more for laughs (from Larry Semon, Oliver Hardy, and an uncredited Spencer Bell) than for thrills (witchless, the picture's dramatic pivot turned on villains yclept Wikked, Kruel, and Vishuss)—may be seen as the nadir of the sub-genre.

This is not to say that supernatural elements toned down and played to the younger set are in any way less genuine or authentic than are those same elements, growed up and out for blood, when played for those who have attained their majority. Most of Lon Chaney's kindhearted-if-misunderstood grotesques made it through this filter because they were aimed at ticket-buyers who were either of the age to drink legally or to vote (with a nod at the 18th and 19th Amendments, respectively), and not at the wee bairn for whom the night light was Horatio at the bridge.

Our endeavor at hand, though, is to reach that same august body.   — *JTS*

The Phantom Honeymoon

The Phantom Honeymoon. J. Searle Dawley productions/Hallmark Pictures Corp. (Famous Directors Series), 19 October 1919, 6 reels, incomplete 16mm print at Library of Congress

CAST: Marguerite Marsh (*Betty Truesdale*); Vernon Steele (*Captain Bob Lambert*); Hal Clarendon (*Henry Claven*); Leon Dadmun (*Professor Tidewater*); Henry Guy Carlton (*Sakee*); Charles P. Patterson (*John Truesdale*); Grace Bryant (*Mrs. John Truesdale*); Harriet Cox (*Vera*); Katherine Perkins (*Caroline*); Edwin Poffley (*Rev. Thomas Peterkins*)

CREDITS: *Director* J. Searle Dawley; *Scenario* J. Searle Dawley

Among our rather tight little circle, J. Searle Dawley is celebrated chiefly for being the director (and scenarist) of the 1910 "Edison" *Frankenstein.* Dawley first showed up for work, though—megaphone in hand—in 1907 and ultimately was credited for some 90-odd short films, including *Bluebeard* (1909), *The House of the Seven Gables* (1910) and *The Ghost of Granleigh* (1913). Thence, he turned his attention and energies towards helming *Tess of the D'Urbervilles* (1913), his first feature and the first of 14 such pictures he directed for Famous Players; however, this didn't include *A Good Little Devil* (see entry), a Mary Pickford fantasy for which Edwin S. Porter got sole screen credit. For a couple of years there, Dawley's name was associated most frequently with that of petite gamin actress, Marguerite Clark, for whom he very nearly served as personal director; together they made *Snow White* (1916), the first live-action, feature-length version of the popular fairy tale, which was adapted from the Broadway stage version that had starred Miss Clark several years previously.

Outside said tight little circle, though, Dawley is best remembered for his role in helping establish the Motion Pictures Directors Association, the forerunner of the Directors' Guild of America. Nicely done, Mr. Dawley!

Nonetheless, to appreciate *The Phantom Honeymoon,* we need dwell neither on the man's earlier cinematic achievements nor on his organizational skills. Nothing else needs be considered for—in every sense of the word—J. Searle Dawley was the *auteur* of the picture highlighted herein.

First, the plot, as taken from the film's press-book:

Prof. Juno P. Tidewater, of the Psychological Research Society, has little faith in the ghost theory and for the purpose of substantiating his disbelief in ghosts, he, who is a kindly old soul, extremely human and a firm disbeliever in all "diabolical stuff," pays a visit to the famous Benmore Castle, which is said to be haunted. The professor and his two pretty nieces, Phyllis and Olive, are touring Ireland.

The story opens with the professor and his nieces seated in an Irish jaunting car, piloted by one Timothy Nolan, official guide and best-informed man in County Cork, Ireland. Timothy is describing the various points of interest when the party are brought face-to-face with the famous Benmore castle, the object of Prof. Tidewater's visit, after Timothy has explained that it is the haunted castle. At the word "haunted," the professor is all interest, and he commands Timothy to stop until he explores the grounds and gains entrance to see for himself the much-talked-about ghosts. Timothy explains that not a living soul goes near the place excepting Sakee, an old Indian servant who lives there alone. The professor and his two nieces start for the castle and are admitted after a long wait by the ghost-like person, Sakee. The two nieces refuse to accompany the professor inside, so he is left alone with Sakee. Sakee tells the professor that if he fears not the shades of death, he may enter.

Once inside the professor is told by Sakee that he is the first one to hear from his lips the true story of Benmore castle and its ghosts. In explanation of this Sakee shows the professor a telegram which reads:

"Sakee, Benmore Castle, Ireland:
At last your lips are unsealed. He died today.
(Signed) Hindlue"

Sakee explains that Prof. Tidewater is to hear what no one has ever heard before. Sakee waves his arm so as to include the wide, spacious walls of Benmore Castle, and explains that within those walls was born a great sorrow, a great love and a great mystery.

And the following is what took place within those halls three years before, during the most violent electrical storm that ever visited the old castle.

Robert Claven, a wealthy explorer and scientist who had spent most of his life in the Orient, had finally settles at Benmore castle, owing to the presence of Betty Truesdale at Truesdale Manor, not far from Benmore.

Three years before the time of the story proper, in the great trophy room at Benmore Castle, Captain Bob Lambert, a young globe-trotter, is seen to enter the hall during a fierce electrical storm without [*sic*]. He is in full evening dress.

Over at Truesdale manor there is gathered wealth and luxury in honor of Betty Truesdale's marriage to Captain Bob Lambert. Returning to Benmore Castle we find Lambert nervously pacing the great hall in darkness. Suddenly the hall is lighted and the door at the head of the stairs opens and Robert Claven, with his Indian servant, Sakee. [*sic*] Sakee is carrying a mahogany box of queer design. Claven apologizes for being late and orders Sakee to bolt the door.

Sakee places the box on the end of a long table and then Claven explains to Bob that he hopes he understands the strange duel that is to take place. Bob nods understanding. Both men proceed to strip themselves of their coats and waistcoats and bare one arm.

Back at Truesdale manor the hour is arriving for the marriage ceremony between Bob and Betty. Betty is waiting when a box arrives addressed in Bob's handwriting. It reads:

"Private — for Betty.
Not to be Opened Until 10:30 P.M.
(Signed) Capt. Bob Lambert"

Her curiosity is stronger than her will. Sending everyone from the room, she proceeds to unwrap the package.

Back in Benmore castle, the two men, Bob and Claven, are prepared for one of the most unusual duels ever fought between two men. Sitting on the opposite sides of the long table with their arm next to the table stripped [*sic*], they await the action of Sakee, who is standing at one end of the table prepared to lift the lid of the box. The word is given, the lid raised and a huge poisonous snake uncoils from its nest in the box and advances toward the two men, their arms resting on the table.

Returning to Truesdale Manor we find Betty's curiosity satisfied. Within the package she finds her future husband's wedding gift and a note which reads:

"Dearest One: This was to have been your wedding gift, but at the hour you will open it, it will be no more. God bless and keep you is the last wish from one who loved you better than anything on earth save his honor.

(Signed) Bob"

She suspects Bob is at Benmore Castle and hurries there through the rain.

At Benmore castle in the Great Hall, the two men are prepared for the strange duel. The snake advances down the table and gradually approaches the arm of Claven. Turning from the arm without setting its poisonous fangs [*sic*], the snake turns to Bob's arm and sinks its fangs into the flesh. The duel is ended as Betty rushes into the room. Sakee returns the snake to its box as Betty rushes to Bob's arms. She notices a look of pain on Bob's face. He tells her that it will be only a few moments before they part for good. As Claven and Sakee leave the room, Sakee grasps Claven's arm and says, "You have tricked him. I recognized the odor of peculiar kind of oil from India — oil that no snake will approach!"

Betty sits down beside the table with her arm resting thereon. By accident the snake leaves its box and, unbeknown to Betty, approaches her arm and sinks its fangs in her flesh. She sees what has happened and a wonderful smile steals over her countenance.

Back in the Great Hall at Truesdale Manor the assemblage is a gay one. But at Benmore Castle all is different. Betty and Bob have passed into the great beyond. Sakee and his mater take the bodies from the castle, place them in an automobile and send the ma-

chine over a cliff. The world believes that they were killed in the accident.

Then into the Great Hall at Truesdale Manor where the wedding guests are assembled comes [*sic*] the ghosts of Betty and Bob. They have one waltz and then start on their trip around the world. Then we follow their phantom car, around the world, into India, Egypt, and along the banks of the Nile.

When Sakee has finished his strange story, he glances at the clock and exclaims that "It is the hour for the phantom car to come." As he says so the old professor is surprised to see drift into the room the white car with its ghost-like occupants, Betty and Bob. They remain awhile and then depart.

The old professor looks up and calls out, "Did I see —!" And so ended the ghost story.

The first and only feature-length production attributable to J. Searle Dawley Productions, *The Phantom Honeymoon* was based on an idea arrived at somehow by Mr. Dawley, who then adapted it for the screen before directing it. Dawley's wits and pen and/or typewriter had served to launch any number of shorts and features prior to this, and if *Phantom Honeymoon*'s idiosyncrasies were typical, those shorts and features must have been doozies. Having one's narrative turn on snakes in post–Saint Patrick Ireland, for example, qualifies said plot-wrinkle for doozy-dom; it also means that the duelists' weapon of choice must have been stashed among the personal effects of Claven's Hindu caretaker from the get-go. Then, too, the number of Hindus staffing Irish castles during the 1910s was probably inversely proportional to the legions of faithful Indian batmen who had (in literature, at any rate) accompanied their inevitably monocle'd-and-mustachioed, retired sergeant-majors home to England from the Raj, so this is at least a minor doozy. And as for the conveyance referred to by the press-book as a "phantom automobile" (*Motion Picture News* called it "a spirit-like limousine"), that's a doozy with a capital D.

The film itself appears to exist only in abbreviated form — a 16mm print with about an hour's worth of footage may be found in the holdings of the Library of Congress — and there are only the sparsest of critical remarks left with which to make breakfast. There is no extant record of the credits crawl (and the Library of Congress print is missing the main titles), but we assume that Dawley must have hired *someone* to help him on the picture, if only to double check that the doors were locked when he called it a night. Said caretaker may also have manned the camera, and it was his double-exposure work that received comment (but not praise) and so revealed how the picture's supernatural element was carried off. And while the pre-honeymoon sequences cited in the above plot précis do sound a bit grim, we can be grateful to the 6 December 1919 *Harrison's Reports* for setting us straight:

> *The Phantom Honeymoon* is an unusual picture. It is entertaining all the way through, except perhaps in the part which shows a snake. This snake is used by the two principal characters to fight a duel for the girl. Snakes are repulsive on the screen equally as much as in real life; but it is possible that the other good qualities of the picture may completely overshadow this repulsiveness. There is good comedy all the way through. Fantastic scenes are introduced towards the end, but in an entertaining manner.

Harrison's "good comedy all the way through" business must have confused more than one exhibitor, though, for the press-book was busily touting the film as having "Great Love — Great

Sorrow — Great Mystery." For all that, the word "Honeymoon" in the title should have tipped everyone to the picture's being geared to the light-hearted side of the afterlife. Still, with the snake garnering more (and better) press than the special effects — which only came into their own in the last reel — we're left in the dark as to whether any shots of that ghostly limo were superimposed over footage of the Taj Mahal or the Great Sphinx, or whether those foreign vistas were merely presented from the defunct newlyweds' POV. No matter which, the 21 November 1919 *Variety* maintained, "At the end there is the use of much double exposure stuff that is so crude that it is almost laughable." Let's face it: when they find your special effects "crude" and "almost laughable" in *1919*, you'd better make sure your snake gets the job done.

Marguerite Marsh — the blushing, if ultimately discorporate, bride of the picture — was a member of the Marsh movie dynasty (such as it was), being elder sister to actresses Mae and Mildred, and to film editor Frances (who worked on 1929's *Darkened Rooms*; see appendix). For Marguerite, who made the majority of her early pictures (mostly shorts) using her husband's name — Loveridge — *The Phantom Honeymoon* sadly presaged an early death: she had scarcely a dozen films left to be made before falling victim to pneumonia in December 1925. Among that dozen, though, was 1920's 15-chapter serial, *The Master Mystery*, wherein she was the romantic interest of Harry Houdini's Quentin Locke. Marsh's leading man in *Honeymoon* was Vernon Steele, whose credentials are briefly recounted in our essay on 1919's *The Firing Line*. As for the bad guys, Hal Clarendon played Henry Claven — the craven, cheating, snake-handling heavy — and Henry Guy Carlton was Sakee — his snake-handling, Hindu sidekick — and neither ever made another genre film (although Carlton made another *Honeymoon* film — *The Place of Honeymoons* — the very next year). Leon Dadmun — the fearless, ghost-busting Professor Tidewater — *may* have been the Leon E. Dadmun who directed a brace of love features (*The Lure of Love* and *The Pearl of Love*) in the mid–1920s. The odds are better that he was than that he wasn't, but, in either case, *The Phantom Honeymoon* was his only genre effort, as well.

None of these folk merited a great deal of attention from the few trade papers that bothered to glance at the film. The best *Variety* could come up with was "Marguerite Marsh is the star of the picture, which is in six reels." Nonetheless, she received about the best notice the "Bible of Show Business" gave *Honeymoon*. "The acting is not out of the ordinary, nor is the direction. The photography is also defective, and the use of exceedingly heavy tints for the night scenes make some of the scenes almost impossible to follow. There is not much to be said in favor of *The Phantom Honeymoon* other than it can play the cheaper houses and get by."

(Having thus pronounced sentence on the actors, director and cinematographer, *Variety* also kicked in the editor's teeth: "A lot of the footage … is padding, and the picture would be just as well off had it been cut to five reels.") On the other side of town, Charles E. Wagner — in the 1 November 1919 *Exhibitors' Trade Review* — opined that "the acting is very well done" and singled out Marsh and Steele for offering "two very pleasing

characters" while maintaining that Clarendon and Carlton "do splendidly." In all fairness, we should point out that Wagner also found the camera work "adequate" and the double-exposure effects "good." So let the buyer beware!

Motion Picture News (25 October 1919) went the safe route and passed on reviewing *Honeymoon*, although the writer did headline his collection of thoughts, "Plenty of Mystery and Suspense Here." In lieu of critique, *MPN* offered exhibitors a few ostensibly catchy taglines, like "She preferred to go with him on a phantom honeymoon rather than remain among the mortals" and "As long as her great love was slipping away into the great unknown she begged to join him." Heady prose, indeed.

It's evident that some small town newspapers — like the *Oil City* [Pennsylvania] *Derrick* — took those prose suggestions to heart, though; in its 12 November 1919 edition, the *Derrick* asked its distaff readership, "What would you do if the man you were to marry was stricken dead one hour before the wedding?" Lest any Oil City woman be befuddled into speechlessness while pondering this deplorable situation, the paper then quickly advised: "The bride-to-be did not allow death to interfere with her happiness." And for the sake of any males whose eyes happened to alight on the movie ad, they cut right to the chase: "A weird story of a honeymoon spent after death." Not the most mesmerizing of ad campaigns, what?

More down to earth were puff pieces like the one featured in the 17 December 1919 *Fitchburg* [Massachusetts] *Daily Sentinel*: "*The Phantom Honeymoon*, the strangest photodrama of romance and mystery ever conceived in which the beautiful Marguerite Marsh is seen in the role of the phantom bride. Although *The Phantom Honeymoon* is strictly a 'ghost story' dealing with the supernatural it is by no means a gruesome tale. On the contrary it is a delightful romance of two lovers whose ghosts haunt the castle of the jilted suitor."

With the press-book awash with rather stilted ad copy (which was probably par for the course in those days) and virtually *none* of the ads found therein depicting the picture's fantastic side, we seem to have before us a perfect example of early 20th Century, genre "under-advertising." Most pictures with fantastic elements that were made in the USA prior to the 1920s usually saw those elements explained away in the last few minutes of screen time. *The Phantom Honeymoon* was not tarred with that brush, but we have to wonder whether a serious-minded publicity campaign that highlighted the film's supernatural aspect would have actually increased revenues or would have doomed the picture, once and for all.

— JTS

The Phantom Melody

The Phantom Melody. Universal Film Mfg. Co./Universal, January 1920, 6 reels [LOST]

CAST: Monroe Salisbury (*Count Camello* or *Federico, Count di Montrone*); J. Barney Sherry or Henry Barrows (*Sir James Drake*); Ray Gallagher (*His son, Oliver*); Charles West (*Gregory Baldi* or *Giorgetto Pisani*); Jean Calhoun (*Mary Drake*); Joe Ray (*Gustavo* or *Antonio Tornelli*); Milton Markwell (*Baron Ferrera*); Lois Lee (*Paulette*)

CREDITS: *Presented by* Carl Laemmle; *Director* Douglas Gerrard;

Assistant Director Rex E. Hodge; *Story and Scenario* F. McGrew Willis; *Cinematographer* Roy Klaffki

Lest anyone think this title yet another arcane rendition of Gaston Leroux's *The Phantom of the Opera*, we repair immediately to a brief plot recap, courtesy of the 24 January 1920 *Variety*:

> An Italian count is nursing in his bosom a viper in the shape of a cousin who steals, borrows, gambles, gets his fiancée's sister [!] into a duel, tells him he has killed his man, gives him his enlistment papers and sends him into the army in his place. He himself goes to Monte Carlo with a courtesan while his manly cousin heads his regiment, returns on leave, falls in love with the abandoned fiancée and becomes engaged to her. At this point the wicked cousin reappears and buries the hero alive. The hero escapes to revenge himself in due time.

And lest anyone, having arbitrarily opened this book to this page and having hacked his/her way — disbelievingly — through that précis, think that we resort to inventing stuff like this from whole cloth in order to wheedle money from unsuspecting genre fans, we repair anon to a slightly longer plot summary (courtesy of *Wid's Daily* from the 25 January of that same year) that will doubtless clear things up.

> An Italian gentleman of title, Federico (the Count di Montrone), a musician, loves an American heiress. She lavishes her affections on his scapegrace cousin, Giorgetto Pisani. Drake, the girl's brother, wounds an opponent slightly in a duel over a gambling game. The villainous cousin makes him believe he has killed him and, war conveniently beginning at that time, gives Drake his army papers and sends him off in his place. He goes to Monte Carlo and enters on a career of licentiousness with one Rosa.
>
> Federico also goes to war. He is captured by Austrians and before the tide of battle turns in favor of the Italians they have seared a cross on his chest with a red-hot iron. He returns to his home to recover from the shock. His cousin is reported killed and he and the girl receive another shock when he returns just as they are bout to be married.
>
> Federico is exhausted in a rain storm and found by Giorgetto and a money-lender. They believe him dead. Later the cousin discovers him still alive but puts him in his tomb anyway. Federico later emerges, his hair now white. He sees his cousin and the girl happy and goes his way back to war. Afterwards he returns, his beard full grown, and enters his cousin's house as a music teacher. The money-lender recognizes him as does the cousin just as Drake comes back from the war and anxious to avenge himself on the villain whose duplicity he has discovered. They fight for possession of the pistol which falls in a fire and discharges, killing the villain.

Now that *that's* settled, we can readily see that the title refers not to the masked musician who ventures up from the cellars of the Paris Opera to seek love and fulfillment, but rather to the hirsute musician who wanders in from the war to seek employment and stay the hell out of the rain. Wid Gunning, over whose name that impeccably written plot recap was loosed on the world, wrote other — and better — things elsewhere, and he gets credit for the better stuff in our essay on Benjamin Christensen's *The Haunted House*. ("Leed," the *Variety* scribe responsible for that first, terser masterpiece, likewise penned more cogent commentary in other editions of the Bible of Show Business, or, perhaps, on other pages in that same number. One would assume.) The film itself is, of course, lost. (One would hope.) Our own commentary, then, is of necessity limited to reflection upon the details provided in those contemporary screeds. This one

went off to war, and the other one returned, and the girl was happy with the cousin, and the brother came back, and the cross on his chest, and the career of licentiousness, and the piano such is all very well and good, but we intend to devote our time to that burial alive. Adieu, M. Leroux! Hallo, Mr. Poe!

Motion Picture News' Laurence Reid, though, saw nothing of Edgar Allan in *The Phantom Melody* — and precious little, either, of F. McGrew Willis, who received onscreen blame not only for the scenario, but also for the original story. In the 31 January 1920 *MPN*, Reid paused during his critique of "Monroe Salisbury's latest expression" to give Willis what-for:

> The author of it has failed to give credit to Marie Corelli since [the picture] is nothing more or less than a visualization of her fantastic tale, *The Vendetta* [*sic*]. However, it has been brought up to date by transplanting the action as centering around the lately deceased war. In developing the romance between a suitor of middle age and his sweetheart, more concentrated situations are unfolded than take place in a half-dozen ordinary features.

In one fell swoop, then, our impression that *The Phantom Melody* was hardly an "ordinary" feature is corroborated, and its plethora of vaguely-described, unlikely events is traced to *another* ersatz–Italian nightmare, one cribbed from the imagination of the late–Victorian Era, ersatz–Italian queen of preposterous prose herself, whose credentials are outlined in our essay on *The Sorrows of Satan* (1926). (We did read *Vendetta*, though — — on line, for free — and have referenced it in our essays on *The Reward of the Faithless* and *Black Orchids*.)

The Poe-fill moment that leaps to mind, of course, is the walling up of Fortunato by his fellow nobleman in "The Cask of Amontillado," and the attendant, desperate plea, "For the love of God, Montresor!" "Yes," answers the trowel-wielding Montresor, dispassionately, "for the love of God." Also leaping to mind (well, to *our* mind, anyhow) is the scene as enacted by Vincent Price and Peter Lorre in the "Black Cat" segment of Roger Corman's 1962 AIP/Poe trilogy, *Tales of Terror*. Yet another mind-leap has us envisioning Ray Milland awakening in his tricked-out sepulcher in *Premature Burial*, Roger Corman's 1962 *anti*–AIP/Poe film wherein the cagey producer/director and writer Charles Beaumont warily attributed the original story to E.A.P. to fool the masses.

Fact of the matter is, we cannot either cite or recapture that moment from *The Phantom Melody*, except to quote the sundry, extant publicity puffs that were aimed specifically at making that moment the highlight of the film. For instance, the following catch lines (reprinted here from the afore-cited *MPN* piece) were crafted to intrigue the cautious movie-goer: "How would *you* like to be buried alive and wake up to find yourself in a vault with no possible means of escape?" Mwa-haa-haaa! (Of course, Federico *did* find a means of escape, but it's to be assumed that Italian noblemen were by nature made of sturdier stuff than moviegoers from Wilkes-Barre or Terre Haute.) "He came back from the grave and when he played the phantom melody his sweetheart recognized him even though his hair had turned white." (His "sweetheart," let's not forget, was the same American heiress who lavished her affections on his "villainous cousin" and who found happiness in His Scapegrace's arms in reel three or thereabouts. And, per *Wid's*, it was the *cousin* [and the money-lender] who recognized the old boy, white hair and beard or no, while the sweetheart was apparently busy borrowing money and learning how to play "Chopsticks.")

There's not much prose devoted solely to the burial alive, but—considering the frank appraisal of the staging of some of the scenes (*Wid's* again), "A number of the moments intended to pass as intense drama will very likely get titters and laughs before audiences accustomed to better pictures…. The part about his hair turning white and the pistol discharging nicely from the fire are events which can't be taken seriously."

We can only thank the gods for small favors. (Harrison wasted far fewer words in his *Report* on the 24 January 1920: "Unbelievable. Impossible.") Nonetheless, proving once again that for every *bop* there is a *bop-she-wop*, Laurence Reid did write: "It will make a sensitive spectator's skin creep to see Salisbury fight for life, rise from his coffin, break the window of his vault and escape. That scene is the outstanding feature in this weird concoction. It is positively harrowing to watch."

The *Exhibitors Trade Journal*, a paper whose very *raison d'être* was to make silk purses out of every sow's ear that came mounted on reels or cores, chose to concentrate on the musical aspects of the picture, aspects which were very much missing from everyone else's coverage of the picture. Cinema entrepreneurs were encouraged to finagle a deal with their local "music stores" whereby the stores' display windows would be filled with musical instruments and sheet music. Inasmuch as one might think the display windows of music stores would *normally* be filled with musical instruments and sheet music, one cannot help but to question the merits of such a suggestion. Oooops! A neatly-lettered sign is to be added to the display, informing potential ticket-buyers that … "Music hath charms to soothe the savage breast. Our instruments are noted for their clear-toned melodies. *The Phantom Melody* is the feature attraction appearing at the _____ theatre."

This tack, *certamente*, would have whet the appetites of the members of the local symphonies, but it offered them (and offers us) not a whit about the role played by any sort of melody—phantom or otherwise—in the picture. Between fighting in the war and catching his near-death of chill during that damned rainstorm (a local newspaper critique had him hit by lightning!), did Federico actually find the time to compose a signature piece that would be recognized by his rather unfaithful ex-lover when played by the organist in the theater pit? If the plot summary above is to be believed (and we're on eggshells there, are we not?), it appears as though Federico may have actually been noodling said melody at the keyboard while Drake and the villain were locked in their mortal struggle, thus making the old pianist little more than yet another musician accompanying the onscreen action. It's tough to tell.

Making it tougher yet to tell is the fact that, according to the 31 January 1920 edition of *The Moving Picture World*, Federico (the Count di Montrone) is, in fact, Count Camello, and his wretched cousin — yclept Giorgetto Pisani elsewhere — is herein reported to be Gregory Baldi. Mary Drake is the American heiress in both accounts, which is nice, although it makes it a tad difficult to understand how her brother, Sir James, can apparently be a British knight. More perplexing is how fully half

of the published commentaries quoted above claim that Sir James was played by actor J. Barney Sherry, while the other half has Henry Barrows in the role.

Basta! as Italian counts would say.

Monroe Salisbury, an actor of some presence — if only per the breadth of some of his roles— was Indiana-born (in early May 1876) and cinema-bound by 1914, when he was hired on for the first of a million versions of *Brewster's Millions* by Jesse Lasky. Prior to that epic, Salisbury had been stage-bound for some years, appearing in a handful of Broadway productions that were already — or would be, subsequently — stabled as theatrical warhorses. The actor received some good press for his deportment in *The Phantom Melody*, with *Wid's* opinion —"Monroe Salisbury, though he poses considerably, gets many points over through his sincere work"— pretty much typical.

The prolific J. Barney Sherry — who *may* have portrayed Sir James Drake — may have numbered the part among the 220-odd roles he did play in the course of his quarter-century-long film career. We know for sure that Sherry *was* in Marshall Neilen's gorilla-man thriller, *Go and Get It*, released a half-year after *Melody*, but his interpretation of "Shut the Door" Gordon is missing, as is the picture. The half-as-prolific Henry Barrows (roughly 110 pictures to his credit) may prove to be even less prolific if it is one day found out that Sir James Drake was not one of his impersonations. Nonetheless, we are tempted to give Barrows the nod here, if only because he was father to actor, George Barrows, who *was* both Ro-Man in the immortal *Robot Monster* (1953) and Goliath (the gorilla) in the almost-as-immortal Cameron Mitchell classic, *Gorilla at Large* (1954).

Director Douglas Gerrard had a second career as an actor, in which he was quite as prolific as was Mr. Barrows. As a director, though, he ran out of gas within 5 years and two dozen pictures. *The Phantom Melody* seems to be his sole genre contribution no matter which hat he wore, although he is listed as having appeared in 1916's *The Dumb Girl of Portici*, the film that may (or may not) have marked the cinematic debut of one Boris Karloff. The *ETR* was the only critique to mention Gerrard and *Melody* by name in the same column, and the journal concluded that "the directorial abilities of Douglas Gerrard have never been placed to better advantage." That having been noted, Gerrard's next picture — Universal's *The Forged Bride* — would mark the last time the man's directorial abilities earned him a paycheck.

— *JTS*

The Phantom of the Opera

The Phantom of the Opera. Universal Pictures/Universal, 6 September 1925 (New York Premiere: 15 November 1925), 10 reels/8464 feet, black and white with Technicolor sequences, available, a Universal Jewel

CAST: Lon Chaney (*The Phantom*); Mary Philbin (*Christine Daae*); Norman Kerry (*Raoul de Chagny*); Snitz Edwards (*Florine Papillon*); Gibson Gowland (*Simon*); John Sainpolis (*Philippe de Chagny*); Virginia Pearson (*Carlotta*); Arthur Edmund Carewe (*Ledoux, the Persian*); Edith Yorke (*Mama Valerius*); Anton Vaverka (*Prompter*); Bernard Siegel (*Joseph Buquet*); Olivia Ann Alcorn (*La Sorelli*); Cesare Gravina (*Retiring Manager*); George B. Williams (*M. Ricard*); Bruce Covington (*M. Moncharmin*); Edward Cecil (*Faust*); John Miljan

(*Valentin*); Alexander Bevani (*Mephistopheles*); Grace Marvin (*Martha*); William Tryoler (*Director of Opera Orchestra*); Ward Crane (*Count Ruboff*); Chester Conklin (*Orderly*)

CREDITS: *Presented by* Carl Laemmle; *Director* Rupert Julian; *Additional Director* Edward Sedgwick [uncredited — Lon Chaney]; based on the novel *Le Fantôme de l'Opéra* by Gaston Leroux (Paris, 1910); *Adaptation* Raymond Schrock, Elliott J. Clawson; *Titles* Tom Reed; *Cinematographer* Virgil Miller; *Additional Photography* Charles J. Van Enger, A.S.C., Milton Bridenbecker; *Art Direction* Charles D. Hall; *Film Editor* Maurice Pivar; *Assistant Director* Robert Ross; *Ballet Master* Ernest Belcher

Universal Studios' 1925 adaptation of Gaston Leroux's pulpy 1910 novel is the one film that we can, without qualification, guarantee every reader of this volume has seen. It is quite possibly the most famous and most seen silent film of any genre and any country. Robert Klepper in *The Golden Age of Silents* calls it "quite possibly the most popular film to come out of the silent era." More's the pity because, despite several wonderful sequences, it's a mediocre film at best and hardly a glowing example of the art of silent filmmaking. Still, most of us have been seeing it in an inferior version — the 1929 part-talkie re-do, stripped of its soundtrack — that does the film no favors at all.

The film was, to resurrect that hoary show-biz cliché, a troubled production, but it didn't start that way. Casting about for a follow-up to their successful 1923 production of *The Hunchback of Notre Dame*, the studio settled finally on Leroux's work. It boasted both a Paris setting and an opportunity for Lon Chaney to showcase his already legendary makeup abilities, both of which were hallmarks of the earlier production and thus considered necessary ingredients to be repeated. (The studio also contemplated another Victor Hugo novel with makeup challenges, but *The Man Who Laughs* was, perhaps fortunately, put aside for another day.) Chaney, too, was enamored with *Phantom* as a vehicle; he was at that time successfully freelancing (a practice he would continue until 1925) and was actively acquiring properties he felt would be suitable for his talents.

According to papers that Michael Blake discovered in the files of Chaney's business manager, Albert Grasso (as outlined in an article in *Filmfax* #52), the actor secured the film rights to the property shortly after finishing up with *Hunchback* and just after it was announced that both Universal and the Carl Anderson Company had tendered contract offers. It remains unknown, though, whether he still retained them in 1925 and sold them to Universal, or acted as a de facto but uncredited producer, as he had on *Hunchback*. Some writers, including Philip Riley, consider Universal's *The Phantom Violin* (see entry) to be an unattributed adaptation, but the studio didn't bother obtaining rights on that occasion as the story was radically revamped even if its inspiration is transparently obvious. In a letter to Grasso, Chaney indicated that Universal initially proposed a budget of $100,000; that was less than what *Hunchback* cost and suggests that the Big U saw *Phantom* as a more modestly budgeted feature than it eventually became.

As they had done previously for *Hunchback*, Universal built one of Paris's landmarks on its back lot; the studio acquired the plans for the Paris Opera House and built a replica of its interior upper stories (at slightly reduced scale) and of the ground level of its façade (extended in long-shots with glass paintings). Not only did the studio thus have a luxurious set but also a dandy publicity-generator. To house the Opera House's cavernous auditorium and its immense foyer, Universal constructed Hollywood's first-ever steel and concrete stage; it was later converted for use as a soundstage and — with some of the auditorium's elements still in place — is in use to the present day. In the intervening years the auditorium has been seen in *Dracula* (1931), *The Raven* (1935), *One Hundred Men and a Girl* (1937), *The Climax* (1944), *Torn Curtain* (1966) and *The Sting* (1973), and, of course, Universal's 1943 remake of *Phantom*.

In conjunction with the massive new-build, the Universal publicity machine went into high gear, and everyone got into the act. While the Hammond Lumber Company of Los Angeles was trucking over 175,000 feet of wood for the stage construction, the studio proudly supplied banners for the trucks that proclaimed, "The largest shipment of lumber for the upcoming production of *The Phantom of the Opera*." (Alas! The machine misfired later. For the film's London premiere, an overly ambitious flack hoaxed British troops into escorting *Phantom*'s film cans off the boat to the theater where they were to be played. When the ruse was revealed there was an explosion of public indignation, and the film was barred from British screen for a number of years.)

Ben Carre — among other things, a production designer for the real Paris Opera — was hired to ensure accuracy of the operatic sets and props; in addition, as Universal had been unable to secure the proper blueprints, he created the theater's lower depths where the Phantom makes his home. Surprisingly, some of Carre's more outré aspects of Erik's lair were based on fact. For example, there really is a lake under the Paris Opera House. While excavating before laying the foundation, the building crews struck an underground spring, and the enormous hole they had dug began filling up with water. Construction was halted (as it would be periodically before the building could finally be completed) until a solution was reached: the underground waters would be utilized in the hydraulic system that operated the theater's scenery-shifting mechanisms. One of the several political upheavals that France experienced in the 1800s brought another halt to construction, when prisoners were incarcerated in the theater's cellars and torture devices were most likely installed. Bones of forgotten prisoners — whose ghosts were said to haunt the labyrinthine catacombs — were still being discovered in Leroux's day. Leroux's novel also answers one of the biggest questions hurled at any film version: how is the Phantom supposed to have gotten that damned pipe organ and all that furniture down there? Per the book, the Phantom is, among other things, a master architect who had become involved in the construction of the opera house, thus allowing him to install his underground, lakeside house and all its amenities.

Since the 1925 version of *Phantom* — which runs 89 minutes — differs in many particulars (especially in the section leading up to the Bal Masque) from the 79-minute version that has until recently been most available, it might be useful to recount the plot in some detail.

"Sanctuary of song lovers" is how the opening title card describes the exterior view of Universal's re-creation of the opera house's façade; at least, in the print we're most used to seeing. [In 1925, the film began with a title card introducing Gaston Leroux to American audiences.] The camera then moves to a lantern-carrying figure in the cellars— presumably the rat-catcher, but unidentified— who gives a brief history of the opera house's nether regions. The action switches upstairs to a crowd entering for a ballet performance. These scenes introduce Vicomte Raoul de Chagny (Norman Kerry) and his brother (John Sainpolis, nearly written out of the reconfigured part-talkie) and the theater's lavish, four-story-high foyer, with its grand stairway, and the equally impressive (and equally tall) auditorium. As the banal ballet progresses, Raoul pays a call backstage on his beloved, Christine Daae (Mary Philbin), who has risen from chorus roles under the tutelage of a mysterious music master.

Meanwhile, up in the offices, management is changing hands, and the departing managers pass on a warning to the new ones about the Opera Ghost. Shortly thereafter, the diva Carlotta sails into the offices with a note from "The Phantom" informing her that Christine is to assume the role of Marguerite in an upcoming performance of *Faust*. La Carlotta finds this arrangement unsatisfactory, to say the least. [In the re-jiggered 1929 version, this character is described as Carlotta's mother; another actress— one who could sing — was engaged for the newly-filmed aria sequences.] But a shadowy figure, lurking behind the walls of Christine's room, promises her that the substitution will indeed transpire. Christine is beholden to this mysterious personage — she thinks him to be the Angel of Music, sent from heaven by her father — and so, at a garden party, asks Raoul to desist in his attentions to her. On the night of *Faust*, Carlotta falls ill and Christine substitutes. During the performance, the managers discover that the supposedly empty Box 5 is occupied by a cloaked figure that disappears abruptly when they decide to confront him. After the opera, Raoul overhears the Angel of Music vowing to Christine that he will soon take her away with him. Meanwhile, property master Florine Papillon (silent comedian Snitz Edwards) discovers the body of Joseph Buquet hanging in a backstage area, a victim of the Punjab lasso. Buquet's brother Simon (Gibson Gowland) swears revenge.

Carlotta soon receives another note, but insists she will not again miss a performance. In the interim, the Persian (Arthur Edmond Carewe), who has been seen skulking about the opera house, pays a visit to the Prefect of Police and warns that catastrophe will occur if Carlotta sings. But sing she does, and on top of that, the managers audaciously occupy Box 5. The Phantom exacts revenge by dropping the gigantic crystal chandelier onto the audience; in the ensuing confusion he lures Christine to him, beckoning her to join him by walking through her dressing room mirror. He sits her astride a black horse, and they descend to an underground lake; placing her in a gondola, the Phantom poles the craft across the lake to his home.

Aboveground, Paris is in an uproar over the missing singer. Down in the Phantom's lair, Christine finds a room outfitted for her, complete with clothing and personalized toilet accessories. There is also a note from the Phantom warning her not to touch his mask. Nonetheless, when she hears him playing at the organ, she is so moved that she is compelled to see his face, with a result that is too famous to bother recounting. The Opera Ghost allows Christine to return to her world for one more performance with the understanding that afterwards she will remain with him forevermore.

Christine's conspiring to meet Raoul at the Opera's Bal Masque was filmed in two-color Technicolor and is the only such scene to survive. [On the picture's original release, many of the opera vignettes were also photographed in Technicolor, while Prizma, another color process, was used for some sequences; these were later scrapped because they looked unimpressive compared to the Technicolor. All color scenes involving the Phantom were also scrapped because Chaney's makeup didn't fare well under the in-

tense lighting needed to expose the film.] The Phantom stalks through the swirling crowd costumed as the Red Death and spots the two lovers together. Later, atop the opera house, he eavesdrops on their plans to escape him. Meanwhile the Persian pays another visit to the police, where we learn about this Phantom: "Erik. Born during the Boulevard Massacre. Self-educated musician and master of Black Art. Exiled to Devil's Island for criminal insane. Escaped. Now At Large."

Despite everyone and everything, Erik kidnaps Christine in mid-performance. The Persian reveals himself to Raoul as Ledoux of the secret police, and they descend to the basements through Christine's mirror [a trek that takes far longer in the 1925 original than in the revised edition]. Ironically, they fall through a trap-door into "the Room of Many Mirrors— an old torture device." Raoul's brother finds his own way below and is drowned by the Phantom. Erik discovers the presence of the two other callers and turns on the lights in the mirrored room, creating intense heat. Christine is offered the choice of staying with Erik — and thus saving her lover — or having the opera house blown up by innumerable kegs of dynamite [the existence of which makes sense in light of the structure's one-time use by the military]. But a mob that has

During the off-season, Erik was known as the Phantom of the Hoedown.

formed under Simon's leadership now storms the cellars, chasing the Phantom out onto the streets. After a furious carriage ride, the mob traps Erik on a bridge, beats him and throws his body into the Seine. The final scene [which some writers allege was cribbed from 1923's *Merry-Go-Round*] shows Raoul and Christine on their honeymoon.

The Phantom of the Opera boasts Lon Chaney's most famous characterization and, arguably, his makeup masterpiece: one he altered in various ways for virtually every camera angle and to suit the emotional (as well as the technical) aspects of the scenes. The performance, one of his best, is extraordinary in that he positively dominates the film even though he doesn't appear — except as a shadow on a wall — until halfway through the film! It is a marvelously judged piece of acting, rising to the outrageous demands of the melodramatic plot yet never tipping over into risibility; Chaney's fluid use of his hands—compensating for the restricted mobility of his face — takes mime nearly to the level of ballet. The unmasking scene is well-known, but the moments following it are equally impressive; immediately after his towering rage at Christine, Chaney crumples and slumps in the realization that the exposure of his face, combined with the exposure of his temper, has doomed all hope of Christine falling in love with him. Chaney's feat is all the more remarkable given that the actor directed his own scenes—having fallen out early with director Rupert Julian — and in those days before video monitors, had no way to view and judge his performance until the dailies were ready for viewing.

Julian (1879–1943), the director of record, was one of the first problems the film encountered. A journeyman director from 1914 — until the firing of Erich von Stroheim from *Merry-Go-Round* promoted him to someone worthy of helming a Universal "Super Jewel"—he took on Von's autocratic ways without possessing a fraction of his talent and reportedly alienated not just Chaney, but most of *Phantom*'s cast and crew. Much of the film's blandness stems from Julian's lack of visual invention. A front-row-center vantage point may be fine for the initial shots of the opera's grand hall and auditorium, recording as it does the fidelity of Universal's reconstruction, but some exploration of its compositional possibilities afterward is in order. Likewise the proscenium-arch nature of the ballet and opera scenes may be fine for an introductory shot, but not for their entire length (particularly when the ballets are as blandly choreographed as the ones herein). Nor should scenes in Christine's dressing room be handled in the same manner.

Many years ago, in his groundbreaking *An Illustrated History of the Horror Film*, Carlos Clarens noted the direct parallels of *Phantom* to "Beauty and the Beast," and compared the Chaney film to Jean Cocteau's 1945 adaptation of the fairy tale, concluding that Cocteau knew the value of his symbols where Universal did not. By refusing to move his camera from a front-row-center perspective, Julian throws away countless opportunities to invest his film with the mythic poetry inherent in the source material. Christine's passing into the underworld through the mirror, for instance — an idea used by Cocteau in several films— is so prosaically visualized it becomes just another secret panel gag. The journey by horse and gondola to Erik's "house" has merely a glimmer of the dark beauty it might have had if

only Julian (or, more likely in this case, Chaney) visually exploited the materials at hand, particularly Ben Carre's evocative set designs for the opera's subterranean levels. The lighting, at least, is more interesting in the catacombs than aboveground — but surely these are sets that could reap the benefit of that old horror movie cliché: cobwebs. And the fall of the chandelier — a potentially exciting scene — is handled in such an offhand way that it has barely any impact, although it was filmed in an unusual fashion: the footage was shot as the chandelier was raised and then shown in reverse.

It is instructive that in most any scene where Chaney (or his shadow) appears, the camera finds more interesting positions from which to record the action. Chaney had an unusual amount of control over his scenes because of his make-ups (and possibly his status as producer), each variation of which was designed for maximum impact with a certain camera angle (he only flattened his nose for profile shots, for instance, or glued back his ears for full-face shots). But Chaney soon fell into an expletive-deleted series of exchanges with Julian, conducted entirely through cinematographer Charles Van Enger, and while Julian's name signed the production, at least half of the footage should be credited to Chaney.

Yet still another director also had a hand in the proceedings. When *Phantom* sneak-previewed disastrously in a nearly two-hour version, the studio eliminated a number of garden parties and duels that were considered inessential. Gone, too, was a sequence, derived from the novel, where Erik hides in Christine's father's tomb and impersonates his ghost in an effort to convince the young woman to abandon Raoul in favor of the Angel of Music; when he is discovered by Raoul, Erik hurls skulls at him and escapes. It and other scenes adjudged too gruesome were discarded for comedy sequences shot by Edward Sedgwick, a frequent collaborator of Buster Keaton's. A comic sub-plot involving a rival to Raoul for Christine's affections was added. Erik's quiet death, expiring as he sits at his organ, was replaced by a wild carriage ride Erik takes fleeing from the mob (according to some sources, that ending was re-shot even before the preview, and Sedgwick merely shot additional footage to Julian's mob pursuit ending). Another preview (according to Blake, this was actually a four-week booking at the Curran Theatre in San Francisco) was every bit as devastating: the added comedy was particularly singled out for drubbing. The film that finally saw release was cobbled together from footage shot for both versions, minus any of the added comic material and with a slew of new title cards to cover the now gaping holes in the story. Per Blake, the two-color opera and ballet sequences were dropped at this point as well, though Riley suggests they remained for the film's first run. (For a more in-depth look at *Phantom*'s troubled gestation, the reader is recommended to Philip J. Riley's *The Phantom of the Opera* [MagicImage Filmbooks, 1999]; the documentary by David J. Skal included on Universal's DVD release of their 1943 production; and the 2005 Image Entertainment DVD of the 1925 film, which includes photo reconstructions of the various versions.)

Julian's career after *Phantom* was brief. The New Zealander directed only eight more films — none of them spectacles; his final assignment was a sound remake of *The Cat and the Canary* entitled *The Cat Creeps* (1931). His early footage was scrapped and he was ordered to re-shoot it in emulation of George Melford's Spanish-language version that was shooting on the same sets at night that Julian was utilizing in the daylight hours. In Peter Principle fashion, his incompetence had caught up with him. His final film was *Love Comes Along* (1930), a low budget comedy. Edward (aka Edgar) Sedgwick (1892–1953), on the other hand, remained active for several more decades; though his output in the 1940s was sporadic, he was still doing megaphone duties on episodes of *I Love Lucy* the year of his death. His last feature film was 1951's *Excuse My Dust*. The closest he came to genre involvement after *Phantom* were two mysteries: *Father Brown, Detective* (1934) and *Murder in the Fleet* (1935).

In what would become standard Universal practice, Norman Kerry's main function as the nominal hero is to be available for the heroine's last-reel romantic swoon; his career is outlined in the chapter on *Hunchback*. Mary Philbin (1903–1993) started in films as a teenager, her debut coming in 1921. She quickly moved up the Universal ladder and within a year was in Erich von Stroheim territory, first appearing (in an uncredited bit) in *Foolish Wives* (1922) and soon graduating to a larger role in *Merry-Go-Round*. With *Phantom* she bade fair to being the Evelyn Ankers of the silents, taking as she did the romantic leads in *The Last Performance* (1927) and *The Man Who Laughs* (1928), appearing opposite Conrad Veidt on both occasions. Her last credits are for the year 1929, the year she returned to the role of Christine to take scenes for the part-talkie release of *Phan-*

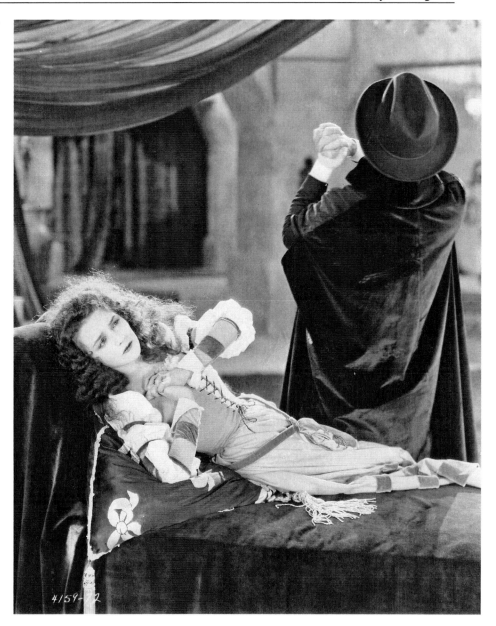

Fun Fact: it was on the set of *The Phantom of the Opera* (with Mary Philbin and Lon Chaney) that isometric exercises came into vogue.

tom. Philbin had invested wisely and lived quietly with her parents, refusing most requests for interviews, though she did respond to fan letters. In her last years she cooperated with several film historians, but her lucid days were numbered; she succumbed to Alzheimer's disease. While both Kerry and Philbin's acting in *Phantom* has been criticized, it's only fair to note that while both were limited talents, neither was given much opportunity to shine, either.

Gibson Gowland (1877–1951)—also credited as T.H. Gibson-Gowland, G.H. Gowland, T.H. Gibson Gowland, T.H. Gowland and T.W. Gowland—made his film debut in Griffith's *The Birth of a Nation* and was yet another von Stroheim favorite, appearing in *Blind Husbands* (1919) and, most famously, as the avaricious dentist McTeague in *Greed* (1924). Possibly his association with that famous disaster put a damper on his career because

he was quickly back to bit parts and extra work with an occasional supporting role such as Simon Legree in 1927's *Topsy and Eva*. His other genre credits include Dmitri in *The Mysterious Island* (1929, see essay) followed by *Secret of the Loch* (1934) and *The Mystery of the Mary Celeste* (1935), made during a junket to his native England. He returned to Hollywood and appeared in *Doomed to Die* and *The Ape* (both 1940), *The Wolf Man* (1942), *A Guy Named Joe* (1943), *Gaslight* (1944) and *The Picture of Dorian Gray* (1945).

Snitz Edwards (1862–1937) was born Edward Neumann in Budapest and began appearing in Hollywood films in 1915, primarily in comic bits such as a bartender in *The Mark of Zorro* (1920). Presumably Douglas Fairbanks liked his work because he brought him back for *The Thief of Bagdad* (1924, see entry). Other of his genre titles include *The Ghost Breaker* (1922), *Tiger*

Love (1924), wherein he played a hunchback, and *The Mysterious Island*. His last role before arthritis—to which he would succumb—forced his retirement, was in *The Public Enemy* (1931).

Arthur Edmond Carewe (1884–1937)—was born in Turkey and began making films in 1919. His looks allowed him to play both heroes and villains; in some cases, as in *Phantom*, he manages to walk the line between the two. Prior to *Phantom* he played Svengali in the 1923 *Trilby* and subsequently he could be found in *The Cat and the Canary* (see entry), *Doctor X* (1932), *Mystery of the Wax Museum* (1933) and *Charlie Chan's Secret* (1936). Sadly, Carewe chose to end his life the following year after suffering a stroke that paralyzed him from the chest down.

Ben Carre (1883–1978), who was so responsible for the look of the film, became intrigued by the painted backdrops used in the new entertainment form pioneered by Georges Méliès and the Lumiere brothers while he was an assistant at Antelier Amable's Artist's Studio in Paris in the early 1900s. By 1906 he was working for Gaumont and traveled to Fort Lee, New Jersey (then the film capital of the USA), when that company opened a branch of their Eclair productions. He became friends with director Maurice Tourneur (see *Trilby*) and followed him to Hollywood, designing many of his productions there. While he was familiar with the Opera House's lower levels and Leroux's novel, his sketches for the cellars, the lake and Erik's abode were drawn as much from his own imagination as from reality. Carre postponed his departure for Nice when the call to work on *Phantom* came from Universal and, as a result, he didn't even see the film until decades later, when he was surprised to discover that the production crew had copied his sketches exactly, even using them to dictate lighting and camera angles. Carre's other genre projects include *The Blue Bird* (1918), *Mare Nostrum* (1926), *The Black Camel* (1931) and *Dante's Inferno* (1935). He returned to the world of opera in quite a different vein when he designed the Marx Brothers vehicle, *A Night at the Opera* (1935).

The final permutation (in 1925, at any rate) of *The Phantom of the Opera* took place in September, at the Astor Theatre in Manhattan. The film was preceded by a lavish stage-show which culminated with a blackened stage; after a pause, a pale light slowly faded up at the rear of the stage and then a white-robed figure appeared, seemingly floating in mid-air. This was the contribution of stage magician Thurston who had answered Universal's $1000 challenge to create just such an apparition. According to *Moving Picture World*, "Despite a continuous rain, traffic was halted in Times Square by the thousands who crowded around the front of the Astor. Police reserves called from the West 47th Street police station had little effect in clearing the situation. The quota of seats allotted to the public for the opening performance was soon used up, but still hundreds pushed their way to the theatre front seeking admittance."

One of the more unusual publicity gambits was Universal's creation of the color "Phantom Red" and having it officially designated by the Textile Color Card Association of America. Universal had the further good fortune to have Phantom Red chosen by the trade as one of its fall and winter shades; otherwise, the designation would have been moot. Products in the new tint were apparently quite popular, running the gamut from Phantom Red Capezio shoes to a Saks/Fifth Avenue Phan-

tom Red Velvet Evening Opera pump. Phantom Red lipstick and other cosmetics also proved quite popular, as did Phantom straw hats, Phantom candy, and Phantom-model radios (there is no record of available colors). Even Kodak leaped on the bandwagon, placing signs in its stores that *Phantom*'s production stills had been made with the company's Eastman Graflex camera.

Eat your heart out, Trilby.

The movie was as well-received by most of the critics as was by the general public. *The New York Times* reviewer proclaimed:

> *The Phantom of the Opera* is an ultra fantastic melodrama, an ambitious production in which there is much to marvel at in the scenic effects.... Lon Chaney impersonates the Phantom. It is a role suited to his liking and one which he handles with a certain skill, a little exaggerated at times, but none the less compelling.... The most dramatic touch is where Christine in the cellar abode is listening to the masked Phantom as he plays the organ. Then she steals up behind him and ... suddenly snatches the mask from the Phantom's face.... In the theater last night a woman behind us stifled a scream when this happened.

Moving Picture World opined:

> The keynote of this picture lies in the element of mystery, spookiness, ghostliness and atmosphere of the unknown and unreal. In fact, apparently having in mind the success of plays like *The Bat*, *The Cat and the Canary* and *The Gorilla*, which cater to similar emotions, Universal has gone them all one better and with the aid of the greater resources of the screen has produced a picture that is undoubtedly a masterpiece of its type.... Due apparently to too-close cutting, the continuity is choppy at times, but the story thrills and intrigues.... We consider it the finest example of sustained tension and suspense we have ever seen.... The story has been produced on a stupendous scale. Among the sets are those representing the interior of the famed Opera House ... and they are said to be authentic in every detail. This effect has been enhanced by presenting many of the scenes in natural color.... Obviously the title role was one for Lon Chaney and he gives a superb performance. Here was another chance to distinguish himself as an unrivaled artist in character make-up and he has done just that. He has made his appearance ugly to the point of repulsiveness, but rather more hideous and grotesque than horrible. To many it will probably not be as revolting as in *The Hunchback of Notre Dame*.

Motion Picture Magazine voiced very similar sentiments:

> Here's an ambitious undertaking which is carried out on a stupendous scale, one surging with eerie, fantastic scenes, one bidding for superlatives in its play of melodramatic action, thru which is shot an uncanny touch of suspense.... It fairly grips you with its suggestion of terror. Lon Chaney plays the Phantom with a real emotional honesty. Mary Philbin brings a wistful appeal to the role of the unhappy heroine, and Arthur Edmund Carewe contributes a cameo characterization. *The Phantom of the Opera* is a complete melodrama—one compact with all the elements which stimulate the pulse and stir the imagination.

Harrison's Reports (17 September 1925) chimed in:

> If you have been looking for a thriller, the kind that will make your patrons' hair stand on end, *The Phantom of the Opera* is the one; it will make them, particularly the women of them, exclaim constantly, "Oh," or stop their blood from circulating.... The Phantom's face is hideous, and yet the picture does not become repulsive; on the contrary, it is fascinating. The suspense in it is the highest felt in a picture in many a moon.... The reproduction of the Paris Opera House is a piece of art. The Prizma scenes showing the multicolored costumes at the masked ball are beautiful. Mr. Lon Chaney's role is terrible; the make-up of his face is

hideous; but he is fascinating. Mary Philbin is charming. In short, *The Phantom of the Opera* has been directed by Mr. Rupert Julian so masterfully that it should prove a real enjoyment to those who revel in blood-curdling mystery dramas…. *The Phantom of the Opera* has been produced on a big scale.

Variety, however, sniffed:

Universal has turned out another horror. This newest of the U specials is probably the greatest inducement to nightmare that has yet been screened…. Lon Chaney is again the "goat" in the matter, no matter if it is another tribute to his character acting. His makeup as the hunchback within the Notre Dame Cathedral was morbid enough, but this is infinitely worse, as in this instance his body is normal with a horrible face solely relied upon for the effect…. It's impossible to believe there are a majority of picturegoers who prefer this revolting sort of a tale on the screen.

Notwithstanding the showbiz trade journal's disbelief — *Variety* was for a good bit of its history notorious for disliking horror films — *Phantom* was a tremendous success. It cost $632,357 (including approximately $50,000 in retakes) and earned $2,014,091 in ticket sales — one of the largest takes of any silent film. In fact, the 5 December 1925 issue of *Moving Picture World* reported:

Box office receipts reaching the Universal home office from theatres of all sizes in all sections of the country indicate *The Phantom of the Opera* is universally topping the excellent records established by *The Hunchback of Notre Dame* its phenomenal successor on the Universal "super" release schedule. Universal officials are elated over the exceptional results … which they hardly dared hope would equal *The Hunchback* figures, much less surpass them.

Theater owners were inclined to view *Phantom* as a picture belonging to a distinct genre, and not as a novelty. The official birth of the Horror Film (and its designation as such) might have been five years away, but in late 1925 the general public was already identifying the outlandish/grotesque, mystery-comedies (*The Ghost Breaker*, et al.) and certain historic melodramas (like *The Hunchback of Notre Dame*) as a distinct movie *type*. And Lon Chaney — for all his care in keeping his roles varied — found himself unofficially crowned king of said productions.

With the coming of sound, Universal toyed with the idea of remaking the film or creating a sequel, but was unable to pry Lon Chaney away from M-G-M where he had become one of the studio's biggest stars. The only other viable option was Conrad Veidt, but he had returned to Germany after deciding that it would be better to handle spoken dialogue in his native tongue, rather than in English. To make matters worse, Universal's horror-specialist, Paul Leni (see *The Cat and the Canary*), died unexpectedly. Left with very few options, Universal instead created a part-talkie by refilming several scenes and dubbing synchronized music and sound effects over the remainder. Chaney constrained the studio from dubbing in a voice for the Phantom, though he did permit the use of a double for the filming of new action, so long as the double was never used for close-ups or seen full-front, three-fourths or in profile. (Chaney thus collected $25,000 for granting permission for a man in a cape to be photographed from the rear!) According to Philip Riley, the footage to be dubbed did not come from the original *Phantom* negative, but from alternate takes and unused

material. The unmasking scene we know so well, for instance, was not the take used for the 1925 release, but was derived from a Technicolor take of the scene that Chaney had vetoed due to makeup flaws made visible by the more intense light necessitated by color stock. For theaters not yet equipped with speakers, Universal released a silent version of this hybrid, and it is predominantly this version that has been seen since.

Even then, the less-than-satisfactory results were noted by *Exhibitors Herald-World*, which groused:

Dressed up with dialog in some of the less important scenes with one Technicolor sequence, plus a musical accompaniment for the rest of the film: that's the new *Phantom of the Opera*. Titles do all the speaking for the Phantom. Perhaps production officials thought they couldn't find a voice to match that hideous countenance. The original picture, as everyone knows, was one of the masterpieces of its day. Had it been entirely refilmed in dialog under modern direction, there is little doubt that it would be a masterpiece today. As it is, half the one, half the other, with the heroine and her lover giving absolutely wooden performances, both as regards voice and pantomime, the original is far to be preferred. Lon Chaney, the phantom, who doesn't utter a syllable, is just as terrifying as he ever was.

— *HHL*

The Phantom Violin

The Phantom Violin (aka *Phantom of the Violin*). Universal Film Manufacturing Co./Universal Film Manufacturing Co. — October 1914 — 4 Reels [LOST]
CAST: Francis Ford (*Ellis*); Grace Cunard (*Rosa*); with Duke Worne, Harry Schumm.
CREDITS: *Director* Francis Ford; *Scenario* Grace Cunard

A crazed musician lurks in the catacombs beneath a theater in Paris and broods over his unrequited love for a young woman. Ultimately his obsession leads to mayhem and murder.

Opera Ghost, anyone?

Paring the story down to these essentials, one might suspect that the story is a reworking of Gaston Leroux's most famous work. Philip Riley, in fact, had no doubt about it at all and wrote in his book on the Lon Chaney *Phantom of the Opera*:

March 9, 1915 — an unauthorized and thinly disguised version of *The Phantom of the Opera* was made by one of Universal's production companies. It was called *The Phantom of the Violin*. The stars were Grace Cunard and Francis Ford. It was described in the trade magazines as "A masterpiece of terror and tragedy." The picture played the usual independent circuit and then disappeared, probably into the bottomless pit. Gaston Leroux's agent would not take the trouble of a lawsuit, to prevent the embarrassment of associating his client with the production [p. 34].

Riley was apparently unaware that *Phantom of the Violin* was a pared-down reissue of the 1914 four-reeler, *The Phantom Violin*. It's unlikely that Leroux or his agent even knew of its existence, either, and no one at the time seems to have even made any connection between the book and the film. It should be remembered that the novel, published in America in 1911, was hardly a sensation. Advance publicity for it was almost apologetic: "admittedly not great literature," "the story is frankly fantastic," etc. In both France and the USA, the book was largely considered inferior to Leroux's earlier thriller, *The Mystery of the Yellow Room* (which was made into a film in 1919 [see appendix] and a number of times thereafter). It took the Lon Chaney film to make the book famous, just as—on a far lesser scale—the prestige of Maurice Renard's *Les Mains d' Orlac* was much enhanced by the Conrad Veidt movie adaptation. Today, when the Andrew Lloyd Webber musical has made Leroux's character something of a household name (without, perhaps, increasing the novel's readership), the basic plot of *Violin* might sound decidedly familiar. *The Phantom Violin* is lost, but the surviving synopses and publicity pieces make its being reduced to a simple rip-off of *The Phantom of the Opera* questionable.

Here's the synopsis of the film as reported by Hanson C. Judson in the 10 October 1914 issue of *Moving Picture World*:

> The film reminds one of Poe, of Hoffman's *Weird Tales* and of Maupassant's. Its authoress, Grace Cunard, and its producer, Francis Ford, play the leading roles in it. It offers us a marked feeling of suspense as to how it will eventually end and bolsters this with an interesting showing of human character and also with entertaining backgrounds.
>
> One of these backgrounds is the room of a musical genius, just such a room and weird strains of violin music might come from to the ears of a girl living across the garden when the night was dark and lightning was flashing out of the sky. Another background is a cabaret, both that part of it which is always open to the public and also what is behind the scenes, that to see one must have business there or be invited. The building of the cabaret was once a monastery but that has been forgotten and under it is a region of darkness and goblin horror-dungeons where white bones lie asleep.
>
> A young girl (Grace Cunard), wakened by a thunderstorm hears the strains of a violin coming from the house across the garden. Next morning she investigates and by accident is caught by the musician. This is the beginning of an acquaintance that soon ripens into love. The musician plays at a cabaret and after the two have been married, the wife one night gets one of his friends to take her there. Soon she is a regular attendant and evens plays her husband's music to add to the entertainment of the place. But she flirts with the friend. The husband finds out and attempts to jump into the Seine but, hindered by the police, goes back to the cabaret and in his madness finds a secret door leading to the old and forgotten crypt. There he lives for some time among the white bones.
>
> The woman also tires of her new lover and takes a third. She plays one of her husband's pieces on the stage but willfully burlesques it. Down in the darkness, he hears it and, ragged and unkempt, comes forth. The man for whom she deserted him is the first victim he seizes on. But after a time he sets the place on fire and also carries off the woman taking her down into the crypt and finally leaping with her into the deepest hole of the lowest regions of the place.

Judson also wrote of the film's Gothic appeal: "Love of a romance whose special properties are such things as a skeleton lying forgotten in some dark and ruined crypt or dungeon, and other goblin, creepy things lives forever in the hearts of many people."

The Phantom Violin was released in October of 1914 and, at four reels, was unusually long for a Universal film of that era (a fact which the publicity for the film noted as being an indication of the movie's above-average quality). Universal President Carl Laemmle much preferred that his movies run between one and three reels; longer than that might upset Universal's "scientifically balanced" program which was sold mostly to small town theaters. Uncle Carl resisted the trend towards features and felt that a variety of short films—say, a two-reel drama, a one-reel comedy and a one-reel Western—would have something for everyone and thus be more appealing to exhibitors, especially as programs changed every couple of days. Showing a feature film as your main attraction would be taking a chance, and who could say what would happen if someone were to come in halfway through it and then have to spend all that time sitting through a picture he couldn't understand? It should be noted, though, that press coverage on the film when it opened in Van Nuys, California (20 November 1914), and New Oxford, Pennsylvania (15 October 1914), had it advertised as being three reels in length and—to confuse matters further—had it entitled *Phantom of the Violin*!

What *is* certain is that Universal decided at some point to edit the film down to three reels and, in March 1915, it was reissued as *Phantom of the Violin*. This wasn't really an unusual practice for Universal, as another Francis Ford/Grace Cunard film, the 1916 *His Majesty Dick Turpin*, was reissued a mere two months later as *Behind the Mask*. In terms of ads and newspaper publicity, *Phantom of the Violin* has left more of a trail as a three-reeler than has its feature incarnation. Sometimes, the grisliness of the story was played down and instead the readers were told that the film was "a brilliant drama of the lights and shadows of Paris' Bohemia" and that "De Maupassant might written such a picture so true is it to the life we might expect in the Bohemian quarters of Paris." Nonetheless, other ads promised the "weird tense story of a crazed violinist who by his uncanny music lures victims to awful death." One rather puzzling blurb (in the *Frederick* [Maryland] *News* on the 12 August 1915) proclaimed: "This is a $5,000 Prize Story of the melodramatic type and tells the story of a musician's weird revenge upon his faithless wife." As the film's star, Grace Cunard, wrote the story, it's anyone guess what the reference to a $5000 prize means.

The film was also novelized—a frequent promotional practice at Universal—and appeared in various newspapers which, in the 1910s, often featured short fiction and serializations of novels (that's largely how *The Phantom of the Opera* circulated at first). The novelization of *Phantom of the Violin* was authored by H.M. Egbert (a *nom de plume* for pulp and science-fiction writer, Victor Rousseau Emanuel), whom Universal kept quite busy in 1915 writing novelizations of such three-reelers as *The Heart of Lincoln, Haunted Hearts, The Sun God, A Woman's Debt, Blood of the Children, Life, Changed Lives,* and *Smuggler's Island*.

Egbert's *Violin* "novelization," though short (just a couple of pages in length), certainly offers more detail than the *Moving Picture World* synopsis and occasionally differs from it (perhaps reflecting the film's reduction to three reels). Ellis is the name of the musician, the woman he adores is Rosa, and she is a naive, convent-bred girl when she meets and quickly marries Ellis. Life with the serious, somewhat withdrawn violinist proves to be dull, and she quickly takes to the excitement of the cabaret. After Ellis teaches her how to play the violin, she starts performing there and is easily seduced by Ellis' actor friend, Caspar. The novelization makes no mention of Ellis' attempt to drown himself when he learns of Rosa's betrayal, or of his rescue by police; nor does Rosa discard Caspar for another lover. We learn that Ellis' own composition—which Rosa burlesques—is titled

"The Phantom of the Violin." At the climax, Ellis strangles Caspar and drags his body to the secret crypt. Ellis doesn't set the theater ablaze, but instead just pulls the fire alarm, causing panic and confusion. He then carries Rosa off, but a crowd spots them and pursues them to the crypt. And there…

> It was the strains of "The Phantom of the Violin" that led them through the darkness, led them to where, with the body of the murdered man between them, Ellis and Rosa rested among the skulls.
>
> He was playing to her as he had never played before and she listened. Whether or not fear had unhinged her own mind also, she showed neither alarm nor eagerness to escape. He played and Rosa listened and nodded sometimes beating time to the music.
>
> The horrified watchers stopped.
>
> Not until the music ceased was the spell broken. The madman looked up and saw them. Instantly he had grasped the girl about the waist and carrying her as lightly as if she were a child plunged into the gloom. The pursuers heard his laughter and hers.
>
> Suddenly the sounds died away. They heard a single scream as though the burden of a lifetime were contained in that one moment's agony. Then — silence.
>
> Somebody struck a match with trembling fingers.
>
> They were standing upon the edge of a measureless abyss.

A photo illustrating the novelization shows Caspar's corpse sprawled out over a slab while Rosa, vacant-eyed, sits besides him, and Ellis saws away on the violin. This grim climax no doubt caused a shudder or two back in 1914.

There are indeed some similarities to *The Phantom of the Opera*: the title, the musical background (here, cabaret instead of opera), Ellis's teaching Rosa how to play the violin (rather than sing), and the madman's lair being located under the theater. One might stretch things a bit and claim the fire (assuming there was one, as *MPW* says) is akin to the chandelier being dropped (though that happens fairly early on in Leroux). Also, while the sundry movie versions have led us to picture the Phantom at the organ, he also plays the violin in the book. (As Francis Ford *was* an accomplished violinist, using that instrument to anchor the title may have just seemed logical.)

Nevertheless, the differences between novel and motion picture are far more extensive: Ellis, though described as wild-eyed and disheveled, isn't disfigured in any way, and Rosa isn't a sweet young virgin under a monster's spell but, rather, an unfaithful wife. *Violin* has at its dramatic core, not a "Beauty and the Beast" motif but, instead, themes touching on the romantic triangle, adultery, and revenge. (Admittedly, the relationship between the Phantom and Christine was hardly a creation of Leroux's, owing a heavy debt to the bond between Svengali and Trilby; *Trilby* was far better known in 1914 than was *The Phantom of the Opera*.) The bloody climax to *Violin* has more in common with *Pagliacci* than bittersweet ending of *The Phantom of the Opera*. What is interesting though is that the mad musician, hearing his own music being played in the theater above him, anticipates the climax of the Claude Rains' *Phantom of the Opera*.

In 1914–1915 Francis Ford and Grace Cunard were the most popular of several boy/girl teams at Universal. They had their own production company where Cunard would write the scripts, Francis Ford would direct, and both would star. Their *Lucille Love: Woman of Mystery*, one of the earliest serials, was

a huge hit. "Beautiful — Daring — Versatile — Magnetic — Lovable — the Acknowledged Queen of the Serials" is how the *Love* ads described Cunard, while Ford was lauded as "Big — manly — dominant — accomplished." Universal kept them very busy with a host of two- and three- reelers, serials, Westerns, comedies, detective thrillers (including a version of Arthur Conan Doyle's *A Study in Scarlet*), and historical dramas: Ford loved playing Abraham Lincoln and did so several times. Sometimes they experimented, as they did with *The Twins' Double*, wherein triple exposure allowed Cunard to play the titular twins (one good, the other a dope addict) *and* their look-alike, a jewel thief. Occasionally they ventured into darker territory: the ad for the three-reeler, *Bride of Mystery* (1914), promised a "story of the occult, of strange mystery and powers, of impending tragedy which penetrates the dark animal part of the mind and arouses vague self pity and terror as when one listens to a ghost ball in the dead of the night."

The film concerned a doctor who tries to save an actress who is under the spell of an evil hypnotist who is also a murderer and master criminal. (As is noted ubiquitously herein, thanks to *Trilby*, the Silent Era was full of sinister hypnotists and their beautiful victims).

In a 1915 interview, Ford — who had worked on the stage and in vaudeville — recalled how he got started in pictures:

> The first job they handed me was that of a fresh drummer. They gave it to me because I looked funny. In that first picture Al Christie and Milton Fahrney were playing parts. Both are directors now for Universal company. I had a good start all right. I started with several different companies until I landed with Meiles doing everything from props to manager, mostly props. I told them I knew more about movies than they did. They wouldn't believe me so they let me go. As they and the Pathe were the first to make moving pictures, I don't blame them [*Ogden* (Utah) *Standard*, 30 October 1915].

At the New York Motion Picture Co., Ford met Grace Cunard. She had been on the stage since age 13 and later worked for Biograph, Pathé and Lubin, where she acted, wrote and directed. (Universal's publicity department claimed Cunard had written some 400 scenarios by 1915). Cunard and Ford hit it off (in more ways than one, even though Ford was married at the time), and made a whole series of popular Westerns. The head man at NYMP Co. at the time was Thomas Ince, who ultimately clashed with Ford over Ince's production methods and his attempt to move Cunard to his own unit. Both Ford and Cunard then headed to Universal, where they achieved their greatest success. In 1914 they were joined by Francis' brother, John, who is as honored today as his brother is forgotten. John Ford later said he learned everything he knew about the movies from Francis and praised his brother as one of the great innovators of the silent screen. He did, however, lament Francis' lack of self-discipline.

Ford eventually left Universal and founded his own independent company; when that failed, he began a film cooperative. That also went under, but Ford had a busy career as a director in the 1920s, when he brought his usual speed and efficiency to a number of serials and action pictures. Ford stopped directing shortly before the coming of sound and spent the rest of his life as a character actor, often in his brother's movies.

Grace Cunard was not so fortunate. An exhausting schedule

and contract disputes lead to friction with Universal. By the end of World War I, the age of the Serial Queen was waning (though it still lasted through the Silent Era), and male heroics more often than not took center stage. Cunard had also entered into a disastrous marriage with Joe Moore, the least of the four acting Moore brothers (Tom, Owen and Matt being the other three) and a drunkard who was so obnoxious that his own mother once had him arrested. The 1920s found Cunard mostly in supporting roles (see entry on *The Last Man on Earth*), as directing and writing assignments for her became scarce. In the Sound Era, she played mainly bit parts. She can be seen in *The Mummy's Tomb* (1942) as the farmer's wife who is awakened by the mummy's shadow crossing her face. It's not likely that anyone would have recognized her as the once celebrated "Queen of the Serials."

Very little of the huge body of work that Cunard and Ford did together has survived: bits and pieces of the different serials, a few cut-down versions of the Westerns and historical dramas (including one with Ford as General Custer). The rest, like Ellis and Rosa, have fallen into the measureless abyss.

— HN

The Poison Pen

The Poison Pen. World Film Corp./World Film Corp, 10 November 1919, 5 reels [LOST]

CAST: June Elvidge (*Allayne Filbert*); Earl Metcalfe (*David Alden*); Joseph Smiley (*Bishop Filbert*); Marion Barney (*Mrs. Filbert*); Jeanne Loew (*Marion Stanley*); George Bunny (*Sims*); Irving Brooks (*Johnson*); John M. Sainpolis (*Dr. McKenna*); J. Arthur Young (*Granville Walters*); Henry West (*Dorgan*); Charles Mackay (*Morton Wells*); Marguerite Gale (*Mrs. Wells*); Dan Comfort (*Boy*)

CREDITS: *Director* Edwin August; *Scenario* J. Clarkson Miller: Based on a story by Edwin August; *Cinematographer* Jacob A. Badaracco

We were tempted to start this one off with a teaser-lead like "Cesare Meets Dr. Mabuse," but common sense prevailed and we decided to tamp down our exuberance for Expressionistic flair and just tell what's what. This 1919 melodrama offered up somnambulists (*a* somnambulist, actually), schizophrenics (the same person) *and* hypnotists (only one of those, too), plus kidnappers, mysterious "heavily robed" figures, and fairly capable detectives— these last being rather novel and infrequently seen on the silent screen.

Our synopsis is courtesy of *The AFI Catalog*:

A furor is created in the village of Queenstead after the discovery of a series of anonymous letters besmirching the reputations of upstanding citizens. Bishop Filbert's daughter Allayne faints at the altar when she receives one of the poison pen letters. Two detectives from the city try to crack the case, but the mystery widens when the infant child of Morton Wells is kidnapped. After the detectives trail a heavily robed figure to the Filbert home, they spend the night inside the house. They later find Allayne in the act of writing a poison pen letter. It is discovered that Allayne has a dual personality and writes the poison pen letters in a

somnambulistic state. A specialist performs hypnosis on Allayne which successfully cures her and allows her to marry. The detectives then arrest the kidnappers and recover the child.

First off, we felt beholden to report on at least one instance of cinematic hypnosis being used for goodness' sake; that is, employed to combat evil. (There are other, equally minor, Silent-Era films wherein a medico uses hypnosis to deal with law-enforcement interrogations and the like, but that sort of thing almost automatically removed said titles from consideration herein.) The evil being fought here is cinematic somnambulism, a state which (low comedy apart) is *never* the sort of thing indulged in by those who live on the side of the angels. One need only consider 1916's *The Witch* (see entry) or 1919's *The Cabinet of Caligari* (nope) to get the picture: no one who ever walked in his/her sleep was up to any good. The fly in the ointment, though, is that the somnambulist in the picture at hand is also described as being the malicious alter ego of the (otherwise) devoted and kind-hearted (albeit schizophrenic) heroine. It's not outside the realm of possibility that a situation like that *could* occur (we assume), but doesn't that mean that every guy who sleepwalks directly to the refrigerator while consciously watching his calories and carbs might therefore be possessed of a dual personality?

Anyhow, this sort of "therapeutic" hypnosis was obviously presented in a different light than were the more flamboyant processes favored by those charlatans and evil geniuses familiar to moviegoers at that stage of the game. The 15 November 1919 *Harrison's Reports* states that "the scenes in the room where the heroine is subjected to the treatment, impress with realism even

How does one hypnotize a somnambulist? "When you awaken, you will fall into a deep sleep…" Original glass slide for *The Poison Pen.*

those who do not believe, either in dual personalities, or in such treatment," and while that's all very well and good, there's really nothing more disappointing to the bona fide genre fan than sensational material (of *any* sort) served up in a sterile or mundane fashion. One can only hope that the scenes wherein the lady's evil psychic twin put the titular poison pen to parchment — or the vignettes centering on that "heavily robed figure" — brought a little pizzazz to this picture. (Otherwise, we're reduced to the sorry state of affairs we outline in our essay on *His Brother's Keeper*.)

Motion Picture News (22 November 1919) admitted that the picture "strains credulity in that it is far removed from life," but — come on — that's pretty much the case with every feature in this book. *MPN* continued, "A surgeon is called in and by using hypnotic suggestion and violet rays [!] and what not, the heroine is cured of her evil personality." You've got our interest now…. Later still: "It is a terrifying moment … for her parents and fiancé when the two personalities battle for supremacy and the evil nature seems to dominate." This statement might very well have referred to some sort of double exposure or soft-focus visual effect, no? (More probably, though, it described June Elvidge's undergoing a series of grimaces, glowers and similar facial contortions before her character comes to grips with her problem and some kind of peace with herself. The *good* herself.) *Sans le film*, we have but the scantest of evidence about what transpired on the screen, and no less an auteur than Akira Kurosawa has proven that any number of folk can absorb the same information and come up with varying conclusions. Therefore, forgive us our trespasses (and our proclivities) and fling open the gates.

Female lead June Elvidge has her resume posted in our chapter on *The Zero Hour*, so make your move now. Joseph Smiley (who played her father) moved out of Beantown and into the movies in 1911 and, by 1927, had appeared in about six dozen films while directing nearly only a handful fewer. His character man's credits include a few shorts (like *The Sorceress*, *The Gray Horror*) that would be discussed herein were it not for their brevity and a couple of features (like *The Face in the Fog* and *Seven Keys to Baldpate*) that likewise missed out on inclusion for having just fallen short of the requisite quality/quantity of frisson. His director's credits elevate him in our eyes, though, as they include *Life Without Soul*, the first, (presumably) epic, lost, feature-length retelling of the Frankenstein story. More on Mr. Smiley may be found in our coverage there.

We're assuming that the character, David Alden, was Miss Elvidge's love interest, but the only clue we can seize on with respect to that is *MPN* — when speaking of the lady — followed immediately with "Earl Metcalfe gives a satisfactory performance in the opposite role," and Earl played David. Metcalfe got into films a year after Joseph Smiley, and he, too, graced the screen (about 12 dozen times) and wielded a megaphone (for about 20 Lubin comedy shorts) for a couple of years in the mid–1910s. His career and his life ended abruptly in late January 1928, when he fell from an airplane during a flying lesson; his last feature, ironically, was Superlative Pictures' *The Air Mail Pilot*. *The Poison Pen* was his only genre movie.

Other than those three actors/characters, we've no idea who played whom and which character did what to someone else; there exist no synopses with enough specifics to fill us in. For example, we might reveal that the part of Sims was played by George Bunny, whose chief claim to fame (at this point, at any rate) appears to be his having been brother to John Bunny, but to what end? Who the hell was Sims? Morton Wells — the chap in the summary whose infant child is kidnapped — was enacted by Charles Mackay, a character man who made about 15 films in a career than spanned half as many years, but… So what? Dr. McKenna, who *might* have been the hypnotist who shears the villainous side off our heroine — we've no idea, really — was played by John Sainpolis, a longtime supporting cast member who gets a tip of the hat in our coverage of *The Mystic Hour*. Et cetera, et cetera, et cetera.

Edwin August, the director, also wrote the story on which J. Clarkson Miller's scenario was based. *The Poison Pen* marked August's only genre work, but Miller's name is printed again in our essay on the 1921 version of *The Case of Becky*.

And so it goes…

Harrison's felt "this is a fairly good program picture. It is well acted and directed." *MPN* found it to be "quite entertaining" and apt to hold the viewer's interest "because of its novelty and its unique characterization." Neither *Variety* nor *The New York Times* spilled any ink on it, poisonous or otherwise.

Upon reflection, we'll admit that there may be those among the readership who will quibble about the inclusion of *The Poison Pen* herein, what with the plot — in all honesty — dealing with the machinations of a sleep-challenged, two-faced woman. To those, we ask to be allowed to play devil's advocate: Consider the direction Robert Louis Stevenson's oft-imitated tale might have taken had Dr. Jekyll's evil self refrained from his sundry violent, lust-filled activities and had, instead, vented his innate wickedness via the blogosphere.

— *JTS*

The Price of Silence

The Price of Silence. G.B. Samuelson/States' Rights and Sunrise Pictures, 1 Jan 1921 (approx. date, taken from trade review), 6 reels [LOST]

CAST: Peggy Hyland (*Beryl Brentano*); Campbell Gullan (*Col. Luke Darrington*); Tom Chatterton (*Lennox Dunbar*); Daisy Robinson (*Leo Gordon*); Dorothy Gordon (*Mrs. Brentano*); Van Dycke (*Frank Darrington*)

CREDITS: *Producer* G.B. Samuelson; *Director* Fred Leroy Granville; based on the novel *At the Mercy of Tiberius* by Augusta Jane Evans Wilson (New York, 1887); *Cinematographer* Leland Lancaster

Perhaps shot at Universal City (there is but one, uncorroborated statement to that effect), there can be no doubt that *The Price of Silence* was produced by Briton G.B. Samuelson in America. Oddly, this independent feature was released in England (in mid–1920) as *At the Mercy of Tiberius* — the title of the film's source novel — before it won distribution throughout most of the USA via the States' Rights system in late 1920/early 1921. We say "most of" the country as the Sunrise Pictures Corporation snagged the distribution rights for "Greater New York and Northern New Jersey." Still, local press coverage in the

Chicago market had the picture playing as *At the Mercy of Tiberius*, so some British prints (identical to their American counterparts save for the title card) may have been pressed into service to offset States' Rights inadequacies. The novel — a strange affair by Augusta Jane Evans Wilson — had previously been mined for its ore by Thanhouser, which released the result of its excavations as *God's Witness* in 1915. One may find additional information of Miss Wilson's master work in that essay, but a comparison of that film's scenario with this one will yield few common elements save for grandfathers and window panes.

Samuelson did not bother to register his picture for copyright with the Library of Congress, so the following synopsis is taken from *The AFI Catalog*, which does not cite its source.

> Beryl Brentano's mother is in need of an operation but is unable to pay for it. Beryl goes for the needed cash to her grandfather, who has disowned her mother for marrying against his will. She obtains it and leaves, unseen by any of the servants; later that night, her grandfather is found dead, presumably murdered. Beryl, thinking her brother is the killer, offers no self-defense and is arrested, tried, and convicted of the murder. A year passes, and the butler tells the prosecuting attorney that the ghost of his master is fighting with his murderer. Upon investigation, it is discovered that lightning had sketched on the window a picture of the death of the grandfather, who met his end by no violence. Beryl, freed from prison, finds that her mother has died and that there is no trace of her brother. Through advertising she communicates with her brother, now a priest, and learns the truth; while he was quarrelling with his grandfather, a bolt of lightning struck him dead.

One might think it odd that Beryl's brother manages to take Holy Orders within the space of a single year, but perchance he is already a seminarian at the time of their granddad's not-so-happy dispatch; either way, it's odder still that a supposed man of the cloth would let an innocent party (especially his sibling) be sent up the river for what is indubitably a tragic accident. (Unless, of course, said priest is covering up for his Boss for an appallingly litigious Act of God!) A tad bizarre, too, is the butler's claim that "the ghost of his master is fighting with his murderer," when subsequent scrutiny reveals that the old boy "met his end with no violence"! We're also a bit confused as to how a bolt of lightning can impress an image of *itself* on a window pane; either the lightning makes the impression or it is, itself, impressed upon the glass; how in blazes does it do *both*? It matters not; we're less interested in what the windowpane wrought (for us, the MacGuffin) than in the fact that the windowpane wrought anything whatsoever. This is the rather watery genre glue that holds this epic within these pages.

Virtually none of the American print advertising for the film (we could locate nothing from its U.K. release) bothered with the business about gramps and the bolt from heaven, treating the story as if it were just another selfless-soul's-self-sacrifice-for-someone-else saga. The oddly capitalized ad copy from the 25 December 1920 edition of *Moving Picture World* is rather representative: "The Prosecuting Attorney was relentless … a Crusher of Women's Souls whose one God was the God Success— She Was Friendless— Circumstantial Evidence was Against Her — She Sealed Her Lips to Shield Another — He Sent Her to the Penitentiary — And Then —*He Fell Madly in Love with Her!*"

Had Beryl *not* ended up romantically entangled with somebody, *that* would have been the element that qualified *The Price*

of Silence* for inclusion in this book. A less predictable (but more satisfying) pairing than the match-up between prosecutor and comely defendant was *Price*'s director, Fred Leroy Granville, falling madly in love with Peggy Hyland (and she with him). Along with his junket from Australia to the States in the mid–1910s and his renouncing the camera to heft the megaphone, marrying the British Hyland in July 1921 was the third of three great career/personal moves for the Victoria-born Granville. In 1916, at the age of 20, he had photographed Universal's fantasy, *Undine* (see entry), his only other genre contribution, and in 1932, scarcely 36 years old, he was dead of Bright's Disease; his last film credit — *Sous le ciel d'Orient* (*Under the Eastern Sky*) — was earned in 1927. Hyland herself (see *Black Shadows*) was out of the industry by 1925.

Among the picture folk who did not fall madly in love with someone else (publicly, at any rate) at about this time was Tom Chatterton. Chatterton's character, Lennox Dunbar, was the stolid prosecutor who found his heart aflutter while contriving to send the object of his affection up the river. More importantly — per Miss Wilson's screed, at any rate — it is Dunbar's resemblance to a bust of the emperor Tiberius (an association made by Beryl while she is still thinking clearly) that provides the otherwise opaque nomenclature of both source novel and British release title.

Anyhow, Chatterton junketed from the remote reaches of upstate New York down to the Big Apple in 1913 (when scarcely in his majority) and thence to Hollywood. From 1913 until the tail end of the 1940s, the strapping actor appeared in well over 150 films, including genre titles ranging from intriguingly entitled shorts (like 1915's *The Secret of the Dead*) to classic sci-fi serials (like *Flash Gordon Conquers the Universe* and *Drums of Fu Manchu*, both 1940) to bits (credited and un-) in "B" and "C" cult favorites (such as 1945's *The Phantom Speaks*). Like so many of his contemporaries, he spent a few of his earliest industry years directing others (and occasionally himself) in forgettable two-reelers; unlike many of his confreres, he seems to have taken a 15-year hiatus from films not long after *The Price of Silence* wrapped. Research has thus far failed to determine whither wentest he. Chatterton died in Hollywood in mid–August 1952.

We pause to note that research has also failed to identify the actor who played Beryl's brother, the priest who lammed it rather than 'fessing up to watching his grandfather fry and thus saving his sister from spending a year rooming with someone named Bubba. (To be fair to the character, in the novel the lightning bolt that did in granddad also disfigured him [as he was quarrelling with the old man], and the newly-highly-unattractive lad ran off to join an order of monks and thus hide himself away from a world that does not appreciate inner beauty.)

For the mainstream crowd, *The Price of Silence* offered yet another variation on how boys and girls who are just meant for each other will ultimately end up in the clenches, even despite the U.S. penal system. For genre aficionados (like us), the film turns on an hysterical butler who sees ghosts and murders that aren't there on a windowpane that — obviously — the upstairs maid hadn't cleaned in a year's time!

Let's face it. It's *always* been hard to get good help.

— *JTS*

Princess of the Dark

Princess of the Dark. New York Motion Picture Corp. and Kay-Bee/Triangle Distributing Corp., 18 March 1917, 5 reels [LOST]

CAST: Enid Bennett (*Fay Herron*); Jack Gilbert ("*Crip*" *Halloran*), Alfred Vosburg (*Jack Rockwell*); Walt Whitman (*James Herron*); J. Frank Burke (*Crip's father*)

CREDITS: *Director* Charles Miller; *Supervisor* Thomas H. Ince; *Scenario* Monte M. Katterjohn; *Story* Lanier Bartlett; *Cinematographer* Clyde DeVinna; *Music* Victor Schertzinger

> "It was a picture called *Princess of the Dark* and Jack (Gilbert) was given the lead. He was absolutely floating on air. He couldn't believe his luck. Not that it was much of a part. I mean, it was awful. He played a hunchback crippled boy in love with a beautiful blind girl who of course, couldn't see that he was crippled, and everything would be perfect as long as she didn't try to give him a back rub. Really corny stuff."
>
> — Rowland V. Lee, quoted in John Gilbert's bio, *Dark Star*

Corny perhaps, but romance between a blind girl and a deformed man is at least as old as Dea and Gwynplaine in Victor Hugo's *The Man Who Laughs*. Such matches also turn up in movies like *The Face Behind the Mask* (Peter Lorre and Evelyn Keyes), *The Brute Man* (Rondo Hatton and Jane Adams) and, in comicdom, *The Fantastic Four*'s Ben "The Thing" Grimm and Alicia. Chaplin's *City Lights* gives us a variation on the same theme, with the beautiful blind girl who doesn't know her hero is the Little Tramp. The blind — at least in fiction — are often depicted as having a kind of moral superiority; they are able to intuit a person's true character since their affliction spares them the handicap of judging others by appearances. (For a cynical antidote to such sentimentality see *Laughter in the Dark* and the Australian film, *Proof.*) While *City Lights* ends on an ambiguous note (Will the newly cured blind girl still love the Little Tramp now that she can see him?), the *Princess of the Dark* is far less merciful to her crippled swain.

Synopsis (drawn from *The AFI Catalog* and contemporary reviews):

> In a squalid mining town in West Virginia, James Herron, a consumptive, lives with his little daughter Fay, who has been blind since birth. He stimulates her imagination by reading her fairy-tales. Fay's best friend is "Crip" Halloran, the hunchbacked son of the town drunkard. They play in an old mineshaft which becomes an enchanted fairyland in Fay's mind. She pictures herself as a princess and Crip as her Prince Charming and the ugly smokestacks of the town as towers bedecked with jewels. One day John Rockwell, son of a rich mine owner, comes to look after his property. By chance he meets Fay and becomes enchanted with her charm and idealism. He is admitted to the magic kingdom, but Crip resents the competition. In love and with pity for Fay's misfortune, John arranges for an operation to restore her sight. The operation is a success and Fay asks that Crip, her Prince Charming, be the first person she looks upon. When she sees the ugly, misshapen man, she is shocked and disillusioned, and shrinks away from him. Later Fay and John find Crip's body in the cavern where he was once happy with his Princess.

It should be noted that the *Variety* review states that Crip dies of a broken heart, but *The AFI Catalog* says he takes his own life.

Princess of the Dark was the first starring vehicle for Thomas H. Ince's discovery, Enid Bennett, and was promoted accordingly. *MPN* reviewer Peter Milne was duly impressed:

> Miss Bennett's popularity seems a thing assured for she has a personality that is most pleasing. Fay was a part hard to portray, no doubt, particularly for a player new to the art. Simplicity and unsophistication [*sic*] are its dominant qualities. That Miss Bennett is never for a moment out of character is a distinct attribute to her ability. Blind girls of the screen so often obviously see [17 February 1917].

Roland V. Lee likewise thought that the film was a good showcase for Bennett, but that Jack Gilbert was wasted "thrashing around like Quasimodo with pimples." *Variety*'s Fred, though, offered a few words of praise for Bennett before going on to say:

> Her work is not of the startling quality that would cause anyone to immediately say, "The greatest find ever in filmdom," and therefore before the sponsors for Miss Bennett can hope that the public will accept their star as such they will have to hammer the fact home with advertising and better pictures from a scenario standpoint than *Princess of the Dark* [9 February 1917].

"Fred" felt Gilbert gave the more memorable performance. Perhaps one thing that made Gilbert's portrayal convincing was that he *had* a crush on Enid Bennett and was later distraught when she married director Fred Niblo. Gilbert's disappointment, though, did not result in suicide or death by broken heart.

Reviewers noted that just the month before *Princess* was premiered, its distributor, Triangle, had released a similar film titled *Nina, the Flower Girl*, in which the blind title character is loved by a crippled newsboy. In the end, both of them are cured. There's no fantasy element in that film, other than perhaps a surgeon of miraculous capability who can give sight to the blind and running shoes to the lame. This marvelous medico was perhaps a disciple of the scientist who straightened out Quasimodo in another 1917 film, *The Darling of Paris* (see entry). Unfortunately, he was not available for Crip, and there was no way Ince was going to let his beautiful new star walk into the smoggy sunset with an impoverished hunchback; instead, Fay acquires a rich and handsome husband and a comfortable new life, while Crip just gets the shaft.

Reviewers don't say a great deal about the fantasy land we see visualized in Fay's imagination (the only reason for the film's inclusion here). Apparently, there were a number of double exposures, probably showing the real world being replaced by the imaginary one, as well as Fay and Crip exchanging their rags for finery. It's not clear what — if anything — happens in this fantasy world. There's no mention of evil wizards or dragons, so presumably this magic kingdom is as benign as Disney's Orlando playground.

Variety felt the film was routine except for the photography (also favorably noted by *MPN*): "The latter is unusual, and the cameraman will be fully as responsible for Miss Bennett achieving stardom as were the author and director." The praised but unnamed cameraman was Ince veteran, Clyde De Vinna, who later won an Academy Award for his work on *White Shadows in the South Sea* (1928).

One ad for the film promised "mystery and thrills," while another claimed the movie was based on the question "Is Ignorance Bliss?" Perhaps more typical of the publicity campaign, though, was an ad describing the film as: "A play for mothers and fathers and sisters and brothers. It will make you laugh and cry. A fairy story of modern life with a little fairy of a star who shines through the play and will make you glad you know her." In the same vein is a rather clumsy blurb that states the film is "for little children of five and big children of 85."

Enid Bennett, "the little fairy of a star" (and at just 5 feet, she was little), was born in York, Australia, and went on the stage as a teenager. Her first success was as Modesty in *Everywoman*. She also had parts in a few movies directed by her future husband, Fred Niblo, who was doing stage and film work Down Under with his then-wife, Josephine (sister of George M. Cohan). In 1915, Bennett went to America, where she played in *Cock o' the Walk* (with Cornelia Otis Skinner) on Broadway and, later, in Los Angeles. It was in L.A. that she met Thomas H. Ince, who persuaded her to sign with him. Bennett later said she was at first reluctant since she had already achieved success on the stage and didn't want to start on the bottom in a new medium, but Ince told her that she was going to begin her film career as a star. When she worried about homesickness, Ince brought her family over from Australia and arranged a screen test for her sister, Marjorie. (Both Marjorie and another sister Catherine, became actresses, though not stars, like Enid.)

Bennett became a popular leading lady and is best remembered for her heroine roles in swashbucklers like *Robin Hood* and *The Sea Hawk*. She also had a very strong part in the underrated *The Red Lily* (directed by Niblo), playing a nice French girl forced into a life of sin in the Paris underworld. She had married Niblo in 1918 (after the death of his first wife) and in 1925 gave birth to their first child, Peter; two more kindern followed. Marriage and motherhood resulted in fewer and fewer screen appearances, although Enid did accompany her husband to Italy to act as his assistant during the very difficult *Ben-Hur* shoot. In 1929 she appeared on the stage with Edward Everett Horton in *The Streets of New York* and made her "comeback" film, *Skippy*, in 1931. A few more film roles followed — including that of Mrs. Wetherby in James Whale's *Waterloo Bridge*— and then she left the screen again. Niblo was no longer directing (he later claimed that he'd been blackballed — presumably by MGM — for refusing an assignment), but the couple was financially secure. In 1939, David Selznick brought Enid back for *Intermezzo* (supposedly he was looking through old fan magazines and saw her picture), but after a couple of minor roles, she retired for good. Besides *Princess*, her only other genre credit is *The Haunted Bedroom* (1919, see entry), directed by Niblo.

As Rowland V. Lee had said, *Princess of the Dark* did little for Jack Gilbert's career, but he did get good notices. In a few years, Gilbert would find his niche as a leading man and matinee idol, but he was never comfortable with that status and always felt character roles were not only more challenging, but also would assure a steadier, more stable career. Time would prove him right.

The leading man in *Princess* was Alfred Vosburgh, who had been a stage actor before achieving some modest film success freelancing at the different studios. A year or so after *Princess*, fans wrote to Vitagraph saying that their new player, Alfred Whitman, bore a striking resemblance to Vosburgh. It turned out they were one and the same; 1917 was not a good time to have a German sounding name, so "Vosburgh" had to go. In 1921, Whitman switched his focus to the stage, working at the

Morosco Theater in Los Angeles. In 1925 Warners offered him a contract which he accepted under the name Gayne Whitman, a moniker he kept for the rest of his career. He ended up doing mostly supporting roles, and his film career dwindled as the talkies came in. Nonetheless, he did extremely well on radio where he originated the character of *Chandu the Magician* (the very popular show was, at one point, getting 8,000 letters a week). In 1933, Sol Lesser announced that Whitman would star in a film version of *Chandu* that would also be broadcast while it was filming! What emerged, though, was the 1934 serial, *Return of Chandu*, which starred not Gayne Whitman, but Bela Lugosi. It may not have mattered to Whitman, who did very well in radio while continuing in the movies in bit parts (often as a radio announcer or a narrator).

Princess of the Dark was based on a story by Lanier Bartlett (whose forte, actually, was Westerns) and turned into a script by Monte Katterjohn. The latter's most famous scenario is for a fantasy of a different sort, 1921's *The Sheik*. Katterjohn, a one-time clerk at the Indiana legislature and later a journalist, had become scenario editor at Universal Film Manufacturing Company by the age of 23. He also started one of the first film magazines, *Motion Picture Topics*; in spite of the scintillating title, the magazine flopped. Ketterjohn was more successful as a press agent for Florence Lawrence and, in 1915, he wrote her biography, *Growing Up with the Movies*.

"Charming" was how *MPN* described Charles Miller's direction of *Princess of the Dark*. Miller had strong stage credentials and, in addition to heading his own stock company, had played leads in New York in plays like *The Squaw Man*, *Bought and Paid For*, and *The Great Divide*. He signed with Ince in 1915 for $8 a day and is supposedly somewhere in Ince's big epic, *Civilization* (see entry). Miller quickly switched from acting to directing, his first film being 1916's *The Moral Fabric*. Miller helmed a number of important movies in the 1910s, including *Flame of the Yukon*, with Dorothy Dalton, and *Ghosts of Yesterday*, with Norma Talmadge, but his career as a director faltered in the 1920s, and he returned to acting. In 1927 he joined the crew of the Hollywood Playhouse and was interviewed by the *Los Angeles Times* (on the 24 July); the article was entitled "Once-Favored Director Acts" and explained how things had gone wrong. Miller related how he had made the huge error of going into independent production: "I decided if I could make money for others, I could make money for myself, so I decided to make my own pictures. I made six in all and they broke me." Further complications ensued when Miller became very ill and was bedridden for a year. When he was ready to go back to work, he found that Hollywood simply wouldn't let him take up where he had left off: "I've made some good pictures, and they know it in the motion picture industry. But I haven't a hit released just yesterday to talk about, and thus I'm not making a picture today." Miller made the best of his return to the boards, but still hoped to direct again. It was not to be, and the last film he acted in was *The Road to Ruin*, in 1928.

Violinist and composer Victor Schertzinger wrote a score for *Princess of the Dark*, just as he had for *Civilization*, and then went on to a long and successful career as a film composer and director.   — *HN*

Public Opinion

Public Opinion. Jesse L. Lasky Feature Play Co./Paramount Pictures Corp., 17 August 1916, 5 reels, Library of Congress
CAST: Blanche Sweet (*Hazel Gray*); Earle Foxe (*Dr. Henry Morgan*); Edythe Chapman (*Mrs. Carson Morgan*); Tom Forman (*Philip Carson*); Elliott Dexter (*Gordon Graham*); Raymond Hatton (*Smith*); with Robert Henry Gray.
CREDITS: *Director* Frank Reicher; *Assistant Director* Roscoe Smith; *Story and Scenario* Margaret Turnbull; *Cinematographer* Dent Gilbert; *Art Director* Wilfred Buckland

This 1916 Lasky film is a melodrama with a mission — to attack yellow journalism and trial by the press — and it owes its presence in this volume to a brief (and entirely unnecessary) supernatural element it would be better off without. The story is unbelievable in other ways as well, but it is so solidly acted and directed that its lapses of realism can be overlooked.

Synopsis based on a viewing of the print at Library of Congress:

> Nurse Hazel Gray elopes with Dr. Henry Morgan but quickly leaves him when she discovers he is married. The story reaches the press, and Hazel leaves town to escape the gossip. Sometime later she is courted by Philip Carson who has left the home of his mother, a wealthy philanthropist, because he dislikes her new husband (who turns out to be Dr. Morgan). Morgan is a shady character whose first wife died under mysterious circumstances. Morgan provides cocaine to Smith, an addict who knows Morgan's past. Morgan begins to poison his new wife.
>
> A new lodger at Hazel's boarding house knows her past and tells the landlady who then asks Hazel to leave. Philip, who has recently been home to visit his ailing mother, suggests Hazel become her new nurse. Hazel consents but is shocked to find that Philip's stepfather is Dr. Morgan. Morgan makes a pass at her that she angrily rebuffs, but it is in the interest of both of them to keep silent about their shared past. Mrs. Carson Morgan becomes very fond of Hazel, but Dr. Morgan sees her presence as a way to speed up his murder plot.
>
> Since his mother is not getting better, Philip insists on another doctor being called in. The doctor prescribes a new medication. Dr. Morgan takes the little box of medication and substitutes a similar one filled with arsenic. He is about to burn the box of medicine when he is interrupted by Smith on another of his unwelcome visits in search of cocaine. Seeing the box in the fireplace, Smith takes it when the doctor's back is turned.
>
> Hazel unwittingly administers the poison to Mrs. Carson Morgan, and the woman dies immediately. The new doctor is highly suspicious and, after examining the body, declares that Mrs. Morgan was poisoned. The police are called and, since it was Hazel who gave her employer the drug, she is arrested and charged with murder. The truth about her earlier affair with Dr. Morgan comes out, and this makes for sensational headlines. People from all walks of life who admired Mrs. Carson Morgan for her good works are furious about the murder and believe Hazel to be guilty. Even Philip's faith in the woman he loves wavers.
>
> At the trial Dr. Morgan tells the jury that Hazel is still in love with him and speculates she wanted his wife out of the way so she could have him — and his inheritance — for herself. On the witness stand, Hazel desperately pleads her case and declares "Men have no justice for a woman they believe to be bad!" At that point, the spirit of Mrs. Carson Morgan becomes present in the courtroom. When the case goes to the jury, the ghost desperately tries to influence the jury in Hazel's favor, but eleven of the twelve men believe her guilty. The only one who has doubts is Gordon Graham, a rich ne'er-do-well who tried to get out of serving on the jury by telling the judge he had plans to go fishing for the week. Graham's

flippancy has faded, and he is very drawn to Hazel and believes her to be innocent. The spirit of Mrs. Carson Morgan focuses on Graham as he looks over the transcript in the hope of finding something that will clear Hazel. Finally, he takes note of the fact that no one actually saw Hazel substitute the poison for the real medicine, and that the whole case against her is likewise circumstantial. Graham is able to sway the other jurors, and Hazel is found not guilty. However, the court of public opinion has already decided she is a murderess, and there is outrage at the jury's verdict.

> Hounded by the publicity, Hazel finds refuge at the house of Gordon's aunt. Philip visits her there, but she no longer cares for him since he didn't support her in her time of need. Gordon has fallen in love with Hazel, but she insists there can be romance between them until she clears her name. She decides to confront Dr. Morgan. Morgan is planning on liquidating his inheritance and leaving town but Smith, not wanting to lose his drug connection, threatens him and reveals that he has still has the packet of medicine. Just as Hazel arrives the two men begin struggling. Smith shoots Dr. Morgan, and Gordon, who has followed Hazel, brings a policeman into the house. Smith is arrested and, as the spirit of his wife lingers in the room, Dr. Morgan confesses just before he dies. The next sensational newspaper headline trumpets Hazel's exoneration.

Publicity for the film described it as a "realistic and gripping presentation of the theory that those who have passed away from this world return in spirit to right wrongs." Well, there you go.

The ghost of Mrs. Carson Morgan is a figure of sorrow and distress, wrapped in a shroud and with a distraught expression on her face. Her situation is not unlike that of the main character in the hit play, *The Return of Peter Grimm* (and publicity for *Public Opinion* did not fail to mention this), in that she returns from the dead to accomplish some purpose, but finds she cannot communicate directly with the living. Unable to move furniture, rap on tables, or write ghostly messages on a blackboard, Mrs. Morgan has to try to get into the minds of the living as a kind of thought or suggestion. Her appearance in the film — accomplished by simple but effective double exposure work — is very fleeting, and when she returns at the ending, she doesn't seem to do anything except observe. Possibly we're meant to think that it's her presence that causes Dr. Morgan to confess or perhaps she's just there to see things through. And even though justice has been done, she doesn't seem any happier! There is no discussion of the supernatural among any of the characters nor is there the slightest indication that anyone has actually felt her presence, all of which makes one wonder why veteran scenarist Margaret Turnbull added this particular element, especially as Gordon's sudden infatuation with Hazel provides reason enough for him to doubt her guilt.

In spite of the surprising emphasis on the supernatural in some of the publicity, the reviews we consulted don't mention the ghost at all. Nor, for that matter, does Kevin Brownlow in his description of the film in *Behind the Mask of Innocence*; Brownlow even quotes a *Photoplay* critic who felt there was certainly sufficient evidence to convict Hazel, and the jury only let her off because of misplaced chivalry. Poor Mrs. Carson Morgan went through the bother of returning from the dead to seek justice, and no one even noticed!

Harvey K. Thaw, in the 2 September 1916 *Motion Picture News*, spends most of his review describing the story rather than critiquing it, but he seems to admire its theme and does mention that it's "an excellent vehicle for Blanche Sweet and a strong supporting cast." Still, "Jolo"—in his 18 August 1916 review in *Variety*—found the story "cheap" and often unbelievable; regarding the latter he writes: "During the trial the fact that it is unethical for a physician to prescribe for his own wife is not once brought out, nor is his name once suggested as an accomplice of the accused." Jolo seems to have forgotten that a second opinion on Mrs. Carson Morgan's case *was* called in, but his other complaint is valid. One would think in fact that, given he has the most to gain from his wife's death, Dr. Morgan would be considered the primary suspect; however, focusing on Hazel allows the film to criticize the double standard of justice for women.

The exposition in the early scenes of the film is a little vague, and it's not clear exactly how much time has elapsed between Hazel breaking off with Dr. Morgan and the subsequent events; presumably enough time has passed for Morgan to dispose of wife No. 1 and then re-marry. We do see Hazel, in double exposure, tearing the newspaper that bears the headline of the scandal, but it's not clear why the doctor's love life would make the news in the first place.

Director Frank Reicher (see *Unconquered* for a rundown on his career) cuts back and forth effectively between Hazel's trial and the growing public resentment against her. There's discussion of the case everywhere, from ritzy private clubs to humble homes as well as on streetcars and in barber shops. Later, when Hazel is released and tries to check into a hotel, she is recognized by one of the staff, and the manager refuses to rent her a room; she withdraws in humiliation as a crowd gawks at her. Of course the happy ending is a bit contrived, and one can't help but note that — after two tries — Hazel ends up with a rich guy after all.

Though promoted as a Blanche Sweet vehicle (see 1915's *The Case of Becky* for more on Miss Sweet), *Public Opinion* is by no means dominated by its star and boasts excellent ensemble work by all concerned. Perhaps best of all is Earle Foxe as Dr. Morgan. Sporting a handlebar moustache that makes him look like a sinister Wyatt Earp, Foxe smoothly underplays his role as a cold-blooded Bluebeard who lacks anything resembling a conscience (which makes his dying confession a bit unlikely). Mr. Foxe can also be found here in entries on *The Last Man on Earth* and *Black Magic*.

An ad for *Public Opinion* in the *Sandusky* [Ohio] *Star Journal* put Blanche Sweet's name over the title and also promised "a powerful portrayal of an intense role. The work of the 'dope fiend' is the best of its kind ever seen in Sandusky." How often dope fiends were to be seen in Sandusky is not known, but the reference is to Raymond Hatton's turn as Smith. While he frequently played dubious characters, Hatton is best remembered for his later, lighter roles and as Wallace Beery's frequent sidekick, but here he sniffles, twitches and gets saucer eyes whenever Dr. Morgan produces the little white packets he craves. Nonetheless, his performance is a veritable model of restraint compared to the spasmodic addicts in films like *Reefer Madness* and *The Cocaine Fiends*.

Elliot Dexter (Gordon Graham) looks much younger than his 40+ years and though his character — the rich idler who reforms because of a girl — is a silent movie cliché, he ably suggests a man with an emerging conscience. Dexter turns up a number of times in these pages and a biographical sketch can be found in our essay on 1923's *Forever*.

In his aforementioned piece on *Public Opinion*, Kevin Brownlow points out that the reviewer for *The New York Dramatic Mirror* found a parallel to the story in the case of Dr. Arthur Waite, a New York dentist who poisoned both his in-laws and then tried to do the same to his wife in order to collect the family's millions. When the evidence began pointing to him, Waite took an overdose of narcotics but recovered to stand trial. There was a great deal of lurid press coverage, and while there was no real counterpart to Nurse Hazel, the press did come up with "the other woman," a beautiful young singer who claimed her relationship with Waite was innocuous. Waite was indicted in March of 1916, but Brownlow states that, curiously enough, Margaret Turnbull had sold her story to Lasky prior to that. Be that as it may, the film was not released until August of 1916 and Turnbull, who also did the scenario, could certainly have embellished her script with details from Waite's trial.

Dr. Waite, who heard himself described as a "Dr. Jekyll and Mr. Hyde" during his trial, confessed and entered an insanity plea. This was rejected and Waite went to the electric chair. Before he died, he said that he hoped that in the afterlife he would be able to serve those he had wronged. Mrs. Carson Morgan would have approved.

— *HN*

Puritan Passions

Puritan Passions. The Film Guild/W.W. Hodkinson Corp., 2 September 1923, 7 reels/6,600 ft. or 6,859 ft. [LOST]

CAST: Glen Hunter (*Lord Ravensbane/The Scarecrow*); Mary Astor (*Rachel*); Osgood Perkins (*Dr. Nicholas*); Maud Hill (*Goody Rickby*); Frank Tweed (*Gilead Wingate*); Dwight Wiman (*Bugby*); Thomas Chalmers (*The Minister*).

CREDITS: *Director* Frank Tuttle; *Scenario by* Frank Tuttle and James Ashmore Creeland; based on the play *The Scarecrow or The Glass of Truth: A Tragedy of the Ludicrous* by Percy MacKaye (New York, 1908); *Cinematographer* Frank Waller, Jr.

Though Nathaniel Hawthorne is best remembered for shining a light on the dark, tortured souls of his Puritan forefathers, the author of *The House of the Seven Gables* was not above an occasional foray into satire: "Feathertop," his last short story, looks askance at a society that values style over substance. The title character is a scarecrow given life and a human appearance as a joke by a witch, who dresses him in fancy clothes, teaches him the manners of a dandy, and sends him out into the world. He's immediately accepted as a gentleman of great refinement by everyone he encounters. Only children and animals shrink from Feathertop, because they are able to see the scarecrow as he really is. Feathertop wins the heart of the local beauty, but when she looks into a mirror with her beloved, she sees not her elegant suitor, but a grotesque scarecrow with a pumpkin for a head. Disillusioned by what his reflection reveals, Feathertop returns to the witch and asks to be made inanimate again. She reluctantly consents, but bemoans her creation's sensitivity in a world where so many who are like him never see themselves for what they are.

Hawthorne's scarecrow was first brought to life in a 1908 Edison one-reeler entitled *Lord Feathertop*, and publicity for the short described it as a tale of "love, disappointment and revenge." Another one-reel version appeared courtesy of Eclair in 1912 and starred Muriel Ostriche. The very next year, Kinemacolor did its own, equally obscure, one-reel adaptation; however, that film wowed them in La Crosse, where the local paper was impressed by the effectiveness of the Kinemacolor process: "Colonial costumes called for by the play give an excellent chance for the display of Kinemacolor's ability in reproducing colors" (*La Crosse* [Wisconsin] *Tribune*, 19 May 1913). A feature-film version appeared in 1916 (see appendix), but had little to do with the original story.

The most enduring adaptation was Percy MacKaye's 1908 play *The Scarecrow, Or, The Glass of Truth, a Tragedy of the Ludicrous*. What had impressed MacKaye the most about the Hawthorne tale was not its rather obvious satirical points, but the poignancy of Feathertop's "ludicrous" situation: a man-made creature who yearns to be a real human being. Feathertop shares this longing with his more famous brethren: Pinocchio, Frankenstein's Monster, the Golem, and Homunculus — not to mention more recent counterparts in *Blade Runner* and *Artificial Intelligence: AI*. MacKaye used the story as a springboard for his play, but made many changes: Feathertop — who assumes the name Lord Ravensbane — is brought to life by the witch, not as a lark but rather as part of her scheme of revenge against the Puritan elder who wronged her. The devil, a mere bit-player in the short story, takes center-stage here as the scarecrow's sinister tutor. At the end, self-sacrifice, not self-loathing, motivates Ravensbane to give up his life, and his act saves the woman he loves. Love trumps the devil, and the scarecrow becomes a real man in death.

MacKaye, who also wrote poetry, pageants, and plays about famous historical figures (like Joan of Arc), was considered to be a bit of a highbrow and there was some reluctance to bring *The Scarecrow* to the stage. However, in 1911 it made Broadway in a production starring Frank Reicher (best remembered as Captain Englehorn in *King Kong*) as Ravensbane and Edmund Breese as the devil. Clever bits of staging were noted, especially the confrontation between Ravensbane and his hideous reflection. The devil displayed not only his usual Mephisthophelean wit, but also a monstrous and rather expressive tail, making him the kind of demon who would have felt hellishly at home in *Häxan*. Nonetheless, the play's mixture of emotion, philosophical asides, and the macabre failed to win over the public, and the show closed after 23 performances.

The Scarecrow found a more receptive audience among the members of the Film Guild, a movie cooperative formed in 1921 and modeled after the Theater Guild. The Film Guild — whose motto was "Fewer and Better Pictures" — was comprised of young firebrands (most of whom had been friends at Yale) who set out to do something different from the usual Hollywood brand of entertainment. Frank Tuttle, one of the few members of the group with a little film experience (as a scenarist for Paramount) hit up family, friends, and former classmates for the $25,000 investment capital needed to shoot the Guild's first film, *The Cradle Buster*. Glenn Hunter, whose own career was on the ascent, became the Guild's star (agreeing to work for a minimum salary), and W.W. Hodkinson acted as the distributor.

The Scarecrow became the Guild's fourth film. Percy MacKaye, who endorsed the project enthusiastically, doubtless asked very little for the rights to his play. He was also doubtless impressed by the Guild's decision to do some of the shooting at the location (Salem, Massachusetts) where his play took place. It's not known how MacKaye reacted when his title was changed to *Puritan Passions*, but even idealists have to consider the box office, and the silly-but-exploitable title was likely to sell more tickets than *A Tragedy of the Ludicrous*.

This synopsis is based on a "fictionization" of the film, as written by Osgood Perkins for *Motion Picture Classic* (July, 1923). The picture's obscurity convinced us not to stint on detail:

> One snowy night outside of Salem in 1680, Gillead Wingate, the town beadle, chides a passing stranger for wearing a fancy plume on his hat: "We frown upon such things as Satan's handiwork." The stranger makes an elegant apology, removes the plume and continues on his way. Wingate's suspicion turns to horror when he sees the man has left a trail of cloven footprints in the snow behind him. The devil has come to Salem.
>
> Satan — in the form of Dr. Nicholas — is visiting Salem at the behest of Goody Rickby, mother of Wingate's illegitimate child. The boy is dying, but the self-righteous Wingate has refused to acknowledge his offspring or even send a doctor. Dr. Nicholas offers to save the boy's life, but Rickby balks when she learns his soul would then belong to Satan ("I have many in my keeping, it would not be lonely," he responds). The boy dies and Rickby asks for the power of witchcraft to destroy the pious sinner, Wingate. Nicholas agrees, but tells her to bide her time: "When he has reached the pinnacle of his career — then he shall now what it is like to fall — from a height."
>
> Twelve years pass. Wingate has become the stern chief justice of Salem and, urged on by the governor, his council wants to go from punishing blasphemers and husbands who kiss their wives on Sunday to seeking out witches and their kin. The mention of Goody Rickby makes Wingate nervous, especially as someone brings up the matter of her son ("The father is unknown — and the child is dead — I think" is Wingate's response). Goody Rickby is suspected of causing some of Salem's recent woes and a letter of warning is sent to her blacksmith shop.
>
> Aside from chastising sinners, Wingate's only joy in life is focused on his beautiful niece and ward, Rachel. Rachel is engaged to Richard Talbot, but she has some doubts about the match. She has arranged to secretly purchase from Goody Rickby the Glass of Truth, a mirror that reflects the true soul of whoever gazes into it. A raven, one of Rickby's familiars, drops a note by Rachel's window telling her the mirror is ready.
>
> At her forge, Rickby is surprised by an unexpected visitor dressed in Puritan garb. The Glass of Truth reveals a monstrous, demonic form, and Rickby realizes Dr. Nicholas has returned. Referring to the warning letter, Rickby tells Nicholas: "They are out to get us kith and kin — If my son were only alive." Dr. Nicholas, spotting a grotesque scarecrow in the shop, is suddenly inspired. He suggests bringing the scarecrow to life and passing him off as Wingate's son to ensnare the chief justice in a charge of witchcraft. Rickby is reluctant: "If you give this thing life, he may get a soul and turn against us." Nicholas dismisses this as nonsense; the scarecrow will believe himself to be a real man, but he will under Nicholas' control.
>
> They are interrupted by Rachel who has come to pay for the mirror. She asks that it be delivered to the cabin in the Black Wood. When she leaves and Nicholas learns who she is, he decides

to include her in his scheme: He will transform the scarecrow into a handsome young man, teach him manners and lovemaking, and send him off to woo Rachel. Once they are married, the scarecrow's true nature will be exposed, and Gilead and Rachel will go to the gallows for witchcraft.

Nicholas carves away at the pumpkin that serves as the scarecrow's head, and the face takes on a human shape uncanny in its detail and gruesome with its yellow color. Nicholas puts a pipe (brimstone is the tobacco),in the scarecrow's mouth, and he slowly comes to life. The Thing calls Goody "Mother" and begins to move unsteadily about the forge, puffing eagerly at the pipe of Life.

Sometime later, Rachel's betrothed, Richard Talbot — who has been suspicious of his fiancée's behavior — follows her into the Black Wood. She tells him about the Glass of Truth and, while he chides her for dealing with Goody Rickby, he has no hesitation to stand before the magic mirror. A mist covers the glass but when it disappears, Richard can be seen smiling out at Rachel: honest, sincere, unaltered. Richard suggests they destroy the mirror, but, while Rachel hesitates, two men on horseback approach. Dr. Nicholas introduces himself and his pupil, Lord Ravensbane of London. Rachel is instantly captivated by Ravensbane's good looks. Rachel asks them for help in disposing of the mirror, so Nicholas and Talbot conceal it in the hollow of a tree. When Talbot turns around, all of his companions have vanished and he is alone.

Rachel, Ravensbane and Nicholas arrive at Justice Wingate's house to find it full of visitors. Wingate is overawed by Ravensbane. The young lord fascinates everyone in spite of his rather uncouth habit of frequently puffing on a pipe, but Ravensbane explains that the practice is necessary because recent illness has left his heart so weak that it demands constant stimulation.

Nicholas takes Wingate aside and the justice suddenly realizes that he's the stranger on the hilltop from many years ago. Wingate is shocked when Nicholas tells him that Ravensbane is the son Wingate thought was dead. Nicholas produces a marriage contract and insists that Rachel marry Ravensbane, or the whole story will be told. Wingate reluctantly assents.

Rachel is quite taken with Ravensbane's charm, coupled with his almost childlike demeanor. When Talbot discovers what's going on, he furiously objects. He strikes Ravensbane in the face with a glove. Ravensbane accepts the challenge and, at Dr. Nicholas' urging, suggests "Rapiers, the blacksmith shop, midnight." Rachel begs Ravensbane to spare Talbot, "if you love me." Ravensbane is confused by the request, but feels strange stirrings within his own breast.

The duel takes place amidst weird shadows dancing on the wall of the blacksmith shop. Ravensbane wounds Talbot slightly and is urged by Dr. Nicholas to finish him off, but Ravensbane instead lowers his sword. Talbot refuses to back off, and the duel continues until Talbot runs Ravensbane through. To the shock of the onlookers, the thrust has no effect. Nicholas quickly pulls the pipe from Ravensbane's mouth, and he collapses into a chair. Nicholas pronounces the wound not serious. Rachel, having witnessed the conflict, agrees to marry Ravensbane. Nicholas suggests the ceremony take place the next day so that Talbot will finally give up.

The next day the church is full for the wedding. Goody Rickby and Nicholas are also in attendance and eagerly await the moment that will seal their revenge. However, when the minister asks if anyone has reason to object to the ceremony, Talbot speaks up and produces the Glass of Truth. When he raises its curtain the congregation is astonished to see a reflection that reveals the beautiful Rachel standing next to a bizarre figure with a pumpkin for the head. Rachel faints and the guests flee in terror amidst cries of "Witchcraft!"

Rickby tells Wingate the only way he can save the situation is to convince the crowd that the mirror lies and is enchanted. Rachel is willing to believe this and go on with the ceremony. However, Ravensbane, who now knows what he really is, becomes dis-

traught, but his anguish turns to fury when he realizes that Nicholas' real goal is the death of Rachel as well as Wingate. A shaft of sunlight falls on a passage from the prayer book abandoned by the minister when he fled: "How shall they which are dirt gain a soul and be saved from Satan and the Eternal fires of damnation? And the Prophet answered 'By Love, Alone.'" Ravensbane destroys his pipe and collapses.

Wingate is arrested for witchcraft, but Rachel is spared. Rickby and Nicholas bow to the now humbled chief justice and disappear into space. With Rachel's help, Ravensbane takes one last look in the mirror: The scarecrow image slowly grows indistinct, and the reflection of the young lord as the world knew him looks out from the glass. Just before dying, Ravensbane tells Rachel and Talbot: "Love one another."

On the whole, Tuttle and co-scenarist, James Ashmore Creelman, remained faithful to MacKaye's play, but did make a few changes. In the play, Wingate survives the plot unscathed and it is Goody Rickby who is arrested for witchcraft after being double-crossed by Dr. Nicholas. Wingate's fall in the film seems more in keeping with the overall tenor of the scenario that tends to stress Puritan hypocrisy a bit more than had MacKaye. Also the play, which takes place on two sets— Goody Rickby's forge and Wingate's house — had to be opened up. It was a rather audacious move for Tuttle to move the denouement to a church with both a witch and the devil in attendance!

The Christian Science Monitor's very favorable review recognized the film's uniqueness:

> The Film Guild has rushed in where screen directors have been cautious into setting foot, the realm of the imaginative and the illusory. To create and sustain the mood and atmosphere of New England in 1680 when Salem Towne was torn between puritan repression and austerity and the secret forces they labeled witchcraft, the Film Guild had to work out its salvation as best it might since there was little precedent to go by. The success of their attempt is unquestionable from every artistic standpoint [22 October 1923].

The trade papers were enthusiastic but uncertain how audiences would respond to the film; it was probable that some viewers would find the supernatural elements unintentionally comic. At that time, films dealing with otherworldly matters were usually either fairy tales or "haunted house" comedies wherein the spooks turned out to be fake. It was highly unusual to center a film intended for adults on events that were unabashedly supernatural while still being represented as real:

> It is so well directed and acted that the spectator at times enters the illusion completely, feels as if being present before a real life occurrence. How popular will, however, the theme prove is problematical.... Pay attention how it will take in the theaters ahead of you [*Harrison's Reports*, 15 September 1923].

> So different is this film story from the majority of productions that it would be best for the exhibitor to see the picture and then decide for himself the extent to which it will appeal to his particular patronage. Persons with imaginative natures who like to get away from the realm of fact at times and into the realm of fancy will be intensely interested and will be held and pleased by the development of the story and the beauty of the idea [C.S. Newell, *Moving Picture World*, undated].

Wid's Film Daily (on the 9 September 1923) found *Puritan Passions* to be an "absorbing, somewhat somber production, splendidly mounted with particular appeal to more intelligent audiences." As had his his colleagues, Wid warned exhibitors that this is "a tricky one" and advised that they see the film first; still, he felt it could be a huge hit with the right sort of audience:

> If you do pick this one get back of it … dwell on the unusual features…. There is an unusualness in the old Salem witch atmosphere that is conspicuous in itself and the transformation of the scarecrow into a London gallant of the period is one of the most interesting things ever recorded by the camera. The many twists and trick photography with the witchcraft background should prove interesting in these days of costume pictures and big sets.

The transformation of the scarecrow into Ravensbane is often mentioned by reviewers, and ads for the film usually showed Osgood Perkins (Dr. Nicholas) sculpting the face of his creation. Actually, the human face emerging from under the pumpkin "wig" makes the scarecrow appear very much like the Golem; this may not have been totally coincidental: the Paul Wegener film had been released to the USA in 1921.

Not surprisingly, critics were taken by the idea of the Glass of Truth. This element, too, owed its debt to earlier stories and films: Count Dracula doesn't reflect in the glass; the ancient Witch-Queen in Frank L. Baum's "Queen Zixi of Ix" is a young woman in the eyes of the world, but not in the mirror; Balduin, the student of Prague, sells his reflection to the devil; the Phantom of the Opera speaks to Christine through a mirror; and who can forget "Mirror, mirror on the wall…" in Disney's *Snow White*?

Another noteworthy aspect of the film was the special score for it composed by F.S. Converse. Such an approach was not standard for the day (though the claim by the film's promoters that this was a first was hardly true) and critics were as enthusiastic about the music as they were about the film, especially at the film's premiere in Boston, where full orchestral accompaniment was provided by the New England Conservatory of Music:

> The score served not as the customary musical accompaniment but rather as the oral complement of the silent picture. By the skilled use of characteristic motives, consistently developed as in an opera or symphonic poem the persons, incidents and dramatic sequences of the play were brought out and intensified. It points a way to a new form of artistic expression [*The Boston Globe*, 19 December 1923].

"Eager, youthful, vibrant with beauty" is how the 19 December 1923 *Christian Science Monitor* described the score. "The music eliminates the need for over action allowing the suggestive element to have full play and giving greater opportunity for attention to detail. It talks but leaves your imagination free." In the big cities, that is; in small towns all of this would have translated to the local music teacher pounding out "Hearts and Flowers" on a beat-up old piano.

Glenn Hunter received very good notices as the scarecrow-turned-nobleman, although some reviewers thought the part was not a strong one and that Hunter was overshadowed by Osgood Perkins' Dr. Nicholas. Hunter made a career out of playing juveniles on stage and screen and was identified with those roles to such an extent that he later refused to give his real age. Ironically, unlike his characters— who at least came of age by the last reel — Hunter seemed stuck in adolescence. Playing a naïve youth who thinks movies reflect real life, he scored a huge hit

A pair of *Puritan Passions* photographs from the October 23, 1923, issue of *The Moving Picture World.*

in George S. Kaufman and Marc Connelly's *Merton of the Movies* (and later did the film role), but squandered his money as quickly as he made it. His Broadway and film careers had both fizzled by the 1930s, and he coasted doing summer stock and radio (at one point, he was reading recipes under a pseudonym). In 1936 he made the newspapers when he was arrested in Chicago for not paying his hotel bill and for giving his tailor a bad check. Friends came to his rescue but Hunter shrugged off his day in jail, and claimed that while he had been shocked by his fellow prisoners' bad language, he was going to write a book based on his experience. No *Shytown Archipelago* was forthcoming, but Walter Winchell reported in his column that Hunter was reduced to selling tickets at the Heckscher Theater in New York. Some years later, Hunter's house burned down and he made headlines again when he claimed that while many antiques and prized theatrical memorabilia had gone up in smoke, what really hurt was the fact that that his new Hollywood contract had also been reduced to ashes. Hunter died in 1945, apparently without ever having looked into the Glass of Truth.

Osgood Perkins' performance as Dr. Nicholas was very highly

praised. *The New York Times'* comment (on the 15 September 1923) was typical: "Perkins is splendid as the saturnine character. His smile is something of which to beware, the conjuring in his crafty face is forbidding, and his wheedling causes one to shrink at its success." Dr. Nicholas was likely Perkins' best film role during the 1920s, for the Massachusetts native generally had small comic parts or was cast as sleazy, somewhat ineffectual villains (as in 1926's *Love 'Em and Leave 'Em* in which he's a cheap crook who gets the stuffing beat out of him by Evelyn Brent). He's best remembered by film buffs for *Scarface*, wherein he plays Tony Comonte's gangster boss who ends up getting rubbed out by his prodigy. Perkins' greatest successes were on the Broadway stage, particularly the 1928 production of Ben Hecht and Charlie McArthur's *The Front Page*, where he won terrific notices as the fast-talking, relentless newspaper editor, Walter Burns. In 1937, during a pre–Broadway tryout of *Susan and God*, Perkins had a fatal heart attack. His son Anthony, five years old at the time, would later achieve greater fame than his father as the star of *Psycho* and many other films.

Mary Astor (Rachel) was only 17 during the filming of *Puritan Passions*, yet had already been in movies for two years. She was pushed into films by her tyrannical father, a German immigrant; Astor later said Erich von Stroheim would have been the ideal actor to play him. What initially brought Astor to Hollywood's attention was a series of photos of her as "The Madonna-Child" done by Charles Albin. These won her a contract at Famous Players–Lasky, which led to a number of bit roles and some work for Film Guild, and then stardom by the mid–1920s. She didn't mention *Puritan Passions* in her autobiography, but had fond memories of the Film Guild members and their kindness to a shy neophyte. Astor worked steadily in the 1930s, but did not achieve top-flight stardom; interestingly, she was somewhat relieved by this, since it meant a picture's success or failure did not depend entirely on her presence. Unfortunately, this also meant that many of her pictures were inconsequential programmers. She did, however, make some undeniable "A" movies, including *The Prisoner of Zenda* and *Dodsworth* (in which she played Mrs. Edith Cortright, her favorite role). The 1940s found her giving an Academy Award–winning performance for a supporting role in *The Great Lie*, as well essaying the part for which she's best remembered today: Brigid O'Shaughnessy, the double-crossing anti-heroine of *The Maltese Falcon*. After these triumphs, Astor settled into "mother" roles and character parts, and turned frequently to TV, as well. Her last film was one of her few genre credits, 1964's *Hush, Hush, Sweet Charlotte*.

Frank Tuttle's Silent Era work was mostly in the realm of smart comedies, like *Love 'Em and Leave 'Em* and *Miss Bluebeard*. Still, *Second Fiddle* (also with Hunter and Astor) has some tense moments involving a brutal killer hiding out in an abandoned house. Tuttle did a wide variety of films in the 1930s and 1940s, the most famous of which are the wacky time-travel comedy, *Roman Scandals* (1933), and the film-noir classic, *This Gun for Hire* (1942).

Following a few decades of well-deserved slumber, Nathaniel Hawthorne's short story was revamped as a television musical with Hugh O'Brian [!?] in 1961. MacKaye's *The Scarecrow* never

made it back to Broadway, but is revived elsewhere from time to time; a very good made-for-television version (with an oddly cast Gene Wilder as Ravensbane) was broadcast in 1982.

Given class "A" promotion by Hodkinson, *Puritan Passions* was both the Acme and the Adios of the Film Guild's brief life. Only one more film followed—*Grit*, based on a short story by F. Scott Fitzgerald—and it was greeted with the worst reviews a Film Guild production had ever received. Shortly thereafter, Glenn Hunter was lured away by a lucrative Hollywood contract, and he set out of the path that led to the comedy of errors that we recounted above. Even the "Let's put on show!" exuberance of the Film Guild could not compensate for the loss of the company's only bankable star *and* the subsequent withdrawal by its distributor, and yet another small studio with a dream quietly went under.

— *HN*

Queen of the Sea

Queen of the Sea. Fox Film Corp./Fox Film Corp. (A Fox Special), 1 September 1918, 6 reels/5350 feet [LOST]

CAST: Annette Kellerman (*Merilla*); Hugh Thompson (*Prince Hero*); Mildred Keats (*Princess Leandra*); Walter Law (*King Boreas*); Beth Irvins (*Ariela*): Philip Van Loan (*Prime Minister*); Fred Parker (*Clovis*); Louis Dean (*The King*); Carrie Lee (*The Queen*); Minnie Methol (*The Duenna*)

CREDITS: *Producer* William Fox; *Director* John G. Adolfi; *Scenario* John G. Adolfi; *based on a story by* George Bronson Howard; *Assistant Director* John William Kellette; *Cinematographers* Frank Williams, Carl L. Gregory

We have to wonder whether realizing (from the reception the film received) that *Queen of the Sea* would most likely be her last mermaid-epic brought any relief to swimming star, Annette Kellerman(n). Neptune only knows, having reached this plateau is a relief to *us*. When you've discussed one of these formulaic aquatic fantasies, you've discussed 'em all, and we've already plumbed the depths with *Neptune's Daughter* (1914) and *A Daughter of the Gods* (1916). When even diehard genre-lovers like us complain a bit about same old, same old, you just know that — way back then — audiences were probably of a similar mind.

This is not to say that the curvy lass did not still hold sway over her male admirers; one of the publicity campaign's key elements was a poster that claimed to be a "full-length picture of star with tabulated index showing comparative measurements between Miss Kellerman and the other two fact [*sic*] and fictional beauties, Cleopatra and Venus." (Warily, we accede to the possibility of discovering the Egyptian queen's vital statistics via spectacular archeological serendipity, but Venus's? We're suspicious of this last.) The dramatic hook (such as it was) upon which Miss Kellerman hung whatever scraps of costuming she would briefly wear had become not only redundant, but also superfluous.

We ought also consider that *Queen of the Sea* was released into theaters whose audiences were somewhat male-challenged. America was (in late 1918) engaged in the Great War, and lots of the men who would have cheerfully preferred ogling the seldom-fully-clothed young woman were off in Europe, doing their patriotic duty. As a result, the pride that distaff ticket buyers had taken in the cinematic displays of the perennially-underdressed star a couple of years earlier was also moved to a mental back-burner by very real (and omnipresent) worry. The Age of Mermaids had passed — for the nonce, at any rate — and Fox Studios keened loudest among the mourners.

Our first précis is taken from the 14 September 1918 *Motion Picture News*, and the trade journal's acknowledgment of the picture's predictable plot points is evident:

> Merilla, Queen of the Sea, is a mermaid who incurs the hatred of King Boreas, Master of Storms, by rescuing three sailors whose ship had been lured to destruction by sirens, the daughters of Boreas. For her good deed Merilla is given mortal shape by the fairy Ariela, when he water queen falls in love with prince hero. She does not find happiness with her lover, however, until she goes through a number of the regulation hardships at the hands of her enemies. She is taken captive by Boreas, and rescued by the prince. An eighty-five foot dive from a wire is one of her sensational acts.

The *Exhibitor's Trade Journal* — published a week earlier — gives further, if not quite complementary, detail:

> Boreas, Master of the Storms, commands his sirens to capture Merilla, Queen of the Sea, who has been rescuing sailors which Boreas has lured to destruction. Prince Hero rescues Merilla and falls in love with her, but, prompted by the fairy, Ariela, goes on to fulfill his engagement with the Princess Leandra. The vengeful Boreas then captures Leandra and shuts her in the tower of swords and knives. Merilla braves the wrath of Boreas to rescue the Princess and is locked in the tower with her with every means of escape shut off. However, a spider spins a gossamer cable [!] to an opposite cliff and Merilla attempts to escape by walking across it. Boreas cuts the cable and Merilla dives into the sea. She brings the Prince to rescue the Princess, who, out of gratitude, releases the Prince from his promise so he may wed the Queen of the Sea.

The *ETR* piece ends its first paragraph of commentary by admitting, "One is not greatly concerned with the accompanying story, which is frail and could never stand on its own legs" (Neat observation about a mermaid flick, no?). *Wid's Daily* (1 September 1918) didn't even bother printing the storyline, as "The plot, if you can call it such, is a series of action incidents hooked together by titles which make it possible for any character to do most anything they like because this happens to be a fairy tale.... Of course, the outstanding item in this sort of a film is the question of how much footage registered the scantily clad mermaids."

Such casual dismissal of the picture's narrative by the Powers That Were may have tipped William Fox to that fact that the light was out at the end of this particular tunnel, but the canny mogul might still have pressed on were it not for the dichotomy posed by those two sentences of Wid Gunning's: how does one sell the picture as a fairy tale (and thus market it to Mom and the kiddies) when anyone with a pulse understands that a good chunk of the running time is really just an inch shy of soft-porn (and the old man is Over There)?

If there is anything like a *definitive* plot summary of *Queen of the Sea*, it must be (must it?) the studio's copyright registration text, on file at the Library of Congress and quoted verbatim in *The AFI Catalog*:

> Merilla, the queen of the sea, learns that if she saves four lives, she will be endowed with a mortal body and an immortal soul.

The kindly queen saves her first lives by rescuing three drowning sailors whose ship the Sirens (the daughters of the wicked King Boreas of the Storms) have been instructed to destroy. Furious, King Boreas confines Merilla in a cave, but she is freed by Prince Hero, a human being with whom she falls in love. Determined to have his revenge, Boreas wrecks Hero's ship and locks up the prince's fiancée, Princess Leandra, in the Tower of Knives and Swords. Following several thrilling adventures, Merilla rescues Leandra, who, in her gratitude, releases the prince from his promise so that he may marry his beloved sea queen.

If things aren't crystal clear by now, they never will be, so let's just plow the waves, full speed ahead.

Herbert Brenon, Annette Kellerman's favorite director, had managed — during the filming of *A Daughter of the Gods* (see entry) — to cheese off William Fox to the point that not only wasn't the director invited to the premiere of his own "Million Dollar Picture," he was also given the gate and told never again to cross any threshold that bore Fox's name. (Okay, okay; by 1922 all was forgiven, but the drama of the moment must have been *something*.) Without Brenon, Miss Kellerman's enthusiasm waned so far as mermaid flicks were concerned. Shopping about for new thrills for her Vaudeville act, the lady was bitten by the high-wire bug and not long thereafter was adept at strutting her stuff up there on the tightrope: the siren of the sea was now also the hottie of the heights.

Meanwhile, finally having finished counting the receipts from *A Daughter of the Gods*, William Fox commissioned yet another take on Fantasy on the Foam, this time from John G. Adolfi, a New Yorker with a number of screenwriting credits under his belt. Refusing to argue with success led to numerous similarities between *Queen of the Sea* and the brace of previous Brenon/Kellerman/briny-deep epics, and the most striking bit of originality in the latest film — the two-legged mermaid's high-wire junket prior to taking the requisite, jaw-dropping dive to the safety of Poseidon's lair — did little to offset the indifference bred by familiarity.

As related in Emily Gibson's biography of Annette Kellerman, *The Original Million Dollar Mermaid*, besides the loss of Herbert Brenon, two other elements contributed to the curvy heroine's less-than-total enthusiastic participation in the project. For the lady star, the decision not to film *Queen* in the delightful waters off Bermuda or Jamaica, but rather in the cooler climes of Bar Harbor, Maine, was a letdown; for the mogul, though, the move meant fewer international bureaucratic headaches, while greatly reducing the expense of getting personnel and materials to on-location shoots. Much more serious — and frightening — was the actress's being injured in a fall from horseback prior to the start of principal photography. Per Gibson, it was initially touch and go as to whether the athletic star would ever walk again, and the production was put on hold for over a year until — "following a physiotherapy regime of her own devising" — Miss Kellerman was once again able to walk, dance, dive, and brave the high-wire.

All, it seems, for naught. Again, per biographer Gibson: "In the two years since the release of *A Daughter of the Gods*, America had joined the war against the Kaiser, and times had changed. It seemed that tales of real people, not mermaids, were what the public wanted to see."

While somewhere in the strata of his subconscious William Fox may have recognized the truth in this statement, the studio chief couldn't very well attribute the film's less-than-stellar reception to his own misreading of the changing public taste. Thus, albeit without the drama he had employed with Herbert Brenon, Fox made it clear that he had signed the last payroll check for John Adolfi. Adolfi— who had directed *Queen* in addition to crafting the screenplay based on an "original" treatment by George Bronson Howard — shrugged and went on with his life. The lion's share of his film credits still lay before him, and these included a couple of lower-shelf early–30s talkies with rising stars Bette Davis and Jimmy Cagney. Genre stuff was not the director's forte, though, and his only other title of interest to us, 1923's *Little Red Schoolhouse* (see appendix), was a marked step down from even the predictable proceedings of *Queen of the Sea*. Adolfi died suddenly, victim of a cerebral hemorrhage, in May 1933; he was only 45 years old.

Miss Kellerman likewise went on with her life. She made but two more feature films—1920's *What Women Love* and 1924's *Venus of the South Seas*— and in neither did she don the fishtail that she doffed during the course of her mermaid triptych. Rather than continue with things cinematic (only a few shorts that might be described as "autobiographical documentaries" remained in her future), she returned to Vaudeville. We cannot do better than biographer Emily Gibson in relating the whys and wherefores:

> Perhaps the strongest reason of all for leaving motion pictures was that theatre was her first and abiding love. She missed the immediacy of the audience and the fact that things could go wrong. When she stumbled and fell running up to perform a dive, she laughed at the hole in her stocking, hobbled up again, made the dive, bowed and limped off the stage to thunderous applause.

Years after retiring from her aquatic theatrical tour, the actress returned to the public eye in association with Mervyn LeRoy's 1952 Technicolor biopic, *Million Dollar Mermaid*, when she had a (reputedly) chance meeting with Esther Williams, who was playing Kellerman in the film. The elder Stateswoman of Swimming later went on record disparaging Miss Williams' abilities as a diver, an indication that age had done nothing to diminish Miss Kellerman's self-confidence or to temper her tendency to tell it like she thought it was. The original Million Dollar Mermaid died on 6 November 1975.

Queen of the Sea came and went without making anywhere near the splash its predecessors had. The above-cited *MPN* had, in fact, suggested that the exhibitors could best advertise the story by ignoring the story altogether: "The best sales angles you have are the photos of Miss Kellerman and the diving girls." Even *ETR*, the trade journal whose very *raison d'être* was to find the pony in the pile of poop, had to admit that "the feature doesn't differ greatly from Annette Kellermann's other exploits in the realm of pictures."

About the only published indication that there were other folk besides the athletic Aussie in the picture was the matter-of-fact "Hugh Thompson, Walter Law, Mildred Keats and Beth Irvins have the leading parts among the supporting company" in *MPN* and a similar, listless recitation (following "In the cast were") in *Wid's*. In the face of such indifference, we hasten to report that Hugh Thompson played Sir Edward Leighton in Essanay's 1916 feature, *Sherlock Holmes* (starring William Gillette), while Walter Law was Inspector Donohue in 1919's *The Thirteenth Chair* (see entry).   — *JTS*

The Quest of the Sacred Jewel

The Quest of the Sacred Jewel. Pathé Frères/Eclectic Film Co., November 1914, 4 reels, Cinémathèque Française (Paris)
CAST: Charles Arling (*David Harding*); Edna Mayo (*May Rowland*); William Rosell (*Joe Marsden*); Ernest Truex (*The Office Boy*).
CREDITS: *Director* George Fitzmaurice; *Cinematographer* William H. Edmond

The sleepy city of Barrnipore one day receives a visitor in the person of an American soldier of fortune, David Harding. The young fellow's good judgment is overruled by his passion for adventure when he learns that a priceless diamond decorates the forehead of the stone god in the Hindu temple of worship, and he determines to become possessor of it. Disguised as a native he enters the temple at night, pries out the stone and is about to make away with it when he is discovered by one of the fakirs who arouses the guards with his cries.

Harding manages to escape to his rooms, changes his clothes, mounts his horse and rides away with the crowd of terror-stricken, howling Hindus at his very heels. The high priest and his assistants follow him to America, board the same train as he when he leaves New York, and, by hanging from the top of the Pullman car, kill him as he sleeps in his berth. One of the Hindus slips as the train passes over a trestle and falls to his death below. The others fail to find the stone, but learn later that it has been willed to Harding's niece, May Rowland.

The girl wears the diamond at a party given at her home in celebration of her engagement to Joe Marsden, and the Hindus, hiding on the veranda, see it. Joe becomes the victim of their plans when he answers their call and goes out to watch them juggle. The old priest exerts his powers of hypnotism upon him, and the rest of the party come to the door just in time to break the charm. That night the Hindus approach the house, and again the priest calls his strange powers into play. Joe responds to the telepathy by rising, entering May's room, and securing the diamond.

On the way back to his room, he drops the stone and it is picked up by one of the other guests who has lost heavily at cards during the evening. He pawns the jewel, and there it is traced by the detective whom the Rowlands have employed at Joe's suggestion. All this time, however, May firmly believes that Joe is voluntarily the thief, having seen him enter her room on the night of the robbery. The detective unravels the mystery and succeeds in convincing May that Joe is innocent of complicity.

The old priest gains possession of the sacred gem although his assistants sacrifice themselves in securing it for him, and returns home to replace it on the god's forehead. As he mounts the altar steps he is seized with an attack of the heart, and, in his agony, accidentally drops the stone into the incense-pot where it is consumed by the fire [*Motography*, 28 November 1914].

Clearly, whoever wrote *The Quest of the Sacred Jewel*— and we don't have a credit for the script — had taken more than a casual perusal of Wilkie Collins' *The Moonstone* and borrowed not just its plot, but many of the secondary elements as well. Some of the latter include: the innocent niece inheriting the coveted jewel from her thieving uncle; the display of said sparkler at a party crashed by the Hindu priests posing as jugglers; the theft of the gem by a hero acting in a trance and witnessed by his uncomprehending fiancée; the party guest who then steals the jewel from him; and, finally, the detective who unravels the case with the assistance of an energetic office boy. The most significant change in the film version occurs at the ending, where the death of the high priest and the destruction of the jewel suggest that the quest of the Hindus was an unholy one rather than an attempt to right a wrong. That — and changing the setting to America — pretty much throws out Collins' critique of colonialism and turns the priests into chapter-play bad guys.

Oddly enough, none of the reviews made any connection between the film and Collins' classic novel. *The New York Dramatic Mirror* critic devoted half his review to deriding the film for its shopworn ideas without even suggesting their literary source:

"And on the forehead of the God is a sacred gem of inestimable value" the adventurous American is told by his host in India and you can guess the rest. Not only can you guess it, but it follows the lines hewed out for it by previous productions of similar nature so closely that one wonders if there be a caste in this sort of subject. It will not allow them to wander far from the fact that the native worshipers send a trio of their brown-skinned brothers to follow and slay the offender or whoever unluckily comes into its possession. They are possessed of marvelous faculties for tracking, are those Mohammedans, seem never to be at a loss for money and invariably bring back the gem to the forehead of the hideous heathen they venerate [18 November 1914].

Other trade papers, while equally unmindful of the influence of *The Moonstone*, were far more favorable.

The story increases in interest and suspense as it unfolds— the last two reels of it reach the point of being gripping. The first half follows beaten lines; but in its continually changing incident, will be pretty sure to please well enough to hold safely till the real mystery begins to be felt by the spectator [Hanford Judson, *Moving Picture World*, 21 November 1914].

Motography's Charles Condon found the film "realistic and impressive" and was particularly taken with the sets:

Pathé features in the past have been noted for their stupendous interior settings, and this one adds to the record by possessing a temple scene that is a masterpiece in studio construction. It represents an East Indian house of worship, and is complete in every detail, even to the half-naked, white-haired beggars who adorn the foot of each of the temple's enormous columns [28 November 1914].

The temple sequence also wowed Clifford Pangburn of *Motion Picture News*:

The views in the temple from which the diamond was stolen are of particular excellence. A great open hall, apparently built out of massive materials and in correct oriental architecture is seen. At the far end of it is an idol in the form of a grotesque elephant seated upon a throne.... [The theft of the jewel] is shown in the dim light of the moon, which shines through a few high windows. It is an exceptionally fine piece of photographic work, and its effectiveness is further enhanced by its attention to details. For example, a Hindu priest with a withered arm is the one who gives the alarm [21 November 1914].

All the reviewers noted the scene where Harding is killed, and the *Motion Picture News* account is typical: "One rather startling scene shows one of the Hindu avengers of the desecrated idol hanging by a rope from the window of a moving Pullman car. Opening the window, he stabs the thief to death but is knocked to the ground by a telegraph pole before he can get the diamond."

The cast was highly praised, especially Ernest Truex as the comic-but-resourceful office boy. Truex would have a long career ahead of him on stage and screen playing trembling heroes and henpecked husbands; more on Mr. Truex can be found in our entry on *A Good Little Devil*.

Edna Mayo (May) enjoyed a brief but conspicuous career in the mid–1910s. Some publicity pieces claimed that the Philadelphia native made her stage debut at age five and was known as "Little Princess Charming," but in later interviews, Mayo asserted she didn't trod the boards until she was sixteen. She landed parts in *Help Wanted* and *Excuse Me Madame* and did some Broadway work before switching to film in 1914. In an interview published in the 16 October 1915 edition of the *Evening Standard* [Ogden, Utah], Mayo claimed she was happy with the change and hadn't liked working in theater:

The terrible and deadly monotony of playing the same piece night after night, week in and week out, almost drives one to madness at times.... It sometimes gets on your nerves so that you hate the production. You want to run away and hide where you never have to go through or see the play again. [In film] you have the satisfaction afterwards of seeing spectators enjoy your finished production on the screen. It gives one the same satisfaction that I imagine a painter gets in having his picture appreciated and admired.

The height of Mayo's film career was in 1915. She made 20 features and shorts and was given the star treatment in the press with numerous interviews—filled with cutesy anecdotes— and publicity puffs about her hobbies, likes and dislikes. She made a few films in 1916, including the serial, *The Strange Case of Mary Page*, wherein she played a woman falsely accused of murder. After leaving Essanay, where she been under contract, Mayo made only one more movie, the 1918 Civil War drama, *Hearts of Love*, before dropping off the Hollywood map. Whether this was due to the unpredictable ups and downs of movie stardom or to some personal issue is not at present known.

Charles Arling (Harding) had been a regular player at Pathé Frères for several years before *Quest*. His skill at applying his own make-up first won him recognition when the then-32-year-old portrayed an elderly man in 1912's *Memories*. The Canadian-born Arling actually began his career as a baritone in the Boston Opera Company, but was no more enamored of opera than Edna Mayo was of the stage, and he later recalled going through a performance of *The Tales of Hoffman* in a complete daze brought on by nerves. Stage fright was not a problem when he moved to the silent drama. After his time at Pathé, he became a freelance character actor and got to go back to his native Canada to play a villain in Nell Shipman's *Back to God's Country* (1919).

A year after *The Quest of the Sacred Jewel*, William Rosell (Joe Marsden) portrayed the villainous Godfrey White in *The Moonstone* (see entry). That time around, Wilkie Collins *was* credited.

Director George Fitzmaurice, who had come to the United States from Paris as a set designer, was little known when he made *The Quest of the Sacred Jewel*, but that would soon change. By 1916 he was famous enough to be interviewed on his opinions of direction and film production (at least by the Xenia, Ohio, *Daily Gazette*) and offered the following:

A comprehensive knowledge of psychology, in all its branches, is a necessary complement of good directorship, for motion pictures have progressed to such a stage that psychology is the base upon which they are all built. The public of today demands something more than mere action; it demands a well developed theme and when you enter upon this you enter the realms of psychology. To incorporate human nature into a picture you must understand the science of mental phenomenon for it is this science that is the guiding hand of realistic action [9 July 1916].

Whether any of this came in handy during the filming of *Quest* is hard to say. Fitzmaurice would deal with nasty Hindoos once again in *The Romantic Journey* (see entry), but would discover a gentler realm of fantasy with *Forever* (see entry, where there is also more on Mr. Fitzmaurice).

There is some confusion about the title of this entry. *The New York Dramatic Mirror* calls it *The Quest of the Sacred Jewel* (and *The AFI Catalog* follows suit), but it is *The Quest of the Sacred Gem* in *Moving Picture News*, *Moving Picture World*, and *Motography*. In addition, ads for the film in venues as disparate as Winnipeg (Manitoba), Lumberton (North Carolina), Victoria (Texas), and Cedar Rapids (Iowa) all give the sparkle to "Gem."

— HN

Rasputin the Black Monk

Rasputin the Black Monk. World Film Corp. Pictures; Peerless/World Film Corp., 8 October 1917 (general release), 7–8 reels [LOST]

CAST: Montague Love (*Grigory Novik, later known as Rasputin*); June Elvidge (*Inez*); Arthur Ashley (*Rodin*); Violet Axzell (*Ilda, as a child*); Lillian Cook (*Ilda, as a grown-up*); Irving Cummings (*Prince Felix*); Julia Dean (*Mme. Vasta*); Pinna Nesbit (*Princess Sonia*); Hubert Wilke (*Czar Andre*); Florence Beresford (*Czarina Katherine*); Charles Crompton (*Paulus*); Frank Beamish (*Choynski, in Russian secret service*); Joseph Granby (*Mikula Dvorkin, leader of Duma*); Robert Fisher (*Varnileff, in Russian ministry*); Edward Elkas (*Pasloff, in Russian ministry*); Henry Hull (*Kerensky*)

CREDITS: *Director* Arthur Ashley; *Producer* William A. Brady; *Scenario* E Richard Schayer; *Cinematographer* Jacques Monteran

NOTE: The script indicates that some of the character names were to be changed — Rodin was to become "Raff," Ilda was to be "Olga" and so on. As most of the reviews we've read use the original names, we are going with them.

Arguing that films about Rasputin be included in the horror genre is somewhat problematic. After all, Rasputin (real name was Grigori Novik; *Rasputin* was a nickname meaning "licentious one") was an actual person who played a part — albeit a minor one — in the fall of the Romanoff dynasty which, in turn, precipitated the great upheavals in 20th-century Russia. What's mainly of interest to horror fans is the *legend* of Rasputin: the master hypnotist who used his powers to bend to his will any woman he desired; the mad monk who succeeded in subjugating the royal family; the monster so full of demonic life that his assassins had to do everything but drive a stake through his heart to finally dispatch him. The real Rasputin, while he was indeed licentious, was neither mad nor (technically) a monk, but was, rather, a complex and tortured individual, more mystic/healer than mesmerist. Even the reports of his death may have been greatly exaggerated; his assassination was little more than treacherous, cold-blooded murder, and his killers may have sought to justify their actions (and their ineptitude) by painting

their victim as some kind of supernatural creature. Still, who can look at photos of Rasputin — with his long beard and hair and Bela Lugosi–like eyes — and not think of Svengali?

It was only a matter of months after Rasputin's death in December of 1916 that Czar Nicholas II fell from power and just a few months later there were not one, but two films about Rasputin and his part in the last years of the Romanoff dynasty. *Fall of the Romanoffs* was a big-budget epic that was directed by Herbert Brenon and that boasted the presence of Illodor (Rasputin's rival) playing himself (although not terribly well, according to the reviews). William Brady, president of World Film, decided to capitalize on all the publicity leading up to the release of *Fall of the Romanoffs* by quickly doing his own version of the tale, *Rasputin the Black Monk*. The script was delivered to director Arthur Ashley on the 24 July and was shot from 2 August until the 30 August for a fall release.

Brenon did not take kindly to this piggybacking on his film, and when *Fall* was sneak-previewed for 600 guests on the 6 September 1917 in New York's swanky Ritz Carleton Hotel, Brenon was not pleased to see Brady in attendance. According to one version of the story, Brenon wouldn't let Brady see the film; another says that Brady made some comment about beating Brenon to the punch, which, technically, was not true since *Fall* was released first. In any event, the two came to blows in the Ritz-Carlton lobby before rolling down a flight of stairs into the street. Friends — among them Adolph Zukor of Famous Players–Lasky — broke up the fight, and Brady made a quick retreat via taxi cab. There was violence of another sort when *Rasputin* premiered less than a week later; riot police had to be called in to control the rowdy crowds that turned up for the showing.

(Even Roscoe Arbuckle got into the act. The 1918 two-reeler, *The Bell Boy* — which he also wrote and directed — saw Fatty shaving a hirsute hotel guest whose makeup was very much patterned on the Svengali-like countenance of the Russian mystic. A title identified the guest as "Rasputin, the Mad Monkey!")

Though *Rasputin* made claims to historical accuracy, it changed the names of most of the principals, including that of Czar Nicholas (Andre in the film) and Czarina Alexandra (Katherine). At one point in the production, there was even a different name for Rasputin, but someone wisely decided that *Keshinka the Black Monk* didn't have much *oomph* to it. We have read the original shooting script (working title: *Russia*) and give the following synopsis based on it.

The year is 1905 and revolution is in the air in Russia. In a small village, a group of radicals led by Rodin plots against the repressive government. Rasputin lives in the same village, but is planning on moving to Petrograd. Rasputin is a scoundrel who often disguises himself as a monk to bilk the peasants. He also has hypnotic powers which he uses to seduce women. He attempts to put Rodin's wife, Inez, under his control, but is interrupted by the timely arrival of Rodin. Rasputin hastily moves on. In a nearby town, Choynski, a secret-service agent ferreting out revolutionaries, hears Rasputin address a crowd in his monk guise. Choynski is impressed, but quickly discovers that Rasputin is a scoundrel. Nonetheless, he approaches Rasputin and asks him to spy for the government. Rasputin knows that Rodin and his group meet in a crypt in the cemetery, so he leads a detachment of troops, commanded by Prince Felix, to the spot. The rebels are arrested and Rodin vows vengeance on Rasputin. When Inez hears what has happened, she realizes that Rasputin will be calling again, so she quickly flees with her little girl, Ilda. Rodin is sent to Siberia.

In Petrograd, Rasputin establishes his own cult appealing mainly to "the fair but frail." Rasputin tells his wealthy female adherents that "All that is Nature is good and all that is against Nature is evil. He that restraineth the natural impulses of his flesh, filleth his heart with evil spirits." One of his most ardent followers is Vasta, a lady-in-waiting to Czarina Katherine.

In the royal palace, Czar Andre and Katherine lament the frailty of their newborn son, Paulus, heir to the throne. The doctors tell them the boy may live but will never be healthy. Vasta brings Rasputin to pray over Paulus. Rasputin tells the deeply religious Katherine that "I can save him, but I must always be near." Katherine immediately makes arrangements for Rasputin to move into the Palace.

Ten years pass. World War I is raging. Russia is fighting the good fight, but the cost is heavy. Rasputin's power and influence have grown considerably. He is sabotaging the war effort and intriguing with the Germans because he knows an Allied victory will bring democracy and the fall of the old regime. Inez is also living in Petrograd, and her rooming house has become a meeting place for radicals. Prince Felix has become sympathetic to democratic ideals. Felix's wife Sonia is a great beauty and captures Rasputin's attention, but she resists the peasant's hypnotic eyes. When he tries a more direct approach, she angrily rebuffs him.

Rasputin oversteps his bounds and is denounced to the Czar by members of the Duma. Angry at stories of Rasputin's claims to authority, the Czar tells Rasputin to leave Petrograd. Rasputin goes but tells the royal couple that Paulus' health cannot be guaranteed if he departs. At Rasputin's behest, the loyal Vasta puts a mild poison in Paulus' tea. The boy at once becomes ill, and Rasputin is immediately sent for. The poison has worn off and Rasputin promptly claims credit for the "miracle." The royal couple is now totally under his sway.

The radicals want Rasputin out of the way, but Inez is against violence. Inez' daughter, Ilda, now a young woman, has ideas of her own. Her beauty and youth gain her immediate entrance to Rasputin's headquarters, but her attempt to shoot the evil charlatan fails. Rasputin orders her locked up with the intention of paying her a visit later. The desperate girl appeals to Vasta who pities her and takes a note to her mother.

Inez is frantic and appeals to Prince Felix. Felix has Sonia send a letter to Rasputin telling him that she wants to see him at once at her palace. Felix gathers all Rasputin's enemies together so when Rasputin arrives he is taken prisoner. Felix assures Rasputin no harm will come to him if he will sign a letter freeing Ilda. Rasputin has no choice but to agree. Meanwhile, Rodin has escaped from Siberia. When he meets Inez, she tells him what's been going on. Rodin rushes to the Prince's palace, confronts the captive Rasputin, and empties his revolver into him. Although Felix regrets the violence, he helps the others wrap up Rasputin's corpse and throw it into the river.

The death of Rasputin spells the end of the old order and a new dawn of freedom for Russia.

Though publicity stressed the film's historical accuracy, that was mostly nonsense (*Fall of the Romanoffs* is no better; it even has Rasputin personally meeting with the Kaiser!). In fairness, though, most of what was written about Rasputin in the press was slander and propaganda from people who had more axes to grind than Henry VIII's headsman, so a film script based on the current headlines was bound to be wide of the mark historically. Stories about Rasputin being a German agent and drugging the Czarevitch were spurious but widely believed at the time. Rasputin *did* oppose Russia's entry into World War I, not out of any anti-democratic, pro–German feeling, but because he knew his fellow peasants would provide most of the cannon fodder (his own son ended up getting drafted). Few knew that the Czarevitch had hemophilia and that the real key to Rasputin's influence over the royal family was his ability to calm the boy down during his attacks. Without that information, there had to be something to explain how an uncouth, lecherous peasant rose to such power. Tales of drugs, hypnosis and trickery filled in the gaps.

The film seems very uncomfortable on how to depict the death of Rasputin. The earliest newspaper accounts of Rasputin's murder claim that he was given a gun and told to commit suicide, but when instead he turned the revolver on his captors, they shot him; something like this happens in *Fall of the Romanoffs*. What became the standard story of Rasputin's death — the poison that didn't slow him down; his "coming back to life" after being shot — didn't emerge until later. The script brings up the option of assassinating Rasputin several times only to have it rejected and is obviously at pains as to how to show the conspiracy to kill him as somehow being heroic, rather than base. The problem is solved none too smoothly by bringing things down to a personal level: the plotters act only to save the virtue of a young girl, and it is her much-wronged father who fires the fatal but unexpected shots. "What has happened, has happened," says Prince Felix regretfully. "We must by our silent allegiance protect one another."

Rasputin, it seems, got around. In this scene from 1917's *The Fall of the Romanoffs*, the old boy (Edward Connelly) even hobnobbed a bit with the Kaiser (Georges Deneubourg).

Publicity for the film assured viewers that "this play is not of the weird uncanny type that will tend to make one have bad dreams, but is of a high plane of historical drama in which the true history of the Russian revolution and the incidents that led up to it are depicted in a more most interesting manner." A somewhat different tack was taken by other ads that described how Rasputin's leadership of "a wicked cult of passion and pleasure exalted him among the royalty, especially the ladies."

Though Rasputin's hypnotic abilities didn't play a major role in the film, they were sometimes mentioned in the ads, and publicity: "It was through Rasputin's hypnotic power over women that he gained his tremendous authority and it was through this hypnotic power over women that his downfall came."

The following segment of the shooting script describes Rasputin's attempted seduction of Inez:

18 — CLOSE-UP of Gregory (Rasputin) and Inez. She slowly raises her head and her eyes meet his. Instantly she starts and stares fixedly into his face.
TITLE: The Secret of Gregory's power over women.
19 — CLOSE-UP of a startling pair of eyes, staring straight into the camera — If possible, get the effect of pupils expanding and contracting.

Montagu(e) Love, character actor par excellence in both the silent and sound eras.

IRIS OFF 20 — CLOSE-UP of Gregory and Inez.
IRIS IN — Inez staring into Gregory's eyes as his arms slowly start to enfold her and his head bends nearer and nearer.

This might very well be a scene from *Svengali* or *Dracula*. (Rasputin uses guile — not hypnotism — in *Fall of the Romanoffs*, and the same is true of his cameo appearance in *The Red Dance* (1928), so both films are excluded from our coverage herein.)

Rasputin the Black Monk received good notices, but mostly for its topicality: *Motion Picture News*' Peter Milne thought the interweaving of dramatic situations with actual facts made for "above average entertainment," but...

Art and Rasputin the Black Monk are things apart.... Mr. Ashley (Rodin) served also as director, but his work in this capacity never approaches in merit his portrayal of the peasant. Possibly, Mr. Ashley was working on a time schedule and, this being the case, one can readily forgive, though not overlook the slipshod direction. The settings are below the average and the placement of the camera seems to have been left to no one but the cameraman, who was as pushed for time as the director [29 November 1917].

Variety's Jolo felt the picture would have been better cut down a reel or two, but...

considering its timeliness it should prove to be the best possible program feature.... Not that it's a wonderful picture but with the interest in the subject of the recent fall of the Russian dynasty, an intelligent picturization [*sic*] of the events leading up to it, patrons of programs houses are certain to flock [14 November 1917].

The 11 October 1917 *Wid's Daily* also found the film's subject worthy:

The life of Rasputin makes fine material for the camera, and the scenario has to draw but little on the imagination in order to weave a melodrama of the most approved villains, heroes and heroines for screen presentation.

Performances were highly praised, especially that of Montague Love as Rasputin. Still, *Variety* had some reservations:

Love is excellent in the earlier scenes, but when later Rasputin is pictured as a resident of the Czar's palace with a Svengali beard and hypnotic eyes, he is altogether too Machiavellian and suave. True, he has by that time lived for ten years in refined surroundings, but no ignorant peasant, unable to read or write, would in an entire lifetime cultivate the manners of a gentleman of society.

Love, who turns up many times herein (see *The Case of Becky*, 1921), was one of the outstanding villains of the silent screen and probably the main reason to regret the loss of *Rasputin the Black Monk*.

Though *MPN* criticized Arthur Ashley for wearing two hats in *Rasputin*, for much of his World Film career he did exactly that: directing and starring in half-a-dozen features, often with his *Rasputin* co-stars, June Elvidge and Montague Love. Ashley (née Ash) went on the stage after graduating from high school. He was leading man in road company versions of *Brewster's Millions*, *Dorothy Vernon of Haddon Hall*, and *Get-Rich-Quick Wallingford*. He signed with Vitagraph in 1913, but enjoyed his greatest success working for World. When he left World in 1919, his film career faltered, so he returned to the stage, did vaudeville, worked as an agent for William Morris and later started his own stock company, the Arthur Ashley Players.

Like Ashley, June Elvidge (Inez) had her best movie years at World. More on the former concert singer-turned-actress can be found in the entry on *The Eleventh Hour*. She also appears in these pages in *The Poison Pen* and *The Man Who Saw Tomorrow*.

Irving Cummings (Prince Felix) became a first-rate director, but started his career as a stage actor and appeared with such notables as Lillian Russell and Henry Miller. He became a leading man at Reliance Film Company in 1913 and worked steadily throughout the 1910s without becoming a major star. As the studios evinced little interest in hiring him on as a director — his first love — Cummings formed his own production company in the early 1920s with the help of his wife, Ruth (herself an actress and writer), and did several two-reel Westerns. Wanting to do a feature, he approached popular writer James Oliver Curwood about adapting one of his stories. Curwood's price was far beyond anything Cummings could afford, so he persuaded the author — for $4,000 — to allow his name to be used on *The Man from Hell's River*. Curwood insisted on script approval, but didn't write a word of it. Apparently, Cummings succeeded in capturing the author's style because Carl Sandburg, in his review of the film for the *Chicago Daily News* (19 December 1922), found it typical of Curwood's work.

Cummings did not continue as an independent, but he *had* established himself as a director. He easily made the switch to sound and his work in *In Old Arizona* earned him an Academy Award nomination. In the 1930s he directed big-budget musicals and Shirley Temple films as well as *The Story of Alexander Graham Bell* and a biography of his old co-star, *Lillian Russell* (1940).

Julia Dean (Vasta) was a distinguished stage actress, but didn't have much of a film career in the silent era. Rasputin likely gave her one of her better parts. She was brought out of retirement in the 1940s and had good roles in 1944's *Curse of the Cat People* (playing the crazy old lady who vividly recounts the tale of the Headless Horseman) and *The Emperor Waltz* (1948).

Henry Hull as Kerensky, the Duma member who tried unsuccessfully to hold the country together after the abdication of the Czar, has only one scene. It may have been added as an afterthought, as it's not described in the original script and Hull's name is penciled in; *Variety* thought he was too young for the role. The youthful Mr. Hull can also be found mentioned in our coverage of *One Exciting Night* and *The Last Moment*.

E. Richard Schayer, author of *Rasputin*, worked as a reporter and war correspondent in the 1910s. In 1914, he spent seven months in active service with the British army at the front lines in France and wrote grim accounts of what he saw there. He became a publicity agent and writer for World Film in 1916, but later wrote scenarios for a number of different companies. Publicity materials stressed his productivity:

> In his 29 months of scenario work, he has written 33 scenarios, in many cases being the author of the original story as well as the screen version. Several of these on the other hand have been novels. During 1919 he wrote an average of one continuity every three weeks, which is believed to be a record in these days of big, carefully wrought productions [*Washington Post*, 15 May 1921].

He also wrote one of Lon Chaney's biggest hits, *Tell It to the Marines* (1926), and contributed to the scripts of such sound shockers as *The Mummy* (1932) and *Devil Doll* (1936).

Rasputin was to prove very popular with filmmakers and was the kind of larger-than-life personality that encouraged many an actor to out–Herod Herod. In films ranging from 1932's *Rasputin and the Empress* to Don Bluth's *Anastasia* (1997), he is portrayed as a villain, but Conrad Veidt makes a sympathetic and rather sad character of him in *Rasputin, Dämon der Frauen* (1932), while the great Harry Baur's performance smacks of Zorba the Greek in *La Tragedie Imperiale* (1938).

— HN

The Raven

The Raven. Essanay Film Mfg. Co./V.L.S.E., Inc., 8 Nov. 1915, 6 reels. Exists in abridged form at the Library of Congress
CAST: Henry B. Walthall (*Edgar Allan Poe*); Warda Howard (*Virginia Clemm/Helen Whitman/The Lost Lenore/A Spirit*); Ernest Maupain (*John Allan*); Eleanor Thompson (*Mrs. Allan*); Marian Skinner (*Mrs. Clemm*); Harry Dunkinson (*Tony*); Grant Foreman (*George Graham*); Hugh E. Thompson (*David Poe, Jr.*); Peggy Meredith (*Mrs. Graham*); Frank Hamilton (*David Poe, Sr.*); Billy Robinson (*Joseph Reed*); Burt Weston (*Negro*); Charles K. Harris (*Mr. Pelham*).
CREDITS: *Director* Charles J. Brabin; *Scenario* Charles J. Brabin; based on the novel *The Raven: The Love Story of Edgar Allen [sic] Poe* by George Cochrane Hazleton (New York, 1909), and his play of the same name (Allentown [PA], 13 September 1904).

As noted in the entry on *The Avenging Conscience*, the first attempt at creating a biopic of Edgar Allan Poe came on the centenary of his birth. This was also the first acknowledged cinematic effort at dealing directly with the author; the previous year had seen the plot of "The Murders in the Rue Morgue"— sans Auguste Dupin — gratuitously handed over to the Great Consulting Detective for *Sherlock Holmes in the Great Murder Mystery* (1908). This was the inverse of what became the standard Hollywood practice of grafting a wholly different story onto a Poe title. The same year that D. W. Griffith filmed *Edgar Allan Poe* and *The Sealed Room* (1909), the Edison Company released an adaptation of "The System of Dr. Tarr and Professor Fether" entitled *Lunatics in Power*, marking a brief flurry of relevant American titles. For the most part, Poe was more profitably explored in foreign films during the Silent Era, but in 1911 the American Eclair Company produced *The Raven* (another biopic, built around the poem), and Thanhauser was responsible for something called *The Mummy*, which definitely was in the debt of Poe's "Some Words with a Mummy": both title characters (Thanhouser's is revealed to be a beautiful woman) are revivified by means of electricity.

As was usual for American product at the time, most of these were one-reel projects (*The Raven* was two reels), and all save *The Sealed Room* and *The Mummy* are considered lost. In 1913, the French *émigré* director, Alice Guy-Blaché, created *The Pit and the Pendulum* in three reels (feature-length for the time) for her company, Solax. The first two reels (back-story build-up) are preserved in the Library of Congress, but the final reel — which contains the visualization of the actual tale — went missing long ago. More's the pity as contemporary reviews praised the film's visual qualities and stills reveal a sumptuously designed and costumed production. In 1914, the same year as *The Avenging Conscience*, producer Sol Rosenberg brought forth a new adaptation of *The Murders in the Rue Morgue*; its fidelity to its source material and its level of quality cannot be ascertained, as it is also lost.

In 1915 Henry B. Walthall returned to Poe territory, this time "officially" portraying the writer in a new biopic entitled *The Raven*, a non-traditional offering from Essanay, a company that usually specialized in comedies and the Westerns of "Bronco" Billy Anderson (the "A" of "S and A"). Given its product emphasis on oaters, Essanay was located, surprisingly, in Chicago. While *The Raven* was in production, Charlie Chaplin signed on with Essanay; together with the Poe feature, the company's having lured him away from Keystone was a clear sign that it was looking to expand its profile. Sadly, Chaplin would depart after but a year and the company's fortunes would decline quickly thereafter. In 1917 this penultimate surviving member of the Motion Picture Patents Company would cease to be, although Vitagraph would continue until 1925, when it was sold to Warner Bros.

Taking its cue from Griffith and the American Eclair production, *The Raven* has a visualization of the title poem forming the centerpiece of the film, although it is primarily a biography — and an often wildly inaccurate one. The picture was based on the play *The Raven: The Love Story of Edgar Allen Poe* by George C. Hazelton (who also scripted the film), and the misspelling of Poe's middle name in the title suggests that Hazelton's scenario might have benefited from more scrupulous scholarship.

The film begins with a series of abruptly edited *tableaux vivantes* depicting Poe's ancestors, concluding with one of his parents performing on stage. [The editing might have been less choppy when the film was new; the print that has survived is somewhat the worse for wear.] The film then briefly depicts the 1811 death of Elizabeth Poe [although only two children are shown to be orphaned, rather than three], and Edgar's "adoption" — as the title card terms it — by the reluctant John Allan, who took Poe into his household but never legally adopted him. It then cuts to a portrait of Poe which dissolves into a close-up of Walthall who, it must be admitted, bore a fair resemblance to the writer.

With this fade, the film thus jumps 15 years to the University of Virginia in 1826 where the 17-year-old Poe is getting crocked, suggesting he is already an alcoholic. [Walthall deploys his trademark cheesy grin every time he contemplates a glass of spirits, unfortunately with risible results.] He passes out and has a dream of playing cards with himself while a group of friends watches, and then of fighting a pistol-duel with his other self. In other words, he has a vision of "William Wilson" which would be published 12 years later.

Back at home, nestled by a picturesque lake, he woos Virginia Clemm (Warda Howard) by relating a fairy tale about a young woman who stays an archer from shooting a buck; woman and archer fall in love, and wood nymphs appear and dance around them. Said sprites are summoned by a pipes-playing figure, unaccountably played by a woman who looks little like the satyr she is surely intended to be. The sequence appears to have been inspired by the same source that provided the ending to *The Avenging Conscience* [or simply by that sequence in that film]. Virginia, by the way, is quite well developed for a girl who would only have been seven at the time [no film biography of Poe to date has dared depict Virginia's age accurately]. Virginia is also portrayed as having other suitors — represented here by the rotund Harry Dunkinson as Tony, a drinking buddy with whom Poe has an ongoing, supposedly comic contest for Virginia's affections — but as she was all

of 13 years old when she and Poe married, the existence of other suitors seems highly unlikely.

Then comes a very odd episode: on the way home from their tryst, Edgar and Virginia witness a Simon Legree–like character whipping an old slave [played by white actor, Bert Weston, in blackface] and Poe halts the beating by purchasing him … with a $600 I.O.U., naturally. The return of this promissory note to John Allan (Ernest Maupain), atop the many bills Edgar has been accumulating [per this account] from drinking and gambling, prompts Poe's ejection from the household.

[The attitude of the film-makers in including this episode seems rather enlightened for the period, and more enlightened than Griffith himself would prove to be in that same year's *The Birth of a Nation*, even if once again we are presented with a Caucasian actor portraying a black character. Still, there is no evidence that Poe had anything other than the typical Southern attitude toward blacks in the first half of the nineteenth century; in fact, his treatment of all non–WASPs in his stories is equally condescending and intolerant. Those few black characters that do appear in his works are usually servants and are generally peripheral to the action — Jup in "The Gold Bug" being a notable exception. At times, one might not even know that there *are* any black characters, were it not for other characters barking orders at them, as in "The Man Who Was Used Up." There is also no evidence whatever that a black servant was ever part of Poe's extended household, as is depicted here.]

When Poe is thrown out by his foster-father, the slave follows along and is still present at the time of Virginia's death. [According to a 1940 article in *The Baltimore Sun*, Poe acted on behalf of Maria Clemm in assigning a slave named Edwin to a freed black for a period of nine years for $40.00. Poe's motives were probably less due to a belief in Abolitionism than to the results of the chronic penury the Poe/Clemm household faced. Edwin seems not to have rejoined the family afterward, but the particulars do not correspond to the film in any case.]

The biggest howler, historically speaking, is reserved for the film's final sequence, where it is inferred that Poe never sold a story in his life. In truth his stories were in great demand and were printed widely and frequently during his lifetime. It is also true that publishers, knowing of Poe's chronic need for money, rarely paid what the stories were worth; they knew all too well the author could not afford to haggle or shop around for a better price. And since the U.S. had no copyright laws at the time, he never saw a penny from the myriad reprints of his works during his lifetime; Poe's poverty, however, was not due to any lack of public popularity.

Director Charles Brabin reserves his most spectacular visual tricks for *The Raven* sequence in which the inebriated Poe conceives of the poem. Moving back and forth between Poe's apparently real chamber, a series of symbolic locales, and, more often, some nebulous region between the two, Brabin conjures up a series of spectacular and frequently gorgeous visuals: a silhouetted Poe climbing a craggy incline with a large rock labeled "wine" blocking his path, Poe holding a goblet of wine over which a skull is superimposed, Poe being denied entry at the gates of heaven. While these images may be considered naive and clichéd nowadays (or at least seen as being overly obvious, if not a suspect reading of the poem as a Temperance tract), they were less so in 1915. If anything, they very much resemble the sort of imagery utilized in newspaper-editorial cartoons well into the 1960s, and they remain strikingly composed and photographed. To his credit, Brabin used a live raven throughout, except for its first appearance as an Arthur Rackham–like silhouette on the door. The sequence's only flaw — aside from Walthall's typically playing to the last row, although he is more controlled here than in *The Avenging Conscience* — is a lack of clarity as to whether Poe's imagination is stirred by the visit of an actual bird, or whether the entire episode is an alcoholic hallucination [the cartoon-ish silhouette that precipitates the sequence suggests the latter]. Okay, the repeated title card of "Nevermore" lettered in bones *is* pretty corny.

Poe scribbles down the poem and rushes off to town, desperately trying to interest someone in purchasing it — or any of his works — but finds no takers — although, in truth, "The Raven" was snapped up by not one, but two publications, one of which was a newspaper that employed him at the time. Virginia dies soon thereafter. Tuberculosis was almost invariably fatal at that time, no matter one's social position or financial situation — medical science simply did not as yet understand it — but, as in Griffith's

biopic, the cause of Virginia's death is chalked up to Poe's inability to earn the money to obtain treatment for his wife.

The film continues to the introduction of Helen Whitman, one of several women with whom Poe became briefly involved after Virginia's death, but before anything much can be made of her character — and indeed before she and Poe even meet — the film oddly and abruptly ends.

There was more to the film once than what has come down to us; some sources cite an original running time of 80 minutes, but the available version runs only a little over half that. Since American features at the time rarely ran more than five reels, it is more likely the film ran the 57 minutes cited by other sources. The AFI and several contemporary accounts place *The Raven* at six reels (approximately an hour), so some footage — at least a reel of it, perhaps all or most of the final one — has gone missing.

An account in the 14 December 1915 edition of the Pennsylvania newspaper, the *Daily Independent*, suggests that Poe loses his mind after Virginia's death, has hallucinations — a *non sequitur* shot of an angel appearing to Poe may be from this otherwise lost footage — and confuses Helen with the late Virginia. Given that Whitman is shown preparing to go out and bestow charity on the needy, there may have been a bit more to it than that. (It should be noted that Poe and Whitman did not meet as the result of the author being one of the lady's charity cases.) Then again, several contemporary accounts seem to suggest that any post–*Raven* footage amounted to very little of the running time, so the missing 12 minutes might just be odd bits from throughout the film.

Confusing the running-time issue somewhat is a 14 December 1915 interview with writer George Hazelton that was printed in *The Ogden* [Utah] *Standard*. Therein, he twice refers to the film's running time as "an hour and a half." Another of Hazelton's intriguing claims was that he was in possession of a pen-holder made from the "headboard" of Poe's coffin. Per his account, when Poe's body was moved so that it would be side by side with the remains of Virginia and Maria Clemm, it was also placed in a new coffin because "the headboard of the old coffin against which the brain of the mighty poet had gone back to dust fell away from moisture and decay." According to Hazelton, this section of wood was taken away by an unnamed prominent editor of an equally unnamed leading journal of Baltimore. Years later, his widow had the pen-holder made from the wood and, because of Hazelton's interest in the poet, presented it to him.

The fact of the matter is that Poe's body was transferred to another coffin — *prior* to his burial — when a relative substituted a more expensive, lead-lined model for the poplar one provided by the hospital. (Poe, after all, had essentially been a charity case, having been removed to the hospital from the sidewalk in front of a tavern where he'd been found unconscious.) But the historical record does not state that he was presented with yet a *third* coffin on the event of his body's exhumation and transfer to its current grave in 1875. Hazelton also refers to Poe's body being removed from "a 'vaulty' place under an old church," whereas, in reality, Poe was laid to rest initially in the plot purchased by his grandfather in the cemetery. From this we can infer that Hazelton is the source of the inauthentic biographical

Artwork from the original stage production upon which this Essanay picture was based.

details of *The Raven*, and thus even that his estimation of the running time might be suspect. Much of the interview with him has the tone of someone spinning yarns; his novel, play and screenplay of *The Raven* were similarly constructed out of whole cloth. Admittedly, Poe scholarship was not then what it is now, but Hazelton gets even simple, easily-verified details wrong. Hell, he can't even spell Poe's middle name correctly!

Charles Brabin (1883–1957) — sometimes billed with middle initial "R" or "J" — was an Englishman who joined the Edison company in 1908 after some experience on the stage. By the 1920s he was a highly-regarded film director and was married to Theda Bara, whose last two films he directed before she retired. Their marriage was considered one of the rare successful ones in Hollywood and lasted until her death from cancer in 1955. Brabin's career hit something of a snag when he was removed from the troubled *Ben-Hur* (1925) and replaced by Fred Niblo. The incident repeated itself — at the same studio — when he was yanked off 1932's *Rasputin and the Empress* (reputedly at the behest of Ethel Barrymore, who feared shooting was progressing too slowly for her to keep a stage commitment). But M-G-M moved him over to another film that was having production difficulties, *The Mask of Fu Manchu* (1932), possibly the movie for which he is best remembered.

Despite a tendency to overuse the front-row-center position for his camera (not uncommon for the period) — though with more variety of distance from his actors than was then usual — Brabin produces a number of memorable images throughout the film. In addition to those in *The Raven* sequence (which begins with a then-highly-unusual dolly-in towards the snoozing Poe), these include shots of Poe and Virginia by the lake; Poe grieving at Virginia's sepulcher (though how the poverty-stricken poet is to have afforded such an elaborate monument is a riddle); a seaside shot of Poe, flanked by rocky abutments, experiencing the vision of an angel; and — in a composition worthy of Vermeer — Mrs. Clemm (Marian Skinner) staring up at a crucifix on the wall, praying for her daughter's life. Brabin made only a few more films after *Fu Manchu* and retired from the screen in 1934; his only other genre credit is the first film adaptation of Thornton Wilder's *The Bridge of San Luis Rey* (1929).

Warda Howard (1880–1943), a very busy actress in 1915–1916, then disappeared from the screen until 1918, when she appeared in a single title before disappearing again, this time for good. As with most of the cast of *The Raven* — save for Walthall — she appears to have been an Essanay contractee, and many of her film credits are shared with others in the cast of *The Raven*.

Ernest Maupain (1869–1944, sometimes credited merely as Maupain) first appeared in films in 1911 in his native France, before relocating to the United States. He returned home in 1920, and his remaining credits up to 1929 are all Gallic productions. His most notable genre role is Professor Moriarty in the 1916 *Sherlock Holmes*. Marian (aka Marion) Skinner began in films in 1915 and racked up scores of credits between then and 1924, when her resume ceases. She also appeared (as a suffragette) in *Sherlock Holmes*.

Harry Dunkinson (1876–1936) began with Essanay when the company was still located in Chicago and continued acting — usually in small, uncredited roles, such as the bartender in *Tillie and Gus* (1933) — until shortly before his death. He is sometimes billed as Harry Leopold Dunkinson or Henry Dunkinson. Surprisingly, given his wealth of credits, *The Raven* seems to be his only genre film. Bert (aka Burt) Weston would seem to be a subject for further study. He has a few credits in the year before *The Raven* and a couple in 1915, and then there's a long break in his resume until two widely separated films in the 1930s. He seems to have been sufficiently well known back in 1915 to appear as himself in *Midnight at Maxim's*, but, then again, he wouldn't be the first or last performer to go from fame to obscurity in the course of a few decades.

In a 15 November 1915 review from *Wid's Daily* — the small trade publication begun that very year by Wid Gunning that would metamorphose into *Film Daily* in 1922 — an anonymous (but quotation-mark-happy) reviewer opines that much of the film is old-fashioned in its technique.

> Where double exposure work is used, it is very noticeable that the director and the camera man … waited too long for their two bits of film to come together properly, thus leaving the effect which we had in "the old days," of the person in the scene "holding" a pose until the dissolve "came in" or "went out"…. If double exposures are to be used they must be made so evenly that there is no "halt" in the action. It can be done and it has been done and for that reason the "old school conservative" methods disappoint. In one place the grave of "leonore" [*sic*] is shown in an exterior on the top of a hill with no trees about. Later the grave is shown in a studio setting which is very, very "stagey"…. Many other scenes were made in the studio which could have been made to much better advantage outside.

Wid, however, was very keen on Walthall's performance which he thought "wonderful" and possessing "remarkable power" even though he felt the technical aspects seriously hampered it. Wid also times the film at "Hour and Half," which he termed "hopelessly draggy at times and surely some of the scenes are truly bad."

Time changes one's perception of everything. It is now the acting technique of Henry Walthall that looks outmoded and stagy, while the allegorical sequences would not be out of place in a Ken Russell film.

— *HHL*

Red Lights

Red Lights. Goldwyn Pictures/Goldwyn-Cosmopolitan Distributing Corp., 30 September 1923, 7 reels/6841 feet [available]
CAST: Marie Prevost (*Ruth Carson*); Raymond Griffith (*Sheridan Scott*); Johnny Walker (*John Blake*); Alice Lake (*Norah O'Neill*); Dagmar Godowsky (*Cherita*)* William Worthington (*Luke Carson*) Frank Elliot (*Kirk Allen*); Lionel Belmore (*Alden Murphy*); Jean Hersholt (*Ezra Carson*); George Reed (*Porter*); Charles B. Murphy (*The Henchman*); Charles H. West (*Conductor*).

---

*The Library of Congress synopsis has "Cherita" while other sources call the character "Roxy."

CREDITS: *Director* Clarence G. Badger; *Adaptation* Carey Wilson and Alice D.G. Miller; based on the play *The Rear Car; A Mystery Play* by Edward E. Rose (New York, 1926); *Cinematographer* Rudolph Berquist.

"The detective appears *after* the crime is committed. The *deflector* appears *before* crime is committed and *de*-flects it."

The above quote is from the character Sheridan Scott, describing his profession in Edward Rose's 1922 play *The Rear Car*. Sheridan drives the other characters crazy with his endless, often absurd banter, but while he does come off like Inspector Clouseau, his eccentric manner hides a mind as sharp as Sherlock Holmes or Mark Twain's Puddn'head Wilson. Rose's play is set entirely aboard the private car of a train and has a variety of characters menaced by an unseen presence with evil designs on the heroine, an heiress going east to meet her father. Author Edward Everett Rose specialized in stage adaptations of famous novels (*Janice Meredith*, *David Harum*) and is not to be confused — though he inevitably is — with British playwright Edward Rose, who did the same sort of thing and whose stage version of *The Prisoner of Zenda* was a huge success in 1895.

The Rear Car was likely the most noteworthy of Rose's original works and a big hit in Los Angeles. Ads promised "a million laughs and a few thrills" ("Forty-three plus" of the latter according to *LA Times* critic, Edwin Schallert). The play's debt to *The Bat*, which had been inducing shivers on Broadway for two years, was duly noted and there was much praise for Richard Bennett's performance as Sheridan Scott. The play had a nationwide tour and while it did play in New York, it never made the Great White Way. A year later it was back in the City of the Angels — with Edward Everett Horton as Scott — and then was revived again in 1929, with Franklin Pangborn playing the crime deflector; (he was the villain in the original production).

The play is an enjoyable read but has many improbabilities even for a thriller; at one point the train is stalled because there's been an accident with a circus wagon and a gorilla has escaped. The beast promptly turns up on the train, but later it's revealed that it's only the bad guy in a costume. Did he pack an ape suit with him for just such an eventuality?

Instead of trying to smooth over such absurdities, scenarists Carey Wilson and Alice D. G. Miller decided instead to compound them when they did their adaptation of the play for Goldwyn Pictures. They added a number of confusing subplots, including an odd science-fiction element, and then made not the slightest attempt to pull them all together and explain exactly what had happened or why. The result is less like *The Bat* than Benjamin Christensen's loopy *Seven Footprints to Satan*.

Synopsis based on a viewing of the film:

Railroad magnate Luke Carson is travelling to Los Angeles on one of his trains to reunite with his daughter Ruth whom he has not seen since her childhood. Ruth was kidnapped when she was a little girl and has grown up unaware of her true identity. Carson's

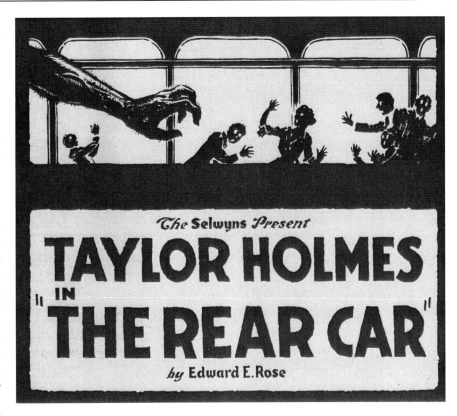

The column "Gossip of the Rialto" — in the May 28, 1922, edition of *The New York Times* — announced that Edward Rose's play was on track for The Great White Way. It was staged, but not on Broadway.

West Coast lawyer Kirk Allen discovered Ruth working as a shop girl and has proof of her true identity and an eagerness to claim Carson's $50,000 reward.

We then see a crazed scientist with wild eyes perfecting his invention: a red light that materializes out of nowhere and projects the voice of the scientist.

In Los Angeles, Ruth is overwhelmed by her new status as an heiress and worries about the strain it will have on her relationship with her boyfriend John Blake. She also feels she's being watched and that "horrible eyes" follow her everywhere. John takes her to his friend Scott Sheridan, the crime deflector. Scott agrees to look into it.

Meanwhile there is tension between Kirk Allen and Carson's East Coast lawyer Alden Murray who arrived earlier to look after Ruth. Allen has given Murray proof of Ruth's identity but Murray, in spite of a fatherly attitude towards Ruth, is skeptical and accuses Allen of being in love with Ruth. In reality, Allen is just after her money and hopes to win her affection before she meets her father. Allen's henchman intercepts a telegram meant for Murray in which Carson, who has had a presentiment of danger, tells everyone to stay in LA until he gets there. Allen destroys the telegram.

Ruth has been put up in a fancy bungalow which she shares with her friend Norah. Murray comes in with a telegram from Luke Carson telling the party to head East in his private car. That night they all go to a nightclub where girls dressed as monkeys do a dance number. One of the other dancers, Cherita, is actually Allen's wife whom he had abandoned in Europe. She stabs the disconcerted lawyer with a rubber knife.

Later, Ruth meets John in a secluded spot and tells him of the plan to travel East in the morning. John agrees to join them and bring a minister so they can be married. Ruth, still feeling the evil eyes watching her, returns to the bungalow. Allen, anxious to get Blake out of the way, has him arrested on a false charge.

Later that night, Ruth is terrified by a strange red light and a sinister voice that tells her to say her prayers. Her friends think she's imagining things but later the red light and its warning appear again. Scott patrols the grounds where he sees a cloaked figure in the shadows. Scott is always asking for a light and when the strange man obliges him, Scott sees that it's a hairy paw that's holding the match. Scott takes time out from his deflecting to romance Norah who thinks he's nuts but is still attracted to him.

The next morning at the train station, a conductor whose face we can't see too clearly shoos reporters away from Carson's private car saying there's still work to be done on it. Cherita, determined to expose her husband, arrives at the station but is kidnapped by Allen's henchman. Allen puts her in a little plane, lands in a desert area and then leaves her there and flies off.

Ruth is puzzled by John's absence but nevertheless consents to leave. Carson's private car pulls out with her, Murray, Norah and Scott aboard. No sooner has it left than Luke Carson's train pulls in. Too late to stop them, Carson decides to follow them on the next train and sends a telegram ahead. However, Allen's henchman overpowers Carson, ties him up and leaves him in his compartment with a "Do Not Disturb" sign on the door.

Meanwhile Cherita has wandered to a remote train station. A conductor — the workman from before — takes charge of her. Allen is able to fly to the next station and joins the private car when they stop there. Allen tells Ruth that Blake is a thief but then Scott, who has somehow sprung Blake from jail, tells the young man to come down from the roof of the car where he has been hiding. Accusations start flying from all parties. Notes threatening Nora appear and the strange voice from the red light warns of her imminent death. A rug begins to move and Cherita, in a daze, emerges from a trapdoor beneath it. At that point Murray staggers into the room and drops dead. Cherita disappears.

Allen thinks Murray died of a heart attack, but Scott claims it was murder done with a hat pin and his theory is confirmed when a porter finds a bloody towel. Murray's body disappears and with it the proofs of Ruth's identity. That night in her room, Ruth is terrified by the hairy claw of a gorilla that emerges to threaten her from a secret panel. Her cries bring help but no gorilla is found.

At the next stop, Luke Carson joins the party. As the train pulls out, Scott chides him for sending the telegram to come East, but Carson indignantly denies sending the telegram. The gorilla makes another appearance and Scott tussles with it in one of the rooms. Scott emerges with a pair of hairy claws — the gorilla was a man in a costume but he's gotten away. An unconscious Cherita, wrapped in a sheet, falls out of a secret panel.

Immediately after we see someone uncouple the private car from the rest of the train. The man emerges and it turns out to be the crazed scientist from before. He reveals himself as Ezra Carson, Luke's brother, who had been a rival for the woman Luke ultimately married. Ezra had been put in an asylum but escaped and has plotted revenge for years. He admits that he sent the bogus telegram, invented the red light to frighten Ruth, rigged the private car with secret panels, and murdered Murray and hid his body.

The runaway car careers down the mountain track and it seems inevitable it will collide with an oncoming train. Seeing a work crew on another track, Blake leaps from the train in the hope that he can get help. Ruth clings to Luke Carson and laments that the day of their meeting will also be the day of their death but the man responds "Hell, I'm not your father! I'm a detective!" He pulls off a false beard, disconcerting Ezra that his revenge scheme has gone awry. Just before the car can collide with the train, a brakeman switches it to another track. The car crashes near a precipice. Ezra falls to his death attempting to escape. The others are rescued.

The real Luke Carson, freed of his bonds, is reunited with his daughter. Scott reveals that he had the papers proving Ruth's identity the whole time. Scott also admits to Norah that he wishes she were blonde. Norah promptly takes off a blonde wig and reveals

she's a detective hired by Murray. The detective and the deflector kiss.

Perhaps rather than pointing out the numerous lapses in logic and muddled motivations, we should simply quote the *Los Angeles Times*'s review of 8 August 1923:

> A plausible plot? Not at all. But the director and the adapter seem to say "Now here's a jumble of impossibilities and absurdities, but the jumble also contains mystery in plenty and lots of fine thrills. Forget about logic and probabilities, follow the sequence of events, guess who the villain is if you can, but enjoy yourself."

To *Variety*'s "Fred," though, the confusing storyline caused the film to just miss "being a wow of a comedy mystery melodrama." Indeed, the film's whole technique added to the obscuration:

> The direction was given too decidedly to middle length shots, so that the audience failed to get the drift of what was going on on the screen, and in the cutting the titles were too short, a fault likewise present in the showing of writing and telegrams in the feature…. Possibly in smaller theaters where the audience is more apt to be close to the screen the picture will stand a better chance of going over for it full value [13 September 1923].

The New York Times found the film a "strange concoction" redeemed by "splendid photography and scenic effects," but doubted that the film's producers "could detail a comprehensive conception of the narrative" (Having read the 19-page summary on file at the Library of Congress, we would agree).

On the other hand, "Mae Tinee" of the *Chicago Tribune* (17 September 1923) felt that viewers knew what was going on all too well:

> This picture was designed for the specific purpose of scaring the spectator to death before the end of the film. It fails in its purpose because the average moviegoer has grown so WISE to claws and detectives with fake beards; so terribly on the JOB where trapdoors and escaped inmates are concerned that it takes an eyeful to make those seasoned pulses beat any faster than the doctor allows.

Critics did agree that the runaway train car finale was stunningly photographed and directed. Runaway trains and action sequences on trains were as common in the Silent Era as car crashes are in today's films, but the climax in *Red Lights* is no doubt one of the best of them. Two oddities to note about it: the hero's attempt to save the day proves irrelevant, and the director cleverly breaks the tension when the gruff detective refuses to play daddy to the terrified Ruth and takes off his disguise.

The railroad sequences were largely filmed in Carrizo Gorge, and publicity provided some details about the five weeks of shooting in that area:

> A special train of ten coaches, carrying a radio, an airplane, a five piece orchestra and a special car on which was mounted an electric generator left Los Angeles for the border with seventy-five members of the company including carpenters, electricians, property men, cameramen, extras, mechanics and technical men. Two immigration officials accompanied the party as representatives of the United States government for the greater portion of the railroad runs through Mexico. The little town of Jacumba Hot Springs was the destination of the Goldwyn special. With the arrival of the Goldwyn Company, the civilians of the town hailed a new era of prosperity. There had not been much excitement since the Mexican revolution when Uncle Sam's soldiers camped about the town.

Seen today, *Red Lights* is not in the same league as *The Bat* or *The Cat and the Canary*. The accent is heavily on comedy and how much of that works depends on your reaction to Raymond Griffith as Sheridan Scott. Nevertheless there are a few spooky moments: the hate-filled eyes that follow Ruth about; the mad doctor in his lab; the moody, noir-ish photography of LA at night; the startling shot of the monstrous paw that strikes a match (though why the villain is walking around Los Angeles dressed like a member of The Nairobi Trio is anyone's guess); and that same claw reaching for Ruth through the secret panel à la *The Cat and the Canary*. The red-lights scenes themselves are less effective since a sinister voice scarcely means much in a silent, and this went right past the *Harrison's Report* reviewer, who thought the device spelled out the words rather than spoke them[!] The red-lights invention is nowhere to be found the play, wherein the villain merely speaks in ominous tones from various hiding places, including a hollow desk.

Reviewers praised Raymond Griffith's crime deflector, but the best we'll say for him is that he's easier to take than is Charlie Ruggles in the 1934 sound version, *Murder in the Private Car* (which, by the way, is more faithful to the play than *Red Lights*). Griffith came from a theatrical family and was on the boards before he could walk; however, as a child he contracted respiratory diphtheria which damaged his vocal cords and resulted in Griffith not being able to speak above a hoarse whisper. In the mid–1920s, *Photoplay* circulated the story that Griffith's voice impediment came about when he was playing a child being viciously beaten in the stage production of *The Witching Hour*. According to the story, Griffith screamed so frantically that he ruined his voice. Griffith, who shunned publicity and wasn't disposed to discuss his voice anyhow, didn't publicly contradict the tale, but it's a doubtful one especially as *The Witching Hour* has no scene of a boy being whipped.

As the young Griffith couldn't do legitimate stage work anymore, he danced, performed a pantomime act, and joined the circus. In the mid–1910s he turned to the movies, working first for Lehrman Knock-Out Comedies and then for Mack Sennett, where he did only supporting roles, as Sennett didn't think he was funny. After some freelancing, Griffith ended up back at Sennett as a gagman, writer and assistant director.

In 1922 Griffith appeared as "Tony the Wop" in Marshall Neillan's gangster melodrama, *Feet First*; it was a small role but, after seeing the early rushes, Neillan was impressed with Griffith's performance and built up his part. Griffith also had a serious role in the Tod Browning fiasco, *The White Tiger*. It was following his move to Paramount that Griffith achieved a measure of fame and it was there that he built his persona as "the man in the silk hat" in films like *Paths to Paradise* and *Hands Up* (both done *by Red Lights* director, Clarence Badger). In the late 1920s, a dispute with Paramount led to Griffith winning release from his contract, but the studio retaliated by not promoting his last two films for them; more disastrous still was the coming of sound. Griffith made a couple of talkie shorts and then did his final film role, the memorable bit part (which he did for nothing) as the dying French soldier in *All Quiet on the Western Front*. Griffith went on to a successful career as a producer and script doctor. While not nearly as well known today as Chaplin, Keaton, or Lloyd, he has an enthusiastic following among fans of silent comedy.

Marie Prevost (Ruth) spends most of the movie screaming and fainting, but apparently didn't do either well enough to impress most critics. The *Los Angeles Times* dismissed her as "pretty, but not much of an actress in this picture. Moreover, the upper part of her arms is too fat — the first sign that diet and exercise have become essential to a woman who would preserve her beauty." Prevost took those last comments all too much to heart; her crash-dieting binges later contributed to a nervous breakdown and then her death.

The Canadian-born Prevost became a Mack Sennett bathing beauty early in her career. Edgar Kennedy, who worked at Sennett, recalled her as her being very beautiful and given to doing funny drawings with titles like "Love is Blind" and "Nature Dances." Prevost eventually left Sennett and won supporting roles in a variety of films. In spite of her lukewarm notices for *Red Lights*, she went on to starring roles in comedies like *Getting Gertie's Garter*, *Girl on the Pullman*, and *Blonde for a Night* (all of which are still extant). She did serious parts as well, notably in *The Racket*, *The Sideshow,* and Cecil B. De

"Wow! I can see your house from here!" Raymond Griffith, in **Red Lights**, seems to suffer not at all from acrophobia.

Mille's underrated (and unsuccessful) *The Godless Girl*. Still, the 1930s saw her career go into rapid decline as her roles grew smaller and smaller; her part as the wisecracking best friend in movies like *Three Wise Girls* was typical. She began gaining weight again and starved herself in an effort to reduce. Depressed over the death of her mother in a car accident and her own declining fortunes, Prevost also took to drink.

By the mid–1930s, Prevost was doing uncredited bits and living in a cheap room with her dog. She had a role in the film, *Ten Laps to Go*, which the movie's star, Rex Lease, described as a scene-stealer, but Marie didn't live to see it released. On 23 January 1937, her dog's continual howling eventually alerted the landlord that something was wrong, and he entered Prevost's room to find her dead, lying face down on her bed with little bite marks from her dog on her arms and legs. She'd been dead for several days and no doubt the faithful beast was trying to rouse his mistress, not eat her, later reports and the song "Marie Provost" [*sic*] notwithstanding; ghoulishly, a photo of her body was printed in a number of newspapers. During the search of her apartment, a promissory note made out to Joan Crawford for $110 was found; earlier that week, Prevost had gone to M-G-M to see Crawford — with whom she worked in *Paid* — but missed her. A bit of mystery was added to the tragedy when police reported that Marie had recently changed her phone number several times to avoid someone who was harassing her, but the empty liquor bottles scattered about the room told the real story, and acute alcoholism was given as the cause of death. Prevost was cremated and her ashes mingled with her mother's. In her heyday, Prevost had been making $1000 a week, but she left an estate totaling barely $300.

The supporting cast of *Red Lights* had happier careers: Jean Hersholt (see entry, *Sinners in Silk*) may have been an odd choice to play the crazed Ezra Carson, but he seems to have had fun with the role. And fans of Universal horror pictures will no doubt appreciate the presence of Lionel Belmore (see *The Return of Peter Grimm*), everyone's favorite burgomaster, as the doomed Murphy.

— HN

The Return of Peter Grimm

The Return of Peter Grimm. Fox Film Corp./Fox Film Corp., 7 November 1926, 7 reels/6,961 feet, Museum of Modern Art
Cast: Alec B. Francis (*Peter Grimm*); John Roche (*Frederick Grimm*); Janet Gaynor (*Catherine*); Richard Walling (*James Hartman*); John St. Polis (*Andrew MacPherson*); Lionel Belmore (*Reverend Henry Bartholomey*); Elizabeth Patterson (*Mrs. Batholomey*); Bodil Rosing (*Marta*); Mickey McBan (*William*); Florence Gilbert (*Annamarie*); Sammy Cohen (*The Clown*); Hank (*Tobe, the dog*)
Credits: *Producer* William Fox; *Director* Victor Schertzinger; *Assistant Director* William Tummell; based on the eponymous play by David Belasco (1911); *Adaptation* Bradley King; *Cinematographer* Glen MacWilliams

"The author does not advance any theory as to the probability of the return of the main character of this play. For *the many*, it may be said that Peter could exist only in the minds of the characters grouped around him — in their subconscious memories. For *the few*, his presence will embody the theory of the survival of the persistent personal energy. The character has, so far as possible, been treated to accord with either thought."
— note by David Belasco at the beginning of *The Return of Peter Grimm* (1911)

Although the above sounds like a disclaimer, Broadway impresario and playwright David Belasco insisted that his play had been inspired by this personal experience with the spirit world: He had just returned to his New York home and had fallen asleep when he was awakened by a vision of his mother, then living in San Francisco. Belasco said the vision spoke to him: "As I strove to speak and sit up she smiled at me a loving reassuring smile ... leaning down [she] seemed to kiss me; then drew away a little and said 'Do not grieve; All is well and I am happy,' then moved toward the door and vanished."

The very next day Belasco received word that his mother had died during the night.

Whatever his personal beliefs on the subject, Belasco was well aware that depicting the supernatural on the legitimate stage was a tricky endeavor. Victorien Sardou, an ardent believer in Spiritualism, had one of his few failures with his 1897 play, *Spiritisme*, despite its starring Sarah Bernhardt; critics had complained that Sardou let his advocacy of the subject override his dramatic sense. In contrast, while Belasco had one of his characters, Dr. MacPherson, act as the spokesman for Spiritualism, the play didn't descend to pamphleteering but instead focused on the conflict going on within the Grimm household and how the deceased patriarch returns to try to set things right and make up for his own failures. Belasco eschewed the usual séance and table-tapping devices and settled for Peter Grimm standing unseen among the other characters. He also used no outré lighting other than having Grimm lit a little more dimly than the rest of the cast. The one special effect occurred when Grimm's spirit pounds on the table in frustration and no noise is heard.

The play was an enormous success. David Warfield received outstanding notices as the title character and special mention was made of Percy Helton, the child actor who played little Willie. Helton grew up to be a familiar, raspy-voiced character actor who played in scores of films and television shows; in the 1960s he appeared on *The Tonight Show* where he did an excerpt from Peter Grimm's moving farewell speech.

In the opening night program for *The Return of Peter Grimm*, Cecil B. De Mille was given credit for the original idea. De Mille, however, claimed that he had done more than just throw out a suggestion, but rather *had written an entire play on Spiritualism at Belasco's request*. This play — which depicts a séance at one point — concerns a ruthless tycoon who has wronged his ward and then comes back from the dead to try to make amends. De Mille was thus quite disenchanted with Belasco, who was a friend of his father's and a mentor to Cecil's brother, William, but — other than making a public complaint — he took no legal action against the "Bishop of Broadway," who had already been accused more than once of taking credit for others' work (see the 1921 *The Case of Becky* for additional info on this artistic larceny).

Complicating matters of authorship still further was a review of the play by Cincinnati critic, Lewis Hillhouse, who claimed *Grimm* was much like *Old Lady Mary: A Story of the Seen and the Unseen*, an 1884 novel by Mrs. (Margaret) Oliphant; if truth be told, *Mary* sounds like a distaff version of *Grimm*. Hillhouse did not accuse anyone of plagiarism, but pointed out a number of remarkable similarities between the two works.

Whoever wrote it, audiences loved the combination of sentimentality and the supernatural, and the play was successfully revived in 1921, again with David Warfield in the title role. In 1922, Metro announced that Warfield would star in film versions of *Grimm* and another of his big stage hits, *The Music Master*; that, however, that may have been wishful thinking, for Warfield had no interest in movies, which he considered "animated photographs" and good only for prepping people to enjoy theater. Mr. Warfield, who retired from the theater in 1924, consistently turned down lucrative offers (as much as one million dollars, according to one source) to do a movie. In 1925 Fox bought the rights to *The Return of Peter Grimm*, and there were subsequent reports that Henry B. Walthall would star; in the end, though, veteran stage-and-screen character actor, Alec B. Francis, won the role. Starlet Duane Thompson was initially cast as Grimm's adopted daughter, but she was replaced by Janet Gaynor, who was just then beginning to win public notice.

The film version of *The Return of Peter Grimm* is faithful to the play — or at least as faithful as it could be, given the limitations of the silent drama.

The synopsis is based on a screening of the print of the film held at MOMA.

Peter Grimm, the kindly but stubborn master of a floricultural estate in New York, is getting elderly and hopes that his only blood relative, his nephew Frederick, will continue the generations-old nursery business. Grimm also wants Frederick, recently returned from Europe, to marry Catherine, the orphan girl Grimm has raised as his own daughter. Catherine, however, is in love with James, and employee at the nursery and also the son of one of Grimm's oldest friends. Completing Grimm's household is Willie, a little boy who is the grandson of Grimm's housekeeper, Marta. Willie's mother, Annamarie, had borne him out of wedlock and still defies public scorn by refusing to name Willie's father.

Grimm's good friend Dr. MacPherson is a fervent believer in spiritualism and shows Peter a book titled, *Are the Dead Alive?* Peter remains a skeptic and considers mediums to be "furniture bouncers." Nonetheless, MacPherson tries to convince Peter to make a bargain with him; whoever dies first will try to come back and manifest himself to the other. MacPherson also attempts to convince Peter to make out a will, but the old man sees no need for it since Frederick will inherit everything and Catherine will have her share as his wife.

It turns out that Peter is gravely ill, a fact that MacPherson has concealed from him. The physician does discuss the matter with the rest of the household as well as with the local minister, the Reverend Bartholomey, and his busybody wife. The conversation is overheard by Willie, who adores Peter. The little boy spills the beans to the old man, but Peter scoffs and says the doctor has been "trying to make a spook of me for years" and makes plans to go to the circus with Willie.

Frustrated by Peter's attempts to marry Catherine off to Frederick, James tries to convince the girl to elope with him, but Dr. MacPherson tells them the shock would likely kill Peter. Later that day, Peter brings Catherine and Frederick together and tries to persuade Catherine to marry his nephew within the next ten days. Catherine, knowing that it will make her benefactor happy, reluctantly promises. Smiling and content, Peter sits in his favorite chair, smoking his pipe and petting his beloved dog. A few moments later, he dies; his pipe drops to the floor and breaks.

Ten days later, the unhappy Catherine is preparing for her wedding to Frederick who knows she doesn't love him but still insists on her keeping her promise to Peter. Frederick also makes plans to sell the nursery to Mr. Hicks, longtime business rival to the Grimms.

That night a storm breaks out, and Frederick is startled by noises at the door; no one seems to be there, but Peter Grimm has returned in spirit form. Observing what is going on, Peter is shocked by his nephew's callousness and desperately wants to contact Catherine and release her from her promise. However, Grimm's incorporeal body cannot disturb any material objects or communicate in any coherent fashion. Catherine, Dr. MacPherson and Willie sense him as a loving presence and Frederick is disturbed and haunted, but there's no way for Grimm to impart any kind of message.

The opportunity arises when Frederick gets a letter addressed to Peter. It's from Annemarie, Willie's mother, who names Frederick as the boy's father. Peter is reading the letter over Frederick's shoulder but is powerless to stop him from burning it. However, the letter includes a photo of Annemarie for Willie, and Frederick merely tears it up and throws it away. Willie has been ill and comes down from his sickbed. Peter manages to influence him to look in the wastebasket, and there he finds his mother's photo. Peter also tries to have Willie remember the days before he lived with Marta and the man who used to visit his mother. Willie can't see or hear Peter, but he knows his friend is there.

Dr. MacPherson, James, Catherine and the Bartholomeys find Willie on the staircase with the picture and question him about what is going on. Willie finally remembers the man who used to make his mother cry and, though too frightened to name him, declares that he is at the outside door. Frederick promptly enters and the others confront him about Annamarie. He becomes angry at their accusations though he doesn't exactly deny them. Catherine announces that their marriage is off but Frederick, who's been increasingly unnerved by his sense of his uncle's nearness, says it doesn't matter: Hicks has agreed to buy the nursery, and there's nothing anyone can do to stop it. "God can stop anything!" Peter declares and a telegram arrives saying Hicks has died in an accident and the whole deal is off. At that moment, Peter concentrates with all his will and one of his pipes falls on the floor and breaks. This proves too much for Frederick, who announces that Catherine can have the estate and then leaves.

Later that night, the dying Willie sees Peter clearly for the first time and asks if he can go with him to the next world. Peter agrees and the boy's spirit joins his beloved friend, and they leave the land of the living forever. Catherine and James are married and the film ends as it began, with shots of the beautiful tulips and roses on the Grimm estate.

In the play, MacPherson not only challenges Grimm's skepticism about the spirit world but chides the conventional piety of Reverend Bartholomey and his "gingerbread house" heaven. Apparently, MacPherson's heaven, while as pleasant as the conventional one, allows its denizens liberal travel privileges while "spiritual energy" becomes the substitute for the soul. (For more on the Spiritualist movement, see the entry on *Earthbound*, a film that does a bit of borrowing from *The Return of Peter Grimm*). God, however, is still in His heaven, but the other place isn't mentioned at all. While such speculations enriched the play, the film largely eliminates them rather than become top-heavy with title cards.

Naturally, Peter's extended monologues also had to go. By necessity, the film has to focus on Peter's desperate attempt to communicate with the living, but it does not overlook his new understanding that he had allowed vanity to eclipse love in his hope for an earthly immortality via the perpetuation of the Grimm name and business.

These changes did not deter most reviewers from saying the film had done an admirable job in catching the essence of the play. C.S. Sewell's review in the 20 November 1926 *Moving Picture World* was typical:

> Fox Film Corporation is to be congratulated on the manner in which this great play has been transferred to the screen.... With Victor Schertzinger directing and Alec Francis in the title role, the result is a profoundly moving, impressive and dramatic offering that holds the attention from start to finish and offers pleasing and decidedly out of the ordinary entertainment.

Harrison's Reports (13 November 1926) predicted it would be a real crowd pleaser: "Good for everywhere. First-run houses of other producers-distributers-exhibitors should not pass it up; it is one of those pictures that add prestige not only to the theater that shows them but also the entire industry. The picture will stand an increase in admission prices."

At least one exhibitor (E.C. Silverhorn of the Liberty Theater in Harrisville, Michigan) took the last bit of advice to heart: "Excellent picture, high moral tone and registered fine with my crowd. I class it as a special and know it will hold up. In fact, we increased our admission price to that of specials."

Paul Thompson's review in *New York Telegraph* (7 November 1926) was favorable but offered some mild dissent, opining that Alec Francis did not have "the wistfulness and charm" of David Warfield in the title role, and that "it is not the play in many respects but it is a highly credible piece of work and reflects credit on Victor Schertzinger, the director, and the Fox Company."

Thompson, like most critics, did concede the film was superior to the play in one respect:

> The credulity of the playgoer was always stretched to the breaking point when Warfield became a spirit yet to all intents and purposes possessed of all the physical attributes of the living man he had been. In the picture through the tricks of photography, either double exposure or by a system of mirror reflections, the spirit Peter is an ectoplasm figure through which the other living, breathing characters pass unconscious of his presence. In this respect the picture is much more convincing and effective.

The double-exposure work is indeed excellent and used to good dramatic effect, as in the sequence wherein Frederick burns Annamarie's letter and Grimm's spirit vainly tries to put out the flames with his phantom hands. Of course, in later years, the use of such tricks to depict ghosts became routine and were often used for comedic effect (sometimes unintentionally, as in the 1940 remake of *Earthbound*), but they were still convincing in 1926. Less effective is having the title cards blur slightly every time Grimm's spirit speaks, a device that soon becomes tiresome.

Grimm's camerawork was done by Glen MacWilliams, who started his career as one of the group of young photographers employed by Douglas Fairbanks Pictures. MacWilliams had a long career, and his other genre credits are *Black Magic* (1929, see entry) and *The Clairvoyant* (1934), but he's best remembered for his Academy Award–nominated work on Alfred Hitchcock's *Lifeboat* (1944).

Victor Schertzinger's direction is very fluid and not in the least stage-bound, though he certainly makes good use of stage devices. With the ghostly Peter's first entrance from the other world (and the terrified Frederick convinced that *something* has come into the room), the front door becomes a symbolic and dramatic focus; then, too, Frederick stands revealed as Willie's father because he's "the man at the door." The dramatic denouement — the delivery of the wire that tells of Hicks' death — is also effected at the door, which again acts as a portal between this life and the next, when all that is seen is the hand of the deliveryman, holding the telegram, outstretched from the darkness.

The director's touch is particularly strong in the irony underlying Peter's death scene: Having extracted Catherine's promise to marry Frederick — and still totally oblivious to the unfairness of his request — Peter asks her to play the piano for him. As he sits in his comfortable chair, he makes a picture-perfect illustration of old-age contentment and satisfaction with a life well-lived; however, Catherine is miserable and stops playing, only to be replaced by Frederick at the piano as Peter dies. The audience knows the truth, but Peter passes away still comfortable in his illusions and it takes his entrance into the spirit world to open his eyes.

Schertzinger had a conspicuous career both as a composer and a film director. Music was very much a part of Schertzinger's background; his mother, Paula von Weber, had been court violinist to Queen Victoria, and Schertzinger himself was a child prodigy, playing violin in the Victor Herbert Symphony Orchestra and later for John Philip Sousa. Schertzinger enjoyed great success as a songwriter, his "Marcheta" having sold some four million copies to date.

His obits claimed he was the first person to compose musical scores for the silents; that wasn't accurate, but Schertzinger was an early advocate for music written for specific films and did scores for *Civilization*, *Peggy*, and a number of others. He also seemed to have had a flair for publicity: For *Civilization*, he arranged for a female chorus representing the "Mothers of Men" to be photographed as they sang, and then hid some singers in a pit beneath the stage at the film's opening at the Criterion Theater. The concealed chorus performed (in perfect lip-synch) during the appropriate scene, and Schertzinger's publicity flacks — who had told the press that *Civilization* was going to be a sound picture with sound coming *right from the screen* — thus grabbed the brass ring. For a few weeks, at any rate.

Schertzinger directed a wide variety of films during the Silent Era, many with the diminutive Charles Ray. When the talkies took over, he became associated, appropriately enough, with musicals like *Love Me Forever* and *The Birth of Blues*; he also started Bing Crosby and Bob Hope's enormously popular "Road" series. In 1941, while directing *The Fleet's In*, Schertzinger granted star Dorothy Lamour's request to leave the set early to attend the funeral of Alma Lockwood, widow of silent star, Harold Lockwood. That same night, Schertzinger died in his sleep. His sudden death was a shock to the Hollywood community by whom he was particularly well liked.

Alec B. Francis doesn't dominate the proceedings the way David Warfield was said to have done in the play but that was inevitable, given the absence of sound and the loss of Peter

Grimm's long soliloquies. Francis, who said he had wanted to play the part of Grimm for years, expressed great admiration for Warfield and, as he told the *Los Angeles Times*, he was making no attempt to copy Warfield's performance:

> Fortunately from the standpoint of my own best interests, I did not see Mr. Warfield in the role of Peter. Had I witnessed his delineation I fancy the memory of it would influence me unconsciously in my own work. No doubt, as would be natural, I would be endeavoring to recall just how Mr. Warfield performed this or that bit of business at a time when I should be concentrating on the action as hand, as directed by Victor Schertzinger [27 June 1926].

Francis skillfully captures Grimm's basic kindness— and his pig headedness— as well as his desperation to make up for his earthly mistakes. The final scene between Grimm and the dying Willie is movingly played by both actors and their subsequent journey to the heavenly realm reminds one of the close of another fantasy, *On Borrowed Time*, where Gramps and Pud skip off together to a happy afterlife (though perhaps not one so very different from what they've left behind).

The actor was apparently as kindly as many of the characters he portrayed, and Janet Gaynor remembers the set of *The Return of Peter Grimm* as being a particularly happy one; heck, even the dog loved Francis. Francis also helped Gaynor with her own performance. Long before he began to specialize in essaying wise and gentle older men, though, Francis toured the United Kingdom playing Cyrano and Hamlet on stage. British-born, Francis— who had briefly practiced as a barrister — also found time to do a stint in India with the British army, serve as a nurse in the Spanish-American War, and even farm a little in the Midwestern USA before settling permanently into the actor's life.

When it came to doing movies, Francis was the polar opposite of David Warfield, as his comments in the 7 August 1917 *Moving Picture World* indicate:

> Five years ago I realized what a future there was before the camera, and I went into picture work when the going was good…. I didn't go into it as a side issue as so many stage people do today. I went into for good and all, giving up the stage entirely. It was quite a leap in the dark you know as most of the actors in those days looked down on picture work as something beneath them.

Although he was a popular supporting player, *The Return of Peter Grimm* and the subsequent Fox film, *The Music Master*, made Francis, as one article put it, "a star at sixty." He easily made the transition to sound, playing in the first all-talkie horror film, *The Terror* (1928), and later in *Outward Bound*; however, he began having health problems. During the filming of *Mata Hari*, he disappeared after hailing a cab and foul play was suspected. Thirty-six hours later, he turned up in a diner, disheveled and confused and seemingly with amnesia. The diner manager recognized him and called the police, and Francis was taken to the hospital; he recovered and later returned to complete his scenes for the film (with his wife by his side). Three years later, though, he fell ill and died after emergency surgery.

The Return of Peter Grimm was Janet Gaynor's breakthrough film. F.W. Murnau watched her during its filming and cast her as the heroine in his masterpiece, *Sunrise*, while Frank Borzage was so impressed with her performance that he made her the star of *Seventh Heaven*. (According to one report it was *Return*'s "wedding scene" that impressed Borzage, but there's no wedding in the film. Possibly the reference is to the bit where Gaynor stands around in her undergarments, looking particularly forlorn and pathetic, while the maid gets her wedding dress ready.) In 1929, Gaynor became the first woman recipient of the Oscar for her work for Murnau and Borzage, and she went on to a successful film career in the 1930s.

John St. Polis played Frederick in the original stage production of *The Return of Peter Grimm* (as John Sainpolis), but here he has the much more sympathetic role of Dr. MacPherson. St Polis turns up in a number of times in these pages (under either version of his patronymic) and his particulars can be found in the entry on *The Untameable*.

Lionel Belmore — a familiar face to horror fans from *Frankenstein* and *Son of Frankentein*— has little more to do than look pompous and long-suffering as the Rev. Bartholomey ("a heavenly body in a constant state of eclipse, the eclipse being his wife" a title card tells us). Still, he does it very well with Elizabeth Patterson providing some mild comic relief as his obnoxious helpmate.

The Return of Peter Grimm was brought to the screen again in 1935 with Lionel Barrymore, just beginning his new career of playing ornery-but-softhearted oldsters. Not only was the play was a bit dated at this point, but the film's direction and script were also lackluster; the RKO Radio Picture didn't even take advantage of the addition of sound by giving Barrymore Grimm's more memorable lines. Three years later, Barrymore did a *Lux Theater* radio production of the play, supported by Edward Arnold and Maureen O'Sullivan.

— *HN*

The Reward of the Faithless

The Reward of the Faithless. Bluebird Photoplays, Inc. [Universal]/ Bluebird Photoplays, Inc. [Universal], 12 February 1917, 5 reels, first reel exists at the British Film Institute

CAST: Claire Du Brey (*Princess Dione*); Richard Le Reno (*Prince Paul Ragusin*); Nicholas Dunaew (*Feodor Strogoff*); Wedgewood Nowell (*Guido Campanelli*); William J. Dyer (*Peter Vlasoff*); Betty Schade (*Katerina Vlasoff*); Yvette Mitchell (*Anna Vlasoff*); Jim Brown (*Karl*); Bill Rathbone (*Cripple*); John George (*Court Jester*)

CREDITS: *Director* Rex Ingram; *Scenario* Rex Ingram; based on a story by E. Magnus Ingleton; *Cinematographer* Ralph Perry

Though Rex Ingram is considered to be one of the master pictorialists of the silent screen, surprisingly little has been written about him. In 1975, DeWitt Bodeen penned a fine article on Ingram and his actress wife Ellen Terry for *Films in Review* and, in 1980, Irish film historian Liam O'Leary did the first and only biography of the great director, *Rex Ingram, Master of the Silent Cinema*. Though exhaustively researched, the book attracted little attention. Of those who did read it, not all were pleased. Michael Powell, who had worked as an assistant for Ingram in the 1920s, recalls Kenneth Anger's reaction to the book: "Thank God for it anyway! It's incredible how one of the greatest directors of the silent screen has been ignored and forgotten! But this book, it's only a sort of record, for God's sake! Nothing about the dwarfs and hunchbacks!" (*A Life in the Movies*, p. 141).

Indeed, O'Leary does take a just-the-facts approach to

Ingram's career and doesn't really capture the color and eccentricity of the man himself. Still, O'Leary had never met Ingram and obviously felt that the man's private obsessions and sometimes disagreeable, autocratic ways, were less noteworthy than were his contributions to cinema (especially as he was a fellow Irishman). And, Kenneth Anger notwithstanding, Ingram's penchant for including dwarfs and hunchbacks in his movies is indeed mentioned, though not dwelt upon.

O'Leary also made another important contribution to preserving Ingram's memory: while rummaging through a Dublin junk shop, he found the first reel of Ingram's 1917 *The Reward of the Faithless*. Not only is this ten minutes or so of footage all that remains of the film, it's all that survives of the twelve movies Ingram directed in the 1910s. O'Leary donated the nitrate footage to the British Film Institute.

Ingram himself had written the stories for his three earlier Universal/Bluebird films, but for *Reward* he left the task to E. (Eugenie) Magnus Ingleton. Ingleton was an actress in Britain who toured the U.K. and South Africa (where, she claims, she also doubled as a secret agent during the Boer War). She came to America in 1911 in the play, *Bunty Pulls the Strings*; afterwards, she went to work at World Film as a reference librarian and then a scenarist. Ingleton, who also directed a couple of films, will turn up here again and again as she wrote the scripts for *The Dark Mirror* (1920), *Trilby* (1915) and *The Moonstone* (1915). She also worked on the scenario for *Life's Whirl*, a 1916 version of *McTeague*; at five reels, *Whirl* was considerably shorter than *Greed*, Erich von Stroheim's version of the book. For *Reward*, Ingleton drew inspiration not from Frank Norris or Wilkie Collins, but from Marie Corelli's *Vendetta* (see *Black Orchids*).

The following synopsis of *The Reward of the Faithless* is drawn from *The AFI Catalog* and contemporary reviews:

> Prince Paul Ragusin wants his daughter Dione to marry the poet Feodor Strogoff, but an adventurer named Guido Campanelli has won the Prince's trust and charmed Dione. Campanelli has also seduced and abandoned a poor girl named Katerina, daughter of the brutal Peter Vlasoff. Princess Dione befriends Katerina in her time of trouble and sends her to a convent. Prince Ragusin dies and Dione marries Campanelli. Katerina joins the household as a servant and becomes Campanelli's lover. The two plot against Dione. She discovers their treachery, but falls victim to their scheme: they with-hold the medicine she needs for her survival. Dione lapses into a coma and is pronounced dead. However, when Feodor kneels by her side in the family crypt, she returns to consciousness. The couple leaves Russia for France where Dione, under an assumed name, becomes the belle of Paris. Campanelli fails to recognize his first wife and is captivated by this strange woman. Dione refuses to submit to Campanelli unless he brings her the emerald ring of his first wife, the ring she was buried with. Guido returns to Russia to get it, unaware that Dione and Feodor are following him. Guido finds the vault empty. He is then accosted by the ghostly figure of Dione, clad in her shroud. Terror stricken, he backs toward the sea cliffs and falls over a precipice to his death. Their revenge extracted, Dione and Feodor are reunited.

We have seen the BFI footage and offer the following description.

There are no opening credits and the footage is a bit disjointed. We are introduced to the Prince and Dione and the conniving Campanelli. Campanelli may have fooled the Prince as to his true character, but an old family servant looks disap-

provingly at the oily conman, especially as the latter rudely drops his cigarette ashes on the castle floor. We switch to a setting of a very different sort, the squalid hovel of Peter Vlasoff and his wretched, cowed family. Vlasoff is played by western heavy William Dyer who here bears a striking resemblance to Gibson Gowland in *Greed*. A policeman warns Vlasoff that the neighbors have been complaining about his drunken rages, and if there's more trouble, he and "his spawn" will be put out into the street. The constable pauses long enough to give a leering once-over to Vlasoff's young daughter, Katerina.

Back at the castle, Campanelli admires the Prince's emerald ring. The Prince tells him the tragic history of the ring: *The Prince's ancestor had coveted the ring which had originally belonged to another ruler. The Prince of old had sent his hunchbacked jester* (John George) *to the nobleman's court. In flashback, we see the jester try to remove the ring from the sleeping ruler's finger, but the man awakens and the jester kills him* (the scene is a little truncated). Because of this ancient sin, the Prince's family is destined to find happiness only after great sorrow.

We see Katerina trying to sell trinkets outside a tavern. Another young girl is hawking flowers and bravely enters the inn, which is full of drunken lowlifes. She tries to disarm them by dancing a little jig, but they mock her and a dwarf climbs on a barrel and does his own dance. She *does* win the sympathy of Feodor who, in addition to being a poet, is a man of action, and he forces the hostile inebriates to buy the girl's flowers and then sends her on her way.

Katerina returns home having failed to sell anything. Vlasoff berates her and then gives her body a very unfatherly appraisal. He rips her shawl away and sends her back out, and there is no doubt of what he expects her to do to fill the family coffers. The distraught girl is comforted by a hunchbacked cripple, who's also a member of the Vlasoff clan.

At the castle, the Prince tells Dione and Feodor how happy he is that they are to be wed. We see Campanelli going out. (Presumably at this point he meets Katerina, an encounter one critic describes as "an assault rather than a seduction.")

Only ten minutes of film and Ingram has convincingly depicted places high and low, introduced a curse, given us a father who pimps his own daughter, and has managed to work two hunchbacks and a dwarf into the mix! The performances are all quite restrained, with the handsome, brooding Nicholas Dunaew (as Feodor) registering a particularly strong screen presence. The mood is sordid and grim rather than macabre, but title card artwork depicting a winged demon pouncing on a victim foreshadows the later Grand Guignol twists.

Not long after laboring at the Big U as a little-known contract director, Ingram became one of the most famous and celebrated directors in Hollywood. In an interview conducted by Hallett Abend and printed in the 8 April 1923 issue of the *Lincoln State Journal*, Ingram made a few comments that no doubt refer to his time at Universal and, perhaps, *The Reward of the Faithless*:

> A few years ago, when I was working for some producers whom I shall not name, I made a scene in a low sort of dance hall dive. I picked my types with care — some cripples, some with faces which denoted crippled souls. The producers objected to the scene. They called it "morbid," told me I had been reading too much Russian

literature. Well, then I made *The Four Horsemen* with the South American dance hall scene. My former producers saw this. Money was rolling in. They were loud in their praises. I told them to look on their shelves and that they'd find the same action and in many cases the same people, in the scene which they rejected as "morbid."

Still, some critics *were* appalled by the unpleasant characters. George Shorey, in the 17 February 1917 issue of *Motion Picture News*, wrote:

> Depressing atmosphere, with the assembling of the most horrible types of the gutter in one single family of which the unfortunate girl is a member, opens this peculiar story in which all of the characters are faithless to one another and useless to themselves. Satisfactory portrayal of these strange and inhuman roles is impossible. None of the characters, except the faithful Feodor and the much wronged Princess, who takes her vengeance in murder, can be expected to attract deep sympathy from the audience.

Ben Grimm, in the 10 February 1917 *Motion Picture World,* was a bit more positive, but still described the film as a "heavy dramatic offering whose somber plot depresses while its very dolefulness fascinates and holds the interest captive."

The 2 February 1917 *Harrison Reports* review was a little lighter: "It's a story of intrigue and death, carrying home the old punch line of 'The Wages of Sin Is Death,' b'gosh." The reviewer goes on to note that "there are moments in the picturization that border on the sensational and there is one scene in particular, showing the seduction of the 'vamp' as a young girl that is cleverly told without the aid of a title. Just how the scene will get by the censors remains to be seen but is done ingeniously and drives home the desired suggestions very strongly."

The critic for the *Manitoba Free Press* (10 May) lifted much of the *Harrison Reports* write-up for his review, but added he was very impressed by the death of the villain: "And it's thrillin' when the adventurer, 'scared green,' jumps over the side of a very high cliff and rolls down and down and down." None of the reviews we found mentioned what "reward" Katerina received for her faithlessness. Perhaps she was let off with no more than a good scare because of her earlier woes. Or maybe there was another airtight chamber left over from *Black Orchids*.

There was criticism of the implausibility of Dione's "death": "We see the wife in her shroud and believe her to be dead. But she isn't. She comes out of her comatose trance when her first lover mourns at her side" (*MPW*). Other reviewers just took the Sleeping Beauty twist at face value.

Ingram's direction was praised, both by *MPW*—"The picture has received careful and artistic production by Rex Ingram; some of the lightings being especially effective"—and by *Harrison's*—"The detail in the early part of the picture is remarkable and the exterior scenes are particularly good."

Occasionally, local press coverage was as offbeat as the film itself. On 10 February, the *Sandusky* [Ohio] *State Journal* ran an ad for *Reward* in which it mistakenly called it "the sequel of *Black Orchids,*" possibly because it went into release barely a month after *Orchids* and both have similar love-triangle/grisly-revenge story lines. Another ad (in the 10 February *Mansfield* [Pennsylvania] *News*) was written by someone who apparently hadn't seen the film: "She Bartered Her Soul That Others Might Live — This Startling Theme is Vividly Set Forth in *The Reward of the Faithless.*" Any viewer expecting such a theme must have indeed been startled by what he saw on the screen. Publicity for the film called it "the kind of a picture that recalls the early 19th-century novels with a flavor of Shakespeare's tragedy, a dash of Poe, and a hint of Lytton." (Everyone, that is, except Marie Corelli).

Though never a big star, Betty Schade (Katerina) was a regular at Universal and received prominent billing in the ads for *Reward*. Back on the 8 January, the *Fort Wayne* [Indiana] *Sentinel* had run an article — supposedly written by the novice actress, herself — that purported to tell how she got into the movies:

> I really didn't break in. I just drifted into the movies. As a school girl in Chicago, I visited the Essanay studio and, just as some other girls, had done, attracted the eye of a director. One day he suggested I take part in a picture…. I supposed it was only a pleasantry on the part of the director and scarcely imagined that I could obtain a permanent place with the company. But I did and have been in pictures ever since.

Just a few months later and, via the publicity for *Reward* (as reported in the 2 June *Reno Evening Gazette*), we get a somewhat different version:

> Miss Schade's picture shows she is a beauty with some eyes. And she knows how to use those eyes too. Betty was born in Berlin so she is German — but wait a minute — she was only two years old when she came to this country in 1896 and she can't speak German or any language except English and, having been educated in Chicago, not too much of that. Her only stage engagement in which she was a success was *A Modern Eve* but after that she went into the movies and she has been there ever since.

Actually, Schade's early film work was for Mack Sennett at Keystone where she worked with her husband, comic actor Fritz Schade. Fritz, sometimes billed as the Human Cork ("So fat, he floats!") remained with Sennett when Betty defected to Universal. There she met handsome leading man, Ernest Shields, and promptly tossed the Human Cork out to sea. She married Shields in 1917, and — America having entered World War I — the publicity people made much of the fact that Schade was one of the first Hollywood "war brides," having encouraged Shields to enlist. She also renounced her German citizenship.

One of Schade's last films for Universal was Jack (John) Ford's *Bare Fists* (1919), with Harry Carey. She freelanced a bit subsequently, mostly in supporting roles. She played Helen Keller's mother as a young woman in *Deliverance* (with Helen Keller playing herself) and in the troubled, much censored, *Night Rose,* she was gangster Lon Chaney's cast-off girlfriend. After that, Betty pretty much disappears from the record.

Playing the passionate poet Feodor couldn't have been too much of a stretch for Nicholas Dunaew (sometimes spelled "Dunaev"), a man *The Washington Post* described as "one of the leading poets of the Russian social revolution" (3 September 1911). A friend of Gorky and Tolstoy, the poet and playwright was very anti-royalist (the *Post* article notes that he brought a miniature monkey to America with him and named the little guy Nicholas II). In the 1910 he worked at Vitagraph both as an adviser on Russian atmosphere and as an actor. In *Snatched from a Burning Death*, Dunaew played with Rex Ingram (then acting under his real name of Hitchcock), who no doubt remembered him when it came time to cast *The Reward of the Faithless.*

Dunaew did some acting, stage work and writing in the 1920s, but fame eluded him. He achieved notoriety of a different sort when, in 1929, theater and vaudeville magnate, Alexander Pantages, was accused of rape by a 17-year-old dancer named Eunice Pringle. Dunaew was Pringle's manager and (perhaps) lover. Pantages suffered through a pair of trials; found guilty (and sentenced to up to 50 years) in the first, he was acquitted following the second. Pringle, who had also sued him for a million dollars, settled for a paltry $3000 (which she could not claim until she turned 21). While she then took a brief stab at a stage career (and marriage to a salesman), Dunaew dropped out of the public eye.

The next time his name found its way into print was in his obituary, which — as printed in the 23 February 1963 *Evening Star* — read as if it had been written by one of Universal's publicity flacks. It reports that Dunaew was an associate of Alexander Kerensky during the first Russian Revolution and was sent by the communists to Siberia, whence he escaped by breaking the iron bars of his prison with his bare hands. Actually, Dunaew was in America during that period, and the closest he ever got to Siberia was his writing a screenplay by that title in 1926. The obit goes on about Dunaew's move to Washington, D.C., in the 1930s and his subsequent career as speechwriter for a number of politicians. No mention is made of the Pantages scandal.

Originally Cleo Madison had been cast as Dione, but, according to O'Leary, she quarreled with Ingram and walked off the set. She was replaced by Claire Du Brey, a novice who had only done a few movies at that point. That would change as the actress, who lived to be 100, went on to a long career, playing socialites and vamps in the Silent Era and numerous character roles right up until the late 1950s. In 1928, she met Marie Dressler, then at a low point in her career, and became her friend, secretary, and nurse. Stories circulated that they were more than just pals, rumors Du Brey always denied. The women had a falling out, but — on her deathbed in 1934 — Dressler sent word of her affection for her friend via screenwriter Frances Marion. The actress was not mentioned in Dressler's will, so she sued the estate for $25,000 for nursing and secretarial services; the court granted her $3,000. Du Brey then took a shot at the casting agency business with silent film star Anna Q. Nilsson, but, when that faltered, she went back to acting for good.

O'Leary mentions the legend that Ingram was finally fired by Universal for putting every hunchback and dwarf in Hollywood on the payroll. Ingram was as handsome as any matinee idol, and he was married to the lovely Alice Terry. He was a sculptor and artist who was fascinated by the beautiful contours of the human form, and his films are a feast for the eye. Paradoxically, dwarfs and hunchbacks — those embodiments of physical imperfection in extremis — pop up again and again in his films. There's no real sympathy for these unfortunates in Ingram's movies, though; they are either comic or criminal and sometimes, as in *Mare Nostrum* and *Turn to the Right*, there is really no logical reason for them to be there. They are Ingram's signature in much the same way one expected Alfred Hitchcock to turn up in his own movies. Alice Terry once groused about "Rex's damned dwarfs" when her husband began fussing over

some bit of business with them on the set instead of paying attention to more important details. Even though Ingram prized their presence in his films, however, he had a condescending attitude towards them as people and treated them as a king would his buffoons.

Most likely it was not his obsession with dwarfs that got Ingram booted from Universal in late 1917; rather, he had gone $2,000 over budget with *Black Orchids*, hardly a fortune but still a mortal sin at penny-pinching Universal. Speed and efficiency, not artistry and temperament, were what was admired most at the Big U, and Ingram just didn't fit in. He did some freelance directing and then served briefly in Canada's Flying Corps just before World War I ended. In 1920 he signed at Metro, and it was there he would make his most memorable films.

— HN

The Right to Be Happy

The Right to Be Happy. Bluebird Photoplays/Bluebird Photoplays, Inc., 25 December 1916, 5 reels [LOST]

CAST: Rupert Julian (*Ebenezer Scrooge*); John Cook (*Bob Cratchit*); Claire McDowell (*Mrs. Cratchit*); Francis Lee (*Tiny Tim*); Harry Carter (*Jacob Marley*); Emory Johnson (*Fred, Scrooge's nephew*); Roberta Wilson (*Caroline*); Francelia Billington (*Scrooge's sweetheart*); Mrs. Titus (*Mrs. Fezziwig*); Wadsworth Harris (*The Ghost of the Past*); Dick Le Strange (*The Ghost of the Present*); Tom Figee (*The Ghost of the Future*)

CREDITS: *Director* Rupert Julian; *Scenario* E.J. Clawson: Based on the novel *A Christmas Carol* by Charles Dickens (London, 1843); *Cinematographer* Stephen Rounds

Back in the days of the giants — those earliest days of cinema, before every other film on the schedule was either a sequel to or a remake of the picture that had preceded it — creativity was pretty much taken for granted. The medium was still novel, the excitement was palpable, and the challenges, ubiquitous and welcome. The cinema underscored the notions that the spectrum of human experience was ever-expanding and that the scope of human imagination was almost without limit. As did life, so also did the flickers find their spice in variety: if one's *joie de vivre* were enhanced, for example, by M. Méliès' bizarre and colorful shorts, there were a couple of hundred out and about by the early 1910s, when the Parisian cinemagician was driven into bankruptcy. If, on the other hand, one had little patience *avec le surnaturel*, there were oaters and weepers and knockabout comedies aplenty that brought more realistic takes (sort of) on the myriad experiences faced by lonesome cowpokes, sadder-but-wiser young women, and clowns adorned with trademark hair appliances. There was lots of great new stuff in those earliest of days; of course, "new" referred to the stuff's being transferred onto film, and not to the stories themselves, most of which had been around since Old Testament Days.

Case in point: Charles Dickens had penned *A Christmas Carol* in 1843. Less than 10 years later, the author read the work aloud in Birmingham's Victoria Square; the event won so much positive press and public reaction, the tale was reworked for audiences (as opposed to readers) and thereafter excerpts from it became part of Dickens' popular speaking engagements. *Carol* turned on avarice, ghosts and conversion, and although those three elements had — separately or as a triad — led to many great moments to ponder since the beginning of recorded thought, Dickens' arrangement was more than conventional; it was magical. The novel was soon thereafter transferred to the stage (the stage as in settings and actors; not as in lecterns and lectors) in any number of variations (faithful, bizarre, anywhere in between) and with all degrees of success.

In 1901, that which was almost six decades old became new again, but not in *les mains* of the aforementioned M. Méliès; rather, it was Briton Walter R. Booth who— working at R.W. Paul's Animatograph Works— shot and released *Scrooge; or, Marley's Ghost*. Listed at 620 feet in Denis Gifford's *British Film Catalogue*, the one-reeler was typical fare for Booth (like Méliès, an ex-prestidigitator), whose other cinematic contributions that year included *The Magic Sword*, *The Devil in the Studio*, and *The Haunted Curiosity Shop*. Scrooge next fussed and fumbled in 1908, when Briton Tom Ricketts portrayed the old reprobate in Essanay's two-reeler, *A Christmas Carol*; seven years and the Atlantic Ocean had separated these dips into Dickens' ghostly well. Only two years later, though, the snowball had begun to … errrr … snowball, and J. Searle Dawley (see *The Phantom Honeymoon*) took a whack at it. The Edison Company opined that Dickens' plot was worth maybe one reel's worth of celluloid, and the resultant epic — released bearing the title of the source novel—featured Marc McDermott (an Aussie; were there no Americans available who could mutter about decreasing the surplus population?) as Scrooge and Charles Ogle as Bob Cratchit (!) (Bringing up the rear in this epic were Brooklynites Viola Dana and Shirley Mason: see *Aladdin's Other Lamp* and *The Eleventh Hour*, respectively.)

Having a citizen of their formal penal colony playing lead in Dickens' cash-cow must have led the Brits to some significant upper-lip-stiffening, and Seymour Hicks (who had come off playing the role a couple of thousand times on stage) was tapped to play Scrooge for his cinematic debut. This time 'round a three-reeler (for Zenith Films), *Scrooge* was based on Hicks' screenplay, which was based on Hicks' familiarity with the property. As both this silent version and the identically-titled Twickenham Film sound feature (1935, made after Seymour was knighted) are out there on DVD, the passionate Scroogeophile can compare the young(er) Hicks and the more mature Hicks in the role. (For the obsessed Scroogeophile — and information on still other silent takes on Dickens' classic — we recommend Fred Guida's *A Christmas Carol and Its Adaptations*: McFarland, 2000.)

For the benefit of that singular individual who might have stumbled this far through life without having encountered Scrooge, Marley, the three Christmas Ghosts, or any of the Cratchits, let us repair to the story itself as it unspooled in Bluebird's *The Right to Be Happy* (as reported by *The AFI Catalog*):

On Christmas Eve, chronic curmudgeon Ebenezer Scrooge endures a visit from the ghost of his late business partner, Jacob Marley. Jacob chastizes Ebenezer for his grouchiness, and then hands him over to the ghosts of Christmas Past, Present, and Future. These spirits take him to scenes from his boyhood and early manhood, and then to his dishonored grave. With his entire life passing before him, Ebenezer finally understands that he has led a

life of selfishness and greed, and so he begs for a chance to repent. Then, Ebenezer wakes up and realizes that his experiences with the ghosts had been only a bad dream. He is sobered and changed by the nightmare, however, and devotes the rest of his life to helping those less fortunate than he.

As history would have it, it fell to Rupert Julian — one of Lon Chaney's all-time favorite people — to engineer das Kino's first feature-length adaptation of Dicken's Christmas tale. From the array of extant contemporary accounts we note that, right off the bat, *The Right to Be Happy* suffered in comparison, fidelity-wise, to the source novel and even to the shortest of the earlier versions. Scenarist Elliott Clawson — who would cap his career with not one, but four Oscar nominations in the industry's Second Academy Award ceremonies (for *Sal of Singapore*, *Skyscraper*, and *The Cop* [all 1928] and *The Leatherneck* [1929]) — was still finding his way, and the 23 December 1916 *New York Dramatic Mirror* elaborated on his sins (and those of director Julian and the uncredited production designer):

While *The Right to Be Happy* is a pretty and highly moral little play, it cannot be regarded as a faithful screen interpretation of the immortal *Christmas Carol* by Dickens. The thousand, almost im-

Original program art.

perceptible details which make up what we vaguely call "atmosphere" are conspicuous by their absence and the scenes and characters fail utterly to suggest the quaint classic which has been associated with the Christmas season as inevitably as holly or mistletoe. For one thing, the Christmas scenes in this production are staged under a blazing California sky amid the luxuriant green foliage of Mid-Summer and without the slightest suggestion of anything resembling snow.

The identically-dated *MPW* coverage — unmistakably derived verbatim from Bluebird Photoplay publicity puffs—crowed that the company "has been careful to impart the Dickens atmosphere to the subject" while referring solely to characterization and avoiding assiduously any mention of sets, locales or the absence of the "thousand, almost imperceptible details" bemoaned by the critic over at the *NYDM*. The *Motion Picture News* opinion — published under Steve Talbot's byline in the 30 December 19196 issue — held that Julian's picture, while "pretentious," "sticks faithfully to the theme."

> The only criticism that could be leveled at the production is that the players seem too cold by far. They fairly reveled in mufflers and top-coats, while the California sunshine bathed everything in its rays. Too, the shrubbery in the exteriors showed green and plentiful, while the juvenile players rolled about on grassy knolls as Scrooge shook and shivered his way along the highway.

Interesting description, this last. Does that "only criticism" stem from Talbot's shock that it's apparently cold in England at Christmastime? Or that it can somehow be cold and sunny simultaneously? Our quibble: how can the *MPN* have attested to the film's faithful stickiness when it reported that said scenario contained scenes wherein "the juvenile players rolled about on grassy knolls"?

The back-and-forth between *MPN*'s Talbot ("Theatres with a semi-refined and well-read class of patrons can pack them in if it is made known that this is really *A Christmas Carol*") and the *Dramatic Mirror*'s "A.G.S." ("Exhibitors should not over emphasize the play's relation to Dickens") ultimately leads nowhere save for madness, so... Humbug!

What's really depressing is the fact that, even in the aggregate, the documents we consulted spilled little ink on the story's more supernaturally-oriented sequences. The 23 December 1916 *Exhibitor's Trade Review* offered the following: "As a screen production, it will probably receive even greater applause than it did in the 'legitimate,' and convey a more potent message, because of the camera resources for developing ghostly effects through the agency of dissolving views." (True or false? The "agency of dissolving views" a] was later bought out by William Morris; b] was a secret code for "double exposure.")

Wid's (21 December 1916) cut right to the chase:

> The production isn't strikingly artistic, and most of the photography and lightings lack the little distinctive touches [ed. note: about a thousand or so?] which do so much toward creating an impressive atmosphere.... It is quite possible that there was a bit too much depressing detail in a few of the sequences, particularly in the scenes referring to Tiny Tim's death. Many people do not like to see deathbed scenes and are certainly opposed to graveyard locations.... The handling of the scenes in which the spirits moved about was rather effective, the camera work in all of these bits being very good, although the average film patron has come to accept this sort of thing without considering it any thing unusual.

Thus, even the damned were but faintly praised....

On the upside, John Cook won universal approbation (if not an Amana freezer) for his portrayal of Bob Cratchit. *Wid's* thought he "gave the best characterization in the offering"; *MPN* felt he "shone in the cast"; and even the *NYDM* opined that "by far the best piece of acting was done by John Cook." Mr. Cook did no acting — best or otherwise — in any other pictures that would be of interest to us. On the reverse of the upside was Rupert Julian, the Actor, who was swatted by journalistic brickbats wielded by every scribe save for *ETR*'s, who wrote that RJ was "immensely effective in the role." (The others offered everything from "A disappointment — his makeup and mannerisms were exaggerated" to "Scrooge is enacted by Rupert Julian.") Julian, who haled from New Zealand, acted and directed up a storm (and scripted a healthy rain) during a movie career that spanned a decade and a half, but his name is forever associated with Universal's *The Phantom of the Opera*, and more on the man Lon Chaney loved to hate may be found there.

Just so you know: Dick Le Strange — the actor who played the Ghost of the Present in this lost feature — also (as Dick *La* Strange) played Maximo, the Ghost of the Castle, in 1914's *The Ghost Breaker*. As Richard L'Estrange, our erstwhile ghost managed production details on a slew of interesting projects from the 1935 Lon Chaney Jr. potboiler, *A Scream in the Night*, to Monogram's *Revenge of the Zombies* (1943), to a brace of that studio's Charlie Chan masterpieces (*The Chinese Cat* [1943] and *Black Magic* [1944]), to the 1954 run of *Rocky Jones, Space Ranger* episodes on the small screen. He also occasionally acted as producer and even helmed a couple of films. A perennially busy man, L'Estrange died in Burbank, California, on November 20, 1963, three days before JFK was assassinated.

— *JTS*

The Road to Yesterday

The Road to Yesterday. De Mille Pictures Corp./Producers Distributing Corp., 15 November 1925, 10 reels/9980 feet [available]

CAST: Joseph Schildkraut (*Kenneth Paulton*); Jetta Goudal (*Malena Paulton*); Vera Reynolds (*Elizabeth "Beth" Tyrell*); William Boyd (*Jack Moreland*); Casson Ferguson (*Adrian Tompkyns*); Julia Faye (*Dolly Foules*); Trixie Friganza (*Aunt Harriett Tyrell*); Clarence Burton (*Hugh Armstrong*); Josephine Norman (*Anne Vener*); Charles West (*Watt Earnshaw*); Junior Coghlan (*Boy Scout*); Iron Eyes Cody (*Indian*); Walter Long (*Extra in the crowd during the burning-at-the-stake*); Dick Sutherland (*Torturer*); Chester Morris (*Partygoer*); Sally Rand (*Flapper*)

CREDITS: *Producer and Director* Cecil B. De Mille; *Assistant Director* Frank Urson; based on the eponymous play by Beulah Marie Dix and Evelyn Greenleaf Sutherland (New York opening: 31 December 1906); *Adaptation* Jeanie Macpherson and Beulah Marie Dix; *Cinematographer* Peverell Marley; *Art Direction* Anton Grot, Paul Iribe, Mitchell Leisen; *Film Editor* Ann Bauchens

> "...he decided to have a train wreck."
> — Mordaunt Hall on a scene in Cecil B. De Mille's *The Road to Yesterday, The New York Times*, 6 December 1925

So, was watching De Mille's picture like watching a train wreck? Let's begin with the notes we took while viewing the film:

> The story opens in the vicinity of the Grand Canyon. Kenneth and Melena Paulton are newly married. Kenneth's arm inexplica-

bly hangs paralyzed from his shoulder. Melena discovers an aversion to her new spouse that she can only dimly associate with something from the past; Kenneth attributes her icy behavior to his disfigurement. Later, Kenneth skeptically picks up a bible belonging to Reverend Jack Moreland, under whose tutelage a local boy's camp is run. After Kenneth expresses bitterness over his defective limb, Jack suggests, "If other surgeons have failed you — give Him a trial!" In spite of being a nonbeliever, Kenneth is ready to try anything.

Elsewhere, Mr. "Rady" Tompkyns — who has proposed to Elizabeth Walsingham Tyrell countless times — finally wins her acquiescence on a coin flip. Meanwhile, Jack Moreland instructs a young boy scout how to use a bow and arrow. The youth, misidentifying his target, shoots a feathered hat from the head of Elizabeth. Jack comes to her rescue, their eyes meet, and she says with deadly seriousness, "Haven't I met you before — somewhere?" "No," he responds but, with a twinkle in his eye, states that he hopes they'll meet again. They kiss. Rady sees this, and the engagement is called off.

At Kenneth's homecoming, Jack appears wearing his minister's collar. Elizabeth sees him this way for the first time. Kenneth tells Jack of his recent prayers but — with his pleas to heaven made solely from self-interest — it turns out that the condition has actually worsened. A doctor informs him that only an immediate operation by a San Francisco surgeon can save him. Elizabeth, after telling Jack (who now realizes that he loved her "in some dim yesterday") that she couldn't marry a clergyman, rebounds back to Rady. He now insists on a quick wedding — also in San Francisco.

The scene shifts and an inter-title appears:

> Rushing through the night —
> No train has ever carried five
> destinies so strangely tangled.

As Melena avoids Kenneth on the train, Jack first offers to be Rady's best man and then scuffles with him. Suddenly, the locomotive collides with another, head-on. Melena is trapped. Elizabeth cries out, "Jack, where are you? I'm drifting away — I'm going *back!*"

Appropriately enough, Elizabeth is transported through time and space to Elizabethan England, as are the others. All are now clothed in wardrobe of the times. However, Elizabeth is the only one with a memory of her prior-future life. Kenneth ("Lord Strangevon" in this incarnation) aims to find Elizabeth and marry her for her family's wealth by any means possible. Aiding Elizabeth are Jack and Melena (who claims to be Kenneth's wife via gypsy rites). In the background, lending comic relief, is Rady, the "wastefulest tapster."

Strangevon captures Elizabeth and brings her to his castle. Jack arrives and, after hero and villain cross swords, Strangevon's men capture Jack. Elizabeth agrees to marry Strangevon to save Jack's life. Melena enters; Strangevon, rather than acknowledge her, accuses her of witchcraft. Jack — in spite of Strangevon's promises — is severely whipped and Melena is burned for her "crimes." Strangevon shows signs of remorse at the sight of Melena writhing in the flames, but both of his victims seek revenge. Jack — who is in his death throes — stabs him, and Melena hurls this curse his way:

> Through lives and lives
> Through hells and hells
> Till the will that made has
> Unmade — thou shalt pay —
> and pay — and pay!

Flashing forward to the train wreck, Melena now pleads, Ken — Ken — save me from the Fire! Ken prays for the strength, his arm is cured, and he lifts the wreckage. Jack's occupation is no longer an obstacle to Elizabeth, nor is anything any longer wrong with Ken in Melena's eyes.

While Elizabeth and the company onscreen were experiencing a case of "déjà vu all over again," many of the older audience

members might have also had a similar feeling, for the theme itself had already been incarnated several times in multiple formats.

The Road to Yesterday originated in 1906 from the collaborative pens of playwrights Beulah Marie Dix and Evelyn Greenleaf Sutherland. Although two decades separated the two in age (Dix being the younger), a close friendship developed between them, and it was the Sutherlands who introduced Ms. Dix to her husband, George Flebbe. Not too surprisingly, a professional collaboration that resulted in 17 plays was the springboard for the camaraderie; what's more, Dix and Sutherland regularly attended the theater together and on several occasions even journeyed jointly overseas to view the fruits of their collective labor. The pair's united efforts worked well. Sutherland, for years a drama critic, provided technical expertise, while Dix — who showed interest in writing plays and novels while still a 16-year-old Radcliffe undergraduate — displayed a knack for historical fiction, something that worked to her advantage in *The Road to Yesterday*.

Yesterday opened in late 1906 at New York's Herald Square Theater and moved subsequently to the Lyric. Star Minnie Dupree, a favorite of Sutherland's, also won the approval of Dix, who described the actress's performance as "charming, both in comedy and pathos" in her journal. The production became a high-water mark for the duo ("A whimsically extraordinary play," said Franklin Fyles in *The Washington Post* on 6 January 1907), and its favorable initial reception led to multiple stock performances and revivals over the years. Tragically, the Dix/Sutherland partnership lasted not nearly as long; Ms. Sutherland died from severe burns on Christmas Eve, 1908, after a gas heater had set her dressing gown on fire. Apart from her collaborations with Ms. Sutherland, Beulah Marie Dix was a writer of children's literature, a novelist (*Across the Border*), and frequent scenarist (as with *The Squaw Man* [1918] and *The Affairs of Anatol* [1921]). Within these pages, her name may be found in conjunction with *Borderland*, *For the Defense*, *The Leopard Lady*, and other genre titles.

In the 1910s, *The Road to Yesterday* became ripe for adaptation, and the first filmed adaptation appeared in 1914. Starring future serial stalwart, Walter Miller, the picture was faithful to the source material — or at least as faithful as was any Biograph short of the period. In 1917, one Edgar J. MacGregor signed a contract ceding him the rights to produce *Yesterday* as a musical comedy; however, MacGregor's option expired (in 1920) before the erstwhile producer could either compose a note or elicit a laugh. George M. Cohan, Mr. "Yankee Doodle Dandy" himself, then expressed some interest in the project, but it was the theatrical Shubert family that next obtained legal dibs. Another four years elapsed until the work — now an operetta entitled *The Dream Girl* — finally raised its curtain in New Haven, Connecticut. The prolific Rida Johnson Young provided *The Dream Girl* with her book and lyrics, while the highly regarded Victor Herbert (*The Fall of a Nation*; see entry) penned the score.

To use the story for his 1925 picture, Cecil B. De Mille compensated Dix and the Sutherland estate to the tune of $15,000. Dix — close enough to the De Mille family that her daughter, Evelyn F. Scott, referred to Cecil as "Uncle" — was brought on board to assist Jeanie Macpherson with the script. Macpherson updated the modern framing sequences, and Dix sketched out the historical scenes. (Just what was it about *The Road to Yesterday* that only women seemed to be ready, willing, and able to deal with the material?). Due (probably) to the success of *The Dream Girl* and publicity about De Mille's upcoming feature film, theatrical publishing house, Samuel French, Inc., ordered a new print run of *Yesterday*, as "rewritten and revised" by Beulah Marie Dix *Flebbe*. (Using her married name professionally was not the authoress/playwright's usual practice.)

The Road to Yesterday — the first motion picture to be created at the new De Mille Studios in Culver City — opened at the equally-brand-spanking-new $1,000,000 Figueroa Theater in Los Angeles on 15 November 1925. As the movie made the rounds, the publicity machine trumpeted loudly that this was a *De Mille* picture, with newspaper advertisements like "The Hand of Fate guided by the hand of the great De Mille" (*The Charleston* [West Virginia] *Gazette*, 24 November 1925) and "Cecil B. De Mille's Gorgeous Melodrama" (*The Lincoln* [Nebraska] *Star*, 31 December 1925) typical of the attention played to the producer. Even one of the film's preview trailers included shots of De Mille posturing behind the camera.

Off the printed page and on the set, *Yesterday* was a De Mille production all the way. Discipline and punctuality were the order of the day when De Mille took to the director's chair and the cameras rolled under his complete and total control. As one scribe on the film set described the situation, "If he [De Mille] walks three paces forward, they [his assistants] walk three paces forward. If he retreats, they go back too."

Enter star actress, Jetta Goudal, stage right. Stories of Goudal's temperamental behavior had followed her to Culver City. While shooting a storm scene in Raoul Walsh's *The Spaniard*, for example, her abrupt exit from the studio premises was the result of a perceived slight: a wrap had not been provided to her quickly enough. It seemed inevitable that Goudal and De Mille would not hit it off ... and they didn't. In his autobiography, Cecil B. summed up their relationship: "She was a good actress, but our professional temperaments did not exactly blend."

Sometimes the actress's personal temperament also got in the way. Per Evelyn F. Scott's *Hollywood: When Silents Were Golden*, Goudal's off-camera opinion of her co-star, Joseph Schildkraut — and his of her — mirrored the sentiments found in the screenplay. "They had brought along a genuine and mutual aversion, never quite explained," wrote Scott, although their mutual antipathy most likely dated back to their days in New York. The pettiness between the two reached epic (but comic) proportions; as Scott reported: "What was more, each of these attractive players felt the same side of his (her) fact photographed the best. Since it is awkward to shoot romantic scenes with both of a pair of lovers always looking to the right, problems grew."

Goudal left acting in the early 1930s for a career in interior design and over 50 years of marriage to art director, Harold Grieve.

One might think that Goudal and Schildkraut's unique brand of "method acting" would register auspiciously with the critical crowd, but the fact is that reviews were so-so. Mordaunt Hall in *The New York Times* (1 December 1925) felt that "Jetta Goudal manifests none of the daintiness she has displayed in other pictures," and Epes W. Sarget (writing in the 12 December 1925 *Moving Picture World*) observed that "Miss Goudal is almost too exotic in the modern-dress portion."

Joseph Schildkraut's sire, Rudolf, had attained renown as one of the greatest European stage actors of the late 19th and early 20th centuries. Following in his father's sizable footsteps, the younger Schildkraut gained his own measure of distinction starring opposite Eve Le Galliene in the original 1921 Broadway production of Ferenc Molnár's *Liliom* and, in 1932, both actors would reprise their roles in a revival staged by Miss Le Galliene. 1921 also marked Schildkraut's American film debut: the Viennese-born actor starred as Le Chevalier de Vaudrey in D. W. Griffith's *Orphans of the Storm*. Come 1925, De Mille's much-hyped train wreck scene must have had Schildkraut yearning for the relative calm of that epic storm. As the actor revealed in his autobiography, *My Father and I*:

> It was not a pleasant feeling to sit there and wait for that crash, hoping the engineer would stop in time. He did stop at the pre-arranged spot, but we had not thought of the hot steam escaping from the engine. It scorched my face and hands. In spite of my pain I did not move, according to the script presumably dead, until De Mille whistled the all-clear signal and I could climb out of the car.

In addition to the hot steam [!] and the scorching, Schildkraut and the company still had to wait on You-Know-Whom. Mitchell Leisen, set decorator on *The Road to Yesterday*, shared his own thoughts on the very unpleasant situation with his biographer, David Chierichetti. As printed in *Hollywood Director: The Career of Mitchell Leisen*:

> We had a train wreck in The Road to Yesterday that was terribly difficult to set up. I had all the bits and pieces wired so that when I pushed a button, it would all fall apart. Jetta Goudal was supposed to jump across the wreck and every time we tried to shoot it, she'd chicken out and not do it and we'd have to spend the rest of the day piecing it back together again. This went on — for I don't know how long — until she finally did it.

Schildkraut didn't fare any better critically than did Goudal, even with all his suffering. The reviewer at *Time* magazine (14 December 1925) was rather representative here as he carped: "His [Schildkraut's] personality and appeal, so valuable in the legitimate box office, do not screen particularly impressively."

On the other hand, hardly anyone complained about William Boyd's efforts. "Sisk" in *Variety* (2 December 1925) easily rated his acting at the top of the heap: "It is William Boyd, apparently a newcomer, who takes the cake and icing away from everyone else," while *The Christian Science Monitor* (17 November 1925) described his work as "quite excellent." After *The Road to Yesterday*, assignments and accolades aplenty flowed in Boyd's direction ... for a time. Aficionados of vintage Westerns are well aware of what happened next: When a Broadway actor of the same name was arrested at a drinking and gambling party, it was *The Road to Yesterday*'s Boyd who took the hit when his photograph was printed in the papers alongside the story of the arrest, and retractions followed too late to rescue his plummeting career. It must have been poor consolation that the guilty party was forced to be billed thereafter as William "Stage" Boyd. Happily, William Lawrence Boyd survived the confusion and achieved Western immortality as the only man to ever play the role of cowboy hero, Hopalong Cassidy.

At times *The Road to Yesterday* brandishes some fair doses of whimsical humor. Casson Ferguson and Vera Reynolds—the first principal cast members hired—provide their share in one early scene wherein the two "sweethearts" take turns switching empty drinks when the other looks away; it's hardly classic comedy, but the actors' timing is excellent. Adding to the mix is Trixie Friganza, whose stout Aunt Harriet is funny just by riding down the canyon on a burro. Even Boyd gets his chance to shine in the comic spotlight: when confronted by a gang of Strangevon's henchmen, he quips with Reynolds in an exchange taken directly from the play:

> Elizabeth: "If you were a man you'd save me!"
> Jack: "If I were *four* men—I might!"

Much of the film is unintentionally camp or "unconsciously amusing" in the 1920s' parlance of *The Times* (of London, that is, on 13 June 1926). Bursting into Goudal/Melena's room to "cure" his new bride of her frigidity, Schildkraut's Ken Paulton acts as deadly seriously as would Clark Gable in *Gone with the Wind*, but the whole thing comes across as a hoot, as one can only imagine the lovers' lack of privacy, what with the boudoir door now possessing a gaping, open gash.

Production values are generally palatable. Strangevon's castle on the hill proved worthy of reuse by De Mille on several occasions, and there is some well-choreographed swordplay. But the effects boys could never quite make Goudal/Melena look like she was actually *burning*, and most shots of the Grand Canyon are as static as an antique postcard. The vaunted train crash provided the promised spectacle, but hardly equaled the subtle lighting and creative camera angles crafted by Robert Weine for a like scene in his *The Hands of Orlac* the previous year.

In his program notes on the picture when it was screened for The Theodore Huff Memorial Film Society on the 18 December 1956, legendary film historian William K. Everson speculated that payola caused overly positive trade reviews. Indeed, *The Moving Picture World, Variety, Motion Picture News* and *Motion Picture Today* all fell in line with good things to say. For all of that, *The Road to Yesterday* made only a modest profit: the film cost $477,479.29 to make and by 1930 had made $522,663.77. It was certainly an inauspicious debut for De Mille's new production company.

Less than favorable reception came from January 1926's *Photoplay*: "Beautiful photography forms the background for a muddled story." In fact, virtually all of the mainstream periodicals seemed short on compliments:

Vera Reynolds and William Boyd in *The Road to Yesterday*. Playing with the space/time continuum demands physical stamina, psychological tenacity, and a decent clothing allowance.

The subtle charm of the original play has been trodden to earth and there arises a chaos of ideas that breaks upon the mind like the staccato sound of a structural ironworker's pneumatic hammer [Mordaunt Hall, *The New York Times*, 6 December 1925].

Somehow or other it does not seem to matter much what the various characters might have been to each other at some remote period, or in what way they settle their various differences of today. They never seem quite real at any time…. In softness of mood or subtlety of narration it leaves much to be desired…. He [Mr. de Mille] clings to gimcracks of a thoroughly outmoded sort, and it does his pictures more harm than he knows ["R. F.," *The Christian Science Monitor*, 17 November 1925].

Cecil De Mille, the prophet of midnight bathing parties and purple society dramas, has suddenly turned serious and to ill-effect [*Time*, 14 December 1925].

Nothing to recommend this picture except Mr. Peverell Marley's admirable photography, which deserves better employment…. One might dismiss with a laugh if it did not include an admixture of religiosity which we found it hard to endure [*The* (London) *Times*, 13 June 1926].

Finally, this prize commentary from L. J. Vandenbergh in the *Los Angeles Times* (22 November 1925):

Unless De Mille prepares a more definite program of reincarnation pictures, the best advice would be to reverse Shakespeare's encouraging lines and make them read:
> "Lay off, lay off, MacDuff
> For you confuse your stuff."

No discussion of *The Road to Yesterday* would be complete without a few what-ever-happened-to words on the rest of the cast and crew.

Chester Morris, small potatoes in *Yesterday*, subsequently thrilled "B" movie fans as the big enchilada in numerous

"Boston Blackie" films of the 1940s and briefly did likewise on the radio. Prior to Blackie, Morris also starred in *The Bat Whispers*, Roland West's sound remake of his 1926 comedy/horror/thriller, *The Bat* (see entry).

Jeanie Macpherson, already an iconic scriptwriter, was one of only three women who helped found the Academy of Motion Picture Arts and Sciences in May 1927.

Iron Eyes Cody — he of Italian blood — leveraged his stint in *Yesterday* into years of employment as a Native American in Westerns. Baby boomers might recollect his 1971 Public Service Announcements on behalf of the environment, wherein he shed a tear at the sight of a littered landscape.

Sally Rand (one of the partying flappers at Kenneth's shindig) might have remained Harriet Helen Gould Beck if De Mille hadn't renamed her. Despite being named one of the WAMPAS Baby Stars in 1927, Sally did not enjoy a lengthy or terribly distinguished film career, but — come the talkie era — she revealed a talent for "fan dancing" that led to her being one of burlesque's most popular headliners.

At a mere nine years of age while in *Yesterday*, Frank "Junior" Coghlan learned archery and got to ride a burro (all at the Grand Canyon, no less, courtesy of Cecil B.). As a young adult, he won lasting fame for shouting *Shazam!* as Billy Batson in one of the most beloved serials of all time, *The Adventures of Captain Marvel* (1941).

The Road to Yesterday reappeared — in an abbreviated form — as a segment in the early 1960s TV series, *Silents Please*. Following the screening, narrator Paul Killiam made these concluding remarks, and no one could have said it better: "Cecil B. De Mille was accused of mixing sex, sadism and religion in overabundant proportions. Some critics called it vulgarity, others showmanship. But it paid off for the colorful producer until his death ended his career."

— *SJ*

The Romantic Journey

The Romantic Journey. Astra Film Corp./Pathé Exhange; Gold Rooster Plays, 24 December 1916, 5 reels [LOST]
CAST: William Courtenay (*Peter*); Alice Dovey (*Cynthia*); Macey Harlam (*Ratoor*); Norman Thorpe (*Broadhurst*).
CREDITS: *Director* George Fitzmaurice; *Scenarist:* Ouida Bergère; *Cinematographer* Harold Louis Miller

In spite of a title more appropriate for a Harlequin novel, this 1916 thriller is still another tale of a sinister hypnotist and his lovely victim. Hollywood may have skipped over Svengali's Jewish origins, but the Orient seldom got a break and, once again, the man with the evil eye wears a turban. In the 1910s, interest in Eastern thought and religion abounded in LaLaLand, and, faddish or not, one would think this would result in *some* celluloid sympathy for its practitioners. Nope; an unnamed reviewer, quoted in *The AFI Catalog*'s entry on the film, cut to the chase: "A story dealing with the pitting of wills of an American against the cunning of a foreigner, especially of a Hindoo, has a natural appeal to the patriotism of an audience.... Keep well before your patrons that it is American wits against Oriental

cunning." Of course, the following year it would be American wits against *Teutonic* cunning in the movies.

Our synopsis comes from the Library of Congress's awkward copyright entry:

> Peter, a social lion, suffering from ennui and wanting trills [*sic*], visits a mysterious antique shop conducted by Ratoor, an East Indian who has, through hypnotism, enslaved Cynthia, a beautiful young girl. Peter notices there is something wrong in the shopkeeper's conduct and decides to investigate. Broadhurst, a millionaire, is in love with Cynthia through whom Ratour [*sic*] plots to get his millions
>
> Under cover of night, [Peter] visits the shop and, discovering Cynthia imprisoned, tries unsuccessfully to liberate her. Ratoor, dominating Cynthia, compels her to accept Broadhurst's proposal, and a wedding day is set. After the ceremony, she warns him against Ratoor and begs him to leave for his own safety. Broadhurst refuses and takes her to an obscure country house to get away from the scoundrels. Peter, keeping Ratoor, who has discovered their abode, under surveillance, arrives too late and he himself narrowly escapes being thrown into the river by Ratoor's henchmen. Cynthia, failing to outwit her former master, is again in his clutches.
>
> Ratoor, suspecting that Peter is spying on him, decides to make an end to Cynthia, who has transferred her husband's property to him. He bids his Oriental followers to bury her alive. In the sepulcher the scoundrels, frightened in their ghastly task by uncanny sounds, flee in terror. Peter, who has followed, rescues Cynthia. The gang are overpowered by detectives and Ratoor, imprisoned, his evil influence over Cynthia is broken and Peter wins the hoped for place in her heart.

Presumably Peter is the source of the "uncanny sounds" that so terrify Ratoor's henchmen into fleeing the supernatural as if they were Hindu cousins to Stepin Fetchit. Peter seems rather laconic for a hero, waiting as he does for the eleventh hour with a watch that's running slow (per the AFI synopsis, "When Ratoor makes plans to bury Cynthia alive, Peter decides that it is time to step in"), and one wonders why he didn't call detectives in earlier. It's certainly to the benefit of Cynthia's oxygen intake that good evil underlings are so hard to find.

Ratoor's hypnotic power over Cynthia apparently doesn't work well from a distance or without the occasional brownout, as she is able to shake it off from time to time. Perhaps that's one reason why Ratoor survives the last reel instead the plot's insisting that his death break the spell, the usual outcome of such situations.

Peter Milne (*Motion Picture News*, 23 December 1916) helped no one with his confusing description of Peter's first attempt to rescue Cynthia: "So he [Peter] climbs up a balcony, fells one of the Hindu's subordinates in a fight, shuffles along window ledges, encounters a black cat by the side of a coffin, enters a tomb and opens the coffin and finds the girl isn't there! The girl wasn't dead after all and the hero has her for his own after the whole mystery has cleared satisfactorily."

More focused was Milne's enthusiasm for George Fitzmaurice's "masterly" and "perfect" direction:

> The touches of the gently grewsome [*sic*], the admirable contrasts between the drama and the comedy and the realistic manner in which he has pictured the Hindu characters all lay stress on his mastery of his art.... And what is most important of all he has managed to keep the suspense sustained at all times. The tension never drops; not even when the story flashes back from one phase to another.

Wid Gunning (21 December 1916) also found Fitzmaurice's touch "classy and interesting," although he thought the director let things run wild at times, calling the film pretty much "serial stuff" and "bordering on the wildest of 'meller.'" Still, the reviewer felt the picture was first-rate overall and would have great appeal for the right kind of audience:

> If your audiences like bing-bing mystery dramas they should eat this up, because there's plenty of mystery, oodles of action…. If your audiences are critical and inclined to favor human stories of characterization, they may think this is rather funny, because of the speed of the action and some of the impossible situations. But even then, they may accept it as interesting entertainment.

As per his usual modus operandi, Wid found one unrealistic minor point to complain about:

> There was one very convenient interior set in this, it being an arrangement of windows in apartments where Mr. Courtenay [Peter] could stand in his home and look directly into the home of the mysterious one, seeing everything that transpired in this "room of terror." I don't know what city this particular apartment was supposed to be in, but, believe me, they don't dare make apartments like that in New York.

Wid also advised exhibitors to play up the leads, William Courtenay and Alice Dovey (and not the story), and Pathé's publicity department certainly heeded his advice: most press releases and ads emphasized the considerable fame both performers had achieved on the stage and what a charming screen couple they made. (Typical: "The tall, straight, slender Mr. Courtenay and the little, tiny Miss Dovey make a wonderful combination.") When the story *was* mentioned, the flacks often mistakenly claimed it was set in India or the Orient!

William Courtenay graduated from Holy Cross College and went directly to the stage, joining a barnstorming troupe in *Ten Nights in a Barroom*. In New York, he appeared in scores of prestigious Broadway productions, among them the 1905 revival of *Trilby* wherein he played Little Billee and fell in love with leading lady, Virginia Harned, who had created the title role in the original production. The two were subsequently married.

Miss Jerry, Courtenay's first film, wasn't exactly a film at all. In 1894, Alexander Black — literary editor of *The Brooklyn Times* and an expert photographer — did a series of stills illustrating a story and then projected them onto a screen, timed to switch so rapidly there was an illusion of movement as the story unfolded. A narrator explained what was going on and the entire showing lasted two hours! Courtenay, who didn't step in front of a camera again until he made *Sealed Lips* in 1915, acted only occasionally in the movies until 1919 and then focused exclusively on the stage (where he also did some directing); he did not make another film until — perhaps not coincidentally — sound came in.

One of Courtenay's notable stage successes was *The Spider*, a mystery in which he played a flamboyant stage magician and mentalist. John Halliday had originated the role on Broadway, but twice fell ill and both times Courtenay replaced him. Courtenay also did the national tour, including a stint in Los Angeles in 1928. Playing Tinsel Town at the same time was another mystery play, *Dracula*, starring Bela Lugosi. It may well have been his performance in *The Spider* that led Universal to consider Courtenay for the title role in the film version of *Dracula*, but

we all know what happened there. Courtenay's role as a suspicious official in the spy drama, *Three Faces East* (1930; perhaps the only one of the actor's films to survive), gives little idea how he might have played the immortal Count had things turned out differently. *The Spider* went before the cameras in 1931, with Edmund Lowe playing the magician, while *Three Faces East* was remade as the Boris Karloff B-film, *British Intelligence* (1940).

Like Courtenay, Alice Dovey's movies were few but her Broadway hits many. Born on a chicken farm in Plattsburg, Nebraska (not, as per the IMDb, in London), the teenage Dovey renounced egg-gathering and headed for New York, where she played in a number of crowd-pleasers (like *Old Dutch*, *Queen of the Movies*, *Stubborn Cinderella*, and *The Pink Lady*) that long ago disappeared into the mist. In 1916 she married comic/playwright Jack Hazzard whose play, *Turn to the Right*, was a long-lasting success. The couple may have had an inkling that their marriage would prove lengthy and successful, for Dovey — despite having scored big with *Very Good Eddie* that very same year — subsequently retired from show biz.

Macey Harlam (Ratoor) had spent years playing heavies — particularly Orientals and "foreigners" — onstage and on the screen, but one happy exception was his portrayal of the benign Yogi in the Chicago production of *Eyes of Youth*. Harlam can be found again in these pages in our essay on *The Witch* (1916), in which he experienced a second happy exception.

The Romantic Journey was one of numerous collaborations between director George Fitzmaurice (see entry, *Quest of the Sacred Jewel*) and scenarist Ouida Bergère. Bergère, who had a brief career as an actress, met Fitzmaurice when they were both writing scenarios at Pathé. Fitzmaurice switched to directing and both their fortunes began to rise as they worked together on a series of popular films with Mollie King. Fitzmaurice and Bergère married in 1917. Bergère became one of the most highly paid scenarists in the business (she later recalled when she got just $25 a script instead of the $10,000 that became her asking price) and Fitzmaurice, a major producer/director. Bergère described their joint efforts together and her own way of writing for an article printed in *The Cumberland* [Maryland] *Evening News* (22 July 1922):

> The nub of my idea comes from simple things which contain the essence of the most thrilling developments and complications. For days I mull it over, writing down not a single note. When pretty well formulated I tell it intact before many people from different walks in life and watch their emotional reaction. Not until then do I talk it over with my husband. We discuss every detail of acting, character, costume, action, fight over the ideas involved, stripping, adding, collaborating.

Bergère insisted that fighting with Fitzmaurice and thrashing out their differences over the story was the secret to their success and that only after the tussle would she settle down and dictate the script to her secretary, adding the titles later on. Perhaps this creative combat became a bit too intense in 1924, for Bergère found herself replaced by Frances Marion for her husband's troubled production of *Cytherea*.

The year 1924 proved to be a very fateful one for Bergère. She and Fitzmaurice separated and, while she insisted there was no third party involved, she soon found herself denying rumors that she had become engaged to actor Basil Rathbone; Bergère also declared bankruptcy. Two years later she did, in fact, marry Rathbone and soon became renowned for throwing lavish parties for the rich and famous (which threatened to bankrupt *Rathbone*). Every so often there was a story published somewhere about her intention to return to writing. In 1938, for example, it was reported that she had spent months researching the life of Franz Liszt and had had Warner Brothers interested in the project when it was announced that MGM had plans to do a Liszt bio with Greta Garbo (*not* playing Liszt) and conductor Leopold Stokowski. Bergère insisted that she had come up with the idea and even shown her script to Stokowski. Nothing came of either project and Bergère spent the rest of her life playing the happy hostess (when Basil's money allowed).

Bergère and Fitzmaurice can be found together again in our entry on *Forever*.

— HN

The Sacred Ruby see The House of Mystery

Saint, Devil and Woman

Saint, Devil and Woman. Thanhouser Film Corp./Pathé Exchange (Gold Rooster Plays), 25 September 1916, 5 reels [LOST]

CAST: Florence LaBadie (*Florence Stanton*); Wayne Arey (*Dr. Gregory Deane*); Hector Dion (*Alvarez*); Claus Bogel (*James Carter*); Ethyle Cooke (*Grace Carter*); Ernest Howard (*William Stanton*).

CREDITS: *Director* Frederick Sullivan; *Scenario* Philip Lonergan

NOTE: In some contemporary publications, Hector Dion's character is referred to as "Alvarez"; in others, as "Miguel Cordova."

This is still another potboiler that deals with the twin obsessions of silent horror — melodrama: hypnotism and split personalities. The movie begins with a statement that it is "founded on psychological facts," presumably referring to the celebrated case of Christine Beauchamp, a victim of multiple personality, whose travails were documented by Dr. Morton Prince in 1905. In 1915, a revival of interest in her story was brought about in part an essay in *Old Pen*, the weekly review of the University of Pennsylvania. Subsequent newspaper articles about the case referred to Miss Beauchamp as being "divided into saint, devil and woman," a description that did not go unnoticed by Thanhouser's prolific scenarist, Phillip Lonergan, when it came time to concoct a new starring vehicle for Florence LaBadie in 1916. Publicity for *Saint, Devil and Woman* praised Lonergan as "an originator of unique plots" while simultaneously (and somewhat curiously) reminding the reader of *The Case of Becky*, *Trilby*, and *Dr. Jekyll and Mr. Hyde*. Oddly (or maybe *not* so oddly), the publicity pieces failed to mention Gelette Burgess' 1907 novel *The White Cat* (see entries on *The Two-Soul Woman* and *The Untameable*), which seems to have had more than a little influence on Lonergan's scenario.

Our synopsis is compiled from *The* [New York] *Morning Telegraph* (10 September 1916) and other contemporary reviews:

Florence Stanton, a young girl whose world has been limited to the confines of a convent, suddenly finds herself amazingly rich through the death of her wealthy uncle. Because of her innocence, she is a gullible fool in the hands of the rascally executor of the estate, a Spaniard named Alvarez. Through an article in the newspaper, she finds that she is being condemned by society because of the terrible conditions which prevail in the tenements she owns

and because of Alvarez's despicable method of securing control of an important railroad. Personally looking into the tenement conditions, she meets Dr. Deane, a settlement worker, and the two become fast friends.

Florence is about to accept her guardian's proposal of marriage when she discovers that he is wanted for murder in Spain. She dismisses him and appeals to the courts for another executor. On the night of a terrible thunderstorm, Alvarez goes to her house to murder her; just then, a bolt of lightning just outside the window affects her mind so that she has no memory of her identity. Quick to see his opportunity, Alvarez ingratiates himself with the girl and, now under his evil influence, Florence becomes a depraved creature whose greatest pleasures are violence and cruelty. At this time the employees of the railroad owned by the estate demand an increase of wages. Florence, under the control of Alvarez, decrees a reduction instead and, surrounding the property with armed men, instructs them to shoot to kill should the employees strike.

Hearing of Florence's illness, Dr. Deane calls upon her and at a glance discovers her condition. Through an effort of will he breaks the hold of the Spaniard over her, bringing back her memory and rendering her normal once more. She then averts the railroad strike by acceding to the demands of her employees. Thereupon follows a battle of wills between Alvarez and Dr. Deane for the control of Florence's personality. Deane emerges victorious, and Alvarez commits suicide.

We'll let *Variety*'s Jolo describe the finale: "With the death of the executor the girl's diabolical impulses depart and she returns to the convent, fearing to face the world. Thither goes the doctor and he says, 'Are you afraid to face it with me?' And then she lays her curly locks on his manly bosom and the picture fades out" (20 October 1916).

Perhaps the only original element in the scenario is blaming labor/capital problems on the evil influence of hypnotism, certainly something Marx had never considered. Everything else must have looked pretty shopworn, even in 1916. The year before, in fact, Thanhouser had produced a kind of dry run for *Saint, Devil and Woman* with their two-reeler, *Duel in the Dark*, again starring Florence LaBadie (once more playing a character named Florence, something she seemed to do quite often) and with a script by Philip Lonergan. The plot concerns a fake clairvoyant named Sardo (Morgan Jones) whose activities are being investigated by D.A. John Gregory (Arthur Hauer). Unfortunately, Gregory's wife (Carey Hastings) is under Sardo's hypnotic control and tips him off whenever a raid is imminent. Gregory's daughter Florence discovers the truth and gets her mother to promise never to see Sardo again. "But his influence proves too strong. Florence follows her mother to the mesmerist's house, where the daughter pits her will power and her love for mother against the hypnotist's control. After a terrible psychic struggle, the girl wins and Sardo is arrested" (from the studio synopsis).

Some publicity for *Saint, Devil and Woman* mentioned the work of Dr. Prince as playing an important part in the story, while Florence La Badie was quoted as having done some research on her own:

I'm learning about dual personality. I have to understand it for my picture, *Saint, Devil and Woman*. I have to play a girl who is normally a saint, but who, through a chain of startling incidents, becomes a fiend and in the end changes to a fine, normal woman. In order to portray the character correctly, I have to read up on dual personalities so that I won't offend any psychologists who might see the picture and be anxious to criticize my interpretation.

Whether the theme (or Florence) offended any psychologists or not, it was discovered early on that multiple personality disorder is usually caused by childhood sexual trauma. As, obviously, this was a subject that was verboten in the Silent Era, the movies conspired to insist that the malady could also be brought about by hypnosis or lightning, although real-life investigations had never turned up a single case attributable thus. Clearly, *Saint, Devil and Woman* owes far more to George Du Maurier than Morton Prince and, just to make sure people made the connection, veteran heavy Hector Dion (Alvarez) was touted as "The Svengali of the Screen."

While *Variety* found *Saint, Devil and Woman* "uncanny and ridiculous," most reviews were a little more favorable, particularly Peter Milne's write-up in the 23 September 1916 *Motion Picture News*:

> The construction of the picture is praiseworthy over most of its length. The hypnotism has not been allowed to overshadow the drama and the drama is very well established. In the latter part of the subject the influence exerted for good and evil over Miss LaBadie in the same part is a little too sudden to result in absolute realism in the action but as a whole this difficult element has been handled convincingly and successfully.

Dickson G. Watts of *The Morning Telegraph* (cited above) was far more critical of the climactic battle of the wills for Florence's soul:

> As presented the incidents are unconvincing and border on the burlesque. Alvarez, returning, subdues her with but a keen glance from his eyes. Then at the entrance of the doctor, with two conflicting wills brought to bear upon her, Florence turns from saint to devil with all the ease and speed of a chameleon changing color while crawling over a patchwork quilt.

Wid Gunning (19 November 1916) likewise found the finale unintentionally funny:

> It must have been that there was not enough footage when this climax was reached, because although the hero conquered and stopped the strike, and the heiress knew that the villain was a murderer wanted by the police, they allowed the villain to nonchalantly remain about the place, with the result that he again influenced the girl, and the hero had to come in and do it over again…. I fear most audiences will be amused rather than convinced.

Wid's was also very critical of the excessive use of title cards in the film:

> The offering is terribly handicapped by many long titles, which explain exactly what is going to happen, this being done so frequently that it puts the production in the "primer" class. It would seem that those who edited this offering have no respect whatever for the intelligence of their audiences. Instead of allowing the characters to put over the dramatic scenes— and I can tell you that the director and artists presented the dramatic scenes in a very acceptable manner — the title writer proceeded to tell just what was in the mind of every character and just what they were going to do….
>
> As a sample of the titling, I might tell you that, when they got to the big scene where the villain and the hero were battling for the swaying of the heroine, the editor stopped the scene at the big moment and inserted a long title telling what was going to happen, instead of allowing the characters to put it over by their acting, which they were truly capable of doing.

All the trade paper critics did agree that Florence La Badie was completely convincing as the troubled heroine. Dickson G. Watts' comments were typical of La Badie's good notices: "The acting of Miss La Badie in her dual role is the best piece of work in the production. With every incentive to overact, she plays with repression and presents a convincing character study."

La Badie was Thanhouser's most important female star in 1916 — and just one year away from a tragic death. Her career is profiled in the entry on *God's Witness*.

Wayne Arey (Dr. Deane) spent almost all his brief film career at Thanhouser. A native of Rock Falls, Illinois, he became an actor in his hometown's opera house (built over a stable!) and made his stage debut as the gravedigger in *Hamlet*. Bigger roles followed, and he paid his dues in stock company work before achieving some success on Broadway, notably in the David Belasco production of *The Rose of the Rancho*. When his leading man days at Thanhouser came to an end, Arey returned to the New York stage and in late 1919 founded the socialist Workers' Theater Guild which put on plays by Theodore Dreiser and Saint John Ervine. Arey died in 1937, while was doing plays for the Federal Theater Project.

Director Frederick Sullivan was the son of a prominent English comedian and the nephew of Sir Arthur Sullivan (of the renowned Gilbert and Sullivan comic-opera team); in fact, Frederick made his stage debut in the first juvenile production of his uncle's *H.M.S. Pinafore*. Sullivan came to Los Angeles in 1884 and became the sports writer for *The Los Angeles Herald*. He worked for various other newspapers, including *The Chicago Tribune* and *The New York Sun* before going into theatrical publicity work; he then turned to acting and directing both on stage and in film. Sullivan signed with Thanhouser in 1913 and stayed there until the company folded in 1917. After that, he freelanced as a director, but that ended with the disastrous 1923 production of *The Courtship of Myles Standish* with Charles Ray. Sullivan spent the rest of his career as an actor, mostly in small roles and uncredited bits.

Ads and even publicity pieces for *Saint, Devil and Woman* had some trouble getting the title right. In addition to the title given in this essay, it sometimes was publicized as *The Saint, Devil and Woman* or even *The Saint, the Devil and the Woman*. Under any title it failed to make much of an impression.

— HN

The Savage

The Savage. First National Pictures/First National, 18 July 1926, 5 reels/6,275 feet (copyrighted and apparently released in spots at seven reels) [LOST]

CAST: Ben Lyon (*Danny Terry*); May McAvoy (*Ysabel Atwater*); Tom Maguire (*Prof. Atwater*); Philo McCullough (*Howard Kipp*); Sam Hardy (*Managing Editor*); Charlotte Walker (*Mrs. Atwater*)

CREDITS: *Supervisor* Earl Hudson; *Director* Fred Newmeyer; *Scenario* Jane Murfin, Charles E. Whitaker; based on a story by Ernest Pascal; *Titles* Ralph Spence; *Cinematographer* George Folsey; *Art Director* Milton Menasco; *Film Editor* Arthur Tavares

Were this chuckler about evolutionary hoaxes to be made today, the title role would be a natural for Vince Vaughan or

Ben Stiller or one of the other dozen or so contemporary comedians capable of delivering clever lines *avec nuance* while clad in animal pelts and mooning the ingénue. Back in the mid–1920s, it was Ben Lyon — Mr. Bebe Daniels — who frequently punched that ticket, but the sight of the Atlanta-born actor's backside was denied audiences here. Sadly, but not consequently, *The Savage* proved less than successful. The following, rather ungrammatical précis is taken from the copyright documents filed with the Library of Congress.

> Danny Terry, wild animal expert for a scientific magazine, goes to the Mariposa islands and plays the part of a white savage to put over a hoax on a rival magazine that has representatives accompanying Professor Atwater who is searching for the lost white savages. He is found and is brought back to New York and placed on exhibition at a jungle ball which Mrs. Atwater gives to celebrate the betrothal of her daughter to Howard Kipp.
>
> At the ball, Terry's editor appears and tries to expose the hoax, but Terry has fallen in love with Ysabel and refuses to expose her father. To save exposure he escapes from the cage and leaps out the window with the guests in pursuit. At the ball, Ysabel has discovered her fiancé with another girl so breaks her engagement. She rushes after Terry and tells him that she knows he is a fake. But Terry grabs her in his arms and carries her with him to a log cabin on a neighboring estate. There he tells her that he loves her, and she shows that it is not in vain. Terry finds a razor in the cabin, shaves off his beard and when the pursuers arrive, he is lying on the floor and Ysabel has her hair down and clothing disarranged as though done by the savage.
>
> They tell the crowd the savage went through the windows and as the crowd goes on the hunt they smile and embrace and the picture ends with Terry and Ysabel finding their real happiness.

The year before Ernest (*The Charlatan*) Pascal wrote this tale of Danny and Ysabel and Adam and Eve, the "Scopes Monkey Trial" — wherein Fredric March and Spencer Tracy's respective grandfathers battled over the right of high-school teacher, John Thomas Scopes, to teach his students about evolution — had drawn the attention of Western Civilization to Dayton, Tennessee. While this brouhaha over monkeys and men was still a hot topic, First National had Charles Whitaker and Jane Murfin extrude a scenario from Pascal's story and penciled in Lyon and May (*The Enchanted Cottage*) McAvoy as the ersatz Tarzan and his Jane.

Shot (and copyrighted) as a seven-reeler, the film was finally released in five, causing no little theorizing as to what was cut from the camera negative and why, and a couple of published comments indicating that the picture may have originally included more spectacular sights than the hirsute Lyon provide the reason for its inclusion in this book. There's the 14 August 1926 edition of *The San Mateo* [California] *Times and Daily News Leader*, which opined, "Those who saw *The Lost World* will easily recognize some of the prehistoric monsters that were seen in this picture except that in *The Savage* they are used for comedy purposes." What's more, the 4 November 1926 *Bioscope* flatly declared that "there is a first-class thrill in the shape of a huge brontosaurus." In Forrest J Ackerman's book on American science fiction films — cited elsewhere in this volume — the author avers that the picture ends as "the affable dinosaur pursues [Danny] back to New York."

Adding fuel to the fire is an "adaptation from the screenplay" written by Virginia Brunswick Smith that appeared in the 5 Oc-

tober 1926 *Moving Picture Stories*. The text relates how, during the scene when the expedition tries to capture Danny — the fake ape-man who's up in a tree — a dinosaur makes an appearance: to wit, "a horrible slimy monster that scrambled rapidly through the jungle like a colossal lizard, its long, snake-like neck and head weaving to and fro through the treetops as its quested its prey." Danny, in trying to escape his perch, ends up on the monster's back as it chases the expedition back to their yacht. The beast plunges into the water and goes after the ship. Prof. Atwater then expostulates: "Undoubtedly a brontosaur, a leftover from antediluvian times, perhaps thousands of years old, the first living specimen to be discovered in the memory of man." As the boat pulls away from the dinosaur, Danny, still on the monster's back, tries to jump onto the deck. He ends up in a net and the brontosaurus retreats. There's no indication in the adaptation that the dinosaur (a "slimy" dinosaur?) turns up in New York; perhaps FJA confused the ending with that of *The Lost World*.

Yet, if all of this dinosaur-related ink was spilled hither, thither and yon, why, then, would the studio's plot summary — filed with two prints of the film at the Library of Congress and reflecting the picture's *seven-reel-long* storyline — not have mentioned this remarkable creature? There's nary a trace of any such beastie in First National's own narrative, save for the titular character impersonated by Mr. Lyon.

If — due, perhaps, to an understandable dread of box-office death because of backlash over an uneasy mix of science and religion — all traces of the prehistoric (those two reels) were cut before national release on the 16 July 1926, how was it that the three periodicals quoted above were able to report on dinosaur footage? If not prior to release, then when were the reels cut, and why? (*Variety*, on the *4 August* of that year, called *The Savage* "a two-reel knock-about comedy, spread out very thin to make a five-reel feature" and repeatedly referred to "monkey-comedy" without even alluding to dinosaurs.) Were there two sets of prints prepared for screening, one at five reels in length and the other at seven?

And if we do consider the possibility of the cuts having been made due to fear of Scopes-inspired backlash, can we for a moment take seriously the thought that a boycott of the picture by the pro–Darwin left in 1926 would have had much impact on revenue? The number of potential ticket-nonbuyers that believed to one extent or another in the Genesis account was far larger than those who subscribed to The Origin of Species. In fact, Professor Atwater's coming across Danny — bearded or not — "coexisting" with the enormous sauropod would have supported the radically Christian-fundamentalist view that the Earth's age is measurable in terms of mere millennia — as quoted above, he announces that the brontosaur is "perhaps thousands of years old" — and where would have been the harm in that? With Atwater portrayed as being fiercely *anti*–Darwin — his expedition sets out to prove that mankind is descended from a race of white savages and *not* from the apes — the idea of the studio might have been fearful of a box-office boycott is dubious at best.

On the other hand, given the success of its 1925 science-fiction adventure, the notion that First National would have scrapped just the sort of dinosaur footage that had proven so popular scant months earlier is even more unlikely. We may never know the truth of the matter, but perhaps it was just that the time was not yet right for a *serious* (if comedic) cinematic examination of evolution, even as Bull Montana was working overtime portraying more ape-men than Carter had Little Liver Pills.

Other than Mr. Lyon (see *One Way Street*) and Ms. McAvoy, the only principal cast member to have lent his presence to more than one genre feature was the prolific Philo McCullough; along with Mr. Pascal, he is showcased in the coverage on *The Charlatan*.

With respect to the technicians, though — apart from Fred Newmeyer, a long-time comedy veteran whose name will forever be associated with that of Harold Lloyd (but not with our beloved genre) — we have a different story altogether. Writing the titles for the picture was Ralph Spence, who spent most of his life writing titles for silent films, stories for talkies, and plays (see the 1927 adaptation of *The Gorilla*) when he wasn't working in movies. Photographing the goings-on was George Folsey, whose career behind the camera would ultimately encompass some 160-plus features; Mr. Folsey's bona fides are to be found in the chapter on 1921's *The Case of Becky*. Editing on the picture was done by Arthur (aka Arturo) Tavares, who is remembered more for his work on the Spanish-language versions of *Dracula* and *The Cat Creeps* than for his constructing (or *de*-construct-

ing) the adventures of a boy and his brontosaurus. And overseeing the whole shebang was Earl Hudson, who had earlier supervised Mr. Lyon in *One Way Street* and (it is supposed) an altogether different brontosaur in *The Lost World*.

Without knowing just why *The Savage* was savaged, we can only point to Warners' take on the missing link business — its aptly-titled *The Missing Link* (see entry) — which was received genially and without hubbub when released less than a year after First National's five- or seven-reeler.

What a difference a year makes!

— JTS/HN

A Scream in the Night

A Scream in the Night. A.H. Fischer Features/Select Pictures Corporation, 5 October 1919, 6 reels [LOST]

CAST: Ruth Budd (*Darwa*); Ralph Kellard (*Robert Hunter*); Edna Britton (*Vaneva Carter*); John Webb Dillon (*Professor Silvio*); Ed Roseman (*Lotec*); Stephan Grattan (*Senator Newcastle*); Adelbert Hugo (*Gloris*); Louis Stern (*Mr. Graham*)

CREDITS: *Presented by* B.A. Rolfe; *Directors* Burton King, Leander De Cordova; *Story* Charles A. Logue; *Cinematographers* William Reinhart, A.A. Cadwell; *Editor* John J. Keeley

WORKING TITLE: *Female of the Species.* Per *The AFI Catalog*, "One source credits A. Fried a co-cinematographer with A.A. Caldwell. Another source lists Leander De Cordova as the scenarist, not the co-director. Some sources list the film as a five-reeler with a Sep. 1919 release."

This elusive 1919 feature, starring the ex-circus and vaudeville performer Ruth Budd as Darwa, the victim of a bizarre experiment in evolution, had us screaming — and not just in the night, either. Our hunt for *any* kind of information took us down several meandering paths, but left us frustrated and only moderately successful, albeit through no fault of our own. The Library of Congress copyright record, the first and often best source for this kind of thing, had suffered so much paper loss that it was virtually useless. Then, the folks at the Allen County-Fort Wayne Historical Society very graciously copied and mailed what they could, but only a personal pilgrimage to their facilities — not feasible due to time constraints and fiscal challenges — could have yielded a comprehensive inventory of their Ruth Budd collection.

The best (or, at least, the most comprehensible) synopsis of *A Scream in the Night* that could be found is taken from the 21 September 1919 number of the *Atlanta Constitution*:

Senator Newcastle is preparing to finance a trip to the Amazonian jungle in search of his daughter who was stolen in early youth. It is reported that an insane scientist is holding the girl a captive until she reaches an age when the scientist will be enabled to prove the Darwinian theory. The night before the search is scheduled to start the senator is killed in his drawing room. Robert Hunter, the senator's prospective heir if his daughter is not found, takes up the search, and with a companion strikes out for the heart of the jungle. Several weeks later they find themselves above Iquitos, over 2,000 miles up the Amazon from Para.

One day, while they are tramping through the heavy jungle growth, they come upon a young white girl, clad in skins, who frolics and leaps among the tree-tops. Hunter and his companion question the girl. They discover that she can speak English, having been tutored and protected by a civilized Indian, Lotec, who

Ben Lyon in the title role if *The Savage*. After a lengthy stint in grad school, his character won everlasting fame as Doc Savage.

agrees to go back to America with them when Hunter produces the proper sign. All doubt of the girl's identity disappears when she tells Hunter that she is Senator Newcastle's daughter.

A report of the girl's discovery is cabled to America and Hunter's friends plan a reception. Many guests are invited, among whom is a strange scientist named Silvio, who has become acquainted with one of Hunter's friends. On the night that Hunter and Darwa return home Silvio recognizes her as the girl who has been chosen for the great experiment, and when the time is opportune he tells the assemblage that the girl is not human. At the same time a sheriff arrives and places Silvio under arrest as the murderer of Senator Newcastle, but the scientist produces a letter written from the senator which proves that he is still living.

While the sheriff and his assistants start for the false address which Silvio has given them the scientist escapes to his hunting lodge. His movements have aroused Hunter's suspicions and together with Darwa he follows Silvio to the lodge. Hunter is disposed of by Sivio and Darwa is dragged to the basement of the lodge. There she finds her aged father, who has been held captive by the scientist. In the next room there is a fierce ape which Silvio has kept in a cage. It is the ape which killed the man who was mistaken for Senator Newcastle. Silvio throws Darwa into the cage with the ape and then leaves the room to await the result of his experiment.

Those partially decomposed Library of Congress records indicate that this rather detailed account of the action is still lacking in two areas. First, *A Scream in the Night* apparently gave us, not a love triangle but, rather, a love *quadrangle*. Vaneva Carter — a character unmentioned in the newspaper précis — initially sets her sights on Hunter but later settles comfortably in with Silvio (after Hunter reveals that he intends to marry Darwa). The jungle gal, unaware that this machinery is chugging along, grows jealous upon seeing Hunter and Vaneva together. Just where all this ends up is anybody's guess, but we'll put up even money that it's lovelorn Vaneva who gets the demented Silvio.

The second loose end was publicity-driven. The *Constitution* critique concludes by hinting at the film's finale with a noncommittal bit of exaggeration: "From that point on the story takes one of the most unusual turns ever seen on the screen." With the film lost, we need not be coy. Darwa has in her possession a small pistol. It has only one shot left and she must make it count. As the beast advances on her, she fires empty chamber after empty chamber at her own eye. In one of the dumbest acts of "monkey-see, monkey-do" ever committed by a (presumably) genuine primate, the ape grabs the gun and shoots himself in the head!

It's unclear whether the scenario for *A Scream in the Night* was authored by credited scribe Charles A. Logue, or whether Charles had merely penned the serialized jungle tale that reputedly ran an ungodly number of weeks in *The Saturday Evening Post*, or whether he had a hand in both. (There is no doubt that Logue was the literary sire of Quentin Locke, the federal agent-cum-escape-artist played by Harry Houdini in the 15-episode chapter-play, *The Master Mystery*.) What *is* clear is that another Charles — surnamed Darwin — had written more famously and at greater length about evolution some 60 years earlier. In 1919, John Scopes of Tennessee began teaching from George W. Hunter's *Civic Biology*, a book very much in the debt of Darwin's *The Origin of Species*. Six years later, Clarence Darrow and William Jennings Bryan would be waving Bibles and pounding

desks during the (in)famous Scopes Monkey Trial. Suffice it to say, without delving further into either trial or theory, Darwin was very much in the public's consciousness the year of *A Scream in the Night*'s release.

Those curious about Mr. Darwin and his theories may have wandered into *A Scream in the Night* in search of answers, but they exited as befuddled as before — the picture was an exploitation programmer all of the way. Sure, the trade journal ads enticed theater owners to cash in on the movie's evolution angle, and some local newspaper campaigns piqued the interest of potential ticket-buyers with taglines ("Did your forefathers spring from treetops?") and come-hither badinage ("The story of this beautiful girl who is accused of being only half human" — both from *The* [Oshkosh, Wisconsin] *Daily Northwestern*), while others (like the Fitchburg [Massachusetts] *Daily Sentinel*) leveraged the notoriety of the recent *Tarzan of the Apes* by declaring the movie "A Sensational Jungle Picture." The winner of the centerpiece was undoubtedly the *Appleton* [Wisconsin] *Post Crescent*, which immodestly promised, "It startled the Universe and will startle you!"

Much of the industry and national press, however, begged to disagree.

Harrison's Reports (11 October 1919) opined:

> There is not a single redeeming feature in the picture. It conveys not a single uplifting moral, or an entertaining element.... The best reward for authors, and remuneration for distributors who dare distribute such pictures, would be to enclose them in a similar iron cage, in company with the same wild ape, — but first get the ape good and hungry.

The 17 October 1919 *Variety* stood firmly on a more middle ground: "Take a little atheism, agnosticism, and a large dose of Darwinism, throw an Episcopal clergyman and a scientist into the potpourri, and you have an unusual picture." Still, the Bible of Show Business declared the film "a good program feature" and concluded that "if the producers of *A Scream in the Night* were striving after sensationalism they have attained their object."

Nonetheless, the reviewer for *The Moving Picture World* wrote of the "repulsiveness" of the material, a clue that he may have suffered from anti–Darwin bias. He predicted that the film "will never appeal to intelligent spectators," that the tale "lacked conviction" and that the story was "poorly constructed and the sensational features do not register." A tad kinder to the film's heroine than to the film itself, he ended with this left-handed compliment: "Ruth Budd as Darwa proves to be a good acrobat and a fair actress, considering the circumstances" (27 December 1919).

It was no coincidence by a long shot that Budd showed she was capable of the cinematic acrobatics necessary for the main role in *A Scream in the Night*; she'd been earning her bread and butter for almost two decades via her gymnastic abilities. In her 1999 study, *Rank Ladies — Gender and Cultural Hierarchy in American Vaudeville*, author M. Allison Kibler writes that Ruth and younger brother Giles started out in the early 1900s as a juvenile trapeze act in fairs and circuses. The two eventually gained fame as the "Aerial Budds," and by 1910 had set their sites on the Vaudeville tour by accepting spots on the lower end of the billing. The novelty of their acrobatic turn lay in the fact that the muscular Ruth and her lighter, younger brother switched traditional roles: Ruth hefted, swung and twirled her smaller sibling up on the wires. When Giles was seriously injured in 1915, Ruth decided it best to finally strike out on her own. Developing and refining her solo routine, she even incorporated a bit of song-and-dance in an attempt to fit better within Vaudeville conventions. In 1916, she and Giles reunited to bring their athletic prowess to the screen via *Building up the Health of a Nation*, which we can only guess was some sort of instructional film.

Although lacking any real talent at song and/or dance, Ruth's acrobatic ability remained the one true card she could play, and she was a headline performer by 1919. There is no doubt that her stage-bound gymnastics were the reason for stardom, as it were, in her feature film premiere. But if her name-value had given her a leg up on her *A Scream in the Night* co-stars, her involvement in the film, the regrettable human-monkey comparisons that followed (Kibler quotes a contemporary news piece wherein Budd even "complained about ... the real monkeys on the set, who

A jungle goddess (Ruth Budd), a great white hunter (Ralph Kellard), *A Scream in the Night*…. How often have we seen this happen?

threw coconuts at her"), and the controversy that accompanied anything Darwinian, caused waves of unwanted publicity. By the late 1920s, Ruth Budd's fame as a performer had faded. Following her announced retirement in 1929, she made several minor comebacks in the early 1930s, but never again appeared on the screen.

As for Miss Budd's fellow actors, Ralph Kellard was Darwa's love interest, Robert Hunter. Kellard, a New Yorker, had appeared on the Broadway stage in *Eyes of Youth* (1918), creating the role that Edmund Lowe would play in the Clara Kimball Young seven-reel feature the following year. *A Scream in the Night* was Kellard's only genuine genre feature, but he did leave a horror legacy, of sorts: That's he in the introduction of the great, old television program, *Silents Please*, being surprised by a giant, crab-like creature emerging from a lake. The whole shebang was cribbed from one of Kellard's big scenes from *The Shielding Shadow*, a Louis Gasnier chapter-play from 1916.

London-born John Webb Dillon had the lengthiest film career of his *Scream* colleagues— he was in the industry since 1911 and was making movies well into the Sound Era. A frequent cinematic heavy, Dillon was the ideal choice for the villainous Silvio, and more may be found on him in the essay on 1916's *The Darling of Paris*. Edna Britton —*Scream*'s "other woman," Vaneva — had but one other screen credit, in which she was once again wonderfully monikered. Britton was "De Luxe Dora" in the 1919 B.A. Rolfe Productions serial, *The Master Mystery*, which starred Harry Houdini as Quentin Locke and which leads us full circle back to Charles A. Logue.

What to think of *A Scream in the Night*? Was there truly a

bond between Darwa and Darwin? Hardly. Kibler cites the 24 October 1919 *Variety* review that "recognized that the film was confusing, pointing out that Darwa's survival in the woods and in high society offers no proof of evolutionary theory." Darwa and Silvio may have been more radical examples of Eliza Doolittle and Henry Higgins, perhaps, but evolutionary bellwethers, leading the masses to lofty — if secular — thoughts? Nah.

Still, there are some early oddities that have achieved "cult movie" status, like *Just Imagine, Sh! The Octopus*, and several of the pictures discussed in this volume. With *Scream* being lost, though, we really can't call it a cult movie. But for that, with a release title that bears absolutely no relation to the film's content, with a killer ape in the control of an evil (and unbalanced!) scientist, a pert yet powerful jungle gal, and an ending unique in the annals of motion picture history, well… Hands down, *A Scream in the Night* would be right up there with the rest of them.   — *SJ*

Seven Footprints to Satan

Seven Footprints to Satan. First National Pictures/First National, 27 January 1929 (silent version), 6 reels/5237 feet, Fondazione Cineteca Italiana (Milan)

CAST: Thelma Todd (*Eve*); Creighton Hale (*Jim Kirkham*); Sheldon Lewis (*The Spider*); William V. Mong (*The Professor*); Sojin (*Himself*); Laska Winters (*Satan's Mistress*); Ivan Christy (*Jim's Valet*); DeWitt Jennings (*Uncle Joe*); Nora Cecil (*Old Witch*); Kalla Pasha (*Professor Von Viede*); Harry Tenbrook (*Eve's Chauffeur*); Cissy Fitzgerald (*Old Lady*); Angelo Rossitto (*The Dwarf*); Thelma McNeil (*Tall Girl*); Loretta Young, Julian Rivero, Louis Mercier (all uncredited)

CREDITS: *Producer* Wid Gunning; *Director* Benjamin Christensen; *Script* Richard Bee; based on the eponymous novel by A. Merritt (New York, 1928); *Titles* William Irish; *Cinematographer* Sol Polito; *Editor* Frank Ware; *Makeup* Perc Westmore. *The AFI Catalog* maintains that there were talking sequences, sound effects and a musical score. We found no evidence anywhere of any talking sequences.

> "I sat through the picture and wept. The only similarity between the book and the picture was the title. The picture likewise killed the book sale of *Seven Footprints*, for people who saw the picture felt no impulse thereafter to read the book."
>   — A. Merritt on the film version of his story, in an interview by Julius Schwartz in *Science Fiction Digest*, January 1933

The author's tears notwithstanding, *Seven Footprints to Satan* was the most financially successful of all Merritt's books, and the Photoplay edition produced by Gross and Dunlap in 1928 also did very well. The story was originally run in five parts in *Argosy All-Story Weekly* from the 2 July to the 1 August 1927, and it was also serialized in the *New York Daily Mirror* before being released in book form. The movie may have been a travesty of the book, but the story actually represented a departure into thriller territory for an author best known for his science fiction and fantasy.

Abraham (a name courtesy of the Quaker heritage he had little use for) Merritt had originally studied law at the University of Pennsylvania, but when his family's sudden financial woes caused him to abandon his plans, he turned to journalism. He got a job covering executions at *The Philadelphia Inquirer* before graduating to night editor. Short, rumpled, bespectacled, and nondescript, the pipe-smoking Merritt would never have been cast as a reporter in a Warners' movie, but an incident early in his career was like something out of a Lee Tracy film: Merritt had witnessed "a violent indiscretion" (he was never more specific) involving a Philadelphia politician, and said politician paid Merritt handsomely to go somewhere beyond the reach of a subpoena. Merritt chose Mexico and Central America where he hooked up with an archaeologist and spent a happy and exciting year exploring Indian culture, an interest that stayed with him all his life. In 1912, after six years on the *Inquirer*, Merritt became assistant editor of the "Sunday Supplement" of the Hearst Sunday newspapers. The supplement would later evolve into *The American Weekly*, which often dealt with supernatural and psychic phenomena and weird science, as well as with violent crime; the occasional "human interest" story was thrown in to lighten things up. The *Weekly* was highly successful and in 1937 Merritt took over as editor, a post he held until his death, six years later.

In between his editing chores, Merritt wrote a number of fantasy and sci-fi tales such as *The Moon Pool* (1918), *The Metal Monster* (1920), *Face in the Abyss* (1923), and *Ship of Ishtar* (1924). These and others were serialized mainly in *Argosy*, a publication quite suited to Merritt's needs. "Possibly, unfortunately, I do not have to write for a living," Merritt said. "I write solely to please myself and those who like to read what I write. The *Argosy* realized this and printed my stories without change of a single word."* Per Sam Moskowitz's biography of the author

(*A. Merritt: Reflections in the Moon Pool*), though, the genesis of *Seven Footprints to Satan* was a bit different: "It was a novel whose general direction was agreed upon in advance by both the publication and the author" (p. 73). Moskowitz argues that, in the mid–1920s, advertisers had discovered that women — who usually made the final decision on the most important household purchases— didn't like science fiction or fantasy; rather, detective fiction was much more popular with the hand that held the purse strings. Thus, Merritt agreed to forgo the mountains of the moon and deliver a straight thriller.

Seven Footprints tells the story of adventurer James Kirham who, in a clever scene worthy of a Hitchcock film, is kidnapped off the streets of New York in broad daylight. He is brought to a Long Island mansion that is honeycombed with secret passageways and torture chambers, and there discovers that he is the prisoner of a master criminal known only as Satan. Satan is no mere gangster, though, and his worldwide empire is cult-like, with members who live in awe of his brilliance, cruelty, and seeming omnipotence. Huge, bald-headed and with piercing eyes, the criminal genius presents himself not just as a devil, but *The* Devil. (Merritt may have based Satan's appearance partly on Aleister Crowley, the cult leader and self-proclaimed magus whose notoriety was at its peak in the 1920s.) Satan's reluctant recruits are made to play a bizarre game in which they must ascend a stairway to Satan's throne by choosing only four of the seven footprints leading to it. The result of this game of chance may be freedom, death, or service to Satan and his criminal plans for a specific period of time.

The lowest of Satan's minions are addicted to a hallucinogenic drug which Satan doles out to them in a ceremony in which they worship him as a god. Most of his gang, though, consists of clever criminals or professionals who are willing to break the law for excitement or wealth. Kirkham plays the game and finds that he must serve Satan for three years. He falls in love with Eve, another of Satan's unwilling accomplices, and they plot to escape from the seemingly all-powerful fiend. Their chance comes when Kirkham discovers the Seven Footprints game is rigged and controlled by Satan. When this is exposed at an assembly of Satan's followers, a riot breaks out just as one of Satan's victims, driven mad by torture, escapes his cell and begins lobbing firebombs into the mob. Satan is blinded and then perishes in the flames that consume his mansion. "In the end, he was just a crooked gambler," Kirkham pronounces, Joe Friday–like, following his ersatz master's demise.

It's hard to say how many washing machines this sold, but it's a crackling good yarn nonetheless. Ayn Rand, of all people, had some good things to say about it: "The story is exciting in the sense that the writer knows how to keep up suspense and mystery and when to introduce the unexpected" (*The Art of Fiction*). For all that, the story was highly derivative: his demonic pretensions notwithstanding, Satan is not very different from Fu-Manchu. The torture chamber with mirrors is not unlike Erik's lair in *The Phantom of the Opera* or the maze in Francis Stevens' 1918 story, "The Labyrinth." Even the Seven Footprints

---

*"A Merritt — His Life and Works," *Scienti-Snaps*, October and December 1939.

game is not entirely original: Moskowitz mentions the 1900 Robert Barr short story, "A Game of Chess," in which players must walk across a giant chessboard in which some of the squares are electrified. Still, the book as written would have made a very good movie, and one could easily imagine Montagu Love or Paul Wegener playing Satan; however, director Benjamin Christensen (again scripting under the name of Richard Bee) had other ideas for this second entry in his "old dark house" trilogy.

Our synopsis of the film, taking from our screening of same:

Having inherited millions from his father, Jim Kirkham prepares to go in search of adventure in Africa, much to the frustration of his lovely fiancée Eve and the dismay of his down-to-earth Uncle Joe. On the night before Jim's planned departure, Eve asks him to attend a reception at her house during which an invaluable emerald will be displayed. Eve fears that one of the invited guests, Professor von Viede is a fraud. Kirkham attends the party but when he exposes von Viede as a fake, a melee breaks out during which shots are fired and the phone lines cut. Jim and Eve go to get the police but are kidnapped by Eve's own chauffeur and forced at gunpoint into a rambling old mansion.

Sheer madness rules inside the mysterious house which seems populated mainly by weird characters and gun-toting criminals in evening dress. A dwarf appears from behind a secret panel and warns Jim to beware the man with crutches. The latter's shadow promptly materializes and we later learn he's a sadistic maniac known as the Spider. An ape-man and a real ape wander the halls. A screaming woman is dragged away to be whipped. Hauled from room to room, Jim and Eve are informed by an old crone that they are prisoners of Satan. A professor who looks like a wolf-man with glasses turns up and promises to help the beleaguered and mystified couple. Jim discovers that he has the prized emerald in his pocket, but it is promptly taken away by a sinister Oriental. Apparently, this criminal gang run by Satan is after Jim's millions and is quite willing to threaten Eve's virtue to get him to cooperate.

After several attempts to escape fail, Jim and Eve are brought into a huge throne room where Satan, a masked man in costume, presides over the assembly. Jim is told his life and Eve's freedom depend on the Seven Footprints game he must play. Jim's choice of which footprints to step into is not unerring, but his life is saved. He is told he must serve Satan for three years. At this point everybody breaks for lunch. An astonished Jim follows the whole crowd into an adjoining refractory and finds he has been the victim of an elaborate hoax staged, not by Candid Camera but by Uncle Joe, who wanted to give his naive nephew the excitement he had been craving, but in a risk-free environment. Jim sheepishly agrees to settle down with Eve and work for Uncle Joe (who had masqueraded as Satan) for the next three years.

Abraham Merritt, who had been overjoyed to sell his novel to First National, was in Guatemala when *Seven Footprints to Satan* premiered. Still, had he seen the coming attraction (in which Creighton Hale spoke directly to the audience from the screen) he would have known what to expect.

Whew! Ladies and gentlemen, please don't think I'm this way all the time, but honest, I've been scared to death ever since I started to rehearse *Seven Footprints to Satan*. That is a First National Vitaphone picture that is coming to this theater in the very near future, which I had the pleasure of playing with Thelma Todd, Sheldon Lewis, William V. Mong, Dewitt Jennings and a very fine cast.

Now, we've had the movies for a long time, and then we got the talkies. Well, now we got the shriekies, and I can guarantee you this is the snappiest, zippiest melodrama that's ever played this theater, but it's done with a little laugh so's you don't even know

Sheldon Lewis examines Footprint number four in *Seven Footprints to Satan*.

till we get to the last foot whether we were kidding you or on the level.

Now, how would you like to see just one or two high points of the picture? Wait, how do you like this for a blood-curdler? [Scene is shown.] How do you like that...

Well, wait a minute now. I'll show you something better: here's Satan giving a party and when Satan gives a party... Well, he gives a party. [Scene is shown.] Hoo!Not bad, eh? Did you notice the little girl that's sitting on his left? Well, the less said about that, the better.

Now, I'll show a flash of the fatal seven steps. [Scene is shown.] Well, I got up there all right, didn't I? But what happened after I got up there... Well, listen, folks. You'll just have to see that in the picture when it plays in your theater. I thank you.

While Creighton Hale may have spoken in the preview, the Vitaphone *Seven Footprints* had a synchronized music/sound effects track (which is lost), but—despite some advance publicity to the contrary—no dialogue, and of course it was released as a silent as well.

Critical response to the film, while not as lachrymose as Mr. Merritt's, was nevertheless quite unenthusiastic. "An utterly moronic sound film ... all hokum" was *Variety*'s opinion. Mildred Martin of Merritt's old paper, *The Philadelphia Inquirer* (19 March 1929), wrote that "after all the screams and creaks and thumps it reaches a somewhat tame conclusion with an explanation of all the wild doings." The *Charleston Daily Mail* (26

February 1929) called it "fairly entertaining" and noted that "the smaller of the boys in the audience whooped and yelled when Alonzo [sic] Rossitto, the dwarf, shoots the gorilla so he must rate a mention." The film's sexual trappings were often mentioned, particularly the bevy of pretty girls and the revealing attire of Satan's female devotees, as well as the (implied) nudity of the girl who is whipped. From *Variety* again: "Patrons grew tense in their seats at the apparently real wickedness. One scene depicts scores of men and women in evening clothes, lying on the floor. This is unquestionably one of the hottest exhibitions done in a long while." The reviewer felt that only the film's "It's all a fake" conclusion saved it from censorship. One can only imagine what these critics would have made of Christensen's *Haxan.*

Modern defenders of the films take different approaches. In his film notes from May 1968, Ib Monty of the Danish Film Institute wrote that he regarded the picture as a joke, ridiculing superstition and including much irony in its "descriptions of the banal and naive dreams of horror and eroticism." Film historian Arne Lund thought the picture could be read as "a parody of its Sax-Rohmer–style source novel" and said as much in his requisite article, "Benjamin Christensen in Hollywood." If the film is indeed a satire of pulp thrillers, it's weak and not very sharply etched. If Christensen was parodying anything, most likely it was the mystery comedy genre — only half serious to begin with — that had been around since the 1910s and was undergoing a revival because of *The Cat and the Canary.* Lund also noted the "striking similarities to the 1997 David Fincher film, *The Game,* starring Michael Douglas." Then, too, the testing of the main character by scripting a bogus adventure had already been done in Eddie Sutherland's *Wild, Wild Susan* (1925). In fact, Christensen's earlier *The Haunted House* also depicted a collection of weirdoes who turn out to be actors hired to explore the worthiness of the other characters caught up in the charade.

To enjoy *Seven Footprints to Satan,* one needs to forget about the Merritt book and foreswear any hope of finding a coherent plot. The "cheat" ending scarcely matters because the story leading up it doesn't make any sense either. The juveniles are trapped in a mansion full of monsters, criminals and grotesques, and try to escape. That's it. Uncle Joe was obviously not much of a writer because none of the action he has thrown at his hapless nephew is pulled together with any kind of logic. What one is to make of the presence of Japanese screen actor, Sojin (who is billed as appearing as "Himself"), caught strutting about in the midst of a constant procession of grotesques is anyone's guess. It's one crazy thing after another without any interconnection, but one still wouldn't call the atmosphere dream-like; it's too frenetic for that. *Seven Footprints to Satan* is like a funhouse ride in which the passenger is jerked about in the dark from one exhibit to the next, some of them frightening, some comical, and still others a combination of the two. If you want an actual story to go with your thrills, you need to ride "The Tower of Terror" at Disney world. Here, one sits back and waits for the next secret panel to open to see what will pop out: A dwarf? A sexy Dragon-Lady? A gorilla? A human skeleton begging for mercy? Shadows are everywhere (great camera work and lighting by Sol Polito), and characters are continually leaping out of them. People and creatures chase each other around the house and in and out of rooms without any real rhyme or reason. And whenever the action even threatens to slow down, somebody is sure to pull out a revolver and start shooting.

Christensen has taken the old-dark-house comedy/thriller clichés and exaggerated them to the point of total absurdity. The nonstop lunacy becomes very entertaining after a while, and Christensen's direction keeps pace with the madness and is often very clever. A good example of this comes early in the film when Jim and Eve arrive at the mansion and are told to go upstairs. The camera appears to crane upward, but actually a smooth optical wipe brings us to the upstairs room as the couple enters. Christensen uses this device twice more, both times to good effect. The sets are appropriately gloomy and imaginatively lit, and particularly effective is the Spider's lair, where the mass of shadows gives the impression of a web. The one disappointment is Satan's throne room which, with

The Christmas formal at the frat house, and just about everybody who's anybody is there…. That's Angelo Rossitto — doing the Mystic — in the lower left-hand corner in *Seven Footprints to Satan.*

its harem girls, Nubian servants, and ornate curtains surrounding the throne like a giant seashell, looks like something out of a Maria Montez movie; one keeps expecting to spot Jon Hall or Sabu somewhere in the crowd. Satan himself is a pretty unimpressive villain and is only glimpsed a couple of times. It's an amusing touch, though, to have the cultists politely applaud whenever he enters.

Creighton Hale, a serial hero in the 1910s, did more and more comic roles as the 1920s progressed but, unfortunately, he didn't do them very well. Every so often he'd be cast against type (he makes a good — albeit somewhat prissy — villain in 1927's *Annie Laurie*) but his role in *Seven Footprints* is more typical. If anything, he's even more annoying here than in *The Cat and the Canary*. In her last silent, Thelma Todd looks very lovely indeed, and that's enough. And of course it's fun to watch such favorites as Sojin, Angelo Rossitto and Sheldon Lewis as supporting ghouls. Lewis, in fact, is more restrained than usual, and his Spider is the one menace in the film that may be meant to be taken seriously.

Another great project that failed to find backers: "Edgar Bergen and Charlie McCarthy; the Untold Story," or Angelo Rossitto (left) and William V. Mong from *Seven Footprints to Satan.*

Time did not soften A. Merritt's feelings about Christensen's *Seven Footprints*: "It was lousy and I made no bones about it. Even though they did pay me well, it didn't mitigate the hurt" (as quoted in *Fantasy Field Fiction*, 31 July 1941). Merritt was also unimpressed with the 1936 *Devil Doll*, an adaption of his *Burn, Witch, Burn!*: "I did not like it. They were forced by English censorship to change the scenario from one of straight witchcraft into a pseudo-scientific one. The movie *Dr. Cyclops* was a steal both from *Burn, Witch* and *Devil Doll*. In my opinion, few motion pictures are worth the trouble of seeing" (Letter to Allen McElfresh, 16 February 1940).

From time to time there was chatter about plans to do a new version of *Seven Footprints*, but no remake was forthcoming and the original silent drifted into the nether regions of the vaults. The occasional odd still in horror magazines of the 1950s and Merritt's "Look what they done to my book, Ma" lament was pretty much all most horror fans knew about Christensen's film. Then, in late 1995, to everyone's amazement and delight, Turner Classic Movies listed a play date for the film on their schedule. For reasons that remain unknown, the movie was not shown; however, it did appear on Italian television under the title *La Scala di Satana* and with a music score cribbed from the Milestone release of the 1920 *Last of the Mohicans*. Video copies made their way to the USA and elsewhere, but more and more collectors found that dealing with the Italian title cards was less frustrating than trying to make out what was happening on the screen as increasingly unwatchable multi-generation copies

began to circulate. Good film elements do exist on this title; a reputedly excellent 35mm copy held by the Fondazione Cineteca Italiana in Milan has been given an occasional public showing. Unfortunately, no plans for a DVD release have been announced, so most fans will have to be content with the bootleg video versions of the Italian telecast. A few hopeful souls have translated the title cards, but found that the film doesn't make any more sense in English than it did in Italian.

People who found *Seven Footprints* too outré may be thankful they were not subjected to a follow-up that could have been even more outlandish. As *Seven Footprints to Satan* was about to be released, the First National publicity team announced that the third film in Christensen's horror comedy trio would be an adaptation of the play, *Sh! The Octopus* (reported in *The* [Zanesville, Ohio] *Sunday Times Signal*, 4 November 1928). It didn't happen, but it's hard to imagine a more appropriate sequel to *Seven Footprints*.

— *HN*

The Shadow of the East

The Shadow of the East. Fox Film Corp./Fox Film, 27 January 1924, 6 reels/5874 feet [LOST]
CAST: Frank Mayo (*Barry Craven*); Mildred Harris (*Gillian Locke*); Norman Kerry (*Said*); Bertram Grassby (*Kunwar Singh*); Evelyn Brent (*Lolaire*); Edythe Chapman (*Aunt Caroline*); Joseph Swickard (*John Locke*); Lorimer Johnson (*Peter Peters*)
CREDITS: *Presented by* William Fox; *Director* George Archainbaud;

Scenario Frederic and Fanny Hatton; based on the eponymous novel by E.M. Hull (Boston, c. 1921); *Cinematographer* Jules Cronjager

There were all sorts of pictures centering on or alluding to shadows shot and released during the 1920s, and we'd be quite safe in saying that just about none of them holds any interest for us. 1922's *Shadows of the Sea* was mermaid-less, 1923's *Shadows of the North* had nothing to do with Yeti, and you can well imagine the dramatic pivot of 1921's *Shadows of the West*. Spoiling that perfect record is *The Shadow of the East*, a Fox Film effort from 1924 wherein *East* meant India, and *Shadow* meant occult spell.

The following synopsis, dated the 3 February 1924, is unattributed:

> Barry Craven, Earl Craven, like his father before him, has a government job in India, and although he has fallen heir to the estates in England, puts off returning from year to year. He has married a native girl, Lolaire, who in the person of Evelyn Brent is plenty of reason for him to remain in India.
>
> Gillian Locke (Mildred Harris), the daughter of an artist and unsuccessful man, turns up in India. Barry falls in love with her and she with him. She returns to England. He goes to Bombay to see her off, and Lolaire thinks he has left her for all time. She kills herself. Kunwar, Barry's servant, in love with Lolaire, swears that he will follow Barry and keep him away from other women.
>
> Gillian and her father, who is an old sweetheart of Barry's aunt, Caroline, visit Craven Towers in England, where Aunt Caroline is keeping the place in Barry's absence. John Locke dies there and Barry is called home. In England he realizes that Gillian means a great deal to him. His attempts to tell Gillian of his love for her are frustrated by Kunwar, who is able to bring Lolaire into Barry's mind whenever he is talking to Gillian.
>
> The ill-health of Aunt Carolina [*sic*] brings the matter to a crisis, and Barry proposes, is accepted, and marries Gillian. On the wedding night, Kunwar interferes again, and Barry rushes away.
>
> He goes to the desert to join a friend of his, Said, who has appeared in the picture before as a suitor of Gillian. There he requests and is granted dangerous positions in the desultory fighting that is always going on among the Arabs. Gillian, loving him, follows him.
>
> Said tells her that Barry is not there, but in Paris with another woman, and makes love to her himself. In the midst of this a messenger rushes in saying that Barry has been surrounded by an enemy band and is in danger of being killed. They rush to the rescue, Gillian in the lead, and all ends happily. Kunwar is killed, thus ending the curse which he has put on Barry.

And Said, properly chastened, enters a monastery and devotes the rest of his life to making really fine Cheddar. (Okay; this last bit is pure fabrication.)

The picture was based on the eponymous novel by Edith Maude Hull, an Englishwoman who began putting pen to paper while her husband was off fighting the Kaiser. Nothing if not the spiritual ancestor of such trend-setting Millennium-Age authoresses as J.K. Rowling and Stephenie Meyer, Hull (real name: Edith Maude Winstanley) is credited with having initiated the Desert Romance/Adventure craze with *The Sheik*, which was published in 1919. An international bestseller, it was followed by *The Shadow of the East* in 1921 and *The Sons* [*sic*] *of the Sheik* in 1925. We're not at all sure how Paramount let that *Sheik* sequel get away from it, or how Fox managed to snag the rights to Hull's page-turner without snaring Valentino as well (more than one reviewer wondered where he had gone off to),

but that's what happened and readers interested in investigating those questions have our earnest best wishes.

Movie buffs that are even remotely into the Silent Era are well aware of the Valentino/*Sheik* features, but cognoscenti of *The Shadow of the East* are fewer and farther between. This is due to the chiefly non-desert-oriented film adaptation's being the least successful—critically and box-officely—of the three pictures, and that lack of success is more probably due to the absence of Mr. Valentino than to the absence of sand dunes. Still, we must mention that—even in the mid–Roaring Twenties—India and scenarios dealing with things, places and personages Indian were generally associated by the public with flim-flam, rather than with romantic adventure. The book you hold is rife with scenarios impacted by nefarious Hindoos, as the Silent Era vernacular had them, and every blessed one represented everything that was simplistic and stereotypical about the polytheistic religious beliefs of about 15 percent of the world's population. Could Ms. Hull really have strayed so far from the swath that she had herself had cut?

Well, no… The action that unfolds in Hull's *The Shadow of the East* takes place in just about every locale on Earth into which an Englishman would venture *except* for India. Opening in Japan, the narrative takes its hero to Paris and then to an Arab camp in southern Algeria, while making numerous references to characters who seem always to be in transit to or from London. Barry Craven's junket onto all that revenue-generating sand doesn't occur until the second half of the book, when Arabs named Omar and Saïd gallop in to grab the flagging interest of those readers who had picked up *The Shadow of the East* looking for more sheikhs. Still, better late than never, right?

Not in this case. Responsible for abandoning the Japans for the slightly less–Far East while still keeping the meaty part of the story away from the Sahara until patrons began to squint at their watches were the Hattons, Fanny and Frederic, the same folks who would work later that same year on Fox Films' idiotic *Curlytop* (see appendix). Much more adept at writing and adapting their own claptrap than fooling with someone else's claptrap, Team Hatton penned over a dozen plays that made it onto Broadway and worked on (some say worked *over*) more than six dozen film projects, including a good handful that were taken from their stage-bound originals. It's anyone's guess as to why our spousal scribes felt that Barry Craven's adventures would be better received by moviegoers if the early exposition were to take place in the land of Vishnu, Brahma, and (genre-favorite) Shiva, rather than within Buddha's broad borders, and the reception the picture received did little but point out how wrong they were.

That intriguing phrase, "The Shadow of the East," then, refers to the mystical positing of Lolaire's image into Barry's mind whenever the earl is trying to make time with Gillian. Some people might call this image the result of *guilt*, but who are we to quibble with the occult? Guilt lasts, if not forever, a really long time, but … the occult? Guilt never really goes away, even though you can find temporary respite in strong drink or a Yankees–Red Sox game; all is takes is a thoughtless word, or even a meaningful glance, and… Bingo! Guilt is back, and with a vengeance! As for the occult, once Kunwar is killed—Presto!—

Barry never gives so much as a single thought to Lolaire ever again, regardless of the fact that she looked just like Evelyn Brent.

Miss Brent brought her (cosmetically-impacted) dusky beauty to only one other Silent Era genre film, 1929's *Darkened Rooms*, but that shared resume space with some 10 dozen other pictures, including 1943's marvelous *The Seventh Victim*. Starting out as Betty Riggs in 1915, the Tampa-born stunner was still emoting with fair regularity up until the end of the 1940s. After retiring in 1960 (her last appearance was in an episode of the then-popular TV series, *Wagon Train*), she became an agent. Perhaps the most intriguing part of Miss Brent's curriculum vitae was her hobby, unusual for a woman: she enjoyed carving pieces of furniture.

Gillian Locke was played by Mildred Harris, the lady whose cinematic talents will always be somewhat obscured by her status as Charlie Chaplin's child bride. Before meeting the Little Tramp, Harris had won roles in a brace of the Oz pictures (*The Magic Cloak of Oz* [1914] and *His Majesty, the Scarecrow of Oz* [1916]), and after the divorce, she went on to appear onscreen opposite most of the decade's most popular leading men. (She also had a brief fling with Edward, the then-current [and fairly randy] Prince of Wales.) Her screen career slowed down appreciably come the 1930s, and she turned to vaudeville to supplement her income. Miss Harris died of pneumonia in July 1944.

John Locke (*not* the British philosopher known as the Father of Liberalism, but rather, the father of Gillian Locke) was impersonated by Josef (here, Joseph) Swickard, and there's more on that august figure in our coverage of *The Young Rajah*. Likewise, there's a list of genre credits belonging to Bertram Grassby (the mind-game-playing Kunwar) in *Her Temptation* (1917) and similar data pertaining to Norman Kerry in *The Hunchback of Notre Dame* (1923). That pretty much leaves Frank Mayo.

Who?

Between the Silent Era and the Sound Era, New Yorker Frank Mayo appeared in well over 300 feature films, shorts and serials, although a good two-thirds were of the "uncredited bits" sort that filled out the resumes of so many film veterans. Of the remainder, fewer than a handful of titles would have us look twice. Had you begun reading this volume in reverse alphabetical order, though, you would have already spotted Frank in his two other silent, genre leading roles: as Bruce Taunton in *The Zero Hour* and as John Woolfolk in *Wild Oranges*. And there's a tad more about Frank in our entry on the latter picture.

Nobody who published anything we could find was crazy about *The Shadow of the East*. C. S. Sewell (in the 16 February 1924 *Moving Picture World*) cut to the genre chase when he kvetched that "the wonderful occult powers of the valet are unconvincing and as the whole story depends on this, its hold on the spectator is weakened." The 9 February 1924 *Harrison's Re-*

ports passed on the occult and moaned about the geographical setting: "Mediocre. It is unlikely that it will draw many people, for the reason that it is tiresome, it shows the hero married to a native of India, and much of the action unfolds in India, a feature which is bad so far as American audiences are concerned — no picture whose action unfolded chiefly in India has ever drawn."

And the 26 March 1924 *Variety* took everything a step further, got the picture's name wrong, and ended up calling *The Shadow of the Desert* "bunk."

Only *Film Daily* — that most loyal of cinematic publications, the trade that would have unhesitatingly recommended looking through the mountain of horse poop to find the pony — managed to find something positive: "As a Whole... Another 'Sheik' picture with story by the author of the original; should be a good number for women patrons. — They'll 'love' the love scenes" (3 February 1924). Unwritten: any men who might be present can, presumably, catch up on their sleep.

Casting a quick glance at the two Valentino/Sheik pictures and comparing them with the UnRudolfo offering at hand leads us to make several inferences with respect to the picture's Un-Success. (1) Duh! No Valentino. *Shadow*'s "love scenes" would have enjoyed geometrically-advanced popularity had the World's Greatest Latin Lover been a part of them. Not only would the women — Bless 'em — have had another hour and a half of Filmdom's most fabulous eye candy, but the guys that had been dragged along could have taken notes on posture, expression, and gesticulation, while assessing how well a caftan or a burnoose could effectively mask paunches and love-handles. (2) Plopping your principal cast anywhere in India while simul-

Both Mildred Harris and Frank Mayo seem mildly surprised at Norman Kerry's sporting a mustache devoid of wax. Blame this aberration on the desert heat... or *The Shadow of the East*!

taneously failing to provide any sign of a pagan idol, a purloined gem, or a fanatical religious cult just doesn't cut the curry. When you already have a formula for success—as did *The Sheik* or any of the scrillion *Moonstone* rip-offs we cover herein—do not screw with it. (3) If you're going to introduce some sort of mystical curse into the proceedings, make sure it has to do with death or, at the very least, dismemberment. Clouding one's mind with images of Evelyn Brent could not have been regarded as anything but a mitzvah by the men who had been forced to accompany their dates into the silent darkness.

Director George Archainbaud did what he could with what they handed him, and he did get some positive back-slapping, along the lines of "George Archainbaud has directed with one eye on artistic detail, but the other, probably his right, even more firmly focused on the box office" *Variety* (cited above)—so much for Show Business's Bible being divinely inspired. M. Archainbaud also contributed to *The Brand of Satan* and *Easy Pickings* (vid., the pair).

Everyone associated with *The Shadow of the East* went on to other—if not necessarily bigger and better—things, and the next project with which the Hattons were involved was Fox's *The Wolf Man*, a melodrama dealing with drunkards and not lycanthropes.

So near, yet so far…   — *JTS*

She

She. Fox Film Corp./Fox Film Corp, 14 April 1917, 5 reels [LOST]

CAST: Valeska Suratt (*Ayesha, also known as "She"*); Ben L. Taggart (*Leo*); Miriam Fouche (*Ustane*); Wigney Percyval (*Billali*); Tom Burrough (*Holly*); Martin Reagan (*Job*)

CREDITS: *Presented by* William Fox; *Director* Kenean Buel; *Scenario* Mary Murillo; based on the eponymous novel by H. Rider Haggard (New York, 1886); *Cinematographer* Frank G. Kugler

By the time this version of *She* went into production, no fewer than four other takes based directly on or "inspired by" the 1887 H. Rider Haggard original had been screened somewhere or another. Earliest of the lot appears to have been Georges Méliès' 1899 *La Colonne de Feu* (*The Column of Fire*; still extant!), followed by Edwin S. Porter's eponymous two-reeler (nope), released in 1908. In 1911, Thanhouser cast Marguerite Snow in the title role, tossed James Cruze (soon to be Dr. Jekyll and Mr. Snow) and Alphonz (*A Message from Mars*) Ethier into the mix, and came up with a three-reeler which is also around and about after all these years. In 1916, the Brits decided that if anyone was going to make a franc, a buck or a pound from their boy, Haggard, it would be they, and so they signed on Henry (*King of the Zombies*) Victor as Leo Vincey and Alice (nothing much else, really) Delysia as the immortal femme fatale for the 1916 Barker feature. (Incidentally, Victor would return to the fantasy field as the title character in Barker-Neptune's *The Picture of Dorian Gray* later that same year. That would be it for the big guy's silent genre stuff, but he portrayed the woeful Hercules in Tod Browning's 1932 oddity, *Freaks*, en route to being the chief zombifier in the 1941 Monogram epic parenthesized above.)

Anyhow, come 1917, Fox decided the time was ripe for a feature-length retelling of the tale aimed at American ticket-buyers, and the studio lined up the exotically yclept Valeska Suratt (from Owensville, Indiana) as Ayesha; the mysterious Wigney Percyval (probably *not* from Owensville, Indiana) as Billali; and New Yorker Ben Taggart (in one of the few film roles for which he received credit) as Leo Vincey. The picture came and went and is still gone as of this writing. The following précis, then, is taken from the copyright records at the Library of Congress:

> Three thousand years ago, a young Egyptian priest was killed by Queen Ayesha when he refused to abandon his young wife for her. His widow gave birth to a son, whom she charged to avenge his father's death. The duty was passed on from generation to generation, until it fell upon Leo, a direct descendant of the priest. Setting out with his friend Holly to fulfill his responsibility, Leo meets Ustane, a young Egyptian woman, and they are married. During a skirmish with some cannibals, Leo is wounded and Holly is taken before Queen Ayesha. Holly implores the queen to heal her friend's wound, and upon entering his cave, Ayesha recognizes in Leo her lost Egyptian priest. Upon recovering, Leo goes to Ayesha to fulfill his vow, but Ayesha kills Ustane and then declares her love to Leo who falls at her feet. She takes him to the Flame of Life to make him immortal, but as Ayesha bathes in the fire, her beauty begins to shrivel and she emerges a hideous ape. Accompanied by Holly, Leo flees the city and returns to civilization, his mission completed.

Pretty dismal, but Haggard's Ayesha suffered an even more ignominious end than did Fox's:

> "Why, what is it—what is it?" she said confusedly. "I am dazed. Surely the quality of the fire hath not altered. Can the principle of life alter? Tell me, Kallikrates, is there aught wrong with my eyes? I see not clear," and she put her hand to her head and touched her hair—and oh, horror of horrors!—it all fell upon the floor.
> "Look!—look!—look!" shrieked Job, in a shrill falsetto of terror, his eyes starting from his head, and foam upon his lips. "Look!—look!—look! She's shriveling up! She's turning into a monkey!" and down he fell upon the ground, foaming and gnashing in a fit.

Not many fantasy-film fans associate the climax of *She* with the titular hottie doing the evolutionary backslide; the sundry sound remakes have usually concluded with Herself but an ashen remnant of what She used to be. Haggard's account of Ayesha's demise is sprinkled with references to simians, so—if nothing else—this 1917 silent feature rings the bell as being most faithful to the source novel.

What we have here, of course, is another instance of the essence of fantasy film: the cocking up of time. While imaginative tales of conquering space—whether the farthest reaches of the most remote galaxy in the universe or an atom's irreducible quarks—are more properly the provenance of science fiction, imaginative tales of overcoming Father Time are, as of now, purely and simply fantastic. The fact that there's technology involved (e.g., *The Time Machine*) or there's evidence of profound human purpose (*The Terminator* mythos) matters not a whit; at present, there is not even any mustard to be cut. On the other hand, one must accede to the contention that much of yesterday's fiction *has* become today's fact. An iPhone to Eisenhower-era teenagers would have been as borderline supernatural as an icebox to Ramses II. A given, then, is that—with the exception of inventing a fountain pen costing less than $200 that doesn't leak all over your good shirt—science continues to come up with that which was formerly considered impossible. Messing with time is fantastic *at this point*; given the geometrically-progressing advances in technology and man's ceaseless thirst for knowledge that might well change.

So ... Ayesha — older than dirt (or, depending on the locale in which a particular reinterpretation of the story has been set, than *sand*) — is required to take a periodic dive into the Colonne de Feu to keep her breasts up and her facial lines down as she is without access to the Nip/Tuck hunks and Botox. Thus, (1) immortality: the time-cheating obsession that has tantalized mankind from time immemorial, that has so far eluded humanity's desperate search, and that will ultimately — when the lads who are even now screwing with cloning, genetic encoding and colon-cleansing miracles will have stumbled onto the secrets of unending life — impact only the super-rich and ultra-famous. Then, too, because Ayesha senses that Leo is, in fact, that same young Egyptian priest in whom She took an interest millennia earlier, we have (2) reincarnation: the mystical belief that the soul survives the death of a body only to be reborn in another body, somewhere down the line. Viewed this way, we're dealing not so much with time as with time-*share*. Either way, it's more than a step up from the chemically-induced schizophrenia of Jekyll and Hyde (who occupy the same body, more or less, simultaneously, more or less) and a mile and a half away from all those hypnotically-engendered behavioral shifts favored by Silent Era screenwriters.

The conventional wisdom holds that Silent Era screenwriter Mary Murillo had crafted her scenario to suit Theda Bara, the movies' reigning vamp, and that when Ms. Goodman was otherwise occupied, the role was offered to Valeska Suratt, who had made quite a name for herself as an actress and fashion plate in London and New York. (La Bara spent 1917 making an even *eight* features — all for the Fox Film Corporation — and one of these, *The Darling of Paris*, is discussed elsewhere in these pages.) Actually, Ms. Suratt had been wooed away from Famous Players–Lasky the previous year, when mogul William Fox agreed to take her on as his second-string — but not lower-shelf — man-killer at a whopping $5000 a week. In addition to *She*, the actress appeared in five other Fox pictures during 1917 and was advertised as "The Vampire Woman" for such films as *The Siren*, *A Rich Man's Plaything*, and *The Slave*.

Suratt left the movies behind her that year, returned to the stage and then turned to religion; in the latter, she was greatly influenced by Baha'i scholar, Mirza Ahmed Schnab (multiple spelling variations out there), who wrote a book on the life of Mary Magdalene. Suratt purchased the rights to same and sent it to film czar, Will Hays, who passed it on to Cecil B. De Mille. Expressing no interest whatsoever in the material, Cecil returned the book to Suratt; when, subsequently, the actress saw *The King of Kings*, she claimed parts of Schnab's work had been plagiarized. She sued De Mille, scenarist Jeannie Mc Pherson, and Will Hays for a million dollars. The suit dragged on for three years but was dismissed in 1930 by Federal Judge Frank Coleman who, per the 12 August 1930 *Oakland Tribune*, ruled that while Miss Suratt's scenario was based on Schnab's life of Mary Magdalene and thus was 95 percent fiction, *The King of Kings* was based on the life of Christ; Coleman also opined that he found no similarity in the two except "in those parts which were already of general knowledge." Presumably the book didn't have Mary Magdalene riding around in a chariot pulled by zebras.

Times and tastes had changed after America emerged from The Great War, and it wasn't long before vamps and Ms. Suratt (and Ms. Bara) were passé. When the 1920s were in mid–Roar, in fact, her style of acting *and* fashion likewise began to fade, and the actress retired from the stage by the end of the decade. Nonetheless, those Hoosiers were (and are) made of stern stuff; Valeska Suratt hung in there for another 30-odd years, although the whys and wherefores of her later life remain the subject of much speculation and argument.

Back on the 27 April 1917, though — at least according to *Variety* scribe, "Fred" — Ms. Suratt was still very much in vogue:

> Never had an idea that Valeska Suratt could be so beautiful with a veil on. As a matter of fact, she is better looking with her face covered than she is at the time when her countenance is showing.... Her characterization [relies] principally on a long piece of gauze in which she enwraps herself, allowing the outline of her form to be strikingly visible, at times permitting the covering to slip to such an extent there is nothing left to the imagination. This alone will be reason enough to establish the box office drawing quality of the film.

Nor did *The Moving Picture World*'s Edward Weitzel rush to Ms. Suratt's defense. After finding Kenean Buel's direction lacking in "eyrie [*sic*] feeling," Weitzel turned his sights on the leading lady: "Valeska Suratt's performance of the ancient queen is also untouched with the same important quality. Her dressing of the character is in keeping with the author's conception, but her entire performance is uninspired a defect for which ease and freedom of movement and close attention to the task at hand does not fully atone" (5 May 1917).

Faint praise, to be sure, but a damned sight better than the mention Ben Taggart received from these two trades: *MPW* dismissed him with "the Leo of Ben L. Taggart is another quite ordinary performance," while Fred concluded that "the men were particularly weak, especially Ben L. Taggart in the role of Leo." This may be just the spot to reiterate that Mr. Taggart had few opportunities after this one to carry either a picture or a gauze-enwrapped glamour girl. *The AFI Catalog* lists *a* Ben Taggart who surfaced in the 1930s and 1940s; his résumé features well over 150 appearances, and he carried a badge in most of them, including such disparate fare as *Monkey Business* (1931) and *Horse Feathers* (1932), *The Thin Man* (1934), *The Longest Night* (1936), *Topper Takes a Trip* (1938), *The Gracie Allen Murder Case* (1939), and *Man Made Monster* (1941); only in this last did his name make the crawl. Still, we've no conclusive proof that both Bens Taggart were one and the same.

Other than Miriam Fouche, whose film debut herein won her a couple of nods, the other cast members that merited a mention of their name received little else than a mention of their name, and a few, scattered sentences indicated that the Egyptian settings didn't pass reviewers' eyes unnoticed. The times being what they were, though, the racial background of some of the extras was thought worthy of inclusion. From the 17 May 1917 *Wid's*: "Quite a lot of husky native coons and a number of pickaninnies figured in the action." Still, the few trades that bothered with the film were pretty much as one with the local papers who took the time to remark on the art direction and settings. The 18 May 1917 *Newark* [New Jersey] *Advocate* praised the settings and the background players without stooping to slang: "The scenic effects are marvelous, the scenes [of] Ancient Egypt, with its wastes of sand, verdant Edens, waving fronds, half-nude savages, black chorus girls is most interesting including Miss Suratt's knees, which play a star part owing to the tropical architecture of her costumes. It is almost, so to say, an undressed role." Full circle, then, to the leading lady's corporeal splendor. (*Wid's*: "That's where that gal lives!")

As the saying goes, those who live by the knees, die by the knees, and Fox's *She* didn't last much longer in the movie-palace circuit than Ayesha did after that second jaunt into the *colonne de feu*. There really wouldn't be any "definitive" American silent version of H. Rider Haggard's cash-cow, although the most elaborate rendition to survive until this day — Great Britain's mid–1920s feature — starred Americans Betty Blythe and Carlyle Blackwell. It would remain for RKO — the company that brought King Kong from Skull Island to 34th Street — to give *She Who Must Be Obeyed* the voice that was needed to take attention away from her knees. Sadly, while Helen Gahagan is remembered by film buffs for her 1935 turn as the immortal Ayesha, students of history still view the woman as one of many who fell victim, not to the Undying Flame, but to Richard Milhous Nixon.

— *JTS*

The Show

The Show. Metro-Goldwyn-Mayer/M-G-M, 22 January 1927, 7 reels/6,309 feet, Turner

CAST: John Gilbert (*Cock Robin*); Renée Adorée (*Salome*); Lionel Barrymore (*The Greek*); Edward Connelly (*The Soldier*); Gertrude Short (*Lena*); Andy MacLennan (*The Ferret*); with Zalla Zaradna, Edna Tichenor, Betty Boyd, Agostino Borgato, Polly Moran, Bobby Mack, Barbara Bozoky, Jules Cowles, Jacqueline Gadsden, Cecil Holland, Ida May, Francis Powers, Billy Seay, Dorothy Seay, Dorothy Sebastian.

CREDITS: *Director* Tod Browning; *Scenario* Waldemar Young; based on the novel *The Day of Souls* by Charles Tennney Jackson (Indianapolis, 1910); *Titles* Joe Farnham; *Settings* Cecil Gibbons and Richard Day; *Cinematographer* John Arnold; *Film Editor* Errol Taggart; *Costumes* Lucia Coulter

"The event everyone has been waiting for! The joint reappearance of John Gilbert and Renée Adorée, the big sensations of *The Big Parade*. And what a picture! Under-world drama! Sideshow life! Romance, intrigue, color!"
— advertisement for *The Show*

"Illegitimate spew."
— John Gilbert's opinion of *The Show*

Much has been written about John Gilbert's fall from stardom and, more often than not, it's been blamed on his boss, Louis B. Mayer. The men despised each other and the hatred was not always cordial; there were at least two reported fistfights between superstar and mogul. On the last such occasion (the day Greta Garbo left Gilbert at the altar), Mayer reputedly told Gilbert he would ruin him even if it cost a million dollars. Some would say *The Show* represented the first step in Mayer's making good on his threat. Yet, while he may have been vindictive, would

Mayer — a shrewd businessman — have deliberately scuttled the career of a star who meant big box office for M-G-M? Or, rather, was *The Show* meant as no more than a one-shot punishment to prove to Gilbert just who was the boss? *The Big Parade*, of course, was a tough act to follow; it was a huge commercial and critical hit and remains one of the great films of the Silent Era. No doubt any kind of follow-up film would have paled in comparison. Still, putting the stars of *The Big Parade* in a modestly-budgeted, Tod Browning crook-melodrama would be comparable to casting Clark Gable and Vivien Leigh in a B-movie right after their triumph in *Gone with the Wind*.

We have seen the Turner print of *The Show* and offer the following synopsis:

A sideshow in Hungary is the scene of romantic rivalry between the barker, Cock Robin, a dancer named Salome, and a criminal known as "the Greek." Salome and Robin were once lovers but Robin — a vain, skirt-chasing scoundrel — has cast her off, and she is now the mistress of the Greek. Salome still has feelings for Robin, a situation the jealous Greek notes with displeasure.

Robin is currently romancing Lena, a naïve country girl whose father has just sold part of his flock of sheep for a hefty sum. The transaction has been noticed by "the Ferret," a pal of the Greek's. The Greek kills and robs Lena's father, but discovers too late that most of the money is being held in safekeeping by Lena.

Distraught at her father's death, Lena goes to visit Robin in his room. She gives him the money and tells him it represents only a part of the income derived from her father's flock. Robin thinks he'll be on easy street, but Salome shows up and tries to stop him from bilking the girl. Robin beats Salome, and the terrified Lena runs off.

The next day, though, it's business as usual at the Show, where the daily fare includes fake women-freaks, a deadly Gila monster, and a re-enactment of the beheading of John the Baptist. In the latter act, it is Robin who impersonates the Baptist and, of course, it's Salome who dances for his head. The Greek plans a different end to the play on this particular day. He overpowers the "executioner" and, disguised in his costume, prepares to use a real sword instead of the fake one on the neck of his rival. The deception is discovered at the crucial moment and the Greek flees. Meanwhile, Lena, accompanied by the police, turns up at the carnival. Salome tells Robin to hide himself in the attic of her apartment.

As the days pass, Robin grows restless, and his nerves are not helped by the frequent appearances of Salome's neighbor, a blind former soldier who's always asking for his son. Salome is kind to the demented old man and reads him letters from his son, who is away in the army. Eventually, Salome tells Robin the truth; the son is soon to be hanged at a nearby prison, and she is making up the letters to comfort the old soldier. The soldier comes to think that Robin is his son and has returned. Robin goes along with the deception, but the excitement gives the old man a fatal heart attack. Robin also discovers that the soldier is Salome's father. Moved by her devotion, Robin tells her he will return Lena's money and go straight.

Meanwhile the Greek, who had earlier discovered Robin's hiding place, has taken the money and replaced it with the Gila monster, which he has stolen from the Show. The unexpected arrival of the police throws off his plans, however, and both Robin and the Greek are trapped in the attic with the venomous reptile. The Greek is fatally bitten, and a policeman shoots the Gila monster.

The authorities let Robin off, and he returns to the show to be with Salome, his true love.

The movie is supposedly based on Charles Tenney Jackson's 1910 novel *The Day of Souls*. Jackson, who alternated penning boys' adventure books and steamy melodramas, is forgotten today, but was sufficiently well known in the 1920s for his name to be mentioned frequently in ads and publicity for *The Show*. Jackson's novel is set in San Francisco and, amid heady ethnic atmosphere, concentrates on the problems its central character has in dealing with a political scandal. The hero does romance a simple country girl who has inherited some money (albeit from the sale of lumber, not sheep), and he is a kind to an old blind man who doesn't know his son is dead. Other than that, nothing is taken from the book. Most of *The Show* covers the typical bases for a Browning film: savvy cons bilking their naïve marks, a tawdry sideshow setting, stolen loot, and a criminal who reforms by the last reel (and doesn't spend a day in jail). Browning is aided and abetted by his usual writing team of Waldemar Young (scenario) and Joe Farnham (a former cameraman and editor, and one of the best title writers in Hollywood; also the man who edited *Greed* down to 10 reels).

What makes *The Show* a bit different from the usual Browning film is that its hero is a real louse, a man who exploits and hurts the women who are drawn to him and cares only for himself. The typical Browning criminal/hero may be larcenous, but never is a brute; hence, we're at least prepared for the inevitable last-reel change of heart, even if it's not entirely persuasive. In the case of *The Show*, we've seen nothing to make us believe the scene where Robin throws himself on the floor and declares he doesn't deserve to live in the same world as the noble Salome. Just a scene or two before, Robin acts with revulsion at the insanity of the old, blind man and berates Salome for putting up with him. Why should the revelation that he's the young girl's father make so much difference? Unfortunately, the father/brother subplot throws whole film off-kilter.

Gilbert's "Cock Robin" is no doubt a variation on the title character in Frederick Molnar's *Liliom*, a womanizing carnival barker who slaps his wife around and becomes a petty criminal but who, in spite of everything, genuinely loves her and seeks to redeem himself in the afterlife. *Liliom* was a Broadway sensation in the 1921 production with Joseph Schildkraut (see *A Trip to Paradise*), and Gilbert had hoped that M-G-M would buy the rights to the play so he could star in a film version. It didn't happen, but *The Show* kept the Hungarian setting of *Liliom* and put Gilbert in the same barker outfit worn by Schildkraut; small consolation, no doubt.

Time noted the influence of *Liliom* on *The Show* before dismissing the latter in six words: "Good cast. Poor acting. Fair entertainment" (28 March 1927). The *Variety* reviewer thought that "something about the story suggests touches of *Merry-Go-Round* and *Liliom*" and wondered if the role would be bad for Gilbert's career (16 March 1927): "It seems to have been a mistake to cast Gilbert as a highly egotistical panderer such as he here portrays. It undoubtedly will hurt his general popularity with the women for while he is a great lover there is nothing romantic in his character, it being a sordid role of the type which tends to degrade."

Moving Picture World's reviewer did not agree: "Gilbert does fine work that will appeal to his fans even though his role is not a sympathetic one" (19 March 1927).

Reviews were mixed. *Motion Picture News*'s Laurence Reid described the film as "novel and weird but not so good" (which might serve as a summary of Tod Browning's career):

> He (Browning) has such a gift for fashioning mystery plays off the beaten path that he has built up a distinct following for them. *The Show*, however, is not in the same class as *The Unholy Three*. In that number he had us staring pop-eyed at the queer doings of the characters and enveloped them in oodles of suspense. The new film shoots wide of the mark…. It has plot but it lacks motivation and characterization [20 March 1927].

The *MPW* reviewer likewise had some reservations: "*The Show* is exceptionally tense, forceful, well constructed melodrama but its reception by the average patron will depend on whether this outweighs the sordidness of the characters and story itself, and the gruesomeness of a number of the situations."

Freudian interpreters of Browning can have a lot of fun with *The Show*. You have a lead character named "Cock" (*Cock o' the Walk* was the film's original title) who is nearly beheaded (castrated); and it doesn't take long to understand that, among the female freaks in the sideshow—a spider-woman, a mermaid, and a woman with only an upper torso—there's not one set of genitalia in the lot. One moment the pundits seem to have overlooked comes early in a film in a confrontation between the Greek and Robin. The Greek looks menacingly at his rival and opens a switchblade knife; Robin slowly unscrews his cane and pulls out a much longer stiletto. Size, apparently, *does* matter in a Browning film.

Joe Farnham's title cards are often snappy and surprising. "How's business?" Robin inquires of a glum prostitute. "You're hired to be freaks, not vampires," Salome says to the sideshow girls when they show an interest in Robin. "That's funny. Two deaths tonight — and good things always come in threes," sneers the Greek while casting an evil glance at Robin. And, most startling, Robin's reaction to the old soldier's demise: "Christ! He's dead!" That kind of expletive would not make the big screen again for decades to come.

Browning's direction also has some clever touches. A simple scene like the Ferret interrupting the Greek's card game to tell him Salome is with Robin has an ominously low-key quality to it. We don't even see the other players and much of the scene is shot with a set of stairs in the foreground. The sequence where Robin beats Salome includes an especially effective camera-angle shot from above the two characters as Robin raises his cane. Browning doesn't get all the suspense he should have out of the Greek's attempt to behead Robin, but he includes a deliciously grisly moment earlier, with the Greek imagining the scene and relishing the moment when Salome realizes that it really is her lover's head on the silver platter.

The latter scene squares with a frequent theme in Browning's films: illusion becoming reality. In *The Blackbird*, a fake cripple ends up really paralyzed by the climax; in *The Unknown*, the phony armless man actually does lose his arms, and in *Freaks*, Cleopatra, made an honorary freak, really becomes "one of us" by the ending. Browning, the cynical carny pitchman, may delight in showing how the illusions are staged in the sideshow and how the rubes are totally taken in, but — perhaps on some level — he wants to *be* one of the suckers, to really believe that the illusions could somehow be real.

The sideshow is particularly bizarre with its female freaks (the spider-lady is played by Edna Tichenor, soon to go from playing a phony freak to a phony vampire in Browning's *London After Midnight*), a disembodied hand collecting tickets, and, of course, the deadly Gila monster. The latter is played by an iguana that is no more convincing in the role than were his cousins as dinosaurs in *One Million B.C.* some years later; still, the "leapin' lizard" is effective enough at the climax. An earlier sequence where the Gila monster fatally bites a patron was perhaps influenced by a similar scene in *The Magician* (1926), where a sideshow snake exhibit turns deadly.

Renée Adorée as Salome received the best notices for *The Show*, but she seems a bit too round and wholesome to be convincing as a sideshow siren. Publicity for *The Show* made much of the fact that Adorée began her career as a dancer, but she apparently doesn't do her own dancing in the movie. *Variety* noted: "The 'blow off' for the chumps is a tabloid version of 'Salome,' which gives an excuse for a cooch dancer. In this spot Tod Browning grabbed off a double for Renée Adorée who could throw a mean wiggle. And boy, what a 'grind' she staged!"

This observation would be seem to be confirmed by the fact that "Salome" is shown almost entirely from the back during the dance sequences.

The French-born Adorée (née Jeanne de la Fonte) was the daughter of circus performers. She joined them under the big top and later recalled an act she did (at age ten) that would have made Tod Browning proud:

> I was billed as the Mysterious Madame X. Every night promptly at 11 o'clock, I would be led blindfolded into the ring. My act consisted of walking up to an aged, toothless and moth-eaten old lion who had trained to open his mouth so I could stick my head into it. This feat made the audience fairly gasp. They thought I was in imminent danger of losing my head ["How I Broke into the Movies," *Renwick* (Iowa) *Times*, 16 November 1933].

Adorée went on to bareback riding, pantomime, and (later) dancing. She was playing in a show in Brussels when the Germans invaded, and she fled to England and subsequently to America. She achieved some success in musical theater and played on Broadway twice. She had a screen test for Fox and, although not pleased with the results, went on to star for them in *The Strongest* (1920). Adorée met — and later married — Tom Moore, brother of fellow actors Matthew, Joe, and Owen, and signed with his studio, Goldwyn, and although she didn't become a big star, she worked steadily and even supported John Gilbert on a couple of occasions before their great success with *The Big Parade*.

Years later Adorée recalled being moved to tears while watching Sarah Bernhardt perform. The great lady asked the little French girl why she was crying, and Adorée responded: "I am crying because I want to be a great actress like you." "If you cry, child," replied Bernhardt, "you will never be a great actress" (*Abilene* [Texas] *Morning News*, 13 October 1933). Nonetheless, it was her weeping and very emotional farewell to Gilbert in *The Big Parade* that most moved the public. On the lighter side, the scene where Gilbert teaches her how to chew gum is equally memorable.

After *The Show*, Adorée worked again with Gilbert in *The*

Cossacks, a hokey but occasionally exciting big-budget adventure that did well. She also played in *Redemption*, one of Gilbert's string of ill-fated talkies. While working on *The Call of the Flesh* (1930) with Ramon Navarro, Adorée collapsed on the set. It turned out she had tuberculosis; she entered in a sanitarium in Arizona and spent two years there. She returned to Hollywood, and there were rumors she had recovered and was about to re-enter films, but more likely she had just come home to die among friends. She passed away just five days after her 35th birthday.

Notices for *The Show* also favored Lionel Barrymore (the Greek) and Edward Connelly (the old soldier). Barrymore goes through the entire film with an evil leer on his face; no great challenge there, but it's all the role requires. Connelly, who turns up in these pages many times, is effective enough, but his character slows the film down so much that viewers are likely to share Robin's increasing annoyance at his every appearance.

As for John Gilbert, his travails during the Sound Era have been much discussed. Perhaps, though, it was a combination of factors that brought about his decline: the end of the type of romantic melodramas that made him famous, the refusal of M-G-M to try to find vehicles suitable for his talent, Mayer's hostility, a voice that — while hardly reedy or high pitched — didn't quite match Gilbert's dramatic persona. The actor would not allow M-G-M buy out his very expensive contract, even though each succeeding film just provided one more nail in his own coffin. The last picture in his contract was the forgettable *Fast Workers* (1933), directed by none other than Tod Browning.

The Show may not have enhanced Gilbert's reputation any, but for Browning it was another in a series of increasingly *outré* crime melodramas that enabled M-G-M's public relations department to declare him the "Edgar Allan Poe of the screen." 1927 saw numerous articles and puff pieces in print about Browning the director. One claimed that, being superstitious, he believed that the whole movie would go well if the first scene was filmed without rehearsing. Another story told how he didn't believe in acting out the parts for the players:

> Browning deliberately assumes an expressionless attitude when explaining a scene. "If I do this," he says, "I can get the actor to visualize it himself; otherwise I would only inspire him to visualize the director trying to play the role" [*Salt Lake Tribune*, 30 June 1927].

Later — if some of the actors Browning worked with in the 1930s are to be believed — he extended this detachment by not offering any direction at all.

The Show played on French TV in the 1990s and in 2006 it was given a showing on Turner Classic Movies, replete with an excellent score that made the film seem better than it was. For a long time, though, *The Show* was hard to find — even to the point of erroneously being labeled as lost — but, when it resurfaced in the 1970s, not everyone was overjoyed by its discovery:

> Alas, it must be sadly admitted that while it is a good and healthy thing when any film resurfaces after years of obscurity, there are sometimes very good reasons for that obscurity and *The Show* is a case in point. It is the kind of film that tends to reinforce the opinions of the unknowing that the silent film was usually turgid, slow and overwrought. If there was ever a wise and criti-

cally astute yet neutral filmic Deity, one would hope that he would contrive to keep films like this in the depths, while bringing out plenty of Tourneurs and Borzages into the sunlight [William K. Everson: Notes for the Theodore Huff Memorial Film Society, 5 November 1970].

Still, it's hard to resist a film which ends with a scene in which the hero (seen as a severed head) and the heroine (a belly dancer) looking lovingly into each other's eyes.

— *HN*

The Silent Command

The Silent Command. Universal Film Mfg. Co./Universal, 2 June 1915, 4 reels [LOST]

CAST: Robert Leonard (*The father*); Ella Hall (*His daughter*); Harry Carter (*The doctor*); Alan Forrest (*The sweetheart*); Mark Fenton (*The coroner*)

CREDITS: *Producer* Carl Laemmle; *Director* Robert Leonard; *Scenario* Robert Leonard; *Cinematographer* Stephen S. Norton

First off, this is *not* the 1923 spy melodrama that marked Bela Lugosi's Hollywood debut; however, the Hungarian Master of the Evil Eye would have been right at home in this 1915 film that sounds a very familiar warning about the power of hypnosis to enslave the human mind.

Public interest today in hypnotism is about nil—after all, next to alien abductions, it's pretty tame stuff—but people in the 1910s were fascinated (and frightened) by this mysterious process that apparently robbed the individual of his will. The benign use of hypnotism in psychotherapy was even then well-known, but the public was more taken by its sinister undertones, best represented by Svengali's domination of Trilby in Georges Du Maurier's famous tale. "Can Hypnotism Force Us to Murder Our Friends?" asks the headline of an article from a vintage–1915 issue of the *Atlanta Constitution*, and stories about hypnotists turning their victims into mindless zombies abounded during that period. Even though many expert authorities maintained that no one could be hypnotized against his will or forced to do something she would not otherwise do in a waking state, hypnotic suggestion was blamed for everything from forced marriages to murder. Other articles contain grisly tales of hypnotized people going mad or failing to come out of a trance. (Of course, this being America, there was the expected "You can do it, too" sales pitch: Flint's School of Hypnotism — founded by Herbert Flint in Cleveland, Ohio in 1915 — offered a book entitled *Flint's Lessons in Hypnotism* which promised that its readers could learn to "cure diseases and bad habits and win and hold the affections of others"— the latter apparently illustrated by the book's cover which depicted an entranced young woman in a low-cut dress.)

Naturally, Hollywood was not going to take the high road in this matter, and sinister hypnotists in the silent era were as plentiful as mad doctors in subsequent movie decades. *The Silent Command* is typical of the lot.

The following sinister synopsis is taken from *The AFI Catalog*:

Unable to pay for the operation that cured his daughter, a man promises to surrender her to the doctor on her eighteenth birthday. Knowing that the physician wishes to make her the subject of his experiments with hypnotism, the distressed father ultimately reneges on his promise, whereupon the doctor attempts to hypnotize the girl from afar. Under his power, she descends the stairs, where, holding a dagger, she stands over her sleeping father. The next day, the girl is accused of murdering her father, but her sweetheart, a lawyer with an interest in hypnotism, believes that she is innocent and sets out to prove it. After finding a button belonging to the doctor's butler, the lawyer places the servant under his own power, learning thereby that the doctor sent his hypnotized butler to murder the old man. Her name cleared, the girl takes her sweetheart's book on hypnotism and throws it into the fire.

Perhaps it was Herbert Flint's book that was consigned to the flames.

It's not clear from the synopsis why the doctor had to use his servant in the murder if the girl was already under his power, unless we are to assume that such a sweet young thing wouldn't kill her daddy even if hypnotized. The doctor's fate is also left in doubt, but suicide was usually the way out for discomfited hypnotists (see both *The Case of Becky* and *Saint, Devil and Woman* elsewhere). One review describes the daughter's initial problem as paralysis which of course can be caused by hysteria, but that can be ruled out here since the doctor operates to restore her to health. Presumably, he is a bit like Dr. Vollin in *The Raven*: a skilled surgeon with an obsessive interest elsewhere. It would also seem that his motives for wanting the girl aren't solely scientific.

The father's deal with the doctor has something of a fairy tale quality to it and is reminiscent of other bargains struck by desperate parents in tales such as "Beauty and the Beast" and "Rumpelstiltskin." We don't know how old the girl is when her father first brings her to the doctor, but a still accompanying a review of the film shows her dressed in little-girl garb while being examined, so presumably some years elapse before the hypnotist tries to claim her.

The legal ramifications of acting under hypnotism also played a part in Augustus Thomas' 1907 play, *The Witching Hour* (twice filmed as a silent; see entries), and the Kalem three-reeler, *An Innocent Sinner*— based on an 1896 play by Lawrence Marsten (who later directed the Broadway versions of *The Monster* and *Eyes of Youth*)— was released just one month prior to *The Silent Command*. Marsten's play told of a young woman accused of murdering her fiancée, a deed actually committed by a rival for her affections, a doctor with an interest in hypnotism. The girl had experienced the murder while in a trance, but had regarded it as a dream. Ultimately, she is acquitted of the crime but is not free of the doctor's hypnotic influence until *he* is stricken with paralysis.

The Silent Command actually beat the much-publicized Wilton Lackaye/Clara Kimball Young *Trilby* to the theaters by a couple of months, but Universal's PR crew didn't hesitate a moment from doing a little publicity piggybacking: "Harry Carter's characterization of the hypnotist is strikingly reminiscent of Wilton Lackaye's famous role of Svengali in *Trilby*." Ad copy for *Command* also promised...

A creepy, thrilling story of love, hypnotism and crime that holds the spectator spellbound. Shows how the machinations of a clever but unscrupulous doctor and his piercing, soul stirring eyes work mischief to his innocent victims…. It grips more and more as it is shown on the screen. A Villainous Doctor loses his head on account of Jealousy. He had been a respected physician but an exposure came. *He was shown up as a Murderer*, made so through Hypnotism.

An effective poster for the film shows the daughter, dressed in a nightgown, standing by her bed and looking up at the bedroom curtains, through which the face of the doctor—with Mephistophelean beard and glowing eyes—glares down at her hungrily. Stars can be seen through the window and on the other side of the curtain is the worried countenance of her father.

Peter Milne of *Motion Picture News* (5 June 1915) found the film engrossing, though he realized some would question the plausibility of the theme:

> Whether or not the feature possesses the faculty of convincing its audience, or merely thrilling it—for the two properties often go alone as well as hand in hand—depends entirely on the audience itself. The picture is based on hypnotism, extreme mental suggestion, in which some persons will believe and others prefer not to. Before the former class, the picture will present a strong, convincing case and realistic story; before the latter, its realism will be lacking, but they will not fail to be highly entertained by it.

Milne also felt the film built up quite a bit of suspense and had the proper mysterious atmosphere throughout, while highly praising actor/director Robert Z. Leonard:

> Robert Leonard, who wrote and directed the subject, as well as playing the father of the girl, may be justly proud of his completed work. The settings are appropriate, the photography good, purposely dimmed in some instances. He has used close-ups effectively, and they would be even more powerful if merely a few were effaced from the film. As the father, Mr. Leonard is excellent.

Leonard was only 26 at the time, a mere seven years older than Ella Hall, who played his daughter. Leonard and Hall were one of Universal's "teams" (like Francis Ford and Grace Cunard) and were usually romantic leads, making their casting in *The Silent Command* a bit offbeat. Leonard had come to Universal in 1913 after a couple of years as a leading man at Selig; prior to that, he had done stock work in his native Colorado, had sung in the Ferris Hartman Opera Company, and had spent a season as leading man to musical-comedy star, Trixie Friganza. Once at Universal, Leonard quickly began writing and directing as well as acting; he did all three for the hit 1914 serial, *The Master Key*, and ads for *The Silent Command* reminded audiences that all the principal cast members had played in the serial.

In 1918 Leonard married dancer, Mae Murray, and directed her in a series of successful films. No matter; the tempestuous Murray divorced him in 1925 after signing with M-G-M; Leonard also ended up at M-G-M, where he spent most of his remaining career directing. "Bringing a fond light to high-class cheesecake" is how one wag described his work; some would call that an apt description in general for M-G-M in its heyday. Leonard won Academy Award nominations for directing such cheesecake as *The Divorcee* and *The Great Ziegfeld*.

As for Ella Hall in *The Silent Command*, Peter Milne found her to be "exactly the type for the daughter as she invests the role with her youthful personality that is sure to attract sympathy." Publicity for the dainty Miss Hall stressed her youthfulness and spread wholesome stories about how Ella—who was 17 when *The Master Key* began filming—lived with her mother in a Hollywood bungalow, where the two would sew dresses and hats. Hall's stage work had included a role in David Belasco's 1907 *A Grand Army Man* (with David Warfield) and a stint at understudying Mary Pickford (to whom she was often compared) in *The Warrens of Virginia*. After some rather inconsequential work at Biograph and Kinemacolor, the young actress moved to Universal where she played fairy princesses and Pollyanna clones (most notably in Philip Smalley's *Jewel*). In the late 1910s she married actor/director, Emory Johnson, and retired from Hollywood for a few years. She returned in 1921 to do *The Great Reward*—a serial directed by another Universal alumnus, Francis Ford—but her film appearances after that were few, among them *The Flying Dutchman* (see entry).

— *HN*

Singed Wings

Singed Wings. Famous Players–Lasky/Paramount Pictures, 18 December 1922, 8 reels/7,788 feet [LOST]

CAST: Bebe Daniels (*Bonita della Guerda*); Conrad Nagel (*Peter Gordon*); Adolphe Menjou (*Bliss Gordon*); Robert Brower (*Don José della Guerda*); Ernest Torrence (*Emilio, a clown*); Mabel Trunnelle (*Eve Gordon*)

CREDITS: *Presented by* Adolph Zukor; *Director* Penrhyn Stanlaws; based on the eponymous story by Katharine Newlin Burt (publication undetermined); *Adapted by* Ewart Adamson, Edfrid A. Bingham; *Cinematographer* Paul Perry

An extremely weird study in that popular sub-genre, portentous dreams, *Singed Wings* is a potpourri of the sort of roundly bizarre, potentially tragic elements that frequently went into the making of a 1920s-vintage Hollywood melodrama. This operatic monstrosity starred Bebe Daniels (of all people), said casting an appalling blunder due, in part, to the misreading of the actress's image and strength. It's not that the cosmically talented Ms. Daniels was incapable of portraying a Spanish type — she would shine as the Zorro-ish, mustachioed, cross-dressing title character of 1927's adventure romp, *Señorita*— but the lady was far more effective working with comics like Harold Lloyd or Wheeler and Woolsey than she was dodging ordnance fired by Emilio, the half-witted, tragic clown impersonated by Ernest Torrence.

The following scenario was based on a short story by Katharine Newlin Burt and is presented herewith courtesy of the Famous Players–Lasky Corp. press-book.

> Bonita della Guerda, a Spanish girl, has a vivid dream which she discusses with her grandfather, Don José. As she talks, the dream is re-enacted. It shows a lovely garden and a fairy castle. The fairies plan to make the Prince and the Princess fall in love. The Prince meets the Princess and retrieves a white rose which has fallen from her hair, kisses it and returns it to her. The King's Jester is jealous and spys [*sic*] upon the lovers. When the princess is alone he draws his bow and discharges an arrow into her breast. As she swoons, the Princess sings a strange song. The Prince, hearing it, turns his horse and starts back to the garden. There the dream ends. Don José tells Bonita that the dreams of the della Guerdas always come true.
>
> In the cabaret where Bonita is a dancer, Emilio, a half-witted clown, worships her. With his wife, Bliss Gordon comes to the Café Rosa d'Espagnol and is struck by Bonita's charm. He learns

that the white rose in her hair is a symbol of her virtue and cannot be bought. Gordon makes a wager that he will get the rose.

Gordon's wife, Eve, is miserable because she has lost her husband's love. His infatuation for [*sic*] Bonita is only one of many other, similar affairs. Eve sends for her husband's nephew, Peter Gordon, in the hope that he will be able to help her in winning back her husband's affection.

While Bonita is dancing, her rose falls from her hair and Peter Gordon, who has arrived and is in the café, picks it up, kisses it and returns it to her. Bonita and Peter both have the feeling that the same thing has happened somewhere, sometime before. Eve decides to obtain a moth costume, similar to the one worn by Bonita, and learns the Dance of the Moth, thus hoping to regain Gordon's love.

Bonita goes to Gordon's country place, determined to pay the price so that she may lift her grandfather and herself out of the toils of poverty. But at the last moment she rebels. Peter enters and Gordon attacks him, pretending to Bonita that he is a burglar. After a fierce fight, Bonita discovers that the "burglar" is Peter. He tells her that he has come to save her from his uncle. She is indignant at his interference and sends him off.

Next day, Peter learns that Bonita loves him and he goes and asks her to forgive him. A church bell rings and Bonita recalls it as the death knell of her dream. She sends him away forever. Meantime, at a house party given by Gordon, Eve, masked and dressed like Bonita, is doing the Dance of the Moth. Emilio observes that the dancer has no rose in her hair. Enraged, he shoots and kills Eve, thinking that she is Bonita and has sold herself to Gordon.

Bonita comes upon the scene and sees a man in a jester costume holding Eve's head, just as it appeared to her in her dream. She realizes that the dream was not intended for her and rushes to Don José. Emilio, thinking her dead, is alarmed, but gaining courage, forces her to dance, threatening to kill her the minute she stops. Bonita, in her desperation, chants the quaint song that she remembered from her dream. In a boat beneath the window, the despondent Peter hears. It is the Princess! He rescues Bonita. Emilio then kills himself. Bonita and Peter go to Don José for his blessing.

And Bliss Gordon — now freed of his ball and chain — is inspired to invent the concept of Club Med.

Okay, so we made that last bit up.

It might be assumed that the "wings" in the title refer to those fairy Yentas of the dream sequence. Or perhaps to the virginal Bonita (her name means *beautiful*), who is an angel in all, save feathered appendages, and whose brief movement toward the Dark Side (then headquartered in Bliss Gordon's "country place") results in her getting slightly burned, metaphorically speaking. If truth be told, the wings that are singed (again metaphorically, unless old Emilio overpacked his pistola with gunpowder) are those of the moth costume worn by Eve (and not, in this instance, by Bonita) in her (Eve's) pathetic attempt to win back the love of her (Eve's) husband, the miserable bastard who was going to get her rose (Bonita's; Eve's forgetting the rose is a MAJOR plot point) while, presumably, still stringing her (Eve) along.

They may not make 'em like *Singed Wings* anymore, but — back in the 1920s — they made 'em like that all the time.

It's not just the dream coming true that wins

Singed Wings inclusion herein — back then there were loads of films in which dreams came true, for any number of reasons, all of which fell neatly into line with the seven basic plots. (And, hell! If the della Guerda dreams *always* come true, couldn't have Bonita arranged — dietetically or via mesmerism or something — to dream of a pile of cash coming her way? Always with the doom and gloom...). Ditto with the fairy business; if we had a dime for every silent film that was visited at some point (here come those dreams again) by gnomes, spirits, malevolent dwarfs, magicians, elves and/or fairies (the Brits were particularly big on fairies), we'd be spending our time conferring with a broker instead of a publisher. Nay; 'tis the notion that Peter and Bonita have somehow, somewhere done all this before that rings the bell. Even though the plot description brings up this "prior lives" business en passant, it must be noted that this smacks of reincarnation, not dreams, and we therefore have — directly in from left field — a supernatural moment.

Singed Wings was directed by Penrhyn Stanlaws, who surely never was a household name anywhere except at his mother's, wherein he was called Stanley Adamson, the name he was awarded at his christening in Dundee, Scotland, back in 1887. Stanlaws got his foot in the industry door via his talent at illustration; subsequent to his moving to the New World, he did free-lance portraits of the theatrical set for the trendier art magazines of the early 1900s. His visual sense caught the eye of Realart, Paramount and Famous Players–Lasky at the outset of the Roaring Twenties — that time of snowballing enthusiasm and gay abandon — when each studio was scrambling to find a guaranteed market share and a readily identifiable "look," and when folks with an artistic bent were granted relatively easy entrée into the world of production. Stanlaws made his way through

Bebe Daniels needn't worry; Conrad Nagel's got a good handle on her... *ummmm...* situation.

the ranks and came to helm seven features, including the Betty Compson favorite, *The Little Minister* (1921). Besides being his swan song, *Singed Wings* took home the centerpiece for its imaginatively named technicians: Penrhyn at the megaphone, of course, was aided by Ewart Adamson (a relative of the director's) and a certain Edfrid A. Bingham, both of whom were charged with making sure that Burt's original story ended up onscreen somewhere in that middle ground that lie between fetched and far-fetched.

Manning the camera for Stanlaws was the more prosaically named Paul Perry, a cinematographer who had first received screen credit for 1916's *Sweet Kitty Bellairs*. Perry's presence on the *Singed Wings* set was due to no random assignment; rather, he and Stanlaws had already worked together on four of the director's half-dozen previous features. Perry's name could be found on three dozen or so serviceable films by 1929, at which point he appears to have vanished from Hollywood only to resurface in Argentina a decade or so later. The 1917 Jack Pickford comedy-thriller, *The Ghost House*, was Perry's only other genre credit.

Bebe Daniels—a vivacious Texan with an undeniable gift for comedy—was in pictures from about 1910 (she was Dorothy in the Selig Polyscope *The Wonderful Wizard of Oz* at age nine), after having been a theatrical presence since the age of four! Her first truly steady film work came as the "love interest" for Harold Lloyd's Lonesome Luke character, and, for quite a while, Daniels and Lloyd's relationship mirrored that of their cinematic counterparts. She continued on in comic one- and two-reelers—again, opposite Lloyd—until the early 1920s, when she slid effortlessly into features. Of the 230+ films Daniels graced over the course of her 45+-year career, only *Singed Wings* nipped into the genre, just barely, and 1925's *Wild, Wild Susan* missed by a hair.

As for her leading men, please consult our coverage on *The Sorrows of Satan* (1926) for information on Adolphe Menjou, *The Brass Bottle* (1923) for more on Ernest Torrence, and *London after Midnight* (1927) for the skinny on Conrad Nagel.

Photoplay cocked an eyebrow at the picture and pronounced:

> We haven't encountered a more absurd photoplay in a year of picture going. Another variation of the simple and honest girl who dances in a wicked cafe, her noble young lover and a scoundrelly [*sic*] man about town. This time it's a Frisco cafe. Added to the complications is an idiot clown. Director Penrhyn Stanlaws saw fit to introduce a fantastic prologue that heightens the absurdity.

Harrison's Reports (16 December 1922) did some similar cocking and pronouncing:

> The interminable walking around and the slowness with which the characters arrive at the point to which they set out, fail to sustain the interest and so tire the spectator. The acting is good, well enough—that of Ernest Torrence, the clown, in particular, being a piece of art; but good acting alone is not enough to grip the interest, when the situations are overburdened with so much trivial detail. Miss Daniel's [*sic*] acting, too, is commendable, being the best piece of work she has ever done in her career.
> The introductory scenes, which comprise a dream, dreamed by the heroine, are extremely artistic; they represent days of Knighthood. But these appeal only to the esthetic senses.

One has to wonder whether the *Variety* reviewer didn't get his titles and his notes mixed up, for—in the 1 December 1922

issue—although he admitted that *Singed Wings* wasn't really a children's picture, he did think it "especially suited for children's matinees during the coming holiday period." All that sexual frustration, infidelity, insanity and murder apart, "Fred" the critic's thoughts turned to the tykes thus: "The picture is well handled in direction, especially the trick stuff in the dream episode where Stanlaws has employed the fairies and witches as aids to his story, which part will please the children."

Although a fairly major Paramount release with a popular cast, *Singed Wings* wasn't covered by *The New York Times*. In contradistinction to this critical default setting, we herewith offer instead the perceptions of Middle America as recorded in the 29 December 1922 edition of *The Lima News*, "Northwestern Ohio's Greatest Daily." After admitting that the film had been withheld by the Ohio Board of Censors [!], the *News* critic provided folk such as us with a jot of usable information and a tad of opinion:

> The production opens with an artistic and charming allegorical tale dealing with fairies and witches and things exceptionally well photographed…. Miss Daniels has one of the best roles of her career as the little Spanish miss, while Conrad Nagel, as always, gives a sincere, realistic interpretation of his role. Adolphe Menjou and Ernest Torrence are fascinating, as are Robert Brower as the old paralytic and Mabel Trunnelle as the lonely wife.

Those witches went unmentioned in the press-book, and only God knows what the "things" were.

Moving further west, toward the San Francisco which served as the setting for our movie, we arrive in Ms. Daniels' native Texas, where the 16 December 1922 *San Antonio* [Texas] *News* spells out the denouement for us: "Peter, floating to the shore in his boat, looks upward and sees the shadow of Bonita as she dances the 'dance of death.' As the shadow of Bonita vanishes, the shadow of Emilio appears, following her; his grotesque form outlined plainly against the drawn shade of the window."

Thanks to that intrepid reporter deep in the heart of Texas, we're now aware 'twas shadows that floated Peter's boat.

— *JTS*

Sinners in Silk

Sinners in Silk. Metro-Goldwyn-Mayer Corp./Metro-Goldwyn Distributing Corp., 6 reels/5750 feet, 1924 [LOST]
CAST: Adolphe Menjou (*Arthur Merrill*); Eleanor Boardman (*Penelope Stevens*); Conrad Nagel (*Brock Farley*); Jean Hersholt (*Dr. Eustace*); Hedda Hopper (*Mrs. Stevens*); Dorothy Dwan (*Rita*); Edward Connelly (*Bates*); Jerome Patrick (*Jerry Hall*); John Patrick (*Bowers*); Miss Du Pont (*Ynez*); Virginia Lee Corbin (*Flapper*); Bradley Ward (*Ted*); Frank Elliott (*Sir Donald Ramsey*); Ann Luther (*Mimi*); Peggy Elinor (*Estelle*); Eugenie Gilbert (*Chérie*); Mary Akin (*Peggy*); Estelle Clark (*Carmelita*)
CREW: *Producer* Louis B. Mayer; *Director* Hobart Henley; *Assistant Director* Frank Smity; *Continuity* Carey Wilson; *Story* Benjamin F. Glazer; *Cinematographer* John Arnold; *Art Director* Richard Day; *Film Editor* Frank Davis

Rejuvenation via the Steinach procedure? *Check.*

An aged American returning from overseas? *Check.*

Society soirees? Gossip? Flappers? *Check. Check. Check.*

If this 1924 item isn't a *Black Oxen* clone trying to cash in on the hoopla from the previous year, we don't know what is. An outline from Metro-Goldwyn Pictures press material demonstrates the connection (as well as a slightly more Faustian flavor):

> The action of *Sinners in Silk* takes place in and around New York, particularly the deck and swimming pool of an ocean liner, a country house in the exclusive Westchester district, a fashionable apartment on Park Avenue, a magnificent villa located on the roof of a downtown skyscraper.
>
> The story is of a man [Arthur Merrill] broken in health and past middle age who returns to America after an absence of twenty years. He meets on shipboard, during a festive swimming party in the ship's swimming pool, a very beautiful and a very modern young lady to whom he is attracted. He is traveling with a distinguished physician, a disciple of Dr. Steinach, the Viennese specialist, who tempts him to undergo a rejuvenation treatment which will restore his youth.
>
> "You will find your country altered since last you were here," the doctor tells him. "A new generation has been reared. Its god is jazz; its slogan speed. Love is free, free for the taking."
>
> Merrill yields to temptation, undergoes the treatment and twenty years are lifted from his life. He immediately enters the gayest set of young people and becomes the sponsor of a succession of "wild" parties. And he does not fail to get himself talked about in scandalous gossip. After a series of stirring episodes and intrigues, Merrill all but succeeds in taking the girl whom he met on shipboard and the one girl he really desires away from the young man who truly loves her.
>
> But in the end he steps aside in the young man's favor and resumes his former and milder ways of life. He has found that there is no free love, that one always must pay for love — sometimes with sacrifice, sometimes with self-respect, sometimes even with one's heart's blood.
>
> It also develops that the young man he wished to cheat of the girl is his own son, whom he had not seen since early childhood when he deserted his wife and the boy's mother. The young fellow has a letter for Merrill from his mother in which is stated that if the father thinks himself worthy, he is to acknowledge his son. This is what makes him to give up the unnatural life of gaiety.

And if the press outline did nothing to make things clearer, we can offer this terse recap from *The AFI Catalog*:

> Aging roué Arthur Merrill meets flapper Penelope Stevens on an ocean liner and decides to undergo rejuvenation surgery so that he may enjoy life again. Transformed, he attends a wild jazz party given by Penelope and persuades her to visit his apartment, but he finds that she is a "good girl" and only flirting. After he gives Penelope a scare and a lecture, her old beau, Brock Farley, enters with a letter to Arthur that reveals Brock to be his son. Arthur gladly steps aside, renounces his wild living, and returns to a simple life.

At least now we have a couple of names to play with....

Like *Black Oxen*, *Sinners in Silk* delved into the mechanics of Doctor Steinach's fountain-of-youth procedure, but only a little. As the camera does a fade-in *for eleven feet of film*, a post-op Merrill (Adolphe Menjou) is shown miraculously youthful in a hospital room while the triumphant Dr. Eustace looks in. (Since the movie itself is lost, this bit of information — and others — is gleaned from the cutting continuity.) If the onscreen procedure (as well as any attempt an explanation) seems to have been left vague, it was done purposefully; both *Oxen* and *Sinners* counted on the average 1920s moviegoer having only most tenuous of understandings with respect to rejuvenation, and so interwove essence of Steinach with a dash of "Monkey Gland" experimentation, this latter activity also being a well-chronicled phenomenon of the time. Norman Haire, in his 1925 book, *Rejuvenation*, tried to set the record straight:

> When one speaks of Rejuvenation even educated people will say, "Oh Yes, I know. Monkey Glands. The thyroid, isn't it?" And express a fear that any resulting children might exhibit and awkward proclivity for nut-cracking and tree-climbing.... Professor Eugen Steinach, of Vienna, is the most important authority in this field, and his researches have nothing to do with the transplantation of the glands of monkeys or of any other animals into human beings. He has attempted, with a considerable measure of success, to improve human health and happiness by transplantation of human sex-glands, or by stimulation of the patient's own sex-glands by means of X-radiation or by the ligature and section of a small duct.

(Dr. Steinach remained noncommittal as to whether a person's life span could actually be increased by his operation in any of its various forms; rather, his intent was to reinvigorate the aging: mentally, physically and sexually. During the 1920s and 1930s — amidst countless debates on the effectiveness of his process — the man somehow was nominated *six times* for a Nobel Prize. He never won. Today, Steinach is largely [and deservedly] forgotten and we have to admit that sifting through commentary on his bizarre pseudo-science via dated treatises like Haire's is akin to experiencing the written equivalent of *Reefer Madness*. Back then, only folks with tons of money and overactive imaginations — and the more delirious members of the Nobel Nominating Committee — paid the doctor much attention in the first place.)

Anyhow, Menjou's Merrill certainly abounds with newfound ... *ummm* ... mental and physical friskiness after undergoing the procedure and provides some spice (after all, these *were* the pre-code years) in a scene strongly suggestive of date rape. Pulling out one of the oldest tricks in the book, he invites the luscious Penelope Stevens (the girl from the ship) to a party that turns out to — that's right! — consist only of the two of them. When his quarry ultimately breaks into sobs and brandishes a knife in his direction, Merrill finally relents, but then goes all self-righteously avuncular: "The next time you use your beauty for the sheer sport of the chase, I hope you will remember this visit."

Later in life — when his natural friskiness had subsided somewhat — Adolphe Menjou occasionally claimed that his image as the screen's most elegant gentleman was one he had chosen himself back in the 1920s: "In the early days everyone was typed. Bill Hart was the big western he-man. I couldn't compete against him. Rudolph Valentino was the handsome sheik. The only type left that I could fill was the debonair habitué of the drawing room." And fill it he did.

Before his white tie and tails days, Menjou had attended Cornell University with an eye to mechanical engineering, but he found his studies less engaging than writing and directing college theatricals. After commencement, he joined a stock company, acted in *their* theatricals, and eventually ended up as a bit player in Hollywood. He worked his way up to good supporting roles in films like *The Three Musketeers* and *The Sheik* before becoming firmly established as Movieland's premier sophisticate. Along with obviously luxurious tastes, finely tailored clothes, the best champagne (and the classiest ladies), a dapper moustache and the wry smile of a man who knows the score became Menjou's trademarks, on display whether he was entering (or exiting) opera houses, first-class restaurants, stately mansions, or imperial palaces.

Sound proved no obstacle for the Pittsburgh-born Menjou (who received his Gallic moniker honestly; his father was an emigrant from France), and he even got to play against type in pictures like *The Front Page* (for which he was nominated for the Oscar) and *Little Miss Marker*. While he made his share of B-movies—he portrayed Fulton [*The Spider*] Oursler's Chief Commissioner Thatcher Colt in *Night Club Lady* and *The Circus Queen Murders*—and there *was* the occasional farrago (like 1934's *The Trumpet Blows*), overall Menjou maintained his high-class Hollywood profile.

An arch-conservative politically, Menjou testified as a friendly witness at the HUAC hearings in the 1950s, claiming he was proud to be a witch hunter if the witches were communists. He denounced Hollywood as a hotbed of communist activity and was willing to name names (Edward G. Robinson's among them) based solely on hearsay. (Menjou was hardly alone in this: Robert Taylor and John Wayne were but two of his ideological colleagues who gave similar testimony.) In addition, the actor was a member of the ultra-right John Birch Society for a while and supported Barry Goldwater's bid for the Republican presidential nomination in 1960. Ironically, one of Menjou's best later performances was in Stanley Kubrick's pacifist film, *Paths of Glory*, wherein he plays a French general who connives in the executions of three innocent soldiers. The actor died on the 29 October 1963.

A scandal-fest like *Sinners in Silk* might have been right up Hedda Hopper's alley had it occurred a decade or so later, and

in real life. Born Elda Furry in Hollidaysburg, Pennsylvania, on the 2 May 1885, the future Queen of Movie Mean became Mrs. Hopper when DeWolf (*Casey at the Bat*) Hopper took her as his fifth wife; she assumed the soubriquet "Hedda" later still. Among her first films was the 1917 *Seven Keys to Baldpate* (in which she was billed as Elda Furry); she went on to appear in more than 100 more, billed early on as "Mrs. DeWolf Hopper." It was as Hedda Hopper, though, that she played Madge Larrabee opposite John Barrymore's Sherlock Holmes in 1922, and appeared as Mrs. Chase in *Men Must Fight*, the 1933 cautionary anti-war picture with science-fiction undertones. The *Sinners in Silk* publicity campaign hyped Hopper's name a bit, but her character did little to warrant the hype, limited as she was to sending out party invitations, greeting guests, and, in general, doting over her thrill-seeking daughter, Penelope.

Hopper's claim to real fame never did take place on the big screen. In 1936, figuring she knew as much about Hollywood as the reigning gossipmonger queen (Louella Parsons), Hopper began contributing to the Tinseltown rumor mill on radio. Within a couple of years, she was challenging Parsons' supremacy on her own turf in the tabloids; the rivalry continued for quite some time. Nonetheless, acting was a profession that Hopper never quit completely and throughout the years she performed in everything from *One Frightened Night* (1935), *Dracula's Daughter* (1936) and *Tarzan's Revenge* (1938) to *Don Juan* (1926), *The Last of Mrs. Cheyney* (1929) and *Alice Adams* (1935). She was famous/notorious enough to play herself in Billy Wilder's *Sunset Boulevard* (1950). Come the mid–1950s, the Hopper mantle fell onto the shoulders of her son, William, who

quickly achieved renown as Paul Drake, the investigative aide to Raymond Burr's phenomenally successful TV mouthpiece, *Perry Mason*. On 1 February 1966, Hedda Hopper died of double pneumonia; her son died of pneumonia four years later.

Eleanor Boardman (Penelope Stevens) lived a long life (she passed on at age 93 in 1991), but her film career barely lasted a decade. After achieving nationwide recognition as Eastman Kodak's poster girl at the outset of the 1920s, Boardman graduated to motion picture film in 1922. She met King Vidor that same year (and became Mrs. Vidor in 1926) and many of her noteworthy assignments occurred working under the celebrated director's control, with *Souls for Sale* and *Three Wise Fools* (both 1923), and *The Crowd* (1928), among others. In *Tell It to the Marines* (1927), Boardman played Nurse Norma Dale, another of those loves that Lon Chaney always seemed to lose. Miss Boardman's on-screen suitor—Conrad Nagel—gets his just desserts in *London after Midnight*.

Jean Hersholt (Dr. Eustace) performed many a medical role before he called it quits. In 1936, he was acclaimed for his

In the silken chemise, Eleanor Boardman; behind the silken tongue, Adolphe Menjou, in *Sinners in Silk*.

work in the title role in *The Country Doctor*, but rights problems prohibited him from reprising that character in a sequel. Thus, in homage to fellow Dane, Hans Christian Anderson, Hersholt invented his own country practitioner: Dr. Christian. The character caught on and, between 1937 and 1954, was the subject of several films and a highly popular radio show. Hersholt's distinguished and varied career saw him in appearing in such disparate fare as *Tess of the Storm Country* (1922) with Mary Pickford, von Stroheim's *Greed* (1925), *The Mask of Fu Manchu* (1932), and Tod Browning's *Mark of the Vampire* (1935). Pertinent to our volume is his participation in *Red Lights* (1923) along with fellow *Sinners in Silk* cast member, Frank Elliott, and *Sinners in Silk* continuity writer, Carey Wilson.

Crafting the *Silk*-en storyline were two Hollywood stalwarts. The aforementioned Wilson also contributed to the excellent silent version of *Ben Hur* (1925) and M-G-M's classic *Mutiny on the Bounty* (1935) before moving up to produce the classic film noir, *The Postman Always Rings Twice* (1946). In addition, Wilson was awarded a special Oscar for his development of the immensely popular Andy Hardy series. Wilson's partner in *Silk* was writer/producer/director Benjamin F. Glazer. A founding member of the Academy of Motion Picture Arts and Sciences, Glazer brought home twice as many Oscars as did Wilson, and both were for excellence in screenwriting: *Seventh Heaven* (1927) and *Arise My Love* (1940). On the fantasy end, Glazer was involved with just about every Hollywood version ever made of Ferenc Molnar's *Liliom*, and a rundown on those can be found in our entry on *A Trip to Paradise* (1921).

For a rather formulaic effort, *Sinners in Silk* did relatively well by the reviewers.

> Although *Sinners in Silk* is snappy and jazzy, neither of those qualities is exaggerated. Their brilliance in natural and at times roams close to the border of the salacious, but never too close or across that line. Under less skillful hands than those of Director Hobart this horizon of discrimination could easily have been made to prominent or too vague … there is a naturalness about the whole feature which should put it in a class above the average of this type [Tom Waller, *Moving Picture World*, 30 August 1924].

> The entire appeal of *Sinners in Silk* may be spurious and fantastic to the last degree, but one thing about it that can be said unqualifiedly is that at no point does it really lag. The scenes have color and variety, an uncanny reality and even brilliance whenever they get going [Edwin Schallert, *Los Angeles Times*, 6 August 1924].

> When one comes to the middle of this picture it is obvious that the narrative is not what one anticipated. Nevertheless there is no denying the entertainment value of this picture, as it is equipped with lavish settings, excellent photography, novel and amusing situations, and the excellent acting of Adolphe Menjou [*The New York Times*, 8 September 1924].

Not everyone was so easily pleased, though. The 13 September 1924 *Movie Weekly* nailed it: "*Sinners in Silk* is *Black Oxen* in trousers," but acknowledged that Menjou and Boardman did make the picture entertaining "in spite of some of the incongruities." *Time* magazine, a couple of days later, opined: "*Sinners in Silk*. Modern youth again fairly amiably concerned with nothing in particular. Profitable only for a great deal of expensive scenery and Adolphe Menjou."

— *SJ/HN*

The Sins of Rosanne

The Sins of Rosanne. Famous Players–Lasky/Famous Players–Lasky Corp./Paramount Pictures, 7 November 1920, 5 reels/4862 feet, incomplete print at Library of Congress (2 reels of 5; reels 3 and 4 only)

CAST: Ethel Clayton (*Rosanne Ozanne*); Jack Holt (*Sir Dennis Harlenden*); Fontaine La Rue (*Rachel Bangat*); Mabel Van Buren (*Mrs. Ozanne*); Fred Malatesta (*Syke Ravenal*); Grace Morse (*Kitty Drummond*); C.H. Geldart (*Leonard Drummond*); Dorothy Messenger (*Precious Drummond*); James Smith (*Hlangeli*); Guy Oliver (*Hlangeli's father*)

CREDITS: *Presented by* Jesse L. Lasky; *Director* Tom Forman: *Scenario* Mary O'Connor; based on the short story "Rosanne Ozanne" by Cynthia Stockley (London, 1918); *Cinematographers* Alfred Gilks, Harry Perry

When the word "sins" is used in a film title nowadays, the default interpretation is "sex." Back in 1920, though, only God, the titular sinner, and the screenwriter knew which way the story would go, albeit even then the odds were pretty good that sex would play a major role. That being said, the bits and pieces we've scraped together on this picture don't allude even remotely to sex, so we've shifted gears to the path wherein the word "sins" raises the possibility of supernatural forces poking around in there somewhere. (Let's be honest — the movies usually tag more mundane infringements as "crimes" [*The Crimes of Dr. Hallett*] and shameful/arcane happenings as "secrets" [*Secrets of the French Police*], while the more bizarre cases of cinematic wretched behavior frequently include "horror" in their titles, no?) Anyhow, *Rosanne*'s a bit of a puzzle because we can't tell whether she was the victim of malevolent mind control, or was subject to that dual-personality disorder that was making the rounds just then, or — worst case scenario — was merely an easily misled malcontent.

Please read the following plot synopsis (reprinted from *The AFI Catalog*), which we present as Exhibit "A."

> Rosanne Ozanne, the child of a wealthy widow living in South Africa, is cured of a serious illness by Rachel Bangat, a Malay servant who returns the infant to her mother after endowing her with a love for bright stones and a passion for hating. In later years, her love for bright stones induces Rosanne to become a diamond thief. Hlangeli, a Kaffir boy, smuggles from the mines uncut stones which she exchanges for cut gems with Syke Ravenal, who is infatuated with her. When young Englishman Dennis Harlenden falls in love with Rosanne and proposes to her, she resists, still under the influence of the Malay woman, until young Hlangeli is arrested during a mission. Her enormous feelings of guilt allow Rosanne to break the spell as the old Malay woman approaches death. Entering Ravenal's room in order to return the diamonds, Rosanne is attacked by him, but Dennis arrives in time to rescue her. Freed from her sins, Rosanne and Dennis are married and sail for England.

That scenario was based on "Rosanne Ozanne" by Cynthia Stockley, one of a quartet of tales collected in the author's *Blue Aloes: Stories of South Africa*. A contemporary review of "Rosanne" classified it as "a weird tale of Malay voodoo magic, the facts of which are at least partially supported by scientific research." While we couldn't find any contemporary newspaper accounts delving into the scientific research on Malay voodoo magic, we did plow through the story, which we bowdlerize thusly:

Rosanne and Rosalie are twin daughters born to John and Sophia Ozanne. A year after the girls' birth, Rosanne falls ill with a wasting sickness. A new Malay cook, Rachel Bangat, makes an offer: "Missus sell baby to me for a farthing; baby not die." The mother is at first shocked but, after realizing the desperate situation, a bargain is struck. It is agreed that for two years, Mrs. Ozanne must stay away from the child. After that point, she may purchase her back.

Fifteen years pass. John Ozanne is fatally injured in a carriage accident. Both girls are not only wealthy from the inheritance, but attractive as well. However, the two differ in demeanor. Rosalie has "a nature as sunny as her hair" while Rosanne's "dark beauty was touched with something wild and mysterious that repelled even while it charmed." Two additional traits mark Rosanne as different: Unfortunate incidents happen to anyone offending her, and she displays an obsession with jewels—often appearing in public wearing diamonds that even the family's wealth cannot afford. This combination fares badly for Dick Gardner (who plans to marry Rosalie). After questioning how Rosanne came to be wearing such expensive jewelry, he is stricken ill.

Rosanne's gem transactions often expose her to unsavory people and places. Worse, she involves herself with stealing from the De Beers diamond compound. Aided by Hlangeli, an African worker, she sneaks near the facility and regularly retrieves small, wrapped packages though a tiny tunnel. After a meeting with Syke Ravenal—a jeweler, her co-conspirator, and fence—she liaises with Denis Harlenden. The two are in love but, realizing her own nature, she refuses to marry him.

Admonished by her mother (who suspects *something* is remiss) for her callousness concerning Dick Gardner's worsening illness, Rosanne lashes back: "It is I who have the right to reproach you for bartering me away to witchcraft...." She is jolted further when the authorities catch Hlangeli. Ravenal and Rosanne meet. The man, who has a fatherly affection for her, determines the game is up. "I *must* have diamonds," she exclaims and adds "I have given up every thing for them—everything!" Followed home by Denis, the two encounter each other. Consumed by love for him, she casts aside the jewelry she's wearing. "Long, bitter sobs shook her frame and seemed to tear their way out of her body."

Rosanne herself becomes ill. Her mother visits the Malaysian woman from years back. There she hears her former cook state: "I tell you missis. Because I love my baby so much and want her be very rich and happy, I give her two good things—*the gift of bright stones* and *the gift of hate well.*" Rachel also reveals that Rosanne's powers will go away when she passes on—predicting the event will be a mere three days hence. Recovering briefly, Rosanne returns all of the stolen goods to Ravenal. However, her condition worsens. Mrs. Ozanne recounts to Denis Harlenden the old woman's whammy and expresses her hope that the woman's death will save her daughter. "Love has already broken that spell," he says. Upon the hour of Rachel's death, a cure for Dick Gardner is announced; Rosanne is well and the memory of "dark things of the past" is removed from her mind.

If we consider the story itself as Exhibit "B," we have no choice but to admit its supernatural undertones (overtones?) and concede that, were the picture more faithful to the story, we'd be of one mind in classifying *Rosanne* as a bona fide genre entry. Unfortunately, the list of *dramatis personae* includes neither her sister, Rosalie, nor her sister's love interest, Dick Gardner, so that bit of business seems to be absent from the film. Without that flagrant display of "the gift of hate well," Rosanne's transgressions appear more along the lines of les affaires du coeur and/or felonies than sins. Still, was our heroine but a lower-shelf Trilby? (The 11 February 1921 *Reno* [Nevada] *Evening Gazette* saw Rosanne as "the most fascinating feminine Jekyll and Hyde that ever broke a man's heart," so *that* critic, at least, was watching a super-charged schizophrenic.) Or was she, as some of the film's publicity puff pieces suggested, a gal who was literally "bewitched, bothered, and bewildered"? *Harrison's Reports*—which pointblank called the five-reeler "a good picture" in its 16 October 1920 edition—declined to mention any cause/effect relationship involving Ranchel Bangat's death and attributed the inevitable happy ending instead to ... what else? "Her love for a man breaks the Malay woman's hold over her."

The incomplete print of this title held at the Library of Congress cannot give the whole story, and the challenge is to determine just which of the several story-possibilities we discussed is supported by the extant footage. Two scraps of reviews, found on www.newspaperarchive.com, are similar in construction and may be paraphrases of the studio's publicity handout, rather than the reflections of the papers' respective critics. *The Mexia* [Texas] *Evening News* held that Rosanne has "received an uncanny craving for bright stones and the gift of bringing misfortune upon those whom she dislikes" (31 May 1921). The *Logansport* [Indiana] *Pharos-Tribune* said Rosanne is "imbued by her with a passionate desire for bright stones and the strange power to cause injury to those whom she might hate" (12 April 1921).

At least we can thank the anonymous reviewer from the *Los Angeles Times*, who had both seen the movie and read Stockley's original. His/her thoughts follow:

> I remember being thrilled by the original story because a spell of words was woven around the theme, while on the screen, the bare bones of the plot look rather serial-ly.... It's a pity the story was not done with more imagination, more emphasis on the psychological side.... There are some awkwardness and ineffectiveness of direction in the scenes alternating between the girl, in her battle of renunciation of her evil ways, and the showing of the Malay nurse, on her death bed, striving to hold her power; but perhaps it was done as well as could be [24 January 1921].

And then again, perhaps it wasn't, or we wouldn't be in a quandary right now. The 17 October 1920 *Wid's* adds its attempt at comprehension, while reflecting a ho-hum reaction:

> A wildly fantastic yarn which is treated so seriously as to look quite ridiculous. It borders upon hypnotic suggestion or some queer hokus-pokus, for the actions of the heroine are guided by a snake charmer who holds a strange power over her.... Just why this story appealed to its sponsors as good screen material will be the thought of more than one spectator after he has seen the word "Finis" at the end of the concluding reel. It may be that they saw in the plot a certain dramatic element which is missing in the finished product.

And an unattributable critique holds a similar perspective: "There is very little incident—very little conflict. And a great deal of far-fetched hokum. The action centers mostly on the countenance of the players."

The title character was played by Ethel Clayton, who is vetted in our chapter on *Beyond*, as is Fontaine La Rue, who appears to have had the genre role of her lifetime in *Rosanne*. Jack Holt—whose background is considered in the essay on *All Souls' Eve*—must have uttered a resigned "Déjà vu, all over again!" when he was cast in 1934's *Black Moon*; like *Rosanne*, it is a tale of a naïve, white girl led to fanaticism by the hate-filled machinations of an older, dark-skinned woman.

If it's of any help to anyone in making up his/her mind on this one, *The AFI Catalog* lists this picture thematically under the heading "Witchcraft."

— *SJ/JTS*

Slave of Desire

Slave of Desire. Goldwyn Pictures/Goldwyn-Cosmopolitan Distributing Corp., 4 October 1923, 7 reels/6673 feet [LOST]

CAST: George Walsh (*Raphael Valentine*); Bessie Love (*Pauline Gaudin*); Carmel Myers (*Comtesse Fedora*); Wally Van (*Restignac*); Edward Connelly (*The Antiquarian*); Eulalie Jensen (*Mme. Gaudin*); Herbert Prior (*M. Gaudin*); William Orlamond (*Champrose*); Nicholas De Ruiz (*Tallifer*); William von Hardenburg (*The General*); Harmon MacGregor (*Emile*); George Periolat (*The Duke*); Harry Lorraine (*Finot*); Calvert Carter (*The Major Domo*)

CREDITS: *Presented by* Gilbert E. Gable; *Producer* Samuel Goldwyn; *Director* George D. Baker; *Scenario* Charles E. Whittaker; *Adaptation* Alice D.G. Miller; based on the novel *La peau de chagrin* by Honoré de Balzac (Paris, 1831); *Cinematographer* John Boyle

As one of history's great Yogis reportedly said, "It's like déjà-vu all over again!'"

In *Slave of Desire*, we have the second feature-length remake of *The Magic Skin* in less than ten years (see that latter title and *The Dream Cheater*, if you think we're kidding). What we haven't is a clue whether the theme's popularity was due to the magical gimmick's novelty (a welcome breath of fresh air from those Old-as-the-Sands-of-the-Desert genie-in-a-bottle pictures) … or to confusion that may have resulted from a misunderstanding of the phrase, "skin flicks" … or to the fact that, by the mid–1910s, source author Honoré de Balzac had been in the bosom of Abraham (where moth doth not corrupt nor thieves break through and steal; thus, there are no lawyers) for well over a half-century. At this late date, it matters little.

What matters is that, come 1923, they were pulling out all the stops and doing the thing up right. "They" referred to Goldwyn Pictures, the outfit founded by Samuel Goldwyn (formerly Samuel Goldfish, né Schmuel Gelbfisz) after he broke off with Jesse Lasky and Adolf Zukor; the organization he left behind there would soon reemerge as Paramount Pictures. (A year after *Slave of Desire* was released, theatrical entrepreneur Marcus Loew would buy out Metro Pictures, Goldwyn Pictures and Mayer Pictures, and Loew's resultant mega-studio would not re-emerge as Paramount Pictures.) Back to the top: Goldwyn Pictures had been named for Goldfish and his partners, Broadway producers Edgar and Archibald Selwyn; Sam had donated half of his anglicized surname, the brothers kicked in their half, and off they went. Almost *ab initio*, Goldwyn's projects—no matter where, when, or under what corporate logo—seemed a bit more polished than those of many of his competitors, and while the nouveau-mogul-cum-Polish-émigré may have achieved notoriety for his English-language malapropisms, he won respect for his vision, his commitment, and his (or, at least, his subordinates') attention to technical detail.

Thus, *Slave of Desire* would represent a coming into fruition for Balzac's by-then-familiar tale, with a top-notch B-level cast, sophisticated effects (this last, vouched for by the contemporary critical press), and first class settings and properties. There are some that might say that this was just a case of putting lipstick on a pig, as Balzac's basic blather remained essentially untouched (and may thus be consulted in our essay on *The Magic Skin*), but — rather than "Americanizing" the production further than had *The Dream Cheater* in order to reflect the zest of the Roaring Twenties—Goldwyn took the high road and "re–Frenchified" it to the point that its Tours-born author might well have gulped an overly-chilled Chardonnay with his *poisson* in his excitement over the film (had he made it to that point, of course). The result was that *Desire* was the most determinedly faithful movie version of *La peau de chagrin* ever produced, for what that was worth.

There was a decided upgrade, cast-wise, from Everett Butterfield et al. Director George D. Baker had George Walsh (Raoul's younger brother) as Raphael Valentine, Bessie (*The Lost World*) Love as Pauline, and Edward Connelly (1915's *The Devil*, himself) as the diabolical antiquarian. Of the three, only Walsh — a sturdy New Yorker active in films for a couple of decades beginning in the mid–1910s— had no genre experience apart from his jousting with the demonic skin here in *Slave of Desire*. Sexy Carmel Myers played Raphael's seductive nemesis, la comtesse Fedora, still hot to trot for her own amusement, but — this time 'round — bearing the nomenclature and title Balzac had awarded her in his novel. (In Charles Whittaker's screenplay, based on Alice D.G. Miller's translation/adaptation of the 1831 original, all the dramatis personae operated under their literary names. Characters that hadn't made the cut in *The Magic Skin*—like Pauline's father—were reintroduced for *Desire*, and with Balzac's spelling [Gaudin—not, as in 1915—

This title was *so* much more marketable to male viewers than *The Magic Skin*....

Gardin] meticulously restored. Gaudin *pere* was played by Herbert Prior, the role an undeniable demotion from that of the satanic antiques merchant he had essayed under Richard Ridgely's direction.)

Incidentally, Alice D.G. Miller (see *Red Lights*) was the daughter of celebrated novelist, poet and screenwriter, Alice Duer Miller.

Considering that *Slave of Desire* was intended to be the upscale interpretation of *La peau de chagrin*, it's odd that we were unable to find even a modestly comprehensive plot summary to present herewith. The copyright registration document is, in this case, less than one page in length and is inadequate at best. The review in the Bible of Show Business gives a bumper-sticker rendition ("the director has modernized the fantastic story of the youth who possessed the magic skin…"), and this seems to have been the rule — and not the exception — when it came to coverage of this motion picture. This may have been due to the then-familiarity with Balzac's tale, due, to no little extent, to the fact that people in those pre-reality-show-TV days used to read as a major source of pleasure. We could have consulted the *Slave of Desire* photoplay edition, but that tome consisted not of the screenplay but, rather, of Balzac's novel. Thus…

The following précis — obviously written with the critic's tongue in his cheek — is taken from *The New York Times* (11 December 1923):

> Raphael Valentin, the hero of this adventure, is played by George Walsh. Valentin is a poet whose verse finds no market. He is shown in his garret, one that looks almost as comfortable as S. L. Rothafel's office in the Capitol.
>
> Valentin's friend, Rastignac, introduces the disconsolate worshipper at the shrine of the Lasses of Parnasses to the beauteous Countess Fedora, played by Carmel Myers. The Countess, whose face and figure are notorious, lets her eyes wander lazily upon Valentin. She even recites one of Valentin's poems, which brings a sale to a publisher who a day before had rejected it. Fedora's eyes and the words coming from her fascinating lips and an invitation to appear the next afternoon, send Valentin away happy. The next day Valentin — acting on instructions from Mr. Baker — attacks the Countess's lips fast and furiously, like a cave-man. She admonishes him. Really Carmel Myers looks very pretty in these scenes, and her costumes, forgotten at the back, with wonderful lines in the skirt, cause one to forgive Valentin.
>
> But Fedora soon tires of Valentin. Her fickleness is also notorious. So Valentin saunters with his last coin to a gambling place, and, after losing, he takes a look at the Seine. A floating body deters him from taking the chilly plunge, and soon he visits an antique dealer, where he finds the Wild Ass's Skin, of which he becomes the owner. This skin grants the owner's wish, but becomes smaller each time and with its disappearance the owner's death must come. In the end Valentin unselfishly wishes that the girl he had known in the garret should be saved. This is so unselfish that he gets rid of the skin and is protected himself from the penalty of owning the skin.

Plot summaries may have been scarce, but reviews were good, albeit several of the usual suspects were as concerned that the picture did not — heaven forbid! — depict any of the titular desire as being desirable as they were that the picture might somehow still be worth seeing. The 29 December 1923 *Harrison's* reported that

> the scenarist and the director have handled the plot so well that the picture contains nothing that will prove objectionable even to a

minister of the gospel; if any, it contains a moral lesson, not in the form of a preachment, but in that of an entertainment; it shows by example that one's abandoning oneself to worldly desires has destructive consequences to health and happiness.

Sounds like a preachment to us. As for the stuff up there on the screen, *Harrison's Reports* admitted: "The plot of the picture is not exactly the same as that of the book; several changes were made. But the changes improved it; the dream idea, though ordinarily it is used to cover a multitude of sins, has in this instance been used to advantage."

The 13 December 1923 *Variety* likewise took two tacks: the first, the sermon: "The moral of the tale is that selfishness doesn't pay — a theme used quite frequently in literature and in pictures, and while it contains amoral the film is not preachy or heavy in its promulgation of its object lesson." The second, the film stuff:

> There's plenty of exciting melodrama notwithstanding the fact of the picture's highbrow antecedents and it's all handled with an efficient directorial method that makes it click…. It is a question whether the allegory that runs through the picture will be penetrated readily by the average picture patron but even if it isn't it should not materially affect their enjoyment of the film.

We're not certain what the film's "highbrow antecedents" were: was the reviewer perhaps astonished by the fact that the source material was written in French? And we're not at all sure just what the "allegory" is to which *Variety*'s "Bell" refers. Other than that, no harm, no foul.

The New York Times — being *The New York Times* — was not cowed by the brow-level of the picture's antecedents but, rather, carped about the screen treatment given those antecedents: "This version of the Balzac narrative is not uninteresting, but it could have been made much stronger if someone familiar with French and France had undertaken to do full justice to Balzac's story." Still, while the review found the actors merely "adequate" and bemoaned the liberties taken for the screen, it concluded that the film was "very entertaining."

Goldwyn Pictures went whole hog when it came to hawking *Slave of Desire*, even providing a set of stills from the film to the A.L. Burt Company for the purpose of issuing that photoplay edition of a translation of Balzac's novel. *The New York Times'* opinion of the picture's Gallic verisimilitude notwithstanding, the book's translation is a good one, with Balzac's characters' diatribes just as longwinded and convoluted in English as they are in French. The problem, as we stated above, is that a reprint of a source novel's text gives no assurance whatsoever that the scenario was to any degree faithful to it.

And, as was pretty much typical for the era, the *Slave of Desire* photoplay contains what must surely have been the most static/least exciting photographs taken on those sets or any others.

— *JTS*

The Sleep of Cyma Roget

The Sleep of Cyma [Cymba] Roget. Lejaren a'Hiller Productions/States Rights; Pioneer Film Corp., July/August 1920, 5 reels [LOST]; aka *The Devil's Angel*— distributed by States Rights; Clark-Cornelius Corp.— 3 Jan 1922

CAST: Helen Gardner (*Cyma Roget*); Templer Saxe (*Chandra Dak*); Marc Connelly (*Paul Bridere*); Peggy O'Neil (*Artist's Model*); with C.D. Williams, Lejaren a'Hiller, Albert Tovell, Jenkyns Dolive, Miss Leli Lanier, Mrs. Harry Davenport, Countess Olga Treskoff, William Anker

CREDITS: *Supervisor* Lejaren a'Hiller: *Director* Charles L. Gaskill (and/or Lejaren a'Hiller); *Story and Scenario* Charles L. Gaskill

Originally released as *The Sleep of Cymba Roget*, this obscure study in mysticism made more waves (all things being equal) when it was reissued as *The Devil's Angel* and publicized vigorously as a "romance of Bohemia." Said publicity was part of the re-titled film's States Rights distribution campaign, so it is not crystal clear whether those potential ticket-buyers in less traditional venues would have regarded "Bohemia" as that specific area of Central Europe bordered by Moravia and Hapsburg Silesia, or to the *mot français* that referred to the squalid lifestyle shared by impoverished *fin de siècle* musicians, artists, scribes, et al., that would be romanticized by novelist, Henri Murger, and then gloriously celebrated by Giacomo Puccini. Someone (somewhere) anticipated this potential thematic muck-up, and it wasn't long before the trade-magazine ads for *Devil's Angel* included clarifying prose, such as this masterpiece, which was printed in the 23 October 1920 edition of *Motion Picture News*:

> A Vivid Drama Of
> Artist Life In
> The Latin Quarter,
> Where Women's
> Conventions And
> Men's Intentions
> Are Cast To The
> Four Winds For
> The Sake of Art

The film was re-titled and re-publicized almost immediately after its initial release (as *The Sleep of Cym[b]a Roget* had proved to be underwhelming), not because it was thought necessary to emphasize the presence of struggling artists and their models and *la vie de Bohème*, but rather because it was thought necessary to de-emphasize the film's true, underlying theme — the perils of social contact with itinerant, evil hypnotists. As will become apparent to the reader who thumbs indiscriminately through these pages, silent thrillers and malevolent mesmerists went together like salt and pepper, point and counterpoint, or Guns N' Roses. Although his deportment became more circumspect (and his appearance, less operatically bizarre) as the years passed, the typical silent-movie hypnotist could rely upon well-crafted key lighting and moody orchestral cues to complement his stock-in-trade paraphernalia (among which twirling watches, swirling fingers, and/or pre–Lugosi eye-googling were *de rigueur*). Thankfully, once its villain had been thus accoutered, the production's budget usually experienced little additional strain: depicting the effects of hypnosis onscreen required nothing other than a modicum of pantomimic talent on the part of the victim. All of this was preeminently do-able, because it was all pretty much formulaic.

And therein lies the crux of the problem. Great things were expected — not only of the cinema, but from the World — what with the end of the Great War and the dawning of the new decade. Novelty for its own sake was sought in dress, in art, in attitude, and in life, itself. The old order had passed away, and

innovation was the key to the future. But nobody told the sleepy Cyma Roget. Like so many other tired clichés and conventions, movie hypnotists' roots extended back to the 19th century — to the great Georges Méliès, even to his first handful of trick films, *pour l'amour de Dieu!* — so the prospect of yet another comely young woman brought very nearly to indulging in naughty behavior was greeted with rabid apathy by novelty-seeking audiences. This led to someone having a quick look 'round the screenplay with an eye to finding something different to exploit.

Here, then, *The Devil's Angel*, by way of *The Sleep of Cym[b]a Roget*, courtesy of the American Film Institute:

> Cyma Roget, a beautiful young woman, has fallen under the influence of evil Hindu scientist Chandra Dak, who can cast her at will into a hypnotic state resembling death. Chandra Dak's power over Cyma wanes as his love for her grows, however, and one night she escapes and takes refuge in the atelier of three young and struggling Bohemian artists. During her stay at the atelier, she becomes an artist's model and forms an attachment to one of the artists, Paul Bridere, but soon Chandra Dak falls out of love with Cyma and sends her into a hypnotic coma. To all appearances dead, Cyma is interred in a vault, but Chandra Dak's death ends her coma, and she is rescued from the vault and restored to the arms of Paul.

(The preoccupation with evil Hindus did not stem from M. Méliès but, rather, came from those unlikely stories of the British Raj that were spun without surcease by retired, monocle'd-and-mustachioed Sergeant-Majors looking to cadge drinks from eager tyros at their Clubs. Exotica have always had their following, and tales of the Raj spread like wildfire.)

Anyhow, if one strove to overlook the business about the nefarious Chandra Dak and the usefulness of his ability to cast flowers of femininity into deathlike states, one wasn't left with much other than the health-challenged heroine, the pack of struggling artists, their "atelier" (a $25 word for studio or workshop), and the inevitable scent of love in the air. In short, Puccini's *La Bohème*! (One can only imagine the musical cues that accompanied the print the second time around to reinforce the so-called "Romance of Bohemia.") Even with the plethora of purposefully misleading ads that peppered the trade magazines, few moviegoers would have been lulled into believing they were watching a story of Paris, painting and passion once their fannies had settled into their seats. The revamped publicity campaign did not work its intended magic, and the resultant misfire — coupled with the usual, threadbare States Rights policies re: the striking and distribution of prints — assured that neither *The Sleep of Cyma* (or *Cymba*) *Roget* nor *The Devil's Angel* was a title that would be embraced, discussed, or even remembered by the time church let out the following Sunday.

The picture was the brainchild of two artisans. The more familiar (Ho, boy!) of the two was Charles Gaskill, a journeyman writer/director whose credentials appear to be as inconsequential as his titles (*The Breath of Araby*, *The Daring of Diana*, *The Lights of New York*) are monotonous. Even the title of Gaskill's earliest genre feature, 1914's *The Strange Story of Sylvia Grey* (see entry), seems somewhat prescient of *The Sleep of Cyma* (let's stick with Cyma, shall we?) *Roget*, although there's no record that *Sylvia*'s peculiar plot — involving an evil hypnotist yclept

Dr. Frankenstein!—was reshaped à la Verdi or Donizetti or some other Italian tunesmith in those earlier, pioneering days. The man did appear to have something of a proclivity for the genre, though: his *And a Still, Small Voice* (1918) is examined elsewhere in these pages, and two of the short films he directed — *The Cave Man* (1912) and *Miss Jekyll and the Madame Hyde* (1915) — dealt with themes that are still near and dear to our hearts. His last film credit was as scenarist on 1924's *Let Not Man Put Asunder* — a J. Stuart Blackton society melodrama that resulted in little credit for either gentleman.— and the North Carolinian left the industry shortly thereafter. Gaskill died in Los Angeles on the 9 December 1943.

The other artisan responsible for *Cyma Roget* was Lejaren a'Hiller; per the 2 October 1920 *Motion Picture News*, he was "an artist of national reputation and the originator of what is known as 'photographic illustration.'" Mr. a'Hiller appeared out of nowhere, returned thence almost immediately, and enjoyed watching his name misspelled no fewer than five times (out of six variations) during the extremely brief flurry of press coverage devoted to *Cyma Roget/The Devil's Angel*. Even today it is unclear whether a'Hiller was (a) only the picture's producer (a credit *does* survive for "Lejaren a'Hiller Productions"), (b) the picture's sole director (in addition to his/her being the producer), or (c) with Gaskill, the picture's *co*-director (in addition…). Ultimately, it matters not a whit, as the man upped and vanished (as did the picture), and our interest here is completely academic. Gaskill indubitably wrote both the original story and the scenario, probably directed it (thus, our schema below), and purposefully maneuvered his actress-wife, Helen Gardner, into the title role (no matter which title one chooses).

Miss Gardner, who haled from Binghamton, New York, made about 50 films in the course of a career that lasted about 14 years, and about 40 percent of those involved her showing up at the studio on her husband's arm. Included in that 40 percent were all of Gaskill's genre titles, plus a handful of Arabian Nights–inspired concoctions (like the 1913 *A Princess of Bagdad*) that may have incorporated a fantastic element or two. As an actress, Miss Gardner was capable, if not roundly acclaimed, and to promote *Devil's Angel* — her last film but one, as was the case with Gaskill — she agreed to tour with the States Rights "road-show." Sadly, confusion reigned once again, as the advance publicity seemed unable to decide just *what* type of picture it was selling:

> Helen Gardner, who plays the feature role in the production, will appear in person in a number of first run theatres in various parts of the country. The unique theme of *The Devil's Angel* is said to offer unlimited exploitation possibilities for the progressive exhibitor. The title, the many unusual settings, and the Oriental atmosphere should also prove an asset to the exhibitors, is the claim [*Motion Picture World*, 6 November 1920].

It would have taken a smooth-talker of the caliber of a used-car salesman or a presidential press secretary to have posited, in November 1920, that "Devil" in a movie title could in any way be viewed as being an asset. That very month of that very year, actress Fritzi Brunette was grousing (for publication in *The Oakland Tribune*) that "Devil films" were no longer even a dime-a-dozen. In the course of her diatribe — she was being interviewed about her current participation in a gem entitled *The Devil to Pay* (see entry) — Miss Brunette snarled rhetorically, "What's next? *The Devil's Goat*?"

Then, too, the "unusual settings" appear to have consisted solely of several rather pedestrian interiors and the recherché appointments of the aforementioned "atelier." Then, three, whatever "Oriental atmosphere" might have been wrung from that mélange of deviltry and essence of attic — perhaps the turban worn by Briton Templer Saxe cast its own spell over the garret wherein turned most of the plot — can't automatically have been considered either helpful to or consistent with the picture's theme, no matter whether one viewed said theme as the dangers of "Hindoo" hypnotism or the portrait of the artist as a young roué.

(We had to add further details on the proposed *The Devils' Angel* road-show, if only because they are too good to ignore. "Some of the states-right men are planning to use a Harem scene with Oriental dancing girls as an entr'acte, others are arranging for the staging of a studio scene with artist models in popular poses, while in one state it is planned to have Peggy O'Neil, who appears in the picture, to stage a prologue in person, depicting a number of famous works of art." It is presumed that Miss O'Neil — herself an artist's model before entering pictures — depicted that flock of famous artworks via "tableaux vivantes," a form of choreographed posturing that was popular in Vaudeville and Florenz Ziegfeld's extravaganzas.)

The 10 July 1920 number of *Motion Picture News* crowed about the picture's cast, which was "reported to be an unusually strong one, including Templer Saxe, C.D. Williams, Marc Connelly, Albert Tovell, Jenkyns Dolive, Miss Leli Lanier, Mrs. Davenport, Countess Olga Treskoff, and William Anker."

The *MPN*, always a bastion of precision reporting, attributed the direction to "Lejarin and Hiller." Apparently Miss O'Neil was not viewed as being one of the picture's strengths, but the name *Marc Connelly* should hop clear of that passel of forgotten impersonators like the dancing chicken in old Coney Island.

Connelly did some film acting in his youth (*Cyma Roget* was his first job in a feature) and returned to the practice in his dotage (for some TV work in the late 1960s, when he was in his late 70s). As notable as his thespic talents may have been, his literary abilities ultimately won him the better notices; the man was a veritable wellspring of good writing. Beginning in 1915 (when he was a still-damp-behind-the-ears 25-year-old), he contributed lyrics for some Broadway musicals (with *Hip! Hip! Hooray!* that inaugural effort), wrote entire books for others (like *The Amber Express* and *The '49ers*), and also penned "straight" plays (such as *Merton of the Movies* and *Beggar on Horseback*, both with George S, Kaufman, with whom Connelly frequently and famously collaborated); occasionally, he staged, produced and/or directed them, as well. In 1930, Connelly won the Pulitzer Prize for *The Green Pastures*, and damned near won the Tony Award for Best Supporting or Featured Actor in 1959 for his performance in Howard Lindsay and Russell Crouse's *Tall Story*. (The McKeesport, Pennsylvania, native had also been hand-picked by playwright Thornton Wilder to create the role of the Stage Manager in the world premiere of Wilder's classic *Our Town* in January 1944.)

Connelly didn't receive good press for *The Devil's Angel*; no one did. In fact, no one received any sort of post-release Yea or Nay, if only because the picture apparently was never reviewed. Virtually all of the press the awkwardly-handled feature chalked up had been purchased by the production company (Mr. a'Hiller's store) or the "states-right men" prior to release. All that baloney about a nation-wide road-show, for naught. Not a critical word anywhere.

Except for the 7 August 1920 *Exhibitor's Trade Review*, which found the supporting cast "unimportant," the direction "satisfactory," and the story "fantastic." "You don't believe a word of all that happens," the critic opined, "but you are interested." But he was writing of the *original* "Lejarena Hiller" photoplay, *The Sleep of Cyma Roget*.

— JTS

A Sleeping Memory

A Sleeping Memory. Metro Pictures Corp. (Special Production de Luxe)/Metro Pictures Corp., 15 October 1917, 7 reels, Eastman House, but unavailable for viewing

CAST: Emily Stevens (*Eleanore Styles Marston*); Frank Mills (*Powers Fiske*); Mario Majeroni (*Dr. Steven Trow*); Walter Horton (*Henry Johnson*); Richard Thornton (*Chadwick*); Frank Joyner (*Angus Hood*); Kate Blancke (*Mrs. Fiske*).

CREDITS: *Producer* Maxwell Krager; *Director* George D. Baker; *Assistant Director* Charles J. Hundt; *Scenario* Albert Shelby Le Vino; based on the eponymous novel by Edward Phillips Oppenheim (New York, 1902); *Cinematographer* Ray Smallwood

For most people, the books of E. Phillips Oppenheim don't conjure up memories, sleeping or otherwise, but the British novelist was extremely popular on both sides of the pond in the first quarter of the twentieth century. His thrillers made good movie material, and his 1920 spy tale, *The Great Impersonation*, was filmed three times: 1921, 1935 and 1942, with the latter two by Universal; the studio also paid Oppenheim $10,000 to write their 1915 sci-fi serial, *The Black Box*. Oppenheim cranked out two novels a year and claimed he got his inspiration by hanging out in the Bohemian section of London or the Latin Quarter in Paris and just listening to people talk. The plot of his 1902 novel, *A Sleeping Memory*, is actually set in motion by an overheard conversation, but the subsequent mishmash of weird science, romance, reincarnation and hypnotism is not likely the results of Oppenheim's eavesdropping. It's outlandish and entertaining, but veddy, veddy British; which means that even in their most passionate or furious moments, the characters retain a certain decorum in their speech. And, of course, the class system is rigorously observed.

In 1917 Metro announced that they would be doing a series of "Special Productions de Luxe" each of which would run more than five reels. All these "super-productions" would be shot at Metro's Quality Studio in New York and were intended for week-long runs. The very first of them was to be *A Sleeping Memory*, which starred famous Broadway actress, Emily Stevens, who was just finishing up on *The Slacker*. One-time journalist Albert Shelby Le Vino did the adaptation of Oppenheim's book and, except for moving the setting from London to New York, he seems to have remained very faithful to the plot.

This synopsis is taken from *Moving Picture World* (10 November 1917):

> Eleanore Marston is summoned from a house party to learn that the dishonesty of her father has been discovered and that he has committed suicide. He has left a large amount of money for her but she uses it to pay restitution to the people he has defrauded. She breaks off her engagement to Angus Hood, and finally obtains work in a department store.
>
> Chadwick, the manager, and Johnson, the floorwalker, both make love to her, Chadwick in an offensive way. Powers Fiske, a young man of wealth, overhears her say that for one day of decent living she would gladly die, and tells her to come to him whenever she makes up her mind to do so. She is discharged for repulsing the advances of Chadwick, and goes to Fiske.
>
> Fiske offers Eleanore a life of luxury if she will consent to have an operation on her brain performed which will completely deprive her of her memory. She consents. Fiske has been asked to take care of Rose Harding, the daughter of an old friend. When the news comes that her ship has been sunk by a submarine, Fiske decides to give Eleanore her name and identity, as she has lost all memory of her life as Eleanore Marston. Henry Johnson has discovered her whereabouts, and thinking Fiske has wronged her, attempts to kill him.
>
> Fiske is soon horrified to learn he has robbed Eleanore of her individuality and she has become cruel, selfish and remorseless.
>
> Dr. Trow, a friend of Fiske's, reminds him of his intention to hypnotize Eleanore and get her to tell of her previous reincarnations. Fiske refuses, and Trow hypnotizes her himself.
>
> First she remembers herself as the mate of Ulric, a Viking of old, who made war on England. She was faithless and Ulric made her kill her British lover. Her heartless nature gloried in the deed. Next, Eleanore's memory seeks out her soul, living in the body of a Borgian princess. To punish a man she has failed to ensnare, she asked the right to take his life, but later, being merciful, urged that his life be spared. The soul was progressing, learning wisdom with the ages. Next the wrongs, instead of being done by the soul, were directed against it, as shown in Eleanore's memory of herself as a persecuted woman in the days of Salem witchcraft. Trow later succeeds in getting her to join him on the brow of the cliff. Johnson has followed them and, upon Eleanore's request for help, leaps upon Trow. The men go hurtling together over the cliff, and sink to the bottom of the water, locked in each other's arms. Fiske has followed Eleanore and leads her back to the house. He appeals to a great scientist, who restores her memory by means of a second operation, and Eleanore becomes the bride of Fiske.

The movie puts more of an emphasis on reincarnation than does the book, where the heroine only experiences one of her previous lives, that of that the Viking's wife. The slow moral transformation of Eleanore through the ages is an interesting idea, unique in reincarnation films. It's not clear why the operation changes Eleanore from a serious, morally-upright young woman to a frivolous, social butterfly — especially after all that good karma — but perhaps it's a nod to Frankenstein and the dire consequences of scientists trying to play God. Still, the "new" Eleanore, while shallow, coquettish and only interested in a good time, is hardly a she-devil like the evil titular character in Hanns Heinz Ewers' later novel, *Alraune*, another tale featuring a female protagonist who is the creation of a cruel experiment.

The "science" in *A Sleeping Memory* is left very vague. In the book, Eleanore's transformation is brought about by a combination of surgery and drugs, a technique Fiske learned in India from another physician who had used it successfully to treat people made inconsolable by grief. One of the latter has lost his family to a murderous maniac on a rampage, but happily has no memory of the event as a result of the surgery. Possibly, the film showed those murders in flashback, as C.S. Sewell (of *Moving Picture World*) complained that the scene "where the Hindoo fanatic runs amuck" was too gruesome. The Indian subjects, however, don't lose their personalities because they belong to "the lower orders"[!] Presumably, Oppenheim considered them less complicated than an upper-class British lady reduced to working in a department store.

The operation itself sounds a bit like a lobotomy but such procedures didn't draw public attention until the 1930s and were, of course, irreversible. The "great scientist" who comes out of nowhere to restore Eleanore to her true self is a pretty feeble plot device, but it puts the heroine safely into the arms of her wealthy lover and restores her to her rightful place in society. Naturally, the poor floorwalker didn't have a chance and, in the book at least, is depicted as a near-psychotic stalker whose main function — other than offering another example of how irresistible the heroine is — rests in disposing of the villainous Dr. Trow, the only male character immune to Eleanore's charms. Trow brings a bit of Svengali to the mix and, unlike Fiske, is untroubled by qualms of conscience, but remains focused solely on the experiment.

Some ads for the film described it as a "startling modern drama" and "the most peculiar idea ever filmed" and asked "would you like to lose your troubles and identity at the same time? Would you care to be alive but without a soul?" Another ad described the film as depicting "good and evil women throughout the history of the world."

While star Emily Stevens and E. Phillips Oppenheim received the bulk of the publicity, occasionally other aspects of the film were mentioned; an article printed in the 22 July 1917 edition of *The Oakland Tribune* called attention to one of the sets: "The production will include a replica of the B. Altman Store in New York. The set, which shows a department or two of that big establishment on Thirty-Fourth St. and Fifth Avenue, required the entire floor space of the Metro Studio."

The climatic struggle between Trow and Johnson — sometimes mentioned in the ads where it's described as a "thrilling fight under water" — was the subject of a piece in *The Fort Wayne* [Indiana] *Daily News* (18 October 1917): "This part of the picture was taken at the Palisades Amusement Park in New Jersey. A specially-constructed glass room was sunk in the large swimming pool, the camera and the cameraman being stationed inside."

MPW's C.S. Sewell praised the performances of Emily Stevens, Frank Mills (Fiske) and Mario Majeroni (Dr. Trow); the direction of George D. Baker, and the photography of Ray Smallwood ("especially fine and there are many beautiful outdoor scenes"). Nonetheless, the reviewer did find some scenes "overdrawn" and "rather gruesome," and the Salem episode "reminiscent of *The Scarlet Letter*." The reviewer in the 19 October 1917 *Variety* found the picture "far above the average of a 'release,' including photography and direction" and was especially impressed with Frank Mills, who he thought "did some corking playing and took away most of the acting honors from Miss Stevens."

Emily Stevens was the cousin of stage legend, Minnie Maddern Fiske (ads for *A Sleeping Memory* mistakenly referred to Stevens as Mrs. Fiske's niece), but achieved Broadway fame in her own right and triumphed as *The Unchastened Woman* (twice filmed, the last time being Theda Bara's attempt at a come-back in 1925) and as the title character in two revivals of Ibsen's *Hedda Gabler*. She also played opposite George Arliss in *The Devil*, another major success, although Stevens had some nervous problems and later confessed to Tallulah Bankhead that she would get physically ill before each performance.

Stevens also had difficulty keeping her weight under control, and the extra pounds drew an ungallant comment from *Variety* in their review of her 1918 film *Kildare of the Storm*. Friends and colleagues warned her that "a fat woman can never be a great actress," so when Stevens started her next film, she began dieting and eventually got to the point where she was eating little more than spinach. She lost the weight, but had a physical and mental breakdown, and in 1920 had to be hospitalized during a successful run of *Foot Loose*. When Stevens recovered her film career — never top-flight to begin with — was over, but she still had great prestige on the stage and did some vaudeville work as well. Unfortunately, she was never able to achieve emotional equilibrium and in 1928 suffered another breakdown, which was complicated further by pneumonia. Servants found her comatose in her apartment, a bottle of sedatives nearby, and in spite of frantic efforts by her doctors to revive her, she died the next day. Early reports indicated that she taken a fatal overdose of sedatives, but an autopsy found she died of natural causes.

Like Emily Stevens, Frank Mills achieved far greater success on stage than in films and was leading man to famed actress Olga Nethersole in the early 1900s; he also played with other notable actresses, including Mrs. Fiske. Mills didn't enter the movies until he was in his forties — a bit late to be a leading man — but in the late 1910s played opposite Ethel Barrymore, Corrine Griffith and Norma Talmadge (*De Luxe Annie*, see entry). Sadly, he seems to have shared Emily Stevens' emotional instability and died in an asylum in his native Michigan in 1921.

George D. Baker was not a director of the first rank and is probably best remembered for his work with John Bunny at Vitagraph, but he turns up frequently in these pages, most notably in *Dust of Egypt*, *Buried Treasure* and *Slave of Desire*.

Rochester, New York's George Eastman House has a copy of *A Sleeping Memory* but, unfortunately, at this writing, it has not been restored and is unavailable for viewing.

— HN

Something Always Happens

Something Always Happens. Paramount Famous Lasky Corp./Paramount Pictures, 24 March 1928, 5 reels/4.792 feet [LOST]

CAST: Esther Ralston (*Diana*); Neil Hamilton (*Roderick*); Sojin (*Chang-Tzo*); Charles Sellon (*Perkins*); Roscoe Karns (*George*); Lawrence Grant (*The Earl of Rochester*); Mischa Auer (*Clark*); Noble Johnson (*The Thing*).

CREDITS: *Producers* Adolph Zukor, Jesse L. Lasky; *Director* Frank Tuttle; *Scenario* Florence Ryerson, Raymond Cannon; *Story* Frank Tuttle; *Adaptation* Florence Ryerson; *Titles* Herman J. Mankiewicz; *Cinematographer* J. Roy Hunt; *Editor* Verna Willis

"The picture that out bats *The Bat*."
— advertisement for the film

This 1928 Paramount comedy thriller was a vehicle for the beautiful Esther Ralston and featured her frequent leading man (and good friend) Neil Hamilton. Oddly enough, the publicity campaign claimed there wasn't as much as a kiss between them during the entire film, as it stressed laughs and scares rather than romance. Director Frank Tuttle, having abandoned the heavier dramas with which he began his career (see *Puritan Passions*), brought a deft and efficient touch to a number of Paramount comedies and, from all reports, did likewise with this fast paced, but highly derivative lightweight chiller.

Our synopsis comes from the film's press-book:

> An American girl, Diana Mallory, in England is driven to desperation through lack of excitement at the home of her fiancé, Roderick Lord Keswick, only son and heir of the Earl of Rochester. Roderick's father shows her the famous Rochester ruby, which will be hers after the wedding.
>
> Diana goes on strike and demands some thrills, her first coming when she learns that Chang-Tzo, notorious Chinese outlaw is after the ruby [other sources mention that he has just escaped from prison].
>
> Diana and Roderick start for London to put the ruby in a safe deposit vault. The car becomes lost in the rain and Roderick goes to the door of a deserted house to get information as to the right road.
>
> When Roderick fails to return, Diana follows him into the house. She encounters doors which open, close, and lock themselves. She sees hideous apparitions, eyes flashing in the darkness, black cats, mysterious hands and feet and chairs that move around for no reason at all.
>
> More than half the story is laid in this haunted house. Diana gets the thrills she is looking for, and then learns Roderick has arranged the whole thing for her benefit. When Roderick calls off his apparitions and ghosts, the excitement doesn't stop, for Chang-Tzo and his gang keep things humming in the same mysterious manner
>
> There are fights, battles with ghosts, and everything else an imaginative brain can conceive. When the constables arrive and take charge of the bandits, Diana agree to return to Roderick's country home, convinced that she has had enough excitement for the rest of her life.
>
> Back to evenings at the country manor, playing chess and retiring at 10 o'clock without even a good night smooch.

The synopsis doesn't mention that when Diana finds out she's been tricked, she tries to turn the tables by disguising herself as a ghost, a device used in an earlier Paramount film, *Ghost House* (1917, see entry). Actually, *Something Always Happens* seems very similar to still another Paramount mystery comedy, the 1925 *Wild, Wild Susan*, wherein thrill-starved socialite Bebe Daniels has a series of adventures with thieves in an old house and, cured of her desire for excitement, finds out it's all been engineered by her boyfriend (there are apparently no fake spooks; hence the film's omission from these pages). Of course, this idea would be trotted out still again most famously — or infamously — in 1929's *Seven Footprints to Satan* (see entry). *Something* does shake up the mix a bit by having the heroine in real danger for the closing reel.

Ads for the film prominently featured Esther Ralston, looking both lovely and terrified, and sometimes holding a gun. A drawing of a comic black cat also turns up frequently, but the publicity materials didn't hesitate to highlight the spooky stuff, as indicated by the following item (printed in the 10 May 1928 edition of *The* [Connellsville, Pennsylvania] *Daily Chronicle*):

> The result was the construction of the house, a stucco affair containing a score of secret passages; doors with springs to close them automatically, great beams from which dangled a myriad of cobwebs— the whole thing being done in an eerie manner. When spotlights were thrown about the set the effect was particularly impressing. Lights play a large part in making the picture unusually effective.

Sojin, the Silent Era's most formidable Asiatic villain (see *Chinatown Charlie* for more info), was cast as Chang-Tzo. Jim Pierce (see *Tarzan and the Golden Lion*) and Johnnie Morris were initially announced for the film, but were later dropped, with Morris's part being taken over by Roscoe Karns. (Publicity unhelpfully described Karns as playing "a crooked dummy," but he was apparently one of Neil Hamilton's co-conspirators.) Mischa Auer (who would number this among his very first film credits) also appeared as a member of the gang, but much of the menace was provided by Noble Johnson, playing a henchman called "The Thing," although presumably no relation to The Thing(s) of *The Last Moment* and *While London Sleeps*. A still from the film shows Neil Hamilton brandishing a chair at Johnson while Ralston cowers in the background. Johnson does appear quite brutish, but hardly monstrous enough to justify his tactless nickname, looking rather as he did in *Vanity* (1927), wherein he played a rapacious sea cook who tries to ravage Leatrice Joy. Nevertheless, he impressed Marquis Busby of the *Los Angeles Times*: "If little Willie doesn't behave, just tell him that Noble Johnson will get him if he doesn't watch out. Incidentally, Johnson appears in the picture briefly but he is as ruffianly looking an individual as you could hope to find. You wouldn't want him as your next-door neighbor" (28 May 1928).

Busby was also wowed by the fight between Johnson and Hamilton, describing it as a brawl that makes "the Battle of the Century look like a bridge-tea. Even Esther Ralston does a high dive from a balcony into the fray." Still, Busby did find some of the humor a bit lame: "Some of the comedy is hard to forgive, notably when Miss Ralston disguises herself as a dummy and precipitates a fight between two men by sticking them with knives. I thought the comedy studios had about exhausted that situation."

While no critic thought *Something Always Happens* was in any way comparable to *The Bat* or *The Cat and the Canary*, reviewers found the film to be good fun with likeable performers and brisk direction. *The New York Times* thought it was "cleverly produced nonsense" though at times it descended into "just nonsense" and was stronger and wittier in the opening scenes that in the closing ones. *Variety*'s "Sid" opined (on the 23 May 1928) that its principal strength was in a brief running time that was just right for the story:

> Short mystery comedy that should serve its purpose as summer fare. No particular kick to the story but they squealed and laughed here over the haunted house idea…. It moves fast, run off here under fifty minutes with enough action, thrills and giggles to hold it up. Mankiewicz's titles no panic but Tuttle has made it a compact example of competent direction.

The "Mankiewicz" is Herman J., still some years away from *Citizen Kane*.

Esther Ralston's show-biz career started when she was a toddler and had become part of her father's vaudeville act. Her dad was a physical-culture advocate as well as an actor, and Esther and her four brothers were alternating acrobatics with Shakespeare as soon as they could walk and talk. By the time Esther had entered her high school years, the family had drifted to Hollywood where Esther and her brother Clarence found work as extras on the Universal lot. In her autobiography, *Someday We'll Laugh*, Esther recalled that, while her brother was working on a Lon Chaney picture, Esther watched Tod Browning direct Priscilla Dean. Noticing the rapt expression on young Esther's face, Browning asked if she could scream, explaining that he wanted a startled reaction from Dean in her close-up and an unexpected shriek might be just the trigger. At the right moment, Browning nudged Ralston who let out a yell so piercing that "the startled cameraman let go of the crank, the star nearly jumped nearly out of her skin, and Clarence came racing in from the Chaney set to see who was raping his younger sister." Browning was happy with the result, and Ralston wrote that he gave her a nice bit in his next movie.

After laboring awhile as an extra, Ralston got a good supporting part in *Huckleberry Finn* (1920) and then starring roles in westerns and serials for Universal. The knockabout atmosphere and occasional danger that was part of such work did not appeal to Ralston, and she was relieved when a starring role in *Peter Pan* enabled her to hang up her spurs for good. Strong parts in *Beggar on Horseback* and *A Kiss for Cinderella* followed, but Ralston really didn't become a star until Frank Tuttle's spoof of beauty contests, *The American Venus* (1926). Ralston was known as "The American Venus" from that point on.

The end of the Silent Era and the resultant upheaval dislodged a number of silent film stars, and even though Ralston had had stage experience and a good voice, Paramount did not renew her expensive contract; worse still, her husband — actor George Webb — had gambled and speculated away much of her fortune. Her beautiful Hollywood mansion was put on the block, and Ralston turned to summer stock and vaudeville to support her family. A brief sojourn in England (where she made *Contraband* with Conrad Veidt) was heartening, and she signed with M-G-M back in the States; however, according to her book, Ralston rebuffed a pass made by Louis B. Mayer, and the mogul retaliated by selling her contract to Universal. After that it was Poverty Row for the American Venus, who finally left Hollywood for the business world, although she did take occasional acting gigs on radio and television.

Neil Hamilton started out as a male model, but he quickly came to prefer theater to posing in Arrow Collar shirts and, at 19 years of age, found himself playing juvenile roles to Grace George, actress-wife of stage/film impresario, William Brady. On one famous occasion, (which he claimed was instigated by Humphrey Bogart), Hamilton improvised a line as a joke onstage and was promptly slapped by George, much to the astonishment of the audience. Hamilton also worked as a movie extra for four years before D.W. Griffith first gave him a good role in *The White Rose* (1923) and then starred him in *America* and *Isn't Life Wonderful?* None of these were among Griffith's more successful pictures, though, and there was little chemistry between Hamilton and co-star Carol Dempster. Nonetheless, Hamilton went on to become a popular leading man.

In the 1930s, Hamilton freelanced and did "A" pictures like *What Price Hollywood?* and *Tarzan of the Apes* as well as good programmers, most notably *Terror Aboard* and *Silk Express*. The actor, who had lost a lot of money in the stock market crash and had made bad investments in the New York World Fair to boot, had little to fall back on financially when his career began to wane. Things got so bad that, in 1941, Hamilton was obliged to take a job as an agent's assistant for $50 a week. He turned to drink and then to thoughts of suicide, hoping his family could collect the life insurance. Years later, Hamilton wrote that he drove up to the mountains with the plan of jumping off a cliff into an abandoned quarry; however, the road to the quarry was blocked and, upon taking another route, Hamilton impulsively stopped at a building he'd never run across before. It turned out to be a club for Catholic students, run by a priest he knew slightly; Hamilton told his woes to the clergyman who advised him to make a novena. After nine days of prayer, Hamilton got in touch with a Universal agent he'd treated shabbily during his salad days, only to find that the man held no grudge and promptly got Hamilton a part. The actor's fortunes improved considerably after that, albeit it was in television he enjoyed his greatest success in his later years: his deadpan portrayal of Commissioner Gordon in the campy *Batman* TV series (1966ff) can still bring a smile in these post–*Airplane* years.

Noble Johnson was no doubt among the 1930s' most menacing movie henchman, offering as he did his loyalty and muscle to the likes of Im-ho-tep, Dr. Mirakle, Count Zaroff, and Fu Manchu, while still taking the time to serve up Fay Wray as a sacrifice to King Kong. Johnson, a boyhood chum of Lon Chaney, didn't come to the movies from summer stock, but instead had spent his formative years breaking horses, training dogs, prospecting, and boxing. According to Bill Cappello's excellent bio of Johnson in issues 199 and 200 of *Classic Images*, Johnson broke into the movies in 1914, replacing an actor who been injured doing a stunt while shooting *Eagle's Nest* for Lubin in Colorado Springs.

Johnson stunted, handled horses and did bit parts throughout the 1910s. In the 1920s his roles became more conspicuous, and he was often mentioned in the publicity releases for his movies, far more frequently than would happen in his talkie days. In the John Gilbert vehicle, *A Man's Mate*, Johnson shared co-billing with Renee Adoree in ads for the film. The son of an African American father and a white mother, Johnson's race was seldom mentioned (except in the black press, which referred to him as a "colored actor"). When he played Friday in the 1922 serial *The Adventures of Robinson Crusoe*, the following item appeared in papers like *The Decatur* [Illinois] *Review*: "All that Noble Johnson wears in his role of Friday is a breech cloth, but it takes him three hours to make up. He has to bronze his body and there are 215 pounds of it" (24 March 1922).

Occasionally, publicity alleged that Johnson was a full-blooded Sioux Indian. Ignored in all of this was his work in co-founding (with his brother) in 1916 the Lincoln Motion Picture Company, a studio which aimed its movies — produced without typical Hollywood stereotypes — at black audiences. Running the studio proved to be an uphill battle, and Johnson resigned in 1920; according to Cappello's article, Universal — which not only had Johnson under contract, but also was cognizant of the competition Lincoln's movies gave to Universal's product in black neighborhoods — pressured him to give up the company. Lincoln folded shortly thereafter. Nonetheless, Johnson may have had a hand in making the 1922 western, *Tracks*, which was described in the press as a "Noble Johnson production."

While he played his share of brutes and villains in the 1920s, Johnson occasionally had a sympathetic role. In *Topsy and Eva* (1927), the further adventures of characters from *Uncle Tom's Cabin*, Johnson played kindly Uncle Tom. It may be worth noting in passing that the film contains a scene wherein Topsy hides out in a graveyard and is startled by "ghosts" who prove to be runaway slaves.

After playing numerous roles in the Sound Era, Johnson abandoned film for real estate in 1950. Shortly before he died in 1978, he destroyed all his movie memorabilia.

— HN

A Son of Satan

A Son of Satan. Micheaux Film Corp., 18 Sep 1924 (NY State license application), 6000 feet; listed variously as 6, 7, 8 reels [LOST]

CAST: Andrew S. Bishop, Lawrence Chenault, Emmet Anthony, Edna Morton, Monte Hawley, Shingzie Howard, Ida Anderson, E.G. Tatum, Dink Stewart, W.B.F. Crowell, Olivia Sewall, Mildred Smallwood, Blanche Thompson, Margaret Brown, Professor Hosay

CREDITS: *Producer and Director* Oscar Micheaux; *Scenario by* Oscar Micheaux, based on his original story, "The Ghost of Tolston's Manor," publication unverified

Oscar Micheaux, the pioneer black filmmaker who finally received his own star on Hollywood Boulevard in 1987 (some 35 years after his death), produced (arguably) a total of 26 silent motion pictures. Only three are known to exist: *Within Our Gates* and *The Symbol of the Unconquered* (both 1920), and *Body and Soul* (1925). While this may seem like a poor survival rate, it's miraculous that anything of Micheaux's silent output (or of that of any of his African American contemporaries) has made it down through the years. First off, *very* few prints were struck. "All-Colored" films may have received wide distribution in the South, but apart from large cities with healthy black population centers, their availability was nearly non-existent in the North. It would probably be fair to posit that more moviegoers in Hispanic countries saw Micheaux's work than did their counterparts north of the Mason-Dixon Line.

In addition to their receiving dreadful distribution, the prints themselves were subject to on-site editing and local censorship. As per *Oscar Micheaux and His Circle*:

> In many cases, a given film varied substantially in length and meaning as the result of censorship directives or anticipated problems. Micheaux sometimes submitted the same film to different censorship boards in different lengths. Thus, New York censors saw a 10,000-foot version of Birthright, while two months later those in Chicago saw one that was only 8,000 feet in length [p. 230].

Such practices did not augur well for preservation of the excised footage, and should one of those 23 now-missing features come

to light at some point, it would probably be safe to bet that it would fall short, footage-wise, of the length it had enjoyed when first released.

Shot under the working title, *The Ghost of Tolston's Manor*, *A Son of Satan* is one of those missing Micheaux titles and one that *probably* merits inclusion in this volume. There is no coherent plot synopsis out there (that we've been able to locate, at any rate), and the sparse commentary on the film makes it difficult to determine the extent to which there was a "son of Satan" in the popular, genre-oriented sense. The AFI's "plot summary," taken from the New York State Archives, is as follows:

> Depiction of the experiences of an ordinary black person going to a haunted house to stay all night as the result of an argument. "This picture is filled with scenes of drinking, arousing and shows masked men becoming intoxicated. It shows the playing of crap for money, a man [Captain Tolston] killing his wife by choking her, the killing of the leader of the hooded organization and the killing of a cat by throwing a stone at it."

Contemporary newspapers and flyers — as quoted in *Oscar Micheaux and His Circle* and elsewhere — add little to the plot description, although the Baltimore *Afro-American* described the picture as "a hair-raising story of adventure in a haunted house, where rattling chains and walking ghosts are as common as parrots and puppies" (19 June 1926).

A disturbing element in the story, though, may be found in the opinion released by the Virginia State Board of Censors, which rejected the film as being inflammatory: "The central figure in the plot is a mulatto whose villainies justify the significant title of the photoplay. By implication at least the audience is led to believe that the criminal tendencies of the man are inherited from his white forefathers." (*Oscar Micheaux and His Circle*, p. 252) If this interpretation was on the money, the whole shebang is an entirely different kettle of fish altogether and while it would be hard to reconcile it with the horror-hijinx promised by the Maryland paper, it would jive more with the scant plot details provided by the AFI. In light of those notes, that phrase, "the leader of *the* hooded organization" (emphasis ours), takes on another, more ominous meaning.

It's not possible to ascertain just how that "adventure in a haunted house" melded with the series of outrages committed due to the title character's racial purity being diluted and/or tainted by white blood. It should be noted, though, that Micheaux did not present the behavior of other of the African American characters in the photoplay — including those who could not lay the blame for said behavior on their mixed heritage — in a wholly favorable light, either. As is stated in the AFI notations:

> Critic D. Ireland Thomas, writing in the African American newspaper *ChiDef*, commented concerning this film, "Some may not like the production because it shows up some of our Race in their true colors. They might also protest against the language used…. I must admit that it is true to nature, yes, I guess, too true. We have got to hand it to Oscar Micheaux when it comes to giving us the real stuff."

Without the film, we cannot continue. Nevertheless, without this brief commentary, we cannot claim comprehensiveness in our work.

— JTS

The Sorrows of Satan

The Sorrows of Satan. Famous Players–Lasky/Paramount Pictures, 12 October 1926 (New York premiere),* 5 February 1927, 9 reels/8691 feet [available]

CAST: Adolphe Menjou (*Prince Lucio Ramirez*); Carol Dempster (*Mavis Clare*); Ricardo Cortez (*Geoffrey Tempest*); Lya de Putti (*Princess Olga*); Ivan Lebedeff (*Amiel*); Marcia Harris (*The Landlady*); Lawrence D'Orsay (*Lord Elton*); Nellie Savage (*Dancing Girl*); Dorothy Hughes (*Mavis' chum*); with Josephine Dunn, Dorothy Nourse, Jeanne Morgan, Claude Brooke, Wilfred Lucas, Eddie Dunn, Owen Nares

CREDITS: *Producers* Adolph Zukor, Jesse L. Lasky; *Director* D.W. Griffith; *Screenplay* Forrest Halsey; based on the novel *The Sorrows of Satan or, The Strange Experience of One Geoffrey Tempest, Million-aire* by Marie Corelli, (London, Methuen, 1895); *Adaptation* John Russell, George Hull; *Titles* Julian Johnson; *Cinematographers* Harry Fischbeck, Arthur De Tita; *Art Director* Charles Kirk; *Miniatures* Fred Waller, Jr; *Film Editor* Julius Johnson; *Music* Hugo Riesenfeld

In a sublime moment in the otherwise ridiculous Richard Burton *Dr. Faustus* (1967), there is a close-up of Mephistopheles weeping as Faustus is dragged down to hell. Marie Corelli's 1895 novel *The Sorrows of Satan* likewise aims at depicting a regretful Lucifer who would rather serve in heaven than reign in hell but, instead of a teardrop, Corelli uses a river of overheated prose and florid speeches to get the point across. D.W. Griffith's film version is wide of the mark thematically and is far from the Master's best work, but it is certainly the most effective of his few forays into horror/fantasy.

Corelli's novel, subtitled *The Strange Experience of One Geoffrey Tempest, Millionaire*, tells of an impoverished London writer who is bitter about life in general and the literary establishment in particular. The writer—Geoffrey Tempest, of course—unexpectedly inherits a fortune and with it comes the patronage of the mysterious Prince Lucio Ramirez. The Prince, who is forever philosophizing about society and religion, tells a skeptical Tempest the legend that Satan gets to spend one hour at the gates of paradise for every soul who rejects the temptation that he is duty bound to offer. Lucio introduces the nouveau millionaire to the decadent British upper class, among whom is the wanton Lady Sybil (corrupted by reading too much Swinburne!) whose father is eager to marry her off for financial gain. Tempest takes the bait and weds Lady Sybil, but she later commits suicide. The newly-minted widower then accompanies Lucio on a yacht trip to Egypt that turns into a phantasmagorical journey to the Underworld, where he sees sights that would make even the most resolute atheist give pause. As the ship founders in a storm, Tempest understandably repents when Lucio reveals himself as Lucifer. Rescued (although the ship sinks and Lucifer rises to the skies for his 60 minutes of respite), Tempest returns to London determined to marry Mavis Clare, the pure-of-heart novelist who had never given in to the Prince's wiles. While in London he spots Lucio hobnobbing with politicians and Cabinet ministers.

Mavis Clare is a none-too-subtle version of Marie Corelli

(the shared initials give it away), who is depicted as being wildly popular with the public, but scorned by the critics. Corelli was indeed one of the most widely read writers of her day, her books usually selling 100,000 copies in spite of many critical barbs; commenting on *Sorrows* from his jail cell, Oscar Wilde wrote that "from the way she writes, *she* ought to be here."

Naturally a stage version of such a best seller was a certainty and, in late 1896, Herbert Woodgate and Paul Berton approached Marie Corelli about just such a project. Initially, Corelli was enthusiastic and wrote three acts to be submitted to the great actor, Herbert Beerbohm Tree (a sensation as Svengali in the London stage version of *Trilby*). Nonetheless, Tree was apparently not interested and Woodgate and Berton, having formed a syndicate to produce the play, came up with their own adaptation (one account of the story says it was *this* version that Tree had rejected). Corelli was not happy, as her comments in the 15 January 1897 *Bristol Time and Mirror* indicate:

> I am perfectly indifferent as to whether the piece is ever produced on the stage or not. It does not interest me in the least as there are many things in the dramatic version I do not like; but I have no time to bother about it as I am more than fully occupied with other work; besides men always think they know better than women even if a woman should happen be the author of the very idea in which they "see capital."

Though Corelli had withdrawn her imprimatur, Woodgate and Berton were still allowed to advertise the play as being based on her book. While their effort received mixed notices, it appears to have amused George Bernard Shaw, who found the story derivative of *The Flying Dutchman*. More to the point, Shaw was a bit perplexed by the climax wherein Tempest drowns and Satan ascends to heaven wearing a suit of armor: "It seems hard that Geoffrey Tempest should be left in the cold water; but the spectacle of Satan ascending in the fifteenth century splendor, with his arms around a gentleman in shirt and trousers, evidently would not do."

Ultimately, the play did not do well, but that did not prevent numerous unauthorized stage versions popping up all over the United Kingdom. Because Corelli had initially failed to follow proper copyright procedures to protect her book from such presumptuous adaptations (a few of which had combined *Sorrows* with other literary sources), she was obliged to take legal steps to try to squelch these productions. And not just in Britain, either. In December 1898, after numerous delays, a stage version of *Sorrows* opened on Broadway; while Corelli's name was used in the advertising, the dramatist was not credited so this was no doubt another pirated production. *The New York Times'* reviewer (25 December 1898) dismissed it as "a crudely made, extravagant and violent sort of thing" that would have little appeal to the cultivated theatergoer. Still, the critic admitted that a few set pieces were impressive, especially the elaborate garden party (a bizarre highlight of the book as well) in which demons mingle with London society:

> It is mounted gorgeously and a picture of a weird, fantastical garden fete, with showy electrical effects, introducing a pan-

---

*Apparently the film was previewed in Middletown, New York, from 31 July until 2 August, 1926, highly unusual to say the least. The ads in *The Daily Times Press* also promised personal appearances by D.W. Griffith and all members of the cast. Clearly this was not the final cut, and there's no indication of what the audience reaction was or if it resulted in further editing.

tomimic dance, in which the dancer, a blonde Gaiety girl, fascinates a bronze statue, warms it to life and disappears clasped in its arms into a pit from which flames presently issue, will surely be much talked off.

Mounted gorgeously or not, the production had financial woes and, two weeks into its scheduled three-week run, the show abruptly closed with sheriffs carting away costumes and electrical equipment, and an embarrassed theater manager trying to explain it all to ticketholders who had arrived for the evening performance

Corelli was outraged to discover that several of these unofficial stage adaptations, for which she received no royalties, were also being sold to different film companies. According to Theresa Ransom's *The Mysterious Miss Marie Corelli*, Britain's Dreadnought Films actually made a film version of *Sorrows* in 1911, but Corelli — having caught wind of it — refused to allow the film to be released without her approval. The quirky authoress, who looked upon movies as being akin to cave drawings, was appalled when she saw it: "The 'film' is simply *awful*! I could not see it through and the man who came with it was fully aware of its inadequacy and said so. It is the most vulgar and commonplace travesty of my work and not for pounds would I 'pass' it."

Apparently this was the only showing, and the 1911 film has disappeared from history, credits and all; intriguingly, the British Film Institute maintains that the Dreadnought Film Company did not become an active corporate entity until 1914. Ransom's claim that Dreadnought tried again in 1916 (either with a new version of *Sorrows* or a revamping of the old one) seems to be an instance of the biographer's muddling her facts; she may well be confusing Dreadnought's efforts with those of producer G.B. Samuelson. The latter did indeed make a film version of *Sorrows* in 1917, but there's no record of how Corelli reacted to it; since it was properly released, she apparently didn't hinder it. Gladys Cooper played Lady Sybil (according to some sources, she was made the main character) and later went on record saying that she had despised the movie and hated making it. With Samuelson's *Sorrows* yet another lost film, we shall never know whether it deserved her condemnation.

Other films — while not direct adaptations — could claim some inspiration from *Sorrows*. In 1912, Italy's Ambrosio Films released *Satana*, a five-reel epic (supposedly costing $200,000) depicting the fall of Satan and his numerous attempts to lead humanity astray, starting in the Garden of Eden and ending in modern times (wherein he appears as an elegant gentleman). The film was released the following year in the United States under the title *Satan or the Drama of Humanity* and — according to a description in an article printed in the 17 May 1913 edition of *The Mansfield* [Ohio] *News*— it was based on several sources: "They have given the pictures a decidedly literary flavor by drawing heavily on material from Milton's *Paradise Lost*, Klopstok's *Messiah*, Daudet's *Letters from My Mill*, and by the most recent popular play, *The Devil*, and Marie Corelli's *Sorrows of Satan*."

Carl Theodore Dreyer's Satan in the Danish master's 1921 film, *Leaves from Satan's Book*, likewise leaves a trail of cloven hoof-prints through the centuries, but although the movie was supposedly taken from a Marie Corelli novel (that Dreyer left unnamed), it has little in common with *The Sorrows of Satan*.

None of this discouraged Famous Players–Lasky from trying to do their own cinematic version of the novel and from offering Corelli $30,000 for the privilege. In the late 1910s, negotiations with Corelli were duly reported in the press and it was announced that Robert Warwick would star; however, in August 1919 it was reported that the film would be shot at the new Lasky studio in London, with Albert Kaufman directing an all–British cast. That proved premature, as author and studio could not come to terms. (Quite possibly, Corelli wanted to write the script herself.) Although the project collapsed, it did mark Alfred Hitchcock's entrance into film; answering an ad, he went to the studio with some title cards he had designed for the proposed film and the producers were impressed enough to keep him on

Corelli died in 1924 and her estate, no doubt in a hurry to cash in on her fading fame, was far more eager than the prickly authoress to strike a deal with Paramount (the banner for Famous Players–Lasky and headed by Adolf Zukor). Cecil B. De Mille was initially assigned to direct, but he was just about to

Fanamet (German/USA film co–op) original-release souvenir card.

board a boat to England to finalize the deal and scout locations when Paramount — with whom he'd quarreling for awhile — terminated his contract.

Next up at the plate was D.W. Griffith. Even though Griffith had not had a solid box office hit for several years, he was still the world's most famous director and his signing at Paramount in 1925 was given considerable fanfare. Griffith did two routine features, but Paramount proclaimed that his third one, *The Sorrows of Satan*, would be a big-budget spectacle along the lines of *Birth of a Nation* and *Intolerance*. Early publicity for the film (as reported in the 27 December 1925 issue of the *Sioux City* [Iowa] *Journal*) also promised it would be true to the novel.

> It may require four to six months to make the picture. A magnificent country house in the Shakespeare country similar to the one described by Miss Corelli is being sought; tropical island locations have already been examined; agents have visited caves in Virginia to study their pictorial possibilities and there has been an engineering estimate made of the possibility of having a yacht pass between two splitting icebergs as described in the closing chapters of the book.

Almost immediately, Paramount began trying to pare down the budget and Griffith butted heads with the studio bean-counters. Concessions were made, but location shooting in England fell by the wayside and the film was shot at the Astoria Studio on Long Island. Later, it was argued that contemporary London looked too different from London of the 1890s, a feeble excuse at best, given that the film seems to be set in the 1920s anyway! Next to be axed was the novel's climax, thus eliminating the need for tropical islands, yachts and icebergs. Instead, the hero is pursued through the London streets by Lucifer's shadow, a highly effective sequence but one that is far from the macabre grandiosity of the novel. When the smoke (and fire and brimstone) finally cleared, what *did* end up on the screen downplayed the sympathy for the devil, in essence the only original element to be found in Corelli's take on the Faust legend. Perhaps this restructuring reflected Griffith's reputed distaste for her book. Unfortunately, what he offered in its place — supernatural trappings aside — was just the old chestnut about a guy who lets success go to his head and rejects his loving sweetheart for a vamp, but sees the error of his ways and returns to the faithful lass who has never stopped adoring him.

Synopsis based on a viewing of the film:

> A prologue shows Lucifer's banishment after his failed attempt to wrest heaven from God. The devil is promised one hour at heaven's doorway for each soul who resists his overtures.
>
> The story proper begins with two impoverished writers, Geoffrey Tempest and Mavis Clare, struggling to survive in a cold, miserable boarding house. They turn to each other for love and companionship and, after spending the night together, decide to get married. Geoffrey then discovers he has lost his low-paying job as a book reviewer. Back in his room, Geoffrey denounces God and exclaims that he would gladly sell his soul for money. Shortly after, the mysterious Prince Lucio arrives telling him that he has inherited a fortune from an uncle he didn't know existed.
>
> Lucio easily leads Geoffrey away from Mavis and introduces him to the swanky fleshpots of London society. Tempest falls in love with the decadent Princess Olga who is actually infatuated with Lucio. However, Olga agrees to marry Geoffrey so she can stay close to his charming friend, who is universally admired by the rich and powerful. Meanwhile, Mavis still pines for Geoffrey and has no luck selling her stories. She meets Lucio at a party for

artists and rejects his offer of literary fame if she will play up to an elderly publisher who admires her. The Prince seems glad of her refusal. Mavis later falls ill.

> Geoffrey's marriage to Olga proves a disaster and he finds himself thinking of Mavis. He catches Olga throwing herself at Lucio who coldly refuses her. Olga then kills herself, causing Tempest to again vent his anger at God. The Prince then assumes his true appearance as a winged demon. The horrified Tempest flees through the streets pursued by Lucio's monstrous shadow. Tempest rushes to Mavis' sickbed and she comforts him and recites the Lord's Prayer. The hellish figure once again becomes the Prince who quietly withdraws into the darkness. "See?" Mavis tells Geoffrey. "There's nothing there."

The finale is a bit reminiscent of *Nosferatu* with the monster thwarted by the heroine's purity of heart.

Though unimpressed by Corelli's novel and no doubt frustrated by having to spar with Paramount over the budget, Griffith threw himself into the production with his customary thoroughness and attention to detail. He worked with writers John Russell and Forrest Halsey to produce a 30-page synopsis of what would be filmed and then began concentrating on sets, casting and costuming. As usual, Griffith worked without a script but required exhaustive rehearsing, a technique he discussed while describing what he looked for in an actor: "An artist must have inveterate perseverance. He or she must have the patience to go over and over the same scene and action time after time until it is perfect and human. I do no doubt but every sequence in *The Sorrows of Satan* will be rehearsed at least one hundred times" (*The* [Massillon, Ohio] *Evening Independent*, 13 April 1926).

One actor who did not think much of Griffith's methods was Adolphe Menjou, who was cast as Lucio. In the book, the Prince is young, tall and strikingly handsome, and early press on the film claimed that was the "type" the producers were looking for. This was hardly a description of the short but dapper Menjou, who had become famous for playing suave cads and cynical men of the world. The actor — also frustrated by the lack of a script and "interminable hours" spent rehearsing and tinkering with "very dull and uninteresting scenes" — predicted the film would be "The Sorrows of Zukor" by the time it was released.

Even more appalling to Menjou was his having to appear in a traditional devil costume, complete with wings and horns, for an elaborate special-effects scene. In his autobiography *It Took Nine Tailors*, he stated that Griffith wanted the demon Lucifer to fly down to earth and transform into Lucio for his first appearance during a garden party. (In the film, the garden party scene occurs much later and thus the actor's recollections may have been a little confused.) Menjou, sometimes billed as the "King of Sophistication," did not feel very debonair dangling from piano wires for four days — flapping a tail rather than wearing tails — while the sequence was being shot. Based on what a friend in the editing department told him, Menjou wrote the following about how the scene looked: "But when it was finally assembled in the cutting room, all the supernatural stuff was out. For when the sky was supposed to open up and the devil come winging down to earth, it just looked phony and ludicrous. And when I was supposed to walk through doors and stone walls, the trick photography was not in the least convincing."

Less spectacular, but still original and eerie, is Lucio's actual entrance in the film; the viewer see him within a huge shadow that retreats as he walks toward the camera. It was, in the words of *Variety*, "a weird effect that made 'em all sit up."

Publicity at the time (as published in the 20 June 1926 *The Lincoln* [Nebraska] *Evening Star*) also described another elaborate sequence involving Lucifer:

> Fred Waller, the camera expert, was responsible for the event. He had to photograph the figure of Satan falling as a tiny figure out of Paradise down through space, increasing to enormous proportions as he falls and splashing right into Hades. The camera was placed on a truck that moved forward on a long track to create the effect of the figure's increase in size and the figure dropped in a slanting line across a large white drop.

Nothing like this can be found in extant copies of *The Sorrows of Satan*, though judging from the praise the prologue received from some critics and several references to scenes of heaven/hell, such a sequence must have at least made it to the premiere. The prologue was the last part of the film to be shot and, in preparation, the studio advertised for non-professionals to play the angels, with Fred Waller demanding the following specific requirements: "All candidates should be six feet tall or over, with even features and as physically perfect as possible. Complexion, age, nationality or previous servitude do [*sic*] not matter." The extras who earned their wings were Francis Maran (playing the archangel Michael), Carl Morton (champion spring board jumper), Ramon Racomar (sculptor), Joe Gluck (manager of a physical-culture school), Albert Kirsch (real estate salesman), Tom Mallinson (Broadway song-plugger) and Ernest Daniels (prize fighter). These gentlemen presumably played the good angels; there *was* no want ad for the bad ones.

Originally, famous scenic designer Norman Bel Geddes was to have created the backgrounds for the prologue, but according to the *Los Angeles Times* on the 24 July 1926, the outspoken Bel Geddes was not happy with the scene and left the production: "His withdrawal from *Sorrows of Satan* was caused by caused by what is euphemistically termed 'differences.' Fred Waller, in charge of trick photography, will be given full credit on the screen for the heaven and hell sequences." Since these sequences were entirely reshot, it's not clear how much — if any — of Bel Geddes' work remains. What's left of the prologue in extant prints of the film is brief and scarcely impressive, especially when compared to similar scenes in F.W. Murnau's *Faust*.

It wasn't just the prologue, though, that proved problematic. Paramount was displeased with the film and Griffith was doing retakes as late as September 1926, a process interrupted by his having to appear in court in a suit against Al Jolson (see entry on *One Exciting Night*). The studio finally took the picture out of Griffith's hands and cuts were being made right up to its New York premiere in October. Some of the supporting characters had their scenes trimmed or were eliminated entirely. Also, almost all of the pre-release publicity about Lya de Putti (Olga) refers to her character as Lady Sybil, making one speculate that the change in nationality was largely a last minute thing achieved through the magic of title cards. This is reinforced by Olga's companion being named Lord Elton (Sybil's father in the book). Possibly, the notion of a father pimping off his daughter

was a bit too distasteful or perhaps de Putti's exotic (and unbecoming) make-up was deemed too outré for a British lady, even for one addicted to decadent literature.

Critics found some merit in the film but thought it uneven and slowly paced. Robert Lusk's review in the 17 November 1926 *Los Angeles Times*— under the headline "*Sorrows* Only Half and Half"— was typical: "The picture is a strange combination of the good and evil in Griffith's equipment as a director. There are moments of exquisite beauty in composition and lighting such as could only come from Griffith's imagination, but on the other hand there are stretches of unrelieved dullness. The story, in fact, is largely boresome."

The Oakland [California] *Tribune*'s Quinn Martin was one of a number of reviewers who, whatever their reservations about the film, felt its sexual content would be a good box-office draw: "The picture will be profitable since in it there are three orgies, large restaurants and a generous sprinkling of sex and near sex." Gene Cohn of the NEA wire service found much to praise in Harry Fischbeck's superb camerawork, but overall found the film a mixed bag and seriously flawed: "Griffith is such an elastic fellow. He supplies so many brilliant touches and, on the other hands, such mindless drivel. He underdoes so little and overdoes

Adolphe Menjou as the Prince of Darkness. The portrait suggests something of the underlying sadness proffered by the film's title, *The Sorrows of Satan*.

so much He can be keen and yet so stilted…. The first thing this picture needs is a ruthless slasher who will deal rudely with interminable close-ups, asides and drawn out duets and trios" (*The* [Frederick, Maryland] *Daily News*, 20 November 1926).

Variety (20 October 1926) was likewise enthusiastic about Fischbeck's camerawork: "And yet Harry Fischbeck's work at the camera dominates the film. Especially in the later footage does this combination of photography and lighting become more prominent. Illumination of a mammoth staircase so that just the tops of the stairs are in relief and down which the figures come only picked out by a 'pin' spot showing the bust of the characters must rate as a great piece of work."

Variety, however, had serious doubts about the film's blockbuster potential and gave it what proved to be the kiss of death: "Limited action comes very close to trying the patience more than once and for that reason it is obvious that this is not a $2 roadshow." Unfortunately, a roadshow hit was exactly what Famous Players–Lasky/Paramount was counting on and, when the public reception proved cool, it was D.W. Griffith that they blamed. It had been earlier announced that Griffith would direct *The White Slave* starring Carol Dempster and Richard Dix, but after the poor receipts for *Sorrows*, the project was dropped and so was Griffith.

Seen today it must be conceded that the reviewers were on the money about both the film's virtues and its flaws. The camerawork and lighting are often striking and much of the movie has the pictorial quality of the German film fantasies of that period. The staircase at Geoffrey's mansion is a great set and shot in a way that may remind viewers of the closing scenes at Carfax Abbey in Tod Browning's *Dracula*. Lucio's entrance, the macabre garden party (a bit similar to the bacchanal in Rex Ingram's *The Magician*), the creepy, erotically charged scene between Lucio, Olga and Tempest, and Lucifer's subsequent pursuit of the hero are among the most unsettling scenes of Hollywood silent horror. Still, everything else — and that's most of the movie — is slow and repetitive with hackneyed situations and a clichéd romance.

In his autobiography, Adolphe Menjou claims he got outstanding notices for his performance as Prince Lucio, but a quick perusal of the reviews indicates that this is a bit of an exaggeration. There's no real demonic force to his Lucio; rather, the prince seems little more than a cynical bon vivant who's pleasantly surprised when he encounters the rare virtuous lady.

If there's a standout performance in *Sorrows* it's clearly that of Carol Dempster as Mavis. Dempster, of course, was better known as D.W. Griffith's romantic interest than she was as a thespian, but he did his very best to promote her as a star; however, Lillian Gish was a tough act to follow. (One is *very* grateful that the plan to have Dempster replace Gish in *Broken Blossoms* when Gish fell ill turned out not to be necessary.) The critics were usually scornful and the public for the most part indifferent, but Griffith carried on with the determination of a Charles Foster Kane forcing his untalented Susan on the opera-going public. In some of her earlier films, Dempster acted like a teenage girl with a bladder problem, but she improved in the course of time and scored in an unglamorous role in Griffith's *Isn't Life Wonderful?* Perhaps her best moment in *Sorrows* comes

when she frantically tries to catch up with Geoffrey when Lucio takes him away in his touring car: the car is billowing satanic exhaust fumes, and Dempster superbly conveys that her desperate attempt to reach Geoffrey stems not just from her pain at losing him, but also her presentment that he is in terrible danger. The purity of her devotion in the final scene is conveyed with such sincerity that one has little doubt that she's more than a match for the Prince of Darkness. Dempster left both the movies and Griffith after *Sorrows* and enjoyed a happy retirement, during which (hopefully) she ignored the occasional spurious accusation that she was responsible for Griffith's decline.

Ricardo Cortez is no more than adequate as Tempest but admittedly the character is a bit of a stiff: whining, weak and unheroic. Ricardo's brother Stanley visited him on the *Sorrows* set and was so impressed with Fischbeck et al. that he embarked on his own highly successful career as a cinematographer. Ricardo's particulars may be found in our entry on 1929's *Midstream*.

Lya de Putti's role as Olga is relatively minor, but her big moment — wherein she tries to seduce a scornful Lucio — was considered pretty hot stuff at the time, and her emoting was thought to be so suggestive that more than one critic felt the scene would likely be censored. In his notes on the film for the Theodore Huff Society, the late, great William K. Everson mentioned seeing stills from the movie that showed de Putti in the semi-nude (and with a different hairdo) and speculated that this might have been for a European cut of the film. The Hungarian born de Putti played in German films for both Fritz Lang and F.W. Murnau, but it was her performance as the sexy waif in E.A. Dupont's *Variety* that brought her to the attention of Hollywood. When her stateside film career quickly faltered, she blamed her producers for insisting that she wear her hair in a boyish bob. With the arrival of sound, the problem was found not to be her hair but rather her heavy accent; while in England making *The Informer*, she discovered that a British actress would be dubbing over her voice. De Putti decided to give Broadway a try in 1930, but her debut in *Made in France* received such scathing reviews that she withdrew after just three days, claiming illness. The very next year she was dead, the result of a combination of blood poisoning, infection and the pneumonia she had contracted after an operation she underwent to remove a chicken bone stuck in her throat. Though there were stories she had been given a huge sum as a settlement from one of her lovers, de Putti left an estate worth scarcely $2,000.

The Sorrows of Satan was D.W. Griffith's last big chance to reestablish himself as a bankable director. A few more films followed and then, unbelievably, he found himself regarded as nothing more than a famous name belonging to Hollywood's past.

— *HN*

Spellbound

Spellbound. Balboa Amusement Producing Co./General Films Co., 17 May, 1916, 5 reels, unpreserved 35mm print at Library of Congress

CAST: Lois Meredith (*Elsie York*); William Conklin (*Harrington Graeme*); Bruce Smith (*Major Cavendish*); Edward J. Brady (*Katti Hab*); Frank Elranger (*Mematu*); Edward Peters (*Azetic*); R. Henry Grey (*Graham*).

CREDITS: *Director* Harry Harvey; *Producers* H.M. Horkheimer and E.D. Horkheimer; *Scenario* Bess Meredyth.

From *The AFI Catalog*: The working title of the film was *The One-Eyed God*. Some sources attribute the direction to H.M. Horkheimer and E.D. Horkheimer

In April of 1916, Balboa Films announced that, in addition to their usual program of serials and two- and three-reelers, they would be launching a series of five-reel features, with one to be released every month. The films would be released under the "Knickerbocker Star Features" banner and the first one would be *Spellbound*, a "drama of modern society" starring Lois Meredith. The publicity flacks claimed that the film had already been previewed to a dozen leading exchange managers and had won "high praise." H.M. Horkheimer, head of Balboa, insisted that exhibitors would find this new product of high quality, yet eminently affordable:

> While no expense is being spared, the introduction of modern efficiency methods into our studios enables us to produce features of exceptional quality for release in the regular service. I'm sure everyone who sees Lois Meredith in *Spellbound* will agree that no recent production of any character has surpassed this extraordinary picture in quality and scope of production, in strength and story [*Moving Picture World*, 29 April 1916].

Actually, *no one* agreed, as the object of all this hype turned out to be no more than a tired variation on *The Moonstone*. Of most interest to us in *Spellbound* is the film's one, overtly supernatural element, which takes place at the climax; nonetheless, it probably drew more snickers than shudders from 1916 audiences. BTW, *Spellbound* was *not* a "Knickerbocker Star Feature"; there was only one of those —1916's *Pay Dirt*.

Our synopsis comes from *Moving Picture World*, 3 June 1916:

> Major Cavendish returns from India, bringing with him an idol he has picked up. His ward, Elsie Yorke, is in love with Harrington Graeme. The major asks her to marry him and she laughs at the idea. Graeme, in ill favor with the major, asks Elsie to elope with him. She is to meet him in the grounds at midnight. As she passes through the library, she is fascinated by the ugliness of the idol. Her guardian enters and startles her. Graeme, through a window, sees the girl in the major's arms and goes away, thinking he has lost her.
>
> Later he returns from abroad and, having learned that Elsie is still unmarried, ventures to call. Elsie is receiving friends whom she has invited to hear a lecture on Indian morals by the noted Yogi, Katti Hab. She is impressed by his statement that even inanimate objects have a strange power. Katti Hab sees the idol and gives a start of recognition. Graeme wins Elsie's forgiveness. The major enters and orders him from the house. He returns that night to walk under Elsie's window. Katti Hab and one of his servants enter the house to steal the idol and kill the major. Graeme puts them to flight and is found on the scene with the knife in his hand. Held for trial, he is freed on the testimony of the Yogi's servant, who bears a grudge against his master.
>
> Graeme and Elsie are married. Elsie undergoes a change. Graeme discovers that she is gambling and pleads with her to stop. She flouts him. An admirer abets her and lends her money. Graeme, also changed, has an affair with an actress. Katti Hab, in hiding, resolves to risk all on another attempt to steal the idol. Elsie's physician informs her she is about to become a mother. She rebels at the thought, and hates her child when it is born. Katti

> Hab, surprised in the house, conceals himself in a closet and is imprisoned by a spring lock. He calls on the idol for deliverance and the idol moves, upsetting a lamp which sets fire to the house. The valet telephones Graeme who rushes homeward.
>
> Elsie, returning from a ball at which her admirer has revealed his true character, sees the fire and her maternal instinct is aroused. She saves the child and is herself overcome. Graeme rescues her. Katti Hab is killed by the fire. The image is broken and Graeme finds jewels in its head. Both feel that a sinister influence in their lives has been removed and they are happy with their child.

Presumably, the jewels provided sufficient cash for the newly reconciled couple to buy a new house, pay off Elsie's gambling debts and perhaps obtain a phone book with the number of the local fire department so that Graeme's valet won't have to call his master first should the smoke detectors fail again.

A rather muddled synopsis in a publicity release states that Katti Hab meets his fiery end in a room rather than in his undignified hiding place in a closet. It would make dramatic sense for the yogi to be in the *same* room as the idol when he invokes its help, but it's not clear this was the case. The statue — described as *small* in *The AFI Catalog* synopsis — "jump[s] around on a table" according to Wid Gunning's account of the "very impossible situation" when the idol comes to life. Whether the statue's brief and clumsy period of animation was achieved by some sort of stop-motion or with the help of a stagehand yanking on some wires may never be known, but audiences likely shared Wid's incredulity in either case.

Also, the idol's motive in causing the fire is rather obscure unless we assume the blaze was an accident. Zapping your devotee when he asks for help seems a rather arbitrary act for a deity, but the gods are crazy sometimes, and the same fate was meted out to the loyal Im-Ho-Tep in 1932's *The Mummy*. Nonetheless, it is possible that Katti Hab was acting out of desire for the jewels rather than piety which would make him guilty of a greater sacrilege than the unbelievers.

The only other variation from the usual *Moonstone* clichés is that the personalities of the main characters change for the worse because of the presence of the idol. Since no one but the villain knows about the jewels, it's not a question of greed dragging people down. The statue functions not as a sacred object that belongs on its home turf but rather as a bad luck charm that brings disaster to everyone in the vicinity. The curse ends when the statue is broken (or melted) and, happily, does not extend to the jewels within.

Wid Gunning felt that most audiences had tired of Hindu idol stories but, for the minority who had not grown weary of sinister Eastern cultists prowling about English manors, Wid thought the film would be of some interest — at least up until the scene of the idol coming to life. Other than that, Wid had nothing remotely positive to say about the movie which he considered to be a "jumbled mass of hackneyed stuff," boring, unconvincing, and poorly paced besides: "Throughout the offering there were many unnecessary scenes, many scenes that ran too long and there was very little which could be called tempo. The story was not put over by the titles. The name *Spellbound* is not accounted for in the film since none of the action clearly defines the reason for selecting the name" (*Wid's*, 1 May 1916).

It seems that the randomness of some geographical play also irked Mr. Gunning: "In the one place we have the hero sent to Africa by means of one title and next we see him return from Africa by means of another title. Why pick on Africa?"

Wid opined that the acting ranged from adequate to painful and was unimpressed with leading lady Lois Meredith: "Miss Meredith was rather pretty but did not register much in the way of emotion that would give any definite idea as to exactly what she was trying to put over. Her expressions are very much alike throughout." More on the woman of one face can be found in the entry on *The Greater Will*.

Perhaps acting on the theory that "if you can't say something nice," et cetera, Oscar Cooper — in his 13 May 1916 review for *Motion Picture News* — doesn't bother to comment on the story and acting. Rather, he offers some praise for the lighting and photography and tells us that the "interior sets are elaborate and the exteriors bring to view some pleasing bits of California scenery." Such blandness makes us grateful that *Wid's*, unlike *MPN*, was not dependent on ads from the movie industry.

Wid may have been sick of *Moonstone* clones, but the Balboa publicity department still felt the public was up for more and ads for *Spellbound*. The adverts promised "an Eastern mystery story of love and deep adventure, having to do with idols and hidden riches" and a tale in which "the mysterious East casts its shadow over an English family." Other PR pieces touted Lois Meredith, while one (7 June 1919's *The Salt Lake Tribune*) claimed that the fantastic story did not preclude at least one nod to reality: "Included among its scene is a wonderfully staged English courtroom, produced under the personal direction of the Lord Chief Justice Howell of Canada who was in California at the time the picture was being taken."

Harry Harvey (how did Harry Houdini miss using that name for one of his characters?) spent most of his brief career as a director at Balboa, starting with the 1915 *Who Pays?*, a 12-part series of three-reel morality plays teaming Ruth Roland and Henry King (before his days as a major director of films like *Tol'able David*). *Pays?* was an odd affair: not actually a serial, it had King and Roland playing different roles in each episode; in support of the disjunct releases, the stories were serialized in newspapers. After *Who Pays?* Harvey worked on a variety of shorts and features for Balboa and other independents until Balboa went belly-up in 1918 and he moved to Universal to direct genuine serials and action films. The very patriotic Harvey — a decorated veteran of the Spanish-American War — spent a good deal of time supporting the war effort, becoming head of the "War Savings, Thrift and Stamp" movement at Universal.

In 1919 a rather puzzling item appeared in the press, announcing that Harvey was going to make an independent production in which he would have the lead; the feature would include the participation of two other directors, James Gordon (mistakenly described as the maker of *The Perils of Pauline*) and George Nichols (formerly of Selig and Lubin). Nothing came of the project and, at that point, Harvey largely dropped off the face of Hollywood's earth. Today, his credits are sometimes muddled with those of actor, Harry Harvey, and his actor/director son, Harry Harvey, Jr. Muddying the waters is the fact that there was also a popular vaudeville comic named Harry Harvey.

Spellbound was far from veteran scenarist Bess Meredyth's finest hour. Meredyth (née Helen MacGlashan of Buffalo, New York) began her career as an extra at Biograph in 1912, but switched to Universal where she eventually got to star in her own series of comic shorts playing "Bess the Detectress." Sometime later, Meredyth recalled those early years:

> After about a year's work I became a featured player at $35 a week. I was in the big money then and aside from acting, had to assist with the writing, cutting and titling. In those days everyone had to help with the entire production…. I soon decided that I liked the writing best of all. At that time you could choose the work to which you thought you were best suited and were usually given the opportunity in the line you desired.

In the 1910s, Meredyth wrote scores of scenarios for shorts, features and serials for Universal, Balboa, and other studios. Perhaps her most noteworthy films of this period were the 1917 Lon Chaney revenge tale, *Pay Me,* and the sequel to Elmo Lincoln's *Tarzan of the Apes, The Romance of Tarzan.* The latter was directed by her husband, Wilfred Lucas, with whom she had acted in her Universal days.

In the 1920s, Meredyth began working steadily for the major studios and became one of the highest paid scenarists in the business, writing the scripts for films like *The Red Lily* and *Ben-Hur,* as well as a trio of John Barrymore movies: *The Sea Beast, Don Juan* and *When a Man Loves.* Meredyth thought her experience as an actress was helpful in her writing:

> Now I am able to get an actor's angle into my stories. I know their abilities and limitations and am able to write my scripts accordingly. Many writers just write their stories and leave it to the director to figure out how they can be pictured. But having worked in front of the camera I have a pretty good idea of what can be done and how to do it [*The Ogden* (Utah) *Standard-Examiner,* 3 December 1927].

In 1924, while working on *Ben-Hur* in Italy, Meredyth got a letter from husband Wilfred Lucas saying that they were through. Five years later Meredyth married director Michael Curtiz, a marriage that was by all accounts stormy and punctuated by frequent separations. Curtiz adopted John Lucas— Meredyth's son by Wilfred — who went on to become a film director himself. Meredyth continued to write into the 1940s, contributing to films like *Phantom of Paris, Charlie Chan at the Opera, Mark of Zorro* and *The Unsuspected.*

Additional dirt on Harry Harvey, H.M. Horkheimer, and H.M.'s brother, E.D. (*and* Balboa), is to be had in our essay on *The Stolen Play.*

— HN

The Star Rover

The Star Rover. C.E. Shurtleff, Inc./Metro Pictures Corporation., 22 November 1920, 6 reels [LOST]

CAST: Courtenay Foote (*Dr. Hugh Standing*); Thelma Percy (*Faith Levering*); Pomeroy "Doc" Cannon (*Inspector Burns*); Dwight Crittenden (*District Attorney*); Jack Carlysle (*Sergeant Andover*); Chance Ward (*Tubbs, a political boss*); Marcella Daley (*Maizie, of the chorus*)

CREDITS: *Director* Edward Sloman; *Scenario* Albert Shelby LeVino; Based upon the eponymous novel by Jack London (New York, 1915); *Cinematographer* Jackson Rose; *Special Art Interiors* Edward Shulter

He was, as a boy, a member of a California outlaw gang, had been captured and condemned to life imprisonment in San

Quentin. Here as he was a high-spirited lad, he rebelled and was as a consequence condemned to years of solitary life in a dark cell with occasional long spells of torture by the brutal jacket. He found that while under torture he could self-hypnotize himself and separate his ethereal body, which used to live a separate life and a very pleasant one, while the poor natural body was cramped and twisted in this horrible machine.

These words of Sir Arthur Conan Doyle, which appeared in his syndicated newspaper series, "Our American Adventures," provide us with the best introduction to the once well-publicized life of Edward M. Morrell. Conan Doyle, who would later became all but obsessed with spiritualism, was writing here about his recent encounter with the ex-convict.

Morrell's autobiography, *The 25th Man*, was published two years after the "Our American Adventures" account, and goes into far greater detail about out-of-body experiences. In the late 1800s Morrell had become a renegade and had fought against the reprehensible treatment of the settlers of the San Joaquin Valley by the railroad companies. When finally captured, he was sent to Folsom Prison whence, along with 24 other of his gang members, he was transferred to San Quentin. After leading an unsuccessful revolt against miserable prison conditions, Morrell became an easy target for a frame-up when a stoolie reported that Morrell had smuggled firearms into the prison. While these accusations were unfounded, the outraged prison warden ordered that Morrell be placed in a straightjacket for long periods of time. Not even torture could enable him to reveal the location of non-existent weapons, but the prisoner claimed to have devised a way to disassociate his mind from his body in order to survive these excruciating ordeals. Morrell was finally pardoned in 1909 and became both a well-known crusader for penal reform and a spokesman for the paranormal.

Morrell's later association with the famed writer Jack London gave the erstwhile convict's notoriety its biggest boost. In 1914, London's novel *The Star Rover* (British title: *The Jacket*) was published. Written in the first-person—from the vantage point of a death-row inmate scheduled to hang—the novel incorporated many of the events that had involved Ed Morrell, although the central character was re-cast as Darrell Standing, a college professor of agronomics who has been tried and found guilty of murder. In homage, Morrell became a secondary character who teaches Standing how to leave his physical body in order to cope with the cruelty of the agonizing straightjacket. Unlike Morrell, Standing discovers that his current life is but one of many and that he can return to prior reincarnations by "star roving" under the extreme duress of torture. In granting Darrell Standing this timeless existence, London may have bestowed the closest thing to immortality to Ed Morrell as well; it's chiefly because of the novel that his name is remembered today.

By 1920, filmed adaptations of two of Jack London's works—*Burning Daylight* and *The Mutiny of the Elsinore*—had made their way to movie theaters everywhere. The films were crafted by the same technicians (scenarist Albert Shelby LeVino and director Edward Sloman), were made for the same producer (C.E. Shurtleff), and were distributed by the same company, Metro. Eager to continue with a winning formula, the team completed the trifecta late that same year with the release of *The Star Rover*. As was (and *is*) often the case, a bit of plot- and character-juggling had to be done to assure a smooth transition to the screen. For reasons now known only to God, convicted murderer Darrell Standing was transformed into Dr. *Hugh* Standing, who was accorded a much kinder fate than the hangman's noose. As was (and *is*) often the case (Part II), the filmmakers managed to squeeze into their picture the requisite happy ending, replete with requited love. Squeezed *out* of the script was any mention of Ed Morrell.

We didn't find a heck of a lot of commentary and/or production information on *The Star Rover*, an odd thing, given that the film was based on the works of an author of Jack London's stature. (An informed theory of ours is that this particular London work suffered for not being cut of the same cloth as other, more "traditional" London works.) We can provide a précis of the film's plot, though, for the following is taken verbatim from the press-book found in the archives of the Library of Congress:

On the evening that Dr. Hugh Standing is attending a performance of the season's musical comedy success, Tubbs, notorious political boss of the city, is present. Seated in the stage box opposite the one occupied by Dr. Standing, Tubbs is in high spirits; for the politician has been interested for some time in one Maizie, a chorus girl in the show. During an encore a hand grasping a pistol is thrust through the curtains in the rear of Dr. Standing's box, and Tubbs is shot dead. Standing picks up the assassin's weapon. While he is holding it he is arrested for the murder.

Standing is taken to Police Headquarters, where Inspector Burns, a hard-heavy-jowled man with a reputation for "Third Degree" methods, and the District Attorney, more intelligent and sympathetic, try every means to obtain a confession from Standing. But he insists he has told them all there is to tell. Faith Levering, Standing's fiancée, is permitted to talk with him and the officers of the law listen in with a dictaphone, but learn nothing. After Faith leaves, Standing is beaten by Inspector Burns and thrown into a dark cell to await further intimidation if he refuses to make a confession.

After several days, Inspector Burns, unsuccessful in bringing a confession from Standing by his usual brutal methods, has him strung up by the thumbs. Standing bravely bears the torture, strengthened by his knowledge of Faith's love and also by his belief in reincarnation; his belief that his soul has lived many lives, fitting him for future existences; that this life is merely another preparation. Although the may hurt his body, they cannot touch his soul.

With a forced smile, Standing tells the Inspector that his soul can feel no pain and that the longer they keep him strung up the more numb his body will become—and his soul will be freed to live again a life he has lived before. Sneering at Standing's belief, the Inspector leaves him alone, and going to his office listens through a dictaphone, confidently expecting that Standing, in the fearful agony of torture, will make an involuntary confession. But as the numbness creeps over Standing's body, his soul roves far from his physical body—and as a Viking he stands in the throes of death, while the Inspector listens to his subconscious, rambling word picture, disgustedly.

Sergeant Andover, the Inspector's aid, is horrified by the brutal performance and tells the Inspector he is carrying things entirely too far—contrary to police rules and the law. But the Inspector angrily ignores him. Faith comes to the Inspector and insists upon seeing Dr. Standing. But he refuses her, absolutely—and walks out of the room, to Dr. Standing's cell. Sergeant Andover, left alone with Faith, tells her the truth. And armed with this weapon, Faith goes to the District Attorney and tells him what the Sergeant has told her.

Upon the Doctor's assurance that Standing can stand still more punishment, Standing is again strung up by the thumbs. And again, he "star roves" as a Korean, whilst the Inspector listens again to Standing's word picture. As Standing becomes unconscious, the vision ends, and the Inspector angrily tosses the dictaphone away and orders Standing taken down until the following day.

The District Attorney, roused to action by Faith's story, goes to the Inspector and demands an explanation. The Inspector denies everything. Then Faith is called in and she accuses the Inspector of cruelty to Standing, but he still denies it. But when he is faced by Sergeant Andover, he confesses.

Faith pleads with the District Attorney that he allow Standing to be tortured again, as a possible way of learning through his subconscious rambling who the real murderer of Tubbs was. The District Attorney reluctantly agrees and they go to Standing's cell. The plan is explained to Standing and he is again strung up by the thumbs. They all watch him as he slowly takes on the appearance of a man in a trance.

With a faint smile and unconscious of his physical pain, Standing haltingly tells the story.

During the first part of Standing's talk, Sergeant Andover, suddenly leaves and at this point he returns to the cell with Maizie, the chorus girl, as Standing describes his subconscious vision of Maizie leaving the chorus on the night of the murder, and from the shadow of Standing's box, shooting Tubbs. As Standing tells this, Maizie screams and hysterically confesses the murder. As the District Attorney angrily turns to the cowering Inspector and tears the badge from his coat, Faith goes to Standing, who has been released and is seated on a bench, exhausted and half-conscious. As he slowly regains consciousness, Faith takes his head in her arms and their troubles vanish.

Familiar as we are with a good deal of London's science-fiction and fantasy output, we herewith opine that *The Star Rover* is not among the author's best work. The many chapters devoted to Standing's other-life escapades seem as if they were arbitrarily tacked onto a much more fascinating prison story, and therein lay the novel's weakness. The film, too, indulged its viewers with a good number of these "star rovings" and, based on the few trade journal items we were able to locate, it seems that these passages worked better interjected as visual vignettes than they did printed on paper. Per the 27 November 1920 issue of *The Moving Picture World*, "The Norse period and the scenes in China [*sic*] are elaborate," although the critic went on to kvetch that the picture "is told in a form that is too involved to bring out the best dramatic effect." Less confused by Asian geography, the *Exhibitor's Trade Review* reported that "the camerawork in the Korean streets and in the temple deserves special mention, the close-ups being especially good" (11 December 1920). The *ETR* review concluded that *The Star Rover* "is splendidly produced, lavishly portrayed."

Both periodicals gave positive mention to Briton, Courtenay Foote, for the man who essayed the film's title character was also the biggest name in its cast. Foote, educated both at his native Oxford and on the Continent, began his career onstage in a variety of parts ranging from Shakespeare to old English comedy. In 1909, at the urging of a friend, he moved to New York City and performed in any number of Broadway engagements including Dickens' *Oliver Twist* and *Little Dorritt* (which was presented as *The Debtors*). Foote quickly found that the stage provided an easy entrée to the world of moving pictures and his screen career began at Vitagraph with such titles as *The Great*

Diamond Mystery and *The Reincarnation of Karma.* The actor would soon toss work with D.W. Griffith and Famous Players into the hopper along with his Vitagraph roles, and the occasional return to the East Coast to tread the boards filled out his schedule.

Thelma Percy, younger sister to actress Eileen Percy, played Foote's love interest, Faith Levering, in *The Star Rover*. Per *The Oakland* [California] *Tribune*— Jack London's hometown newspaper — the Belfast-born Percy had won this major role "with but a few months of motion picture experience." Our research indicates that Thelma's *entire* movie career lasted only a few months in toto, but among her handful of titles were the 1920 Eddie Polo serial, *The Vanishing Dagger*, and Max Linder's classic comedy, *Seven Years Bad Luck* (1921).

Everything we consulted listed Edward Sloman's first directorial effort to be *Faust,* a 1915 Lubin two-reeler which starred — as Mephistopheles— Edward Sloman! Sloman went on to direct Irving Pichel in the bizarre, buried-alive thriller, *Murder by the Clock* (1931), and between that one and *The Star Rover* came *The Lost Zeppelin* (1929). Cinematographer Jackson Rose was also involved with *The Lost Zeppelin*, which marked for Rose (and for that industry niche in which he had cut his teeth) a shift from decent, if pedestrian, silent programmers to entertaining, if unremarkable, B-talkies. *Behind the Door* (1924) is an example of the former and *Midstream* (1929)— released as a silent and as a silent hybrid, with talking/singing sequences— is an instance of *both*.

As for the possibility of a person's "star roving," one must consider the book, the film, and the two media's flesh-and-blood template. Are there such things as out-of-body experiences? Many of the details in Morrell's autobiography may be found, in essence, in London's novel; were Morrell's claims factual, or merely embellishments of sequences from the earlier fictional work? Objectively, it's impossible to determine whether Ed Morrell actually believed that he had participated in authentic psychic phenomena, whether he was guilty of fabricating an elaborate hoax, or whether the circumstances in which he found himself made him delusional. The novel, of course, celebrated the preternatural. Per the extant publicity pieces and critical commentaries, so did the film, although not every anecdote on the motion picture can be taken as gospel: It was reported, for example, that Mr. Foote was a victim of a faulty prop during the scenes in which he hung by his thumbs, and that his "acting" was anything but — a claim that most probably came directly from the typewriter of a *publicist* who was delusional.

The 27 November issue of *Motion Picture News* covered the picture under the headline "Artistic Production, but Disappointing for a London Story," arguing that

> because it is a fantastic, impossible story, based on the theme of reincarnation of the soul, which few, if any, can take seriously, *The Star Rover* falls down as pure entertainment. It has none of that appeal for which other Jack London stories of the sea and far north were noted.... The elaborate production can hardly make up for the lack of story interest. The theatre scene in the beginning is a corker, and the Oriental sequence is artistic to a high degree, presenting some beautiful photography.

Without a print of the film, our knowledge of Edward Sloman's *The Star Rover* is limited to conjecture and second hand accounts such as this and those cited above. Would that we could "star rove" and see the picture for ourselves.

— *SJ*

The Stolen Play

The Stolen Play. Falcon Features/General Film Co., September 1917, 4 reels, print at Library of Congress, but unavailable for viewing

CAST: Ruth Roland (*Sylvia Smalley*); Edward J. Brady (*Leroux*); William Conklin (*Charles Edmay*); Lucy Blake (*Alice Mason*); Harry Southard (*Foster*); Ruth Lackaye (*Mrs. Edmay*); Makoto Inokuchi (*Togo*)

CREDITS: *Supervisors* H.M. and E.D. Horkheimer; *Director* Harry Harvey; *Story* D.F. Whitcomb. The copyright documentation filed by General Film Company lists the author of the story as H.O. Strachhan (aka H.O. Stechhan). It is unclear whether this credit should be taken to mean that Strachhan was the scenarist or whether there was a contractual obligation to give Strachhan a writer's credit as part of the distribution deal.

Edmay, a famous blind playwright, is engaged to marry Sylvia, his amanuensis. Leroux, a dramatic producer, is anxious to produce a play that Edmay has just finished, but the playwright is reluctant to sell. Leroux plans with his agent, Alice Mason, to secure the play. Working over the play, Sylvia has become nervous and Edmay morbid, and presently the story, as filmed, begins to develop startling situations. Leroux sends Alice to steal the script, and he also abducts Edmay and Sylvia. In attempting to steal the script, Alice has an encounter with Togo, the playwright's valet, and he is accidentally killed by Alice. Leroux has hypnotic ability and, placing Sylvia in a trance, gets from her subconscious memory a dictation of the completed play, while Edmay is concealed in a secret wine cellar under the house. Leroux learns to love Sylvia which leads to a stormy scene with Alice who is infatuated with him. Alice starts to leave Leroux's house but is persuaded by him to remain for the sake of preserving the propriety as a caretaker of Sylvia.

Leroux discovers in the meantime that in a hypnotic state Sylvia is capable of great dramatic powers, and at the play's premiere she takes the leading role with success under his hypnotic direction. The effort is too great, however, and she succumbs to exhaustion and is taken back to Leroux's house. He revives her, whereupon she realizes her position and so reproaches him that he releases Edmay from his prison and permits her to escort him home. Overheard by Alice, Leroux plans a dramatically remorseful end of his evil career; placing a tool of his, Foster, under hypnotic control, Leroux commands him to wall up the entrance to the underground prison and leave the country forever. Leroux enters the vault and is walled up alive. At the approach of his death throes, Alice discovers herself to him in the vault where she had secreted herself to die with him through devotion. At this apparent climax the story suddenly takes a totally different turn and concludes in an explanatory manner.

We can only hope that neither D.F. Whitcomb, the fellow who penned the original story on which this picture was based, nor the Horkheimer brothers (H.M. and E.D.), who took Daniel's masterwork and scenario-ized it, had a hand in writing the copyright registration synopsis we just quoted. Whitcomb served up three dozen or so stories and screenplays in the dozen or so years he earned a regular paycheck from the movie industry, and the Horkheimer brothers wrote more than their fair share of claptrap while keeping their Balboa Feature Film Company chugging along. (The film at hand was shot under the masthead "Falcon Features," but ... Falcon, Horkheimer,

Knickerbocker, Balboa ... they all boiled down to H.M. and/or E.D. no matter how you sliced it.) All things being relative, the three men were just too good at what they did to write that badly. Has it really been some 90 years since anyone "discovered herself" to anyone else without an English teacher going off somewhere to die? Or since one character's name reeked of ersatz Pig Latin, while another's was stolen from the author of the wildly popular novel, *The Mystery of the Yellow Room*? Or since a last-reel dream ending could be called a "totally different turn"? And come on ... was there ever *anyone* other than James Boswell or Archie Goodwin for whom the title "amanuensis" truly fit?

To start anew: brothers Herbert M. and Elwood D. Horkheimer were born about a year and a half apart (E.D. was the elder) in Wheeling, West Virginia, at the outset of the 1880s. In the *very* early 1910s, Herbert set about looking to stage *The Strugglers*, a drama on which he reputedly collaborated with one Lucile Sawyer. Exactly who wrote what and how much is not known, but, inasmuch as available records show that, in November 1911, NYC's Bijou Theatre briefly (a week or so) hosted said *Strugglers*— a production of the H.M. Horkheimer Amusement Company — we are led to hypothesize that Ms. Sawyer was the principal playwright and that Mr. Horkheimer made whatever literary addenda were deemed necessary by Mr. Horkheimer so that Mr. Horkheimer would fund the whole shebang. When the play's run ended, so, too, did any and all ties between H.M. Horkheimer and the stage.

Herbert moved cross-country, rented an office in sunny California, and — in a self-effacing move — rechristened his corporate entity the Balboa Amusement Producing Company. It appears that Herbert came up with "Balboa" as a tribute or a debt or something to the intrepid Spanish explorer who, like him, had sojourned west and had discovered the Pacific Ocean. In 1913, with a reputed starting capital of some $7000, H.M. started cranking out cheap one- and two-reelers, and he was soon joined by brother, Elwood, who started crafting publicity pieces to accompany Balboa's product. Said product begat sufficient money for the Horkheimers to expand (they bought the old Edison Studios and some adjoining lots in Long Beach the following year) and to begin to crank out serials and *three*-reelers. The Horkheimer empire soon encompassed 15 buildings and a stable of stars and artisans that included such names as Baby Marie Osborne, Ruth Roland, Henry King, Thomas Ince and William Desmond Taylor.

In 1914, four-reel (or longer) feature films underwent outcranking, and the BAPC (along with corporate clones Balboa Amusement Company, Balboa Feature Films Company, and — watch closely, now — Balboa Amusement Producing Company; a Fortune Photoplay) became the nation's Number One independent production company, at least with respect to feature films. In an effort to imply diversity, films were occasionally shot under different mastheads (see Knickerbocker et al., above) and distributed by different releasing companies. It may well be that the studio's product oversupply led to the Horkheimers declaring bankruptcy and closing down operations in 1918, a move that flabbergasted fans and critics alike. Both H.M. and E.D. galloped off into the cinematic sunset shortly thereafter, and they left few tracks. Fans looking to follow the brothers' trail would do well to acquire McFarland's *Balboa Films: A History and Filmography of the Silent Film Studio* by Jean-Jacques Jura and Rodney Norman Bardin II (shouldn't that be *Junior*?).

Among the Balboa, etc. films in which we'd have an interest are *Spellbound* (1916), *The Inspirations of Harry Larrabee* (1917), and, of course, *The Stolen Play*; comments on all three pictures are contained herein. We did have a look around, naturally, but plunging into the uncertain waters of *The Devil's Bait* (also 1917) left us nothing but wet, as the feature contains no devils of any kind, nor worms, squid, or guppies. And we became positively vituperative about the duplicitous nature of the company's succulently titled *Vengeance of the Dead* (which we screened — every last frame — at the Library of Congress). Our rant on same may be found in the introduction to this book.

There's not much to rant about where *The Stolen Play* is concerned, though. There doesn't appear to be anything of a critical nature on this title in any of the usual collected print materials, nor — other than the plot summary (word for word from the copyright materials) in the 8 September 1917 *Moving Picture World* — is there any sign of more mundane, non-critical screeds, either. None of the online sites devoted to silent films offers much (if any) mention, and that includes the sites that specifically target the genre. Thus, as Casey Stengel used to say in the early 1960s (while throwing up his hands in disgust), "What you see is what you got!" What we *can* see — the film being lost and all — is a bit of *Trilby*, a tad of "A Cask of Amontillado," and a fairly early instance of the climactic cop-out we've all come to know and loathe. (Actually, it's unclear whence cometh the AFI's revelation of the last-reel dream ending. The studio's prose [which opens our discussion, above] opts for that "totally different turn" phrase and — as we've said once already — there's nothing else to be had. Queries to the AFI have gone unanswered, so perhaps someone there dreamt up the whole thing.)

Genre-stuff-wise, more impressive than most of the early, routine, mesmeric nonsense is Sylvia's detail-oriented subconscious, which can retrieve from its depths an entire script — all parts, presumably (with stage directions?) — when Leroux looks at her, just so. The audacity of the scope of this contrivance is as breathtaking as it was novel. Not so the lady's promenade down Trilby Avenue, a stroll which consisted not in her recall, but rather in those "great dramatic powers" which leads ultimately to "exhaustion" for her, but to increased revenue potential for her evil genius. Still, Whitcomb's less predictable turn of *that* screw lay in Sylvia's surviving both the stress of her stage successes and the lust/love of her hypnotist, and in Leroux's choosing to be walled up ("For the love of God, Foster!" — guess at possible title card) rather than succumb to the sort of all-purpose heart attack that had removed Svengali from the scene late in the game. The descriptive shift between paragraphs in the sole, extant publicity puff — from "secret wine cellar" to "underground prison"/"vault" — may reflect either Whitcomb's taking Poe's tale and running with it, or (more likely) the literary extravagances of the flack who wrote the plot summary.

Ruth Roland — the hypnotically remarkable Sylvia — vied with Pearl White's for claim to being the Queen of the Silent Serial; both women had chapter-plays entitled for them (albeit White had but one: 1916's *Pearl of the Army*), with Roland's including *The Adventures of Ruth* (1919), *Ruth of the Rockies* (1920), and *Ruth of the Range* (1923). The competition has endured to the present, with aficionados of both women and their adventurous output still engaged in debate over which woman won the top prize and which was the also-ran. It appears that — *The Stolen Play* apart — Roland had something of a propensity for playing eponymously named characters (then again, many of her wares were manufactured by her own company, Ruth Roland Serials); her first appearance in an "extended series" (12 three-reel, tenuously related shorts, not quite the same as a serial), though, was for H.M. Horkheimer's Balboa Pictures' *Who Pays?* in 1915. Roland had also starred as Ruth (Girl Detective) in a mid–1910s series of two-reelers directed by James W. Horne for Kalem. As had White, Roland made over 200 films, saw her film credits virtually ended during the Silent Era, and shuffled off this mortal coil before the end of the 1930s.

Edward J. Brady, the lecherous Leroux, appeared in well over *three* hundred films in his career, with much of the overage due to 1) his surviving until 1942, and b) his playing dozens of those "uncredited" bits during the 1930s and early 1940s that put food on the table for otherwise-forgotten silent-film thespians. A New Yawka, Brady also provided the villainy in the Horkheimers' genre epic, *Spellbound* (he was Hindu heavy, Katti Hab), his only other true genre role. William Conklin (Edmay, the AywrightPlay) mirrored Brady's Manhattan origins by debuting in Brooklyn, but the actor was out of the industry by the end of the 1920s, with fewer than one hundred pictures on his résumé. Among those pictures, though, may be numbered *Spellbound* (yup; again) and *The Haunted Bedroom* (1919, see entry).

The remaining cast members were all either flashes in the pan or Horkheimerites, with the exception of Nipponese actor, Makato Inokuchi, who played Togo, the unfortunate valet. We came upon a mini-biography of Inokuchi (in the 13 December 1914 number of *The Atlanta Constitution* and thus predating *Stolen*) which revealed a multi-talented Samurai of letters. For those readers possessed of eyesight ever attuned to political incorrectness, the puff piece summed up thus: "Mahotoo Inokuhi [*sic*] … is a well educated Jap."

— *JTS*

The Stolen Voice

The Stolen Voice. William A. Brady Picture Plays/World Film Corp., 9 August 1915, 4–5 reels, 28mm print at the Eastman House

CAST: Robert Warwick (*Gerald D'Orville*); Frances Nelson (*Marguerite Lawson*); Giorgio Majeroni (*Von Gahl*); Violet Horner (*Belle Borden*); Bertram Marburgh (*Dick Leslie*).

CREDITS: *Director* Frank Crane; *Scenario* Paul McAllister

As is mentioned a number of times in this volume, George Du Maurier's *Trilby* had more influence on silent horror than many other, more notorious tales of terror; the most famous early film version of the story was done by Maurice Tourneur in 1915 (see entry). Oddly enough, just a month before Tourneur's movie premiered, *The Stolen Voice* was released. The short feature had been written by Paul McAllister, who would appear as Gecko, Svengali's servant, in the Tourneur *Trilby*, and who had played Svengali himself on the stage. *The Stolen Voice* is a clever pastiche of *Trilby*, as well as an amusing behind-the-scenes look at movie-making in 1915; however, it's not quite clear just who was in on the joke. Reviewers took the film quite seriously on its own merits and did not mention *Trilby* at all. For all that, it was also quickly forgotten in the wake of the very successful Tourneur film. *The Stolen Voice* survived in 28mm (an early format aimed at the home-movie market in the 1910s), but was transferred to 35mm by Eastman House in 2005. We have seen this version and we offer the following synopsis:

Gerald D'Orville is a popular opera singer who plays the music hall circuit. He attracts the attention of Belle Borden, an adventuress, who is less interested in his voice than in the fact that he makes $2,000 a week. Belle's boyfriend, Dr. Von Gahl, is none too pleased by this, but reluctantly goes with her backstage to meet D'Orville. Belle gives Gerald a beautiful flower for his buttonhole, and the three agree to dine later on. Gerald is also much admired by a pretty shop girl named Marguerite Lawson. Outside the theater, Marguerite gives him a little flower, and the singer takes it to replace the one Belle gave him. Later at dinner, Belle notices this and throws the flower off the roof of the restaurant. When Gerald leaves the restaurant later, he happens upon the flower again and puts it in his wallet.

Gerald's friend Dick Leslie is a drunkard and often hits Gerald up for money. One night, Dick helps himself to some funds from Gerald's wallet. When Gerald discovers the theft, he gives Dick the rest of the money and tells him to use it to straighten out his life. Touched by his friend's devotion, Dick promises to change his ways.

As the relationship between Gerald and Belle grows closer, Von Gahl becomes increasingly jealous. Von Gahl is also a master hypnotist and begins to plot against his rival. After an all-night party, Gerald, Belle, Von Gahl, and the other revelers go to the beach. Belle dares Gerald to jump into the water in his evening clothes. Gerald does just that and, goaded by Belle, Von Gahl follows. However, he cannot swim, and Gerald has to save him. Von Gahl nearly throttles him in the process.

That night, Gerald has a cold from his impromptu swim and worries a bit about his voice but goes on stage nonetheless. From the balcony, Von Gahl casts a hypnotic spell on Gerald, causing him to lose his voice. Von Gahl's energy is drained by his efforts, but they have worked very well indeed; not only is Gerald unable to sing, he can no longer talk.

Doctors are baffled by Gerald's condition. When it starts to look hopeless, Belle gives up on him and sends him a note telling him "You can hardly expect me to carry on a one-sided conversation." A despairing Gerald goes to Europe in search of a cure. After two years and no success, he returns to America, totally broke.

Meanwhile Dick Leslie has become a successful film director with his own studio. He runs across Marguerite in her shop and tells her that she has beautiful eyes and should come to his studio for a test. Gerald is desperately looking for work but has no luck. He tries Dick's studio and is being turned away when he's spotted by his former friend. Dick immediately signs him up for the movies. Marguerite comes in for her test and is astonished to see Gerald. Gerald proves that he remembers her by showing her the flower he has always kept.

Gerald and Marguerite do very well as co-stars and become increasingly popular. While filming on location, Gerald, playing an Indian warrior, is left stranded on a ledge as a joke while the crew breaks for lunch. Marguerite is dozing in a canoe in the river below him, but the boat becomes untethered and begins drifting towards the nearby waterfall. Gerald sees the danger and jumps into the rapids in time to save Marguerite. Their love for each other continues to grow.

Belle and Von Gahl pass by a movie theater showing Gerald's latest two-reeler. Belle insists on going in, although Von Gahl is extremely nervous at the prospect. The film turns out to be about hypnotism. As Gerald puts a spell on Marguerite on the screen, Von Gahl drops dead of a heart attack. At that moment, Gerald, attending a ball game, instinctively cheers and is astonished to find his voice has returned He telephones Marguerite and "he talked and he talked and he talked." The two are next seen as bride and groom on top of a wedding cake.

The Svengali of Du Maurier's novel, Paul Potter's play and all the subsequent films gives the heroine — who can't sing — a beautiful voice through his hypnotic powers, while in *The Stolen Voice*, the Svengali character does the opposite and stills a great voice with his mesmerism. In both cases, a public performance provides a crucial scene. Like Svengali, Von Gahl finds that exerting his hypnotic power weakens his heart. In *Trilby*, the evil hypnotist dies of a heart attack while the heroine is on stage; in *Voice*, he is similarly stricken when his victim is on-screen before him. Von Gahl's death scene has a further parallel to the stage Svengali (and the subsequent Tourneur film), where, in death, the villain's head is tilted back toward the audience, with his eyes open and staring. Von Gahl assumes a similar pose on the floor of the movie theater. Perhaps these pictorial quotations would have been more obvious to reviewers had the Tourneur *Trilby* been released first.

There are a couple of differences between the 28mm film and the AFI synopsis. In the former, the hypnotist is not named Von Gahl, but rather, Dr. Luigi Brosio. The rather confusing *Variety* review (20 August 1915) refers to Belle's relationship with "an Italian doctor of a jealous disposition. At least the jealous one looks like an Italian and the captions admit he is a doctor." Also, according to AFI notations, Gerald's heart-attack-inciting two-reeler is entitled *Sevengalleys, the Hypnotist*; in the 28mm print, the fatal short has the much less satirical title of *The Unseen Power*.

Like most film hypnotists, Van Gahl's powers are more akin to black magic than to any type of real hypnotism. When Van Gahl first conceives of his plan, he passes his hand over his throat; in another room, Gerald reacts and clutches his own throat for a moment. Von Gahl casts his potent spell from his box at the opera without having any face-to-face contact with Gerald whatsoever. Then, while Belle is watching the performance, Von Gahl stands back in the shadows and begins gesturing with his hands. Of course, as in all sorcery, the spell ends with the death of the necromancer. Critics found the hypnotism angle unbelievable, but didn't feel it feel it did any real harm to the film:

Paul McAllister, author of this most novel production, is evidently possessed of an imagination that soars to great heights so high, in fact, that we are inclined to doubt the credibility of some of the story's situations. But believable or not as the case may be, *The Stolen Voice* as a whole is a most thrilling drama…. The marvelous hypnotic power exercised by the heavy is apt to strike one as untrue or impossible, but outside of this the story develops in a pleasantly convincing style. It contains many incidents of a sort that thrill by their human qualities and others that thrill because of their sensationalism [Peter Milne, *Motion Picture News*, 14 September 1915].

The *Variety* review — which was also very favorable — also noted that the hypnotism angle was the "weakest point and beyond a stretch of 'picture license' even." However, the reviewer seemed more put off by the very idea that a sophisticated celebrity of the sort Warwick was playing could be taken in by the adventuress, even to the point of jumping into the water in his evening clothes: "At least give a headliner credit for a little more common sense than that implies." The reviewer also shed a good deal of ink mulling over the fact that the story was an original scenario and not adopted from a play.

Director Frank Crane, who stumbled in *The Moonstone* (see entry), seems more in his element here, especially in the film-within-a-film sequences. During one of these, hero Robert Warwick just can't seem to beat the villain down, so, finally exasperated, he tosses him out a nearby window and then turns to the heroine with an apologetic shrug for his violence; a few moments later the scene ends, and the defenestrated heavy reappears behind the fake window-frame. The Indian and Svengali films also seem to be tongue-in-cheek, though they are not much different in content and/or style from typical two-reelers and serials of that era.

Star Robert Warwick was the big selling point of *The Stolen Voice*, and his publicity harped on how amazing it was that Warwick was playing an actor, "a manly hero of a photoplay within a photoplay." Other puff pieces claimed that there was a parallel between actor and character, and that Warwick had once been an opera singer, but had turned to the stage after he lost his voice! Warwick did indeed study opera in Paris, but switched to the stage early in his career; there's no evidence that anything went wrong with his singing voice or that he fell victim to a jealous hypnotist. Judging by later reviews of Warwick's occasional forays into musical comedy, his voice simply lacked the timbre necessary for an opera singer. Some would say, however, that there *was* a real-life parallel to the situation in *The Stolen Voice*— with *Hobart Bosworth*'s career! Bosworth had achieved great success on the stage and scoffed at movies, but had to do an about-face after bouts of tuberculosis had damaged his speaking voice.

Variety commented on Warwick's sex appeal and that he was "stripped to the waist in the dressing room, quite unnecessarily, but the girls will likely appreciate his sacrifice to art." Additional beefcake is on display later on when Warwick, clad only in a loincloth, dives into the drink to save the heroine. *Variety* recalled Warwick's matinee-idol days and felt "this picture will be accepted by all of the public, those who believe that Warwick is as big a favorite, if not bigger, on the screen than he was and is with the matinee girls and those as well who like only pictures."

Warwick's patrician good looks had indeed made him a big matinee idol in the 1900s, and he often appeared with such distinguished stage actresses as Mary Mannering and Virginia Harned. He signed with World in 1914 and played in a number of popular films, including two for Maurice Tourneur: *Alias Jimmy Valentine* (Warwick played the reformed safe-cracker) and *A Girl's Folly*, a lighthearted look at filmmaking in which Warwick gently kids his movie-star image. Unsatisfied with his World films, he started up his own production company in 1917; however, when America entered World War I, Warwick quickly enlisted. Promoted to major, he worked in intelligence under General Pershing at the Central Command. When the conflict ended, Warwick focused on Broadway rather than Hollywood and only made a handful of films in the 1920s.

When Warwick returned to movies at the dawn of the Talkie Era, he found that he no longer was considered a bankable star. Possessed of a rich, stentorian speaking voice, he was in demand for small roles as authoritarian figures, like generals, mayors, wardens, and police commissioners. He did get to reprise his Jimmy Valentine role (though now a supporting character) in *The Return of Jimmy Valentine* (1936), but was more frequently found doing uncredited bits. The 1940s were kinder to him, as he became a favorite of Preston Sturgess's, who gave him good roles (and prominent billing) in a number of his films, notably *Sullivan's Travels*. Humphrey Bogart remembered Warwick's kindness to him in his early Broadway days and insisted on his being cast as the washed-up Shakespearean star in *In a Lonely Place*; some felt that Warwick stole the show.

Warwick continued to work steadily in the 1950s. On the set of *Sugarfoot* (1951), he amused his co-workers by showing them the budget sheet for *Alias Jimmy Valentine*: an eight-week shooting schedule at a cost of $27,000; the latter would barely have covered the Technicolor expenses for two days' work on *Sugarfoot*. He also kept busy with TV work (appearing in such popular series as *Peter Gunn*, *Maverick*, *Wagon Train*, and *Dr. Kildare*) and kept acting right up into his 80s.

Frances Nelson was *The Stolen Voice*'s likable and charming heroine. (*Variety* also thought she was good, but didn't seem to know her name!) A graduate of stage-musical comedy, Nelson worked first for Brady Picture Plays and later Metro, but her film career seems to have petered out in the 1920s. A 1925 article about an extortion attempt in which she was victimized described her as a "former actress." Perhaps she devoted herself to aquatics as her early publicity made much of the fact that she had swum New York's Ausable Chasm.

Giorgio — aka George — Majeroni (Von Gahl) makes a suitably lean and green-eyed villain and bears a resemblance to Osgood Perkins in *Scarface*. Majeroni came from a theatrical family and his aunt was the great tragedian, Adelaide Ristori. Both on stage and screen, Majeroni was evil more often than not. In 1918's *King of Diamonds*, playing another jealous lover, he eliminated his rival by giving him a drug that creates the appearance of leprosy! Majeroni reflected on his villainy during the filming of the serial, *Patria*:

> I smile and smile and am a villain still. Throughout my stage career I have plotted crimes and murders without end and have killed and slain until this hand is redder than that of any Borgia. When there was no one else left to kill I have had to kill myself a score of times, proving myself to have more lives than the proverbial cat [*Elyria* (Ohio) *Evening Telegram*, 20 April 1917].

Scenarist Paul McAllister was likewise a stage actor and played in various stock companies as well as on Broadway. He usually did light comic or juvenile roles, so his turn as Svengali in a Washington revival of *Trilby* could have been a fiasco, but the *Washington Post* found his performance "brilliant, genuinely convincing, an artistic, even a powerful interpretation of the role that made Wilton Lackaye a star" (26 August 1913). A pen-and-ink artist as well as an actor and writer, he did his own make-up which, he claimed, followed the novel's original illustrations more closely than did the traditional stage conceptions of Svengali. McAllister was also seen to good effect as the conniving Baron Sartoris in Maurice Tourneur's popular *The Whip* (1917). McAllister wrote only other feature, *One Hour* (1917), which he also directed.

At least some showings of *The Stolen Voice* experimented a bit with sound:

> The Phonograph provides music during intermissions in a great many motion picture houses, but its practical possibilities in connection with the silent drama were carried further recently when it was used to add an impressive touch of realism to the presentation of *A Stolen Voice*, featuring Robert Warwick. In the picture, Mr. Warwick is shown singing before a large audience and just as this scene commenced the lights were turned out, the projector stopped, and a rendition of an aria from *Pagliacci* came from an Edison phonograph on the stage. When the song was ended the picture again was flashed on the screen and the performance continued [*Edison Phonograph Monthly*, August 1915].

It's not recorded how audiences reacted to this interruption, but *The Jazz Singer* was a long way off.

— HN

The Story Without a Name

The Story Without a Name aka *Without Warning*. Famous Players–Lasky/Paramount Pictures, 5 October 1924, 6 reels/5912 feet [LOST]
CAST: Agnes Ayres (*Mary Walsworth*); Antonio Moreno (*Alan Holt*); Tyrone Power (*Drakma*); Louis Wolheim (*Kurder*); Dagmar Godowsky (*Claire*); Jack Bohn (*Don Powell*); Maurice Costello (*Cripple*); Frank Currier (*Admiral Walsworth*); with Ivan Linow
CREW: *Producers* Adolph Zukor, Jesse L. Lasky; *Director* Irvin Willat; *Screenplay* Victor Irvin; based on the serialized novel *The Story Without a Name* by Arthur Stringer (New York, 1924); *Cinematographer* Hal Rosson

"Radio Fans Ought to Like This Film"
— *Chicago Daily Tribune*, 12 October 1924

During the 1920s, the number of American households with radio sets increased exponentially, and science fiction, eager for an innovative theme, pounced on the new technology. In 1924 — the same year that *The Story Without a Name* (more on that odd title later) hit the nation's screens— Wisconsin state senator, patent-law author, and engineering/mathematics teacher, Roger Sherman Hoar, indulged in a bit of intellectual slumming. As Ralph Milne Farley, he began his popular series of "Radio" tales (*The Radio Man, The Radio Beasts, The Radio Planet*, etc.) for pulp magazine, *Argosy— All Story*. The movies were also quick to recognize radio's exploitation possibilities, and at least one genre feature (1923's *M.A.R.S.*, see entry) owed its shift from red to black ink to its being re-titled (as *Radio-Mania*) to cash in on the new craze. Serials-wise, enthusiasm about the nouveau medium ran so high that chapter-plays involving wireless dictographs, retrievable radio broadcast signals, radio compasses, radio-hydro airplanes, radio-air torpedoes— just about everything this side of radio-potato-peelers— titillated the imaginations of (mostly younger) fans each and every week.

At first, the love affair between radio and science fiction was one-sided. While there had been some (admittedly crude) ability to record audio genre presentations decades before the cinema arrived in town, for reasons that are still not completely clear, mechanically-aided sound drama took a while to catch on. While a plethora of recordings of minstrel shows, clarinet solos, singing duets, etc., has survived from the last decade of the 1800s, there was a long draught between Len Spencer's brief wax-cylinder recording of the transformation scene from Robert Louis Stevenson's *Dr. Jekyll and Mr. Hyde* (circa 1905, extant) and the B.B.C. Radio's lost 27 May 1927 broadcast of Karel Capek's *R.U.R.*, the first acknowledged science-fiction radio broadcast. Nonetheless, during Radio's "Golden Age," the trickle ultimately turned into a flood. Throughout the 1930s, listeners thrilled to regular space opera episodes featuring Buck Rogers and Flash Gordon. Arch Oboler's creative programming — highlighted by his masterpiece *Rocket from Manhattan*— entertained audiences well into the 1940s, and, in the 1950s, performances of the celebrated *Dimension X/X Minus One* brought a measure of maturity that early, televised science fiction generally lacked.

Radio also almost immediately impacted the political scene. Warren G. Harding's was the first "presidential" voice to traverse the airwaves, but it took Calvin Coolidge to regularly mine the media's possibilities. As "Silent Cal" admitted: "I can't make an engaging, rousing or oratorical speech ... but I have a good radio voice." Mr. Coolidge little realized that one of his deliveries would provide a window of opportunity key to saving the Land of the Free! This summary of the ... ummm ... radio action in *The Story without a Name* (thanks to the *Moving Picture World* of 18 October 1924) explains more:

> Alan Holt, radio expert, perfects for the government an electrical ray capable of causing death. Drakma, an international spy, seeks to learn the secret and has his minions seize Alan. Mary Walworth, daughter of an admiral, who is with Alan in his laboratory, smashes the machine. Alan and Mary are taken on board Drakma's yacht and he places Mary on a rum-runner, while Alan is put on a lonely island with only a workshop and he promises to complete the apparatus to save Mary. Instead, he goes to work and completes [an] apparatus necessary to broadcast a call for help when the air is clear just before the President delivers a message. The call is received by Mary's father, who is en route to Cuba for target practice. He immediately rushes to Mary's aid, and has an aeroplane sink Drakma's yacht. Alan in the meantime escapes on a raft and paddles out to the rum-runner off shore and manages to hold off the crew until the sailors arrive.

(Moral of the story: under no circumstance should an aspiring, villainous, would-be world conqueror ever provide a resourceful heroic weapons inventor with his own workshop facilities. Anyone the least bit familiar with the origin of Marvel Comics' Iron Man will attest to this.)

MPW augmented its synopsis with a helpful who's who: "Antonio Moreno [see *Dust of Egypt*, 1915] and Agnes Ayres [*Borderland*, 1922] ... handle the leading roles, with Tyrone Power as the arch-spy, Dagmar Godowsky as the vamping accomplice, Louis Wolheim as the rum-boat captain, Maurice Costello as one of the spy's henchmen, and Jack Bohn as the hero's friend in the Marines."

Reviews were as might be expected.

In *The New York Times* (6 October 1924), motion-picture beat writer Mordaunt Hall opined that the picture "begins with considerable mystery, then grows into an exaggerated melodrama and finally dies off as something so absurd that it seems like the work of a novice." As for the players… "Mr. Wolheim is as usual the acme of villainy…. Miss Ayres was handicapped by the stupidity of the character and Mr. Moreno, judging from the easy way in which he pummeled Mr. Wolheim, ought to challenge Dempsey."

"Sisk" in *Variety* (8 October 1924) recorded fairly much the same: "It is all very childish and obvious. It is, however, exceptionally well produced, without being well acted, save for Louis Wolheim's part." Displaying the type of geographical bias that *Variety* was known for, Sisk concluded: "Because it is so very melodramatic the impression is given that the big cities won't take so kindly to it, but in the wheat and corn belts they will probably sit in open mouthed amazement and applaud at the proper time. This one was strictly built for the sticks."

Roberta Nagle, writing for the afore-cited *Chicago Daily Tribune*, felt that "the director somehow failed to inject any human interest into it, and the character portrayals are rather weak. Antonio Moreno is fairly convincing as the hero, but Agnes [Ayres] never loses a self-consciousness which detracts from her role. If you're an ardent radio fan, *The Story Without a Name* may thrill you; if you're not, it may bore you."

"It has enough melodramatic action crowded into its six reels to make at least several exciting serials," said the December volume of *Photoplay* in a short and complimentary piece.

Photoplay's brevity was more surprising than its lack of adverse comment, considering that for the months preceding and following the release of *The Story Without a Name*, the magazine beat the drums for a national contest to rename the movie.

That's Agnes Ayres as Mary Walworth, Admiral's Daughter. Public relations for *The Story Without a Name* claimed that this scene inspired the invention of the classic carnival game, Whack-a-Mole. Who can say for sure?

And the prizes offered weren't something to sneeze at … especially in 1924 dollars: First Prize, $2,500; Second Prize, $1,000; Third Prize, $500, five $100 and $50 prizes, ten $25 prizes with a chance to win one of four "De Forest Reflex Radiophones," and additional cash from sponsoring broadcast stations. That sure brought 'em in; over 100,000 entries were reportedly submitted, with the winning entry the brainchild of Laverne Caron, a factory worker/alleged aspiring writer. His suggestion, "Without Warning"—which acted as an alternative release title in some venues—was thought to fit the bill because, per Mr. Caron, "Alan's invention strikes its victims without warning; because foreign spies have conspired against Alan and the American government." Second prize was awarded "Phantom Powers," which came with an even hokier explanation, courtesy of Texan runner-up, Pauline Pogue: "In this story there are two powers—the power of radio, and the power of love, both of which are phantom."

Tyrone Power—neither the first nor the last thespic "Tyrone Power"—took top bad-guy billing in *SwaN*. Tyrone Power #1 (1795–1841)—grandfather to our Drakma—was an Irishman who had written for and appeared on the London stage. (*Father* to our Drakma was Harold Power, a brilliant concert pianist whom we're glossing over because he hadn't been christened Tyrone by *his* father.) When "our" Tyrone's son (Tyrone Power #3) entered films in the early 1930s, "our" Tyrone then became known (more or less unofficially) as Tyrone Power, *Senior*, although he had already expired of a heart attack (literally in his son's arms) following a day of shooting on the 1931 genre remake, *The Miracle Man* (see entry on the 1919 original). Coincidentally, Tyrone #3 would also die of a heart attack while shooting a motion picture. Grandson (Tyrone #4)—somewhat awkwardly billed as Tyrone Power, *Junior*—is working in films as we write this.

Anyhow, Mr. Tyrone Power may have received the higher billing, but Louis Wolheim—he of the unmistakable broken nose—won the bulk of the critics' favor. Wollheim's trademark kisser (the result of a football injury at Cornell) had prompted Lionel Barrymore to entice him away from his math lectures at Cornell Prep into a career as a character actor ("With that face, you could make a fortune in the theater!"). In addition to *SwaN*, his having a bit part in John Barrymore's *Dr. Jekyll and Mr. Hyde* (1920) and providing the original story for *The Greatest Power* (1917; see entry, both) complete Wolheim's genre credits. Like Power, Louis Wollheim also passed away in 1931.

Burly Ivan Linow was also (probably) a lower-shelf heavy in *The Story without a Name*, but we've no clue as to how villainous he was onscreen, or for how long. Linow became a minor-league genre favorite during the early Sound Era, when he portrayed the doomed Hercules in the 1930 Lon Chaney talkie, *The Unholy Three*. The Latvian-born actor frequently played strongmen, wrestlers and pugs (or lugs) before and after *The Jazz Singer* turned the movies upside down, but most of his post–1930 appearances saw him uncredited.

Not missing any tricks, *The Story Without a Name/Without Warning* tapped into the ongoing press coverage of H. Grindell-Mathews (see *Laughing at Danger*, also from 1924). However, due to all of the radio-hoopla hardly anyone took notice.

— *SJ*

(The Strange Story of) Sylvia Gray

(The Strange Story of) Sylvia Gray. Vitagraph Co. of America and Broadway Star Features/General Film Co., by arrangement with Broadway Star Features Co., 26 October 1914, 4 reels [LOST]

CAST: Helen Gardner (*Sylvia Gray/Silvery*); Charles Kent (*Henry Gray*); Mary Charleson (*Margy*); Charles Eldridge (*Uncle Adam*); Gladden James (*Mr. Lennox*); Charles Dietz (*Dr. Frankenstein*); Arthur H. Ashley (*Vanveldt*); Evelyn Dumo (*Vivette Frankenstein*); Phyllis Grey (*Lucy Reynolds*); Edward Elkas (*Mr. Cohen*)

CREDITS: *Director and Screenplay* Charles L. Gaskill

They don't come much stranger than this. To prove our point, we shall reprint the picture's narrative gist — courtesy of the 31 October (Halloween!) 1914 *Variety*— adding [in brackets] only those details that might add to the overall lunacy of the thing. As always, we mourn the loss of films like *Sylvia Gray*.

Henry Gray and his wife Sylvia are reduced to poverty (although they still keep a nurse for the baby), and all depends upon the sale of Henry's play. When a manager's letter of rejection arrives, Sylvia — tired of poverty — elopes with Mr. Lennox, a wealthy clubman, who smokes cigarettes and keeps his hat on in the house. Subsequently, another manager — the cigar-chewing one — arrives and pays $5000 for the play as related. Henry hides the $5000 (in five bills) in the wall. Then he learns of the elopement, goes out of his mind, and vanishes, while the nurse-girl takes charge of the baby [named *Silvery*]. Sylvia learns that Lennox is about to wed Lucy Reynolds and promptly stabs him to death.

Twenty years elapse in two flickers and a light flash, and behold the Gray baby has grown up and is working as an artist's model, in love with her boss, [Vanveldt]. But she becomes involved with a hypnotist [Dr. Frankenstein] [!] working the small time. By a curious coincidence, Sylvia and Henry return home from their wanderings, Sylvia having beaten the murder case (you are permitted to fill in this detail from imagination). By another striking illustration of the fact that the world is a small place, their child, now grown, visits the village and her hypnotist learns of that $5000 in the wall, forgotten by Henry, who is lucid at intervals, but remembers nothing.

So the hypnotist sends the girl under his mesmerismic [*sic*] influence to get the roll, handing her a large dirk to work with. In the nick of time, the hypnotist's jealous wife [Vivette] appears on the scene and stabs him in the back so that his psychic power over the girl goes flop and she doesn't use the dirk on her father. The artist arrives on the scene to fold the girl in his arms and all is well.

[All ends happily in the betrothal of Silvery and Vanveldt and the reunion of Mr. Gray and Sylvia, who remorsefully and penitently (*sic*) admits the justice of all her punishment and determines that the past shall be forgotten in the happiness of the future.]

This last bit in brackets was brought to you by *The Moving Picture World* on the 26 December 1914. From *The Lima* [Ohio] *Daily News* (23 August 1915), we toss in the hitherto unreported fact that — upon his return to Stately Gray Manor, some two decades after having wandered off into the Great Unknown — not only is Himself intermittently lucid and completely memory-free, but he is also blind. BLIND. Somehow.

Those readers who have been thumbing through this volume, following devotedly our meticulously arranged alphabetical order, have already bumped into scenarist-director, Charles Gaskill, a few pages back (in *The Sleep of Cyma Roget*). Mr. Gaskill wrote and directed that one, much as he did here, and we have to admit that he didn't seem to improve much between *Sylvia Gray* (his first, definite genre turn — we're hedging our bets on his 1913 *A Princess of Bagdad*) and *Cyma Roget* (his last). If truth be told, though, we wouldn't have had it any other way.

Sylvia Gray (and *Cyma Roget*, and lots of other Charles Gaskell pictures) starred Helen Gardner — in real life, Mrs. Gaskill. Not a bad actress at all — if even half of these old press clippings are to be believed — Gardner received most of the few more positive adjectives that emanated from the trade press, which otherwise was quite bad. The critic for the aforementioned *Lima Daily News*, for example, felt constrained to admit that Mrs. Gaskill's double-role (she played the adult Silvery, too) demonstrated acting "at its very best." Also lending their names and presences to the Vitagraph production were Charles Eldridge, Charles Kent, Charles Dietz, and a handful of other folks not named Charles, chiefly because they were women. (Intriguingly, one was the aptly monikered Mary *Charles*on.) These women (and others) were left with the critical crumbs (and nothing from the otherwise perspicacious *Lima Daily News*), all of which were along the lines of "and the strong cast includes…" and "in supporting roles are…"

Fittingly, the one supporting Charles who *did* merit the occasional, semi-individual mention (like "The hypnotist and other characters are wisely cast" from *The New York Dramatic Mirror* on the 4 November 1914) was Mr. Dietz, who played Dr. Frankenstein. This may not have been the Dr. Frankenstein essayed by Augustus Phillips for J. Searle Dawley (whose Monster was yet *another* Charles — and an unbilled one, at that — Mr. Ogle), but would anyone care to question the likelihood of Mr. Gaskill's having reached into the air, only to pluck "Frankenstein" from his own, personal muse? By the bye, *Sylvia Gray* marked Mr. Dietz's only appearance in a major motion picture.

Charles *Kent*, on the other hand, had been in motion pictures (and had directed his fair share of them) since 1908. Born in London in 1852, Kent became a mainstay at Vitagraph during the 1910s, where he helmed (and acted in) everything from Shakespeare to … well … Gaskill. By the time *Sylvia Gray* was released, New York–born (he haled from Saratoga Springs) Charles *Eldridge* had appeared in about 100 films for Vitagraph. Both Kent and Eldridge would die with their boots on, within eight months of each other, in the very early 1920s.

We put *The Strange Story of* in parentheses because we found the film was referenced that way — and as plain old *Sylvia Gray* — without betraying rhyme or reason for doing so. It doesn't appear to have been a case of a different reissue title; we could find no evidence that the film was ever reissued. (In fact, we were hard-pressed to find much evidence that the film made it out of the can the *first* time!) None of us and no one with whom we have communicated in the writing of this tome has ever seen a poster or a press-book from this film, so we can only assume that it was released under its long(er) name and then (maybe gradually, maybe not) came to be known by its shorter, more casual title. At some point.

There's virtually nothing we can say about hypnotists at this juncture that we haven't already said within these pages, except to note that — even in 1914 — they were neither deemed trustworthy by air-headed young damosels nor faithful by jealous middle-aged wives.

There's a lesson to be learned in there. Somewhere.

— JTS

The Stranglers of Paris

The Stranglers of Paris. Motion Drama Co./Victory Film Co., 3 December 1913, 6 reels [LOST]
CAST: James Gordon (*Simmonet, later Jagon*); Jane Fernley (*Mathilde*); Anna Lehr (*Jeanne Guerin*); Stella Kibby (*Sophie*); Robert Broderick (*Lorenz*)
CREDITS: *Producer* J Parker Read, Jr.; *Director* James Gordon; based on the serialized novel *Les Estrangleurs de Paris* by Adolphe Belot (Paris, 1879), its adaptation by David Belasco, and the drama, *A Grip of Steel*, by Arthur Stanley.

Like that of Victor Hugo and Gaston Leroux (although neither as prolific as the former, nor as celebrated as the latter), Guadeloupe-born scrivener Adolphe Belot's reputation nowadays is based largely on his tales of violence and grotesquerie. Belot was a novelist, a playwright and — when money was tight — a writer of magazine serials, and it was in this latter capacity that he penned *Les Etrangleurs de Paris* in 1879. A tale of revenge, murder and secret societies, *Les Etrangleurs* was *de rigueur* escapism for the French working class and the bourgeoisie, alike. For a large number of Francophiles in foreign climes, the serial may not have raised an eyebrow; for David Belasco, though, it raised dramatic possibilities. The man who would one day be known as the "Bishop of Broadway" adapted the magazine piece for the stage, and *The Stranglers* opened in San Francisco in 1881.

Fast forward to 1898, when Arthur Stanley — a British playwright with a penchant for Paris — cranked out his own version of Belot's story. Retitled *A Grip of Steel*, the melodrama opened during Thanksgiving week at Broadway's Star Theatre; the length of its run is unknown and there is no evidence that the play was ever revived in a professional venue. Fast forward (again) to 1913: Back in the UK, Stanley was hired to adapt his own handiwork to the cinema, and *The Grip of Iron* — a Brightonia Production, starring H. Agar Lyons, the man who would go on to become the screen's first Fu Manchu — was released at 3250 feet. Come 1920, Britain's Famous Pictures would traipse back to the Stanley well. *The Grip of Iron* — this time 'round, a full-blown, 5000-foot feature — was directed by Bert Haldane, who also helped Stanley concoct the new scenario. If renowned for nothing else, this latter *Grip* was among the first films to

showcase the talents of Moore Marriott, a comedian who — along with Graham Moffatt and Will Hay — would come to personify British hi-jinks for decades to come.

In this midst of all this forcible asphyxiation, The Motion Drama Company — a one-shot entity, if our research is not faulty — came to grips with Belot's original, Belasco's adaptation, Stanley's variation, and the theme in general:

> Following his wife's untimely death, a French peasant named Simmonet takes his daughter Mathilde to Paris, where, unknown to the girl, he adopts the name of Jagon and becomes the leader of the murderous "Stranglers of Paris." After tampering with the will of Mathilde's wealthy suitor, Claude Guerin, Jagon strangles the old man, but the innocent Blanchard is convicted of the crime. A second murder is committed, whereupon Jagon is named as Blanchard's accomplice and imprisoned, leaving Lorenz, a member of the gang, to care for Mathilde. In attempting to prove Blanchard's innocence, Guerin's daughter Jeanne and her sweetheart Robert succeed in convincing Mathilde that her father is involved. Lorenz, angered by her denunciation, tries to strangle Mathilde, but the escaped Jagon appears to save her life. After killing Lorenz, Jagon reveals Blanchard's innocence and dies in his daughter's arms.

The above copyright précis — provided by "The Stranglers of Paris Co., Inc.," a corporate name that was definitely a trifle odd for the time — would have us believe that the City of Lights was at one time infested with stranglers much as the mattresses of no-tell motels might be rife with vermin. Even a perusal of Belasco's English-language adaptation wasn't much help in the long run, as we were unable to determine which elements of the play were derived from Belot's original (which eluded our best efforts at tracking it down), which were of Belasco's own invention, and which may have actually ended up embellishing the six-reel feature that saw release.

Forced to rely solely on that brief paragraph for plot points, we are thus in the dark as to whether there was a "Stranglers of Paris" society or gang or loose-knit band of brothers or whatever *before* Simmonet became Jagon and Jagon then became its "leader," or whether the ex-peasant somehow founded the organization and recruited from the available societal outcasts via their reputation, a talent search, or competitive examination. We know not the circumstances of his wife's passing, nor whether her death unleashed the fury of the man's vengeful nature or merely inspired him to move to the big city and ....errr ... try his hand at something completely different. It's not clear whether the Stranglers strangled passionately, yet indiscriminately — per that terse narrative, there are no attendant robberies — or passionately, but with a canny and purposeful plan in mind. Was Mathilde a moll who was merely stringing along Claude Guerin, her wealthy but elderly suitor? Or did she — presaging Anna Nicole Smith and her ilk — honestly love her old darling? Did the SoP survive Jagon's dying after strangling Lorenz following Lorenz's attempted strangulation of Mathilde? Or, bereft of leadership, did they disband and disperse, to strangle no more?

We've no idea, actually, but this effort by Pennsylvanian James Gordon — who also essayed the role of Simmonet — *was* the first, feature-length, USA-made thriller to deal with the terror to be caused by organized stranglers, French or otherwise. Gordon's resume (which included *The Haunted Sentinel Tower* [1911],

Hoodman Blind [1913], *The Mystery of the Poison Pool* [1914], and *The Sea Wolf* [1920]) shows that the man had a definite affinity for the offbeat and the adventurous during his two-decade career.

None of his colleagues did much genre-wise, though, and the identity of the picture's cinematographer has not yet been found. There's not much out there on the film, other than some passionate argument to have it suppressed and recalled. The 13 December 1914 edition of *Moving Picture World* spilled its ink, not in critiquing the film, but rather in an effort at destroying it.

> While the photography, scenic effects and acting in this production are praiseworthy, the picture presents one of the strongest arguments for censorship that we have yet witnessed. Reeking with the depiction of crime it will probably be thrown out in its entirety by every known board of censorship, official or otherwise. As a production it has not one redeeming feature and the exhibitor who will have the hardihood to offer it to his patrons will merit all the condemnation its exhibition will certainly drawn upon him.... Notwithstanding whatever sum *The Stranglers of Paris* may have cost The Motion Drama Company, the best disposition that concern can make of it will be to destroy the negative and charge the whole transaction off to profit and loss.

Nonetheless, a couple of weeks later, that same trade journal revisited the controversy and indicated that — in the interim — The Motion Drama Company had paid some serious attention to the *MPW*'s chastisement:

> A few weeks ago the *Moving Picture World* had occasion to condemn, in unmeasured terms, a motion picture production entitled *The Stranglers of Paris*.... The depiction of crime was altogether too realistic to be presented to the public. Whether the producer recognized this fatal defect himself, or whether the criticism of the *Moving Picture World* brought him to a realization of the fact that the subject in its original form was not suited for public exhibition, does not matter. The more important consideration is that he has very materially changed it from its original form, eliminating all of the more objectionable features and toning down others until he has now a feature production to which serious objection cannot be made.
> *The Stranglers of Paris* was directed by James Gordon, who also plays the leading role of Jagon, the Strangler. Not only is Mr. Gordon's work as director excellent, but his delineation of Jagon is most convincing. Jane Fernley, long a picture favorite, takes the part of his daughter. The other members of the cast provide excellent support throughout. The scenic effects are well chosen and form an interesting part of the picture, and the photographic quality is above average. All of the elements of good picture making are there.... The producers deserve credit for having done their work well and their willingness to eliminate the more objectionable features indicates that they recognize a limit beyond which they may not go with propriety or profit [27 December 1913].

See? *Somebody* reads movie reviews.

— *JTS*

Sylvia Gray see *(The Strange Story of) Sylvia Gray*

Tarzan and the Golden Lion

Tarzan and the Golden Lion. R-C Pictures/Film Booking Offices of America, 2 January 1927, 6 reels/5807 feet [available]

CAST: James Pierce (*Tarzan, Lord Greystoke*); Frederic Peters (*Esteban Miranda*); Edna Murphy (*Ruth Porter*); Harold Goodwin (*Burton Bradney*); Liu Yu-Ching (*Cadj, High Priest*); Dorothy Dunbar (*Lady Greystoke*); D'Arcy Corrigan (*Weesimbo*); Boris Karloff (*Owaza*); Robert Bolder (*John Peebles*); Jad-Bal-Ja (*Himself, the Golden Lion*)

CREDITS: *Producer* Joseph P. Kennedy; *Director* J.P. McGowan; *Assistant Director* Mack V. Wright; based on the eponymous novel by Edgar Rice Burroughs (Chicago 1923); *Adaptation* William E. Wing; *Cinematographer* Joe Walker; *Art Direction* F.J. Franklin

The only known print of the film is from French sources, so our summary is based upon the Grapevine Video release of same (which, fortuitously, bears an English translation).

> The tale takes place in equatorial Africa. There Tarzan (Lord Greystoke) is the de facto leader of the Wazari tribe. Tarzan's pet, Jad-Bal-Ja the Lion, warns of an intruder approaching. It's a haggard-looking white man, called by his African name, Weesimbo. Weesimbo, an explorer, tells of his capture and eventual escape from the Tangani people.
> While this is occurring, an entourage consisting of Jane Porter (aka Lady Greystoke), Ruth Porter and Tarzan's long-time friend and companion Burton Bradney, is en route to Tarzan's African dwelling. (It's obvious that there is an attraction between Burton and Ruth.) On yet another front, "Having been assured of rich spoils, Owaza, defector of the Wazari tribe, leads a band of plunderers toward the house of Tarzan." They are prodded on by the European, Esteban Miranda, and his subordinate, John Peebles. On the way, Miranda's forces discover Lady Greystoke's party. Miranda signals for an attack, but it is thwarted by the arrival of Tarzan and his Wazari warriors.
> Once back safely, the group hears Weesimbo reveal more: "Ten years ago I was captured by the Tangani, a tribe of the giant rocky mountains at the edge of the jungle.... This temple was built on top of a stunningly rich diamond mine, in which I was forced to work in the company of a few other captives." Despite his earlier setback, Miranda has not given up on his plans and sets up camp near Tarzan's home. Eavesdropping on the conversation, he decides to kidnap Weesimbo in order to find the treasure's location. As insurance against deceit by the old man, Ruth is taken hostage (but not before Burton is overcome).
> In the land of the Tangani, "Cadj, the giant fills the all-important role of high priest and sorcerer," but the status of a god is reserved for Numa, the "sacred lion." Shocked at a sudden earthquake, Cadj promises the superstitious natives a sacrifice to appease Numa. The cowardly Miranda forces Ruth to be the first up the Tangani cliffs and Weesimbo, second. The woman is immediately chosen for sacrifice; Weesimbo is injured.
> Tarzan, in pursuit, finds Weesimbo who courageously maps out in — his own blood — a shorter, easier route to an underground entrance. Esteban watches the exchange from afar, but cannot make out the directions. He disguises himself as Tarzan to dupe the delirious Weesimbo into (re-)revealing the secret.
> In the nick of time, Tarzan makes his way through the subterranean maze and kills Numa. Outside, Burton Bradney leads the Wazari against the Tangani. Ruth's safety is completely assured when Jad-Bal-Ja attacks the lone priest standing in the way of her freedom. Esteban finally finds his treasure, but his victory and life are both short-lived thanks again to Jad-Bal-Ja.
> Burton and Ruth reunite. The end title reads: "Long live Tarzan, long live the King of the Jungle" as Jad-Bal-Ja, the Golden Lion, sits atop Numa's throne.

Before going any further, it should be pointed out that in the French print character names differ from those apparently used in the initial U.S. release, and we've opted to change them back to the originals. (By way of example, the French-language print had transformed "Ruth Porter" into "Betty Greystoke," Tarzan's *sister.*) Adding to the confusion is the fact that many of the players in Edgar Rice Burroughs' source novel go by still other monikers, or are depicted significantly differently onscreen, or have been jettisoned completely.

In Burroughs' original prose, plot convolutions ruled the day. A woman by the name of Flora Hawkes—once employed by the Greystokes and thus aware of the treasures of Opar—heads up the band of European intruders; she enlists two Brits (the picture's John Peebles being one) and Adolph Bluber, a thickly accented German, as members of her coterie. As ERB conceived him, Esteban Miranda is a moving-picture actor capable of impersonating Tarzan, which ability will play a key role in the Europeans' master plan. Nonetheless, as deceitful as they are toward the King of the Jungle, the group members are treacherous to each other. Another key difference between the book and the film is that Burroughs' work includes no returning caravan of friends and family but, rather, does feature several brief appearances by Korak (aka Lord Greystoke, Jr.) and La (Queen of Opar, a reoccurring character in the series).

Besides Tarzan, Burroughs' rich imagination hatched a host of unsophisticated but popular fictional series starring the likes of John Carter of Mars, David Innes of underground Pellucidar, and Carson Napier of Venus. In *Edgar Rice Burroughs: Master of Adventure*, author Richard A. Lupoff describes Burroughs' collection of fictional heroes as "completely human and the reader of any age has no trouble identifying himself with them." Our 1927 film adaptation of Burroughs' ninth Tarzan novel received a not too dissimilar array of commentary:

> *Tarzan and the Golden Lion* is an extraordinary picture; the suspense in it is tense.... The story material is interesting and has been constructed into a plot intelligently.... This picture should take well everywhere, and in all types of theatres. It should please adults as well as children, particularly children [*Harrison's Reports*, 12 March 1927].

> This will undoubtedly furnish great amusement for the children but you will have to sell it to their elders on the utterly weird angle.... It is a wildly impossible story, Tarzan conversing with apes ... the mystical blah-blah in the hidden Temple—all that sort of thing [Harold Flavin, in *Motion Picture News*, 25 March 1927].

> The picture is decidedly out of the ordinary. It has that much in its favor but the weird concoctions that make up its situations are quite farfetched and require an overdose of imagination if they would be properly enjoyed. The thrills are of a fairly new order and the introduction of wild animals will undoubtedly make the picture doubly appealing for the younger element [*The Film Daily*, 26 March 1927].

And, reporting in from the local scene...

> *Tarzan and the Golden Lion* delighted the children and many grownups yesterday at the Phell [a local theater]. One little girl stayed through the picture twice and even then did not want to leave [*The* (St. Petersburg, Florida) *Evening Independent*, 28 May 1927].

Millennium viewers of all ages would unlikely buck the above opinion. If fast-paced adventure is the goal, *Tarzan and the Golden Lion* definitely provides interest for everyone. James Pierce makes for an acceptably athletic Tarzan, with his prowess at climbing hand-over-hand on branches, swinging convincingly from vine to vine, and punching out natives evident all the way through. The same cannot be said for the stout Frederic

Peters as the bogus Jungle King, though, and one wonders how old, wounded Weesimbo didn't just roll over and die laughing at the impersonation, even given his extreme mental state. Solid action (there's a *lot* of fighting), decent scenery, and some unintentional silliness permeate the picture. Initially, shots of the Tangani temple have a nice exotic feel to them, but credibility deteriorates a bit when the same static view is reused several times. And if Peters' portrayal causes some eye-rolling, horror icon Boris Karloff is wasted in a small part as a villainous native. What's more, his poor make-up makes him look like he has grey skin. Nevertheless, in the final prognosis, these maladies cause no real harm when swallowed with that "overdose of imagination" alluded to by *The Film Daily* above.

American James Pierce was neither English noble nor King of the Jungle, but he did make his way into the *real* Tarzan royal family. It turns out that Pierce, a Hollywood actor with a lingering career, met Burroughs at a party given by the author. After one glance, E.R.B. selected the tall, well-built, former All-American center for the next Tarzan movie. A year after the film's debut, the cinema's newest Jungle King wed Burroughs' daughter, Joan.

To hear Burroughs tell it, all did not go smoothly for Pierce on the set of *Tarzan and the Golden Lion*. As he recounted several years later in *Screen Play* (May 1934):

> It was the end of a long and tiresome day. The lion was tired, nervous and irritable. Furthermore his cage was inside the bungalow and he wanted to get to his cage far more than he wanted to go on any mission [as the script called for]. Ten or twelve times in succession he turned and ran into the bungalow instead of obeying the trainer's command.
> Pierce was tired, too, and wanted to get the thing over, so the last time, instead of stepping out of the lion's way as he had previously, he stood directly in the doorway, and when the lion tried to go between his legs he brought his knees together and stopped him.
> When Pierce stopped him, he backed off in surprise, bared his fangs and commenced to growl.
> [Charlie] Gay [the lion's owner] rushed in, shouting to Pierce to stand still, and with prod and chair held the lion off while Pierce edged his way slowly to the gate and safety.

Before the Silent Era ran its course, Frank Merrill took on the title role in two serials (1928's *Tarzan the Mighty* and 1929's *Tarzan the Tiger*), and this helped keep Burroughs' most lucrative character in the public eye. *Tiger* technically brought the Jungle King to the public's *ear* as well by boasting an optional partial soundtrack with Merrill providing the famous jungle yell. Still, it remained for Johnny Weissmuller—most folks' choice as the all-time definitive Tarzan—to ice the process when he began his vine-swinging legacy in filmdom's first, all-sound Tarzan feature, *Tarzan the Ape Man* (1932). That same year, *Golden Lion*'s Pierce also gave voice to the Ape Man on radio. In the broadcasts, Dorothy Dunbar—the Jane in Pierce's *Golden Lion*—was replaced by Joan Burroughs Pierce.

Pierce, Merrill, Weissmuller and all later Lords of the Jungle followed the lineage of the "Adam" of the cinematic canon, Elmo Lincoln, who starred in the very first film entry, *Tarzan of the Apes* back in 1918. Or did they? While it's true that Lincoln took on most of the acting chores in portraying the first Jungle King, the 10-year-old Gordon Griffith did cop the brass ring, technically; he played the Ape Man as a prepubescent boy. Further, there is strong evidence that a 6' 4" novice actor named Stellan S. Windrow was first handed the adult role. Windrow was forced to bow out after a few weeks of production when drafted into military service; however, some long shots of him swinging through the trees reportedly made the final cut.

These three Tarzans thus joined forces— along with Enid Markey (see *Civilization*, 1916), the screen's premier Jane— in what was a rather loose adaptation of ERB's eponymous first Tarzan tale. The film — one of the first features of The National Film Corporation (which also was responsible for *The Romance of Tarzan* and the subsequent — and biologically inevitable — *The Son of Tarzan*, a chapter-play)— is extant and readily available to Tarzan fans. Spoiler Alert! (and Animal Lovers Beware!): in one of the scenes, a tame, aged lion was stabbed to death by Lincoln in a display of "realism" that came well before the American Humane Society put a damper on such butchery with its *Guidelines for the Safe Use of Animals in Filmed Media*. Lincoln, Griffith and Markey all reprised their roles the very same year in the aforementioned *The Romance of Tarzan*; in the main, said sequel took place outside of Africa and differed significantly from Burroughs' source novel. Lincoln's last hurrah as the Ape Man appeared in chapter-play form with *The Adventures of Tarzan* (1921), in which he joined forces with the young serial queen, Louise Lorraine.

Sandwiching Lincoln's later efforts, Gene Pollar became the second (or fourth, depending on one's viewpoint) cinematic Tarzan in 1920's *The Return of Tarzan*, which, once again, did away with lots of Burroughs' storyline and most of the Dark Continent action. Pollar had the physique for the role, but not the thespic chops. Prior to the production, he had been a member of New York City's Bravest; filling out the loin cloth

constituted his first, last, and only acting experience. Burroughs once opined, succinctly: "As an actor, Gene was a great fireman."

Despite Pollar's best efforts, Tarzan silent-screen portrayals had not yet reached their nadir. In the serial, *The Son of Tarzan* (1920–21) — re-released as the feature-length *Jungle Trail of the Son of Tarzan* in 1923 — the role fell to P. Dempsey Tabler, a toupee-wearing, middle-aged actor with a decidedly un–Tarzan-like physique. Luckily, most of the action centered on Tarzan's titular offspring, played (at varying ages) by two actors, the first of whom was Hawaiian, Kamuela Searle. The presence of the second — Gordon Griffith — must have given the Tarzan faithful pause, what with the actor's apparently having skipped forward a *generation* from his first appearance five years earlier.

Edgar Rice Burroughs often brought Tarzan into the realm of the fantastic. In his *Tarzan at the Earth's Core*, the hero crosses over to meet up with David Innes, the protagonist in ERB's Pellucidar series. Judging by its source material, *Golden Lion* may be the most fantastic of the silent Tarzan features. In the novel, the treasures are to be found in Opar, an ancient colony of fabled lost Atlantis, and a good portion of the prose centers upon the "Bolgani," a half-human/half-gorilla race. Be that it may, the entire Tarzan concept itself stretches the boundaries of known science with the idea that a feral child could be raised by animals and subsequently adapt to *any* kind of society, let alone take on the duties of an English Lord.

— *SJ*

The Temptations of Satan

The Temptations of Satan. U.S. Amusement Corp./Warner's Features, Inc., November 1914, 5 reels [LOST]

CAST: Joseph Levering (*Everyboy*); Vinnie Burns (*Everygirl*); James O'Neill (*Satan*); Fraunie Fraunholz (*Justice*); Mr. Morton (*Avarice*). The actor playing *Avarice* is referred to only as "Mr. Morton" in the above-cited publications. *The AFI Catalog* opines that the actor may have been Walter Morton.

CREDITS: *Producer and Director* Herbert Blaché

An odd bit of stuff concerning His Infernal Majesty's pursuit of a gal who wouldst be an opera singer, *The Temptations of Satan* is part morality play (the heroine goes by "Everygirl"), part Charles Gounod, and mostly treacle. The most cogent plot element may be traced back to Genesis; not a one of the other details has survived the decades since the film's original release in any sort of intelligible form. None of the (dreadful) "synopses" we've found have left us with anything other than a vague notion of the movie's narrative flow and a paucity of specifics.

The ebb in that narrative flow is most evident in the 31 October (Halloween!) 1914 sort-of-summary from *The Moving Picture World*. We have kept reviewer Hanford C. Judson's language intact so that the reader might be simultaneously edified and frustrated.

James Pierce as Tarzan, with Jad-Bal-Ja as the Golden Lion. Mr. Pierce and Mr. Bal-Ja's furs are by Armani.

Satan rehearses his cast of helpers (semi-theatrical, cabaret characters and the like) before sending them up to Metropolis to snare and ruin the pretty Everygirl who has a voice and is ambitious. Then Satan, having got the show started, becomes human, and follows to see the fun and take part as the double villain. He fits in perfectly.

[Then Everyboy strives] to rescue his sweetheart who, at first, almost becomes a white slave and, later, as poor working girl, has to be rescued from foreman and then from owner and then from a sweatshop fire.

And that, as they say in Missouri, is that. Peter Milne, commenting on the movie in the 7 November 1914 *Motion Picture News*, adds the following "details" to the ebb (or maybe it's the flow): "Everyboy and Everygirl are the characters with whom we are most concerned.... The story woven about the two young people is one of great interest, nothing unusual, but always absorbing.... A fine fight is staged in a café, and a good fire scene comes near the end of the picture."

Hmmmmmm… One might think that satanic interference in the aspiring operatic career of an Everygirl would be a textbook example of "unusual." In that dim light, Mr. Milne also mentions, en passant, "the subsequent losing of [Everygirl's] mind," without apparently considering *this* condition as being somewhat out of the ordinary. (An additional tantalizing tidbit, courtesy of Mr. Milne, reveals that "when Everygirl lets go of the end of a rope and falls to the ground, she drops only a few feet, yet the fall completely unbalances her mentally." Ye Gods! Unlikely? Certainly. *Unusual?* Naaah.)

Following immediately is *The AFI Catalog*'s description, which (usually) is drawn from the copyright registration. *Temptations* was never registered for copyright, though, as it was a production of the U.S. Amusement Corp.—run by the Blachés—and the paperwork on many of their features never made it to Washington, D.C. The AFI staff, then, must have exuded this "plot recap" from a judicious (albeit random) selection of words and phrases that appeared in either (or both) of the critical journals cited above. "Satan and his helpers decide to ruin the innocence of Everygirl, who has a beautiful singing voice and desires to be on the stage. Satan takes on human form and follows her in Metropolis to make sure that she accepts his terms."

Logical considerations of those terms may include, but not be limited to, assumptions that (1) the Devil arranges for the wench to sing at—where else?—the Metropolis-alitan Opera à la the sort of machinations later immortalized by Otis B. Driftwood, or (2) after determining preternaturally that the gal *can't* cut the vocal mustard, His Nibs finds her other employment, better suited to her temperament, skills, and education. Nor is she merely relegated to the chorus. Nay; the reported storyline suggests that, with her not possessing sufficient vocal magnificence to be borne on the shoulders of an adoring public or to inspire the creation of a "Peaches Everygirl," the young darling's only recourse is to wield a washboard or steam iron 24/7 in a converted tenement in the Lower East Side.

Admittedly, this *is* but a theory. The scenario may, in fact, have been a masterpiece of unparalleled genius, with our heroine's descent from Verdi and Puccini's celestial ether to Dante's Seventh Ring-around-the-collar sending audiences home,

moved to rededicate their lives to selfless charity and pure vegetarianism. We don't know. If we can't quite put our fingers on the pulse of the picture's plot, though, let us instead have a gander at the dramatis personae.

Satan—in any and all of his guises, including that intriguing, non-human form referred to by Mr. Judson—was portrayed by James O'Neill, a Philadelphian who was born a couple of weeks after the Battle of Gettysburg. A Vaudeville song-and-dance man before entering the flickers (via Alice Guy-Blaché's Solax Company in the early 1910s), O'Neill would late in life claim that he had appeared in over 200 films with the selfsame lady producer/director. Whether or not that claim rang true, one of his first appearances in a feature (if not his first) was in *The Star of India*, a 1913 example of that popular sub-genre—covetous gem-snatchers vs. exotic repo squads—directed by Alice's husband, Herbert. Records show that O'Neill's feature credits were sparse—fewer than two dozen in 15 years—although he did work for Vitagraph and Universal in addition to his aiding and abetting the Blachés, in any of their corporate identities.

As for the actor's performance in the picture at hand, Mr. Judson offered a terse paean: "Satan is acted by James O'Neill." In speaking of the cast to his *MPN* readership, Mr. Milne admitted that James O'Neill is the most important. He embodies the popular idea of Satan and is constantly changing from one character to another, but in all of the parts he retains the same evil countenance which stamps him always as Satan.

Neither the film nor still photos of O'Neill in full, diabolic gear can be located, so we are left to our presumption that the "popular idea" of the Old One would have included horns and a tail. His "constantly changing from one character to another" is what really intrigue us, though, as the image of his retaining "the same evil countenance" while taxing the resiliency of the Blaché wardrobe department brings a wry smile to our lips. There's not much else we can offer on Mr. O'Neill's devil, or on Mr. O'Neill, himself. His professional history has become inadvertently entwined with that of another, more renowned James O'Neill—the Irish actor who was also father to playwright, Eugene O'Neill—and even the most astute of research facilities (e.g., the Academy, the AFI) admit to not being altogether certain as to which O'Neill essayed what part in a number of early cinematic concoctions.

Fraunie Fraunholz, Vinnie Burns (a gentleman and a lady, respectively, their Christian names notwithstanding), and Herbert Blaché had also partnered to provide the masses with *The Woman of Mystery* (1914; see entry), while Fraunie and *Satan* co-star, James Levering, added their names and avoirdupois to the aforementioned *The Star of India*. Mr. Levering, by the way, directed more frequently than he acted, and his *Luring Shadows* (1920)—a sort of murder mystery colored with a touch of spiritualism—is covered elsewhere in these pages. As for Miss Burns, she reappears, arm in arm with Mr. Blaché, in our entry on 1914's *The Mystery of Edwin Drood*.

Mr. Blaché, his arms folded, is considered at greater length in our essay on *The Untameable* (1923).

In addition to accounts of *Temptation*'s storyline being things of shreds and patches, critical coverage on the film is equally unintelligible. Mr. Judson, upon whose quirky prose we must rely for the essence of our knowledge of the plotline, works himself into a near-unfathomable lather in his subsequent analysis of this allegorical melodrama. "Mr. Blaché," he starts, calmly enough, "has succeeded in getting a higher degree of melodramatic power by ... frankly admitting that his heroine and hero are as individual as every boy and girl and no more so." At neither first, nor second, nor thirtieth glance does this even begin to make sense. Mr. Judson continues, "The atmosphere of the morality brings out distinctly some of the qualities that are inherent in the melodrama. Melodramas are nothing if not moral. This picture will suggest to thoughtful spectators the seed from which melodramas grew — and, if the mind wants to dwell on it, it will start one on many an interesting cogitation."

Another interesting cogitation would center on this man's receiving a regular paycheck from *The Moving Picture World*. Amazing? Yes. *Unusual?* Hell, you know the answer to that.

— *JTS*

Terror Island

Terror Island. Famous Players–Lasky Corporation/Famous Players–Lasky Corp. and Paramount-Artcraft Pictures, April, 1920, 5 reels, partial print at Library of Congress

CAST: Houdini (*Harry Harper*); Lila Lee (*Beverly West*); Wilton Taylor (*Job Mourdaunt*); Jack Brammall (*Ensign Tom Starkey*); Eugene Pallette (*Guy Mourdaunt*); Edward Brady (*Captain Black*); Frank Bonner (*Chief Bakaida*); Ted E. Duncan (*First Officer Murphy*); Fred Turner (*Henry West*); Rosemary Theby (*Stella Mourdaunt*)

CREDITS: *Presented by* Jesse L. Lasky; *Director* James Cruze; *Assistant Director* Cullen B. Tate; *Scenario* Walter Woods; *Story* Arthur B. Reeve and John W. Grey; *Cinematographer* William Marshall; *Art Director* Wilfred Buckland

Harry Houdini — who appeared as himself in short films as early as the beginning of the 20th century — almost got his first crack as an actual cinematic *actor* in, of all things, the silent production of *20,000 Leagues Under the Sea.* Negotiations with Universal broke down, though, and the world never did get to watch the famed "self-liberator" as Captain Nemo. Nor did anyone ever get to view *Houdini and the Miracle,* an aborted collaboration with the Williamson Brothers, the underwater film team that made *20,000 Leagues* possible. Instead, it was Famous Players–Lasky that finally got him under the oceans in *Terror Island* — as Harry Harper, intrepid inventor of a new type of submarine.

Although most of the film is intact at the Library of Congress (from a 35 mm Realart re-release) and sufficient to get the gist of the action, as of this writing reels three and four have gone missing. Without further fanfare, the full copyright synopsis dated 26 March 1920 to help fill in the gaps:

Harry Harper is an inventor of enormous strength who uses his strange powers to entertain his friends. He invents a deep-sea submarine by the aid of which he plans to salvage valuable cargoes of sunken ships. Despite his efforts to keep his invention a secret, an account of it appears in one of the big newspapers.

Among those who read the article are Beverly West, the ward of Job Mourdaunt, and his son, Guy Mourdaunt. Job is held to be the meanest man in town and his son is little better. They are commission merchants and have a warehouse on the waterfront. Beverly is interested in Harper's invention because she has just received a letter from her father informing her that he is a prisoner on an island and is destined to die unless she delivers in person a black pearl given her by the chief on the occasion of her visit to the island with her father five years previously.

West advised his daughter to induce Mourdaunt to organize a wrecking company and after taking her to the island, salvage a wrecked vessel containing vast treasures, the location of which lies under the lining of the jewel case in which the pearl is secured. Job and Guy have fitted up a schooner to salvage the wreck, and when Beverly tells of her father's plight and her desire to save him from being sacrificed on the next feast day, they plan to obtain the jewel and chart from her and make the voyage without her. They tell her that they cannot find anyone to make the voyage.

Guy Mourdaunt has read about the submarine and he decides to double-cross not only his father, but Harper as well. He seeks to induce Harper to join him in the enterprise, but Harper refuses. Beverly appeals to Harper for aid and he agrees to carry her to the island in the submarine. The Mourdaunts try by every means to obtain the jewel and chart, they even resorting to fire, but Harper rescues Beverly who slips the jewel box to him. Stella Mourdaunt tries her wiles on Harper without success, and in revenge, the Mourdaunts smash the model of the submarine and disable the deep-sea vessel itself.

Convinced at length that they cannot obtain the jewel case or the chart, the Mourdaunts sail for the island. Discovering that Harper has returned the jewel case to Beverly, they bundle her on board the schooner, but Harper goes to her rescue. He is compelled to battle the chains, locks and fires. He escapes and gets into a box which is thrown into the sea. He escapes from the box and rises to the surface only to find the schooner outward bound, carrying Beverly, whom he now loves, with it. He repairs his submarine and starts in pursuit. He finally overhauls the schooner and after a desperate battle rescues Beverly and carries her to the submarine. But the jewel case and chart were in the possession of the Mourdaunts, so that the submarine is compelled to trail the schooner to the island.

Both vessels reach the island on feast day and the natives under Chief Bakaida are celebrating in anticipation of the sacrifice of Mr. West. The natives have salvaged the wreck and carried a heavy safe to the top of a cliff. Guy, Job and Stella land, the latter presents the jewel to the chief, and in accordance with his promise Bakaida turns over to them the property salvaged from the wreck. But it transpires that Stella, who claims to be West's daughter, must be sacrificed in place of her reputed father, a bit of news that terrifies the Mourdaunts. West is released and meeting Beverly and Harper, he introduces Beverly as his daughter, whereupon the chief orders that Stella's bonds be transferred to Beverly.

Harper battles valiantly in Beverly's behalf, but he is imprisoned and she locked up in the ship's safe and thrown into the sea. The Mourdaunts send down a diver to dynamite the safe, but Harper releases himself and then rescues Beverly. He carries her to the submarine just as the safe is blown to atoms. Harper makes a second trip to the safe, obtains the jewels, encounters the schooner's diver and beats him under water. The Mourdaunts, on learning that Harper has the jewels, decide to kidnap Mr. West and they go ashore only to engage in a fierce battle with the natives who are infuriated because some sailors have captured five native girls. Job is slain in the battle.

Harper realizes that only magic will be able to save Beverly's father as the natives are determined to kill every white man they find. He and Beverly swim ashore and Harper does a rope trick which awes the natives who proclaim him king. Harper orders West released and Guy and Stella make a dash for the submarine. Guy accidentally shoots Stella and to save Harper, his friend Starkey shoots Guy. The party then make its escape from the island in the submarine.

In the states Harper and Beverly give a party to a party of waifs.

It is announced that Harper purposes to devote the treasure he has won to financing a great charity, in which work, it is made evident, Harper and Beverly will work as one.

An introductory inter-title assured audiences that Houdini "actually performed the amazing feats here pictured" (as if they didn't already know). Most of the feats consisted of his escaping from something, rescuing someone, or battling somebody, but when Harry wowed the natives in the last reel with his rope trick, he literally took a page from the book of his namesake, Jean Eugene Robert-Houdin. In his 1859 autobiography, *Memoirs of Robert-Houdin*, the French conjurer recounted how three years earlier he had served as a special ambassador in Algeria for the French Foreign Office. At the time, Marabout priests performing phony acts of sorcery had prompted the native Kabyle people into sporadic rebellion; Robert-Houdin was called in to outdo them so as to debunk their powers. He obliged by rendering a strong man "weaker than a woman" and incapable of lifting a simple box, catching bullets in his teeth from a gun fired point blank, and performing other assorted acts of "magic."*

The science-fiction elements in *Terror Island* took a back seat to Houdini's demonstrations of proficiency as an escape artist and magician, yet at least one such element played a crucial role in the story. Harry Harper's invention of an "electric periscope" (a circular TV-like screen wired to a transmitting device) was instrumental in saving at sea the beauteous Beverly West (Lila Lee; see *One Glorious Day*). *Moving Picture Stories* (16 April 1920)—a fan-oriented publication specializing in elaborate plot synopses—enticed potential ticket-buyers with a description of Harry's advanced sub in its *Terror Island* adaptation: "The machinery was very compact. It consisted of a mechanism for driving the boat on the surface by a gasoline engine. When he [Harry Harper] wished to submerge, the engine was run by a system of storage batteries, as the gas engine required oxygen to run it and none was available underwater."

What's more, *MPS* continued, the submarine's interior was "automatically sprayed with a solution of lime, to purify the air" and illuminated with electric lights.

Clearly, *Terror Island* was mindless fun intended for the American hinterlands, which may be why *The New York Times* passed on reviewing it. It was left to the New York tabloids to sell the Houdini feature to its citizenry, while newspapers in "less sophisticated" venues (like Wisconsin, Tennessee and Iowa) ran multiple publicity pieces and large advertisements in their entertainment sections. As for the trades, *Wid's* felt that "they've gone very wild on both story and thrills," the critic for the *Motion Picture News* suggested that the picture "resembles a wild serial in incident and action," and *Moving Picture World* found it "really entertaining." *Billboard*, on the other hand, testified that audiences laughed out loud, while the 4 April 1920 *Variety* passed sentence thusly:

> Despite the scenario by Arthur B. Reeve and John W. Gray, and the direction by James Cruze, there is little in this picture apart from the interest in Houdini that offers any substance in the way

of a rational story.... It has a very able cast, among them being the beautiful Lila Lee and Wilton Taylor as a deep, dyed-in-the-wool villain. But their abilities cannot here be taken into consideration for criticism, for in that event it would mean endorsing their efforts in a vehicle which does neither the first nor second party any good.

Per Harold Kellock's *Houdini: His Life Story* (an early biography liberally drawing upon the documents of Mrs. Beatrice Houdini), gross domestic receipts for the movie through the end of 1926 were $111,145; with worldwide distribution, the figure reached $165,003. Had the film actually appeared in serial form, as *Motion Picture News* suggested, receipts might have been much worse. Crucial for the financial success of any chapter-play was the word of mouth generated by the first few episodes, and the action in *Terror Island* bogs down severely in its initial minutes. Not helping matters is a plethora of inter-titles, character-intro cards, close-ups of letters and newspaper headlines—in short, all of the silent film devices necessary to unfold a convoluted tale. The storyline was hatched by Arthur B. Reeve and John W. Grey (gagman for Mack Sennett and Harold Lloyd), who were aided and abetted by scenarist Walter Woods.

Of these, Reeve's is the most recognizable name, if only due to his popular series of books featuring scientific detective, Craig Kennedy, and filled with everything from electro-magnetic weaponry to cheap atomic energy. Reeve's Kennedy had already appeared on screen in the entertaining trio of "Elaine" serials and would endure long enough to be featured (in a lesser capacity) in the juvenile serial, *The Radio Detective* (1926); in the incredibly abysmal 1936 chapter-play, *The Clutching Hand*; and in *Craig Kennedy — Criminologist*, a mainly mediocre TV show from the early 1950s. Of perhaps greater importance is the influence that the fictional hero had on similar characters throughout the 20th century.

Arthur Benjamin Reeve was born in Patchogue, New York, in mid–October 1880 and went on to graduate from Princeton. Although he studied law for a while, Reeve turned to writing and — before entering the film industry — did some serious work on criminology. In 1912 and 1913, *McClure's Magazine* published his *Great Cases of William J. Burns* (a readily known detective of the day) and, in the early 1930s, he wrote a series of articles for NBC's Radio Crime Prevention Program. Reeve also collaborated with *Terror Island* partner, John Grey, on both *The Grim Game* (1919) and on the novelization of *The Master Mystery*, aka *The Houdini Serial*.

James Cruze's surname referred to the Battle of Vera Cruz. Born Jens Vera Cruz Bosen ("Bosen" was a name he kept for his private life) on the 27 March 1884 near Ogden, Utah, Cruze maintained that one-quarter of his lineage was Ute Indian; still, he was raised early on as a Mormon. A youthful stint as a fisherman in Alaska brought him enough money to afford acting lessons, but he spent some time as a hawker in Billy Banks' traveling medicine show before joining up with a theatrical company in Boise City, Iowa; later, he formed his own troupe.

---

*In the first trick, the befuddled fellow was unaware that the box that he was charged to lift was connected to a sizeable electro-magnet that could be activated at Robert-Houdin's discretion. Wax bullets and sleight-of-hand saved the Frenchman in the second trick.

Progressing through the ranks, Cruze eventually attained membership in David Belasco's prestigious company. Filmmaking seemed the next, natural step, and Cruze later recalled: "The Thanhouser film *She* was the first picture in which I appeared. I had done some big stuff on the stage just previous to that, so I came into the company as lead and played opposite Marguerite Snow."

The 1911 *She* was most likely not the first picture in which he appeared but, nonetheless, he turned in a commendable job in the dual roles of Leo Vincey and the ancient Kalikrates. James Cruze — who easily attained prominence as *the* Thanhouser leading man — then made *the* ultimate dual performance an actor could make in the titular role(s) of 1912's *Dr. Jekyll and Mr. Hyde. Reel Life* (5 September 1914) stated that the performance "was one of the strongest pieces of acting Cruze ever did."

Cruze left Thanhouser for California in 1915 and, in 1918, began a new career as a director. While he would go on to be named twice as one of the world's Top Ten in his craft, this did not translate into popularity with his fellow technicians. Karl Brown, the cameraman on Cruze's 1924 triumph, *The Covered Wagon*, described the director as "a drunken, obscene, lecherous individual." Still, the man could exhibit a Jekyll-like counterpoint to his Hyde-like behavior, and thus he was one of the few to publicly rise to the defense of Roscoe Arbuckle (the ill-fated, would-be star of the Cruze-directed *One Glorious Day*). Thrice-married (his first was Marguerite Snow, his co-star in *She*), Cruze left to his third wife (Alberta Beatrice McCoy) an estate valued at a mere $1000 when he died of a heart ailment on the 4 August 1942. His contributions to silent genre films were few, but noteworthy, and his *Waking up the Town* (1925) is discussed elsewhere in this volume. And what might have been! Shortly after Fritz Lang gave the world *Metropolis*, Cruze started planning to adapt Karel Capek's *R.U.R.* for the silver screen, using Eugen Schüfftan as his special-effects man. Sadly, his plans fell through.

Given the choice, we'd have taken that over Houdini's Captain Nemo in *20,000 Leagues Under the Sea*. The real pity is that we have neither.   — *SJ*

The Thief of Bagdad

The Thief of Bagdad. Douglas Fairbanks Pictures/United Artists, 18 March 1924, (New York premiere at 14 reels/12,933 feet); released 1 January 1925at 12 reels/11,230 feet [available]

CAST: Douglas Fairbanks (*Ahmed, The Thief of Bagdad*); Snitz Edwards (*His Evil Associate*); Charles Belcher (*The Holy Man*); Julanne Johnston (*The Princess*); Sojin (*The Mongol Prince*); Anna May Wong (*The Mongol Slave*); Brandon Hurst (*The Caliph*); Tote Du Crow (*The Soothsayer*); Noble Johnson (*The Indian Prince*); Sam Baker (*The Sworder*); Mathilde Comont (*The Persian Prince*); Charles Stevens (*His Awaker*); Charles Sylvester, Jess Weldon, Scotty Mattraw (*Eunuchs*); with Winter Blossom, Jesse Fuller, Sadakichi Hartmann, Eugene Jackson, Jesse Lasky Jr., Etta Lee, K. Nambu, Jack Parker, David Sharpe

CREDITS: *Produced by* Douglas Fairbanks; *Director* Raoul Walsh; *Scenario* Lotta Woods; based on a story by Elton Thomas (Douglas Fairbanks); *Cinematographer* Arthur Edeson; *Assistant Photographers* P.H. Whitman, Kenneth MacLean; *Art Director* William Cameron Menzies; *Consulting Art Director* Irvin J. Martin; *Technical Director*

Robert Fairbanks; *Film Editor* William Nolan; *Musical Compositions* Mortimer Wilson; *Assistant Director* James T. O'Donohoe; *Production Manager* Theodore Reed; *Costume Director* Mitchell Leisen; *Master of Wardrobe and Props* Paul Burns; *Director of Mechanical Effects* Hampton Del Ruth; Consultant: Edward Knoblock; Research *Director* Arthur Woods; *Associate Artists* Anton Grot, Paul Youngblood, H.R. Hopps, Harold Grieve, Park French, William Utwich, Edward M. Langley; *Master Electrician* Albert Wayne; *Technicians* Howard MacChesney, Clinton Newman, Walter Pallman, J.C. Watson; *Still Photographer* Charles Warrington

Douglas Fairbanks' *The Thief of Bagdad* was the most ambitious, lavish and expensive fantasy film made in Hollywood up its premiere in late March 1924, and it would remain so (even in non-adjusted dollars) for many decades. As it turned out, the picture, while critically lauded, was not a big hit with the hoi polloi and so studios were reluctant to invest enormous sums in fantasy films for some time to come. The large-scale genre pictures that *were* successfully mounted between *Thief* and *2001: A Space Odyssey* came from England and Europe, and — ironically — included Alexander Korda's 1940 quasi-remake.

The Thief of Bagdad of 1924 — the movie that put the skids to the high-budget flight of fancy — is out and about all over the place, and our synopsis is based on our viewing same: Ahmed — the happy-go-lucky and audacious thief of the title — hangs his turban in a subterranean hideaway off the side of a well. One day, while escaping pursuers, he takes refuge in a mosque and hears The Holy Man (Charles Belcher) preach that happiness must be earned. (This bit of ersatz-pragmatic philosophy must come directly from the heavens, as it is spelled out in the stars that fill a tableau at the beginning and end of the picture.) Ahmed scoffs at this notion. Back on the job, he steals a magic rope, decides to rob the palace of the Caliph (a nigh-unrecognizable Brandon Hurst — see Barrymore's *Dr. Jekyll and Mr. Hyde*), but settles for stealing the slipper of the lovely princess (Julanne Johnston), who is, at that moment, taking a siesta. When she awakens, the princess is put up on marriage block, and a soothsayer has already foretold that she will wed whichever suitor touches the rose tree in the courtyard. Ahmed has decided to kidnap the princess, so he and His Evil Associate (as Snitz Edwards is billed) purloin garments and quadrupeds from the marketplace and present themselves, suitably accoutered, alongside the other suitors (which include Noble Johnson's Indian Prince). A convenient bee stings Ahmed's horse, it bucks, and the thief is sent into the rose bush. The princess — who has been watching the arrival of the would-bes and who has already been struck by Ahmed's roguish good looks — is now certain that he is to be her husband and, in due course, her betrothal ring is presented to him by the Caliph.

Despite having been given the ring, Ahmed *still* plans on kidnapping the princess. Once he has climbed into her chambers, though, love works its magic, and the thief confesses his lowly status. Said deception becomes known to the Caliph, Ahmed is captured and flogged, and the order is given that he be thrown to the great ape (a chimpanzee, photographed on reduced-size sets) so that he might be torn to pieces. But the princess bribes the guards, and Ahmed is not only spared this severe punishment, but he is tossed out of the palace to his freedom via a secret door (and, as the film unspools, we discover that there are secret doors everywhere). Given that the princess's first choice is no longer a contender, the three bona fide princes are tasked with going forth and finding the rarest of all treasures (whatever *that* might be) and returning it to the princess, who will then choose a husband based on what she thinks of their swag. Ahmed, in a deep funk, consults the same holy man he had ridiculed earlier. The Imam encourages him to join the hunt for magical doodads and thus win the princess's hand, fair and square. ("Happiness must be earned," remember?) Obviously not one to hold a grudge, the old boy even gives Ahmed some pointers on what he should look for and where he might find it.What no one knows—aside from one of the princess's servants (Anna May Wong)—is that the Mongol Prince, Cham Shing (Sojin), has secreted thousands of his men in Bagdad and is prepared to take the city by force if he cannot win the princess on the up and up.

Among them, the three scavengers manage to collect a flying carpet, a magic crystal gazing-ball, and a magic apple that can cure all ills and possibly (this is less than clear) reverse the effects of death. Ahmed, after battling monsters galore, acquires a cloak of invisibility *and* a magic chest whose glittery contents can conjure up one's heart's desires. When the princes regroup after their travels, Cham Sing suggests the crystal be used to view the princess who, it transpires, lies dying. (The Mongol Prince had sent ahead orders that she be poisoned so he could use the magic apple to heal her.) The three hop onto the flying carpet and the princess is revived. Nonetheless, when each of her suitors declares that she should choose him because his gift was responsible for saving her, she maintains they are all in a dead heat. She argues that they would not have known that she was

close to death without the crystal, they would not have arrived in time without the carpet, and she would have died without the apple; on its own, each gift was inadequate without the other two. Cham Sing reacts poorly to this observation and decides to take over the city. In a sequence that burlesques the climax of D. W. Griffith's *The Birth of a Nation*, Ahmed arrives on the scene with *his* magic stuff, foils the heavy, saves the day, and marries the princess.

The Thief of Bagdad's chief flaw may be found in its second half: those quests for the rarest of all treasures are, for the most part, rather formulaic and perfunctory. To wit, upon showing up wherever, two of the princes almost immediately encounter someone who knows of a merchant's stall where there's a flying carpet for sale or a spot where one might well find a magic apple. Only the magic crystal—located in the eye-socket of a gargantuan statue—presents any challenge or poses any peril whatsoever: the servant sent off to retrieve it falls to his death. In a similar, fairly flat fashion, Ahmed vanquishes all the monsters he encounters within a minute or so of screen-time and without (apparently) breaking a sweat. These "battles" are suspenseless, as the thief does not display a moment's hesitation in confronting flying bats, dragons, or aquatic arachnids. What he *does* display is the sort of combat savvy and "can do" spirit one usually does not associate with near-homeless petty criminals. On the other hand, this section of the film underlies (without hammering at it incessantly) the theme that one must earn happiness: the princes send underlings to acquire their treasures while Ahmed goes the distance entirely alone.

Douglas Fairbanks had gone the distance entirely alone, too—sort of—having moved within the space of five years from being an athletic comedian in a hugely successful series of short films that spoofed then-current fads to an athletic romantic hero, prone to dashing about while colorfully attired in a series of popular motion pictures based on classic adventure literature. His early, stock portrayal of the milquetoast who must become a man to win the girl may very well have been the template for the timorous lead roles in such films as *The Monster* and *The Cat and the Canary*. Still, Fairbanks' most famous (and bizarre) short—1916's *The Mystery of the Leaping Fish*, wherein he played hopped-up detective, Coke Ennyday—is not exactly typical of this role.

By 1920, Doug had shed his first wife (Anna Beth Sully, mother of Douglas Fairbanks, Jr.) and married Mary Pickford (who had similarly shed her first husband) and the pair became Hollywood's "Royal Couple." (That this did not cause scandal rather than adulation is an indication of just how popular the two were and how Americans have always been able to cherry-pick moral matters.) They joined with Charlie Chaplin and D. W. Griffith to form United Artists, the company that was intended to distribute their films. Ever since Griffith had unveiled *The Birth of a Nation*, American

From the expressions on Douglas Fairbanks and Julanne Johnston's faces, Ahmed might succeed in stealing more than a kiss in ***The Thief of Bagdad.***

movies had gotten bigger and longer and every studio had its epic or two. By 1923 Cecil B. De Mille, until then known for lavishly produced but still comparatively intimate domestic dramas, made the move and worked a Biblical flashback into the otherwise modern-day *The Ten Commandments*. That same year, even the notoriously parsimonious Universal would spring for beaucoup bucks and released *The Hunchback of Notre Dame* as a Super Jewel (see essay). In 1920 Fairbanks would take his own cautious step into the same territory with *The Mark of Zorro*. While modestly produced and careful not to stray *too* far from Fairbanks' usual modus operandi, *Zorro* took the actor's established All-American persona and recast him as a swashbuckler — arguably the first to be concocted purely for the screen. After *Zorro* (with the exception of 1921's *The Nut*), Fairbanks not only abandoned that All-American persona for exotica and contemporary settings for history's more flamboyant

eras, he would not again portray an American citizen (or, save for *Thief*, a commoner) until the coming of sound. *Zorro's* box office success led to *The Three Musketeers* (1921) and *Robin Hood* (1922), each film more extravagant than its predecessor.

For many decades *Robin Hood* held the honors for having the largest set constructed for a Hollywood film, and Bagdad was constructed on the skeleton of that set. (Multiple sources refer to *Thief* being built on the "foundation" of the *Robin Hood* castle and that this was one of the film's few economies.) Much of the credit for the success of the six-acre *Thief* set must go to William Cameron Menzies, who was working herein on his first art direction assignment. The picture contains numerous instances of what would be seen as his trademark use of large foreground objects to make a shot more interesting or to lend added depth to a set (and which would work from one *and only one* camera angle). Menzies prevented the massive sets from dominating the actors by having the walls essentially bare save for a telling detail here and there, such as a tiny window or a modestly proportioned balcony or an enormous vase. The light-colored walls, combined with highly polished black floors, keep the tall sets from seeming too substantial for the lighter-than-air fantasy that plays out on them. The art director was also responsible for designing the special effects, with some simply shots of humans framed within compositions that contained massive objects (such as the idol from whose eye the magic crystal is stolen). In 1924 — with matte work still in its infancy — such visual effects were accomplished with glass paintings or meticulously placed miniatures, tricks that dated back to Méliès. Only the flying horse — filmed on a treadmill against a black background and then superimposed on footage of clouds — fails to impress today, because the horse is so obviously galloping on something solid. (Still, this didn't keep Menzies from repeating the same effect for Alexander Korda's remake.) Others effects remain intriguing. The giant bat that attacks Ahmed is a man in a suit who's flown on wires (and who looks like something out of a K. Gordon Murray import), while the undersea arachnid is a large marionette. But is the dragon an optically enlarged alligator with makeup appliance? or a puppet? or both? It seems far too limber to be a full-scale model (à la the impressive-looking but fairly inert dragon of Fritz Lang's same-year *Die Nibelungen*) yet, for certain action sequences, a full-scale critter must have been tinkered together.

William Cameron Menzies (1896–1957) was possibly the most influential designer in the history of cinema. He was master of all territories: capable of meeting the expansive demands of epic productions (such as *Thief* and *Gone with the Wind*); the more cramped, paranoiac

Saturday night at the Palace: First prize at the costume ball to Ahmed, left, as Scarlett O'Hara (rumor has it the sultan chuckled when he recognized his drapes) and runner-up is the unnamed Evil Associate (Snitz Edwards) as Carmen Miranda.

settings required of films noir; or the faithful reproductions needed for such intense historical dramas as *Reign of Terror* (aka *The Black Book*). He was de factor director of Korda's *Things to Come* (1936), although that picture — like much of his directorial output — is more notable as a series of set-pieces and compositions than as a film. Two of his earliest directing jobs, the sadly neglected *The Spider* (1931) and *Chandu the Magician* (1932), may be instances where he was given a co-directing credit because of his extensive design rather than for his time on-set. (This co-credit was the then-standard acknowledgment for an art director whose visual design was so spot-on that his sketches would have sufficed for the production crew to shoot the movie.) The visual marvels in the hard-to-find *Trick for Trick* (1933) also bear Menzies' unmistakable touch. The most curious item on Menzies' resume is his credit as screenwriter for the 1933 *Alice in Wonderland*; it is only writing credit to be found in his long career and the film has a distinctly Menzies-esque look. Among his other genre titles is the 1929 *Bulldog Drummond*, the silly (but beloved) *The Maze* and *Invaders from Mars* (both 1953). Tobe Hooper's 1986 remake of this latter picture reportedly incorporated some of Menzies' original designs.

Menzies' assistant art director on *Thief* was Anton Grot, in films since 1917 and the designer of the sets for *Robin Hood*, and it was he who designed the stunning poster (depicting Ahmed on the flying white horse) for *Thief* — not Maxfield Parrish, to whom the art is extraneously attributed in some texts. The Polish-born Grot (1884–1974) gets genre props for the bizarre sets he created for Warners' *Svengali* and *The Mad Genius* (both 1931) and *The Mystery of the Wax Museum* (1933), and First National's *Doctor X* (1932). While he produced some notable work in the Silent Era, he only came into his own in the 1930s, designing films that ran the gamut from the aforementioned classics to Busby Berkeley musicals to the William Dieterle biopics starring Paul Muni. Also contributing to *Thief*'s imaginative visuals are the costumes of Mitchell Leisen (1898–1972): all towering turbans and flowing capes that fall into Art Nouveau swirls that mimic Aubrey Beardsley drawings. Leisen worked in advertising art and architecture in Chicago before moving to Hollywood in 1919, where he spent his time designing costumes for De Mille and Fairbanks before shifting to set design: *The King of Kings* and two of De Mille's most delirious projects — *Madame Satan* (1930) and *The Sign of the Cross* (1932) — were photographed on Leisen's sets. The artist turned director in the early 1930s, and his *Death Takes a Holiday* (1934) is a little-seen and underrated gem of the fantastic cinema.

Preproduction on *The Thief of Bagdad* began in November 1922, and some eight months were spent on research (mostly conducted by playwright Edward [*Kismet*] Knoblock), scenario creation and problem-solving. Fairbanks tapped Raoul Walsh to direct; this proved to be an interesting choice as Walsh — a director since 1915 (and a protégé of Griffith) — was still the occasional actor. He was only just beginning to make a name for himself, and *Thief* would launch him into the front ranks of Hollywood. Like Grot and Leisen, cinematographer Arthur Edeson had been with Fairbanks for several pictures, though *Thief* would be his last. Edeson entered the movies in 1911 (he had been a portrait photographer to that point) and went on to

lens James Whale's early-1930s genre triumvirate: *Frankenstein*, *The Old Dark House*, and *The Invisible Man*; the trick work needed to make Ahmed's invisibility cloak credible definitely helped Edeson vanish Claude Rains in 1933. And 1925's *The Lost World*, 1926's *The Bat*, and 1927's *The Gorilla* were recorded by Edeson's camera before the Silent Era came to a close.

With respect to all the requisite visual trickery, Fairbanks wanted to out-do the magic that was then being performed by the German Expressionistic film wizards. In some cases the simplest of solutions was the best. The army raised from scattered magic powder, for example, was helped along with exploded flares. The magic rope was simply lifted up by piano wire; the same material was used to flap the flying horse's wings (albeit not very convincingly) and to make the magic carpet airborne and swoop over the city, though this latter effect involved more intricate engineering. In his biography, *Douglas Fairbanks*, Jeffrey Vance reports how Fairbanks' brother Robert (who often solved the mechanical problems for the star's films) "decided that it was best to use a crane, the highest camera stand ever built up to that time."

> Constructed of steel by Llewellyn Iron Works and operated on a derrick and hoist, the crane was ninety feet high, with platforms for the camera operators ... the carpet itself was "a three-quarter-inch flat piece of steel, five feet by eight feet in size and covered with a Persian carpet with an eight-inch fringe hanging down around the edges." It was suspended by six "invisible" piano wires and moved at twenty-five miles an hour; undercranking the cameras made it appear to move much faster.

And naturally a certain amount of pre-production was devoted to Doug working through the stunts he was to perform. For the bit where he jumps into and out of a series of oversize crockery jars, for instance, hw was aided by hidden trampolines; the star practiced with trampolines and hurdle sticks raised higher and higher until he'd mastered the stunt. Production officially started on the 5 July 1923 and lasted a bit over 28 non-stop weeks (excepting Sundays and Christmas Day), finally wrapping on the 26 January 1924.

There's no doubt that *Thief* is often astonishingly beautiful to behold and much of this is attributable to its being entirely studio-bound; even a scene at sea is created with a boat rocking on billowing silk, the obvious artificiality of which only increasing the charm. As such, *The Thief of Bagdad* is one of the most ravishing of the Hollywood silents, bypassing even many a Hollywood film made in the Sound Era. It is the visual equal of the great German fantastic films of the time, the pictures Fairbanks and Menzies studied for inspiration on how to achieve certain technical effects. The scene at sea appears to have had its inspiration in Conrad Veidt's *Wilhelm Tell* (1923). There are allegations that Fairbanks bought the American rights to Fritz Lang's *Der müde Tod* (1921) and held up its release so he both could copy (and hopefully out-do) the effects and then have his film in theaters first. Fairbanks was known to have advised the United Artists board not to distribute German fantasy because he felt its tone was too dark and would thus prove to be unsettling to film-going Americans. He did admire their technical effects, though, and reportedly chatted with Fritz Lang during the latter's visit to the USA in 1924 for the premiere of the first part of *Die Nibelungen*. The Germanic influences on *Thief*, though, came not from any particular film, but rather from the whole of German cinema in the early 1920s. As Richard Schickel notes, German films "influenced nearly everyone involved in film production at the time…" and that country's spectacle films sought to "blend the values of the modernist tradition in the plastic and architectural arts, with a narrative tradition borrowed from folk material." For all the effort and emulation, the picture itself was not universally beloved. Quoting Alistair Cooke, Schickel wrote that the film, "made at prodigious cost," succeeded only in suffocating "the beloved old sprite in a mess of décor." Alexander Walker adds that in *Thief*, as well as in the other films of the 1920s,

> the armies of period historians, costume designers, special effects men, and art directors … do not support their leader so much as swamp him…. Where once he danced on air, Doug now stands on ceremony…. [The settings] were extraordinary … we expect something wondrous to occur in such contexts, and would be quite let down if it didn't happen. But in employing them he lost the value of contrast between his own unique gifts and the dull, normal world he had, in his earlier films, seemed to share with us.

While it is true that the Fairbanks athletics resonated differently in more fantastic climes than in contemporary settings, this criticism misses on two points: the swashbucklers were lighthearted, not outright comedies, and that may have caused problems for contemporary audiences of the time and critics writing later on. (Curiously, it is the adventure films that have kept Fairbanks in the public consciousness and Millennium-Age viewers are sometimes surprised to discover that the actor had a different persona early in his cinematic career.) It should be noted, too, that Fairbanks was 41 at the time of *Thief* and was thus less likely to dance on air, though he (and, at times, his stunt double Richard Talmadge) still managed to perform some remarkable acrobatics. Fairbanks' doctors were already advising him of the need to slow down (he was developing circulatory problems, most likely brought on by his heavy cigarette habit) and perhaps the switch from numerous shorter films every year (almost eight a year between 1916 and 1919) to one feature per annum was his way of dealing with medical admonitions. Still, what *Thief* lacks in gymnastic display (which is really to say it is not an endless series of such set-pieces), it make up for in celebrating the Fairbanks' physique. Stripped to the waist and either tanned or darkened with make-up, Doug is photographed repeated while in repose or while stretching, images that are as sexually charged as any Robert Mapplethorpe photo. Reportedly Fairbanks worked out daily to get even more buff than usual; *Thief* would mark his first shirtless role in several years and he wanted to display an enviable torso. (An early costume test for his outfit during the first few reels lacks the gauzy pantaloons he ended up sporting throughout; had the test outfit been retained, Doug would have been cavorting in only briefs and a waist-sash.) One aspect of the Fairbanks package that certainly changed with the onset of spectacular productions was his acting, if it can be called that. In the shorts so unendingly and insufferably cheerful and hyperactive as to threaten diabetic shock and exhaustion on the part of the audience members, in the costume features he adopted a grandiloquent style that he doubtless thought more appropriate considering the subject matter, but which can only

be described as embarrassingly hambone. His overdone mime must have looked cornball even at a time when film acting was far less subtle than it is today. For example, in a scene wherein Ahmed detects the aroma of food, the actor desperately needed someone to rein him in and to edit the inserts: he sniffs about in close-up and there's a cut to the food; cut to Doug still sniffing and cut yet again to the food; a final (please, Allah!) cut to Doug still sniffing, and then finishing everything off with a shot of him leaning back and rubbing his stomach with an exaggerated circular motion. This is typical of Fairbanks' performance and the film. What's exasperating is that Fairbanks can be very effective when he isn't posturing. He is nigh-heartbreaking in the scene where he surreptitiously climbs into the princess' chamber, confesses his charade, and then tries to return the betrothal ring. And, happily for the viewers' dental work, his performance becomes less teeth-grindingly obnoxious once he realizes what the princess means to him and shifts the happy-go-lucky business into lower gear. Nonetheless, we readily admit that there are folks who possess a higher tolerance for Doug than we do. His performance aside, it is regrettable that Fairbanks (1883–1939) never again attempted a fantasy film.

The real acting honors in the film go to Sojin and Anna May Wong, both of whom give deliciously understated portraits of evil. Sojin's most memorable moment comes when he directs an underling to deliver a snake-bite to some poor unfortunate, who's conveniently nearby, just so the curative powers of the magic apple can be tested. Similarly, Wong can be seen dispassionately wafting the fumes from a poisonous concoction toward the sleeping princess while taking care to shield herself from their effects. Of the two, Sojin (né Mitsugu Mita, 1884–1954) was the luckier, career-wise. Although frequently cast in villainous or red-herring roles in Hollywood, he did enjoy the occasional breath of fresh air: he was one of three authentically Oriental actors to be cast as Charlie Chan (in 1927's *The Chinese Parrot*). Come the Sound Era, limited English and his thick accent pretty much tore it with the movie industry, but between *Thief* and then, he tallied such genre credits such as 1925's *The Bat* (see entry) and *The Road to Mandalay*, and 1929's *Seven Footprints to Satan* (see entry) and *The Unholy Night*. Sojin thereafter returned to Japan and continued an active movie career, capping it with an impressive performance in Akira Kurosawa's *The Seven Samurai* (1954).

It is impossible to discuss Anna May Wong (née Wong Liu Tsong, 1905–1961) without addressing the sad role racism played in her career. Marshall Neilan (see *Come and Get It*) gave Wong her first credited role in 1921's *Bits of Life* wherein she played Lon Chaney's abused wife, and she has the distinction of playing the lead in the first two-strip Technicolor feature, *Toll of the Sea* (1922), an adaptation of *Madame Butterfly*. *The Thief of Bagdad* was her breakout role, but she invariably was otherwise cast either as a femme fatale or in support of Caucasian actresses (such as Myrna Loy) who were themselves dolled up in Oriental drag. On decamping for Europe in search of better roles she told a journalist, "I was so tired of the parts I had to play. Why is it that the screen Chinese is always the villain? And so crude a villain." In London she appeared on stage with Laurence Olivier and it was while there that criticism of her voice led her to hire a Cambridge University tutor, which resulted in her acquiring an upper-crust British accent. Moving to Germany, she became acquainted with Marlene Dietrich, Leni Riefenstahl, et al., and appeared in E.A. DuPont's *Picadilly* (1929). Lured back to Hollywood by Paramount (with the promise of leading roles), she discovered that Paramount's conception of leading roles for Chinese actresses meant impersonating Fu Manchu's offspring in *Daughter of the Dragon* (1931). She tested for both the wife *and* the mistress of farmer Wang Lung in *The Good Earth* (1937), but lost out to Caucasians Luise Rainer and Tilly Losch because Irving Thalberg's assistant, Albert Lewin, supposedly didn't feel that she fit his concept of what a Chinese woman ought to look like. (Wong may not have looked Chinese to Albert Lewin, but the same year *The Good Earth* was released, the actress appeared on the cover of *Look* magazine and was proclaimed "The World's Most Beautiful Chinese Girl." Naturally, she was holding a knife.) Adding to the foolishness at the time were California's miscegenation laws that forbade marriage between Asians and Caucasians, and M-G-M feared that by casting an Oriental woman opposite studio star, Paul Muni, they might be charged with promoting inter-racial marriage. What's more, in 1932 Wong had lost a role in M-G-M's *The Son-Daughter* to Helen Hayes because she looked *too* Chinese. The treatment by M-G-M sent her off to England again where she starred on both stage and screen until she was required to return to Paramount to fulfill the balance of her contract. For once, she appeared in a non-stereotypical role (in Robert Florey's *Daughter of Shanghai*, 1937) and had major roles in the mysteries, *King of Chinatown* and *Island of Lost Men* (both 1939). Anti-Oriental fervor brought on by World War II effectively quashed her career, and her final two starring roles (in 1942) were for PRC — Producers Releasing Corp.— the bottom of Hollywood's barrel. Wong went unseen onscreen for the next five years, but turned to television in the 1950s and starred in the short-lived 1951 Dumont mystery series created for her, *The Gallery of Madame Liu-Tsong*. Given all this, it is not surprising the actress came to be known as a heavy smoker/drinker and this probably explains her death by heart attack at the age of 56; sadly, she seemed on the verge of career revivification as a result of her role in the Lana Turner vehicle, *Portrait in Black* (1960). Wong never married, for wedding one of her white lovers would have led to criminal prosecution, and she feared an alliance with a Chinese man would have forced her out of her career and into the role of dutiful wife, as actresses and prostitutes were thought to be on a par by Chinese culture. Some of the unlucky lady's hitherto unmentioned appearances of note include *Mr. Wu*, *The Chinese Parrot* (both 1927), *A Study in Scarlet* (1933), and *Ellery Queen's Penthouse Mystery* (1941).

Charles Belcher (1872–1943) may be seen in several other Douglas Fairbanks' swashbucklers, and his name will also be found herein in our essays on *Fools in the Dark* and *Midnight Faces. Thief* seems to have been Julane Johnston's only leading role and reportedly she was picked for the role only when Evelyn Brent abruptly departed from the production. (It is rumored Miss Brent's abdication was at the behest of Pickford, who suspected the actress was having an affair with Doug.) Johnston (1900–1988) appears, albeit uncredited, in *The Young Rajah* and

The Brass Bottle (see entries), but her resume in the main consists of entries like "Miss Conning Tower" in *Madame Satan* (1930) and "Lady-in-Waiting" in *The Scarlet Empress* (1934).

Hungarian-born Snitz Edwards (né Edward Neumann, 1868–1937) was wed twice, and the second time (in 1906) was the charm; his bride was actress Eleanor Taylor (who was 20 years his junior) and together they had three daughters. The entire Edwards family appeared in a series of short subjects produced in the late 1920s by Universal, and the movies played a large role in the future of all three girls: Cricket became a producer, Marian married writer Irwin Shaw, and Evelyn worked as a staff writer at RKO. See our essay on *The Phantom of the Opera* for more on old Snitz. Noble Johnson (1881–1978) may have racked up more credits in less time in genre films than any other African American actor, and he is profiled in our essay on *Something Always Happens*. Raoul Walsh (1887–1980) mostly avoided the fantasy genre in his long Hollywood career, admitting later in life that it wasn't quite his thing. Still, in addition to *The Thief of Bagdad*, he also helmed Jack Benny's wonderfully infamous *The Horn Blows at Midnight* (1945) and his name appears again in our chapter on *The Monkey Talks*. As for the official commentary on the picture: In the 26 March 1924 edition of *Variety*, "Ibee" offered…

> Doug has come forth with an absorbing interesting picture, totally different than any of its predecessors. Never once does the present day commonplace intrude … not so much a story as it is a presentation of mystical events…. The wealth of magic that is applicable to pictures has finally been adapted by Fairbanks…. There is a profusion of fine long shots and the maze of strange settings are great aids in keeping interest balanced throughout the showing. Many of the scenes are tinted, designed to picture the spirit of the incident or event…. Fairbanks as the Thief gives a corking performance. Not so much of the athletic stunts [*sic*] of his earlier pictures are resorted to. He makes his hero more the dream lover of the story…. *The Thief of Bagdad* is the finished product of trick photography, a magical tale brilliantly picturized.

The 19 March 1924 review in *The New York Times* went unsigned, but the critic (probably Mordaunt Hall) was enthusiastic:

> Imagine a clever satire on the Arabian Nights' with marvelous photography and you have an inkling of Douglas Fairbanks's new picture…. For the time that one is beholding the miraculous feats of the photographer, the remarkable sets and costumes that are a feast for the eye, one forgets all about the humming, buzzing, brilliantly lighted Broadway, and for the time being, if you will, becomes a child again. Douglas Fairbanks is his happy-go-lucky self throughout the picture, in which he shows his dexterity and agility…. There are some wonderfully well-worked-out double exposure photographic effects and even to an experienced eye the illusion in nearly every instance kept up to a state of perfection.

On 23 March, Thos. B. Hanly weighed in for the *New York Morning Telegraph*, calling the picture "a fantastic series of scenes depicting magic ropes, jinns and genii, magic crystals, horses, dragons and bats, employing trick photography with skillful effect to create the illusions." Hanly went on to predict that "every youngster in the country will want to see the picture and their parents will want to take them." Nonetheless, the *Telegraph*'s reviewer oddly claimed that, in its road-show format, "the picture runs a full three hours," which is "much too long for the ordinary motion picture theater." While *Thief* did go out at a road-show length of 15 reels (approximately 150 minutes) and was later edited down for standard exhibition, it never ran for three hours. Either Hanly — knowing the number of reels delivered up to the booth — did some facile (and incorrect) math, or he caught a showing where the projection speed had slowed to a crawl.If Mae Tinee (1 September 1924, *Chicago Daily Tribune*) also sat through a three-hour-long screening, she didn't let on. If anything, she indicated that she hadn't been worn out by the picture but, rather, was quite taken with it.

Mr. Douglas Fairbanks asks that you "please believe in fairies" when you see *The Thief of Bagdad*. Watching his individual performance I should say you had better believe in Darwin. However, *The Thief of Bagdad* does take you out of the land of always, always is into the land that never, never was— and for this— poor slaves of the prosaic — be grateful!

Over at the *Chicago Daily News*, Carl Sandburg liked the film so much he reviewed it twice. On the 31 December 1924 (during *Thief*'s second engagement in the Windy City), he wrote:

Probably no photoplay since the motion picture business and art got going has been greeted so enthusiastically in the circles known as highbrow and lowbrow…. There is both intelligence and fine art quality, and the picture has won large audiences…. Douglas Fairbanks is the producer of it, also the leading player, and it represents the quintessence and distillation of what he has learned since he started in, among the first of the film workers…. Magic and fantasy of the tales of the Arabian Night entertainments are woven through the silversheet [*sic*] story. The telling of the story would be impossible in ordinary theatrical stagecraft. It is precisely the kind of story that the movies can deliver where other media fail…. We say it is one of the rare movies worth seeing. This reviewer is going for a third look at it this week.

Nearly four months later, on the 20 April 1925, he added,

It may be 10 times, possibly 100 that we have made reference to *The Thief of Bagdad*. However many times it may be, there is no reason for apology or explanation, because the simple fact is that *The Thief of Bagdad* is one of the few pictures that ought to be mentioned over and over. This reviewer has gone to see it three times and if he lives he will go again that many times more.

Writing in the 11 July 1924 *Los Angeles Times*, Edwin Schallert expressed his awe:

I have no words to evoke its magic. Veritably it needs some sort of sorcerer's incantation to do this…. *The Thief of Bagdad* is, I think, the ultimate of its kind. I can see why now a majority of producers did not follow Doug as they did in the instance of *The Three Musketeers* and *Robin Hood*. There will be no reign of fantasies following it…. This one is the last word…. The effects are almost unimaginably enchanting … [and] are simply unforgettable and almost unimpeachable, too, in their proof of the perfection of the photographic art….

Counterbalancing these critical huzzahs, though, was the 6 December 1924 issue of *Harrison's Reports*, wherein an unsigned article (on the front page!) warned, "Beware of Modern Greeks Bearing Gifts." The report continued:

It has been learned that United Artists are to release *The Thief of Bagdad* to the picture theaters, instead of continuing to road-show it, as was the original plan. The United Artists salesmen may tell you that the reason they are going to give [it] to the picture theaters is the love they have for you and their desire to help you make some money; my own information is to the effect that such reason is the failure of the picture to hold up the receipts in Chicago and the subsequent cancellation of road-show bookings.

This revelation is followed by a week-by-week tally showing sales dropping by about a thousand dollars every week, starting at $16,188 and ending up with $6,558 in the ninth and final week. *Harrison's* blamed *Thief*'s failure on the fact that "the people do not want costume plays; no one can force such plays down their throat." The article cites the failure of Pickford's recent *Dorothy Vernon of Haddon Hall* and predicts a dire reception for Rudolph Valentino's upcoming *Monsieur Beaucaire*. A month or so later (in the 31 January 1925 edition), *Harrison's* recurring column "What the Picture Did for Me" contained comments from a theater-owner based in an un-named town of some 28,000 people: "Failed to draw at this house first-run at 25c and 50c. Paid a fat price for it but lost heavily."

In his book *The Film Till Now*— published some 40 years after the picture was released — Paul Rotha wrote that *The Thief of Bagdad* "was a poor film, badly designed and conceived with false artistry." Still, the author found it "impossible not to appreciate the motive that underlay its production" while bemoaning that "there has been too much Fairbanks the producer and too little Fairbanks the acrobat." Almost two decades prior to Rotha's book, New York's Museum of Modern Art levied it own assessment, with the following appearing in the museum's bulletin (Vol. 16, No. 2/3, 1949):

[Fairbanks] meant *The Thief of Bagdad* to dwarf both his own past and the German present. In the huge Pickford-Fairbanks studio he outdid the Germans to the extent of creating a dream picture unrelated to any known reality. And it seemed he had outdone them in spectacle and trick illusion, which many people in 1924 thought were the best novelty the movies had to offer. A second generation of movie-goers, then growing into adolescence, enjoyed the new thrill of seeing fairy tales set in motion. The Fairbanks of *The Thief* became their Fairbanks for keeps.

First-generation film lovers who were still buying tickets in 1924 had thus sat through Fairbanks' transformation from the exuberant small-town lad who had to prove himself to others to the suave and self-assured action hero who never made a misstep. As Arthur Lennig states in his *The Silent Voice*:

In *The Thief of Bagdad* Doug's character of good-natured hero is apparent only in the beginning of the film. We see him in a mythical Bagdad stealing from others, tricking the local merchants, and creating general mayhem. But as soon as he meets the princess, the engaging role of wild and carefree thief leaves him. Smitten with the girl's charms, he converts into becoming a serious hero…. And as his roguishness ends, so does his interest as a character…. What has taken over in *The Thief of Bagdad* are the production values, two-Process Technicolor, spectacle, gigantic sets…. The more his films were pre-planned and carefully constructed … the less Doug was able to act spontaneously…. Alas, poor Doug began his career making off-beat films and ended up making conventional ones.

Perhaps it was the freshness of the effects work that made contemporary critics wax so enthusiastic about the film; latter-day scribes— heirs to more sophisticated (and credible) techniques— have been less taken with it. Still, even in our own, jaded, CGI-filled Age, we have to admire the fact that Fairbanks' Arabian magic was created from little more than inspiration and determination, and we have to admit that the quaintness of the realization is part of the picture's charm; it's akin to reading a book from the early 20th century that's illustrated with paintings, rather than photographs. *The Thief of Bagdad* has been remade several times, with the aforementioned 1940 Alexander Korda production justly considered the best and most famous. Even Millennium-Age viewers still enjoy the charm, the flamboyance and the color of the British wartime production. Nonetheless, for all of Fairbanks' overreaching and for the film's comparative creative shortcomings, the 1924 original is well worth the time spent.

— *HHL*

The Thirteenth Chair

The Thirteenth Chair. Acme Pictures Corp./Pathé Exchange Inc., 31 August 1919, 6 Reels/5,598 feet [LOST]

CAST: Yvonne Delva (*Helen O'Neil*); Creighton Hale (*Willy Crosby*); Marie Shotwell (*Madame LaGrange*); Christine Mayo (*Mrs. Philip Mason*); Suzanne Colbert (*Helen Trent*); Georges Deneubourg (*Edward Wales*); Marc McDermott (*Stephen Lee*); Walter Law (*Inspector Donohue*); Fraunie French Fraunholz (*Philip Mason*); with Alice Calhoun (uncredited)

CREDITS: *Director* Léonce Perret; *Scenario* Léonce Perret; based on the eponymous play by Bayard Veiller (New York, 20 Nov 1916); *Cinematographer* Alfred Ortleib

The complaint nowadays is that more films than you can shake a stick at are merely remakes of earlier pictures or adaptations of older TV series, but — back in the 1910s — they were shaking that same stick at celluloid takes on Broadway plays. The adaptation process back then was simplicity itself. Someone affiliated with a movie studio would buy a theater ticket and then spend two or three acts checking the house for empty seats and taking copious notes on audience reaction, while envisioning all those live actors flattened to two dimensions. He/she would then file a report for perusal by the suits. Said suits would proceed to estimate the actual costs of bringing the gist of the play to the screen, finagle the charging of virtually everything under the sun that shone on the studio lot to that photoplay, and then prognosticate public acclaim, personal triumph and production profit. If all went well, things would probably go even better the second time around, as most of those initial steps could be skipped, and the first picture's scenario could serve as the foundation for the remake. Thus, while the 1929 remake of the 1919 *The Thirteenth Chair* has always received more press than the 1937 remake of the 1929 remake, the silent "original" — usually ignored completely in the course of discussing the Tod Browning rendition — owed *its* flesh and bones to nothing other than Bayard Veiller's eponymous, long-running melodrama that opened late in 1916 at the 48th Street Theatre.

For reasons known only to them and to their gods, the producers of this first motion picture version thought it best to bring on board absolutely no one from the Broadway cast, that "no one" including Margaret Wycherly, widely acclaimed by New York theater critics for her interpretation of Madame LaGrange (and, incidentally, Bayard Veiller's wife). Thankfully, Tod Browning would rectify the oversight at MGM a decade later and — because there were silent prints of the 1929 remake struck for theaters that had not as yet rewired for sound — you'll find more data and opinion on that particular production in the appendix.

The woman who impersonated Madame LaGrange for the 1919 Acme Pictures Corp. release was Marie Shotwell, who had made her genre debut as C. Aubrey Smith's old flame in the original photoplay of *The Witching Hour* (1916), itself based on a Broadway play *and* remade twice. (*Zounds!*) As Madame LaGrange is the catalyst for the play's (and the movies') denouement, we're in perfect position to launch into the plot, courtesy of the copyright registration synopsis.

> Mrs. Philip Mason commits suicide after she has had an affair with Stephen Lee, a disreputable stockbroker, and has sold her husband's securities so that her lover could buy stocks. When Lee subsequently goes bankrupt, he blackmails Helen Trent by threatening to reveal silly love letters that she had written to him before she married her husband. Helen's brother, Willy Crosby, and his fiancée, Helen O'Neil (who lives with the Crosbys), go to retrieve the letters. While Willy waits outside, Lee is knifed to death as he attacks Helen. Lee's friend, Edward Wales, attempts to have Helen accused of the murder by having Madame LaGrange, a clairvoyant, conduct a séance. In the darkened room, Wales — through whom Lee's spirit is supposedly speaking — is about to name Helen as the murderer, when he himself is murdered. After Helen confesses to Inspector Donohue that Madame LaGrange is her mother, the medium — while conducting another séance — tricks Philip Mason into confessing to the killings.

The copyright registration piece — from which *The AFI Catalog* synopsis was crafted — alternates between calling Shotwell's character LaGrange and LaFarge. Contemporary reviews do likewise. As the character in the Veiller text is LaGrange, and as both Wycherly and Dame May Witty's characters were named LaGrange in the 1929 and 1937 film releases, respectively, we have opted to bow to the majority opinion, and LaGrange it is. A less important inconsistency in the existing documentation on the 1919 feature film is that Creighton Hale's character is referred to variously as either Grosby or Crosby. A *glaring* omission to the aggregate of information that has survived is the identity of the actor who played Philip Mason (Fraunie Fraunholz) and any sort of clue to just where Mr. Mason was for the body of the photoplay.

What separates *The Thirteenth Chair* from the zillions of other pedestrian mysteries that were cranked out since the invention of cranks is Madame LaGrange's being a professional medium/clairvoyant (bogus or otherwise) who conducts a pair of séances during the course of the plot's unfolding. As is mentioned hither, thither and yon in this volume, the always-intriguing possibility of communicating with the dead added pizzazz to quite a few otherwise dreary silent melodramas. Spiritualism's toys — rather than its tenets (see *Earthbound*) — were inexpensive to replicate onscreen: Ouija boards had been sold in novelty shops across America since 1890, circular tables could be found in most parlors, and double exposure cost nothing save for time and a sure hand. (It was also less perilous, both business- and litigation-wise, to cock an eyebrow at those toys, or at spiritualism's fraudulent or incompetent practitioners, than to snicker at spiritualism — Arthur Conan Doyle's "psychic religion" — itself.) Draped with props and costumes that were readily identifiable with the extrasensory set by audiences everywhere, scenes wherein confessions of guilt were obtained due to interference from Beyond the Grave quickly became the hoariest of Dei-ex-machina (if said interference was legitimate), or the most predictable of plot devices (if contrived). During the hey-day of silent films, genuine messing-about by supernatural forces in the affairs of mortals was a darned sight less common-place than the last-reel revelation that the whole thing was either a dream or an elaborate hoax propagated by the forces of right-eousness. Either way, the element could be counted on to lift the most mundane of scenarios at least a notch or two in most folks' estimation.

Anyhow, as there is no set number of sitters (so far as we know) who must be present for a proper séance to really take off, Veiller's insisting on thirteen chairs introduces the added element of triskaidekaphobia: the fear of the number 13. (In the play, Mrs. Erskine makes a comment about the number of par-ticipants, and Wales remarks, "I don't mind those little super-stitions." Determining just which of the thirteen chairs is the thirteenth would be quite a mystery were it not that Wales' chair is accorded that number solely because his cadaver occupies it at the end of the first act. Big formula to be found in plays and films such as these: superstition + coincidence = irony.) Also feeding into the ambience is a knife in the ceiling which hangs, à la the sword of Damocles, over the assemblage before falling — to great consternation on the part of the hereto mystery vil-lain — moments before the final curtain.

Bayard Veiller's play is situated in the "Italian Room" of a wealthy businessman's home in New York City as, presumably, is the 1919 photoplay. The two MGM remakes inexplicably shift the action to Calcutta. No matter which locale she's medium-izing in, though, Madame LaGrange is supposedly an expatriate Irishwoman, a contrivance with which the London-born Ms. Wycherly had no problem. (Nor had Mrs. Patrick Campbell, the Madame LaGrange in the play's West End debut in 1917. Mrs. Campbell, for whom Bernard Shaw had written the role of Cockney Eliza Doolittle in *Pygmalion*, was said to be "remarkable in her ear" for accents, brogues, and burrs, so long as they could be found within the confines of the United Kingdom. Following the advent of sound motion pictures, Mrs. Campbell packed her valise, moved to LaLaLand, and set up shop as a dia-logue coach.) Of course, while the Mme. LaGrange of the Acme Pictures Corporation's interpretation, Marie Shotwell, hailed from that greatest of Melting Pots — New York City — and her ability to do a Brogue was thus never in doubt, the mere act of speaking in any way, shape or form whatsoever was foreign to that era's film industry, so the point was moot. A murky re-view — dated 24 August 1919 and published over the byline of Helen Pollock, yet with no other, discernible attribution — went into a little detail about the Gaelic-ness of the medium: "In the original play the clairvoy-ant was a wistful old Irish woman, but in the photo-play she is a regular Cleopatra." We've no idea whether the title cards attempted to replicate an Irish lilt.

To aficionados of the thriller genre, the biggest name in *The Thirteenth Chair* — all things being equal — remains that of Creighton Hale, the set-upon juvenile whose presence is surely better remembered in pictures like *The Cat and the Canary* (1927) and

Seven Footprints to Satan (1929). Hale, a *genuine* Irishman, had no worries about vocal intonation for the first third of his film career (which started in 1914), and few for its remainder, as — once sound reared its inevitable head — most of his many on-screen appearances were in uncredited bits. On Broadway in 1913 (in *Indian Summer*, a nothing of a drama penned by *The Witching Hour*'s Augustus Thomas), the young actor soon found that the motion picture industry in America paid better and more regularly than did the stage. (Hale's last Broadway credit was in 1915's *Moloch*, another here today/gone tomorrow effort, crafted by Beulah Marie Dix, a writer whose name will be found here and there in this volume.) Almost the first film production he worked on was Thanhouser's 23-episode serial, *The Million Dollar Mystery*, shot back in the days (1915) when a million dol-lars was still a lot of money. A brief period followed in which he supported Pearl White in each of her three *Elaine* serials, as he also did in the 1916 chapterplay, *The Iron Claw*, wherein Miss White was menaced by gargoyle, Sheldon Lewis, as the titular villain. (Miss White had first been menaced by Mr. Lewis — as The Clutching Hand — in her first Elaine serial, *The Exploits of … * in 1914.) Ironically, Hale's only "Pearl-less" serial was 1917's *The Seven Pearls*, but at least the presence of the Parisian-born director who had helmed the three *Elaine*s — Louis Gasnier — provided some sort of continuity as the young actor shook the dust of the serial world from his brogues and headed exclusively into feature films.

A puff piece from the picture's press-book had Hale, whose serial experiences had left him at one time or another with a fractured knee and broken rib, a natural for the picture, if only because of a sort of reverse-triskaidekaphobia:

"This is just the chance I've been waiting for," said the actor. "This play is going to change my luck — and change it quick. My

Philip Mason (Fraunie Fraunholz in *The Thirteenth Chair*), at first cha-grined to learn that he was assigned no chair whatsoever, is speechless at finding that he's won the door prize.

lucky number is thirteen; and inasmuch as Veiller, the author, is a member of the same club as myself, I will get the greatest pleasure out of working in *The Thirteenth Chair*."

As some 200-plus motion pictures fell Hale's way after Léonce Perret's thriller, it's a cinch that he must have regarded *some* of them as reflections of his new-found luck.

The *least* familiar names on the cast crawl are probably those of the actresses entrusted with playing the two Helens: Yvonne Delva and Suzanne Colbert. *The Moving Picture World* (in its 6 September 1919 edition) revealed that Mlle. Delva "has the reputation of being one of the most talented, as well as most beautiful personages on the [French] stage or in the [French] cinema," and the *MPW* would never lie. The online *AFI Silent Film Catalog* claims *The Thirteenth Chair* was Miss Delva's first film, but we've come up empty trying to discover the title of her second, whether made here or in France, and that goes for Miss Colbert, as well. Unless these young women both changed their professional names and then disavowed any participation in this particular motion picture, they probably lasted no longer in Hollywood than those two plays featuring Mr. Hale lasted on the Great White Way.

The name Marc McDermott may be slightly less familiar than that of Mr. Hale, but the Australian character man made over 170 more motion pictures than did Miss Delva and Miss Colbert put together. In films since approximately 1909, McDermott is more readily remembered by silent cinemaniacs as Baron Regnard in Victor Sjöström's *He Who Gets Slapped* (1920), Sir John Killigrew in *The Sea Hawk* (1924), or Count von Rhaden in Clarence Brown's *Flesh and the Devil* (1926), than as the despicable Stephen Lee in *The Thirteenth Chair*, and that would probably remain true even if *Chair* weren't lost. Sadly, cirrhosis of the liver cut short McDermott's career — and his life — during the first week of 1929.

The whole shebang was directed by Léonce Perret, like Mlle. Delva (and possibly Suzanne Colbert), on loan from *le cinema français*. The 11 January 1919 *The Moving Picture World* reported that *The Thirteenth Chair* would be Perret's fourth American film, but the sundry data lists available from the AFI and elsewhere throw a shadow on this. The same issue of *MPW* revealed that "Mr. Perret has not quite mastered the English language and it is necessary for him to use [his secretary] in translating instructions to the cast." This linguistic shortcoming is doubly disturbing in that Perret was also responsible for the scenario of the picture. In the 12 July 1919 *MPW*, a rather self-effacing M. Perret pooh-poohed the notion that he had scripted a masterpiece: "I do not flatter myself insofar as *The Thirteenth Chair*, for example, is concerned, that I have written something particularly wonderful. It is simply that I have sounded a sympathetic note which is caught by those who go to see either the play or the screen presentation of it."

We infer from all this that his modest dismissals of genius were made with his arm around the shoulder of his truly bilingual secretary. Picking the guilty party out of a roomful of purposefully guilty-looking possibilities is, of course, one of the SOP's of detective movies, and by 1919 a touch of the supernatural or some other bizarre element was necessary if the humdrum was indeed to hum. Most of the reviews, then, found

Chair's séance(s) worth particular mention, with the 16 August 1919 *Harrison's Reports* opining the sequence to be "as realistic and impressive as has ever been put in pictures." There hadn't been all that many cinematic séances by *Harrison's* publication date, actually, and in only one picture — 1919's *The Firing Line* — did the activity produce genuine spiritualistic results. Still, even a fraudulent séance could be counted on to give a static plot point a bit of a shake, provided that the business could be adjudged "realistic and impressive" by the average ticket-buyer who, of course, was in a position to know.

The New York Mail — gone a half-century, easily — was taken in by the séances and everything else, and wholly, if ungrammatically, recommended the photoplay: "Have you sat up, of a midnight or later, absorbed in some baffling mystery of the detective world, that never revealed the whole truth until the last chapter? Have you read, enthralled, preferring to read on forever to missing a link in the development of the case? If so, you have that in store for yourself if you see *The Thirteenth Chair*."

The New York Sun — also removed these many years — chose to home in on triskaidekaphobia: "See it or you'll be sorry. All your friends will tell you so. Thirteen will not be unlucky to those who see *Thirteenth Chair*."

The *Sun*'s 24 August 1919 review by Helen Pollock did more than report of the comeliness of Marie Shotwell; it went into a little detail about the production itself:

> The facilities which the screen offers for presentation of detail and the amplification of incidents increases the suspense and mystery…. The production of the photo-play is of a high order. No expense has been spared in providing first-class settings, and the cast, too, is thoroughly competent…. The lighting effects are quite striking during Madame LaGrange's séance and the entire film has been carefully staged.

As the one trade publication that seemed on top of every move *The Thirteenth Chair* may have made, *The Moving Picture World* closed out its file on the film by reporting on press-book-inspired ideas that a couple of enterprising exhibitors were following in order to fill all the *other* chairs in their theaters. The following is from the 30 August 1919 edition:

> Taking advantage of the exploitation possibilities offered by *The Thirteenth Chair*, a Milwaukee exhibitor … will turn over his theater each morning during the week's run to a spiritualist who will conduct séances for all interested…. Another exhibitor in Milwaukee has made arrangements with a mind-reader to give an exhibition of her skill just prior to each showing.

In addition to the two talkie remakes, *The Thirteenth Chair* worked its magic as an episode of *Climax*, a mid–1950's television anthology devoted to the dramatic and the mysterious. Adapted from Veiller's original by Walter Brown Newman, the hour-long teleplay — which first aired on the 14 October 1954 — featured Dennis O'Keefe and Arthur Franz in support of Ethel Barrymore, whose performance as Mme. LaGrange was deemed worthy of an Emmy nomination.

— *JTS*

The Thirteenth Hour

The Thirteenth Hour. Metro-Goldwyn-Mayer Pictures/M-G-M, 13 October 1927, 6 reels/5252 feet [available]

CAST: Lionel Barrymore (*Professor Leroy*); Jacquelin Gadsdon (*Mary Lyle*); Charles Delaney (*Matt Gray*); Fred Kelsey (*Detective Shaw*); Polly Moran (*Polly*); Napoleon (*Rex, the dog*)
CREW: *Director* Chester Franklin, *Scenario* Chester Franklin, Douglas Furber; based on their eponymous play; Continuity: Edward T. Lowe Jr., *Titles* Wellyn Totman; Settings: Eugene Hornbostel; *Cinematographer* Maximilian Fabian; *Film Editor* Dan Sharits

To the young flapper, stepping out to a school party for the first time *The Thirteenth Hour* is the zero hour — unless she is home in bed by that time, she'll get a warm reception from her folks next day.

To the milkman, it is the start of his day — the hour for him to pile out of bed and start delivering his milk. To the radio fan, it is the hour that reception of distant stations is the best....

But in the story *The Thirteenth Hour*, it is that hour when the majority of people are asleep — when thieves and murderers roam about. It is that hour, commonly known as one A.M., when the murder in the story is committed and its psychology is carried throughout the picture to sustain suspense until the last scene.

The above quote from *The Kingsport* [Tennessee] *Times* of 28 March 1928 is from the lips of Chester Franklin, director of *The Thirteenth Hour* and co-creator, with Douglas Furber, of the play of the same name. Some eight decades later, few flappers are still around, we know of no one who makes a living by delivering milk door to door, and — thanks to modern technology, the internet and XM radio — poor reception is hardly the downer it once was to some folks. Thankfully, what *has* survived this bygone era is Franklin's cinematic recording of *The Thirteenth Hour*. This summary is taken from a viewing of that footage:

A master criminal who invariably attacks exactly one hour past midnight baffles the police. A member of the force, Matt Gray, is on patrol with his police dog and "best friend," Rex. The two spot a perpetrator hurrying away from a scene of the crime. Rex chases after the crook and jumps into the villain's car. Nonetheless, the criminal manages to return home safely and is revealed to be Professor Leroy in disguise The next day, Mary Lyle (Leroy's secretary) discovers the injured Rex even as the morning's headlines read: "Professor Jacques Leroy, Noted Criminologist, Offers Ten Thousand Reward for Capture of Mystery Killer." Aided by the canine's identifying tags, she returns the dog to Gray at the local precinct. Gray — who's enamored with Mary and feeling his oats — boldly offers to bring the dog to call on her.

Leroy becomes suspicious of Mary and orders his henchmen: "Watch Miss Lyle closely. She is not to leave the house. Report all her actions to me." As promised, Matt and Rex drop by Leroy's in order to see Mary. Gray introduces himself to the butler and then is somewhat startled to see the door automatically closing behind him. In the meantime, Rex sneaks in through a window, recognizes Leroy as the man from the previous night, and becomes agitated. Leroy, in turn, spots the dog and leaves the room in haste.

Mary is now held captive even as the butler tells Gray that she is not at home. Rex finds her and she manages to flip Rex a note to "Get help!" After reading the message, Gray speeds away for reinforcements while Rex stays back.

Rex adroitly navigates a ledge to return inside. Leroy watches Rex on an internal television monitor and electronically triggers several barriers to trap the dog. The professor's accomplices place the canine in a sack and throw him into a chamber that's rapidly flooding. As Gray is returning with backup, Rex — pulling a canine Houdini — escapes from the cloth bag and makes his way into a series of underground tunnels.

Leroy espies the approaching cops and takes further pains to hide Mary. Mary somehow escapes, meets up with Gray and states the obvious: "This is a den of crooks, and Leroy's their leader!" Their reunion, though, is short-lived; while Gray investigates an intruder in the hallway, a man abducts the girl through a secret passage.

Matt now has a look-see on the grounds. Rex has found his way almost to the surface under an outdoor drain, where Matt lifts the drain cover to free him. Meanwhile the police posse (accompanied by the pesky "Polly" from the Evening Press) poke around inside. The clueless Detective Shaw, in the lead, is unaware that one by one each member of the group is being grabbed from behind and abducted.

The wonder dog rescues the cops. The liberated lawmen then think they've found Professor Leroy sitting calmly at a desk, but, this turns out to be a dummy. But ol' Rex has the scent. He follows the fleeing criminal through a series of secret passageways. Leroy makes his way back to the room with the desk where he poses as the dummy. Therefore, he's ignored when the cops reenter the room. All of the policeman leave except for Matt. When Matt puts his gun down, Leroy gives himself away trying to grab it and has to make a run for it. Matt finds Mary. The fearless Rex follows Leroy onto the roof. Both fall. Rex limps away triumphantly and the crook is finally cornered.

The cops clean up the rest of the gang.

Matt and Mary drive off in a car. Rex pulls down the rear window shade.

The End.

Well, now... The Silent Film Universe had already unveiled *The Man of Mystery* and *The Woman of Mystery* (see entries, 1917 and 1914, respectively) and was *that close* to *A Dog of Mystery*, the planned title of M-G-M's *The Thirteenth Hour*. For whatever reasons, the studio decision-makers decided to buck this "mystery" trend in favor of the title the Messrs. Franklin and Furber had originally chosen for their unpublished (and presumably un-produced) play. In any event, the thespian career of Napoleon the Dog does evoke a mystery or two, for about the only other credit we have for him — if indeed we're speaking of the same Napoleon — is the 1922 Metro vehicle, *Peacock Alley*.*

Norbert Lusk in the *Los Angeles Times* (4 December 1927) typified reaction to the role Napoleon played in the show: "It is distinctly his picture." And doggone it, if our canine hero doesn't display a wide array of talent: crawling, climbing, running and escaping into and out of all kinds of mischief. His acting range, likewise, is first rate, as he waxes quizzical at Matt's tentative advances towards Mary, fakes injury like a pro, and is downright menacing when chasing down the Professor. Although veteran headliner, Lionel Barrymore (see *The Bells*, vintage 1926), capably mugs his way through as the campy criminologist-cum-criminal, it's clear who is the real star of *The Thirteenth Hour*.

Working in animal movies became one of Chester M. Franklin's staples and his film work showcased incarnations of ultimate and penultimate dog superstars (Lassie and Rin Tin Tin) and included such animal-world fare as *Sequoia* (1934) and *The Yearling* (1946). Franklin's other talents were many and diverse. In addition to crafting the storyline with Mr. Furber — a man better known for his musical lyrics than his prose — and direct-

*All rumors that Napoleon the dog retired to obscurity in the '30s due to a bark unsuitable for the talkies are unfounded!

ing the picture, it was he who did the knife-hurling in one of *The Thirteenth Hour*'s more action-filled scenes. Prior to latching on with Griffith and Sennett in the 1910s, he earned his keep as a newspaper cartoonist; his art soon matured enough to warrant serious exhibitions, and one of his paintings graced Sid Grauman's theater in San Francisco, coincidentally Franklin's city of birth.

Like Franklin, comedienne Polly Moran got started with Mack Sennett as one of his many bathing beauties, and she, too, shared an affinity for canines. Moran often took in strays and one part of her campaign platform for City Council in Laguna Beach was the avowal: "I'm for dogs!" (She lost.) Dogs apart, Polly was given but one properly comedic scene in *The Thirteenth Hour*— she was not helped by some decidedly unfunny title cards— and her lone triumph occurs when, investigating on her own, she backs into a would-be abductor hiding behind a black curtain, miraculously escapes entanglement, and then shakily calculates that it's time to sit down and pour a drink.

Aiding in the comic relief department, Fred Kelsey (see *The Gorilla*, 1927)— the quintessential stumbling, bumbling, Hollywood flatfoot— also finds his moment in the sun. As Detective Shaw, his "leadership" display over his ever-disappearing gang of subordinates registers for a hoot or two.

Charles Delaney discharged his typical B-level male-lead responsibilities, while Dorothy Sebastian — an early choice for the heroine — saw the role eventually taken over by Jacquelin Gadsdon (aka Jane Daly). In a 30 November 1927 review, *Variety*'s "Sid" speculated that the vehicle was launched to break out Ms.

Gadsdon's career; while her career did encompass another couple of dozen films, none was memorable enough to keep her name in the minds or on the lips of audiences.

Overall, Sid pigeonholed the picture thusly: "It figures a good cheap admission fare, but what it'll do in the handsome chalets is something else again," and observed, "One youngster was muffling shrieks of delight during the picture and a balcony laugh sounded raw enough to be a 'plant.' But that can easily be the tip-off as on this reel opus. Its forte is in the balcony."

The *Moving Picture World* (3 December 1927) wasn't nearly so cocksure where *The Thirteenth Hour* fit in:

> It seems a sort of Mulligan stew in parody of mystery thrillers in general. However, there can be no certainty of this, for that is where the picture errs— it lacks definition. It's hard to make up one's mind about this one. If it's to be taken seriously, it will divert minds of smaller stature. The mental blue-bloods will laugh at it regardless.

Reflecting a schizophrenic point of view until the very end, *MPW* supplied its own report on viewer response: "A cross-section of audience reaction registers the fact that some persons laughed gleefully in spots while two persons spoke of getting their money back."

From *The New York Times* (28 November 1927) sprung the obvious— "the only pity is that the story is not saner or more logical"— and the *National Board of Review Magazine* (December 1927) stated matter-of-factly, "It is more a film of action than of acting, with dungeons and unexpected exits and entrances to provide plenty of surprises and mystery."

With the enigmatic and nefarious criminal identified by the end of the first reel, *The Thirteenth Hour* can't honestly be labeled as being much in the mystery department. Still, it was not for nothing that the picture was filmed entirely in the absence of daylight; in so doing, the film incorporated the best trappings of old-dark-house thrillers. With a plethora of secret passages, eerie chambers, strange silhouettes, hands appearing out of nowhere, knives whizzing unexpectedly in the dark, camouflaged trap doors, and even a couple of eyes peering through a stuffed gorilla head (!), the whole thing's all logically illogical offbeat fun.

And what's not to love about a loyal companion like Napoleon, anyway?

— *SJ*

Well, no matter what this original glass slide says, the only way *The 13th Hour* could be *tomorrow* was if one started keeping time at noon.

Tin Hats

Tin Hats. Metro-Goldwyn-Mayer/M-G-M, 28 November 1926, 7 Reels/6,598 feet. Incomplete print archived by Turner Classic Movies

CAST: Conrad Nagel (*Jack Benson*); Claire Windsor (*Elsa Von Bergen*); George Cooper (*Lefty Mooney*); Bert Roach (*Dutch Krausmeyer*); Tom O'Brien (*Sergeant McGurk*); Eileen Sedgwick (*Frieda*)

CREDITS: *Director* Edward Sedgwick; *Story* Edward Sedgwick; *Adaptation* Lew Lipton, Donald W. Lee; *Continuity* Albert Lewin; *Titles* Ralph Spence; *Director of Cinematographer* Ben Reynolds; *Film Editor* Frank Davis; *Sets* Cedric Gibbons, Frederic Hope; *Wardrobe* André-ani

Edward Sedgwick's name may be most frequently associated with Buster Keaton's, but for genre fans, Sedgwick is best known as the (uncredited) director who stepped in when Lon Chaney had his fill of Rupert Julian, the helmsman assigned to 1925's *The Phantom of the Opera*. And just as Keaton was not the only comic to work under Edward, so also was *Phantom* not the only thriller to require his services (credit or no); additional info on Mr. Sedgwick and his genre contributions may be found in the chapter on *The Haunted Pajamas* (in which he had a supporting role).

Tin Hats was first and foremost a service comedy, with its genre elements— a haunted castle and a ghost — secondary to the body of the action, if not to the laughs. Said body of action took place just after the Great War, so none of the plot incidentals involved the Kaiser, but were concentrated rather on the sort of "Awkward American Fumbling about Europe" vignettes that well-rested veterans might have longed for (or even lied about having).

The plot recap from *The AFI Catalog* centers on the haunted castle sequence as though it were the picture's dramatic pivot, but other sources indicate that much (if not most) of the film was spent leading up to these climactic episodes.

> At Armistice time, three members of the A.E.F. become separated from their regiment attempting to retrieve some souvenirs. Looking for their company, they cycle into a Rhenish village and are accepted by the burgomaster as the new overlords. Jack Benson takes an interest in Elsa von Bergen, a wealthy aristocrat; and another personable girl becomes enamored of the hard-boiled Lefty Mooney. With his friends, Jack invades Elsa's castle with the intention of "rescuing" her from some danger. She arranges a welcome with mysterious doors, traps, and other surprises, culminating in a battle with a ghost in ancestral armor. The trio is arrested, but through Elsa's influence they are released and the couples are happily married.

The two members of the A.E.F. (American Expeditionary Forces) referred to in the above summary were played by Conrad Nagel (who replaced Tom Moore in the role at the last minute) and George Cooper, respectively, but Bert Roach's "Dutch" Krausmeyer was as nearly ubiquitous as the romantic leads. Roach's avoirdupois gained him frequent (if unbilled) screen time in short comedies throughout the 1910s and 1920s, and his ability to do a frightened take was recorded in two Universal horror classics: *The Last Warning* (1929) and *Murders in the Rue Morgue* (1932). The Washington, D.C. native did a ton (Sorry) of uncredited bits (including *Think Fast, Mr. Moto* [1937] and *Mr. Moto's Last Warning* [1939]) up until the early 1950s, and the sharper-eyed among us can spot him in *Dr. Renault's Secret* (1942). He can also be seen to advantage — even by the less keen among us— as Athos in James Whales' rendition of *The Man in the Iron Mask* (1939). Bert Roach made nearly 350 films in a career that spanned almost four decades; details surrounding his last two decades (he died early in 1971) are fuzzy, to say the least.

Leading man Conrad Nagel shares a bit of film history with Tod Browning and Lon Chaney, as his most notorious film — 1927's *London After Midnight*— is on just about everyone's list of Most Wanted Lost Films. Nagel, one of the founders (and first presidents) of the Academy of Motion Picture Arts and Sciences, broached the transition to sound as an actor, an industry official, and an "interlocutor": a host who introduced acts in early talkie musical/dramatic compilation films, like *The Hollywood Revue of 1929*. Apart from the lost Chaney/Browning epic and *Tin Hats*, Nagel graced *Singed Wings* (1922) and *Sinners in Silk* (1924), but most of his genre credits were grounded in the talkies. Mr. Nagel is covered in greater depth in our essay on *London after Midnight*.

George Cooper's pertinent credentials are covered in the essay on *The Dark Star* (1919), and Tom O'Brian — who shared screen time with Bert Roach in Paul Leni's *The Last Warning*— has his bona fides (such as they are) outlined in the chapter on that picture. Eileen Sedgwick was Edward's younger sister, and she enjoyed a decent enough career, starring as she did in a healthy slumgullion of Westerns, shorts, and serials during the Silent Era. Claire Windsor was born Claire Cronk in the heart of the Wheat Belt, and among her first pictures (in which she, too, went uncredited) was the Clara Kimball Young edition of *Eyes of Youth* (1919). Along with Lila Lee, Bessie Love and Colleen Moore, she was named a WAMPAS (Western Association of Motion Picture Advertisers) Baby Star in 1922, and a contract with Goldwyn Pictures coincided with the honor. Although she *was* featured in a handful of early 1930s sound films shot by independent studios, Windsor's star eclipsed with the waning of cinematic silence, although she was awarded (in essence for a series of middling features released throughout the Roaring Twenties) her own star on the Hollywood Walk of Fame.

Tin Hats was photographed by Ben Reynolds, the cinematographer of choice of Erich von Stroheim. As such, he was associated with that auteur's scope and attention to detail and, consequently, remained behind the camera on big pictures for most of his career. Dr. Arthur Lennig, author of the requisite biography, *Stroheim*, told us,

> Reynolds must have been a patient man to have worked so often with Stroheim. He also must have proved his worth, for Stroheim was very demanding about photographic detail — hazy, misty scenes of dawn; light, filtered through shutters and piercing dusty gloom; and sometimes arduous location work (running the gamut from mountains to swamps to deserts) — and Reynolds obviously gave him what he wanted.

Other of the *Tin Hats* techies have their names mentioned elsewhere in these pages. Donald W. Lee, for example — who adapted Edward Sedgwick's story to the screen along with Lew (*Mummy's Boys*) Lipton — penned the screenplay for 1924's *The Last Man on Earth*, while Albert Lewin (in charge on continuity here) adapted Oscar Wilde's prose for — and directed — M-G-M's *The Picture of Dorian Gray* in 1945. Oddly, Ralph Spence (of *The Gorilla* fame) got screen credit for the titles but, according to the 11 December 1926 *Harrison's Reports*, "Many of the laughs that the picture causes are due to the subtitles by Katherine Hilliker."

Reviews were good, if not exceptional, with *Harrison's* observation that "Conrad Nagel, George Cooper and Bert Roach

… have never done better work" pretty much typical, although the 4 December 1926 *Moving Picture World* groused, "Conrad Nagel is rather weak in his comedy and yet enough of a comedian to make his acceptance by Elsa something to wonder at. He would have been better had he been all comedian or all hero."

Film Daily took the time to alert exhibitors to the ethnic mix of the picture's protagonists, using language that would hardly pass the P.C. test nowadays:

> Edward Sedgwick seems chiefly responsible for *Tin Hats* which he wrote and directed. It is a post-war story, not extensive or even logical for that matter — but sufficiently well stocked with good comedy incidents to make a thoroughly fine entertainment. The buddy idea is used again and the result is a doughboy trio — a Yank, a "Mick" and a "Heinie" — all U.S. boys pledged to the Stars and Stripes…. There are some great gags in this. Their search through mystery castle is a little bit too long but, on the whole, *Tin Hats* has few quiet moments [5 October 1926].

The *Manitoba Free Press* obviously didn't find the "mystery castle" search "a bit long," and the paper's 18 September 1927 recap of the film gave it a more traditional, old-dark-house comedy slant.

> There is not one episode in *Tin Hats* that can honestly said to be exciting or thrilling but for all that it is one of the most delightful little comedy war pictures one could hope to see. Fancy three brave American doughboys … see a German girl, Elsa, whom they had previously met…. Elsa invites the hero and his comrades to the castle.
>
> They go fully armed. Established in their separate rooms for the night, each experiences a group of surprising adventures: one finds a pair of boots filled with blood; another sees a black cat playing under the covers of his bed; the third sees a terrible visage at an opening in the ceiling. Jack has made a rendezvous with Elsa for midnight; they meet and are frightened by more funny adventures.

Is being frightened by funny adventures any less peculiar than being amused by scary adventures?

— JTS

The Tip Off

The Tip Off. Universal Pictures/Universal, 2 June 1929, 5 reels/4,109 feet [LOST]

CAST: Bill Cody (*Jimmy Lamar*); George Hackathorne ("*Shrimp*" *Riley*); Duane Thompson ("*Crystal Annie*"); L.J. O'Connor (*Captain McHugh*); Jack Singleton (*Confidence man*); Robert Bolder (*Duke*); Monte Montague (*Negro*); Walter Shumway (*Stock salesman*)

CREDITS: *Producer* William Lord Wright; *Director* Leigh Jason; *Story-Continuity* Basil Dickey; *Titles* Val Cleveland; *Cinematographer* Charles Stumar; *Film Editor* Frank Atkinson

At some point herein — we'll get more plot-specific in a moment — "Crystal Annie" gazes into her you-know-what and actually sees someone planning injury to someone else. As the surviving documentation on this film reads as though this is all on the up-and-up, we ask your indulgence: *The Tip Off* may well be one of the least-known ventures into the Silent-Era psychic world.

Or it may not.

Many of the films that may be found in our appendix are there only because the genre elements they contain are operat-

ically fraudulent (but still of great visual interest); genuine, but of little import (a dream comes true; a feeling of unease is spot-on); or vague (quite probably due to poorly-crafted studio materials/critical pieces), and thus open to interpretation. Quite a few films were left out of this book because the majority of the publicity pieces we were able to consult either made no mention of any genre element, or greatly downplayed the role said element played in the storyline. And, at the risk of repeating ourselves once too often, inasmuch as most of the films discussed herein are lost, in many cases we literally had nothing on which to go except for the contemporary reviews and publicity materials, and those were colored to a large extent by the cinematic prejudices of the critics and by wishful thinking on the part of the studios.

Thus, as to whether or not the psychic powers on display in Universal's *The Tip Off* were authentic, let us consider the following synopsis, taken from *The AFI Catalog*:

> Crook "Shrimp" Riley and his wounded pal, Jimmy Lamar, hide out at the home of fortune-teller Crystal Annie, Shrimp's girl. Although Shrimp's friends warn him that he will lose Annie to Jimmy, he scoffs at the idea. When the inevitable happens, Shrimp begins to plan his revenge by arranging a frameup for Jimmy. He persuades Jimmy to join a robbery, although Jimmy has promised Annie to go straight, and tips off the police, intending himself to escape. Annie sees the danger in her crystal ball, hastens to the scene of the crime, and helps Jimmy escape. Shrimp realizes the futility of his actions and allows the couple to escape while he dies ensuring their getaway.

First off, the use of "fortune teller" rather than "clairvoyant" bodes ill, authenticity-wise. We haven't had a chance to count 'em up, but the odd are good that every plot-synopsis in this book that mentions "fortune tellers" uses said phrase as a synonym for "con artists." Still, number two, that plot précis comes right out and says that Crystal Annie "sees the danger in her crystal ball," so that's a nod to the genre, right there. If you're keeping score, we're tied.

The picture's working title was *The Stool Pigeon*, and that's the name the copyright registration synopsis still bears, over at the Library of Congress. The relevant lines from that synopsis read as follows: "At home Annie, gazing into her crystal ball, sees Jimmy and the others. She dashes out, commandeers a taxi at the point of her gun, and forces the driver to take her to the apartment." If nothing else, it was the intent of the scenarist to have Annie a legitimate crystal-gazer (see *The Crystal Gazer* for more on the subject), and her legitimacy vindicates this essay. (And we remain unsure whether the fortuitous arrival of the taxi was also due to her clairvoyant powers, or just to the sort of impossible Hollywood coincidences — like the hero's always finding a parking space right in front of his building — that continue to pepper the cinema.)

Jimmy was played by Bill Cody, a fairly petit, Canadian-born, Western-action star who was no relation to Buffalo Bill Cody, who was neither petit nor Canuck. One of the online movie chat sites refers to Cody as the "silent Alan Ladd" with respect to his onscreen toughness being in inverse proportion to his mass, and another draws a parallel between our Bill Cody and old Buff, both of whom headlined with Wild West Shows that toured the country to enormous popularity and profitability early in the 20th century. Any number of surviving publicity pieces give credence to both observations, and Cody — who started out in the movies as a stuntman — was definitely more at home in horse operas than in crook-melodramas with supernatural undertones. Typical of the actor's press (with respect, at least, to the film at hand) was "This picture gives Bill Cody a chance to do some of his thrill stunts" and "Cody is the he-man type and knows how to get his stuff over with a punch" (*Film Daily*, 9 June 1929).

Crystal Annie was portrayed by the unfortunately-named Duane Thompson, an Iowan lass who (like almost every other possessor of XX chromosomes that entered films during the decade) was at one point a WAMPAS Baby Star. The young lady began in shorts (films, not pants) in the early 1920s, graduated to the principal cast of features that impressed no one save for the families of the principal cast members later on, and was — for all intents and purposes — out of the industry with *The Tip Off*. Nonetheless, she did return to play herself in the Busby Berkeley musical, *Hollywood Hotel*, in 1937. After that, silence, industry-wise.

The fact that *The Tip Off* was released by Universal only as a silent in June 1929 pretty much showed that the company thought the programmer to be little more than ... well ... a programmer; no extra bucks were budgeted to allow Crystal Annie's taxi-driver-threats to be heard aloud. Nor did the critical "Usual Suspects" think enough of the picture to waste ink on it; that *Film Daily* piece was about the biggest fish in the pond. Small-town America talked up the movie, though, if only to fill column-inches in local papers, and more than once we came away unsure of just what in hell the local scribes intended to say. For instance...

> *The Tip Off*, a Universal thrill picture, starring William Cody, is here Saturday. It is one of those good news stories that never get in the paper. Written by Basil Dickey, a former reporter, *The Tip Off* tells of one of Dickey's assignments in a large American city. Rather than run the story, which Dickey had exclusively, the writer quit his job in order to save the reputations and happiness of two people [*The* (Frederick, Maryland) *Daily News*, 28 September 1929].

Does anybody out there — crystal ball or no — know what in blazes that means?

Another local piece (from the 10 November 1929 *Cleveland Plain Dealer*) had Inez Wallace (a Cleveland native who would go on to pen the story on which was based Curt Siodmak's screenplay of *I Walked with a Zombie*) go on — pointlessly — about small-theater fare, using *The Tip Off* as an example: "Life, stripped to realities — right down to bed-rock — that's *The Tip Off*, in a crook setting. My heart stood still, a condition which, after seventeen years of movie work (more or less), is hard to imagine." Harder to imagine is what the woman was getting at. Impossible — which trumps even "harder yet" — was finding any credits for Inez Wallace during the 17 years (more or less) of movie work that preceded the publication of these comments.

One of the least of the films in this book to feature even a glimpse of a "genuine" genre element, *The Tip Off* (the hyphen came and went, per available publicity) was considered a throwaway effort even at the time of its release. Director Jason Leigh's greatest triumphs (such as they were) came during the 1950s and on the small screen, so his vision might not be missed due

to the picture's absence as much as is the camera magic of Charles Stumar, who would go on to work on Karl Freund's *The Mummy* (1932) and Kurt Neumann's *Secret of the Blue Room* (1933). Vying with Stumar for title of *The Tip Off*'s Genre Shining Star has to be scenarist Basil Dickey, around since the mid–1910s and Serial-Screenplay-Sire of everything from 1915's *The Perils of Pauline* to 1933's *Tarzan the Fearless* and 1934's *The Vanishing Shadow* to 1945's *The Purple Monster Strikes* and 1946's *The Crimson Ghost* (and loads of others, betwixt and subsequent to these titles). *The Tip Off* was the gentleman's only silent genre feature, and that tortured account from The Frederick, Maryland, *Daily News* may explain why.

— *JTS*

Trifling Women

Trifling Women. Metro Pictures Corporation/Metro, 2 October 1922 (New York premiere); 6 November 1922 (general release), 9 reels/ 8,800 feet [LOST]

CAST: Pomeroy Cannon (*Leon de Severac*), Barbara La Marr (*Jacqueline de Severac/Zareda*), Ramon Novarro (*Henri de Maupin/Ivan*), Edward Connelly (*Baron Francois de Maupin*), Lewis Stone (*Marquis Ferroni*) Hughie Mack (*Pere Alphonse Bidondeau*), Gene Pouyet (*Colonel Roybet*), John George (*Achmet*), Jess Weldon (*Caesar*), Hyman Binunsky (*Hassan*), Joe Martin (*Hatim-Tai, an ape*)

CREW: *Director* Rex Ingram; *Story* Rex Ingram; *Cinematographer* John Seitz; *Editor* Grant Whytock; *Production Manager* Starrett Ford; *Art Director* Leo E. Kuter; *Technical Assistance* Jean de Limur and Robert Florey

In 1922, Metro hired a young Frenchman named Robert Florey to insure that the atmosphere of the new Rex Ingram production, set in Paris, was authentically French. When Florey arrived on the set of *Trifling Women*, then called *Black Orchids*, he was greeted by the sight of director Ingram, dressed in his Royal Canadian Air Force uniform, playing soccer with a group of dwarfs and hunchbacks. On a subsequent visit Florey encountered a veritable menagerie: Siamese cats, a tank full of fish, an owl, a parrot and Joe Martin, the orangutan. Though at first nonplussed by such sights, Florey quickly came to admire Ingram and realize that each bizarre bit of business was an essential part of the mood Ingram was trying to create.

In the space of a few years, Ingram had gone from being a little-known contract director at Universal to fame and great critical success at Metro. He owed this to his 1921 mega-hit, *The Four Horsemen of the Apocalypse*. Not everyone, however, was convinced he was a genius. Metro had paid a hefty sum for the rights to the play, *Turn to the Right*, a popular, but very old-fashioned, comedy/melodrama. Though he had little enthusiasm for the task, Ingram agreed to direct the film version as a favor to his Metro patron, Richard Rowland. Reviews were lukewarm, and there was muttering that perhaps *Four Horsemen*'s success was due more to the work of scenarist June Mathis than to the volatile Irish director. Ingram largely dispelled such rumors with his 1922 *The Prisoner of Zenda*, which was a big hit with both audiences and critics. He now had pretty much a free hand to direct whatever he liked. His choice was a rather curious one: a remake his 1917 Universal film, *Black Orchids* (see entry), which he himself had written. The new version was almost double the length of the original but, other than some changes to the characters' names and a few, new grisly touches, the story remained the same.

This synopsis was drawn from contemporary reviews:

> Jacqueline de Severac is a fickle little thing who is really in love with Henri but who hates to admit it, even to herself. She makes sport of Henri to her father, a novelist, who then tells her the story of Zareda, the crystal gazer.
>
> Zareda is a most beautiful woman who is cunning in her power over men. The fashionable of Paris come to her for readings of the future for which they pay handsomely. The blades of Paris also come to Zareda for readings of her heart for which they also pay handsomely, but do not get.
>
> The lecherous old Baron de Maupin is infatuated with Zareda, but his courtship is complicated by the fact that his son, the dashing young Ivan, also loves her. Zareda tolerates the vain old man because of the wonderful gifts he bestows on her, but privately she mocks him and even hangs around the neck of her pet ape the strand of pearls the Baron has just given her.
>
> War breaks out and the Baron contrives to have his son enlist; he soon realizes, though, that the pain of parting threatens to precipitate marriage between Zareda and Ivan. The baron decides to distract Zareda by introducing her to the Marquis of Farroni, a man of great wealth who lives in a castle as magnificent as one of medieval legend. Zareda is quite taken with Farroni's wealth and nobility. The baron connives with the Marquis to arrange for Ivan's hasty departure to the front without even giving him the opportunity to say farewell to Zareda.
>
> Having gotten his son out of the way, the baron plots to have the marquis poisoned at a banquet, but Zareda becomes aware of the scheme and, with the help of her pet ape, arranges to have the goblets switched so it is the baron who ends up dying. Zareda subsequently marries the marquis.
>
> Ivan returns from the war and is furious to hear of Zareda's marriage, but Zareda contrives to bring about a duel between Ivan and her husband, knowing that Ivan is the best swordsman in Paris. As the marquis is cut down on the field of honor, he sees Zareda take Ivan in her arms.
>
> The marquis arranges his own funeral by having a bag of stones placed in his shroud. Zareda and Ivan go to the tomb to place a wreath of black orchids; the marquis removes it. A codicil to marquis' will insists that on the night of the funeral, Zareda should go to a deserted tower. She arranges a tryst with Ivan there.
>
> As Zareda primps before a mirror in the tower, she sees the specter of her husband. Backing away from the mirror, she faints when he clasps his hand upon her shoulder. He drags her downstairs to a dungeon. Ivan arrives and hears her cries, but is met by the marquis who shoots him dead and casts his body into the dungeon with Zareda. The avenger's strength fails. He places the wreath of black orchids upon the locked door of the dungeon and falls dead.
>
> Chastened by this tragic tale, Jacqueline de Severac accepts the love of Henri.

According to Michael Powell (in his autobiography, *A Life in the Movies*), *Trifling Women* was Ingram's favorite film. A perceptive review in *The New York Times* (4 October 1922) perhaps captures what drew Ingram to it:

> But it was not this story which caught Mr. Ingram's fancy. At least it does not seem so. It seems rather that pictures haunted him, pictures of a Circean woman, of men made foolish and mad by her, of queer medieval towers and castles, of dark dungeons and cellars, of duels and murders, and of characters, definitely stamped and oddly real characters, passing through it all to give it the passing semblance of reality.

The *Times* review was echoed in Robert Sherwood's assessment: "I can't say much for him (Ingram) as an author, for

Trifling Women possessed an unnecessarily trifling theme. The picture's merit, however, was not dependent upon its plot. It was filled with strong drama which was derived from the pictorial qualities and not from its situations." (*The Best Moving Pictures of 1922–23*; it didn't make Sherwood's Top Ten list, but he gave it an honorable mention.)

Perhaps one reason Ingram remade *Black Orchids* was his desire to do it right. Instead of having to contend with economy-minded Universal, he had all the considerable resources of Metro at his disposal and a budget of $250,000. He had a first-rate cast, including his discovery, Ramon Novarro (touted in the ads as "the only true rival to Valentino"), and the screen's premiere vamp, Barbara La Marr. He also had, in John Seitz and Grant Whytock, his favorite cameraman and editor, respectively. The sets were lavish and ornate, and created by newcomer, Leo Kuter, who would go on to a long career as a set designer and special-effects artist. Stills from the film show Zareda's lair as something out of a hashish smoker's delirium: the elaborate floor designs appear to form a giant spider-web, leading to Zareda's crystal ball in the center, and the huge room is replete with glass tables, erotic statuary, and flowing curtains. The interiors of the sorcerer's tower have a more traditional Gothic appearance, and even Ivan's lonely military outpost has a slightly Expressionist look. The miniatures of the tower and the marquis' castle were created by Billy Bitzer, D. W. Griffith's cameraman.

Ingram was even able to procure from France the favorite bed of the notorious Gaby Delys—the singer, erotic dancer, and spy—who died in 1920. The bed was shaped like a giant gondola, and publicity stills showed a provocatively-garbed Barbara La Marr lolling about on the bed, like Theda Bara channeling Lucretia Borgia. Publicity puffs claimed that over $20,000 had been spent on La Marr's gowns alone.

Originally, Alice Terry was supposed to star in *Trifling Women*. An item in the 14 April 1922 *Lima* [Ohio] *News* announced that "Rex Ingram and Alice Terry will film *Black Orchids* when they return from their honeymoon." When the honeymoon was over—and it was mostly spent going to the movies, according to the lovely Alice—it was La Marr who ended up being cast as the enchantress. Terry, who was weary of playing noble virgins, had earlier wanted the role of the sexy Antoinette de Mauban in *The Prisoner of Zenda*, but had lost that part to La Marr, as well. Eventually, though, Ingram would give Terry the role of her career, as the elegant and seductive spy in *Mare Nostrum*.

In spite of his wanting her for *Trifling Women*, Ingram did not get along particularly well with La Marr. Nevertheless, the only major problem on the set came from the orangutan, Joe Martin. Joe was smitten with Miss La Marr, and when Edward Connelly as the old baron put a pearl necklace around La Marr's neck, Joe attacked him. It took three of the crew to pull the beast off (by "twisting his balls," according to Grant Whytock). Connelly, who was pushing seventy at the time, refused to be in any more scenes with his hirsute rival, so matte shots (of which John Seitz was a master and pioneer) were used for the remainder of their scenes together.

Trifling Women did well and the reviews were generally good, though no one was inclined to put the film in the same league with *Four Horsemen of the Apocalypse* or *The Prisoner of Zenda*. Some found the lurid storyline too gruesome and distasteful, and felt it was redeemed only by Ingram's great pictorial sense. The reviewer in *The Indianapolis Star* (28 February 1923) compared *Women* favorably to *Foolish Wives* (directed by Ingram's friend, Erich von Stroheim), but noted that in both films, "Their perfection in unsavoriness smacks of Baudelaire's best poetic efforts, *Flowers of Evil*; they are beautiful in their ugliness." Reviews often mentioned the scene of the old baron sitting dead at the banquet table, while the ape raises his glass in a toast.

Ingram's attention to atmospheric detail was also noted by *The Indianapolis Star*'s reviewer:

> Ingram paints in little miniature portraits that are gems. He slips in a close-up of the corpulent proprietor of the wine shop. He inserts a shot of the baron's careful manservant. He puts in a glimpse of two soldiers at the front, jointly celebrating the birth of a son and heir to one of them. He pictures an admiring group of fencers in the gymnasium. There is the old novelist amusedly watching his flirtatious daughter spurn the advances of her handsome suitor.

Ingram's obsession with getting small things right — not unlike von Stroheim's — was caught in this bit of publicity, as reported in the 2 June 1923 *Appleton* [Wisconsin] *Post Standard*:

> For adding realism to the interior of a Paris dive, Ingram found "genuine Apache gangsters," exiled desperadoes from France who, attracted by the fame and glitter of Los Angeles, had drifted west to California. Rex Ingram turned them loose on the set and let them scrawl over the walls the ribald wit and queer humor of the Montmartre "rat." The result is lurid realism.

While Edward Connelly and Lewis Stone (the marquis) received uniformly good notices, the reception to La Marr's performance was mixed. *The New York Times* found her only "sufficient," while, in the *New York Morning Telegraph*, Louella Parsons commented that "it is surprising that a young woman who can be so good in some of the scenes can be so bad in others. She is much better as the sorceress although I did wish she wouldn't feel it necessary to get over her scenes by the aid of her lips." Novarro's reviews were favorable, though the part certainly appears to have been a rather routine juvenile role, a comedown after his turn as the flamboyant, monocle-flipping scoundrel in *The Prisoner of Zenda*.

While critics had taken the story's framing device in stride in 1917, the reviewer for *The New York Times* felt it was "absurd" in 1922 and went on to write: "To attach a moral to this pure shocker is make the moral look foolish. The effort was made, apparently, for the sake of the censors and the twelve-year-old minds among movie fans, but it is inconceivable that even such as these will be impressed."

Still, James W. Dean in the *Reno Evening News* (14 October 1922) thought that, given the outlandishness of Zerada's story, "the device enabled Ingram to deal with improbabilities that would hardly have been digestible had they presented as situations in real life." The device also obviated the need for Ingram to film an alternate happy ending, a practice that became increasingly common for major productions in the 1920s, usually to the annoyance of their directors. Ingram had been obliged to

film a happy ending for *The Prisoner of Zenda* and was delighted when most exhibitors preferred the bittersweet one. Given that all the characters in *Trifling Women* are pretty despicable, finding a positive wrap-up would have indeed been a challenge. Metro apparently had some misgivings about this sordid horror story and, after the film was previewed under the title *Black Orchids*, insisted on the change to *Trifling Women*. (In Germany, it was titled — more appropriately — *The Serpent of Paris*.)

Ads were varied and plentiful: one depicted a haughty-looking flapper admiring herself in the mirror, unmindful of the sword pointing at her heart. Another promised a "clean, uplifting, moral and truthful photo-drama that every mother and daughter should see." Danville, Virginia's *The Bee* reported an ad that made the rather strange claim that "96% of women in New York who saw *Trifling Women* were married within 30 days." Another ad, aimed directly at men-folk, asked, "Have you ever been the victim of a Trifling Woman?" Still others played up the romantic angle and showed Novarro and LaMarr locked in passionate embrace: "A tale of how three men sought one woman and one woman sought everything — and what they all got" (*Mansfield* [Pennsylvania] *News*, 9 January 1923). Virtually all ads and publicity pieces highlighted director Ingram and his earlier accomplishments, especially *Four Horsemen*.

What's more, some of those ads and puff pieces were not shy about playing up the more outré aspects of the film. An illustration showing Zareda cowering at the feet of the vengeful marquis was captioned, "It pleased the Marquis of Ferroni to show the wreath of Black Orchids to the woman who had placed them upon his sepulcher." A similar drawing in another ad was headlined:

> In the Sorcerer's Tower! There was no way out.
> Zareda was cornered and knew it.
> Ferroni's heart was like the stones of the tower.
> He would lock her in — in that dungeon where the air was chill as a dead man's breath!

Another promised excitedly (if a bit ungrammatically): "Atmosphere exotic, settings; a gorgeous story, like a legend — a modern Arabian Nights of Paris; plots sinister, passion overwhelming, destiny swift and inexorable." Still another featured a drawing of Zareda, her gown half off, cradling Ivan's corpse. The suggestion of necrophilia in the film's finale was not lost on the New York censor, who insisted that the scene of Zareda caressing the boy's dead body be cut. The censor was also unhappy with the shots of Zareda being dragged into the dungeon, and Ivan's body being thrown down the stairs. Metro shortened the shots, but did not eliminate them.

Barbara La Marr was ascending to the height of her popularity when she made *Trifling Women*. La Marr, who had enjoyed considerable success as a dancer in her 1910s, initially broke into the movies as a screenwriter. "The girl who was too beautiful" soon turned to acting, though, catching the public notice with her performance as the scheming M'Lady in Doug Fairbanks' *The Three Musketeers*; it was typical of the parts that would make her famous and which would win her legions of captivated fans. She was just as celebrated overseas and, four years after her death, was still the most popular actress in Russia, at least according to Sergei Eisenstein.

La Marr's personal life, however, was quite another matter. She was married three times before she turned 21, and — in what sounds like something right out of *Alraune*— her first two spouses met untimely deaths, while the third went to prison for forging checks in his attempt at keeping his lovely wife in the style to which she had become accustomed. Two more marriages followed, less disastrous, perhaps, but still unsuccessful. Along the way, La Marr had a series of love affairs, but remained something of a mystic about romance. She wrote a poem about reincarnation, part of which reads:

"Perhaps, adored that centuries ago
I knew things that I now don't know.
Perhaps on primitive, desert shores
I found you, loved you, was truly yours."

In addition to her great capacity for love, La Marr also developed an insatiable taste for partying, cocaine, and alcohol. Her drug problem is sometimes blamed on the studio doctors who gave her morphine when she injured herself on the set of *Souls for Sale*, but it seems like she needed little encouragement to indulge herself beyond the limit. She also developed a weight problem and countered it with bouts of crash-dieting.

The actress's stamina finally broke, and she collapsed during the shooting of *The Girl from Montmartre.* Too ill to return to the set, her scenes were completed by look-alike starlet, Lolita Lee. La Marr lingered for several weeks before dying on the 30 January 1926. The cause of her death was apparently pyelitis (inflammation of the pelvis of the kidney), but there were also rumors that she died of tuberculosis which had developed when her body was weakened after a round of starvation dieting. She left no will and only a small estate. Her adopted son was taken in by her good friend, ZaSu Pitts.

La Marr had requested a Christian Science burial service, and the brief ceremony was attended mainly by her Hollywood friends. Outside the little chapel, it was a different matter. Thousands came to view La Marr's body and, in ugly scenes similar to those depicted in *The Day of the Locust*, riot police had to be called in to quell the disturbances. This hysteria was to be repeated on an even grander scale just a few months later at the funeral of La Marr's onetime dance partner, Rudolph Valentino.

Gossip sometimes linked La Marr with Ramon Novarro, but that was purely for publicity purposes as Novarro was gay, a fact that, of course, could not be made public. Novarro was no mere Valentino clone and was a far better actor than sometimes given credit for; his intensity as Ben Hur is much more convincing than Charlton Heston's teeth-grinding — but Academy-pleasing — histrionics in the remake. Ingram and Novarro had a relationship of great mutual respect and worked together a number of times; Ingram's failure to land the director's job for *Ben Hur* was as painful for Novarro as it was for Ingram. Sound brought a decline in the kind of romantic, costume movies that had made Novarro famous, so he retired in the mid–1930s though he made an occasional return to the screen. He had sensibly saved his money and invested in real estate and thus was able to live comfortably throughout the succeeding years, although he was largely forgotten by the public. That changed on 30 October 1969, when the aging, former matinee idol was tortured and murdered by the two young men he had invited to his Laurel Canyon home. They mistakenly believed he had a fortune stashed away, but they found only $45. It was all prime Hollywood-Babylon material and overshadowed the genuine accomplishments of his career.

Lewis Stone, best known as the insufferably wise Judge Hardy in the popular-but-saccharine Andy Hardy series, played a wide variety of roles in the Silent Era. A writer for the *Indianapolis Star* (28 February 1923) summed this up very well: "Mr. Stone with rare exception has done everything he ever tried very capably, whether it be the tired businessman, dissipated heir, suave foreigner, stately backwoods priest, Mountie, or what-not. Memory fails only in an attempt to recall when he has put on the hardy chaps and sombrero and sat himself astride a bronco."

The silver-haired, distinguished-looking Stone was also very popular with the flapper set; (perhaps they were looking for a father figure). For Ingram, Stone played the hero in *The Prisoner of Zenda* and the villain in *Scaramouche*, and he lived long enough to play small parts in the 1950s remakes of both films. Stone died of a heart attack in 1953 while confronting some teenage prowlers who clearly were not from the Andy-Hardy-mold of wayward youth.

A few words should be said about the career of erstwhile orangutan "actor," Joe Martin. Martin was discovered by "Daredevil" Curley Joe Stecher, who also brought Charlie (the Elephant) and Elsa (the Educated Lioness) to Universal City. Joe had his own series of one-reel comedies and was pal to both Elmo Lincoln (in the serial *The Adventures of Tarzan*, 1921) and Harry Myers (in the serial *The Adventures of Robinson*

Zareda (Barbara La Marr) accepts a trifle from Hatim-Tai (ape-star Joe Martin), who knows how to treat a woman, in this scene from *Trifling Women*.

Crusoe, 1922). While usually benign, Joe was sometimes used as a menace, as when he was called upon to do a Murders-in-the-Rue-Morgue bit in *Merry-Go-Round*. His bad behavior in *Trifling Women* marked the beginning of the end of his career, and Universal sold him to a circus in 1924, after giving him a big farewell party. Unfortunately, there was no happy ending for Joe, who ran amuck doing a performance and had to be shot. Michael Powell considered *Trifling Women* one of the few, true, Hollywood horror films of the Silent Era, and perhaps should have the last word on this regrettably lost film: "It was all moonlight on tiger skins and blood dripping onto white faces, while sinister apes, poison and lust kept the plot going."

— HN

Trilby (1915)

Trilby. Equitable Motion Pictures Corp./World Film Corp., 20 September 1915, 5 reels [available]

CAST: Clara Kimball Young (*Trilby O'Farrell*); Wilton Lackaye (*Svengali*); Paul McAllister (*Gecko*); Chester Barnett (*Little Billee*); with D.J. Flanagan

CREDITS: *Director* Maurice Tourneur; *Assistant Director* Clarence L. Brown; *Scenario* E.M. Ingleton; based on the eponymous novel by George Du Maurier (London, 1894) and the play of the same name by Paul Potter (New York, 15 April 1895); *Art Director* Ben Carré; *Editor* Clarence L. Brown

"I hate it! I have always wished to gain a reputation through my drawing and it is rather bitter for me to get success by what I consider my worst work."

— George Du Maurier

The "worst work" that so vexed Du Maurier was *Trilby*, very likely the best-selling novel of the 19th century, far surpassing anything by Dickens or Twain. It also influenced more films in this volume than *Dracula*, *Frankenstein*, or the stories of Poe.

The Anglo/French Du Maurier was an artist who spent most of his career doing illustrations for the satirical magazine *Punch* and only turned to writing during the last few years of his life, first with *Peter Ibbetson* (see entry), then *Trilby* (which he also illustrated) and finally *The Martian*. Trilby was first serialized in *Harper's New Monthly Magazine* and then released as a novel in 1894. The book was a phenomenon and sold 200,000 copies within the year. Libraries couldn't keep up with the demand; a Chicago librarian remarked that "every one of our 54,000 card holders seemed determined to read the book."

Trilby is a long, rambling potboiler about life and love in the Latin Quarter in Paris, while focusing on the painter, Little Billee, and his friends, the Laird and Taffy, the "Three Musketeers of the Brush." Du Maurier had lived in the Latin Quarter during his youthful artist days, but what separates the tale from being just another variation on *La Vie Boheme* is the sinister music teacher Svengali and his bizarre relationship with Trilby, a sculptor's model who is loved by Little Billee. Trilby reciprocates Billee's love, but his wealthy family doesn't approve and convinces Trilby to give Billee up. Trilby disappears, and the heartbroken Billee returns home to England where he becomes a successful artist. To the amazement of Billee and his friends, the tone-deaf Trilby later resurfaces as a great diva and Svengali's wife. Trilby doesn't even recognize her old friends, and they are

baffled by her behavior. Svengali dies of a heart attack during Trilby's London debut, and Trilby cannot sing without him. She reverts to her normal self, but with confused memories of the last few years. Despite the best efforts of her friends, Trilby wastes away and expires, calling out Svengali's name. Little Billee, too beautiful for this world anyway, dies soon after. Gecko, Svengali's pupil and minion, reveals that Svengali used hypnotism to dominate Trilby and to turn her into an extraordinary singer.

According to Paul Potter, the playwright who adapted *Trilby* for the stage, Du Maurier's children told him that their father wrote the concluding chapters of *Trilby* without the elements that ultimately made it successful: Trilby dies without becoming a great prima donna, and Svengali is just her music teacher, not her master. The children objected to such a lackluster finale: "Then we all opened fire on him at once. We pointed out how out extravagant he had been to let poor Trilby take all those lessons and then never do anything with her voice." Du Maurier, "fearfully tired of the story," locked himself in the library and supposedly reshaped the tale into the form that made it famous.

Du Maurier's children were not the only ones concerned about Trilby's fate. While the story was being serialized, some readers begged Du Maurier not to kill her off. (Shades of Dickens and Little Nell!) Every detail of the book was relished and debated, sometimes even from the pulpit. Du Maurier was besieged with letters asking all kinds of questions about the book's characters (e.g., did Trilby and Svengali have a sexual relationship?). Du Maurier was appalled by such inquiries and couldn't understand why the public had taken the story so much to heart. "Trilbymania" swept England and the United States: there were Trilby hats, Trilby soap, Trilby sausages, Trilby headache pills (Svengali first hypnotizes Trilby to alleviate her headaches), Trilby shoes, Trilby "beautiful feet" contests (Little Billee thinks Trilby has the most perfect feet in the world and does an impromptu sketch of them), Trilby calendars, Trilby artwork and music (the old sailor's tune, "Ben Bolt," Trilby's favorite song, made a comeback), Trilby trivia contests, stage acts using the names Trilby and Svengali (including a circus act featuring a whip-cracking Svengali and a beautiful bareback rider Trilby), and, perhaps most appropriately of all, Trilby sleeping pills. There was a racehorse christened Trilby, and the little town of Macon, Florida — tired of getting mail intended for Macon, Georgia — changed its name to Trilby, complete with Svengali Square and Little Billee Lake. No doubt there would have been Trilby and Svengali action figures had anyone thought of it.

None of this put so much as a brass farthing in Du Maurier's pocket, but he did turn a good profit by selling the stage rights. The aforementioned Paul Potter turned the novel into a four-act play which premiered in Boston in 1895. Whereas the literary Svengali is a fleeting presence, off-stage much of the time (much like Count Dracula in Stoker's novel), Potter put him into the forefront of the action. The "Hebrew hypnotist" (Du Maurier's work is decidedly anti–Semitic) and mad genius became one of the most colorful of stage villains. Wilton Lackaye, a specialist in larger-than-life studies, was the theater's first Svengali; the character became Lackaye's *de facto* signature role, one he played in three subsequent Broadway revivals of the play (1905, 1915 and 1922), as well as in the 1915 movie.

Virginia Harned essayed the part of *Trilby* in Boston, and she reprised the role in the 1905 production. In the audience at the Boston premiere was famed British thespian, Sir Herbert Beerbohm Tree, who immediately brought the UK rights to the play; his turn as Svengali became a huge success for him back in Old Blighty. Tree's Gecko? None other than Du Maurier's son Gerald, who was on his way to becoming a famous actor and to fathering Daphne, the mystery writer who is much better remembered today than either her father and grandfather. Some critics may have thought the play a "vulgarization" of the novel or found it "full of melodramatic excess" (especially Svengali's prolonged death scene), but the public disagreed and before long there were dozens of theater companies touring with *Trilby*, as well as parodies like *Thrillby* and *Thilby*.

Of course, the movies couldn't neglect such a gold mine. Shorts like *Trilby and Little Billee* (1896) featured a scene from the novel and *Svengali and the Posters* (1899, aka *The Poster Girls and the Hypnotist*) depicted a hypnotist who brings to life the figures of two ballerinas on a poster. Norway adapted the story to film in 1908, and Austria did likewise, twice (in 1912 and 1914). In 1913, the impresario Daniel Frohman had Virginia Harned photographed while enacting Trilby, perhaps as a test for a possible film version. Nonetheless, the most notable, early cinematic rendition of *Trilby* was a British production (done by American director, Harold Shaw) highlighted by Sir Herbert Beerbohm Tree repeating his stage triumph. About two reels of the film survive at the British Film Institute.

Trilbymania had peaked before 1915, but the story was still one of the best-known in America, and Equitable/World was confident it had a sure moneymaker when it signed Wilton Lackaye and the very popular Clara Kimball Young to star in *Trilby*, with Maurice Tourneur set to direct. Publicity for the film said it took three months to shoot at a cost of $71,000 (at least twice the likely cost of the average feature for that day), but considerably more far-fetched was the claim that the five-reel film featured a cast of 50 principals, 700 supporting players, and was comprised of 250 scenes. No doubt something along those lines would have been necessary had an attempt been made to be doggedly faithful to the novel, but Tourneur and writer E.M. Ingleton wisely decided to follow the play instead and simplified the plot further still as well as eliminating many minor characters.

This synopsis of the film is taken from contemporary reviews and from viewing the print as it stands on video. It must be noted that the character is called "Billee" in Du Maurier's novel, and "Billie" in the film; from here on in — in the interests of preserving the reader's sanity — he is Billie.

In the Latin Quarter, model Trilby O'Farrell befriends three British artists: Taffy, the Laird, and Little Billie. Svengali, an eccentric music teacher who lives in the same building, hears Trilby amuse her friends with an out of tune rendition of "Ben Bolt." Svengali joins in the mirth, but a quick inspection of Trilby's mouth convinces him that she has the potential to be a great singer. Trilby and Little Billie fall in love. When Trilby complains of headaches, Svengali hypnotizes her and she awakens free of pain, but her friends are furious with Svengali and warn Trilby not to let him hypnotize her again. Svengali tells his pupil Gecko that by using hypnotism he can turn Trilby into a great singer and make millions.

When Little Billie sees Trilby posing in the nude for an art class, he becomes disillusioned with her but, much to Svengali's chagrin, the two become reconciled and a Christmas-night party is planned to celebrate their engagement. On the night of the party, Svengali hypnotizes Trilby and makes her write a note telling Billie that she's unworthy of him and is thus leaving Paris. Svengali and Gecko spirit her away, and the despondent and ill Billie returns to London to be cared for by his mother and sister.

Under Svengali's power, Trilby becomes a great diva and they tour the world. However, Svengali's heart suffers from the strain of exerting his will on Trilby and, whenever he's ill, she returns briefly to her normal self. Svengali and Trilby travel to London for her grand debut there as La Svengali. He also has a life-size portrait of himself painted and arranges to have it delivered to his hotel. Little Billie has recovered and Taffy and the Laird are visiting. Curious about what kind of person could possibly have married someone like Svengali, the trio attends opening night and is shocked to find out that La Svengali is Trilby. During intermission they go backstage and quickly realize that Trilby is in a trance. Trilby returns to the stage, but Svengali scuffles with her friends in the dressing room and suffers a fatal heart. Trilby, released from his spell and understandably confused, begins singing "Ben Bolt" in her old voice and is hooted off the stage. Back in the dressing room, Billie and the others shield her from the sight of Svengali's body and take her back to the hotel where they celebrate their reunion. The friends take their leave, but while they are waiting for the elevator they hear Trilby scream. She has seen reflected in her mirror the great portrait of Svengali and has died of shock.

The film opened in New York with full orchestral accompaniment and a score written especially for the film by Dr. Hugo Riesenfeld; everything fell into place under the direction of master showman, S.L. Rothapefel. "A wonderful production, wonderfully presented," enthused Longacre of *Motion Picture News* (25 September 1915), describing the premiere. The reviewer went on to praise all involved for giving the public a screen version of one of the most famous plays of the century in a way which makes the superiority of the speaking stage over the screen seem ridiculously small even in the speaking stage's particular precinct, pure drama.

While most of the reviews were equally laudatory, *Variety*'s Jolo had some reservations which he expressed in a rather peculiar review: "It is not an adaptation of the play, following more closely the story as laid out in the book. For instance, in showing Little Billie, Taffy and the Laird walking through a street in the Latin Quarter of Paris, they pass an English 'bobby' or policeman…. Once more, some of the titles were hard to read."

Actually, the scene with the bobby is set at the London docks where Billie is greeting the newly-arrived Taffy and the Laird, but perhaps the title card explaining that Billie has gone home was one of those that the reviewer found hard to decipher. Jolo concluded his review by equivocating that "one might continue indefinitely recounting the pros and cons of this feature, saying a lot which meant little or nothing. The one thing that counts and means anything is that the picture is worthy of being played in the best picture houses throughout the world."

Still, in a moment of near coherency, Jolo did manage to zero in on the problem with Wilton Lackaye's portrayal of Svengali: he saw it as being "most intelligent and not exaggerated," and therefore disappointing. "He might have disregarded a modicum of consistency and contributed a bit of sensationalism." Jolo no doubt would have been more impressed with the 1914 British film, wherein Beerbohm Tree is clearly not toning down his performance for the camera.

Clara Kimball Young's Trilby won much praise, but again there was one dissenter—Julian Johnson in the December 1915 *Photoplay*: "She was pert rather than innocent and childish; there was little variation between Trilby and La Svengali, and when she died it seemed not because the demonic vitality of her master had passed from her, but because she fell down and bumped her pretty little head."

Apparently Young showed far more restraint in her death scene than did Virginia Harned, whose Trilby stumbled to and fro across the stage for quite some time before finally collapsing. Time-wise, this was still an improvement over the novel wherein Trilby—who seems determined to break Camille's record for the longest death scene in literature—spends chapter after chapter s-l-o-w-l-y expiring.

Extant copies of this picture appear to come from the 1917 reissue, which is missing the ending. The reissue closes on a happy note, with Trilby biding farewell to her friends and presumably ready to resume a normal life. The missing climax is a particularly unfortunate loss as Tourneur had gone to some lengths to set it up: Svengali inspects the portrait at the shop and orders it delivered to the hotel on the night of Trilby's London premiere. We see the picture arriving at the hotel and the maid grimacing in distaste as she sets it up not far from Trilby's mirror, the mirror into which Trilby does not so much as glance just before she has dinner with her friends. Trilby's first glimpse of the portrait is the fatal one at the climax.

Also missing is the quarrel between Svengali and Gecko that includes "the introduction of the vision of Death," a figure *Motion Picture World* dismissed as "not too impressive" (18 September 1915). Gone, too, is a series of dissolves—described in the 15 September 1915 *New York Dramatic Mirror*—that depict "Svengali's wanderings with Trilby." What's left now is a long shot (in silhouette) of Svengali dragging Trilby along on a hillside as Gecko follows, a moment that's both macabre and melancholy. Other than that, there's only a scene showing Trilby singing for a crowd of peasants and then, after a title card informs us that Svengali has realized his dream, we see Trilby performing in a grand theater.

There exists a still that shows Clara Kimball Young's Trilby enmeshed in white nets (meant to be symbolic of Svengali's hold over her), but there's no sign of any such scene in the extant copies of the picture. It's surprising that Tourneur used nets rather than a spider web, as one of the book's most famous illustrations (again, by Du Maurier) shows a giant spider with the head of Svengali (perhaps this inspired the image of Hyde as a monstrous spider in the 1920 *Dr. Jekyll and Mr. Hyde*). There is, however, a title card showing a vulture with Svengali's head.

Viewers familiar with later Svengalis—particularly John Barrymore's in the eponymous 1931 film—may be surprised to learn that Tourneur doesn't include even a single close-up of Svengali's eyes exerting their evil power. At one point, Trilby attempts to resist Svengali by turning her face away from him until he forces her to look at him—all in one medium shot of

the two of them. Close-ups were used more sparingly in the mid–1910s than just a few years later, and Tourneur was praised for keeping them to a minimum in *Trilby*. Svengali's power seems mainly in his hands, and it's through gestures that he usually exercises his control over Trilby. This is in keeping with traditions of mesmerism in which precise hand movements over the subject's body are supposed to stir up magnetic forces that are directed to various ends. One of the most eerie moments in *Trilby* occurs in a shabby, shadowy room wherein Tourneur shows Svengali crouching over the headboard of Trilby's bed as she sleeps in her trance. He moves away and sits in a nearby chair, but continues to makes passes with his hands in her direction as though he's building a barrier around her to keep her prisoner; here, he seems more sorcerer than hypnotist.

Tourneur had already directed half-a-dozen American films by the time he got to *Trilby* and was being acclaimed as a director equal in importance to D.W. Griffith (for a career overview of Tourneur, see entry on *The Brass Bottle*). From this early period, film historians like William K. Everson and Kevin Brownlow tend to single out the 1914 *Wishing Ring* as his most innovative and noteworthy accomplishment. *Ring* is certainly a lyrical and charming film and seems more in keeping with Tourneur's style of fantasy than the much grimmer *Trilby*.

On the surface here, though, Tourneur seems less interested in the macabre aspects of *Trilby* than in the Latin Quarter atmosphere. The Christmas Night party is one of the best sequences in the film and contains a particularly beautiful moment, lit entirely by candlelight, where the guests toast Trilby and Little Billy, who are seated in the foreground and gazing happily into each others eyes. Despite this, Tourneur doesn't let the audience forget what's afoot, and the joyous party scenes are intercut with shots of Svengali making his preparations to take Trilby away.

The climax at the concert hall seems a bit rushed, and one wishes that there were some sort of earlier encounter between Trilby, Svengali and the Three Musketeers before things came to a head. Trilby's posing in the "altogether" (a word that Du Maurier coined in his book) is actually better done in the Beerbohm Tree film, wherein Svengali craftily arranges for Little Billie to see his beloved undraped before a roomful of men. In the Tourneur film, the disrobing is witnessed inadvertently and is over in a flash. Reviewers thought the scene tastefully done, but it supposedly elicited gasps from Chicago audiences. At least they did have something to gasp at; in the play, the incident is talked about, but not shown.

Tourneur *does* introduce interesting bits of business here and there: Trilby playing with some caged songbirds is a nice bit of foreshadowing of her own fate. When Trilby first meets the Musketeers and Svengali, the sequence achieves a pleasing symmetry by beginning and ending with Trilby standing in the foreground at the door looking at the other characters within. Mirrors turn up at key points; when, for example, Svengali enters the room where Trilby is dressing for the party she first sees him approach in a mirror. Later, in the dressing room of the London concert hall, a fearful Trilby sits in front of her mirrors as Svengali works his magic on her. Shortly thereafter, those same mirrors reflect Svengali's corpse as a heartbroken Gecko looks on.

And, of course, it's in a mirror that Trilby sees the reflection of the portrait that ends her life.

Clara Kimball Young was a big star when she made *Trilby* (for her triumphs and travails, see the entry on *Eyes of Youth*), but the characters she usually played were more likely to be found in high society than Bohemia. She was an attractive woman, but not very sexy; ads often described her as "queenly." Her Trilby seems like one of the boys, more of a good sport and pal than a love object. Nevertheless, she makes the hapless model likable and funny, impishly blowing smoke into Svengali's face when he flirts with her or gamely choking down a salad that her beloved Little Billie has over-seasoned. As La Svengali she's appropriately vacant eyed and docile, but—in more disturbing moments—she seems like a sleepwalker experiencing a bad dream from which she's struggling to awaken. Young later said that she threw herself heart and soul into the character: "I felt Trilby's every emotion, and approached the final climax forgetful of all else save the character itself." According to Eve Gold (*Golden Images*), Young was so immersed in her role that she overturned a candle and set her hair on fire. Fortunately a stagehand who was not in a trance threw a rug over her head to smother the flames.

In his book *The Matinee Idols*, David Carroll writes that women crammed the matinees to see Wilton Lackaye on the stage as Svengali in spite of the fact that Lackaye's character was "ugly and disgusting and everything a Victorian lady fainted over and professed to despise." This was no Dracula, no saturnine seducer in the Lord Byron mold, but a physically repulsive character. Nevertheless, many female patrons were apparently drawn to the "merciless manner by which he rendered women helpless to his will." None of this charisma is really evident in the film. Lackaye's relatively restrained performance suggests little more than a brutish scoundrel out to exploit Trilby for cold cash. There's no intimation that he has a (perhaps sublimated) sexual obsession with her. Likewise, little is done with the notion of Svengali's being a frustrated artist: he himself has only a "croaking, raven's voice," so it's only through Trilby that he can express his talent; hence, he needs her to be whole. He has made her a part of himself so it's only naturally that when he dies, she must follow him to the grave. Svengali's perverse genius just doesn't come through in Lackaye's performance though, in fairness, the scenario—and the necessity of cramming the whole story into five reels—must share part of the blame.

Svengali's being Jewish had been transferred from novel to play (critics refer to him making entreaties in Yiddish to the God he doesn't believe in,) but has largely been dropped from the film except for a possible reference in the brief prologue: After a title card—"Out of the mysterious East"—we see Svengali putting Trilby under his spell while wearing a garment over his shoulders that suggests a prayer shawl. Lackaye's make-up, true to the book's illustrations, is something of a Semitic caricature in the Fagin/Shylock tradition.

Lackaye is effective in Svengali's death scene, which is taken from the play rather than the book. In the latter, Svengali dies quietly in the special box whence he's watching Trilby's performance, as he does in the 1954 film version with Donald Wolfit. As there was no way that the stage Svengali was going to go so gently into that good night, he would rage at Little Billie and the others until he felt the fatal spasms in his chest. Continuing his venomous rant, he would finally keel over backwards onto a table, his head over the edge and his dead—but still-hate-filled—eyes glaring out at the audience. Reviewers of the play marveled that Lackaye managed to pull off that little stunt at every performance without breaking his neck.

Lackaye's well-to-do Virginia family had intended him for the priesthood, but on his way to a seminary in Rome, he stopped in New York and attended a performance of the play *Esmeralda* (which had no connection to the Victor Hugo character). It was his "Road to Damascus," and he put aside his vocation faster than John Barrymore doffing his cassock after getting a look at Dolores Costello in *When a Man Loves*. Appalled, Lackaye's father tried to persuade him to go into law instead, but the young man persisted and was soon traveling with different stock companies. After some years of apprenticeship, he won his first significant notices while playing Leo Vincey in a William Gillette production of H. Rider Haggard's *She*. He was particularly noted for his villains and played Nero in a production that included a stage filled with lions, and Simon Legree in *Uncle Tom's Cabin* (wherein the animal support was more than likely provided by bloodhounds). A year after *Trilby* first opened, he was playing a hypnotist again in *Dr. Belgraff*, a melodrama in which he keeps a young woman under his spell to prevent her from revealing that he has committed murder. While *Trilby* is his only genre film credit (and perhaps the most significant movie of his rather limited screen career), his stage work includes *The Monster* (1922; playing Dr. Ziska, a role taken by Lon Chaney for the film version), *The Monkey Talks* (1925; as Lorenzo), and *The Curious Conduct of Judge Legarde*, in which he impersonated both personalities of the title character. The cinematic counterparts to all these productions are covered in this volume.

Lackaye was known for his acid wit and his frequent public quarrels, often with theater producers. When asked if he'd found a backer willing to produce his proposed *Les Miserables* project, Lackaye responded: "To produce it! I haven't been able to find one who can pronounce it!" The exchanges weren't always just verbal; on one famous occasion, Lackaye was knocked down a flight of stairs by John J. McGraw, manager of the New York Giants and, like Lackaye, a member of the famous Lamb's Club. Lackaye had a particularly nasty set-to over the leadership of Actor's Equity and, perhaps coming full circle in a way, he founded a guild for Catholic stage actors. He developed heart trouble in the late 1920s and went into semi-retirement while remaining busy—and feisty—until his death in 1932. His obituaries always mentioned Svengali first of all.

Chester Barnett makes an appropriately sensitive Little Billie. His most dramatic moment probably comes when he recognizes Trilby as La Svengali; his amazement and horror turn to near hysteria, but—once his friends have calmed him down—he begins to laugh, presumably that the bitter joke is on him. Barnett was a popular juvenile lead in the 1910s and was frequently paired with Pearl White (just before her *Perils of Pauline* success). He was also directed by Tourneur in *The Wishing Ring* and *The Pit* (which also featured Wilton Lackaye). He seems to have retired from films in the early 1920s and to have spent his later years running a music store in Jefferson City, Missouri.

Paul McAllister, who himself played Svengali on the stage, is rather poignant as Gecko, a man totally devoted to his master and in thrall to his genius. McAllister also wrote a spoof of *Trilby* called *The Stolen Voice* (see entry).

Trilby was extremely successful and revived with much hoopla in 1917 (with "art nouveau" titles) and again in 1920, with the latter production no doubt capitalizing on Clara Kimball Young's comeback with *Eyes of Youth*. Ads for these reissues tended toward the sensational: "Eyes— Eyes— Eyes— Wherever she went they followed her and searched her soul with a pitiless scrutiny." Kimball Young's "altogether" scene was also prominently featured (and, probably, pitilessly scrutinized).

— HN

Trilby (1923)

Trilby. Richard Walton Tully Productions/First National Pictures, 29 July 1923, 8 reels/7321 feet [LOST]

CAST: Andree Lafayette (*Trilby*); Arthur Edmund Carewe (*Svengali*); Wilfred Lucas (*the Laird*); Maurice Cannon (*Zouzou*); Gordon Mullen (*Durfen*); Martha Franklin (*Mme. Vinard*); Gilbert Clayton (*Rev. Bagot*); Edward Kimball (*Impresario*); Creighton Hale (*Little Billee*); Philo McCullough (*Taffy*); Frances McDonald (*Gecko*); Max Constant (*Dodor*); Gertrude Olmsted (*Miss Bagot*); Evelyn Sherman (*Mrs.Bagot*); Rose Dione (*Laundress*); Robert De Vilbiss (*Jeannot*)

CREDITS: *Presenter* Richard Walton Tully; *Director* James Young; *Scenario* Richard Walton Tully; based on the eponymous novel by George Du Maurier (London, 1894) and the play of the same name by Paul Potter (New York, 15 April 1895); *Cinematographer* Georges Benoit

Trilby, toiling in a French laundry, comes to the notice of an artist who wants to sketch her beautiful foot. She meets an English boy, studying art in the Latin Quarter of Paris, and calls him Little Billee. He falls in love with her, but on the night of their betrothal party, Svengali, one of the lodgers in the house, hypnotizes Trilby and takes her away, presenting her as a concert singer. One night Billee and his companions hear her and rush to see her. Svengali has a fatal attack, and Trilby sings without his influence — ruining her reputation. She is united to Billee, but the strain of her career under Svengali has been too much and she dies.

— *Moving Picture World*, 4 August 1923

At one time, George Du Maurier's 1894 novel *Trilby* was, in the words of a literary critic, "a license to print money." By the 1920s, though, the story had become the victim of its own success. Hypnotists— larcenous or lecherous or both — had become the standard villains of silent melodrama. The public was still interested in hypnotism, especially since it often played a part in the new science of psychiatry, but trances and characters acting under the influence of the evil eye had become movie clichés, something hack writers readily added to the mix when their imaginations had reached their limits. The 1922 Broadway revival of *Trilby*— with the great Wilton Lackaye as Svengali (and Edmund Lowe as Little Billee)—closed after just twelve performances.

Still, even though the book was no longer a sensation, the public was still familiar with the plot and the main characters. Stories of "real life" Svengalis and Trilbys turned up regularly

in the early 1920s. A widely-circulated newspaper article told of a young woman named Mimi Nizarri who couldn't sing a note until hypnotized by music teacher, Leon Ardin. The article drew many parallels to the DuMaurier story and was illustrated with a large, rather crude drawing of a sinister, bearded man waving his claw-like fingers in front of a woman singing under his command. There was also a fair amount of publicity about the singer, Mme. Ganna Malska, who was hypnotized to enhance her debut as Gilda in Verdi's *Rigoletto* at the Paris Opera House. (While the audience didn't approve of her performance, thankfully she didn't break into "Ben Bolt" as a result). A series of stories about Italian dictator Benito Mussolini called him a "strange, new kind of Svengali," with Italy playing the role of Trilby and much being made of Il Duce's piercing, hypnotic eyes. Even a simple case of a Cincinnati housewife's disappearance was given the Du Maurier slant, with the distraught husband claiming his missing wife was" likely in a trance" and under the spell of a local Svengali.

No doubt such stories helped convince the playwright and theater impresario, Richard Walton Tully, that the old warhorse could still be turned a cash cow. Tully, who had switched his attentions from Broadway to Hollywood, certainly realized that the tale had indeed been told once too often, but he reasoned that the public might still be entranced by it with the right kind of publicity. Tully's idea was to mount a campaign to find an unknown actress to play Trilby and then promote her as a new superstar.

Tully had a string of Broadway successes behind him, mostly romances set in exotic locales (one of them, *The Flame*, even has a bit of voodoo thrown into the mix). Critics were often scornful, but the public was enthusiastic, and Tully's biggest hit was undoubtedly his 1912 *The Bird of Paradise*, which popularized Hawaiian music. Theater audiences were also captivated by his *Rose of the Rancho*, *Omar the Tentmaker*, and *The Masquerader*. The latter two starred Guy Post Bates, who reprised his roles in the subsequent film versions when Tully landed a contract with First National to produce his own movies. Both films were directed by James Young, former husband of Clara Kimball Young. *The Masquerader* was later remade as a talkie with Ronald Colman, and *Omar the Tentmaker* features Boris Karloff in a small role; without the presence of these actors, both films would be as totally forgotten as the plays. Even though Bates had failed to click with moviegoers, Tully nevertheless announced that he would play Svengali in the new film version of *Trilby* and that James Young would again direct.

But who would play the beautiful but childlike Trilby? Early publicity for the film stressed that Richard Walton Tully was not going to be easy to please: "He will be adamant in his reserve and cannot be 'vamped' by mere tricks or special pleading." This admirable rejection of the casting couch was supplemented by James Young's description of the ideal Trilby:

> She must be tall and very young, or at least able to "look" very young. She must also have tiny feet. The general racial appearance must be Irish, for, you will remember in the book, Trilby was of Celtic parentage. She must also possess a very large mouth, the mouth of a singer. Of course she must be pretty and, quite as important as anything else, she must be portrayed by a young woman

who can act [*Indianapolis Sunday Star*, 7 January 1923].

This is one of the very few times Young is mentioned in the publicity. Tully may have picked him as director because of his success in transferring the George Arliss play *The Devil* (see entry) from stage to screen in 1921. Young wasn't a big name,

Andree Lafayette is all plaintive and pretty as she graces this trade ad from the September 15, 1923, issue of *Motion Picture World*.

though, and Tully might have simply preferred a competent but low-key craftsman who would have no problem staying in his producer's shadow. Young could be a bit volatile — he once stabbed Clara Kimball's boyfriend in the neck when he encountered them together on the street — but that was in the past. He also apparently had no problem directing his former father-in-law, Edward Kimball, who was given a small role in *Trilby*.

With much fanfare, Tully and his crew departed for France in the winter of 1923; there were exteriors to be shot, a cast to be assembled, and the search for the new Trilby to be continued. Guy Post Bates was among the entourage, but — somewhere along the way — he was dropped from the cast. (Nevertheless, a 1938 *New York Times* article about a proposed new film version of *Trilby* — to star Joan Fontaine — credits Bates as having played Svengali in the 1923 film!) Bates was replaced by Arthur Edmund Carewe; this proved to be a most astute move as Carewe was the only of the cast to receive uniformly excellent notices when the film came out.

Tully later reported that many of the scenes were shot in Du Maurier's exact locales, although — according to the director — the author "… had camouflaged the names of streets and buildings he described. I finally discovered his 'Cirque Bashibazooka' to be the 'Cirque Boom Boom,' now called the Cirque Medrano. The square in which the boys of the story lived was called 'Anatole des Arts' and is in reality the 'Andre des Arts.'"

Presumably these scenes were shot by veteran cameraman Georges Benoit, who was originally from Paris but had been in the USA since the 1910s, lensing such notable films as *Regeneration* and *Carmen* (with Theda Bara). In an article published by the *Oakland* [California] *Tribune*, Tully claimed that "at the Cirque Medrano we took some of the circus scenes, using 4000 people, all in the costumes of 1860" (21 March 1923). The matching of the location footage with the studio scenes was highly praised when the film was released.

And, of course, it was in France that Tully found his Trilby, Andree de la Bigne who — he claimed — first came to his notice when he saw her on a poster. Blonde, blue eyed, 5'8" tall, Mlle. de la Bigne was strikingly beautiful and seemingly an exact match for Du Maurier's Trilby. But what clinched the part for de la Bigne so far as Tully was concerned were the woman's "perfect" feet! This was the beginning of a rather bizarre emphasis in the extensive publicity over the new Trilby, including a claim that Tully had insured her feet for $1,000,000! With a plethora of publicity like that, people not familiar with the original story may well have assumed it dealt with an evil podiatrist and his attempt to control the daintiest tootsies in the world.

Mademoiselle de la Bigne admitted her parents were "poor Normans," but confessed that she did have a famous grandmother, Valtesse de la Bigne, a noted beauty of the 1860s and the model for several magnificent portraits. Valtesse had also served as the inspiration for Zola's *Nana*, the story of an elegant courtesan. Although this sort of thing seemed a perfect fit for a tale of the Latin Quarter and artists' models, fairly early on in the publicity campaign Tully decided it was all a bit too risqué for America. He rechristened Andree de la Bigne as "Andree Lafayette," and in an instant she went from being the granddaughter of a whore to a descendant of that friend of the American Revolution, the Marquis de Lafayette! The ballyhoo boys even came up with a cutesy story about her wandering through New York City in search of the statue of her illustrious ancestor.

Though Tully's publicity machine referred to Lafayette as "the celebrated French actress" and made much of her being a beauty-contest winner, it was noticeably shy on providing any prior stage or film credits. Lafayette later said, "I had been in a few pictures in France — just for fun." One of these fun pictures was supposedly a version of *Cinderella*, another tale in which the heroine's feet play an important role.

Tully wanted his film to be closer to the play than the 1915 Clara Kimball Young version and so brought back a number of colorful characters, like Zouzou and Dodor, who previously had been excluded. In attempting to make things authentically Gallic, Tully enlisted other French actors for the cast, including Maurice Cannon and Max Constant. Rumors that circulated during filming suggested a romantic link between Lafayette and Cannon, but shortly after *Trilby* was completed, the reconfigure actress married Monsieur Constant.

When Tully returned to the USA in March, he was also accompanied by scenic designer, Conrad Tritschler, who, he claimed, was the "Urban of England" (the reference being to Joseph Urban, the famous Viennese architect and set designer). Tritschler's American film credits are elusive, but he did create the rendition of Murder Legendre's castle for the glass shot in *White Zombie* (1932).

With the film being released in July, Tully's publicity machine went into overdrive. He arranged for the novel to be serialized again in newspapers across the country, with stills from his movie being used as illustrations. It turned out that the newspapers were provided with an edited version of the book that ended with Trilby's death.

Lots of the film's publicity pieces were devoted to the transformation of Arthur Edmund Carewe into Svengali: "The Svengali nose is made of putty — an hour's job," reported the 19 July 1923 *Olean* [New York] *Evening Herald*. "Three more strenuous hours with grease paint and false whiskers and things and Svengali is ready for his evil doing." While this amount of time may seem exaggerated to us, we should recall that early film and stage presentations of Svengali did tend to give him an ogre-like appearance (in contrast, say, to the later Barrymore version, where he's unkempt and sinister but hardly grotesque). The end product of that lengthy makeup session certainly impressed the critic from *The New York Times*: "His make-up is true as steel. He has the long fingers; the sharp, aquiline nose;the hollow, cadaverous cheeks; the black, matted beard and unkempt hair of the Svengali of the book. He dark eyes are scintillating and gruesome. He is the sleek, sloppy greasy Svengali. He wears shapeless trousers, a filthy shirt and an Inverness cape" (30 July 1923). This same reviewer called Carewe's performance a "revelation."

Most of the publicity of course centered on Trilby and Andree Lafayette. "The romance of an artist's model whose modesty was her shield and whose feet were her fortune," proclaimed one of the ads, appropriately illustrated with a shot of Mlle. Lafayette's feet. A number of articles attributed to Lafayette had her describing the proper way to care for your feet, emphasizing that Trilby's feet were not really small, just perfectly formed. Lafayette also endorsed Walk-Over shoes: "Mlle. Lafayette is a constant wearer of Walk-Over shoes, having first become acquainted with their desirability through a visit to the Walk-Over shop at 21 Rue de Italienne in Paris." Many theaters showing the film held contests for free stockings: Ladies were invited to put their stocking size down on a card and submit it to the "Trilby girl" at the theater. If their size matched Miss Lafayette's, they were winners!

Occasionally there was an ad that was not aimed at foot fetishists. One showed Mlle. Lafayette in the altogether, with a discreetly-placed blurb promising: "The story of a career influenced by five loves— one, pure and honorable; the second, a fatherly affection; the third, hopeless infatuation; the fourth, like the worship of a dog for its master; the fifth, sinister." The comparable scene in the film was considered tastefully done, but the New York censor insisted on the removal of a title card that depicted a nude figure.

Reviews were generally enthusiastic. The aforementioned *New York Times* reviewer called the film "wonderfully good" and gave much of the credit to Tully. The critic was also impressed by the ending: "Trilby is seen in her room, appealed to by Little Billee. A picture is brought into the room after he has left. She unwraps it and before her eyes sees the Saturnine Svengali. The picture comes to life and then fades down to a mere photograph, with Trilby attacked by its spell and dying."

Variety critic "Rush" likewise was likewise taken by the finale: "The screen version holds to the original ending. A manufactured happy ending would have been a crime, and, although the death of the heroine is not the best ending for a picture, it was here inevitable." Crime or no, an alternate happy ending was offered to exhibitors.

The one dissenting voice came from the ever-grumpy *Time* reviewer: "Inspection of this film makes one wonder why movies aren't convicted as a public nuisance. The producers have taken Du Maurier's story (which is not far from the fringes of the classics) and, wringing its neck, have served the dead body. The semblance of Trilby remains— but spiritless…. They have retained Svengali's whiskers and some of the Parisian atmosphere" (6 August 1923).

There was some enthusiasm for Lafayette's Trilby, notably in the *New York Telegraph* ("An outstanding picture with the perfect actress"), the *New York Tribune* ("She is the best Trilby we ever saw") and the *Detroit Free Press* ("She was chosen for her perfect feet, but she will remain in future productions, we predict, because of her charm, beauty and splendid acting"). *The New York Times* thought she made "a Trilby full of fun" and that she "catches the spirit of Du Maurier's fascinating Parisian character."

Other critics, though positive, were a bit more guarded. *Variety* thought she was good in the lighter and sentimental scenes, but "her management of the more emotional moments was not so convincing. The scene where Little Billee finds her posing in the altogether was not very strongly acted." The *Moving Picture World* reviewer (in the 4 August 1923 edition) was, like all the others, struck by Lafayette's beauty and good figure, but seemed a little uncertain about her acting talent: "She flashes alluringly through the gay scenes of Parisian revelry and, whether her dramatic ability is impressive or not, anyone will admit she is a picturesque camera subject. It is probably her appearance rather than her performance that will cause comment."

The public, though, was far from impressed. Some "Straight from the Shoulder" comments reported:

"The star is unknown and, as my patrons say, she needs practice" [Irvington, Ca.].

"Some walked out and some came back to ask if she died or went to sleep. We told them she died of course; had to after acting in such a picture as that" [David City, Nev.].

"Lafayette to me is beautiful but dumb" [Benoit, Miss.].

Lafayette's next film was *Why Get Married?* (original title: *The Vital Question*), a low-budget drama done by a Canadian concern that least offered a part for Lafayette's husband, Max Constant. Publicity for that film admitted that Lafayette was "a type distinctly different from anything on the native screen; it is going to be hard to find suitable vehicles for her." The actress apparently thought those suitable vehicles might be more likely parked somewhere in Europe, where — subsequently — she was able to parlay her modest fame from *Trilby* into (increasingly smaller) roles in some French and German films, including *Glanz und Elend der Kurtisanen* (released in the United States as *Survival*) with Paul Wegener.

It was announced that, after *Trilby*, Richard Walton Tully would begin work on a film version of his greatest theatrical success, *Bird of Paradise*. That never came to pass, though, possibly because Tully was involved in seemingly endless plagiarism lawsuit over the play. At one point, he was assessed a half-million dollars in damages; in 1930, after 18 years of litigation, he won the suit. (*Bird of Paradise* was subsequently filmed twice, but Tully was not involved in either version.) Tully made one more film after *Trilby*—*Flowing Gold* (1924)— and then retired from the movies. He had failed to conquer Hollywood or to create a brand-new star, but he finally had the time and money to devote to another hobby: breeding Arabian horses.

In 1927 Du Maurier's story came to the screen again, this time in Germany with Anita Dorris as Trilby and the great Paul Wegener as Svengali. Wegener eschewed the traditional "Semitic" look of the villain and played the part without the usual long hair and beard, but perhaps the most significant change was in the film's title, which was not *Trilby*, but *Svengali*. Subsequent film versions usually followed suit. It is Du Maurier's sinister music teacher whose name has passed into popular culture as a synonym for the behind-the-scenes-manipulator, the man who pulls the strings— whether his puppets are rock stars or politicians.

It seems that his poor innocent victim has been forgotten, perfect feet and all.
— *HN*

A Trip to Paradise

A Trip to Paradise. Metro Pictures Corp./Metro, 5 September 1921, 6 reels/5800 feet [LOST]

CAST: Bert Lytell (*Curley Flynn*); Virginia Valli (*Nora O'Brien*);

Brinsley Shaw (*Meek*); Unice Vin Moore (*Widow Boland*); Victory Bateman (*Mrs. Smiley*); Eva Gordon (*Mary*)

CREDITS: *Director* Maxwell Karger; *Scenario* June Mathis; based on the play *Liliom, a Legend in Seven Scenes and a Prologue* by Ferenc Molnar (English text by Benjamin F. Glazer, New York, 1921); *Adaptation* Benjamin F. Glazer; *Art Director* Julian Garnsey; *Cinematographer* Arthur Martinelli

It shouldn't take long to realize that we're familiar with this story.

Curley Flynn is a successful barker at Coney Island near the entrance of the Widow Boland's "Trip to Paradise" concession. Nora O'Brien, whose aunt operates a photo gallery, captures Curley's Heart, and he loses his job when the widow learns she has a rival. When Curley and Nora are out late one evening, she accepts his offer of marriage rather than return home. Mrs. Smiley makes him her partner, but the business does not thrive, and he is about to accept the widow's offer to leave his wife and return to his former job when he learns his wife is with child. Desperate for money, he is shot while helping to rob a house; in the hospital he has a vision of heaven, where his case is tried; he is sent back to Earth to live for his wife and child.

Ferenc Molnar's play *Liliom* (1909) not only has a strong theatrical presence in its own right, but also served as the inspiration for Rogers and Hammerstein's famed musical, *Carousel* (1945). Molnar's original tanked in his native Hungary, but saw a limited-run, English-language production on Broadway every ten years or so for the three decades that preceded Oscar Hammerstein's adaptation. The playwright had his carousel barker, Liliom — the name is Hungarian slang for "tough"— run afoul of the law while trying to support his pregnant wife. Choosing suicide over capture by the police, Liliom is granted the right to return to Earth for one day sixteen years later in order to help his teenage daughter — whom he had never even held in his arms— to do a good deed.

The traditional staging of *Carousel* contains scenes in which Billy Bigelow — the Liliom/Curley doppelgänger — interacts with otherworldly agents, and it's assumed that Bert Lytell's character did likewise in this 1921 feature, the first cinematic take on the tale. (Hungarian director Mihaly Kertesz — who would become the famous and more pronounceable Michael Curtiz when he emigrated to the States— started up his own production on *Liliom* in 1919, but the film was never completed.) The picture, no está aquí, though, and no details regarding the supernatural settings are available except for comments made en passant in film critiques. The 27 August 1921 *Harrison's Reports*, for example, sniffs that "the scenes of the Heavenly Court may be taken exception to by religious people," but also gives us a tad more information on the staging of that scene:

During the attempted looting, the hero is accidentally shot and seriously wounded. While the surgeons are probing for the bullet, the unnatural physiological effects of the anesthetic cause him to have a queer dream about dying and being summoned before the Heavenly Court. He recovers and, with his returning consciousness, there is born in him a determination to make good.

And while we've no idea whether that particular plot wrinkle had any influence whatsoever on the renowned British director, let us just note for the record that Michael Powell used the same hospital bed/Celestial Court angle when his protagonist sought to cheat fate in *A Matter of Life and Death* (1946).

Bert Lytell was the biggest name in *Paradise*, although Virginia Valli (née McSweeney) had her fans, as well. The actress, a native of the Windy City, was kept busy throughout the Silent Era, retired when sound took over, and then married actor Charles Farrell, who would take his turn as *Liliom* in the eponymous talkie filmed by Frank Borzage for Fox in 1930. Valli — not to be confused with the Italian star, Alida Valli [the "next Garbo"] — had her fair share of genre features, and her name will rise again in discussions of *The Devil Within* (1921) and *Wild Oranges* (1924), among others. The few sound films she was involved with include *The Isle of Lost Ships* (1929) and *The Lost Zeppelin* (1930). *A Trip to Paradise* was one of four pictures in which Ms. Valli appeared opposite Bert Lytell.

Lytell, a New Yawka, debuted in the movies as Michael Lanyard, *The Lone Wolf*, under the watchful eye of Herbert Brenon, and returned to the role sporadically during his career. Born in 1885, Lytell was also the screen's first Boston Blackie (in *Boston Blackie's Little Pal*, 1918). In addition to fighting crime, the handsome star spent most of his onscreen time performing heroics and wooing available ingénues in a series of enjoyable, if usually lower-shelf, productions. Few of those heroics and little of that wooing went on in Bertram's genre movies, though, as he didn't appear in many: *A Message from Mars* (1921) pretty much rounds out his pertinent credentials. Late in his life — following a hiatus of nearly 20 years — Bert Lytell returned to the fold and got into television. He was still enjoying his successes when he died in late September of 1954.

As Curley and Nora, Lytell and Valli were put through their paces by Maxwell Karger, a competent artisan who made a slew of pictures, most of which have vanished from polite conversation and cinematic consideration. Karger went east to the Big Apple from his Cincinnati birthplace and got into pictures — the Metro Pictures Corporation — around the mid–1910s. Moving easily from writing to directing to supervising production, he looked to have a lock on a bigger role in the company when it moved west and the sign over its doors came to read Metro-Goldwyn-Mayer, but he died of heart failure in mid–1922. The critiques of *Paradise* and the other films that we've been able to track down don't make mention of Karger except as the recipient of sundry left-handed compliments. The anonymous reviewer at the *Mansfield* [Ohio] *News* pretty much typified this when he observed, "It is cleverly done, but still when one knows the original Franz Molnar story one feels that Maxwell Karger, the producer, did not live quite up to the possibilities found in the original" (6 December 1921).

Most genre fans are familiar with the name Arthur Martinelli because the Italian cinematographer put the visual coup de grâce on such supernatural thrillers as *White Zombie* (1932), *Revolt of the Zombies* (1936), and ... errr ... *Supernatural* (1932). If Martinelli displayed, even in rudimentary form, any of the atmospheric savvy that marked these early talkie features in *Paradise* and *A Message from Mars* — his only other silent film herein — the offbeat sequences would have been dramatic standouts.

Scenarist June Mathis was as experienced as they come when pre-production began on *A Trip to Paradise* and she would go on to involvement in projects (*The Four Horsemen of the Apocalypse* [also 1921] and *Ben-Hur* [1925]) that would cast *Paradise* into the shadows. Nonetheless, notice was taken of Miss Mathis'

working her magic with regard to the locale of the piece, and for metamorphosing Molnar's band of Hungarian social misfits into more typically American social misfits. As Gertrude Chase remarked in her 21 August 1921 *New York Telegraph* critique:

> Adapted by June Mathis, that remarkable writer who filled in the awkward spots in "The Four Horsemen," with such effective innovations, we may say that she has given us an Americanized version which leaves out the Viennese complexities of character and makes the best use of the story, which is laid in Coney Island. Her Lilliom [*sic*] is the typical, shiftless American boy to be found on any street corner, a swaggering, pathetic figure. He never sinks to the moral slough of the original. He loves his wife and puts up a good fight before he is inveigled into the robbery. The scene before the Heavenly Court Police occurs while his body is on the operating table under an anaesthetic. The handling of this scene, while missing the satire of the play, has a real beauty of its own that to the average public, will be far more impressive. Unlike Lilliom, the stubborn, untuned soul who remains unregenerate, Curley Flynn, as he is called, finds justice in Heaven and is given strength to go back to Earth and make good for the sake of his wife and child.

Great things were expected of the Colorado-born Ms. Mathis, but this was not to be, as the lady, an audience member during a Broadway presentation of Jean Bart's *The Squall* (staged by Lionel Atwill!), announced to her mother — and everyone else in attendance — that she was dying. And die she did, moments later, in the alley behind the 48th Street Theater. Her other genre assignments included *The Conquering Power* (1921) and *The Young Rajah* (1922), and we will attempt to honor her memory in our discussion of the latter.

On the whole, *A Trip to Paradise* was greeted tepidly, even when individual actors or technicians were cited for commendable work. *Variety* critic Jolo noted that "the picture runs about 70 minutes, is carefully acted and directed throughout, but with nothing distinctive in any department to individualize it from an ordinary program feature" (7 October 1921). One of the few basically positive notices the picture received was from the afore-cited Gertrude Chase, who concluded that, "The cast throughout is excellent. Bert Lytell does a very fine piece of acting, and Virginia Valli is wistful and sweet as the wife. The settings are well done and the photography good. On the whole, it is a picture with a strong popular appeal. It is interesting, impressive and uplifting."

Liliom has been brought to the screen several times since Metro Pictures produced and released *A Trip to Paradise*. After the un–Americanized 1930 Fox production with Charles Farrell and Rose Hobart made some money, Fritz Lang went to France in 1936 and worked his trademark magic with Charles Boyer, certainly one of the least likely carousel barkers imaginable. Both Austria and Germany tried their hand at the tale, and the two television specials that resulted won good reviews and large audiences. For American viewers, though, the 1956 motion picture musical, *Carousel* — itself remade for small-screen consumption a decade and a bit later — takes the cake. That Rogers and Hammerstein masterpiece — acted and sung beautifully by Gordon McCrae, Shirley Jones and a pip of a supporting cast — is all the exposure to *Liliom* that most Millennium-Age folk will ever have.   — *JTS*

The Triumph of Venus

The Triumph of Venus. Victory Film Mfg. Co./General Film Co., May 1918, 7 reels [LOST]

CAST: Betty Lee (*Venus*); Phyllis Beveridge (*Diana*); William Sherwood (*The Sculptor*); Hussan Mussalli (*Pannas*); Grace Hamel (*Nea*); Bonnie Marie (*Cupid*); Percy Standing (*Vulcan*); John Fedris (*Jove*); Carl Dane (*Mars*); Beatrice Armstrong (*Juno*); A. Freeland (*Mercury*); Don McDonald (*Apollo*); Ruth Bradley (*Hebe*); M. Paul Roche (*The Oracle*)

CREDITS: *Director/Scenarist* Edwin Bower Hesser; *Cinematographer* Otto Brautigam; *Editor* Juliet Bradley

Mythology is among the strangest of ducks found in that great pond that we call life. The great mythic systems (including, but not limited to, Roman, Greek and Norse) may have lost their religious import ages ago, but they have nonetheless maintained to this day a hold on the hearts and minds of men. If never as sophisticated or as sober an academic discipline as theology, mythology was always more readily understandable (for its relative simplicity), more popular (no risk of being burned as a heretic or slain as an infidel), and more romantic (emphasizing man's corporeality over his spirituality). Way back when, any Viking not liking exposure to the elements (especially during dark and stormy nights) might find comfort — and no more scientific explanation than he could handle — in the saga of Thor, short-tempered son of Odin. Stories of Thor and his hammer wended their way down through the centuries and across the oceans and, if anything, enjoyed greater popularity with the passage of time and the traversal of space. Nowadays, the Thunder God has his own comic book, has appeared in cartoons and movies, and is as familiar a topic of conversation for young boys as dinosaurs, robots and Play Station.

Still, Ares and Bellona apart, for us Americans Greek and Roman mythologies somehow seem more genteel and less threatening than their Nordic counterpart, and they play a larger part in our everyday lives. Our planetary system owes its nomenclature to the Roman deities (with a nod to Uranus, as the sole Greek god who made it in under the wire; Earth came from an Old English/Germanic meld), rather than the Norse. And when 1990s' literature and pop psychology hypothesized that their bedroom behavior proved that men and women shared an ontological bond with Mars and Venus — and not with Tyr and Freya — we don't recall this causing anyone grief or consternation. It just seems that, over the years, the U.S. educational system has made its students more cognizant of Rome's fabled deities than with any other (albeit Greece's run a respectable second), and we can probably chalk that up to the fact that English owes a greater linguistic debt to Latin than to any other language.

Thus, it's supposed that few moviegoers back in 1918 would have had to consult their encyclopedia for the low-down on the title character of *The Triumph of Venus.*

This Victory Film Manufacturing Company's production was a costume epic, entirely set in whatever past represented the Olympians' collective salad days, and resplendent with the sort of magical goings-on that one has come to expect from tales of gods and goddesses.

The following two précis — taken, respectively, from the copy-right registration information provided the Library of Congress by the production company and from *The New York Times*' online archives — illustrate an amusing disparity in tone.

Angry with Venus for having rejected his love, Jove gives the beautiful goddess of love to the ugly blacksmith, Vulcan. Venus escapes, and Vulcan, seeing her with Mars, entangles them in his magic net, much to the delight of the jeering gods. Apollo releases them, and Venus takes refuge on the island of Milo, where she falls in love with a young sculptor. Venus bears the sculptor a daughter named Nea, but soon afterward, when she sees him watching Diana bathing in a stream, she kills him. Nea grows into a lovely young woman and falls in love with Pannas, a fisherman. Diana, who also loves Pannas, imprisons the girl in a rock. Cupid releases her, but the two are forced to undergo several more ordeals before Venus intercedes with Jove on their behalf. His anger now turned toward Diana, Jove forces her to hand the lovers the cup of immortality while the radiant Venus looks on [copyright registration, Library of Congress].

Venus, goddess of love, falls for a "mortal" sculptor, who pays for his blasphemy when he is shot full of arrows by Venus' rival, Diana. Flash-forward about seventeen years: Nea, the half-human daughter of Venus, falls in love with another mortal, a fisherman named Pannas. Once again, Diana tries to sabotage the romance, but this time Venus manages to get the OK from Jove to bestow immortality on her future son-in-law [movies2.nytimes.com/gst/movies/movie.html?v_id=114501].

Regardless of whether the first account paid the film's mythological elements the respect the producer felt was due them, or whether the second did likewise (although the *Times*' reviewer had adjusted for inflation), it's plain that *The Triumph of Venus* served to remind its audiences that a wandering eye, the fruits of lust, and major-league hissy-fits were by no means ever restricted to the terrestrial plane. That's the story, amigos.

Savvy American audiences might have quibbled with regard to the name of the king of the gods, for they knew him as Jupiter, rather than Jove, which was the name favored by the British. (Supplemental, boring pedagogical point: In Latin, the deity's name is declined Iuppiter, Iovis…, so both are technically correct.) A major adjustment that *should* have been made was the reconciliation of the locale — much of the picture is set in ancient Greece — and the ethnos: the gods all sport Roman names. The faux Grecian exteriors were photographed (per *The AFI Catalog*) in and around "the White Mountains of New Hampshire, as well as at locations in Maine and Florida." The interiors were most likely shot — this being the *only* film listed as a Victory Film Manufacturing Company production — in rented facilities either in Hollywood or New York.

Director/screenwriter Edwin Bower Hesser's industry experience was only slightly more extensive than was Victory's, for — including *Venus* — he was involved in exactly two (2) motion pictures. (For the record, the other Hesser effort was 1917's *For the Freedom of the World*, a drama of the American Legion of the Canadian Army during the Great War.) The "veteran" technician on the credits list (with a *pair* of films under his belt before *Venus*) was Otto (aka George) Brautigam (aka Brautigan). The earlier of Otto/George's two titles was the 1915 *Vanity Fair*, which starred the 50-year-old Mrs. Fiske as Becky Sharpe, a role suited more to actresses of Reese Witherspoon's vintage. Most of his post–*Venus* work (and we could find none after

1922) saw him monopolized by Eileen Percy for lightweight woman's pictures over at Fox. As for *Venus* itself, the 1 March 1918 number of *Variety* had some nice words for Mr. Brautigam's efforts: "It is only fair to note that the production has scenes of frequent photographic beauty. It is this photographic beauty rather than the development of the fanciful theme or the work of any player which is the saving grace of *The Triumph of Venus*."

Cast-wise, none of the female principals (and that included "Bonnie Marie," who bore Cupid's wings) was in anything else that left a vapor trail, although the IMDb asserts that "Betty Lee" graced a sound feature (1934's *Pecos Dandy*) that is curiously absent from the AFI listings. (Both women seem to have jettisoned their family names in an effort to appear more marquee-friendly.) A contemporary review reports that "Betty Lee is starred as Venus, but her work does not stand out. She photographs indifferently and no special dramatic ability is apparent." With no mention made at all of Bonnie Marie, apparently that lady's work stood out even less.

A few of the men's names were spotted (more) frequently on title cards, even if most of their faces remain blank nowadays and most of their credentials, like those of the ladies, consist solely in the picture under discussion. The biggest name (saith we) was that of Percy Darrell Standing (Vulcan), the British thespian who ascended to the genre pantheon via his portrayal of the "Creation" in *Life without Soul* (1915; more on Mr. Standing there). Next up (in the race for genre recognition) would be Karl Dane, a (Yup) Dane whose career enacting guys listed as Swenson or Swanson or Swede in the titles would end in suicide with the coming of sound and his inability to play down his thick accent. Dane (Mars) — billed here as Carl — was probably best regarded for his low comedy roles, but he is forever a part of Bela Lugosi–world for his turning out to be the surprise villain in *The Whispering Shadow* (1933), the worst serial Lugosi (or nearly anyone else) ever made. It must be noted that Karl Dane played Von Hellweg in 1918's *To Hell with the Kaiser* (see appendix) and was reputed to have been involved in 1929's *The Mysterious Island*, although we have been unable to corroborate this.

Of the lesser lights among the male cast members, William Sherwood (the nameless, mortal sculptor) may have shared some screen time with the Great Profile, for Sherwood appeared somewhere in *The Lost Bridegroom* (1916) when Barrymore was on his way up. After a run of pictures in which his character was afforded a name, Sherwood made his last film, *The Triumph of Venus*. Sources indicate the young man (in his very early twenties when *Venus* was released), died as the result of a fall. Despite his possessing a handful of silent film credits, we could find nothing of note on the Pannas of the piece, one Hassan Mussalli.

The aforementioned *Variety* critique makes a salient observation that other available publicity pieces do not:

> The production, with its many glimpses of wood nymphs dancing in the abbreviated attire popularly attributed to dryads, and of their deporting, diving and swimming in pools and rivers minus even this scant attire, will probably give the production a certain box office pulling power. After observing some of the bathing scenes with nude girls swimming about and the various scenes of Grace Hamel in a veil and the character of Nea, it might be ob-

served that the National Board of Review has broadened its viewpoint in the last five years.... *The Triumph of Venus* is likely to stir the risibilities [*sic*] of a thinking audience, On the other hand it would crowd a theater with the kind of fan who goes to the Kellermann fantasies or such films as *Sirens of the Sea*.

It's a shame films like this end up lost.

— JTS

20,000 Leagues Under the Sea

20,000 Leagues Under the Sea. Universal Film Mfg Co. and Williamson Submarine Film Corp./Universal and States Rights, c. 9 October 1916, 8 reels [available]

CAST: Allan Holubar (*Captain Nemo, also known as prince Daaker*); Jane Gail (*A Child of Nature/Princess Daaker*); Dan Hanlon (*Professor Aronnax*); Edna Pendleton (*Aronnax's daughter*); Curtis Benton (*Ned Land*); Matt Moore (*Lieutenant Bond — referred to as Gideon Spillett on copyright records*); Howard Crampton (*Cyrus Harding*); Wallace Clark (*Pencroft*); Martin Murphy (*Herbert Brown*); Leviticus Jones (*Neb*); William Welch (*Charles Denver*); Lois Alexander (*Nemo's daughter, as a child*); Joseph W. Girard (*Major Cameron*); with Ole Jansen

CREDITS: *Director and Scenario* Stuart Paton; based on the novels *20,000 Leagues Under the Sea* (Paris, 1870) and *Mysterious Island* (Paris, 1874) by Jules Verne; *Art Director* Frank D. Ormston; *Cinematographer* Eugene Gaudio; *Assistant Cameramen* Friend Baker, Milton Loryea; *Underwater Cinematographer* "Brulatier"; *Assistant Director* Martin Murphy; *Orchestra arranged and conducted for Broadway Theater showing* James C. Bradford

Jules Verne, arguably the first man to make a living writing what came to be called "science fiction," was born on 8 February 1828. Son of a maritime lawyer, Verne spent his youth around the French port city of Nantes and his young adulthood in reluctant pursuit of his father's profession. In 1863, while at one of life's crossroads, Verne met established publisher, Pierre-Jules Hetzel, thus beginning both a lasting, personal relationship and a full-time writing career that gave Verne the outlet that his adventurous side had always demanded. Said outlet was launched with the novel *Five Weeks in a Balloon*.

Twenty Thousand Leagues Under the Sea was begun in 1865, but debates between Hetzel and Verne over the origin of Captain Nemo resulted in delays in publication. The author had originally conceived Nemo as a Polish aristocrat seeking vengeance for Russian brutality to his family. The publisher, objecting to anything offending Mother Russia (and her mother lode of avid readers), won the battle and Verne was forced to revise his prose in order to make Nemo a more enigmatic figure. The tale was introduced finally to the public as a magazine serial between March 1869 and June 1870. *Twenty Thousand Leagues Under the Sea* was not the first novel to deal with underwater travel, but — thanks in no small part to Hetzel — it became the most popular. Realizing the visual splendor and sheer wonder inherent in the tale, he commissioned well over a hundred illustrations to accompany the first text issued in book form in 1871. Quickly capturing the imagination of legions of fans in Europe and the United States, the story cried out for a sequel: Verne obliged in 1874 with *Mysterious Island*.

If Hetzel had felt that Verne's *voyages extraordinaires* called for interpretation that transcended the printed page, Jules felt likewise and began a second — and more lucrative — career as a playwright. Collaborating time and again with theatrical veteran, Adolphe d'Ennery, he watched merrily as such fare as *Around the World in 80 Days* (1874) and *Michael Strogoff* (1880) met with critical acclaim and box-office success. Among the partners' other notable productions was a fanciful, original work called *Voyage Through the Impossible* (1882), wherein Captain Nemo himself was reincarnated in the second act. Several of Verne's plays — as well as an unauthorized Jacques Offenbach adaptation of Verne's *From the Earth to the Moon* — even made it to America, where they were produced by the famed Kiralfy Brothers, Bolossy and Imre.

Early filmmakers were quick to use the Verne name as a selling point for their wares. Foremost was, of course, Georges Méliès, who, like Offenbach, adapted bits and pieces of *From the Earth to the Moon* into his tour de force, *A Trip to the Moon* (1902). Méliès' short pastiches also included *The Voyage through the Impossible* (1904) and *200,000 Leagues Under the Sea*

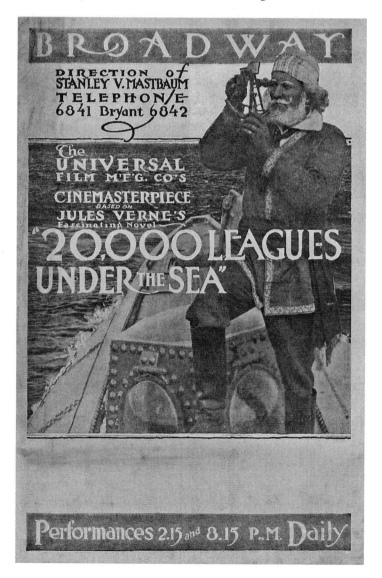

Original window card.

(1907) — that's right; *Two Hundred Thousand Leagues* — with neither film bearing much resemblance at all to its source, and Captain Nemo absent from both. *Voyage* was a rehashing of sorts of the formula used in *A Trip to the Moon*, while *200,000 Leagues Under the Sea* — long on title but short on characters — reduced down its narrative complexities into the dreams of one, lone fisherman. It's interesting to note that, while Méliès had only scratched Verne's storyline in *200,000 Leagues*, he succeeded in depicting his background sets — with their many sea creatures — almost exactly as they had been envisioned more than three decades earlier in the book's original illustrations.

One man who had every right to exploit Jules Verne's oeuvre was Michel Verne, the renowned author's son. In the 1910s, Verne the younger had helped bring to the screen a series of adaptations called "Les Films Jules-Verne," although apparently the only film in the series that was exported to America was made before Michel's involvement: a 1914 adaptation of *The Children of Captain Grant*, based on a novel from 1868. The film was renamed *In Search of the Castaways* for U.S. theaters.

Other than the above-mentioned French output, only a Biograph short from 1905 preceded the picture under discussion. The first cinematic rendition to be titled *20,000 Leagues Under the Sea*, the two-reeler was a surprisingly recognizable bowdlerization of the novel. Also known as *Amid the Wonders of the Deep*, it too opened with the search for a huge sea beast, which led to a strange submarine voyage by the captured expedition of one Captain Sam Whaler.

Intriguingly, the 1916 feature-length *20,000 Leagues Under the* Sea was less faithful to the book than had been the short, deriving two-thirds of its plot elements from *Mysterious Island* and the imagination of scenarist, Stuart Paton. The following synopsis (culled from the lengthy copyright summary and peppered with original wording from a theater program and the film's inter-titles) tells us more:

The time: 50 years ago. The civilized world is in a panic over the depredations of a mysterious "sea monster" that attacks vessels in mid-ocean, sometimes sinking them with all on board.

Because of the menace to navigation, Uncle Sam sends the frigate, *Abraham Lincoln*, to locate and destroy the terror. In America at this time is Prof. Aronnax, a distinguished French scientist, with his daughter. The Government of United States will with pleasure see France represented in the enterprise. Foremost among the members of the exposition is Ned Land, the "prince of harpooners." Searching the sea thru the green waters of the Atlantic a strange shape is seen. Within the bowels of the strange creature, men are to be found working in unison and harmony under the careful direction of a man, a veritable genius. This man is none other than Captain Nemo, and the Monster over which he holds dominion is naught else than a monster submarine — the "Nautilus."

Silently the monster rises from the deep. Immediate attack is in order. Capt. Nemo, "The Wizard of the Sea," curtly orders the *Abraham Lincoln* rammed and the frigate drifts away like a wounded animal. In the haste of the departure, it is not noticed that the professor, his daughter, and Ned Land have been thrown over the rail by the force of the collision. Captain Nemo orders his men to rescue the castaways.

Meanwhile, five daring men, prisoners of the Confederacy, make their escape from Richmond, Virginia, in a giant balloon which has been moored near the walls of their prison. They are carried out to sea. A mysterious island is sighted. Four men make for the island. The fifth is rescued without explanation and put ashore. The men make themselves comfortable in a cave and discover floating in the surf a large box of supplies which Captain Nemo has intended for them.

Meanwhile, in the submarine, Captain Nemo has extracted a promise from Professor Aronnax and his party that they will not try to escape. In the days that follow Captain Nemo regales his guests, perforce, with submarine gardens of indescribably beauty. From the heavy glass windows of the submarine, they are enabled to observe the various denizens of the deep and the coral caverns which they inhabit. Nemo takes the men on an odd hunting trip over the floor of the sea.

On the island, the castaways discover a woman … a child of the jungles. The "child of natur" meets a friend. She relates to Lieutenant Bond how, when a child, she was dragged from her dying mother's arms and taken to sea on a boat. Pencroft, a rough member of the group, conceives a passion for the little wild thing of the jungle. The jungle maiden is rescued from his unwelcome embrace by Bond.

Charles Denver, a wealthy English ocean trader, haunted by memories of a crime in far-off India, takes to the sea in his yacht to escape mental torture. Twelve years before this time he had forced his attentions on the wife of Prince Daaker, of India. Drawing a concealed dagger from her bosom, the wife quietly took her own life rather than suffer disgrace.

After days of sailing, Denver sights the same island upon which the former prisoners of war are living. Aboard Denver's yacht is a professional pearl diver, who decides to try his luck by diving for the valuable mollusks. A terrible scene is enacted when a gigantic octopus seizes him. Nemo, donning his diving suit, goes to the man's assistance with an axe and drives away the monster.

Denver goes ashore to explore. Wondering if the child of Princess Daaker still lives, he decides to search for her. Separated from the remainder of the party, he loses his way in the jungle and is finally on the verge of madness. Captain Nemo sends out two spies to the island with an order to obtain the identity of the owner of the yacht. Denver is finally located, half-demented, by members of his search party. Pencroft, the brute in him uppermost, determines to have the girl and, with the aid of the men from the yacht, carries her away by force.

Captain Nemo's spies have learned the yacht belongs to Charles Denver. At last Nemo sees his plans for revenge taking form. Bond has been a witness to the girl's abduction and impetuously swims out to the yacht. A struggle ensues between him and Pencroft in which he is victorious. He succeeds in leaving the yacht safely with the girl. Thus it is that he narrowly escapes the death that Nemo plans for his enemy. A marvelous torpedo blows the yacht sky high.

A wonderful scene follows in which the father recognizes his long lost daughter. Nemo, realizing his death is near, relates the tragic story of his life as the Indian Prince, tenderly entrusting his daughter's future to the man she has learned to love.

Despite the startled reaction of the mariners aboard the *Abraham Lincoln*, submarine technology was not unknown even in Verne's time; in fact, his wasn't even the first sub to be dubbed *Nautilus*: Robert Fulton had built two, primitive, underwater crafts by that name at the start of the 19th century. Thus, when *20,000 Leagues Under the Sea* was released, it wasn't the wonder of undersea navigation but, rather, the illusion of plumbing the ocean depths that drew huge crowds into the darkened theaters.

One family's pioneering efforts brought these groundbreaking effects to the screen, and Captain Charles Williamson had laid their foundation with his invention of a device to aid in inspection and retrieval in deep-sea salvaging. The forward to the photoplay novel issued in conjunction with the picture described Williamson's tube-like device as being "composed of a series of strong, interlocking iron plates or hinges joined together and covered with a watertight fabric." Still, it took the ingenuity of the captain's son, John Ernest, to realize the true potential of his father's discovery. It was "J.E." who enlarged the observation chamber and hung banks of powerful electrical lights from the vessel above; this enabled him in 1913 to make underwater photographs. The Williamson name might have remained a mere historical footnote had he stopped there, but J.E.'s goal wasn't mere photography: he wanted to shoot the world's first underwater film footage.

In 1914, J.E. and his brother, George Maurice Williamson, founded the Submarine Film Corporation. Their first film was a feature-length documentary (working title: *The Williamson Submarine Expedition*) that was released as both *Terrors of the Deep* and — in an obvious homage to Jules Verne — *Thirty Thousand Leagues Under the Sea*. Famed poet (and occasional movie critic) Carl Sandburg lauded the picture's hair-raising finale in a tribute entitled "In a Breath — *To the Williamson Brothers*":

> A naked swimmer dives. A knife in his right hand shoots a streak at the throat of a shark. The tail of the shark lashes. One swing would kill the swimmer…. Soon the knife goes into the soft under-neck of the veering fish…. Its mouthful of teeth, each tooth a dagger itself, set row on row, glistens when the shuddering, yawning cadaver is hauled up by the brother of the swimmer.

It should come as no surprise that the swimmer was J.E. Williamson.

Williamson's next project was *20,000 Leagues Under the Sea*, the picture that would become his most ambitious, most challenging and most famous. For the joint production with Universal Film Manufacturing Company, J.E. was charged not only with filming an underwater spectacle, but also with shooting it on location in the Bahamas; he encountered obstacles to almost every facet of the assignment.

For the undersea scenes, for example, Williamson enlisted the services of George D. Stillson, who for years had been tapped by the U.S. government for important diving work. With Stillson's help, diving suits were procured from an English factory just before the facility was commandeered for the war effort, but plans to have the veteran diver and his crew do the requisite underwater work went awry when a Hawaiian salvage operation drew them to the Pacific. Fortunately, Stillson and his men returned from their expedition just after an accident had scared off a group of locals from being trained as substitute divers.

To duplicate the *Nautilus*, J.E. constructed his own sheet-metal submarine, well over 100 feet in length. Capable of being controlled by one man, it could submerge just below the water's surface by filling a series of tanks. J.E. saved his sub unwanted damage by simulating the ramming of the *Abraham Lincoln*— an actual frigate, brought down from New York — and having barrels rolled within the hold of the "wounded ship" in order to make it list heavily. Another scene, calling for the Nautilus to torpedo Denver's yacht, was postponed when an already-damaged vessel, also being brought down from New York, sank while in transit. After J.E. had revamped a second boat (to the tune of some $25,000), a premature signal caused it to be detonated too soon, and the shot was almost ruined. What's more, curious passers-by — including the Governor of the Bahamas — had been sailing in the vicinity and quite possibly had been in camera range. It was not until the footage was developed in the States that J.E. found that a costly retake would not be required.

The celebrated octopus battle was originally conceived with an actual giant cephalopod in mind. When none was found, J.E. constructed his own, using a model from the Brooklyn Museum. With a child's toy as inspiration, springs were put inside hollow tentacles and compressed air was used to extend them. To complete the effect, rubber balls cut in two served as the "sucking-disks," sticky swamp marl was deemed a good substitute for ink, and a diver was placed inside the head to control the eight-legged monstrosity. Workable underwater firearms were then jury-rigged from Springfield army rifles, loaded with wax plugs instead of bullets.

Even some of the non-ocean footage was done under J.E.'s supervision. A Nassau public square was chosen as the launching point for the castaways' balloon, and J.E. was granted a permit to film there overnight. Required to vacate the square by sun-up, however, Williamson arranged for a huge fire pit — necessary to fill the bag with hot air — to be dug after dark … by gravediggers!

Of course, not everything was shot on location. Per H. H. Van Sloan in the 23 February 1917 *Moving Picture Stories*:

> After spending six months at Nassau the company returned to New York and worked at the studios at Leonia. From there they went to Universal City, where the remaining scenes were taken. Over 300,000 feet of film were taken in making this picture and its cost was nearly half a million dollars.

The premiere of *20,000 Leagues Under the Sea* was held at Chicago's Studebaker Theatre. Trade magazines such as *Motion Picture News* had announced the release of the movie as early as the 23 September, and short, illustrated, newspaper blurbs appeared thereafter (like the 2 October 1916 *The Fort Wayne*

[Indiana] *Daily News*), but these most likely publicized advance screenings that were not open to the general public. In his *Twenty Years Under the Sea* (1936), J.E. Williamson recalled that the picture premiered on the exact day that a German submarine "had torpedoed and sunk half a dozen British ships just outside New York," i.e., 9 October 1916. Although some of Williamson's facts are off (two of the vessels were not British, and the attack took place off of Nantucket), that date seems as probable as any.

The advance screenings continued virtually until the day before the film officially opened in New York on Christmas Eve. While the Chicago showing had served more or less as a trial balloon, Uncle Carl Laemmle was taking no chances in the Big Apple. He arranged to take over the Broadway Theatre on December 10th and personally oversaw the preview screenings for the local and tri-state press. For some days afterwards, anyone holding the proper press credentials (and the sort of positive attitude that lent itself to good publicity) was invited over to Universal's offices to preview the movie.

Primary sources printed conflicting information on the film's original length: it was either 10 or 11 reels when first released. Somewhere between the screening of the picture's preview print and its debut on Broadway, the footage was pared down to eight reels and there it remained. J.E. Williamson's autobiography again offers some clues:

> Captain Nemo's adventures began with the story of the Sepoy Rebellion, therefore, argued the potentates, there must be scenes of war. Accordingly, nearly $50,000 was added to the cost of the picture by staging a terrific battle. It was money thrown away. When shown on the screen, the fight between the soldiers on land seemed false and commonplace beside the undersea battles between men and monsters of the deep. Most of it was scrapped after the opinion of a famous newspaper critic was read: "If the rest of the picture were discarded, the undersea scenes alone would be worth three times the price of admission."

As it was, it appears that many exhibitors had second thoughts about charging the price of admission once. The 23 June 1917 *Trenton* [New Jersey] *Evening Times* reported, "This picture is always shown to high admission prices, and when the agent insisted on getting the usual admission at the State Street Theatre, Manager Wahn declared that he would not ask his patrons to pay 50 cents." Other newspapers had a higher opinion of the picture's worth. The 23 June 1917 *Fort Wayne Daily News* crowed, "This is an entertainment of the most extraordinary kind, which will prove distinctive among all motion pictures of the present day," while an earlier (3 June) critique from *The Oakland* [California] *Tribune* had raved, "Battles in the air and battles under the water are common every-day occurrences nowadays, and this eight act submarine picture is chuck a block with thrills that surpass the

The game of "chicken," Jules Verne-style in *20,000 Leagues Under the Sea*: last one down the hatch before this thing sinks is *un oeuf pourri* (*Motion Picture Stories*, February 23, 1917).

wildest dreams of those who would peer into the mysteries of the deep."

Some reviewers praised the film while lamenting the similarity between the battle footage at sea and the real-life warfare then underway in the Atlantic. The 5 June 1917 number of *The Newark* [Ohio] *Advocate* grimly related that "the whole appalling truth of the submarine and its white-headed torpedo are pictured to the very minute in this seemingly impossible screen production," but concluded, on a more upbeat note, that "no man, woman or child can afford to miss this spectacle."

The trades held off until the film's N.Y.C. debut had come and gone. *Variety*'s "Jolo" opined on the 29 December 1916 that "it is at once educational, scenic and melodramatic, not to mention its value as a film spectacle, and heretofore untried novelty of showing innumerable scenes under water…. Suffice it to hazard the statement that Universal's *Twenty Thousand Leagues Under the Sea* photoplay will prove an unqualified artistic and financial success."

George N. Shorey of *The Motion Picture News* (6 January 1917) echoed Jolo's screed:

> Submarine gardens of indescribable beauty, "tigers of the sea," ravenous looking sharks, one of which actually attacks one of our adventurers, and other novelties, work into a credible plot, which includes a fight with a devilfish and the rescue, all on the ocean's bottom. Torpedoing a good sized yacht, and the destruction of an East Indian Walled City over which Captain Nemo formerly ruled, furnish excellent spectacular effects in addition to the undersea wonders, and it can be surely said no one will be disappointed who makes proper allowance for the fanciful material from which this film story is constructed.

Exhibitor's Trade Review checked in that same day with a difference of opinion:

> The story has ceased to be the striking imaginative creation it was at the time of its publication, for submarine travel has long since lost its novelty…. It is certain that picture patrons as a whole will find *Twenty Thousand Leagues Under the Sea* satisfactory, and in spots thrilling entertainment, but it cannot be said that Captain Nemo, nor any of the story's other characters or incidents contribute to this condition.

Edward Weitzel (*The Moving Picture World*; 13 January 1917) also found the adaptation somewhat lacking:

> The remarkable story written over fifty years ago which, in view of present day knowledge, seems nothing short of prophetic, contains no female characters and supplies but a third of the material used in the photoplay. To piece out this shortage of plot the make of the scenario has gone to another tale by Verne, *The Mysterious Island*, and taken freely of its characters and incidents. To this blend of the two Verne stories has been added considerable original matter whose mission is to furnish the love motive necessary to all properly constructed screen romance. The result of this amalgamation of material is not a perfect product.

Weitzel found the picture's lead lacking, as well:

> Allan Holubar is the Captain Nemo. He works faithfully at his task, but does not measure up to

the imposing figure of the East Indian Prince drawn by the French novelist. Jane Gail as the heroine of the story … is graceful, makes a fascinating appearance in her garment of skins, and leads the entire cast in excellence of acting. Dan Hanlon, Edna Pendleton, Curtis Penton and William Welch are the other members of the cast who materially assist in gaining the picture's good repute.

Allan (aka Allen, Allen J. and Alan) Holubar had a relatively brief career as an actor, and while Captain Nemo in *20,000 Leagues Under the Sea* remains his best-known role, Holubar's place in cinema history is inexorably linked to that of his actress wife, Dorothy Phillips. The two met during a theatrical production of *Every Woman* wherein she played the role of "Modesty" and he, appropriately enough, that of "King Love." In 1913, the pair joined the fledgling movie industry for a brief period with Essanay, but Carl Laemmle, acquainted with the duo's stage abilities, quickly spirited them away for his Independent Motion Picture (IMP) Company. Holubar took on a few acting assignments while at IMP, but quickly turned to directing — often with his spouse appearing in his films. In 1920, the couple struck out on their own to form Allen Holubar Pictures. The First National Company released the Holubar features, all of which were produced and directed by him and enacted by her. Allan Holubar's career as artisan lasted not much longer than his career as actor; sadly, he passed away at 33 years of age on the 20 November 1923.

Donning not only a "garment of skins" opposite Holubar as Nemo's stranded daughter, Jane Gail also took on the chore of doubling in the role of his wife, the Princess Daaker. Born Ethel Magee on the 16 August 1880, in Salem, New York, Gail had taken an early interest in the performing arts. Study at the

Captain Nemo in *20,000 Leagues Under the Sea* decided to build the *Nautilus* only after his plans for the world's first underwater railroad hit a snag (*Motion Picture Stories*, February 23, 1917).

Frohman Dramatic School was followed by various stage and then film roles—the first of which were under Sigmund "Pop" Lubin of The Lubin Film Company. Moving on to Carl Laemmle's IMP, Gail appeared alongside King Baggott in *Dr. Jekyll and Mr. Hyde*. After a brief stint with the London Film Company, she returned to Laemmle, now Rex/Imperator of Universal, for the making of *20,000 Leagues*. As happened with many a film career, Gail's fortunes took a downward turn soon after this point; by 1920, when said turn finally skidded to a halt, she was being billed in poverty-row productions. The final curtain fell on Ms. Gail on the 30 January 1963.

Being billed seventh in the cast did not stop Matt Moore, brother of silent film actors Joe, Owen, and Tom, from once reportedly declaring to an interviewer that he had been the "lead" in *20,000 Leagues*. While, as Lieutenant Bond, Matt was the romantic interest for Gail (in her role as Nemo's child), perhaps he had confused his participation in *20,000 Leagues* with any number of films in which the two appeared together—including a highlight of both careers: *Traffic in Souls* (1913), an exposé of white slavery. With one of the lengthier careers of the four Moores, Matt's credits include 1919's *The Dark Star* (see essay) and the 1933 adaptation of S. Fowler Wright's *Deluge*.

Rounding out the cast was Edna Pendleton (also in *The Curious Conduct of Judge Legarde*, see entry), Curtis Benton (writer for J.E. Williamson's 1924 color motion picture *The Uninvited Guest*), Howard Crampton (see 1917's *Black Orchids*), and Wallace Clark (1916's *Elusive Isabel*).

Writer-director Stuart Paton was born in Glasgow in 1885. Following stints as chemist and painter, the multi-talented Scot turned to acting on the English stage. His film career began in 1912, and he would eventually direct about 50 films and write for a half-dozen more. Among his directing achievements were the above-mentioned *Elusive Isabel* and Lon Chaney's *The Scarlet Car*. Yet another victim of what we might be tempted to term "The *20,000 Leagues* Curse," Stuart Paton was subject to a freak accident in 1930, when someone in a crowd hurled a silver dollar his way, shattering his glasses and leaving him blind for months. While Paton did subsequently recover his sight well enough to paint landscapes, he never rejoined the movie industry, although he passed away at the Motion Picture Country Club in Woodland Hills, California, on the 16 December 1944.

When it comes to U.S. science fiction films of the 1910s, *20,000 Leagues Under the Sea* ranks right up there as one of the best received. One measure of the picture's popularity was the spate of parodies generated in 1917. Details on these farces are as scarce as hen's teeth, but we have verified—through brief newspaper blurbs—the existence of *Twenty Thousand Legs Under the Sea*, *Twenty Thousand Feats Under the Sea* and *Twenty Thousand Laughs Under the Sea*. All three, hereafter referred to as "*Legs*," "*Feats*" and "*Laughs*" to save us some ink, were animated shorts. *Legs* featured "The Katzenjammer Kids," characters that originated in a turn-of-the-century newspaper strip and were subject of more than a couple of silent cartoons. Described only as "1,000 feet of special cartoon comedy" by *The Fort Wayne* [Indiana] *Journal-Gazette* (17 June 1917), *Feats* likely had limited distribution; in fact, the only other reference we can locate is in *The Daily News*, another paper from the same burg. Last but

not least, Universal decided to cash in themselves with *Laughs* and hired Pat Sullivan—sometimes credited as the creator of Felix the Cat—to provide the animation.

Like 1925's *The Lost World*—perhaps the definitive 1920s American sci-fi movie—the fascination with *20,000 Leagues* lay chiefly in the special effects. Willis O'Brien's stop-motion dinosaurs still hold up reasonably well today, though, and help move along the action in what is still a thrilling film. In contrast, when viewed from Millennium perspectives, J.E. Williamson's painstaking underwater photography in *20,000 Leagues* seems passé and occasionally grinds the narrative to a halt.

Twenty Thousand Leagues Under the Sea may not be the perfect choice with which to introduce the silent film to the CGI fanatic, but its wonders are still to be had for those with active imaginations and an appreciation for history.

— *SJ*

Twisted Souls

Twisted Souls. ?/?, 1 September 1920 (?), 6 reels (?), fragment survives
CAST: Howard Thurston (*The Spiritualist*); Tarah Ben Mahamet (*The Hindu Philosopher*); Eric Mayne; Horace Braham; Agnes Scott; Evelyn Sherman; Miriam Nesmith
CREDITS: *Director* George Kelson (?)

Like *The Call of the Soul* (1916), *Twisted Souls* may or may not have made it into release. A fragment of footage (under 3 minutes; summarized below) is available commercially, but this—like the sheaf of stills that supposedly survived the 1916 mystical film—is no proof that the production ever started in earnest or that there ever was a finished product that subsequently vanished like one of Howard Thurston's levitated lovelies.

For those of us who are not cognoscenti of the magical fraternity, Mr. Thurston (1869–1936), illusionist and magician extraordinaire, was one of a plethora of conjurors who greeted the dawning of the 20th century with the hopes of continuing the grand traditions of their magical predecessors and of raising the art of legerdemain to ever higher planes. These hopes were realized during Mr. Thurston's lifetime, but, as seems to happen sooner or later with all entertainment trends, the medium (here, large stage shows) gradually lost favor. *Very* few touring spectaculars (especially those booked in major venues, like Doug Henning's 1974 Broadway hit, *The Magic Show*) survived the dawn of the Television Era, as the small screen shrank prestidigitators to fit into a corner of one's living room. Magic remained a popular hobby, but the opportunities to make one's living from it dwindled, as did the popular appreciation for the Past Masters of the Art. A unique exception—Harry Houdini—is *still* a household name for readers of this book, while Jean-Eugène Robert-Houdin (the renowned escape artist's inspiration) has faded into the shadows of cultural history, as have (to a greater or lesser extent) names like Blackstone, Chung-Ling-Soo, Okito, Alexander, Herrmann the Great, and Harry Kellar.

Kellar toured the world in the late 1800s/early 1900s with (arguably) the largest stage-illusion show in existence. His signature effect was his "Levitation of the Princess of Karnak," a reputation-building illusion which (say some) Kellar purloined from British magus, John Neville Maskelyne. Regarded as the first Dean of American Magicians, Kellar capped his extraordinary career by the ritual passing on of his magic wand (and the private sale of just about everything else he owned, including the Karnak Levitation) to Thurston on the 16 May 1908, whence Thurston took over as the touring-est magician to ever hit the U.S. skids. Unfortunately, none of this did anything to displace Houdini — the aforementioned household word, yesterday AND today — in the hearts, minds and Q-factors of the masses, and Howard Thurston was thus up against it.

Houdini was seemingly forever in the public eye, escaping from strait-jackets, caskets, miles of rope and/or eye-popping lengths of chain after first being hoisted into the sky, dangled from a precipice, or dropped into the frigid waters of the East River. These widely-seen displays of his prowess kept his name on the lips of those who could never have afforded tickets to his vaudeville magic shows, which were running parallel to the muscular marketing efforts of Mr. Thurston. The two men also found themselves on opposite sides of the great Spiritualism "debate": Howard was a believer, while Harry — albeit desperate to cling to any indication of his mother's having survived her death — was compelled finally to debunk it. It has been reported that Houdini, Thurston, and Arthur Conan Doyle made a pact in which the first of the triumvirate to pass beyond the Veil would seek to get a message across to the survivors, and — between themselves — Mrs. Houdini and her husband arranged a code in order to guarantee the authenticity of any such message. Houdini was the first of the three men to die; Bess Houdini never acknowledged any communication from beyond the grave.

Both Houdini and Thurston were products of their times, and the art of magic has evolved and adapted since. The message has metamorphosed to fit the medium. As this book is being written, the two most popular stage magicians of recent years — Doug Henning and Harry Blackstone, Jr., both of whom had full-length stage shows on Broadway — are deceased. Still, Penn and Teller — a madcap duo given as much to political commentary as to illusion — enjoy a hip (if limited) following. Siegfried and Roy — the wildly successful and flamboyantly gay illusion-team from Las Vegas — are just back from the road to professional recovery, following an appalling attack on Roy Horn by one of the company's Siberian tigers. And Criss Angel — the "Mind Freak" of cable television — has reduced down the illusory wonder of stage magic to the intimacy of the all-seeing lens. What's more, among the most successful, recent motion pictures has been a brace of magic-themed features, set in the Victorian Era: *The Prestige* and *The Illusionist* (both 2006). If we add in the Harry Potter novels and films — easily the most popular works of fiction to hit the streets since God-knows-when — we may readily maintain that we are still living in a "magical age." And, for all that, Houdini remains a timeless icon in post–Millennium America, and Howard Thurston does not.

It's impossible to determine whether the idea for *Twisted Souls* originated with Howard Thurston, or was dreamed up by his handlers following the release and success of 1919's *The Grim Game*. *Game* was the first of the Houdini film canon, and was, essentially, a series of death-defying stunts wrapped around an

unremarkable plot saddled (even then) with an all-too-predictable outcome. The picture concentrated on Houdini's reputation as a physical marvel in an otherwise ordinary world, while completely ignoring other areas of his professional resume, like vanishing elephants or investigating higher planes of existence. (Ergo, *Game* is not included herein, whereas Harry's *Terror Island* [1920], *The Soul of Bronze* [1921], and *The Man from Beyond* [1922] all grace these pages.) Thurston's career was less segmented than Houdini's, an attribute that was at once an advantage and a liability. Whether viewed as an astounding illusionist or a masterful practitioner of sleight of hand, Howard was first and foremost a conjurer; his talents — albeit profound and undeniable — were thus not as diverse as his rival's. Posters depicting Houdini, billed as the "King of Handcuffs," emphasized the man's physicality and the testosterone-laden overtones of the situation. Artwork of Thurston that illustrated his frequently used title, "King of Cards," may have captured Howard doing impossible things with pasteboards, but neither that action nor the soubriquet itself offered much promise in the way of thrilling motion pictures.

Thurston's interest in Spiritualism was as well-known as Houdini's, though, and it might have been argued that money could be made (and publicity had) from a film that revolved around the role of mysticism in what was otherwise everyday life. Whatever the rationale, the film fragment that exists — whether comprised of outtakes, floor-sweepings from some long-forgotten projection booth, or sample segments shot to entice backers — doesn't give us much room in which to maneuver.

The fragment has been conserved by William McIlhany, a much-appreciated, magic-oriented film historian who, some years back, provided us with help with minutiae for several chapters in *Of Gods and Monsters*. Mr. McIlhany opines that the story of *Twisted Souls* "may have been based on a treatment co-authored by Charles Fulton Oursler." Oursler, aka Anthony Abbot, was a playwright (*All the King's Men*, *The Walking Gentleman*) and novelist (*The Circus Queen Murders*, *The Greatest Story Ever Told*) with an affinity for magical-themed theatrics. A contributor to the screenplay of Fox's *Trick for Trick* (1933), he had seen his drama, *The Spider*, open on Broadway in 1927 before helping reshape it for the screen (in 1931). Born in 1893, Oursler was himself a professional magus (performing as "Sandalwood, the Magician" — named for his home in West Falmouth, Massachusetts — and as "Samri Frickell"), but his participation in helping shape Thurston's movie would have pre-dated all of the above.

Just about everything known about *Twisted Souls* that does not stem from the surviving film clips may be traced to the briefest of mentions in the 28 August 1920 *Motion Picture News*: "*Twisted Souls* is a six-reel picture just completed by Howard Thurston, the magician. It will be released on September 1. The scene [sic] shows where Thurston, who plays the part of a spiritualist, murders his best friend, a Hindu philosopher who tries to keep him in [sic] the straight and narrow path."

Following this plot revelation, Howard Thurston was to have been the villain in his own movie. Talk about a contrast to/departure from Houdini's portrayal in *The Grim Game*!

Herewith is the sequence of segments as they exist in the *Twisted Souls* fragment:

Shot A (approx 30 seconds): Thurston gesturing to 1 woman and 2 men sitting and one woman standing in a parlor or dining room. Thurston points at man.

Shot B (approx 5 secs.): 3 women standing and 2 men standing. Man in mustache holds hand of 4th woman sitting. It appears that she just saw something odd. All are dressed in nightgowns, robes and such.

Shot C (approx 5 secs.): 3 men and 4 women sitting on chairs and sofa. Thurston puts hands on knees and gestures.

Shot D (approx 2 secs.): Thurston standing, woman sitting.

Shot E (approx 2 secs.): Same scene as above. Thurston sees something by fireplace.

Shot F (approx 10 secs.): Man and woman sitting on separate chairs in front of table. He's slouching and looks distraught. She holds his hand, apparently trying to comfort him.

Shot G (approx 5 secs.): Close-up of brown-haired woman, looking earnest.

Shot H (approx 10 secs.): Close-up of Thurston talking and looking more and more distressed.

Shot I (approx 10 secs.): Continuation of Shot C (?). Woman in center rises; then other 2 woman rise. They see something (probably are also looking at fireplace).

Shot J (approx 20 secs.): Thurston sees Ghost (undoubtedly Tarah Ben Mahamet) by fireplace. Ghost fades out.

Shot K (approx 2 secs.): Different angle of Ghost and Thurston.

Shot L (approx 2 secs.): Quick close-up of Thurston.

Shot M (total approx 20–30 secs.): Takes of group in front of large (perhaps 10 feet in height), obviously fake skull. The eyes are window-like and in the nose sits a Swami-ish figure.

Shot N (approx 5 secs.): Woman looking over dead body (perhaps by fireplace).

Shot O: (approx 20–30 secs.): Closer shot of group in front of skull.

Some of the shots are preceded by a person (or a hand) holding a clapboard on which is written *Twisted Souls*/G. Kelson. If G. Kelson was George Kelson, we're looking at a man who directed several features (including *The Strong Way* [1917] and *Stolen Orders* [1918]), helped direct another (1919's *Bolshevism on Trial*), while doing tech work and acting in yet another (1918's *Little Women*). We've been unable to find biographical data on Mr. Kelson, and any credits beyond these and *Twisted Souls* are likewise beyond us.

Nothing else is known of the technical crew. As for the cast, Evelyn Sherman appears to have had a brief film career, with a couple of dozen (more or less) pictures under her belt. While *Twisted Souls* was her first film credit (such as it is), she can be seen in the 1923 *Trilby* (see entry). Dublin-born Eric Mayne had Sherman beat by some ten dozen pictures, and his genre titles include *The Conquering Power* (1921), *Black Oxen* (1923), and *Behind the Curtain* (1924; the latter two are discussed at length herein). Mayne's onscreen importance waned with the coming of sound and virtually all of his post-silent performances were in uncredited bits. Londoner Horace Braham barely put his toe into silent-cinematic waters before withdrawing same and heading to the stage; he resurfaced for a few television appearances in the early 1950s. *Twisted Souls* is his only genre "feature," as well as being the *only* film credit we could locate for his cast-mates, Tarah Ben Mahamet, Agnes Scott, and Miriam Nesmith.

And for Howard Thurston.   — JTS/SJ

The Two Natures Within Him

The Two Natures Within Him. Selig Polyscope Co./Selig, 1915, three reels [LOST]
  CAST: Tom Santschi, Bessie Eyton, Franklin Hall, Lafe McKee
  CREDITS: *Director* Tom Santschi; based on a story by Jules E. Goodman.

Too much of a good thing department: Our collective obsessive-compulsive nature requires that we point to yet *another* Jekyll-Hyde, dual-personality, blow-to-the-head, cure-via-neurological-operation film: *The Two Natures Within Him*. In this lost three-reeler, it is a *clergyman* who's knocked silly, only to assume a criminal mien; he goes so far as to attempt to rob his own house and to strangle a former girlfriend before undergoing one of those restorative surgical sessions that apparently are available down the block and around the corner, no matter where you live. Apparently, cinematic surgeons back then were eons ahead of their real-life counterparts (*Variety* [28 May 1915]: "The usual operation by the doctor brings the minister-crook back"). For the credits mavens among our readership, Ecce!

The Two-Soul Woman

The Two-Soul Woman. Bluebird Photoplays, Inc./Bluebird, 6 May 1918, 5 reels [LOST]
  CAST: Priscilla Dean (*Joy Fielding/Edna*); Ashton Dearholt (*Chester Castle*); Joseph Girard (*Dr. Copin*); Evelyn Selbie (*Leah*)
  CREDITS: *Director* Elmer Clifton; *Scenario* Elmer Clifton; based on the novel *The White Cat* by Gelett Burgess (New York, 1907)

The 1950s had Eve with her three faces and—come the 1970s—Sybil had upped the ante by ten. In the early 1900s, though, the most famous case of multiple personality was that of Miss Christine Beauchamp. Miss Beauchamp's therapist, Dr. Morton Prince, told the story of her travails in his 1905 book *The Dissociation of a Personality*. Dr. Prince discovered that four separate personalities were at work in Miss Beauchamp, but only one of them — Sally — was fully aware of the others. Sally was a mischief maker and delighted in causing problems for Christine: running her into debt, sending nasty letters to her friends, and leaving boxes of spiders around for her arachnophobic alter-ego to discover. When she was "herself" once again, Miss Beauchamp would have no recollection of what Sally had done. Ultimately, Dr. Prince used a combination of therapy and hypnosis to get rid of Sally and integrate the other personalities into a viable whole.

Not everyone, however, was convinced that Miss Beauchamp's ills were the result of some psychological malady; believers in spiritualism, reincarnation and demon possession had their own explanations and were not shy about publicizing them. "The Case of Sally" became the inspiration for books, plays and films, and even though hypnotism played a benign role in Miss Beauchamp's recovery (at least according to Dr. Prince), the evil eye à la Svengali invariably was worked into the fictional mixes. The film under consideration here, *The Two-Soul Woman*, was based on the 1907 Gelett Burgess novel *The White Cat*, and was made by Universal/Bluebird as a vehicle for its upcoming star, Priscilla Dean.

Synopsis of the film courtesy of the 11 May 1918 *Motion Picture News*:

> Chester Castle (Ashton Dearholt) sustains injuries when his automobile overturns which render him unconscious. When he comes to, he finds himself in a strange house tended by the sympathetic Joy Fielding (Priscilla Dean). Before he fully regains his health, he witnesses a great change come over her. All her good characteristics drop from her and she becomes a cruel, fierce, shameless girl, calling herself Edna. It does not take Chester long to discover that she is in the power of a crooked doctor, Dr. Copin, (Joseph Girard) possessed of hypnotic power. When Joy assumes her bad character, she gives him money and shows love for him. When her good self returns, Chester marries her. The doctor, furious, once again sets to work to bring about the changes and does so with success. Leah (Evelyn Selbie), Joy's servant, determining to end it, shoots the doctor at this point and, with his death, Joy regains her natural manner for all time.

The AFI account of the climax seems to suggest the villain's death was accidental: "When Dr. Copin enters, Chester struggles with him and, in the confusion, the doctor is shot with his own revolver."

In the Burgess's novel, Copin isn't harmed at all and withdraws from his failed attempt to assert control over his meal ticket with little more than a "Curses! Foiled again!" Chester saves Joy from Edna by taking a crash course in psychology and, after concluding that the split in Joy's psyche is the result of some terrible fright, attempts to reverse the process by terrifying Edna out of existence. He shoots at her (with blank cartridges), sics the household dogs on her, and enlists the crazy Chinese gardener to perform an impromptu exorcism. Even though Edna fires back with real bullets, Chester's strategy ultimately prevails and Edna retreats into oblivion. Universal might well be forgiven for thinking that, on film at least, such a finale would be more risible than dramatic. Nevertheless, it's a bit more imaginative than breaking the spell by simply killing off the villain.

Humorist, illustrator, author of children's books, and master of linguistic word-play and nonsense, author Gelett Burgess has claims to fame more lasting than *The White Cat*: he invented the word "blurb" and also wrote the following immortal verses:

> I never saw a Purple Cow,
> I never hope to see one,
> But I can tell you, anyhow,
> I'd rather see than be one.

There is decidedly little humor in *The White Cat* (the title refers to a fairy tale in which the enchanted cat tells the hero he may have to kill her to set her free), but it works as an entertaining melodrama. The characters are intelligent (the depiction of Leah, the black servant, is without condescension) and the differences between Joy (refined, poetic, musical) and Edna (flirtatious, volatile, mannish) are intriguing enough to see why Universal thought they would make good star material for Priscilla Dean.

According to publicity for the film (as related in the *Sheboygan* [Wisconsin] *Press* on 9 August 1918), Miss Dean threw herself into the role a bit too much and declared that she would never again consent to appear in a dual role in any picture. The article goes on to say that, in order to play Edna more convincingly, "Miss Dean sought out the detested and remained with them until her nerves were on edge and as she put it 'was as hateful as she appears' in the picture. During her lapses she insulted several of her friends without meaning to do so, and lost them." It's not clear from the article just who these detested folks were, but apparently Miss Dean was ultimately able to sever her identification with them without resort to Dr. Prince.

Such method acting, though, did not impress *The New York Times*' reviewer, who allowed only that "Miss Dean's acting in a few of the scenes is effective to a moderate degree" (29 March 1918). The anonymous reviewer panned the film, writing that "improbabilities and impossibilities are expected in melodrama but should one be asked to accept absurdities?" Then, apparently not being familiar with *The White Cat*, he went on to claim that the film was … "no doubt derived from *The Case of Becky* which David Belasco produced some seasons ago and which, in turn, was suggested by a scientifically reported case of dual personality. Mr. Belasco's play departed considerably from the scientific record in search of theatrical effect but its departure was only the slightest deviation compared to that of *The Two-Soul Woman*."

This did not prevent the Universal publicity department from proclaiming the film "a dramatic analysis of one of the most remarkable women who ever lived" (*Fort Wayne* [Indiana] *Journal Gazette*, 15 June 1918).

Other reviewers, however, were easier to please than *The Times'*. The 11 May 1918 *Moving Picture World* thought that Dean did "some remarkably interesting work in this weird double role." The review also noted that "but four characters appear in the story from first to last but there is no cessation of interest in the problems that confront the hero" and "the film rounds up with an exciting climax." *The Motion Picture News*, published that same date, likewise praised Dean and felt the film achieved "some fairly good suspense considering there is only one situation in the whole five reels." Frances Agnew (in the *New York Telegraph*) noted that the film traded on *Dr. Jekyll and Mr. Hyde*, *The Case of Becky*, and other, dual-personality stories, while opining that such stories "really offer but one satisfactory ending, the disposition of the evil influence and dominance of the more genuine and amiable self."

Once debate on the merits of the storyline was out of the way, the film's special effects won praise from virtually all the critics. *The New York Times* approved of "the photographic tricks used to represent the transition of the woman from one personality to the other," while *MPW* also took note of "the intelligently employed double-exposure photography." Presumably this was the same, rather simple effect Universal employed when they remade the film as *The Untameable* five years later: one sees the image of Edna entering Joy like a spirit and then Joy "becomes" Edna, a process arguably better conveyed by performance (like Sybille Schmitz' transformation in *Vampyr*) than by photography.

Marketing-wise, the 18 May 1918 *MPW* advised potential exhibitors to play up the mesmerism angle: "Newspaper controversies on the subject of hypnotism are recommended as a means to advance interest. Follow this up with advertising designed to capitalize on the discussion. If you desire to pull a "fake" hypnotic display in the lobby, a man dressed to resemble Svengali and a woman to duplicate Trilby would attract attention."

One would think from all this that Dr. Copin was *causing* Joy's dual personality rather than just taking advantage of it, but such oversimplification played to the public's lack of understanding and perhaps skepticism of the "split personality" phenomenon. And, of course, the fascination (and suspicion) of hypnotism could always be counted on to help sell a few tickets.

The Two-Soul Woman was a hit and added to the growing reputation of Priscilla Dean, who became Universal's major female star. The daughter of famous stage actress, Mae Preston Dean, Priscilla began treading the boards as a toddler and, by the age of ten, was sharing the stage with such notables as Joseph Jefferson and James A. Herne. As a teenager, she began playing at Les Folies Bergère in New York and, in 1912, she attracted the attention of D.W. Griffith, who invited her to try the movies at Biograph. After a short stay there, Dean freelanced at bit before ending up at Universal, where she played in a number of two-reel comedies. As was usually the case with the Universal ladies of the 1910s, it was a serial that brought Dean to serious public attention: 1917's *The Gray Ghost*.

Dean was no great beauty, but she was feisty, fun loving and independent. She was as game and agile as any stunt woman, and those qualities came across on the screen and endeared her to the public; (the tam she often wore in her films became a fashion rage). Director Tod Browning led Dean's mischievous persona into somewhat darker territory and she became the star of his "crook melodramas." But whether jewel thief, pickpocket or con artist, Priscilla's characters always reformed by the last reel. Wallace Beery and Lon Chaney (whom Dean much admired) alternated as her villains, and the somewhat tepid heroics were provided by Matt Moore, Wellington Playter or Wheeler Oakman (to whom Dean was briefly married). Typical publicity for a Dean film: "You'll know her instantly by her tricky eyes, dangerous smile, exquisite gown and nimble fingers." Occasionally, Dean stayed on the right side of the law, as when she scored one of her most memorable roles as Cigarette, the half–Arab camp-follower in the Foreign Legion romance, *Under Two Flags*. (*Flags* probably would have been a better picture if directed by someone other than Browning, who was obviously more at home in sleazy dives than he was among sand dunes.) Nevertheless, Dean was so successful as a "bad" girl that Gelett Burgess himself sent her the following ditty:

> There was a young star named Priscilla
> Who at home was as sweet as vanilla,

> But you never can tell,
> For she acted like hell
> When she played in a cinema thrilla.

In 1923, Dean temporarily walked off the set of Browning's *Drifting*, complaining that she was being forced to play an "immoral woman." The role — that of an opium dealer who falls in love with the agent sent to smash her business — doesn't seem any different than the parts she usually played, but her reaction indicated her growing dissatisfaction with the Big U.

Dean left Universal and tried to recapture the fiery persona of old that had somehow gotten lost while she was filching jewels and picking pockets. Unfortunately, films like *A Cafe in Cairo* and *The Siren of Seville* — exotic melodramas in which Dean dived into rivers and fought bulls to save the hero—failed to win public approval, perhaps because the films lacked the humor found in similarly-themed efforts, like Bebe Daniels' *Señorita*. When one of her biggest hits—*Outside the Law*— was reissued in 1926, the advertising had co-star Lon Chaney's name above the title, and not Priscilla Dean's. By the late 1920s, Dean's film career was back where it had begun: doing two-reel comedies.

Personal problems may also have played a part in her career decline. Dean became engaged to Lieut. Leslie Arnold, who, as one of a crew of aviators, had thrilled the nation by circumnavigating the globe in 1924. Not so thrilling was the revelation that the lieutenant, in spite of his many assurances to the contrary, had been married previously and never properly divorced. Mrs. Arnold surfaced and fiercely fought his subsequent efforts to make the divorce legal; Dean was even forced to request police protection from her. Ultimately, the actress got to marry her aviator, but only after a much-publicized court battle.

Dean made a few talkies and finished her career playing a reporter in the dismal Poverty Row melodrama, *Klondike*, which also featured Henry B. Walthall and Tully Marshall; they, like her, were on their way down. Moving east, she settled in Leonia, New Jersey, where whatever excitement she needed was provided via her volunteering in the ambulance corps. Though she occasionally answered inquiries about her career, Dean largely shunned publicity or declined any offer to participate in documentaries about the era in which she was famous. She died at 91 years of age in late 1987.

Leading man Ashton Dearholt injured his arm during the auto-crash sequence at the beginning of *The Two-Soul Woman*. As the picture was being shot under the title *The White Cat*, the actor purportedly quipped, "Even the white ones are unlucky." Dearholt later switched cars for horses and starred in a number of low-budget Westerns in the early 1920s, including a stint as the whip-cracking, masked hero, Pinto Pete. More than a few of those Westerns were made by Dearholt's own production company (incorporated in 1923) and co-starred his wife, Florence Gilbert.

In the latter part of the decade, he was introduced to Edgar Rice Burroughs; the two became friends and business partners. It devolved that Burroughs was not happy with the way his famed Tarzan character was portrayed on the screen and, in 1934, formed his own film company, with Dearholt as manager. Shortly before the new manager left for Guatemala to film *The New Adventures of Tarzan*, Florence Gilbert filed for divorce.

Some months later, Burroughs divorced his own wife (after 34 years together) and married Florence. Dearholt, in the meanwhile, had wed Ula Holt, the heroine of *The New Adventures of Tarzan*. Somehow, the Dearholt/Burroughs partnership survived this soap opera. Dearholt, who was also billed as Richard Holt (his birth name) and Don Castello late in his career, died in Los Angeles in April 1942.

It's not known from the synopses whether Leah (the devoted maid) was black, as she was in the book, but Evelyn Selbie often played non–Caucasians, notably in such films as *Without Benefit of Clergy*, *Omar, the Tent-Maker* (the latter two with Boris Karloff), *Lord Jim*, *Mysterious Dr. Fu Manchu* and *Return of Dr. Fu Manchu*. (In addition, the actress also received some very good reviews as the East Indian, Mammy Pleasant, in a roadshow version of *The Cat and the Canary*.) Selbie was very successful on the legitimate stage in the early 1900s before turning to film in the 1910s, where she often appeared as Bronco Billy Anderson's sweetheart. While never really achieving star status, she often got good and conspicuous supporting roles in the Silent Era. Selbie's career in the talkies, like that of so many of her contemporaries, consisted mostly of bit parts.

Director Elmer Clifton, a D.W. Griffith assistant who sometimes acted in the Master's films (*Birth of a Nation*, *Intolerance*), became a well-known director. He did a series of very successful comedies with Dorothy Gish that was profitable enough to help fund Griffith's weightier projects. Clifton's most famous film is probably *Down to the Sea in Ships* (1922), a good whaling melodrama that gave Clara Bow her first big break. Later Clifton went the way of another Griffith alumnus, Christy Cabanne, and spent his talkie career directing B-movies (*Captured in Chinatown*, 1935), exploitation films (*Assassin of Youth*, 1937), Westerns (*Deep in the Heart of Texas*, 1942), and serials (*Captain America*, 1944).   — HN

Unconquered

Unconquered. Jesse L. Lasky Feature Play Co./Paramount Pictures Corp., 31 May 1917, 5 reels [LOST]

CAST: Fannie Ward (*Mrs. Jackson*); Jack Dean (*Richard Darcier*); Hobart Bosworth (*Mr. Jackson*); Tully Marshall (*Jake*); Mabel van Buren (*Mrs. Lenning*); Jane Wolfe (*Voodoo Queen*); Billy Jacobs (*Little Billy*).

CREDITS: *Director* Frank Reicher; *Assistant Director* Charles Watt; *Scenario* Beatrice C. De Mille and Leighton Osmun; based on their original story, "The Conflict"; *Cinematographer* Dent Gilbert

It is a well known fact that voodooism still exists among the most ignorant Negroes in the south although the strange cult has been stamped out in most places. Tully Marshall gives a wonderful portrayal of the half-crazed Negro who is frightened into making a sacrifice to the voodoo in *Unconquered*.

The bit of PR quoted above pretty much sums up Hollywood's take on voodoo in the 1910s. When fans of classic horror think of voodoo, they naturally conjure up visions of zombies, dolls being used as pin-cushions, and the magic island of Haiti, but such elements are absent in these early films. Back then, strange rituals that would culminate in human sacrifice (if not — almost inevitably — stopped in the nick of time) were the norm for celluloid voodoo, and the stories were set in the American South or in Africa, but never in Haiti. The lack of interest in this latter locale seems particularly odd as the United States invaded Haiti in 1915 and occupied the country for another 17 years; however, it was the *politics* of those events that made the news and articles on voodoo in Haiti didn't begin appearing in the popular press until several years into the occupation.

Voodoo (or, more correctly, *vodou* or *vodun*) was a West African religion that was transported to Haiti, Cuba and North America along with the poor souls who fell victim to the slave trade. The religion — which involves spirit- and ancestor-worship — developed differently in each of these places (merging with traditional Catholic practices in Haiti) and, of course, was subject to violent suppression by slave owners who considered it not only a depraved superstition but subversive, as well.

While many a chicken or goat ended up on the sacrificial altar rather than the Sunday dinner table, voodoo rituals did not involve *human* sacrifice despite a few notorious cases wherein charismatic Haitian or Cuban fanatics exhorted their cult followers to slay "the goat without horns." To Hollywood, though, an orgiastic ceremony of chanting and dancing non–Caucasians had to culminate not in a hen getting its throat cut, but with a human being (a white one, invariably) facing death. 1916 proved to be a good year for such grisly enterprises: In the three-reeler, *The Lion's Ward*, Betty Schade is saved from being offered to the spirits by the intervention of her pet lions, while the title character of the serial *Miss Jackie of the Navy* rescues a young sailor from being sacrificed to a python by voodoo worshippers. In another serial, *The Secret Kingdom* (based on a story by Louis [*The Lone Wolf*] Vance), the main characters find themselves in the clutches of a powerful voodoo priestess. On the stage, Richard Walton Tully worked a Central American variation on voodoo into the melodramatic mix of *The Flame*.

Unconquered may be the only Hollywood silent *feature* that has voodoo as part of its plot. Still, its main concern is less with human sacrifice than self sacrifice, here represented by Silent Cinema's most enduring martyr, the loving mother.

Synopsis taken from the Library of Congress copyright entry and contemporary reviews:

Mrs. Jackson, wife of a millionaire, married this man when she was too young to know his cruel nature. Her whole thought and life are devoted to Billy, her little son.

Mrs. Lenning, a designing widow, gives Mr. Jackson the idea that his wife is weaning Billy's affection from him and he tries to buy the boy's love with toys and candy. Jackson commands his wife to call upon Mrs. Lenning and invite her to visit them at their Florida home, threatening to take Billy away with him if she refuses.

Richard Darcier, a writer, is ordered to Florida by his physicians, and he and Billy become firm friends. Darcier's caretaker, Jake, a half-crazed Negro, is a voodoo worshiper and has been warned by a voodoo queen that he must provide their group with a victim or he himself will die. Jake is about to kill Billy when Richard and Mrs. Jackson rescue him, but the Negro stabs Richard and is taken to an asylum.

During Richard's convalescence, a wonderful friendship grows between Mrs. Jackson, Billy and Richard. In the meantime, Mrs. Lenning is gradually winning over Jackson, who demands a divorce from his wife and the custody of Billy.

Jackson and Mrs. Lenning purposely allow Mrs. Jackson to overhear a conversation which will induce her to run away with

Billy, and they surprise her in Richard's house. Jackson secures a divorce *and* the boy. Mrs. Jackson kidnaps Billy as he is out with his nurse. Jake, who has escaped, secures a knife and enters the cave where Mrs. Jackson leaves Billy in order to go to Richard's for food. The nurse gives the alarm just as Jackson is married to Mrs. Lenning. Jackson and his men rush to Darcier's home, and Mrs. Jackson steals away to the cave. Word comes that Jake has escaped. Jake is about to kill Billy when Billy's mother comes upon them. She insists a white woman, not a child, must be the sacrifice, and bares her breast to the gleaming knife when her husband and his men and Richard come to the rescue, and the father gives up the custody of Billy to his more worthy mother.

Presumably, "bares her breast" should not be taken too literally.

Only in the movies does the winner of a custody case give up the child to the loser. Since it's Mrs. Jackson who puts her son in danger in the first place by kidnapping him and hiding him a cave — on her ex's wedding day, no less — one could argue that she loved little Billy well, but not too wisely. One might also think that Mr. Jackson's dalliance with Mrs. Lenning (why are these characters known only by their surnames?) would have given his wife some potent ammunition in the courtroom but, apparently — unlike her millionaire husband — she couldn't afford a good lawyer. The synopsis doesn't indicate Jake's fate, but most likely the rescue party, not wanting to take a chance on his escaping again and menacing little Billy a *third* time, gunned him down.

Voodoo queens were much more common than male priests in depictions of voodoo in the 1910s, and this may have been due in part to the fame of a certain Marie Leveau, a hairdresser who doubled as a voodoo priestess and attracted a big following in New Orleans in the mid–1800s; her lookalike daughter (also named Marie) kept up the tradition after her mother's death. There was also the case of Clementine Barnabel (like Leveau, a Louisianan), a fanatical voodoo practitioner who was brought to trial in 1912 for urging her followers to butcher a number of local families. Barnabel's story was well publicized, and audiences in 1917 may have recalled it with a shudder as they watched *Unconquered*'s voodoo queen working her evil magic on Jake.

In spite of the occasional nod to voodoo in the publicity, most puff pieces and ads described the film as a testament to mother love and focused on the film's star, Fannie Ward. An ad printed in *The Lowell* [Massachusetts] *Sun* was typical: "A powerful drama with motherhood as the theme and Miss Ward as the charming star. The display of morning, afternoon and evening gowns worn by Miss Ward in this production will delight the heart of every feminine patron."

In an interview, Fannie Ward talked about the dilemma of keeping and, when necessary, getting rid of husbands and the heroine's plight in *Unconquered*:

> The wife doesn't care so much whether she loses the husband or not, but she doesn't want to lose her little boy, and when she hears the child is to be stolen from her, she is in an unusual position. She doesn't know which way to turn nor what to do and it is only by seizing an opportunity at a psychological moment that she is eventually made happy. I think Mrs. De Mille and Mr. Osmun (the two scenarists) have handled this problem in a most charming manner and I am sure that everyone who sees this photodrama will say that the wife did just exactly right.

The "Mrs. De Mille" was Beatrice, mother of Cecil and William, and Ward's description of the climax — if we can assume that it came from her in the first place — sounds more like one of Cecil's sex comedies than what actually happens in *Unconquered*. More on Fannie Ward, who is best remembered for being on the receiving end of Sessue Hayakawa's branding iron in *The Cheat*, can be found in the entry on *The Fortune Teller*.

George Shorey of *Motion Picture News* (2 June 1917) was considerably less impressed than Ward with the De Mille/Osmun collaboration and found the principal characters under-written:

> Hobart Bosworth, supposed to be a villain, had to be labeled as such. He gave little evidence in the character he portrayed of being the "bad man" the part called for…. But there is no leading male role opposite Miss Ward. Darcier, the character played by Jack Dean, is intended to be the hero … but he does absolutely nothing but be "present." We have never seen anything like this or even approaching this character in any previous dramatic creation. He is a gentle and loving soul but not even romantic.

Perhaps Darcier was David Manners' role model for the useless heroes he played in horror films of the 1930s.

Shorey did think Ward's depiction of a loving mother was a success. However, the unnamed reviewer of *Moving Picture World* (2 June 1917) found her work uneven: "A lack of repose often deprives Fanny Ward's acting of the recommendation it would otherwise merit. This criticism does not apply however to the moment at the end of the trial after the boy has been taken from her. She is the heart-broken mother, numb with despair."

The reviewer also found the story "not very attractive" and "taking a long time in gathering force, and approaches dangerously near an anti-climax at the end of the third reel." Presumably, the writer is referring to Billy's rescue from Jake in the middle of the picture and then the repetition of same a couple of reels later.

Tully Marshall (Jake) got good notices, but it's a bit hard to imagine him in blackface and while he played his share of sleazy characters, a knife-wielding psychopath wasn't his usual brand of villainy. Marshall's career bona fides can be found in our essay on *The Brass Bottle*.

Like Marshall, Jane Wolfe (the voodoo queen) was also praised for her performance in blackface. This was not Wolfe's first impersonation of a black woman, though, as she had earlier played Roxy (again for Frank Reicher) in an adaptation of Mark Twain's *Pudd'nhead Wilson*. Wolfe began her film career at Kalem and, though very attractive, was more at home in character roles than she was as a leading lady. More intriguingly (for us), publicity about the actress during the 1910s focused on her interest in architecture and her success in designing bungalows without so much as a mention of her growing obsession with the occult. Understandably.

At about the same time she was doing *Unconquered*, Wolfe discovered the writings of the notorious Aleister Crowley, self-styled high priest of "Black Magick." Crowley claimed magical powers and while he couldn't pull a rabbit out of a hat, he did attract a following with his teachings — a mixture of Eastern philosophy, magical lore and blasphemy, with a heavy emphasis on drugs and sex. Wolfe, who had a vision of Crowley, began corresponding with him; in the early 1920s she put Hollywood behind her and headed for Crowley's cult headquarters, located in a villa in Cefalu, Sicily, and dedicated to the principles of Thelema (the Greek word for "will"). Like most communes, it was appallingly unclean (Crowley himself sometimes referred to the "mystery of filth," certainly an original reason for not mopping up), and this disgusted Wolfe. Nonetheless, she remained fascinated by Crowley — the role model for Maugham's *The Magician*, the film version of which is covered elsewhere — and became his lifelong devotee.

A very curious article later circulated in American papers:

> After some harrowing experiences in the "mystery house of Cefalu," Miss Jane Wolfe, an American actress who played film mothers in early Mary Pickford pictures [actually just one, *Rebecca of Sunnybrook Farm*] has returned to her home in Hollywood, California to seek complete recovery from injuries received from Sicilian peasants who tried to stone her to death…. She travelled to Sicily to follow the teachings of Sir Aleist [*sic*] Crowley, "high priest of Therama." While practicing asana, remaining absolutely motionless for long periods of time in a rigid position, she was attacked by natives who believed her possessed by evil spirits [*New Castle* (Pennsylvania) *News*, 22 May 1928].

Aside from its misspellings and its granting Crowley a knighthood (though the old boy *did* make that spurious claim at one point), the article's oddest aspect was its timing: Crowley's cult had been expelled from Sicily by Mussolini five years earlier. Everyone had been ousted due to the publicity that followed the death of one of Crowley's disciples, whose widow was interviewed by none other than William Seabrook, subsequently the author of *Magic Island*, which popularized the word "zombie."

Wolfe did indeed return to Hollywood where she continued to preach Crowley's doctrine and became an important part of the Los Angeles branch of Crowley's magic society, the Ordo Templi Orientis, which took the rather innocuous name of "Agape Lodge." Crowley never set foot in the house but, rather, pulled the strings from England where, desperate for money, he urged the Society to attract the wealthy and influential. Given the spiritual supermarket that was Los Angeles, the competition was fierce and, except for rocket scientist John Whiteside Parsons (whose involvement wasn't known until after he'd accidentally blown himself up), the Lodge made no notable conquests. Supposedly, though, the house was visited by John Carradine at the time he was doing a bit part in *The Black Cat* (wherein Boris Karloff played a devil worshipper who was, coincidentally, based on Crowley). The Agape group went on to establish a commune at a larger house and Wolfe, then 64 years old, found herself not high priestess but *housekeeper* for a group beset by jealousies, quarrels, and deranged behavior. Crowley died in 1947, a pathetic, impoverished heroin addict, but Wolfe retained her faith in his teachings until her own death in 1958.

Director Frank Reicher, the son of stage-great Emanuel Reicher, took up his father's profession in their native Germany. Reicher *fils* recalled his one instance of stage fright when, playing Rodrigo in *Othello*, he completely froze and did not snap out of it until his father, standing in the wings, hissed "Idiot!" at him. On a trip to America with his father, Reicher liked what he saw, determined to make good there (and perhaps get out from under the shadow of his famous *vati*), and became the stage manager of the Henry B. Harris repertory company. Later

he did the same for David Belasco. Onstage, he created the role of Lord Ravensbane in the Broadway production of *The Scarecrow* (see *Puritan Passions*).

In the mid–1910s, Reicher turned to film directing, initially at Lasky, then at World, and he was quite vocal about what he perceived to be some of the shortcomings of silent film:

> It's difficult enough for an actor to play a scene through facial play without his attempting to impart to the audience just what he is trying to do by mouth play. This tends to distract the audience who thinks they are missing something if they do not try to follow the lips and thus gather a word here or there…. I recall a picture where the actor was dying as a result of a knife wound. The audience saw the blow and who struck it yet the actor insisted on saying "You killed me, John Morgan." Instead of the scene being taken seriously, a big laugh went all over the house as someone exclaimed "You fool, I know he stabbed you." … Many times I have sat out in the front and been simply bored at actors who continuously read lines as he was acting the scenes. This sort of scene retards the action [*Bridgeport* (Connecticut) *Standard Telegram*, 7 July 1919].

This pet peeve did not prevent Reicher from experimenting a bit with sound, and his 1918 *The Claim* contained a synchronized sequence in which heroine Edith Storey sings "Annie Laurie."

Reicher returned to Broadway during the 1920s and it was there that he did most of his acting and directing chores, staging the original hit productions of *Liliom*, *He Who Gets Slapped* and *The Monkey Talks*, as well the experimental Expressionist drama, *From Morn to Midnight*. According to one report, Reicher began having health problems in the 1930s and this meant an end to his demanding work as a stage director. He became head of the Pathé Junior Stock Company, wherein young actors were trained for the movies — Carole Lombard and Lew Ayres were among the graduates — but today is best remembered by horror fans for his roles in *King Kong*, *The Mummy's Ghost*, *Night Monster*, et al.

— *HN*

Undine

Undine. Bluebird Photoplays Inc./Bluebird Photoplays, Inc., 7 February 1916, 5 reels [LOST]

CAST: Ida Schnall (*Undine*); Douglas Gerrard (*Huldbrand*); Edna Masion (*Lady Bertheida*); Carol Stelson (*The Duke*); Caroline Fowler (*The Duchess*); O.C. Jackson (*The Fisherman*); Josephine Rice (*The Fisherman's Wife*); Elijah Zerr (*Kuhleborn*); Jack Nelson (*Waldo*); Thomas Delmar (*Father Heilmann*); with Eileen Allen, Grace Astor.

N.B. The copyright registration lists Elijah Zerr as *Father Heilmann* and Thomas Delmar as *Kuhleborn*.

CREDITS: *Director* Henry Otto; *Assistant Director* Scott Beal; *Scenario* Walter Woods; based on the eponymous fairy tale by Friedrich de la Motte Fouqué (Germany, 1811); *Cinematographer* Fred Granville; *Music* M. Winkler

In late 1915 Fox announced that they would be filming *Daughter of the Gods*, another spectacular fantasy starring champion swimmer, Annette Kellerman(n), whose earlier *Neptune's Daughter* had proven to be a big hit. No doubt very much aware of the receipts for *Neptune's Daughter*, Universal decided to beat Fox to the punch by doing their own aquatic romance, *Undine*. The film would be based on the novel of the same name by Fredrich de la Motte Fouqué, who had written it in 1811; this placed the book safely in the public domain, which was just swell with Universal. (No slouch in their own right, Thanhouser had discovered the royalty-free property a few years earlier and had, in fact, produced a two-reel version with Florence La Badie in 1912.) Universal didn't have Annette Kellerman, of course, but they did have Ida Schnall who—though saddled with a name that didn't inspire any poetry—had won the title "Champion Female Athlete of America" and was a noted diver.

Anyhow, around the time that Fox was putting forth a good deal of hoopla about the filming of *Daughter* in Jamaica and the huge expenses it entailed, Universal announced they would be sending director Henry Otto and the cast and crew of *Undine* to Catalina to shoot exteriors for three weeks. Obviously, the economy-minded Big U wasn't going to attempt to match Fox's budget (even the suggestion probably would have given Uncle Carl Laemmle a stroke), but it *was* a big film by their standards and when the company returned from location, Universal issued a rather breathless description of what they had accomplished:

> Pictures of caves and deep-creviced caverns whose hundred-foot arches cut through towering walls of malpai rock that rise in silent grandeur from the futile beating of surf at their base; pictures of sea nymphs, garlanded with strings of kelp and sea-weed, sliding from half-submerged rocks in the breakers or riding through the surf on dolphins and sporting about in the water among the seals; pictures of wood fairies shifting about from tree to tree and disappearing down the semi-lighted archways of giant pines that grow straight to the water's edge; pictures of underwater swimming and of dives from unbelievable heights; pictures of elves and gnomes and woodland spirits that come and go in a twinkling, coming from nowhere and disappearing into thin air — these and a hundred other effects are seen on the screen [*Motion Picture News*, 14 April 1915].

The same press release also mentions that the camerawork was done by Fred Granville "who went with the Steffansson expedition to the Arctic regions and whose camera work has occasioned such favorable comment with the releasing of those films." No doubt Granville found the shoot of *Undine* much more pleasant; more on his career can be found in the appendix entry on *The Price of Silence*.

Barely two months later, the results of these endeavors were seen on the big screen, released under Universal's Bluebird label (and well ahead of the release of *Daughter of the Gods*). Our synopsis comes from the 12 February 1916 *Motion Picture World* and *The AFI Catalog*:

> The story begins in the realm of Queen Unda, mistress of the undersea, surrounded by her nymphs, sylphs and mermaids, who disport themselves on the sands and in the waters of the deep. Bertheida, daughter of a fisherman and his devoted wife, has been stolen by the mermaids one day when the child was playing on the sands. Queen Unda rules that little Bertheida shall be left to roam in the Enchanted Forest, because her parents have taken fishes from the ocean much to the annoyance of Queen Unda and Neptune.
>
> Undine, the most skillful aquatic nymph in the kingdom grows up and marries a mortal, Waldo, who shoots a sacred deer with his crossbow. Kuhleborn, the king of the Enchanted Forest, slays Waldo for this transgression. Before Undine dies of grief she bears a daughter also called Undine. Little baby Undine is taken to the shore near the fisherman's cottage, to be discovered by the fisherman and his wife. It is Undine's mission on earth to marry a mortal and thus atone for the sins committed by her mother.

> Undine is welcomed by the fisherman and his wife who consider she has been sent by the gods to take the place of little Bertheida. Fifteen years pass. Bertheida has been adopted by the Duke and Duchess and among those who pay her court is Huldbrand, the bravest of knights.
>
> To test his love, Bertheida sents Huldbrand into the Enchanted Forest and bids him return with proof that he has explored its wonders. Huldbrand drinks from a fountain in the Enchanted Forest which causes him to immediately fall in love with Undine [or at least his drinking from the fountain is a sign that he's the one destined to marry her; it's not quite clear from the various synopses]. They are married by a shipwrecked priest, whom Undine has rescued from the sea.
>
> Going with his bride to the castle there is great rejoicing. At the celebration in honor of Huldbrand's marriage, there appears a messenger from Queen Unda who tells Undine her earthly mission is fulfilled and she returns to the waters under the sea. Huldbrand is reconciled to Lady Bertheida and the story ends.

It's not clear though why Undine and Huldbrand's match would cause "great rejoicing" in the castle since the knight has jilted the princess for the gill-girl, although maybe no one's too upset because Bertheida is not really of royal blood. The movie also jettisons the book's unhappy ending (which the 1912 Thanhouser version kept) wherein Undine shows up at Huldbrand's wedding to Bertheida and gives her former lover a (literal) kiss of death. Publicity for the film admitted that scenarist Walter Woods did not follow the original too closely and gave the rather weak reason that the fantasy was not pictorial enough.

It's also unclear as to why Undine repeating the "sin" of her mother in falling for a mortal man somehow clears the slate. In the folk tales the book is derived from, marrying a human being and bearing his child gives the nymph/mermaid a soul. In the legends, the Undine character is often a mermaid and, in one version, she reverts to her real state one day a week and keeps it a secret from her human lover. In *Undine*, though, she's a nymph and has no tail (albeit one gathers she's often bottomless).

The film has a framing device wherein a mother and father read the story of Undine to their daughter. The film returns to them five or six times, and they even turn up as characters in the main narrative. Some found this device very clever, but others felt these frequent interruptions were distracting and unnecessary, as surely no one needed a reminder that they were watching a fairy tale. However, Universal must have wanted to stress to viewers that *Undine* was based on a classic children's story, for some of the publicity for the film was certainly not aimed at the kiddies as this example from the 30 March 1916 issue of *The Clearfield* [Pennsylvania] *Progress* illustrates: "The incidents in the realm of Queen Unda will be found to be particularly attractive There are a score of maidens clad mostly in wisps of seaweed (when they are not encased in nature's bathing suits) disporting themselves in the sea and upon the sands."

Small wonder that *Variety*'s "Fred" cracked that *Undressed* would be a better title for the film.

Naturally, some censors were not happy with all the cavortin' and disportin' going on in Unda's kingdom. *The Chicago Tribune* (21 March 1916) printed an account of what happened when censor Mrs. Grace Brooks arrived a little late for the preview of *Undine*:

As she entered and took her seat she encountered a dozen or fifteen women marching indignantly up the darkened aisle. She noted an air of pleased, even vociferous appreciation on the part of a number of well groomed youths down in front. Then she looked at the screen…. They [the nymphs] were disporting themselves in the waves and their forms glistened alluringly as the spray flung itself upon their flowing hair. Not to put too fine a point on it, they didn't have anything on. Just as one of the mermaids flung caution to the wind and jumped astride a sea serpent, Mrs. Brooks found her voice. "Stop that picture!" she cried. "Stop that picture!"

Undine did play in Chicago much later, but *The Chicago Tribune* reviewer Kitty Kelly had found it more saccharine than suggestive, likely to charm some while putting others to sleep. In the 24 January 1916 edition of the paper, she also wondered whether Shytown audiences were getting a heavily censored version: "Two or three [of the nymphs] might have worn their chiffons more discreetly but they are easily forgotten. This is after a session with the censors however, concerning which the Universal people say no harm was done to the picture and the machine operator says the longest reel he has is three-fourths of the regulation 1,000 standard feet."

Kelly thought the film was full of beauty and grace but lacked "punch" and, from the various descriptions, *Undine* doesn't sound terribly dramatic. The Annette Kellerman movies may have been equally insipid, but at least contained plenty of sword and sorcery to make for a little more excitement.

Virtually every review we consulted mentioned the nudity and near-nudity but insisted there was nothing salacious about its use in the film. Harvey Thew's comment about the nymphs in *Motion Picture News* (12 February 1916) was typical: "Although their clothing is scanty (and in some cases entirely absent), there is nothing about the scenes that will give offense. Censors will look in vain for something to cut out (Which does not mean they will cut nothing)."

Variety was less optimistic on whether the film would beat the local censors, but felt an uncensored version would do well at the box office if the picture were given a longer than normal run to be properly exploited. Critics were also in agreement on film's striking pictorial quality and the excellence of the photography and lighting. *MPW's* George Blaisdell, after calling the film "a thing of beauty," offered some complimentary though rather muddled comments: "The photography is unusual. While most of it is in black and white, the exceptions are marks of laboratory judgment. Especially true is this statement in the coloring of the sunset call. It is the sunset."

Advertising and publicity for the film were not shy about comparing it to *Neptune's Daughter* or proclaiming it superior to the Kellerman film. Naturally, Ida Schnall, "The Girl with the 100% Figure," garnered much of the publicity, and a good deal was made of her dive of 175 feet from the top of a wall of rock straight into the sea below.

Schnall was not a born athlete. A native of Austria, she was a sickly child but — at eight years of age — became inspired by watching the training and exercises of the new army recruits at the barracks near her home. She became the regimental mascot and, by the time her family moved to the USA and settled in The Bronx, Ida had become healthy and strong; she soon developed a fascination with all sports, especially baseball and div-

ing. She began winning diving contests even before she knew how to swim — she had to be pulled out of the water by attendants with hooks — and was soon racking up medals and awards in a variety of sports while championing the cause of permitting U.S. women athletes to compete in the Olympics.

One day in 1911/12, Annette Kellerman — while appearing in a musical version of *Undine* at the Winter Garden — had a tiff with the management and absolutely refused to go on. In true *42nd Street* fashion, Schnall was called in to replace the star for the night and did all her diving stunts superbly. This led to more show biz aquatics and ultimately brought her to the attention of Universal when the studio was planning *Undine*. (Once out in LaLaLand, Schnall wasted no time in organizing baseball teams made up of actresses.) No doubt Schnall would have made a great serial queen (and one who perhaps *really* would have done her own stunts), but she found filmmaking dull compared to leaping out of airplanes into the ocean or jumping from tall buildings into firemen's nets. Schnall also found the time to marry and raise two children. In the 1930s she took up tennis, boxing, weight lifting and wrestling, winning many awards (and a mention in "Ripley's Believe It or Not"). She died in 1973, probably of exhaustion.

More on director Henry Otto can be found in the entry on *The Willow Tree* while some particulars on the career of Douglas Gerrard (Huldbrand) are outlined in *The Phantom Melody*.

In the 24 July 1920 issue of *Motion Picture News*, an ad from New York company, Wilk and Wilk, announced the release of *The Answer of the Sea*, "a dream of fair women — a marvelously staged sea picture" which had been "reproduced from the famous motion picture classic *Undine*." The ad was accompanied by a drawing of naked nymphs splashing happily about. Apparently Universal had sold the rights to *Undine* to Wilk and Wilk, who then released the film via States' Rights under its original working title of *The Answer of the Sea*. When it played in Chicago in 1921, *The Chicago Tribune* reviewer "Mae Tinee" mistakenly thought it was a new film. Her review, nonetheless, echoed the remarks of her predecessor, Kitty Kelly: "Pretty and artistic" with little action and no punch. Mae's comments on Schnall are interesting: "Miss Schnall may be all that it said of her. The picture, however, gives her little chance to display beauty or prowess. Now you see her in the water, and now you catch a glimpse of her on the shore. The lady may be a great actress, too, but in the present production all she needs to do is to kick a shapely leg and keep her head above water."

Apparently, in spite of the tantalizing ad, the Windy City was once again getting a censored version of *Undine*.

In 1924 Thomas Ince produced *The Galloping Fish*, a six-reeler starring Louise Fazenda as Undine (Wow!); mercifully, the film contained no fantasy elements. On a more serious level, the legend of Undine (alternate spelling, Ondine) became the subject of operas, ballet, plays (Audrey Hepburn won a Tony for her performance in the Jean Giraudoux play) as well as TV productions and movies. As we write this, yet another retelling (of sorts) has been filmed and put into release: *Ondine* (2010), starring Colin Farrell (as Syracuse, the fisherman), and Polish actress-singer, Alicja Bachleda, as the mer-nymph. The first review we consulted grumped, "Not seaworthy."

We stopped there.

— HN

The Undying Flame

The Undying Flame. Jesse L. Lasky Feature Play Co./Paramount Pictures, 24 May 1917, 5 reels [LOST]

CAST: Madame Olga Petrova (*The Princess/Grace Leslie*); Mahlon Hamilton (*The Shepherd/Captain Paget*); Edward Mordant (*The King*); Herbert Evans (*The Architect*); Warren Cook (*General Leslie*); Charles W. Martin (*Col. Harvey*); Violet Reed (*Mrs. Harvey*)

CREDITS: *Director* Maurice Tourneur; *Assistant Director* Philip West; *Scenario* Charles E. Whitaker; *Story* Emma Bell; *Cinematographer* John van den Broek; *Art Direction* Ben Carre; *Production Miscellany* Albert Kaufman

Between 1916 and 1920 at least a dozen Hollywood films were made that touched on the theme of reincarnation. The Great War was taking its terrible toll on the world's youth, so was it wrong to hope that death in the trenches was not the absolute end for boys who had barely had a chance to live and would never return to the sweethearts they had left behind? There was also a great public interest in hypnosis and psychoanalysis and the times produced the occasional offbeat theory, such as the one which wondered whether the victims of multiple personality weren't actually experiencing past lives, and not just present fragmentation. In any case, most reincarnation films owe a heavy debt to H. Rider Haggard's *She* (first filmed in 1908), the tale of an immortal queen and the great white hunter who is the reincarnation of her ancient lover. *She* established two basic rules about reincarnation stories: (1) The principal characters were always reincarnations of lovers, and not enemies, family members, etc. (2) At least one of the lovers would be royalty or of noble blood; apparently no one saw much value in the romance between a farm girl and a fishmonger or in seeing their love bridge the centuries. Filmed in Florida under the working title *The Scarabaeus*, Maurice Tourneur's *The Undying Flame*— done as a vehicle for Olga Petrova — sticks to the rules.

Synopsis from *Motion Picture News* (9 May 1917) and other contemporary reviews:

In ancient Egypt a Princess loved a simple Shepherd, to the great displeasure of the King, who ordered the offending lover buried alive, for he had promised his daughter to the Builder of the Temple. Breaking a double scarab in twain, the Shepherd and the Princess each kept a broken half, a pledge that their souls would be reunited in death. The princess called upon Isis to turn her to stone before she can be made to wed the architect.

Centuries later, Captain Harry Paget of the English garrison at the Soudan, is greatly attracted by Grace Leslie, daughter of Sir Hector Leslie, in command of the garrison. Though a newcomer to Egypt, Grace feels she has been there before and that she is in familiar surroundings. A fortuneteller gives Grace half of the scarab and explains the legend about it. Mrs. Harvey, wife of a brother officer, is also in love with Paget, and while he is called to a false meeting on the desert by the jealous woman, a surprise drill is called. Grace hears from her father of the intended surprise and saves Paget from disgrace by notifying him, thus interrupting the meeting with Mrs. Harvey. Paget volunteers for a dangerous outpost duty in desperation, but Mrs. Harvey explains and Grace falls into her lover's arms and announces she will go to the desert with him, alone; when it is singularly discovered that each possesses a

piece of a broken scarab which just match. Are these "souls reunited"?

We don't learn from the synopsis where Paget got his half of the scrarab; perhaps he visited the same Egyptian Yenta.

One major problem with this type of film is that the ancient story, full of exotica and cruelty, is usually a good deal more compelling than the modern one. Scenarist Beulah Marie Dix solved the problem in De Mille's *The Road to Yesterday* by putting the flashback in the middle and wrapping the thrilling train-wreck sequence around it. Nothing very exciting appears to happen in the second half of *The Undying Flame*, and the romantic triangle and stiff-upper-lip melodramatics seem weak substitutes for the *Aida*-like goings on in the first half.

Another difficulty is the inevitability of the outcome of the second half. Since the Princess/Grace Leslie is played by Olga Petrova and the Shepherd/Paget by Mahlon Hamilton, we know how the modern story must turn out. Obviously the adulterous Mrs. Harvey isn't the reincarnation of the Princess, so there's not much suspense in waiting for the lovers to discover what the audience already knows.

Reviews and publicity for the film sometimes mentioned H. Rider Haggard and — in regard to the depiction of colonial Egypt — threw in Rudyard Kipling as well. Haggard was actually an ardent believer in reincarnation and tried (with questionable results) to convert Kipling.

The PR boys also issued press releases about reincarnation:

[In the film] one of the strangest facts of human experience is touched upon and in fact forms the basis for the whole weird and mysterious story which has been woven around it. This is the very common sensation of having been in a place before or having performed exactly the same actions in relation to the same persons, whom perhaps one has never seen before. Who is there who has experienced this baffling sensation? The Egyptians, thousands of years ago, worked out a theory to explain all this in their religion of the "Transmigration of souls".... Thus an Egyptian in experiencing this feeling would merely say to himself: "I have known this person or have been in this place before in one of my previous incarnations" — and then go about his business [*Lowell* (Massachusetts) *Sun*, 31 May 1917].

The article made no mention of the fact that modern Egyptians, being predominantly either Muslim or Coptic Christians, don't believe in transmigration, or that worshippers of Isis and Osiris are pretty uncommon nowadays.

One person experiencing a sense of déjà vu while watching *The Undying Flame* was author Frances E. Jackson, who claimed the film's plot was swiped from her novel *The Two Diamonds*. Jackson sued Famous Players–Lasky, Paramount, and scenarist Emma Bell Clifton. We have no information on the outcome of the case, but such suits became increasingly common as the 1910s wore on.

Variety scribe Jolo found *The Undying Flame* "a tiresome and uninteresting affair" and, as usual, seized on a minor point to rib the filmmakers:

The world is indebted to Olga Petrova for many things in the past, and with the presentation on the screen of "The Undying Flame" it is revealed that she is so learned in the lore of archaeology as to have discovered that modern corsets were worn in ancient Egypt. The female servants or maids in waiting, it is observed, did not affect this style or physical adornment-only princesses. That is, it is presumed all princesses did and, as the one portrayed by Miss Petrova is the only royal female in the picture, one must accept her as the standard [25 May 1917].

George Shorey (of *Motion Picture News*) was much more positive, though he did have a few reservations:

> It does not reach the tensest pitch of dramatic realism, and what might have been one of the most effective scenes of all was spoiled to the writer by a too obviously " "staged" closing of the tomb, burying the hero alive at the close of the first act; but artistic beauty as a production, with Madame Petrova in the most impressive role we have yet see her, clearly entitles this picture to first rank.

Edward Weitzel (of *Moving Picture World*, 9 June 1917) thought the film had "the leisurely pace of a novel" and seemed a bit halfhearted in his praise:

> This highly romantic tale never reaches any great dramatic moment, but it will serve to entertain the spectator who does not demand anything but present-day realism. The scenes in ancient Egypt are architecturally imposing, but some of them betray their recent origin by the brush of the scene painter. The modern scenes in the land of the Pharaohs are cleverly counterfeited.
>
> Madame Petrova is more convincing as the princess than in the later character. Her daughter of Egypt contains no suggestion of the modern woman, the actress having the stately grace that is associated with Cleopatra, but not her warmth of passion. Most of the time she seems to have stepped down from a fresco in the palace and as usual her impersonation is a piece of finished art.

One could interpret all this to mean that Petrova looked the part but was rather wooden. In any case, evaluating her film acting is impossible, as almost all of her movies are lost, including a few that she wrote.

The flamboyant Petrova — who insisted on always being addressed as *Madame* Petrova — was actually British (née Muriel Harding), the daughter of a proprietor of a fish-and-chips shop. Shortly after she embarked on her stage career, the red-haired actress took the advice of an agent and reinvented herself as Olga Petrova, a Russian refugee who arrived in London with only the clothes on her back and $25 in cash. Petrova even affected a colorful accent that was described as a combination of Russian and French. After some success in England, she came to New York in 1911 to star in Les Folies Bergère, an attempt to imitate Parisian cabaret; it was a disaster, but Petrova drew both crowds and great reviews for her subsequent stage and vaudeville work. A prototypical feminist and very unconventional, she often made the news for saying things like "My ideal would be a woman's soul in a man's body," and for claiming women were more polygamous than men, but were too timid to leave the cocoon of marriage. At one point Petrova claimed to have discovered that, as she wanted to stay in the United States, her getting married was the only way to break her English theater contract; she thus advertised for a "temporary husband." Hundreds of men responded ("Never did I dream there were so many fools in the world," the actress declared); a year after this particular publicity stunt, the lady really did get married — to a New York surgeon.

In 1914 Petrova turned to the movies, played in a number of films directed by Alice Guy Blaché for Popular Plays and Players, and then moved to Lasky, where *The Undying Flame* was her first film. After several more films for Lasky, she started her own production company, but gave up the film business in 1918, say-

ing the studio lights were damaging her eyes. She did more stage work, lectured on women's issues, and wrote poetry, novels, short stories and plays (one of which, *What Do We Know?*, concerns spiritualism). Petrova retired in the 1930s and spent her time alternating between New York and Paris. In 1942 she wrote her autobiography *Butter with My Bread*.

Mahlon Hamilton got good notices for his dual role in *The Undying Flame*. Before entering film, Hamilton spent a number of years on the stage and won attention for his support of musical comedy star, Blanche Ring, in *When Claudia Smiles* (1914). His film debut came the same year with *Three Weeks*, an adaptation of an Elinor Glyn romance. Hamilton soon joined Olga Petrova at Popular Plays and Players, and became her regular leading man. When Petrova moved to Lasky, Hamilton was hired as well. He did not go with Petrova when she started her own company, but instead freelanced and won a number of good roles, notably the title character in Mary Pickford's *Daddy Long Legs* (1919). His popularity waned in the 1920s and by the 1930s he was doing bit roles.

The great Maurice Tourneur turns up many times in these pages, notably for *Trilby* and *The Isle of Lost Ships*. *The Undying Flame* was no doubt one of his minor works.

— HN

The Unfaithful Wife

The Unfaithful Wife. Fox Film Corp./Fox Film Corp., 5 December 1915, 5 reels [LOST]

CAST: Robert B. Mantell (*Fabiano Romani*); Genevieve Hamper (*Juliet, Fabiano's wife*); Stuart Holmes (*Arturo Durazzi*); Warner Oland (*Rigo, an outlaw*); Henry Leone (*Domenic, a butler*); Doris Wooldridge (*Theresa, a flirt*); Phillip Hahn (*Pedro, her lover*); Charles Lewis (*Monk*); Anna Leona (*Nurse*); Groof, a St. Bernard dog (*Himself*).

CREDITS: *Director* J. Gordon Edwards; *Scenario* Mary Murillo; *Cinematographer* Phil Rosen.

Synopsis from contemporary newspaper accounts and *The AFI Catalog*:

> Count Fabiano Romani, a studious Italian nobleman, is married to Juliet, beautiful and frivolous. The Count lives happily in his love of his wife in whom he believes implicitly. Absorbed in his scientific research, Romani does not notice the disgraceful intrigue existing between the Countess and his good friend Arturo Durazzi, an artist. When cholera strikes the little Italian village where they all live, Romano develops symptoms of the dread scourge but in reality his indisposition is nothing other than sunstroke. When the Count is brought home comatose, Juliet and Durazzi, though they realize he is still alive, have him hastily buried, using the plague as an excuse. With scarcely concealed delight they follow the procession while the coffin, containing his remains, is interred in the family vault.
>
> The Count awakens from his coma and escapes from the coffin. He then discovers that brigands have been using his family vault as the hiding place of a vast treasure in stolen jewels and gold. In his efforts to escape from the vault the Count discovers both the treasure and their concealed entrance and emerges at last, his hair turned white by his terrifying experience. Returning home, Romani is stupefied at finding Juliet in the arms of Arturo. He withdraws without disclosing himself and, all his love transformed to hate, he swears to be avenged upon his betrayers.
>
> Assisted by his changed appearance, Romani assumes the guise of Count Cesare, a wealthy nobleman, and worms himself into the

good graces of his false wife and Arturo. Tutored by hatred, he sets himself to the task of winning Juliet's love from Arturo and, by dint of flattery and costly presents from the bandits' horde, he finally succeeds. Furious at his rejection, Arturo challenges Romani to a duel but before he can fire a shot, Romani reveals his identity and slays him.

Still ignorant of his disguise, Juliet marries Romani and then begs him to take her to the treasure of family jewels she believes will be hers. Romani leads her to the very vault in which he was buried and then unveils his secret. Juliet pleads for mercy but the Count turns an unhearing ear to her entreaties and locks his unfaithful wife, now a raving maniac, in the crypt.

If the story sounds a little familiar, it's because bits and pieces of it turn up in three Rex Ingram films covered in these pages: *Black Orchids*, *Reward of the Faithless*, and *Trifling Women*. Those movies are rife with premature burials, conniving lovers and vengeful spouses returning from the grave. Here, Ingram was no doubt inspired by Marie Corelli's 1886 novel *Vendetta, a Story of One Forgotten*, and reworked a number of incidents from it. On the other hand, Fox Films' *The Unfaithful Wife* is outright plagiarism, even to the point of keeping the same name for the central character. There are only two significant changes: in the novel, the wife and lover don't realize that they have buried the Count alive and, at the ending, Romani relents a bit when he sees his wife has gone mad, but a convenient cave-in disposes of her anyway. By making the lovers (would be)-murderers, the film increases their culpability and make Romani's vengeance more justifiable.

The fact that *Vendetta* was never copyrighted in the United States presumably gave Fox the necessary loophole to rip it off so blatantly. The downside was that the studio couldn't use Corelli's name in the publicity even though, given the fact that she was very well known, it would have been a plus to do so; instead, Fox's chief scenarist, Mary Murillo, was given the credit although some of the reviewers did recognize the source material. This shouldn't have been hard to do because a French film-version of the novel — a feature-length offering from Eclipse that retained the book's title — saw a wide release in the United States in 1914. The success of the picture, which had been filmed in Italy and which starred Regina Badet and Jean Angelo, may have inspired Fox to do their own version as a vehicle for legendary Shakespearean actor, Robert B. Mantell.

Corelli, whose life and career are discussed in the entry on *The Sorrows of Satan*, did a little borrowing of her own for *Vendetta*, mainly from Dumas' *The Count of Monte Cristo*. In the latter, Edmund Dantes is "buried alive" in a notorious prison, but escapes and discovers a fabulous treasure that he uses to finance his complex scheme to wreak vengeance on his enemies. He assumes a new, aristocratic identity and relishes the moment when he can reveal his secret to his astonished victims; however, he does falter a bit when one of them goes insane. *Vendetta* covers much the same ground although Romani's motives are strictly those of the cuckolded husband. Just to make sure we get the idea, Corelli has just about every character Romani encounters tell him some tale of infidelity. It's all operatic, overwritten and florid, but cut down to its essentials — and in a silent film there's rarely any choice but to do that — it might well have made a fine bit of Grand Guignol melodrama.

No doubt Corelli was also influenced by Poe's tales of living entombment: "The Premature Burial," "Fall of the House of Usher," and especially "Cask of Amontillado," another story of vengeance that ends in a cavernous burial vault. Corelli claimed to have drawn upon true stories of infidelity and retribution in Italy, but her inspiration was more likely drawn from the sort of Gothic novels that turned on nightgown-clad, décolleté heroines being chased across the fog-laden countryside by swarthy, Italianate villains. Corelli (née Mary Mackay), who hailed from England, may have shared Archie Bunker's opinion that Italians are best known for "spaghetti and revenge."

The Unfaithful Wife was the second of six Fox films starring Robert B. Mantell, and all co-starred the aging matinee idol's much younger wife, Genevieve Hamper. The half-dozen gems were all directed by J. Gordon Edwards (see entry, *The Darling of Paris*) and photographed by Phil Rosen (see entry, *The Faker*); only one other entry, *The Green-Eyed Monster*, is grisly enough to win a mention in these pages. The premier effort, *The Blindness of Devotion*, reads like a warm-up for *The Unfaithful Wife*: An elderly count marries a vamp who promptly seduces her husband's adopted son. The lovers meet violent ends, and the count throws his wife's body onto the corpse of his son. The scenario was by Rex Ingram — soon to leave Fox for Universal — and he later recycled a few of its ideas (like the switching of a poisoned chalice) for *Black Orchids* and *Trifling Women*.

It's not known what Mantell thought of having to repeatedly play an older man cuckolded by his young wife, but he had praise for Fox: "I am content to enter 'photoplay' and I stake my reputation on whatever I may achieve in this new realm of art. I believe the photoplay as produced by Mr. Fox offers greater opportunities for histrionics than does the so called legitimate stage of the present day"(16 February 1915). Perhaps Mantell was channeling Othello while going about his melodramatic business as Romani.

Mantell, of course, was the big selling point of *The Unfaithful Wife*, as is evident from the following, typically overheated hype:

> Unquestionably one of the greatest of screen pantomime seen in this city. In it the distinguished tragedian, one who has dominated the very pinnacle of his profession for thirty years, rises to the heights of dramatic eloquence of unparalleled power and appeal. We have heard, but with incredulous mien it must be confessed, of actors holding the audience spellbound, but after watching the six [sic] tremendous acts of this play, one knows that it is possible for a single man, possessed of naught but personal magnetism, to so draw an audience into the web of his personality that they sit like mutes, dumb in admiration at his powers and breathless in record with his emotions.

"Breathless" certainly describes that last sentence. Apparently, though, not everyone was dumbstruck by Mantell's performance in *The Blindness of Devotion* and thought *The Unfaithful Wife* was actually a better vehicle for him (maybe because he got to play a "dual" role):

> We may have been disappointed at Mr. Mantel's first appearance on the screen some weeks back, but *The Unfaithful Wife* justifies the shrewd business mind of William Fox who has signed the famous tragedian with his beautiful young wife to a two-year contract. Here Mr. Mantell has a role giving boundless scope to the ability which has made him famous these many years. I am

unable to think of any other player now engaged in screen work who could have done the "coffin" scene so brilliantly as he [*Syracuse Herald*, 7 December 1915].

Ads for *The Unfaithful Wife* trumpeted blurbs from the New York press:

"Mr. Mantell a triumph in the movies" [*New York World*].

"Extraordinary display on the screen off dramatic prowess by Mr. Mantell and Miss Hamper" [*New York Evening Mail*].

"A revelation in moving-picture acting" [*New York Telegraph*].

Please note: The title of the film itself was never mentioned.

Oscar Cooper of *Motion Picture News* joined in the effusive praise of Mantell: "In his rendition of cunning, cold blooded revenge, thrown against a background of pathos which completely commands sympathy, Mr. Mantell is unsurpassed by any screen actor we have seen" (18 December 1915). Cooper was likewise impressed by Genevieve Hamper: "We knew of course that Miss Hamper's beauty would grace any photoplay, but we had not realized before that she could portray so well the full extent of emotions like that of horror. She portrays it with great impressiveness in the final tomb scene."

Stuart Holmes — who played villainous roles in five of the six Mantell films and didn't make it through the last reel in any of them — also won critical praise. (More on Mr. Holmes can be found in the *Body and Soul* [1920] entry.)

While Cooper found the scenario of *The Unfaithful Wife* "gruesome but satisfying," he did have a few reservations: "Some of the early scenes moved almost too rapidly for clear understanding and occasionally the photography was a little dark." Be that as it may, Phil Rosen's camera work had already received a good dollop of publicity in an earlier issue of *MPN*:

Spirit photographs and ghost photographs are common. They are common for the reason that they are fakes — with all due respect to those who believe that departed spirits pose for the camera. Double exposure is the answer.

No everyday photographer, however, and but a few of the so-called experts can furnish you with a picture of the human breath…. In *The Unfaithful Wife*, a mirror is held before the face of Count Fabio Romani to ascertain whether or not life is extinct. The Count, it develops, is not dead; hence his breath is supposed to be revealed on the mirror. How to make a close-up photograph of so intangible a quality as the human breath at first non-plussed Phil Rosen, but by calling into play ingenuity and the proper arrangement of lights, he secured the desired effect [27 November 1915].

Publicity for the film also mentioned that much of it was filmed at "Shadow Lawn," an estate that served as the summer home for President Woodrow Wilson. (There was also the less likely claim that $17,960 worth of real jewels were used to represent the Count's treasure. What? They couldn't spring for $18,000?)

After their Fox contracts were up, Mantell and Genevieve Hamper returned to the stage. They would make only one more movie, 1923's *Under the Red Robe* (with Mantell playing Cardinal Richelieu); more on the famous couple can be found in our essay on *The Green-Eyed Monster*.

Not much is known about prolific screenwriter, Mary Murillo, other than the fact that she was born in England and was — according to studio publicity — of Irish rather than of Hispanic descent. It was claimed that she had passed both her bar and medical exams, but never practiced as either lawyer or physician. Apparently, somewhere along the way she took acting lessons too, as she shows up in small roles in four Broadway plays. The last of these was in 1913 and it was the following year that she began writing scenarios for both Vitagraph and Universal. Murillo thrived at Fox and became their chief story editor, writing scripts for Theda Bara and, later, Norma Talmadge. In the 1920s, she worked on several British productions. She kept writing right until the 1930s, and one of her last scripts was for Maurice Tourneur's first sound film, *Accusee, levez-vous!* Murillo's work can also be found here in our chapters on *The Green-Eyed Monster* (1916) and *She* (1917).

In 1917, *The Unfaithful Wife* was released to Canada, where it was sometimes shown as *The Living Death* and where references to its source novel were more frequent. An ad from the *Lethbridge* [Alberta] *Herald* (23 October 1917) tied it all together nicely: "*The Living Death* or, *The Unfaithful Wife*. In other words, a real vendetta."

— *HN*

The Unknown

The Unknown. Metro-Goldwyn-Mayer Pictures/M-G-M, 4 June 1927, 6 reels; 5,517 feet [available]

CAST: Lon Chaney (*Alonzo*); Joan Crawford (*Estrellita**); Norman Kerry (*Malabar*); Nick De Ruiz (*Zanzi*); John George (*Cojo*); Frank Lanning (*Costra*); John Sainpolis (*Doctor*); Louise Emmons (*Gypsy Woman*)

CREDITS: *Director* Tod Browning; *Scenario* Waldemar Young; based on a story by Tod Browning; *Titles* Joe Farnham; *Cinematographer* Merritt Gerstad; *Art Direction* Cedric Gibbons and Richard Day; *Film Editors* Harry Reynolds, Errol Taggart; *Wardrobe* Lucia Coulter

Fans of Lon Chaney often mention that *The Unknown* is the perfect film to show to friends who think that silent movies are all Mary Pickford and the Little Tramp; the uninitiated are usually amazed to discover that the Age of Innocence had such a dark and perverse underside. *The Unknown* is perhaps Tod Browning's best silent film as, while many of his movies start to falter about half way through and then sputter on to tepid finales, this one has a steady build-up of mystery, eroticism, pathos, and the grotesque, plus a thoroughly satisfying final reel.

Lon Chaney had played supporting roles (read: thugs) for Tod Browning in *Outside the Law* and *The Wicked Darling*, but actor and director didn't become a real team until 1925's *The Unholy Three*. By then, Chaney had gone from bit player/character actor to leading roles, à la *The Hunchback of Notre Dame* and *The Phantom of the Opera*; he had become "The Man of a Thousand Faces" and a big star. At the same time, Browning was still probably best known as a director of crook melodramas, often starring Priscilla Dean.

---

*The character's name is Nanon in the extant prints of the film, and she is so called in the *Variety* review. Other reviews (*The Los Angeles Times*, *The New York Times*, *The Chicago Tribune*) and publicity for the film refer to her as Estrellita.

The Unholy Three was basically just another Browning crime film, even though it was distinguished by a gang with an unusual modus operandi (courtesy of the Tod Robbins novel) and a gimmick — ventriloquism — that would be miles more effective in the talkie remake. The ape was thrown into the mix for villain-disposal purposes, and Chaney — who spends much of the film disguised as an old lady — must once again love the heroine enough to give her up; this was the reverse of the narrative pivot of many of Browning's Priscilla Dean movies, wherein the good-bad girl/heroine always got her man.

Still, *The Unholy Three* was a hit that convinced M-G-M to produce a series of quickly-made, modestly-budgeted (by that studio's standards) thrillers with Chaney starring and Browning directing. The follow-up, *The Blackbird*, featured Chaney as a Limehouse criminal whose modus operandi sees him operating under two identities: his own, and that of his brother, a crippled preacher at a mission. (That premise might remind horror fans a bit of two later Bela Lugosi films, *Dark Eyes of London* and *Bowery at Midnight*.) Chaney's contortions and false smiles are pretty much the whole show in *The Blackbird*, but even he wasn't able to save the next collaboration, *The Road to Mandalay*, a melodramatic hodgepodge wherein the actor played a one-eyed gangster trying to protect his beautiful daughter.

In a 9 January 1927 interview in *The New York Times*, M-G-M writer and director Paul Bern described how the studio was shying away from buying plays and books that often proved to be unfilmable and was instead looking for original works specifically written for stars like John Gilbert, Ramon Navarro … and Lon Chaney. As one example, Bern mentioned the latest Chaney project, *Alonzo the Armless*, and described Chaney's portrayal: "He [Chaney] knows how to use a typewriter with his toes. He sews and handles his knife, fork and spoon with his feet. It is a typical Chaney role." *Alonzo the Armless* went on to become *The Unknown* (though we cannot recall any instance in the film in which Chaney pecks at a typewriter with his tootsies). Oddly enough, Bern didn't mention anywhere in his interview that the original story came from Tod Browning.

Our synopsis is based on a viewing of the film:

"This is a story they tell in old Madrid…. It's a story they say is true."

Alonzo, an armless knife thrower, is one of the big attractions at a gypsy circus. Alonzo is in love with Estrellita, his partner in the act and the daughter of Zanzi, the circus's brutish owner. The beautiful Estrellita considers Alonzo her friend and confides in him that she finds the touch of any man revolting. Malabar, the circus strong man, is attracted to Estrellita and asks Alonzo for advice. Jealous and knowing what will happen, Alonzo suggests he take the young girl in his arms. Estrellita is, predictably, disgusted by Malabar's advances.

It turns out Alonzo isn't really armless. With the help of his assistant, the hunchback Cojo, Alonzo straps his arms into a kind of strait-jacket underneath his clothes. Alonzo's real problem is not the lack of appendages but an excess of them; he has double thumbs on one hand. Since Alonzo is a criminal such a distinction would make him easily recognizable. Zanzi discovers Alonzo's secret and the knife thrower strangles him. Estrellita witnesses the murder but her view is obstructed and all she can see is the killer's freakish hand. The police investigate but of course Alonzo is above suspicion because of his supposed infirmity.

When the circus is sold to pay off debts and then leaves town,

Alonzo convinces Estrellita to stay behind. He tells Cojo that he simply must have the girl and intends to propose to her. Cojo reminds him that she will then discover that, not only does he have arms, but that he killed her father. Alonzo comes to realize that he is so accustomed to using his feet for everything that he really doesn't needs his arms. He blackmails a doctor into amputating them.

While Alonzo is secretly recuperating, Malabar courts Estrellita once again and she comes to accept his love and his touch. When Alonzo returns, he is shocked to discover this new development and plans revenge. Malabar has a new act in which he holds the reins of two horses who are running on a treadmill while Estrellita whips them. Alonzo realizes that his rival's arms will be torn off if the treadmill gets jammed, so he attempts to make that happen on the show's opening night. The helpless Malabar is saved when Estrellita, seeing what Alonzo is doing, jumps onto the stage. Alonzo pushes her out of the way of the rearing horse and is himself crushed underneath its hooves.

In the interview quoted above, Bern mentions that Alonzo conceals his arms because he has "great hands" that would make reveal his true identity, but Browning — or scenarist Waldemar Young — decided double thumbs might work out better than prosthetic mittens.

Browning told the *Los Angeles Times* (in a piece published in the 5 June 1927 edition) that his characters weren't as farfetched as people thought:

When I am given a script the first thing I do is to fit some person I remember into each character. Sometimes many interesting changes take place. The character Chaney plays — the man masquerading as a sideshow freak to evade the police — really lived once. He was an acrobat rather than an armless wonder — I faked that much — but he stayed in hiding by performing before thousands of people in two years and then the detectives grabbed him in a little country town.

(Browning's account also fits Jimmy Stewart in the 1952 Cecil B. De Mille film, *The Greatest Show on Earth*, wherein the laid-back actor plays a man fleeing a murder rap who hides his identity by performing as a clown.)

Chaney had already played a legless criminal in *The Penalty* so perhaps having him lose his arms this time around was not much of a stretch. At the end of *The Blackbird* the fake cripple becomes the real thing due to an accident; Browning recycled this idea but added the perverse touch of deliberate self mutilation.

Publicity for the film tended to play down the bizarre love triangle in favor of the crook melodrama angle, as is evident in this piece from the 21 June 1927 *Cumberland* [Maryland] *Evening Times:* "It is a strange mystery tale revolving around a circus freak with Chaney as a sinister armless circus freak ruling an underworld from his hiding place among the hundreds in a tented city. The audacity of this is amazing — an apparently harmless sideshow freak controlling the criminal underworld."

For all that, Chaney's "underworld" consisted only of him and one (diminutive) minion, and a scene depicting Alonzo and Cojo looting a safe didn't even make the final cut. As things stand now, the only reference to Alonzo's criminal activity comes when the police investigate Zanzi's death, and a title card refers to the circus leaving a trail of robberies in its wake.

Naturally, the film's main selling point was and has always been Lon Chaney, himself. Chaney fans tend to gnash their teeth when their favorite actor is described as a "horror star" like his own son, Lon Jr. or Karloff and Lugosi; of course, they're correct inasmuch as there was no "horror genre" per se in the Silent Era. Still, many of Chaney's contemporary admirers were no doubt drawn to his films by the macabre aspects of some of his characters and by a simple, straightforward desire to be scared (just like their counterparts in the 1930s). Consider a couple of reviews of *The Unknown*:

> A dramatic if unpleasant theme, colorfully presented, with an undercurrent of sinister, spine-tickling thrills is what the Chaney followers cry for. They won't be disappointed in *The Unknown*; they'll shudder to see their hero, cast as an armless wonder, using his pedal extremities instead of his hands; they'll writhe with horror as he depicts the vicious workings of a tortured and perverted mind and yet their hearts will go out to him as, with the frustration of his astounding plot, he painfully shuffles off this mortal coil [Roberta Nangle, *The Chicago Tribune*, 1 August 1927].

> The unholy two are together again and there is great rejoicing throughout the land. Now they [Chaney and Browning] are joined in evil once more, and there come the welcome rattle and clank of rusty chains and the merry screams of the walking dead, as only these two can evoke them…. In script form [it] must have read like the last word in horror [*Los Angeles Times*, 6 June 1927].

Of course, Chaney's "straight" roles—like *Tell It to the Marines, While the City Sleeps,* and *Thunder*—were also very popular, and some think those are the types of parts Chaney would have gravitated towards in the 1930s had he survived his bout with cancer. And while he was no John Gilbert or Rudolph Valentino, he had his female admirers as well. One of them, a "Miss D," gushed about Lon to "Mae Tinee" in the 16 October 1927 issue of *The Chicago Tribune*: "Isn't Lon Chaney wonderful? I just saw *The Unknown* and I can't get over how perfectly—O—I just can't explain how I feel about him. I just adore him. Don't you, Mae? I stayed to see it three times *and the next* chance I get I'm going to see it again."

A good deal was made of Chaney learning to do so many things with his feet—eat, drink, shave, fire a rifle, and throw knives at his lovely co-star, Joan Crawford. This bit of publicity, printed in the 11 September 1927 number of *The Florence* [Alabama] *Times Daily*, was typical: "Miss Crawford smiled while Chaney hurled the knives. She says she has absolute confidence in him, after his two months of practice for the queer role he plays and she wasn't a bit nervous. Chaney adds that this helped him too, because if she was nervous, he might have been too—and perhaps with disastrous results."

Most critics swallowed whole the studio line that Chaney accomplished these feats with his own limbs, although *Variety*'s "Sid" did comment that sometimes they were "obviously not Chaney's legs." Today we know that Sid's skepticism was justified and that most of the work was done by a real armless man whose legs doubled for Chaney's with the help of some clever props and astute camera placement. Unfortunately, all the praise for the things Chaney didn't do might have distracted critics from what he *did* do; namely, deliver one of his most intense performances. His discovery that he has amputated his arms for nothing and has lost the girl he is infatuated with makes for one of the most wrenching moments in silent cinema, and the whole sequence is certainly one of Tod Browning's finest hours. When, at first, he thinks Estrellita is talking about marrying

him, there's a tight close-up of Chaney, his face smiling, adoring, and full of hope (like Chaplin's at the end of *City Lights*). Then, upon discovering the truth and seeing Estrellita in Malabar's arms, his expression goes from puzzlement to a fixed grin. As the lovers caress, with Malabar's arms holding Estrellita close, Chaney whole body begins to shake with laughter; it's as though the lovers are mocking him and their healthy physical affection becomes a taunt, a vision of hell. They innocently join in his laughter, not understanding what's really going on. Chaney's face seems ready to explode and his convulsive laughter ends with a scream; then, his collapse. One thinks of the climax of *The Blue Angel*, wherein degraded schoolteacher Emil Jannings is obliged to crow like a rooster as part of a tawdry night club act, and his resulting cries seem torn from a damned soul whose suffering is beyond all human endurance. Chaney's pantomime captures the same sense of naked anguish. Interestingly enough,

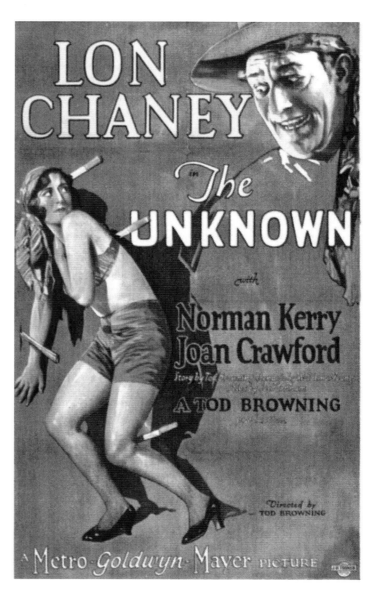

What remains unknown — even to this day — is how Joan Crawford can look so damned good with three knives sticking out of her. Original one-sheet artwork.

Variety thought the film should have ended right at this ironic point, feeling that the closing sequence was something of an anti-climax.

Many critics shook their heads at the film, and "unpleasant" was the word they most frequently used to describe it. The negative comments from the reviewer in *Harrison's Reports* have often been quoted, but that august journal loathed anything with a sadistic theme. "No one can be entertained with the doings of a perverted mind" was the critic's summing up of another 1927 film: *Body and Soul*, wherein crazed physician Lionel Barrymore brands the heroine with a hot iron. Such feelings were also reflected in a terse comment about *The Unknown* from Ward Marsh in the 16 June 1927 edition of *The Cleveland Plain Dealer*: "a wild and frequently repulsive melodrama considerably below the usual Chaney–Tod Browning standard."

Despite the critical carping that has the film seem like a silent gore movie, not a drop of blood is shown on the screen. In fact, Alonzo's plan to have his arms amputated doesn't even get a title card (though there's no doubt what he's up to). The only overtly sadistic scene is at the climax wherein Malabar nearly has his arms torn out by the horses, a variation on a particularly grisly method of medieval execution in which the condemned had all his limbs pulled off by horses yanking in four different directions. Some odd sexual sparks are added to the scene by Joan Crawford gleefully cracking the whip in her skimpy costume; however, Browning and Co. were more likely just trying for irony — her enthusiasm could inadvertently lead to her lover's dismemberment — rather than commenting on female sexuality. The sequence is actually very exciting, with a variety of shots (unusual in a Browning film) and perfect staccato editing.

While some reviewers may have admired Chaney's supposed skill in using his feet in *The Unknown*, they still found the sight of him doing so rather distasteful, and that may be the main reason they were so put off by the film. "Some of his toe feats are rather disgusting" is how Roberta Nangle of *The Chicago Tribune* phrased it in her otherwise favorable review. *Harrison's Reports* (15 June 1927) put the case more bluntly.

> The sight of an armless freak cleverly doing everything with his toes that the average person does with his hands may pass as amusement for a few idle moments when one looks at him in his proper setting in a circus. But when one is compelled to watch a freak doing tricks with his feet for several reels of film, it becomes not only revolting but monotonous. And when the freak is shown as an absolute demon of viciousness, without a redeeming quality, one wonders by what strange reasoning the men responsible for the production were led to believe that the American people would accept him as a fit subject for the screen.

No doubt critical revulsion would have been increased had it been known that a real armless man was doing the work.

Still, the reviewer in the *Los Angeles Times* had a different perspective on the film's shortcomings: "Certainly it is a tale to be told around a crackling hearth fire in an old house with the shutters banging an obbligato and the wind howling a dolorous refrain but it is told on the screen at Loew's State, and something is lost from it. Probably it is all too real, too concrete; there is horror in the pictures, but not in the atmosphere."

One thing that prevents *The Unknown* from being a great

film — instead of merely a very good one — is the cinematography; the famous M-G-M "gloss" is already present, and it works *against* the gloomy mood of the story. Cameraman Merritt Gerstad shoots some scenes with gauze over the lens to give them a soft look, and while that would be fine for a Garbo/Gilbert romance, it seems out of place here. He does far better in the scene wherein Alonzo and Cojo visit the doctor: the latter is first shown standing alone in a huge operating room shot and lit like some unholy, cavernous cathedral; right after that, there's a cut to Alonzo and Cojo approaching through a shadowy corridor on their grisly errand. More such Expressionist touches would have complemented the macabre tale, and it's not that Gerstad was incapable of these; he worked with Tod Browning a number of times, most notably in *London after Midnight* and *Freaks*.

Whatever reviewers thought of the film, no one remarked on its sexual undertones. (The Freudian implications have taken center stage for some commentators nowadays.) Inasmuch as Browning probably never finished high school — and most likely did not have a copy of *The Interpretation of Dreams* tucked away in his coffin when he was playing "The Living Corpse" in sideshows — his having provided such touches intentionally is a matter for discussion. Still, Waldemar Young — the unsung partner in the Chaney/Browning collaborations — was a graduate of Stanford University and could well have perused Herr Doktor Freud's writings. We don't know, of course, how much of the finished film came from him and how much from Browning, nor do we have Browning's original story to compare with what ended up on the screen.

In any case, Estrellita's complaint that men have tried to grope her all her life obviously reflects a fear of physical intimacy. When Malabar flexes his muscle for her, Estrellita reacts as though he had exposed himself. Frigidity is sometimes attributed to incest, so, since Estrellita's mother is not in the picture and her father — whom she fears — is a brute, is some such suggestion being made? Again, at one point Zanzi viciously tears from her body the shawl Alonzo has given her. This could be a sexual suggestion or may be no more than a demonstration of Zanzi's bullying nature.

(Despite all this possible suggestiveness, the only thing that invoked the ire of the New York State censor was a bit where the gypsy Costra apparently makes a pass as Estrellita, and she tells him, "Keep your pawing hands off me." The censor didn't object to *that* but, rather, to Costra's response, which the censor decried as "an indecent action of lips." The entire scene is actually missing from current copies of the film. In fact, Frank Lannon as Costra is barely in the film at all and is seen only when telling Zanzi that Estrellita is with Alonzo again.)

In 1962's *Walk on the Wild Side*, whorehouse madam Barbara Stanwyck complains about the awful lusts of men to her husband, a cripple who pulls himself around on a cart (something you'd expect in a Chaney film), and who assures her that her company is enough for him. Miss Stanwyck is meant to be a lesbian, though, and there's no way anything like that was going to pass muster in Hollywood's Silent Era. In place of such a revelation, *The Unknown* offers the then-usual understanding that even the most complex psychological issue can be settled if one can only find the right mate, and Estrellita does so, in the person of the patient and gentle strong man. Some would say that Alonzo's lack of arms represents castration and thus his being acceptable to a woman who fears sex; however, Estrellita's relationship with Alonzo is not much different from the usual Chaney situation: he loves a young girl who sees him as a friend and/or a mentor, but not as a romantic partner.

The continuity in *The Unknown* is occasionally ragged. Early on, Estrellita is alone in her wagon, raving about men and how God should take their hands away, and then — quite abruptly — we see Alonzo reacting and realize that we are suddenly and inexplicably in *his* cabin. Later, when Alonzo leaves to have his arms amputated, it's odd that there's no farewell scene with Estrellita or even a title card stating what he would have told her to explain his absence. Malabar's return to the scene would make a little more sense were it to occur after Alonzo leaves, but instead he turns up *before* the knife-thrower has departed. Intriguing, too, is the fact that Cojo vanishes from the film entirely after Alonzo reappears after his operation.

Some of these problems can perhaps be explained away as resulting from the film's having been cut from seven to six reels, the current length of extant copies. The picture was copyrighted at seven reels and was submitted to the New York State censor at seven reels, but — according to the trades— appears to have played only in a six-reel version. The fact that the *Los Angeles Times* critic mentioned Polly Moran's being in the supporting cast (she played Alonzo's landlady and has completely disappeared from extant prints of the film) may indicate that the movie had premiered at seven reels, or it may have merely been an error.

Publicity for the film made much of the circus scenes and claimed that a thousand extras watched a full performance featuring tight rope walkers, clowns and bareback riders. The *Times'* critic writes that the picture opens "with a series of dissolves showing the various acts of the circus in the manner of *Variety*," but as it stands now, we see very little of the circus footage, so much of that too must have ended up on the cutting-room floor. Nevertheless, *Variety*, noting that the film clocked in at under an hour, rightly observed that the short running time was an asset: "Browning has chopped to the bone in the cutting room. It's logical to suppose that there was ample footage 'shot' on this yarn. And that's smart too because it crams the picture with action and interest."

As for Cojo's surprising disappearance from the film, in his commentary on the DVD of *The Unknown*, Chaney scholar Michael Blake states that one draft of the script had Chaney murder the doctor who had amputated his arms and then poison Cojo, thus eliminating the only two men who knew he did indeed once have arms. It's not clear whether this sequence was actually ever shot, but Cojo's last appearance in the film sees him drinking a glass of wine offered him by Alonzo. Because killing his loyal little friend would have destroyed all audience sympathy for Alonzo, the idea of constructing of the scene to suggest this was wisely dropped.

Cojo was played by John George, and it was the diminutive actor's most substantial role for which he justly received his share of good notices. Even though Cojo wears a devil costume

as part of Alonzo's act, he really isn't playing the tempter but, rather, the voice of reason, always cautioning Alonzo and warning him to be sensible about Estrellita. George, the Dwight Frye of the Silent Era, was often identified with the films of Rex Ingram. Ingram biographer Liam O' Leary wrote that George's real name was Tufei Fatella and that he was a Syrian who illegally immigrated to the States in 1911 to join his mother and sisters in Nashville. He ended up in Hollywood where Ingram, who had an odd obsession with dwarves and the deformed that rivaled Tod Browning's, frequently used him in films and may have considered him a kind of good luck charm (See *Reward of the Faithless*). When Ingram set up his film headquarters in France, he insisted on George joining him there just to do a very brief part in *Mare Nostrum*, most of which was edited out. George might have stayed on — and probably would have played the sorcerer's assistant in Ingram's *The Magician* — but the little man had a big gambling problem and Ingram sent him back to the U.S.

Back in Hollywood, George got into trouble of a different sort: he reputedly got fresh with a married woman in — of all places— a movie theater. When the lady's husband confronted him, George knocked him down and took off, running right into the arms of a passing policeman. According to an article in the 23 June 1926 edition of the *Los Angeles Times*, George was found guilty, but sentencing was postponed until two character witnesses— G.H. Robinson (the cameraman?) and G. Barsow (an extra)—could testify on his behalf. We don't know the outcome, but it couldn't have been too dire as George was subsequently kept quite a busy on a number of films, including Browning's *The Road to Mandalay*. George went on to a long career as an extra and is lurking in the background in a score of horror classics, including *Dracula*, *Island of Lost Souls* and *The Black Cat*.

Joan Crawford looks stunning as Estrellita, and her lovely figure played a prominent part in ads and publicity for *The Unknown*. It's surely her best performance in the Silent Era and one which seems a predecessor of all the neurotic types Crawford played in the 1940s and 1950s. (One recalls the actress's real life phobias; while she certainly had no problems with men's arms, bathrooms and wire hangers were another story.) Crawford was one of the grand stars of Hollywood's Golden Age and survived any number of professional ups and downs, including being labeled "box office poison" at one point. Her performance opposite rival Bette Davis in 1962's *Whatever Happened to Baby Jane* revived her film career late in life and led to the considerably less memorable genre credits of *Strait-Jacket*, *Berserk* and *Trog*.

The New York Times thought Norman Kerry was excellent as Malabar, but the *Los Angeles Times* critic opined that he was miscast. In any case, according to the publicity boys Kerry suffered for his art because he had to appear stripped to the waist in some scenes and thus developed a bad case of "indoor-sunburn" because of the hot studio lights. More on the man who needed suntan lotion can be found in the entry on *The Hunchback of Notre Dame*.

Waldemar Young originally was a newspaper reporter in his native Salt Lake City (he was the grandson of Mormon pioneer, Brigham Young, and the brother of famous sculptor, Mahonri

Young). In 1903, he moved to San Francisco and worked on several different newspapers there, first as a sports writer and then a drama critic. A half-dozen years later, he was living in New York City, working in publicity for Charles Fogarty and Associates, and on his way to becoming the press agent for dancer Gertrude Hoffman. Having written amateur theatricals since his days at Stanford University, in 1914 he co-authored a skit entitled *When Caesar Ran a Paper* and then acted in it on a vaudeville tour; the play was later adapted as a short film starring Raymond Hatton. In 1917 he signed with Universal as a scenarist and there had his first collaboration with Tod Browning; the men worked together on several vehicles for actress Mary MacLaren.

In an interview published in the 18 October 1923 *Sioux City [Iowa] Sunday Journal*, Young defended screen writing against those who dismissed it as easy work:

> I wonder if most folks realize that about the same number of words are required for a scenario as are included in the average novel. By that I mean for both the detailed synopsis and the continuity.... You first do the synopsis to get the story properly arranged from a dramatic standpoint. And then you break the story into scenes for the camera. This means a continuity.... About 75,000 words are pounded out before the job is complete.

Two films Young worked on in those early days are of some interest here. *The Little White Savage* (1919) is about a reporter trying to find the back story on a carnival wild-woman. Two of the carnies tell him she was found on an island inhabited by descendants of Sir Walter Raleigh's lost colony. When she was brought back to the States to be exhibited at a sideshow, she escaped and fell in love with a minister, thus scandalizing the community with her uninhibited ways; in the end, we learn the story isn't true. Young also did the scenario for *If You Believe It, It's So* (1922), a variation on *The Miracle Man* featuring two of that film's stars, Thomas Meighan and Joseph Dowling. Young later did the script for the sound remake of *The Miracle Man*.

While Browning stayed at Universal, Young freelanced and wrote a number of big pictures, including a couple for Mary Pickford. Both Browning and Young ended up at M-G-M at about the same time and collaborated on nine movies, seven of them starring Lon Chaney. Young and Browning worked closely together; a reporter for the *Los Angeles Times* observed the two often thrashing out their ideas in a garden outside one of the M-G-M lots, Young pacing back and forth, and Browning seated on a fire hydrant.

Young thrived in the Sound Era and wrote such "A" films as *The Sign of the Cross, Test Pilot, Lives of a Bengal Lancer,* and *Desire.* In 1933, a book of his poetry—much of having it to do with San Francisco—was published as *The Lace of 1000 Trees and Other Lyrics.* Young's most famous genre credit from the 1930s is, of course, *Island of Lost Souls.* The much-traveled screenwriter died of pneumonia in 1938 and was buried in Salt Lake City.

— *HN*

The Unknown Purple

The Unknown Purple. Carlos Productions/Truart Film Corp., September 1923, 7 reels/6980 feet [LOST]

CAST: Henry B. Walthall (*Peter Marchmont/Victor Cromport*); Alice Lake (*Jewel Marchmont*); Stuart Holmes (*James Dawson*); Helen Ferguson (*Ruth Marsh*); Frankie Lee (*Bobbie*); Ethel Grey Terry (*Mrs. Freddie Goodlittle*); James Morrison (*Leslie Bradbury*); Johnny Arthur (*Freddie Goodlittle*); Richard Wayne (*George Allison*); Brinsley Shaw (*Bill Hawkins*); Mike Donlin (*Burton*)

CREDITS: *Director* Roland West; *Scenario* Roland West, Paul Schofield; based on the eponymous play by Roland West and Carlyle Moore (New York, 14 September 1918); *Titles* Alfred A. Cohn; *Cinematographer* Oliver Marsh; *Settings* H. A. Jackson

The idea that science could make a man invisible triggered the imagination of more than one early filmmaker, and it's very likely the first such instance in which invisibility was actually central to the plot (and tossed in not merely to show off some camera trickery) came from Biograph back in '08. *The Invisible Fluid,* which featured a young actor by the name of D.W. Griffith, still survives in the Library of Congress paper-print collection and is, all things considered, a cute little film. But *Fluid*—as almost all "science fiction" back then—was played for nothing but laughs. The invisibility theme got a more serious treatment and was also developed for the first time in the United States in full-feature form with *The Unknown Purple* (1923).

When it comes to the origin of *The Unknown Purple,* there's no lack of contemporary sources on the subject. All accounts agree that the storyline was authored by Roland West (see *The Monster,* 1925) and staged on Broadway before being filmed; however, there the agreement ends. According to the *Syracuse [New York] Herald* (31 August 1919), it all started from a piece of *magazine* fiction:

> In the first place, Mr. West wrote the story for a magazine. When it appeared in print it consisted of about 2,000 words, and according to the editor of the magazine it had the same number of thrills. At this time West was devoting his stage efforts to dramatic vaudeville acts. Just to keep his hand in at stage work, he dramatized the short story, with the result that the vaudeville stage enjoyed the thrills of "The Unknown Purple."

The *Los Angeles Times* (24 November 1923) corroborates parts of this story but has things starting off with the vaudeville performance: "The life history of 'The Unknown Purple' is interesting. In its infancy it was a vaudeville sketch, a one-act playlet, and a promising child." On the other hand, *The New York Times* (22 September 1918) declared that the tale began as, of all things, a motion picture scenario*: "The central idea of 'The Unknown Purple' had been West's for some half a dozen years before he wrote and produced the play. In its original form it was a motion-picture scenario called 'The Vanishing Man,' and it was when a movie concern offered $10,000 for it that the author decided that perhaps it was too valuable to sell."

According to the *Times*, West then solicited assistance from several men in order to help develop his concept into the play. He first approached playwright Carlyle Moore, who was cool

---

*The Washington Post (23 June 1918), in a much less detailed report, concurred that West rejected the $10,000 for "The Unknown Purple" in movie scenario form. At least somebody agreed with someone!

to the proposal. A couple of years later, West commissioned a draft from a certain Jasper Ewing Brady, but then turned it down as not being up to par; subsequently, Edward Clark — of *De Luxe Annie* fame — went on record as declining to collaborate on the project. It was only then that West finally convinced Moore (who had balked at the invisibility element!) to change his mind and pitch in.

The chain of events gets a little clearer from this point on, with West bankrolling the play's production to the tune of $50,000 of his own money. (Among those turning down the chance to buy in early was heavyweight theater producer, A. H. Woods, whose objection to purchasing a bargain-priced 60 percent interest was that the story featured an imprisoned man [Peter Marchmont] returning to his wife after a number of years only to find that she'd betrayed and swindled him with the aid of another man. Woods thought the notion of Marchmont being unrecognizable by his own wife was too unbelievable; *invisibility*, on the other hand, didn't seem to give him much pause.)

Despite any perceived flaws, the play picked up out-of-town steam during the summer of 1918 in Long Branch (New Jersey), Atlantic City and Washington, D.C. Potential investors now came a-knockin' in anticipation of the September opening at the Lyric Theater on Broadway, but West began to dole out pieces of his pie cannily, and it was actress Norma Talmadge that managed to gobble up the biggest slice. West had just left the Norma Talmadge Film Studios — where he had directed her in the film version of the aforementioned *De Luxe Annie* (1918, see entry) — and Norma leveraged their relationship to obtain 5 percent at $5000. Smaller stakes were also granted to Talmadge's better half, Joseph M. Schenck, and to two office assistants.

First among the cast members of the Broadway production of *The Unknown Purple* was leading man Richard Bennett (sire of performers Barbara, Constance and Joan), whose performance *The Washington Post* (25 June 1918) found to be "a remarkably well-balanced and well conceived impersonation of a picturesque role." Other notables — especially to the classic genre crowd — were Edward Van Sloan and Frank McCormack, who would appear on The Great White Way as Abraham Van Helsing in *Dracula* (1927–28) and "Red" Mackenzie in Crane Wilbur's *The Monster* (1922), respectively. Critic George Jean Nathan referred to the Lyric's production of *The Unknown Purple* as "the most ingenious yokel show, the trick melodrama height," but his words were meant more affectionately than caustically; Nathan thrice joined the audience during the play's eight-month run.

After *The Unknown Purple* closed on Broadway, it took to the road with George Probert — a man more known for playing heavies — taking over the lead. Performances were given in Philadelphia, Chicago, Cleveland, Hartford, Syracuse and Boston, and the *Boston Daily Globe* seemed prophetic when, in the course of its 23 December 1919 review of the Beantown production, referred to "tricks of modern photoplays" and noted the use of motion picture–like cut-backs. The paper was enthusiastic, calling the show "capital entertainment." And others agreed. In Bridgeport, Connecticut, for example, traditional

liturgy took a backseat to theatrical thrills when the Rev. Henry Rose and his brother captivated their congregations via an *Unknown Purple* slide show, replete with the pastor's personal commentary.

Research has failed to uncover a written copy of *The Vanishing Man*, Jasper Ewing Brady's rejected draft, Reverend Rose's observations, or any publication of *The Unknown Purple* in full form. An abbreviated version of the play — found in *Hearst's Magazine* (April 1919) — does little but raise the same old question: could this have possibly been confused with the magazine article that supposedly served as the genesis of *The Unknown Purple*? Might it have been an account of the alleged vaudeville version? Or was it merely another of the "play-condensations" that were so popular back in that day? What *can* be gleaned from the Hearst artifact is that *The Unknown Purple* was seemingly full of vintage melodramatic dialogue. This from the mouth of the haunted James Dawson, co-conspirator in ruining the unseeable protagonist:

> It follows me! It isn't this house alone, but in my office, the street; anywhere. At times I have the uncanniest feeling that there is someone behind me. I can feel their presence, almost hear their breathing, yet when I turn around there is no one. In my room at

Lorraine Frost, who played Jewel Marchmont in *The Unknown Purple*, the play.

night I have heard footsteps approach my bed. I could swear there was someone there. I've struggled to see something; anything; but if I did, I know I should go mad.

In any event, a half-decade and another media variation later, *Variety*'s "Skig" (26 March 1924) seemed pleased about the celluloid rendition of *The Unknown Purple*: "Roland West has taken his stage play, which he wrote in conjunction with Carlyle Moore, and given it able screen presentation. It is an exceptionally well-made picture — among the best of its type." Our detailed synopsis comes courtesy of the Library of Congress, guardian of the movie's original copyright registration:

Buried in the grey walls of a penitentiary were two men who never had seen each other but who nightly argued about … women! Bill Hawkins believed there was only one kind … rotten — so he hated them all! The other prisoner argued that there were good women upon the earth and one of them was his wife, who was waiting for him with their little son. Hawkins laughed and told him a story of a wife who had betrayed her husband.

Hawkins told of an experience in a little one-horse burg called Higsby, where years before he had been hired by the lover of a trusted wife to steal a valuable formula from the husband. The husband, an inventor, was at the time perfecting a purple light which would make the human body invisible.

Bill Hawkins, after stealing the formula, was obliged to hide in the house to escape discovery and saw the unfolding of the drama which sent the husband to prison because he took the blame for the stealing of money from his employer because he thought his wife was guilty of having taken the money to send their child to the country. In reality the lover had stolen the money and urged her to place the blame on the husband so they would be rid of him. Even Bill Hawkins admitted he was fooled by the wife's tearful story to her husband and left the formula which he had stolen because the husband said it would keep him out of prison.

When Bill Hawkins finished the story he passed a newspaper to the other prisoner in which was a picture of the wife and the lover, now Mr. and Mrs. James Dawson, wealthy from the returns on the inventor's dye formula.

The prisoner looked at the paper and then asked Bill Hawkins what he would do if the woman was his wife. Bill told him he would get her alone in some dark room and choke her and he would pull the man down step by step … down … down.

Then the prisoner said "That is just what I am going to do…. I am Peter Marchmont … the husband!"

Mrs. James Dawson was entertaining at her Long Island home. Her husband was getting into financial difficulties through the mysterious thefts of formulas and other valuables from his office. Dawson was anxious to get in touch with Mr. Cromport, a mysterious financial and diplomatic power from abroad.

Cromport is finally persuaded to come to the dinner party at the Dawsons. In Cromport no one would recognize the former Peter Marchmont, jailbird, inventor and possessor of the mysterious purple ray. At the Dawson house Cromport meets his little son, now grown up, and Ruth Marsh, Mrs. Dawson's sister, who has always loved Peter Marchmont. A mysterious servant in the house is Hawkins, placed there through the scheming of Cromport and acting as his colleague. Before the dinner a mysterious message is received from the Unknown Purple that at the stroke of midnight Mrs. Dawson's diamond necklace will be stolen. William J. Allison, a detective of international fame, with his assistants is there to capture the Unknown Purple, who has been responsible for the thefts at the Dawson office.

At the stroke of midnight a purple haze appears about those seated at dinner, the curtains are thrown back by an unseen hand — a purple ray of light travels about the room and behind Mrs. Dawson a hand issued from the purple ray and snatches the diamond necklace from about her neck.

A month passes — Dawson, broken and desperate — a victim of the Unknown Purple, is preparing to steal the securities entrusted to him by one of his friends interested in his company. He is going to leave Mrs. Dawson. But Cromport has intrigued his former wife — the now Mrs. Dawson — and he learns from her what her husband plans. And so he schemes with her — she is fascinated by this apparent strange foreigner — she agrees to give Dawson the poison which Cromport gives her and also learns where the securities are that her husband plans to steal, forcing her to agree to take them herself. She and Cromport are to steal away that night.

The fatal hour arrives and then Dawson and his wife learn who Cromport really is. Allison is on hand to catch the Unknown Purple having learned that he will be at the Dawson's that night. Mrs. Dawson has given her husband the poison and before she can steal the securities from the safe they have already been taken by the Unknown Purple — who returns to them to their rightful owner.

Cromport — Peter Marchmont — takes his vengeance on the two — tells them that it was not poison he took but only a harmless sleeping powder. Then Cromport leaves — made invisible by his purple ray — laughing at Allison's effort to catch him. With Peter Marchmont go his little son and Ruth, with whom he finds happiness in a foreign land, away from the memories of a former shattered life.

James and Jewel Dawson are left alone — broken, ruined — together, each hating the other. Peter Marchmont had meted out a greater punishment in this, than he could by separating them — in death, or otherwise.

Quinn Martin in the *Oakland Tribune* (1 April 1924) concurred with the above-cited *Variety* review, concluding, "It is fair to report the picture will amuse and entertain you." Film reviewer Aileen St. John–Brenon fell in line with, "The picture has been excellently produced as well as ably cast." *Harrison's Reports* (1 December 1923) felt everything was "first-rate": "The production end of it is high class, direction, acting, settings, photography — all being of a high order. The action holds one in keen suspense." He concluded: "Because of the fact that it is different, it should prove refreshing to almost every picture-goer."

That uniqueness — as well as the unusual title — might have led to some of those picture-goers to avoid coughing up the coin at the box office. While the *Moving Picture World* (15 September 1923) reported that *The Unknown Purple* was received well at the California Theater (in Venice, California), a quick survey of letters sent in to *The Reel Journal* and *MPW* by exhibitors generally reveals that *The Unknown Purple* (a) was considered a worthwhile picture and (b) not enough people in the nation's smaller venues realized that fact. As one theater operator from Braddock, Pennsylvania (who described his burg as a "mill-class city of 20,000") stated in the 2 August 1924 *MPW*: "Star cast. Good Picture but no business. Well liked by those the few people who saw it."

Harriette Underhill, writing for *The New York Herald Tribune* (24 March 1924), admitted being thrilled by *The Unknown Purple* on stage but being disappointed with its originality on film: "On the screen one has been seeing these things for years…. When the surface was first scratched in the new art it was to produce pictures where furniture moved around by itself and tables were laid out for supper without the aid of human hands."

Still, Underhill conceded: "It may be, however, that those who did not see the play will be well pleased with the picture." "Mae Tinee" in the *Chicago Daily Tribune* (23 January 1924) was also more qualified in granting her approval: "Despite the photography, which is at times poor, it registers as a fairly exciting program film.... The so-called 'comedy touches' failed to move me to laughter. The costumes, sets, etc. are pretty good."

As for those photography problems hinted at by Ms. Tinee, once again clues come from exhibitor feedback mailed in to the *Moving Picture World*. "Some scenes very dark," reported one theater manager from Illinois; "the color hurts your eyes," said another from South Dakota. This explanation on the matter is from *The New York Times* (24 March 1924): "The sequences in which the cone of purple light is shown are much more effective than those where the whole screen is tinted purple." *The Times* also didn't think much of the humor element laying blame at the "rather amateurish performance" of comedian Johnny Arthur (see *The Monster*, 1925).

This is not to say *The Times* totally knocked the film, either: "This picture furnishes attractive and sometimes thrilling entertainment." As for the picture's star, the Grey Lady opined, "Mr. Walthall, one of the screens veterans, is thoroughly at home as M. Cromport." More on Henry B. Walthall (who also played Peter Marchmont) is found in our essay on *The Avenging Conscience* (1914). Readers interested in biographical sketches of Alice Lake (Jewel Marchmont) and Stuart Holmes (James Dawson) need look no farther than our piece on *Body and Soul* (1920). — *SJ*

Unknown Treasures

Unknown Treasures. Sterling Pictures/Sterling Pictures Distributing Corp. of America, 1 September 1926, 6 reels/5643 feet — incomplete/unviewable footage at the Library of Congress

CAST: Gladys Hulette (*Mary Hamilton*); Robert Agnew (*Bob Ramsey*); John Miljan (*Ralph Cheney*); Bertram Marburgh (*Cyrus Hamilton*); Jed Prouty (*Remus*); Gustav von Seyffertitz (*Simmons*).

CREDITS: *Director* Archie Mayo; *Adaptation and Continuity* Charles A. Logue; based on the story "The House behind the Hedge" by Mary Spain Vigus (publication undetermined); *Cinematographer* Harry Davis

Bob Ramsey is desperately in love with Mary Hamilton, niece of the banker, Cyrus Hamilton, but will not propose to her because she is rich and he is poor. He has spent nearly everything he had searching for the missing securities belonging to his uncle who had been mysteriously killed some years before. He has made a living by running a public garage with the assistance of Remus, a devoted colored man.

The story opens with the murder of a man who had driven past the deserted house in which Bob's uncle had lives. The mysterious murder heightens the evil reputation which had become attached to the lonely dwelling.

Bob receives a letter from his lawyers stating that their search for the missing securities had been in vain. They advise him to make a thorough search of the walls and floors of the house, now tumbling into ruins. Bob determines to go and takes Remus with him.

Ralph Cheney, a cousin of Bob's, who is also in love with Mary, reads the lawyer's letter over Bob's shoulder when he shows it to Mary, and sets out to find the hidden treasure. Mary does not believe in the existence of the certificates, or at any rate, that they will ever be found, and advises Bob not to spend the rest of his

money in the search. He is determined, however, and Mary conspires with her uncle to drive to the deserted house ahead of Bob and "plant" a lot of securities there. She thinks that when he has once found these securities he will propose to her in the belief that he is bringing money to their marriage and not accepting money from her.

Mary and her uncle reach the house and hide a package of securities behind some loose bricks in the fireplace chimney, but are surprised by the arrival of Bob and Remus before they can escape. They hide in the house.

Bob finds evidence that someone else has been hunting for the treasure, and the Negro is paralyzed with fear when the door is heard to close or seen to open. His rabbit's foot is worked overtime. A crouching figure is seen occasionally slinking along the passages in the building.

Cheney covers himself with a sheet to frighten Remus, while he is left alone in the building while Bob goes for a crowbar. He gets the key to the door when Bob sends it up to a string to Remus, in hopes of making a getaway at an opportune moment. Bob, finding the door locked on his return, smashes it in at a cry of fear from Remus, who declares that he has seen a ghost.

Bob discovers Cheney, Mary and her uncle when Cheney, endeavoring to hide from him, takes refuge in the closet which conceals Mary and Hamilton. Her cry brings Bob to the rescue. He tears the sheet from Cheney's face and locks him up in the closet. Bob accepts Mary's explanation that she and her uncle followed him to the deserted house to make certain that nothing untoward happened to him. They all retire to various rooms to try to get some sleep.

Cheney breaks out of the closet and discovers the securities in the chimney, but just as he reaches for them he is attacked from behind by a gigantic ape and strangled to death. Bob, aroused by his cries, finds him still clutching one of the lost securities in his lifeless fingers. He follows the crouching, shadowy figure of the ape and sees it disappear through a hole in the floor. He looks down to find that Simmons, the man who had had charge of the house and to whom he had gone to get the key, is counting over a big pile of securities. He jumps down and confronts Simmons, with pointed revolver. He is not aware of the ape, creeping up behind him. Simmons commands the brute to kill Bob, but it revolts against Simmons, attacks and kills him. Before dying, Simmons confesses that he had murdered Bob's uncle for the securities. Mary has "discovered" the bonds she had hidden and now offers them to Bob. He gives them to her for spending money; he has enough for both.

That synopsis, taken from the film's press-book, contains so many typical 1920s old, dark house elements — deserted mansions, lawyers and securities, the hero's rival for the heroine's affections, apes, devoted Negroes (this one named *Remus*, yet!), last-reel turnabouts, and the inevitable fade to the intertwined juveniles — that *Unknown Treasures* might have served as a blueprint for any cinematic architect looking to darken an old house on his own. We'll be honest: the story is *so* typical that, had the project not included heavy-hitter Gustav von Seyffertitz as the slouch-hatted gorilla-meister, we wouldn't have dismissed it without much more than a weary sigh. (What is it with those silent-movies apes and their formulaic, last-reel treachery, anyhow?) Hell, even *with* the presence of old Gus, we don't feel we have to do the sort of archeological dig needed in order to find an undespoiled tomb.

This most familiar of tales was adapted from "The House behind the Hedge," an unpublished work by Mary Spain Vigus, a Southern belle whose poesy, essays and stories for the most part fell into the cracks left when the 20th century strode past the nineteenth. "Hedge" was adapted to the screen by Charles Logue, a fairly prolific adaptor whose talents seem to lay in extra-genre, alliterative piffle (like *Even as Eve* [1920], *Devil's Dice* [1926], and the film that must have inspired Al Franken to aspire politically, 1927's *Cheating Cheaters*). Logue's only other genre title (excluding the 1920 Houdini serial, *The Master Mystery*) was 1919's *A Scream in the Night*, and our entry on that epic offers more detail on the Beantown scribe.

Hero Bob Ramsey was essayed by Robert Agnew, a Kentuckian who basically shot his cinematic wad as the male lead (or the male lead's best friend) in such other alliterative fare as 1923's *The Marriage Maker*, 1924's *Broken Barriers*, and 1926's *Dancing Days*. The crème of Agnew's cinematic crème coincided with the Roaring Twenties, and he was out of the industry before the mid–1930s. Agnew's squeeze herein was played by Gladys Hulette; like her leading man, she showed her face in dozens of so-so features during the Silent Era and was out of the picture(s) by 1934. Miss Hulette's "big" genre title was 1925's *The Mystic* (see entry), a Tod Browning thriller in which—despite her being the plot-pivot—she didn't make much of an impression; her "other" genre title was 1923's *Whispering Palms* (see appendix), an independent thriller that didn't make any kind of impression, either. Appearing in blackface as Remus, the "devoted colored man," was Caucasian, Jed Prouty, whose greatest claim to fame would be his capacity to stutter disarmingly for the sound camera.

The human villain was, of course, Gustav von Seyffertitz, the gaunt old goblin whose angular kisser had been giving youthful moviegoers nightmares since 1917 (and *The Devil Stone*, see entry). Born in Bavaria the month before George McClellan moved too slowly to prevent Harper's Ferry from falling into Stonewall Jackson's hands, the middle-aged thesp came to America in the late 1910s, and his distinctive face was soon up there onscreen, even if his name in the cast scrawl occasionally read "G. Butler Clonbough." It was as G. Butler Clonbough, in fact, that he added his formidable presence to 1919's *The Dark Star* (see essay), and there's more on him—in any either and any of his aliases—in our coverage of *The Wizard* and the 1926 version of *The Bells*. John Miljan's name was never anything other than John Miljan, but the prolific character man from Lead City, South Dakota, was himself anything—and everything—in the course of his nearly-40-year-long career. (Given the actor's rather severe demeanor, though, it's unlikely he was ever the romantic lead but—inasmuch as we noted in the aforementioned essay on *The Devil Stone* that even Tully Marshall ended up with lookers like Geraldine Farrar and Gloria Swanson on occasion—we cannot write with absolute certitude that never once, over the course of some 200-odd pictures, did Mr. Miljan get lucky.) Other than *Unknown Treasures*, his silent-genre credentials are sparse: he appeared briefly—and without screen credit—as Valentin in Lon Chaney's *The Phantom of the Opera*. Once sound slithered into the picture, though, his creepy credits gradually grew and he could be seen in 1928's *The Terror*, 1929's *Stark Mad* (see the appendix for notes on the silent versions of these talkie thrillers) and *The Unholy Night*, 1930's *The Unholy Three*, and a host of other offbeat, if not unholy, offerings throughout the ensuing decade and a half.

Try as we might, we can't pin the crouching, slinking gorilla on Charles Gemora or Bull Montana.

Director Archie Mayo came to be known as a "pushy New Yawka" for the zeal (and single-mindedness) he displayed while at the helm of many of his pictures. In films since the mid–1910s, Mayo had put his time in onstage before heading west to break into the industry by directing a couple of dozen unremarkable two-reel comedies. *Unknown Treasures* was one of his first features, and neither it nor any of the others were in any way remarkable, either. Mayo first came on the genre fan's radar with the 1931 *Svengali*, and he left the director's chair behind following the release of *Angel on My Shoulder*, the 1946 diabolic fantasy starring Paul Muni and Claude Rains; nonetheless, his most memorable feature may have been the decidedly mainstream *The Petrified Forest* (1936). One of Warners' house directors during the 1930s, Mayo freelanced thereafter, and opinion on the Manhattan-born technician has since run the gamut from faint praise as a "competent craftsman" to outright dismissal as "a fat slob."

At present, we have only vintage reviews and commentaries to consider in order to form our opinion of *Unknown Treasures*; although five (of six) reels are archived at the Library of Congress collection, only the first reel is in any condition to be viewed, and following is our recapitulation of same:

> The opening title card informs us that "the haunted house had been hastily deserted after it's owner's gruesome murder—still an unsolved mystery." We then see an ape loping across the front porch of the old house. Another title relates that people from the nearby town give the house a wide berth. An "agent" (presumably some sort of salesman, not a talent scout), who is a stranger to the region, is passing through in his carriage when he hears some weird noises coming from the house and pauses to listen. There's a close-up of the ape peering at him through the bushes and then the creature jumps into the carriage. As man and beast struggle, the startled horses move on (rather casually).
>
> The scene then shifts to the general store of the village. The owner is played by Gustav von Seyffertitz, surely the most unlikely purveyor of beans and molasses one is apt to encounter. A title card introduces him: "Elijah Simmons was named after a man in the Bible—but that was no protection for his customers." We then see him casually cheating a lady by putting his thumb on the scales. The customers and idlers at the store are startled by the arrival of the agent's carriage, bearing the body of its driver. There's a grisly close-up of the agent's blood-streaked face. Simmons tells an onlooker to get the sheriff and speculates that this is yet another murder committed near the old Ramsey place. Then there is a tight close-up of Simmons looking particularly sinister (one eye even droops in a kind of macabre wink). Is it possible that he knows something about these strange events?
>
> We are then introduced to Bob Ramsey, nephew of the late owner of the old house. Bob runs a gas station. (A poster for White Owl Cigars is prominently featured indicating that product placement in the movies is not a recent phenomenon.) Bob's helper, Remus, is a typical Silent-Era black character; he is more interested in shooting craps than doing his job, speaks in a dialect rarely heard outside the movies, and provides excruciatingly unfunny comic relief. Mary Hamilton drives up, accompanied by friend Ralph Cheney (played by John Miljan, with his usual smarmy sneer). Mary is sweet on Bob and a title card tells us that she can't get near him "without developing engine and heart trouble." She stops the car—in front of a Christian Science reading room—and then pretends she can't get it started. Bob comes to check it out and gets grease on Ralph's coat. Ralph is indignant,

but Mary chides him and goes for a walk with Bob. Bob tells her that he's heard from his uncle's lawyer who has advised him that he should search the old house for some missing bonds. Meanwhile, Remus tries to clean Ralph's coat and deliberately makes it worse. When Ralph gets angry, Remus tells him (in dialect) "Don't rile me, white faces, my razor's got a fast temper!"

The film has the feel of a 1930s Poverty Row forgotten horror. All it needs is some stock music from Abe Meyer and Wallace Ford as a wisecracking reporter....

The body of available criticism pretty much holds that *Unknown Treasures* was not a bad melodrama. ("Not a bad melodrama," *Harrison's Reports*, 16 October 1926.) And while we're happy that the opening reel is available to anyone with a little drive and about 10 minutes of free time, most of the genre-related critical noise centered on the last reel. *Harrison's* offered, "Some of the scenes are very strong. These are near the end, where the villain is shown killed by an ape." (None of that "Spoiler Ahead" nonsense in those days, what?) A short, unattributable review from 26 September 1926 likewise makes special mention of the closing minutes: "The identity of the man-sized ape and the reason for his presence in the haunted house finds full explanation in the denouement."

We'll have to take that on faith.

— JTS

Unseen Forces

Unseen Forces. Mayflower Photoplay Corp./Associated First National Pictures, 29 November 1920, 6 reels, New Zealand archive
CAST: Sylvia Breamer (*Miriam Holt*); Rosemary Theby (*Winifred*); Conrad Nagel (*Clyde Brunton*); Robert Cain (*Arnold Crane*); Sam De Grasse (*Captain Stanley*); Edward Martindel (*Robert Brunton*); Harry Garrity (*Peter Holt*); James O. Barrows (*Joe Simmons*); Aggie Herring (*Mrs. Leslie*); Andrew Arbuckle (*Mr. Leslie*); Albert Cody (*Henry Leslie*); with Fred Warren, May Giraci
CREDITS: *Producer* Sidney A. Franklin; *Director* Sidney A. Franklin; *Story* Bennett Cohen; based on the novel *Athalie* by Robert W. Chambers (New York, 1915); *Cinematographer* David Abel

There's not much to report on this one — the one print of which we're aware is nestled in an archive in New Zealand, and we can't come up with the carfare — but make what you can of the following brace of plot particulars (the first paragraph is from the 16 July 1921 *Harrison's Reports*, and the second, from *The AFI Catalog*):

The story deals with the heroine, who from her childhood showed signs of possessing the power of seeing things long before they happen. Once she cautions an explorer, who is about to go to South Africa on a wild-animal hunt, to provide himself with the necessary drugs to cure himself from an accident that was to befall him. The explorer heeds her advice, and when, while hunting, a tiger springs on him and bites him on the arm, he is well provided with antiseptics, which save his arm from amputation.

At a small inn kept by her father, and frequented by wealthy hunters, Miriam Holt meets the son of a sportsman, Clyde Brunton. The two young people are attracted to each other, but years later when Clyde visits the inn expecting to marry Miriam, he mistakenly believes her to be interested in someone else. Clyde later marries the shallow Winifred, which leads to unhappiness. Meanwhile, Miriam has become famous for her psychic powers, which she uses to benefit humanity. When Miriam discerns that one of her suitors, the dissolute Arnold Crane, has wronged a

woman, he promises to reform. Although Clyde's father and Winifred brand Miriam a fraud, Miriam intuits that it is Winifred whom Arnold has wronged. Miriam's purity and good character are now evident to all. Winifred wants to make restitution, and the way is cleared for Miriam and Clyde to find happiness together.

Wow! Another of the researcher's joys: two accounts— one, semi-vague; the other, unhelpfully explicit — and neither taken separately nor together are they anything other than sloppy and imprecise. The *Harrison's* scribe must have hit his head moments before writing of an "explorer" going on a "wild-animal hunt," or in reporting that the "antiseptics" use to ward off amputation were, in fact, the very "drugs" needed to effect a "cure" from an "accident." (We feel that such profligacy with quotation marks is, in this case, justifiable.)

In the latter screed, the woeful timeline (set down by a studio hack, as this prose was taken from the copyright registration summary) has Clyde (the "explorer," we assume) meeting Miriam, and then heading off—following her caveat about soap and iodine — to be savaged by the tiger. Years later (it says, above), he returns to that small inn and, with both arms waving about wildly, proposes to propose to the woman who had saved his bacon (his arm, actually) from deadly infection. At that moment, she (we are led to believe) is busy recommending vitamins or daily baths to benefit some other participant in humanity, and Clyde — mistaking her good intentions for lifelong commitment — goes off and marries the shallow Winifred, who had earlier (when unattached) canoodled with Arnold. Surely the film can't have unfolded *that* way?

Still, Miriam's famous psychic powers— even if little more than a knowledge of first-aid, the capacity to put two and two together, and the much-vaunted "women's intuition"— have worked their magic yet again, if only by winning a spot for this picture in this book. As none of the commentary on the film reveals that any special lighting or optical effect was employed to signal whenever Miriam revved up her psychic engine, we are led to believe that any such displays were understated at best. And lo! More proof that non-prestige pictures pandering to the passions of people prone to a proclivity for the paranormal pretty much always pass on pyrotechnics. (Due, we hypothesize, to lack of funding, lack of expertise, or even a perceived lack of need on the part of the production staff: how better, easier, and cheaper to demonstrate psychic influence than by alternating extreme close-ups of psychic and psych*ee* glaring and reacting à la the standard silent-film-acting mores? Harrison *did* report that "one is given a genuine thrill watching things seen by the heroine with her mental eyes, long in advance, come true," but we remain hard pressed to envision just how her visions were visualized onscreen.)

Unseen Forces' scenarist was one Bennett Cohen, a prolific writer/adaptor who concentrated in the main on horse operas (not surprisingly, as he haled from Colorado), and who, mid-career, dabbled now and again in production and direction. For *Unseen Forces*, Cohen focused on dabbling in *Athalie*, a novel with paranormal overtones written by Robert William Chambers, an artist-cum-author born in Brooklyn, New York, during the last year of the War Between the States.

Undeniably prolific — the man wrote over 70 romance and/or adventure novels, in addition to several dozen short-story collections and non-fiction works— Chambers lived to see a number of his pieces adapted to the screen, including four of his genre-oriented stories: *Athalie*, *The Dark Star* (1919), *The Firing Line* (1919), and *Between Friends* (1924; see essays on all). His most renowned horror work was *The King in Yellow*, a short-story amalgam that turned on the premise that the reading of the material would result in the death of the reader. (And you thought *The Ring* was an innovative concept!) A slew of modern horror writers (including August Derleth, Abraham Merritt, James Blish, H.P. Lovecraft, and Lincoln Carter) went on to cite *The King in Yellow* as having had influence on their style and output. Many of Chambers' titles are back in print, thanks to the dedication of publishing firms like Rockville, Maryland's, Wildside Press, which guarantees that reading its edition of *The King in Yellow* will not, in itself, lead to the buyer's demise.

We put the eye to *Athalie*, and the plot summary that follows demonstrates the much stronger supernatural leanings of Chambers' original.

Athalie, a beautiful, sensitive girl, lives with her parents who run a modest hotel. Growing up, Athalie discovers that she has extrasensory abilities. She can also see dead people. They make brief appearances, unbidden, sometimes with a message but usually just mute. Athalie has no control over this but is not unduly disturbed by her power. After the deaths of her parents, Athalie moves to New York City and becomes a stenographer, but spends more time preserving her virtue than taking notes. Her two sisters room with her and try to break into show business.

Clive Bailey, a rich young man who met Athalie briefly a few years before, is fascinated by her. He meets her again, and the two become friends. Their feelings really run deeper than that, but both are reluctant to go there, especially as Clive's parents are constantly reminding him that he cannot marry outside of his class. Nevertheless, Clive showers Athalie with expensive gifts and puts her up in a luxury apartment even though their relationship remains chaste. Finally, Clive does tell Athalie he loves her and asks her to marry him, but she refuses, knowing that he will have to break with his family. When Athalie sees Clive's father in the room, she realizes that he must be dead and sends Clive home where he finds the old man has just expired.

Athalie's sisters go on the road with a show sponsored by one of Clive's playboy friends. Athalie's kind-hearted boss dies, and his junior partner makes a pass at Athalie. She promptly quits and has great difficulty finding another job. An explorer named Captain Dane befriends her. One night she sees the spirit of Dane's partner standing next to him. The ghost describes the location of a lost city he and Dane were searching for. When he gets the message, Dane goes off to continue the quest (This may be the origin of the episode in the film about the mauled explorer in need of meds). Meanwhile, not certain whether he has a future with Athalie, Clive gives in to pressure from his mother and becomes engaged to Winifred, a blue-blooded but cold-hearted socialite. Athalie is shocked to read of the engagement in the paper, and she is not mollified by Clive's written apology in which he assures her that he had intended to tell her in person, but his mother jumped the gun. Athalie leaves the fancy apartment and strikes out on her own. Clive marries Winifred, and they go to England.

Down on her luck, Athalie finally finds a nice apartment available at a suspiciously low rent. It turns out the former occupant was a medium who was murdered there. Athalie finds the medium's hidden equipment for staging seances. One of the medium's clients pays a visit and, sensing Athalie is the real thing, urges her to try to contact his dead grandchildren. Athalie succeeds and is paid handsomely for her trouble. Now able to invoke her power at will, Athalie becomes a rich and famous medium.

Clive's marriage to Winifred proves unhappy and childless. He wanders the globe not certain what to do and even goes on one of Captain Dane's expeditions. When Clive returns to New York, he is amazed to hear of Athalie's success. He sees her again and, in spite of the impossible circumstances, their love is rekindled. Clive asks Winifred for a divorce, but she refuses and warns him she will name Athalie as a correspondent if he brings the case to court. This causes Clive to exclaim "Is there anything lower than a woman — or anything higher?" (This line was used in publicity for the film.) Clive is unwilling to risk Athalie's reputation, but nonetheless the two of them move to the old hotel Athalie's parents once owned, and they dream of starting a farm nearby. They neck a lot, but there's no sexual intimacy. They are just ecstatic to be in each other's company unhindered and talk about it constantly. Surprisingly, Athalie sees children in their future; however, she falls ill and dies. Athalie's spirit visits Clive in the garden they once loved. He doesn't know she's there, but with her is their child. Apparently, poor Clive is going to have to wait until the afterlife to get any.

Sidney Franklin, tapped to direct *Athalie* (the picture would be renamed *Unseen Forces* during post-production), is another of those movie vet-

Original glass slide depicts Sylvia Breamer and Conrad Nagel struggling with the world's largest magnifying glass. Can they find New Zealand on the map?

erans whose career spanned decades and whose talents were many and varied. Besides directing everyone and everything from "Baby" Carmen De Rue in 1915's short, *The Rivals*, to both Norma Shearer and Jennifer Jones as Elizabeth Barrett in the 1934 and 1957 productions, respectively, of *The Barretts of Wimpole Street*, he shared in screenwriting chores, produced, and — a half-dozen times or so, during the silent days — tried his hand at acting.

As for the principal cast of *Unseen Forces*, Conrad Nagel's background is available for perusal in our chapter on *London after Midnight* and Rosemary Theby's is in our essay on *A Connecticut Yankee in King Arthur's Court*. Sylvia Breamer (Miriam) was a stage actress in her native Australia before coming to the States to make her fortune on Broadway. We can't vouch for the fortune and can't find reports of her performing on Broadway, but Miss Breamer is said to have joined the New York–based Grace George Acting Company, where she was quickly approached with offers to leave the boards behind and to embrace the beaded screen. In films since 1917, she made a good handful under the eye of the "Commodore" himself, J. Stuart Blackton, although she never appeared in any of Blackton's genre features. (She *was* Mimi in the 1921 "George Arliss" take on *The Devil*, though.) Praised often and effusively for her beauty, Miss Breamer continued in the industry full time until 1926 when — in the classically clichéd words of mini-biographies — "she went on to pursue other interests."

Robert Cain, who portrayed "the dissolute Arnold Crane," moved from the Windy City to the Big Apple while still in his early 20s and *did* make it onto Broadway. During the mid–1910s, Cain also began to work in the flickers, with his earliest credits courtesy of Famous Players and Lubin Studios. Together with *Unseen Forces*, 1921's *The Witching Hour* comprised his genre canon and, as was the case with so many of his silent-film colleagues, Cain's movie career and the Silent Era pretty much left the dance together. Industry-wise, Canadian-born Sam De Grasse outlasted Robert Cain by a couple of years and even spoke a few lines in a brace of talkies. De Grasse was usually hired to portray secondary heavies and weasels, but he hit the jackpot as the weaselly King James II in Paul Leni's epic *The Man Who Laughs* (1928, see essay). The previous year, he had again tormented Conrad Veidt, when — as the district attorney who hauled Erik the Great to trial — he provided the magician with an impressive setting for *The Last Performance* (1927; see entry).

Variety (18 November 1921) heralded the film as "a program feature of merit," and the aforementioned *Harrison's Reports* opined that the picture would "no doubt, give satisfaction." Nonetheless, the column "What the Picture Did for Me" (in the 31 December 1921 *Exhibitors Herald*) arrived at a different verdict: "Very improbable picture, and one that failed to please. Not much good. Very poor business."

Before closing, a word on some of the decade's other pictures that snuck clairvoyance into the mix; not all were done so wisely or so well as to earn them a place in this Pantheon of Genre Achievement. Legion (okay; *semi*-legion) are the titles of 1910s films that had a fortune teller pull some malarkey from out of her crystal or tea leaves that influenced the plotline not at all —

except to start things off. Either the seer is a fake and stuff happens coincidentally (1915's *Buckshot John*); he/she pronounces and then manipulates the gullible soul's actions to bring about the desired result (1916's *A Fool's Paradise*); or — Shades of Real Life! — the prognosticator accepts a pile of sponduliks, tells whomever that a fabulous future awaits him/her, and then departs the scene. The plot then becomes nothing more than a succession of action-oriented details leading to a self-fulfilling prophecy (as in *Sylvia on a Spree*, 1918).

There are also numerous instances wherein the fortune teller's dictum comes up aces, and the cards are played out according to Hoyle. In *The Social Leper* (1917), for example, a divorcée is warned (by the "clairvoyant") to beware an admirer she has previously spurned. She doesn't and tragedy ensues. We had considered devoting space to *Leper*, but decided not to after we agreed that (a) the caveat on staying away from jilted lovers might just as likely come from the young woman's mom, and (b) once the fateful imprecation was hurled, said seer vanished like day-old pizza in a collegiate dorm. Even Agnes Smith — reviewing *Leper* in the 15 March 1917 New York Morning Telegraph —found the semi-supernatural stuff too sparse to have any impact: "If the predictions of the medium and the premonitions of the victim of the murder had been dwelt on at greater length the situations which lead up to the crime would have been more impressive."

As we repeat with Raven-like constancy herein, the absence of most the films we're dealing with means that our choices for inclusion are pretty much guided by conclusions we've drawn from vintage 1910s–1920s printed materials. The more pronounced the mention of the genre-oriented element in these published implications and inferences of long-departed movie critics, the more likely the picture's inclusion, either in the appendix (1918's *The Magic Eye*) or the main body of the book (1915's *The Cowardly Way*). Were there not other Silent-Era features that included somewhere in their dramatis personae a "clairvoyant" yet which we ignore with passion and resolve? You betcha. But we've made every effort at determining (rightly, we hope) that those films — like many faith-healing movies, quasi fairy tales, ersatz haunted house flicks, etc. — do *not* merit consideration by genre fans for reasons recounted above and elsewhere.

And so, being unable to junket off to the other side of the world, we're at a loss to offer our assessment. Mayflower Photoplay — genre-friendly, having already produced *The Mystery of the Yellow Room* and *The Invisible Foe* — hyped the paranormal angle, rather than its bizarro-world love story. Newspapers advertised it as "A Drama of Life's Mysteries" and, presaging Universal's *Dracula* by a decade, as "The Strangest Love Story Ever Screened." Ads had Miss Breamer striking a mystic pose, carrying a wand and bathed in light, an image not even hinted at in the plot summaries that saw print.

All, it appears, for naught.

— JTS/HN

The Untameable

The Untameable. Universal Pictures/Universal, 10 September 1923, 5 reels/4776 feet, available

CAST: Gladys Walton (*Joy Fielding/Edna Fielding*); Malcolm McGregor (*Chester Castle*); John Sainpolis (*Dr. Copin*); Etta Lee (*Ah Moy*)

CREDITS: *Director* Herbert Blaché; *Continuity* Hugh Hoffman; based on the novel *The White Cat* by Gelett Burgess (Indianapolis, 1907); *Cinematographers* Howard Oswald and Ben Kline

"She Turned on the Man She Loved, and Loved the Man She Hated!"

— advertisement for *The Untameable*

Universal had filmed Gelett Burgess' novel *The White Cat* in 1918 under the title *The Two-Soul Woman* (see entry) as a star turn for Priscilla Dean. Perhaps believing that a good vehicle was worth reselling, the Big U decided to do it again, this time with its new star, Gladys Walton. The athletic Miss Walton was best known for circus pictures, and her fans may have expected more of the same with a title like *The Untameable* and ads that described her as playing the "White Cat." However, while there are no lions in the film, Walton does get to use a whip.

The following synopsis is based on the current VHS edition of the film:

Chester Castle, an architect, has an auto accident in the country. When he awakens he finds himself in the house of Joy Fielding, a rich heiress. Chester is cared for by Joy and by her devoted servant, Ah Moy. Joy's physician, Dr. Copin, comes to visit and seems anxious for Chester to recover and be on his way. During Chester's convalescence, he and the refined, shy Joy fall in love.

One morning Chester hears the sound of breaking dishes. Investigating, he witnesses Joy beating Ah Moy with a whip because she has served eggs for breakfast. Joy is dressed in a revealing kimono, wears an anklet, and has her hair down. She also torments her two beloved English mastiffs, smashes furniture, puffs frantically away at a cigarette, and swings from the drapes. "She seems so unlike herself today," remarks the ever-observant Chester to Ah Moy. Joy tells Chester that her name is Edna and seems to remember him only vaguely. Dr. Copin arrives and is greeted affectionately by "Edna" who—at Copin's urging—sends Chester packing. The old man who drives Chester to town remarks that Copin is after Joy's money.

Chester has Copin investigated and discovers he has been barred from the medical profession for unethical conduct. It turns out Joy has a split-personality and has only dim memories of what she does as Edna, who loves Copin and gives him whatever he asks for. Copin begins to hypnotize Joy so he can make Edna appear whenever he likes. When he discovers that Chester is on to his scam, Copin secretly marries Edna.

Chester visits Joy, who can't believe that her late father's friend Dr. Copin would behave so treacherously. At Chester's suggestion, Joy pretends to be Edna at the doctor's next visit, and she then discovers the truth. When Copin leaves, Chester decides that the only way to save Joy is to marry her. Joy, of course, has no memory of her earlier wedding and willingly goes off with Chester in search of a justice of the peace.

Copin returns and hypnotically invokes Edna. Chester confronts the conniving medico, and the two try to settle their competing marital claims with a fistfight. Edna acts as the doctor's cheerleader, but when Copin is about to hit Chester with a shovel, Ah Moy releases the mastiffs, who attack and kill the physician. At Copin's death, Edna vanishes forever. Chester and Joy are free to be together, though how they'll explain bigamy and one chewed-up husband to the authorities isn't part of the story.

Seen today, *The Untameable* is less psychological thriller than campy melodrama, and with a few changes in the already risible title cards, it could almost pass as a comedy. Gladys Walton's hyperactive antics make Edna seem like a drunken, teenage brat badly in need of a whack across the keister, rather than a dangerously disturbed woman. Copin, mustachioed and dignified, appears understandably embarrassed by her attentions and, while their scenes together are no doubt meant to invoke Trilby and Svengali, viewers who remember *The Carol Burnett Show* will be reminded more of Burnett and Harvey Korman. Joy is so negligible as a dramatic character that the poignancy of her double life — so important in the novel — is completely lost.

Since Edna is ridiculous rather than threatening, the menace is left up to John Sainpolis as Dr. Copin. Sainpolis is more Adolph Menjou than Bela Lugosi, but close-ups of his eyes exerting their power over Joy are sufficiently malevolent. The doctor is also given a hawk-faced assistant who helps him with some unexplained experiments. "As you expected, the nerve cells are changing completely," the assistant announces, while showing Copin a slide fresh from the lab; busy reading up on hypnotism, Copin pays little attention. The doctor is equally nonchalant when his helper threatens blackmail; he just promises him more of Joy's money when the three of them high-tail it across the border. Copin's death-by-dog is far less brutal than similar scenes in *The Man Who Laughs* and *Wild Oranges*, and while it's established that Copin doesn't like the beasts, it's not clear why they should savagely attack him so readily at the climax. Maybe it's in response to Ah Moy's repeated prayers that Buddha save her sweet mistress.

It doesn't seem entirely logical that Copin's death should mean the end for Edna, especially as she pre-existed his hocus pocus, but — thanks to *Trilby* — it became standard in hypno-movies of the 1910s and 1920s for the fair-but-entranced maiden to be set free by the demise of the sorcerer. Nonetheless, it's possible that, as Edna does love Copin, his death traumatizes her into oblivion. Being an older man, he also may be a stand-in for Joy's father, perhaps indicating either an Electra complex or incest as an explanation for Joy's split personality and Edna's feelings for Copin. More likely though, the hypnotist's death was simply an easy and accepted way of wrapping things up.

The latter scene does contain one of the few effective shots in Herbert Blaché's otherwise nondescript direction: Copin lies dead and Joy, having fainted, is a few feet away from him, in front of the wall where he has met his end. Via double exposure (used several times throughout the film to indicate Joy becoming Edna), Edna rises from Joy's body, slowly approaches the corpse of her lover, and then lies next to him before disappearing entirely. Unfortunately, this surprisingly touching moment is marred by having Chester in the background appearing as if he can actually see this transmigration happening and is waiting until it is over before he rushes to Joy's side.

While Hugh Hoffman's script couldn't have been much inspiration, Blaché still should have found a few good possibilities. There could have been more of an unreal, ethereal quality to the early scenes when Chester first awakens after his accident and meets his beautiful but sad and mysterious hostess. However, Blaché treats it as a routine boy-meets-girl set-up, cutesy and bland though, perhaps, with Walton playing the part, it couldn't have been otherwise. Nor is there any mention of the "white cat," Joy's self-description taken from an enchanted but doomed fairy-tale character; Blaché is more interested in getting right to the "hell cat," Edna.

Some ads for the film showed Copin waving his arms hypnotically at Joy while Edna hovers behind her, like a specter. Less effective — but certainly kinkier — was another ad depicting Edna brandishing her whip over a cowering Dr. Copin! "Do you believe in hypnotism?" asked another blurb. "Do you believe in the power of one mind over another? Are there two sides to all of us, one good, the other evil?"

"Mae Tinee" of *The Chicago Tribune* addressed the last question in the first line of her review (12 August 1923): "The dual personality we are, it seems, always going to have with us in the movies. The pleasant urbane Dr. Jekyll and the ferocious Mr. Hyde; the lovely ingénue who, at a moment's notice, insists on tearing off her clothes or throwing the furniture about." Ms. Tinee found the film an "ordinary program picture" with a trite story and only so-so acting (except for John Stainpolis): "Mr. McGregor (Chester), as a perturbed lover who has his hair yanked out by the roots when he is expecting a kiss, will probably please the ladies. Miss Walton has grown a bit stouter. No must do if she is to keep up the peppy roles that usually fall to her lot."

As for the film's strange title: "It hasn't a great deal to do with the picture but may serve as a drawing card for shy souls who would learn how to kick up their heels."

The *Harrison's Reports* reviewer (1 September 1923) was much kinder: "It keeps on the spectator's attention a pretty good grip all the way through; its air of mystery is mostly responsible for this. Gladys Walton handles the dual role well, shifting easily from the one personality to the other…. *The Untameable* should please fairly well."

Herbert Blaché spent most of the 1920s as a contract director at Universal and was put in charge of Walton's vehicles. His main claim to fame, of course, is as the husband of film pioneer Alice Guy Blaché. It's debatable whether Alice Guy was a great director in addition to being an historically important one, but no one would make either claim for Herbert Blaché. He was, however, quite willing to take risks in the course of making a film. In her autobiography, Alice Guy recalls:

> For my film, *Dick Whittington and His Cat*, in order to illustrate the sinking of a pirate ship, we transformed a big old unused sailboat into a magnificent caravelle. The gunpowder and the fuse to provoke the explosion being ready, my husband, arguing that women lacked the sangfroid for this, insisted on executing the task himself. But when the wind had three times extinguished the fuse, he lost patience and tossed the match directly into the powder. The blast was thunderous…. I saw my husband regain the bank in the little boat into which he had fallen back, fortunately. Worried, in spite of that, I begged my assistant to go get news of my husband. He had taken refuge in a bar, where he lost consciousness. Seriously burned on face and hands. It took him weeks to mend.

Blaché was equally reckless with the family purse and made some bad investments, though he cannot be held responsible for the collapse of the Solax Company, a production company he and Alice started in 1910. Alice Guy and Blaché divorced in

1922, and Guy returned to France, but could not find work there as a director. Herbert Blaché's career lasted until 1929, when he retired from film. In 1951, Hollywood writer Richard Collins (*Cult of the Cobra*) went before the House Un-American Activities committee and named a number of Tinseltown people as being communists or former communists; among them were Herbert Blaché and his second wife, Norma Hallgren. One can't imagine such an accusation meant much at that point in Blaché's life. He died two years later, the same year Alice Guy received the Legion of Honor from the French government.

Malcolm McGregor, a Yale athlete and diving champ, was the son of a millionaire clothing manufacturer in Newark, New Jersey, but he chucked it all to become a $7.50-a-day extra in Hollywood. His first film was *The Lightning Raider* (1919), a Pearl White serial, but he was largely invisible until Rex Ingram gave him a chance in *The Prisoner of Zenda* (1922), with a conspicuous supporting role as the dashing Captain Fritz. This won him a contract at Metro, and he went on to play opposite Colleen Moore, May McAvoy, and Norma Shearer. Metro loaned him out to Universal for *The Untameable*, which certainly didn't advance his career any, but didn't harm it either. After many good roles in the 1920s, McGregor's career began petering out as sound came in; however, his family hadn't disowned him and in 1932 he inherited his father's fortune. After that, his biggest worry wasn't employment but, rather, the tax man. Probably as a lark, he continued to appear in the movies for awhile (including the serials, *The Whispering Shadow* and *Undersea Kingdom*). He died in 1945 of burns suffered after he fell asleep holding a lit cigarette.

Before he turned to film in 1914, John Sainpolis (sometimes billed as John St. Polis) was a veteran stage actor who played with Shakespearean great, Walker Whiteside, and who was a cast member of the original Broadway production of *The Return of Peter Grimm*. Although he essayed mostly character roles during the Silent Era, he was occasionally tapped to be the star (as in 1920's *The Great Lover*). As the Sound Era dawned, he had a good role as Mary Pickford's father in her first talkie, *Coquette*, but his career in the 1930s and 1940s largely consisted of small roles and unbilled bits. Silent horror film buffs may remember him as the hero's brother in the 1925 *Phantom of the Opera* and as the doctor who amputates Lon Chaney's arms in *The Unknown* (1927).

Etta Lee plays the small role of Ah Moy with delicacy and grace. Lee was born in Hawaii and was the daughter of a Chinese doctor and a French mother. She was trained as a schoolteacher but, on a visit to Los Angeles, became interested in the movies and began her career as an extra in the 1921 *Without Benefit of Clergy* (which also featured Boris Karloff). Lee continued to teach in LA in between acting chores and had roles in *The Remittance Man*, *Cytherea*, *One Night in Rome*, and *The Thief of Bagdad*. In an interview printed in the *Lima* [Ohio] *News* (15 July 1924), Lee lamented the fact that her parts weren't more substantial: "By heritage, temperament and the trend of self culture, I am equipped to depict odd, bizarre, exotic, extravagant gesture-thoughts; interpret the reality of mood rather than the realism of fact; to show oriental impulse and emotional complexities. But in this field I have not yet had opportunity."

The article concludes with the writer complaining about the tendency of Hollywood to cast Caucasians in Oriental parts rather than use authentic Asians like Lee and Anna May Wong: "Directors can't convert an American movie star into a Chinese, Japanese or East Indian woman with grease paint and penciled eyes." That wasn't about to change and, in 1927, Lee left Hollywood to star in the play *The Scarlet Virgin* and then went on to do a Vaudeville tour. In 1932 she married radio-news commentator, Frank Brown, and — except for the occasional bit part — retired from the screen.

As for Gladys Walton, 1923 was pivotal year for her and not because of *The Untameable*, either. She didn't enjoy being a movie star, particularly at the Big U, where her schedule was grueling and even getting a vacation was an issue. She was also tired of husband, Frank Liddle, Jr., and had become enamored of Henry Herbel, a district sales manager for Universal. Her divorce from Liddle became final on the 9 June, and she married Herbel three weeks later (albeit she had some trouble finding a clergyman who would marry them so soon after her divorce). Walton left Universal and made a few low-budget films, the last one being *The Ape* (1928, see entry). Her marriage to Herbel was a happy one, and the couple had six children. For good or ill, *The Untameable* is the only one of her films available on video.   — HN

Up the Ladder

Up the Ladder. Universal Pictures/Universal, 3 May 1925, 7 reels—available

CAST: Virginia Valli (*Jane*); Forrest Stanley (*Van*); Margaret Livingston (*Helen Newhall*); George Fawcett (*Judge Seymore*); Holmes Herbert (*Bob Newall*); Patricia Moran (*Peggy*); Olive Ann Alcorn (*Dancer*); Lydia Yeamans (*Housekeeper*); William V. Mong (*Richards*)

CREDITS: *Director* Edward Sloman; *Adaptation by* Grant Carpenter; *Scenario* Tom MacNamara; based on the eponymous play by Owen Davis (New York opening, 6 March 1922); *Cinematographer* Jackson Rose

Though he is not at all well known today, one of the most prolific American playwrights in the early 1900s was an indefatigable New Englander named Owen Davis. Between 1894 and 1917, Davis turned out about 150 plays, the majority of which were melodramas with titles like *The Burglar's Daughter*, *The Power of Money* and *The Opium Smugglers of Frisco*. By the end of the First World War, though, American theater had seen considerable change. Stage audiences for melodrama had switched their allegiance to the movies, and a greater seriousness was needed if theater was to thrive. This proved to be no problem for Davis, who scarcely needed to change the ribbon in his typewriter to make the switch to real drama; in fact, his 1923 *Icebound* even won the Pulitzer Prize. Davis still continued with thrillers and farces, but balanced them with weightier fare and later did much-praised adaptations of *The Great Gatsby*, *Ethan Frome*, and *The Good Earth*. March 1922 saw the Broadway premiere of his four-act play, *Up the Ladder*, a light-hearted critique of the Jazz Age and the success-at-any-price business mentality.

Courtesy of Gerald Boardman's *American Theater: A Chronicle of Comedy and Drama from 1914–1930*, the legitimate version of *Up the Ladder*:

Davis' hero and heroine were Jane (Doris Kenyon) and John Allen (Paul Kelly). At the time of their marriage, Jane had been the more financially secure of the pair and moving into the cheap apartment John had selected was something of a comedown. But John, a bond salesman, is a driven man. His ruthless pursuit by day and wild socializing by night, though it helps them move to a fine home in Westchester, nearly wrecks their health and their good name. They pull themselves together in time for a happy ending.

The play was a success and, in November 1922, Universal announced that they were scheduling a film version, with Virginia Valli in her first starring role for the studio. A.P. Younger and Hobart Henley were penciled in to adapt Davis's play and to direct it, respectively. The two had just collaborated on *The Flirt* (based on a Booth Tarkington story) and would team up the following year for *The Abysmal Brute*, a reworking of a tale by Jack London. When *Up the Ladder* finally *did* make it to the screen — as a Universal Jewel in May of 1925 — Younger and Henley had been replaced by the decidedly second-rate team of Edward Sloman (director) and Grant Carpenter (adaptation). Valli remained the picture's star, although at that point her playing a starring role was hardly a novelty.

The following synopsis of the film is courtesy of our assimilation of the Grapevine Video release, which may be missing some footage:

Wealthy Jane Cornwall returns to her mansion after a six-month world cruise. She ignores the attempts of her lawyer and friend Judge Seymore to have a serious talk and rushes to see her childhood sweetheart, James Van Clinton. Van's family was once well off, but now Van lives in a small house adjoining Jane's estate. He is an inventor and has been working on a device called the Tele-Visionphone, a phone with a screen that allows you to see the person with whom you're talking. Van is quite discouraged because no one will back his idea and he needs $25,000 to perfect the invention. Jane offers to give him the money, but he turns her down, saying that if he took money from a woman, his ancestors would turn over in their graves.

Undaunted, Jane goes to Judge Seymore and tells him to take $25,000 from her accounts and invest it in Van's machine without telling him the source of the money. Seymore informs Jane that her investments have all gone bad and she has no more fortune. She could undoubtedly raise the $25,000 by selling the house, but that would leave her broke. Nonetheless, Jane insists on doing just that and Seymore reluctantly assents. The mansion sold, Jane goes to live in the old servants' quarters while Van continues to work on the Tele-Visionphone. He finally runs a successful test and immediately asks Jane to marry him.

Five years pass. The invention has done well and Van heads the corporation that mass produces the machine. He still thinks that it is Judge Seymore who is his partner, but it is Jane who controls a large number of the shares. Van and Jane have a little girl, Peggy, and seem to be happy and prosperous. However, Van has gone from workaholic to slacker and the business is suffering. Helen Newhall, a friend of Jane's, is attracted to Van and one night, at a party in Van's mansion, the flirtation turns serious and the two become lovers. Helen's husband Bob has always admired Jane, but has never acted on his feelings. Neither Jane nor Bob have any idea of what's going on between their spouses.

Van and Helen plan a weekend together since Bob is going to be out of town. It is Jane's birthday but Van has completely forgotten about it. However, Peggy, searching his coat pocket for candy, finds a beautiful diamond pendant and an affectionate card. She shows it to her mother who naturally assumes it is a surprise birthday present for her. She puts the package back together and has Peggy secretly return it to Van's pocket. Van leaves the house saying he has an unexpected business appointment to keep. Jane is puzzled and hurt and doesn't know what to think. Not wanting to be alone on her birthday, she calls Helen on the Tele-Visionphone. When Van realizes who is calling, he ducks out of the screen's range, but Jane sees his image in a nearby mirror. Shortly after that, Bob returns home unexpectedly, bringing the attempted tryst to a hasty conclusion.

The next day Helen goes to Jane's for tea. Jane manages to keep her composure until she sees Helen with the pendant. Jane furiously orders her from the house: "You're just one of those women who'll play with any man — just because you know most men will play!" Judge Seymore, ever the bearer of bad financial news, tells Jane that Van has accumulated so many debts that he is in danger of losing the business and going bankrupt. He tells her that she must immediately sell her shares of the Tele-Visionphone to Mr. Richards of the Electrical Trust. Jane agrees to meet Seymore and Richards the next day to sign the appropriate papers. When she arrives at the office, though, she changes her mind and refuses to sign, feeling that Van needs the shock of losing everything to return to his old self. Van arrives at the office and is amazed to discover that it is his wife who has been his business partner all along.

Richards takes control of the Tele-Visionphone Corporation and Van becomes one of his managers. He and Jane separate. After a year, Richards is impressed with Van's hard work and offers him a very lucrative contract. Van signs and Richards calls in someone to witness the contract. The witness is Jane, and she and Van are reconciled.

Obviously, virtually nothing from Davis's original made it into the film although perhaps the trite and unoriginal story is a tribute of sorts to the kind of hokum Davis had churned out in his melodramatic heyday. And the one thing lacking in the play — the science fiction element represented by the Tele-Visionphone — is the only reason the film is included herein.

The notion of transmitting images either electronically or mechanically had been bandied about by both Edison and Bell, but the 1920s saw great progress made in the development of what would become known as television. (That word, by the way, was coined at the First International Conference on Electricity, part of the World's Fair held in Paris in 1900.) Charles Jenkins, John Baird and Vladimir Zworkykin all were doing important pioneering work at about the time *Up the Ladder* was released, and perhaps we should also note the contribution to the cause by Universal's chief engineer who, per the studio's publicity department, actually constructed a "practical televisionphone." (For whatever reason, Universal chose not to share this discovery with the scientific world.) Television — depicted as a sort of visual phone — also turns up in *Metropolis* (1927) and *High Treason* (1928) and was, of course, the preferred means of communication (and spying) of many a serial villain in the 1930s.

In addition to its lack of interest in the science that underscores its plot, *Up the Ladder* doesn't even give a nod to the economic repercussions of Van's machine. No footage is spent in showing the kind of impact the Tele-Visionphone has on society. (Apparently, it doesn't replace the standard phone as even Van has one of those in his mansion.) Is his invention just a fancy toy for the rich? Other than adding a little novelty to the hope-

lessly corny tale of a self-sacrificing woman and the clueless ingrate she loves, the Tele-Visionphone is there simply to provide an unusual way of catching someone in adultery. And as the business with the pendant proves to be the most damning evidence against Van, his invention doesn't prove to be crucial in that respect, either. MacGuffin, anyone?

What's more, even the poster artwork for *Up the Ladder* ignores the damned thing. One-sheets depicted Van climbing up a ladder with Jane bolstering him from beneath, or Jane confronting Helen with the diamond pendant in the foreground and Van in the background sheepishly entering the room. A typical blurb for the film can be found in the *Nashua* [New Hampshire] *Reporter* (21 April 1926): "He climbed up so rapidly he forgot his wife in the rush! Every woman faces this tragedy-to-be left at the bottom of the ladder. His wife found out after she had sent her husband to the top of the ladder that he was only climbing for another woman! See her gallant fight for his love — you will hope for her, cry for her, love her." None of the extant ads so much as mentions the miracle of the Tele-Visionphone. Perhaps Van should have just built a better mousetrap; it really wouldn't have changed the plot at all.

The performances in *Up the Ladder* are adequate, and one could hardly expect much more given the clichéd material. Virginia Valli is sprightly enough in her early scenes, but her noble suffering and dutiful silence become a bit maddening after awhile, especially as she has to impoverish herself not once but twice for the sake of her man. It *is* nice, though, to see her purposely spill tea on her snooty rival. Forrest Stanley as Van is off-putting even when he's *supposed* to be likable. Stanley had a busy (if not especially noteworthy) career in the Silent Era and did a turn as Boston Blackie in *Through the Dark* (1924) with Colleen Moore, while also being featured in *The Young Diana* (1922) and *The Cat and the Canary* (1927; see our essays on both). Margaret Livingston, who was probably the worst thing about Murnau's great *Sunrise* (1927), makes for a rather campy-looking vamp, replete with frizzy hairdo. George Fawcett, a Griffith favorite who made a career out of playing grumpy old men, does his usual curmudgeonly act here to good effect. Veteran character actor Holmes Herbert has little to do as Bob Newhall, and although he's not listed in the AFI entry on the film, William V. Mong appears briefly as Mr. Richards.

The role of Little Peggy was played by one Priscilla Moran, whose story merits a brief recounting, resembling as it does a Shirley Temple movie (albeit one without a typical Shirley Temple ending). Priscilla Dean Moran was born in 1918 (in Sedalla, Missouri) to a woman whose favorite actress should be obvious and a man whose involvement in an oil scam in Roundup, Montana, had caused him to seek other climes, and fast. When both parents contracted tuberculosis, they were told by their doctor to move to a yet healthier climate, so the Morans made for Hollywood where dad, Leo, was soon making the studio rounds with adorable little daughter, Priscilla, in tow.

The little girl made a big hit with the Tinseltown community and was cast in *The Toll of the Sea* (1922). When assistant director Archie Mayo learned of the family's dire financial circumstances, he had his wife hold a bridge-party fundraiser for them that netted them $200 in cash, plus the attention of Constance Talmadge, Dorothy Dalton, and none other than the moppet's namesake, Priscilla Dean.

Soon thereafter, little Priscilla got a contract at Universal for $300 a week, and the three-year-old went to work, supporting her family. When, tragically, Mrs. Moran died shortly thereafter, Leo placed the girl with Jackie Coogan's parents and then disappeared. Resurfacing six months later, he reclaimed his daughter and formed something called "Priscilla Moran Productions" after convincing Ella Schraber — a theater owner in Tulsa, Oklahoma — to invest $3500 in it. Leo agreed to Schraber's terms — the theater owner was named the child's guardian in order to protect her investment — after which he hit the road again. A couple of months later — his health failing — he reappeared once more and ran off with Priscilla, whom he took to John Ragland, a film-exchange executive. Schraber be damned, this time around Leo named the Raglands as Priscilla's guardians, consented to their adopting her, borrowed $500, and then headed off to Arizona where he died three days later.

When Priscilla's grandmother turned up, demanding custody of the child as next of kin, a court battle ensued, with the Raglands and Ella Schraber also seeking custody. The trial was attended by Mary Pickford, Priscilla Dean and Dorothy Dalton, all of whom wept when Priscilla was given into the care of her grandmother. Eight years old by the time the smoke cleared, the moppet saw her career as a child star ended as she went to live with her grandmother in Long Beach, in circumstances far removed from the high life of Hollywood and the riches-rags-riches-back again nonsense of *Up the Ladder*.

In contrast to that convoluted tale, we may note, simply, that director Edward Sloman was a Universal contract employee, and that he did a competent enough job with the material he was given here. Perhaps the most egregious of the British import's dubious distinctions lay in his inadvertently turning the great Russian actor Ivan Mosjoukine into the spitting image of Larry Semon in Mosjoukine's only American film, *Surrender* (1927). On a more positive note, Sloman did a good job with the creaky (but still creepy) *Murder by the Clock* (1931).

Reviewers were not kind: "An atrocity… The acting is rather unpleasant and the total ends up minus" (*Time*, 18 May 1925). *The New York Times* write-up was less harsh and did mention the Tele-Visionphone: "While the idea is depicted cleverly, more might have been made of it to the benefit of the production, as the story itself does not hold water…. One finds perchance more interest in the manipulation of the 'vision telephone' and its possibilities than in the love affairs of the faithless young inventor."

Decades later, the *Overlook Encyclopedia of Science Fiction Films* delivered a scathing indictment of the film's sexual politics, based on a totally inaccurate synopsis of the film in which Van marries Jane for her money! Perhaps, though, the fairest assessment came from *Harrison's Reports* (31 January 1925): "It may get by with such movie-goers as are not hard to please."

Besides *Up the Ladder*, Davis wrote four other plays that were made into movies covered herein: *Chinatown Charlie*, *The Haunted House*, *Lola*, and *Blow Your Own Horn*. Intriguingly, there is no mention of any of these film versions in either of his two, long, rambling accounts of his career: *I'd Like to Do It Again* (1931) and *My First Fifty Years in the Theater* (1950). In some

ways, this is surprising since Davis himself did a three-year stint as a screenwriter for Paramount in the late 1920s, and one would think it natural that he remark on film adaptations of his own work. Then again, considering what Universal did to *Up the Ladder*, perhaps his silence is appropriate after all.

P.S. A version of Davis' play was televised on 9 March 1951 as part of the anthology series "Pulitzer Prize Playhouse." It starred Barbara Britton, Constance Dowling and Howard St. John. It's safe to assume the Tele-Visionphone was not added to the drama.   — HN

Vanity's Price

Vanity's Price. Gothic Pictures/Film Booking Offices of America, 7 September 1924, 6 reels/6,124 feet [LOST]

CAST: Anna Q. Nilsson (*Vanna Du Maurier*); Stuart Holmes (*Henri De Greve*); Wyndham Standing (*Richard Dowling*); Arthur Rankin (*Teddy*); Lucille Rickson (*Sylvia*); Robert Bolder (*Bill Connors*); Cissy Fitzgerald (*Mrs. Connors*); Dot Farley (*Katherine, Vanna's maid*); Charles Newton (*Butler*)

CREW: *Director* Roy William Neill; *Assistant Director* Josef von Sternberg; *Writer* Paul Bern; *Cinematographer* Hal Mohr

Vanity's Price was just one in the spate of 1920's rejuvenation films that invariably found the Fountain of Youth in Vienna (home of The Steinach Procedure; see *Sinners in Silk*, 1924) and that usually featured Anna Q. Nilsson (*One Hour Before Dawn* [1920], *Between Friends* [1924]) — undisputed queen of that long-ago fad — in need of the Procedure or something similar. A year after *Vanity's Price* was released, Nilsson was again transformed (this time, from a washed-up, aged opera singer to a popular, young Society belle) in *One Way Street* (1925, see entry), a second stab at the theme taken by the Film Booking Offices of America. Nilsson's career later led her down the long and winding road to Billy Wilder's *Sunset Boulevard* (1950) for a poignant cameo role, as herself. In the famed *Boulevard*, aging actress Norma Desmond (portrayed by Nilsson's contemporary, Gloria Swanson) never, of course, quite regained her youthful looks and fame — at least not in the reality outside of Norma's mind.

This synopsis from the Library of Congress copyright records is by Paul Bern, scenarist for *Vanity's Price*:

Vanna Du Maurier, a great actress, has been overtaxing her strength and living on her nerve for months in an exacting role. She promises Dowling, her faithful suitor for many years, that she will give it up and rest as soon as she has achieved her lifelong ambition to have her own theatre. As the story opens Bill Connors, theatrical manager, has as his guest in a stage box at Vanna's performance Henri De Greve, a polished man of the world whom he expects to use as an "angel" to fulfill Vanna's ambition. Connors takes De Greve back stage to meet the famous actress after the performance; but on seeing him Vanna's smile changes to an expression of fear, and she tells Connors she does not really want the theatre. De Greve simply smiles his enigmatic smile while Dowling, who is waiting to take Vanna home from the theatre, and Connors are both completely mystified.

Vanna's son Teddy comes home from the university. Sylvia, his sweetheart, has been in Vanna's play, and the elder woman has displayed a touching solicitude for Sylvia, watching over her while the boy is away. Mother and son are very devoted to each other. His return, however, finds Vanna feeling the strain of her work and beginning to show her age, as her mirror cruelly informs her every morning. Not all her will nor all her art can retain the youth which she sees slipping away from her.

While Teddy, his mother and his sweetheart are holding a reunion in Vanna's boudoir, the maid comes in with the portable telephone and tells her mistress someone wishes to speak with her. It is De Greve, and he asks if he may come over to see her that afternoon. Vanna says "No" emphatically, almost hysterically, and hangs up. De Greve, however, appears, forces his way in, and in an intimate boudoir scene it is revealed that he is the father of Teddy. Vanna has left him fifteen years because of his revolting animalism.

De Greve's visit and the harrowing scene in which it results is the last straw, and that evening the great actress is unable to leave for the theatre. The physicians tell Connors that her nerves are shattered and that she must have absolute rest and quiet. After months of lingering illness a changed Vanna is found at her country estate; a Vanna too old and haggard to again appear before the public in the roles to which she has been accustomed. When she asks Connors why he has not brought her new play, the manager is obviously embarrassed, and finally says that the stage wants youth. All around her is youth; the middle-aged female hypocrites who pretend to be her friends are all talking youth, and the famous rejuvenation process in Vienna. Vanna at length determines to regain her youth and tells the maid to pack immediately for Vienna.

Vanna's return from Vienna is a triumph. She is again the glorious, blazing creature of twenty years before. De Greve, who has meanwhile been paying court to Youth in the person of Sylvia, despite Vanna's protestations, is again drawn to Vanna's side by her charm; and to the surprise of her friends and the horror of Teddy and Sylvia she accepts his attentions. Meanwhile, De Greve has financed Sylvia in a play and is going to build her the theatre he considered for Vanna. In the sweep of her return to sex, Vanna is all woman, no longer a mother who is watching over her son's sweetheart. She demands that De Greve close Sylvia's show, which he does. Dowling attempts to pierce De Greve's armor of polished worldliness, but he is no match for this accomplished rake. Teddy in vain pleads with his mother to break with De Greve.

Vanna finally discovers that Sylvia feels she can not now marry Teddy because of her relations with De Greve, and acting a part she allows De Greve to come to her boudoir where she horsewhips him with a riding crop. Teddy, breaking in on this scene, rushes to De Greve with a bronze figure as a weapon, but is floored by the elder man before Vanna can interrupt and tell the boy he is attacking his father. Sylvia tries to commit suicide by leaping into the river at night, but is saved by Dowling who has been trailing her. Dowling goes to De Greve's rooms and administers a terrific beating to the man. He finally persuades Vanna to marry him, and Teddy and Sylvia are happily re-united.

Vanity's Price surely had its share of grit and violence (did anyone *not* want to give a beat down to poor Stuart Holmes playing Henri De Greve?). Maybe it was due to the strange mores enforced by the censors in Kansas who—while readily objecting to such egregious offences as a shot of a girl's bare leg, a title card with the word "God," and the screen appearance of a flask of booze—didn't apparently give a hoot about De Greve getting a fair pounding, not once but twice—and almost thrice. Or maybe they watched the film and simply decided that he deserved his lecherous comeuppance no matter how severe. Alas, we'll never know for certain as the footage is long gone.

Without giving specifics, Roberta Nangle, opining on behalf of the *Chicago Daily Tribune* (31 October 1924), returned from the theatre a tad disturbed by what she saw: "The theme of second youth is a delicate one at best, and unless it is skillfully han-

dled it becomes unpleasant and slightly disgusting. *Vanity's Price* goes to some vulgar lengths in order to say that those who accumulate wisdom with age will be resigned to grow old gracefully." Nangle signed off with: "Most movie fans will term *Vanity's Price* an unnecessary picture, with a good cast and good photography wasted on a worthless plot."

Summer Smith in *Moving Picture World* (20 September 1924) concurred in the main on the quality and tone of the movie: "Lavishly produced and excellently acted, it nears technical perfection. But the story does not deal with ordinary people and the general atmosphere it creates is somewhat abnormal." Smith, in her (his?) closing arguments, left the final verdict at the mercy of the jury's demographics: "This review can't undertake to tell how the picture will please all the varieties of people to be found in the U.S. melting pot."

The *Los Angeles Times* (6 October 1924), via the typewriter of reviewer Kenneth Taylor, reported a bit of unevenness in the production:

> Spasmodically flashing bits of excellent photoplay between sequences which are only poor or fair…. There are moments when you'll swear *Vanity's Price* is mediocre. There are others when you awaken from a state of mental slumber when something happens upon the serene with the discovery that there are other than certain bromidic ways of presenting a situation, even though so few directors use them.

One reasonable theory is that assistant director Josef Von Sternberg managed to add some of the stylized touches alluded to above. Be that as it may, Mordaunt Hall, writing for *The New York Times* two days after the review of its L.A. namesake, felt that director Roy William Neill had not yet hit his stride and there was another directing choice that was missed:

> The costumes and stage settings of this production are quite promising, but the direction appears to be inexperienced, certainly so far as this type of narrative is concerned. R. William Neill, the director has some of his characters often standing in awkward and stiff poses…. While this is not a film that is going to set the world on fire, it is an entertainment which is not badly done. The story was written by the imaginative Paul Bern, and it would have been a superior effort if he had directed it.

Hall's commentary is a trifle odd considering that Bern had in fact no more directing experience back then than had Neill, who went on to direct any number of programmers, most famously those featuring Basil Rathbone and Nigel Bruce. Bern, on the other hand, had less time to hone his craft at directing, splitting time as he did with screenwriting; nor would he advance his career as long; as did Jean Harlow (his sex-pot bride of 2 months), as he died at an early age, allegedly a suicide, on the 5 September 1932.

The New York Times piece also provided some choice details on a few scenes … and a minor plot hole. The Grey Lady expanded on the risks that Vanna took for vanity by recounting that in the operating room, one of the observing physicians "shakes his head, knowing that the woman's vanity is bound to suffer by the effect the Steinach treatment will have on her mentality." And, as *The Times* further noted, Du Maurier had a house in which "armies can be hidden," replete with "Russian dancers and Ethiopian underlings"; but how, then, was it that she couldn't afford her own theater?

Nilsson was in her prime when the *Vanity's Price* was photographed, so playing a vibrant young actress probably was no great shakes; most accounts indicated she handled the flipside of her role admirably too. Representative of her reception is this quote from *The Washington Post* (22 September 1924): "Miss Nilsson gives a very good interpretation of the part intrusted [sic] to her. Seldom has she been seen in a role which shows her to better advantage." *The Post*'s paradoxical take on Stuart Holmes (see *Body and Soul, 1920*) was that he was "admirable" as the villain and succeeded in "making himself thoroughly hated." As for the younger generation, *The Post* declared: "Lucille Rickson (see *Behind the Curtain*, 1924) and Arthur Rankin, as the youthful lovers, gave fine characterizations."

— *SJ*

Voices

Voices. Victor Kremer Film Features, Inc./States Rights, 26 September 1920, 5 reels [LOST]

CAST: Corliss Giles (*John Vance*): Diana Allen (*Mary Vance*); Gilbert Rooney (*Tom*); Henry Sedley (*Justin Lord*); Gladys Coburn (*Marion Lord*); Harold Foshay (*Frank Mears*); with Gaspard Hicks

CREDITS: *Presented by* Victor Kremer; *Director* Chester De Vonde: *Story and Scenario* Chester De Vonde

Visions! We've got visions!

Odd way to start an essay on a film entitled *Voices*, no? Still, (a) the picture was made in 1920, so technically, there were no voices to be had, and)b) the sole reason for inclusion in our volume is a series of visions (of his mom, transmitted from Beyond the Veil) had by the juvenile. The visions did entail his mother's voice (and said visions were thus also *auditions*), but as the vocal element was conveyed via title cards, we're back to being righteously persnickety. Considering all the silent films made that either starred or dealt with opera singers, we *are* being a bit anal here....

Before we're all reduced to talking to ourselves, let's repair to the plot précis, provided by *The AFI Catalog*:

> Venturing to New York to study music, Mary Vance makes the acquaintance of a girl posing as a student and through her is drawn into questionable society where she apparently becomes a victim in the white slave traffic. One day, Mary's brother John has a vision in which his dead mother appears and tells her son that his sister is in danger. Alarmed, John goes to New York where he discovers that his sister has disappeared. Suspecting that profligate womanizer Justin Lord may be responsible for his sister's disappearance, Tom kidnaps Lord's daughter Marion in revenge. Soon after, Mary is brought home by her fiancé Tom and explains that she had been in hiding, fearful that Lord had killed himself when he tripped and fell during a seduction attempt. The mystery satisfactorily explained, Lord reforms and John realizes that he has fallen in love with Marion.

As those depraved New York music students might sing, "Gran Dio!"

Hang up the plot; we don't want to go there: who's kidnapping whom, white slavery, reverse–Stockholm syndrome ... who in hell can keep up with all that? The 23 October 1920 *The Moving Picture World* review revealed that "throughout the story the voice of John's dead mother influences him at critical moments." When even the cast members need supernatural help to get things straight, it's time to skip the message and concentrate on the medium. (No; there are no mediums in this film.) Anyhow, it's mom's *voice* that motivates John to do whatever it is he does — honestly, all he seems to do is grow alarmed and then fall hard for Marion; Tom is the picture's get-it-done guy — hence, the title.

Back on the 10 July 1920, *MPW* ran a full-page advance ad on the picture — doubtless in an effort to set some plot parameters up front — and it will definitely prove helpful to us to ponder same in order to fully understand what the *Voices* are saying.

Prologue
Out from the width of the Great Beyond — out from the depth of the Inner Deep —from the turmoil of Life or from the Peace we know not whence, come *V o i c e s*.
They speak to us with recurrent sound — ever reminding us that we are guided or misled, dominated or crushed by the Spirit of their unseen Power.
Let us then, with mind attuned, take heed —casting out each discordant note — basking in the harmony of Light and Love.
He that hath an ear, let him hear.

V
Will   O
Open   I
Eyes   C
Closed   E
to   S
Sights

Ears
Sealed
to
Sounds

Chester De Vonde's Supreme Effort

Portrayed by Superlative Stars including
DIANA ALLEN
CORLISS GILES
HENRY SEDLEY
GLADYS COBURN

Presented by Victor Kremer

Epilogue
Who there us now that will dispute
With scoffing sound and manner rude
That *V o i c e s* in us do not speak
Guiding strong — protecting weak,
The voice of her who life us gives
Though dead, withal, forever lives

Well, maybe not...

If the names Chester De Vonde, Victor Kremer, Diana Allen, et al. don't jump off the page and hit you between the eyes, you've a lot of company. Devoted fans of the Man of a Thousand Faces will probably recall Mr. De Vonde's indirect participation in Chaney's *West of Zanzibar* (1928, see entry), as he was the gentleman who co-wrote the play (*Kongo* — on Broadway for four months in mid–1926) upon which Elliott Clawson and Waldemar Young's scenario was based. Mr. De Vonde was likewise involved with M-G-M's 1932 sound remake of *Zanzibar*, entitled *Kongo*. Obviously, the 1926 stage drama and the 1928/1932 celluloid takes on same ought to be considered Mr. De Vonde's "supreme effort," if only by virtue of name recognition. Still, half-a-dozen years prior to *Kongo* hitting The Great White Way, *Voices* marked the first time the man wrote anything that required the price of admission and the second (and *last*) time he was paid to direct a movie. As a glance at the credits section that follows will show that *Voices* was essentially a one-man operation, we offer plaudits to the shade of Mr. De Vonde.

It's likely that none of the actors listed in the above ad never again saw their names linked in print with phrases like "Superlative Stars," but — save for Corliss Giles (spiritual conduit/man of inaction, John Vance) — all had reasonably decent runs as featured players in other, more notable productions ("more notable" being a relative term). Actually, Swedish-born Diana Allen copped her share of leads in the course of a couple of dozen shorts and features between 1918 and 1925. *Voices* was the lady's second venture under the guidance of Chester De Vonde (*Even as Eve*, a six-reeler based on a non-genre Robert W. Chambers novel, had been released a few months prior to our tale of mother hens who just can't let go). Henry Sedley's map graced over 50 pictures from 1917 until the early 1930s (when he slipped into doing those inevitable "uncredited bits"), and — other than *Voices* — the closest he came to a genre feature was 1923's *The Devil's Partner* (which featured not a devil of any kind) and 1929's *The Ghost Talks*, which had talking, but no ghosts. At 11 films in her resume, Gladys Coburn is only up two on the aforementioned Corliss Giles, but those two are genre titles *The Black Crook* (1916) and *The Firing Line* (1919; see entries). There's a bit more on Miss Coburn in our coverage of the former.

From comments in *MPW*'s feature, "Consensus of Published Reviews," it's evident that hearing, seeing, or otherwise experiencing *Voices* wasn't everyone's cup of tea: "Crude production of familiar story," moaned "N," while "W" found the production to be an "inferior melodrama." In his 23 October 1920 review of the picture for *MPW*, Jesse Robb opined:

> Striking a modern appeal, *Voices*, a Victor Kremer production with Corliss Giles in the leading role, deals with spiritualism in a fairly striking, but perhaps too morbid a fashion. The situations are highly melodramatic and therefore untrue to life, but it offers the lover of thrills emotional appeal and the heroine, beset by many dangers is saved from unkind fate in time for the demanded happy ending…. Throughout the spirit of a dead mother influences the life of the hero and this aspect will appeal to dabblers in spiritualism. The production is made with a number of costly sets, but the direction is somewhat cramped and the players are given little chance to show their caliber.

Those costly sets were courtesy of the pockets of Victor Kremer, a mini-mogul who had (prior to *Voices*) distributed a slew of pictures (mostly oaters, but also including Chaplin's *The Champion* [1915] and *Burlesque of Carmen* [1916]) before he turned to making the damned things in 1919, starting with the immortal Shorty Hamilton World-War-I-drama-with-horse-opera-underpinnings, *When Arizona Won*. Kremer had earlier been the GM for the W.H. Clifford Photoplay Company and, inasmuch as that company (in an earlier "incarnation" as W.H. Productions) had, in 1918, re-cut and reissued Thomas H. Ince's *The Devil* (1915; see entry), some tenuous genre props must be

given Mr. Kremer. Still, other than 1919's *Stripped for a Million* (a five-reel Crane Wilbur comedy), *Voices* marked the only non–Western notch on his gun-belt.

Despite semi-poetic publicity puffs that bordered on the Baroque…

> A Production Wide as the Universe, Condensed to Find Lodgement [*sic*] in Your Heart's Chambers. Carressing [*sic*] in its Tenderness, Stirring in Its Appeal, Firing the Imagination to Unprecedented Heights of Admiration

… and some interesting observations couched by local reviewers in idiomatic — if somewhat ungrammatical — phraseology…

> *Voices* … supplies the audience with glimpses of scenes never seen before, for that play treats of that unseen world about which there has been lately much controversy, especially by scientists.

… audiences on the whole resisted the picture's siren-like call. (Maybe they were more discerning than we give them credit for. *The Trenton* [New Jersey] *Evening Times* — which printed the comments immediately above — also claimed that "*Voices* has one of the best casts seen at the St. Regis in a long time"; that, in itself, may go a long way in explaining the public's indifference to the film. The 15 December 1920 *Naugatuck* [Connecticut] *Daily News* gave only a brief and ambiguous mention with respect to the supernatural, when speaking of Corliss Giles' dealings with "the onslaught against his enemies, both seen and unseen." Were savvy audiences to assume that John's mom was the "unseen enemy"?)

In spite of all the press touting the treatment of Spiritualism, it seems that the picture was too clever by half in its presentation of the late Ma Vance. As the 3 October 1920 *Wid's Daily* disclosed, there was a very good chance that viewers would have taken the apparitions as nothing more than timely dreams:

> *Voices* opens up with a very interesting main title composed of good lighting and cloud effects. Following come [*sic*] a string of subtitles suggesting that the picture is to deal with some sort of spiritualism. The only times when this suggestion becomes a fact are the scenes in which the hero drops off to sleep and is visited by the spirit of his departed mother. This happens four or five times throughout the picture and each time the hero drops off to doze in the same pose — each time he awakes with the same start after his mother has stood by his side in double exposure.

And if *that* didn't take the wind out of some moviegoers' sails, Mr. Gunning's thoughts on direction ("inferior") and acting ("the cast isn't exceptional") may have moved at least a handful of potential ticket-buyers away from thoughts about the Great Beyond and into movie palaces offering tales of horses, cowpokes, and distressed schoolmarms.

If *The New York Dramatic Mirror* (3 October 1920) didn't say it briefest, it said it strangest: "The basic theme is fair enough if you believe in that sort of thing, but we feel that it was used merely as a cloak with which to conceal from the unwary the obvious intent of getting away with some unpleasant scenes."

Like a mother standing at her son's side…

— JTS

Waking Up the Town

Waking Up the Town. Mary Pickford Company/United Artists, 14 April 1925, 6 reels/5800 feet, partial print at the Library of Congress

CAST: Jack Pickford (*Jack Joyce*); Norma Shearer (*Mary Ellen Hope*); Claire McDowell (*Mrs. Joyce*); Alec B. Francis (*Abner Hope*); Herbert Pryor (*Curt Horndyke*); Ann May (*Helen Horndyke*); George Dromgold (*Joe Lakin*); with Malcolm Waite, Mike Donlin

CREW: *Director* Vernon Keays (per intro cards); *Story* James Cruze, Frank Condon; *Cinematographers* Arthur Edeson, Paul Perry; *Art Director* Edward Langley

NOTE: Most print sources consulted in preparing this essay credited James Cruze as director.

The lowdown on this comedy is from *Exhibitor's Trade Review* (18 April 1925):

> Jack Joyce works in old Abner Hope's garage, has a grand project for utilizing nearby waterfall for electric power, but cannot obtain backing. Mary Ellen Hope comes to stay with her grandfather. She and Jack fall in love. Abner Hope predicts the end of the world and gives Jack all his money, telling him to spend it. With these funds Jack realized his electric project and opens a plant, waking up the town. In a dream he sees the end of the world, with destruction on all sides. He wakes up to find himself prosperous and the accepted suitor of Mary Ellen.

When it comes to inventive whiz kids, Jack Joyce (Jack Pickford) might just be the king of gadgetry, most of which gets stirred into the mix to help trigger some humor, although — with a good chunk of the proceedings missing — that's a hard case to prove. Mary Ellen Hope abruptly rolls into town on the tail end of a poor man's Keystone Kops chase, and it's Jack's handy-dandy elevator (conveniently installed in Abner's country garage) that's used to hide her car. Later, Jack seeks to impress Mary Ellen with an escalator built into his mansion, downplaying his nouveau-riche status with weak, not-so-witty dialogue like "A little invention of mine — a mere trifle — nothing at all." Perhaps the funniest (or the least unfunny) sequence is when Jack seeks to grabs the attention of financier, Curt Horn-

dyke: invited to play "stunts" at the banker's daughter's party, he brings along his miniature, prototype war tank. When it's his turn up, instead of making an impression, he accidentally shoots his would-be benefactor in the kisser and, after a bit of requisite slapstick, summarily gets his keister booted out the door.

These are some of the "highlights" that can be gleaned from the 35 or so minutes of the picture held at the Library of Congress (said footage donated by the Mary Pickford Foundation) and, on that basis, none of Jack's contraptions really exceeds the limits of 1920's technology. Unfortunately gone missing from *Waking Up the Town* is a bit of primo footage — at least according to afore-cited *Exhibitor's Trade Review*:

> The most important scene is that in which Jack dreams that the end of the world has come and sees our planet destroyed, with floods drowning out town after town, volcanoes blazing, mountains collapsing and hurtling into the ocean, etc. Not even little old New York escapes, for the island of Manhattan takes a header into the sea, skyscrapers and all, a very effective bit of trick photography.

That's an imposing description of the only true sci-fi element the movie offered, but how this finale might stack up against other early end-of-the-world disaster flicks is open to conjecture. Evidence points to at least some stock footage. *Variety*'s "Lait" observed (on April Fools' Day 1925) that "towards the end there are some end-of-the-world bits (some looked like as though filched from the newsreels)." Laurence Reid of *Motion Picture News* (on 11 April 1925) echoed: "The concluding reels featuring the destruction of our planet in miniature scenes through the devastating effects of a tornado resemble library shots."

Meanwhile, *Time* (magazine) noted on 6 April 1925: "There is at one point a fairly ingenious sequence stolen from the recent end-of-world scare." *Time* was most likely referring to Robert Reidt, one of the many Prophets of Doom who came to the forefront of the collective attention throughout the centuries. Reidt apparently had convinced himself that the he had the Armageddon scoop directly from the Archangel Gabriel himself: the world would surely end on his stipulated date in February of 1925 (a Friday the 13th by some accounts). A true zealot, Reidt even tried to persuade others to heed his prediction via a number of newspaper advertisements, and on the day *after* the proscribed doomsday — when the sun rose and those very same papers rolled their presses — he just revised his forecast and started anew.

The printed prognosis for *Waking Up the Town*'s future was, on the whole, almost as dim, with critiques ranging from the charitable to the horrendous. The short version of the 14 February 1925 *Harrison's Reports*: "Duck it." As for the longer version…

If a contest were held to determine what are the ten worst pictures of the year, this one should hold

Highly respected financier Curt Thorndyke (Herbert Prior, right) refuses to hear a word about the end the world from a guy with a clip-on tie (Jack Pickford) in *Waking Up the Town*. À gauche is George Drumwold, lending a black tie, wing collar, and muscle to the argument.

indisputable rights for a place in the list. It is about as boresome a picture as can be produced. The characters undertake to do things that are too trivial to arouse even mild interest. It is evident that the producers depended on the destruction of the world, seen by the hero in his dream, to put it over; but when the time comes for the spectator to see the deluge, the swallowing up of a big city, the collision of moon and earth and the resulting fire, he is too wearied to be impressed with these sights.

"Harry Carr's Page" in the *Los Angeles Times* (6 May 1925) — after blasting away with adjectives like "senseless," "pointless" and "stupid" — expanded: "If Jack Pickford really wishes to commit professional suicide, I should think it would be better for him to put all his make-up together in a pile, set them on fire and go out with a grandstand finish. Thus would the public be spared the slow agonies of pictures like *Waking Up the Town*."

The above-quoted *MPN* called the plot "sketchy" and the material insufficient for more than a three-reeler. *Variety* (also cited above) conceded that "there is much that is pleasing." but then (quite correctly) added a qualifier: "in all, *Waking Up the Town* can scarcely be rated as an important or outstanding contribution, the less so in view of the several impressive screen-world names attached to the various departments responsible." Considering that the team included James Cruze (see *Terror Island*, 1920), Arthur Edeson (*The Devil's Toy*, 1916) and — receiving top-billing — star #1 Jack Pickford (*The Ghost House*, 1917), that proviso seems spot on.

Star #1A in the film's publicity campaign was actress Norma Shearer. How she was assigned to this particular picture is not clear, but her entree into the movie industry *is*: "I guess it was just a dogged determination," she once admitted, "that got me my first chance in motion pictures." Migrating south from Canada, Norma and her sister, Athole, both followed the allure of the cinema to the Big Apple. Sis dropped out early to get married (to Howard Hawks), but Norma persevered; first came bits, then small parts and then, well… Come 1930, Miss Shearer received an Oscar for her role in *The Divorcee* — quite a step up from cavorting with Jack Pickford's gadgetry back in '25.

— *SJ*

West of Zanzibar

West of Zanzibar. Metro-Goldwyn-Mayer Pictures/M-G-M, 24 November 1928, 7 reels/6150 feet [available]

CAST: Lon Chaney (*Flint*); Lionel Barrymore (*Crane*); Mary Nolan (*Maizie*); Warner Baxter (*Doc*); Jacqueline Gadsdon (*Anna*); Roscoe Ward (*Tiny*); Kalla Pasha (*Babe*); Curtis Nero (*Bumbo*)

CREDITS: *Director* Tod Browning; *Scenario* Elliot Clawson and Waldemar Young; based on the play *Kongo* by Chester De Vonde and Kilbourn Gordon (New York premiere, 30 March 1926); *Titles* Joe Farnham; *Cinematographer* Percy Hilburn; *Film Editor* Harry Reynolds; *Set Decoration* Cedric Gibbons; *Costumes* David Cox

The film was released both as a conventional silent and as a silent with a Movietone sound effects and music score.

"The sordid and the sublime!"
— advertisement for *Kongo*

The name, Chester De Vonde, like the names of many stage greats of old, is mentioned only in theater histories, but in his day (the beginning of the 20th century), he wrote, produced and starred in a score of melodramas that were as popular then as their creator is forgotten now. De Vonde retired a couple of times, occasionally dabbled in the movies (see *Voices*), and settled down for a while to run a brass factory in New Jersey. Tiring of that, he sought a bit of adventure and headed for the Belgian Congo where, according to an article in the 8 September 1926 issue of the *Oakland Tribune*, he got more excitement than he bargained for:

> He ran afoul of one King Jamokis, head of a popular tribe, who learned that a white man had invaded the sacred precincts of his domain and was excessively annoyed, for at that point he was engaged in bitter warfare with neighborhood tribes. De Vonde was captured and although ultimately cleared of blame, he was forced to remain eighteen months within the confines of the state.

De Vonde returned to America with a case of tropical fever (which ultimately led to his death in 1928), but also with plenty of material for a play. Nonetheless, it took the Broadway success of *White Cargo* (1923) — a stew of sex and sweat set in Africa — to inspire De Vonde to deliver more of the same by writing *Kongo* (in collaboration with Kilbourn Gordon, producer of *The Cat and the Canary*). *Kongo* tells the tale of Flint, a crippled magician who sets himself up as a powerful witchdoctor in an ivory-rich backwater of the Congo. It's revenge and not money that motivates Flint, who is obsessed with getting back at the man (another ivory trader) who had crippled him and had stolen his wife many years before. To do so, Flint has taken his enemy's infant daughter and has had her raised in a convent, only to have her delivered to a brothel upon reaching womanhood. (Erich von Stroheim appropriated this idea for *Queen Kelly*.) He then has the syphilitic, broken girl brought to his hellish, jungle stronghold where he further degrades her. Ultimately, Flint discovers that she is really *his* daughter.

While no one saw great art in *Kongo*, critics found it to be an effective melodrama while noting that it owed a debt to *Rain* and *The Emperor Jones*, as well as to *White Cargo*. (Surprisingly, no one seems to have drawn a connection between Flint and the unreliable Mr. Kurtz, the ivory trader-turned-native god in Joseph Conrad's *Heart of Darkness*.) The play, starring Walter Huston as Flint, ran four months on Broadway and then went on to successful road show engagements. De Vonde and Gordon collaborated again the following year and came up with another convoluted revenge drama, *Tia Juana*. It flopped.

In 1928 M-G-M's Tod Browning was still casting about for vehicles with which to showcase the talents of Lon Chaney. Most of the six films they had already done as a team were in-house affairs with Browning and his scenarists concocting the stories. Perhaps Browning, who frequently drew inspiration from his days as a carnival pitchman to provide atmosphere for his films, developed an interest in *Kongo* because of the character of Flint, a magician who goes from gulling the suckers for a few pennies to holding an entire tribe in thrall with the same bag of tricks. First and foremost, though, the story allowed Chaney to do what he often did for Browning: display a physical deformity that was the outward manifestation of some moral or criminal vice. (Actually, that formula had originated, not with Browning, but with an earlier Chaney film, *The Penalty*, wherein the Man of a Thousand Faces played a legless cripple who becomes a feared gang leader and plots vengeance against the doctor who he believes needlessly amputated his legs.) All Browning really added to the mix was a heightened sense of the macabre and the sleazy show-biz background he knew so well.

One problem facing Browning in doing a celluloid version of *Kongo* was that the Will Hays Office, guardian of the nation's morals when it came to the movies, had forbidden any film adaptation of the play. Still, this was a few years before the Production Code had any real bite; Hays had likewise proscribed *Rain*, *West of the Water Tower* and *They Knew What They Wanted*, but all of them had gone before the cameras anyway. As a sop to the film czar, M-G-M let it be known that their new production, ultimately titled *West of Zanzibar*, was not really based on *Kongo* at all, and the play was not mentioned in the ads (though occasional publicity blurbs forgot this). Browning kept the basic premise, but changed those elements most likely to cause offense: Flint's half-caste mistress disappeared; Flint's crony, Doc, became a drunk rather than a dope addict; the heroine's venereal disease was not mentioned; and various acts of sadism directed at the girl and Flint's underlings were softened or jettisoned entirely. Some critics apparently didn't recognize the film's source, but others weren't fooled, notably *Harrison's Reports*, whose contempt for the movie we will presently consider.

Our synopsis comes from a viewing of the film.

Anna, wife of the stage magician Phroso, is in love with a man named Crane and plans to run away with him to Africa. Crane tells Phroso the bad news and the two of them fight. Phroso falls and is badly injured, losing the use of his legs. Later Anna and her baby girl return. Phroso finds Anna dead in a church. He swears vengeance on Crane and the child, whom he presumes is the offspring of his rival.

Eighteen years pass. Phroso, now known as "Deadlegs" Flint, lives in a remote Congo village, where the natives are in awe of his powers [actually his old stage magic tricks]. His helpers include Doc, once a physician, Tiny; the hulking Babe, and Bumbo, one of the Africans. Crane is now an ivory trader, and Flint delights in robbing his convoys by disguising Babe as a demon and frightening off the bearers. Flint has had Maizie, Crane's daughter, raised in a brothel but now that she's a young woman, he has her brought to his compound as his revenge scheme nears completion.

Flint treats Maizie abominably and encourages her dissipation in alcohol. Doc is her one friend and the two fall in love. One of the native customs is, when a man dies, to burn either his wife or daughter along with him on the funeral pyre. Flint gleefully participates in these rituals. Flint sends word to Crane that he is the one who has been robbing him and suggests that they meet. His scheme is to tell Crane about his daughter and then have him ambushed by Bumbo on his way back; this would result in Maizie being immolated by the tribe.

Crane arrives at Flint's dwelling and is amazed to find out that he's really Phroso. Flint shows him the drunken, disheveled Maizie and informs him that the wretched girl is his daughter. However, Crane bursts into laughter and tells Flint that Anna, hating him for crippling her husband, never ran away with him at all. Maizie is really Flint's daughter. Crane leaves and is shot by Bumbo before a shocked Flint can call his killer off. The natives prepare a funeral pyre for Crane with the expectation that Maizie will be sacrificed. Doc knows the truth about the girl's parentage, but Flint makes him promise never to tell her. Flint holds the natives off with his magic tricks allowing Doc and Maizie to escape. Enraged at being cheated of their victim, the natives burn Flint alive instead.

Variety's "Waly," in a largely negative review of the film, found the transition from music hall to jungle jarring and unconvincing:

An excellent basis for a story is sacrificed apparently for background and the theme in jumbled episodic way that reduces continuity to shreds.... Then [after the opening scenes] the action is transferred to another world. Chaney, too hurriedly, is shown as an ivory robber and just as mysteriously Barrymore [Crane] suddenly develops to have quit the stage and become a white trader in Africa [9 January 1929].

Actually there originally were some scenes setting up Phroso becoming Flint. A number of production stills bear this out, and Michael Blake, in his *Lon Chaney, the Man Behind the Thousand Faces*, describes a deleted scene wherein Phroso first meets Doc and Babe in Zanzibar, where they are running a scam in a low-class dive. The most famous missing scene, though, shows Chaney in a bizarre "duck man" getup, wherein he passes himself off as a freak to gull more suckers. (Presumably, the fact that Phroso has no feeling in his legs makes it possible for him to cram himself into the outfit; Browning, of course, later used a similar costume for Olga Baclanova at the end of *Freaks*). Nonetheless, the omission of the scene from the film did not extend to its elimination in the advertising. Per the 8 December 1928 *San Antonio* [Texas] *Light*: "The old Chaney of *Hunchback* and *Phantom of the Opera* fame — in all his glory as the 'Duck Man'.... Back in make-up: Weird, Grotesque make-up." No doubt there were some disappointed Chaney fans when they discovered that his "weird" make-up consisted of an unshaven mug and cropped hair.

There's also a still showing Kalla Pasha (Babe) holding down Warner Baxter (Doc) while Chaney pierces his back with a knife. Something like that happens in *Kongo*, with Flint cutting Doc to prepare him for his drug cure from the leeches, but Doc is an alcoholic, not a dope addict, in the silent. As per usual with Browning films, the continuity is a little ragged. Apropos of nothing, Doc tells Flint: "You're a puzzle, Dead Legs. One moment you're a fiend and the next — you're almost human." (This, right after the human sacrifice scene!) Maizie, apparently clean and sober, tells Doc he should lay off the hootch, but the very next scene shows Maizie addicted to the booze and Doc apparently shocked at this development. (Where has he been?)

Like the other Browning/Chaney silents, the focus is on melodrama, not horror, but there are a couple of eerie moments. The early swamp sequence is typical Browning: snakes, spiders, lizards, scorpions, crocodiles ... all things that crawl — like Flint himself — appear in rapid succession to produce maximum audience revulsion. (There are, however, no armadillos.) The masks worn by Babe, the witchdoctors, and Flint are effective in suggesting an ancient, primitive evil. The human sacrifice sequence is over quickly; the comparable scene in the 1932 remake *Kongo* pulls out all the stops and achieves a kind of delirium, switching from one scene of horror and lust to another. In the Browning film, this is conveyed largely by Mary Nolan (Maizie), who watches the ritual with a mixture of horror, disgust, fascination, and finally hysteria; some footage from the swamp scene and the human sacrifice later turn up in *Kongo*. As far as the human sacrifice goes, De Vonde — in spite of his sojourn in Africa — seems to have turned to India for inspiration and concocted a variation on the practice of *sati* (widow burning). There *was* a tradition of human sacrifice in the Congo, but it was usually practiced after the death of a chief and involved the killing of slaves. Such savagery however, pales in comparison to what the Belgians did in the Congo, but colonial atrocities are peripheral to *Kongo* and not part of *West of Zanzibar* at all.

While *Variety* complained the Chaney/Browning films were becoming repetitious and hastily conceived, most reviewers gave the film guardedly favorable notices. Whitney Williams' comments in the *Los Angeles Times* (14 October 1928) were pretty typical:

> Those who favor an element of weirdness, a suggestion of the grotesque, will thoroughly enjoy *West of Zanzibar*.... It is a picture that will arrest attention more for its novelty than for its dramatic or plot strength. It is this very essence, however, that will make it a box-office success.... Chaney gives to his portrayal the same conviction that generally characterizes his work in role of sinister nature, and while the part is striking, it lacks the customary force. This is by no means a contradiction — Chaney has imbued the role with real life but the part is not up to his usual standards.

Harrison's Reports, hardly a fan of the grimmer Browning/Chaney vehicles to begin with, was appalled by *West of Zanzibar* and devoted several articles to denouncing it, describing it (in the 5 January 1929 number) as "horrible" and "a piece of filth." *Harrison's* was also scornful of the Hays Office for its weakness and its chumminess with the producers they were supposed to be monitoring. The magazine urged support of the Brookhart Bill, which would have ended the blind-booking practice whereby the exhibitors were obliged to take a series of films from the studios rather than just one. The bill's supporters claimed that if the theater owners could pick and choose which films they wanted, they would reject the more morally questionable ones.

Recognizing the dilemma that blind-booking forced on the exhibitors, *Harrison's* also had a suggestion for theater owners who were being forced to show a film like *West of Zanzibar*:

> You may not be able to avoid either playing it, or at least paying for it even though you may not play it; but as not many of you can afford to pay for a Lon Chaney picture and not play it because of the price you are charged for it, I suggest that, should the distributor refuse to eliminate it from your contract, you call on every priest, minister and rabbi in your locality and lay the facts before them.... Have him write either to the exchange or the home office demanding that the picture be shown to a committee of clergyman before they force you to play it.

Several times *Harrison's* insisted that part of Flint's revenge scheme involved Maizie getting syphilis but, unlike the play, there's no direct reference to this in the film unless one simply assumes that Maizie, having been brought up in a brothel and having (*presumably*) become a whore herself, *must* therefore have contracted syphilis. Nonetheless, there is a scene where

Flint tells Maizie to smash the cup she's just drunk from because he doesn't want to take the chance of accidentally drinking from it himself; this could be a suggestion that she has a social disease. *Harrison's* had nothing against the revenge motif in the film; after all, they felt the skinning alive of the U-Boat commander in *Behind the Door* was quite justified. However, taking vengeance on an innocent child was something else again and put the film in a different category:

> But what had the little girl to do with the wrong, even if she were the offspring of an illicit union of his wife with the villain, which she is not? She had done nothing to deserve the horrible punishment. So the construction of the plot does not follow the laws of the drama and therefore *West of Zanzibar* is not art.... I am giving you this opinion so the distributor may not induce you to play the picture under the pretext that it is a piece of art [19 January 1929].

The writer apparently was unfamiliar with *Wuthering Heights*, wherein Heathcliff avenges himself on the Earnshaws and Lintons through their children. Still, it must be admitted that Flint's treatment of Maizie is so obscene that the sheer distastefulness of the idea takes away from the pathos and irony of the finale. There's also an odd element of blasphemy in the film, as the vow of vengeance is made in a church in front of a statue of the Madonna and child.

It is safe to assume that *Harrison's* would also have been horrified by the special treat the *Oakland Tribune* arranged for its paperboys: a free showing of *West of Zanzibar*! The paper thought it was a particularly good choice because, as the paper put it, "Lon Chaney and his funny faces and queer actions has [*sic*] always been a pleasure for the youngsters" (16 December 1928).

Compared to the 1932 sound "remake," *Kongo*, *West of Zanzibar* is pretty tame stuff. The former takes the play's trashy mix of sex and sadism and runs with it, allowing Walter Huston to

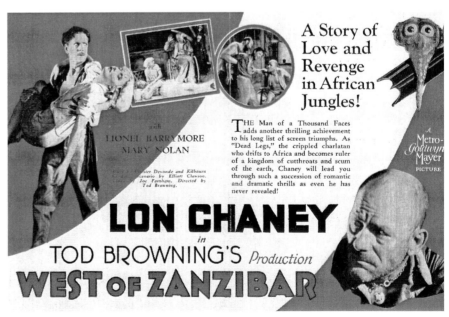

Original movie herald. The critter in the upper-right corner is "Man of a Thousand Faces Elmo," marketed when "Apatosaurus Elmo" finally ran out of gas.

repeat his stage role to create one of the most memorable movie villains of the 1930s. His Flint is a megalomaniac, unpredictable and vicious; a ruthless dictator that his underlings and the natives are quite right to fear. Chaney, on the other hand, suggests little more than a gruff gangster. And since this was a Lon Chaney picture, did anyone in the audience back in 1928 really think he'd stay a rotter until the very end? Nor was it likely that anyone was surprised by the revelation that Maizie is really Flint's daughter. In addition to the film's rather clumsy set-up, Chaney had already gone that route in his earlier Browning film, *The Road to Mandalay*, wherein he plays a Singapore criminal whose daughter, unaware that he's her father, despises him. There, he likewise sacrifices his life for her happiness (which he does *yet again* in Browning's *Where East is East*). Before one attempts to analyze Browning's interest in this situation, it should be pointed out that parent/children issues were the subject of more movies in the Silent Era than at any other time, and the plot contrivance dealing with a son/daughter who doesn't realize that another character is their father/mother was standard melodrama. Browning most likely just took the easy way and drew on the clichés of the day, and not on something more personal.

West of Zanzibar does have the benefit of a good supporting cast. Besides Mary Nolan — managing to be both hardboiled *and* vulnerable, the actress pretty much steals the show from

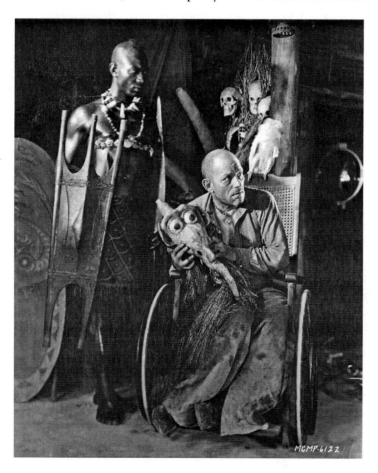

Lon Chaney holds a singularly unfortunate native mask in an otherwise wildly atmospheric scene in *West of Zanzibar*.

Chaney, at least in the swamp scene — there's Warner Baxter bringing his usual innate decency to the role of Doc (even though the part is underwritten) and, of course, Lionel Barrymore as a sneering, sardonic Crane. The final confrontation between Flint and Crane doesn't play quite as well as one might expect, but it doesn't in *Kongo*, either, nor even in the original play, according to *The New York Times*. Part of the problem here is Barrymore's reaction at being told the pathetic Maizie is his daughter: He seems totally shaken and moves slowly, almost painfully away from Chaney as though in shock; i.e., the reaction you might expect if he really *did* believe Maizie to be his child. He then begins laughing and tells Chaney the truth, but the initial phony theatrics throw the whole scene off. Jacqueline Gadsden (see entries, *The Mysterious Island* and *The Thirteenth Hour*) is seen only very briefly as Anna, but brings a sad-eyed poignancy to the role. As per usual, Browning rounds up just the right sort of faces for the music hall scene and, later, the brothel sequence.

Mary Nolan (née Mary Imogene Robertson) began modeling (under the name Imogene Wilson) in New York City when she fourteen. Her face was described as "angelic," and she went on to become a famous Ziegfeld Follies girl (nicknamed "Bubbles"); Flo Ziegfeld himself pronounced her the most beautiful of the Ziegfeld girls. Still, Nolan had the misfortune to fall in love with popular blackface comedian, Frank Tinney, a married man whose idea of "indoor sport" was beating his girlfriend. Nolan staged a well-publicized, phony suicide attempt and then charged Tinney with assault (she said he beat up her maid too!) and filed a lawsuit. The court case was a circus and, in stark contrast to how a situation of domestic abuse would be treated in the press today, became something of a media joke. The charge was dismissed and Tinney headed for England, but, when Ziegfeld learned that Tinney and Nolan had reconciled, he fired her.

After some stormy times with Tinney in Old Blighty, Nolan headed for Deutschland where she appeared in a string of movies under the name Imogene Robertson. One of them, *Die Abenteuer eines Zehenmarkscheines* (*Adventures of a Ten Mark Note*) became something of a minor classic. Still, she gained a reputation as a prima donna, faking fainting spells and breaking contracts. Facing court cases and unpaid bills, Nolan left Germany in a hurry in 1927. Back in Hollywood, she did a bit part in *Topsy and Eva* and changed her name to Mary Nolan, telling the press she was breaking totally with the past.

Besides *West of Zanzibar*, Nolan had good roles in *Sorrell and Son* and *Desert Nights* (with John Gilbert), but her sound movies, including Tod Browning's terrible remake of his *Outside the Law*, were inconsequential. After a few Poverty Row quickies, she supported herself singing in night clubs; a failed marriage to a stockbroker, frequent brushes with the law, and drug problems added to her woes. In 1935, she sued M-G-M honcho Eddie Mannix (according to some, M-G-M's version of Luca Brasi) for a half-million dollars, claiming they had a relationship from 1927 to 1931. Nolan charged that Mannix, another married man, had beaten her and later had her blacklisted from the movies when she refused to get lost. Mannix settled with her out of court — the terms were kept secret — but before long

Nolan was broke and ill. In 1941 she sold her life story to *The American Weekly*; it was syndicated in a number of newspapers under the title "Confessions of a Follies Beauty" which featured an illustration of a naked girl sitting in a bathtub which was being filled with champagne by fancy-dress partygoers. This brief flurry of publicity did Nolan little good; her remaining few years were spent in poverty, illness and the throes of addiction. In 1948 she wrote her autobiography, *Yesterday's Girl*, and had high hopes of selling it to the movies, but she died of an overdose of sedatives at the age of 42.

Warner Baxter had a far happier career. After a stab at selling insurance, Baxter became a hoofer in 1910 and — in true *42nd Street* fashion — got to replace the lead dancer when he broke his ankle. A stint in vaudeville was followed by stock-company work as a juvenile lead and then a 1917 appearance on Broadway in Oliver Morosco's *Lombardi, Ltd*. After doing his bit in the Navy during the Great War, Baxter broke into the movies and achieved some notice as leading man to Ethel Clayton and later to Betty Compson. He played good supporting roles as often as leads, but starting coming into his own in the mid–1920s, notably in Herbert Brenon's *The Great Gatsby* (lost, unfortunately). When a car accident prevented Raoul Walsh from taking the role of the Cisco Kid in *In Old Arizona*, Baxter took over and won the Academy Award.

Baxter thrived in the 1930s (he made nearly $300,000 in 1936 alone) and put in a particularly strong performance as Dr. Samuel Mudd in John Ford's *The Prisoner of Shark Island*. Genre fans might be most interested in his role as the murdered diplomat brought back to life in the offbeat sci-fi/romance, *Six Hours to Live*. He also starred in two films featuring Bela Lugosi: the rather screwy *Such Men Are Dangerous* and the Foreign Legion drama, *Renegades*.

Health problems and other interests — mainly real estate — saw Baxter turn to "B" movies in the 1940s, including a weak remake of the ghost drama, *Earthbound*, and the *Crime Doctor* series for Columbia. In the latter he played criminal psychologist, Dr. Ordway, who solved many a puzzling case, but always looked like he'd rather be napping. As the 1940s came to an end, Baxter's health problems took a grim turn for the worse. A terrible case of arthritis was so painful he was finally unable to eat. A lobotomy was performed to ease his suffering, but pneumonia set in resulting in his death in 1951.

In *The New York Times* review of *Kongo*, the critic wrote that acting honors for the play should go to black actor, Clarence Redd, who portrayed Fuzzy, Flint's (hench)man Friday. Curtis Nero received no such accolades for playing the comparable role, Bumbo, in *West of Zanzibar*, but he did get to reprise the part in *Kongo*. Nero, who also did bits in films like *Tarzan of the Apes* and *The Sign of the Cross*, came to a demise that sounds like something out of *Zanzibar*: In 1932 Nero got into a fight over a card game with a man named Jack (Blackjack) Woods. Nero gouged out one of Woods' eyes. A full ten years later, Woods got his revenge and shot Nero dead while he was playing pool.

No doubt Dead Legs Flint would have approved.

— HN

When Dr. Quackel Did Hide

When [Dr.] Quackel Did Hide. The Gold Seal Film Corporation/States Rights via Aywon Film Corporation, July 1920, 4/5 reels, two-reel cutdown available
CAST: Charlie Joy (*Dr. Henry Quackell*); Tom Findlay (*Sir George Kerchew*); C.R. Churchill (*Mr. Uttermum*); James Renfroe (*Doctor Laudunum*), Edgar Jones
CREDITS: *Directed and Written by* Charles Gramlich

Ho, boy…
This is the most obscure J&H film to hit the screens during 1920, a banner year for the sundry Doctors Jekyll and Messrs Hyde if ever there was one. A production of the Gold Seal Film Corporation — per our research, its *only* production —*Quackel* was distributed via the States Rights system, under the auspices of the Aywon Film Corporation. It may be remembered that Aywon Films likewise handled the release of *The Evolution of Man*, which starred everybody's favorite man-ape, Jack. Aywon, which was also responsible for the production of a baker's dozen features (mostly Westerns) from the late 1910s to the mid–1930s, was headed by Nathan Hirsh, a businessman whose professional *raison d'être* was the rapid movement of 35mm prints throughout the country's less notable venues. During that same time frame, Hirsh juggled over 140 motion pictures (again, mostly Westerns) that would have gone forever unseen had there been only the studio-owned theater chains. Thus, the man made his living. (Hirsh personally produced a handful of features — yet again mostly Westerns, several for Aywon, at least once as "Robert Curwood" — during the first half of the 1930s.)

Besides being Aywon's president, Hirsh was also its publicist, and if the *extremely* limited number of news items on *Quackel* was typical of an Aywon publicity campaign, the man could have used some help. Although virtually all the trackable press the film received was concentrated within a period of some eight weeks, problems still arose, both with the title (the film was aka *When Quackel Did Hide*) and the running time: the picture was alternately tagged a four- or five-reeler. Other notices we were able to find led to our feeling confidant in concluding that the information contained in a typical Aywon press release was pretty much as vague and unreliable as said press releases were infrequent. One puff piece (in the 6 November 1920 *Motion Picture News*) was headlined "Three Aywon Pictures Find Ready Buyers," although the body of the first paragraph listed FOUR such Aywon pictures, and it's impossible to determine at this late date whether one of the titles mentioned ever made it to the screen. None of the press the film enjoyed was generated by anyone other than Hirsh — we could locate no reviews of any kind — and in none of *der Hirshtext* was there any inking of story details, save for pithy, anticipated stuff like "A travesty on Dr. Jekyll and Mr. Hyde." And if *Quackel* was even *once* promoted via an illustrated ad during its limited run, only Hirsh and the Shadow knew for sure.

Starring in *Quackel* was the aptly stage-named Charlie Joy, who —*Motion Picture News* revealed — was bringing his "Miami beauties" along to join in the "laugh-provoker." A full-page ad (text only) in the 3 July 1920 number of *The Moving Picture World* promised that the Joy-ful feature —"a real comedy sensation with plenty of thrills"—was a harbinger of bounteous Joys yet to come: there were already six (6) two-reel Joy comedies awaiting release, the ad averred, with others ("one every month for fifteen months") to appear soon thereafter. Try as we might, we could none of us locate any information whatsoever about the six two-reelers that were already in the can, and Mr. Joy—afforded the appositive "well-known comedian" in the 17 July 1920 issue of *The Motion Picture News*—appears to have vanished as utterly as did prints of *Quackel*. When even renowned silent-comedy historian and author, Ed Watz, confessed his ignorance of Charlie and his angels, we gave up the ghost.

The only other cast member named in any of the picture's bountiful publicity was one Edgar Jones, a New Yorker who appeared in about 80 early (1910s) Westerns while directing about half of them. Per *The AFI Catalog*, in 1922 Jones not only directed and appeared in Playgoers Pictures' *Lonesome Corners*, he wrote and produced it, as well. *Quackel* appears to be the man's sole genre credit, but some sources list him as having directed a short for Lubin in 1915—*The Beast*—and the lack of plot info may leave the door open on that one.

When Dr. Quackel Did Hide was never copyrighted, so we have no registration summary or other incidentals to share. Film historian Richard M. Roberts reports that a two-reel condensation was available in both 8mm and 16mm Kodascope formats to the collectors' market some years back, and Grapevine Video's release, "Hollywood Spoofs," includes the cut-down, entitled *When Quackell Did Hide*. Courtesy of film historian/author/webmaster, Don Glut, we were able to screen the cut-down and thus can report…

In the *Quackell* bowdlerization, Sir George Kerchew, Attorney Uttermum, and Doctor Laudunum (substitute Sir Danvers Carew, Mr. Utterson, and Dr. Lanyon for authentic Stevenson nomenclature) are engaging in philosophical discussion. Kerchew declares that "there's not a man alive who hasn't skidded at least once in his life from the straight and narrow," but Dr. Laudunum—once Henry Quackell's college "chump"—singles out his ex-schoolmate as an exception.

Enter Quackell: "A little more holy than a saint—famous for doing good and making liver pills." In the mood to socialize, Doctor Q. opts to go slumming with the boys (albeit qualifying his participation with "But—gosh, how I hate it"), and the entourage saunters over to the "Bucket of Blood," a local pub. There follow a few, short, weak gags.

Cut to new scene and title: "For weeks Henry Quackell experimented, trying to discover a drug that would moult [*sic*] the wings from his shoulder, grow horns on his head, and make him BAD." Quackell dips his fingers inquisitively into his elixir, tastes it, and transforms immediately into his sought-after alterego; straightaway, he changes back. (The transformations in the film—effected either via the intrusion of title cards or the crudest of editing-room cuts and splices—are hardly special-effects highlights. Quackell's monstrous self sports little more than fangs, wild hair, and ripped clothing, but we feel that the substandard makeup application would pass muster [if only barely] with most genre fans. In one unfortunate shot, though, he is eerily reminiscent of a toothy Michael Jackson.)

Cut to the doctor paying a professional call at hospital. After offering a patient several of his "famous 32 caliber pills," the good physician promptly and inexplicably whacks him over the head with a large rubber hammer and—in a sequence reminiscent of George Méliès on a bad day—said patient explodes in a puff of smoke. After the man's remains are casually swept up by a "wrecking crew" of hospital attendants, Quackell's evil self again emerges. Proceeding to a nearby watering hole, he realizes that he now needs a name; he decides on "Hide" since that's what he is now trying to do. Feeling his wicked oats, Hide accosts a youth (actually an obese adult dressed like a child) and steals his candy. Moments later, restitution is made to the youngster's father (actually a child in adult garb) in the form of a check drawn on the "National Sand Bank" and handed over with the accompanying title, "Here's my check for 400 pounds—I hope they all fall on you at once." Again, moments later, he then scares an African American boy chalk white, and the close-up of Hide at this point may be the nearest thing to horrific to be found in the entire picture.

Ultimately, Hide takes up lodging at a tannery while his comrades display concern over the Quackell/Hide association. Kerchew follows Hide to his new domicile where the villain forces a liquid down Kerchew's throat and—in what may be the funniest part of a generally unfunny comedy—a title card reads "Just a moment's intermission, folks, while Hide changes back into Quackell."

Kerchew's daughter tells Quackell that she fears her father has been killed; Quackell then (for some reason) summons the police, who begin a Keystone Kop–like chase after Quackell, who has transformed once again into Hide. As all converge on Quackell's lab, Hide searches desperately for an antidote (which is revealed to be Seitletz Powder, an early 1900s supposed cureall). Kerchew—hung over, but not nearly dead—produces some of the powder and Quackell's condition is (at least for the nonce) remedied.

We can't imagine the wonders that vanished along with the missing two (or three) reels.

—*JTS/SJ*

Where Is My Father?

Where Is My Father? Exclusive Features, Inc./Exclusive; States Rights, July 1916, 7 reels [LOST]

CAST: May Ward (*Mathilde/Therese*); William Sorrell (*Dieudonne de la Graveries*); Ed. F. Roseman (*Dumesnil*); Harold J. Jarrett (*Gratien/Henri*); Agnes Marc (*Maid*); George Henry (*Baron de la Graveries*); with Roy Pilcher

CREDITS: *Director* Joseph Adelman; *Scenario* Joseph Adelman; based on the short story "Black, the Story of a Dog," by Alexander Dumas, père, in *Histoire de mes bêtes* (Paris, 1868).

This tale of reincarnation was adapted from the story, "Black: The Story of a Dog," by Alexander Dumas, père (of all people). The nominal phrase, "Dumas père," of course, conjures up visions of *The Three Musketeers*, *The Count of Monte Cristo*, and *The Man in the Iron Mask* (actually the renamed fourth volume of *Le Vicomte be Bragellone*), all of which have survived the years (and the movies) better than has "Black." Be that as it may, the story served as the underpinning for one of the half-dozen or so features produced by the short-lived Exclusive Features. With no swords to be flashed or swashes to be buckled, the most demanding of the roles fell to a certain May Ward, and the film unreeled thus:

> Dieudonne de la Graveries, a well to do young man in Paris, meets and falls in love with Mathilde, a young orphan living with her aunts. The couple is married, but Mathilde wearies of her good-natured husband and becomes fascinated with two handsome, French officers. Through an accident, Dieudonne learns of his wife's unfaithfulness and leaves for a trip around the world with his friend, Dumesnil. They settle on an island in the South Pacific Ocean. In a fight with the natives, Dumesnil is wounded and dies, after assuring Dieudonne that, if he needed him, he will come back some day in the shape of a dog, according to the Pythagorian idea of soul-transmigration. In the meanwhile, Mathilde has died in Paris, leaving an infant daughter, whose father is unknown.
>
> Years later, the child has grown to the young girl, Therese, who keeps a flower shop. She loves a wealthy young man, who is betrothed to another; he sends a farewell message to Therese, by his twin brother, who taking advantage of the resemblance, finds means to betray the young girl. When she discovers the deception, she drives him from her. Dieudonne de la Graveries living in retirement in Paris, is visited by a black dog that recalls the prophecy of his old friend, Dumesnil. The dog leads him to Therese, who in her despair, is about to commit suicide.
>
> Dieudonne learns who she is, and on hearing her story, demands that the twin brother, a lieutenant in the army, shall marry Therese. The officer refuses, and falls fatally wounded in a duel with Dieudonne. Before his death, the officer marries Therese and gives her his name. A year later, Therese, her child and the family dog are seen happily living under the protection of Dieudonne, while the spirit of Mathilde, the erring mother, is seen in the background, giving her blessing.

(The quaint phraseology and suspect punctuation of the synopsis meticulously transcribed from a contemporary herald on the film, held at the archives of the Library of Congress.)

It's obvious that were it not for that "Pythagorian idea of soul-transmigration," *Where Is My Father?* would still be perched in some obscure corner of the collective unconsciousness. (Okay; we'll throw in Mathilde's double-exposed presence at the last-reel fadeout, but that's really just a case of gilding the lily.) Pythagoras, the Greek philosopher and mathematician who is still roundly cursed out by high-school students befuddled by the length of the hypotenuse, did indeed believe in soul transmigration. The old boy (he did most of his best work from around 560 B.C. on) held that, unlike the body, the soul is immortal and thus moves from body to body, stopping only to refresh itself in the Underworld between moves. After a number of these spiritual junkets, the soul is so purified that it can skip further transmigrations and head to its reward. (Hey, it *could* happen.) Still, despite our poking about in *res philosophicae*, we could nowhere find mention of Pythagoras insisting that one must come back at some point as a dog.

An interesting discussion may be had in determining just where and how Dumesnil and Dieudonne became so caught up in this particular "Pythagorian" theorem; it's unlikely that the two picked up the idea while beachcombing in Tahiti. "Well to do young gentlemen" in 19th-century Paris *might* have come across a theory or two of reincarnation in the course of their

university education, and *might* have opted to board that train of thought rather than succumb (as did the less- or uneducated) to the rites and rituals of Catholicism. No matter where or how they latched onto it, though, it's a given that they did, and the fact remains that Dumesnil must have been keeping an eye on his friend during one or more of those myriad refreshment stops in the Underworld. How else to explain that he waited 20 or so years before donning fangs and fur to help Dieudonne in his hour of need? Dieudonne himself had no idea that Therese was being deflowered, or that there even *was* a Therese with whom he might want to become involved. The fact that good ol' Dumesnil led him to the scene of Therese's undoing *must* mean that Dieudonne was the girl's biological father. Otherwise, Dieudonne — having lammed it to the South Pacific back when Mathilde had started hawking her wares — would have had no vested interest in the waif's fate and would, thus, not have been in any sort of "need."

Deep stuff.

The Moving Picture World (15 July 1916) wasn't having any of it. After admitting that its story was entertaining and that one could follow the plot without difficulty, it lowered the boom:

> It is not an artistically produced film. There is not one of the players who consistently holds to a character with convincing ability. The backgrounds are now and then almost amusingly unconvincing. In the costuming one won't find any special effort to attain realism…. The coming back of the husband's friend in the form of a dog, because, as Pythagoras taught, he took that doom upon him for his sin, is, in the tale, a startling thing; but in the picture, is more amusing than effective. It is hard to get that kind of thing over in a picture, and the director of this one is no Griffith.

A full-page, fully-illustrated advertisement for the film accompanied the above-cited review, and the title was bracketed with sensational, purple prose:

> Of all Vampires
> Here is the Cruelest,
> Subtlest, Most Alluring.
> — the woman in —
> WHERE IS
> MY FATHER?
> (The untold secret)

The New York Dramatic Mirror (14 October 1916) made no mention of "vampires" and took no notice of either the reincarnated Dumesnil or the disembodied Mathilde, preferring, rather, to comment on the production design:

> Judging from this play, people dressed in the novelist's time much as they do today and about the only differences in the household furnishing was an abundance of candles and candlesticks in place of electric lights…. While the story of intrigue seems rather sordid and unredeemed by much nobility until the last act, it is not depressing, as it might seem from a recital of its incidents. This is because there are so many pretty outdoor scenes in parks and private gardens and sea and shore views in the South Seas. Flowers abound all through the play and their appearance adds a sort of festive appearance.

May Ward seems to have made her motion picture debut in 1915 (appearing, as she did, in both *A Continental Girl* — in which she was first billed as the "Dresden Doll" — and *Virtue*) and pretty much called it a career with *Where Is My Father?* Prior to her stint in the flickers, the lady was a singer/comedienne who put out elaborate song-and-dance revues through the usual vaudeville circuits. Originally the act was called "May Ward and the Eight Dresden Dolls," but at some point her eight sidekicks vanished, and May became "*The* Dresden Doll" by default. Two of her more memorable musical revues were entitled *The Cash Girl* and *The Garden of Love*, whence came such unforgettable tunes as "Put Your Arms around Me, Honey" and "Hands Up."

Beyond these fragmentary bits, we enter the world of speculation. There was *a* May Ward (along with a Lizzie Ward and a Harry Ward) featured among the cast members of *In New York Town*, an unremarkable musical that played on Broadway for less than a month in 1905. And there was also a May Ward*e* on Broadway once — for 80-odd performances — in a bit part in the 1903 adaptation of Tolstoy's *Resurrection*. The smart money says it was our May in the 1905 tune-fest, but someone altogether different hacking her way through the translation from the Russian.

Joseph Adelman probably would have agreed that he certainly was no Griffith (Who was?), but he did direct 100 percent of May Ward's cinematic output (which also represented 100 percent of Mr. Adelman's cinematic output), and not even David Wark himself could make that claim. As was the case with Ms. Ward, there are legitimate theatrical credits for *a* Joseph Adelman, but the "Broadway Adelman" was an actor, pure and simple, in ten different productions presented between 1903 and 1918. And as for *Father*'s leading man, William Sorrell, he was on hand for ⅔ of all the May Ward features (he was curiously absent for *Virtue*), but he was on the payroll for some two dozen *other* films, including Edwin S. Porter's 1909 *Faust* (Sorrell was Mephistopheles) and the King Baggott version of *Dr. Jekyll and Mr. Hyde* (1913). Mr. Sorrell seems to have had as many onscreen variations to his name as he did onscreen appearances.

Exclusive Features, Inc. was both a production company (briefly) and a distribution company (briefly) in its (brief) existence. With its New York City office(s) manned by Joseph M. Goldstein (both president and treasurer of the concern), Exclusive made features exclusively (a whopping six of 'em in toto), but distributed only one — *Where Is My Father?* — and that one, only in New York City. Outside of the City limits, *Father* — and the other features — fell victim to the inadequacies of the States Rights system. Between 1915 and 1919, though, the company was also responsible for distributing a different handful of pictures, but whether those features (like *The Victory of Virtue* or *Pamela's Past*) vanished by accident or by design remains anybody's guess.

Yet another mundane weeper ginned up by a dose of the supernatural, *Where Is My Father?* had so little going for it that its quick disappearance from the scene left no one asking *Where Is that Picture?*

— *JTS*

While London Sleeps

While London Sleeps. Warner Bros/Warner Bros., 27 November 1926, 6 reels/5,810 feet [LOST]

CAST: Rin Tin Tin (*Rinty*); Helene Costello (*Dale Burke*); Walter Merrill (*Thomas Hallard*); John Patrick (*Foster*); Otto Mathieson (*London Letter*); George Kotsonaros (*the Monk*); Dewitt Jennings (*Inspector Burke*); Carl Stockdale (*Stokes*); Les Bates (*Long Tom*)

CREDITS: *Director* Howard Bretherton; *Story and Scenario* Walter Morosco; *Assistant Director* William Cannon; *Cinematographer* Frank Kesson; *Assistant Cameraman*: Fred West

No one will argue that dogs haven't played their part in an admittedly good number of horror films (or whatever stuff like *Where Is My Father?* is), but usually only in supporting roles, on scene (or just out of frame) to gin up the creepy atmosphere by baying in the fog or by barking out a warning as the mummy shambles through the backyard. In most of these movies, Rover is just one of the boys, as it were, adding his two cents to the mix at its noisiest or putting in his oar when the moment is right, and settling for having his ears scratched and lying on a rug in front of the fireplace for the rest of the unreeling. There *has* been the odd picture featuring a dramatically significant, canine menace (*The Most Dangerous Game*) and even the odder (if not downright *rare*) film that centers on Man's Best Friend come straight from hell (*The Hound of the Baskervilles*), but doggie heroes of the horrors have been fairly rare, especially in the cinema's Golden Age. One heroic pooch that leaps to mind is the noble Thor from 1935's *The Black Room*. At the climax, while the useless two-legged hero (Robert Allen) stands around sulking, Thor bounds into the church and disrupts the ceremony mere moments before the heroine is irrevocably tied to her bridegroom, a villain who has assumed the identity of his brother for nefarious purposes. The villain's plans thwarted, he flees from the angry mob and makes for the safety of the titular chamber where, due to Thor's noble instincts and a well-timed leap, he is toppled into a pit and impaled on a knife wedged in the still, cold arm of his brother's cadaver.

Rin Tin Tin would have been proud.

Rinty was a particularly resourceful dog. If Timmy was trapped in the old mine, you could count on Lassie to go off somewhere to get help, but Rin Tin Tin would have thrown the boy a rope and pulled him out and perhaps even chastised the mine owner for not taking good care of his property. Rin Tin Tin was discovered by Corporal Lee Duncan, who rescued him and his sister Nanette from a bombed-out kennel in France during the First World War. Duncan took the two pups back with him to America, where Nanette died of distemper. Rin Tin Tin (the name comes from a doll French children used to give to the American soldiers for good luck) survived and thrived and Duncan was so impressed by the German Shepherd's intelligence and agility that he envisioned a career for him in the movies. After some skepticism Warner Brothers gave Rinty a chance; it proved to be a wise move as the dog's subsequent popularity kept the studio afloat in troubled financial times.

Rinty's adventures usually took place somewhere in the Great Outdoors; *While London Sleeps* is atypical in both its urban (and foreign) setting as well as its being the only Rin Tin Tin film to have a horror element.

Our synopsis comes from *The AFI Catalog*:

Inspector Burke of Scotland Yard concentrates all his forces on the capture of London Letter, a notorious criminal leader in the Limehouse district who possesses both Rinty, a splendid dog, and a man-beast monster that ravages and kills at its master's command. Burke almost apprehends the gang, but Rinty's uncanny perceptions foil Burke's coup, and Foster is killed for betraying the gang. When Rinty loses in a fight against another dog, Burke's daughter, Dale, rescues Rinty from London Letter's abuse, and he becomes devoted to his new mistress. At the criminal's order, the monster kidnaps Dale and imprisons her. Burke and his men wound London Letter while on his trail, and Rinty finds him dying. In a ferocious battle, Rinty kills the monster.

Oddly enough, when the film was released to Germany in 1928 (under the title *Rin Tin Tin Unter Verbrechern*; *Rin Tin Tin Among Criminals*), the trade journal *Film Kurier* didn't even mention London Letter's monstrous helper in the course of its synopsis. In fact, the review changes the villain's name to the Hawk (as does Paul Thompson in his write-up of the film for *Motion Picture News*) and gives the following description of the climax:

> It comes to a fistfight between Hawk's gang and the police. An unlucky shot hits a kerosene lamp that starts the house on fire.... Now it is the dog's turn to rescue the girl who is tied up in the burning house. The dog shows the girl a secret passageway that leads to the roof. The girl is exhausted and falls from the roof into the Thames. The dog jumps in after her and rescues her.

None of the other reviews we consulted mentions any such climatic fire, which leads us to speculate whether an alternate version of the film was made for the foreign market. In any case, when the film played in England, the beast-man disappeared not just from the reviews but from the movie itself. The British censors were not alone, however, in questioning the inclusion of horror scenes in a film likely to draw many patrons who were still in short pants. Under the headline "Better Not Let the Children See This," "Mae Tinee" (in the 14 December 1926 *The Chicago Tribune*) wrote the following: "Some of the children who attended the same performance I did got terribly excited over the actions of the hideous brute man as portrayed by George Kotmarof [*sic*], and will probably be afraid to go to bed alone for a long, long time."

Paul Thompson, in the aforementioned *Motion Picture News* review, thought the beast-man's presence stretched credulity to the breaking point and that the producers tried "to send chills up and down the spine by the imminence of this monster's ravishing of the heroine, Helene Costello, but somehow it didn't seem to click."

Variety's "Rush," who panned the film, thought directorial ineptitude ruined any possible scares: "At one point there is what should be a thrill-inspiring shock when a savage ape-man from the Indian jungle climbs into the bedroom of the sleeping beauty to abduct her. The thrill is cancelled when anyone can see that the ape-man is being hoisted through the trees to the bedroom window by a cable hooked to the back of his coat."

Nevertheless, the critic in *Harrison's Reports*— writing the only favorable review we found — thought that "the scenes in which the ape-man, chained to the wall, tried to break his chains in order to lay hands on the heroine are extremely suspensive."

London Letter's brutish helper is known as the Monk; presumably this is short for monkey and not a reference to an earlier religious vocation traded in for a career as a henchman. Rush's comment that the creature hails from the Indian jungle is the only indication as to his origins, and publicity for the film always refers to him as an "ape-man." Clearly he's not the result of a sinister scientific experiment, nor can we assume he's some sort of evolutionary throwback. Perhaps he's meant to be a Tarzan-type whose adopted ape-family was rougher than the one who took in the Lord of the Jungle. Mae Tinee describes the Monk as shining "like a hunk of jet." He doesn't seem particularly monstrous in the stills: short, stocky, seemingly bald, he has neither claws nor fangs. Still, publicity for the film made much of his climactic battle with Rinty:

> Rin Tin Tin, canine screen star, has enacted death struggles with many creatures, from men to crocodiles but never before has he fought a more thrillingly dramatic fight.... Rinty, after an enmity that lasts throughout the story, pits his ninety pounds of flashing energy against the 180 pounds of George Kotsonaros, the world's light-heavyweight wrestling champion, who portrays a ferocious ape-man. The dog is fighting for her possession while she, weak with horror, beholds the evenly matched struggle which will decide her fate [*Alton* (Ohio) *Evening Telegraph*, 31 December 1926].

Kotsonaros would play a bona fide ape man in *The Wizard*, and the particulars of his career appear in our chapter on that picture.

The Monk didn't turn up in ads for the film, which tended to depict the canine star striking a noble pose or snuggling with Helene Costello. Naturally, publicity for the film focused on Rinty, who—interested readers were informed—became a father during the shooting; tellingly, he didn't let this blessed event detract from his performance. Nonetheless, Otto Mathieson (London Letter) *did* rate a mention in one piece printed

"Who's a good boy?" George Kotsonaros scares the hell out of Rin-Tin-Tin, whose tail can be seen between his legs, in *While London Sleeps*.

in *The Mansfield* [Ohio] *News* (on the 21 August 1927). After recounting the number of hazards the actor faced during filming, the article revealed that the biggest one came when Mathieson was obliged to fall backward from a dock twelve feet to the water below:

> Mattissen [*sic*] does not swim a stroke nor has he ever dived, and even for an expert the business of slowly becoming unconscious and falling — not diving — limply over backwards is no small feat. Five cameras were stationed at various advantageous angles; and although he had to repeat the performance twice, he claims his nerves were steady but the "thrill" was right on the job as he leaned backward for the second time.

No doubt had stagehands not dived in to assist him, Mathieson would have been saved by Rinty (assuming the dog was not on his lunch break). More on the man who took a dive can be found in the entry on *Whispering Wires*.

Reviewers found the film very old fashioned, a throwback to the two-reelers of the 1910s (already regarded as campy in the sophisticated 1920s). "Rush," commenting that the heroine's clothes were as out of date as the plot, speculated that the film may have been made a few years earlier and shelved because it was a "weak sister." Rush found the film's technical aspects likewise primitive: "The photography is not even passable and most of the action is timed like slow-motion film so when the butler walks to the door to answer a ring he seems to float through the air."

Sources differ as to whether Howard Bretherton or scenarist Walter Morosco actually directed the picture, although given the notices, either might have preferred "Alan Smithee." Morosco, whose main claims to fame come from being the son of Broadway impresario, Oliver Morasco, and the husband of Corrine Griffith, has no other directorial credits — though he did go on to a career as a producer — so most likely former film editor Bretherton must take the blame. If so it was his first film and, while he never developed into a notable director, his subsequent work must have been at least acceptable, as he labored steadily for Warner Brothers and Paramount until the mid-1930s. A publicity piece for his work at Warner Brothers in the early talkie days describes how he would insist that his actors give up smoking while on a film as it could cause "husky voice" and thus result in inconsistent sound recording. Bretherton also turned up in ads for Lux Toilet Soap, wherein his experience as a director of beautiful actresses meant he was also an expert on what it takes to have lovely skin. Bretherton's most notable genre credit is the still-extant-but-elusive *The Return of the Terror* (1934). Not long after that, the director-cum-toilet-soap-spokesman turned to westerns — notably the Hopalong Cassidy films — and pretty much stayed with that genre for the rest of his career.

Playing the romantic leads in a Rin Tin Tin movie was a thankless task, so such roles often went to second-stringers like John Harron and June Marlowe, or Carroll Nye and Audrey Ferris. Here, Helene Costello and Walter Merrill get the honor of being upstaged by the charismatic German Shepherd and, judging from their subsequent careers, Rinty didn't break a sweat stealing scenes from them. Helene was the daughter of matinee idol and early film star, Maurice Costello — who had

enjoyed his heyday in the 1910s at Vitagraph (*While London Sleeps* was shot there, Warner Brothers having purchased the studio in 1925) — and the sister of Dolores, who would marry John Barrymore in 1928. Though both sisters had been child actresses in films with their father, Dolores' career took off in the 1920s while Helene's sputtered. Perhaps her most notable movie was the first all-talkie (and all-awful) *Lights of New York*, but even that proved a mixed blessing, as some critics found her voice inadequate for sound movies. She then did bit parts, racked up four unhappy marriages, and became addicted to drugs before dying in poverty in 1957.

While London Sleeps was probably the highlight of newcomer Walter Merrill's career; at least his name is mentioned in the ads and publicity although no one was likely to have heard of him. Merrill went from romantic lead to bit player almost overnight and spent the rest of his career doing walk-ons.

While we have no figures on how well *While London Sleeps* did at the box office compared to Rinty's other films, the heroic dog's next movie was *In the Hills of Kentucky*, and he didn't venture into the urban jungle again. Obviously, he couldn't retain his incredible appeal (10,000 fan letters a week at one point) forever, but a popularity contest held by Eastern theaters still named him as one of the top two favorite actors in 1930. Still, Moviedom's Best Friend was getting old and a bit temperamental; he'd occasionally nip his fellow actors in addition to the villain. In 1932, at age fourteen, he died; a weeping Jean Harlow (Lee Duncan's neighbor) held Rinty's head on her lap as he expired.

Not a bad way to go.   — HN

While Paris Sleeps

While Paris Sleeps. Maurice Tourneur Productions/W.W. Hodkinson Corp., 21 January 1923, 6 reels/4,850 feet [LOST]

CAST: Lon Chaney (*Henri Santados*); Mildred Manning (*Bebe Larvache*); Jack Gilbert (*Dennis O'Keefe*); Hardee Kirkland (*His Father*); Jack McDonald (*Father Marionette*); J. Farrell MacDonald (*Georges Morier*)

CREDITS: *Director* Maurice Tourneur; *Cinematographer* René Guissart; *Lighting* Floyd Mueller

NOTE: In Harry Waldman's *Maurice Tourneur, The Life and Films*, the author attributes the script for Tourneur's film to Wyndham Gittens. Gittens worked for Tourneur later, while at First National, but we can find no corroboration for Waldman's claim that he participated in *While Paris Sleeps*. Also, Waldman is flat out wrong when he writes that Tourneur's film was adapted from Basil Woon's "disturbing story," *The Glory of Love*. Woon was responsible only for the script of the 1932 Victor McLaglen talkie, *While Paris Sleeps*. As was stated above, *The Glory of Love* — Leslie Beresford's novel — was the basis for Tourneur's film, which was released in 1923 (almost 3 years after shooting had finished) as *While Paris Sleeps*.

It was reported that during a performance of the *Eumenides* of Aeschylus, staged around the year 400 B.C., the entrance of the hideous goddesses provoked a veritable panic in the crowd. "Women aborted, children died, and several spectators were struck by madness," maintained Andre DeLorde.

Playwright Andre DeLorde, known as the "Prince of Terror" over 2000 years later, was justifying the grisliness of Paris' Grand Guignol Theater to which he was a primary contributor (with over a hundred plays to his credit). It is uncertain whether the *Eumenides* really did cause such mass-audience terror, or if the story was merely some exaggerated publicity concocted by a toga-clad ancestor of William Castle. In any case, no such extreme reactions were ever reported at Grand Guignol performances or at wax museums, other outlets for people looking for a good but harmless scare. Unlike the Grand Guignol, though, wax museums often claimed respectability by insisting their waxen mannequins and tableaux were educational. After all, they depicted historical figures and great events, and surely many of the wax figures were works of art. Still, there was never a wax museum without a Chamber of Horrors, and that appealed to the same fear and sadism that drew people to the Grand Guignol in order to watch severed heads roll and eyes, gouged out.

One of DeLorde's plays, *Figures de cire*, became the basis for a one-reel film made by Maurice Tourneur in 1914. The film tells of a man who takes a bet to spend a night locked in a wax museum. The experience drives him mad and he kills the man he placed the bet with when he turns up in the morning. The film was later re-released with its title changed from *Figures de cire* to *L'Homme aux figures de cire*. Tourneur was at the early stages of his career as a director but had previously done another adaptation of a DeLorde play, a particularly grisly version of Poe's *The System of Dr. Tarr and Professor Fether* (1913).

A mere three years after helming *Figures de cire*, Maurice Tourneur was among the top directors in America. One of his greatest successes was *The Whip*, whose title character is a racehorse that attracts the attention of a number of unscrupulous plotters when he's entered in an important race. At one point, the heroine and her friend are spying on the villain, who stops for dinner at a cafe inside the Eden Musée (a real wax museum on 23rd Street in Manhattan). It's almost closing time at the museum and the two women, attempting to avoid being seen by the heavy, retreat back into the Chamber of Horrors and are accidentally locked in for the night. The build-up to this is chilling enough, with one burglar-proof door after another automatically slamming shut and trapping the two panicky friends in the dark; however, nothing very scary happens, and this is in keeping with Tourneur's light, slightly tongue-in-cheek approach to the material. The wax figures— Marat in his bath, being stabbed by Charlotte Corday; an execution; a prison scene — are barely glimpsed. (Of course, the Eden was one wax museum that prided itself on avoiding the sensational, but that changed when the museum burned down and one of the owners used the insurance money to build a far more lurid version on Coney Island.)

In 1920, Tourneur once again returned to the wax-museum setting. He took *The Glory of Love*, a trite romantic novel set in the Latin Quarter, and grafted onto it both a Chamber of Horrors and its mad curator who dreams of torturing flesh, not wax. The stars were Lon Chaney and John (then Jack) Gilbert, whose careers were both on the ascent. For some reason that is still not clear, the film was not released until 1923, when it was re-titled *While Paris Sleeps*.

The following synopsis is drawn from several contemporary reviews:

Henri Santados, a sculptor who has a studio in the Latin Quarter, harbors an unrequited passion for his model Bebe Larvache. Bebe meets a rich young American named Dennis O'Keefe and the two fall in love. O'Keefe's father opposes the match and tries to convince Bebe to give his son up since they come from two entirely different worlds. Bebe agrees, but only if she can have one night of happiness with Dennis during Mardi Gras. Santados' neighbor, Father Marionette, is a demented creature who has spent his life making wax figures depicting the horrors of the Inquisition. Father Marionette also has an electric torture device he yearns to try out on a human being. Santados convinces him Dennis would be the perfect subject.

In order to disillusion Dennis, Bebe places herself in a seemingly compromising situation with Santados just as Dennis enters the studio. Heartbroken and believing Bebe to be unfaithful, Dennis leaves. Father Marionette lures him into his chamber of horrors and subjects him to his torture machine. Santados makes Bebe listen to her lover's groans on the phone while he holds her prisoner. Suddenly, Santados is seized with remorse and sets Bebe free so she and her friend Georges can rescue Dennis. The seriously injured man is brought to the hospital, but Father Marionette attempts to kidnap him from his sickroom and is shot by the hospital guards. Dennis recovers and his father, having seen how much Bebe and Dennis are in love, gives his consent to their marriage.

The Glory of Love was written by Leslie Beresford (using the *nom de plume* "Pan") in 1919. Beresford wrote adventure tales for boys and also dabbled in science fiction; his novel, *The Great Image*, was reprinted extensively following its 1921 debut. Nonetheless, the man's literary stylistics in *The Glory of Love* are very much the prose equivalent of Father Marionette's torture machine: "The humans have passed reasonably through Winter and evaded the tricky plots of Spring (which is but a spiteful jade at best) and are come to Summer, when everything seems to necessitate a bubbling of jollity, and cares matter nothing."

And so on. Father Marionette is not, of course, in the book at all, nor is there a wax museum or any horror element whatsoever. Rather, it's a train wreck that reconciles the insufferably virtuous grisette with her American dullard and opens the eyes of his millionaire papa. Santados lusts after Bebe, but he is hardly obsessed with her. He skulks around, mouthing insinuations and trying to get in the way of the lovers' happiness, and all he gets for his trouble is a good thrashing from one of Bebe's admirers.

Reviewers found the film's combination of romance and Grand Guignol decidedly odd and were mostly unenthusiastic: "The plot suggests the familiar 'penny dreadfuls' of a bygone day" and was rather "unwholesome" (Laurence Reid, *Motion Picture News*). Reid did think that Tourneur's "realistic production was far superior to the story" and that the Latin Quarter atmosphere invited comparison with "the best of the high class pictures," but he still felt that the plot was still "bald melodrama, highly improbable, and not good picture material."

Variety's Fred, writing for the 19 January 1923 edition, found the story "weird" and felt the film's box office potential was limited: "The best that can be said is that it is of the type usually the weak sister on the average double feature bill."

Dorothy Day of the *New York Telegraph* (21 January 1923) commented that "the plays of Grand Guignol Theater are modest little romances compared to this story." Day admired

Tourneur's attention to detail and felt that "the settings are interesting and the carnival scenes brilliant." Day also thought Bebe's role was hopelessly cliché: "Like the good little follower of Camille that she is, she makes the supreme sacrifice (whatever that is)" and decided that "for those who like their drama gruesome, this picture will be sure to appeal."

The Moving Picture World (27 January 1923) echoed the *MPN* review in its admiration for Tourneur's direction as well as the sets, the photography, the colorful Mardi Gras festival and the "expert lighting of scenes," but had little praise for the "unwholesome atmosphere" or the story which is aimed at those patrons with a "strain of morbidity." Referring to the torture sequences, the anonymous critic wrote: "Fortunately for those who do not enjoy these scenes, they are not drawn out nor are they as horrifyingly realistic as in some pictures of this type…. The director seems to have surrounded the exact practices of

"WHILE PARIS SLEEPS"
A
Maurice Tourneur Picture
for Hodkinson.

the artist [presumably, the critic means Father Marionette] with enough mystery to keep the scenes from being extremely real."

Nor were these journals alone in their sensitivity to the theme:

Commonplace story with several sordid incidents that will repel many [*Exhibitor's Herald*].

Gruesome story but if shown in a house where melodrama is enjoyed, it should give fairly good satisfaction [*Exhibitor's Trade Review*].

Very good production accorded commonplace theme that has some gruesome twists [*Film Daily*].

The grisliness of the wax museum sequences did not sit well with the New York Censors, who demanded that the following cuts be made:

- Close-up of girl on rack (after some discussion, the shot was retained)
- Close-up of man in stocks with feet burning
  - Close-up of girl on wheel
  - Eliminate the three views of the rat in a cage (the producers complied but insisted on keeping one shot of the rat where no torture is shown)
  - Close-up of man hanging from rope after subtitle ("Father Marionette, secretly gloating, etc.")
  - Santados dragging Bebe across the floor — All views of man lying on floor of torture chamber with vapor coming from his body and cut down time on two scenes which show man in chamber.
  - Eliminate subtitle: "Following Dennis in his unbalanced mind the thought that he would secure a living victim and serve his friend at the same time." (The censor was satisfied with just dropping dropped the word "living.")

The producers were also obliged to change several subtitles which were thought too salacious in their original form: "Bebe whose glorious body is the inspiration for all artists" became "Bebe, who is the inspiration for many artists." Another subtitle, spoken to Santados probably by either Georges or Dennis' father, went from "Before you go I want a letter from you that will clear Bebe of any insinuation of her relation with you" to "Before you go I want a letter from you that will clear Bebe of any insinuation on your part."

Publicity and ads for the film made absolutely no mention of the chamber of horrors or torture scenes; instead there was an emphasis on Tourneur as the great poet of the screen, the Latin Quarter atmosphere, and the Mardi Gras sequence.

A typical ad:

WHAT WOULD YOU DO?
If you were an American youth with unlimited funds at your disposal and your found yourself suddenly involved in the night life of Paris, surrounded by beautiful models and dancing girls, amid an atmosphere of romance, intrigue, mystery and charm…. And you met the girl of your dreams, posing for a sculptor of questionable character, who harbored a wild and unrestrained love for her.
WHAT WOULD YOU DO?

A photograph spread published in the February 24, 1923, *Motion Picture World* depicts Lon Chaney, Mildred Manning, and J. Farrell MacDonald (left to right). In the lower photograph, Chaney explains to Mildred that her plan contains unlimited minutes only when she makes calls *While Paris Sleeps*.

As for Lon Chaney, the reviewers were nothing if not disappointed. *MPN* found the role of Santados "unimportant insofar as making his presence in the action felt to any degree…. He doesn't have much to do. True, he starts the melodramatic wheels revolving, but with the exception of a few scenes he is absent from the action." The *New York Telegraph* critic agreed: "It seems a pity that Lon Chaney doesn't have more of a chance to do something. He does the best he can with the role of a wicked artist, but the part is sadly deficient in opportunity."

The brevity of Chaney's role was a tip-off to *Variety* that the film "had been lying around for some little time, finally patched up and released to salvage whatever could be got from it." Rather surprisingly, the reviewer then proceeded to opine that "Chaney is better in this picture than he has been in some of his more recent efforts." *Film Daily* thought Chaney better suited to play the role of Father Marionette than was character actor, Jack McDonald, a Tourneur regular: "Just to think what Chaney could have done with the madman character certainly detracts greatly from the role he does play." However colorless it may be, Santados is a typical "Lon doesn't get the girl" role. Even his character's backtracking on his evil scheme is not unlike what happens in *The Unholy Three, The Unknown,* and *West of Zanzibar,* though in those films Chaney makes a personal sacrifice to set things right. In the 1919 *Victory,* Tourneur had given Chaney one of his best villainous roles, so it's surprising he didn't cast him as Father Marionette or combine the two characters in some way. A few years later, though, in *The Monster,* Chaney did get to play with an electrical torture-machine and delivered a fun, but way-over-the-top, performance.

John Gilbert's role as the lovesick American sounds even more nondescript than does Chaney's. The two stars did *not* become friends and, years later, Chaney contributed a couple of negative remarks about Gilbert to a hatchet job on him published in *Vanity Fair.* In truth, Chaney did not care for most other actors, particularly matinee-idol types who, he felt, were not sufficiently dedicated to their craft and just coasted along on their good looks (something Chaney could never be accused of). However, Gilbert, who was all of 21 when he was hired by Tourneur for *While Paris Sleeps,* was very serious indeed about movies, but he wanted to write and direct, not act. He idolized Maurice Tourneur and was thrilled when he was asked to become a part of the great artist's team, which was then working under the auspices of Paramount. Gilbert worked on scripts for several of Tourneur's productions, including *The White Circle, The Great Redeemer,* and *Deep Waters;* he also acted in all three films. According to *Dark Star,* the excellent biography of Gilbert written by his daughter, Leatrice Gilbert Fountain, and John R. Maxim, Tourneur gladly allowed Gilbert to direct most of *The Bait,* a vehicle for Hope Hampton (an actress with flaming orange hair, no talent, and a very important husband, Paramount executive, Jules Brulatour).

Brulatour has been described as "film importer/manufacturer," but the multi-millionaire's most important job was as the general manager of Eastman Kodak and, hence, the provider of raw film stock to all the studios: a man who could stop the cameras very quickly if someone got on his wrong side. Very pleased with Gilbert's work on *The Bait,* Brulatour offered him

a lucrative director's contract on condition that some of the pictures star Hope Hampton (who was called "Hopeless" Hampton behind Monsieur Brulatour's back). Gilbert accepted, an act which Tourneur considered disloyal and which ended their friendship. Gilbert did but one picture for Hampton before breaking his contract to return to acting. Undaunted by his beautiful (and much younger) wife's failure to captivate the movie-going public, Brulatour launched her on a career as an opera singer [!], a fiasco that perhaps influenced the Charles Foster Kane/Susan Alexander match-up in *Citizen Kane.*

Mildred Manning, a "Louise Glaum–type" according to one reviewer, played Bebe Larvache. The *MPW* critic noted that "she answers the picturesque requirements of her role," a comment likely typical of the reviews Miss Manning received in her brief film career, as she was a dancer in musical-comedy theater before she signed up at Biograph in the mid–1910s. Fleeing the small parts offered her at Biograph, she moved on to Vitagraph where, for most of 1917, at least, she was a leading lady. After that, she free-lanced until her film career faded in the early 1920s. Perhaps Manning's oddest credit is her co-authorship (with Biograph co-star, Lillian Langdon) of the book *Kultur — or the Devil's Tool; Synopsis of a Motion Picture Scenario* (1918). *Kultur* (also 1918), with Gladys Brockwell, was one of a number of virulently anti–German films made during the War years.

Cameraman Rene Guissart had worked with Tourneur since their days together at the Eclair/Brady Studio in Fort Lee, New Jersey, although it was the cinematographer's work on Fred Niblo's *Ben-Hur* (1925) that won him his greatest acclaim. Guissart had attracted some attention in 1921, when he had refused an offer of $500 a week to lens *Fate,* an account of the life and murder trial of Clara Smith Hamon that was to star the lady, herself. The mistress of Oklahoma oilman and Republican bigwig, Jacob Hamon (who had arranged a marriage of convenience for her with his nephew), Clara was arrested for killing the elder Hamon, but got off, following a sensational trial. Guissart was so indignant about the proposed film that, as a member of the American Society of Cinematographers, he successfully made a motion that any cameraman who participated in the film would be expelled from the Society. The Hamon movie ended up being made, but there's no indication that anyone's career suffered as a result. In the early 1930s, Guissart returned to his native France and there switched from cinematography to directing.

The year 1920 was a pivotal one for Maurice Tourneur. He was growing increasingly weary of working through Paramount and putting up with studio interference. "It's like three or four people giving a sculptor their ideas on how he should mold the statue of his own creation," he lamented. He was tired also of the aforementioned Jules Brulatour, who had acted as his patron since Tourneur's days at Equitable-World in the early 1910s. Looking for more artistic freedom, Tourneur joined with Thomas Ince, Mack Sennett, Alan Dwan and George Loane Tucker to form the production/distribution company, Associated Producers, in 1920. (The fiercely independent Marshall Neilan was also supposed to join, but the deal fell through.) Between 1920 and 1921, the company distributed 20 films before going bankrupt; Tourneur then resigned himself to freelancing.

Possibly because of the unsettled situation during those last months with Jules Brulatour and Paramount, *While Paris Sleeps* was never copyrighted and was allowed to linger unreleased. Perhaps Tourneur himself finally bought the rights to the film in 1923, when it was distributed by W.W. Hodkinson. Whatever the reason, it's not likely the film was shelved due to any major artistic shortcoming.

Still, a "Straight from the Shoulder" comment from a theater owner in Fresno, California, indicates that there might have been some disagreement on that front: "A hunk of A-1 cheese. Booked it on account of Lon Chaney in the cast. Played it on Sunday and Monday and would have welcomed death to facing patrons."

— HN

Whispering Shadows

Whispering Shadows. Peerless Feature Producing Company/Peacock Pictures; States Rights, June 1921 (?), 6 reels/5800 feet, 28 mm diacetate positive (nonviewable) at Library of Congress

CAST: Lucy Cotton (*Helen Bransby*); Charles A. Stevenson (*Richard Bransby*); Philip Merivale (*Stephen Pryde*); Robert Barrat (*Hugh Brook*); George Cowl (*Dr. Latham*); Alfred Dundas (*Morton Grant*); Marion Rogers (*Margaret Latham*); Mabel Archdall (*Aunt Caroline*); Mrs. Celestine Saunders (*The Medium*)

CREDITS: *Director* Emile Chautard; *Scenario* Walter Hackett; based on the play *The Invisible Foe* by Walter Hackett (novelization by Louise Jordan Milne; New York, 1920); *Cinematographer* Jacques Bizeul; *Scene Arrangements and Subtitles* Harry Chandler, William B. Loeb

"Harrumph! Hypnotism only!" harrumphed Bela Lugosi's Roxor (the heavy) at one point in *Chandu the Magician*, a glorious piece of cinematic claptrap from 1932. The following year Lugosi enacted the role of Professor Strang (the *apparent* heavy) in *The Whispering Shadow*, an early sound serial that oughtn't to have failed as badly it did, what with such surefire elements as a wax museum, a radio-death ray, and Bela Lugosi. (To be completely fair, Bela's Strang had not one single line as quoteworthy as Roxor's sound bite, and his black-clad, eyebrow-cocking eccentric spent the better part of any number of the chapters stretched out, unconscious, on the wax museum floor.) Be that as it may, the savvy (if opinionated) genre aficionado generally regards *Chandu the Magician* as an unadulterated joy, while finding *The Whispering Shadow* something of a guilty pleasure, cherished most by those superannuated remnants of the Karl Dane Appreciation Society.

Ten-plus years prior to that indie chapterplay, other shadows had whispered onscreen, and without the support of wax museums, radio-death rays, or Bela Lugosis. This earlier production had confined its sotto voce (as it were) goings-on to spiritualism, circling 'round the sort of timely providential sagacity that all too seldom follows timeless temporal stupidity. *Whispering Shadows* whispers no longer, being but a memory due to its being misplaced along the way, but the plot (as it were) may be extruded from sundry contemporary, local screeds. Thus:

> Youth and sweetheart attend party at which a séance is given, both disbelieving in spiritualism. Girl joins circle to be sociable and is told to warn sweetheart someone is trying to harm him.

Warning is not taken seriously, but later it is discovered that unscrupulous member of firm where youth had worked is plotting to make it appear as though the latter had embezzled large sum of money. The unscrupulous one is foiled and forced to sign a statement, admitting he is guilty of the embezzlement. Father of girl places statement in book. Later, father dies and statement is lost; the youth joins the army and the unscrupulous one is about to marry the girl when the youth is drawn to her [girl has the psychic power of hearing the voice of her father, who has died, and she seeks and secures his advice to free her lover from the villainy of a conspirator], returns and finds the statement, and marries her [*Motion Picture News*, 25 March 1922 (bracketed addition: *Mansfield* [Ohio] *News*, 2 June 1922)].

King Mongkut of Siam may (or may not) have actually admitted that, for him, much of life was "a puzzlement"— Rex Harrison and Yul Brynner definitely did — but he *was* fortunate enough that the vagaries of time and space saw him at least a half-century and half-a-world removed from *Whispering Shadows'* headache-inducing improbabilities. The précis not only starts out seriously short on definite and indefinite articles (we suspect Charlie Chan may have been filling in for the vacationing house reviewer), but also is positively bereft of both the sort of sense that Mark Twain claimed was "not all that common" and the kind of ratiocination that buttered Sherlock Holmes's toast.

To elaborate: Father of Girl puts signed confession in a book; is there blackmail on his mind? No matter; no apparent witnesses to this act of profound denseness assures Father's demise, and sooner rather than later. Is the signed confession then discovered to be missing *from* the book, or does the book *itself* go missing, the way stuff is apt to go missing when one's house is full of one's relatives? How does the Unscrupulous One avoid arrest and trial for his embezzlement? Girl, apparently, is not aware Unscrupulous One is a rotter (Did Father not spill beans to Daughter?), as she doesn't hesitate to queue up to wed same once Youth is in basic training. Was not Youth already drawn to Girl in reel one? Or is his being "drawn to her" in the last-reel effected by some sort of ectoplasmic fishing line? Is discorporate Dad now in a position to give stock tips to honest, yet evidently clueless, future son-in-law?

Inquiring minds don't give a hoot.

Whispering Shadows was (probably) shot as *The Invisible Foe*, the name of the play upon which the unlikely scenario was (probably) based; the reasons for our hedging our bets will be made clear anon. Said masterwork reputedly played to the West End audiences before crossing the Pond and opening on Broadway, where — per a United Press release printed in the 21 March 1919 *Fort Wayne* [Indiana] *News and Sentinel* — "practically every theatrical critic condemned it in unmeasured terms." One might think — with some justification — that such a reaction would put the kibosh on any plans to preserve the literally deathless drama for posterity. But, no. *Foe's* Broadway producer, Bartley Cushing — whose investment was even then being plowed under by the weight of the negative critical mass — swore that the play would ultimately prove a success, for the spirits themselves were het about it. From that same Indiana newspaper:

> I positively affirm that spiritualistic assurance was given us in making the play ready for the public. I repeatedly felt strange in-

fluences guiding me and directing me in my efforts to secure certain novel effects. I cannot explain it, but I think everyone connected with the play felt that extramundane influences were hovering over the Harris Theater.

Such stalwart American spirits as Johnnie Walker or Jim Beam may have indeed contributed to Mr. Cushing's take on his production, and his (and everyone else's) being under the influence of *something* at the Harris Theater may serve to account for his rather odd discounting of the critical drubbing even then being given to his troupe.

Anyhow, *Foe* (with a decent-enough run of 112 performances) may not have set the world on fire, but it was another feather in playwright Walter Hackett's chapeau. Hackett — husband of ditsy comedienne, Marion Lorne — authored a dozen or so shows that made it onto the Great White Way, one of which (1917's *The Barton Mystery*) was filmed so frequently — in silent and sound versions, both in the USA and in Europe — that the man could have lived comfortably off the royalties from that title alone. Only one of *Foe*'s cast made it onto the screen when the drama went "illegitimate" as *Shadows*: New Yorker Robert Barrat showed up in both renditions, and he went on to grace (in distinctly minor roles) a handful of genre features, including *Secret of the Blue Room* (1933), *Return of the Terror* (1934), and *Strangler of the Swamp* (1946). *Shadows* was one of only several silent films in which Barrat appeared (in a six-decade career that included over 150 motion pictures), as the actor preferred speaking aloud before several hundred enthusiastic patrons to indulging in pantomime for the all-seeing lens. The IMDb lists a Marion Rogers as having participated in *The Invisible Foe*, and a Marion Rogers played (per the above-cited *MPN*) the role of Margaret Latham in *Shadows* (and not the earlier *Foe*), but we are unable to find any additional credits for the lady — either legitimate or cinematic — anywhere.

It is with the introduction of *Shadows*' leading lady, Lucy Cotton, into the mix, that things begin to get interesting. Miss Cotton, who would also lend her youth and beauty to *Life Without Soul* (1916) and *The Devil* (1921, see entries), wrote (in her 1920 entry in the *Motion Picture Studio Directory*) that her performance in *The Invisible Foe* (Huh?) had been the result of the masterful direction of Emile Chautard. M. Chautard, in *his* entry in the directory, claimed the film had been produced (at least in part) by the Mayflower Photoplay Corporation, the same bunch who claimed responsibility for *The Miracle Man* (1919), *The Mystery of the Yellow Room* (both 1919), and *Unseen Forces* (1920; see entries for all three). Leaving M. Chautard's bona fides to our essay on *Yellow Room*, let us take a moment to examine as best we can the admittedly semi-confounding intertwining of *The Invisible Foe* with *Whispering Shadows*.

The Invisible Foe — The Movie — may well have begun production for Mayflower and the Emile Chautard Pictures Corporation, but there's no record that the film was ever completed; that there is no extant copyright registration offers evidence of this, but there were more than a few motion pictures that made the rounds back then without ever having had any of their pertinent data cross the transom at the Library of Congress. Most likely, after a few reels of something or another were in the can, the money dried up: Mayflower disappeared by the end of 1920

and Chautard's own "Pictures Corporation" had produced but one movie prior to *Foe*—1919's *Yellow Room*. Using the SOP of Edward D. Wood, Jr., as a model, one can readily look back and envision old Emile, film cans under his arm, making the circuit in his quest for further funding and guaranteed distribution deals.

Somehow, the footage must have ended up on a desk (and Emile in front of one) in the offices of the Peerless Feature Producing Company, an outfit that had managed to match the solitary-picture output of Chautard's ego-driven company with the 1916 *Sally in Our Alley* before being snapped up by the ever-expanding World Films. As the vestiges of World Films' archives contain no acknowledgement of *Whispering Shadows*, it may be supposed that the completion of the hitherto-entitled *Foe* project was left to Peerless' own resources. (Given that *Shadows*—like *Foe*, copyright registration-less— may have finally been released by Peacock Pictures [a company that has NO traceable record] together with the usual States Rights mishegas, it's also likely that no expense was met in Peerless' effort to see the project well and truly completed.) That confusion reared its ugly head somewhere along the line is undeniable: an illustrated advert for the film in the 18 January 1922 *Mansfield News* bears the lead-in, "The Medium told Ruth to warn Hugh." There *is* no Ruth among the list of dramatis personae.

It's also uncertain who, beside Miss Cotton, had been photographed previously by Chautard's cameraman (longtime Chautard colleague, Jacques Bizeul, received credit for the light-and lens-work on *Shadows*), as no cast or credits list from the cinematic *Foe* was either registered or mentioned in print anywhere. None of the actors who took part in *Shadows* (other than Mr. Barrat) had a terribly lengthy film career, although several did wander through a genre title or two (e.g., Philip Merivale can be spotted in the 1935 *The Passing of the Third Floor Back*, Charles A. Stevenson impersonated General Petrie in the 1929 *The Mysterious Dr. Fu Manchu*, and George Cowl was onscreen during 1923's *Fashionable Fakers*). For what it's worth, Mrs. Celestine Saunders—credited with playing the Medium herein — was a professional seer and was widely advertised as a card-carrying member of the Psychic Research Society of America.

When all is said and done, we're not absoltively, posolutely certain whether *Whispering Shadows* was ever seen by any audience save the one including critic Eugene Carlton, the fellow who provided that comprehensive plot recapitulation we reprinted, above. In an effort to stir the pot a bit, let us conclude with Mr. Carlton's appraisal of this missing magnum opus:

> *Whispering Shadows* is the possessor of a "kick," the kind of a "kick" which creeps through your veins when you are anticipating something unwelcome while enshrouded in darkness…. The picture is so different from the average production, plunging into metaphysical science one minute, and portraying a love story the next, that it is indeed unique. Suspense abound [*sic*] throughout the entire story, but enough human interest element, in the form of a scheming, unscrupulous young man, is injected to serve as a barrier against any possible monotony. The story leads up to a peak of interest, then breaks all at once.

Harrison's Reports (30 July 1921) opined that the peak of interest had broken much earlier: "Instead of the interest increasing as the end approaches, it is all but lost." Whether the peak was broken or lost, we cannot say.

— *JTS*

Whispering Wires

Whispering Wires. Fox Film Corporation/Fox, 24 October 1926, 6 Reels/5,096 feet [available]

CAST: Anita Stewart (*Doris Stockbridge*); Edmund Burns (*Barry McGill*); Charles Clary (*Montgomery Stockbridge*); Otto Matiesen (*Bert Norton*); Mack Swain (*Cassidy*); Arthur Housman (*McCarthy*); Charles Conklin (*Jasper, the Butler*); Arthur Campeau (*Morphy*); Scott Welsh (*Triggy Drew*); Mayme Kelso (*Ann Cartwright*); Charles Sellon (*Tracy Bennett*)

CREDITS: *Director* Albert Ray; *Producer* William Fox; *Scenario* L.G. Rigby; based on the eponymous novel by Henry Leverage (New York, 1918) and the play *Whispering Wires* by Kate McLaurin (Boston, 1934); *Adaptation* Andrew Bennison; *Titles* William Conselman; *Cinematographer* George Schneiderman; *Assistant Director* Horace Hough

"It was an uncanny voice! It whispered!"

The above words, repeated again and again throughout the course of six reels, illustrate the movie's basic flaw: *Whispering Wires* is a thriller that *has* to have sound to be really effective. Its scare devices are all aural: the ringing telephone that summons the next victim; the sinister, whispered threats on the line; and the gong of the clock that announces that the threats have been carried out. Tight close-ups of the villain's mouth and terrified reaction shots of the victims are rather weak substitutes. And the fact that the film gives away almost immediately the surprises that enlivened its book-and-play source material makes the whole project even more ill-conceived. Basically a "locked room" thriller — how the murders are committed is every bit as important as who committed them — *Wires* reveals both the killer's identity and his method barely ten minutes into the picture. All that's left is to wait for the various clueless characters to finally catch on and, until that moment finally arrives, we have to endure excruciatingly unfunny comedy inflicted by the usual "old dark house" stand-bys: frightened servants and dumb detectives.

Ruthless financier Montgomery Stockbridge has succeed in blocking the parole of a former business partner, Andrew Morphy, whom Stockbridge has railroaded into prison. Stockbridge has even taken over Morphy's mansion, located in "a lonely section of Westchester." Stockbridge's equally crooked lawyer, Tracy Bennett, warns Stockbridge that Morphy, the inventor of a "flying boat," is a vindictive man who has sworn vengeance on them both. The two men are unaware that Morphy's best friend, Bert Norton, is living in the secret basement beneath the mansion and has rigged up devices to control the house's electricity and phone. Bert calls upstairs to Stockbridge's study and warns Bennett that he will be dead at five o'clock. Stockbridge dismisses the threat as a crank call, but then receives a letter telling him that "the grave you ordered dug in your family plot is now ready and waiting." Stockbridge decides to call in the Drew Detective Agency. The nervous Bennett heads for home but is ambushed on the road and dies at exactly five o'clock.

Stockbridge has more mundane problems to deal with: namely, his niece Doris's desire to wed Barry McGill in spite of the young man's modest means. "Your income wouldn't keep her in powder-puffs," sneers Stockbridge when Barry asks for Doris's hand. De-

tective Drew arrives, accompanied by his two incompetent helpers, Cassidy and McCarthy. The ticker tape machine in Stockbridge's office starts up and delivers the message that Bennett is dead.

Meanwhile, Morphy has escaped from prison. He joins Bert in the basement and makes a call to Stockbridge, telling him that he will be dead by midnight. Bert has finished testing a device that can fire a bullet from inside a telephone receiver.

Intercepting Stockbridge's call to the phone company about odd noises on the line, Bert poses as a "trouble hunter" (repairman) and shows up at the front door to fix the phone in Stockbridge's study. He installs the device in the phone as his intended victim banters with the detective. Stockbridge decides he will lock himself in the study near midnight, while Drew and his detectives stand guard outside. Just before midnight, Morphy calls and when Stockbridge answers, Morphy sends an electronic signal to his deadly invention and Stockbridge is shot dead. Drew questions everyone, including Doris and Barry, but is completely baffled.

Searching through the house, Drew spots Morphy looking down at him from a ceiling trapdoor but, before he can act, Bert pulls him through another secret panel and ties him up. Bert installs another of the gun devices in the phone in Stockbridge's secretary's office. Bert and Morphy then turn out all the lights in the house except the one in the office. When everyone converges there, Morphy calls and tells Doris she will be dead at 1:00am. Cassidy and McCarthy get their bloodhound, Herman, in the hope he can track down Drew but the dog seems more interested in chasing Jasper, the superstitious butler.

Investigating on his own, Barry finds the secret passageway leading to the basement. He and Bert fight while Morphy watches from hiding. Barry knocks Bert out as and drags him upstairs to the office. Just before one o'clock, Morphy calls the office. Barry makes Bert answer the phone but Morphy recognizes his voice. Bert says the call is for Doris and when she takes the receiver, Morphy prepares to trigger the device but, noting Bert's wolfish anticipation, Barry knocks the phone out of Doris' hand just as it explodes. Meanwhile, Drew has worked himself free and comes upstairs in time to find Morphy holding everyone at gunpoint. With an assist by the timely arrival of Herman, the detective and Barry overpower Bert and Morphy. Drew tells Doris her worries are over as the two villains will no doubt get the chair for their crimes.

Henry Leverage's *Whispering Wires* originally appeared in *The Saturday Evening Post* in March 1918. That same year, it made the rounds in various Sunday supplements (luring in readers by quoting the creepy letter about the grave in the family plot being ready and waiting) and was published as a novel; we found it a fairly readable potboiler. One major departure from the film is that the literary Morphy orchestrates the whole scheme from prison and leaves its enactment to his inventor brother. The book also displays an anti–German bias, not surprising given the year of its publication. Herman the bloodhound does not make an appearance in the book, but there is a talking bird that witnesses the murder. (There's a parrot in the film, but he's no wiser than the rest of the principals.)

Author Leverage spoke about his career to the *Middletown Daily Herald* on the 17 May 1923, while visiting his wife's parents in Middletown, New York. Born in London but raised in the States, Leverage told the interviewer that he was an electrical engineer by profession and that the USA sent him to England at the outbreak of the Great War to install several electrical devices of his own invention on British submarines. While in England, he began writing sea adventures before turning to thrillers. All this may have made a good story for the hometown folk, but other sources say that Mr. Leverage spent most of World War I, not overseas, but under guard stateside. In fact, publicity for *The Twinkler* (1916), a crime film made from one of his novels, notes that author Henry Leverage is "a prisoner in Sing Sing prison" (*Warren* [Pennsylvania] *Evening News*, 22 September 1917). Whatever the cause of his misfortune, Leverage did have the wisdom to deal it with by writing rather than by booby-trapping telephones.

Playwright and short-story author, Kate McLaurin, turned Leverage's book into a play in 1922, although her effort didn't see print until 1934. *Whispering Wires* was a solid hit, running from August 1922 to January 1923, and while promoters ballyhooed it as a successor to *The Cat and the Canary* and *The Bat*—other long-running Broadway mysteries—critics found it less satisfying than those earlier thrillers. The *Wires* cast included Ben Johnson, Jane Houston, Louise Swanson and Malcolm Duncan (as the "trouble hunter"/killer). In the play, the telephone-gun is activated by the human voice, and the ending sees the murderer fall victim to his own device. The film of course, stops just short of that, but perhaps makes up for it with some presumably unintended humor ("Someone wants to speak to Miss Stockbridge"). The play was so successful that numerous companies took it on the road and it was also presented in England and Australia.

Ads for the film promised "A mansion of horrors! Mysterious doors, strange panels and whispering wires." Of course the mysterious doors and strange panels make the whispering wires almost unnecessary as the murderers can freely wander the mansion and stalk their victims at will, making their ingenious killer-phone seem more effort than it's worth. They dispense with it entirely in the case of the lawyer who is simply shot dead in his car. Paul Thompson, reviewing the picture for *Motion Picture World*, called the film a "melodrama of the mello-ist," and wrote:

> The picture suffers because it is almost impossible to maintain the secret of how the murders are committed which is one of the biggest assets a play of this kind possesses. The baffling of the spectator as to the manner and method until almost the final curtain almost always intrigues the theater-goer…. In the film that becomes difficult as the scenarist and director have to tip their hand early.

Thompson also had little use for the ("so-called by courtesy") comedy though "there is doubtless a large audience for that sort of thing."

Artwork for the ads show a man answering the phone just as a scantily clad woman rushes in to warn him. The woman is presumably meant to be the film's star, Anita Stewart, who, at the height of her very considerable popularity, was said to be drawing $127,000 a year, an astronomical sum for the times. Born Anna Stewart, she entered films while still in high school and, upon graduating in 1912, went to work full-time for Vitagraph. It helped, of course, that her brother-in-law was Ralph Ince (brother of Thomas), but she achieved great success very quickly and scored a huge hit with *The Goddess*, a serial in which she plays a child raised on a desert island (thus justifying some very skimpy outfits).

According to Charles Higham's *Merchant of Dreams*, Stewart became almost a caricature of a shallow, spoiled superstar, throwing tantrums when she couldn't get her way and even faking nervous break-downs. Her popularity drew the attention of Louis B. Mayer—just beginning his rise to movie moguldom—and in 1917 he tried to woo her away from Vitagraph. Giving in to Mayer's flattery and promises, Stewart broke her contract with Vitagraph, but they took her and Mayer to court over it. Mayer, whose machinations would make Cesare Borgia look like Francis of Assisi, lost the protracted battle but ultimately won the war by taking advantage of Vitagraph's financial woes to take over Stewart's last films for the company. Stewart did well with Mayer and even made one of her biggest hits, *In Old Kentucky* (kind of an early *National Velvet*), for him.

Come 1923, Stewart decided to try her hand at Vaudeville (she could sing and play the piano), and thus did not renew her contract with Mayer. Unfortunately, her act closed after just a week and resulted in still another lawsuit: her co-star, Louise Sydmoth, sued Stewart, claiming that the star had promised her a career in the movies if the act failed. Stewart did finally return to film (minus Louise) but found that, even though she had been absent from the big screen for less than a year, she was virtually a has-been. Freelancing, she even returned to Vitagraph for *Baree, Son of Kazan* (1925; in which she was no doubt mortified to find that she was billed under her co-star, Wolf the Wonder Dog) and, following some work at Hearst's Cosmopolitan Pictures and at Tiffany, she was reduced to doing a serial, *Isle of Sunken Gold* (1927), that featured Olympic medalist, Duke Kahanamoku, as the "Devil Ape." In 1932, Stewart made a sound musical short, *The Hollywood Handicap*, and then retired from film to busy herself with painting, writing and traveling. Though she made close to 100 pictures, next to none of them survive. She's scarcely impressive in *Whispering Wires*, but it would be unfair to attempt to judge her talent or charm by such a thankless, ingénue role.

The only effective performance in *Whispering Wires* comes from Otto Matiesen as Bert, the murderous inventor. Matiesen, thin-lipped and heavy-lidded, has dead eyes that flicker to malicious life only when a dastardly deed is near completion. He comes off like a restrained Dwight Frye (or at least like a Frye just beginning to come down from his meds) and easily eclipses the more mundane villainy of Frank Campeau as Morphy. The Danish-born Matiesen was a fine character actor in the Silent Era and turns up in such noteworthy films as *Scaramouche* (1923; as the unfortunate divinity student killed by Lewis Stone in a duel), *The Salvation Hunters* (1925) and *General Crack* (1930; as John Barrymore's traitorous lieutenant). He also plays the master criminal in *While London Sleeps* (1926; see entry), but perhaps his most notable genre work is in the 1928 Expressionist short film, *The Telltale Heart*. Made up to look like Edgar Allan Poe, Matiesen delivers a restrained but highly effective performance in a part that readily invites frenzied overacting. He easily made the transition to sound, but, on 19 February 1932, the car in which he was traveling with fellow actor, Duncan Renaldo, skidded and overturned. Renaldo was only slightly injured, but Matiesen was killed.

The rest of *Whispering Wires*' cast is adequate but without distinction. Edmund Burns seems to have been the David Manners of silent horror, a hero whose presence is nearly invisible. Burns suffered a mishap during the filming of the climax, when his hand was scorched because technicians miscalculated the planned telephone-explosion and used too much powder. Charles Clary — the decidedly unsympathetic Stockbridge — is perhaps best known for his portrayal of the evil Marquis de Evermonde in the 1917 version of *A Tale of Two Cities* (though he hardly erases memories of Basil Rathbone in that role).

The then-requisite inept detectives are played by former Keystone Kop, Mack Swain, and perennial inebriate, Arthur Housman, who's sober here. The duo fumbles around with notebooks, makes dumb comments, and accidentally handcuffs each other. Jasper, the Negro butler, is played by Heinie Conklin in blackface. In a publicity puff piece on the film, he's quoted as saying: "Harry Houdini has established himself as an artist in escaping from contrivances where escape seemed impossible, but in *Whispering Wires* I found a place where Houdini would have stayed put." It's unlikely Houdini would have found himself in such a place to begin with.

Whispering's director, Albert Ray, achieved some modest success as a film actor in the 1910s, but in the 1920s, under contract to Fox, he switched to directing (usually comedies). If he had any feel for horror, it's not obvious in this particular effort, but, given the script, creating any kind of tension must have been an uphill battle. (He did take another whack at some marginal genre material, though, with 1928's *A Thief in the Dark*, see appendix) Still, in the 1930s he helmed a pretty good Poverty Row thriller, *The Thirteenth Guest* (1932) and then returned to the genre with *The Intruder* (1933) and *A Shriek in the Night* (1933). Ray ended his career doing B-Westerns.

The film's cinematographer was George Schneiderman, cameraman on such John Ford epics as *The Iron Horse* and *Three Bad Men*. Even though he later gave a nice Gothic look to the horror western, *Mystery Ranch* (1932), his work here is largely banal. Perhaps part of the problem are the nondescript sets: Bert's basement lair is so clean and clear of cobwebs that one suspects he must be equal parts mad inventor and Felix Unger. And although a title card describes the mansion as "standing gloomily aloof from the world," the brief exterior shot it's given isn't lit or photographed in an especially sinister manner. Schneiderman manages a menacing dolly-in on Matiesen spying on the couple from the garden, and there's one very unsettling moment when Detective Drew, looking down on a mirror on a table, sees not his own reflection, but that of Morphy glaring at him from above.

The booby-trapped telephones — nouveaux here — later turn up in the 1931 *Murder at Midnight* (a needle in the receiver), the aforementioned *The Thirteenth Guest* (an electrified phone), and the 1978 John Frankenheimer *Black Sunday* (wherein an explosive in the receiver is triggered by a signal from the other line). The latter device was actually used by Israeli agents to kill suspected terrorist leaders. It's unlikely, though, that anyone in Mossad was actually inspired by *Whispering Wires*.

— HN

The White Flower

The White Flower. Famous Players–Lasky/Paramount Pictures, 25 February 1923, 6 reels/5731 feet [LOST]

CAST: Betty Compson (*Konia Markham*); Edmund Lowe (*Bob Rutherford*); Edward Martindel (*John Markham*); Arline Pretty (*Ethel Granville*); Sylvia Ashton (*Mrs. Gregory Bolton*); Arthur Hoyt (*Gregory Bolton*); Leon Barry (*David Panuahi*); Lily Phillips (*Bernice Martin*); Reginald Carter (*Edward Graeme*); Maui Kaito (*Kahuna*).

CREDITS: *Producer* Adolph Zukor; *Director* Julia Crawford Ivers; *Story and Adaptation* Julia Crawford Ivers; *Cinematographer* James Van Trees; *Art Director* George Hopkins.

Hawaii has rarely provided the setting for horror.

Let's be honest: the setting is w-a-y less likely to inspire nightmares than dreams of gentle island breezes, ukulele music, and smiling maidens in grass skirts. Even the old Hawaiian native religion with its gods and spirits is usually depicted as being pleasantly pagan and in sync with the laidback rhythms of island life. Still, the old ways did have a less benign aspect: a long tradition of ritual cannibalism and human sacrifice as reflected in the familiar conceit of the young woman being tossed into the live volcano to placate those gods and spirits. This cliché can be traced back to Richard Walton Tully's popular 1912 play *The Bird of Paradise*, but had no basis in reality; sacrificial victims were actually dispatched by either stabbing or strangling. Thus, when it came to depicting tropical terror, Hollywood usually bypassed the Pacific isles and turned to Haiti and voodoo, perhaps feeling that the only real danger Hawaii presented to Westerners was the temptation to put aside work and duty and "go native."

Nonetheless, the very first movie shot in Hawaii — the 1913 two-reeler, *The Shark God* — depicted the snit thrown by the eponymous deity after Christian missionaries failed to completely stamp out his/its worship. The first feature set in Hawaii — though not shot there — was the 1915 *Aloha Oe*, which was also the first film to have the heroine face the prospect of jumping into a volcano without a bungee cord. 1917 saw the cinematic version of *The Bottle Imp* (see entry); while the picture's publicity campaign claimed some scenes had been filmed in Hawaii, native viewers were skeptical. In 1922, popular Famous Players–Lasky star Betty Compson starred as *The Bonded Woman*, a melodrama set in the islands though again not shot there; later stories to the contrary, the company got no further than San Francisco. *Woman*'s director, Julia Crawford Ivers, anxious for a change of scene after the murder of her good friend, William Desmond Taylor, and the resulting scandal (see entry on 1921's *The Witching Hour*), took a vacation in Hawaii and mulled over the possibility of doing a film there. Her initial thought was to involve the goddess Pele (who abided — where else? — in a volcano on Kilauea), but eventually her script for *The White Flower* — though still concerned with Hawaiian lore and magic — evolved into something completely different. Ivers confessed to having fallen in love with the beautiful setting, and the very next year she returned to shoot the film along with her son, the cinematographer James Van Trees, and a company of 25 actors and technicians, including Betty Compson and Edmund Lowe.

From all descriptions, *The White Flower* was mostly

concerned with romance and island atmosphere, but it did contain a bona fide and effective curse

Synopsis from *The AFI Catalog* and contemporary reviews:

Konia Markham, the daughter of an American father and a Hawaiian mother, is told by a sorceress that the man who presents her with a perfect white flower will be her true love. However, the sorceress has been bribed to say this by David Panuahi who loves Konia and plans on presenting her with the flower. Before Panuahi can complete his scheme, Konia meets Bob Rutherford, an American who runs a ranch in Hawaii. He gives her a white flower from his buttonhole. Konia believes he is her intended and they subsequently fall in love. Unfortunately, Rutherford is already engaged to Ethel Granville, who soon arrives with her aunt and uncle. Panuahi convinces Konia to consult the kahuna (priest) to put a death curse on Ethel. The priest burns a lock of Ethel's hair and the woman falls ill. Touched by Bob's devotion to a failing Ethel, Konia decides to call off the curse. The kahuna is about to throw the ashes into the ocean, sealing Ethel's fate, but Konia overtakes him in a rowboat and retrieves the ashes. Ethel recovers and, learning of Konia's devotion, releases Bob from their engagement. Konia meanwhile is preparing to throw herself into a volcano when Bob finds her and declares his love.

The screenplay has the Hawaiian magic taken at face value and thus it seems to be authentically supernatural. The efficacy of the curse does not depend on the victim believing in it but, rather, is due to the invocation of sinister powers. And, even though the sorceress is suborned, her prediction nevertheless comes true.

The hero dallying with a native girl while he has a fiancée back home is the usual *Madame Butterfly* stuff, though, in this case, there's a happy resolution due to the self-sacrifice of both women. Still, given the racial politics of the Silent Era, had Konia been a full-blooded Hawaiian, the volcano would probably not have gone without a victim.

Naturally, much of the publicity touted the Hawaiian location shooting even though, as the *Variety* reviewer pointed out, this was no longer much of a novelty by 1923. Periodicals were also filled with cutesy articles on Betty Compson's learning to dance the "hula hula" and to surf. A typical puff piece ad showed a grass-skirted Compson gyrating while taglines trumpeted: "See her bathing on the beach of Waikiki or dancing the hula at the Suav— Tropic Splendors— Intoxicating perfume — The crash of green combers On the Beach at Waikiki — Surf boats— Hula maids dancing in the moonlight." Irresistible, no?

According to another bit of publicity, the missionaries had done their task of teaching the islanders to be modest all too well:

Julia Crawford Ivers wanted the men and women to appear in their native costumes. But the Hawaiians regarded picture-taking as an affair of state. The Hawaiian women absolutely declined to put on the "malo" or native skirt or let their hair fall around their faces…. Out of the entire group, one woman was finally found who was willing to sit in the dirt and do anything she could be made to understand through an interpreter.

And it took days to find a native man who was willing to take off his clothes and wear just a scarf. They were willing to do it, but insisted on having their underclothes on under the scarf! At last one talented amateur actor was discovered in the person of an aged "newsboy" of Honolulu who was cast in the role of the "kahuna" or sorcerer. Incidentally, for sufficient remuneration he was willing to wear anything or fail to wear anything that was ordered [*Manitoba Free Press*, 31 March 1923].

Cameraman James Van Trees had better luck photographing the titular flower, but that too required patience:

The flower — a gorgeous white blossom — blooms but once and then at midnight. The bud remains open for only a short time and the flower dies immediately after it has blossomed. James Van Trees selected a promising bud and then set his camera in position. Lights were placed so that enough illumination to photograph would be available at a moment's notice. And then it was necessary to sit down and wait until the blossom opened. Just before dawn of the third nightly vigil the crocus blossomed and the record of it was secured [*The Lethbridge* (Alberta) *Daily Herald*, 7 July 1923].

Such attention to detail failed to impress the anonymous critic who reviewed the film for the 23 March 1923 *Harrison's Reports* and who was appalled by the "very unpleasant" curse and the behavior of the heroine: "There is no worth-while moral conveyed by the story. While the sacrifice for love may be considered a good thing, this is obscured by the murderous intention of the heroine who loses the spectator's sympathy on account of her damnable act. Moreover, it is not in the nature of true love to plot against life." The reviewer did admit to finding the Hawaiian backdrop "enchanting."

Variety's "Fred" was not enchanted by the scenery, though, and felt there was way too much of it at the expense of the action, a fault he blamed on the direction in his 8 March 1923 critique:

While not particularly interested in the cause of its lack of punch from the box office angle, it might be well to state in passing that this is an author directed picture. That may account for it and again it may not. It is true, however, that about two reels of the opening of the feature are spent in laying the atmosphere of the islands as a background to the story.

Fred did find some good words to say about the acting, but griped about the make-up used on Arline Pretty (Ethel) in her sickbed scenes, finding it "very bad," especially in the close-ups.

Still, Fred's words were absolute raves when compared with the pig-roasting NEA's James W. Dean gave the film: "*The White Flower* is such a weak thing that the critic feels it would be cowardly to attack it. It could be tackled at the neck for its subtitles, at the ankles for its continuity, at the knees for its direction or even at the waist for its story and thrown for a substantial loss. *The White Flower* should have been kept on the sidelines. It has no business in the game" ([Hornell, NY] *Evening Tribune Times*, 9 March 1923).

Be that as it may, *The Chicago Tribune's* "Mae Tinee" found the film to be out of the ordinary, colorful and charming. Per her 21 February 1923 review,

It was made in Hawaii and is a composite of excellent photography, good acting and a story that appeals to your emotions (though it doesn't exactly do the same to your common sense)…. It is rarely in one film that two women are given the chance to prove themselves nature's noblewomen. The stars usually hog the big scenes where purity, self-sacrifice or martyrdom of any kind is required. In *The White Flower*, Miss Pretty is allowed to stick in her finger and pull out a plum. Miss Compson, of course, is accorded most of the plums, but her co-player does get one big one.

The film also played well in Hawaii, though audiences snickered at the sight of the workers at the pineapple plantation going around in grass skirts.

Betty Compson got favorable notices, though usually with a caveat or two. Mae Tinee opined that she was an actress who really needed good direction to show what she could do. *The Evening Tribune Times'* John Dean felt she had real screen presence whatever her limitations:

> Any film in which Betty Compson appears is not a total loss. She is not always a great actress. Sometimes she is not an ordinarily good actress, but there's always something magnetic about her appearance. She is like Priscilla Dean in that respect. One can keep an eye on the screen while either of these two are on it, even though they may not be doing much of consequence.

Yet, could even the kahuna have foreseen that one day lovely Betty would exchange her grass skirt for an old bathrobe and engage in staring contests with Bela Lugosi in *The Invisible Ghost*? More on the highs and lows of Miss Compson's career can be found in the entry on *The Miracle Man*.

Mae Tinee swooned over Edmund Lowe: "He's of the Richard Dix type and he sure do know how to make love." Lowe didn't set Fred's heart aflutter, but the *Variety* scribe found his performance "really clever" and "one that registered with the audience." Fred also thought Lowe resembled John Barrymore in his younger years. The particulars on this Dix/Barrymore clone can be found in the entry on *The Wizard*.

Arline Pretty's supporting part in *The White Flower* was typical of her roles in the 1920s. Pretty — and that was her real name, though at one point she considered allowing a fan magazine to conduct a contest to change it — started her working life as a secretary, laboring for a Louisiana senator as well as the American Conservation Society. At night, though, she attended drama school and upon graduating put down her stenographer's pad and joined the Columbia Stock Players in Washington, D.C. She entered the film world in the mid–1910s and became King Baggott's leading lady in a whole series of films for Imp. The actress later played opposite Doug Fairbanks in 1917's *In Again, Out Again* and opposite world-heavyweight champion, Jess Willard, in *The Challenge of Chance*. For all that (and more), she is/was probably best known for serials like *A Woman in Grey* and *The Hidden Hand*; in the latter, she was the vampish assistant to the eponymous villain.

Pretty's film roles declined as the 1920s progressed, but she had a champion in Louella Parsons, who penned the following, which was syndicated and then printed in the 16 November 1927 *Oil City* [Pennsylvania] *Derrick*:

> They all come back, that is if they have real talent and ability. That's why the friends of Arline Pretty aren't surprised that she has been invited by Darryl Zanuck of Warner Brothers to play one of the important feminine roles in *Tenderloin*, Dolores Costello's next picture. Arline for a time wrote scenarios. A worthy ambition we admit but all the time she had a hankering to return to the screen and when Michael Curtiz, who is the directorial genius of *Tenderloin* saw her, he decided he wasn't making a mistake.

Somewhat anticlimactically, Pretty didn't get the part in *Tenderloin*, but she no doubt appreciated Parsons' efforts; many years later — in 1965 — she shot off an angry letter to *Life* magazine, in which she criticized the periodical's less-than-flattering-article on Parsons. Pretty, who died in Hollywood at the age of 92, may also be found herein in the entries on *The Girl on the Stairs* and *The Dawn of Freedom*.

While James W. Dean may have hated *The White Flower*, he was nonetheless impressed with Edward Martindel (John Markham): "It's a rather negative role, as his roles usually are. Yet Martindel is one of the best actors on the screen. He never appears to be an actor." In a piece dated 28 March 1923, "Chatty," the reviewer for Madison, Wisconsin's *The Capital Times*, agreed: "We feel that Edward Martindel who played the part of the father was a better actor than the hero. His facial expressions were such that they did not require the accompaniment of hand gestures to understand them."

Martindel began his show biz career as a singer and eventually became known for his roles in musical comedies, like *Naughty Marietta*; he also scored in dramatic parts in *The Commanding Officer* and *The Alaskan*. Martindale made his film debut in *The Foundling* (1916) playing Mary Pickford's father, who initially rejects his infant daughter because his wife died giving birth to her. Tall and distinguished-looking, Martindale played mostly authoritarian types during his Silent Era career. He continued his stage work as well and, although he had prominent roles in early talkies like *The Singing Fool*, he was soon doing uncredited bits.

Julia Crawford Ivers was mostly known as a writer, but she also directed and produced, had managed Bosworth Studios in the mid–1910s, and — during her tenure at Famous Players–Lasky — worked with William Desmond Taylor on a number of important films. While Ivers preferred to maintain a low profile and usually shunned publicity, oddly enough — on one of the few occasions when she did allow a brief interview (in the 16 October 1920 *Motion Picture World*) — she seemed to agree with Fred's putdown of writers who had directorial ambitions: "The writer is only a helper and sometimes very poor help. More stories have been spoiled than made by writers who tried to put them in picture form, and if many of the writers who are yelping for credit on the screen should be debited with the lack of imagination and lack of vision the display, they would have no more to say."

By the time of *The White Flower*, Ivers was willing to step into the spotlight a bit in order to publicize the film; however, after *Flower* her credits are few and ill health forced her to retire in the late 1920s. She died in 1930, and her obits identified her (incorrectly) as only the second woman to direct Hollywood films. In addition to *The Witching Hour*, Ivers is also represented here in *Beyond* and *The Intrigue*.

— HN

The White Rosette

The White Rosette. American Film Company/Mutual Film Corp.; Mutual Masterpieces De Luxe Edition, 5 February 1916, 5 reels [LOST]

CAST: E. Forrest Taylor (*Sir Errol/Thomas Eric*); Helen Rosson (*Lady Maud/Joan Long*); Eugenie Forde (*Lady Elfrieda/Frieda Carewe*); Harry Von Meter (*Baron Edward/Pierpont Carewe*); William Stowell (*Lord Kerrigan/Van Kerr*); Richard La Reno (*Sir Longson/Ben Long*).

CREDITS: *Director* Donald McDonald

> The incidents I have related are difficult of belief and it is a matter of material indifference to me who thinks or does not think I am the reincarnation of some other man. I am not subject to hal-

lucinations and if these incidents were mental delusions, I would like to know why they are all related to the incidents of one man's life, and why I have never had any others.

— Edward Wodiska, a Florida businessman who claimed to be a reincarnation of Louis XIV, in *The Ogden* [Utah] *Standard*, 5 February 1915

In the 19th century, stories like the above would likely have been treated as a joke or as a matter for the analyst's couch, but, by the mid–1910s, belief in reincarnation — while hardly widespread — had piqued the public's interest and posed still another challenge to the assumptions of traditional Western religion, already under siege by Darwin's theory. In fact, advocates of reincarnation claimed it was quite consistent with evolution and the idea of continual change and also theorized that the belief could explain the split-personality phenomenon; in order words, maybe the guy who claimed to be Napoleon *wasn't* crazy after all. Naturally, this was not a subject that popular literature and films were going to ignore.

Still, perhaps because the notion was too easy to ridicule, Hollywood shied away from depicting the great and powerful figures of the past taking on human form once again in the present (with *Civilization* the one exception). Bunker Bean, on stage and screen, might have believed he was the reincarnation of Napoleon, but he found out otherwise by the curtain or end titles. Publicity for *The Dark Road* (1917) claimed that Dorothy Dalton's Cleo was really a reincarnated Cleopatra, but extant synopses seem to indicate a Mata Hari clone and not a literal reincarnation of the Princess of the Nile.

When it came to reincarnation, the movies took their cue from books like *The Gates of Horn* by Beulah Marie Dix (see entry, *The Road to Yesterday*), in which a young woman dreams of previous lives and the man who has loved her through the centuries; when, finally, she meets this literal "man of her dreams," in spite of a few obstacles (he's married), they eventually get together. Short films like *The Reincarnation of Karma* (1912) and Edison's *The Tragedies of the Crystal Globe* (1915) did not shy away from sad endings, but features always made sure the lovers were locked in happy embrace by the last reel. *The White Rosette* follows the formula to the letter as indicated by this synopsis from *The AFI Catalog*:

> In the eleventh century, Lady Elfrieda, who married Baron Edward for expediency, falls in love with the victorious knight Sir Errol, and arranges for his betrothed Maud, a lady-in-waiting, to be sent away. Before leaving, Maud pins a white rosette over Errol's heart, and he vows fidelity. Lord Kerrigan and other nobles plot with Elfrieda to kill Edward and replace him with Errol, who succumbs to Elfrieda. Maud returns disguised as a knight to warn Edward. Errol accidentally kills Maud and when he recognizes her, he puts the rosette on her breast and swears to atone for her even if it takes a thousand years.
>
> In the present, Frieda, wife of railroad magnate Pierpont Carewe, falls in love with Carewe's engineer, Thomas Eric, and sends his sweetheart, Joan Long, to Bermuda with her father, Carewe's head engineer. Although Eric almost succumbs to Frieda, Sir Errol appears in his dream and Eric stops an assault on Carewe by his business rivals at a dress ball, where Eric is reunited with Joan, who wears a white rosette.

Apparently the attempt by Carewe's rivals to usurp his business is a hostile takeover in the most literal sense since they physically attack him but, of course, they're acting on atavistic impulses.

Taglines for the film promised "a strong drama of love and intrigue" involving "the expiation of an ancient sin." Occasionally, the publicity flacks got a bit carried away: "There is all the romance, the singing of soft guitars, the gentle sighing, the artful coquetry which one has been led to believe existed in these days of your. But it is more convincing than literature because the life is made real again by the aid of the camera" (*Bismarck* [North Dakota] *Daily Tribune*, 9 September 1916). Presumably, this means Sir Walter Scott belongs on the scrapheap.

One ad for the film was written by someone who apparently couldn't follow the story:

> The young knight and the civil engineer meet at Lady Maud's coming out reception. Both are in love with Lady Maud and become rivals. Both lay traps to get each other out of the way. Lady Maud also takes a hand which ends in the temptress' death. A desperate fight and the mysterious return of the man who had been exiled, making this one of the greatest plays put on by the company [*The Titusville* (Texas) *Herald*, 28 February 1916].

No doubt it would have taken Monty Python to do justice to the meeting of the civil engineer and the knight at the medieval lady's coming-out party.

The film also elicited some fawning comments from *The Middletown* [New York] *Daily Times-Press* in a 21 April 1916 review that often sounds like a rewritten publicity handout (it was penned by someone with the appropriate moniker of "Brownie"):

> E. Forrest Taylor as "Sir Errol" was exceptionally good…. He is usually cast in western roles, is an expert at riding and shooting and usually wears chaps and sombrero and his work in *The White Rosette* suggests the typical happy, carefree disposition of the cowboy.
>
> [Helen Rosson] is a very vivid blonde beauty. In fact her features are so vivid it is not necessary for her to "paint" her eyes and for this reason her screen beauty is more satisfactory than most of the more famous painted beauties. Miss Rosson's natural coquetry is also a valuable and inimitable possession that cannot be acquired successfully.
>
> The scenery was wonderful. We understand that the castle entrance, drawbridge and moat were especially built for the picture…. The ballroom was a big scene and with a few glimpses of that big orchestra, we knew the music was good too.

On the other hand, Kitty Kelly — in the 23 March 1916 number of *The Chicago Tribune*—found the retelling of the story in the modern section a bit boring….

> The same villain struts the stage, raising his eyebrows, rolling his eyes. The same adventuress coils her arms around the same hero, happily divested of his flowery locks, which were unbecoming in one who is none too handsome at the best.

…the medieval segment a bit better, but still not very convincing…

> One doesn't feel at home in these houses as in others in picture land. They consist of collections of furniture not welded together in spirit as it should be. Nor do the people feel wholly at home in their costumes. They put themselves in them, but they don't succeed in wearing them as to the manor born — a common difficulty with costume pictures.

…and, sounding a bit like *Variety*'s Jolo, the lady was amused by a few unrealistic details:

> It should be noticed by all who are cultivating their manners from the movies that the civil engineer coming back from his railroad survey kisses the hand of his employer's wife when he is in-

troduced to her, and also that as soon as he reaches the pale of civilization, his life is incomplete without a valet, which should inspire the youth of the land to civil engineering ambitions.

In the 12 February 1916 edition of *Motion Picture News*, Harvey F. Thew opined that the film, while having some merit, was less than it should have been:

> Reincarnation comes again to the fore as a motif in motion pictures. It has been used by the American studios to produce an interesting and really dramatic, though frequently unconvincing effort, and it opens up great vistas of possibilities— possibilities which have not always been taken advantage but which are hinted at strongly enough to start many minds to thinking. The use of two periods, a thousand years apart, has made possible unusual versatility in settings, costumes and character drawing. One could wish that something more poetic or possibly mystic had been used to link the two ages than a mere subtitle.

Some of the publicity for *The White Rosette* revolved around Helen Rosson, one of American Film Company's most prominent stars, to the extent that the copy seemed to have been written by her mother. For example, the reader is told that the old silk gown Ms. Rosson wears in the film had been in her family for five generations and that the jewels she's adorned with are likewise old family heirlooms. The scene wherein she dons a suit of armor (presumably *not* an old family heirloom) is mentioned solely to point out that the woman's great appeal transcends even that unfeminine get-up. More on the gal who looked good in chainmail can be found in the entry on *The Light*, wherein will also be found information on actress Eugenie Forde, *Rosette*'s Lady Elfrieda/Frieda.

E. Forrest Taylor (Sir Errol/Thomas Eric), like so many Silent Era stars, had had quite a bit of stage experience before turning to film. Still, even at so late a date as the end of his college days, Taylor was uncertain as onto which career path — that of actor, travelling salesman or Episcopal rector — he ought to embark. All was fortuitously settled when a travelling repertory company came to his Bloomington, Illinois, hometown and advertised for extras for their production; away flew any idea of sales or sermons. Taylor applied and was not only accepted, but the company's manager was so impressed with the good-looking, athletic youth that he offered him a permanent place in the company. Taylor toured with this troupe and others before forming his own company in 1912; however, the endeavor failed and, several years later, the erstwhile impresario switched to the movies, where he came to have a particular love for the Western genre (he even wrote poems about the Old West). Despite this, Taylor took a cinematic sabbatical and returned to the stage for a few years. When he returned to Hollywood in 1926, he found that his starring days were over. He had a long career ahead of him nonetheless, playing small roles and bits in numerous westerns and serials, and he kept working right up to the Television Era.

Richard La Reno (Sir Longson/Ben Long) — also associated largely with westerns — had been for many years a circus performer whose specialty was lifting a 130-pound wagon wheel with his chin, a feat he was still able to accomplish in his sixties. Leaving the circus for less strenuous work in vaudeville and the stage, La Reno would recall late in life making his first movie, *Humpty Dumpty* (most likely Selig Polyscope's *Humpty Dumpty*

and the Baby), in Chicago in 1903; he was doubtless reminded of this milestone by his wife, Mae Bennett, who had co-starred with him in the film. Later in the decade, La Reno moved to Hollywood and later still began his work in the industry; he was, for example, the first sheriff in feature-length motion pictures (in Cecil B. De Mille's *The Squaw Man*) and went on to play small roles in numerous films, including two covered in this volume, *Black Orchids* and *Reward of the Faithless*. La Reno also founded the Trouper's Club, an organization dedicated to vaudeville and circus performers.

Like many of his peers, director Donald McDonald had started out onstage — he had appeared, for example, in support of Frank Craven in the Cohan and Harris production of *Going Up*— and then moved on to both acting in and directing films in the 1910s. World War I interrupted McDonald's film career and he found on his return that he was more in demand as an actor than as a director. While the demand lasted, he scored in films like Charles Ray's *Forty-Five Minutes to Broadway* (based on another George M. Cohan play) and Maurice Tourneur's *Lorna Doone* (wherein he played villain, Carver Doone). Again, like many of his peers, he watched his roles grew smaller and smaller as the 1920s progressed and this may have led McDonald (who once supposedly held the world's record for most rummy games played in one year) to try his hand at cards once more.

Reincarnation films continued to be made in the 1920s despite the fact that even the most notable of them, *The Road to Yesterday* and *The Love of Sunya* (see entries on both), failed to draw big audiences. Now, if they had them to do all over again…

— HN

Why I Would Not Marry

Why I Would Not Marry. Fox Film Corp./Fox Film Corp., 24 November 1918, 6 reels [LOST]
CAST: Lucy Fox (*Adele Moore*); Ed Sedgwick, William Davidson
CREDITS: *Presented by* William Fox; *Director* Richard Stanton; *Story and Scenario* Adrian Johnson; *Cinematographer* H.G. Plimpton, Jr.

The Internet Movie Data Base, while listing *Why I Would Not Marry*, also lists another, earlier 1918 Fox picture entitled *Why I Should Not Marry*, also starring Lucy Fox and with some of the same cast and crew as *Would Not*. However, no copyright exists for anything entitled *Why I Should Not Marry* and there is no evidence that any such film was ever made.

> "That's a mighty big proposition, isn't it? How many of you said you would not marry but never gave a definite reason why? Now Adele Moore did the same thing but she showed why she would not marry. Come and see her reasons and compare them to yours. Might be interesting."
> — advertisement for *Why I Would Not Marry*

No doubt the producers of the hit Broadway play *Eyes of Youth* would have indeed found the Fox production of *Why I Would Not Marry* very interesting, as it is clearly a take-off (or, more precisely, a rip-off) of their story. The play — a triumph for Marjorie Rambeau that captivated audiences throughout 1917 — would go on to be filmed twice (see entries on the Clara Kimball Young *Eyes of Youth* and the Gloria Swanson *The Love of Sunya*), both times openly and above-board. With *Marry*, Fox apparently managed to avoid plagiarism charges by semi-spoofing the original and sending their little *homage* in under the radar by giving it a minimum of publicity and a star (Lucy Fox, no relation to the boss) who was practically unknown to the public.

We turn to *Moving Picture World* (14 December 1918) for our synopsis:

> A lawyer, a banker, a physician and an impecunious youth each seek the hand of the heroine in marriage. Her father favors the banker — the richest of the quartet. She slightly favors all four. But a crystal globe is given her to look into the future. In the globe she perceives what the fates have in store for each marriage. The lawyer would cast her off for an adventuress. The banker's financial sins find him out. The physician neglects her for his studies and the impecunious youth would sacrifice her to his employer to advance his fortunes. She rejects them all and seeks engrossment in business, but here fresh troubles arise and once more the Swami presents the crystal globe and shows her the path to happiness.

The synopsis from *The AFI Catalog* shows us that path in more detail: "Adele moves to Vermont and opens a store. Business is slack until a passing salesman assumes management of the store and transforms it into a booming success. Happy at last, Adele agrees to marry him." Presumably, dear old Dad is happy too.

One major difference between *Why I Would Not Marry* and *Eyes of Youth* is that the latter is not exclusively concerned with the heroine's matrimonial prospects, but with the different paths her life could take (career, devotion to family, marriage). Of course, marrying for money to please the parental units is one of the big clichés of Silent Era melodrama, but one has to wonder what kind of person Adele is to attract such poor husband-material not once, but four times.

Why I Would Not Marry also apparently jettisoned the mysticism of the play and the Oriental wisdom preached by the yogi with the crystal. Here, according to the *Moving Picture World* review, the swami is a woman who tells Lucy she too has psychic powers, sells her the crystal and takes her money and runs, leaving Lucy to look into the magic globe all by herself. This being the case it's not clear why (per the *AFI* synopsis) the swami needs to make a return visit to help confirm the enterprising hero's worthiness. Perhaps the swami's crassness is meant as a jab at *Eyes of Youth*.

MPW's Walter K. Hill (30 November 1918) didn't know what to make of the film: "In this new Fox presentation drama struggles for recognition while comedy protests — and finally broad farce prevails in bringing to belated ending one of the most unusual of recent film endeavors…. Who shall get the worst or the best of the 'spoofing' we cannot say — with no crystal ball at hand we cannot foretell the future like Lucy could."

Apparently in keeping with the spirit of the film, Hill offered his own version of how the story should end:

> Our instant guess at the outcome was in effect that we should in the next and final reel find Lucy in Marion, Ohio, in possession of a glass furnace making the big, round glass balls that sorceresses gaze into and vision the future for girls who are considering the matter of marriage. While a member of the Society of Projectionists was rewinding the fifth reel we had time to figure it all out for Lucy, planning sales drives and laying out a campaign of national advertising for the glass bowling balls that would make a ten-strike with the lovelorn millions.

Though publicity for the film stayed pretty low key, Fox did suggest some taglines:

> — Four Times Had She Been Deceived by Men Who Professed Undying Love for Her.
> — Every Woman Thinking of Marriage Will Like to Know How to Choose a Husband.
> — Four Kinds of Husbands Reflected in Mysterious Crystal Ball.
> — The Art of Crystal Gazing Reduced to Science in Photoplaying.

In regard to the latter, the publicity boys had an additional suggestion: "By all means, have a crystal globe for the lobby. If you cannot obtain a fairly large crystal invert a small fish globe. If you can rig it so that the stills appear below the level of the stand so much the better."

In an oddity noted by reviewers, Fox promised "a carefully chosen cast," but disclosed none of their names except for Lucy Fox. A later newspaper article about William Davidson's induction into the service noted that he played "the juvenile lead" in *Why I Would Not Marry* so one would guess he was the "impecunious youth." He was at that time a fairly well-known leading man, so it's odd that Fox ignored him, PR-wise, in favor of Lucy Fox, whose brief flurry of fame did not occur until the 1920s. Edward Sedgwick was also in the film and, while there's no indication as to what part he played, one can hope that Sedgwick — who resembled a tall Bert Roach — was the salesman whose pitch wins the heroine's heart. Sedgwick's particulars can be found in our entry on *The Haunted Pajamas*.

Although Lucy Fox's career *was* at its height in the 1920s, with the exception of a couple of serials and westerns she was more likely than not to be found in supporting roles. Fox was beautiful and photogenic and did receive a great deal of publicity, but that didn't quite add up to top flight stardom. Since she did a number of action pictures, there were the inevitable stories about how her hardiness belied her dainty appearance:

> Miss Lucy Fox who is a member of the company in *Sonny* in which Richard Barthelmess is starred, is the daughter of a New York City battalion fire chief.
> "My father says it takes more nerve to be a motion picture actress than to be a fireman," Miss Fox relates. "In one of my earlier films, I was called upon to drive an automobile at a fast rate straight through a plate glass window. In spite of trepidations, I did it. When I got home my father asked me how I cut my hand. I told him. 'Well, you're the daughter of a fireman,' he exclaimed. 'And you go a bit farther too. I would never have had the nerve to do that'" [*Oakland Tribune*, 14 May 1922].

In 1923 it was announced that Fox would star in a series of films for producer Max Graf, but nothing came of it. In 1925, Fox married wealthy, New York silk manufacturer, Jules Forman. It was reported that Cecil B. De Mille wanted Fox to star in his production of *The Golden Bed* and to sign a five-year contract with him, but Fox — not wanting to stay in Los Angeles while her husband lived in New York — declined and retired from show biz.

William Davidson was head of his class at Columbia University in 1909; popular and athletic, he also had a good singing voice, composed music and acted in college musicals. After graduating, he worked on Wall Street for a while, drifted around a bit, and then ended up in the movies; appropriately enough, in his first film, *For the Honor of the Crew* (1915), Davidson played a college athlete. He subsequently free-lanced, appeared with Ethel Barrymore a couple of times, and took a villainous part opposite Lionel Barrymore in *The Weakling*, all the while writing tunes, including "Gypsy Moonbeams" and "I Want to Go Back to Blighty." In 1918 Davidson enlisted in the field artillery and won a commission, but the Armistice was signed before he could see active service. Davidson returned to both civilian life and life at Fox where he frequently appeared opposite Theda Bara.

Davidson's leading-man status declined in the 1920s, and he found himself cast more frequently as villains in films like *Women and Gold* and the Tom Mix western, *The Last Trail*. Come the Sound Era, he was reduced to doing small roles (the captain in *The Most Dangerous Game*, the crooked politico who employs thug Boris Karloff in *Graft*) and kept busy right up until the late 1940s, although mostly in uncredited bits.

Both director Richard Stanton — a one-time actor at Universal — and scenarist Adrian Johnson enjoyed their brightest days at Fox. Stanton helmed a couple of dozen ho-hum features between 1914 and 1925 (directing Dustin Farnum as Sir Percy Blakeney in 1917's *The Scarlet Pimpernel* may well be his most impressive credential), but Johnson had a somewhat more conspicuous career; he was even known as the "Theda Bara Man" since he frequently churned out her scenarios. He also wrote for foreign sirens like Francesca Bertini and, in his spare time, composed poems praising the arms of women (especially when they — the arms — were in motion). He also penned *The White Brother*, a book concerned with split personality; one brief review described the opus as being "autographic." Assuming *auto*biographical is meant, perhaps it was Johnson's darker self who was responsible for *Why I Would Not Marry*.

— HN

Wild Oranges

Wild Oranges. Goldwyn Pictures/Goldwyn Cosmopolitan Distributing Corp., 20 January 1924, 7 Reels/6837 feet, Turner Classic Movies
CAST: Virginia Valli (*Nellie Stope*); Frank May (*John Woolfolk*); Ford Sterling (*Paul Halvard*); Nigel De Brulier (*Lichfield Stope*), Charles A. Post (*Iscah Nicholas*)
CREDITS: *Direction and adaptation* King Vidor; based on the eponymous novel by Joseph Hergesheimer (New York, 1919); *Editorial Director* June Mathis; *Cinematographer* John W. Boyle; *Settings* Cedric Gibbons; *Costumes* Sophie Wachner; *Titles* Tom Miranda

In a lengthy career-interview director King Vidor gave to David Shepard and Nancy Dowd, he barely mentioned his 1924 Goldwyn production, *Wild Oranges*. He recalled that it got good reviews (which it did) and that his later *Bird of Paradise* had a similar plot (which, perhaps, was a bit of a stretch). Possibly Vidor had so little so to say about the film because it was his first financial flop. A Michigan exhibitor groused, "I only hope the balance of the Goldwyn pictures is better than this one. I had thirteen people the second night so draw your own conclusions" (*Oakland Tribune*, 21 December 1924).

Vidor was barely in his thirties when he made *Wild Oranges*, but his earlier films had scored with the public and critics con-

sidered him something of an innovator. He had become a recognizable name to moviegoers so that in itself should have been a draw. The film's two stars, Frank Mayo and Virginia Valli, may not have been of name-above-the-credits caliber, but were certainly had a following. Including them, though, the cast consists of only six players (one of whom is killed off in the first scene), and the movie was shot almost entirely out of doors, mostly in a dismal swamp setting. The film's few interiors are set in gloomy rooms of a dilapidated old mansion, hardly a banquet for the eye (unless you're Edgar Allan Poe). One ad for the film showed a drawing of a topless maiden picking an orange. Audiences expecting an exotic romance were no doubt disappointed by the macabre atmosphere and the rather odd story.

We present the following rather odd plot summary following our viewing the film:

After his bride is killed in a carriage accident, John Woolfolk leaves his native Boston on his yacht and spends the next three years sailing aimlessly from place to place, estranged from society and life. His only companion is his cook, Paul Halvard.

Anchored off a desolate inlet on the Georgia coast, Woolfolk notices a decaying and seemingly deserted mansion near the shore. He also sees a young woman swimming nearby. Woolfolk goes ashore and finds the old house is located near an orange grove. He samples one of the oranges and finds, though bitter at first, it has a satisfying aftertaste. He also meets the young woman, Nellie Swope, who lives in the old house with her grandfather, a man driven into seclusion by pathological fear triggered by the horrors of the Civil War. Nellie has lived in the house all her life and, inspired by all the books she has read, dreams of seeing the world even though she has inherited some of her grandfather's fear of people. She is drawn to the taciturn Woolfolk and he, in turn, is moved by her fragility and beauty though he is wary of developing any kind of attachment to her.

It turns out, though, that Nellie and her grandfather do have a legitimate object of fear: a hulking, half-witted giant named Nicholas, who has forced himself upon the family. Nicholas' sexual attentions toward Nellie become increasingly more aggressive as he observes her attraction to Woolfolk. After a couple of nasty encounters with Nicholas, Woolfolk is puzzled as to why they tolerate the man in their house. Woolfolk takes Nellie for a sail and, though she is initially delighted, the vastness of the waters terrifies her and she begs to go back. Woolfolk puts her ashore and decides to leave the inlet; however, though torn over the risk of loving again, he quickly returns.

Nellie shows him a wanted poster that reveals that Nicholas has murdered a woman and is a fugitive from justice. Nellie tells Woolfolk that Nicholas has threatened to kill her grandfather if she runs away. Woolfolk convinces Nellie to get her grandfather and bring him to the dock later that night and he will take them both away. Nicholas learns of the plan, kills the old man, and ties Nellie to her bed. A fierce storm arises and, when Nellie does not show up at the appointed hour, Woolfolk goes to the house. He has a ferocious battle with Nicholas, during which the mansion is set on fire. Woolfolk manages to escape to the dock with Nellie, but loses his revolver in the process. Back on the ship, Halvard tells them that the storm makes negotiating the sandbar very dangerous. Nicholas finds the gun and begins shooting from the shore, and Halvard is wounded. He is too injured to help steer the ship but, with Nellie's aid, Woolfolk is able to sail the yacht out of the inlet to safety A savage dog that Nicholas has been tormenting breaks its chain and tears Nicholas' throat out. The storm ends and a peaceful dawn finds Woolfolk and Nellie looking forward to the future together.

If, despite the obvious melodrama, *Wild Oranges* sounds a bit artsy and pretentious, it must be remembered that those are exactly the qualities movie producers were looking for in the early to mid–1920s. There was an ongoing rush to buy plays, books, and stories that could be transformed into "prestige" projects, regardless of their ultimate suitability for film. For example, the rather hefty sum of $5000 was paid to Catholic Worker founder, Dorothy Day, for *The 11th Virgin*, her semi-autobiographical account of her bohemian days and love affairs. The producers rushed in and *Virgin* ended up — albeit completely unrecognizably — as the 1925 Warner Bros. release, *The Woman Hater*!

Famous-Lasky Players and Sam Goldwyn competed fiercely to land the rights to such now-forgotten little masterpieces and, so far as "land" was concerned, the works of Joseph Hergesheimer were the *Boardwalk* and *Park Place* of desirable, contemporary literary properties. Goldwyn bought the rights to Hergesheimer's *Wild Oranges*, which was serialized in 1916 in *The Saturday Evening Post* before being released in book form, two years later, as part of *Gold and Iron*, a trio of the author's novellas.

Although nearly forgotten today, Hergesheimer was one of the most popular writers of the 1920s— in fact, he was rated the *best* American writer in a poll of book critics taken by *Literary Digest* in 1922 — and won the praises of H.L. Mencken, James Thurber and F. Scott Fitzgerald, even if Mr. Fitzgerald's praise was begrudging. The patrician Hergesheimer was a disciple of the "aesthetic" school of art (which held, more or less, that art should be devoted to some ideal of beauty rather than merely reflect moral concerns), and he saw a number of his stories turned into films during the 1920s: *Java Head* and *The Bright Shawl* (both 1923, with the latter, one of Edward G. Robinson's first films), *Cytherea* (1924, also produced by Goldwyn), and *Flower of the Night* (1925). The most notable film adaptation of Hergesheimer's output was doubtless *Tol'able David* (1921), the Henry King classic that, like *Wild Oranges*, climaxes in a savage David vs. Goliath battle. Still, as the 1920s waned, so did Hergesheimer's popularity. The disillusionment caused by the Great War and a growing trend toward social realism made the typical Hergesheimer hero— an upper-class, middle-aged man facing a crisis in an exotic setting — decidedly irrelevant, and Hergesheimer's once-praised, ornate prose was increasingly seen as flowery and overwritten, especially when compared to the taut, lean styles of a Hemingway or a Fitzgerald. Joseph Hergesheimer found himself consigned to the dustbin of literary history, where he has remained ever since.

It was different, though, in 1924. In addition to being courted by the studios, Hergesheimer also became friendly with stars like Lillian Gish, Douglas Fairbanks, and Richard Barthelmess. He even gave some thought to writing directly for the movies, but, as he wrote to Lillian Gish in 1921, he abandoned the idea because scenarios were the "mere statements of acts rather than the creation of emotion." As a published author, he was extremely particular as to how his works were adapted for film. He recognized in Henry King's *Tol'able David* a personal triumph for the director and for star, Richard Barthelmess, but ultimately felt that the film relegated his story to a back burner. When his novel *The Three Black Pennys* was optioned for film, Hergesheimer insisted upon contractual approval of scenario, cast, location, and final production. As for *Wild Oranges*, the Goldwyn publicity department claimed that the author had sent a letter to King Vidor — who was credited with the adaptation as well as the direction — saying that Hergesheimer was "speechless with delight" at the result and thought "the production is perfection" and "without an inch of bunk in it." Hergesheimer did indeed approve of the film, but he actually gave accolades to Hollywood's Girl Wonder, June Mathis—credited in the film as "editorial director"— and not to Vidor. In a letter to publicist (and, later, lyricist) Howard Dietz, Hergesheimer elaborated:

> My story was changed from one medium to the other without any loss of its spirit and that was a difficult and important accomplishment. Miss June Mathis, who had made the transposition, understood to the finest shade of meaning my exact purpose and followed it in such a manner that put me forever in her gratitude [The University of Calgary Special Collections, February 1924].

Mathis, of course, was a prolific writer and one of the most powerful women in 1920s Hollywood.

Frank Mayo and Charles A. Post (depicted left, right) battle it out while Virginia Valli, eschewing violence, implores the deity's advice on orange futures.

Whoever was responsible for the final scenario did indeed adhere closely to the original story. There were a few minor changes: in the novel, the heroine's name is Millie, not Nellie (although *The New York Times* film review does refer to her as Millie), and it's her father — not her grandfather — who's a prisoner of his fears. Some blood and thunder were added to the climax of the film, mainly in the form of the fire that consumes the mansion and Nicholas' graphic death by dog. Also, in the novel, Halvard dies of his wounds, but onscreen — as he provides some mild (but necessary) comic relief and is played by former Keystone Kop, Ford Sterling — he survives to keep on mugging. Some of Hergesheimer's prose is preserved in the title cards, including the funniest line in the book: When Nellie comes aboard the ship, she is impressed by the cleanliness of the cabin and remarks, "Why, it couldn't be neater if you were two nice old ladies." (We shall let braver souls than we delve into the subtext there.) The only other amusing line to be found in the picture is writ on the description on Nicholas' wanted poster: "He has a large nose and a stupid expression."

Virginia Valli tries hard as Nellie and looks lovely but is never completely believable in the role of a neurotic innocent who's terrified of people but who nonetheless falls immediately in love with a stranger she has just met; indeed, no one could be. Valli, a popular ingénue who worked primarily at Universal, saw her career decline with the waning of the Silent Era. No matter; she retired from film and married actor Charles Farrell. Frank Mayo makes for a stalwart and stoic John Woolfolk until the contrivances of the plot oblige him to become infatuated with Nellie. His best moment, though, is in the first scene of the film, wherein his bride is killed. His shock, panic and despair are wrenching, and his utter helplessness in the face of such a bolt out of the blue is reminiscent of Lillian Gish's whirling about in horror in the closet just before her murder in *Broken Blossoms*. Like Valli, Mayo was a leading player at Universal, but he suffered a less happy fate than his sometimes co-star and was reduced to doing bit parts, mostly uncredited, in the 1930s and 1940s. He did get billing in one memorable film, though: In Robert Florey's 1937 tribute to forgotten actors, *Hollywood Boulevard*, Mayo played himself.

For all this, the most memorable portrayal in the film is Charles A. Post's Nicholas. Post plays the giant as if he were Steinbeck's Lenny Smalls, but with a mean streak. Nicholas is as pathetic as he is menacing, rocking back and forth while weeping in frustration when things go wrong for him. He's dangerous, though, and there's one particularly unsettling shot of him rushing toward the camera, knife in hand. Elsewhere, wearing a dirty apron as he kills and plucks a chicken, Nicholas more than slightly reminds the viewer of Leatherface, from *The Texas Chainsaw Massacre*. Still, the fact that he's so childlike takes him out of the hissable-villain category, in contrast to the equally dim-witted but completely monstrous Luke Hatburn in *Tol'able David*. Post, who also wrote and produced a number of westerns in the 1920s, ended his acting career playing Earthquake McGoon in 1940's *Li'l Abner*.

As Nellie's tormented grandpa, Nigel De Brulier — gaunt, wide-eyed, with a shock of tangled gray hair protruding from under a wide-brimmed hat — looks like a scarecrow haunted by visions of hell. A fine character actor and a frequent face in silent and sound genre features, De Brulier was a put to especially good use in costume dramas like *The Three Musketeers* (1921 and 1935), *The Hunchback of Notre Dame* (1923), and *Ben Hur* (1925). His most iconic film appearance may have been as Shazam in the 1940 Republic serial, *Adventures of Captain Marvel*, and, coincidentally, one of his last roles was providing the model for the sorcerer in "The Sorcerer's Apprentice" segment of Disney's *Fantasia*.

The New York Times reviewer found *Wild Oranges* "exciting and entertaining," though he had some (understandable) doubts about the story's plausibility. Hergesheimer claimed that the theme of his book was fear and the overcoming of it through heroism and love, but everything is far too pat and schematic. Woolfolk loses his fear of life by loving Nellie and saving her from Nicholas; Nellie conquers her fear of the world by loving John and steering the yacht to safety; her grandfather breaks free from *his* all-consuming fear by standing up to Nicholas and dying a hero. It was as though Hergesheimer had rewritten Joseph Conrad's *Victory* and had given it a happy ending by having Heyst first change from philosopher to action hero and then save Alma by plugging Mr. Jones and his criminal pals. (Nonetheless, Woolfolk's plan to rescue Nellie — especially in the movie — is almost laughable: "OK, dear, you go back to the house, convince your crazy, paranoid grandpa to leave with you, and then sneak out without the giant lunatic spotting anyone, and I'll just wait here for you on the wharf!")

Vidor keeps the book's obvious symbols (the titular fruit, the sandbar, etc.) but doesn't seem particularly drawn to the romantic angle. In fact, his treatment often borders on the trite when he deals with it: double exposures of Nellie and Woolfolk's late bride in the cabin as Woolfolk ponders what to do is too commonplace a device for a director with such an imaginative visual sense. What's more, Vidor seems less interested in Hergesheimer's lofty thoughts on conquering fear than in rendering his viewers helpless before it. What remains memorable about the film is its focusing chiefly on horror at a time when audiences expected their thrills to be mitigated with laughs. Strip away the symbolism, the hero's angst, and the improbable romance, and what you have left is the story of an isolated handful of people terrorized by a homicidal maniac. The old mansion has no sliding panels, butlers in black face, terrified maids, or guys in ape suits. Instead, the images of the slowly opening door in the shadowy corners of the mansion, the flapping roof tiles, and the recently vacated rocking chair that creaks back and forth are meant to induce fear and tension, and they very nearly involve *all* the viewer's senses. *Wild Oranges* is a silent film you can almost hear. The Germans might have taken a more Expressionist approach to material such as this, but Texas-born, Christian Scientist Vidor keeps things on an earthier, more fundamental level.

The horrific images start in the very first scene. The blowing newspaper that startles Woolfolk's horse and causes the carriage accident may be a symbol of Fate (or absurdity), but what is most memorable about the sequence is the close-up of the dead girl's face, her eyes open and vacant in a fixed and terrible stare. When Woolfolk's yacht pulls into the inlet, Vidor cuts to the different reactions of the observers: Nellie's fear, mingled with curiosity; her grandfather's abject terror; Nicholas' emergence from the swamp like a startled animal. The purely visual sequence is so eerie that the subsequent explanation via title cards is almost a letdown. Later, in a scene that might have inspired *Sparrows*, Nicholas puts Nellie on a stump in the middle of the swamp and watches with delight as alligators circle the poor girl. His price for saving her is a kiss. Then, too, when Nellie shows Woolfolk the wanted poster, the scene is set in a musty old outbuilding that is crammed with odd items that look scavenged from Mrs. Bates' sitting room and is alive with spiders, birds, rats and bats. The final sequences of the film are truly terrifying and contain one of the most brutal fights of the Silent Era (too brutal for the New York censors, who insisted on cutting a close-up of Woolfolk sinking his teeth into Nicholas' arm and the resultant spurt of blood). Nicholas seems like some unstoppable, mindless force of nature: implacable, relentless and more terrible than the storm. Woolfolk hits him repeatedly with a club, but the brute recovers again and again and keeps on coming. Nicholas' own death is especially grisly (and a forerunner to Brandon Hurst's demise in *The Man Who Laughs*) and there are two macabre shots of the approaching dog in which all that can be seen is its eyes, glowing in the darkness like some terrible avenging hound from Hades.

Ads for the film promised "A Kiss in the Dark, a Raging Fire, a Thrilling Escape — and then some" and "Virginia Valli as the girl of Florida's jungle in this tender love story" (here, from an August 1924 number of *The Manitoba Free Press*). More than one ad, in fact, confused the place where the film was shot (Florida) with where it was set (Georgia). In a misguided effort at adding its own personal touch to the canned publicity sent out by the studio, the 25 June 1924 *Chillicothe* (Ohio) *Constitution Tribune* stated that the picture was photographed "along the mouth of the St. John's River near Jacksonville. The old Harriet Beecher Stowe estate figures prominently in one of the backgrounds." The estate is actually located, appropriately enough, in Mandarin, Florida.

Wherever the film was shot or set, audiences weren't buying it. Its failure, though, was not even a bump in King Vidor's road to success. His great silents — *The Big Parade* (1925) and *The Crowd* (1928) — were still ahead of him, and he would have a long (though perhaps not quite as interesting) career in the talkies. In spite of his seeming lack of affection for *Wild Oranges*, he did try, in the 1940s, to interest David Selznick in a remake to star Gregory Peck and Ingrid Bergman.

The story was also performed as an episode of the radio anthology, *Escape*, in 1947. Shortly thereafter, Horror Meister (and man of refined tastes) Val Lewton found to his dismay that scripting a remake of *Wild Oranges* was to be his first assignment at MGM. In a letter to his sister (written in July of 1948 and quoted in Joel Siegel's *Val Lewton: The Reality of Terror*) Lewton lamented, "I ran the old picture and it looks very dated and very bad today. Also a re-examination of the values and motivations of the novel itself distressed me." Disagreements with producers over the script ultimately caused the project to be scuttled.

Wild Oranges is not available on home video, but it is occasionally revived at silent movie festivals. Most recently a beautiful 35mm print was shown at Capitolfest 3, in Rome, New York. Audiences in 1924 may have regarded the film as odd or distasteful but, in 2005, as the finale unreeled in all its frenzied violence to the thundering accompaniment of Dr. Phil Carli at the organ, the Capitolfest audience seemed totally caught up in the tension and horror on the screen. Perhaps Joseph Hergesheimer might have preferred a more profound response to his philosophical thriller, but one suspects King Vidor would have found it immensely satisfying.

— HN

The Willow Tree

The Willow Tree. Screen Classics/Metro Pictures Corp., January 1920, 6 reels, Eastman House

CAST: Viola Dana (*O-Riu*); Edward Connelly (*Tomotada*); Pell Trenton (*Ned Hamilton*); Frank Tokunago (*John Charles Goto*); Harry Dunkinson (*Jeoffrey Fuller*); Alice Wilson (*Mary Fuller*); Togo Yamamato (*Itomudo*); George Kuwa (*Kimura*); Tom Ricketts (*The Priest*); Jack Yutaka Abbe (*Nogo*)

CREDITS: *Supervisor* Maxwell Karger; *Director* Henry Otto; *Scenario* June Mathis; based on the eponymous play by J.H. Benrimo and Harrison Rhodes (New York, 6 March 1917); *Cinematographer* John Arnold; *Settings designed by* M.P. Staulcup; *Set Painting* George M. Carpenter

Based on one of those venerable Oriental myths of which most contemporary Orientals are ignorant, yet which most romantic Occidentals find fascinating, touching, and not a little incomprehensible, the theme of *The Willow Tree* resurfaces now and again throughout the first half of the era of silent features. Although he is not the story's pivotal figure (as in Thanhouser's *The Image Maker*, 1917), the sculptor (here, Tomotada) remains very much in control of the actions of the rest of the dramatis personae; indeed, there is always something godlike about him. In some films, this perception is undeniable evidence of the intrusion of the supernatural into whatever "real" world the picture is depicting. In others, it serves to put the other characters off their game: they must proceed as if the hitherto immutable laws of the Universe might give way at any moment.

> While seeking the seclusion of Japan in order to forget an unhappy love affair, Ned Hamilton chances upon a shop owned by Tomotada, an image maker. There Ned falls in love with the carved figure of a beautiful girl which Tomotada refuses to sell because of the mythical legend connected to the tree from which it was carved. However, when Tomotada's daughter O-Riu runs away from an arranged marriage and her brother spends the money paid for her by the would-be groom, the image maker is forced to sell the figure of the princess of the willow tree. After it is delivered to Ned's home, O-Riu wanders in and takes the place of the image in the cabinet. Having been told that a mirror placed in the hands of the image will endow it with life, Ned tries the experiment and is pleased when O-Riu pretends to come to life. The two fall in love, and when war breaks out, Ned refuses to leave his princess to return home to England and defend his country. Rather than have her lover disgrace himself, O-Riu contrives to make him believe that she has returned to her image state, and Ned leaves for England. Returning to Japan after serving his country, he finds the princess waiting for him [*The AFI Catalog*].

The Willow Tree is pretty much a straightforward woman's picture — traces of *Madame Butterfly* are interwoven with the arduous boy meets girl, boy loses girl, etc.— with the fantastic element being represented by the conceit of the inanimate somehow coming to life because of love, duty, honor, outrage, and such.

The picture's *Japanese* element was represented by the usual handful of lesser lights: Nipponese expatriates who had come to the USA to find employment in the movies as secondary (or tertiary) cast members playing generic Oriental types meant to lend verisimilitude while wandering about in the background. It's impossible to determine how important were the roles played by any of the genuine Japanese assigned to the actual supporting cast, but it's not surprising that the only Oriental characters crucial enough to warrant mention in the plot précis were portrayed by Occidentals. Cast-list inspectors will doubtless smile at the sight of George Kuwa's name; besides *The Willow Tree*, the screen's first Charlie Chan was involved in *The Bottle Imp* (1917), *Curlytop* (1924), and *Chinatown Charlie* (1928; all discussed in this volume), while providing support for countryman, Kamiyama Sojin, in *his* turn as Earl Derr Biggers' Honolulu police inspector, in 1928's *The Chinese Parrot*.

The Willow Tree had its origin, not in some Nagasaki garden, but rather on Broadway, courtesy of the collaborative efforts of sometimes actor, J.H. Benrimo, and fulltime author/playwright, Harrison Rhodes. Their *Willow Tree* had a decent run — 100+ performances during the winter of 1917 at the (George M.) Cohan and (Sam) Harris Theatre on 42nd Street — before being adapted by June (*Aladdin's Other Lamp*, *A Trip to Paradise*, etc.) Mathis for Screen Classics late in 1919.

Director Henry Otto was yet another of those multi-tasking,

early-cinema jacks-of-all-trades, with credentials in the fields of writing (the 1923 mythological fantasy, *The Temple of Venus*; see appendix), directing (1924's *Dante's Inferno*, see entry), and acting (he's Dr. Hayden in 1929's *One Hysterical Night*), and producing (once only), with respect to 1916's *Undine* (see entry). This is not to say that he did any of this terribly well, but the fact that the man was gainfully employed — in any and all of these occupations; at times, simultaneously — indicates he was at least competent at his craft(s).

Variety's opinion of *The Willow Tree* saw print on the 24 January 1920, and the reviewer ("Leed") saw fit to single out Mr. Otto for mention: "Henry Otto directed." So much for superlatives. Actually, *Variety* damned much of the production with faint praise (or casual mention), when not outright grousing about the way the picture turned out.

> It is badly cast to begin with and Viola Dana is completely lost in the part. Tough, smashing roles are her forte, but this was something for a more delicate and accomplished actress. Helen Jerome Eddy could have done it wonderfully and there are a dozen cuties in pictures who could have gotten a hundred percent more out of it. The Japanese showing did well, but otherwise Mr. Karger seems to have thought the most ordinary work would do and so the amazingly elaborate scheme of settings and photography are comparatively wasted.

For more on Miss Dana and her "tough, smashing roles," please consult our thoughts on *Aladdin's Other Lamp* (1917).

Mr. Karger's Christian name was Maxwell, and he received credit (here, however, a dismissive snort) for supervising the project. Leed led off his mass of disappointments with a couple of positives (for the visual technicians) before bemoaning the way the picture ended up…

> Jack Arnold is responsible for the nearly perfect photography. The art settings and inserts designed by M.P. Staulcup are the kind to arouse unlimited enthusiasm, but Maxwell Karger in passing this product has loosed on the market a "beauty" picture for the benefit of the artistic, not a rousing story calculated to set the hearts of the masses on fire. Somehow, the story misses fire.

Harrison's Reports (3 January 1920) admitted to missing Fay Bainter in the role (O-Riu) she had created on stage, but had some kind words for Miss Dana and the production's artfulness: "Quite the best thing … is the legend that is incorporated into the story. It is a tale of old Japan and it gives Miss Dana an opportunity to play the real goddess of the Willow Tree. Director Otto has produced it with poetic effect and it is beautifully acted by the star. It is one episode that is in the full spirit of the stage play."

The New York Times, never the sort to reduce nuance to "Hix Nix Stix Pix," was also more amiable than had been *Variety* in its 2 February 1920 assessment:

> There is beautiful photographic work in *The Willow Tree*, at the Capitol this week. The Japanese setting of the story gave Henry Otto, the director, and his associates exceptional opportunities, and they did not seem to have missed any of them. Also they made a number

Edward Connelly is the arthritic old darling on the left and Pell Trenton is the slightly embarrassed juvenile on the right. Perched in a flower pot 'twixt the two men is Viola Dana, a Miracle-Gro experiment gone awry. From the film *The Willow Tree.*

of pictures which revealed a mastery of camera technique as well as artistry of setting. Their dream and moonlight scenes were especially good. It was by its pictorial quality that *The Willow Tree* achieved distinction. With all its admitted accuracy of detail, and despite the fact that its cast included several natives of Japan, the photoplay was not impressively Japanese. Perhaps it wasn't meant to be. It was probably intended to be what it was, simply a romance employing an idea of Japan familiar in popular fiction, with costumes, settings and customs serving rather to give it fanciful colors than to identify it with the country across the Pacific.

Still, apart from giving Henry Otto's work a bit of acknowledgement, the *Times*' critique also began by praising the visual stuff and then lowering the boom on the way the story just sort of sat there. If nothing else, though, the commentary succinctly recounted the fantasy element that was at the heart of the story: "The narrative gets out of the rut, and becomes charming, when a supposed, and perhaps actual, Japanese legend is introduced in which the personified heart of a willow tree destroys her mortal life so that the warrior she loves may be free to answer his country's call to arms." Well, we managed to see the picture at the 2007 *Cinesation* in Massillon (Ohio), so our opinion is that while *The Willow Tree* is not without charm, it owes less to Puccini and more to Gilbert and Sullivan. The idea that educated men — both Japanese and English — could fall for a simple ruse reduces the light drama to lightweight farce. Still, as was mentioned above, it is a beautiful movie.

— *JTS*

The Witch

The Witch. Fox Film Corp./Fox Film Corp., 27 February 1916, 5 reels [LOST]

CAST: Nance O'Neil (*Zora*); Alfred Hickman (*General Mendoza*) Frank Russell (*General Hernandez*); Macey Harlam (*Pedro*); Ada Neville (*Isha*); Jane Miller (*Dolores*); with Sadie Gross, Stuart Holmes, Harry Kendall, Robert Wayne, Jane Janin, Ada Sherin.

Strangely, the important role of Riques isn't credited to anyone; Stuart Holmes would be the best guess.

CREDITS: *Presented by* William Fox; *Producer* William Fox; *Director* Frank Powell; *Scenario* Frank Powell; based on the play *La Sorciere* by Victorien Sardou (Paris, 1903); *Set Decoration* J. Alan Turner and William Bach

Working title: *The Sorceress*

While his plays are rarely performed today, French author Victorien Sardou provided high-class fodder for silent-movie melodrama. Sardou's operatic plots were full of passion and retribution and often featured the sort of unlikely coincidences much beloved by scenarists of the 1910s. On the downside, they also contained the sort of political and social criticism that was not likely to make the final cut of any film of that era. His tragic endings also presented a problem, but onscreen they proved to be nothing that couldn't be handled by a last-minute rescue or a fifth-reel change of heart on the part of a betrayed lover. Regarding the latter bit of business, writer/director Frank Powell altered the ending of his adaptation of Sardou's *Fedora* (in his 1915 film, *Princess Romanoff*) by simply having the title character resuscitated by her now-forgiving lover after she takes poison. And if this seems like a particularly corny device, remember how many contemporary romantic films seem to end unhappily

with the lovers parting only to have them improbably reunited (usually at the airport) just before the final credits start to roll. Boy meets girl, boy *loses* girl, boy ... etc., remember?

Powell seemed to have had some difficulty coming up with a coherent scenario for his subsequent adaptation of Sardou, this one based on the playwright's *La Sorcière*, and, like *Princess Romanoff*, promoted as a vehicle for stage great Nance O'Neil. *La Sorcière* is set in Spain during the time of the Inquisition and concerns the love affair of a Moorish woman with a Christian, a liaison that was forbidden under penalty of death. To complicate matters further, the heroine, Zoraya, has hypnotic and healing abilities that make her a suspected witch. Her powers lead both to her condemnation as a sorceress and the means of her rescue, but an enraged mob — urged on by the clergy — causes the deaths of both lovers. Obviously, the anti–Catholicism that runs through the play was the first thing to go, and the whole setting was shifted from medieval Spain to Mexico (with the time-frame being left a bit hazy). Political unrest in Mexico and the escapades of Pancho Villa were much in the news of the day, so perhaps the change of scene was meant to be topical. In its opening reel, the film seems to lose track of the play altogether, as is evident in the following synopsis from the 4 March 1916 *Moving Picture World*.

> Dr. Fernandez, a physician, is believed by Mendoza, the military governor of Mexico, to possess hypnotic powers. Mendoza is in love with Dr. Fernandez's daughter, Zora. When Zora displays no love for him, Mendoza assumes her father is responsible for the failure of his suit. So great becomes the hatred between the two that when a faction of insurrectionists arises, the doctor places himself at its head and leads it against the government.
>
> Dr. Fernandez is killed in battle. In the meantime, Dolores, the daughter of the Governor, is suffering with somnambulism. While she is anxious to be cured, she dislikes to inform her father or her lover that she is so afflicted. Finally, her old nurse makes the fact known to Zora, who possesses the hypnotic power that was her father's. Dolores submits to treatment at the hands of Zora and is cured.
>
> At the same time that Zora brings about the cure of Dolores, the former does not know that Dolores is engaged to be married to Riques, Zora's sweetheart. When she does learn that the wedding day is set, she goes into a rage and contrives to get into the palace at night and hypnotizes Dolores. Shortly thereafter, Zora is denounced as a witch and is carried away by an angry mob to be burned at the stake. Just before the torch is applied, the old nurse makes known to the Governor that his daughter has the habit of walking in her sleep and that she is in a trance from which she cannot be aroused.
>
> Also the old nurse informs the Governor that the only person who can cure his daughter is Zora. At the last instant, the Governor stays the burning of Zora and promises her freedom if she will bring Dolores from her lethargic state. Zora, believing the Governor is acting in good faith, goes to the palace and wakens the girl. When Dolores is found to be safe, the Governor goes back on his word and commits Zora to prison.
>
> [At this point *MPW* describes an ending much in keeping with the play's tragic denouement]: She escapes, however, and Riques, who realizes he loves Zora more than Dolores, runs away with her. The two are captured after a fight and in the end Zora is put to death.

This précis most likely came from an advance studio synopsis and is not the finale audiences in 1916 would have seen. According to the AFI rundown, Zora survives but is driven from the village. This puzzled *Variety*'s "Jolo," who wrote (on the 3 March 1916): "Just what becomes of Zora in the end is left to the imagination, nothing being told. She is simply shown being cast out. The impression is created that a more definite finish was made and proved unsatisfactory and was discarded in the assembling of the feature." Of course, had the film been just a few years later, happy *and* sad endings might have been filmed and the exhibitors given their choice.

Hypnotism, that staple of silent horror, plays only a secondary role in *The Witch*. Victorien Sardou was himself fascinated by hypnotism and speculated that auto-suggestion explained all that the medieval world thought of as witchcraft. His Zoraya is herself seemingly cynical about real magic and, in both play and film, she confesses to bewitching her lover only to save him from the stake.

Hoopla for the film made much of the authenticity of the Mexican settings. Supposedly the village — which was built on four acres of ground in the Fox Studio at Fort Lee — was an exact reproduction of the "town of Tuarepec in the province of Chihuahua." The publicity flacks couldn't decide whether it all cost "several thousand" or as much as $10,000, but they did all agree that it was the work of J. Alan Turner ("noted as a builder of expositions") and Fox technical director, William Bach. Whatever its cost, the set did pay off in numerous favorable comments from reviewers.

Hanford Judson of *Moving Picture World* was enthusiastic about the early action scenes, but seemed disappointed when the film reverted to the more static parameters of the play. Under the headline "Bustle and excitement a-plenty makes good in spite of weak story," Judson offered the following in the 11 March 1916 edition:

> In the opening scenes, the bass drum and the big noise are as important as anything else. We are shown regiments rushing madly as in a dream and those scenes are mixed in with firing and cannonading which often blasts the bowels of the earth till the rocks and stones are flung up all over the screen, and great trees are shattered and fall with a crash. This is very exciting stuff; the rest of the picture is not so convincing nor so exciting; but none of it is dull and none of it drags.

It's all but certain that Mr. Judson saw the film with lively musical accompaniment, and perhaps after providing all that sound and fury for the battle scene, the musicians were too tuckered out to play anything but "Hearts and Flowers" for the remainder of the film.

Peter Milne, writing in *Motion Picture News* on the same date, likewise found the battle scene exciting but thought the exposition in the early scenes unclear: "A number of characters, easily mounting up to two numerals, are introduced in rapid succession without the clarifying medium of close-ups. And also the beginning of the picture launches out on a number of plots. Confusion is very apt to result from this overcrowding."

Overall, though, Milne found the film strong in "most respects" and appreciated the visuals: "The photography furnished by Director Powell's cameraman is excellent and besides there are not a few equally fine light effects. The value of lights and shadows in increasing the strength of a scene is aptly demonstrated."

Variety's Jolo was likewise mostly positive about the film, but thought Nance O'Neil's costumes anachronistic: "Just why Miss Nance O'Neil, the star, should be clad in Cleopatra fashion and sleep in her BC regalia is not explained."

Miss O' Neil's notices were respectful, but accolades were noticeably light. Milne felt that Powell could have done better by her: "Miss O'Neil is seen to fine advantage when she steps within close range of the camera. Director Frank Powell has, however, chosen to award his star with few close-ups and sometimes one is apt to wish that there were more of them for the sake of bringing out the true force of the salient points of the story."

Publicity for *The Witch* claimed that Nance O'Neil had played the title role on stage for "so long and carried it to such triumphant heights in the world of stage art that it has almost become a part of her." Actually, while the lady did receive acclaim for another Sardou play, *Fedora*, it was Sarah Bernhardt who was most identified with the role of Zora (Zoraya in the play); O'Neil did play the part from time to time but never in a major venue. Fox promoted the Oakland, California native as the "Queen of Passion" and the "Empress of Strong Emotions," but the American movie-going public was less interested in tragediennes than plucky heroines, vamps, and sweet young things. Had O'Neil lived in Italy she could have a film career as a diva, suffering exquisitely in front of marble columns and wearing magnificent flowing gowns. In America, however, she became a famous name with little box-office appeal.

Nance O'Neil (née Gertrude Lamson) first came to New York in 1896 to play in the lavish Music Hall established by Weber and Fields, two burlesque comics-turned-impresarios. O'Neil's star began to rise when she hitched it to actor/manager McKee Rankin, and the two formed their own company. Their production of *Oliver Twist* apparently played like a horror show, with the murder of Nancy (O'Neil) by Bill Sykes (Rankin) being the grisly highlight. O'Neil went on to triumph in *Magda* and *Camille*, but there were questions about her relationship with Rankin, who was twice her age and married; thus, to escape the constant queries, O'Neil set off on a worldwide tour that included such far-flung venues as England, Australia and South Africa. The tour was hardly a success, garnering mixed notices and running into financial difficulties, due both to the actress's extravagances and Rankin's growing mismanagement. Stories circulated comparing O'Neil and Rankin to Trilby and Svengali, with even Lionel Barrymore commenting that Rankin was constantly looking at O'Neil as if to keep her under his spell. Whatever Rankin's hypnotic powers, his managerial skills were on the decline and, in spite of the enthusiastic personal notices O'Neil received and her great popularity, the company slipped ever downward, became embroiled in lawsuits, and finally went bankrupt. The actress was reduced to appearing in vaudeville. In the end, she broke with Rankin and returned to great success in the legitimate theater under David Belasco.

O'Neil made a series of films in the 1910s, but their failure to excite the public caused her to return to the stage where, though no longer a phenomenon, she was still a big star. She did continue to make the occasional picture, with the most notable perhaps being the John Gilbert disaster, *His Glorious Night* (1929). Oddly enough, O'Neil is remembered today less for her career as a thespian than for her friendship with Lizzie Borden, she who was acquitted of giving her mother and father "forty whacks." Borden had inherited a considerable fortune from said butchered parents and, being very much stage-struck, lavishly entertained theater people, but her relationship with O'Neil cooled when Borden announced that the actress would star in a play that she, the nouveau playwright/notorious criminal, was going to write.

Alfred Hickman (General Mendoza) did mostly light comic work in his early years on the stage, but achieved a measure of fame as the original "Little Billee" in the 1895 production of *Trilby* that starred Wilton Lackaye. In another production of *Trilby*— staged and presented the very next year — Hickman fell in love with actress Blanche Walsh who, appropriately, was playing the title character. Walsh was much better known than Hickman, and they kept their subsequent marriage a secret, the truth not coming out until their divorce seven years later. Major stardom eluded Hickman, but he signed on with David Belasco and played opposite Nance O'Neil in one of her biggest successes, *The Lily*, in 1910. O'Neil and Hickman married six years later (there was no secret this time around) and co-starred onstage and onscreen (though Hickman was rarely the leading man in her movies). Hickman died unexpectedly in 1931, not long after he and O'Neil had played in *Death Takes a Holiday*.

Witch helmsman Frank Powell had both directed and acted when he worked with D.W. Griffith at Biograph, although it was Powell's switch to Fox in the mid–1910s that led to his biggest hit, the 1915 *A Fool There Was* with Theda Bara, in which the director himself played a small role. Credited with "discovering" Blanche Sweet, Powell tried to duplicate his success by promoting the career of young actress, Veta Searle, but nothing came of it. Subsequently, he started his own production company and brought Nance O'Neil over with him from Fox; however, after only a couple of films — when Powell declined to renew the contract of her husband, Alfred Hickman — O'Neil walked away. That may not have initially worried Powell, for he also had Marjorie Rambeau, another great star of the stage, under contract; after a half-dozen films, though — when once again a Stage Legend failed to translate into a Screen Legend — Powell's new venture went under. Undaunted — and perhaps thinking he'd been a bit too high-brow in his artistic aims— Powell decided to switch to westerns and helped start still another new outfit, Sunset Pictures. With a big ranch in San Antonio serving as both the company's headquarters and its principal standing set, things were looking up. When Sunset's very first production was plagued by bad weather and the ranch was put under quarantine, things slid downhill once again. The third — and last —feature of Sunset Pictures was the appropriately titled *You Never Know Your Luck*. Powell directed a couple of shorts for Mack Sennett before dropping off the screen-history radar.

And a similar fate befell *The Witch*.

— *HN*

Witchcraft

Witchcraft. Jessie L. Lasky Feature Play Co./Paramount Pictures Corp., 16 October 1916, 5 reels [LOST]

CAST: Fannie Ward (*Suzette*); Jack Dean (*Richard Wayne*); Paul Weigel (*Makepeace Struble*); Lillian Leighton (*Nokomis*).

CREDITS: *Producer and Director* Frank Reicher; *Assistant Director* L.W. O'Connell; *Scenario* Margaret Turnbull; *Story* Robert Ralston Reed; *Cinematographer* Dent Gilbert

Breaking into the movies was a pretty casual affair in the free-wheeling pioneer days of early cinema: directors and writers often had no background at all in the arts and while a number of actors hailed from the stage, others stepped in front of the camera with zero in terms of prior experience. By the mid–1910s, though, the notion that you could actually train for a career in the movies enjoyed a brief vogue. There were "How to" books for writing, acting, and directing, and a number of schools — most of them little more than con games — began luring in star-struck men and women dreaming of fame and fortune in glamorous Hollywood. It appears that there *was* one course that was entirely legitimate; started by Elizabethan scholar, Victor O. Freeburg, at Columbia University in 1915, the course provided students with training at writing photoplays. Sixteen pupils enrolled the first year, but the number grew to sixty in a couple of semesters, and some of the students successfully sold their scenarios at prices ranging from $100 to $700.

The course drew the attention of Samuel Goldfish (later Goldwyn) of Famous Players–Lasky, who was probably less interested in snagging budding authors for his studio than exploiting the course for publicity purposes. Goldfish sponsored a writing contest for the students and promised that the winner, in addition to being paid handsomely for his work, would get a free trip to Hollywood to see his story turned into a film. After the usual hoopla in which the public was told "hundreds"(!) of photoplays were submitted, a panel of judges led by director William De Mille picked *Witchcraft* which was written by Dr. R. Ralston Reed, a physician from Morristown, New Jersey. The good doctor got his check (a middling $350) and his vacation to LaLaLand, where he watched his little masterpiece being shot and met the film's star, Fannie Ward.

We don't really know how much of Reed's story actually made it to the screen as his contest entry does not survive. However, the final scenario, written by veteran scenarist, Margaret Turnbull (see *Public Opinion*), is still extant and we turn to that for our synopsis:

> Salem has become the home for two French Huguenot refugees, Suzette and her ailing mother. Fear of witchcraft has gripped the village and the two women are regarded as suspicious because they are foreigners. It doesn't help that Suzette befriends a strange old Indian woman named Nokomis whom the village children believe is a witch.
>
> The beautiful Suzette catches the eye of young Richard Wayne and his guardian, town miser Makepeace Struble. Struble is particularly interested in Suzette's dowry of precious jewels, which he sees while spying on the two newcomers through their window. Not wanting competition from his ward, Struble agrees to let him leave Salem and take a military commission with the Governor.
>
> Suzette's mother gives a neighborhood girl a cookie. Later, when the girl falls ill, her father accuses Suzette's mother of witchcraft. The town minister tries to reassure Suzette, but Nokomis warns her that the village is in a hanging mood. Struble tells Suzette that if he agrees to marry him, he will use his influence to protect her mother. Suzette reluctantly agrees but, shortly after the

unhappy wedding, Suzette's mother dies. Struble proves to be a brutal husband and often beats Suzette.

When Richard comes back to Salem, he is shocked to hear of the wedding and treats Suzette coolly, figuring she married his uncle for his money. Suzette is hurt by his attitude and, when she tells Nokomis of her troubles, the old woman gives her a beaded necklace which she says will makes her wishes come true. Though she really doesn't believe in the talisman, Suzette wishes on it that Richard, whom she loves, will be friendly to her again. When Richard discovers why Suzette married Struble, he declares his love for her but, realizing they cannot be together, he returns to the Governor's office.

A village girl spies on Suzette and Nokomis while they are making soup in Nokomis' hut and even though nothing sinister is happening, the girl lets her imagination run wild. Back at home she describes the two women as hideous witches toiling over a bubbling cauldron. Her brothers and sisters become hysterical with fear. Their mother declares that they have been bewitched.

Struble is about to beat Suzette again, but his wife denounces him and, declaring the power of her talisman, wishes him dead. A little later, Struble collapses and, helped to his bed, tells his companions that Suzette has cursed him. Meanwhile, Nokomis hears that an Indian uprising is imminent. She tells Suzette who disguises herself as a man and goes to warn Richard. When she returns, she is shocked to discover that Struble has died and that she is accused of witchcraft, a charge bolstered by her wearing men's clothes. Even though she used her necklace merely to frighten Struble, Suzette begins to wonder if she really is a witch.

At Suzette's trial, the village girl who was spying on her and on Nokomis begins twitching and screaming, and declares Suzette is torturing her. Another child follows suit and Suzette is condemned to be hanged. Nokomis rushes to alert Richard, who informs the Governor that the woman who warned the colony about the Indian revolt is about to be executed as a witch. The Governor signs a proclamation ending the witch hunts. Meanwhile, Nokomis has returned to Salem just in time to see Suzette brought out to be hanged. An angry mob is pelting the accused woman with rocks. Nokomis tries to shield her and is seriously injured. Richard arrives with the Governor's proclamation and Suzette is saved. Nokomis tells Suzette that the talisman has no special power and that Struble's death was natural. Reassured, Suzette is comforted by Richard.

It seems likely that either Dr. Reed or Margaret Turnbull had taken a gander at H. Wiers-Jenssen's 1910 play *The Witch*, and reworked it. *The Witch* is an English version of the 1909 play *Anne Pedersdotter*, by Hans Hagedorn, which itself was based on a real incident in 1575 Denmark. *The Witch* starred Bertha Kalich ("The Sarah Bernhardt of the Yiddish Theater") as a Portuguese woman who marries an elderly minister in Salem. The minister keeps from his young bride the fact that her mother was executed as a witch. The minister's son returns from a long sea voyage and falls in love with his father's new wife. When the woman discovers the truth about her mother, she begins to believe she too has the power to make things happen merely by wishing them. She confronts her husband and curses him and he promptly dies. However, there's no proclamation from the Governor or last minute rescue; instead, the minister's son, prompted by his grandmother, turns against his lover who, broken-hearted, accepts her condemnation as a witch. *Anne Pedersdotter* was also the basis for what may be the cinema's finest study of witchcraft, Carl Dreyer's *Day of Wrath* (1943).

The script for *Witchcraft* has several scenes in which the demons of the children's imaginations are depicted on the screen. From the sequence of Nokomis making soup:

> As the child tells it, Nokomis is a terrible, impossible old witch with a pointed cap and a long hooked nose and claw fingers. Likewise what she drops into the stew is not meat and vegetables but toads, little snakes or long worms— dead birds with all their feathers on, and a kitten or two. Suzette is also a witch, but not so ugly, and a talisman she fingers, instead of being composed of beads, is a little skull— the eyes gleaming like pinpoints of fire (If this is possible to get over). Instead of a black cat, a little devil with horns is watching the two.

How much of this actually made it to the screen remains unknown, but it's a clever way of giving the audience a shiver while disparaging the notion of real black magic. Suzette's skepticism about witchcraft and then her gradual doubts make good psychological and dramatic sense, but the way Nokomis' character is written simply seems inconsistent: One minute she's depicted as believing in magic (in a harmless, "folk medicine" way) and, the next, she's debunking it. And, for an old lady, she's a pretty fast traveler, getting back and forth from the Governor's manse quicker than if she had flown on a broomstick.

George Blaisdell, in a very favorable review for *Moving Picture World*, praised director Frank Reicher for doing a "studious, unexaggerated portrayal of the days of witchcraft in New England. Of the several producers who have essayed to treat this subject he is, so far as this writer has observed, the first to avoid the egregious historical error of burning his victims at the stake— an ending which, as a matter of fact, never befell a white person in New England" (28 October 1916).

Publicity for the film seems to have overlooked that fact as at least one ad informed the public that "once in New England people were actually burned, hanged and drowned because they were accused of having business dealings with the devil."

Variety's "Jolo" derided the whole contest gimmick:

> The judges decided his (Reed's) story was the best example of photoplay technique of all the scenarios submitted. In spite of their learned judgment, *Witchcraft* will not prove to be the most successful of all the Lasky productions nor yet the best thing Fannie Ward has done in pictures. True, it tells a straightforward story with very few side lights but that is its very weakness for a five-reeler…. There does not appear to be a sufficient variety of scenes which makes this photodrama a trifle monotonous nor is the gloomy subject lightened by any comedy relief…. The Lasky company had been more fortunate in its selection of scenarios when it didn't resort to school contests. And this being so, why not continue to seek where it discovered "pay ore" in the past? [20 October 1916].

Jolo was grateful at least that the titles weren't written in the Puritan vernacular.

On the other hand, Theodore Osborn Eltonhead's review in *Motion Picture News* sounded more like publicity than criticism and is so full of sunshine it's hard to believe he actually saw what must have been a pretty grim little film:

> *Witchcraft* is a thoroughly delightful picture in every particular and as such will not fail to please any audience that is so fortunate as to witness it. It is a picture that has an almost universal appeal, containing as it does a good wholesome story, most excellently acted and produced. Fannie Ward is a delight, presenting a series of charming scenes that are a distinct pleasure to witness [28 October 1916].

Nothing like bigotry, hysteria and wife beating to bring a happy smile to the face of the average moviegoer.

The (then) husband and wife team of Fannie Ward (Suzette) and Jack Dean (Richard) can be found herein again in our coverage of *Unconquered*, while the particulars of their careers are laid out in *The Crystal Gazer*.

Lillian Leighton received good notices as Nokomis ("a fine interpretation of a strong character, one that bulks in the story": *MPW*). Leighton began her career in stock companies and vaudeville and entered films in 1910 playing Madame Frochard in Selig's *The Two Orphans*, a role she had previously done on the stage. Selig kept her busy in the 1910s, supporting dwarves in the Katzanjammer Kids series and giving her comic roles in many two-reelers. She got more substantial parts when, in 1916, she switched to Famous-Players Lasky where she became a popular character actress. Some publicity for *Ruggles of Red Gap*—printed in *The Davenport* [Iowa] *Democrat and Leader* (22 July 1923)—praised Leighton's versatility: "Other pictures yet to be released which present her performances are *Crinoline and Romance*, *The Grubstake* and *The Eternal Three*. In them she plays respectively: a Negro mammy, an Indian squaw, and an Irish housekeeper. It is said in Hollywood that Lillian Leighton's versatility has depicted a representative of every race and nationality now existent."

Leighton's most conspicuous role in the 1920s may well have been the aforementioned *Ruggles of Red Gap* where she played Ma Pettingill, a tough ranch-lady who rolls and smokes her own cigarettes and doesn't take guff from anybody. It's the part most often mentioned in Leighton's obituaries, but it is mistakenly attributed to *The Covered Wagon* (in which she did not appear). Leighton was reduced to doing bit parts when the talkies came and largely retired from the screen in 1941. She ended her days in the Motion Picture County Home but, according to Billy Doyle's article in the March 1990 (#177) *Classic Images*, she remained upbeat and gracious in her twilight years.

Director Frank Reicher (see *Public Opinion* and *The Crystal Gazer*) directed both on stage and screen before offloading Carl Denham and Ann Darrow on Skull Island in *King Kong* (1933) and unwisely brewing tana leaves in *The Mummy's Ghost* (1943). More on his career can be found in the entry on *Unconquered*.

On the other hand, Dr. R. Ralston Reed's film career began and ended with his scenario for *Witchcraft* even though pr claimed his story was the unanimous first choice of all the contest judges. The notion of professional schooling for a career in film quickly faded and was not revived for many decades.

— HN

The Witching Hour (1916)

The Witching Hour. Frohman Amusement Corp./Frohman Amusement Corp. and States' Rights, December 1916, 7 reels [LOST]

CAST: C. Aubrey Smith (*Jack Brookfield*); Marie Shotwell (*Helen Whipple*); Robert Conness (*Frank Hardmuth*); Jack Sherrill (*Clay Whipple*); Freeman Barnes (*Tom Denning*); Lewis Sealy (*Justice George Prentice*); William Eville (*Lou Ellinger*); Robert Ayerton (*The Judge*); Helen Arnold (*Viola Campbell*); Etta De Groff (*Mrs. Campbell*).

CREDITS: *Presenter* William L. Sherrill; *Director* George Irving; *Scenario* Anthony P. Kelly; based on the eponymous play by Augustus Thomas (New York, 18 November, 1907); *Cinematographer* William A. Reinhart

"If a thought is a dynamic force, a man has a heavy responsibility as to his kind of thoughts. If my malignant thoughts are going to affect my family, my friends, my acquaintances and then drift out into—perhaps impotence—why, then I want to know it."
— Augustus Thomas

Playwright Augustus Thomas was fascinated by telepathy and considered it to be a scientific fact. In 1888, Thomas, who had worked for the railroad and then later switched to journalism, became the manager of Washington Irving Bishop, a vaudeville mind-reader who apparently originated the blindfold gimmick that became standard for stage mentalists. While Thomas thought some of Bishop's routine was strictly show biz, he believed him to have genuine powers which were apparently triggered by auto-hypnosis: Bishop often finished his act by dramatically falling into a faint. After one such swoon, doctors on the scene pronounced him dead and immediately did an autopsy, outraging Bishop's mother who claimed he was subject to cataleptic episodes and thus may have been cut up while still alive!

After that bizarre finale to his career as a manager, Thomas turned to writing and producing on the legitimate stage and eventually achieved considerable success doing regional dramas like *Arizona* and *Colorado*. While he did not lose his interest in telepathy and hypnosis and continued to do research, he was wary of putting the results in play form as he was uncertain of public reaction. He originally wrote *The Witching Hour* as a one-act play and presented it to members of the Lambs Club. It went over well and in 1907, Thomas redid it as a four-act play and showed it to Broadway impresarios, Daniel and Charles Frohman; although they had backed Thomas' earlier plays, they didn't care for the subject matter of this one. Undaunted, Thomas went to the Schubert brothers who were far more amenable. *The Witching Hour* ran for over 200 performances on Broadway, became Thomas' biggest hit, and established him as a serious playwright more interested in ideas than melodrama. The following year Thomas turned the play into a novel.

In the 1910s Thomas took an interest in motion pictures; he was especially impressed by Giovanni Pastrone's *Cabiria* (1914), which he watched with President Woodrow Wilson at a special White House showing. Becoming the director general of The All Star Feature Film Corporation, Thomas helmed the movie debuts of Dustin Farnum and Ethel Barrymore as well the first cinematic adaptation of Upton Sinclair's *The Jungle*, which proved so controversial that Thomas claimed—in spite of much evidence to the contrary—that he *hadn't* directed the picture. In 1915, Thomas put the megaphone aside and took over as art director for the Frohman Company after Charles Frohman went down with the Lusitania.

While at All Star, Thomas had directed the film version of one of his own plays, and there was talk that *The Witching Hour* would follow, but nothing came of it. Instead, Thomas sold the rights to the play to an independent company called, ironically enough, the Frohman Amusement Corp. Gustave Frohman, the least known of the famous brothers, initially had some involvement in this new company and his wife Marie wrote and directed their first film, the 1915 Mary Miles Minter tearjerker, *The Fairy and the Waif*; it was Minter's first feature and it still survives. Gustave (or perhaps it was Frau Frohman) then had second thoughts about this new venture and severed all connections with Frohman Amusement, threatening legal action if the name "Frohman" were not removed from the company's title. For all that, it stayed Frohman Amusement Corp. right up to the company's dissolution in the early 1920s.

C. Aubrey Smith, who starred in four films for Frohman, recalled that the company's two studios, one on Tenth Ave in New York City and the other in Flushing, Long Island, were both former churches. Smith felt "they served our purposes very well; in those days actors were not held in high regard and the fact that we were working in churches somehow boosted our morale." The company's early efforts were adaptations of famous books and plays but, as the 1910s wore on, they turned to serials, Westerns and the occasional oddity like *The Birth of a Race*.

The Witching Hour was made during their prestige period and it was announced that the upcoming production would be faithful to the famous play and recruit as many of the original Broadway cast as possible: "John Mason who starred in the play as head of the original company is soon to appear in *Common Clay* on the speaking stage but it is believed he can divide his time between the theater and the studios in order to appear in the proposed picture. C. Aubrey Smith will be seen as the gambler and Edith Taliaferro in the ingénue role if present plays carry" (*La Crosse* [Wisconsin] *Tribune*, 16 September 1916).

Since Mason played the gambler in the play and certainly wouldn't have taken a secondary role in the film, the whole story sounds like an invention. In the end, none of the movie's cast hailed from the Broadway production though ads occasionally claimed otherwise.

However, the film did remain faithful to the play (though

A postcard sent out in conjunction with the picture's release featured a scene from the 1908 stage production, and *not* from the film itself. It baffles science.

less slavishly so than the 1921 version; see entry) as the AFI synopsis indicates:

Jack Brookfield, a gambler with telepathic powers, becomes reacquainted with an old flame, Mrs. Helen Whipple, a widow with a son named Clay. The Whipple family is cursed with a peculiar fear of the cat's eye and one day Clay kills Tom Denning when Denning taunts Clay with a cat's eye stickpin. Clay is prosecuted for the murder by District Attorney Hardmuth, who has political aspirations, and who is Clay's rival for the affections of Brookfield's niece Viola. Jack inadvertently shows Hardmuth a way to assassinate the governor, and Hardmuth hires a down-and-out gambler named Raynor to do the job. By force of will power, Brookfield makes Raynor confess the murder scheme and the public reaction against Hardmuth results in Clay's acquittal. Clay proves his courage to Viola by assisting in the escape of Hardmuth, whom Brookfield considers an innocent victim. Brookfield convinces Helen that he will quit gambling, and both couples are reunited.

In the play, the political assassination is two years past when the story begins; making it part of the current action was probably a good move though it gives the scheming Hardmuth rather a full plate. The assassination subplot may well have been inspired by the murder of governor-elect William Goebel of Kentucky (the play's setting) and the subsequent trial and conviction of Secretary of State Caleb Powers.

While we know little about *The Witching Hour*'s budget, publicity for the film claimed that it was a lavish production:

The Witching Hour is in seven parts with 2567 super scenes and is staged with a pretentiousness and with a refinement never attempted in any screen production. As an example of the technical detail employed in this production there are used eight paintings that are valued in excess of $18,000; one Corot which plays a part in the production upon which a valuation of $5,000 was placed on loan to the Frohman Amusement Corporation by a famous art gallery in New York.

The producers were also quick to assure audiences that they, like Augustus Thomas, had done their homework: "A deep element of hypnosis and psychology prevails in the story and in order to obtain logical and correct effects, Mr. Irving [George Irving, the director], who will stage the picture, will confer with Hugo Mustenberg and Professor James B. Hyslop, the foremost authorities in America on the subject."

One ad for the film showcased one of the dramatic highlights of the play: Hardmuth confronts Brookfield with a gun but is helpless before the gambler's hypnotic power. Another ad shows a rather crude drawing of the Clay Whipple character cowering before a menacing black cat.

The film garnered some very good notices. The reviewer for *The New York Times* (on the 11 December 1916) was a bit less enthusiastic than his fellow critics but felt it was a worthy adaptation of the play and handled the telepathy theme very well: "It does not gain in probability but that is the last thing a photoplay needs and it abounds in dramatic situations, which is more to the point."

"Jolo" of *Variety* wrote (on the 24 November 1916) that the film was "one of the finest bits of screening ever done anywhere" and that while previous efforts to put "psychology" on the screen were disasters, *The Witching Hour* succeeded admirably, largely due to the actors, especially C. Aubrey Smith: "Smith's depiction of the gentleman gambler possessed of psychic power was not attended with exaggerated physical gyrations so dear to the average stage portrayer of such a role. All through the piece (it did not seem like a film, but actual life) you felt his 'strength' and fine sincerity of purpose."

Peter Milne of *Motion Picture News* (9 December 1916) likewise heaped praise on Smith and the other actors but also gave Augustus Thomas and director Irving their due:

> Perhaps if Mr. Thomas had submitted *The Witching Hour* first, and only as a scenario, the editor would have rejected it because of its episodic arrangement. The suspense rises and falls and results in one or two obvious anti-climaxes, but after all each of the episodes is so strong and so well presented that the scenario editor might have taken it. Mr. Irving has worked in some masterful touches. The double exposure work, for instance, by which he pictures the thought running through the mind of a man, is excellent.

The anonymous reviewer for *The Fort Wayne* [Indiana] *Sentinel* (6 February 1917) raved about the film and felt that it had handled its unusual subject matter perfectly:

> It is full of tense situations and action is an uppermost virtue. Dealing with mental telepathy, the mental realm was not invaded by the author in any superficial way and at no time does he manufacture psychological "truths" which some film writers have been as adept in as they have been in conjuring up new "inventions" in machinery and the like…. The director has taken advantage of every big moment in the play which he has followed with considerable fidelity. There are three or four climaxes and it is a matter of individual opinion which is the most effective. The metaphysical and psychological effects are admirably secured by quick flash methods and effective close-ups.

And of course the reviewer found C. Aubrey Smith's performance a stand out: "C. Aubrey Smith's particularly strong and expressive features lend themselves to such a role and there is an almost hypnotic effect in his steady gaze, even as seen upon the screen."

A Bela Lugosi–like stare set in those craggy features which were more familiarly employed in the service of the British Empire may discomfit the more ardent film fan; it is hardly what one would expect from the man who later became one of Hollywood's most beloved (and busiest) character actors. However, before becoming Tinseltown's face of the Raj, Smith had a long and varied career on stage and screen.

C(harles) Aubrey Smith first attained fame as a cricket player in his native England. After heading the Cambridge team, Smith — who became known as "Round the Corner" Smith because of his style — began playing professionally in Australia and South Africa. He switched from sports to the equally competitive (but less gentlemanly) financial sector and worked for the Johannesburg Stock Exchange. Nevertheless, he maintained a lifelong love of cricket and named his Hollywood estate "Round Corner." Returning to England in 1890, he again changed careers and turned to the stage.

In the mid–1890s, Smith went to the States and appeared in supporting roles in a number of Broadway productions (such as the 1904 revival of *Hamlet* and *The Light that Failed*). While starring in the hit play, *The Lie*, that Smith signed his contract with Frohman Amusement; however, after finishing his requisite four pictures for them, Smith, who always said he preferred the stage to movies, went back to England to do plays and films there. One of his British movies, *The Bump* (1920), is still extant; in it, Smith plays an intrepid but befuddled explorer who can't seem to negotiate his way across London. Smith also starred in one of the many film versions of the stage-horror melodrama, *The Face at the Window*. The actor returned to the States — and to Broadway — several times in the 1920s, but his only American film from that period is *The Rejected Woman*, which co-starred Bela Lugosi.

The 1930s saw Smith cast in films like *Lives of a Bengal Lancer*, *The Four Feathers*, *Little Lord Fauntleroy*, and it was in these and in many others that his portrayals of dignified and honorable upper-class Brits became so firmly established in the minds of moviegoers that it made effective propaganda for the notion that "there will always be an England," Herr Hitler notwithstanding. Hollywood was delighted when the 80-year-old actor was knighted in 1944 (the British consul had to stand in for King George since overseas travel was perilous at that time). Four years later, after finishing his role in *Little Women*, Smith signed up to play in an adaptation of *The Forsythe Saga*, but he died after a brief illness.

Marie Shotwell (Helen Whipple) had a notable stage career working for the Frohmans, during which she acted as James O'Neill's leading lady and did a lot of heavy breathing in roles like that of Antoinette de Mauban in the 1895 revival of *The Prisoner of Zenda*. Shotwell made much less of an impression in the movies where she usually played supporting roles for independent companies. In 1919 the actress had a very conspicuous part, as the medium in *The Thirteenth Chair* (see entry), but according to a later newspaper article excoriating some Hollywood editing practices, her big chance was muffed by a director with ideas of his own:

> Marie Shotwell, a highly capable actress, was cast for the role of the medium, the logical important part. But the ingénue was to be starred and the scenario was so constructed that her role assumed proportions equal to that of the medium. When the picture first was viewed it was discovered that Miss Shotwell, by reason of her opportunities and ability, had dominated the picture. The ingénue was decorative but merely that. By the director's order and despite the frantic objections of others interested in the picture, much of Miss Shotwell's excellent performance decorated the cutting room floor. The production was reduced materially in worth. Close-ups of the ingénue replaced the fine acting of Miss Shotwell [Hallett Abend, *The Lincoln State Journal*, 12 August 1923].

Shotwell continued to work steadily in the 1920s and twice supported W.C. Fields (*Sally of the Sawdust* and *Running Wild*), but perhaps her less-than-stellar film career did not worry her unduly after she had a stroke of extraordinary good fortune: in the 1910s, Shotwell had befriended an elderly schoolteacher named Mary Pierson, who lived in very shabby surroundings but resisted Marie's attempt to offer her financial assistance. Pierson died in 1921 and left all her worldly goods to Shotwell, said goods being securities and valuables worth over $100,000.

As the Sound Era dawned, Shotwell faded from the film scene. Nonetheless, in 1934, she attempted a comeback in the George

M. Cohan vehicle, *Gambling*, but, during the filming, the actress suffered a cerebral hemorrhage and died.

Like his two stars, director George Irving (see entry, *Body and Soul*) had been a well-known stage actor before going into the movies, having been a member of Maude Adams' company for seven years. By the mid–1920s, he focused entirely on acting and became well known for playing exasperated fathers in movies like *The Goose Hangs High*; when the talkies came in he, like so many others, played small roles and bits in countless films. Horror fans may perhaps George from 1943's *Son of Dracula*, wherein he played a Southern gentleman with the bad habit of smoking in bed and the misfortune of having a daughter who was a vampire wannabe.

A number of Augustus Thomas' plays went before the camera, including *The Copperhead*, a Civil War drama that became one of his biggest successes. (Lionel Barrymore played the lead in the play — which was counted among *his* biggest successes — and the subsequent film.) *The Witching Hour* remained Thomas's only foray into the macabre.

— HN

The Witching Hour (1921)

The Witching Hour. Famous Players–Lasky/Paramount Pictures Corp., 10 April 1921, 7 reels/6734 feet, Library of Congress

CAST: Elliott Dexter (*Jack Brookfield*); Winter Hall (*Judge Prentice*); Ruth Renick (*Viola Campbell*); Robert Cain (*Frank Hardmuth*); Edward Sutherland (*Clay Whipple*); Mary Alden (*Helen Whipple*); Fred Turner (*Lew Ellinger*); Genevieve Blirn (*Mrs. Campbell*); Charles West (*Tom Denning*); L. M. Wells (*Judge Henderson*); Clarence Geldart (*Colonel Bailey*); Jim Blackwell (*Harvey*).

CREDITS: *Producer* Jesse L. Lasky; *Director* William D. Taylor; *Assistant Director* Frank O'Connor; *Scenario* Julia Crawford Ives; based on the eponymous play (New York; 18 November 1907) and novel (1908) by Augustus Thomas; *Cinematographer* James Van Trees

Although Augustus Thomas's play *The Witching Hour* had already gotten the Hollywood treatment in 1916, Paramount felt that audiences were ready for a new film version a mere five years later. This wasn't at all unusual as quite a few films from the 1910s were remade in the Jazz Age (like *Tess of the Storm Country*, *Black Orchids*, and *Stella Maris*). The 1916 film had been well received (see entry), but it was an independent production, its stars were not of the first rank, and it could not compete with the Grade-A technical resources available at Paramount. The fact that Augustus Thomas was still a famous name whose work often made it to the Great White Way was yet another reason to do it all again. William Desmond Taylor, one of Paramount's top directors, tackled the assignment with his usual team and, with the aid of a very good cast, produced an entertaining film that was actually more stylish than one might expect from him. Unlike the later sound version (1934) which radically reworked the play, Taylor's film remained faithful to its source. This, however, was not entirely a virtue and resulted in a movie with too many subplots.

Synopsis of the film based on our viewing of the Library of Congress print:

A quote from *Hamlet* begins the film: "There are more things in heaven and earth than are dreamt of in your philosophy." Another title card continues: "And one of these things is surely the great unexpected power of thought, the never ceasing wonder of its power and accomplishment, its far-reaching influence and absolute domination over the realm of the material."

Jack Brookfield, an elegant gentleman and art collector in Louisville, Kentucky, also runs a private gambling establishment for well-heeled acquaintances. Late one night he is visited by Judge Prentice, a Supreme Court justice. Prentice wants to buy a painting from Brookfield but knows the exact price Brookfield will ask without being told. Prentice tells the astonished Brookfield that he was able to do this by means of telepathy. He also senses Jack has considerable psychic powers of his own and promises to send him two books on the subject.

Brookfield is very devoted to his lovely niece, Viola, who is being courted both by Clay Whipple, son of Brookfield's old flame Helen, and Frank Hardmuth, the district attorney. Viola clearly prefers Clay, which is fine by Jack since he's aware that Hardmuth had some involvement years back in the murder of the governor-elect.

Jack gives a dinner party which is crashed by the obnoxious Tom Denning. Denning and Clay take an immediate dislike to each other. Clay reacts with terror when he sees that Denning is wearing a cat's-eye lapel pin. Clay has a horror of the jewel, a phobia he has inherited from his mother. The intoxicated Denning torments Clay with the cat's eye, and the hysterical youth grabs an ivory tusk paperweight and strikes Denning over the head with it. Denning dies and Hardmuth, also at the dinner, sees the opportunity to get rid of his rival and build up his own campaign to be governor. He has Clay charged with murder, and the youth is arrested.

Hardmuth prosecutes the case relentlessly and with all of his oratorical skill. Clay is convicted and sentenced to death. His lawyers appeal the case and it ends up in the Supreme Court where Judge Prentice presides. Helen Whipple remembers that her mother Margaret was at one time courted by Judge Prentice. She finds some old letters which indicate that Prentice even fought a duel over Margaret with a man who had frightened her with a cat's-eye jewel. Helen and Jack pay a late night visit to Prentice who has actually been thinking of Margaret earlier in the evening. After seeing the letters, Prentice admits there was more to the case than he thought and rules in Clay's favor, granting him a new trial.

Hardmuth again is merciless in his prosecution of Clay and, when the case goes to the jury, it's quite unclear how they will vote. Jack has read the two books Judge Prentice has sent him and amazes his crony Lew with his ability to read what cards Lew is holding. Lew wants to capitalize on Jack's power, but Jack refuses and insists he has never used this talent to win at cards. Jack releases to the press information about Hardmuth's involvement in the earlier murder, hoping that the jury will reject Hardmuth and thus his case against Clay. Lew points out that the jury is sequestered and won't see the newspapers, but Jack insists that the message will be communicated to them telepathically by the entire community and their outrage at Hardmuth. Clay is acquitted.

Hardmuth is indicted for murder and he confronts Jack with a gun to make good on an earlier threat to kill him if he said anything to the press. However, by means of his mental powers, Jack makes Hardmuth drop his revolver. Hardmuth goes into hiding.

When Clay is released from prison, Jack makes him confront his fear of the cat's eye ("Show Viola you're not a neuropathic idiot") and he is cured of his phobia and so is Helen. Jack also decides to help Hardmuth escape across state lines because he was not totally responsible for the murder of the governor-elect. Jack had also despised the man and had mentally concocted a plan to kill him, a scheme that Hardmuth had followed to the letter via a hit man, indicating that it was Jack's mental powers that inspired and guided the commission of the crime.

Jack and Helen rekindle their romance and the film ends with the couple and Lew helping Hardmuth escape.

That last reel is top-heavy with explanations that zip by with inadequate preparation, and so the viewer is as puzzled as the other characters when Jack decides to help Hardmuth escape and when — totally out of the blue — he confesses to his link to the political assassination. Jack seems to be a psychic superman; not only can he read minds and render guns useless with a look, but he also can project his thoughts elsewhere (though inadvertently). The latter is perhaps the most interesting idea in the story — and one that became central in the 1934 version — but here it's just a throwaway. Earlier flashbacks might have helped clarify things a bit and surely there should have been *some* explanation as to why the governor-elect aroused the deadly enmity of such morally-opposite characters like Hardmuth and Jack.

Jack's waiting until the jury retires before exposing Hardmuth and then counting on the community's anger to be telepathically transferred to the twelve good men seems like a big risk, though, even for a gambler. Albeit the film is awash in Southern chivalry, Jack's sense of honor stills seems a bit exaggerated; he won't even use his abilities — which he doesn't fully comprehend until he reads Judge Prentice's books — to win at cards. Nonetheless, an early scene shows him playing cards and giving an inscrutable look to his opponent (who then folds). Does his close-up indicate merely a poker face, or is he reading his opponent's hand? The viewer tends to share Lew's skepticism when Jack tells him he's never won through his mental powers.

When the film is not dealing with psychic judges, juries, and gentlemen gamblers, it takes time to ponder the power of suggestion. Jack's black servant, Harvey, tells him that a romantic rival has "hoodooed" him (this is shown in flashback), but Jack assures him that curses are only effective if their victim believes in them (assuming, of course, that the hoodoo man isn't a gifted mentalist like Jack). Later, Jack cures Clay of his cat's eye obsession by telling him that he has the dreaded jewel in his closed fist and insisting that the youth touch his hand. Though frightened, Clay complies and exclaims that he can feel the jewel's evil power. Jack then opens his hand and shows that it's empty; Clay is cured and so is his mother. Clearly, if Jack puts gambling behind him, he has a future as a psychologist.

Whatever weaknesses in the narrative, the film is never dull and it keeps the viewer off balance with one oddball revelation after another. It's often a bit contrived, but the cast plays with such total conviction that the mounting improbabilities aren't too distracting until they reach critical mass in the last reel.

Taylor's direction includes a number of macabre touches. When, for example, Clay looks into the cat's-eye pin we see in the jewel an unsettling close-up of a hissing cat, its one visible eye glaring demonically. Later, when Clay is in prison, he comforts himself by imagining his wedding to Viola. We see the ceremony enacted, but no sooner does Clay say "I do" then a noose descends from above and encircles his neck!

Adding to the outré atmosphere is a number of unusual title cards. The quote from *Hamlet* is accompanied not by a drawing but by two actors doing the tower scene between Hamlet and his father's ghost. Whenever "Blind Justice" is mentioned, an actual woman, complete with blindfold and scales, is shown (she has a hard time keeping still, though). When we're told that

Hardmuth is hiding out in a "rat hole," we see real rats creeping about in front of the words. A mysterious lady dressed in Grecian robes and studying the stars appears in an earlier title card. She puts in another appearance, flapping the folds of her gown this time, when "The End" flashes on the screen.

The film's title is never explained, but three significant events happen at 12:15 A.M.: Judge Prentice makes his initial visit, Jack and Helen appeal to the judge, and Jack takes delivery of the second book on psychic phenomenon. Still, none of these things has the sinister connotation one associates with the "witching hour."

"Mae Tinee" of *The Chicago Tribune* (31 March 1921) gave the film a good review and praised the acting and direction, but was mostly impressed by Elliot Dexter (Jack). Miss Tinee wrote the following under the headline "Elliot Dexter's Back, Girls, Three Cheers! All Together!": "It's been a long time since we've seen Mr. Dexter and people have been considerably exercised because of the fact. Feminine fans have all but wept and the more hardy male has condescended to question. Well, Mr. Dexter's been ill. He's better now, tough, and 'comes back' giving one of the best impersonations of his career." More on the man who made Mae's heart flutter can be found in the entry on *Forever*.

The *Harrison's Reports* write-up (5 March 1921) didn't gush over Elliot Dexter, but it did praise the film as giving "good satisfaction" and as one that "interests, and awakens sympathy." The critic also felt it was superior to the 1916 version "because all gruesomeness has been eliminated" (which is probably not much of a recommendation to readers of this book); however, *Variety*'s "Rush" thought the whole project was misbegotten from the get-go because of its subject matter which even the play had not been wholly successful in depicting:

> The story doesn't lend itself to picturization anyhow. There is too much explaining to do. That was a defect in the play. It was all argument and not much action…. On the screen the task of covering the abstract subject of "mental telepathy" upon which the whole tale hangs is beyond the power of the printed titles, be they ever so skillfully devised [4 March 1921].

As per usual, *Variety* found a couple of minor points to complain about for their lack of realism and was particularly annoyed by one scene: "More serious was the interpolated bit of Lew Ellinger, presumably of some rank in the community and a white man engage in a game of craps with a group of darky boy ragamuffins. The film people seem to be held in no restraint by any laws of probabilities."

Unlikely as it may have it seemed to Rush — who also groused about the flashback to a "Cakewalk" dance that's part of the black servant Harvey's story — this is actually a rather funny scene. Rush's dissing the dance sequence didn't discourage the Paramount publicity department from issuing a lengthy press release about the Cakewalk and explaining how "two hundred colored persons of assorted sizes were secured, wearing gorgeous dresses and spike tailed coats and turned loose on a set representing a Louisville dance hall" (*Wisconsin Rapids Daily Tribune*, 14 December 1921). The newspaper piece went on to say that none of the colored persons knew how to do the Cakewalk (a dance that, in fact, originated in the days of slavery) and had to be taught by assistant director, Frank O'Connor, who had once managed a Negro Minstrel troupe.

The lighthearted scenes mentioned above were more typical of William Desmond Taylor's Paramount films than were those featuring heavy drama. Taylor (*see All Soul's Eve* and *Beyond*) was never considered a great director, but he was a popular one whose name was often used in Paramount's advertising. He was best known for turning out crowd-pleasing vehicles for Mary Pickford, Jack Pickford, and Mary Miles Minter. Today, of course, he's remembered mainly for his untimely demise, a subject that's beyond the scope of this book, though we must pause to note that there was, in fact, a harebrained attempt at inducing a suspect to confess to murdering Taylor by staging a fake séance, complete with a ghostly appearance by the director! (Obviously whoever came up with that idea had seen too many of the films covered in this volume.) Exhaustive information on Taylor's career and murder can be found on Bruce Long's website, Taylorology (www.taylorology.com).

Taylor's scenarist Julia Crawford Ivers was one of the few Hollywood people not to be considered a serious suspect in his slaying, although Mary Miles Minter thought she should have been. Ivers worked with Taylor many times and was such a close friend that she — along with her son, James Van Trees (cinematographer on *The Witching Hour*) — went to Taylor's house at Paramount's behest (right after his murder and before the police arrived) to remove love letters and anything else that might have made the director and his studio look bad. More on writer, director, and evidence-filcher Ivers can be found in the entry on *The White Flower*.

Edward Sutherland (Clay) played a number of juvenile roles in the 1910s and early 1920s but was far more interested in directing. He became good friends with Charlie Chaplin (who was best man at Sutherland's wedding to actress Marjorie Daw; Mary Pickford was the maid of honor) and assisted Chaplin on *The Kid* and *The Gold Rush*. Sutherland finally got to direct on his own with *Coming Through* (1925) — which starred his uncle, Thomas Meighan — and came to specialize in bawdy comedies like *Behind the Front* and *We're in the Navy Now*. If the following remarks to *Liberty* magazine (as quoted in the 10 April 1927 issue of *The Syracuse* [NY] *Herald*) were any indication, the director was a bit sensitive about his choice of subject matter:

> I have made two very successful comedies but you know the highbrows, the critics, never pay any attention to you as a director until you have made a picture they can call "stark," "sheer," "poignant" or "bitterly ironic" something about which they can unlimber the adjectives…. As for prestige as a director, I'm afraid I haven't any because with the exception of *Love's Greatest Mistake*, I have done nothing but comedy. No high art at all.

By the 1930s Sutherland had given up on acting entirely to focus on directing. He did two films that, while not comedies, weren't exactly high art, either, but are fondly remembered by horror buffs today: the twisted *Murders in the Zoo* and *Secrets of the French Police*. After these two uncharacteristic forays into the macabre, Sutherland went back to doing comedies (*Poppy, Flying Deuces, The Invisible Woman*) and the occasional musical (*The Boys from Syracuse*).

The lovely Ruth Renick (Viola) gives her ingénue role a certain wistful sadness that makes one wish she had a little more screen time. In spite of publicity that claimed Renick began her stage career when she was but four years old, it wasn't until her high school days in Phoenix, Arizona, that she found professional work as an actress, when she joined the Maitland Davis stock company and stayed with them for four months. She then returned to Phoenix, finished high school, and studied drama and music. According to a biography she submitted to *The Oakland Tribune*, she then sought work in the movies:

> My next step was to join the Balboa Film Company in Long Beach where I embarked on a career as a motion picture actress. My first picture was *Neal of the Navy*, made with William Courtleigh, Jr.; following with *The Pink Lady* and other serials. I was making quite a success in this line when I was recalled to Arizona by the illness of my family.

Renick supported herself as a church organist during that time and, when her family situation stabilized, returned to stock company work. After several years on the stage she again tried the movies, drawing attention as Doug Fairbanks' leading lady in *The Mollycoddle*. This led to a contract with Paramount in 1920, but after a number of pictures there, Renick returned to the stage with Edward Everett Horton in *The Nervous Wreck*. That was followed by another brief sojourn in Hollywood before Renick became the leading lady at the Fulton Theater in Oakland.

While appearing there in the play *The Notorious Colonel Blake*, Renick found herself in a real-life melodrama. Her husband, Major Wellington Belford, was arrested on charges of impersonating an army officer. In addition, despite Renick's insistence to the contrary, there was no official record of them ever having been legally wed. It turned out that Belford was a con man who was wanted elsewhere on various fraud charges; Renick refused to believe it, and her family came forward saying they were convinced Belford had hypnotized Renick. Articles appeared in the Oakland press with drawings of Belford striking a Svengali-like pose. The bogus major jumped bail and fled to Canada where he became a faith healer and attracted a following until the authorities caught up with him. Belford may not have had hypnotic powers, but he did have a way with the ladies, as a number of women staged a protest at the police station when he was extradited back to the United States. Renick finally cut all ties with him and continued her successful work at the Fulton Theater.

The 1930s found Renick's career on the decline. In 1931 it was reported that she was going to make a comeback in the upcoming Paramount film, *Silence*, but the part went to stage legend, Marjorie Rambeau. Next, Renick was supposed to get a significant role in the film adaptation of Edgar Selwyn's melodrama, *The Mirage*, but when the film was released (as *Possessed*, with Joan Crawford and Clark Gable), Renick had only a bit role. A few more bit parts followed, and then nothing; thus, Ruth Renick has disappeared from Hollywood history.

As for William Desmond Taylor, his murder and the subsequent scandal guarantee that his place in Hollywood history is assured; however, only a handful of his films is still extant. *The Witching Hour* may well be the best of them.

— *HN*

The Wizard

The Wizard. Fox Film Corporation/Fox Film Corp., 11 December 1927, 6 reels/5629 feet [LOST]

CAST: Edmund Lowe (*Stanley Gordon*); Leila Hyams (*Anne Webster*); Gustav von Seyffertitz (*Dr. Paul Coriolos*); E. H. Galvert (*Edwin Palmer*); Barry Norton (*Reginald Van Lear*); Oscar Smith (*Sam*); Perle Marshall (*Detective Murphy*); Norman Trevor (*Judge Webster*); George Kotsonaros (*The Ape*); Maude Turner Gordon (*Mrs. Van Lear*); with Richard Frazier

CREW: *Presented by* William Fox; *Director* Richard Rosson; *Assistant Director* Park Frame; *Scenario* Harry O. Hoyt, Andrew Bennison; based on the novel *Balaoo* by Gaston Leroux (Paris, 1911); *Titles* Malcolm Stuart Boylan; *Cinematographer* Frank Good

On 7 November 1927, *The Los Angeles Times* announced "*The Wizard* has been selected as the new title for *Balaoo*, a Fox Films production ... this is a screen version of a thrilling mystery by Gaston Leroux." That's how it was promoted, but to see just how faithful a version *The Wizard* really was, let's first turn to this summary of the picture from the 3 December 1927 *Harrison's Reports*:

> The master villain [Dr. Paul Coriolos] in this instance is a criminologist who, having grafted the face of a friend of his on the face of an ape, makes the ape appear like a human being. He teaches him to recognize the smell of cigars, the scent of perfume, and so on; by either giving his victims cigars to smoke or spraying perfume on them, he makes them recognizable to the man-ape, who pulls his victims to the demented man's haunt, there to be tortured and then killed.
> The hero [Stanley Gordon], a reporter, is told that unless he gets a story about the mysterious murders he is going to lose his job, and sets about to get a story. He tricks a stupid detective [Detective Murphy] into handcuffing himself. The hero then answers the phone calls and learns from the heroine's [Anne Webster's] father [Judge Webster], who had called up, that a friend of his had disappeared from his house while at dinner with other guests, asking that the matter be investigated.
> Thus the hero rushes to the heroine's father's house. There is he told that the heroine and her father had gone to spend the night at a certain criminologist's. The hero calls on them. Soon he suspects the criminologist and eventually brings to light the fact that he was the murderer. He also saves the heroine and her father from a horrible death. The demented man, having enraged the man-ape, is torn to pieces by him. The heroine shoots and kills the ape just as he was to tear the hero to pieces.

According to other contemporary accounts (like the 3 December 1927 *Moving Picture World*), Coriolos' motive is vengeance on everyone involved in sending his son to the electric chair. Part of his modus operandi is to inform his victims of their impending demise via mysterious warning notes. And, *oh!*—per the cutting continuity submitted for copyright—hero and heroine lock lips in the end (as they are often wont to) although it took some 89 title cards and 742 scenes (many inexplicably tinted lavender) to get them there.

Well, now... *The Wizard* surely registers a notch or ten down the complexity scale when contrasted to its 1911 source. First of all, Leroux's Balaoo is no mere ape; he's a living, breathing, thinking and *feeling* pithecanthrope ("missing link" to most of us) discovered by Professor Coriolos Boussac Saint-Aubin in the forests of Bandong. Balaoo is proud that he's a step up, evolution-wise, from apes and monkeys and yet is continually self-conscious that he's not a member of the "race." Anthropomor-

phic enough to pass to the people of the village as "Monsieur Noel," the Professor's "boy," his vocal chords are capable of speech thanks to an operation performed by the scientist. In a perverse way the professor, although often treating him like a mere specimen, loves Balaoo like a father. In turn, it's Balaoo's devotion to Coriolos' daughter Madeleine that helps to keep the man-ape in control.

Then there are Hubert, Simeon, and Elie Vautrin, aka the "Three Brothers"—triplets fathered by a convict—who live with their old-hag mother in the Black Woods. Hubert, the only non-albino of the trio, is the leader and all are "trained by the very animals which they hunted." "Never happy among men," they readily accept Balaoo for his true nature and befriend him. The brothers even suggest that little sister Zoe, who loves Balaoo, would be a good candidate for matrimony! However, this camaraderie does not come without a price for Balaoo; the Vautrins exploit his unique abilities—including great strength and agility as well the capability to speak animal language—to further their criminal ends.

As was typical, Gaston Leroux constructed a bizarre and intricate tapestry in weaving these characters together. In the final chapters, Balaoo and the group move to Paris. There he studies law (!) and befriends Gabriel, a great, zoo-bound Asiatic Ape. Madeleine weds secretly to avoid upsetting the ever-attached Balaoo. When she is kidnapped, Balaoo is unjustly blamed and, it's Gabriel who's shot mistakenly in his stead. Ultimately, Balaoo discovers that it was the albino Elie who had coveted Madeleine and had whisked her away; he comes to her rescue and kills all three of the brothers.

Although now "civilized," Balaoo becomes deadly morose over the loss of Madeleine to his human rival and his alienation in the world of men increases. Thus, the scientist, his maid and Zoe return with Balaoo to Bandong to rejuvenate him. There all but Balaoo eventually lose the gift of language. He eternally relishes the letters he receives from Madeleine, but his opinion of mankind is summed up by what he tells his animal brothers: "men are gods spoilt in the making!"

The year 1913 marked the first movie adaptation of Leroux's novel: a three-reeler entitled *Balaoo, the Demon Baboon* (he's still no pithecanthrope), that still exists, in part. While the screenplay for such an abbreviated picture was of necessity brief, the Éclair film zeroed in on more key plot points and characters than did *The Wizard*. For example, the three Vautrin brothers are condensed into one: Hubert, a notorious poacher. Still, those looking for *Balaoo* to be recognized as a still-undiscovered horror/sci-fi gem will most likely come away disappointed. We viewed the surviving footage and must report that, in spite of his being patterned after early-edition book illustrations, our simian protagonist unfortunately comes across as rather clownish.

Dr. Renault's Secret (1942), the third take on Leroux's screed, failed once again to explore the Missing Link aspect of the novel, and no one with a scientific bent was in the least bit surprised. Although reports of skeletal findings that purportedly connected modern man with other forms of primates had been forthcoming since 1891 (when Eugene Dubois discovered the Java Man in Indonesia), and the crux of the controversy extended back to 1859 (when Charles Darwin penned *On the Origin of Species*), programmers such as this were made for a fast buck, not to reflect anthropological breakthrough. Regarding the film under discussion, even its choice of a title is baffling; would one look for even the *trappings* of science in a motion picture called *The Wizard*? Despite this, few watching Coriolos graft a face on an ape back in 1927—even as the Great Missing Link Debate raged on—could have imagined that, come December 2008, modern medicine would enable the world's first near-total facial transplant.

Since *The Wizard* is lost, the usual trade magazines, newspapers and other assorted paper scraps left for posterity are the only hope for assessing what might have been the movie's high and low spots. And it appears (as is so often the case) that those were predominantly a matter of taste and point of view. Here are some good words from the *Moving Picture World* (3 December 1927): "In *The Wizard*, William Fox offers an excellent ensemble of high-class fantastic mystery, sometimes of the 'creepy' sort, with romance woven into the skein of things in liberal measure. Differing quite from the average run of 'mystery thrillers,' this one brings a sustained interest coupled with laughs, excellent direction and a well told story."

Pseudonymous "Sid" from *Variety* (30 November 1927) disagreed big-time: "Silly and a waste of time…. This picture hasn't got enough sense to it to even create an illusion of horror. All it can do is keep some imaginative youngsters awake for a couple of nights…. Write and play down to your audience."

From the *National Board of Review* (December 1927), we get a glimpse at what some of the scenes were like and a reassurance that Sid needn't have worried much about all of those young'uns

Original glass slide.

getting upset: "The plot is replete with many thrills calculated to give you the creeps, and innumerable trick doors and subterranean chambers, and everything ends happily with a big fight between the reporter and the gorilla. For the family audience including young people."

On the other hand, something must have stuck in the craw of the Kansas censors, who instructed, presumably for the benefit of family audiences that included young people: "Reel 6: Eliminate close views of fight with man appearing as ape."

Like the *N.B.R.* above, *The Washington Post* (23 January 1928) made it sound as though *The Wizard* were just another old dark house thriller by tagging it as "an especially eerie picture so packed with ominous episodes and appalling apparitions prowling around the home of a renegade scientist at midnight that nobody's nerves are safe." Meanwhile, *Harrison's Reports* (3 December 1927) duly noted that there was a grisly scene or two, but concluded "So what?" "A thrilling mystery melodrama…. It is a 'wee bit' gruesome…. Yet those who love strong melodramas should get their life's enjoyment out of it, for in most of the film one is made to hold his breath and gasp now and then from fear lest the characters be seized by the man-ape and killed."

The *New York Times* had been known to skip this kind of fare, but The Grey Lady decided that, by publishing not one but two reviews, it could pan the humor element twice as much. This lengthy analysis from their 28 November 1927 edition:

> It is quite a good entertainment weakened by the levity forced upon it. This subject really has enough of a story to deserve more serious treatment. It has a motive and could have been fashioned into a genuinely exciting shadow yarn. The producers have been far too eager to touch more or less gently on the ruddy portions of their chronicles and then leap quickly to a rowdy comedy…. This story has an interesting denouement, but it is brought out too abruptly…. The scene with a mad surgeon and a queer gorilla are quite cleverly pictured, especially when the spectator if taken through a room by means of the camera.

One week later, on 4 December 1927, *The Times* reiterated its stance: "This subject possesses some good ideas, but the comedy is a bit too low to suit the story."

Just about the only non-anonymous comment about the film came from writer, Robert E. Howard, and even his mention was but a brief note in a letter (c. July 1928) to one Harold Preece: "I saw *The Wizard* and thought that it was 'red hot.'"

We can't tell what Howard's contemporary, Monsieur Gaston Louis Alfred Leroux—onetime theater critic and founder of his own movie company—would have thought of *Balaoo*'s second cinematic reworking; Leroux passed away weeks before his 59th birthday and a half-year or so before the picture's wizardry was screened in local theaters. In his younger days, the Frenchman had studied law to appease his father (and perhaps thereby inspiring the "any-ol'-monkey-can-be-a-lawyer" theme in *Balaoo*). However, he rejected this safer, potentially lucrative career-path and, in the course of squandering his inheritance, pursued other interests: dramatist, poet, world-traveler, reporter (something he stuck with for a considerable period) and, of course, novelist. Literature had always been a passion of his, and the young Leroux freely admitted to being an admirer of Victor Hugo and Alexander Dumas. When it came to his own writing triumphs, *The Mystery of the Yellow Room* (1907) may have been a breakout novel, but it took *The Phantom of the Opera* (1910) to bring the sort of lasting fame that his illustrious role models had achieved. (Both works reached the screen before Leroux's death, and both are covered within these pages.)

Wizard lead Edmund Lowe was born into a large family—he was one of 13 kids—and his mother (like Gaston Leroux, a Dumas aficionado) named him after *The Count of Monte Cristo*'s Edmund Dantes. Quite the scholar, Lowe was a mere 18 years old when he received his diploma from Santa Clara University, and this was followed by a masters' degree in pedagogy some time later. As an actor, he was as successful as he'd been as a student and became a triple-threat man in theater, film and television. On the screen, he contributed to *Eyes of Youth* (1919), *Madonnas and Men* (1920), and *The Devil* (1921) (see entries). Continuing on a pace of one genre-offering per annum, Lowe appeared in the 1922 revival of *Trilby*, one of his dozen or so Broadway credits, while fans of magic and hoo-hah fondly remember him as the titular *Chandu the Magician* (1932), in which epic he outfoxed Bela Lugosi's wild-eyed Roxor. In later years, Lowe was *The Strange Mr. Gregory* (1946), yet another magus, but one who fakes his own death. In addition, he was top-billed in the short-lived, early 1950s Dumont TV series, *Front Page Detective*, and starred—with just about everyone else worth his or her salt at the time—in the enjoyable *Around the World in 80 Days* (1956).

Lowe's turn in *Wizard* garnered him middlin' press notices. "Mr. Lowe does good work," declared *Harrison's Report*,* albeit *The New York Times* (4 December 1927) didn't much appreciate his mugging for the camera: "The hero of this yarn is the over-smiling Edmund Lowe." At least the *Moving Picture World* found him up to his own standards: "Lowe has a role that, while it calls for nothing exceptional from him, brings out, nevertheless, all of the qualities for quick action and sudden fights that have endeared him to audiences throughout the world."

Harrison's felt that Leila Hyams was "a pretty girl" and that was essentially all *The New York Times* (28 November 1927) had to say, too, describing her only as "graceful and attractive." The former model had failed in her effort at success as a stage actress—somewhat surprisingly,

in view of the fact her parents were the vaudeville team of "Hyams and McIntyre"—but thrived onscreen by playing the perennial ingénue for the remainder of her 12-year career. Besides *The Wizard*, her other works of interest are the 1929 remake of *The Thirteenth Chair* (see appendix), Tod Browning's cult classic, *Freaks* (1932), and the H. G. Wells–inspired *The Island of Lost Souls* (1932), in which only loosely could she be described as "the ingénue."

George Kotsonaros was from that certain Old School that taught that wrestlers were for real *inside* the ring, but could be actors *outside* of the ring—especially if they played wrestlers or … lower primates. A wrasslin' heavyweight, George specialized in lightweight (if testosterone-heavy) roles that carried names like "Battling Roff," "Butch" or "Iron Mike." Back in the day, wrestlers also found cinematic employment as ape-men and such and, like fellow pro-grappler Bull Montana in *Go and Get It* (1920) and *The Lost World* (1925) (see entries), Kotsonaros donned the make-up and suit to appear not only in *The Wizard*, but also in *While London Sleeps* (1926). Both of Kotsonaros's careers were cut short by a car accident (on the 13 July 1933) that claimed his life as he and another wrestler were on their way from Nashville to New Orleans for a match.

By all accounts, George was effective in *The Wizard*. *Variety* rated him the picture's highlight: "Kotsonaros gives the best performance in the picture. He waddles, glowers, fights and gets shot." *Moving Picture World* and *The New York Times* (28 November 1927) echoed these sentiments: "George Kotsonaros has the role of the ape, and does everything well" and "George Kotsonaros, in a fuzzy skin, makes the most of the gorilla's share in this photoplay" claimed the journals, respectively.

Rivaling Kotsonaros for accumulating accolades was Gustav von Seyffertitz. *The New York Times* critique declared that "Gus-

Original movie herald for *The Wizard*.

---

tav von Seyffertitz, who impersonates the mad surgeon, does some capital acting," while *MPW* alluded to his well established reputation for dastardly performances: "Mr. von Seyffertitz has a role that was cut to his measure, and, if anything he is just a wee bit more diabolical as 'the heavy' in *The Wizard* than we have noted in some time." *Harrison's Reports* dittoed "Gustav von Seyffertitz makes an excellent villain." More on the full breadth of von Seyffertitz's villainous film career is found in our essay on the 1926 version of *The Bells*.

Playing Reginald Van Lear was Argentine, Barry Norton, whose place in the Genre Hall of Fame was firmly secured by his role as Juan Harker in George Melford's *Drácula*, the Hispanic take on Universal's trendsetting Browning/Lugosi epic. Norton—born Alfredo Carlos Birabén—made the leap from silent movie title cards to English- and Spanish-language talkie features throughout the 1930s. (In 1939, Norton was in *Should Husbands Work?*, one of the "Higgins Family" comedy features that starred the Gleason family [James, Lilian and Russell]; his role?—Ronald McDonald. It was all downhill from there.) From the outset of the 1940s until his death in Los Angeles on the 24 August 1956 (a week and a day after Lugosi), the actor was usually seen onscreen doing the sort of "uncredited bit" so many of his Silent Era colleagues had been forced to settle for once *The Jazz Singer* cast its long shadow.

Harry O. Hoyt, who co-wrote the adaptation, was no newcomer to man-apes, having directed the prior mentioned *The Lost World* (in which entry his bio is to be found); this go 'round, Hoyt handed the megaphone/baton over to Richard Rosson. As an actor back in the early days, Richard had performed in front of the camera for L. Frank Baum in *The Patchwork Girl of Oz* (1914). He was brother to Arthur Rosson, also a director, and Harold (Hal) Rosson, cinematographer.

In its use of an ape-man as its means of mayhem and its pegging a reporter as its hero, *The Wizard* somewhat resembles 1920's *Go and Get It* (see entry; while the idea that the monster is drawn to scents planted by the villain more than foreshadows Mr. Lugosi and his fatal cologne in PRC's delirious *The Devil Bat* [1940]). Still, despite its hokey nature, *The Wizard* had enough going for it to pique the interest of classic film fanatics. We'd love to see von Seyffertitz and Kotsonaros in action once again, so count us among that number.

— *SJ*

Wolf Blood

Wolf Blood. Ryan Brothers Productions/Lee-Bradford Corporation, 16 December 1925(New York State license), 6 reels/5,800 feet* [available]

CAST: Marguerite Clayton (*Edith Ford*); George Chesebro (*Dick Bannister*); Ray Hanford (*Dr. Eugene Horton*); Roy Watson (*Jules Deveroux*); Milburn Morante (*Jacques LeBec*); Frank Clark (*Pop Hadley*)

CREDITS: *Directors* Bruce Mitchell, George Chesebro; *Story* Dr. C.A. Hill; *Adaptation* Bennett Cohn; *Cinematographer* R. Leslie Selander.

This 1925 independent production is sometimes referred to as the first werewolf movie; however, fans hoping for hairy claws, a full moon and sinister gypsies will be disappointed: it's the power of suggestion and some human manipulation that convince the hero that he's a lycanthrope, and this development doesn't take place until just past the midpoint of the film. Much of the story is devoted to action and romance, and though set in contemporary times, it could almost pass as a Western, an appropriate assessment given that cast and crew spent much of their careers in Gower Gulch or its later equivalents.

For all that, the first honest-to-goodness werewolf movie (entitled—what else?—*The Werewolf) was* a Western two-reeler, produced in 1913 by Bison 101, a company devoted exclusively to Westerns and "Indian" pictures. The now-lost film has a bit more in common with *Wolfen* and the 1912 *Reincarnation of Karma* than the classic Universal werewolf movies, but the supernatural element is completely straightforward. A bit of PR helps confirm this:

> Against a backdrop of powerful emotions and strong action a touch of wild fantasy weaves in and out like a silken thread. Phyllis Gordon, the daring "101 Bison" favorite, will play the half-breed Indian girl who is cursed by the monks and changed into a wolf. She resumes human form at will, returning to wreak vengeance upon those she thinks have wronged her. William Clifford plays first the young monk who sins and a hundred years later comes back as the miner who reaps yesterday's sins [*The Frederick (Maryland) Post*, 13 November 1913].

While there is nothing as unabashedly horrific in *Wolf Blood*, fans will still find a few familiar elements. Our synopsis is based on a viewing of the Grapevine Video VHS which was taken from a nice tinted and toned 35mm print.

> Deep in the Canadian wildness, there is a bitter rivalry between two logging companies. Dick Bannister, manager of the Ford Logging Company, is getting increasingly exasperated by the strong-arm tactics of Jules Deveroux, head of the rival company. Deveroux has even resorted to having his henchman shoot and wound some of Bannister's loggers. Though he has a good rapport with his men, Bannister finds they are growing restless and are increasingly willing to indulge in the bootleg booze sold by the "half-breed," Jacques LeBeq. Bannister decides to appeal to the owner of Ford to provide a clinic for the wounded and to come down to the camp to get a first hand look at the trouble.
>
> The owner turns out to be Edith Ford, a socialite who is being romanced by Dr. Eugene Horton. Responding to Bannister's appeal, she journeys to the camp with Horton who agrees to run the clinic temporarily if Edith will marry him upon their return home. Edith is impressed by Bannister who, though very shy, is quickly smitten with her. Trouble with the loggers continues and Bannister angrily throws LeBeq off the property.
>
> Bannister is outraged to find that Deveroux has put up a dam in the river to obstruct log shipments coming from the Ford mill. In an angry confrontation with Deveroux and his chief thug, Bannister is hit on the head with a rock and rolled down a hill. He awakens later, groggy and confused and sees a wolf pack nearby. He is found by Dr. Horton who takes the seriously wounded man to the nearest shelter which turns out to be LeBeq's cabin. Dr. Horton says that only an immediate blood transfusion can save Bannister's life and while LeBeq has no interest in being a donor he does sneeringly offer his she-wolf in his place. Horton remembers read-

ing of an experiment in which animal blood was successfully transfused to a human being though there was worry that the human recipient would then develop the animal traits of the donor. Horton decides to forge ahead anyway and transfuses some of the wolf's blood to Bannister.

Bannister lives and slowly recovers, nursed by Edith who has fallen in love with him. LeBeq spreads the word that Bannister has wolf blood in him and is no longer fully human. Legends of the loup-garou still hold sway among the loggers and when Bannister returns to the job, he is confused at the frightened, standoffish attitude of his workers. Later he finds Dr. Horton's book about animal/human transfusions and comes to realize LeBeq's story is true. He overhears a conversation between Edith and Horton in which Horton, now jealous of Edith's affection for Bannister, tells her that Bannister shares the traits of a wolf as well as its blood. Bannister confronts Horton: "Why didn't you let me die!— You've made me a thing that is neither man nor beast." Bannister rushes off into the wilderness.

Deveroux is found dead, his throat torn open as if by wolves. Rumors spread that Bannister, the man wolf, is responsible. Bannister returns but has no memory of where he's been. He has a vision of himself killing Deveroux and sees a pack of phantom wolves. Bannister follows the imaginary pack into the woods right to the edge of a cliff. Edith saves him at the last moment and brings him home. It turns out Deveroux was really killed by wolves; LeBeq was a witness. Horton tells Bannister that he has nothing to fear from having wolf blood in him; the jealous physician was just trying to frighten Edith. Bannister and Edith forgive him and plan their marriage.

Had the film been made in the 1940s, no doubt Dr. Horton would have killed Deveroux and put the blame on Bannister, a plot wrinkle we find in films like *She-Wolf of London* and *Devil Bat's Daughter* (both 1946). And, budget willing, perhaps we would have had a posse of torch-bearing loggers in pursuit of the beast-man before the truth were revealed. As it stands now, the wrap-up of *Wolf Blood* seems much too hurried, as if the writer didn't know quite where to go with this action picture-turned-horror melodrama.

The idea of a blood transfusion causing a change in the personality of the recipient was also used in *Her Surrender* (see entry). It was pretty silly in that picture, but becomes even more absurd herein, since one also has to accept the premise that a human being would survive a blood transfusion from an animal. The story was attributed to *Doctor* C.A. Hill, and we can only hope that said medico never tried putting his theory into practice.

The hero's increasing horror at his predicament, his memory lapses, and the possibility that he might hurt his girlfriend all became clichés of werewolf flicks. Bannister's hallucination that he is killing Deveroux is very brief — but well done — with Bannister (George Chesebro) looking appropriately disheveled and wild-eyed. There's also a well-played scene between him and Edith (Marguerite Clayton) wherein the girl-shy Bannister seizes the young woman and kisses her aggressively, causing her to shrink back in fear. Unfortunately, the title cards are rather risible: "Man or beast — I love you!" and "I don't care what you are! I love you!"

The blood transfusion scene is nondescriptly directed and doesn't convey a real sense of horror, but is nonetheless weirdly effective by the very strangeness of the sight of beast and man lying side by side, connected by tubes. Such scenes would be re-hashed in later mad doctor movies like *Captive Wild Woman*, but the medico in *Wolf Blood* (played by Ray Hanford) looks more like a rumpled college professor than John Carradine with a maniacal glint in his eye.

The "wolves" in the film are not particularly menacing and one wishes there could be at least one close-up of them snarling or even looking slightly displeased. The ghost pack is done via double exposure, but again the animals just seem to be trotting along nonchalantly, rather than being actively on the prowl.

George Chesebro is stalwart enough in the early scenes and appropriately agonized later on, when he thinks he's become a lycanthrope, although there's no danger that he'll make anyone forget Lawrence Talbot. Chesebro started his career in musical comedy and vaudeville. Entering films in 1915, he quickly became identified with action movies and Westerns, played opposite Olive Thomas and Viola Dana, and — in a short entitled *The She Wolf* (*not* a werewolf movie)— worked with Texas Guinan, then billed as "the female Bill Hart." In 1918 the actor was cast as the male lead in the Ruth Roland serial, *Hands Up*, but was drafted during the shooting when hostilities broke out. While the still-extant promo shows Chesebro doing the requisite heroics, George Larkin was signed to take over the part for the chapter-play itself.

After the Great War, Chesebro resumed his career in Westerns and serials, with the more notable among the latter including *The Lost City*, *The Jungle Princess*, and *The Hope Diamond Mystery*; still, his career began to falter in the mid–1920s. There was occasional talk of his starting his own production company, and that might possibly explain his co-director credit for *Wolf Blood*; Chesebro may have wanted to get his feet wet, as it were, with an experienced director, Bruce Mitchell (see *Love's Whirlpool*), still at the helm. In any case, the actor did not branch out on his own, but spent the rest of the Silent Era doing supporting roles.

The Sound Era brought Chesebro a whole new career as a villain in "B" Westerns. Scores of sagebrush sagas saw his affable smile replaced by a scurrilous scowl, as the erstwhile hero was now condemned to play gunslingers, outlaw gang leaders, and crooked ranchers. His villainous mug became so familiar that — according to B Western fan extraordinaire, Boyd Magers — it became an in-joke in the 1950 Roy Rogers film, *The Trail of Robin Hood*: "I know you! You're always the meanie!" exclaims one character when Chesebro, playing a good guy for once, offers to help haul Christmas trees. (It is only after Chesebro assures the other characters that he has reformed that his assistance is accepted.) The Minneapolis-born actor spent virtually the rest of his career in the saddle and is said to have chalked up over 300 films.

Marguerite Clayton won her greatest fame at Essanay as "Broncho Billy"Anderson's leading lady, and according to one story she got the job by simply answering an ad in the paper. Clayton played in dozens of one- and two-reel Westerns with Anderson and reputedly became an expert horsewoman and lasso artist. She decided to freelance when Essanay folded in 1916, and appeared in both mainstream productions for established independents as well as oddball stuff (like starring as "Lotta Nerve" in 1919's *Bullin' the Bullsheviki*) for obscure outfits (like the Eff and Eff Producing Company, for which *Bullsheviki* was the sole offense). Mixed in among her shorts and features were a few serials, and it was while filming *Go Get 'Em Hutch* (a 1922 chapter-play) that Clayton was hit with a pipe while Charles "Hurricane Hutch" Hutchison tried to rescue her when a water stunt went awry. The actress sued the production company for $50,000 claiming the accident had left her with a permanent facial scar. While the outcome of the suit is uncertain, we do know that *Hutch* was Clayton's last serial. By the time of *Wolf Blood*, Clayton's film career was largely over and she retired before the coming of sound, dying in an auto accident many years later in 1968.

The cinematography for *Wolf Blood* was handled by Lesley Selander, a name that might ring a bell or two with genre buffs as Selander went on to direct two, fairly unappreciated, Sound Era horror films: *The Vampire's Ghost* (1945) and *The Catman of Paris* (1946). (We rank *Ghost* a couple of points up on its colleague for being offbeat, though.) Most of Selander's long career was spent — like practically everyone else involved with *Wolf Blood* — in Westerns.

Selander, a Los Angeles native, started in Hollywood around 1920 as an extra, earning a buck a day, plus lunch. He had no interest in acting, but learned the technical side of the movie business quickly and began working in the lab for $18 a week; subsequently, he served a long apprenticeship as assistant director. Selander later told Kevin Thomas (in an interview published in the 10 August 1966 issue of the *Los Angeles Times*) that it was W.S. Van Dyke — of *The Thin Man* fame — who broke him in and taught him more than anyone else. Selander began directing on his own in the mid–1930s, his first film being a Buck Jones Western; numerous other oaters followed, many of them Hopalong Cassidy films with Bill Boyd. Naturally, Selander had to be quick and on the ball to complete a whole film on a two-week schedule. As he recalled to Thomas:

> I'll be starting at 7:15 tomorrow morning and I'll be working until 10 or 11 tonight, planning the next day's work, figuring the most efficient way of shooting it. I don't want to take the time on the set.... When you see the sun coming down and you've got only a half hour left you start cutting out as many scenes as possible while making sure the story still makes sense — making sure that you have enough to cement together.

In addition to movies, he did quite a bit of TV, including 52 episodes of *Lassie*. Leslie Selander died in 1979, his name still largely unknown, even to the masses that had frequently spent their Saturday afternoons at matinees, watching his films. Despite this, the moviemaker's death attracted more notice than did Chesebro's or Clayton's.

As for his cinematography in *Wolf Blood*, Selander's camerawork takes good advantage of the location shooting, but the woods are just there as a magnificent backdrop; there are no shadows or suggestions of the uncanny. But this is as it should be, for — no doubt — Selander thought he was doing a Western, and not a horror movie.

— HN

The Woman of Mystery

The Woman of Mystery. Blaché Features, Inc./Blaché Features, 10 May 1914, 4 reels [LOST]

CAST: Vinnie Burns (*The Woman of Mystery*); Fraunie Fraunholz (*Detective Nelson*); Claire Whitney (*Norma*)

CREDITS: Producer, Director, Scenarist: Alice Guy Blaché

Athough this 1914 title is an alphabetical latecomer, it was one of the first feature-length servings of the formulaic ham cured with sinister Hindus, snakes, and psychic powers to hit the movie theaters. We have to thank the 9 May 1914 issue of *The Moving Picture World* for providing the details on this long-lost epic.

Norma, an actress, receives many presents from admirers. Among them she finds a peculiar-looking box, out of which spring several poisonous snakes. Nelson, a detective, is called upon to solve the mystery. On the box, he finds a peculiar trademark, which he seizes as a clue. At his home he finds the same odd mark on an ashtray bought by his mother in a Hindu curio shop, and he learns that the box containing the snakes was purchased by a Hindu woman.

Calling upon the woman, he is surprised to find himself in the home of a Priestess of Buddhaism [*sic*]. The Priestess tries to fascinate him with her beauty and, not succeeding, drops a powder into an incense burner, the fumes of which begin to throw him into a stupor. He fights his way to a window, blows a police whistle, and is attacked by three giant Hindu attendants. But the police arrive in time to save his life, and the priestess is arrested and thrown into prison.

The dancer, Norma, is attracted to Nelson by his bravery, and they become friends. Meanwhile, the Priestess succeeds in working a psychic miracle in which she goes into a trance and, while her earthly form remains in prison, her soul is freed and appears before the horrified detective in his study. His nature is changed immediately by the Priestess's mystic influence, and his face becomes the face of a hardened criminal.

Changing his clothes for one of the rough suits used in his detective work, he visits a den of crooks and aids them to rob a bank. Later he is called by the bank to investigate the robbery and, not knowing of his dual personality, makes every effort to find the man who had committed the crime. He finds his own scarf among the scattered papers taken from the safe. A threatening letter, which he receives from the followers of the Priestess, is seen by Norma, who is so greatly concerned for his safety that when he asks her to marry him, she quickly consents to the engagement, so that she can do all in her power to protect him.

His old mother is puzzled by seeing him leave his own house through the window, when he is again visited by the spirit of the Priestess and influenced to aid the same band of crooks in the robbery of his own home. When his real personality returns, he finds himself in his own office, where he has been discovered by his mother, sleeping in a chair, dressed in his old clothes.

Upon discovery that his house has been robbed, he calls the chief of police and is seen by the companions of his criminal personality, who think that he is acing as an agent of the authorities merely to place them in the hands of the law. When he is again transformed by the spirit of the Priestess and returns to the thieves' den, they regard him as a spy and plan to do away with him, leaving him bound and gagged in the care of an old hag, while they celebrate his capture.

But Norma, who, with his mother has been watching him, follows him to the den of thieves and, overpowering the old woman, helps him to escape. Meanwhile, the followers of the Priestess succeed in rescuing her from her prison cell and are speeding away in an automobile when Nelson, who still retains his criminal personality, asks them to assist him to escape from the crooks, who are closely [*sic*] upon his trail. Thus he unwittingly places himself and his fiancée in the power of the Priestess, who makes them prisoners in a temple of Buddha.

Norma faints, and when Nelson's real personality returns, he finds himself bound hand and foot in the temple. Norma quickly explains the situation to him and, by burning the ropes that bind his wrists with the fire in the incense burner, he frees his companions and makes his way to the roof by the aid of a heavy chain from which a large oriental lamp is swung from the ceiling. He succeeds in helping Norma to the roof by the same method and they reach the ground with the aid of a large tree.

The chief of police, who has been summoned by Nelson's mother, overtakes the crooks and arrests them after a desperate struggle. But the Priestess cheats the majesty of the law by the aid of a poisoned ring with which she does away with herself during one of her wild fanatical dances. Her death marks the end of her influence over Nelson, and he at last feels free to marry Norma.

We shall not comment on the obvious confusion over Hindus and Buddhists and such suffered by producer/director/scenarist Alice Blaché, as keeping the minutiae of exotic religions straight was probably not a strict priority in those politically incorrect days. Nevertheless, because Buddha *is* afforded a place in the Hindu pantheon — he is considered the ninth incarnation of Vishnu — if Mrs. Blaché wasn't exactly spot on, she certainly gets high marks for giving that gaggle of celestial hangers-on a more-than-casual glance.

We must comment, though, on the similarity of certain elements of the scenario to those of *The Curious Conduct of Judge Legarde*, which film was first released the year after *The Woman of Mystery*. Since *Woman* was on screen first, should we not look at *Legarde* as being derived from it — post hoc, ergo propter hoc, and all that — rather than the other way around? Nay. Prior to its being recorded on celluloid by the Life Photo Film Corporation, *Legarde* had been adapted (from a German work by playwright, Paul Lindau) for the stage back in February 1912, and it would not be beyond the realm of possibility that Mrs. Blaché had obtained a ticket to and was impressed by same, and proceeded from there.

Most of the non–*Legarde* elements of the screenplay stemmed, of course, from R.L. Stevenson and his masterwork — That Which Need Not Be Named, for it appeareth every forty or so pages throughout the length of this magnum opus. So frequently was the ol' schizophrenic ploy worked into thrilling motion pictures during the Silent Era that — in a critical commentary on *Body and Soul*, which appeared the same year (1920) along with no fewer than *five* treatments (serious, comic, whatever) of *Dr. Jekyll and Mr. Hyde* — a reviewer whined right off the bat that "there is nothing original about these stories of dual personalities" (*Motion Picture News*, 23 October 1920).

Mrs. Blaché (see more of her bona fides in our entry on 1914's *The Dream Woman*) received sole screen credit for the story, no matter its obvious antecedents. A less obvious source for the goings-on of Nelson and Norma may have been a novel by Wilkie Collins, although that claim — set forth in print in a contemporary trade magazine per *The AFI Catalog* — is somewhat marred by its not identifying which of Collins' books was thus tapped.

No matter who wrote what, *Variety* wasn't having any of it. In his 29 May 1914 review, "Sime" complained:

Picture makers might be a bit more descriptive in their "mystery" films. *The Woman of Mystery*, a feature, runs along on mysterious lines, and ends without explaining either to the players themselves or the audience what it was all about…. The acting and the settings in this picture are quite commonplace. A couple of "hairbreath [*sic*] escapes" and lots of matter to fill out the number of reels, resulting in one of those impossible detective stories that mean nothing after it has been run off, is never logical, has dull photography at times, and closes without having left an impression.

Particularly upset that the picture did not explain "why the East Indian had a grouch [*sic*] against the actress," Sime also reacted poorly to Nelson's propensity to kiss — frequently and with great show — the digits of his fiancée's hands; indeed, fully half the review was spent in grousing about the cinema's tendency to overindulge in displays of affection.

On the other hand (*Sorry!*), Hanford Chase Judson, who critiqued the picture in the 30 May 1914 edition of *MPW*, was a willing victim to seductions by veiled women, discorporate adventures, and hand-kissing. Apparently also seduced by his Thesaurus, Judson waxed eloquently from the very start:

The newest Blaché feature, a four-reel picture, written and produced by Madame Alice Blaché, gives a strongly woven yarn of sublunary powers. We human beings live in this, our eupeptic, sunlit world as very material persons. We are awake and we see everything that goes on around us. But let us fall asleep for a time and things that were not existent before seem to be there now. These things are to us vague, wholly imaginative. Can we, wide-awake folk of the occident, be sure that our imaginative Oriental brothers are not more awake than we? It matters very little in our Western daylight.

He goes on for a full, page-length column and a half, coming up for air only at the end of it all, opining that "it is a good melodrama and makes entertainment of a high order. The offering is desirable [?] The staging and photography are careful and adequate."

The role of Norma was enacted by Claire Whitney, a young (24 at the time) New Yorker who entered motion pictures after having taken a whack at the stage. Miss Whitney's first feature was 1913's *The Star of India*, another thriller that definitely included Buddha, sinister Hindus, and the oddly-named Fraunie Fraunholz as the actress's love interest, and that one, too, *may* have featured unfettered hand-kissing, as it was produced and directed by Herbert Blaché, Alice's husband. Her first couple of years in the industry, Miss Whitney was the juvenile in ten or so productions shot and released by Blaché Features, Inc., and she remained a presence onscreen (although, like so many of her contemporaries, with ever-waning luster) virtually up until the cusp of the 1950s.

The aforementioned Mr. Fraunholz — a Canadian by birth, he was occasionally billed as Fraunie *French* Fraunholz, doubtless to forestall any confusion between him and *other* … errr … ummm… — was pretty much out of films by the end of the 1910s, but he did figure in with some features discussed herein: *The Temptations of Satan* and *The Dream Woman* (both 1914), and the 1919 version of *The Thirteenth Chair*.

The titular *Woman of Mystery* was played by Vinnie Burns, an actress also known as June Day(e). Per available materials, we see that Miss Burns entered the industry in 1911 (she portrayed the title role in 1912's *Oliver Twist*, one of the earliest-known American feature films) and was in her last credited picture by 1921. We've not much else to offer on her. Like her co-stars, she lent her presence to several other silent genre features: *The Mystery of Edwin Drood*, *The Chimes*, and *The Temptations of Satan* (all, intriguingly, released in 1914).

— *JTS*

Womanhood, the Glory of the Nation

Womanhood, the Glory of the Nation. Vitagraph Co. of America/Greater Vitagraph (V-L-S-E, Inc.), A Vitagraph Special, 8 reels, 19 March 1917 [LOST]

CAST: Alice Joyce (*Mary Ward*); Harry T. Morey (*Paul Strong*); Naomi Childers (*Jane Strong*); Joseph Kilgour (*Marshal Prince Dario*); Walter McGrail (*Count Dario*); Mary Maurice (*Julia Strong*); James Morrison (*Philip Ward*); Peggy Hyland (*Alice Renfrow*); Templar Saxe (*Baron Reyva*); Bobby Connelly (*Little boy*); Edward Elkas (*Ortos*); Bernard Siegel (*Carl, the spy*); John Costello (*Prime Minister*); Theodore Roosevelt (*Himself*); Woodrow Wilson (*Himself*)

CREDITS: *Producers* J. Stuart Blackton, Albert E. Smith; *Supervisor* J. Stuart Blackton; *Directors* J. Stuart Blackton, William P.S. Earle; *Scenario* Helmer W. Bergman; based on a story by J. Stuart Blackton and the Reverend Cyrus Townsend Brady; *Cinematographer* Clark R. Nickerson; *Artistic Effects* Ferdinand Earle; *Film Editor* Albert J. Ohlson; *Military Advisor* Captain George W. Johnston; *Pyrotechnician* Herman Rottger

Traveling in Europe, Mary Ward meets Count Dario of Ruritania, who falls in love with her. She promises to give him an answer later. Returning to America by way of the Philippines, Mary meets Paul Strong, United States representative there. There she learns that her mother and younger sister have been killed in an air raid over the United States. She and Strong return together. Mary's brother, Philip, has been in action with his regiment and has been blinded. His fiancée, acting as a nurse, has been scarred about the face. The invading army is headed by Marshall Prince Dario and his son, the Count. Mary gains their confidence and enters their ranks as an American spy. Strong is made Master of Energies of the country, and tours it, arousing that portion of the states not under the head of the invader to action. His sister, Jane, dressed as Joan of Arc and carrying the flag, is brought out to inspire the public. She does such a tremendous good that Prince Dario captures her and has her shot in public. But finally Strong's untiring efforts bear fruit. An army is raised, and after battles on land and sea, the Ruritanians are driven out [*Motion Picture News*, 21 April 1917].

Womanhood's tone provided an upbeat sequel to the incredibly dismal finale of the cautionary *The Battle Cry of Peace* (see entry). To the undoubted approval of American audiences, Count Dario, the nefarious foreign suitor of their heroine, met his villainous just-desserts at the hands of his own father for disobedience of orders. Even Philip's unfortunate loss of sight was slanted as a "blessing in disguise" (*Variety*, 6 April 1917) vis-à-vis his true love's disfigurement.

The sequel also showcased more science-fiction trappings. "A new invention, the 'aerial torpedo,' is demonstrated," touted *The San Antonio* [Texas] *Light* on 22 April 1917, and Mary's spying efforts were aided by a "clever secret wireless telephone" according to the same column. *The New York Times* (2 April 1917) hinted at a bit of futuristic warfare: "A fleet of wireless-controlled 'firebugs,' which are full of an inflammable substance that surrounds the enemy fleets and consumes them, conspire to rout the 'Ruritanians.'" Decades before the advent of heat-seeking missiles, cellular phones, and the like, these devices surely caused 1917 viewers to sit up and take notice.

Nonetheless, it was the topical theme that once again grabbed the greatest attention. April 1917 — mere weeks after the film's debut in Philadelphia on the 19 March — marked the end of United States military neutrality; America finally had entered The Great War on the side of the Allies. Indeed, *Womanhood* would have been called *The Battle Cry of War* but for one thing: *The Battle Cry of Peace* — re-edited and re-issued to a nation bracing for the upcoming all-out conflict — had already laid claim to that title.

Like *Battle Cry* before it, a "Who's Who" again turned out for *Womanhood*'s New York City (at the Broadway theatre) debut on 1 April 1917. Notables primed to soak in the message of J. Stuart Blackton's latest Vitagraph preparedness picture included opera singer, Enrico Caruso; E. H. Sothern (see *The Man of Mystery*); movie executives William Fox and Carl Laemmle; Thomas (*Birth of a Nation/Fall of a Nation*) Dixon; and Daniel Frohman, famed theatrical producer and manager. This time around, the crowd also got to view *two* presidents on the big screen: Teddy Roosevelt (whose appearance was met with thunderous cheers) and Woodrow Wilson. Roosevelt — who had been a staunch supporter of Blackton's *Battle Cry* — had been apprehensive about participating in that earlier picture lest he be accused of using it as a springboard to yet another presidential campaign. The appearance by Wilson — whose isolationist position had by now become untenable — caught most audiences unaware. Adding to the premiere's political fervor, during the intermission Blackton provided a patriotic speech in which he harshly criticized pacifist holdout, Williams Jennings Bryan, himself a three-time presidential candidate as well as Wilson's ex–Secretary of State.

Those who had paid close attention to both films might have been a bit surprised to see Mary Maurice and James Morrison — two actors whose characters had died in *Battle Cry* — "reincarnated" in *Womanhood*. Unsurprisingly, Marshal Prince Dario's uncanny resemblance to George Washington (as he had appeared in *Battle Cry*) was due to the fact that both roles were played by Joseph Kilgour.

Luckily, the rest of the major characters wore "fresh" faces. *Exhibitor's Trade Review* (14 April 1917) found that the actors cast as the juveniles not only were credible as the love interest, but also underscored the film's message: "Harry T. Morey makes the role of Strong stand out as a fine example of American manhood, his natural acting standing him in good stead. Alice Joyce as Mary, in addition to being a joy to behold, brings to the part that sincerity of purpose which has made her the gifted star she is."

Joyce had earlier won fame as the "Kalem Girl," the Kalem Company's biggest attraction. Following a short hiatus, she joined up with Vitagraph and, after starring in a Big V film or two with Morey, played opposite him yet again in *Womanhood, the Glory of the Nation*. Leaving Vitagraph, she made for the greener pastures of Paramount, United Artists, and Warner

Brothers. Married in May 1914 to Tom Moore (a frequent leading man in many of her early pictures and of the famed quartet of acting Moore brothers), Joyce later moved to greener *marital* pastures, first wedding millionaire, James B. Regan, then M-G-M director, Clarence Brown. Ms. Joyce's more notable credits included *Stella Dallas* (1925), *Dancing Mothers* (1926), *Beau Geste* (1927), and both silent and sound renditions of *The Green Goddess*.

Harry T. Morey was playing against type as Paul Strong; for much of his lengthy silent film career, he was the heavy. Morey was featured in a couple of talkies, but even they brought no great relief from this pigeonholing; in 1929's *The Return of Sherlock Holmes*, he portrayed the redoubtable Professor Moriarty. In real life, though, Harry was a "good guy" all the way and, during the war, he aided the enlistment effort via a countrywide tour on behalf of the navy.

Sequels seldom capture lightning in a bottle twice, and *Womanhood, the Glory of the Nation* failed to match its predecessor's reputation or revenue. As Marion Blackton Trimble wrote in her biography of her father, director J. Stuart Blackton: "Surprisingly, the public showed enthusiasm for this production, but, after the explosive power of *The Battle Cry*, it was like sticking a spoon into a whirlpool to try to stir it faster."

Critical opinion was more or less split fifty-fifty. This from *Variety*:

> Vitagraph in *Womanhood* has overshot the mark, and overplayed the game, thereby weakening the effort as a whole…. Preparedness is sorely needed, but much stronger arguments can be made for it than *Womanhood* presents…. As propaganda of a certain kind it is excellent, but in spite of all its hurrah it leaves a feeling of disappointment that no more powerful argument has been presented for the cause than has been shown along not dissimilar lines many times before.

In a piece entitled "Feeble War Film Shown," *The New York Times* (cited above) declared that "*Womanhood, the Glory of the Nation* is an inartistic and ineffective picture." Peter Milne, in what may have been the most poignant critique of all, added:

> There is no semblance of continuity…. There are bits of extreme pathos, such as the meeting of the sweethearts after the girl's face has been disfigured and after the boy has lost his eyesight and there are immense panoramas of fighting men, with mine explosions, and the hurling of gas bombs as indicative that no expense was spared in bringing them up-to-date. But the story runs amuck. Characters are picked up and dropped at will [*The Motion Picture News*, 21 April 1917].

On the asset side of the ledger were words such as these:

> The photography is clear throughout and the scenes effective. The direction results in the swift and inspiring development of a story which is fraught with calamitous moments, but which ends with America triumphant, as she must ever be. There is a tone of sincerity to the film which deserves the success it will undoubtedly achieve [*The New York Dramatic Mirror*, 7 April 1917].

Meanwhile, *Moving Picture World* (21 April 1917) actually found the second film *superior* to the first:

> *Womanhood* is in very respect a finer example of artistry than *The Battle Cry of Peace*, primarily because the story is not continually broken by preachment…. With the same obvious purpose in view, *Womanhood* reaches deeper into the sympathies of an audience, and will on that very account make a more profound impression. *The Battle Cry of Peace* was an intellectual argument.

ALICE JOYCE
IN THE SPECIAL VITAGRAPH BLUE RIBBON FEATURE
"WOMANHOOD"
"THE GLORY OF THE NATION"
LYRIC THEATRE   MATINEE AND NIGHT
WEDNESDAY AND THURSDAY   JUNE 27 & 28

Alice Joyce as the comely Mary Ward, soon-to-be national heroine. *Womanhood* marked the second time in two years that J. Stuart Blackton had the U.S. invaded by Ruritania.

Womanhood is an inspiring appeal to chivalry, to manhood, to ennobling sentiments which lie deep and strong in the American heart....

Doing MPW one better, the aforementioned *Exhibitor's Trade Review* even ranked it at the top (!) of the entire Vitagraph oeuvre: "It is the finest piece of work that has ever come from the Vitagraph studios. It is a picture that, although timely, will live long after hundreds of other features have fallen by the wayside. It will provide exciting entertainment for years to come."

Unfortunately, these claims (likely exaggerated, owing to the subject matter) can never be fully verified nor dismissed. Like the majority of Vitagraph films, *Womanhood, the Glory of the Nation* is presently classified as missing in action.

— *SJ*

The Young Diana

The Young Diana. Cosmopolitan Productions/Paramount Pictures, 7 reels/6744 feet, 7 Aug 1922 [LOST]

CAST: Marion Davies (*Diana May*), Maclyn Arbuckle (*James P. May*), Forrest Stanley (*Commander Cleeve*), Gypsy O'Brien (*Lady Anne*), Pedro De Cordoba (*Dr. Dimitrius*)

CREDITS: *Directors* Albert Capellani, Robert G. Vignola; *Scenario* Luther Reed; based on the novel *The Young Diana: An Experiment of the Future* by Marie Corelli (New York — London, 1918); *Settings* Joseph Urban

Seven reels of *The Young Diana* were deposited with the Register of Copyrights for review on 29 June 1922; as was the policy of the day, they were returned several days later. Those reels are now long gone, but the following summary, filed along with the copyright application, is still at the Library of Congress:

Diana May is a young English girl, engaged to marry Commander Cleeve. Mr. May, her father, manifests an interest in science by maintaining a laboratory in his home where a Dr. Dimitrius is seeking the "elixir of youth." Dimitrius wishes to marry Diana. He sees Cleeve arrive at the house and notices Lady Anne, a friend of Diana, hold a whispered conference with him.

Cleeve tells Diana he must go away, and Dimitrius whispers that the Commander is eloping with Lady Anne. Diana, watching from the window of her room, sees Cleeve and Lady Anne leave, and she falls faint.

It is twenty years later. Diana is a spinster and her father, irritable because she is not married, makes her life miserable. She sees an advertisement that a famous scientist in Switzerland wishes to experiment on a brave women. She leaves indications that she has killed herself by drowning and goes to the Swiss laboratory where she finds Dr. Dimitrius. He restores Diana to youth and beauty, and she becomes the rage of European capitals and watering places. Diana meets Cleeve, now married. He wishes to desert his wife for her, but she spurns him. Dimitrius, too, wishes to marry her. Overcome with emotion, Diana falls into a faint.

When she awakens, learns she has been dreaming and is still young and lovely without the need of rejuvenation. It is morning. Cleeve returns and explains that his sudden departure was necessary because his ship was sailing under sealed orders, but that the orders had been revoked. Lady Anne had accompanied him because she had been secretly married previously to the captain of the ship, and Cleeve was taking her to say goodbye to him. The picture fades out with the wedding of Diana and Cleeve.

The movie was derived from *The Young Diana: An Experiment of the Future* by Marie Corelli (see entry, *The Sorrows of*

Satan, 1927). Corelli, much like Gertrude Atherton (see *Black Oxen*, 1924), appeared to *believe* in the rejuvenation craze of the era, stating in *My Little Bit* that she "wanted to be one of the first in the field to suggest a discovery which is approaching us in the near future; which is, so to speak, 'glimmering' ahead of our scientists like a brilliant streak of sunrise in a summer sky." For her efforts, in addition to book royalties, Corelli received a sweet serialization deal with the Hearst newspaper chain.

In its 24 November 1919 review, *The New York Times* labeled Corelli's new novel as another example of her "usual and somewhat grandiloquent style." It's hard to deny — no matter what feelings might be stirred by a word like "grandiloquence"— that Luther Reed's screenplay dumbed-down the human complexity of the novel's central focus in almost every respect. For one thing, the Diana of the Printed Page out-swooned her celluloid counterpart by a margin at least two to zero, the latter figure underscoring the fact that the movie heroine merely *dreamt* that she had fainted. Then, too, the novel had no love triangle involving Diana, Anne and Cleeve; Corelli's Diana — rejected outright — had to deal with this head-on, as she was never given the usual deus-ex-machina cop-out of escaping her fate by awakening.

Corelli was certainly familiar with rejection. *The Young Diana* was written when she was on the rebound from an unhappy infatuation with a married man. Corelli was in her fifties and the man, an artist, was ten years her senior; after trying to use her fame for his own ends, he shunted her aside. Corelli had something else in common with the young Diana: the ability to reinvent herself. She had been born Mary Mills, the illegitimate daughter of the married poet/writer, Charles MacKay, and his mistress. After his wife's death, Charles married his lover and Mary became Minnie Mackay. As an adult, the would-be writer discovered that the era's literary magazines had no interest in publishing anything by Minnie MacKay, but gave virtual carte blanche to Minnie's alter-ego, "Marie Corelli," a supposed Venetian noblewoman of illustrious ancestry (and of already-published literary achievements) who had spent time in France and England. Mary/Minnie/Marie successfully hid her origins throughout her life and when the truth did come out after her death, it remained muddled and ambiguous.

Marie's first novel, *A Tale of Two Worlds*, was about a young woman who, by means of electricity, is able to visit other planets and has various mystical experiences. It was a huge success and before long Corelli became the most popular novelist in England, even counting Queen Victoria among her fans. Her books ranged from wildly romantic tales like *Thelma*, to religious fiction like *The Sorrows of Satan* and *Barabbas* (the passion of Christ told from the point of view of the criminal who was pardoned in Jesus' place; a rather offbeat take on the traditional story, it depicts Judas' sister Judith as Christ's real betrayer!), to Gothic Grand Guignol (*Vendetta*), and even to science fiction (*The Secret Power* foretells the atomic bomb and germ warfare). She frequently lambasted the hypocrisy of societal mores, the political and literary establishments, and the Christian churches, feeling that the latter were lukewarm in their devotion. Also outspoken on the place of women in society (although she opposed giving women the vote until much later in her life), Marie was a pacifist until Britain entered the Great War, when her jingoistic support of the conflict came to light.

However popular it may have been with the public, Marie's work was often derided by reviewers, and the author was engaged in lifelong warfare with the press. Ditto with the Victorian equivalent of the paparazzi, whom she avoided like the plague due to her somewhat dwarfish stature and frumpy appearance (her official portrait was heavily retouched). Referring to her fame as her "crown of thorns," Marie and her faithful companion, Bertha van der Vyer, moved to Stratford-upon-Avon, birthplace of William Shakespeare. Bertha and Marie lived there until the latter's death in 1924, albeit the pair — ardent believers in preserving historic cottages and locales—clashed with prominent townspeople who were less interested in history than "progress." It still is debatable whether the Mademoiselles Corelli and van der Vyer were, in fact, lovers. Marie left her historic house, Mason's Croft, to be kept in a trust as a residence/meeting hall for distinguished people in the arts (except for actors!)

The *Times'* analysis saw the *The Young Diana* as having two distinct halves, and quite rightly stated: "The Diana of this first part of the book, plain and middle-aged and love-starved, is a real and pathetic person, even though her too angelic disposition does make the reader a little impatient with her." The newspaper's inference about the second half — that Corelli regarded the new Diana as "something more, and the reader is inclined to consider a good deal less than human."— is likewise difficult to

contest, considering Diana's admonishing Dimitrius, as quoted here:

> You, who have studied and mastered the fusion of light and air with elemental forces and the invisible whirl of electrons with perpetually changing forms, must I, your subject, explain to you what you have done? You have wrested a marvelous secret from Nature — you can unmake and remake the human body, freeing it from all gross substance, as a sculptor can mould and unmould a statue, — and do you not see that you have made of me a new creature, no longer of mere mortal clay, but of an ethereal matter which has never walked on earth before?— and with which earth has nothing in common? What have such as I to do with such base trifles as human vengeance or love?

The picture's syncope-prone title character was played by Marion Davies— a move that offered little surprise, considering the hop, skip and jump that separated Hearst newspaper fiction, the film output of Cosmopolitan Productions, and a Davies starring role. (For more on this topic, see *The Dark Star*, 1919.) As a spinster, Davies donned a plain black dress and slicked her hair back while wearing bone-rim spectacles. As Hearst couldn't resist almost literally gilding his lily, in non-spinster scenes she was decked out in heavy satin gowns, dresses made of silver ribbons and strings of pearls, and other, assorted over-the-top costumes.

By more than one account, Davies managed to turn in a worthy portrayal; thus she began to turn the corner on a film career that had been marked by missteps due — at least in part — to Hearst's interference. *Photoplay* (November 1922) deemed she performed credibly while *Variety*'s crystal ball forecast (on the 1 September 1922): "The vogue of Marion Davies in screendom's realm will be augmented materially." In a piece printed in the *Logansport* [Indiana] *Pharos-Tribune*, reviewer James W. Dean addressed Davies' maturation from movie star to actress:

> Indeed, until the present her ability to act has deserved little consideration…. However in all fairness to Miss Davies, it must be recorded that she does act in *The Young Diana*…. Perhaps the best indication that Miss Davies has acting ability is that upon several occasions in the film she forgot she was beautiful. She pouted and twisted her features into expressions of anger. She was really attractive then [12 September 1922].

When Knighthood Was in Flower (1923), a breakout film for Davies, reunited the actress with two of her *Diana* onscreen alumni: Forrest Stanley (see *Up the Ladder*, 1925) and Pedro de Cordoba (see *The Dark Mirror,* 1920). Director Robert G. Vignola — who shared directing credit with Albert Capellani

Diana May (Marion Davies) considers being kept by Dr. Dimitrius (Pedro De Cordoba), who has promised her eternal youth in *The Young Diana*. Her upstairs neighbor, Ed Norton, has offered her a string of polo ponies.

in *The Young Diana*—guided the trio on his lonesome in *Knighthood*.

If anything, the most talented of the *Diana/Knighthood* group was Viennese set-designer, Joseph Urban (b: 26 May 1872). During his early career as an architect, Urban had designed the interior of the Rathaus (the municipal building in Vienna), built the Czar Bridge in Saint Petersburg, and helped construct a palace in Egypt. As an artist, he displayed equal proficiency; in 1897, Urban was awarded the Kaiser Prize for illustrating Edgar Allan Poe's *The Masque of the Red Death*. It was Urban's artistic prowess (among his other achievements, he illustrated the fairy tales of Hans Christian Andersen and the Brothers Grimm) that had led to notice by theatrical managers. This, in turn, created yet another opportunity by enabling him to establish himself as a prominent European scenic decorator and stage designer.

Having first visited the United States in 1901, Urban was commissioned to build and decorate pavilions at the St. Louis Exposition in 1904 (decades later, he was the director of color and lighting for the 1933-1934 Chicago World's Fair). He moved to

Dust-jacket illustration from the source novel.

the U.S. permanently in 1911 at the invitation of the Boston Opera Company for whom he furnished settings and effects for *Hansel and Gretel, Tales of Hoffman, Don Giovanni, Othello, Parsifal* and many more. Between 1915 and 1918, he produced the Ziegfeld Follies, and among the performers with whom he worked during this time was none other than Marion Davies. In 1917, the Viennese expatriate became a naturalized American.

Urban signed on with William Randolph Hearst in early 1920, and the healthy salary he received overcame any reservations he may have had about working in a purely black-and-white medium; the newspaper magnate's largesse eventually helped finance Urban's architectural studio. Once on board with Hearst, Urban charted his own course, outlining his approach for the readers of the 3 July 1920 *Evening Post*: "I want to make pictures that are moving compositions in the same sense that a great painting is an immobile composition." In this spirit, he had his staff cap a discussion on the "problems of art" by viewing Robert Weine's *The Cabinet of Dr. Caligari*. After leaving Hearst (and the film industry) in the mid–1920s, Urban returned to the fold for a brief time in the Talkie Era, but passed away of a heart attack on 10 July 1933 at the Hotel St. Regis, the interior of which had been designed according to his plan.

The loss of Joseph Urban's work in *The Young Diana* is lamentable as evidenced by this contemporary commentary:

Joseph Urban designed the settings for *The Young Diana*, which assures the fact that the feature will appeal to the eye attuned to the artistically bizarre [Fritz Tidden, *Moving Picture World*, 12 August 1922].

The Corelli reasonings are beautifully amplified through the artistic settings of Urban, odd and bizarre, as usual especially in the dream portion ["Samuel," *Variety*, 1 September 1922].

The laboratory scene in which the middle-aged spinster is restored to youth and beauty through the application of condensed light energy is the best executed of its kind to be shown on the screen [James W. Dean, *Logansport Pharos-Tribune*, 12 September 1922].

Overall reception for the motion picture itself was more mixed. *Exhibitors Herald* projected, "It should prove a big attraction," *Variety* opined, "*The Young Diana* shines forth one of the real regular releases of the year," and *Motion Picture News* readily assented that "One could go on indefinitely enumerating the wonders of this production." On the other hand, *Film Daily* declared that "the production as a whole is stretched beyond capacity and not over-convincing" and *Photoplay* agreed: "A style show, perhaps, but not a good motion picture." Sitting on the fence was *Exhibitors Trade Review*: "Here is an unusual story, one that presents difficulties for the person who would attempt to estimate the popular view of the production as motion picture entertainment."

— *SJ/HN*

The Young Rajah

The Young Rajah. Famous Players–Lasky/Paramount Pictures, 12 November 1922, 8 reels/7705 feet, 16mm fragments survive

CAST: Rudolph Valentino (*Amos Judd*); Wanda Hawley (*Molly Cabot*); Pat Moore (*Amos Judd as a boy*); Charles Ogle (*Joshua Judd*); Fanny Midgley (*Sarah Judd*); Robert Ober (*Horace Bennett*); Jack

Giddings (*Austin Slade*); Edward Jobson (*John Cabot*); Josef Swickard (*Narada*); Bertram Grassby (*Maharajah*); J. Farrell MacDonald (*Tehjunder Roy*); George Periolat (*General Gadi*); George Field (*Prince Musnud*); Maude Wayne (*Miss Van Kovert*); William Boyd (*Stephen Van Kovert*); Joseph Harrington (*Dr. Fettiplace*); Spottiswoode Aitken (*Caleb*).

CREDITS: *Presented by* Jesse L. Lasky; *Director* Philip Rosen; *Adaptation and Scenario* June Mathis; based on the novel *Amos Judd* by John Ames Mitchell (New York, 1895) and the play, *Amos Judd: A Play in a Prologue and Four Acts*, by Alethea Luce (New York, c. 26 July 1919); *Cinematographer* James C. Van Trees.

An undated clipping from *The Washington Post* (which might be a review, but is more likely ballyhoo) outlines the story of *The Young Rajah*:

> *The Young Rajah* is one of the most colorful offerings that Mr. Valentino has brought to the screen. It is a picturization of *Amos Judd*, which was adapted in turn from the novel by J. A. Mitchell. A company of talent, including the charming Wanda Hawley in the role opposite him, supports the star.
>
> *The Young Rajah* offers a tale of East and West which is dynamic with action. It reveals the story of a boy who is left with New England folks by two East Indians with money and jewels to provide for his support. He grows to manhood, enters college and at a great college boat race, he meets the girl he loves. Gifted with a strange ability to see into the future, he foresees an attack upon his life and at the same time he learns that he is an heir to an Indian principality and that his duty calls him back to India.
>
> True to his vision, he is attacked by assassins but through the timely intervention of friends his life is saved and he sails for India without the girl, to take up his new life. The later scenes of the story reveal him in his new role of an Indian potentate, and there is revealed to the audience a dream he has by the shores of a beautiful Indian lake. He sees himself the chief actor in a wedding procession and the bride suddenly lifts her veil and behold, it is the American girl he loves and sighs for. And in view of the infallibility of his visions, one is assured that happiness is eventually in store for him.

If the story seems like a lot of tosh, it is; it's all too typical of the kind of nonsense Hollywood worked up in the Silent and Golden Ages for stars who had become such because their appeal was unorthodox and exotic. They were cast over and over again in vehicles that showcased their narrowly-defined roles (which, admittedly was what the public expected of them) until the public grew tired and moved on. It was not for nothing that the standard Hollywood contract in the Silent Era was for five years; the studios had (fairly accurately) determined that period as the typical career arc for the public's fascination with/wearying of most stars. It didn't seem to occur to the Powers That Were that pushing the boundaries a bit further with each film might have resulted in additional longevity; of the "exotics," only Greta Garbo appears to have grasped this in terms of choosing and vetoing material. The studios likely didn't care; unknowns were arriving daily in Tinseltown, and any one of them might be the next breakout star.

Such was certainly the case with Rudolph Valentino (né Rodolfo Alfonso Raffaello Pierre Filibert Guglielmi di Valentina, 1895–1926), who had been playing bit parts in films for six years without attracting very much notice. Prior to that, he had been a gardener, a dishwasher, a taxi-dancer, and (allegedly) a gigolo. A few in Hollywood (such as actress Geraldine Farrar) had taken notice of him, but it wasn't until screenwriter June Mathis campaigned for him to star in her adaptation of *The Four Horsemen*

of the Apocalypse (1921; see essay on *The Magician*) that Rudy— as he came to be referred to by his adoring fans— was launched into the Cinematic Stratosphere. Metro was a bit slow in realizing the fortune *Horsemen* was raking in — and why — and so it was Paramount who snapped up Valentino and starred him in a series of empty-headed, formulaic vehicles that showcased his exotic and carnal appeal. The most famous of these remains *The Sheik* (1921), directed by George Melford, who would gain genre fame of the footnote variety by helming the Spanish language version of *Dracula* in 1931.

The Young Rajah, long considered a lost film, was rediscovered a few years ago when a 16mm nitrate print was found in the holdings of a private collector. Most of the film had suffered decomposition, though; only the final third was intact, and it was in no great shape, either. A digital compilation —created using that final third, plus a few other snippets, plus elements from Coming Attractions trailers and production stills, plus several newly-created photographic inserts— gives us what remains of the film; the arrangement is based on Paramount's cutting continuity. It is this Flicker Alley creation that we viewed in preparing this essay.

It is difficult to judge a film by a remaining fragment, but based on the evidence of the remaining third of *Rajah*, Paramount was not putting all that much thought into Rudy's vehicles by 1922. The story is a slim one, despite its origins in a novel and a dramatic adaptation of same. There is a series of incidents (somewhat more convoluted that the *Post* article suggests), but no very compelling plot urging them forward. That Valentino not only is the adopted son of Joshua Judd (Charles Ogle), but had also been transported from India into his care by Judd's brother — the boy's potentate father had been overthrown by a usurper — is revealed early on. Nonetheless, little more is made of this for some time, as Amos heads off to Harvard immediately after declaring, "I don't care who I am or where I belong. I am perfectly happy here." Four years pass in the space of an inter-title, with old Joshua giving up the ghost in that interim.

Amos helps the Harvard team win the scull race (rowing stroke). At a victory party afterward, another student — infuriated that he didn't make the team — attacks Amos who decks him with a single blow. Undeterred, the student tries to brain Amos with a chair but Amos has one of his psychic flashes and steps aside, causing the attacker to fall through a window to his death.

Amos next meets Molly (whom he has seen in his dreams, according to an inter-title), but she is also being wooed by the best friend of the chap who fell to his death; additionally she can not overcome her bigotry toward anyone of a duskier skin tone. In a "Meanwhile, back in India" moment, the usurper sees Amos' picture in the newspaper and recognizes him as the son of the prince he deposed and sends out a squad of assassins. But all this is divined by the old mystic, Narada (Joseph Swickard), who also departs for New England to bring Amos home and depose the usurper. Then, it's back to more of Amos' romantic travails which find resolution when Molly's fiancé brains him with a rock from behind (Amos' psychic powers apparently having taken the day off). Molly witnesses this, calls off the engagement, and agrees to marry Amos. But, on the very day before the wedding, the assassins pass Amos a drugged cigarette, abduct him, and are on the verge of whacking him with a very large knife, when Narada and his crew burst through the doors and thwart them before whisking Amos off home. Molly receives a telegram from Amos explaining how a man's gotta do, etc., etc.

What a romantic.

All in all, *Rajah* takes a very simple story and stretches it out with a series of sometimes absurd complications. Why, for instance, do the assassins drug and abduct Amos before attempting to kill him except to eat up footage? The most peculiar part of the film's construction is that while it expends a great deal of time on the banal romantic tribulations in the USA, the potentially richer storyline — not to mention the more visually interesting possibilities — hinted at by the India sequences is given short shrift. Paramount *may* have dropped a bundle on those sequences — Alas! a battle in the beginning of the film only survives as stills — for there is some impressive surviving footage of Krishna's temple, an Indian city and some richly appointed interiors (although the possibility exists that these were standing sets); however, these scenes account for only a few minutes of screen time. Take, for example, what there is of the film's climax: after Narada and his followers take Amos back to Mother India, we are shown the usurper being informed that the prince has returned and the army — taking the young rajah for Krishna — has rebelled. The usurper kills himself, there is a procession through the streets with Amos at the head, followed by a few seconds of footage of Amos in his throne room. He then wanders out into a garden where he has the vision referred to

in the *Post* article. The End! The possibility of some exciting battle footage, a confrontation with the usurper, the spectacle of a coronation … all just tossed blithely away.

Likewise, very little is made of Amos' precognitive abilities; they're little more than a trait — like astigmatism — that he happens to have and are thus so incidental to the forward motion of the plot (what little of *that* there is) that the component could have been eliminated with little difficulty. Inasmuch as that element is the main reason the film is even included in this tome, it's off-putting to realize it is so marginal; again a terrific thematic possibility is simply tossed away. Curiously, aside from the sequence involving the rowing contest — where he is bare-chested in revealingly snug shorts — Valentino's sexual appeal is not exploited, nor is his persona as the courtly but dangerous lover. Instead he portrays the kind of lover who deposits his amour on the doorstep with a chaste kiss on the cheek — exactly the kind of harmless screen hero his emergence had mostly banished from the screen. Perhaps making Rudy a more passive, All-American boy was Paramount's (or Valentino's) idea of stretching his appeal, but it makes for an unexciting film; he rarely takes the initiative in anything. In fact, he must be saved from being murdered by Narada and is then relieved of the necessity of confronting the usurper by the miscreant's suicide.

Prior to Valentino, leading men were, to quote Richard Griffith and Arthur Mayer in *The Movies*, "strong, silent he-man, Arrow-collar heroes [who] were deliberately awkward in their movie romancing; it was their badge of self-respect, or perhaps of virginity." Valentino might be courteous, but his eyes promised that the evening would end in the boudoir … and that he would be very knowledgeable in what he would do there. By comparison, such squeaky-clean, boy-next-door types like the recently departed Wallace Reid (off the scene, ironically, while being treated for drug addiction) and Douglas Fairbanks "who seemed to be all the time doing all the things that adolescent boys are recommended to do to take their minds off sex" (David Robinson, *Hollywood in the Twenties*) were abruptly passé, as every studio vied to have its own Latin lover … or several, if possible. Valentino's own brother was briefly pressed into service, and actors such as Jacob Krantz — who simply *looked* ethnic enough — found themselves rechristened Ricardo Cortez or some such. (Amusingly, Jacob's brother Stanley also adopted the new surname even though he worked as a cinematographer.)

To an extent, it is this image to which *Rajah* returns Valentino, although it allows for some sex-appeal in the scull race (photos of Valentino in the contour-hugging shorts were stolen from movie theaters displaying them), and there are photos extant of Valentino in a costume consisting ropes of pearls barely concealing his nudity, inspired by Bakst's costume for Nijinsky in *Scheherezade*. Where the latter was placed in the film is unknown; it does not ap-

Title character Amos Judd (Rudolf Valentino), in *The Young Rajah*, considers whether he might be overdressed for the Harvard scull race.

pear in any of the footage that remains and that footage seems complete so far as the return to India portion is concerned.

It is difficult — if not impossible — to discuss Valentino's appeal without some reference to the rumors about his sexual persuasion. David Ehrenstein, who delved deeply into the Hollywood sexual underground for his book, *Open Secret*, is convinced the performer was "essentially heterosexual," but there are speculations about his relationships with Norman Kerry (see *The Hunchback of Notre Dame*) and his chief rival for the undisputed title of Latin Lover, Ramon Novarro. Valentino seemed attracted to strong women and married two lesbians (Jean Acker, who locked him out of the bedroom on their wedding night, and Natacha Rambova [née Winifred Hudnut], who reportedly took off for Paris after their wedding and never moved into his house, Falcon's Lair). Reportedly, he was involved in a romance with still another at the time of his death. The marriage to Rambova may have been more than the usual "beard" set-up, as she designed the costumes for his films and tried — with limited success while Rudy was at Paramount — to exert even more influence, though she never managed the goal of directing his films. Rambova had designed the sets and costumes for Alla Nazimova's contemporary *Camille* (1921), where she and Rudy likely met. At the time, she was Nazimova's lover, and — given that Nazimova's screen success after a brilliant stage career started the trend for the "exotics" — there is a certain irony to Nazimova's ending up playing Tyrone Powers' mother in his remake of one of Valentino's biggest successes, *Blood and Sand*. Both women surely knew Rudy's appeal was to gay men as well as to women, and his costumes (or lack thereof) — a dressing or (preferably) an *undressing* scene was *de rigeur* in his films — were calculated to play to both segments of the audience.

Possibly less calculated was the ambiguity Valentino registered with the camera; perhaps it was due to his extensive career as a dancer, but there is something undeniably feminine in the grace of his pantomime. This is not a case of hindsight; accusations of his lack of "masculinity" were made at the time, culminating in the infamous "Pink Powder Puff" editorial in *The Chicago Tribune*: "When will we be rid of these effeminate youths, pomaded, powdered, bejeweled and bedizened in the image of Rudy — that painted pansy?" it ran in part. Valentino challenged the anonymous writer to a boxing match. It never took place, as Valentino died from a perforated ulcer before it could be scheduled.

The day of the exotic leading man were fast waning; even Pope Pius XI assaulted the "vogue for effeminacy" brought on, he claimed by "effeminizing influences in post-war Europe and the United States." As early as 1923 Herbert Howe — ironically, a gay man who was reputedly one of Ramon Navarro's lovers — had predicted the backlash in a piece written for *Photoplay*:

> From the moment Valentino hoofed that tango in *The Four Horsemen* ... the movie boys haven't been the same. They're all racing around wearing spit curls, bobbed hair and silk panties.... The public can stand just so many ruffles and no more. Some of the boys better walk up one flight and get some blue serge nifties. It's a cinch if they don't change their panties some of the producers are going to lose theirs.

Initially, Valentino may have been happy to do *The Young Rajah*. He was always happy to be working with June Mathis, who had crafted the script from "the play by Althea Luce, from the novel by J.A. Mitchell" according to the onscreen credits (though numerous other sources claim the book was by one William Henry Giles Kingston, published in 1876). Soon, though, he was complaining about the "cheap sets, cheap casts, cheap everything." He hated director Phil Rosen (Yes! Phil Rosen!). He was convinced Paramount was stinting on the budgets for his movies, and he was probably right; the studio was not in a good way financially at the time and was, in addition, growing weary of their demanding star and his interfering wife. Adding to Valentino's stress is that he was in the process of divorcing that interfering wife — Acker — and her lawyers were proving to be tough negotiators; the lady would eventually get a hefty sum from the star for removing herself from his life. Valentino's performance in *Rajah* was doubtless affected by this ongoing animosity: "Some of my scenes had to be cut because of my bad appearance on the screen," he wrote, "as a result of some of the messages I had from Mrs. Valentino in New York."

Self-medicating (with baking soda) to treat the stomach distress caused by the ulcers that would eventually kill him, Valentino bolted from the studio shortly after finishing *Rajah* and would only return after a protracted legal battle. (The fact that the studio had him in four pictures a year did little to calm his dyspepsia or improve his view of Paramount.) By the time he finished out his contract, he and the studio were probably glad to see the backs of each other, even though that period included another one of his big hits, *Monsieur Beaucaire* (1924). His last few films were all independent productions over which he and Rambova could exert maximum control. Cruel though it may sound, Rudolph Valentino may have died at the right time. The vogue for his type of star was nearly over; he was reportedly getting pudgy (like most Italians, Rudy loved his pasta) and, as was common with many other exotics, his accent might not have been a happy marriage with the primitive sound technology that was just around the corner. Intriguingly, his stardom was exactly five years from *Horsemen* in 1921 to his last film, *Son of the Sheik*, in 1926.

Still, his death set off a national frenzy that made the orgy of lamentation over Michael Jackson's passing seem like, as they say, a vicarage tea party. Women are said to have committed suicide; his funeral in Manhattan turned into riots when frustrated mourners couldn't be squeezed into Campbell's funeral home fast enough. (Footage of these riots turned up in — of all places — the Bela Lugosi vehicle, *Black Dragons* [1942], purportedly as an example of Nipponese sabotage.) Pola Negri, reputedly romantically involved with Valentino at the time, gave rise to the supposition that theirs was an affair designed purely for publicity when she fainted at his casket, said display of inconsolable grief dutifully recorded by the publicist she had thought to bring along. Valentino's body was then shipped to the Coast for another funeral, every bit as well attended but less riotous. For years a mystery woman left a rose on his grave on the anniversary of his birth/death.

Valentino's instincts about *The Young Rajah* were correct; the film was the most commercially and critically unsuccessful of his motion pictures. *Moving Picture World*'s Mary Kelly was possibly being kind in her 18 November 1922 review:

> Similar in style rather in motive to the production which have made Rodolpho Valentino the screen hero of the hour, *The Young Rajah* makes an appeal that is slightly new. It is a sumptuous production of many moods. Compared to his recent achievement in *Blood and Sand* it leaves a decided impression of being less virile…. Instead of relying on an intensely physical theme, as this did, the picture resorts to mysticism as the strongest appeal. This much expression of the supernatural has not found expression in religious passages, but rather in spectacular features such as have proven popular in other pictures…. There are a number of brilliant episodes that are executed with a dash and finesse that do the director and the entire cast credit. The production is a pompous spectacle with many contrasts, as for instance, the simple New England home scenes and the elaborate construction of the Maharajah's palace in India…. Valentino's performance is remarkably smooth. The close-ups are many, and his art in emotional expression was never more accomplished. Less vigorous than his roles in the past, he gets fine results with more subtle efforts. One of the most vivid personalities in the excellent supporting cast is Joseph Swickard as the Indian mystic.

Theater owners were weighing in with a slightly different opinion by the 4 August 1923 issue. One from the "Y" Theatre in Nazareth, Pennsylvania, wrote, "There certainly wasn't very much to this one, but it seemed to please our audience. Not as good as *Blood and Sand*." Another exhibitor in the same issue complained that the print he had gotten was so worn and re-patched "that really few of us knew what the thing was all about," suggesting Paramount was being stingy with striking prints.

A November 1922 review, penned by Suzanne Sexton but without further identification on the clipping, claimed that *Rajah*

> has to recommend it a good scenario by June Mathis and the fact that the magnetic Rodolpho wears rings on his fingers, jewels on his toes, and enough ropes of pearls to have hung Bluebeard's eight wives. He also has an automatic spotlight between his eyes which works on the "stop and go" schedule like Fifth avenue traffic … it has the romantic costume appeal and a "Song of India" prologue, either of which is nearly always irresistible. Photographically and from the standpoint of direction, it cannot approach *Blood and Sand*, or some of Rodolph Valentino's lesser successes. Very little seems to have been spent on production.

It will be noted that Valentino was at this point being billed as "Rodolph"; his billing shifted a good deal over his brief career, and one can find him credited as Rudolph, Rodolph or Rodolfo, Valentino, Volantino, Valentina, Valentini or Valentine and even, extravagantly, as M. Rodolpho De Valentina. It can also be noted from Ms. Sexton's review that the Indian scenes are somewhat more extended than is apparent in the digital restoration and that the string-of-pearls costume was onscreen at some point.

An unsigned review in *Motion Picture Magazine* came close to siding with Rudy in his dispute with Adolph Zukor:

> After witnessing *The Young Rajah*, in which he is starred, we begin to understand many things, principally among them why Mr. Valentino desired to select his own casts. And if it wasn't that we remembered from our nursery days that, "Two wrongs don't make a right," we would be sorely tempted to applaud Rodolph Valentino for refusing to continue with his contract. At any rate,

while we may disapprove of him ethically, we sympathize with him emotionally. All of which has probably led you to believe it is a pretty bad picture. It is. It is about as satisfying as a cheap serial. As a matter of fact, it is the concentrated essence of those things which has composes serials since time immemorial…. Even the Valentino is submerged in the mediocrity of this production. Of the supporting cast Charles Ogle is the only one who stands forth with any degree of effectiveness.

This Charles Ogle (1865–1940) is, of course, the same Charles Ogle who played the creation in the 1910 Edison *Frankenstein*. Surprisingly, in his 300-plus films (many of which were one-reelers, hence the astounding number he appeared in between 1908 and 1926), his only other brush with genre was playing Bob Cratchit in a 1910 production of *A Christmas Carol*. Wanda Hawley (née Selma Wanda Pittack, 1895–1963) was one of the biggest stars of the Silent Era, if only for a moment or two; she is all but forgotten today. Rising to stardom in Cecil B De Mille films, she reputedly she received as much or more fan mail than Gloria Swanson. *Rajah* was the closest thing to a genre credit that she'd have in her career, which sputtered and died shortly after the onset of talkies. The rumor that she paid her rent in the 1930s by renting herself out is repeated on the IMDb, though she is known to have worked for a beauty-cream company during that decade and made numerous public appearances on its behalf. In 1942 it was erroneously reported that she had died. In fact it was another now-forgotten silent actress, Ormi (*The Nation's Peril*) Hawley, who had shuffled off the mortal coil; when corrections were printed they noted that Wanda was not only alive, but also happily married and living in Seattle.

Joseph Swickard was a veteran stage actor who began in films in 1912 and was playing supporting roles for Mack Sennett by 1914. He made over 200 films, most of them in the Silent Era; among his genre credits during this time were *The Four Horsemen of the Apocalypse* and the 1925 version of *The Wizard of Oz*. By the Sound Era, Swickard was firmly relegated to B productions and serials, like Dwayne Esper's *Narcotic* and *The Perils of Pauline* (both 1933), *The Return of Chandu* and *The Man Who Reclaimed His Head* (both 1934), the delirious *The Lost City* (1935), *The Black Coin* (1936), *Lash of the Penitentes*, *The Sheik Steps Out* (with Ramon Novarro), *Zorro Rides Again* (all 1937), *The Secret of Treasure Island* (1938) and *Dick Tracy's G-Men* (1939). It was in 1939 that Swickard's ex-wife was murdered by their son. The actor himself died from natural causes a year later, although some accounts (falsely) claim that he threw himself from atop the Hollywood sign.

June Mathis (1892–1927) barely outlived her famous discovery, succumbing to a heart attack only a year after Rudy passed away. Mathis was watching a performance of a Broadway play (shopping for productions, no doubt) when she suddenly cried out, "Oh, mother, I'm dying!" Needless to say, the performance was brought to a screeching halt as the woman was carried out into the theater alley where she was pronounced dead; it was an exit worthy of one of her own dramatic scenarios. Mathis was one of the most highly prized writers/executives of the Silent Era. She was hired away from Paramount by Irving Thalberg, who wanted her to adapt that company's film of *Ben Hur* (1925). Thalberg and Mathis intended to star Valentino, but Ramon Novarro ended up wielding the reins in the famous chariot race.

The Zero Hour

Mathis' first writing credit dates back to 1916 and while her interest in spiritualism often surfaces in her scripts (as it does in *Rajah*), she rarely created a full-blown genre offering. Her scripts for the Valentino/Rex Ingram collaborations *The Four Horsemen of the Apocalypse* and *The Conquering Power* (1922; see entry on *The Magician* for both) offer some terrifying sequences (which may have had as much or more to do with Ingram than with Mathis), but are otherwise realistic studies. Mathis is often blamed for cutting down Erich von Stroheim's alleged masterpiece, *Greed* (1924), from its eight- or ten-hour length (depending on the source consulted) to the shorter form in which it survives. The tale of the snipping is quite complicated and recounting it would require our moving beyond the parameters of this book, but Mathis created a detailed memo for M-G-M editor, Joseph Farnum, who did the actual cutting. Mathis, who was in fact in sympathy with von Stroheim and who admired the themes in the work — she'd done the adaptation and dialogue for the film — no doubt was trying to salvage it.

One of the joys of working on this book is the opportunity it brings to note that certain Poverty Row directors of the Sound Era were often helming "A" productions before the flickers learned to talk. There is William Nigh, for instance, who went from Lon Chaney's *Mr. Wu* (1927) to Bela Lugosi's *The Mysterious Mr. Wong* (1935) in the space of a decade or so. Or William Beaudine, who ended his movie-directing career with such notorious (but fun) stinkers as *Jesse James Meets Frankenstein's Daughter* (1966) but four decades earlier was putting Mary Pickford through her paces in *Sparrows* and other "A" productions.

Such is the case with East Prussian–born Phil Rosen (1888–1951), who started as a cinematographer with Thomas Edison in 1912. Rosen also photographed Theda Bara in *The Darling of Paris* (1917) and Lon Chaney in *The Miracle Man* (see essays on both) before moving on to calling the shots in such respectable productions as *The Dramatic Life of Abraham Lincoln* (1924) and *Rajah*. (During the overlap between solely being either cinematographer or director, Rosen was elected president of the American Society of Cinematographers [ASC].) When Erich von Stroheim was fired from *Exquisite Sinner* in 1926, it was Rosen who was called into finish the job, which included re-shooting some of the film. It is in the 1930s, however, that our man Phil is of more interest to most readers of this tome, with his participation in films such as *The Sphinx* (1933), *Beggars in Ermine* (1934), *It Couldn't Have Happened — But It Did* (1936), *Phantom of Chinatown* (1940), *Spooks Run Wild* (1941), *The Mystery of Marie Roget* (1942) — a Universal B that must have felt like a big-budget epic in comparison to his then-recent assignments — then back to the depths for *Charlie Chan in the Secret Service*, *The Chinese Cat*, the immortal *The Return of the Ape Man* (look quick for the five seconds of George Zucco!), *Black Magic* (all 1944), *The Jade Mask*, *The Scarlet Clue*, *The Strange Mr. Gregory*, *The Red Dragon* (all 1945) and *The Shadow Returns* (1946). On another note, Rosen's second wife was the dancer, Joyzelle, who may be spotted in the sound (1935) version of *Dante's Inferno*.

And, yes — way down in the cast crawl — that *is* Hoppy (William Boyd), bringing up the rear.

— *HHL*

The Zero Hour

The Zero Hour. World Film Corp./World Film Corp., 16 December 1918, 5 reels [LOST]

CAST: June Elvidge (*Fanny Craig/Evelyn Craig*); Frank Mayo (*Bruce Taunton*); Armand Kaliz (*Esau Brand*); Henry Warwick (*Micah Parrish*); Grace Henderson (*Mrs. Taunton*); Clio Ayers (*Hilda*); Nora Cecil (*Mrs. Winslow*); Dorothy Walters (*The cook*); Reginald Carrington (*Paul Warren*).

CREDITS: *Director* Travers Vale; *Scenario* Harry Hoyt and Reginald Smith; based on a story by Paul West; *Cinematographer* Philip Hatkin

This is yet another warning against consorting with fake mediums, a peril really quite foreign to the average Silent Era moviegoer, but one which film producers apparently felt was as widespread and dangerous as influenza. Perhaps an even greater danger — again, according to Hollywood — involved encountering identical twins and then being unable to determine which one is the good one and which, the nasty. The 1910s were full of movies about twins, identical cousins, and doubles — more often than not, female — and while one might wish to talk about duality, the doppelganger motif, and *Dr. Jekyll and Mr. Hyde*, in reality most of these films offered little more than an excuse to have a prominent actress play a one-dimensional good girl *and* a one-dimensional bad girl, each with appropriate costume changes. In *The Zero Hour*, it was June Elvidge who did the smiling and frowning, and it was she who gave cameraman Phil Hatkin the opportunity to demonstrate the increasing sophistication of double-exposure work. *The Zero Hour* had a few twists, but reviewers found them more ridiculous than surprising.

The following synopsis is copied from *Motion Picture News* (14 December 1918):

Fanny and Evelyn Craig, sisters who closely resemble one another, are students at a fashionable school due to the saving exercised by their stepfather, Micah Parish, a fake clairvoyant. Fanny, the more serious-minded of the two, is constantly at odds with her sister because of her extravagance. Business is poor with Parish and, when he is unable to pay the tuition he owes, the girls are sent home. Parish doesn't want his charges to know of his profession, but Evelyn finds it out and is eager to assist him. She shows no hesitation in aiding to fool the many rich people who believe in the power of the medium to foretell the future.

Fanny, disgusted by her stepfather and sister, leaves their home and acquires the position of stenographer to Bruce Taunton, a young lawyer who has started a war against fake clairvoyants because one of them, Esau Brand, caused the death of his mother while pretending to summon before her the spirit of her dead husband. Brand is close to Parish and, in fact, has the old man in his power. One by one, Taunton attacks the mediums with the aid of the police and finally comes to Parish's place. Fanny, not wanting to see her sister and stepfather jailed, goes to warn them but finds them already flown. Taunton discovers her there, but she explains it away with a lie.

Later Taunton proposes to her and she accepts. While they are on their way to the church, Taunton loses control of the car and it crashes over an embankment, killing Fanny. Taunton becomes mentally unbalanced. Brand sees a chance to make the lawyer confess his belief in spiritualism by using Evelyn as a decoy. Dressed in black she visits him every night, pretending to be the spirit of her dead sister. On the last night, Taunton pulls a revolver, declares his intention of committing suicide and — according to *The New York Telegraph* review — cries "Darling I love you more now than when I knew you in the flesh. I'm going to join you." Evelyn rushes forward and stops him. At the same time Brand is caught by Taunton's chauffeur and the game is up. Evelyn is a changed girl since Fanny's death, and she readily accepts Taunton's love.

No doubt the hastily reformed con-lady and the unbalanced, *very* forgiving lawyer live happily after. Apparently Taunton has no trouble switching his affections from one twin to the other, a convenience that springs up more than once in such movies. Of course he marries Fanny — apparently without inquiring too much into her background — and she, in turn, neglects to inform him of her lookalike sister and the racket in which she's involved. (Perhaps she was saving that for after the wedding night.) On the plus side, Evelyn throwing in the shroud in the middle of the climatic con reminds one of a similar sequence in the best film ever about phony spiritualists, 1947's *Nightmare Alley*.

Per this undated review, we learn that *The New York Telegraph*'s Frances Agnew felt last-reel metanoia quite unlikely and found *The Zero Hour*'s climax completely implausible: "The inconsistency of the conclusion is the attempt made to divert sympathy to Evelyn after Fanny's death. The story, it would appear, could have been carried out more logically by keeping Fanny alive and reforming Evelyn if desired or keeping her true to form by giving her the fate she would deserve, according to the first delineation of her character."

Peter Milne, in the afore-cited number of *Motion Picture News*, admitted to being unimpressed: "The plot is filled with situations of the frankest sort of melodrama and is rather involved.… As a piece of pictorial skill as applied to the dramatic side of the story, the film has several shortcomings, being in more than one case quite inconsistent in fact and travelling beyond the prescribed limits of fancy."

And while both Agnew and Milne managed some kind words for June Elvidge's performance, *Variety*'s anonymous scribe wasn't giving even that much:

> In many scenes of the picture Miss Elvidge takes a dual role as the Craig sisters. The story opens with the girls at a finishing school. Neither Miss Elvidge nor the young woman who takes the part of the other sister in the early reels looks like young schoolgirls. While they play their parts well, it is easy to see "they are made up to look young" and as a result the picture loses much of its interest [6 December 1918].

It's not clear what the reviewer means by "the young woman who takes the part of the other sister" since Elvidge played both sisters. The producers may have used an actress who resembled Elvidge for a few long shots (to save on double-exposure costs), but one wouldn't think she'd have been shown clearly enough for *Variety* to critique her make-up. Elvidge, by the way, was all of 25 when *The Zero Hour* was shot.

Variety also found the farfetched story less irritating than it did a lack of realism courtesy of the wardrobe department: "There are also errors of direction which are particularly noticeable. The girls and their father are in poor circumstances, he eking out a living by telling fortunes and holding séances yet Fanny, who gets a position as a stenographer goes to business all dressed up like a Fifth Avenue society woman and Evelyn is changing her clothes in every scene."

Inasmuch as Elvidge often played socialites and elegant ladies, the producers were not about to disappoint her fans by skimping on the fancy clothes.

The press-book advised exhibitors to push the film's anti-medium stance thus:

> Your strongest advertising point as regards this production is its attack against the fake mediums and clairvoyants that invest any city of size. You might get endorsements from city officials on this subject and so get in considerable free advertising.… People are usually interested in the subject of mediums and will more than likely be interested enough to come to your theater and discover the methods they use.

Perhaps wanting to have it both ways, the PR boys also suggested the following tagline: "Dealing with a love that bridged the chasm between the living and the dead."

The film's title proved somewhat problematic. "Zero Hour" is probably meant to be taken in the same sense as "Witching Hour," but the former had become heavily identified with military operations. To complicate matters further, the First World War had ended just one month before *The Zero Hour* was released. Ads for the film hastened to point out that it was *not* a war movie, a wise move since war movies quickly became box-office poison. Still, the film's working title — *The Love Wraith* — was scarcely an improvement.

The Zero Hour's main attraction was MIss Elvidge, then at the peak of her fame as one of World Film Corporation's most popular stars. Elvidge, a one-time singer, chorus girl and vaudeville performer, joined World in 1915 and worked her way up through the ranks. Standing 5'9" tall in her silk-stockinged feet, she was perhaps the tallest female star of the Silent Era and her height made her ideal for imperious society ladies and the occasional villainess (as in Maurice Tourneur's *The Whip*). Elvidge left World in 1919 but had difficulty finding starring roles at the other major studios. More often than not, she was given supporting parts, her role in *Beyond the Rocks* starring Rudolph Valentino and Gloria Swanson being typical. In 1922 it was announced that Elvidge would star in the remake of *A Fool There Was* — the film that had brought fame to Theda Bara — but it was Estelle Taylor who ultimately got the part. Elvidge then turned to supplementing her screen work with stage appearances, notably in *The Crystal Gazer* and *Miracle Maid*. Her film roles continue to diminish and, when she found herself playing in low-budget hokum with titles like *Pagan Passions*, she retired. Happily, the inevitable "Where Are They Now?" articles found her a successful businesswoman, rather than an extra living on the crumbs tossed to her by Hollywood. Her third and final marriage, to stockbroker Briton Busch, was a happy one. The statuesque Miss Elvidge can be also be in these pages in entries on *The Man Who Saw Tomorrow, The Poison Pen, The Eleventh Hour* and *Rasputin the Black Monk*.

Frank Mayo (Bruce Taunton) was a reliable, if somewhat uncharismatic, leading man and action hero. His particulars can be found in the entry on *Wild Oranges* where he again plays a groom whose bride is accidentally killed on their wedding day.

Director Travers Vale was born in Liverpool, England, but spent a good deal of his life in Australia and India. His family wanted him to study medicine, but Vale — more interested in photography and the stage — found himself the owner and manager of a theater in Melbourne, Australia, by the age of eighteen; he then started the Travers Vale Stock Company which toured the UK. Later publicity stories about his harrowing adventures in the British Army as a photographer are dubious at best. Around 1900, Vale brought his stock company to the United States where he met and married an actress named Loise St. George. "Loise" became "Louise" and the company was renamed the Louise Vale Stock Company. Many of the plays they performed were not standard pieces, but melodramas written by Vale himself, and one of his most successful was *When the Bell Tolls*, a tale of vengeance set in a monastery.

In the 1910s, Vale switched to the movies, working mainly for small companies (like the Pilot Company, whereat he one of only two directors). He found steadier work at Biograph and labored mainly on two- and three-reelers before he signed on with World Film Corp. Louise also entered the movies, but with the occasional exception of films like *Girl of the Sunny South* (which her husband directed from a script adapted from one of their stage hits), she was found in the supporting cast; she fell victim to the influenza epidemic in 1918. Travers soldiered on, but after his stint at World, he found jobs as a director hard to come by and had to resort to the occasional acting gig. The last film he directed was the 1926 Art Acord Western for Universal, *Western Pluck*. Vale died the following year.

The Zero Hour is based on a story by Paul West (see entry, *De Luxe Annie*), written not long before his suicide, a tragedy mentioned in the publicity to perhaps tie in with the film's morbid theme. The scenario was written by Harry Hoyt (see *The Lost World* and *The Wizard*) and Hamilton Smith. The latter wrote scores of two-reel thrillers for Kalem, among them another tale of crooked mediums, *The Clairvoyant Swindlers* (1915), and *The Vivisectionist*, a mystery centered on an operation involving arm-grafting.

— HN

Appendix of Tangential Films

The horror film, per se, did not (of course) come into its own until Universal put Dracula onscreen in mid–February 1931, but — as we have attempted to show herein — there was a large number of feature films that did the horror genre proud for a good decade and a half prior to that. The same is true of science fiction and fantasy though the "starting point" for those genres is harder to pin down. In addition, there were more than a few pictures that came close, falling short only in that their genre element either played a profoundly minor role or was totally tangential/superfluous to the goings on of the narrative. Be that as it may, most of those movies are at least worth a mention in the context at hand, so we offer our thoughts on those films that came that close to true genre recognition. We have also chosen to include in this section a handful of efforts that were primarily sound films but had released silent versions as well for the many theaters still not equipped for sound in 1928–1929.

Blow Your Own Horn

Blow Your Own Horn. R-C Pictures/Film Booking Offices of America, 11 November 192–, 6 reels/6315 feet. Extant at Gosfilmofond.

CAST: Warner Baxter (*Jack Dunbar*); Ralph Lewis (*Nicholas Small*); Derelys Perdue (*Anne Small*); Eugene Acker (*Augustus Jolyon*); William H. Turner (*Dinsmore Bevan*); Ernest C. Warde (*Gillen Jolyon*); John Fox, Jr. *("Buddy" Dunbar)*; Mary Jane Sanderson (*Julia Yates*); Eugenie Forde (*Mrs. Jolyon*); Dell Boone (*Mrs. Gilroy Yates*); Billy Osborne (*Percy Yates*); Stanhope Wheatcroft (*Timothy Cole*)

CREDITS: *Director* James W. Horne; *Scenario* Rex Taylor; based on the play *Blow Your Own Horn: A Merry Adventure in Three Acts* by Owen Davis (New York, 1926); *Cinematographer* Joseph Dubray

This brief synopsis is from the 10 November 1923 *Moving Picture World.*

> Returning from the World War, Jack Dunbar, unable to land a job, is discouraged. On a country road he meets Nicholas Small, a war millionaire, and fixes his auto for him. Out of gratitude, Small tells Dunbar the way to succeed is to "blow you own horn" and tell everybody how great you are. Later, Dunbar wanders into an estate where Small is a visitor. To demonstrate his theory, Small introduces Dunbar as a millionaire. So successful is Dunbar in keeping up his end and adapting Small's slogan that he succeeds in convincing capitalists that young Augustus Jolyon has a great thing in his apparatus for the wireless transmission of power, helps him to perfect it, and, despite crooked work on the part of Small to prevent it, finally demonstrates its success. He also wins the love of Small's daughter, saves her from an explosion which Small's villainy has brought about, and even wins Small's consent to the match despite the fact that Small has other plans for her.

We made sure to include *Blow Your Own Horn* in these pages since it completes the body of playwright Owen Davis's more

fantastic work that had been adapted to the silent screen: *Lola* (1914), *Up the Ladder* (1925), *Chinatown Charlie* (1928) and *The Haunted House* (1928; see entries) We've relegated it to appendix status, though, because the man-invents-better-mousetrap aspect, while technically qualifying as science fiction, struck us as a wee bit too marginal.

Still, invention-wise, wireless energy transmission is a major step up from what Augustus Jolyon had concocted in Davis' source play, where said "invention" was revealed in the very first lines: "THE PHONOGRAPH: At last it is a fact accomplished! This is the 'Phono-recorder,' an improvement upon all phonographs, phonophones and dictographs invented and improved by –e–e–*ouch!* –e–e–."

Those are Jolyon's exact words, of course, and that "–e–" screeching at the very represents his attempting the name "Edison." The young man is apparently better (although not much) at inventing than he is at reading the current technological journals, as both he and his financial partner, Dunbar (portrayed by Warner Baxter in the film), are ultimately disappointed to discover that the wizard of Menlo Park has indeed developed a phono-whatever that is equal — if not superior — to their own. *Oops!* Dunbar must now wrestle with his conscience over returning to the townsfolk the money they have invested in Jolyon's over-hyped invention. His choosing to do the right thing finally wins him the love of the fair Ann Small and "All's well that ends well," as they say.

Variety's "Skig" didn't think much of the play's transference to celluloid:

The tale does not impress as having received an over-abundance of attention for screen presentation.... There is nothing in the production to make it especially stand out, although an attempt at a thrill has been included in the happening of a cut wire crossing and electrifying a cabin where the "invention of the age" is contained.

Although he hadn't seen fit to include it in his plot précis, *Moving Picture World* scribe C. S. Sewell also singled out the cabin scene as a highlight while tempering Skig's lofty expectations by opining "It belongs to the type of productions that are built to entertain." In the exhibitors' opinion column, "Straight from the Shoulder Reports," in a later (15 December) issue of the *MPW*, Iowan theater owner H. Aldinger checked in with the faintest of praise: "You will hear as little adverse comment on this one as any moderate priced picture."

As for the principals... Star Warner Baxter is still best known (to us, at least) as the Cisco Kid, for which role (in *In Old Arizona*, 1929) he won the second Best Actor Academy Award ever. (We're also partial to his "Crime Doctor" series. And... uhhh... to *42nd Street*.) Ralph Lewis (the nefarious Nicholas Small) is profiled in our entry on 1924's *Dante's Inferno*. A brief biographical sketch on leading lady, Derelys Perdue, may be found in our essay on *The Bishop of the Ozarks* (1923), and the write-up on *One Glorious Day* (1922) has more on John Fox, Jr., *Blow Your Own Horn*'s chief comic relief. Director James W. Horne's only other claim to genre fame came as a bit player (as in *piano player* — we did say "bit") in 1914's *The Invisible Power* (1914, see entry).   — SJ

Brace Up

Brace Up. Bluebird Photoplays, Inc./Bluebird Photoplays, 18 March 1918, 5 reels [LOST]

CAST: Herbert Rawlinson (*Henry Court*); Claire Du Brey (*Ellen Miles*); Alfred Allen (*Colonel Court*); Sam De Grasse (*"National" Jim*). The *Moving Picture World* review gives Claire Du Brey's character the name "Clara Tirayton" and gives Rawlinson's character the first name of "Dick."

CREDITS: *Director* Elmer Clifton; *Scenario* Waldemar Young; *Story* Elmer Clifton; *Cinematographer* Virgil E. Miller.

Our synopsis is an amalgam crafted from *The AFI Catalog* and contemporary reviews:

Colonel Court, an agent in the Secret Service, is distressed by the occasional lapses in courage in his son Henry, a college athlete. Henry is in love with Ellen, a college widow, whose comings and goings are sometimes mysterious. Henry is deliberately hurt during a football game and finds he cannot finish the game. To help heal his son's shattered spirit, Colonel Court enlists him in the Secret Service and puts him on a case involving a radium smuggler known as "National" Jim. Unbeknownst to Colonel Court, Ellen is also a secret agent and is working on the same case. When Henry's courage fails him once again, he goes to an employment agency and hires three men to meet at midnight and communicate power and courage to him through intense concentration. The scheme works and Henry enters Jim's house in time to defeat him in a fight, locate the hidden radium and save Ellen.

This sounds like a plot more appropriate for a Harold Lloyd vehicle but, in spite of a few flashes of humor, it was apparently played straight. PR for the film describe the foundation of the film as "thought transmission," while a title card that opens the movie claims it deals with "mental inspiration," which is not necessarily the same thing.

Some publicity pieces for the film state that it's Colonel Court who is behind the "communication of power" idea: "The idea of mental suggestion is cleverly carried out by the father of the boy and his friends in their endeavor to bring back to life the spirit which has been broken by the fatal game of football" (*Wisconsin State Journal*, 24 March 1918).

Other press mentions (like that of the 9 August 1918 *Daily Kennebec* [Augusta, Maine] *Journal*) reported that "The Colonel decided to adopt an experiment of a professor of psychology." This would suggest that there was likely no real telepathy at all but rather just a charade to restore Henry's self confidence. Of course if that is the case, the film doesn't even merit a place in this appendix but, without the film itself, we can't be sure and the reviews we consulted yielded no definite answer. For example: "There is a sort of vagueness about the main idea which at first keeps the observer in a state of wonderment as to what is intended, but it is all cleared up as the story proceeds (Robert McElravy in *Motion Picture World*, 23 March 1918). Or...

In Bluebird's feature, *Brace Up*, story and direction of Elmer Clifton, scenario by Waldemar Young, starring Herbert Rawlinson, just one attempt at "psychology" — or some such thing — has been essayed for screen depiction. There must be a peculiar fascination for experimenting with psychology, allegory and the like; possibly for the very reason that the percentage in favor of putting it over is infinitesimally small ... Very praiseworthy attempt at visualizing in the matter of cast, production and direction, but there is small likelihood of the average picture patron "getting" exactly what is meant to be conveyed ["Jolo" in *Variety*, 15 March 1918].

Jolo *did* like the midnight meeting of the chosen three: "The men are shown 'communicating' at the stated moment with one very funny flash showing a couple of them standing up a bar clinking glasses and saying, 'More power to him.'"

British-born Herbert Rawlinson could have gone to Cambridge but opted to join a Shakespearean touring company instead. Coming to the States in 1910, he performed in various repertory companies before switching to film. Rawlinson made for Universal in the mid–1910s and occasionally played with Jack P. Pierce, who would later become famous as the creator of that studio's classic monster make-ups. Rawlinson became one of Universal's most popular leading men and, years later, described the trajectory of his career to columnist Bob Thomas: "When you reach a certain age the face changes, the hair turns color and you are a different person. When I was around 35, I found I couldn't play romantic leads anymore. So I went back to the stage. When I returned to pictures my hair was white and I began playing characters." White hair notwithstanding, Rawlinson retained his patrician good looks and kept busy in the movies until his death from lung cancer in 1953.

More on director Elmer Clifton can be found in the entry on *The Two-Soul Woman*, while scenarist Waldemar Young turns up here and there numerous times as one of Tod Browning's key collaborators.   — HN

Brain Cinema

Brain Cinema. Film-Lore Congressional Productions, Inc., 1920(?), length undetermined [LOST?]
CAST: Unknown

CREDITS: *Supervisor* Alexander A. Stuart; *Director* J.A. Fitzgerald; *Story* Alexander A. Stuart; *Cinematographer* E.J. Cederberg

This film is called a "hypothetical," so our write up won't be long, if only because there aren't many facts about the damned thing in the first place.

Per *The AFI Catalog*, "In Jul [*sic*] 1920, the Film-Lore Productions Co. announced that it would film the story 'of love, mystery and science,' its first production, near Edinburgh and the Scottish Highlands, where the story was set." The "love, mystery and science" angles may well indicate that this feature could be right up our alley, as all three elements pitched in to fill the bill with respect to, say, *Frankenstein*. As did brains.

Shortly after that announcement, Film-Lore Productions went to stump for *Brain Cinema* again, but, the second time 'round, was signing off as "Film-Lore Congressional Productions, Inc." Either a merger had been struck in the interim, or the company now had some serious governmental ties. The 20 July 1920 *Motion Picture News* cited a certain Alexander Stuart as the company's president and manager (as well as the "supervisor" for this picture and "all future Film-Lore productions"), and a full-page ad for the film (hailed as a "Super Production" in the 24 July 1920 edition of *The Moving Picture World*) lists Mr. Stuart (as "Alex. A. Stuart") as also being responsible for the picture's original story.

Both trade magazines repeated what was essentially the same information (with the addition of "Congressional" into the mix, of course) in September 1920, and then nothing more was heard from this county on love, mystery, science, film, or lore. Or Alexander Stuart. (At least, not *that* Alexander Stuart.) It is currently being argued as to whether nothing more was heard of Congress, either.

Stuart being a bonnie, braw (good) Scots name, it cannot be discounted that the multi-talented author-cum-mogul *may* have, indeed, crafted a humdinger of a tale — incorporating all of those aforementioned factors and set up there in Alba, where Men are Men and Women are Women, but only the Men wear kilts — but we can't be sure. And neither can anyone else.

The credits listed above were culled by us (and the AFI compilers) from the four, rather redundant PR pieces cited or referred to, above. The man listed to direct the film — J(ames) A. Fitzgerald — has exactly one (other?) credit to his name: the ironically-titled *Ignorance* (1916), the only cinematic offspring of the so-called "Private Feature Film Manufacturing Company." *Ignorance* was then released via the States Rights system and promptly disappeared. Mr. Fitzgerald sure knew how to pick 'em.

There doesn't appear to be anything else out there on this, the sole production — if, in fact, anything *did* come to pass on this — of Film-Lore Congressional Productions, Inc.

It is, therefore, only for the sake of comprehensiveness that we herewith include *Brain Cinema*.

Shame, though. It's a great title.   — *JTS*

Castles for Two

Castles for Two; *Rich Girl-Poor Girl*. Jesse L. Lasky Feature Play Company/Paramount Pictures Corp., 5 March 1917, 5 reels. Library of Congress.

CAST: Marie Doro (*Patricia Calhoun*); Elliott Dexter (*Brian O'Neil*); Mayme Kelso (*Patricia's secretary*); Jane Wolff (*Brian's sister*); Harriet Sorenson (*Brian's sister*); Lillian Leighton (*Brian's sister*); Julia Jackson (*Brian's mother*); Horace B. Carpenter (*Neough*); Billy Elmer (*Callahan*); Marie Mills (*Nanny*)

CREDITS: *Producer* Jesse Lasky; *Director* Frank Reicher; *Assistant Director* Charles Watt; *Story and Scenario* Beatrice C. de Mille and Leighton Osmun; *Cinematographer* Dent Gilbert

Our synopsis is from the Library of Congress:

Brian O'Neil, a poor Irish lord, has recently come into the title and lands of Kilcuddy, and his sisters decide that he must marry for money to save the estates.

Patricia Calhoun, a wealthy American heiress, tiring of the butterfly-life which her position forces her to lead, leaves suddenly for Ireland with her Irish nurse. She conceives the idea of changing places with her secretary. She hears from Lord Brian O'Neil's tenants tales of poverty caused by his high rents, and gives them money, forming a great dislike for the man who is supposed to be so oppressive.

Nagged continually by his sisters, Brian endeavors to propose to the supposed heiress, but fails dismally. In the meantime, he rescues Patricia from a tree where she has taken refuge from a cow. She airs her views of Lord O'Neil's methods, and he finally discloses his identity. However, Patricia and the secretary keep up the deception and the innocent Brian falls into the snare of the roguish Patricia and, also in love with her, still believing her to be only a menial. In a burst of confidence, Brian tells Patricia he must marry the rich American to save his estate.

Patricia plans a party for the O'Neils. Brian steals a few moments with her alone, then presents himself at the front door and is admitted with all due formality by Patricia herself in maid's uniform. Excusing himself a little later, he again seeks out Patricia, or Clutie, as she is known to him, tells her that he wants to marry her, goes back and breaks the news to his mother and sisters, who are horrified. Patricia hurriedly slips in a beautiful evening gown and jewels, enters the room with great dignity, and Brian, taking in the situation, withdraws his offer of marriage. Patricia takes Brian's mother into her arms and tells him that she and his mother will decide the matter.

Perhaps Brian would have been better off by climbing up that tree himself.

The synopsis obviously fails to mention the plot element that is the reason for the film being included here: the presence of fairies throughout the story. In Irish folklore, fairies are not always benign and sometimes indulge in some not-very-loveable behavior (like kidnapping babies from their cradles or causing insanity); however, we are in Hollywood's Eire here — full of castles and romance and with nary an IRA man or Black and Tan in sight — so it's hardly surprising that the fairies are depicted as mischievous, but not malicious.

Gary Don Rhodes, film scholar *extraordinaire* (and our good friend), has seen *Castles for Two* and has kindly saved us the trouble of making still another trek to Library of Congress to do likewise. Gary tells us the fairies are first shown when described to Patricia by her nurse. Later, in Ireland, Patricia is able to see the fairies, but the nurse cannot, and so tells her charge, "I can't see them, Clutie, darlin'. I'm not fey like you." (The suggestion that only the pure in heart can see the fairies also turns up in *Little Lady Eileen*; see entry). Later, after a title card reading "The Witching Hour," the fairies join Patricia up in the tree and show her an image of Brian. At the same time, Brian is sitting in a chair in his castle when the fairies — invisible to him — swirl around him. One of them punches him in the stomach, causing him to get up and go for a walk, and thus leading to his finding Patricia on her leafy perch. Having brought the future lovers together, the fairies apparently withdraw from the action and allow nature (and the various script contrivances) to take their course.

Reviewers praised the double-exposure work used to create the fairies. Per Gary Don Rhodes, "The fairies are regular actors superimposed into the shot with the resulting effect that they appear short…. They wear little costumes with little fairy hats; one of them clearly has wings. The use of superimposition gives them a slightly otherworldly look (due, I think, to a little different lighting on them)."

Publicity for the film claimed the fairies were played by children who were so taken with the actress who played Patricia (Marie Doro) that they were unhappy when the cameras stopped rolling.

Variety was likewise taken with Miss Doro and the film, describing the latter as "dainty, winsome and full of charm." More to the point, the trade's 13 April 1917 number claimed that "there is nothing of the mysterious, gloomy, bloodthirsty or vampire sort of play in *Castles for Two* and its clean wit and picturization should carry it far as a program feature of a fine order."

Still, the critic for *Current Opinion* opined that the actress was pretty much the whole show: "But for Marie Doro this might be more of a castle for one than two…. Miss Doro makes up for what the cast lacks in animation" (19 May 1917). The reviewer did feel that the fairies gave the film a certain "eery [*sic*] charm," but was annoyed by the character of the "quasi hero," feeling that his meekness was "hardly true to the Irish spirit of independence."

Not surprisingly, most of the publicity for the film centered on Marie Doro, with mention of her elaborate gowns pulling up a close second. Thankfully, there *was* a word or two about director Frank Reicher and his ability to get the cow that chases Doro to perform on cue, and more on the cow whisperer can be found in our entry on *Unconquered*.

Marie Doro's notable stage career was by no means matched by her relatively short stay before the cameras. A beautiful actress with raven hair and big, soulful eyes, Doro captured the adulation of thousands, including the 16-year-old Charlie Chaplin, who appeared with her in a London production of *Sherlock Holmes* in 1905. Despite her marked femininity, one of her biggest hits found her donning male garb to play the title role in *Oliver Twist*, a part she repeated for the 1916 Lasky film version. After *Castles for Two*, Doro made one more film for Lasky (the still extant *Lost and Won*) and then left Hollywood for Europe, where she made films in England and France. When she returned to America in the mid–1920s, it wasn't to Hollywood or Broadway, but to a quiet life of intellectual pursuits, including studying religion at both Union Theological Seminary and Princeton. Doro died in 1956 and left $90,000 to the Actors Fund.

Publicity for the film invariably referred to Elliott Dexter as "the husband of Marie Doro." The two co-starred together on stage and screen, but Dexter later became a star in his own right (see *Forever*).

Jane Wolfe (who played one of Brian's sisters) may not have known much about fairies during production, but she would—as an acolyte of the notorious Aleister Crowley—later become well acquainted with "Magick." Some particulars on her career can be found in our chapter on *Unconquered*, while a bit on the writing team of Beatrice De Mille (Cecil's mom) and Leighton Osmun may be found in our essay on *The Devil Stone*.

— HN

Circe the Enchantress

Circe the Enchantress. Tiffany Productions/Metro-Goldwyn Distributing Co., 6 October 1924, 7 reels/6882 feet [LOST]

CAST: Mae Murray (*Circe, mythical goddess/Cecilie Brunne*); James Kirkwood (*Dr. Wesley Van Martyn*); Tom Ricketts (*Archibald Crumm*); Charles Girard (*Ballard "Bal" Barrett*); William Haines (*William Craig*); Lillian Langdon (*Sister Agatha*); Gene Cameron ("*Madame*" *Ducelle, modiste*)

CREDITS: *Producer and Director* Robert Z. Leonard; *Assistant Director* David Todd; *Adaptation* Douglas Doty; *Story* Vicente Blasco-Ibáñez; *Titles* Frederick Halton and Fanny Halton; *Cinematographer* Oliver T. Marsh; *Art Director* Cedric Gibbons

Synopsis courtesy of *Moving Picture World* (13 November 1924):

> Cecilie Brunne, convent-bred and gently reared, loses many positions through her endeavors to live up to the high standards of morality inculcated by the good sisters. On the death of her mother, left alone in the world, the struggle becomes more difficult and she turns against all men, luring them, Circe-like, to a sudden infatuation in which they give lavishly and get nothing in return. So skillfully does she dig into the golden prospects that she is able to maintain a handsome home on Long Island and a private lawyer to keep her enterprises safe, but barely within legal bounds. She becomes infatuated with her next door neighbor, a famous surgeon, whose grave disapproval of her life piques interest into real love which he repulses. Seeking forgetfulness of her repulses, she plunges more deeply into dissipation which she has hitherto encouraged but not shared and in a mad moment gambles away even her home. She has but one way to regain her possessions—to be as generous to the winner as he will be to her—and she scorns this overture. There is a tumultuous scene culminating in a drunken riot and Cecilie, making one last appeal to the physician, steals back to the old convent where presently the doctor finds her, just in time to save her from paralysis as the result of an automobile accident.

The only reason this Mae Murray vehicle is included herein is that there was apparently a prologue in which the famous clothes-horse-and-dancer played the sorceress who met her match in Ulysses. Supporting this are the credits which list Murray as playing both Cecilie Brunne and Circe the goddess; however, information about what actually happens in this sequence is scarce. There's a bit of studio PR printed in the *Appleton* [Wisconsin] *Post-Crescent* (12 February 1925) which confirms the prologue's existence, but offers little more: "This episode of the picture has been transferred to the screen in a very colorful way and is an interesting novelty as well as furnishing a foundation for the real story that follows."

Still, while all the reviews we consulted—*The New York Times*, *Variety*, *Moving Picture World*, and *Motion Picture News*—note the connection between the ancient Circe and the modern one, they say nothing about the prologue. Did it contain state-of-the-art special effects showing Circe's admirers double-exposed into swine? If so, one would have expected that would have been worth a line or two in the reviews. There are plenty of publicity stills showing Murray in dazzling Jazz-Age outfits, but none in any kind of ancient garb. All this would lead one to suspect that the sequence must have been very brief and may have consisted of no more than Murray dressed in an exotic harem outfit and batting her eyelashes at the camera, while a title card or two tells us the legend of Circe.

The general critical consensus about the film was that, while it was handsomely mounted, it was strictly for Mae Murray fans. *Variety*'s Sisk was apparently not one of the latter:

> The wild party scenes are very much like others and the bits wherein Mae gets hot feet and dances with a colored jazz band trumpeter are none too pleasant. Another bit shows Mae doing one of those cheesecloth dances in slow motion — with neither enough motion nor cheesecloth. At all times, Mae tries emoting — and gets a hand on her dancing [10 December 1924].

Someone who *did* admire Mae Murray's talents was author, Vicente Blasco-Ibáñez, who supposedly wrote *Circe* especially for the actress. It's hard to see much of the passion of *The Four Horsemen of the Apocalypse* in *Circe*'s trite story, but one element that does seem like typical Ibáñez is the linking of a mythological seductress to a real one: much the same thing happens in his *Mare Nostrum*, wherein Freya, the Mata Hari–like spy, is a kind of incarnation of the goddess Amphitrite.

— *HN*

The Crimson Cross

The Crimson Cross. Fanark Corp./Pioneer Film Corp. and States' Rights, 22 April 1921, 5 reels [LOST]

CAST: Van Dyke Brooks (*Richard Gromley*); Edward Langford (*Buddy Billings*); Marian Swayne (*Mary Wallace*); Eulalie Jensen (*Mrs. Otto Fischer*); William E. Hallman (*Otto Fischer*); Augustus Phillips (*Bill Billings*); Archie Clarke (*Jim Hawkins*).

CREDITS: *Presented by* D.J.H. Levett; *Producer and Director* George Everett; *Story and Scenario* N. Brewster Morse

This one's gonna be short and sweet as the theme — human behavior may be impacted by divine power, but not by other human behavior — is so dotty as to be unbelievable. From *The AFI Catalog*:

> Buddy Billings, adopted son of the dean of detectives, uses hypnotism to extract confessions. Richard Gromley, a welfare worker who has redeemed many prisoners through love and kindness, warns Buddy against the use of hypnotism. Buddy does not listen and uses his power to make Mrs. Otto Fischer, an anarchist, confess. Mr. Fischer, furious over his wife's treatment, reveals that Buddy has just convicted his own mother and father and proves it by the crimson cross on Buddy's arm. Fischer escapes, and Buddy becomes depressed to the point of almost committing suicide. Gromley, however, using a divine power, redeems Fischer, who reveals that Gromley is Buddy's real father and that he had stolen the baby to revenge Gromley's use of hypnotism to get a confession. Buddy becomes convinced of his past errors and all ends happily.

In most of the hypnotist-at-large pictures in this book, the Master of Mind Control has larceny in his heart when he hasn't lust in his… errr… wherever, and so this title represents a most novel turn: the Mesmerist as Crime Buster! (The concept — although not the hypnotist, himself — got additional work in 1924's *The Girl on the Stairs*; see entry in appendix) Any excitement those capital letters and exclamation point might have generated, though, was effectively stifled by that vague and poorly written précis, and — upon reflection — the whole thing seems a farrago to us. We doubt whether one could *ever* legally use confessions obtained under hypnosis to convict anybody of anything in the American Judicial System — Lionel Hutz isn't answering our phone calls— but, let's face it: lie detector transcriptions aren't admissible, "confessions" due to sodium pentothal aren't admissible, and the legal weight of information gained through torture seems to vacillate depending upon which TV news station one chooses to watch. Thus, you can see which we we're leaning.

But we're careful not to lean too far, because we've no idea either where we are or just where in the heck we're headed. Where — per the above synopsis— is the beef, anyhow? In the first sentence, we're talking about the use of hypnosis to "extract confessions" (and, therefore, put people away), while the second talks about "prisoners" (those who *have already* been put away) being reformed through love and kindness. Seems sort of sequential, no? Once you get the bad guys behind bars, you love 'em until their badness evaporates and then you let 'em go. The latter does not seem (to us) to be in any way, shape or form the diametric opposite of the former. Why, then, the fuss?

As to who can claim Buddy on his/her income tax, that's a puzzlement, too. Buddy uses his hypnotic prowess to find out that the woman in question is an anarchist, and a stool pigeon to find out that the anarchist is his mother. The screed is unclear from that point on. His mother lams it (surely a sign that her hypnotically-elicited confession was a mistake, no?) and —following some Love from Above — Mr. Fischer tells Gromley who tells Buddy that he (the anarchist's husband; is he also an anarchist?) isn't his (i.e., Buddy's) father, although he's currently married the woman he (Mr. Fischer) claims is his (i.e., Buddy's) mother), or maybe she's not. Buddy has a crimson cross on his arm, which could mean any number of things, including (a) it's a birthmark (proving what, exactly?), or (b) it's a tattoo (pointing to Buddy's biker-like childhood with Mrs. Anarchist), or (c) it's a long-forgotten sign that the remains of Mary Magdalene are buried under the Louvre. It must mean *something*, as the bloody picture took its title from it.

Anyhow, Gromley's divine power slips into overdrive just before Buddy — despondent over mom or dad or anarchy or his arm or something — does himself in. Fischer, now a font of truth and light, reveals that *Gromley* is Buddy's real dad and that he (Fischer) "had stolen the baby to revenge Gromley's use of hypnotism to get a confession." Well, this is the first time we've heard that Gromley is himself a reformed hypnotist — like father, like son; we should have seen this coming — but, we now have another problem. If Fischer is only now telling the truth about Buddy's father, how do we know he was earlier telling the truth about Buddy's mother? Gromley may have converted from hypnotist to brotherly lover at some point years back, but is The Light still in his eyes to the extent that he cannot recognize the woman who (supposedly) had birthed his own son?

Never has so little, written so poorly, screwed up so many so much.

The Crimson Cross was the Fanark Corporation's one shot at the big time, and the picture misfired badly. *The AFI Catalog* lists the epic as having been distributed by the Pioneer Film Corporation, and its having been filed for copyright at least gives a tad of credence to this claim. Nonetheless, the 22 April 1922 *Harrison's Reports* maintains that Fanark dropped the picture into the States' Rights system, and that claim — given the film's no-name indie birthright — also strikes a solid chord. Not that it makes any difference. *Cross* was produced and directed by someone named George Everett, and we couldn't find any evidence anywhere of his ever getting within meddling-distance of another movie — silent or otherwise. It's unlikely that Pioneer would have picked up this *Cross* purely on Everett's potential, and it's also doubtful that the story/scenario of N. Brewster Morse — who *would* contribute to a couple of decent 1930s features (like *The Perfect Specimen* with Errol Flynn and *The Lady with Red Hair* with Claude Rains and Miriam Hopkins) — had any of the Pioneer folks singing Hosannas.

Cast-wise, it's worth mentioning that the part of Bill Billings (?) was played by Augustus Phillips, the venerable actor who had enacted the role of Dr. Frankenstein in Edison's 1910 cinematic classic, which was Phillip's first film credit. *The Crimson Cross*, sadly, was Phillips' *last* film credit. In between, the Hoosier State character man could be seen in *Aladdin's Other Lamp* (1917) and there are few more lines on him there.

The Crimson Cross is long gone, and we've paid more attention to it in our coverage here than did any trade or fan publication during its initial release. Fanark's subsequent disappearance from the scene implies that the picture didn't have much of a following (*Harrison's*: "It may get by with the cheaper class of theatres"), but — again — we felt that the novelty of having a mesmerist castigated for operating on the side of the angels merited its inclusion in the appendix.

And, come on... a hypnotist named *Buddy*?

— *JTS*

Curlytop

Curlytop. Fox Film Corp./Fox Film Corp., 28 December 1924, 6 reels/ 5828 feet [LOST]

CAST: Shirley Mason (*Curlytop*); Wallace MacDonald (*Bill Branigan*); Warner Oland (*Shanghai Dan*); Diana Miller (*Bessie*); George Kuwa (*Wang Toy*); Ernest Adams (*Sproggs*); Nora Hayden (*Hilda*); La Verne Lindsay (*Annie*)

CREDITS: *Presented by* William Fox; *Director* Maurice Elvey; *Adaptation and Scenario* Fanny Hatton, Frederic Hatton; based on the short story, "Twelve Golden Curls," by Thomas Burke (collected in *More Limehouse Nights*, New York, c. 1921); *Cinematographer* Joseph Valentine

Shirley Temple cute-sied her way through a picture entitled *Curly Top* for Fox in 1935, but — despite the virtually identical title and the same production company — the similarities between that film and this one end there. Our feature has a darker scenario, a malevolent (and Oriental!) hypnotist — essayed by that great faux Oriental, Warner Oland — and a not-nearly-as-cute Shirley (Miss Mason), who was then in her mid-twenties, which meant that *her* "cuteness" lay, essentially, in the regard of post-pubescent males. Cuteness be damned; we feel that Miss

Mason's *Curlytop* is worth a look at this point only because of the genre-oriented avocation of Mr. Oland's character.

Had we paused to print the words *hypnotist* and *mesmerist* herein in Day-Glo ink, the pages of this book would (under proper lighting) more than resemble one of the psychedelic effects of, say, a Virgil Fox concert at the Fillmore East, back in the days when your authors were young and movies like *Curlytop* were the absolute last thing on their minds. This tome is positively rife with films that number eyebrow-heavy (often hirsute), glowering mind-controllers among the dramatis personae, there (usually) to ensure that the picture's requisite "boy-loses-girl" business would prove to be the most interesting third of the old formula. That's precisely where we have here — Mr. Oland has positioned himself between Miss Mason and her fella, Wallace MacDonald — and that's why *Curlytop* is in the Appendix.

The picture's plot was contrived by the Hattons — Fanny and Frederic — erstwhile playwrights, theatrical adaptors, novelists, scenarists, and storytellers. F & F were inseparable partners, professionally as well as personally (Frederic was Fanny's second shot at connubial bliss), and together they may be held responsible for over five dozen of the Silent Era's less memorable films, including genre offerings *The Shadow of the East* and *Circe, the Enchantress* (both 1924; see entries). In this instance, the Hattons were assigned to take the *Curlytop* source material — a short story by Thomas Burke, whose "The Chink and the Child" had earlier been the foundation for Griffith's *Broken Blossoms* — and arrange that it be captured truly and well on celluloid. The film's casual reception may be have been due to the fact that (1) not everything Mr. Burke wrote was on a par with "The Chink and the Child," (2) the Hattons' adaptive magic worked best on their own screeds, and/or (3) Maurice Elvey and William Fox were no D.W. Griffith and D.W. Griffith.

And herewith, courtesy of *The AFI Catalog*, is *Curlytop*:

> Curlytop, an attractive, naive girl who works in Sprogg's department store in the Limehouse district of London, meets Bill Branigan, a charming but feckless young man, and falls in love with him. Bill casts aside his sweetheart, Bessie, and, reformed by Curlytop's love, goes to Hammersmith to find work. In his absence, Bessie gets Curlytop drunk and cuts off her twelve golden curls. Shanghai Dan, a sinister, halfcaste Chinese hypnotist, then hires the shorn Curlytop as a waitress on his floating barge-restaurant. Bill returns; but not finding Curlytop, he renews his relationship with Bessie, until, by chance, he discovers the golden curls among Bessie's belongings. Forcing her to tell him where he can find his lost love, Bill arrives on the waterfront just as Dan's barge is sinking after a collision with a schooner. Bill rescues Curlytop from the water, but Dan, who at the time of the accident was below decks hypnotizing the unwilling girl in a locked cabin, is lost in the Thames.

Burke's short story, "Twelve Golden Curls," had been collected in 1920-21's *More Limehouse Nights*, the follow-up assemblage to *Limehouse Nights: Tales of Chinatown*, which had first been published in 1916. Just as title cards and a modicum of foreign-language ability could enable American studios to reach out economically to international audiences, so also could silent stock footage, nondescript standing sets and a touch of chutzpah on the part of the art director transform the most modest of back lots into London's most intriguing — and notorious— neighborhood. The cinema's capacity to metamorphose realism into romanticism had been evident even back in Méliès' day, of course, and the industry's genius at whipping up counter-realities, alien worlds, and alternate dimensions would expand exponentially in the ensuing years. Still, the most flamboyant examples of this mind-numbing ability to twist time and space per the whim of the film crew owe their credibility to these early, more mundane exercises wherein a world that was known not so much by experience as by reputation would, in the end, be replicated more by the power of suggestion than by its meticulous duplication.

Our piece on *The Eleventh Hour* offers a bit more insight into Miss Mason, and Wallace MacDonald — who played her hero— was another of those "five-tool" players (actor, director, producer, writer, miscellaneous crew member) who did lots of stuff, just not anything that might hold our interest. (Still, MacDonald's *name* may be found in the cast list in our essay on *Darkened Rooms*.) Other than his portrayal of *Curlytop*'s Shanghai Dan ("the most impressive on the screen," per *Variety*'s "Sisk"), just about every genre role Warner Oland played was a product of the Sound Era; still, we did manage an overview of the great Swedish Charlie Chan-impersonator in our coverage of *The Faker*. Speaking of Charlie Chan, let us also note the presence in *Curlytop* of George Kuwa, the cinema's first peripatetic Honolulu police lieutenant.

The *Curlytop* alumnus who went on to win kudos in conjunction with a few of Alfred Hitchcock's signature thrillers (*Saboteur*, *Shadow of a Doubt*, *Rope*) was cinematographer Joseph Valentine, who also lensed James Whale's *Remember Last Night?* and George Waggoner's *The Wolf Man*. New Yorker Valentine made his industry debut in 1924, so *Curlytop* was among the first films to bear his stamp, but he went on to receive five Oscar nominations— and cop the award for 1948's *Joan of Arc*— in a career that was cut short by his untimely death in May 1949; he was 48 years of age.

The most intriguing *Curlytop* contributor has to be director Maurice Elvey, a Briton whose fairly sparse American credits are bracketed by some prolific — and genre-heavy — English titles. Like Wallace MacDonald, Elvey wore a number of hats during his career (except for "miscellaneous"), but it was as helmsman that he won the most plaudits. It was he who directed Eille Norwood as the Great Consulting Detective in features like *The Hound of the Baskervilles* and in Stoll Pictures' fabled short series, *The Adventures of Sherlock Holmes;* he who directed Montagu Love in Stevenson's *The Suicide Club* in 1914; he who helmed the first film adaptation of *Mr. Wu* and both versions— silent and sound — of *The Wandering Jew*; he who directed *High Treason*, Gaumont's first talkie feature-length film; the first sound remake of Alfred Hitchcock's remarkable Jack the Ripper tale, *The Lodger*; Claude Rains and Fay Wray in *The Clairvoyant*; and *The Tunnel*— aka *Transatlantic Tunnel*— one of Britain's signal 1930s science-fiction blockbusters. Coincidentally, none of these titles is covered herein, but we do bow from the waist to Mr. Elvey, whose career spanned more than a half-century (active until 1958, he died in 1967). We can only hope that this most productive of British cinematic pioneers may soon receive the appreciative biographical treatment he deserves.

In the 22 April 1925 *Variety*, the aforementioned "Sisk" felt that "some liberties have been taken with the story as Burke wrote it, but as it stands it makes nice picture material, and in the hands of Director Elvey is finely handled." The colorfully named reviewer concluded that the picture was "entirely up to scratch," a somewhat apropos description for a mundane film set to play nowhere save for the neighborhood "itch."

Moving Picture World's Laurence Reid likewise felt that this was little more than a "program feature," but suggested that the exhibitor enliven things a bit by playing up the advantage of "girls having hair bobbed in view of what happens to Curlytop's tresses in picture."

You can't make up stuff like that.

— JTS

Darkened Rooms

Darkened Rooms. Paramount–Famous Lasky Corporation/ Paramount, 23 Nov 1929, no footage available (silent), 66 minutes/7 reels/6066 ft. (sound), UCLA and Library of Congress

CAST: Evelyn Brent (*Ellen*); Neil Hamilton (*Emory Jago*); Doris Hill (*Joyce Clayton*); David Newell (*Billy*); Gale Henry (*Madame Silvara*); Wallace MacDonald (*Bert Nelson*); Blanche Craig (*Mrs. Fogarty*); E.H. Calvert (*Mr. Clayton*); Sammy Bricker (*Sailor*)

CREDITS: *Director* Louis Gasnier; based on the eponymous novel by Philip Hamilton Gibbs; *Adaptation and Dialogue* Melville Baker, Patrick Kearney; *Titles* (silent version): Richard H. Digges, Jr.; *Sound* Movietone System; *Cinematographer* Archie J. Stout; *Film Editor* Frances Marsh; *Original Music* Karl Hajos

This Paramount production was one of those "Cusp o' Sound" features that were released both as a talkie and a silent. As it stands now, prints of the sound version are archived both at UCLA and The Library of Congress, but no copies of the silent release are known to exist. The following recap reflects the sound version; there is no apparent difference between this and the précis on its silent partner, à la *The AFI Catalog*.

Emory Jago runs a small boardwalk photo shop, but dreams of making it big as a spiritualist, having read up on the medium racket as well as on hypnotism. Madame Silvara, a crystal gazer in the adjoining arcade, comes to Jago to ask that he fake some "ghost" photos for her customers, who are willing to shell out $25 for a picture of their dear, departed relatives. Jago complies, but tells Silvara that he plans on becoming a spiritualist himself and asks that she send a rich sucker his way. She agrees in return for a piece of the action.

Ellen, an unemployed chorus girl, comes to the photographer in the hope of getting him to take some publicity stills of her, but she ends up fainting in his shop. Jago revives her, gives her a bite to eat, and asks her to come back that evening. He does try to hypnotize her, but she laughs it off and leaves. Realizing that her prospects are pretty grim — and sensing that Jago is basically a decent guy — she returns to his shop. He gives her a job as his assistant so he can spend more time boning up on how to be a phony medium. Ellen falls in love with Jago, who half-heartedly clings to the harebrained notion that she is under his hypnotic control.

Madame Silvara finally turns up a gullible mark for the fledgling spiritualist, a rich girl named Joyce Clayton. Although newly engaged, Joyce still pines for her erstwhile love, an aviator who was killed in a plane crash. Deciding to have Ellen pose as the medium — an idea the girl agrees to without much enthusiasm — the pair go off to Joyce's house, where they stage a séance. Joyce's current fiancé, Billy, is enraged at what he calls shenanigans, but

Joyce falls for it completely and makes for Jago's shop for an additional consultation with the spirit world. Billy also shows up, knocks Jago down, and promises him jail time for fraud and extortion if he tries to see Joyce again.

Billy succeeds in keeping Joyce away from Jago who continues to plot to lure her back and make a big score. Ellen tries to discourage him, but Jago won't give up and even begins to wonder whether there might not be some reality to the spirit world after all. He reads that Joyce is preparing to leave for Europe and is able to get her to agree to return to the shop for another séance. Fearing that Jago will end up in prison, Ellen comes up with a scheme of her own: She enlists her friend Bert, an out of work actor, to pose as the dead aviator during the séance. As Jago invokes the spirits for Joyce, he is shocked to hear the sound of an airplane (it's Ellen running a vacuum cleaner) and see a man in an aviator's outfit appear out of the dark (he's at the top of the stairs). The "spirit" warns Joyce that Jago is no good and she should run off to Europe and be happy with her new love. She leaves and the "ghost" vanishes (out a back door). Chastened by his encounter with a real spirit, Jago gives up the spook business. He settles down with Ellen and decides to stick to photographing tourists.

Announced from the get go as a "one hundred percent dialog picture," *Darkened Rooms* plays like a typical early talkie, with a static camera glumly surveying a few dreary indoor sets; most of the plot takes place in the photography shop. The sound effects connected with the séance shtick are rudimentary and some — table tapping, miscellaneous creepy noises—could

"That fool. He queered it for us~~~~~~~~"

1224·84

Emory Jago (Neil Hamilton) and Ellen (Evelyn Brent) begin to suspect that they're not very good at being up to no good in *Darkened Rooms*.

probably have been replicated by a creative accompanist. Others, like Uncle Edgar's spooky voice from beyond, would have suffered in the silent medium: squiggly writing on the title cards doesn't quite capture the effect. That having been said, *Darkened Rooms* doesn't do anything creative with sound effects and the séance sequences don't even attempt to be frightening. The appearance of the aviator's "ghost" could have been played for thrills if the audience hadn't been tipped off in advance to Ellen's scheme. As it is, the scene — like the entire film — is neither funny nor dramatic.

Tod Browning would have been our choice for director of this material, rather than Louis Gasnier. To be honest, *Darkened Rooms* probably wouldn't have been much better, but at least Browning would have injected a bit of the macabre into the séance scenes, captured something of the sleazy boardwalk atmosphere, and expressed a genuine empathy for the con artists. By 1929, Gasnier — a Parisian by birth — had already made his greatest genre splash by co-directing (with different partners) the sundry *Pauline* and *Elaine* and other serials that were popular in the mid–1910s. A rundown of his output following *The Perils of Pauline* reveals that the chapterplay and the woman's picture appear to have been his twin fortes, and *Darkened Rooms* was neither. Gasnier's most memorable outing, though, was the delirious *Reefer Madness* (1936), the definitive (if inadvertent) paean to marijuana that just *had* to be considered as bizarre in its initial release as it was deemed camp in each and every of its subsequent appearances.

As it stands, lovely Evelyn Brent's charm is all the film has going for it. A 1923 Wampus Baby Star, the petit actress was in films from 1915 (billed as "Betty Riggs," in Herbert Blaché's take on Robert Service's *The Shooting of Dan McGrew*). More on Miss Brent may be found in the chapter on *The Shadow of the East* (1924). The part of Jago was originally intended for William Powell, who had recently worked with Miss Brent in *Interference*, Paramount's first talkie. Between essaying Philo Vance for a brace of features and getting involved in the first sound version of *The Four Feathers*, Powell opted to pass, so the role fell to 30-year-old Neil Hamilton, who usually played likable stalwart types. Hamilton is miscast here as the scoundrel wannabe. The rest of the cast is adequate although Doris Hill makes Joyce seem like such an irritating simpleton that it's hard to know whether we should pity her or laugh at her.

The plot is so wafer-thin, dramatically, that it might have been reworked (for the better) as a Three Stooges short, with the resolution more appropriate for a *Honeymooners* episode. (Alice teaches Ralph a lesson when he tries to break into the medium racket....) We can't be sure, but we suspect that there was some sort of humor intended in the title: photography — darkroom — darkened rooms? Of course we never see a darkroom in the film, but there could be a halfhearted joke there somewhere.

We hacked our way through Philip Hamilton Gibbs' eponymous source novel, and we found that the book seems to straddle the fence as to whether there is something to the paranormal or not. Both Jago and Laveray (another medium who isn't in the film) believe that they have some abilities, but they embellish them with lots of hocus-pocus to bring in clients. The ending wants you to still see the door open on the issue. Unlike the film, which is rather straightforward in screening its oddities, the novel contains various random references to H.G. Wells, Darwin and religion, a dead fictional Indian (who channels a warning about the Yellow Menace!), *Orphans of the Storm*, the Lusitania, the world of science since the discovery of relativity, and so on. All mentions are made en passant and may have been thrown in to make the novel more contemporary.

Or to pad the page count.

— JTS/HN

The Dead Alive

The Dead Alive. Gaumont Co./Mutual Film Corp., Mutual Masterpieces De Luxe Edition, 17 February 1916, 5 reels, incomplete print at MOMA
CAST: Marguerite Courtot (*Jessie/Mary*); Sydney Mason (*William H. Stuyvesant*); Henry W. Pemberton ("*Doc*" *Ardini*); James Levering (*Old Jim*)
CREDITS: *Director* Henry J. Vernot; *Assistant Directors* Edwin Vail, Fred N. Schierbaum; *Scenario* Henry J. Vernot

Fake spiritualists and gimmicked séances abound in *The Dead Alive*, included herein (despite the depressing qualifiers just used) as we've no idea as to the atmosphere of the piece, the creativity with which the table sessions were approached, or the extent to which the mechanics of the scam enlivened (*Ouch!*) the picture.

The storyline (immediately below) is courtesy of the *Lima* [Ohio] *Time Democrat* (from the 28 April 1916) which obviously copied same from the press book. It's interesting to note how this précis varies from that of the copyright registration materials (which follow) in terms of the apparent importance of the ersatz supernatural:

> *The Dead Alive* is the story of twin sisters, Mary and Jessie, whose father is employed in a gambling house. Jessie, who works in a department store, is seen and admired by Stuyvesant, a young millionaire. When she learns that her father is a gambler and that he has just been arrested for murder, she declines Stuyvesant's offer of marriage, but finally consents. Her father is sent to the penitentiary for ten years, and Ardini, the proprietor of the gambling house, is sentenced to three months.
>
> When the latter is discharged, he forces Mary, a chorus girl, to secure money from Jessie by threatening to reveal Mary's stage career and her father's disgrace. Jessie is killed in an automobile accident and Ardini wins Stuyvesant's friendship, and tells him that it is possible, through spiritualistic powers, to see his dead wife. Mary is to pose as Jessie.
>
> Ardini's plan is to rob the safe in the millionaire's house during the scene [*sic*]. Mary warns Stuyvesant and Ardini is killed by an automatic device attached to the safe. Mary reveals the family secrets to Stuyvesant and the two are married.

The picture was also known as *His Wife's Double*, although it's not certain whether that was an alternate-release title, the film's re-release title, or the working title. What *is* certain is the unlikely nature of some of the story's elements: Jessie (apparently) almost denies herself the happiness of marriage because her father is a *rotter* and then is almost tossed under the marriage bus because her sister is a *chorus girl*. (Thank God for that fatal car accident!) Sister Mary is not above scamming her

still-grieving brother-in-law — playing on his sympathies so that he can be robbed — because a) she (Mary) is a *chorus girl*, and b) Stuyvesant's deceased wife's father is a *gambler* (and a *rotter*). As outlined above, the denouement sees her moving in on the newly-minted widower before her sister's body is even cold, and that doesn't say too much about old Stuyvesant, either, although bedding both twins is, we guess, about as close to cloning as 1916 sexual fantasy could get.

The copyright stuff (courtesy of *The AFI Catalog*) puts it all less repulsively:

> Jessie has married millionaire William Stuyvesant without telling him that she has a twin sister, Mary, or that her father, Old Jim, is in jail on a murder charge. When Jim's accomplice, "Doc" Ardini, is released, he tries to extract money from Jessie in exchange for silence about Jim, but hits on a better scheme to get rich after Jessie dies in a car crash. Taking Mary with him and posing as a psychic, he tells an inconsolable William that he can make Jessie materialize. Then, while William is preoccupied with his wife's "spirit," Doc starts cracking his safe. A contrite Mary quickly exposes the plot to William, however, and Doc dies when he triggers an automatic revolver that guards the safe. Finally, William and Mary decide to get married, and she tells him all the family secrets.

Well, *slightly* less repulsively…

Motography's hack (on the 26 February 1916) has a few plot details differently:

> The twin sisters come to the city to keep house for their father. He is employed by Doc Ardini, a crook and the owner of a gambling resort. The girls are not aware that their father is employed in such a place. Jessie finds work in a business office and Mary becomes an actress. Jessie attracts the attention of William Stuyvesant, a millionaire. His love for her is honest and he asks her to marry him. Before she gives her deferred answer she learns that her father has been arrested under an assumed name for murder. The father is convicted and sent to jail for ten years.
>
> This disgrace upon her family caused Jessie to refuse Stuyvesant, but he insists that she marry him. A few years later Ardini is in need of money. He has a hypnotic influence over Mary and he plans to be on friendly terms with Stuyvesant, who is now a widower, Jessie having met death at sea [?] He informs Stuyvesant that he can call back the spirit of his dead wife. When Mary comes upon the scene Stuyvesant is overcome and she tells her brother-in-law of the plot to rob him. Stuyvesant, later, proposes marriage to Mary, and she accepts.

In this version, the stigma of Mary's occupation — she's been promoted from chorine to legitimate thespian — bears no weight on her decision to help Ardini screw Stuyvesant, who is still reeling from the image of his wife in her Bentley, going down for the third time somewhere in the Briny Foam. Ardini no longer is represented as "posing as a psychic" or fudging "spiritualistic powers"; rather, he now "has a hypnotic power over Mary" which is not the same thing by a long shot. No matter which combination of particulars one chooses, though, the bottom line is that all three accounts imply some sort of supernaturally-oriented scene, and again, mes amis, that is why this chapter is here.

If it didn't actually get worse via additional press coverage, it didn't get any clearer: The 4 March 1916 edition of *The New York Dramatic Mirror* found *The Dead Alive* "quite an intensive picture" and spent a goodly portion of its prose mulling over Marguerite Courtot's playing opposite herself, as the twins.

Again, there was not a word there (or in the *Lima Time Demo-crat*, or the Library of Congress materials, or in *Motography*) about the visualization of the séance or epiphany or whatever in which we've the greatest interest (although the reviewer recalled that Jess "is drowned while yachting with her husband"). Nor was there any mention in the 19 February 1916 *Moving Picture World*, which did, at least, flesh out the character of the girls' apparently murderous, gambling-addled pater: "Old Jim loses his money in the gambling house of 'Doc' Ardini, an international crook. Feeling sorry for the old man, Ardini gives him a job. He will not write his motherless twin daughters that he is down and out…. Word comes that [their] father has killed a man when the police raided Ardini's resort."

The *MPW did* helpfully add that "Jessie is killed in an automobile accident," while the *Motion Picture News* (dated three days earlier) claimed "Jessie falls overboard from her husband's yacht and is drowned." All this leads us to believe that maybe researchers ought not to rely too heavily upon the perspicacity of 1910s-vintage film reviewers for the skinny on *anything*.

Thank God we saw the surviving reels (1–3) at the Museum of Modern Art and can elucidate.

The film begins with Old Jim losing all of his money in "Doc" Ardini's gambling house. Jim takes out a picture of his twin daughters, Jessie and Mary, and prepares to shoot himself. Doc has been looking over his shoulder at the photo and then stops Jim from shooting himself. He offers Jim a job in the gambling house. Since Doc is depicted as a pretty bad egg, it's not clear why he's being so nice to this washed-up loser, and his looking at the picture plays no further part in the story. Jim begins sending money to Jessie and Mary and they decide to come to the city to keep house for him. He hasn't told them how he makes his living.

Jessie gets a job in a department story. Mary becomes an actress but all we see of the theater is a pretty threadbare dressing-room; likewise the whole department store set is the little corner where Jessie works. (This is obviously a pretty low-budget production.) Jessie attracts the attention of millionaire William Stuyvesant. She plays hard to get but secretly dreams of becoming his wife. Stuyvesant falls in love with her.

One night a couple of customers at Doc's establishment get too rowdy and they are roughly shown the door; they complain to the police who then raid Doc's place. Jim begins struggling with one of the cops in an adjoining room when Doc comes in and, for no discernible reason, fatally stabs the policeman. Doc then exits by a secret passage elevator and Jim is arrested for the cop's murder; however, Doc gets arrested too and gets three months in jail. A newspaper article in a later scene informs us that Doc got his nickname from his medical studies and his hypnotic abilities.

Jim writes to Jessie that he's been arrested (under the alias O'Connor). Jessie writes to Stuyvesant that there's been a family tragedy and she cannot possibly marry him and she is quitting her job and moving. However, the persistent millionaire tracks her down, tells her he will never so much as ask about the family disgrace and practically drags her to a justice of the peace. After their marriage, Jessie finds that she really likes the good life.

Mary goes to visit her dad in prison. He gives her a letter from Jessie wherein she states she has never told her husband about her father or her twin sister. As Mary leaves the prison, she tears up the letter and drops it, but lo and behold, Doc has just been released and sees her drop the letter. (They don't make it clear whether he remembers her from the photo or if he just likes reading other people's mail.) He picks it up, pieces it together and follows Mary to the theater, where she gives him money to buy his silence but he's not satisfied for long. He returns and demands $100. Mary doesn't have the big bucks and heads for Jessie's house

("Mary goes on her loathsome errand" reads the title card). Doc follows her.

Jessie is furious with Mary and angrily berates her. (This is the one and only scene in which the two sisters are shown together facing the camera. In all the previous scenes, one of them always has her back to the camera. This obvious subterfuge becomes amusing after awhile. They're introduced in flashback at their mother's grave, both kneeling and wearing veils. One sister stands up and raises her veil — then a cutaway to the grave — then a shot of the one sister standing with her back to the camera, and then the kneeling sister raising her veil. And so on. It's surprising the director didn't stretch his obviously meager special-effects budget at least enough to show them *once* together earlier on.)

So, Jessie gives Mary the money and flounces off for a car ride with her sugar daddy. A little bit later, she and hubby are together on their yacht, "The Jessie." Jessie has been drinking heavily and, when Stuyvesant tries to grab the bottle she's holding, she struggles and falls off the yacht. Even though the water is calm and her husband and three crewman jump in to save her, she still drowns. Stuyvesant is distraught.

Meanwhile Mary is doing well at the theater and has received a raise. Doc shows up at her apartment, where he takes her by the hand and makes her look into his eyes. A few mesmerizing passes later, she is under his spell. Presumably this will absolves her for her part in Doc's subsequent fake ghost scheme. The footage ends here.

As we stated above, the better part of the ink spilled about this picture were devoted to Marguerite Courtot and her double role. The *NYDM*'s comments are quite representative: "[The picture's] main feature is the marvelous double exposures, some of which are the best that we have seen in pictures, especially those resulting from blocking out. Marguerite Courtot plays the dual role of the twin sister [*sic*] and the doubling is truly remarkable, although another girl who from the back appears exactly like Miss Courtot is often used in the scenes with her face from us."

Miss Courtot's next feature film — *Feathertop* (see essay in appendix), her only other genre credit — also had her playing a double role. Coincidentally, her director in that one was also Henry Vernot, and these two titles likewise comprised Mr. Vernot's entire genre canon. James Levering's name may be spotted in the cast list in our Appendix entry on *Feathertop*.

— *JTS/HN*

Destiny; or, the Soul of a Woman

Destiny; or, the Soul of a Woman. Rolfe Photoplays Inc./Metro Pictures Corp., 5 reels, 6 September 1915
CAST: Emily Stevens (*Mary Gadman*); George le Guerre (*The boy*); Walter Hitchcock (*The connoisseur*); Theodore Babcock (*Standish*); Fred Stone (*Parishioner*); Howard Truesdale (*Father Anthony*); Henry Bergman (*Avarice*); Effingham Pinto (*Lust*); Del DeLois (*Rum*); Florence Short (*Passion*); Vivian Oakland (*Beauty*); Ralph Austin (*The neighbor*); Edwin Martin (*Father Time, Death*); Baby Field (*Baby*)
CREDITS: *Director* Edwin Carewe; *Producer* B.A. Rolfe; *Scenario* Anthony Paul Kelly; based on the play, *Destiny*, by Anthony Paul Kelly (unpublished); *Cinematographer* W.C. Thompson
Metro re-issued the film in 1918. Publicity incorrectly stated it was Emily Stevens' first film.

Allegories have their place — but not here.

There will be no discussion herein of full-blown allegories like *Everywoman* (1919), or even of partial ones, like *The Slacker*

(1917), which bolsters its pro-war propaganda with embodiments of Columbia, Liberty and other patriotic symbols. Nonetheless, we must make exception when the macabre is introduced into the lesson: a whiff of hellfire, a cameo by His Satanic Majesty, or a walk-on by Weary Death himself guarantees a place in these pages, if only in the Appendix. This particular entry deals with suffering and redemption, but it has a couple of outré elements that nudge it into our purview.

Our synopsis comes from the 10 October 1915 *Delmarvia Star* (Wilmington, Delaware) and was likely taken from the press book.

> Standish, an artist, uses Mary, his wife, as a model for his painting of the Madonna. When the Connoisseur and the Parishioner come to inspect the picture, the Connoisseur recognizes in the model an old paramour and tells the husband so. The husband, while surprised, fails to disclose his identity and the visitors purchase the picture. After their departure the artist upbraids his wife. She tells him of her long acquaintance with the Connoisseur and how, for five years, she believed herself legally married to him. But the husband, unforgiving, turns her and her infant son out into the street.
>
> The mother leaves the baby on the steps of a monastery with a crucifix bearing her name. Then she enters a brothel known as the "House of Lost Souls."
>
> Seventeen years later the boy is a novice in the monastery. Before becoming a monk he wants to see the world. Father Anthony gives consent. The lad wanders into the "House of Lost Souls" of which his mother is now proprietress. There the boy meets Lust, Rum, Avarice, Passion and Beauty who tempt him in vain, but finally he succumbs to Beauty. The proprietress enters, leads the boy to her room and learns by the crucifix he wears that he is her son. She begs him to go back to the monastery. Then she renounces her companions forever and falls into a faint.
>
> Eight years later the boy is a parish priest. In a fearful storm, an old hag enters the church. It is the mother. She kneels at the altar and recognizes the picture of the Madonna for which she posed and her son by the crucifix he still wears. Unknowing, he gives her absolution as the Angel of Death descends and takes away her spirit.

Elsewhere we learn that the Angel of Death descends from the portrait of the Madonna to carry off the heroine's soul; this must have made for an eerie moment, especially if the double-exposure work was as striking as the reviews indicate.

While the symbolism is heavily Catholic, Greek mythology was not ignored. Per the 18 October 1915 issue of *The Independent*: "At each crisis in the play the movement is interrupted by a picture of the three Fates spinning the destinies of the characters and, at the last, Atropos is shown severing the thread of the woman's life with her shears." (With the Death Angel hovering and the Fates snipping away, the poor lady didn't stand a chance.)

We're not at all sure how Death was depicted, but we know that the role was played by Edwin Martin, who may have been billed elsewhere as Ed and/or Edward Martin, and who, therefore, *might* have featured into Houdini's *The Grim Game*. Or not. We're certain that Mr. Martin also played Father Time in the picture at hand, though. Emily Stevens (who receives more attention in *A Sleeping Memory*), the star of *Destiny*, actually posed for the picture of the Madonna that caused all the fuss in the film; said painting was done by a young artist named Paul Rosseau who subsequently gave the painting to Stevens. The

idea of an "unworthy" woman posing for a portrait of the Madonna also turns up in Frank Borzage's *Street Angel* (1928), which likewise sets its climax in a church, with the real model face to face with her idealized picture.

The film was a hit in religious circles and was even shown after mass in one New York City church (probably a first). Nevertheless, some exhibitors considered it adult fare and prohibited anyone under18 from attending.

Critics were enthusiastic about *Destiny*, particularly with respect to the direction of Edwin Carewe (see entry, *The Greatest Power*) and the camerawork. "F" of *The New York Dramatic Mirror* wrote (in the 9 September 1915 issue) that the preview audience applauded frequently during the film and was very moved:

> If instinctive feelings engendered by a series of touching effects that directoral camerawork bring about be the gauge we should say that this offering must have a moist time ahead of it. For it might be as well to state here that it is not of the "and they clinched at the end type".... The arrangement of the subtitles, the wording and consensus of camera strategy is a novelty not to be passed over in silence. Striking it surely is.

The critic for *The Independent* called the film "a happy blend of the conventional melodrama with is neatly dovetailed plot and the symbolic morality play of the *Everywoman* type." The reviewer was also impressed by the climatic storm sequence: "The finest scenic effect is the thunderstorm in which the performance for once oversteps the limits of the screen and the landscape setting of the stage is illuminated by flashes of lightning."

Harvey Thew (in the 4 September 1915 *Motion Picture News*) praised the film as "real art" with "magnificent settings, scenery and photography." He also joined in the accolades for director Carewe: "The director who can look through his company and see his public is predestined to success. This is just what Edwin Carewe appears to have done in this case."

Edwin Carewe was born Jay Fox, but early in his stage career decided that his real name wasn't distinguished enough (he was part Chickasaw Indian), so he borrowed "Edwin" from his favorite actor, Edwin Booth, and took "Carewe" from a stage play; his fortunes as an actor subsequently improved. Carewe spent some 13 years on the stage before turning to film in 1912. After a few years as a leading man at Lubin, Carewe switched to directing for Rolfe Photoplays, and became successful enough to start his own production company in 1920.

In 1925, while on a trip to Mexico as part of the Bert Lytell/Claire Windsor wedding party, Carewe married his fiancée, actress Mary Akin. The Carewes then met the beautiful Dolores del Río and her husband Jaime, a rich man who dreamed of writing movies. Carewe thought Dolores could be a female Rudolph Valentino and persuaded the del Ríos to come to Hollywood. While Señor del Río's aspirations came to naught, Dolores did become a star under Carewe's tutelage, but both she and the director ended up in divorce court; reputedly, only a substantial bribe kept Mary Akin Carewe from naming Dolores as a correspondent. Del Río starred for Carewe in *Resurrection* (1927) and *Ramona* (1928); both were hugely successful and were said to have netted Carewe over a half-million dollars.

The 1930s proved disastrous for Carewe. Not only did he become estranged from del Río (who subsequently called him "my worst enemy"), but an opera star — who claimed Carewe had promised her a film career — sued the director for breach of contract and won a $75,000 settlement. Worse yet, the beleaguered director was arrested for tax evasion, as the government charged that he owed Uncle Sam over $100,000; in 1933, Carewe would declare bankruptcy. When his 1931 sound version of *Resurrection* was dismissed as a fiasco and various proposed Hollywood projects failed to materialize, Carewe — perhaps remembering *Destiny*'s showing in a church — declared that he was going to reach the "25 million people who never attend the movies" by making films that would be played instead in lecture halls, schools and churches. (His thinking was that such films would actually be outside the jurisdiction of the Hays Office.) In spite of many ambitious proposals per this plan (including a life of Christ to be shot in the Holy Land), he directed only one other film, the 1934 *Are We Civilized?*, which takes place in a mythical country clearly meant to be Nazi Germany and features cameos from every great man in history from Buddha to George Washington). Edwin Carewe died of heart trouble six years later.

Destiny's screenplay was written by Anthony Paul Kelly, who based it on his unproduced play. Kelly would score a big hit on Broadway in 1918 with the spy melodrama *Three Faces East*, which would be filmed three times, the last version being *British Intelligence* with Boris Karloff. Kelly tried again with *The Phantom Legion*, in which the ghosts of slain veterans fight alongside their living counterparts; it flopped and was thus a great financial blow to Kelly, who had also produced it. Kelly also wrote a number of scenarios worth mentioning: the bizarre *Birth of a Race* (1918); the 1916 version of *The Witching Hour* (see entry); the Edmund Lowe/Bela Lugosi tribute to the U.S. Navy, *The Silent Command* (1923); and *Way Down East* for D.W. Griffith. In 1932 Kelly, beset by ill health, asphyxiated himself in a New York hotel room. A copy of *Three Faces East* was by his side.

— *HN*

The Devil's Bondwoman

The Devil's Bondwoman. Universal Film Mfg. Co./Universal, Red Feather Photoplays, 20 November 1916, 5 reels [LOST]

CAST: Dorothy Davenport (*Beverly Hope*); Emory Johnson (*Mason Van Horton*); Richard Morris (*Prince Vandloup*); Adele Farrington (*Daria Manners*); William Canfield (*John Manners*); Miriam Shelby (*Aunt Barbara*)

CREDITS: *Director* Lloyd B. Carleton; *Prologue written by* Fred Myton; *Scenario* Maie Harvey; based on an original story by Willis Woods (the pen name of the team, F. McGrew Willis and Walter Woods). There is a discrepancy over writing credits between the extant, published critical commentary and the copyright description documents.

Working Title: *The Devil's Die*

The synopsis/thank-you note this time goes to the 25 November 1916 *Moving Picture World*.

> Mason Van Horton, a young millionaire in good society, owns the Van Horton bank in the tenement district, but he has so little care for the business that the bank — and the hundreds of poor

workers who have entrusted their hard earned savings to it — is on the verge of ruin.

> John Manners is responsible for this condition of affairs, for he has business ability and has taken advantage of Mason at every turn. His wife, Doria, has social aspirations and is a typical vampire. She does her best to ensnare Mason and he is easily charmed until he meets Beverly Hope, who has come to visit her Aunt Barbara.

> Doria is infatuated with Prince Vandloup. One night, after a party in the Manners' home, Mason goes to Doria's apartment, where she is waiting to receive him. But — as he starts towards her — the face of Beverly comes before him, and he rushes madly from the room, passing Manners on his way out. Doria tells her husband that Mason has forced his way to her room and that she had to fight for her honor. Manners is angry enough to kill Mason, but she begs him to ruin him instead.

> Manners does not take long to accomplish this feat. Beverly promises to marry Mason and to help him in every way. Doria gives a reception to which she invites Mason; he goes, intending to have a talk with Manners. One of the women whose earnings have been lost by the bank appears, but Doria orders her from the house. Instead, the woman slips unnoticed into Doria's room and stabs herself. Later, while all the guests are assembled at dinner, Doria is startled by a drop of blood which falls from the ceiling, thus causing much consternation.

> Mason talks with Manners in the library, and the two are advised of what has happened. Manners goes to the woman upstairs and, as he is returning to the library, he overhears his wife and the Prince making love. He denounces her and tells the astonished guests that *she* is the one who is really responsible for the failure of the bank and the ruination of Mason. The Prince, after trying to besmirch the reputation of Beverly by reporting that he saw her coming from Mason's apartment late at night, takes Doria away with him. His form changes to that of the Devil, and she is knows that she is in his power.

Sounds like this was one heck of a dinner party. One supposes the only thing that might cause more consternation than blood dripping from the ceiling and into one's soup would be seeing one's lover transformed into Satan himself. Interesting that Doria faces damnation for being a vamp and social climber, but her husband merits a "Get-out-of-hell-free card" even though his sharp business practices and desire for revenge have ruined hundreds of innocent people.

Bondwoman contained a prologue set in hell, as well as the occasional flash of the inferno, but we've been unable to find more specifics. Peter Milne, in the 25 November 1916 *Motion Picture News*, felt that such scenes had little to do with the story and the picture would have been better without them. Still, such touches were enough to sell the film as an allegory, although its contrived, melodramatic plot doesn't really yield any moral other than "bad things happen to bad people."

Even had the hell footage been excised, it's not likely Milne would have liked the film a whole lot better:

> The main plot is of a commonplace sort and is not founded on basically convincing situations.... Lloyd B. Carleton directed the production and his direction falls quite far below the standard he usually maintains. The double exposures and dissolves are not well done. The exteriors were chosen with little care and the interiors are not appropriate.

Prior to making it in the movies, Adele Farrington (Daria) had been a burlesque- and vaudeville-actress and singer. She had scored a hit as a destroyer of men in the 1912 stage production of *A Fool There Was*; however, when the play was adapted for film in 1915, it was Theda Bara who did the destroying. That may very well have been for the best if Milne's assessment of Farrington's performance in *The Devil's Bondwoman*—"Adele Farrington is an unconvincing vampire and over-acts so strenuously that one can never take her appearances seriously"— was credible in the least.

Dorothy Davenport (Beverly) was the most famous name in the film. She would soon be abandoning her film career to devote herself to her husband, movie idol Wallace Reid, and their child. After Reid's tragic death from drug addiction, she returned to film, but mostly to direct and write stories that were focused on social problems.   — HN

The Devil's Confession

The Devil's Confession. Circle Film Attractions/Circle Film Attractions, 5 March 1921, 5 reels [LOST]
  CAST: Frank Williams (*Bob Perry*); Lillian Ward (*Kate Perry*); Mary Eberle (*Ma Perry*); Louise Lee (*Rose Hill*); Harold Foshay (*Neil Drake*)
  CREDITS: *Director* John S. Lopez; *Cinematographer* Frank Perugini

Since, as Stan Laurel used to say, honesty is the best politics, let us admit up front that the Devil plays no part in this indie feature, but that there *is* some messing about with a Ouija board. (*The AFI Catalog* lists this one under the heading, *mental telepathy*, but — as with the film itself — we can't see it.)

Speaking of *The AFI Catalog*, here is its plot précis:

> Bob Perry loses his temper and threatens to kill a scandalmonger who is spreading gossip about the affections paid by Neil Drake to Bob's girl, Rose Hill. When the man is found dead, Bob is arrested and convicted for murder while the actual killer, Neil Drake, goes free. The sentence of death is about to be executed when two children find Drake's cap in a nearby brook. Kate, Bob's sister, feeling certain that Drake is the murderer, entices him to use a Ouija board and forces a confession through its revelations. She rushes the written confession to the governor, who at the last minute pardons Bob.

Before going any further, allow us to point out that Rose Hill is a neighborhood in the Bronx that is occupied by Fordham University. Allow us also a moment to cogitate as to how a woman "entices" a man to use a Ouija board....

Circle Film Attractions— the corporate sire to *The Devil's Confession*— neither produced nor released any other movie; hence, with this film, Circle Film Attractions came full circle.... Where could it go from there? (An online source claims that the picture was distributed via the States Rights system, and while logic impels us to go along quietly with this statement— no advertisements and no critiques are pretty much the negative hallmarks of States' Rights products— we could find no corroboration; all other information about CFA supports the assertion that it was both production company and distribution arm for one picture and one picture only: this one.

Bob Perry was played by Frank Williams, and we're not at all sure how much further we can take that one. What with "Frank Williams" being a fairly commonplace set of nomenclature, we must consider the possibility that there were *two* Frank Williams: the man who acted in *The Devil's Confession*, and the man who— using the middle initial "D" to differentiate himself from our guy— photographed both *Queen of the Sea* (1918) and *The*

Devil's Claim (1920; see entries for the pair) and was responsible for the process shots in 1932's *Murders in the Rue Morgue*. There is also the off-chance that Frank, the *Confession* thesp, had always been a photography nut at heart and that his middle initial debuted onscreen to herald his making new industry inroads behind the camera. We simply do not know.

Kate Perry, the enticing Ouija board wielder, was impersonated by Lillian Ward, an actress of brief tenure whose most memorable film —1932's *A Woman Commands*—featured genre favorites Basil Rathbone, Roland Young, Reginald Owen, Roy Barcroft, and Frank Reicher. *Command*s marked Miss Ward's last film appearance (of four); it was an uncredited bit. Louise Lee (Rose Hill) appeared in *six* movies, in toto, while the production's Grand Old Man — Harold Foshay (Neil Drake, the heavy)— had been Edward Utterson to Sheldon Lewis's *Dr. Jekyll and Mr. Hyde* the year before *Confession* was released. Mr. Fo(r)shay's other two-dozen Silent Era appearances were of more mundane theme, although commentary on 1920's *Voices* is to be found in our appendix, and 1916's *The Tarantula*— which is *not* discussed herein — may have had its moments.

John S. Lopez is on record as having written two stories for the screen —*The Sins of the Children* (1918) and *Out of the Past* (1927)— both "typical" Silent Era mellers, with the latter evincing no advancement whatsoever of style and/or substance over the former. Besides *Confession*, Lopez directed his *Sins of the Children* and a 1922 indie comedy featuring Harold Foshay, *Why Not Marry?* Cinematographer Frank Perugini likewise came and went without cashing a paycheck drawn on a major studio. Besides *Confession*, he photographed 1923 *The Valley of Lost Souls*, a promisingly-titled five-reeler that delivered cowpokes (Canadian Mounties, actually) investigating killings that involved ghosts the same way that Old West ghost towns involved ghosts. Mr. Perugini also directed *The Scar of Shame*— a convoluted tale of drunken stepfathers and gals who deserve better —for the Colored Players Film Corporation in 1927; he then disappeared from the scene.

That may have been a good career move.

                                — JTS

The Empire of Diamonds

The Empire of Diamonds. Léonce Perret Productions/Pathé Exchange, Inc., 19 December 1920, 6 reels, Library of Congress (unviewable), Cinémathèque Française, Lobster Films
  CAST: Robert Elliott (*Matthew Versigny*); Lucy Fox (*Marguerite Versigny*); Henry G. Sell (*Paul Bernac*); Leon Mathot (*Arthur Graves*); Jacques Volnys (*Trazi d'Aricola*); L. Morias (*Andre Zarnoff*); M. Mailly (*Baron de Lambri*); Ruth Hunter (*Esther Taylor*)
  CREDITS: *Director* Léonce Perret; *Scenario* Léonce Perret; based on the novel *Le empire du diamante*, by Valentin Mandelstamm (Paris, 1914).

Dreams of striking it rich via the manufacturing (rather than the mining) of precious substances goes back centuries. As chemistry gradually replaced alchemy, the true nature of matter became clearer, and thus— by the last couple of decades of the 1800s— men like James Ballantyne Hannay and Ferdinand Frédéric Henri Moissan were reporting breakthroughs in (for example) transforming simple carbon into potentially valuable diamonds. Such experimentation continued into the early 20th century.

Where science would tread, science fiction would usually follow. In 1909, Jacques Futrelle (see *Elusive Isabel*) penned *The Diamond Master*, in which he explored the "soft science" aspect of the sociological impact on a global market flooded with synthetic jewels. The first verifiable adaptation of Futrelle's novel came in 1914 with *The Diamond-Maker* (not to be confused with similarly-themed shorts, like 1909's *A Maker of Diamonds* or 1913's *The Diamond Makers*). A later pair of Universal serials— *The Diamond Queen* (1921) and *The Diamond Master* (1929)— was drawn along the same lines. In the midst of this cycle of interest lay our picture, *The Empire of Diamonds*, which had its antecedents in the 1914 novel, *L'Empire du diamant*, by Valentin Mandelstamm.

The following synopsis is taken from the 25 December 1920 *Moving Picture World* and may be considered a Christmas present from reviewer, Robert C. McElravy:

> Matthew Versigny … is head of an American diamond house which has been imposed upon, with others, by the distributors of fake stones, so cleverly made as to almost defy detection. Versigny suspects the gems come from Paris and he arranges to go there, taking his sister, Marguerite, with him. In Paris they join forces with Paul Bernac, a special agent of the French Secret Service. Versigny also takes into his confidence Andre Zarnoff, who invented the formula from which the false stones were made.
>
> The trail brings them into contact with Arthur Graves, a dealer in fake diamonds on a large scale, who is assisted by Trazi d'Aricola. At Monte Carlo Graves also meets Baron de Lambri, who is angry with Versigny, having been discharged from his service for reasons. The Baron enters Graves' employ.
>
> In the course of exciting events both Versigny and Zarnoff are made prisoners. The formula passes between several hands and both Graves and the Baron are murdered. Bernac finally comes to grips with Trazi, the third villain, and brings him to justice. Versigny and Zarnoff are released and Bernac weds the former's sister.

Even when taking this *MPW* précis together with the other documents available to us, it's still unclear whether the word "fake" implies that Zarnoff's formula created: (a) synthetic diamonds with all of the properties of natural diamonds found in nature, or (b) ersatz diamonds capable of fooling experts.

In any case, the *Motion Picture News'* Frank Leonard fawned over the production (also on Christmas day, 1920), but waxed indifferent to the storyline:

> From a production stand point *The Empire of Diamonds* is one of the best pictures we have ever seen. Excluding the story, which is of the average mystery variety, the feature is a combination of wonderful shots which begin in London, take in Paris and its suburbs and the jump to Monte Carlo.
>
> The production is another illustration of the artistry which is possessed by French directors in building beautiful backgrounds for their pictures, and Léonce Perret is no exception to the rule.

"Average mystery variety" seems to push "fake" over to the "fraudulent" side of the fence, but more head-scratching resulted from *MPN*'s questioning whether American viewers would be interested in a movie story of the "French variety"[?] An earlier *Harrison's Reports* (on the 11 December 1920) had pronounced the *filming techniques* were New World, as "Part of it has been produced in America, and most of it in France; but

with American methods," while agreeing with other commentaries that "The photography is sharp; the exteriors, artistic; the locations, well chosen."

The Christmas edition of *Exhibitor's Trade Review* made it three-for-three on the picture's technical aspects and simultaneously applauded the cast:

> Léonce Perret has made a beautiful picture out of the crook story *The Empire of Diamonds*. The excellent acting and the fact that almost the entire picture has been filmed abroad, with no faked foreign locations, help to cover the few improbabilities of the plot…. The interiors are well filmed and well chosen and the exteriors beautiful. There are some excellent long shots and very effective close-ups. The lighting is good throughout.

MPW's McElravy also favored both aspects: "There are many good thrills in this, some magnificent scenic snatches such as are not often pictured, and some superior acting of its type. As a high-class melodrama this stands out strongly."

Finally, *Photoplay* (March 1921)— never a journal big on in-depth critiques— noted tersely that *Empire* had "all the elements of an educational [film]." Including, we assume, melodrama.

— SJ

The Eternal Mother

The Eternal Mother. Tribune Productions, Inc./United Picture Theatres of America, Inc., 18 April 1920, 5 reels [LOST]

CAST: (per *Motion Picture News*): Florence Reed (*Laura West, a society girl*); Lionel Atwill (*Stephen Rhodes, the adventurer*); Gareth Hughes (*William Marsden*); Jere Austin (*Howard Hollister*); Margaret Seddon (*Mrs. Marsden*); with (per *The AFI Catalog*) Robert Broderick

CREDITS: (per *The AFI Catalog*): *Director* William Davis; *Producer* A.J. Bimberg; *Writer*: John K. Holbrook

Indiscretion (reissue title). A.J. Bimberg/Pioneer Film Corp., 1921, 6 reels— Reel four exists at the UCLA Film and Television Archive, but it's not available for viewing.

> Shortly before her marriage to Howard Hollister, socialite Laura West meets Stephen Rhodes, recently returned from India, who introduces her to the cult of the goddess, Gaia, the personification of Nature, the Eternal Mother. Though Laura is fascinated, she shies away from Rhodes' efforts to initiate her and make her the earthly personification of Gaia. Laura and Howard marry, and they spend happy newlywed days, but Laura's continued interest in Gaia and frequent daydreams of herself leading the cult upset Howard, who angrily urges Laura to return to reality and her work in the slums. Falling asleep after their quarrel, Laura dreams she becomes queen of the cult — richly adorned and ardently worshiped. She has a child by Rhodes, but comes to realize that Rhodes' purpose is his own sensual gratification. Laura abandons the baby and leaves the cult, but Rhodes threatens to kill the child unless she returns. Laura wakes up screaming. Howard comforts Laura who assures him that her only desires are motherhood and his love [*The AFI Catalog*].

While India may have many mother-oriented cults and female deities, Gaia is actually an ancient Greek goddess. This theological distinction is irrelevant because, as the *Harrison's Reports* reviewer astutely points out, "This Gaia philosophy is really nothing less than the doctrine of free love, but it is handled so delicately that it should get by without offending" (15 November 1921).

Of primary interest to readers here is probably not the goddess— or even the doctrine of free love — but rather the presence of horror great, Lionel Atwill, in one of his few silent film appearances. It is only natural for fans to assume that Atwill played Rhodes the cult leader, but the film's muddled history has left contradictory credits.

The Eternal Mother was the last of a series of films that Broadway superstar Florence Reed (see *The Cowardly Way*) made for Tribune Productions, a low-budget, New York–based film company that distributed its films through United Picture Theaters of America. After the release of *The Eternal Mother* United Picture went belly up, and the film was purchased by Pioneer Film Corp., who withdrew it from circulation and then reissued it — under the far less exotic title, *Indiscretion*— in 1921. (Example of typical non-exotic publicity puff: "Does the unbending law of conventionality permit a wife to be indiscreet even under the most trying circumstances?" Exciting, no?) It's not clear how Pioneer altered the film (perhaps they added some outtakes), but available information has *Indiscretion* at *six* reels (*The Eternal Mother* is documented at five), and *The AFI Catalog* has two entirely separate listings for the two "versions."

Per the listing for *Indiscretion*, Atwill played the husband, and Rhodes was portrayed by Gareth Hughes (see *Eyes of Youth*, 1919). The baby-faced Hughes, a specialist in juvenile roles, not only would be an unlikely high priest (imagine Mickey Rooney in his Andy Hardy days as Hjalmar Poelzig in *The Black Cat*), but also too young to have played Florence Reed's husband. Laurence Reid, in his review of *Indiscretion* for *Motion Picture News* (undated), lists Atwill as Rhodes and — muddling things further — has the husband played by Jere Austin, with the much-better-known Hughes in the supporting role of William Marsden.

Lionel Atwill, who was becoming well known on the American stage, had already played cads not unlike Rhodes in a couple of films, *Eve's Daughter* (1918) and *The Marriage Price* (1919), so it's not unreasonable to suppose he played the cult leader. While the word "cult" conjures images of black-robed devotees and unspeakable rites, *The Eternal Mother* likely featured no such exotica, but focused on a rather traditional, romantic triangle between a nice, normal guy, a glib pseudo-intellectual on the make, and the destined-to-be-disillusioned girl who preferred mystery to the mundane. Laurence Reid labeled the film "a woman's picture" and, in language not likely to make the cut today, wrote: "The verisimilitude is emphasized because it is an inherent weakness of women to give their undivided attention to a resourceful figure who has become steeped in the gewgaws of Oriental philosophy and hokum."

An unsettling ad for *The Eternal Mother* pictures Florence Reed in the foreground, while behind her is a drawing of the Grim Reaper holding a baby. It's likely that the ad was far creepier than anything to be found in the film.

— *HN*

Feathertop

Feathertop. Gaumont Co./Mutual Film Corp., Mutual Masterpieces De Luxe Edition, 17 April 1916, 5 reels [LOST]

CAST: Marguerite Courtot (*Elsie Green/Polly Goodkin*); James Levering (*Tom Green*); Gerald Griffin (*Captain Dick Green*); Mathilde Baring (*Sarah*); Charles Graham (*Henry Green*); John Reinhard (*Percy Morleigh/Feathertop*); Sidney Mason (*Ward Roberts*)
CREDITS: *Director* Henry Vernot; *Scenario* Paul M. Bryan; based on the eponymous short story by Nathaniel Hawthorne in *The International Monthly Magazine* (1 February and 1 March 1852)

The following synopsis has been crafted from *Moving Picture World* (5 April 1916) and other contemporary reviews.

The Green brothers have taken different courses in life: Tom, the eldest and a lover of flowers, has become an owner of nurseries and the father of a lovely girl, Elsie. Henry, the youngest, won a fortune but not contentment. Dick found happiness in a South Sea home and a good wife, Sarah.

Henry decides to pay Tom a visit, taking with him Grace Lawton, a society girl and Percy Morleigh, an affected fop of to-day. The two young people with their fashionable clothes and affected manners make a deep impression upon simple-hearted Elsie.

Shortly after the visit, Elsie goes to the city to spend time with Uncle Henry. Here she becomes completely inoculated with the froth and glitter of the social world and develops into an ultra-society butterfly. In the meantime, Percy has made a wager that he will kiss Elsie. The knowledge of what Elsie has changed into breaks her father's heart, and he dies.

After her father's death, Elsie becomes discontented with the simple life among the flowers. She also decides she cannot marry Ward Roberts, who had been in charge of the nurseries for her father. She returns to reside with her Uncle Henry and is again completely carried away with the glitter and glamour of society. Uncle Henry, who had grown disgusted with Elsie's behavior, dies and leaves his millions to his brother Dick on condition that he and his wife Sarah come to New York to live. Elsie has been willed only a copy of Nathaniel Hawthorne's "Feathertop."

Dick and Sarah are not happy in their new environment. Dick insists that Elsie read "Feathertop." She does and in her mind's eye she sees in the man of straw and pumpkin-head, the social fop, Percy. Later she learns of his wager to kiss her and is completely disgusted. She leaves with Dick and Sarah on a trip on their boat. There, one of the crewmen pulls off a phony beard and reveals himself as Uncle Henry; the millionaire had faked his death to teach his niece a lesson and to find a simpler life for himself. Ward is also on the boat, and the girl once more returns to the protection of a true man. Presumably, Elsie's father stays dead.

Feathertop enshrines a theme much beloved by Silent Era writers: the superiority of simple country (or seagoing) life to the corruption of the big, bad city ("Just about the same old stuff that was in vogue for thrills at the time the Civil War started," groaned *Variety*'s Fred). It also features a familiar character rarely encountered outside of the movies: the rich uncle/father/grandfather who stages his own death to bring an erring relative back onto the right path.

None of this, of course, has much to do with Hawthorne's satire about a scarecrow animated by magic and sent into Puritan society where his fancy manners and flowery phrases awe everyone he meets. *Feathertop* is included here only because Hawthorne's original story is briefly depicted on the screen:

The scenes that have been interpolated from *Feathertop* have been very nicely done [*Moving Picture World*, 5 April 1916].
The only pictorial allusion made to Hawthorne's original story is a brief picturization and this is most beautifully done. It is exceedingly picturesque and forms the basic theme of the whole plot [*The New York Dramatic Mirror*, 22 April 1916].
The few feet of advance announcement added to the last Gaumont release, showed Miss Marguerite (Courtot — playing Elsie)

in the costume of the Louis Fifteenth period much more attractively than she was given a chance to appear in the few short scenes from Mr. Hawthorne's book [*Motion Picture News*, 29 April 16].

Fred (of *Variety*) seems to have missed the scenes entirely:

> The producers and the publicity department of the Mutual had no idea as to what the picture was going to be, judging from the prepared-in-advance story and billing matter that was handed out. The mimeograph "copy" stated that Marguerite Courtot was to play a dual role. If she did the other half of the role, it must have been cut and thrown into the discard before the picture came into the projection room for there was only one role that Miss Courtot displayed on the screen. [14 April 1916].

Whether the film was praised or roasted, most reviewers agreed that its central asset was the lovely Miss Courtot, then at the height of her popularity. We will encounter her again (along with *Feathertop*'s director Henry Vernot) in *The Dead Alive* (1916). One of her last films was *The Cradle Buster* (1922) in which she played opposite Glenn Hunter who the following year would play Feathertop in *Puritan Passions* (see entry).

— HN

Fig Leaves

Fig Leaves. Fox Film Corp./Fox Film Corp., 22 August 1926, 7 reels/ 6498 feet, B&W with Technicolor sequence

CAST: George O'Brien (*Adam Smith*); Olive Borden (*Eve Smith*); Phyllis Haver (*Alice Atkins*); Andre de Beranger (*Josef Andre*); William Austin (*Andre's assistant*); Heinie Conklin (*Eddie McSwiggin*); Eulalie Jensen (*Madame Griswald*)

CREDITS: *Director* Howard Hawks; *Scenario* Hope Loring and Louis D. Lighton; *Story* Howard Hawks; *Titles* Malcolm Stuart Boylan; *Cinematographer* Joe August; *Gowns* Adrian; *Sets* William Cameron Menzies and William Darling; *Editor* Rose Smith

Our synopsis is based on our viewing of the film:

> In a prologue set in the Garden of Eden, Eve complains to Adam that she has nothing to wear. They argue and Adam leaves for work in a huff. The serpent promptly enters to encourage Eve's unhappiness.
>
> In the modern world, Eve, married to plumber Adam Smith, is likewise discontent with her lack of fine clothes. Alice, her neighbor, urges her to ignore Adam's reluctance to buy her luxuries. However, Alice is after Adam for herself and works to undermine the relationship between husband and wife. Adam is hardly a caveman and Eve can usually get her way so she stops by at his shop to get money for a new hat. En route to the store, Eve is knocked down by the car belonging to Josef Andre, owner of a fashionable boutique. Andre brings the ruffled but uninjured Eve to his ritzy shop where she is impressed by all the finery and the lovely models. Andre offers Eve a job as a model, but he is mostly interested in making her another of his romantic conquests.
>
> After a tiff with Adam, Eve decides to secretly take the job at Andre's boutique. Adam later has second thoughts about Eve's desire for a new coat and decides to buy her one at Andre's shop. He is shocked to find Eve there modeling a skimpy gown. They argue and Adam storms out. Andre makes a pass at Eve, but she clobbers him and quits. Back at home, Eve reconciles with Adam and, having discovered Alice's real intentions, chases her out of their apartment with a broom. Back in the Garden of Eden, Eve likewise takes a broom to the serpent and then makes up with Adam. Adam suggests going to the slaying party at Cain and Abel's, but Eve protests she doesn't have a thing to wear.

Of interest here of course is not the thinly plotted modern story, but the prologue that seems to anticipate *The Flintstones* with its loopy combination of the contemporary and the prehistoric. The daily paper is a stone tablet and is hurled up to Adam and Eve's tree house by an overburdened paperboy. At the breakfast table, Adam is reading the sports page ("Mastodon race today") and, annoyed that Eve keeps looking at the fashion news on the back, simply breaks the tablet in two and gives her half. Adam rides to work on a wagon resembling a subway car, complete with strap hangers, but pulled by a triceratops. At another point, Adam — like at any homeowner protecting property values — yells at a brontosaurus for eating the foliage off a nearby tree. Adam (played by George O'Brien) certainly strikes a finer figure than Fred Flintstone, but for all his bluster he's just as easily wrapped around his wife's little finger as his cartoon counterpart. And since said shapely digits belong to the beautiful Olive Borden, his pliability is understandable.

The Garden of Eden sequence and the fashion show in a later scene were both filmed in Technicolor, but only black and white copies of the film are extant. PR often treated the film as though it were a drama rather than a comedy and made a good deal of the prologue, building it up (*way* too much) as a spectacle. The following, under the headline "True Version of First Man and Woman Striven For," appeared in the 29 December 1926 edition of *The Ukiah* [California] *Republican Press*:

> In this story director [Howard] Hawks has endeavored to bring to the screen a carefully planned version of certain events associated with the Garden of Eden. The Garden sequence, as may be imagined, offered endless opportunities for the reincarnations of jungle animals, ranging from the mighty brontosaurus and the ridged triceratops to the slow-moving stegosaurus and the huge-legged dinosaur about which the man of today thinks a great deal but knows very little.

We are also told that experts on pre-history were consulted, but all of this seems a bit serious for a film whose first title card reads "In the beginning was created heaven and earth … but the Garden of Eden was the only fashionable part of town." We don't recall dinosaurs being mentioned in Genesis, although Hollywood-like Christian fundamentalists — often ignored archaeology and had man and dinosaur co-exist. The film doesn't seem to worry about giving offense with its lighthearted treatment of the Biblical Adam and Eve, but ads for the movie make mention that 6000 years have passed since the appearance of the first couple and the dawn of the modern world, which pretty much jibes with how Biblical literalists calculated the age of the Earth. Nonetheless, within the film a title card cracks that "896 or 7 million years have passed and woman hasn't changed a bit."

Anyone expecting a dinosaur show like *The Lost World* was no doubt disappointed at the big mechanical puppets shambling through *Fig Leaves* like large-scale versions of the creatures in a Méliès film and played strictly for laughs. They are not unlike the creatures of 1957's *The Land Unknown* or *Unknown Island* (1948), but with goofy expressions and batting eyelashes. At one point, a real chimp is blown up to King Kong proportions via trick photography, but that's just for giggles too. And for the record no stegosaurus — slow moving or otherwise — appears in the film, nor is there any "huge-legged dinosaur."

None of this mattered to 1926 audiences, and the movie was a huge hit; director Howard Hawks later claimed that the receipts from one theater alone paid for the cost of the film. *Va-*

riety accurately called it "a conspicuous winner" and "expensively and beautifully mounted" with attractive players, original comic situations, and full of "subdued horse-play for those who like their laughs rough" as well as "certain subtleties the discriminating will appreciate." The *Harrison's Reports* write-up, quoted in ads for the film, likewise agreed that *Fig Leaves* would appeal to high brows and lows brows alike.

There was a good deal of publicity about the fashion show in which Borden modeled outfits purportedly worth $50,000. One ad showed a drawing of Borden in lingerie with the tag line, "With some women, clothes are next to Godliness— and with some —*next to nothing.*" In keeping with the sex theme, the studio released a series of racy stills showing Borden and O'Brien as the Biblical Adam and Eve and wearing a bit less than they do in the finished film. Borden and O'Brien *were* an off-screen couple for a while, but it didn't last and Borden's story had a tragic last act (see *The Monkey Talks*).

The success of *Fig Leaves* gave a big boost to director Howard Hawks' career, but the rest of his silent-film output wasn't particularly noteworthy. It wasn't until the Talkie Era that Hawks became a major director, with films like *Scarface* and *Bringing up Baby.* Apart from *Fig Leaves,* Hawks' only other genre credit is 1951's *The Thing from Another World.*

Movie herald artwork with the lovely Olive Borden. The light should now go on for those who thought this movie dealt with horticulture.

When viewed today, *Fig Leaves* is still clever and funny, with O'Brien as likeable as ever doing his regular-fella routine while Borden, with her soulful eyes and sweet pout, is at her very best. Mention should also be made of Andre De Beranger's waspish performance as the boutique owner given to histrionics and flights of corny poetry. Certainly the sexual politics of the film are outdated, but it's hard not to smile when a female passenger on the dinosaur trolley, forced to give up her seat to O'Brien, sighs and tells her friend that "someday we women will get our rights."

— HN

Finger Prints

Finger Prints. Warner Brothers Pictures/Warner Bros., 8 January 1927, 7 reels/7031 feet [LOST]

CAST: Louise Fazenda (*Dora Traynor*); John T. Murray (*Homer Fairchild*); Helene Costello (*Jacqueline Norton*); Myrna Loy (*The Vamp*); George Nichols (*S.V. Sweeney*); Martha Mattox (*Mother Malone*); Franklin Pangborn (*The Bandoline Kid*); William Demarest (*Cuffs Egan*); Robert Perry (*Hard-Boiled Ryan*); Edgar KIennedy (*O.K. McDuff*); Jerry Miley (*Chicago Ed*); Joseph B. (Doc) Stone (*Cabbage Head McCarthy*); Warner Richmond ("*Annie Laurie*" *Andy Norton*); Lew Harvey (*Secret Service Agent*)

CREDITS: *Director* Lloyd Bacon; *Scenario* Graham Baker, Edward Clark; based on the eponymous story by Arthur Somers Roche (publication undetermined); *Assistant Cameraman* Edward Cronewealth; *Assistant Director* Ted Stevens

We'd bet dollars to crullers that if we were to list all the silent films that centered on crooks trying to scare non-crooks out of their "haunted" hideouts, this book would be twice the size it is now. Heck, if we were to concentrate only on the haunted-crook films of Louise Fazenda, we might come close, as La Fazenda made damned near 300 pictures in the three-and-a-half decades she kept herself— and legions of ersatz country bumpkins, sidekicks, and foils— busy. Her more serious genre credits (in which, of course, she was inevitably the comic relief) included *The Bat* (1926), *The Terror* (1928), *Stark Mad* (1929) and *House of Horror* (1929) (see entries).

The film at hand, though, is one of those crooks-frightening-the-innocents-out-of-the-old-dark-house things, and we're adding it here only because we've an interesting and atmospheric still that demonstrates beyond a reasonable doubt that there was at least *one* quasi-scary sequence in the film. This is not to say that none of those other CFtIootODH films didn't have their share of hair-raisin' thrills, but— as most were programmers not targeted for conservation or considered likely candidates for film retrospectives— we've no way of knowing whether each did or did not. One title that was made numerous times (all of which are extant) and which has proven each time to have *zero* "quasi-scary" sequences is *Seven Keys to Baldpate*. After watching the brace of silent versions and mulling over the handful of stills we have from both productions, we've decided to let *Finger Prints* serve as the template for all these many, routine, predictable-yet-usually-enjoyable movies.

Our synopsis is taken from the copyright registration documents.

Andy Norton, chief of a gang of mail thieves, is captured and imprisoned, though he does not reveal to the other gang members the hiding place of the loot. They plot to obtain the secret from him, but to no avail. Inspector Sweeney of the Post Office Department, posing as a criminal, suspects that the stolen property is hidden in the house of Mother Malone, a clairvoyant. There he finds the gang members who have escaped and who threaten Norton's daughter, Jacqueline, thus forcing Norton to divulge the secret. After a series of mysterious and comic adventures, the gang is arrested with the aid of Doris, a servant who turns out to be a Secret Service agent, and the booty is retrieved.

Miss Fazenda, *naturellement*, was Doris, and the accompanying photograph reflects that "quasi-scary" sequence that has you reading this essay; more on the perennially popular comedienne may be found in our essay on *The Bat*. Other funnymen in the picture who transcended the Silent Era to find glory (well … at least steady employment and fans) were Franklin Pangborn, William Demarest, and Edgar Kennedy.

Appearing as the Vamp ("booty" meant something different in those days) was Myrna Loy, a few years shy of her appearances in *The Mask of Fu Manchu* and *Thirteen Women*, and a couple of years shyer still of her iconic Nora Charles in *The Thin Man* et al. The sloe-eyed beauty was Montana-born, and it took the wonders of sound to have moguls and moviegoers alike understand that Loy could deliver bon mots as readily as she could come-hither glances (her vamp here was pretty much typical for her during the 1920s). Helene Costello was the daughter of Maurice (*The Man Who Couldn't Beat God*) Costello and sister of Dolores (Mrs. John Barrymore) Costello; genre-wise, her story is found in our coverage of *While London Sleeps*.

Martha Mattox, whose Mother Malone was *said* to be clairvoyant but we've no further detail, entered films in 1913 and spent most of her pre–*Finger Prints* days in shorts and small (usually credited) bits. As luck would have it, one of her *un*credited bits was in *Red Lights*, an entry in this tome. Fortunately, the lady's plum Silent Era genre role — Mammy

Pleasant in 1927's *The Cat and the Canary* — survives, as does our chapter on that film. Early on in the Sound Era, Miss Mattox hit the thriller lottery, winning parts in *Murder by the Clock* (with Irving [*Dracula's Daughter*] Pichel), *The Monster Walks* (with Sheldon [*Dr. Jekyll and Mr. Hyde*] Lewis) , and *Behind the Mask* (with Boris [What? Are you kidding?] Karloff).

Finger Prints was directed by Lloyd Bacon, and *Stark Mad* (see entry, appendix) also bore his (ahem) visionary stamp.

"Rush" at *Variety* (26 January 1927) was not impressed and called it "a cross between the custard pie comedy technique and the methods they use in building up melodramatic serials. That is to say, no device is too crude or violent to serve its purpose. There is not a legitimate laugh in all seven reels, and the best of the picture is in the gag titles."

Harsh. Still, *Harrison's Reports* (15 January 1927) wasn't much kinder…

> Silly burlesque. So silly, in fact, that picture patrons should poke fun at it…. At the beginning one is led to believe that it would be a detective melodrama, with hair-raising melodramatic situations. But after a reel or so it turns into a Sunshine comedy, with trap doors, people disappearing behind them, and with everything that goes with such action.

Let's be honest. The really good CFtIootODH films couldn't be made until after Universal had filmed *Dracula*, and Gower Gulch discovered it could afford Bela Lugosi.

— *JTS*

The Fool and the Dancer

The Fool and the Dancer. Abraham Bloom (?), October 1915, 4 reels [LOST]
CREDITS: *Story* H. Wolkof

Don't get your hopes up. There is literally nothing out there on this 1915 four-reeler other than the following plot summary, which was taken from the copyright registration materials at the Library of Congress. *The AFI Catalog* notes that the Library of Congress received 49 stills along with the summary, so there was at least that much evidence that somebody had photographed *something* in conjunction with this title. There *was* that much evidence; the photos are long gone. (God bless film researchers with sticky fingers.)

Anyhow…

Dr. Smith falls in love with Mademoiselle Dazie, a dancer in a variety theater, and convinces her to leave her foster father, Sergeant. Although Sergeant, who desperately loves Dazie, threatens to kill her if she goes to Smith, she escapes early one morning, but Smith, because of his social standing, refuses to allow her to stay with him. She refuses his money and finds refuge with Madam Dupont, a famous dancing instructor. Dazie studies hard, and in a few years she becomes known as a great dancer. Dazie accepts the proposal of John Hamilton, a wealthy businessman, and repulses Smith when he propositions her after he visits the theater with Hamilton.

This is the "quasi-scary sequence" of *Finger Prints* about which we wrote.

After learning that Sergeant has been confined to Smith's sanitarium for the insane, Dazie tries to visit. Smith, in revenge for Dazie's rejection, takes Sergeant to Dazie's home, and by hypnotic suggestion causes Sergeant to strangle Dazie and Hamilton, now Dazie's husband.

While it's obvious that we're compelled to include this film because of the existence of evil hypnotist, Dr. Smith, we're on less firm footing with respect to who's who in the story. The smart money says Mlle. Dazie is the dancer, but who is the fool? (It cannot also be Mlle. Dazie; otherwise, the title would be *The Foolish Dancer*. The logic is irrefutable.) Sergeant, Dazie's foster father and would-be lover (*Wow!*), is the last-reel throttler of both his foster daughter (nice, huh?) and her husband, but is he the titular fool? Might it not be, rather, her late husband, who—after all—had married the devotee of Terpsichore in the first place, mindless of the inherent danger? Or, just possibly, could the fool be Doctor Smith himself? After all, he sweet-talked Mlle. Dazie out of the comfort and security of her hearth and homicidal guardian and into a Motel Six or onto the street or something, and all because of his "social standing"? Sounds mighty foolish to us. Lastly (if only because we've run out of dramatis personae), might the title not refer to Madame Dupont, who took in the presumable penurious Mlle. Dazie and turned the erstwhile variety-theater dancer into a "great dancer," only to see her strangled before either she or her businessman husband could pay back the old lady for the training?

The scribe responsible for this quandary was one H. (as in Herman) Wolkof, who is on record as having also written *Hearts Aflame* (another story that must be read—and can be, on the online AFI Silent Era searchable site—to be believed) at some point in 1915. (The IMDb goes so far as to maintain that the cast of *Hearts* included a Dorothy Rosher [later known as Joan Marsh, owner of "the smallest feet in Hollywood"], but the AFI listings offer no corroboration on this. Her participation in the "film," not the size of her feet.) Anyhow, Wolkof apparently penned these two pips before someone or something put an end to his screenwriting career, and we hope he blowed up real good.

Hearts Aflame and *The Fool and the Dancer* were presented to the Library of Congress for copyright on the 26 October 1915, and the films were registered under the name, Abraham Bloom. When we noted that, intriguingly, the pictures didn't bear consecutive copyright numbers (*Hearts* is LU7183 and *Fool*, LU7185), we backpedaled and checked "Bloom, Abraham" in *The Catalog of Copyright Entries, Motion Pictures, 1912–1939*. Voila! Mr. Bloom's name appeared, yet again, as claiming copyright on *The Lure of the White Lights*, which had been awarded copyright number LU7184. On the 26 October 1915. More intriguingly, we can't find evidence of any picture entitled *The Lure of the White Lights* anywhere, including the IMDB, *The AFI Catalog*, or the online archives of the Library of Congress. (By the way, *White Lights'* author is listed as Oscar Liebof, and it doesn't take a genius to figure out that, with respect to a Herman Wolkof, an Oscar Liebof is not Very Faroff.)

We've no idea what any of this means, but the chase was a great deal more fun than copying down the absurd plotline of this picture in our quest for comprehensiveness.

— JTS

Fools in the Dark

Fools in the Dark. R-C Pictures/Film Booking Offices of America, 4 August 1924, 8 reels/7702 feet [LOST]
CAST: Patsy Ruth Miller (*Ruth Rand*); Matt Moore (*Percy Schwartz*); Bertram Grassby (*Kotah*); Charles Belcher (*Dr. Rand*); Tom Wilson (*Diploma*); John Steppling (*Julius Schwartz*)
CREDITS: *Director* Al Santell; *Writer* Bertram Millhauser; *Cinematographers* Leon Eycke, Blake Wagner

This is appendix-fodder, pure and simple. A spoof of the sort of ersatz-spooky melodramas that would find their apotheosis in *Seven Footprints to Satan*, *Fools in the Dark*—lost though it may be—is more memorable for its cast than for its pedigree. The three leads of said cast—Patsy Ruth Miller, Matt Moore, and Bertram Grassby—are covered fairly extensively in our essays on *The Hunchback of Notre Dame*, *20,000 Leagues Under the Sea*, and *Conscience*, respectively.

Story-wise, the following is a slumgullion crafted from bits taken from *The AFI Catalog*, the 18 August 1924 review from *The New York Times*, Janiss Garza's online "All-Movie Guide," and the 20 July 1924 *Motion Picture News* critique:

> Young Percy Schwartz, an aspiring screenwriter who is mired as heir apparent in his father's garbage-can business, is in love with the comely Ruth Rand. Ruth, whose uncle (some accounts have Dr. Rand her father) has apparently invented some sort of death ray, regards young Percy as a milksop; thus, with the aid of Kotah, his Hindu henchman (who also has set his sights on Ruth), Dr. Rand finagles an adventure to test Percy's mettle.
> Percy quickly finds himself in the clutches of a clutch of madmen (and very nearly a guinea pig in the testing of Dr. Rand's death ray), but escapes with the help of his friend, Diploma, a street cleaner who happens also to be a 1920s, stereotypical, cinematic Negro. While all this is transpiring, Ruth—who was to have been kidnapped as part of this charade—ends up having been kidnapped for real, by Kotah, the Hindu turncoat. Procuring a seaplane, and receiving help from some nearby marines, Percy rescues Ruth. Dr. Rand, seeing the error of his ways, gives his blessing.

That death ray is really all that we needed to stick this entry here in the Appendix. Nor can the presence of that traitorous Hindu servant be discounted, especially when one considers that the ever-watchful Kansas censors apparently found some sequences with Bertram Grassby's character a bit too horrific for the Kansas citizenry: "Elim close-up of Kotah's face when attacking girl and elim close-up of Kotah pushing on Matt's eyes while on floor." Nothing like telling an actor his close-ups had to end on the cutting room floor, what?

In neighboring Oklahoma, the proprietor of the Victory Theatre in Shawnee was more concerned with the receipts than the censors and reported (in the 11 October 1924 *Moving Picture World*) that "this is a pleasing picture and can go in my house any day of the week…. Good Attendance."

As for more cosmopolitan locales, Grace Kingsley (in the 28 July 1924 edition of the *Los Angeles Times*) assessed: "The spooky stuff put over in the scenes in which the hero stays at the home of the heroine and her doctor uncle, are as creepy as anything ever seen, with weird dead faces lying on tables, trick furniture, death rays and all other mystery scenery."

The New York Times found the whole enterprise "to cause chuckles, grins, smiles, smirks and full explosions from the lungs," while admitting that the plot bore more than a passing resemblance to D.W. Griffith's *One Exciting Night* (covered herein), which had hit neighborhood screens a couple of years earlier. Mae Tinee of *The Chicago Tribune* (8 September 1924) tried her best to find the same high points, but concluded "My earnest prayer is that all of you will find *Fools in the Dark* more mystifying — and funnier than I did."

While Griffith's film bore the most comparisons to *Fools* (*Variety* and *Harrison's* likewise saw the similarity), other publications found kinship to similar send-ups like *Red Lights* (see entry, 1923), and the yet-to-be-adapted-to-the-screen plays, *The Cat and the Canary* and *The Bat*. As *MPN*'s Laurence Reid summarized, "All the old stock tricks are satirized to the tune of fast and vigorous action."

The cleverest part of *Fools in the Dark* may have been its title, which refers simultaneously to the madcap adventures of the sundry dramatis personae and to the moviegoers for whom Percy Schwartz is seeking to write. The most deplorable element of the picture was definitely its use of Tom Wilson — a Caucasian actor (from Montana!) — as Diploma, the black street cleaner. In his earliest professional days, Wilson seems to have found gainful employment due to burnt cork, shufflin' feet, and eyes opened wide, and the establishment back then had no problem with that. *The New York Times* review mentions a sequence in which Wilson, as Diploma, "is frightened and the caption, as he stands gazing into the glistening orbs of a stuffed tiger, has him saying: 'Feet, don't fail me now!'" Surely, back in the 1920s, that saying was crocheted onto samplers everywhere. Taking its celebration of the "burnt cork Negro" a step further, The Grey Lady reports:

> His most terrified period is where he inadvertently steps into a pool of glue, his substantial pedal extremities becoming stuck, without his being aware of it, to some calico attached to Dr. Rand's pet skeleton. Hence one sees the skeleton following Diploma's every step. This goes on for quite a stretch, when through clever manipulation the cold bone fingers reach out and touch Diploma on the shoulder. As the Negro is not accustomed to medical research or ethnological studies he is quiveringly surprised at the lightness of the tap and the coldness and hardness of the fingers. He dare not look around, so feels behind him with trepidation, getting his fingers on about the location of the skeleton's fourth rib. Then slowly he turns his head, and the second his eyes light on the skull he flees for dear life.

Yes, we're aware that the portrayal in question was pretty much run-of-the-mill for the Roaring Twenties and, yes, we're aware that we're that ethnic humor and racial stereotypes extended encompassed groups other than African Americans. Elsewhere in this book, we speak of Chinese and/or Japanese actors who found that making a living in Hollywood often meant sucking it up, walking it off, and stiffening one's resolve (and upper lip). Still, we can't help but decry the situation: *Not* the stereotypes, for comedic stereotypes became popular and ubiquitous before the ink was dry on Thespis's first contract, and every conceivable social group pokes fun most readily at every other conceivable ethnic group along stereotypical lines. We decry the temperament that denied industry jobs to African American actors, or to Oriental actors, or to *any* actors whose ethnic Sitz-im-Leben prevented them from portraying charac-ters of their own ethnos due to convention, short-sightedness, or downright prejudice.

This is not a condemnation of Tom Wilson, for this propensity to blackface occupied but a fraction of his lengthy career, which spanned six decades and numbered over 250 onscreen appearances. In fact, the 26 July 1924 *Harrison's Reports* singled out Wilson, maintaining that "The [scenes] in which he is shown in the mystery house followed by a skeleton will make the audience roar with laughter; at times they should scream." It was Wilson's talent and not his artificially enhanced skin hue that won him this praise. (For another such appearance in a genre offering, see our essay on D.W. Griffith's *The Greatest Question*.) In addition, it has been argued that — during the industry's Silent Era — a white actor's donning blackface was no more offensive to the black community than was an actor's indulgence in flexible collodion offensive to those who suffered facial scarring. We wish only to go on record on the issue and, the moving fingered having pointed this out, we move on.

The unlikely story and scenario came from the fertile mind and manual typewriter of Bertram Millhauser, yet another New Yorker with genre ties. Millhauser was producer of 1928's *The Leopard Lady* (see entry), production supervisor of 1929's *Black Magic* (see entry), and the scenarist who brought William Gillette's Great Consulting Detective — and Basil Rathbone's — to the screen during the first two decades of the Sound Era. The eponymous *Sherlock Holmes* (1932) was based on Gillette's renowned play, of course, while the sundry Rathbone–Nigel Bruce adventures (like 1944's *Pearl of Death* and others) were derived directly from Conan Doyle, more or less, sort of, to one extent or another. Regardless, they were entertaining stories, cheerfully (if cheaply) told, and they forged an unbreakable link between genre lovers and the Master of Deduction from Baker Street, no matter the details of any particular scenario. Millhauser's Silent Era resume as scenarist also included a number of serials in which he readily brought wacky sci-fi and other, more outré elements, like *The New Exploits of Elaine* (1915), *The Romance of Elaine* (1915), and *Plunder* (1923), all of which starred female serial deity, Pearl White.

Director Al(fred) Santell had but one Silent Era genre bullet left in his gun following *Fools in the Dark*, and that was 1927's *The Gorilla*. His was a varied career with notable talkies such as *The Sea Wolf* (1930) and *Winterset* (1936). Santell once looked back nostalgically over his early days as a writer and said "With a good story and a good cast any director can turn out a successful motion picture." It appears that with *Fools in the Dark* at least, he may have been true to his word.

— *SJ*

The Ghost in the Garret

The Ghost in the Garret. New Art Film Company/Paramount Pictures, February 1921, 5 reels/5037 feet [LOST]

CAST: Dorothy Gish (*Delsie O'Dell*); Downing Clarke (*Gilbert Dennison*); Mrs. David Landau (*Dennison's wife*); William Parke, Jr. (*Bill Clark*); Ray Grey (*Oscar White*); Walter P. Lewis (*Dennison's butler*); Mary Foy (*Dennison's cook*); Frank Badgley (*Detective O'Connor*); Frank Hagney, Tom Blake, William Nally, Porter Strong (*Crooks*)

CREDITS: *Director* F. Richard Jones; *Scenario* Fred Chaston; *Story* Wells Hastings

Faux haunted houses in the movies during the 1920s were as plentiful as the proverbial flowers that bloom in the spring, but there were some in which the spooky stuff was so minimal as to verge on the nonexistent (like either of the silent *Seven Keys to Baldpate* features), and those films will be mentioned only in passing. (Like that.) This 1921 effort may not have been all that much better than the two Earl Derr Biggers adaptations, but inasmuch as the ghost stuff won comment from a few reviewers, without the film on hand we have to assume that it might have gotten at least a thumbs-up or two from our genre-loving forebears.

Our synopsis is taken from the copyright registration materials filed with the Library of Congress:

> Lucy goes from a poverty-stricken home to visit her aunt and uncle and takes along her bull dog and her parrot. The aunt receives her with misgivings and her cordiality does not increase when Lucy's bull dog breaks up a fashionable tea party and sends all the guests wildly climbing the furniture. Billie, the uncle's secretary, is attracted to the little girl [!] and takes her to a dancing party, lending her a string of imitation pearls which are an exact paste counterpart of a $75,000 string belonging to the aunt.
> Percy, the aunt's secretary who is in reality a crook, steals the real pearls and in trying to hide them gets them mixed up with the imitation pearls that Lucy has hidden. Lucy is accused of the theft of the real ones which are found in her pocket through a trick of Percy's and is about to be arrested. Seeing his sweetheart in danger, Billie takes the blame upon himself and goes to jail.
> The aunt discovers her own mistake and Bill and the girl are freed from blame. Lucy then traces the wicked Percy to a haunted house which is being used as a hang out and rendezvous for a gang of crooks.
> The unexpected return of the crooks while she is investigating the house places Lucy in terrible peril. She saves herself by scaring the crooks into blue fits by pretending she is a ghost. She then lowers her faithful bull dog out the window on a rope made up of torn sheets and he brings her help — Billie and the police.

Virtually every one of the plot elements in the above précis may be found in other of the many faux haunted house films listed in this book, with most to be found earlier than 1921 and all done better after 1921. *Variety* (1 April 1921) opened its commentary on the picture by blowing just that whistle:

> That good old hoke classic standby of burlesque and vaudeville in the variety days, when no show of that character was complete without an afterpiece, "Ghost in the Pawnshop" has been dug from the musty archives of the theatrical past, embellished, modified and modernized, and blossoms forth as *Ghost in the Garrett* [sic].

Obviously a romantic comedy first and a haunted house thriller seventh, somewhere between the time the studio was granted copyright (on the 31 December 1920) and the picture was premiered (in February 1921), the nomenclature of Dorothy Gish's character had changed from Lucy (the "poor relation") to Delsie O'Dell. (More cloudy whether also concerned actor Ray Grey, who played either *Percy* White or *Oscar* White but, either way, was the pic-

ture's primo heavy.) It's not clear why the change in the heroine's name was effected, but it's unlikely that a class action suit, brought on by any number of poor relations yclept Lucy, figured in the switch. Just another of those "curious, but ... *so what?*" observations which dot the research.

The big name (we're not far from claiming the *only* name) in *The Ghost in the Garret* was Dorothy Gish's, and the pert actress — who had always hoped for a career in cinematic tragedy, but who had proven herself to be an excellent light comedienne — took home the critical centerpiece. Miss Gish, whose early cinematic career always seemed to be linked with that of her older sister, Lillian (the siblings shared screen credit in over two dozen pictures during the Silent Era), had most of her screen appearances behind her by 1921. After calling it a day in 1928, the lady shifted her attention to the legitimate theater and was quickly on her way to becoming a mainstay of the Broadway stage. Interspersed among the dozen-and-a-half Great White Way plays in which she appeared over the next two decades were a very few movie roles, and the 1950s found her making an occasional television foray. None of her ten dozen movie credits was genre fodder save for *The Ghost in the Garret*, and it ought to be obvious that *that* film has only the most tenuous of ties to any of our favorite themes.

The only other "name" in the picture's cast crawl was that of Ray Grey, whose character — like Miss Gish's — apparently had *two* names. Grey started in the industry with Mack Sennett — the San Diegan's first screen credit was 1916's *A Movie Star* for Keystone — and ended with Hal Roach (*Hired and Fired*, 1926); this last credit was posthumous, as Grey died in1925, a victim of the Los Angeles pneumonia outbreak. He was 35 years old. Grey was father to Virginia Grey (*House of Horrors*, 1946; *Unknown Island*, 1948; *Target Earth*, 1954), and the popular character actress may well be regarded as her father's genre legacy.

Well, there's no ghost in evidence anywhere here, but we're pretty sure that this is the titular garret. Still from *The Ghost in the Garret.*

The picture was directed by F. Richard Jones, another Mack Sennett veteran who ended up deceased way ahead of his time (Jones died of TB in Hollywood when he was thirty-*seven* years of age). A native of the "Show Me" state, Jones quickly showed the Keystone cognoscenti that he was more than capable of holding his own with the likes of Hale Hamilton, Slim Summerville, Polly Moran, Louise Fazenda, Heinie Conklin, Ben Turpin, et al, whom he directed in dozens of shorts from 1915 on. Like Ray Grey, Jones moved on to Hal Roach's Lot o' Fun in the mid-1920s, and there he assumed the producer's mantle and worked with everyone from Babe Hardy and Jimmy Finlayson to Stan Laurel and Charley Chase to Roach's Rascals, on classic comedy shorts ranging from *Yes, Yes, Nanette* to *Thundering Fleas* to *Long Fliv the King*. Jones' last film credit was his only talkie — 1929's *Bulldog Drummond*, with Ronald Colman — and, unlike poor Ray Grey, Jones lived long enough to see his last motion picture released and lauded.

Review-wise, the usual suspects were polite enough, with Dorothy Gish's comic capability earning her kudos in virtually every critique. In one of the local newspaper pieces (the *Lima* [Ohio] *News*, 15 April 1921) we tracked down, though, it's obvious that the movie reviewer tossed the press-book copy and called it as he saw it:

> The picture is a little jerky and suggests many encounters with the censors — tho what there could have been eliminated, I can't imagine. And Dorothy needs a new wig — if a wig she will wear. These faults excepted, *The Ghost in the Garret* is really good fun — and a good picture.
>
> There are a number of people in the cast whom you have never seen before. Most of them you won't miss if you never see them again. Ray Grey, however, as the polished villain, is splendid. And Porter Strong, as a colored gentleman pursued by the ghost, is quite the hit of the piece.

Need we mention that Porter Strong (see *One Exciting Night*) was playing in blackface?   — JTS

The Girl on the Stairs

The Girl on the Stairs. Peninsula Studios/Producers Distributing Corp., 16 November 1924, 7 reels/6214 feet [LOST]
CAST: Patsy Ruth Miller (*Dora Sinclair*); Frances Raymond (*Agatha Sinclair*); Arline Pretty (*Joan Wakefield*); Shannon Day (*Manuela Sarmento*); Niles Welch (*Frank Farrell*); Freeman Wood (*Dick Wakefield*); Bertram Grassby (*José Sarmento*); Michael Dark (*Wilbur*); George Periolat (*Dr. Bourget*).
CREDITS: *Presented by* Elmer Harris; *Director* William Worthington; *Supervisor* Elmer Harris; *Adaptation* Elmer Harris; based on the eponymous short story by Winston Bouve (*Ainslee's Magazine,* March 1924); *Cinematographers* Joseph Walker, Charles Kaufman

Sigmund Freud made good use of hypnotism in psychoanalysis, but Silent Era Hollywood considered dredging up childhood traumas on the couch pretty tame stuff next to mesmerizing beautiful maidens and bending them to your every desire. Taking a page from *Trilby* and *Dracula*, hypnotism was depicted as a sinister, quasi-supernatural form of mind control, a kind of sorcery that could be broken only by the death of the hypnotist. However, in the interest of equal time for good hypnotists, we offer this particular entry (as well as the more ambiguous *The*

Crimson Cross), a courtroom melodrama which takes a more benign view of the subject.

Our synopsis comes from the 2 June 1925 edition of the *Cumberland* [Maryland] *Evening Times* and was undoubtedly taken from the press-book:

> Under great emotional stress, Dora Sinclair has, since childhood, walked in her sleep. At a select girls' finishing school, she has been carrying on a flirtation with Dick Wakefield. Franklin Farrell, a rising young attorney, is ardently in love with her. Later she discovers that Dick is married to an old friend of hers, Joan. Dora is furious at Wakefield and decides to marry Farrell.
>
> A swimming party is given at the Wakefield home and Dora attends in the hope of getting back several silly love letters that she has written to Dick. Present at the party are José Sarmento, a wealthy and insanely jealous Portuguese, and his pretty and flirtatious wife, Manuela, who concentrates her attentions on Wakefield.
>
> During the afternoon, Dora asks Wakefield to return her letters. He tells her that he will if she gives him a kiss for each one. She refuses and a struggle ensues that is interrupted by Joan. Dora leaves without her letters. Joan tells Dick she can stand his attentions to other women no longer and leaves him, going to her mother's home.
>
> That night Dora is restless and walks in her sleep. We see her enter the Wakefield home. We next see her descending the stairs. Then she returns to her home and to bed.
>
> In the meantime, Joan has been advised by her mother to return to her husband. On arriving at the house she goes directly to Dick's room and discovers that her husband has been stabbed in the back. He is dead.
>
> In horror, Joan phones for the police and on their arrival, they find Dora's love letters and on the floor near Wakefield the dagger with which he had been stabbed. The police then go to Dora's house. On being awakened, Dora can recall nothing since retiring. She is arrested. The evidence is sufficient to have her indicted for the murder of Wakefield.
>
> At the trial, she is defended by Farrell and he is apparently carrying on a hopeless fight. Finally, in desperation, he asks her if she has ever walked in her sleep and Aunt Agatha recalls an incident in her childhood. Farrell at once sends for Dr. Bourget, the specialist who attended her. On the witness stand, the doctor testifies that, on awakening, sleepwalkers never remember anything that has happened during their sleepwalking. There is only one way of learning the truth and that is by putting the subject to sleep artificially and probing the subconscious mind.
>
> After hypnotizing her, Dr. Bourget asks Dora why she went to Wakefield's room on the night of the murder and she replies, "To get my letters." He asks her to describe what she saw and in retrospect the scene of the murder is revealed. This shows Wakefield with Manuela in Wakefield's room. They have been drinking champagne and Wakefield draws her into an embrace just as José, her husband, enters. He stabs Wakefield and then leaves with Manuela.
>
> José and Manuela hear this recital in the courtroom and at its conclusion José admits that he is the murderer. Dr. Bourget then wakes Dora and the district attorney withdraws the charge against her. The fadeout is of Farrell and Dora's honeymoon on a transoceanic liner.

The real murderer confessing in court is one of the great clichés of courtroom drama and one that was followed with slavish fidelity on television every Saturday night in *Perry Mason* with Raymond Burr. Of course, in *Girl*, José's confession saves the judge of having to rule on the doubtful admissibility of Dora's spellbound recollections.

Another source tells us that Wakefield's maid spotted Dora

going down the stairs and mistook her for a ghost. Perhaps her fear caused her not to notice the comings and goings of José and Manuela (who apparently ignore the sleepy-eyed Dora taking in the whole show).

In the 24 March 1925 issue of *Variety*, "Con" judged the film "a corking good feature for the second run houses." Con also felt the credibility of the sleepwalking/hypnotism angle would likely determine one's reaction to the film but, plausible or not, it was still engrossing and well acted, especially by Patsy Ruth Miller as Dora. More on the actress Con thought "girlishly appealing" can be found in the entry on *The Hunchback of Notre Dame*. Other than Miss Miller, "the" genre name connected with *Stairs* belonged to Bertram Grassby, whose presence may be noted (even if his face goes unrecognized by all save the most silents-savvy) in such titles that may be found herein as *The Circular Staircase*, *Even as You and I*, *Her Temptation*, *Rasputin the Black Monk*, and *Conscience*— and those are just the titles produced and released before 1918! Mr. Grassby receives more attention in our essay on *Conscience*.

"Fend" of *The Cleveland Plain Dealer* (2 February 1925) had mixed feelings about the film:

> The psychology and the legal tactics both get pretty thick.... Still the detail and completeness in which both are pictured add some interest to the film.... It is rather farfetched material and murder and courtroom scenes must be getting very monotonous for many film fans. This film excels many others in that both the murder and the courtroom scenes are done a little better and more convincingly.

Variety (cited above) also felt the picture's appeal was somewhat skewed:

> If one accepts the theory that the subconscious mind directs the activities of sleepwalkers and that the somnambulists do not remember anything they do while in the coma, but if put to sleep by artificial means, will reveal the promptings of the subconscious mind, the picture is credulous.

We note same without pausing to wonder if the reviewer mean *credible* instead of *credulous*.

Some ads for the film made it seem more like a society drama than a mystery; one showed a young woman in evening dress descending an elegant staircase to a party below. Needless to say, the sex angle was hardly downplayed with tag lines like "She walked in her sleep into Wakefield's room."

The Girl on the Stairs was the last directorial effort of William Worthington, best remembered for his films with Sessue Hayakawa. Worthington, a former stage actor who had been directing and acting in films since 1913, became interested in developing a multicolor camera. An article in the *Los Angeles Times* (8 December 1929) claimed that he had retired from the screen to work on it and had achieved positive results: "With the success of the new color process the secret is out. He has passed the last four years perfecting the invention, which now bids fair to revolutionize color photography on the screen."

Actually, Worthington hadn't invented anything but had, along with son-in-law, Rowland V. Lee, started up a company to utilize the work of Harry K. Fairall, who had done the 3-D film *The Power of Love* in 1922. Worthington and Lee found that Fairall's process could be adapted to color film, something far more practical than 3-D (or stereoscopic film, as it was then

known). In any event, Worthington's company failed, and he spent the rest of his career acting in small roles and uncredited bit parts.

The Girl on the Stairs was also one of the last of the handful of films done by Peninsula Studios, a company that took its name from the rental studio at which the film was shot. The studio, originally called Pacific Studios, had opened in San Mateo in 1920 with the intention of challenging Los Angeles' domination of the film industry. A number of movies were filmed there, but there was not enough activity to keep things solvent and the huge facility was idle by the late 1920s. The facility was utilized for several other purposes— including functioning as a homeless shelter during the Depression — and it did experience a revival of sorts in the 1950s, with the arrival of television.   — HN

Gli Stregoni del Mare see *Those Who Dare*

The Gray Mask

The Gray Mask. Shubert Film Corp./World Film Corp., 13 December 1915, 5 reels [LOST]
CAST: Edwin Arden (*Jim Garth*): Barbara Tennant (*Nora*); Frank Monroe (*Silas Howlett*); Georgio Majeroni (*Foreign Agent*); Buckley Starkey; Hugh Jeffrey (*Burglars*); John Hines
CREW: *Director* Frank Crane; *Scenario* Charles Wadsworth Camp; based on the eponymous short story by Charles Wadsworth Camp (*Collier's National Weekly*, 17 August 1915)
Per *The AFI Catalog*, the film was released in some areas as *The Grey Mask*.

A great number of authorities point to George Méliès' *Le Voyage dans la Lune* as *The* first Science Fiction film. Others are wont to contend that an early —(hold on to your dictionary, here)— *sausage-making* picture (Lumiere's *Charcuterie Mechanique*) fits the definition and should thereby win the honor. For whatever reason, a plethora of such turn-of-the-century shorts were concocted wherein some apparatus or another would directly convert a poor canine into kielbasa for the amusement of easily-pleased audiences— often, through simple trick photography. The reasoning had it that such devices presaged the mechanical age, automated production, and so on and so forth and ... Voila! Instant Science Fiction, no?

Maybe so; but the authors of this volume prefer a more flexible — and practical —categorization; something like, to paraphrase S. F. great Damon Knight, "Science fiction is what we point to when we say it." Even encompassing so broad a scope as that posited by Mr. Knight, the fickle finger wavers when it comes to *The Gray Mask*. We include the title here, in the appendix, for the sake of comprehensiveness.

The synopsis:

> The Hennion gang of crooks having killed Joe Kridel, a police inspector, and, fearing discovery accept the aid of Simmons, who wears a gray mask that covers wounds caused by an explosion. Jim Garth, another inspector, is placed on the trail of the gang of which he becomes a member. Nora, the daughter of Garth's inspector, is beloved by Garth. She appears to be one of the gang. Although Jim loves her deeply, she is cold to him. She has sworn to avenge the murder of Kridel, and believes the murderer to be one of the gang.

The Hennions attempt to steal a valuable explosive and penetrate to a steel room in which the chemical is placed. Nora learns the name of Kridel's murderer. When the gang has gathered in the steel room, Garth reveals himself and calls in the aid of the police.

The gang is arrested; the murderer secured, and out of gratitude, Nora accepts Jim Garth as her lover [*The Moving Picture World*, 4 December 1915].

The *MPW* didn't pull a spoiler, but it should come as little shock to anyone who has seen a couple of million pictures like this one that Garth had disguised himself as Simmons (an explosives expert needed to handle the dangerous material) — replete with gray mask — in order to infiltrate the conspirators. And as for that "valuable explosive" — *The Gray Mask*'s sole basis for consideration as science-fiction fodder — the eponymous source short story (published in the 7 August 1915 *Collier's Magazine*) provided crystal-clear explication:

The fellows tearing themselves to pieces in Europe have put the price up, and their agents seem to think whoever gets the stuff will make the rest look like Tod Sloan fighting Jack Johnson. The inventor thinks Uncle Sam ought to have it if anybody, but he's been holding off. It's new, and he's either afraid of it himself or he thinks he can perfect it.

Crystal clear, that is, to anyone catching the references to the Great War; to the recently-deposed heavyweight champ, Jack Johnson; and to then-famed, early 1900s jockey, Tod Sloan.

Charles Wadsworth Camp (vide: *The Last Warning, Love without Question*), the Philadelphia-born scribe who wrote the picture's scenario, had adapted his own short story (illustrated for *Collier's* by renowned artist, Frederic Dorr Steele) to the screen, making several additions in the process. The promise that "You'll gasp at the terrible dash of the loaded auto into the river, or the horrifying explosion in the chemical laboratory" — per an advert printed in *The Decatur Review* (on the 28 December 1915) — was fulfilled only for ticket-buyers; the magazine's original text offered no such thrills. Intriguingly, another issue of *The Moving Picture World* (15 November 1915) concerning male lead Edwin Arden's part in the upcoming film seemed to indicate inspector Jim Garth was something along the lines of a Craig Kennedy (Arthur B. Reeve's fictional sleuth who often used the latest technology to solve his cases): "He must play in this picture a scientific detective who finds himself in predicaments of more than ordinary complication and danger. It is none of the swaggering, heavy set detective who dogs the footsteps of the villain with the usual murderous air."

However, turning to the short story, is again of no help. At best, Garth does use a piece of paper specially treated to be susceptible to a form of invisible ink in order to signal for help. But, it's the inspector chief who gives even that to him.

Arden was a man of far more stage credits than film ones. His limited film career was cut short by a fatal heart disease a mere three short years after appearing as Jim Garth.

Yet a third installment of *The Moving Picture World* (11 December 1915) summed up *The Gray Mask* with: "The plot is rather ingenious and the picture profits by fast action. Edwin Arden gives an able portrayal of a resourceful detective and Barbara Tennant does very well as the heroine who assists in avenging the death of her lover."

— *SJ*

The Hands of Nara

The Hands of Nara. Samuel Zierler Photoplay Corp./Metro pictures, c. 26 August 1922, 6 reels/ 6997 feet (copyright at 7 reels) [LOST]

CAST: Clara Kimball Young (*Nara Alexieff*); Count John Orloff (*Boris Alexieff*); Elliott Dexter (*Emlen Claveloux*); Edwin Stevens (*Connor Lee*); Vernon Steele (*Adam Pine*); John Miltern (*Dr. Haith Claveloux*); Margaret Loomis (*Emma Gammell*); Martha Mattox (*Mrs. Miller*); Dulcie Cooper (*Carrie Miller*); Ashley Cooper (*Gus Miller*); Myrtle Stedman (*Vanessa Yates*); Eugenie Besserer (*Mrs. Claveloux*)

CREDITS: *Presented by* Harry Garson; *Director* Harry Garson; based on the eponymous novel by Richard Washburn Child (New York, 1922); *Cinematographer* L.W. O'Connell

Nara Alexieff, daughter of a wealthy Russian landowner, escapes to this country after her parents die in the Bolsheviki [*sic*] Revolution. In New York, she is patronized by Mrs. Vanessa Yates, a wealthy widow, at whose home she becomes acquainted with the secretary, Emma Gammell; Adam Pine, a sculptor; Dr. Emlen Claveloux, eminent physician; and Connor Lee, the latter an ex-actor and fake spiritualist. Pine becomes fascinated with Nara's beautiful hands and reproduces them in marble. Lee persuades Nara that she is a medium and induces her to join him in experiments in healing the sick with her wonderful hands.

Nara is successful as a healer. Emlen believes she loves the sculptor and they separate. Emlen's father is a strong foe of spiritualists, but she changes his views by curing his sick wife. Emlen, however, insists that her power is fraudulent and due to his opposition, she leaves the patient. Nara returns to the tenement district whence she originally came. During a paralysis epidemic, her aid is implored by the people, but she is powerless to help them. She is attacked by an angry mob, but rescued by Emlen, who tells her that she has made him believe that faith is an important factor in healing and that he loves her.

That plot recap was taken verbatim from the 2 September 1922 *Exhibitors Trade Review*. The following appraisal comes word-for-word from the 22 September 1922 *Variety*:

This picture is frankly and purely a bit of propaganda for the Christian Science faith. So much so that the title might better have been that of *The Miracle Woman* than *The Hands of Nara*. The latter title means nothing, the former would have at least been in keeping with the story, and, further, it would have linked the picture with that great success of the past in filmdom, *The Miracle Man*.

Variety's "Fred" was not the only scribe to see the film as little more than a second trip to the dairy barn to milk a cash-cow. The 19 August 1922 *Harrison's Reports* was equally sour on the whole project:

It is a crime to think of the money that has been wasted in trying to make a picture of a story that violates almost every known law of the drama, and every unknown. The man who wrote the scenario seems not to understand the first principles of construction, otherwise he would not have tried to unify material that admits of no unification.

If one is to guess right, in making a picture out of Richard Washburn Child's story the intention no doubt was to make it *A Miracle Woman*, on the pattern of *The Miracle Man*....

The Hands of Nara are no longer with us, so we can't ascertain how much screen time was devoted to Connor Lee's fraudulent spiritualism racket — the one aspect of the film that would have held our interest — and when said hokum would have been situated in the scenario. Neither half of the picture seemed to appeal to anyone who had access to a typewriter and a publisher.

Harrison's went on to moan about the disjointed hodge-podge of dramatically unnecessary baggage that encompassed the first few reels. If the whole point of the movie was Nara's ultimately becoming a faith healer, the reviewer argued…

What in the name of common sense was the necessity of starting the story in Russia to show the heroine's father was murdered by the Bolsheviki, that the heroine was carried away as a chattel, and that she escaped "unscathed" and later ran away and came to the land of the free? And what was the need of the passionate love affair between the heroine's patroness and an artist. Why the shooting, which has no bearing at all upon the rest of the story?

The 19 August 1922 *Motion Picture News* agreed with respect to the picture's lack of coherence, then dismissed the whole she-bang as "one of the many following in the well worn trail of *The Miracle Man.*" *The Film Daily* (13 August 1922) found the trouble to be the miracle-story's being "taken too seriously."

> There have been any number of "miracle" pictures since George Loane Tucker's now famous *The Miracle Man* and Richard Washburn Child's *The Hands of Nara* is just another despite the apparently sincere effort of all concerned to make it distinctive and unusual. In this case in point — power of faith to heal bodily ills — is argued pro and con in numerous conversational titles that lessen the picture's value as entertainment and make it draggy and uninteresting.

Basically then, we have the story of a woman whose undeniably effective healing power is based on her faith (in God? In Christian Science? In Mother Russia?) until the guy whom she loves loses *his* faith (in her), at which point *her* faith (in him? In God [still]? In something else we're not getting right now?) collapses, causing her to head back to the slums. Legions of people in those same slums begin getting paralyzed due to an "epidemic," and Nara is now powerless to help them because her faith (in whatever), which was dependent upon his faith (in her, presumably), is no longer sufficiently strong to permit her to do so. Thus, all those angry and frustrated paralyzed people begin chasing her down the street until — at last — he appears, his faith (in her, one can only assume at this point) has returned because his mother (who was cured by her — i.e., Nara's — power, which had flowed through her — i.e., Nara's — veins due to her — i.e., Nara's — faith [in him, in God, in Christian Science, in Mother Russia, etc.]) is now okay, and — per the *MPN* — "this accomplishment of Nara's brings about a deep love between her and the man." There is no information available on whither went the paralyzed multitudes.

For the skinny on Clara Kimball Young, please see our entry on *Lola* (1914).

— *JTS*

The Heart of the Hills

The Heart of the Hills. Thomas A. Edison, Inc./K-E-S-E Service, 30 October 1916, 5 reels, Library of Congress

CAST: Mabel Trunelle (*Hester*); Conway Tearle (*Redgell*); Bigelow Cooper (*Sir Christopher Madgwick*); Ray McKee (*Eric*); Marie LaCorio (*Edith*); Herbert Prior (*Ali*); George Wright (*Sani*); Robert Conness (*Karaji*); Edith Strickland (*Natali*); Crawford Kent (*McInnes*); Charles Sutton (*Dr. Pettigrew*); Henry Leone (*Darton*).

CREDITS: *Director* Richard Ridgley; based on the novel, *The Girl from the East: A Romance*, by David Whitelaw (London, 1912); *Cinematographer* George Lane

This ought not be confused with the 1919 Mary Pickford vehicle, *Heart o' the Hills*, nor are we dealing with a film set in the Ozarks and populated by good country people. Instead, we are again in *The Moonstone* territory: the India of fiction, an exotic and sinister land teeming with rare gems, Brits out to filch them, and fanatical cultists determined to get them back. There *is* a Grand Guignol subplot, but it's unlikely that it was enough to persuade audiences that they hadn't trod this ground a bit once too often.

Our synopsis comes from *The La Cross* [Wisconsin] *Tribune* (11 November 1916) and was likely taken verbatim from the press-book:

> In India, Sani, a seditionist, steals the sacred ruby, "The Heart of the Hills," for the love of Natali, a beautiful Eurasian. But Natali loves and marries Sir Christopher Madgwick, an Englishman, and Sani swears vengeance. Later Sani kidnaps Hester, Madgwick's infant daughter, after a terrible struggle with Natali during which she tears the Heart of the Hills from the chain about his neck. Natali dies and, after a fruitless search for the child, Sir Christopher returns to England, bearing the sacred ruby with him. Hester is consecrated as a priestess and sworn to the cause of the seditionists.
>
> Years later, Madgwick, who has remarried, is the father of a grown son and daughter. Eric, the boy, is a dissipated scoundrel and Edith, his sister, haughty, proud and cold. Sir Christopher suffers from heart attacks, and his doctors urge great care.
>
> Hester, sent to England to recover the ruby, is revealed to Madgwick as his daughter and received with open arms. Eric and Edith are both hostile to Hester, fearing to lose their inheritance from their father. Edith's hatred is heightened by the attentions which Dennis Redgell, a young lawyer on whom she has set her heart, pays to the girl from the Orient. Hester is overcome by her father's affection and repudiates her vow to regain the sacred ruby in spite of threats of Karaji and Ali, London representatives of the East Indian seditionists. This is the situation in the Madgwick household when Sir Christopher suddenly dies, leaving the bulk of his fortune to Hester.
>
> But Ali and Karaji refuse to allow Hester to forget her vow. When she refuses to search further for the ruby, which has suddenly disappeared on the very night of Madgwick's death, they lure her to Karaji's house where she is held prisoner under heavy guard.
>
> Eric learns that the sacred ruby is buried with his father. Assisted by his crony, a dissolute physician, he rifles the family tomb. The physician is horrified to discover that Sir Christopher did not die a natural death, but was the victim of a mysterious Indian poison. This gives Eric and Edith a weapon against their hated half-sister, and they procure a warrant for her arrest, charging her with having murdered her father when she learned she was the chief beneficiary of his will.
>
> How Hester escapes from the clutches of the Hindu chief; how, aided by the faithful Redgell, she proves her innocence; how the seditionist band is broken up and their leader brought to justice; and how Eric and Edith are made to pay the price for their plot on the eve of Hester's marriage to her lover — all this makes one of the most fascinating stories ever seen on film.

We can't answer all of those questions but, not being too worried about spoilers, we can reveal that other sources tell us that Sir Christopher had a terror of premature burial and had the poison buried with him. Waking up in his coffin to find his worst fears realized, he took his own life. The poison was provided by Ali, apparently acting as Sir Christopher's servant while moonlighting as a seditionist. And Hester, though heavily guarded, escaped the bad guys by jumping out the window of their lair and then managing to direct the police to raid the place. We *don't* know the just desserts meted out to the wicked step siblings or, perhaps more importantly, what became of the ruby.

Sir Christopher's precaution in case of living entombment is a bit like Ray Milland's last resort in AIP's *The Premature Burial*, but it is curious that Sir Christopher, who apparently never shared his obsession with anyone except his treacherous servant Ali, didn't come up with a more practical safeguard like the alarm system in the tomb in *Murder by the Clock*.

The miscegenation element is typical of the times. Natali is only part Indian, but she still has to die because she's married a white man. Edith and Eric even try to discourage their father's attentions to Hester by telling him that she is "a Negress!" Presumably, Hester and Redgell are allowed to live happily ever only because Hester is *mostly* white.

The *Variety* reviewer (13 October 1916) could barely stifle a yawn:

> It all straightens out satisfactorily as they always do. All during the story they are looking for the stolen gem which is supposed to ad interest. Some fairly attractive interiors are brought into play. The cast fits the piece nicely with the picture giving a fair amount of satisfaction.

Theodore Osborn Eltonhead (in the 30 December 1916 *Motion Picture News*) was more positive, but felt the pace dragged:

> We believe this could have been obviated, to a large extent, by the elimination of a number of the scenes. In fact, we believe the whole production could have been made more gripping and more intense had the continuity been handled in a different manner.

Eltonhead did have some kind words for star, Mabel Trunnelle, whom he found "attractive throughout, but especially so in the scenes showing her as a vestal virgin in the temple." More on Trunelle can be found in the entry on *The Ghost of Old Morro* which also contains some info on her husband and frequent co-star, Herbert Prior (Ali). Conway Tearle (Redgell) is profiled in *The Mystic*, while director Richard Ridgley's career is sketched out in *The Mystic Hour*.   — HN

The Hellion see *Infidelity*

Hell's 400

Hell's 400. Fox Film Corp./Fox Films, 14 March 1926, 6 reels/5,582 feet [LOST]

CAST: Margaret Livingston (*Evelyn Vance*); Harrison Ford (*John North*); Henry Kolker (*John Gilmore*); Wallace MacDonald (*Marshall Langham*); Marceline Day (*Barbara Langham*); Rodney Hildebrand (*Bill Montgomery*); Amber Norman (*Vivian*)

CREDITS: *Presented by* William Fox; *Director* John Griffith Wray; *Scenario* Bradley King; suggested by the novel, *The Just and the Unjust*, by Vaughan Kester (Indianapolis, 1912); *Cinematographer* Karl Struss; *Assistant Director* Buddy Erickson

The above title had us all envisioning the Netherworld's Elite (blood-red in color, and replete with horns and tails) cackling diabolically over the arrival of the latest batch of the Damned. (Had we evoked that image along the lines of Millennium-Age cinema, we would have had to add washboard abs and bulging biceps to the demonic mix.) With respect to the 1926 feature film, nothing could be farther from the truth.

Its tempting title apart, *Hell's 400* is but another of those tales of larceny and gold digging and murder that, over the years, helped keep overworked, apathetic, or uninspired screenwriters from going on the dole. We're tucking it into this corner of the book solely because of its reel-six dream sequence which (a) featured "monsters" (their word, not ours), and (b) was shot in color, so it (reel six) was regarded as something of a big deal. The film, she is gone, so we couldn't take the time to count those monsters—we're doubtful there were even *close* to 400, if you must know—and no one can say for sure whether the title referred to them, anyhow. Our synopsis, which doesn't help at all with respect to interpreting the title or filling us in on the names of the dramatis personae, is taken from the 26 March 1926 *Cumberland* [Maryland] *Evening Times*:

> *Hell's Four Hundred* ... tells the story of Evelyn Vance, "refined gold digger" of "The Back Stage Café," who goes out for real big game. Marshall Langham is the villain of the story, the squanderer son of a rich father, whose villainy develops only after he has met and decided to marry the "gold digger."
>
> Marshall forges a check to pay for an engagement ring and the real trouble starts with complications that lead to murder of the man whose name he forged. Langham flees and runs into an iceman friend of the gold digger. The murder results in the arrest of the district attorney who is engaged to the slayer's sister and the next day Marshall starts out in his fast roadster. As the car dashes across a narrow bridge, he almost runs down the iceman.
>
> In the clash that follows, the iceman threatens to tell all he knows about the murder and a fight starts that carries both men onto a railroad trestle. In avoiding an approaching train, they swing down under the trestle, hanging to the ties. Both men fall into the water.
>
> The iceman escapes but the slayer is so badly injured he confesses before he dies and clears the murder mystery, but his death leaves the gold digger a widow in the same position in life as that from which she started.

Hmmmmmmmmmmmm... Monsters? We don't see no stinkin' Monsters! For them, mes amis, (and for more fun facts and nomenclature) we must repair to the 30 May 1926 *Film Daily*:

> Evelyn [Vance, a chorus girl] marries the rich Marshall Langham thereby double-crossing Gilmore, her boss, who had employed her to rope Langham into a scandal because of debts he owed Gilmore. The latter is killed and John North, district attorney and sworn enemy of Gilmore and his gambling house, is held on circumstantial evidence. Evelyn could clear North but in so doing, she would expose Langham, the guilty one. When he is dying, he clears North who is engaged to his sister. At this point, Evelyn sees a vision in which her sins take the forms of monsters. For a fade-out you have Evelyn waking from a bad dream and all set to go on the iceman's picnic instead of hunting a rich papa.

Okay; the guy who is killed is John Gilmore (and we had to go to a third source, *The AFI Catalog*, to get his Christian name), while the district attorney set to take the fall is John North. In this second account, Evelyn is more than a mere gold digger: she is partner to a shakedown attempt that leads to murder. Hence, some guilt. Thence, her nightmare. Thus, the Monsters. Inevitably, it was *All a Dream*, and The Iceman Cometh. Finis.

Crap.

Prior to revealing his detail-filled lowdown, the *Film Daily* scribe put everything into perspective when he noted that Margaret Livingston played the part of Evelyn, whom he described as "a spirited young lady of the chorus who has a very bad dream." And there you have it. That very bad dream was not only a life-changing experience for our young Evelyn, but also an example of two-strip Technicolor. And also, we aver without having screened said dream, an example of allegorical cinema.

We have sought to avoid like the plague movie allegories in their purest form, while at the same time offering a sampling that is both representational and strongly genre-oriented. Acting within these parameters, we have included stuff like *The Temptations of Satan* (1914), *Black Fear* (1915), *The Lust of the Ages* (1916), and *Conscience* (1917), and we would be lying if we didn't acknowledge that these particular genre-slanted treatments are — on the face of it, at least — also more fun than films in which Everyman is allegoried mercilessly until he buys into Patriotism, Chastity, Truth, Justice, and/or the American Way. Numerically-minded readers will have noted that those titles were all thrust upon the Movie World during the 1910s; the flipside of that observation ought to be equally obvious: during the Roaring Twenties, allegories saw their popularity drop until it lay somewhere between that of the late Kaiser and the average man's support of both the Volstead Act and the ratification of the 18th Amendment of the Constitution.

Thus, the color-filled cauchemar of *Hell 400*'s Evelyn represented a content-area throw-back arrayed in a technological innovation. Say *that* three times, fast.

Evelyn was played by Margaret Livingston, about whom you may read further in our piece on 1929's *The Charlatan*. Harrison Ford (see *The Crystal Gazer*) played John North, the dynamic D.A., and Henry Kolker was the double-crossed and not-much-liked John Gilmore. (Why were they both named "John"?) Anyhow, Kolker had been in the movies for over 10 years by the time *Hell's 400* came out without drawing much genre attention, although he did portray the damned-if-only-in-a-dream hero in 1915's *The Warning* (see entry in appendix) and he did helm a good dozen and a half features (including 1921's *The Fighter*, see entry). Come the Sound Era, though, his name would be found in the cast scrawls of such well-regarded (by us) talkies as *Black Moon* (1934) and *Mad Love* (1935). Having abjured directing in 1924 — but having acted 'til the very end — Kolker died with his movie boots on in 1947.

Wallace MacDonald was Marshall Langham, the squanderer son with the fast roadster and the knack for forgery. MacDonald proved to be one of those industry multi-taskers, displaying some talent at acting (see *Curlytop* and *Darkened Rooms*), producing (1941's *The Face behind the Mask*), writing (the 1935 serial, *The Phantom Empire*), and directing (okay; no genre gold in this pan). Working in one job or another between 1912 or so and the tail end of the 1950s, MacDonald made his mark on middlin' movie fare. Still, he also deserves special mention for the spate of Boris Karloff films with which he was associated, but which bore no onscreen mark of his: *The Man They Could Not Hang*, *The Man with Nine Lives*, and *Before I Hang*. For Edward Dmytryk's offbeat *The Devil Commands*, though, he was given screen credit as producer. Retired in 1959, Macdonald passed away on Halloween eve, 1978.

Hell's 400 was "suggested by" *The Just and the Unjust*, a novel from the typing machine of Vaughan Kester, a New Jersey–born writer whose estate probably handled the sale of literary rights to the Fox Film Corp., as the man himself had died on the Fourth of July, 1911. Screenwriter Bradley (*The Return of Peter Grimm*) King did whatever he did to the posthumously published novel to come up with *Hell's 400* (aka *Hell's Four Hundred*), and we'd be willing to bet the farm's back forty that the film's last-reel parade of guilt-inspired grotesques arose from King's imagination, and not from Kester's.

It's that last reel that forced our hand, inclusion-wise, here, even though the footage's being in Technicolor may well have worked against its survival over the years. And as for the first five, black-and-white reels? Frankly, dear, if it weren't for the presence of the beauteous Miss Livingston and the fact that the picture was photographed by Karl (*Ben-Hur*, *Sunrise*) Struss, we wouldn't give a damn.

— JTS

An Hour Before Dawn

An Hour before Dawn. Famous Players Film Co./States Rights, 20 October 1913, 3 or 4 reels [LOST]
CAST: Laura Sawyer (*Kate Kirby*), House Peters (*Kate's father*)
CREDITS: *Producer* Daniel Frohman; *Director* J. Searle Dawley; *Scenario* J. Searle Dawley; *Cinematographer* H. Lyman Broening

It's uncertain whether *An Hour before Dawn* exhibited at three reels or four, but inasmuch as that straddles the border for inclusion as a feature, the picture finds itself here in the Appendix. It's fairly certain that the reader may confuse this long-lost epic with *One Hour before Dawn*, and that's certainly understandable. Most certain is the fact that our summary originated from publicity material printed as it was in both *Moving Picture World* (18 October 1913) and *The Wichita* [Kansas] *Daily Times* (18 November 1913):

> Prof. Wallace, a scientific authority, strenuously objects to his son, Richard's romance with Violet Dane, a chorus girl in the "Red Rose" Company. Prof. Wallace tells the girl that unless she abandons every relationship with his son, he will completely disinherit him. That night a servant hears a heated altercation between father and son, and the next day the professor is found dead with a mysterious wound in his side. Kate Kirby, the girl detective, is engaged. All the arts of modern criminal detection and many unique methods are introduced, which prove futile until Miss Kirby finds a carbon sheet the impression of which is a letter from the professor to Violet, asking her to call after the performance, as he wishes "to settle." Blood stains are discovered leading to the observatory, where other disclosures prove the professor was shot. A notebook found in the professor's pocket indicates that he had been engaged on an experiment until an hour before dawn, which stamps the time of his death. The son is arrested on strength of motive. Following the clue disclosed by the carbon, Miss Kirby secures a position in the "Red Rose" Company and becomes intimate with Violet in an effort to gain her confidence. The son is subjected to a grueling third degree and collapses under the ordeal. These facts are graphically told in the evening paper which Miss Kelly reads in an intensely dramatic manner to Violet in hopes that she will admit her guilt.
>
> Later, Miss Kirby overhears her praying for the fate of Richard so earnestly as to force the conclusion that she is innocent. But Miss Kirby is absolutely mystified when she receives a telegram

from police headquarters advising her that Violet has confessed to the murder. Miss Kirby, suspecting Violet's motive, cross examines the girl, who adheres to her confession. The boy is released in Violet's presence. It is the first time that the two have met since the professor's death, and the pathos of the meeting, tragic in extreme, is intensified when the boy hears the confession and recoils in horror, renouncing Violet, who, with stoic fortitude, abandons herself to her fate. Miss Kirby re-examines the effects of the deceased professor, and discovers a note referring to the perfection of a wonderful invention an hour before dawn. A gleam of new hope enters the mystery, she enlists the interests of her father — a paralyzed detective introduced in "Chelsea 7750" — and they discover that the professor was killed by a terrific explosive force (technically known as infra red ray, the discovery of which Signor Ulivi, an Italian engineer, has so lately startled the scientific world).

Two concluding references in our synopsis — the first to *Chelsea 7750* and the second to one Signor Ulivi — interweave fiction and reality.

The Fiction... Regular moviegoers would have recognized *Chelsea 7750* as the title of the first feature-length cinematic adventure of girl detective, Kate Kirby. Edison had planned 1913 to be the year of "Kate Kirby's Cases," a series of short films written and directed by J. Searle Dawley and starring Laura Sawyer as the distaff detective. The first film — all 1000 feet of it — was *The Diamond Crown*, released on the 12 July 1913. A week later, *On the Broad Stairway* hit the screens and, not long afterward, Dawley and Sawyer hit the road; they moved — lock, stock, and Kate Kirby — over to Famous Players, where Kate's adventures took longer to unfold. *An Hour before Dawn* found itself sandwiched between the aforementioned *Chelsea 7750* (released the 20 October 1913) and *The Port of Doom* (the 20 December); if Edison could show ... ummm ... Kirby's shorts one week after another, Famous Players could display her features at precise, monthly intervals.

Both Sawyer and Dawley had been familiar faces at Edison, and their joint departure can't have slowed the studio's gradual dissolution more than the sound and fury effected by the collapse of The Motion Picture Patents Company (the "Trust"), the worst and most self-serving idea ever attributed to the Wizard of Menlo Park. Sawyer would remain in films for several years after *An Hour before Dawn*, with no confirmable credits after 1915. For more on J. Searle Dawley, please see our essay on *The Phantom Honeymoon*. As for character man, House Peters — star of Universal's *Raffles, the Amateur Cracksman* (1925) and father of House Peters, Jr., perennial B-movie henchman — those regular moviegoers mentioned above may have found themselves a tad confused when viewing *An Hour after Dawn*: in that Famous Players feature and *The Port of Doom*, Peters — the villain of *Chelsea 7750* — replaced popular stage star, Henry E. Dixey, as Kate's resourceful father. Quite a promotion.

The Reality... Much as H. Grindell-Matthews (see *Laughing at Danger*, 1924) would a decade later, Ulivi claimed to have invented a ray that could destroy enemy weapons at a distance; dubbed the "F Ray," the device supposedly drew upon the infra-red portion of the spectrum. Although Ulivi's announcement was greeted with acclaim initially, things went downhill quickly. Pressured to explain sizeable theoretical holes and faced with a demand for additional controlled experiments, Ulivi caved and

he and his invention were met with ever-increasing derision. Nonetheless, movie studios cashed in on his hoax — and that of Grindell-Matthews — more than the two charlatans ever could, despite their best efforts.

We can only hypothesize as to the amount of footage devoted to the science-fiction elements of *An Hour before Dawn*. Did, in fact, Prof. Wallace's startling ray ever even see action on the screen? Kate Kirby — she of "modern criminal detection and many unique methods" — was, despite the novelty of her gender, only one of the era's never-ending series of scientific detectives. Was the film replete with the sort of pseudo-scientific gadgetry that such sleuths needed to operate? No evidence one way or the other survives. On the other hand, *mystery* fans may have been tickled by the finale which, per the afore-cited *MPW*, left open the door as to exactly *who* might have fired up that fatal explosive ray after all.

Coverage on the film in another issue of *Moving Picture World* (23 October 1913) found it to be "different," its settings "elaborate," and its acting, direction and photography "excellent." And, in spite of opining that "apart from the introduction of a new scientific marvel, the story offers nothing new," the 29 October 1913 *New York Dramatic Mirror* concluded that "Director Dawley has presented a masterpiece."

— *SJ*

The House of Mystery

The House of Mystery. William Steiner Productions/Arrow Film Corporation; States Rights, September 1921, 5 reels [LOST]
CAST: Glen White (*Tex*); John Costello (*John Raby*); Ethel Russell (*Alice Raby*); Cecil Kern (*Marion Lake*); with Harold Vosburgh
CREDITS: *Producer* William Steiner; *Story* Alexander F. Frank

This epic — supposedly involving séances and communication with/from the Beyond — was but one of a series of features made centering on the character, "Tex, Elucidator of Mysteries." The Tex films were not chapters of a serial but, rather, nine five-reel features that pitted the wits of the Elucidator (played by Glen[n] White; see: *The Darling of Paris*) against various agencies of darkness.

First off, let's get the plot recap of the film under discussion out of the way. (Another tip of the hat to *The AFI Catalog*.)

> When cardsharp Ellis Gale threatens to disclose that Charles Dunn forged his uncle John Raby's name on a check to pay for losses at cards, Dunn promises to repay Gale after he marries Raby's daughter Alice, but Alice, who loves Ralph Crane, refuses Dunn's proposal. After Dunn learns that Raby is attempting to communicate with his dead wife Miriam through a medium, Madame Kautsky, Dunn bribes Kautsky, and during a séance a vision of Miriam tells Raby that Alice must marry Dunn. Meanwhile, Gale, who has stolen love letters from Marion Lake, Ralph's married sister, to Dunn, is murdered. After Marion's husband, Dr. Lake, is accused, Tex, "Elucidator of Mysteries," investigates and learns that a veiled woman was seen at the murder site. During a séance, he captures the veiled woman, who looks like Miriam, and reveals that the woman really is Dunn, Miriam's nephew, who killed Gale when he went to retrieve the forged check. Dr. Lake and Marion are reconciled, while Raby agrees to Alice's marriage to Ralph.

It wasn't hard retyping that from *The AFI Catalog*; understanding what we typed, well ... that's a different story. We are left to surmise that Miriam is still dead, that the titular house was either the murder site or the scene of the fraudulent séance, and that Charles Dunn occasionally cross-dresses. The rest of it — who's bribing whom, whose heart belongs where, and all that sort of thing — is depressingly mundane. Given the equally tepid themes of most of the eight other entries* in the series, our hoping that Mrs. Raby might have actually penetrated The Veil to offer discorporate (but sound) advice to her husband is truly a case of clinging at straws.

Still, the Tex series offered early 1920s audiences one of the first, feature-length series devoted to the continuing adventures of a gentleman detective. Granted, the films had a limited release due to the Arrow Film Corporation, the folks who distributed 1920's *Dr. Jekyll and Mr. Hyde*. (No, not *that* one, *or* that one…. The two-reeler starring Hank Mann … plus 1923's *The Little Red School House* and about 300 shorts.) But the reason not a one has survived may be found in the fact that the series' main distribution arm was the States Rights system, which may have done all right by the states, but was the wrong way to go for pictures looking for a Life after Initial Release. Sometimes, though, indie studios had no other choice.

Other than 1920's *Sky Eye* — an aerial feature made in conjunction with the U.S. Army Air Services — the fortunes of the William Steiner Production Company were viscerally intertwined with the Tex series. As a low-budget independent, Steiner (see entry, *The Hidden Menace*) looked to cut costs wherever he could — Hello, States Rights! — and several times either took on a co-producer (The Empire State Film Corporation) to split expenses or — in the case of *The Unseen Witness* — sold 100 percent of the project to Empire State. With the nine Tex features all produced and released within a year and a half, standing sets were frequently employed, location shooting was restricted to the most local of locations, and actors were asked to supply as many of their own props and costumes as possible. Steiner put a number of inexpensive character persons (like Jane McAlpine, David Wall, Joseph Striker and Alexander F. Frank, none of whom appeared in *Mystery*, at least per our extremely limited cast list) under contract and, while they usually essayed different roles and did *not* play recurring characters, their presence gave something of a sense of continuity to the series on the whole. The few critiques we were able to find (no "usual suspects" reporting here) were almost unanimously unenthusiastic, and when Tex went south after *The House of Mystery*, so did Steiner.

Try as we might, we couldn't find one domestic review on *The House of Mystery*, and it was only with the help of Library of Congress librarian, Josie L. Walters-Johnston, that we could get our hands on a *British* critique. Following, then, are some thoughts on *Mystery* from the 28 September 1922 (yes; 1922) *Kinematograph Weekly*:

> Originality … is not one of the qualifications of the plot, but it is certainly intricate and narrated with a view to complicating

things as much as possible…. Moderate, but not much, entertainment is provided, and what there is is likely to appeal to audiences who favour a detective story, and who do not mind it being dull in other respects…. The setting is mediocre and is chiefly interior. The scene where the spiritualistic medium horrifies Raby succeeds in being moderately creepy; the others are chiefly futile.

As for the character, Tex… There isn't a body of research that we could consult on this issue (there isn't so much as a *digit* of research, actually), but it seems that the ol' Elucidator was a creation of someone named Tom Collins. Inasmuch as the sum total of Mr. Collins' cinematic presence was also viscerally intertwined with the series, one theory (and there aren't really *multiple* theories on this) is that Tom Collins may have been a *nom de plume*, and that director/writer Pierce Kingsley (see *The Magic Toy Maker*) may have assumed the nom de Tom when dealing with Tex. The sundry credits that have survived on the series' entries show Mr. Collins as having directed all of them, except for *The Sacred Ruby*† — another of those gem-stolen-from-the-Eastern-cult jobs — helmed by Glen White; *The Bromley Case*, which was directed by David Wall (an actor in all the Tex features save this one), with Collins "supervising"; and *The House of Mystery*, which bears no director's credit per the surviving documents. In addition, Collins wrote the lion's share of the screenplays. Proving or disproving this hypothesis would require the sort of effort akin to researching one's PhD dissertation and, when the smoke cleared — as is the case with most PhD dissertations — it wouldn't make a damned bit of difference. Whether there really was a living, breathing writer/director named Tom Collins who rose and fell, as it were, with the "Tex, Elucidator of Mysteries" series, or whether Pierce Kingsley came upon the name while sitting in a bar in late 1919, wondering what in hell to do next, we may never know.

Or choose to care about.

The Sacred Ruby. William Steiner Productions/States Rights; Arrow Film Corp., October (?) 1920, 5 reels/4905 feet [LOST]
CAST: Arthur E. Sprague (*High Priest*); David Wall (*Chundra Lal*); Glenn [*sic*] White (*Tex*); Jack Newton (*Mr. Van Tuyl*); Mrs. Jane Drake (*Mrs. Van Tuyl*); Willard Cooley (*Travers*); Ethel Russell (*Grace Van Tuyl*); Marie Treador (*Mrs. Blythe*); Walter Dowling (*The butler*)
CREDITS: *Producer* William Steiner; *Director* Glenn White; *Story* Alexander F. Frank

> Hindu Chundra Lal arrives in America intent upon recovering the sacred ruby that was stolen from his people. The ruby is now in the possession of Mrs. Van Tuyl, the wife of a millionaire whose daughter Grace is engaged to Ray Travers. With the assistance of Mrs. Blythe, a widow who has been spurned by Travers, Chundra Lal steals the gem and places an imitation ruby in Travers' pocket, thus casting suspicion on him. Even Grace doubts her fiancé's innocence, but Tex, a detective, remains skeptical about Travers' guilt. While attempting to unravel the mystery, Tex is captured by Chundra Lal and his henchmen and is about to be sacrificed to the idol Kali when the police rescue him. Eventually Tex uncovers the stolen ruby and Travers, now cleared of charges, reconciles with Grace.

The Wall Street Mystery; The Bromley Case; Circumstantial Evidence; The Scrap of Paper; The Unseen Witness; The Sacred Ruby; The Trail of the Cigarette; The Triple Clue.

†With this tome already heavy with tales of rubies and the like stolen from Indian temples and such, we present herewith an abbreviated entry featuring the plot and cast/credits lists of *The Sacred Ruby*.

The 18 September 1920 *Harrison's Reports*, one of the *very* few periodicals to afford any space to *Ruby*, viewed the film as a clear-cut case of theft and recovery, with no cultish or supernatural elements worth the mention: "The sympathy instead of going to the American owners of the jewel, goes to the Hindoos [*sic*]. One feels that, since the jewel was stolen from them, they are its rightful owners."

— *JTS*

The House of Whispers

The House of Whispers. Robert Brunton Productions/W.W. Hodkinson Corp. through Pathé Exchange, October 1920, 5 reels/c. 5800 feet [LOST]

CAST: J. Warren Kerrigan (*Spaulding Nelson*); Joseph J. Dowling (*Rufus Gaston*); Fritzi Brunette (*Barbara Bradford*); Marjorie Wilson (*Clara Bradford*); Myrtle Rischel (*Mrs. Bradford*); Herbert Prior (*Edward Thayer*); Myles McCarthy (*Henry Kent*); Claire Du Brey (*Nettie Kelly*); Fred C. Jones (*Roldo*)

CREDITS: *Presented by* Robert Brunton; *Director* Ernest C. Warde; *Scenario* Jack Cunningham; based on the eponymous novel by William Andrew Johnston (Boston, 1918); *Cinematographer* Arthur L. Todd

> "You heard whispers," she cried excitedly, "whispers that seemed to come from up near the ceiling?"
> "I thought I heard them. I wasn't sure."
> "I know," she said, shuddering. "I've heard them — twice."
> We looked at each other despairingly. We both of us realized that we must be surrounded with some potent evil forces working to accomplish our ruin.

Silent films and old, dark houses went together like Liederkranz and onions, but silent films and *whispers*? Erik at the organ, Quasimodo at the carillon, Matthias and his bells, phantom melodies and violins — even the House of the Tolling Bell — all these sound-oriented fantasies had their backs covered (as it were) by the musicians in the pit. But … whispers? Let's have a look.

> *The House of Whispers* is haunted at irregular periods by uncanny whisperings, muffled screams and sound of shuffling feet. The uncle of Spaulding nelson leaves the place with a bad case of nerves, Spaulding accepting the task of occupying the apartment. Soon after he starts an investigation, Spaulding meets Barbara Bradford, whose sister, Clara, is being subjected to a strange persecution. Whispers are heard in the Bradford apartment — whispers that are identical with the voice of Roldo, an Italian chauffeur whom Clara married years before, but who had been reported killed during the war. Mysterious notes are left in the Bradford and Nelson apartments. Nelson, who has become interested in Barbara, determines to solve the mystery.
> Roldo — who is actually alive and associated with Henry Kent, a half-crazed crook who erected the House of Whispers and lined it with secret passageways to enable him to rifle apartments — is persuaded to murder Daisy Lutan, an actress. Spaulding meanwhile locates the secret panel doors, but is arrested on suspicion of the murder. He eludes the detectives, escapes through the panel and down the secret passageway where he discovers the kidnapped Clara and the quarters of the gang. He breaks his way into the apartment and forces Kent, Roldo, and Nettie Kelly, whom Roldo had married prior to his illegal wedding with Clara, and causes their arrest. By the confession made by Nettie, Clara is left free to marry her fiancé, while Barbara accepts Spaulding [*Exhibitor's Trade Review*, 2 October 1920].

Let's face it: whispers coming from "up near the ceiling" are a lot more eerie than whispers coming through the walls, so the brief excerpt that opened this chapter — taken directly from William Johnston's eponymous source novel — had us suited up, onboard, and headed for Genre Island. Then the *ETR* summary opened with "haunted," and added "muted screams" and the "sound of shuffling feet" to the mix — more effects that couldn't be replicated by the guy at the Mighty Wurlitzer. Still, not a bad way to start.

As is evident in a lot of other elsewheres in this book, though, movie reviewers were as individual in their tastes and propensities in 1920 as they are now, and one man's meat was even then another man's *poisson*. Thus, as promising as things may have seemed for the *ETR* readership, the folks who put their faith in *The Moving Picture World* got a whole other viewpoint. To wit:

> Shortly after Spaulding meets Barbara Bradford, the girl in the park, who lives in the next apartment. She confides in him that her sister, Clara, who is engaged to be married, *is being subjected to a strange persecution*. [Same peculiar phraseology used in the above *ETR* recap. Coincidence?] She has been secretly married to Roldo, an Italian chauffeur, who was reported killed in the late war. Whispers in Roldo's voice are heard in the Bradford apartment and notes signed by Roldo are found in the rooms. He threatens to divulge his existence to Clara's fiancé unless a large sum of money is paid him [2 October 1920].

This *MPW* critique — replete with details about gals hesitant to mention defunct husbands to new prospects and "otherworldly" demands for cold, hard cash — let all the wind out of our sails, and our junket to Genre Island has become about as likely to happen as our seeing a balanced budget within the next couple of weeks. Once again, then, we are led down the primrose path: teased with the promise of supernatural goings-on, only to be disappointed by the almost inevitably mundane denouement.

Murders and secret passages and unexpected noises and all that were as much a part of that old, dark house subgenre as Doris Day was a mainstay in 1950s movie musicals, but — almost from the very dawn of the cinema — the frissons that were so carefully established in the first couple of reels were, more times than not, meticulously debunked, come the last. Save for genre buffs (like us), who raged through clenched teeth whenever the hoped-for supernatural element was exposed as hoo-hah, most audiences came to expect that somebody — the hero, the police inspector, the gentleman detective — would provide not only a rational explanation for the spooky goings-on, but also the motive for them. Nonetheless, it was the playing out of the piece that appealed to the majority of ticket-buyers, who found that trying to solve (e.g.) the *Secret of the Blue Room* before the "official" solution was unveiled was a fun by-product of a Saturday night at the movies.

In this regard, though, *The House of Whispers* failed — at least per Laurence Reid, who, in his *Motion Picture News* coverage of the picture, complained that "Ernest Warde, the director, places his cards upon the table too early. It transpires that the guilty are established by the simple process of planting them firmly as crooks. And when they glide about in mysterious channels one is certain that this apartment house is built with secret staircases" (2 October 1920). (For the record, the *Exhibitor's*

Trade Review cited above found Warde's *Whispers* work "Splendid" and hailed it as "An achievement in the line of mystery pictures." What did we say about meat and *poisson*?)

J. Warren Kerrigan played Spaulding Nelson; for reasons unknown, scenarist Jack Cunningham gave Nelson a "u" in his Christian name that had been denied him by novelist, William Andrew Johnston. Kerrigan, an enormously popular actor with well over 300 pictures to his credit (in less than 15 years!), saw his career falter and his professional future dim when the fact of his being gay somehow eluded the studios' best efforts at concealing it. The Louisville, Kentucky, native had earlier weathered a storm when some offhand remarks he had made about America's participation in the Great War — plus his refusal to enlist — resulted in a raft of unfavorable publicity. Still, his last couple of years in the industry (he called it quits in 1924) saw him back in the first cast of a good handful of better pictures, including *The Covered Wagon* and *The Girl of the Golden West* (both 1923), and a turn as the title character in the classic action/adventure tale, *Captain Blood* (1924).

MPW praised his portrayal of Nelson (played with "evident enjoyment, vigor and force"), *Wid's Daily* (26 September 1920) found him "adequate," and Helen Pollock — writing on the same date for the *New York Dramatic Mirror*—confessed that, "Of the motion pictures which this reviewer has seen featuring J. Warren Kerrigan — and there have been a great many — *The House of Whispers* is by far the best." It's interesting to note that *Whispers* is about as close to a genre feature that the actor ever got, despite his lengthy resume. And pretty much ditto with respect to his healthy output of shorts; 1913/1914's *The Magic Skin*, a Victor three-reeler based on Balzac's novel, and 1915's *The Shriek in the Night* (another Victor short), seem to be about it. Kerrigan managed to get by quite nicely for the next couple of decades without the hypocrisy he had found in Hollywood and died in June 1947.

Fritzi Brunette (see *The Dream Cheater*) was the beauteous Barbara Bradford, and Claire Du Brey (see: *The Magic Eye*) was the villainous Nettie Kelly. The most genre-friendly name among the remaining cast members belonged to Herbert Prior, an Oxford-born Briton who emigrated to involve himself in the American flickers back in 1908, and whose face was seen in such favorites of ours as *The Magic Skin* (1915), *The Ghost of Old Morro* (1917), and *The Monster* (1925; see entries), although his name wasn't seen on the cast crawl for that last one.

The House of Whispers was directed by Ernest C. Warde, another Brit who had come west looking for his path through life. Warde started out as an actor and kept his hand in even after being promoted to keeper of the megaphone, albeit his genre roles were limited to a bit in *Blow Your Own Horn* (1923). Behind the camera, though, the Liverpudlian pushed 'em this way 'n' that in for 1918's *The Bells* (vintage 1918), *The Devil to Pay*, and *The Dream Cheater* (the latter two, like *Whispers*, released in 1920).

A frequent collaborator of Warde's was cinematographer, Arthur L. Todd, and a more comprehensive list of the genre debt we owe that man may be found in our essay on *The Devil to Pay*.

The picture was marketed more as a mystery than a thriller —

even the publicity pieces printed before the film's release gave away the business about the secret passages — perhaps because Johnston's novel was also prominently featured in the adverts. One of the lesser "house" pictures that peppered the 1920s, *Whispers* had its moments, and it's for those isolated vignettes that we lay the film to rest in the Appendix.

— JTS

Indiscretion see *The Eternal Mother*

Infidelity

Infidelity. Erbograph Company/Art Dramas, Inc., 11 January 1917, 5 reels [LOST]
CAST: Anna Q. Nilsson (*Elaine Bernard*); Eugene Strong (*Ford Maillard*); Miriam Nesbitt (*Dorothy Stafford*); Warren Cook (*Clifford Wayne*); Fred Jones (*Ali Delna*); Elizabeth Spencer (*Mrs. Maillard*); Arthur Morrison (*John Griswold*)
CREDITS: *Director* Ashley Miller; *Scenario* Ashley Miller

We're talking sex here — and talk is all we can do; the film is lost — because the title refers to the state of being unfaithful. Had the title been *Infidel*, we'd be talking about God and the supernatural and stuff. Still, as much as we all like sex, we wouldn't even be talking about this particular film were it not for the fact that, once again, we can isolate the cause of many Silent-Era studies in infidelity: not the XX chromosome, but — rather — the HHH character: the Horny Hindu Hypnotist.

In a nutshell (per the 27 January 1917 *Moving Picture World*): "A Hindoo gentleman possessed of remarkable powers of mesmerism is shown in the act of compelling a young girl, by the mere exercise of his will power, to leave her home and join him in a distant studio."

For those requiring more detail, *The AFI Catalog*:

> When Clifford Wayne is found standing over the body of John Griswold, his wife Dorothy's rejected suitor, he is sent to prison for murder. Years later, Dorothy is running a millinery shop when one of her patrons, Mrs. Maillard, notices her daughter Elaine's artistic ability and insists upon sponsoring her in art school. Elaine enrolls in a class taught by Frank Mayne, who unknown to her, is actually Wayne, her father. Also in the class is Mrs. Maillard's son Ford, who falls in love with Elaine, and Hindu student Ali Delna, who practices hypnotism on the girl. One evening, while Mayne is away from the studio, Ali exerts his hypnotic influence over Elaine and forces her to come to the studio. Ford discovers the two struggling and accuses Elaine of infidelity. At that moment, Mayne returns and explains Delna's hypnotic powers, freeing Elaine from all suspicion. Soon after, Elaine's mother arrives and recognizes Mayne as her husband, and thus the family is finally reunited.

Readers for whom English is the first language will come away from that paragraph realizing that, in terms of infidelity, the picture offers zilch. The moviegoer who had plopped down fifteen cents in the hopes of seeing anybody caught *in flagrante delicto* with anybody else came away woefully disappointed, and that's how the Better Business Bureau was born. The first line readily identifies John Griswold as Dorothy's *rejected* suitor, and that adjective leads one to believe that, in terms of John and Dorothy knowing each other in the biblical sense, we have more zilch.

Then, too — years and years later — when young Ford barges in on young Elaine, she is (apparently) engaged in *fisticuffs* with (young, we assume) Ali, and is not doing not the horizontal tango. Where is the infidelity there? we hasten to ask. Zilch once again. Better they should have named this picture *Misunderstanding* or even *Jumping to Conclusions*. In its 19 January 1917 issue, *Variety* had zilch to say about Ali, sneered at the scenario's understanding of "infidelity," and spilled most of its ink kvetching about the absolutely ludicrous plot-pivot. To wit: "The story is based on one of the milder meanings of the word infidelity having as its central figure an artist who accuses his wife of infidelity and takes a prison sentence of 20 years for killing a man, a crime which he did not commit, in order to sever all relations with his spouse."

Now, if you can believe *that*, you should have no problem whatsoever believing that the United States in the first quarter or so of the 20th century was awash with oversexed Hindus who were here (ostensibly) to study medicine, architecture or art, but — in truth — were just awaiting their chance to deflower American Roses. Seems like a whole lot of crazy to us, but that little catalyst was used over and over and over....

Still, the afore-cited *MPW* critique opened by advising that "Occultism plays a rather important part in *Infidelity*" before admitting that, "The story ... is not as highly spiced as the title suggests." The assemblage of plot bits we've quoted tend to show that the picture was not only low on spice, it was tepid in terms of occultism, too, and while we care not a fig at this point that the onscreen hi-jinx were neither hot nor steamy, we are again disappointed to discover that one can't ever leave hypnosis and hormones (and Hindoos!) alone for five reels without things getting ugly.

Ali Delna, the Hindu with the hots for Elaine, was essayed by Fred Jones — better known as Fred C. Jones — an actor born on the Isle of Manhattan and active in the film industry from 1915 until 1925. Fred had made his debut in Edison's *The Destroying Angel* — a five-reeler that told the typical tale of actors and actresses, death and dying, chauffeurs, auto accidents, rape, and nervous breakdowns — and exited the movie scene (so far as we can tell) after playing a small part in Fox's *The Fool* (an elaborate tale of faith healing and ... infidelity!) a decade later. There was a Fred Jones (and a Fred C. Jones) who dabbled in the legitimate theater on Broadway and elsewhere during the 1910s–1920s, but we can't be certain that he was (they were?) our man.

Dorothy Stafford, the woman who did *not* canoodle with John Gilmore, was impersonated by Miriam Nesbitt, for whom *Infidelity* was her last motion picture, but one. On Broadway (in *At the White Horse Inn*) as early as 1899, Miss Nesbitt made the move from stage to screen in 1908, and the picture under discussion was the lady's 125th or so: between the two performing media, a very good run. Miss Nesbitt's husband (in real life) was Australian character actor, Marc McDermott, who had a small part in 1919's *The Thirteenth Chair*, and who frequently played opposite his wife in vintage 1910s movies. Miss Nesbitt's husband (in *Infidelity*) was played by Warren Cook, a Bostonian who did all of his screen-work during the Silent Era, and whose name may be espied herein in the cast lists of 1917's *The Undying Flame* and 1923's *Dark Secrets*.

Anna Q. Nilsson (*One Hour before Dawn* [1920], *Between Friends* [1924]) starred as Elaine, the gal who really did nothing wrong, and Eugene Strong (*wonderful* name for an actor playing a hero) played her hero. *Infidelity* was directed by Ashley Miller, a gentleman who flourished as a Silent-Era animator (1916's *Why the Sphinx Laughed*), director (well over 100 films, including stuff like 1911's *The Ghost's Warning* [a short with Nesbitt and McDermott] and 1912's *Fog* [another short, with McDermott and Nesbitt]), and scenarist (over two-and-a-half-dozen screenplays other than *Infidelity*). Available information indicates Mr. Miller accomplished all of this between 1910 and 1918, and — similar to our experience with Fred Jones (above) — we've caught sight of an Ashley Miller who performed on the Broadway stage in the early 1900s, but cannot say for sure whether the two men were one and the same.

Ali Delna turns out to be as big a letdown to us as *Infidelity* was to the critics who reviewed it and — most likely — the viewers who sat through it. Still, Eastern-practitioners-of-mesmerism-working-their-magic-on-nubile-young-virgins *is* a winner, thematically, and we've got to consider the theme.

As for stuff within spitting distance of said theme, some brief mention needs to be made of the 1919 *The Hellion* which, like *Infidelity*, arbitrarily throws a hypnotist into its melodramatic mix.

Our synopsis comes from *The AFI Catalog*:

> Joseph and Helen Harper, who have spent their niece Blanche's inheritance, worry that Blanche's fiancé, wealthy George Graham, will no longer want her when he finds out that she has gone insane from grief after hearing a report of his death in the war. When George returns and learns of the situation, he hires detectives to investigate. The Harpers convince cabaret dancer Mazie Del Mar, who resembles Blanche, to impersonate her. Mazie, wanting to escape from cabaret owner Signor Enrico — called the "Hellion" — who uses hypnosis to control her, agrees, but she falls in love with George and feels deceitful. After Enrico kidnaps Blanche, thinking she is Mazie, and unsuccessfully tries to hypnotize her, they fight and Blanche is killed. George tells Mazie, about to confess, that his detectives told him who she was, but that he loves her anyway. He forgives the Harpers since their scheme resulted in love for him and Mazie.

Elsewhere we learn that the "Hellion" is also the name of Signor Enrico's cabaret; maybe it sounded better than "Rico's Place." In spite of a trade paper ad showing a sinister Signor Enrico making mesmeric moves on the heroine, the reviews we consulted scarcely mentioned the villain's hypnotic powers (which apparently can work — if just barely — on only one person at a time). Making Enrico a simple gangster would have been more logical, but the producers may have felt that tossing in a pinch of Svengali couldn't have hurt an already ridiculous story. Without consulting the receipts (and we didn't), only le bon Dieu can advise as to whether the added ridiculousness added to the revenues.

Margarita Fisher, who also starred in *The Miracle of Life* (see essay in appendix), played both Blanche and Mazie, but her performances weren't enough to keep the *Harrison's Reports*' scribe from complaining (in the 16 October 1919 number) about the whole concept: "Dual role themes are like an epidemic. They come and go. While they are here, however, enough damage is done to make one dread their reappearance."

Reviewers were particularly appalled at the fate of poor Blanche: crazy, defrauded, abandoned and then murdered. Helen Pollock of the *New York Morning Telegraph* (5 October 1919) put it best:

> Seeing the poor, helpless creature, the victim of scheming relatives, is not an altogether pleasant turn and when in the end the girl is killed it is too pitilessly apparent that the author decided he had to get her out of the picture in order to marry the other two off. But why make her the "goat" because a supposed tragedy results in the loss of her mind?

Variety (30 March 1919) opined that the film had a feeble, predictable plot and weak direction, but nonetheless found the scene of Mazie's escape from the cabaret impressive: she throws a valuable jewel into the crowd of miscreants and slips away in the resulting melee. The anonymous critic goes on to praise "a peculiar lighting effect in the exterior of this café resilient under its many arc lights, while the area about it is in almost total blackness."

While *The Hellion* may have been forgettable, it wins points with us for having *not* had its lecherous hypnotist be a "Hindoo." — *JTS*

The Hellion. American Film Co./Pathé Exchange, Inc., October 1919, 5 reels [LOST]

CAST: Marguerite Fisher (*Mazie Del Mar/Blanche Harper*); Emory Johnson (*George Graham*); Charles Spere (*Larry Lawson*); Henry Barrows (*Joseph Harper*); Lillian Langdon (*Helen Harper*); George Periolat (*Signor Enrico*); with Frank Clark, Bull Montana.

CREDITS: *Director* George L. Cox; *Story and Scenario* Daniel F. Whitcomb; *Cinematographer* S.A. Baldridge

— *HN*

The Inspirations of Harry Larrabee

The Inspirations of Harry Larrabee. Balboa Amusement Producing Co.; a Fortune Photoplay/General Film Co., March 1917, four reels [LOST]

CAST: Clifford Gray (*Harry Larrabee*); Margaret Landis (*Carolyn Vaughn*); Winifred Greenwood (*Madame Batonyi*); Frank Brownlee (*Batonyi, a.k.a. "The Wolf"*); William Ehfe (*Dr. Stettina*); Charles Blaisdell (*Dr. Seward Wendell*); Tom Morgan (*Hallboy*)

CREW: Producers: H.M. Horkheimer, E.D. Horkheimer; *Director* Bertram Bracken; *Scenario* Douglas Bronston; based upon the eponymous novelette by Howard Fielding (*The Popular Magazine*, 1 February 1914)

GET THE PULMOTOR — QUICK!
HE'S DYING!!

Prepare for such an extremity. Serious accidents will happen in spite of every precaution. Don't stand helpless and watch a life ebb away when there is a good chance of saving it. Have a Pulmotor ready and be prepared to render the only service which can save a life.

— Advertisement in *Safety Engineering*, July 1914

The pulmotor, a device in vogue during the early years of the last century, was a respiratory apparatus for pumping oxygen into the lungs of an asphyxiating individual; while perhaps capable of *saving* a life, no record exists of a pulmotor actually ever reviving the dead. Nonetheless, the idea of restoring life to inanimate bodies was also in vogue during the early years of the last century and it proved to be an oft-played entertainment chord. Thus, Owen Davis's *Lola* (see essay on the 1914 movie)

rejoined the living via nothing more than some pseudo-scientific hocus-pocus and, in *Legally Dead* (1923, see entry), the deed was done via nothing more than a slug of adrenalin.

Small wonder then that Charles Witherle Hooke — a New York newspaperman who took on the moniker "Howard Fielding" when crafting his fiction for the masses — would slip into his 1914 novelette, *The Inspirations of Harry Larrabee*, the inexplicable medical revival of his mystery's departed heroine. The quirkiness of Fielding's tale is further increased by the titular Harry's shaky deductive powers (he's often right for the wrong reason) aided by — take your pick — either strong intuition or something that smacks of the paranormal.

Harry Larrabee was a perfect fit for producers H.M. and E.D. Horkheimer, whose master plans included adapting to the flickers stories from the pages of Street and Smith publications. It fell to scriptwriter Douglas Bronston to pad the story to four reels, and, in the course of doing just that, he renamed the villainous Batonyi (onscreen, he was "The Wolf") and introduced the pulmotor as the miracle device of choice. Cobbled together from *Exhibitor's Trade Review* (10 March 1917) and *Motion Picture News* (31 March 1917) is this summary of the result:

> Harry Larrabee, playwright, loves Carolyn Vaughn who lives in the same apartment house. Her companion, Madame Batonyi, is related in some mysterious way to Dr. Stettina, who resides on the ground floor. These two live in mortal fear of "The Wolf," who shortly puts in an appearance and proceeds to force them into a scheme to rob Carolyn of her jewels. He enters her apartment by way of the dumbwaiter. In resisting him Carolyn is killed. The plans of The Wolf go wrong owing to the interference of Dr. Stettina. Harry, under the spell of one of his "inspirations" learns that a crime is being committed and hurries in to rescue his future wife from the hands of the crook. Larabee rushes Carolyn to the home of a doctor friend and there proceeds to restore her life by means of the pulmotor. Harry is later arrested, but while in jail waiting trial he again has an "inspiration" and learns who the real culprit is. Madame Batonyi clears up the rest of the mystery by disclosing The Wolf as Batonyi, her husband, who had previously forced her into a life of crime.

One week after offering their summary, *Exhibitor's Trade Review* opined that the Wolf's unveiling came across as a bit anticlimactic, but — other than that — found the programmer "quite admirable" with a "realistic setting" and "a very good brand of photography." Peter Milne, in the above *MPN*, declared the show "a rapid-fire mixture of mystery and melodrama" but didn't care for the sensationalism, bemoaned the "little attention" given to the settings, and gave a "fair" to the photography and lighting.

Harry Larrabee, like *Legally Dead*, was something of an askance variation on the larger, "spiritually-oriented" genre theme that was popular after The Great War (see *Earthbound*), in that it dealt not at all with souls, spirits, ghosts, or Life Beyond the Veil, but concentrated solely on getting whomever back up off the table and onto his/her pins once again. Avoiding the ersatz-religious dimension to tales such as these meant also avoiding controversy, local censorship, and (probably the most daunting of all), expensive visual effects. Thus, in this case, budgetary considerations may well have been among the Inspirations of the Horkheimer Brothers. — *SJ*

The Isle of Lost Ships (1929)

The Isle of Lost Ships. First National Pictures/First National, 29 November 1929 (sound); 10 November 1929 (silent), 9 reels/7,576 feet (sound); 9 reels/ 6949 feet (silent), 6814 feet of the silent version at the Library of Congress

CAST: Jason Robards (*Frank Howard*); Virginia Valli (*Dorothy Renwick*); Clarissa Selwynne (*Aunt Emma*); Noah Beery (*Captain Forbes*); Robert E. O'Connor (*Jackson*); Harry Cording (*Gallagher*); Margaret Fielding (*Mrs. Gallagher*); Katherine Ward (*Mother Joyce*; as Kathrin Ward); Robert Homans (*Mr. Burke*); Jack Ackroyd (*Harry*); Sam Baker (*Sam*); Frank Chew (*Wong*); William Holden (*A Passenger*)

CREDITS: *Presented by* Richard A. Rowland; *Director* Irvin Willat: *Scenario* Fred Myton; based on the novel, *The Sea of Dead Ships*, by Crittenden Marriott (Philadelphia, 1909); *Titles and Dialogue* Fred Myton, Paul Perez; *Cinematographer* Sol Polito; *Film Editor* John Rawlins; *Special Photography* Fred Jackman; *Music* Cecil Copping, Alois Reeser

> "You'll find life pretty comfortable here. We have our laws ... some of them queer, perhaps, but ... but necessary. And, in everything, I'm the final authority."
>
> — dialogue from New York Censorship records

These ominous words welcome three shipwrecked travelers to *The Isle of Lost Ships.*

The rest of the twists and turns of this 1929 picture are outlined below:

The S.S. Queen, Porto Rico to New York, bears Lieut. Frank Howard, prisoner of Det. R.L. Jackson. Howard is accused of wife murder. The handcuffed prisoner meets Dorothy Renwick, society girl, who with her aunt is a passenger on the boat. She is attracted to the man, but repelled by the idea of his crime. The ship is nearing the Sargasso Sea, that great sea-weed-and-wreckage-cluttered eddy in the central Atlantic. It strikes a derelict, begins to sink by the bow, and is abandoned.

Jackson, however, has forgotten his prisoner, handcuffed to a bunk on the sinking ship. Accompanied by the girl, he dashes back to get him. When they reach the deck, the life-boats have deserted them and are far across a strip of rough water. The Queen's bulkheads hold and she does not sink. They drift, and reach the Sargasso Sea's interior, stranding after many days in a whole world of ships of all ages and stages of wreckage and decay.

On the unique "island" they find a colony of more than fifty human beings, only two of which are women. The colony is dominated by Cap'n Forbes, an ex–whaling ship master, who immediately wants Dorothy as his wife. It is the rule of the colony that any woman who drifts in with the wreckage must be married immediately to prevent quarrels between the men. Forbes is confident that she will choose him. She chooses Howard instead. Before they are married, Forbes exercises another right, that of challenge. He and Howard fight, and the latter whips him.

Howard, Dorothy and Jackson then retire to the Queen, knowing that a battle with the other faction is inevitable, for one poor woman of the colony has been a widow four times. However, an Irish mechanic, Burke, who operates the engines of a stranded submarine to run the electric lights of the "island," leads them to the undersea craft. Howard finds it in perfect condition, and they plan an escape on it.

They are very nearly caught by Forbes and his gang, who arrive and shoot at them with rifles as they are pulling off, and even manage to rope the sub. It escapes, however, goes deep under the seaweed, and arrives at the surface clear of danger.

Jackson and Howard, now friends instead of officer and prisoner, head for Porto Rico for evidence to clear Howard of the false charge against him. And the "marriage," Dorothy decides, is going to be a real one [Copyright synopsis which also appeared in the film's press-book].

Like the 1923 Maurice Tourneur–directed film of the same name (and from the same studio), 1929's version was derived from *The Isle of Dead Ships* by Crittenden Marriott. Unlike that earlier version, it's was primarily released as a talkie with subtitled reels made only for those theaters still not equipped for audio. It should not be surprising, then, to learn that most still-available contemporary material concentrated on the sound film.

There is debate as to the extent to which the silent and sound versions differed. William K. Everson — after viewing the sound version* on 30 January 1962 with The Theodore Huff Memorial Film Society — opined:

> The whole film is constructed so exclusively on visual terms that it is like watching a wholly silent film. Even the conversations which run a little longer than they would normally in a silent are consistently broken up into long shots, two shots, close-ups; the camera moves in and out; there is never any sense of staginess or equipment-bound inertia.

Virginia Valli and Jason Robards try to rekindle the ol' spark while touring *The Isle of Lost Ships*. Things had started falling apart following their visit to *The Archipelago of Lost Trains*.

---

*Everson viewed the film sans sound discs, which have escaped discovery to this day. He also thrice exhibited for his film groups *An Adventure to Remember*, Robert Youngson's narrative-embellished 10-minute condensation from the talkie footage of *The Isle of Lost Ships*.

Time magazine (11 November 1929) had a contrary opinion, alluding to "…stolid sequences of dialog explaining the locale…." Of little help is *Harrison's Reports* (2 November 1929), which contended that the remake exceeded its 1923 predecessor solely "…because of the fact that the actors now talk…" while offering a brief but cryptic nod to the soundless footage: "silent values excellent."

Not many modern-day film buffs would probably lament the loss of the song performed over the intro titles: "Ship of My Dreams," with words by Alfred Bryan and foxtrot music by George W. Meyer. The bawdier among us, though, haven't given up hope on a press-book story about Caesar, the parrot, letting loose "with a flood of good old-fashioned sailor swearing." Outtakes of Caesar's soliloquy — if the publicity tale spun is to be-lieved — were once held in the First National/Vitaphone Studios private archives.

A specially constructed armada of vessels populated the wrecks held captive in the Sargasso Sea. Per *The New York Times* (27 October 1929), these ranged from Norse ships to sailing yachts to English frigates to "a full-sized destroyer built partly of metal and shell-riddled…." Most of the fleet were merely partial builds, of course, having nothing below the water line except for wooden supports, and the camera was judicious in its choice of angles. *The Times* went on to describe the efforts taken to attain realism: "All of this movie miracle of wreckage was built of new lumber, which was subsequently aged artificially, wrecked, sprayed with salt and rust paint, 'weather beaten' with torches, festooned with sea-weed and glued over artistically with barnacles."

Ken Strong, who screened the film at the Library of Congress, opined on the armada: "It seems they dreamt up every conceivable piece that makes up a ship and then collapsed them all upon each other, making a gnarled work of art. The combined glass shots and still images of the wrecked ships are all marvelously handled. There are nice foreground details such as ropes on the edges of decks that set the perspective for the viewer. Sol Polito's [see *The Bishop of the Ozarks*] camera rocks with the ship, early on, giving the feel that we are on the ship with them. In addition, there's nice lighting when Jackson investigates below decks and light creeps in through the broken wood into the room, as well as when the ship crashes and the ocean blasts through. One shot has terrific depth as the foreground shows a hallway filled with water and in the background outside is the vast sea."

The New York Times found the Frank Howard of Jason Robards — who added "Sr." after his name when his son attained acting fame in his own right — to be "manly and natural" in its 26 October 1929 edition, and Noah Beery (*Go and Get It*, see entry) by all accounts performed very well as the sleazy Captain Forbes. Virginia Valli was the love-struck debutante; and more on her is to be found in *A Trip to Paradise* (1929) and *Wild Oranges* (1924). Robert E. O'Connor played Detective Jackson for laughs. Director Irvin Willat's bona fides may be found in this volume's entry on 1916's *Civilization*.

The Los Angeles Times (1 November 1929) summed the whole thing up as "Capital adventure stuff. Woven on a fantastic pattern, the film packs a sturdy punch and steadily mounts to a thrilling melodramatic climax."

— *SJ*

The Jungle Child

The Jungle Child. New York Motion Picture Corp./Kay-Bee, 8 October 1916, 5 reels [LOST]

CAST: Dorothy Dalton (*Ollante*); Howard Hickman (*Ridgeway Webb*); Gertrude Claire (*Laila*); Dorcas Matthews (*Madeline Travers*); Frederick Vroom (*Señor Grijalva*); Elsa Lorrimer (*Chaperone*); Leo Willis (*Galeche*)

CREDITS: *Producer* Thomas Ince; *Director* Walter Edwards; *Writer* Monte M. Katterjohn; *Cinematographer* J.D. Jennings; *Art Director* Robert Brunton

Synopsis from contemporary reviews:

A Spanish girl's family dies in the South American jungle leaving her, an infant, to be picked up by an Indian woman who raises her as her own child. The girl, Ollante, grows up to be a powerful Amazon, possessed of wonderful physical strength. Ollante rescues Ridgeway Webb, a scoundrel who has become lost after deserting a party of travelers and stealing their supplies. Ollante's foster mother has papers proving the girl's identity and that she is heir to a vast fortune. Webb reads the papers, marries Ollante and takes her back to New York. He does everything in his power to obtain control of her fortune and by deception he at length succeeds. On the night of his success Webb gives a party to disreputable friends in his own house. His wife comes to the door to listen to their revelry and hears him denounce her as a "damned savage" and expresses his desire to be rid of her. Heart-broken, Ollante retreats to a room in the top of the house that has been fitted up as her jungle hut. She dons her jungle clothes and towards morning she commences the dance of death. Her husband hearing the noise and still half-drunk comes into the room and starts to mock her. Infuriated, she seizes him and strangles the life from his body.

Ads for this odd variation on the Tarzan theme described the title character as "Half savage — Half civilized — But with a heart of gold." Of course, her husband may not have agreed with the latter part of that assessment. The synopsis doesn't tell us what happens to Ollante after she throttles her cad of a spouse. Does she commit suicide? Return to South America? Turn her jungle-hut penthouse into a night club? A still from the film with the caption "A savage setting in the midst of civilization" shows Dorothy Dalton (Ollante) cavorting about in leopard skins in her jungle room while her foster mom beats away on the drums and her soon-to-be-choked husband, in full evening dress, watches disapprovingly. Nonetheless, it's a bit difficult to imagine the diminutive Dalton strangling anybody

Surprisingly, *Variety*'s Jolo, usually good for a snide remark or two, liked the film:

A production of uncommon interest, in that a goodly portion of the story is laid in the South American jungle. This is reproduced with every appearance of being the real thing, even to cut-ins of wild animals appearing in their native heath…. Good dramatic construction along regulation lines, with an unconventional background, well acted, directed and photographed, and sure to please anywhere [22 September 1916].

Jolo's only criticism was the lack of explanation as to where in the jungle Webb would find a source for the cigarettes he's continually puffing away on.

However, to Peter Milne of *Motion Picture News*, the absence of a jungle 7–11 was the least of the picture's deviations from reality: "*The Jungle Child* is based on a story which however original in its make-up fails to ring true to life. Its climaxes are unable to create conviction in the spectator. The one place to affix blame is with the author. His story is impossible and therefore it is unreal" (30 December 1916).

The Jungle Child proved no dance of death for Dorothy Dalton, who, in a later interview about how she broke into the movies, credits her performance in *The Jungle Child* and the favorable reception of the film as launching her career as a star. More on that career can be found in our entry on *The Dark Mirror*.

— HN

The Jungle Trail

The Jungle Trail. Fox Film Corp./Fox Film Corp., 1 June 1919, 5 reels [LOST]

CAST: William Farnum (*Robert Morgan*); Mary Lamar (*Anna Luther*); Lyster Chambers (*Philip Garson*); Mrs. Sara Alexander (*Mrs. Morgan*); Anna Schaeffer (*Mrs. Lamar*); Edward Roseman (*Portuguese Joe*); Henry Armetta (*Grogas*); G. Raymond Nye (*Ebano*); Ana Lehr (*Wanda*); George Stone (*Haja*)

CREDITS: *Director* Richard Stanton; *Assistant Director* Edward Sedgwick; *Scenario* Adrian Johnson; *Story* George V. Hobart; *Cinematographer* Horace Plimpton, Jr.; *Set Decoration* Edward Bach

Our ungainly and awkward synopsis (most likely from the press-book) was first printed in the *Fort Wayne* [Indiana] *Journal-Gazette*, 20 April 1919.

> All that stands between Robert Morgan and happiness is money. For Mary Lamar is Robert's definition of happiness and Mary is rich. So is Philip Garson, which fact makes him favored of Mary's mother, but not of Mary. Garson knows his unpopularity and resorts to scheming. He concocts a story about a tiger for which a museum offers a big reward. Reward to Robert means money — and Mary. So Robert goes to Africa and with him go two of Garson's men — sworn to lose Robert in the jungle.
>
> Before the departure, Mary gives a locket to Robert which, the latter tells her, should it be restored by other hands than his, will be an indication of his death.
>
> "Out of sight, out of mind" is what Garson hopes. But the love of Robert for Mary isn't that sort. However, when African natives burn Robert's hut over his head and he runs to the bank of a lake, is shot and falls into the water, dropping the locket on the shore and Portuguese Joe takes the trinket back to New York, reporting to Garson that he has accomplished his mission — well, then Mary gives up hope.
>
> After that matter progress more favorably for Garson — until one day a friend induces Mary to visit an Oriental seer who tells her that her sweetheart is not dead. The seer explains that when Robert falls into the African lake, he takes refuge under the bank and remains hidden until his pursuers depart. After a long wandering, he reaches a city where a strange people reside. By a remarkable feat of strength he escapes burning at the stake and earns honors as a god. Later he wins the gratitude of Wanda, a native girl, and the enmity of Ehano, a chieftain.
>
> He conquers the latter in a contest, man to man, but is followed by Ehano into the Temple of Light, which he enters in violation of religious law. Robert saves himself by overturning an idol onto his praying adversary and eventually escapes to America.
>
> All this Mary hears from the seer. Subsequently, Garson visits the Orient and also learns that Robert is alive — that the seer is Robert. The timely entrance of Mary after Robert reveals himself restores her to his arms and dramatically concludes *The Jungle Trail*.

It's not clear why Robert (played by William Farnum) pulls this Count of Monte Cristo routine, since surely he doesn't require

further evidence of Garson's duplicity. Perhaps he's just testing the sincerity of Mary's love. In any case, it's hard to believe that the hulking, square-jawed Farnum would be able to pass himself off as some kind of mystic. (Imagine John Wayne in a turban!)

The film is included here because of the "lost city/civilization" angle, but we're not told a good deal about it. Ads describe the place as "a garden of Eden" within the jungle and full of weird temples, magnificent palaces and jewels (presumably Robert scooped up a few of the latter during his escape to finance his renewed courtship of Mary). The city's inhabitants are "wealthy, cultured, but superstitious." They are also black, which is a bit of a switch from the usual lost-cities-in-the-jungle stories (like *She* or *Tarzan and the Golden Lion*).

Like his brother Dustin, William Farnum had a long and distinguished stage career, but in the movies he was an action hero not unlike Arnold Schwarzenegger in his *Conan the Barbarian* days. *Variety*, in fact, compared Farnum to Sandow, the Victorian-Era Prussian bodybuilder who is said to have been the father of the physical culture movement. Farnum appealed to both male and female moviegoers, but critics found his acting less than subtle. One wag thought he was "like a well-fed St. Bernard tearing around a yard and then pulling up and attempting a dignified pose." Along the same lines — but more kindly — Peter Milne of *Motion Picture News* wrote that "the star is at his best in his scenes of repose or repressed emotion. His occasional outbursts of frenzied expression are rather too pointed to gain realistic effects in the present instances." It didn't matter; audiences loved watching Farnum throwing people through the air while displaying his soft, sensitive side to the heroine. Reviewers had no doubt that *The Jungle Trail* would be another crowd-pleaser in spite of its rather predictable story.

Farnum first came to moviegoers' attention in the 1914 *The Spoilers*, wherein his fight with villain, Tom Santschi, became a cinematic legend and was talked about for decades. Reputedly, Santschi lost three teeth in the brawl, and Farnum suffered a broken nose, a fractured hand, and a blood clot in his cheek. Many years later, Farnum sneered that "nowadays they won't even let you pare a fingernail yourself." However, it was Farnum's face — and not his hands — that concerned Fox when he became a superstar for them in the late 1910s. Fox had Farnum's handsome kisser insured for $100,000, and his contract forbade him to participate in any sport that could cause a facial disfigurement. Of course this did not stop Fox from issuing the usual stories about Farnum doing his own stunts as indicated by the following bit of PR for *The Jungle Trail*:

> At a spot about fourteen miles north of Miami there is a natural stone bridge crossing the Brackish river at a height of nearly thirty feet. Mr. Farnum's assignment consisted of having a fight with cannibals on the bank of the river, fleeing to the bridge, making a thirty foot dive into the river and swimming underwater to "safety." The dive in itself probably would have been enough to dampen the ardor of the average actor but it was made especially thrilling for Mr. Farnum because of the information reaching him, quite accidentally, just prior to the dive, that the sluggish river was inhabited by alligators [*Centralia* (Washington) *Daily Chronicle*, 9 October 1919].

In 1924, Farnum left Fox for Famous Players–Lasky, but made only one film for them, *The Man Who Fights Alone*, before withdrawing from the movies altogether. There were stories that he wanted to return to the stage or that he was ill with rheumatism but, in 1928, Farnum told *Photoplay* that he had physical problems as a result of being hurt while filming *The Man Who Fights Alone*. The injury (probably to the head) was considered minor at first but, a few weeks later, Farnum fell into a coma that lasted eleven weeks; however, it seems strange that there was no newspaper accounts of this at the time. In any case, Farnum did return to the stage and toured with *The Buccaneer*, as well as playing Banquo in *Macbeth*.

The early 1930s found Farnum coping with a messy divorce and the loss of his $2 million fortune in the stock market crash. Still, Farnum was popular with the Hollywood crowd, and his personal generosity during his salad days was no doubt remembered. He had no trouble getting small roles and, unlike most fallen stars, he usually received billing and was more than just a blurred face in the background. Horror fans perhaps best recall his brief (but conspicuous) part in *The Mummy's Curse*, wherein he plays the wild-eyed, self-appointed caretaker of the tombs who becomes the revived mummy's first victim.

— HN

The Kaiser's Shadow

The Kaiser's Shadow. Thomas H. Ince Corp./Famous Players–Lasky Corp. and Paramount Pictures, 1 July 1918, 5 reels [LOST]

CAST: Dorothy Dalton (*Paula Harris*); Thurston Hall (*Hugo Wagner*); Edward Cecil (*Clement Boyd*); Leota Lorraine (*Dorothy Robinson*); Otto Hoffman (*Frederick Fischer*); Charles French (*William Kremlin*)

CREDITS: *Producer and Supervisor* Thomas H. Ince; *Director* R. William Neill; based on the serial story, "The Triple Cross," by J.U. Giesy and Octavus Roy Cohen, in *All Story Weekly* (30 March–20 April, 1918); *Cinematographer* John S. Stumar; *Art Director* G. Harold Percival; *Art Titles and Special Effects* Irvin J. Martin.

The AFI Catalog refers to the film as *The Kaiser's Shadow or The Triple Cross*, but the reviews and ads we've consulted make no mention of *The Triple Cross* in the title. Also per the AFI: "Contemporary reviews list the name of the Dorothy Dalton character as Paula Harris and Thurston Hall's character as Hugo Wagner. Paramount studio records, however, list these character names as Martha Gerhardt, also known as Doris Gray, and Hugo Mueller, respectively."

Synopsis from the 6 July 1918 *Motion Picture News*:

Paula Harris is seen at a reception in Berlin in 1915. She is a highly rated member of the German Secret Service, and a still higher rated member of the United States Secret Service. Hugo Wagner of the German service, is in love with her and she with him.

The United States in 1918. Paula is maid to Dorothy, an American girl, engaged to Clement Boyd, an inventor, whose new machine gun is prized by the United States Ordinance Department. After the wedding he secures his plans, intending to take them with him on the honeymoon in order to protect them. Hugo is Boyd's chauffeur. Frederick Fischer, one of the heads of the German spy service, has commissioned the two to kidnap the bride and groom. So they are taken to a mysterious house used by the Germans and searched. But the plans are not to be found. Paula has concealed them. She is searched. When she goes to take the plans from the hiding-place she cannot find them. Fischer threatens Boyd with inoculation with a racking disease unless he discloses the whereabouts of the plans. As he is about to insert the needle, Paula cries out. All seems lost, but at that moment the

United States Secret Service arrives in force and a hot battle ensues. When the smoke has cleared away, Paula discovers that Hugo was in reality working for the United States as she was.

Some sources describe the secret weapon not as an advanced machine gun but rather a "ray rifle," and it's this modest science-fiction touch that renders the film eligible (though just barely) for inclusion here. There's no indication from the reviews that the rifle or machine gun or whatever is ever demonstrated or has even gotten past the inventor's drawing board, but since it's just a MacGuffin, that scarcely matters.

The film was based on a magazine serial story ("and has all the earmarks of such a concoction" sniffed *Variety's* Jolo) entitled "The Triple Cross." Since 1918 was the peak year for Hate-the-Hun propaganda — there was nothing too outlandish for the public to swallow — anti–German literature proliferated and there were even stories from official sources that the influenza epidemic was the result of germ warfare conducted by enemy agents from the Fatherland. *The Kaiser's Shadow* apparently had more than its share of such patriotic fervor, as was noted in Peter Milne's review in the 6 July 1918 edition of *Motion Picture World*: "The Hun is damned again and again. One can picture the audience loudly proclaiming approval. And when the inventor refuses to be terrorized by threats of slow death he sees only the honor of the Stars and Stripes!" Nevertheless, Milne found the film "full of thrills" and "intense physical action" though no more believable than your average serial.

While Jolo (writing for the show-biz bible's 28 June 1918 number) thought the photography excellent, he opined that the story was much too conventional: "People signal with shades pulled up and down, a woman is chloroformed in a taxi and spirited away, there is a lot of 'Who's got the papers?' stuff, wiretapping and a quantity of maudlin patriotic propaganda."

The film was a Dorothy Dalton vehicle and "her exquisite show of vitality" drew her usual good notices (more on Dalton in *The Dark Mirror* entry), while *MPW* found some nice things to say about the man with the megaphone: "R. William Neill, Miss Dalton's director on all her Paramount subjects, has demonstrated his ability to handle this type of picture with the same good results he shows in his other work." R(oy) William Neill, of course, is better known to readers of this book as the director who brought style and pace to a number of thrillers in the 1930s and 1940s, such as *The Black Room*, *Frankenstein Meets the Wolf Man*, and the Rathbone-Bruce Sherlock Holmes series. His work in the Silent Era is much harder to track down and only *The Viking* (1929) has had frequent revivals. Nonetheless, Neill's name may also be found in our essays on *Radio Mania* and *Vanity's Price*.

— HN

Keep Moving

Keep Moving. George Kleine, 14 November 1915 (NY trade showing), 5 reels [LOST]

CAST: Harry Watson, Jr. (*Musty Suffer*); George Bickel (*Willie Work*); Cissie Fitzgerald (*Cissy*); Rose Gore (*Dippy Mary*); Dan Crimmins (*Burglar*); Snitz Edwards (*Hypno Jake*); Ruby Hoffman (*Royal governess*); Alma Hanlon (*Queen*); Tom Nawn (*King*); Frank Belcher

(*Lord Chamberlain*); Maxfield Moree (*Fairy tramp*); H.H. McCullum (*Tony*)

CREDITS: *Director* Louis Myll

Our synopsis is from *The AFI Catalog*:

Gloom pervades the kingdom of Blunderland because the royal child longs to see the world. After a ceremony in which the king and queen rollerskate to the throne, the fairy tramp appears and sends the royal child into the wicked world. Dippy Mary gives the child, now a tramp known as Musty Suffer, a mansion where he bathes in beer and is cuddled by six beautiful women, but when Mary serenades him with a German band, he throws himself out of the window and lands in a military ambulance. Musty is taken to prison and because he refuses to drink water is ordered to be shot but he stops several cannon balls with his chest and escapes through rubber bars. After the fairy tramp returns Musty to the mansion, Musty is abducted by burglars who force him to fight champion Willie Work. Although Willie beats Musty unmercifully they set off together in search of adventure. At a barber shop hair restorer is put on Musty's face. In a saloon Musty's new beard gets saturated with gasoline and an explosion rids him of his whiskers. After other adventures Musty wishes to be sent back to the palace. The fairy tramp accomplishes this and Musty becomes the royal child again.

The fairy tramp was described by one of the trade papers as "a tall cadaverous Weary Willie Tramp, with three day's growth and baggy trousers, who wears a ballet skirt and carries a wand with a huge star at the end."

This slapstick fantasy was previewed as a feature in November 1915, but was then apparently cut and made part of a series of one-reelers entitled *The Mishaps of Musty Suffer*. The short films were shown serial-fashion once a week, although they were meant to stand alone without any connection between the shorts. Given the episodic nature of *Keep Moving*, it probably wasn't difficult to divide it into one-reelers with perhaps the helpful addition of a title card or two. One chapter of *The Mishaps*— under the title *Keep Moving*—is still extant at the Library Congress; however, from the Library of Congress description it's hard to say how much (if any) of that reel was taken from the feature. In any event the series, showcasing the talents of vaudeville team Harry Watson, Jr., and George Bickel, did well and spawned two sequels. Watson and Bickel parted company in the late 1910s but, given the imminent arrival of Prohibition, any further adventures of Musty Suffer would have been unlikely anyway.

In the 4 December 1915 issue of *Motion Picture News*, William Ressman Andrews gave the picture a rave review, describing it as "a delightful extravaganza, a medley of absurd incidents offering a wealth of opportunity for seasoned fun makers to keep a theatreful of people laughing until their sides ache." *Variety*'s "Fred" was equally amused: "It is a comedy feature that has been threaded together with a lot of bits that are as old as the bills on the stage and include vaudeville, burlesque and musical comedy but so skillfully are the bits worked into the picture no one expects them as they come along" (19 November 1915).

The supporting cast includes a number of vaudevillians, including Dan Crimmins and his wife, Rose Gore. In black face, Crimmins played the part of helpful witch doctor, "old Pierre," in 1932's *White Zombie*; the entertainer's diction is so garbled therein that one mourns the lack of title cards. Crimmins and Gore—once described by *The New York Times* as a "grotesque pair"—started their act in 1887 (the year they were married), became big-time headliners (according to one source, they were the first to be so billed), and toured Europe and South America. Both entered the movies at about the same time, with Crimmins debuting in *Feeney's Social Experiment* (1913); however, the success they had had in vaudeville eluded them in the flickers, and many of their subsequent appearances in film were uncredited bits. Crimmins had a rather conspicuous one in *Seven Footprints to Satan* (1929), wherein he plays the lunatic who pulls Creighton Hale's ear on his arrival at Satan's mansion.

— HN

The Kid's Clever

The Kid's Clever. Universal Pictures/Universal, 17 February 1929, 6 reels/5729 feet [LOST]

CAST: Glenn Tryon (*Bugs Raymond*); Kathryn Crawford (*Ruth Decker*); Russell Simpson (*John Decker*); Lloyd Whitlock (*Ashton Steele*); George Chandler (*Hank*); Joan Standing (*Girl*); Max Asher (*Magician*); Florence Turner (*Matron*); Virginia Sale (*Secretary*); Stepin Fetchit (*Negro man*)

CREW: *Supervisor* Harry Decker; *Director* William James Craft; *Scenario* Ernest S. Pagano, Jack Foley; *Story* Vin Moore; *Titles* Albert De Mond; *Film Editor* Charles Craft; *Cinematographer* Al Jones; *Art Director* Charles D. Hall

From a technological perspective, amphibious vehicles go back at least as far as 1791, the year Samuel Bentham constructed an amphibious carriage while on an official visit to Russia. Progress has ever since produced new and improved designs, making this piece of film fiction tenuous *science* fiction at best:

[Bugs Raymond] the hero, a mechanic, had invented a fuelless motor, which ran on land and in the water. After meeting the heroine at his garage, where he showed her his new automobile, she is impressed with the invention and persuades her father, an automobile manufacturer, to come and look the machine over. On the day the demonstration was to take place, the villain, a rival salesman, bribes the hero's helper to tamper with the machine, and naturally the demonstration is a flop. The villain obtains the father's signature to a contract and flies away. But the hero, finding out about the trickery, attempts to interest the manufacturer through the heroine once more, but, unsuccessful in their efforts, he, the hero, drags the father, his sweetheart and his father's secretary, into the machine and they pursue the villain's plane on land and over the water in a hair-splitting race. Catching up to the plane, the villain makes his escape, but the hero had torn off his coat which contained the contract. The heroine's father, convinced that the machine was wonderful, naturally purchased the rights, and, of course, the young couple are made happy.

The above summary is from *Harrison's Reports* (9 March 1929) whose reviewer opined, "The acting is good and the action is fast with plenty of thrills and some comedy," but confessed a bit of boredom by elaborating that star Glenn Tryon's act had worn a "trifle tiresome" due to the "sameness of the stories." That's not surprising. A fast hunt-and-peck into the oeuvre of Mr. Tryon uncovers that less than two years prior, Universal was peddling him in a similar farce under the title *Painting the Town* (1927). In that one, Tryon — playing a small town inventor— develops an automobile capable of both rapid acceleration and deceleration; after a temporary setback suffered via a sabotaged demonstration of his wonder machine, the hero ultimately sells the vehicle and wins the girl. Sound familiar? Undoubtedly it did to *Clever*'s William James Craft (director), Vin Moore (story man), Albert De Mond (title card guy), and Max Asher (actor), all of whom aided and abetted Tryon in *Painting the Town* as well. (Lovers of this overused formula might look up 1925's *Super Speed*, as well; we sure did, and we determined that, as a clone of *Clever* and *Painting*, this is all the mention it deserves. Ditto with 1926's *Speeding Venus*. If said overused-formula lovers *insist* on more of the same, we refer them to our essay on 1924's *The Speed Spook*, also here in the appendix.)

Anyone perusing Asher's credit herein and wondering how it came to pass that he portrayed a "magician" may quit in his or her quest to discover any further genre angle. This magician, per several sources, is of the parlor-prestidigitator variety; his sole *raison d'être* in the film is to be shown up by Bugs at the colonial ball.

Glenn Tryon performed as a comedian (in tent shows, stock companies and the like) from the tender age of ten. Enlisted by Hal Roach in 1924 as a sub for Harold Lloyd, his film career — almost exclusively involving comedy — subsequently evolved over the next decade or two from acting to screenwriting to producing. Co-star Kathryn Crawford made her film debut in *The Kid's Clever*. Bit player Lincoln Theodore Monroe Andrew Perry — better known as Stepin Fetchit — achieved more fame (or infamy, depending on one's point of view) than any of the bunch.

Variety (15 May 1929) thought little of *The Kid's Clever*: "Photography poor. Picture a replica of all the traffic chase cinemas seen before. Only novelty is the freak [auto-]boat which has been done in short comedies. Good for small town audiences."

— *SJ*

The Land of the Lost

The Land of the Lost. Sterling Camera and Film Company/?, 6 August 1914, 4 reels [LOST]

CAST: Arthur Donaldson (*Baron de Coverly*); James Vincent (*Gilbert Hastings*); Violent Stuart (*Miriam Bradley*); Roy Sheldon (*The Hermit*).

CREDITS: Author: Leon Wagner

The following is an edited (for length) synopsis that originally appeared in *Moving Picture World* on the 25 July 1914.

John R. Bradley, a wealthy ship builder, seeks a title for his daughter Miriam. Mr. Bradley introduces Baron de Coverly, a fortune hunter, to Miriam. The baron becomes an ardent suitor and Miriam consents to be his wife. They start for a long cruise on Mr. Bradley's new schooner, *Carpathia*. Captain Hastings is taking his son, Gilbert, a young artist, on the cruise. Miriam and Gilbert become friends and the jealousy of the baron is aroused. During a drunken frenzy, the baron sets fire to the schooner. Mr. Bradley and Miriam escape in a boat. The baron jumps into the sea and causes the disappearance of the father. The girl is left helpless, but Gilbert grabs a piece of wreckage and binds her to it.

Miriam, Gilbert and the baron all end up on a desert island. The baron attempts to kill Gilbert by severing a rope while Gilbert is using it to cross over a chasm. Gilbert survives the fall and, though he realizes who cut the rope, he does not tell Miriam of the baron's cowardly act. The selfishness of the baron causes Miriam to break off their engagement and seek the protection of Gilbert.

Exploring the island, Gilbert and the baron discover a very old recluse, the only inhabitant of the island. Later, after the old man tells them his story, the baron follows him and discovers that he has a treasure. The baron kills the hermit with a stick and throws his body off a cliff into the sea.

The baron, running from the cliffs, his mind aflame with the deed, is confronted by the form of the old hermit. In fear and terror, the baron flees from the form of the old man who follows him to the treasure and points an accusing finger at him. The baron runs from the place as the old man fades away. Encountering Gilbert on the way, the baron makes a murderous attack on him, but Gilbert overpowers him. At this point, Gilbert hears Miriam calling him and, when he rushes to the beach, he finds that a rescue ship is at hand.

The baron hears what is going on and watches from the cliff. When he sees the ship, he shouts and calls and tries to go to the shore, but the form of the old man rises to bar his way. The baron becomes a raving maniac. On the vessel we leave Miriam and Gilbert flooded in light from a beautiful sunset, watching the fading of the land of the lost.

It is probably no coincidence that Bradley's schooner shares the same name as the ship that rescued the *Titanic* survivors, the *Carpathia*. *The Land of the Lost* is a story of survival, so the supernatural element at the end — the only reason for the film's inclusion here — seems a bit forced after all that adventure and romance; it serves only to explain the villain's remaining on the island. Still, the *MPW* plot synopsis intimates that the hermit's ghost arises not from the Other World, but, rather, from the baron's imagination — presumably fanned by guilt over his crime. For all that, the baron does not seem like a character prone to remorse.

Silent films (like *Down to Earth* and *Male and Female*) dealt with desert-island survival tales semi-humorously, a treatment still in favor as late as 1974 and *Swept Away*. More serious viewpoints — including those involving sexual tension over the scarcity of the fair sex in such circumstances — wouldn't come into play until much later, post-apocalypse films like *Deluge*; *Five*; *The World, the Flesh and the Devil*; and *Last Woman on Earth*. In that sense, *Lost* was something of a trailblazer.

The Land of the Lost received little press, but did get a very favorable write-up from Peter Milne in the 25 July 1914 *Motion Picture News*:

Not one slow moment in the entire four reels; fine acting from beginning to end replete with thrilling incidents and, above all, excellent photography.... It would be hard to find a picture that is more beautifully photographed. Not one glaring white scene appears. The whole film is tinted with a pretty brown color, pleasing to look upon, and, moreover, it does not strain the eyes.

High praise for a product from such an obscure film outfit (Sterling-Camera and Film Company). Unfortunately, Milne does not name either the cameraman responsible for the easy-on-the-eyes photography or the director who helmed all the thrills. Nor are their names to be found in the *Moving Picture World* synopsis or — apparently — anywhere else. The script *may* have been written by the Leon Wagner who *might* also have been the president of Sterling-Camera, who *may* be the same Leon Wagner who had his appendectomy filmed for later exhibition! (And try finding *that* one in *The AFI Catalog*!)

Ads for the film promised "Beautiful scenes in Maine and New York." While not exactly exotic locals, they may perhaps serve to explain the cryptic comment that closes Milne's review: "In the last scene it is obvious that the island is not uninhabited, but this fact may not be noticed by all and, if it is, the fault is not glaring enough to be severely criticized."

— HN

Life or Honor?

Life or Honor? Ivan Films Production, Inc./States Rights, March 1918, 7 reels [LOST]

CAST: Leah Baird (*Helen West*); James Morrison (*James Manly/Aquinaldo*); Violet Palmer (*Peggy Harmon*); Harry Burkhardt (*Robert West*); Edward MacKay (*Sidney Holmes*); Ben Hendricks (*Martin Cross*); Mathilda Brundage (*Mrs. Harmon*); Joseph Burke (*J.T. Manly*); Florence Sottong (*Molly West*).

CREDITS: *Director* Edmund Lawrence; *Story* Betta Breuil; *Cinematographer* Marcel Le Picard. *Alternate title The Window Opposite*

Our synopsis is taken from the 6 April 1918 *Motion Picture News*:

> J.T. Manly, retired merchant who has spent several years of his life in the Philippines is murdered, and his son Jimmy is arrested. Testimony offered by Aguinaldo, Manly's Filipino servant, convicts Jimmy of the murder. In the house next door live the Wests. Helen West, sister of Peggy Harmon (whom Jimmy loves), is married to an inebriate, Robert. His friend, Holmes (who loves Helen), has seen the murder, but even after Jimmy's conviction refuses to come forward with any information. Peggy eventually goes to Martin Cross, a retired detective and woman-hater, begging him to take the case. She persuades Holmes to visit him to relate the facts. Holmes, exacting Martin's oath of secrecy, tells his story. The night of the murder he had remained at the West home because Robert was seriously affected by drink. He had watched over him until he fell asleep, but on waking had discovered that his charge had escaped. Helen, walking in her sleep because of nervousness, had stumbled and fallen. Holmes carried her to her room and there, from her window, saw the murder ['Holmes had seen the deed committed through the shadow of the killer's arm through a window shade' was the way *Variety* put it]. As this was the only window in the West house where a view of the disaster was possible, he had kept silent to save Helen's good name. Cross then proceeds to hunt up Aguinaldo and, employing a fake hypnotist, so plays on the servant's conscience with light effects, mysterious faces and skeletons that he confesses his crime. It develops that Aguinaldo was also Manly's son, by a Filipino woman he had betrayed. This releases Jimmy, and Robert's death leaves nothing standing between Helen and Holmes.

The film is included here only because of the fake spook-effects conjured up by detective Cross, who must have spent his retirement studying magic. *MPN*'s Peter Milne thought the sequence "raises the interest because of the skill with which it has been staged," but *Variety*'s "Ibee" had a different opinion: "The scenes are naturally quite filled with 'hokem' and there are many lantern flashes with the bull's eye tinted purple for some reason" (29 March 1918).

Publicity for the film stressed the hero's dilemma, though a modern viewer might look askance at the ethics of allowing an innocent man to be condemned for murder so your girlfriend's reputation can remain intact. Even the Victorians might have found the idea a bit quaint, but audiences of the 1910s no doubt merely shrugged it off as just another device to keep the action moving. The *Variety* review mentions that Holmes doesn't even consult Cross until 24 hours before Jimmy is scheduled to die! Luckily the misogynistic gumshoe is a fast worker and Holmes is spared having to at least consider a mad, last-minute dash to the governor's office to save poor Jimmy's life. Then again, perhaps Holmes — true to his surname — was the *real* detective here, given that he was able to identify Aguinaldo by just the shadow of his arm.

Peter Milne's review was mostly favorable, though he found the murderer's long confession "perhaps the only faulty place in the entire picture." Other of Milne's comments indicate that the picture's special effects may have also been faulty: "The double exposure stuff, however, does not attain the excellence which most cameramen have reached in this type of work. There is a shadow spreading itself on either side of the joint."

Variety's Ibee was equally critical of the camerawork: "The photography by Marcel le Picard is in and out. The earlier scenes lacked sharpness which may have been due to poor lighting. Better results were attained later on." Le Picard got to work on only one "A" picture, Griffith's *America*, and spent most of his long career on Poverty Row lensing films like *Voodoo Man* and *Scared to Death*. Some would say he did not in fact attain better results later on.

Life or Honor? was produced by Ivan Films, a company specializing in what would later be termed "exploitation" films, with titles like *Married in Name Only* and *The Sex Lure* and dealing with topics like abortion, prostitution, and genetic defects. Although *Life or Honor?* was pretty much presented as a straight mystery, it still managed to drag in the controversial subject of miscegenation. Of course, per the "standards" of the day, the plot wound up correctly: Manly pays with his life for dallying with a person of another race and the offspring of that relationship grows up to be a murderer.

— HN

Little Lady Eileen

Little Lady Eileen. Famous Players Film Company/Paramount Pictures Corp., 10 August 1916, 5 reels [LOST]

CAST: Marguerite Clark (*Little Lady Eileen Kavanaugh*); Vernon Steele (*Stanley Churchill/George Churchill*); John L. Shine (*Dennis Cavanaugh*); J.K. Murray (*Father Kearney*); Harry Lee (*Powdein*); Maggie Holloway Fisher (*Lady Gower*); Russell Bassett (*Mike Cafferty*).

CREDITS: *Director* J. Searle Dawley; *Story and Scenario* Betty T. Fitzgerald; *Cinematographer* Lawrence E. Williams.

Our synopsis is taken from the entry at the Library of Congress.

> At Miss O'Harahan's school for girls, near Dublin, there is a mischievous pupil with the awe-inspiring name of Lady Eileen Kavanaugh who is barely large enough to sustain the burden of so cumbersome a name. Her pranks are far from pleasing to Mistress O'Harahan, and she is punished many times until the sudden discovery that her father is penniless leads to her being withdrawn from the school.
> Dennis Kavanaugh spends his entire time delving into the hundreds of massive volumes which line the walls of his library from floor to ceiling. While perched on his ladder searching for a musty tome he discovers a will, yellow with age. The contents of the will state that the entire estate of Terrence Kavanuagh amounting to a

vast sum, will descend to the eldest daughter of the House of Kavanaugh provided that she marry the eldest son of the House of Churchill.

On the train homeward bound Eileen meets a handsome young man who as fate will have it, is Stanley, the eldest of the Churchills. During his stay in Eileen's home town, Stanley and the little maid become deeply interested in each other, though he never tells her his name. Meanwhile George, his scapegrace [twin] brother discovers the terms of the will, presents himself at the Kavanaugh home as the eldest of his family and insists that the marriage be arranged at once, despite Eileen's very evident distaste for him. The little girl is tricked into marriage, but fortunately her lover rescues her from George on their wedding day. George, believing he has killed Stanley in the fight which ensues, flees on horseback, but is killed by a huge boulder which rolls down the mountain.

Of course Stanley thinks he found Eileen all by himself and that his brother was killed by accident, but Eileen knows that it was the fairies who showed her her true lover and who rolled the giant boulder down upon the miscreant George.

In spite of the ambiguity in the synopsis, most of the reviews and PR material indicate that the fairies Eileen sees throughout the film are real, but visible only to her, presumably because she's so pure of heart. The fairies turning murderous at the finale is a bit of a surprise, but is perhaps all that remains of a somewhat darker tone suggested in pre-release publicity for the film, as indicated in this curious puff piece about director J. Searle Dawley's (see entries, *Conscience* and *Phantom Honeymoon*) research for the film:

> J. Searle Dawley is delving deep into the subject of the black art, alchemy, necromancy, fairy lore, witchcraft and all other kindred subjects in preparation for the producing of *Little Lady Eileen*. It is an Irish story starring Marguerite Clark in which fairies play an important part. Mr. Dawley is seeking ways and means in gaining control of the spirits of the air as they are essential to the success of the undertaking [*Salt Lake Tribune*, 23 July 1916].

In the end, Dawley relied on the special effects department rather than an Irish version of *The Necronomicon* and that proved to be a wise choice as the double exposure work depicting the fairies was highly praised by reviewers. "The Film Girl," anonymous critic for *The Syracuse Herald* (10 August 1916) wrote the following about the little creatures:

> The story abounds with them [fairies] and in pictures one often sees the dainty creatures of Kathleen's [*sic*] imagination dancing within a magic circle. One also sees some of the hob goblins with queer, distorted faces who conspire to work ill to others that "Kathleen" may be happy.

An article in *The New York Times* (30 July 1916) gave some behind the scenes info on the special effects and how "a startling assortment of huge *papier-mache* heads" depicting the fairies were photographed against a black back drop:

> The dead-black background is used in superimposing the eerie ones upon the actual scene which had already been filmed out of doors. This is done by running the film through the camera a second time and having the hobgoblins prance before the black curtain which does not photograph and then leaves them apparently cavorting in the green fields of the original scene.

The Gray Lady was quite enthused about the film, calling it "much above average" and expertly capturing the Ireland of myth and romance. *Variety*'s "Jolo," on the other hand, thought the film was pretty much just for the kiddies though "maybe grown-ups will accept it as a relief from the usual dramatic fea-

tures." "The Film Girl" agreed, calling it "a regular fairytale, subtitles and all, a regular children's piece and less enjoyable to staid grown-ups than some of the previous releases starring the winsome and diminutive Miss Clark." Inasmuch as these bastions of print criticism found time to quibble between themselves (and with the Film Girl) over who would get the most out of sitting through this, we felt we had better not include this one out. (Good night, Mr. Goldwyn, wherever you are...)

Marguerite Clark was inevitably described as "charming," "irresistible" and "rhapsodical" [*sic*] and millions of fans agreed with those adjectives. Clark had also wowed them on Broadway before she signed with Famous Players and made a series of hits for the studio, always portraying dreamy and high-spirited youngsters (like Little Eva *and* Topsy in 1918's *Uncle Tom's Cabin*). She rivaled — and sometimes surpassed — superstar Mary Pickford in popularity and, like little Mary, was bedecked in pigtails and pinafores even when she was in her thirties. Clark actually didn't like making movies and, after she married a wealthy Louisiana businessman, the road to retirement was not far away. She formed an independent company, starred in one movie — *Scrambled Wives* (1921) — and then left the screen at age 38. Though she was still very popular at the time, Clark later said "I knew enough to go home when the party was over and the guests were gone." In Louisiana, she devoted herself to charity work and died of pneumonia at the age of 53. Only a couple of her films survive.

— HN

The Little Red Schoolhouse

The Little Red Schoolhouse. Martin J. Heyl Productions/Arrow Film Corp., May 1923, 6 reels/5760 feet [LOST]

CAST: Martha Mansfield (*Mercy Brent*); Harlan Knight (*Jeb Russell*); Sheldon Lewis (*Matt Russell*); E.K. Lincoln (*John Hale*); Edmund Breese (*Brent*); Florida Kingsley (*Hired Girl*); Paul Everton (*Detective*)

CREDITS: *Producer* Martin J. Heyl; *Director* John G. Adolfi; *Scenario* James Shelley Hamilton; based on a play by Hal Reid (publication status unknown); *Cinematographer* George F. Webber

The AFI Catalog avers that this film was distributed via the States Rights system.

This Indie six-reeler was the last — and least — of the Silent Era's efforts at claiming that lightning bolts + windowpanes = irrefutable proof of guilt. The best things about the film were its ingénue, Martha Mansfield (see 1920's *Dr. Jekyll and Mr. Hyde*) and its villain, Sheldon Lewis (see 1920's other *Dr. Jekyll and Mr. Hyde*). Osiris knows, its plot — following, courtesy of *The AFI Catalog* — was nothing to write home about.

> Bootleggers secretly operate in the basement of the school where Mercy Brent teaches. Her sweetheart, John Hale, and his revenue agents succeed in breaking up the bootlegging activities and solving the murder of Jeb Russell with the aid of a strange phenomenon: a bolt of lightning causes the face of Matt Russell to be pictured on a schoolhouse window, thus proving Matt to be the murderer of his bootlegging partner –his father.

Viewers watching *Schoolhouse* may have been upset that Matt Russell would have killed his dad, Jeb, over demon rum (or bathtub gin; the type of bootlegged stuff the Russells peddled is unclear), but Harlan Knight (the Jeb of the film) must have been truly aghast: at 47 years of age, he was seven years *younger* than Lewis, who was playing his son. From all accounts, that fact was the most horrifying facet of the picture. (The write-up in the 26 May 1923 *Harrison's Reports* enthused, "A wild melodrama, with much of its action arbitrary." That's tellin' 'em.)

Schoolhouse (aka *School House*) was reputedly based on a play (that, apparently, went unpublished) by one Hal Reid. It's abundantly unclear as to whether this possible playwright was the same Hal Reid as the fellow who cranked out a few screenplays during the 1910s or the fellow who appeared onscreen in the films that did not bear the imprimatur "Hal Reid" as writer. It matter little, as the lightning/window device *had* been published — in 1887 — as part of the grand denouement of the novel *At the Mercy of Tiberius*, and the particulars of that rendition may be found in our chapter on *God's Witness*. The fellow who adapted Reid's play or Augusta Jane Evans Wilson's novel — or whatever — to the screen for Arrow was James Shelley Hamilton, and this will be the only time you find his name in these pages.

That's also true for Martin J. Heyl, whose eponymous production company produced exactly one film … and you've just read about it. Director John G. Adolfi also helmed *Queen of the Sea* — and penned the screenplay — but that title and this one are about all he wrote (for genre-happy folk). Actor Edmund Breese merits more exposure, though, and gets it: see *The Speed Spook*. Photographer George Webber — sans his initial "F" — is listed in the credits of our essay on 1917's *The Image Maker*, but his other genre project, 1929's *The House of Secrets*, was released only as a talkie and thus is not discussed herein.

— *JTS*

Lord John in New York

Lord John in New York. Gold Seal/Universal Film Manufacturing Company, 14 December 1915, 4 reels [LOST]

CAST: William Garwood (*Lord John*); Stella Razetto (*Maida Odell*); Ogden Crane (*Roger Odell*); Walter Belasco (*Paolo Tostini*); Jay Belasco (*Antonio Tostini*); T.D. Crittenden (*Carr Price*); Doc Crane (*L.J. Calit*); Grace Benham (*Grace Callender*); Laura Oakley (*Head Sister*); Albert MacQuarrie (*Dr. Rameses*); with Gretchen Lederer

CREDITS: *Director* Edward Le Saint; based on the short story, "Lord John in New York," by Charles Norris Williamson and Alice Muriel Williamson in *McLure's Magazine* (December 1915); *Scenario* Harvey Gates

It's going to take a moment to explain this one, so be patient, please.

We have to start with Harvey Gates, a Hawaiian-born scribe of prodigious output (easily more than 200 confirmed film credits; probably another 50 or so that are iffy) whose curriculum vitae opens our essay on 1923's *Legally Dead*. As we indicated there, Gates spent most of the Silent Era tossing out ideas that were made into two-reelers of varying quality, plus the occasional serial. One of those occasional serials was 1915's *Lord John's Journal*.

Journal was a rather peculiarly appointed chapter-play, what with its first chapter (*LJ in NY*) four reels in length and the remaining four episodes each three reels long. What's more, chapter one — under discussion herein — was released in 1915 as a

stand-alone feature, while the remaining chapters — *The Grey Sisterhood, Three-Fingered Jenny, The Eye of Horus*, and *The League of the Future* — all hit neighborhood screens the following year. What's even *more*, said 16 reels of Lord John's peregrinations were all supposedly reworked by Gates from a *short story*, penned by C.N. and A.M. Williamson in the December 1915 issue of *McClure's Magazine*. Due to the fact that *LJ in NY* debuted in theaters on the 6 December of 1915, we are forced to wonder whether Gates did, indeed, adapt the Williamsons' tale (which would have been set in print some months prior to the magazine's December delivery) or whether, rather, the Williamsons "novelized" Gates' screenplay. In the cosmic scheme of things, this matters little, but the question is as fascinating as it is academic.

The précis that follows is taken from the Library of Congress registration file.

> Lord John, a detective novelist and the Marquis of Haselmere's brother, receives word that the stage adaptation of one of his stories will not be performed because Roger Odell, a millionaire, has spoken against him. After tracking him down, Lord John joins his foe on an ocean liner along with Grace Callender, an heiress, and Dr. Rameses, a hypnotist and Egyptian cultist. While the evil Dr. Rameses is trying to steal a gold-filled mummy from Maida, Odell's adopted sister, Lord John confronts Odell, who reveals that his anger stems from a disservice that the Marquis once committed against Maida. To make reparations, Lord John offers to clear up the mystery surrounding the untimely deaths of Grace Callender's fiancés. Because she believes that she is guilty and cursed, Grace refuses to marry Odell, but after Lord John's exhaustive investigation in which Marian Callender, Grace's guardian aunt, is shown to have connections with members of Rameses's gang, Marian confesses to murdering the fiancés for her own gain. Exposed, Marian jumps from a window to her death.

We pause (a) to note that Grace did, indeed, have more than one "unlucky" fiancé; at what point would a savvy, would-be heiress-chaser pause to take stock of the odds of surviving until the wedding? (b) to question how a given woman's aunt could reap any financial benefit whatsoever from doing in said woman's boyfriends? Surely Grace didn't have the lawyers in to change her will the first morning one of these guys woke up with his shoes under her bed … did she? (c) to wonder at the lady's considering *herself* to be "cursed" when she's still swanning about, dishabille, lugging bags of cash, be it on ocean liner or in megalopolis. Did Dr. Rameses dabble in insurance fraud when he and his gang were not otherwise nefariously engaged?

As for the good doctor, if the plot summary deposited by Universal took the time to list the man's occupation as hypnotist, he must, then, have done the deed at some point with somebody, right? And his also collecting a weekly check as an "Egyptian cultist" leads us to image said mind control being effected via wonderfully picturesque means. We just have no idea what they might have been. As for his dramatic *raison d'être*, the awkward phrase "gold-filled mummy" conjures up misunderstandings along the lines of chocolate rabbits, wrapped in gold foil, but it was the custom to insert charms, amulets and similar tchochtkes (usually of gold or precious/semi-precious stones) among the wrappings of the mummies of noble or royal personages. We have been unable to locate any sort of illustration at all depicting Dr. Rameses, but in order for Albert MacQuarrie (the San Francisco–born brother of the better- [but not well-] known character actor, Murdock MacQuarrie) to successfully impersonate an Egyptian mesmerist for 1915-vintage viewers, he doubtless would have been bedizened with a turban, prodigious eye makeup, and an acre or two of crepe hair. (May we not assume that the later "chapter"— *The Eye of Horus*— gave Dr. Rameses center stage?) Let's be honest: it is due to Dr. Rameses' machinations that *LJ in NY* is on display here in the appendix, and due to lack of any further information of substance on him, his gang, and Marian Callender that the whole lot of them is not either in the main body of this work, or the hell out of here entirely.

Grace Callender was played by Grace Benham, and about the most we can say about the serial's unlucky ingénue was that the actress mouthing her title cards was pushing 40 while bemoaning the staying power of her fellas. Can anybody say "Cougar"?

Maida Odell — she who had once been … *errrr* … disserviced by the Marquis— was enacted by Stella Razetto, a stage actress of some celebrity who once had her own troupe. When illness forced her early retirement from the boards, she turned to film and changed her name to Le Saint via a ceremony involving a ring; however, she kept Razetto/Razeto for all professional dealings and ran up a pretty hefty string of cinematic credits (albeit mostly shorts). Stella's husband, Edward Le Saint, directed her in *LJ'sJ*, as he did in about a half-hundred other early (1912–1916) pictures. As had a number of her colleagues, Stella withdrew from films when talkies became the order of the day only to resurface (as it were) in a number of uncredited bits in the 1930s and 1940s. Husband Edward likewise had spent his salad days on the stage, moving to the Bastard Art around 1912 as an actor (over 300 appearances; ditto with the uncredited stuff in the Sound Era, although these bits comprised the bulk of his film career) and director (well over 125 shot with a megaphone in his hands). The Lord John mélange was pretty much the totality of genre participation for both the Le Saints, but the scope of their work is a matter of record.

Speaking of records, Edward Le Saint went on one (if only for *The Victoria* [Texas] *Daily Advocate*) to set the stage, as it were, for his latest cinematic project:

> "As a rule," says Mr. Le Saint, "I believe there is no other work that picture producers dislike to handle more than the filmization of novels, however popular those novels may have been in book form. The reason is obvious to picture people for they realize just how difficult it is to picture all the action which is told so simply in the words of the writers, C.N, and A.M. Williamson…
>
> "In 'The Journal of Lord John,' however, I must admit that I have run into the exception to the rule. There is present throughout the entire story exactly the type of action that lends itself most readily to film presentation. It is especially strange coming from these authors, for in the rest of their works this particular type of action is far from predominant, which would make it appear that they had studied the requirements of the screen before attempting to write for it — a process, by the way, which might be emulated to good advantage by other prospective scenario writers, whatever literary experience they may have had" [28 December 1915].

The production's title role was awarded to William Garwood, an actor/director from the "Show Me" state who had already rubbed elbows with Egyptologists (in Thanhouser's 1911 short,

The Mummy) in the course of the 150 or so pictures that preceded *Lord John's Journal*; fewer than 10 of those were feature-length releases. Unlike everyone else we've mentioned to this point, Garwood didn't outlast the Silent Era; although the second date on his headstone reads 1950, his last cinematic credit is from 1919. Of dubious historic value (but worthy of a brief snort) is our noting the intriguing casting coincidence wherein two actors with the same surname (Belasco) play two characters with the same surname (Tostini). Walter was the brother of David Belasco, the Bishop of Broadway and mover-and-shaker behind numerous motion pictures (see *The Case of Becky*); Jay was cousin to Walter and David. We're not sure what it says about either of the men's thespic ability, but David never had his brother or his cousin so much as show his face in one of his films. (For the record, Walter *did* grace the stage once — he doubled, in fact —for his brother's 1901–1902 Broadway hit, *Du Barry*.)

Peter Milne, writing in the 11 December 1915 issue of *Motion Picture News*, spent the better part of his commentary on this first part of the "serial" promising that things were going to get better later on:

> Evidently the unusually large number of characters that are introduced during the first 2 reels of this first number is responsible for its length. This fact entails confusion on the part of the spectator until the real action gets under way and the characters are formally presented in the 3rd reel. It is to be surmised from the clear and compact appearance of the concluding parts, that the installments to follow will be as defined as one might ask for. It is a difficulty not to be underestimated to start a serial without confusion and although *The Journal of Lord John* pictures have not been able to overcome this natural handicap, the character of the story finally presented is proof enough of the interesting nature of those to follow…. The series is under the direction of Edward Le Saint, who so far has been retarded by a confusing scenario, but his staging of the story proper is entirely adequate, and in the 2nd installment, where there will be no large numbers of characters to introduce, he will undoubtedly make a satisfactory film.

There weren't many other critical paragraphs devoted to Lord John's sundry adventures. The 25 December 1915 issue of *Motography* basically recounted the plotline, as was the S.O.P for early (i.e., pre–1916 or so) "reviews." Other than the cast members listed below, credit information is scant. The copyright registration synopsis at the Library of Congress features the name of one "Robert Lusk," but research has failed to determine who was this man and on what other projects he might have worked.

Still, it's better to have Lusked and lost…

— *JTS/HN*

The Lost Zeppelin

The Lost Zeppelin. Tiffany Productions, Inc./Tiffany, 20 December 1929, 8 reels/6,882 feet, Photophone Sound, only sound version survives

CAST: Conway Tearle (*Commander Hall*), Virginia Valli (*Mrs. Hall*), Ricardo Cortez (*Tom Armstrong*), Duke Martin (*Lieutenant Wallace*), Kathryn McGuire (*Nancy*), Winter Hall (*Mr. Wilson*)

CREDITS: *Director* Edward Sloman; *Scenario* Frances Hyland; based on a story by Frances Hyland and John F. Natteford; *Dialogue* Charles Kenyon; *Cinematographer* Jackson Rose; *Art Director* Hervey Libbert; *Set Decoration* George Sawley; *Effects* Jack Robson and Kenneth Peach;

Film Editors Martin G. Cohn and Donn Hayes; *Sound Technician* John Buddy Myers; *Recording Engineer* Jerry Eisenberg

The story deals with Commander Hall, explorer, who, on the eve of his departure for the South Pole, finds his wife in the arms of his lieutenant. Hence complications.

This briefest of descriptions of 1929's *The Lost Zeppelin* comes from *The Charleston* [West Virginia] *Gazette* of the 2 February 1930, and it pretty much sums things up.

Only by the narrowest of definitions does *The Lost Zeppelin* warrant inclusion in this volume. First off, the film's science-fiction elements are marginal at best: a zeppelin is sufficiently advanced to be able to travel to the then-largely-uncharted regions of the South Pole while maintaining radio contact. Second, it qualifies as a silent feature because the Library of Congress copyright records—in the form of press materials filed on the 11 December 1929—clearly state:

An ALL-TALKING Picture
Recorded by RCA Photophone
Available on sound film — Or on DISC — *Or Silent*

Emphasis ours.

That very last word piqued our interest and sent us scrambling to discover just where, by late 1929, *The Lost Zeppelin* would have been screened silent; we seriously doubt that it was ever distributed as a silent in any major venues. A perusal of the New York State Archives' Motion Picture Scripts Collection (which doesn't actually contain "scripts" but, rather, printed copies of dialogue once used for censorship purposes in New York State) failed to uncover any record of *title card* dialogue for the picture, which would have surely been the case had *The Lost Zeppelin* been shown anywhere in New York in silent form.

We can only hypothesize that silent prints were made available to those venues which had not yet rewired for sound. As the various critical writings (both contemporary and modern) agree that the first half-hour or so of the extant sound version is static and talky, we can also hypothesize that the silent version might have been edited to alleviate a bit of this verbiage. Likewise, we are probably safe in assuming that, other than this expository footage — which seems to be yet another example of the sort of gabbing-for-gabbing's-sake in which many extremely early talkies indulged — there would have been no need to cut or amend the more action-oriented segments of the plotline to fit more readily into the "silent format."

Thus, resisting the temptation to stand pat with the above West Virginian synopsis in spite of the marginal status of *The Lost Zeppelin*, we present the full Library of Congress summary:

The night before Commander Hall, world-famed explorer, is to take off for the South Pole in a giant Zeppelin, he is the guest of honor at a farewell banquet. He prefers to spend the evening quietly at home with his beautiful wife, Miriam, whom he worships. His deeds of greatness are to him only worthwhile as laurels to lay at her feet. And that night at the banquet, he unexpectedly comes upon her in the arms of handsome young Lieut. Armstrong — his best friend and a partner in the hazardous trip to be started on the morrow.

The pair suspects that he has discovered their secret but Hall says nothing during the remainder of the evening. Finally Miriam can stand the suspense no longer, confesses to Hall her love for Tom, and asks him for a divorce, but he suggests that she wait until after the South Pole voyage.

Before departing the next day Hall takes Miriam in his arms for the benefit of the world looking on, but her heart is with Tom, as Hall well knows. During the trip Hall tells Tom that he will give Miriam her freedom. He blames the boy for not fighting against his love for her, but still feels compassion and tenderness for him.

The Zeppelin has a voyage filed with exciting moments that are heard back home on the radio by Miriam. Then comes the fateful hour when the ship falls. It is short of gasoline, the weight of the ice on the envelope is too great — and it crashes into a frozen mountain in a terrific gale. There is nothing but bleak ice on all sides of the gallant adventurers.

Their last radio tubes burn out in an effort to send word back to civilization — the last was the message that they were falling, which Miriam heard! Fabric from the ship supplies the only fuel for warmth. Food rations get down to enough for eight days. Hall divides the men into groups to go out in different directions to help any possible rescuers.

Finally, there are only two men left — Hall and Tom. An airplane finds them, but there is room in it for only one passenger, and Hall insists that it shall be Tom.

Some time later Tom is welcomed in Washington as the only survivor of the Zeppelin. After the ceremonies he goes to Miriam — to find that she has discovered, during all those ghastly days of waiting that her real love is for her husband, and she sends Tom away.

Later news comes of Hall's rescue — of a miraculous recovery and when Miriam hastens to him filled with deep affection he feels that the Zeppelin expedition may have been a failure in the eyes of the world, but to him it was the greatest of all triumphs.

Cineastes rarely rave about *The Lost Zeppelin* and there are no Oscar performances here. *The Lost Zeppelin* started the beginning of a spate of early science-fiction/adventure talkies, such as 1933's *FP-1* and *Transatlantic Tunnel* (1935). Like those films, *The Lost Zeppelin* can be an entertaining way to while away some time.

Fog, Blizzard, Sleet, Darkness in a Frozen, Cruel Land—Then crash! Headlong into a mountain of ice! A crew of gallant adventurers stranded at the South Pole!

Melodrama Startling Spectacular♦ With a throbbing love theme of two men who laid siege to the heart of a woman.

"Hey! *The Lost Zeppelin* is not lost! It's right *there*!"

More information on the cast's genre contributions to the Silent Era is to be found elsewhere. Conway Tearle, with the hero's role as Commander Hall, also starred in M-G-M's *The Mystic* (1924). Virginia Valli, who played the ever-fickle Miriam Hall, is mentioned in the entries on *Up the Ladder* (1925) and 1929's *The Isle of Lost Ships,* while Ricardo Cortez's bona fides may be found in the chapters on *The Sorrows of Satan* (1926) and *Midstream* (1929).   — SJ

Lotus Blossom

Lotus Blossom. Wah Ming Motion Picture Company/National Exchanges, 1 December 1921, 7 reels, Reel 5 exists at UCLA Film and Television Archive

CAST: Lady Tsen Mai (*Moi Tai*); Tully Marshall (*Quong Foo*); Noah Beery (*Tartar Chief*); Jack Abbe (*Quong Sung*), Goro Kino (*The Emperor*) James Wang (*Professor Lowe Team*)

CREDITS: *Director* James B. Leong, Frank Grandon*; *Scenario* George Yohalem, Charles Furthman; based on a story by James B. Leong; *Cinematographer* Ross Fisher

Our synopsis is from the copyright entry at Library of Congress:

> Centuries ago Leong Chong was sentenced to life imprisonment by the Emperor as he had invented the first clock which would do away with the use of the sacred bell. On his way to exile, Chong is met by Quong Foo and his little daughter, Moy Tai, who gives him a lotus flower.
>
> Moy Tai grew to beautiful womanhood and was loved by Quong Sung, a youth whom her father had adopted. Sung is sent to Professor Lowe Team to complete his studies. He falls under the spell of the light woman, Taze Sin. Moy Tai is grieved.
>
> The sacred bell cracks. Foo is bade by the Emperor to cast a new bell. The metals refuse to mingle and Foo is given one more chance under penalty of death. Meanwhile a Tartar horde besieges the city. Sung kills the chief but is himself fatally wounded. He is found by Moy Tai. The second bell is worthless and Foo is sentenced to death. But Moy Tai remembers Chong. She goes to him and learns that the metals will fuse only by the addition of flesh and blood. Moy Tai makes the supreme sacrifice for her father's honor and the new bell is cast.

Based on an old Chinese legend, *Lotus Blossom* was meant to be an illustration of filial piety, one of the Confucian virtues. Our own aims being a bit less lofty, we have included the film here because of the human sacrifice and its supernatural result at the climax. From an unidentified newspaper clipping, we learn that only a virgin would be an acceptable candidate for bell-fusion procedures — good thing Sung got killed off in time — and that the young woman actually throws herself into the vat of boiling metal.

Only reel five of the film's seven reels still survives. In it we watch Quong Sung (Japanese actor, Jack Abbe), disguised as a woman, gain entrance to the headquarters of the Tartar chieftain (Noah Beery). Sung doesn't make a particularly lovely maiden, but Beery's character, perhaps a bit nearsighted (or, being a Beery character, desperate), is nonetheless receptive; he quickly finds himself on the receiving end of his own dagger.

Sung escapes but is himself stabbed by one of the pursuing guards. We watch as Moy Tai (the strikingly beautiful Lady Tsen Mai) worries about her father, Quong Foo (played by the not-so-beautiful, but barely recognizable Tully Marshall), who is getting nowhere with his attempts to make a new bell and is beginning to accept his execution as inevitable. Moy Tai risks her life by visiting the exiled inventor, Leong Chong, who has never forgotten her kindness and has kept the lotus flower she gave him. A flashback shows the younger Chong becoming frustrated as *he* (apparently) tries to cast the sacred bell. We see him and his helpers dig up a grave (presumably to use a corpse for the metals mixture, though this is not explained at this point). Back in the present, Chong gives Moy Tai a parchment with the information she needs, and she makes a safe escape.

Though the editing a bit clumsy, the sequence is well directed and acted, and it's certainly regrettable that we have only one reel.

Lotus Blossom was the brainchild of James B. Leong (birth name: Leong But-jung), who had come to America from Shanghai in 1913. The young man went to college at Muncie, Indiana, and entered the movie business in the late 1910s, where he worked as an interpreter, a technical advisor (he helped on D.W. Griffith's *Broken Blossoms*) and an occasional actor. Leong was appalled at how the Chinese were reduced to stereotypes in American films; they were seen only as opium smokers, serial villains, criminals, and pursuers of innocent white women. According to a supportive article published in the 27 November 1921 edition of the *Los Angeles Times*, Leong convinced a group of Chinese businessmen to finance the Wah Ming Film Company, which set out to make movies with Chinese themes that were intended for mainstream American audiences. Leong planned a whole series of films in which American actors would appear alongside the mainly Chinese casts.

The follow up to *Lotus Blossom* was to have been *The Blood of Matrimony*, set in Korea and having to do with ancestor worship; this was to be followed by a picture shot in China and dealing with the virtues of honesty. None of these projects came to pass. In spite of its fine acting and technical proficiency, *Lotus Blossom* apparently failed to score with American audiences. Perhaps the story was too downbeat with both the hero and heroine dying (and the beautiful young woman meeting an especially grisly end). The leads — however attractive and talented — weren't famous, and viewers may have assumed that it was an ethnic film made mainly for Chinese audiences. More likely, viewers preferred the Lotus Blossom who appeared in another 1921 film, *Shame*. In that one, hero John Gilbert believes he's the son of a Chinese woman, Lotus Blossom (Anna May Wong, who's killed off early in the film), but — much to his relief — finds that she's not his *real* mother, so he's not a half-caste after all and can marry the white heroine. No doubt it was plots like this that drove Leong to create his own company.

Leong went on to act in small parts in the movies while producing plays in the Los Angeles area and became a United States

---

*It's possible that Leong was uncertain of his own directorial abilities at this early stage and enlisted Grandon, another Griffith alumnus and the director of *The Adventures of Kathlyn*, to lend a hand.

citizen in 1958. At that time he was still doing bits in films like *Around the World in 80 Days* and *Tea House of the August Moon*. He had also become an anti-drug crusader, producing and directing a picture entitled *Dope over America* and authoring the book, *Narcotics — the Menace to Children*. According to the book's introduction, Leong — as a youth in Shanghai — had had a minor involvement himself in the opium trade until his mother, a devout Christian, objected. Perhaps of more interest here is *The Devil's Paradise*, an anti-drug play Leong wrote and produced in 1956; its star was recovering addict, Bela Lugosi.

— HN

The Love Girl

The Love Girl. Bluebird Photoplays/Bluebird Photoplays, 10 July 1916, 5 reels, UCLA

CAST: Ella Hall (*Ambrosia*); Adele Farrington (*Her Aunt*); Betty Schade (*Her Cousin*); Harry Depp (*The Boy Next Door*); Grace Marvin (*The Maid*); Wadsworth Harris (*The Swami*);

CREDITS: *Director* Robert Z. Leonard; *Scenario* Robert Z. Leonard

For what's it's worth, the working title of this masterpiece was *Ambrosia*.

According to Webster's Third New International Dictionary of the English Language Unabridged, "swami" is "a form of respectful address to a Hindu religious leader or monk" or "an initiated member of a Hindu religious order." According to Silent-Era-genre movie convention, a swami is any swarthy guy in a turban who covets white women, cash, gold, jewels, golden bejeweled idols, or any combination thereof. One may see an example of this latter understanding in *The AFI Catalog*'s plot précis on this 1916 Robert Z. Leonard epic.

> After her mother dies, Ambrosia goes to live with her austere, unloving aunt, whose only eccentricity is her devotion to an Indian swami. As a result, she naturally enlists the swami's aid when her daughter decides to marry a man who has no money. The swami hypnotizes the daughter and orders her to break the engagement; and then, seeing a chance to collect a fortune, he kidnaps her. Ambrosia, however, with the help of the boy next door, discovers where the daughter is being held captive, after which she turns the swami over to the police. Aware of how Ambrosia has helped her, the aunt becomes loving and, after accepting her niece into the family, finally consents to her daughter's marriage.

Ambrosia? *Really*? It augers ill when the only character given a name is saddled with something like *Ambrosia*, while everybody else has to settle for stuff like Her Aunt or The Boy Next Door.

Anyhow, the odds are decent that, should the reader plunge a finger anywhere into these pages, he/she will come across randy Oriental types (a swami by any other name...) who usually are hypnotists, but who doubtlessly are not to be trusted. As our plot recap indicates, it is the very essence of eccentricity (and eccentricity = madness + money) for an American matron to demonstrate devotion to a swami of any stripe, and eccentricity almost always leads to tragedy. Thankfully, Ambrosia (the distressed damsel's cousin) — together the boy next door — saves both auntie's bacon and auntie's daughter's honor. It's not clear whether the boy next door ends up with Ambrosia on his arm — or with so much as a fiver from old moneybags — but *another* of those Silent-Era-genre conventions is that sweet young things

almost always are altar-bound just before the lights are turned up. (Of course, with cousin Nameless headed up the aisle, maybe Ambrosia's reward is getting to bunk down on clean sheets in the gal's old room.)

Only the swami knows for sure.

Some of the local press coverage the picture garnered is worthy of mention, if only for its being rather bizarre. As part of its savvy campaign to lure patrons into the silent dark, *The [Massillon, Ohio] Evening Independent* revealed that the movie was "An idealistic drama of sunshine and love which only aims to make you happy." It takes a real pro to come up with stuff like that.

Then, too, the 17 September 1916 number of *The Syracuse Herald* dropped the following spoiler: "There is a novel subject for photo-playing introduced during the progress of *The Love Girl*, when Hindu mystics well-nigh upset the calculations of everybody concerned. Just how the Buddhist faith is misapplied and made the subject of villainy comprises an element that is said to life this Bluebird feature out of the ordinary."

In fact, this feature *is* extraordinary in that it may well comprise the only example of Silent Era cinematic villainy practiced by Hindu Buddhists. (The *Herald*'s anonymous movie reviewer gave us another gem a paragraph later, when he/she wrote of the "two splendidly equipped children.")

The Love Girl didn't get much coverage from the Usual Suspects, but — in 1916 — the Usual Suspects were still getting their acts together. We've nothing with which to infer that the swami's gesturing hypnotically would have caused early genre fans to sit up and take notice, or whether the Austere Auntie remained the most picturesque of the dramatis personae. Fans of Robert Z. Leonard and Etta Hall (and they're out there, somewhere) should repair to our coverage on *The Silent Command*. Fans of Betty Schade (ditto) should flip to our essay in *The Reward of the Faithless*, followers of Adele Harrington (ditto, again, we suppose), to our piece on *The Devil's Bondwoman*, and relatives of Harry Depp, Grace Marvin, and Wadsworth Harris, to the IMDB.

— JTS

The Lust of the Ages

The Lust of the Ages. Ogden Film Corporation/States Rights, August 1917, 7 reels [LOST]

CAST: Lillian Walker (*Lois Craig*); Jack Mower (*Byron Masters*); Harry Revier (*Edmund Craig*); with Mrs. Nellie Parker Spaulding, W.J. Everett, Frances Sanson, Betty Mack

CREDITS: *Director* Harry Revier; *Scenario* Aaron Hoffman; *Cinematographer* Joseph Seiden; *Art Direction* Thomas Brierly

And just when you thought you knew what lust was all about...

The following synopsis is taken from the 8 September 1917 *New York Dramatic Mirror*:

> The story gets into its stride with the engagement of a young girl to a man who, like her father, has the lust for money and its power. The lesson she had at first hand from the unhappy home life of her parents in consequence of her father's neglect of her mother in his ceaseless attention to business, prompts her to break her engagement when she finds out the man is of the same type. She gives him a book she has written [which has the same title as

the film] and, on completing it, he is so impressed with the truths it contains that he gives proof by changing his worship of money into something finer, and he is accepted again as fiancé. The things contained in the book that reformed him are really stories within a story and from the time the man starts the book what he is reading is pictured on the screen.

One is a love story set in a time when the world was very young. Everything is progressing happily in the Valley of Contentment until the dwellers there are driven into despair by the entry into the world of the first avaricious men, who swoop down upon them and confiscate all properties. The book further proceeds to record the mad craving for wealth at a later period when in the Hall of Mammon, people followed the Money God. Then it jumps to a period about forty years ago when a European warlord determines to lay a foundation of a war of conquest to be forced upon the world at such time when the war chest is filled with gold. The last chapter of the book reveals the present time when this war lord's successor engages upon a war to monopolize the world's wealth and possessions.

The synopsis doesn't indicate whether or not the heroine's book became a bestseller.

The time when people lived in peace and harmony is one of mythology's Top Ten favorite settings, and two of the most prominent examples of that idyllic existence may be found in the stories of the Golden Age of Greek legend and the Garden of Eden in the Bible. Said Utopias always ended poorly, though, and the ancient Greeks and Hebrews watched everything fall apart when Pandora opened the box and the serpent slithered onto the scene with his promises. The net (and inevitable) result was "The Fall" with its endless cycles of greed and violence.

In modern times, the idea of a peace-loving community being overrun by money-grubbing exploiters has become clichéd, turning up in everything from the song "One Tin Soldier" to mega-money-making movie, *Avatar*. While *The Lust of the Ages* certainly skewered the Ebenezer Scrooges of its day, there can be little doubt that the villain of its last chapter is meant to be the Kaiser, the bête noir of that time period, as least so far as American audiences were concerned.

The Lust of the Ages was filmed in Ogden, Utah, and was the fledging effort of a film company called, appropriately enough, Ogden Pictures Corporation. The city fathers, perhaps imagining their town becoming the Hollywood of the Southwest, were delighted. The Ogden press did its part by printing numerous favorable articles about the shooting: hundreds of locals happily appeared as extras; an entire village was constructed in a park on the shore of the Ogden River to represent the Valley of Contentment; and the Temple of Mammon was built on the stage of the huge Alhambra Theater. (And a local reporter then indulged in a bit of understandable local pride when he claimed that only the Babylon set in *Intolerance* was more magnificent.)

Director Harry Revier was equally impressed with his citizen extras, according to a piece that appeared in the 7 May 1917 issue of *The Ogden Standard*:

Such a day… We filmed 132 scenes and say these people out here worked great. They would register "come" and "go" better than a New York crowd would have done with ten days training. Of course we had a little trouble, some [one] passing in front of the camera with a white hat and modern clothes on just as Lewis (the cameraman) was ready to "shoot" and once an old lady wearing a pair of spectacles with her primitive costume, came into line. These were little things however and the people did a big day's work.

Revier was no stranger to the area having managed the Playhouse Theater in Salt Lake City in 1912. He departed rather abruptly, leaving the movie theater shut down and owing the power company (and others) money; all this after a project to make westerns flopped. This was duly reported in the Ogden press at the time, but was tactfully forgotten five years later.

A publicity piece for *The Lust of the Ages* praised Revier as a director anxious to experiment rather than follow conventional filmmaking:

One bold innovation is the elimination in certain parts of the production of the "cutback" and the employment in its stead of dual scenes thrown upon the screen at the same time. These are not double exposures in the common acceptation of the word, but in fact consists of two separate sets if scenes and independent action filmed at the same time.

We're not altogether sure what exactly the above means, but "Jolo" of *Variety* wrote (in the 24 August 1918 issue) that the film contained "some corking fadeouts and double exposures." Jolo was quite impressed with the picture, calling it "one of the most important photoplay productions of the present day" and "ingeniously directed and photographed."

"F.T." of *The New York Dramatic Mirror* was equally enthusiastic:

At the beginning *The Lust of the Ages* sets out to prove that money is the root of all evil, and has been for all time, and when the last of its seven reels has been run, you realize that it has never swerved from its premise. It proves this old lesson conclusively but in an entirely new and absorbing way…. The action moves at an even tempo throughout and the interest is not permitted to lag for a moment. The settings furnish picturesque backgrounds for the various stories. In fact the scenic detail and beauty is one of the outstanding points in the picture. The titling is especially attractive.

We don't know how much gold *The Lust of the Ages* made at the box office but, in spite of many optimistic announcements in the press, Ogden Picture Corp. made only one other film — *The Grain of Dust* (1918) — before disappearing entirely.

Lillian Walker played the authoress of the titular tome as well as the heroine in each of the episodes. Walker was a onetime model and stage actress who made scores of shorts for Vitagraph, often teamed with John Bunny. Petite and pretty, Walker was so well known by the nickname "Dimples," that she made several films with "Dimples" in the title. Perhaps tired of such mostly light fare and feeling that, pushing 30, she was outgrowing "cutesy" roles, Walker left Vitagraph for Ogden Picture Corp. She got good reviews for *The Lust of the Ages* and appeared in *The Grain of Dust* as well, but then Ogden went under. Walker decided to start her own production company, but that proved disastrous and she lost much of her own money in the venture, forcing her to sell her Brooklyn home. She did a serial — *The $1,000,000 Reward* (1920) — but didn't care for that kind of work ("You do stunts, that's all," she later said). Retiring to the family farm in Saratoga Springs, New York, she apparently suffered a breakdown (or some undisclosed illness). When she recovered, she did summer stock and went on to several appearances on Broadway as well, but her subsequent film roles were few.

Harry Revier cast himself as the heroine's greedy father (who dies of a heart attack while pulling off a big business deal) in *The Lust of the Ages*. Around the time of his hasty departure from Salt Lake City, Revier and a partner rented part of an orange grove in Hollywood, on which spot they set up a studio and lab. In 1913, Jesse Lasky rented the studio and filmed *The Squaw Man* there and ultimately bought the whole property. Revier went on to produce and direct — mostly westerns and action films — including the serial, *The Son of Tarzan*, as well as the occasional oddity like 1919's *What Shall We Do with Him?* (based on the scant info that survives on this film, we believe Revier suggested that the Kaiser was the Anti-Christ and that a World Court — presumably, a court in *this* world — should deal with him.)

In 1921, Revier saw dancer Dorothy Valegra perform in a San Francisco cabaret and cast her in his Mountie melodrama, *Life's Greatest Question*. The following year he married her, made her Dorothy Revier, and promptly got jailed for bigamy when another lady claimed that *she* was Mrs. Revier. Harry directed Dorothy in a few films before their short-lived marriage ended; subsequently Dorothy went on to become Columbia's B-movie queen.

In the 1930s, Harry Revier made that most bizarre of serials, *The Lost City* (1935), as well as the exploitation films, *Child Bride* (1938) and *The Lash of the Penitentes* (1937). In 1953, he worked on *Planet Outlaws*, a feature version of the 1939 *Buck Rogers* serial with some narration added. Four years later, he died of a heart attack while directing a TV program called *Jenny, Jerry and the Chimp*.

What the latter was about, we shall never know.

— HN

Madonnas and Men

Madonnas and Men. Jans Pictures, Inc./States Rights., June 1920, 7/8 reels, Print at Eastman House

CAST: Edmund Lowe (*Gordion/Gordon Turner*); Anders Randolf (*Emperor Turnerius/Marshall Turner*); Gustav von Seyffertitz (*Grimaldo/John Grimm*); Evan Burrows Fontaine (*Nerissa/Ninon*); Raye Dean (*Laurentia/Laura*); Faire Binney (*Patsy*); Blanche Davenport (*Mrs. Grimm*).

CREDITS: *Director* B.A. Rolfe; *Scenario* Violet Clark; *Story* Carey Wilson and Edmund Goulding; *Cinematographer* A.A. Cadwell; *Technical Director* W.G. Smart; *Film Editor* J.J. Kiley

Our synopsis is taken from *The AFI Catalog* and contemporary reviews:

> In the Roman Coliseum at the beginning of the Christian era, the Emperor Turnerius, accompanied by his favorite, Nerissa, watches the bestial games in the arena. His son Gordian is asked by Grimaldo the magician to save the life of a Christian girl about to be thrown to the lions. He refuses, whereupon Grimaldo prophesies the fate of the Empire by telling the Prince a story of the future.
>
> The story: Laura Grimm is kidnapped by ruthless millionaire, Marshall Turner, who — years before — loved Laura's mother and was rejected by her. Turner plans to force Laura to marry him. Laura's mother, distraught at her daughter's disappearance, dies. Her husband John, while digging her grave, strikes oil. This new-found wealth enables him to conduct a search for Laura. John meets Ninon, a cabaret dancer, and she agrees to help him. It turns out Ninon is in love with Marshall Turner's son, Gordon. However, Gordon has fallen in love with Laura. John finally locates his daughter and struggles with Marshall, who shoots him.

Marshall then dies of a heart attack, leaving the way clear for Gordon to marry Laura.

> The prince is so deeply affected by the injustice of the story that he plunges into the arena to save the girl, causing the Emperor to die in a fit of rage, thus precipitating the coronation of his son as the new emperor.

The moral of the story is given in the film's final subtitle: "Remember a nation with unrestricted moral standards cannot endure; and no civilization is permanent which is founding on the debasing of womanhood."

Variety's "Fred" hooted at that one:

> Just how this hits at the mode of life of today as compared to that of 2,000 years ago is a question. That is, a question outside of the picture business itself, for offhandedly, one can think of not a single industry or amusement where the exploitation of womanhood is carried on to a greater degree than the so-called "infant industry" [18 June 1920].

Parallel ancient and modern stories were common enough in the Silent Era (with *Intolerance, Manslaughter,* and *Man-Woman-Marriage* but a few) but *Madonnas and Men* is included herein because the whole contemporary tale is cast as a prophesy of the future. Granted, this is all pretty absurd; what, for example, would Gordian have made of "oil"? ("What's this oil stuff, again, and why is it valuable?") And what did the Roman mob do while Grimaldo was spinning his tale? Head for the snack bar?

The Arena sequences were considered rather gruesome. In a bit of sadism that sounds worthy of the Coliseum finale of *The Sign of the Cross*, Nerissa dances on the gory ground where the gladiators have just died and then leaves a trail of bloody footprints as she ascends the stairs to rejoin the applauding Emperor.

Madonnas and Men was no doubt the most expensive and elaborate film made by Jans Pictures, Inc. (see *Love Without Question*), and the company made the most of that in publicity for the film: it took ten weeks to shoot, the titles were modeled in clay, it had the size and scope of *The Birth of a Nation*, and so on. A special showing was arranged for States' Rights buyers, exhibitors, distributors and the press, and an onstage chariot presentation preceded the film.

Representative of local press opinion, Esther Wagner of *The Lima* [Ohio] *Evening News* was impressed with the sets, but found fault elsewhere: "Photographically the production could have been much better. The subtitles are hopelessly stilted. Still, *Madonnas and Men* should please you mightily and if you don't care for the story the effects alone should be worth something" (11 April 1921).

Variety's "Fred" thought the picture had the potential to be a big hit but found it lacking in most respects: 'The direction leaves much. There is at all times a lack of action that becomes tiresome after awhile. The tempo is wrong and needs to be speeded up satisfactorily to hold the interest. The photography is also far from satisfactory...." He went on to praise Anders Randolf (as the Emperor/Marshall Turner) and Gustav von Seyffertitz (in a rare sympathetic role as Grimaldo/John Grimm), but panned Edmund Lowe as the hero: "He does not seem to know what it is all about.... All that Lowe seemed able to have was a deep sigh and trouble with his hands and arms." (Fred also thought it amusing that Lowe's character just stands and watches while the two old guys duke it out at the end of the modern sequence.) On the other hand, Fred was enthusiasm itself about Ziegfeld Follies dancer, Evan Burrows Fontaine, as Nerissa/Ninon: "As a vamp, she absolutely outvamps anything ever seen on the screen before…. She is a find for this type of role."

Find or not, Fontaine's film career amounted to very little. Most of the publicity she received in the 1920s concerned several unsuccessful breach-of-promise lawsuits she filed against Cornelius Vanderbilt Whitney: the actress claimed the millionaire was the father of her child. Whether this was justice or just another case of the debasement of women condemned by the film remains unknown.

— HN

The Magic Eye

The Magic Eye. Universal Film Mfg. Co./Universal, 1 April 1918, 5 reels [LOST]
CAST: Henry A. Barrows (*Captain John Bowman*); Claire du Brey (*Mrs. Bowman*); Zoe Rae (*Shirley Bowman*); Charles H. Mailes (*Sam Bullard*); William Carroll (*Jack*); Elwood Burdell (*Cordy*)
CREDITS: *Director* Rea Berger; *Scenario* Frank H. Clark; based on a story by Norris Shannon; *Cinematographer* John Brown

The inclusion of clairvoyance in the mix is enough to assure the presence of this title in the table of contents, but not enough to push this essay out of the appendix.

During World War I, John Bowman, the captain of a tramp steamer, refuses to allow his wife and daughter, Shirley, to accompany him on a long voyage because he fears that the ship may be torpedoed. Before his departure, he entrusts his life insurance policy to shipping agent, Sam Bullard, who, unknown to John, once courted Mrs. Bowman. Shirley, a clairvoyant, has a vision in which her father's ship is torpedoed and the next day, Sam reports that the ship has been sunk and John killed. As Sam, using indelicate tactics, tries to acquire both Mrs. Bowman and the insurance money, Shirley, who has seen her father rescued in her vision, sends a wireless message that leads to John's rescue. Upon his return, John rescues his wife from the hotel room in which Sam had locked her and then puts the villain out of commission [Copyright registration document, Library of Congress].

Several of the trade publications that critiqued the production referred to Shirley's extrasensory experiences as happening in a dream, rather than a vision, but we're over a barrel, detailwise, what with no prints available, and all.

Playing the pivotal role of Shirley Bowman was Zoe Rae—more than occasionally billed as "Little Zoe Rae"—a Chicagoan of some eight years of age when *The Magic Eye* was readying itself for release. As may be expected, the trades fawned a tad over the young lady, whose movie career seems to have ended rather abruptly when she hit the wall at age ten. Henry A. Barrows—celebrated by us chiefly for having been father to cinematic-gorilla specialist, George Barrows—was Captain John, whose fear of torpedoes indicated that the man himself was no slouch at peering into the future.

From the standpoint of sheer movie output, the biggest name was that of Charles H. Mailes. Mailes, whose name was written on title cards with no fewer than seven (7) variations, appeared in over 300 shorts, features and in-betweeners (albeit mostly shorts) in the course of his nearly three-decade-long movie ca-

reer. The vast majority of those titles were silents, of course, but Mailes' genre-feature catalogue includes only one other legitimate entry, 1920's *Haunting Shadows.* Claire du Brey, the actress whose character was chased all over the lot by Mr. Mailes', ran a close second so far as the sheer volume of cinematic product is concerned. Possessed of over 250 films bearing her name (or any of *her* four alternate versions), Miss du Brey weathered the Talkie storm better than did Mr. Mailes, and fully two-thirds of her screen credits reflect her success in that medium. The lady was active professionally very nearly into the 1960s, and was fortunate (or hardy) enough to be able to stick around and reminisce beyond her 100th birthday.

Last-billed in the cast list is Elwood Burdell, for whom *The Magic Eye* would serve as the omega-feature, acting-wise. A Londoner by birth, Burdell would rise from his cinematic ashes a decade or so following the release of this Universal mishegas, and reestablish himself at the House that Carl Built as an ace cameraman for this same studio. Now answering to Elwood (soon Woody) Bredell, the ex-actor went on to frame and shoot any number of Universal's most beloved early–1940s series entries and horror programmers, among them: *Black Friday* (1940), *The Mummy's Hand* (1940), *Horror Island* (1941); *The Ghost of Frankenstein* (1942), and *Mystery of Marie Roget* (1942). Woody left Universal mid-decade and continued working for various studios over the course of the next decade. He subsequently returned to Blighty and died, at home in London, in late May 1976.

None of the surviving commentary on *The Magic Eye* provides enough detail to allow comment on the dream/vision scenes, so we've no idea how young Shirley's clairvoyant exercises were visualized for the audience. It's a lead-pipe cinch that ship-sinking footage was begged, borrowed, stolen, or shot, but whether that same vignette was used to illustrate Captain Bowman's ominous prescience, or Shirley's real-time psychic experience, or both, or neither, we cannot tell.

— JTS

The Man Who Couldn't Beat God

The Man Who Couldn't Beat God. Vitagraph Co. of America (A Blue Ribbon Feature)/V.L.S.E., Inc., 18 October 1915, 5 reels [LOST]
CAST: Maurice Costello (*Martin Henchford*); Robert Gaillard (*Elmer Bradford*); Denton Vane (*Leslie Gilman*); Estelle Mardo (*Elizabeth Bradford*); Edwina Robbins (*Lady Mary*); Thomas Mills (*Lord Rexford*); Marion Henry (*Nellie Rose*); Naomi Childers (*Hilma Lake*); Mary Maurice (*Old Woman*); Charles Eldridge (*Mr. Henchford*); Harry Morey (*Actor as Bill Sykes*); Florence Natol (*Actress as Nancy*); Mae Halpin (*Maid*); with Gladden James
CREDITS: *Directors* Maurice Costello, Robert Gaillard; *Story* Harold Gilmore Calhoun; *Cinematographer* William H. McCoy

The above title could refer to every man and woman who has ever drawn breath, so why this particular guy's story merited a movie is beyond us. *Except* that the picture—a mid–1910s thriller with repeated visions of corpses driving the killer 'round the bend—owes a debt to Dostoevsky and Poe and, in turn, is one of the cinematic forbears of a very widespread and lucrative Sound Era subgenre: the psychological horror picture.

Our synopsis is taken from the 23 October 1915 *New York Dramatic Mirror*:

> Martin Henchford, an English peasant of exceedingly strong will power, resents with every fiber of his being the arrogant treatment of the nobleman who employs him as a gardener. After suffering several affronts in silence, he meets the nobleman in a lonely wood where a quarrel ensues, resulting in Martin murdering his employer. He hurries back to the tavern to establish an alibi. The body is discovered but, as the nobleman's horse is standing near, the general supposition is that he met his death in a fall. Martin packs his clothes and emigrates to America. There he obtains a job as a sandhog in a tunnel that is being constructed under the river, and by a heroic piece of work rescues one of the other laborers from a cave-in. This conduct brings him to the notice of the head of the company and his advancement is rapid. But he cannot rid himself of the vision of the murdered man. Every time he sees a person in a prone position, the vision of his foul deed returns to him. With an enormous effort of the will he throws it off, resolving that his crime shall not in any way interfere with his success. He rapidly advances in his work and at the end of several years has become a wealthy contractor and successful politician.
>
> By now, through constant fighting and strenuous work he has weakened his body both mentally and physically. The vision recurs with greater frequency and at last he suffers a complete mental breakdown. While at the theater one night, he sees a murder being enacted on the stage. It is the last straw. His conscience can stand no more and with a cry he collapses in the arms of his wife. The doctor orders a long rest and an ocean voyage and Martin insists upon visiting his old home in England. There on the scene of his murder he sees the accusing vision of the man he has killed and with a last despairing cry, he sinks to the ground and dies.

Again, since everyone since the beginning of time has at some point or another sunk to the ground (literally or not) and died, it is Martin's *conscience* (and not life itself) that beats him up before beating him down. Nowadays, the underlying point of many "psychological horror" films is that the killer *has* no conscience and is thus free to commit mayhem with no restraint on him/her at all, save for box-office indifference. They used to call folks like those sociopaths, but there was no way the reel-life Martin could have been pegged a sociopath in 1915, as (a) ever-newly-minted psychological terminology was only then making its way through the more erudite of audiences; (b) the more erudite of audiences were at the theater or the opera, and not at the flickers; and (c) "sociopathy" wasn't one of those terms, anyhow, although doubtless there were proportionally as many sociopaths running around the streets then as there are now. The term itself has fallen out of favor, having been replaced fairly recently by "Antisocial Personality Disorder," but lack of remorse is a key factor to that disorder (or pathology, or whatever you choose to call it), and no screen character back in the mid–1910s could do something that was de facto dastardly and be depicted as suffering from lack of remorse.

Now, the fact that our antihero chooses to cruise off to his (literally) old haunts when he could have junketed anywhere in the world seems to show that he suffered, not from conscience, but, rather, from an excess of stupidity. Said stupidity is, of course, plot-driven, and in the days when virtue in the movies was always rewarded while vice in the same venue was inevitably punished, the hammer would fall only following an act of profound foolhardiness, a conversion experience, or a fortuitous circumstance (read: deus ex machina) presented in a manner that would seldom leave doubt in the viewer's mind that Higher Powers were at work. Nothing, it seemed, ever happened because of chance, as the moral of the dramatic turnabout — either implied or printed there in black and white — was that either "Everything happens for a reason" or "What goes around, comes around."

The guy whom God beat up had these visions via camera trickery, of course. That *Dramatic Mirror* piece is quite laudatory in that vein, and cameraman William McCoy must have cut out the review and put it on his refrigerator: "The photography throughout was up to the usual Vitagraph standards with some good double exposures and fades." *Beat God* seems to be McCoy's first cinematography credit (he had photographed fewer than 12 films in toto, if what we've found can be believed) and his only genre picture; to have met a studio's "usual standards" first time out must have been a feather in his cap. Even less is known about Harold Gilmore Calhoun — the author of the story and quite possibly the scenarist, as well — than is known about McCoy, but said author had only two film credits (this and the 1913, non–Charlie Chaplin short, *The Cure*) to his mellifluous name. (Attempts on our part to link this Calhoun to the more renowned Algonquin J. Calhoun have proven fruitless.) The 30 October 1915 *Motography* reveals that Harold had won second prize in the "Vitagraph-Sun Scenario Contest"; he might have won the damned thing had he used a bit more imagination with respect to his dramatis personae, half of whom have surnames ending in *–ford*. *Motography* does not reveal who came in first, and we shudder to think about all those entries that placed lower than *Beat God*.

We do know quite a bit about Maurice Costello, the titular beaten man, including the fact that this was his first feature-length performance to be released by V.L.S.E. (the short-lived Vitagraph-Lubin-Selig-Essanay distribution conglomerate). And that Costello was born in Pittsburgh in late February 1877 and is said to have made his film debut as Sherlock Holmes in a vintage 1905 J. Stuart Blackton/Vitagraph short devoted to some of the briefer adventures of the Great Consulting Detective. Still, books have been written about Costello and/or his daughters (Dolores and Helene; see: *While London Sleeps* for more on the latter), and — because of Dolores— the old darling has also received coverage and/or extended mention in most everything out there that deals with The Great Profile. Thus, let us confine ourselves to stating that Maurice appeared in over 250 silent films (80 percent of which were produced before the end of the 1910s), did the uncredited-bit routine when sound entered the scene (and supposedly was up there somewhere when Claude Rains did *Here Comes Mr. Jordan* and Boris Karloff achieved *The Climax*), and made no feature-length, silent, genre picture other than this. The actor, who had made his name in vaudeville before ever considering the flickers, also directed a slew of silent films, of which *The Man Who Couldn't Beat God* was the *last*.

Actually, Costello co-directed *Beat God* with Robert Gaillard, a Michigander with whom Maurice shared the megaphone on some three dozen Vitagraph films, and — like his frequent partner — he also acted in the lion's share of the films he also directed (as he did here). As an actor, though, he graced a good 12 dozen more, although apart from a few, succulently-entitled 1910s shorts, *The Man Who Couldn't Beat God* is Gaillard's only genre credit.

Buried deep in the cast list are Harry T. Morey — there's more on Morey (another Michigander) in our essay on *Womanhood, the Glory of the Nation* — Mary Maurice (a brief note in *The Battle Cry of Peace*), and Naomi Childers. Miss Childers' name was buried deep in the cast-list of Vitagraph's *The Dust of Egypt* (see entries), too.

The *NYDM* gushed over every aspect of the film, while *Variety* — which decided that the picture "just misses being great" — groused about the set-up for Costello's death scene: "He goes to his old home and in delirium, rises from his bed and goes to the scene of the crime, where he dies. It is all wrong to have a man in delirium rise from his bed, don his shoes and trousers and drop out a window. His death also makes an unsatisfactory finish." Apparently the real-life deliriously sinful (or is it the sinfully delirious?) abjure clothing and, using more traditional means of egress, wander off haphazardly to find themselves back at the scene of the crime, due to fortuitous circumstances. Or to God, who's lying in wait.   — *JTS*

The Marble Heart

The Marble Heart. Imp/Universal Film. Mfg. Co., 2 July 1915, 4 reels [LOST]

CAST: King Baggot (*Raphael/Phidias*); Ned Reardon (*The Viscount/Georgias*); Jane Fearnley (*Marco/Aphasia*); Frank Smith (*Volage/Diogenes*); Edna Hunter (*Marie, the Sculptor's Servant/ Thea*); Marie Wierman (Clementine/Lais); with Yona Landowska (*Dancer*)

CREDITS: *Director* George A. Lessey; *Scenario* George A. Lessey; based on the eponymous play by Charles Selby (New York, 1854)

Sit around a table with any genre fans who were born around the time George Romero *first* went to the zombie well, and the conceit of statues coming to life will immediately conjure up images of the Golem, in any of his sundry guises. Stone monsters such as this were the very stuff of myth and legend, and their inexorable plodding to destroy those who dared play God presaged Frankenstein and his kith. There is little out there that is as solid, real, or basic as stone, and visualizing it — anthropomorphized, animated, and angry, stomping menacingly toward one — is the stuff of nightmares. This sort of thing is an upper of major-league proportion for older genre fans, and the ensuing discussions, critiques, and opinions are usually worth following, even to the point of buying the next couple of rounds yourself.

On the other hand, tossing in the proviso that walking stonemen — or any such fantastic element — ought to be imprisoned within the dreaded four walls of "It's All a Dream" immediately introduces vulgarity into the conversation and pique into the mix. Dreams are not (usually) nightmares, and while one may legitimately seek inspiration from dreams (cf. Mr. Stevenson or Mrs. Wollstonecraft Shelley), one should at all costs avoid using them as solutions. Dreams have proven to be the fiction writer's hardiest deus ex machina — much more durable and stolid than the rockiest of Golems — and the reader/viewer's most dreaded surprise. Dreams are the unimaginative scribe's

mitzvah, the lazy writer's "Get out of Jail Free" card. Never raise the specter of this topic if you're hoping for a buy-back.

There were two feature films yclept *The Marble Heart* released within a year of each other in the mid–1910s, and considering how they managed *that* one would probably make for a more intriguing few minutes than our poking and prodding the viscera of the earlier (1915) release, even though it concerns statues coming to life. For there be dreams, as well. Maybe.

The following synopses are taken from two sources, neither of which agrees *in toto* with the other. The original, flavorful language and construction have been retained.

> [There is] a very clever comparison between the lives of the ancient Greeks and the people of [modern times]. Briefly, both stories demonstrate the triumph of money over love. In the first a sculptor carves a statue of a woman so perfect that it lives. The sculptor falls in love with his own creation, but the woman spurns his love and smiles favorably on a rich man. In the modern version the sculptor's heart is lost to a societywoman who poses for him, but she also prefers wealth to love without wealth, and so the broken-hearted artist marries the girl of his mother's choice [*Motion Picture News*, 3 July 1915].

> Raphael, a modern sculptor, dreams that in the days of Phidias, about five hundred years before Christ, he lived as Phidias, the sculptor [!], and was the friend of Diogenes and that he made some beautiful statues on commission for Georgias, the richest man in Asia. His female statues come to life and, disdaining his love, smile upon the wealthy man [The précis continues with the modern-day segment] [*The Moving Picture World*, 26 June 1915].

If one believes the *MPN* précis, the statue *de facto* comes to life, thumbs its perfect nose at the momma's-boy artist, and heads out the door for a life of Cosmos, shopping, and running around behind her husband's back. If one subscribes, rather, to the *MPW* version, any number of carved cuties (the copyright registration tract has the number at three) bail out on Raphael (Raphael? Come on…) for a sugar daddy, but he then awakens and realizes that the mousey little thing his mother has pre-selected is, in fact, the girl of his dreams. Well, she's not actually — *they* are — but she's the package he takes home after work.

Thus, we either have a genuine Pygmalion and Galatea rehash (with a wrinkle), or a trio of Galateas who opt for a pre–Common Era Hugh Hefner, albeit only in Raphael's tortured dreams. One may choose whichever one likes, with the understanding that either element is sufficient for the picture to be found in this book, if only in this section. (If one opts for neither, one may repair to that storied attic in Burkina Faso, wherein all lost films are stacked neatly, awaiting rediscovery, and there screen the 1913, two-reel Thanhouser version, starring none other than James Cruze.)

Per Sally A. Dumaux's biography of King Baggot, famed Russian danseuse Yona Landowska (aka Madam Landuska) cavorted choreographically in a couple of scenes laid in ancient Greece. Per coverage on the picture in the 23 December 1915 *Alton* [Illinois] *Evening Telegraph*, though, it was "famous Russian dancer, *Sandowska*" pirouetting her way into the marble hearts of the hoi polloi. As the *Telegraph*'s spelling-challenged reviewer also exhorted potential ticket-buyers to "See the greatest chariot race ever staged," we're at a loss as to understand what's going on or who's on first.

We tried laying hands on the Charles Selby play that inspired this cinematic epic, but with no luck; the drama, quite popular during the latter half of the 19th century, has exited, stage left. (Fama est that John Wilkes Booth added a feather to his thespic cap with multiple performances as the sculptor and that Honest Abe himself watched his future assassin vivify the statue[s] at Ford's Theater in 1863.) We looked for other trade-journal mentions of this King Baggot vehicle (he played both Raphael and Phidias), and came up empty there, too. What you see is what we found and, as Ethel Barrymore once famously said, "That's all there is. There isn't any more."   — JTS

The Market of Souls

The Market of Souls. Thomas H. Ince Productions/Famous Players–Lasky Corp.; Paramount-Artcraft Pictures, 7 September 1919, 6 reels/5852 feet, Gosfilmofond

CAST: Dorothy Dalton (*Helen Armes*); Holmes E. Herbert (*Temple Bane*); Philo McCullough (*Lyle Bane*); Dorcas Mathews (*Evelyn Howell*); Donald McDonald (*Herbert Howell*); George Williams (*Dr. Rodney Nevins*)

CREDITS: *Presented by* Thomas H. Ince; *Supervisor* Thomas H. Ince; *Director* Joseph De Grasse; *Scenario* C. Gardner Sullivan; *Story* John Lynch; *Cinematographer* John S. Stumar; *Film Editor* Duncan Mansfield; *Art Director* C. Tracy Hoag; *Art Titles* Irvin J. Martin

This is a weeper — a multi–Kleenex women's picture — that finds redemption (with us genre fans, that is) in the last reel, when one of those marketed souls finally shows up in all his glorious transparency (transparent glory?).

This summary is taken from the 13 September 1919 *Harrison's Reports*:

> A young man slanders a girl to his elder brother, who, though he has lost faith in women, loves this girl. In defending her name, the elder brother is struck by the younger brother with a candlestick and blinded. The blind man's doctor induces the heroine to assume a new name and nurse him. The younger brother, made to feel remorse by the girl, goes to France to fight. The blind man recovers his eyesight, but when he learns the identity of the girl who nursed him, he scorns her. Broken-hearted, she decides to go away. In leaving the house, she meets the butler who points to the name of the young brother in the list of those killed. She is asked to break the news to the elder brother.
>
> When she enters the room, the man comes to her asking forgiveness. He tells her that his brother has come black to clear her name, and that he is now sitting in the chair. The heroine is unable to see anyone in the chair, so she tells him it is only his spirit come to vindicate her. As they speak, the spirit is seen gradually disappearing. Complete reconciliation now takes place between them.

Okay, even allowing for the chuckle to be had as we read of the blinded brother being nursed, we must ask ourselves: Why would the woman for whom the blinded man fought his brother *change her name* in order to care for him? What physician with any common sense and concern for the welfare of his patient would advise lying as part of home care? Dr. Phil? And where does love come in when the pinheaded heroine agrees to deceive the blind guy? A plot like this one requires reviewing by Ann Landers, not Harrison or Wid Gunning. The summary below — taken from *The AFI Catalog* — puts names to those characters and a bit more detail to an otherwise preposterous narrative:

> Helen Armes, a trained nurse from the country, spends New Year's Eve with her cousin Evelyn Howell and her husband. They

go with Lyle Bane, Mrs. Howell's lover, to a Broadway cabaret where Lyle's brother Temple, a quiet man who has lost his faith in women, sees Lyle's attraction to Helen. When Lyle tries to kiss Helen, the jealous Mrs. Howell, seeing this, orders Helen to leave. After Lyle lies to Temple, saying that Helen forced the embrace, their quarrel ends with Temple blinded by a blow on the head from a candelabrum. Under an assumed name, Helen nurses Temple and later persuades Lyle, planning to rob Temple, to join the army. When Temple regains his vision, he curses Helen. Upon learning of Lyle's death at the front, Helen breaks the news to Temple who apologizes and reveals that Lyle's spirit came to him and confessed his lie. Temple and Helen marry.

In this précis, we can't surmise that Temple (the older brother) felt anything at all for Helen before Lyle gave him what-for, so his being upset with the young woman who lied so that she could … *ummmm* … keep an eye on him while he couldn't keep an eye on anything makes a bit more sense. The only fly in this latter ointment is that the summary reads as if Lyle's spirit had visited Temple before the Great Apology scene, and not during it. Yet *Harrison's* is quite plain in its description of the visual effect, so…

Anyhow, just like the characters' credibility, the film is lost. We are left, then, to suppose that the only genre tie in the whole bloody thing is the spirit of the younger brother in the Barcalounger. Double exposure, followed by a slow fade. Now, none of the reviewers of this picture opted for a logical explanation: that there *was* no spirit in the chair — after all, the heroine didn't spot one and we've seen that she's quite easily led — and that it was a guilty conscience, plus the residual effect of getting clocked with the candlestick, that had the elder brother seeing double exposure. Since the folks who were paid to think these things out settled for a real-life (*Ooooops*) spirit, so have we, and that's about all we can say at this point.

Harrison's reported that "*The Market of Souls* is unquestionably the most dramatic picture ever released with Dorothy Dalton," and we're not sure how to take that. Miss Dalton played the much put-upon girl in the above synopsis and is profiled at decent length in our essay on *The Dark Mirror*. Holmes Herbert was the fickle and visually-challenged elder brother, while Philo McCullough (see *The Charlatan*) was the younger brother whose transparent form *may* only have been in the chair in his sibling's mind. The idiot doctor was impersonated by George Williams, a character man with about three dozen silent movie credits, including an "uncredit" for a bit (as M. Ricard) in 1925's *The Phantom of the Opera*.

— JTS

The Miracle of Life

The Miracle of Life. American Film Company/Mutual Film Corporation, A Mutual Masterpiece, 21 October 1915, 4 reels [LOST]

CAST: Margarita Fischer (*Eleanor Seawell/Woman*); Joseph E. Singleton (*Danforth Seawell/Man*); Lucile Ward (*Mrs. Gerald Fels-Martine*)

CREDITS: *Director* Harry A. Pollard; *Cinematographer* John A. Brown

We have to wonder if this early, Bizarro-world version of *It's a Wonderful Life* did for director Harry A. Pollard even a fraction of what the 1946 classic did for Frank Capra. The Kansas-born filmmaker (another of those writer/producer/director/actor types) was only a couple of years into his two-decade-long career in 1915, yet he had already multi-tasked his way through well over a hundred short subjects. It's unclear whether Pollard was responsible for the story here, as was Capra — at least in part — for his "What if?" epic some 30 years later. Existing documentation is given over to regurgitating the press-book synopsis, and the only other definite credit we have is that of cameraman John W. Brown.

Our choice of the regurgitated press-book synopsis is taken from the 30 October 1915 *Motography*:

> A man and a woman who have long been sweethearts are married. The man brings his bride home and they are very happy in each other's love. One night while in attendance at a ball the wife feels a sudden revulsion against her husband. He cannot understand her actions, but she knows the revulsion means — the coming of a child.
>
> The young wife is horror-stricken at the thoughts of becoming a mother and at last goes to the home of an elderly woman friend and asks her aid. From the friend she obtains a deadly potion which will extinguish the young life about to be brought into the world.
>
> The wife returns home, slips past her husband into the boudoir and places the bottle on her dresser and lies down on the bed sobbing with grief. She falls asleep and then gets up places the bottle to her lips and lies down to await its results. She swoons away and when the doctor is called in he tells the young husband the true state of affairs.
>
> Later the husband gets a divorce form his wife, marries another woman and establishes a very happy home. The young divorcee for a short time is happy spending her time at dancing, clubs, and gay, after-theater parties. Then comes old age andloneliness. One night the old woman is sitting before her grate fire when there appears a little child who says she is the child that might have been.
>
> The little one takes the old lady by the hand and leads her through the world. Everywhere in the kingdoms of animals and plants she is shown happiness which attends the rearing of young an then she is taken through "Babyland." Later comes a vision of death and the old woman sees herself refused entrance at the gates of Heaven and ordered to the region of everlasting punishment.
>
> Then comes the awakening and once more she is the bride of a few months and she is clasping in her hands the bottle which contains the deadly potion. With a cry she rushes to an open window, pours out the contents of the bottle and then calls her husband and tells him the secret. We last see the couple admiring a precious baby which is cooing in the cradle.

(A longer version of the press-book blather — published in the 16 October 1915 *Moving Picture World* — mentions "a stairway to heaven, up which angels are leading mothers and children." It also reveals how the "hateful contents" of that defenestrated deadly potion "fall into a bed of flowers, withering and killing the plants it touches." Nice.)

Clearly an anti-abortion rant done up in a mélange of spirituality, sentimentality ("Babyland"?) and stupidity ("the scene of Cupid at his telephone switchboard" — *Motography*), *The Miracle of Life* the does contain elements that are near and dear to our hearts (like that "region of everlasting punishment") and thus we pause, respectfully. (There is no indication in any of our documents that there are *fallen* angels, hanging about the Gates to Perdition, but hope springs eternal, *n'est-ce pas?*) And despite its concentrated Christian iconography (the review also dwells on a scene "showing the Three Wise Men going to see the Christ Child"), the picture is not so much another instance of faith healing (see *The Miracle Man*) as a decoupage of Goodness and Light (and Eros, sitting by the phone) meant to underscore the relationship between the natural and the supernatural.

The picture was well received by most contemporary commentators, albeit — in all honesty — what else might we expect from a motion picture designed to edify *and* make money in the c. 1915 American milieu? Can any educated person realistically maintain that a mid–1910s *pro*-abortion movie would have lasted longer than the time it took to burn down the theater showing it? John C. Garrett — the *Motography* scribe — went to such lengths to laud the film that he foreswore grammar and comprehension to do so: "With a story which if not handled properly and carefully all of the beauty and appeal would be lost in it, to work upon, Harry Pollard directed the four-reel American Mutual Master-Picture *The Miracle of Life* and obtained exceedingly satisfactory results."

Louis Reeves Harrison, paid to see the film by the folks at *The Moving Picture World*, likewise came across strong (in the 9 October 1915 issue): "A triumph of motion picture art is every story like *The Miracle of Life* when its strong theme is impressed by methods peculiar to story visualization on the screen.... This delicate subject is delicately and beautifully handled through an actual story and through some exquisite symbolism."

And so it goes.

It's not jut a tad ironic that the review published in the "Bible of Show Business" was the least impressed with the angelic hoo-hah that surrounded the film. "Fred" admitted that the picture's subtitle — "The Divinity of Motherhood" — would draw in the fair sex like moths to the flame, but otherwise wasted few words: "It is pleasant enough but that is about all." As was the custom with trade reviews during the mid–1910s, the 8 October 1915 *Variety* piece concentrated in the main on repeating the plot synopsis, with critical observations scant and not always to the point: "The woman who played the role of the family friend was far from being an ideal picture actress. There is one thing certain, that she was carrying weight for age, and in one of the scenes in which she appeared in a dressing gown it was remarked that the gown would readily serve as a circus tent, so great was its proportions." Not much help in that one, is there?

Other than its being dropped *en passant* into the *Motography* introduction, no one so much as whispered Harry Pollard's name, but the *MPW*'s Mr. Reeves Harrison did spare a moment from his fawning over the sanctity of birth to note: "Even the scientific work deserves special mention. Minute attention to details of lighting is brought out by fine work in the laboratory, and the tinting leaves no jarring note on the long series of spiritual double exposures."

By "scientific work" Harrison was referring not to the deadly potions that destroy plants and fetuses without physically discommoding the adult females who quaff them, but, rather, to the cinematography. It took the 1 July 1916 *New York Dramatic Mirror* to identify the photographer as John W. Brown, a Scot from Aberdeen who would leave the industry before the end of the Silent Era, and who would become better known as "Jack"

Brown and more widely associated with Oaters (rather than with "symbolic features") before that would come to pass. It is doubtful that Mr. Brown worked his lighting/double exposure magic without *some* input from director, Harry A. Pollard, but what you've read is what there is. *Sic semper gloria mundi...* For what it's worth, Mr. Brown (as "John") photographed *The Magic Eye*, another item to be found in our Appendix.

The young wife was enacted by Margarita Fischer, wife to Harry A. Pollard. Miss Fischer received little press this time around (*Variety*: "Miss Fischer is charming in a role that does not deserve much sympathy"), but the critical regard she won for the170+ other cinematic roles she would play in the course of the next dozen years doubtless proved to be adequate compensation. Aussie Joseph Singleton made about a hundred fewer pictures than did his Iowa-born co-star, and neither he nor she did anything that remotely resembled a genre feature other than *The Miracle of Life*.

No film, no stills (other than a poorly conserved rendition of an angel standing above a cradle in the Library of Congress's *Motography* microfiche), no question-posing- or -answering screeds; only the bare-bones proof of the existence of this picture that dragged creatures usually more comfortable Beyond the Veil (and Cupid?) into the unconscious mind of a woman who would not be a mom. *The Miracle of Life*— sans the sundry double-exposures and angelic/demonic hallucinations— was remade in 1926, when it starred Nita Naldi and Mae Busch, two actresses internationally renowned for their portrayal of loving mothers.

What *does* exist is a similar film made a little less than a year later by the Universal Film Manufacturing Company. A five-reeler, *Where Are My Children?* was written and directed by Lois Weber, the Pennsylvania-born, female multi-tasker (producer/director/actor/scribe) usually credited with being the first woman to helm a feature-length motion picture (1914's *The Merchant of Venice*). Weber worked her magic in well over a hundred shorts and features from 1911 or so (including 1911's *Sherlock Holmes, Jr.*, 1913's *The Picture of Dorian Gray*, and 1918's feature-length *Tarzan of the Apes*) through the end of the Silent Era, and 1934's *White Heat* marked her Sound Era alpha and omega. (Despite all else, Weber's place in genre history is assured by her having written and directed 1916's *The Dumb Girl of Portici*, claimed always and everywhere as his film debut by Boris Karloff. She also helmed *Even as You and I*, and a more extensive look at her credentials may be found there.) Weber crafted the screenplay for *Children* from an original story by Lucy Payton and Franklyn Hall, and co-directed the "Universal Special Feature" with her then-husband, Phillips Smalley.

Our plot rundown is taken from *The AFI Catalog*:

> The souls of unborn children behind the "Portals of Eternity" are of three groups: the army of "Chance Children," the morally or physically defected "Unwanted Souls," and the fine, strong souls that only are sent forth on prayer. District attorney Richard Walton, a believer in eugenics, grieves because his wife is childless and takes pride in the child of his sister, who contracted a eugenics marriage. When a doctor is convicted for sending a book through the mail that advocates birth control, Walton supports him. After Walton's wife, a social butterfly, takes her friend Mrs. Brandt to Dr. Malfit for an abortion, Mrs. Brandt is again able to attend house parties. Lillian, the Waltons' housekeeper's daughter, is seduced by Mrs. Walton's visiting brother. She dies during an abortion performed by Malfit, and Walton prosecutes. Sentenced to fifteen years, Malfit throws his account book at Walton, who then discovers the many times his wife and her friends have had abortions. Walton calls his wife a murderess and imagines their home with children. Mrs. Walton, now repentant, tries to bring about conception, but learns that she can never bear children.

Although we include this title solely for the vista of the supernatural milieu, we admit sitting open-mouthed at the picture's admission that a) behind those "Portals of Eternity" there's some serious segregation of unborn children going on; we demand a full and immediate investigation. Stupifying, too, is b) our hero's belief in eugenics—"a science that deals with the improvement (as by control of human mating) of hereditary qualities of a race or breed," per Merriam-Webster — and we ask that the readership not fully familiar with the ramifications of this noble scientific pursuit Google same in conjunction with "National Socialist German Workers' Party."

— JTS/HN

My Friend, the Devil

My Friend, the Devil. Fox Film Corp./Fox, 19 November 1922, 8 reels/9,555 feet, LOST

CAST: Charles Richman (*George Dryden*); Ben "Bunny" Grauer (*George Dryden as a boy*); William Tooker (*Dr. Brewster*); Adolph Milar (*Dryden's Stepfather*); John Tavernier (*The Old Doctor*); Myrtle Stewart (*Dryden's Mother*); Barbara Castleton (*Anna Ryder*); Alice May (*Mrs. Ryder*); Peggy Shaw (*Beatrice Dryden*); Robert Frazer (*The Artist*); Mabel Wright (*The Governess*)

CREDITS: *Presented by* William Fox; *Director* Henry Millarde; *Scenario* Paul H. Sloane; based on the novel, *Le Docteur Rameau*, by Georges Ohnet (Paris, ca. 1889); *Cinematographer* Joseph Ruttenberg

Calling upon God to strike his brutal stepfather dead because of his treatment of his mother, little Georgie Dryden sees his mother killed by lightning instead. He renounces faith in God and becomes an atheist. The lad later becomes a prominent surgeon, who believes only in science. He marries. His wife becomes involved in an affair with an artist whom he has aided. The event is kept quiet by Dr. Brewster, a friend.

Fifteen years later, Dr. Dryden finds the truth in his dead wife's diary. In a frenzy, he turns his daughter away. The girl becomes seriously ill. The famous doctor exhausts his knowledge in trying to save her. Unsuccessful, he calls upon the Almighty. The girl becomes well. So he acknowledges God.

We opted to use the telegraphic-language précis of the scenario from *Wid's*, rather than the slightly more fluid prose recorded in the copyright registration synopsis, as the former description — for all its grammatical shortcomings — contains more detail than does the latter. Little Georgie asks for divine intervention, gets it — albeit partnered by one of the great *Whoooops!* moments in the silent cinema — and then becomes piqued.

Asking for supernatural aid and then having to deal with the cosmic screwing that inevitably accompanies it serves as the basis for most of the "Deal with the Devil" literature that has ever seen print, and elsewhere in this volume (*The Devil*, 1915) we offer a brief rundown on this. As for the film at hand, though, we've no idea where/when the Devil enters into the picture, nor whether he ever does (in any form whatsoever) in order to get the traditional machinery going. Our suspicion is that he never does; that his presence is meant to be suggested to average, not-fanatically-religious, movie-going types solely because of the absence of allegiance-to-the-Deity on the part of the principal cast member; and that the title is yet another cheat foisted upon audiences eager for excitement and exploitation. As the film is lost, we might well be very wrong, but the extant critical screeds do nothing to disprove our theory.

Georges Ohnet's source novel, *Doctor Rameau*, has no personal devil, but neither does it have a little Georgie Dryden, an abusive stepfather, or an inept, thunderbolt-hurling Jehovah. Little Pierre Rameau lived with his semi-peasant parents until he was one day whisked away to university to turn upside down conventional medical knowledge, humble his professors, and save whichever lives and limbs appealed to him at the moment. Even without heaven-sent pyrotechnics, he did not believe in any sort of god. He *did* marry, though, and his wife *did* have a wandering eye, and their daughter *did* catch some sort of all-purpose, deadly disease a few pages before the endpapers, and he *did* have a just-in-time epiphany/conversion away from the Dark Side that resulted in roses back in his baby's cheeks, a bridal bouquet in her hands, and the words, "My God! My God!" on his lips. Zzzzzzzzzzzzzzzzzzzzzzzzzzzzz.

Just for the record, the artist who lead wifey astray (don't they all, in pictures like this?) was played by Robert Frazer, who would get *his* most famously when trying to lead Madge Bellamy astray in the Halperin brothers' *White Zombie* (1932). Also, Ben Grauer (billed here as "Bunny")—who would later win fame and a following for his radio and TV work with Arturo Toscanini (and for the 1956–1957 radio mystery program *Sleep No More*)—had also played the protagonist as a lad in the 1921 *Annabel Lee*.

We have to be completely honest. This picture wouldn't even make it into the appendix here if it weren't for two, disparate circumstances. (1) The still unclear status of the Devil in the picture's title. As a quick once over of this volume's table of contents will show, there was no dearth of pictures that suckered in audiences by at least hinting of diabolical goings-on up there on the screen. The review published in the 28 October 1922 *Moving Picture World* praises the cinematography "*with the possible exception of the prologue*" and said prologue *may* have featured Evil Incarnate. Or it may have *not*, which means the title was just another instance of "truthiness" in advertising. (2) As the picture ends with the existence of a loving, merciful God apparently proven beyond all doubt, that errant lightning bolt that killed off old lady Dryden *must have been diabolic in origin*, no? If not, we're forced to ask: Can that undeniably accommodating God still be considered omnipotent if, from time to time, His aim is off?   — *JTS*

The Mysterious Dr. Fu Manchu

The Mysterious Doctor Fu Manchu. Paramount Famous Lasky Corp./ Paramount, 10 August 1929, Sound (Movietone) 8–9 reels/7663 feet and Silent 7695 feet [available]

CAST: Warner Oland (*Fu Manchu*); Jean Arthur (*Lia Eltham*); Neil Hamilton (*Dr. Jack Petrie*); O.P. Heggie (*Nayland Smith*); William Austin (*Sylvester Wadsworth*); Claude King (*Sir John Petrie*); Charles Stevenson (*General Petrie*); Noble Johnson (*Li Po*); Evelyn Selbie (*Fai Lu*); Charles Giblyn (*Weymouth*); Donald MacKenzie (*Trent*); Lawford Davidson (*Clarkson*); Laska Winter (*Fu Mela*); Charles Stevens (*Singh*); Chappell Dossett (*Reverend Mr. Eltham*); Tully Marshall (*Ambassador*)
CREDITS: *Director* Rowland V. Lee; *Screenplay-Dialogue* Florence Ryerson; Lloyd Corrigan; based on the novel, *The Insidious Dr. Fu Manchu*, by Sax Rohmer (Arthur Sarsfield Ward; London, 1913); *Comedy Dialogue* George Marion, Jr.: *Cinematographer* Harry Fischbeck; *Editor, Sound Version* George Nichols, Jr.; *Editor, Silent Version* Bronson Howard; *Recording Engineer* Eugene Merritt

Given his popularity in print, it is somewhat baffling that Sax Rohmer's super-villain, Dr. Fu Manchu, has had rather a spotty history in films. The first attempt (1923–1924) consisted of two series of inter-locking shorts from Britain's Stoll studios that starred Harry Agar Lyons as the arch-fiend. These two-reel productions did not feature cliff-hangers, so they can't properly be called serials, but each of the two series told a continuous story roughly approximating Rohmer's first two books, *The Mysterious Dr Fu Manchu* (*The Insidious Dr. Fu Manchu* in the USA) and *The Return of Dr. Fu Manchu*. The latter, appropriately enough, had first seen print serialized in *Colliers Magazine* before being collected between hard covers. The property then lay dormant for a half-decade until Paramount Pictures decided to tackle same with Oriental impersonator extraordinaire, Warner Oland, in the title role. Why, during the Silent Era, it had not occurred to anyone to cast Sojin—a specialist in villainous and red-herring roles, his looks alone made him a perfect candidate for the devil-doctor—is a question that lacks an answer.

Hot on the heels of the Oland films, M-G-M released the most sumptuous Fu film adaptation to date, thanks to the company's production deal with William Randolph Hearst's Cosmopolitan Productions. Hearst's *Cosmopolitan Magazine* (a very different publication at the time from what it would become under the stewardship of Helen Gurley Brown) was serializing *The Mask of Fu Manchu*, and Hearst snapped up the film rights as well. 1932's *The Mask of Fu Manchu* starred Boris Karloff and probably remains the best-known film adaptation. Almost a decade then passed before Republic Pictures turned *The Drums of Fu Manchu* (1940) into one of their best serials, although the plot owes nothing to Rohmer's novel of the same name; in fact, it seems more a remake of M-G-M's film, which—in turn—had strayed substantially from its source material. Republic planned a sequel, but didn't follow through, and the doctor lay dormant cinematically until British producer Harry Alan Towers launched his five-film series with Christopher Lee. As for the "comedic" 1980 version with Peter Sellers, perhaps the less said, the better. Along the way the character's popularity was such that Fu was featured in a daily comic strip, at least one ongoing radio program, and a television series.

The Paramount films may not have boasted quite as much obvious production gloss as the better-known M-G-M picture (whose torture devices are so loaded with gleaming chrome one half expects the cast to break out in a Busby Berkeley–esque musical number on them at any moment), but onscreen application of money is evident in the opening scenes of the 1900 Boxer Rebellion in *The Mysterious Dr. Fu Manchu* and in some of the sets in both pictures. As in Rohmer, Paramount's Fu has the origins of his transgressions in the Boxer conflict, but here he starts out as a friend of the white man and a benefactor to mankind; when his house is shelled — killing his wife and infant son — Fu swears vengeance on those responsible. (How he determines just which particular soldiers are to be the focus of his wrath, though, is not addressed.) He determines to use a young white baby girl — over whom he has established hypnotic control — as a tool in his plans when she grows up (and when she does, she is played by a very young Jean Arthur).

Those wondering where all those plans for world domination went might recall that, in Rohmer's first novels, Fu was less evil genius and more crime boss — an Oriental Moriarty to Sir Denis Nayland Smith's Sherlock Holmes and Dr. Petrie's John Watson. It is only with the third novel (*The Si-Fan Mysteries* in the U.K. and *The Hand of Fu Manchu* in the USA) that Rohmer reveals the doctor to be working within an organization that has far grander plans that managing a string of opium dens and other such criminal activities; even so, the movie ventures far from the eponymous novel wherein Fu is a shadowy figure who puts in a proper appearance only in the closing chapters. And whereas the novel is notable for a collection of ingenious methods of delivering death to those who stand in Fu's way, the film's most diabolical touch is a canister of poison gas hurled through a window. The first departure may be seen as Rohmer's having started to give the doctor a more prominent role in the books, as it is bad showmanship to build a film around a character who

barely features in the action. As to the second, who knows? Still, the Zayat Kiss and other diabolical methods of homicide are AWOL.

One interesting touch is having Fu re-gild a dragon tapestry that had been stained with the blood of his wife and child; with each murder he retouches another of the dragon's scales. This may be the first appearance of a device that director Rowland V. Lee would utilize time and again in such films as 1939's *Tower of London* (wherein Basil Rathbone as Richard III removes a doll representing each of his victims from a diorama of the royal family and tosses it in his fireplace) and the 1945's *Captain Kidd*, where — more prosaically — Charles Laughton simply crosses names off a list as he eliminates his enemies.

Paramount released its first Fu Manchu film in both silent and talkie versions, the silent print most likely being nothing other than the talkie — sans soundtrack — but with additional title cards. Indeed, the extant sound version has several title cards at the beginning, during the sequence that depicts the fighting of the Boxer Rebellion. Some sources contend that Paramount's first two Fu Manchu films were shot back-to-back. Inasmuch as they almost function as a two-part film — in the manner of such European productions as Fritz Lang's *Dr. Mabuse* (1922) — it is possible that the second was also planned to be released in the same manner, but sound took a firm enough hold on audiences so quickly that such a measure was apparently deemed unnecessary.

Rowland Lee (1891–1975) started in films as an actor for Thomas Ince, and — after the First World War — he began directing for Ince's company. Lee's work remains somewhat uneven, but horror and adventure thrillers (such as those noted above) seemed to bring out the best in him, although some might argue that it his more romantic, Frank Borzage–like films (such as 1933's *Zoo in Budapest*) reflect the man at his apex. Warner Oland (né Werner Ohlund, 1880–1938) will always be known as the definitive film Charlie Chan, but he played nearly every known nationality (except for his native Swedish) during his career. He would repeat the role of Fu in a comedy sketch in the 1930 *Paramount on Parade* and in the first reel of 1931's *Daughter of the Dragon*. Genre fans take especial pleasure in his role as Henry Hull's antagonist in *Werewolf of London* (1935). Jean Arthur (née Gladys Georgianna Greene) made her screen debut in 1923, but was cast in a series of standard ingénue roles in indifferent films until 1935, when she was first allowed to show her ability with comedy. Arthur is known more for these unpretentious but often screwball heroines (in Frank Capra films as often as not) than for such offbeat fare as Fu Manchu's adopted daughter.

— *HHL*

THE MYSTERIOUS DR. FU MANCHU

A Rowland V. Lee Production ~ A PARAMOUNT PICTURE ~

Charlie Chan keeps Jean Arthur (who later played Peter Pan) at arm's length from Neil Hamilton (who later played Commissioner Gordon on television's *Batman*).

The Mystery of the Yellow Room

The Mystery of the Yellow Room. Mayflower Photoplay Corp.; Emile Chautard Pictures Corp./Realart Pictures Corp., 19 October 1919 — 6 reels, elements at Cinematheque Française

CAST: William S. Walcott (*Professor Stangerson*); Edmund Elton (*Robert Darzac*); George Cowl (*Frederic Larsan*); Ethel Grey Terry (*Mathilde Stangerson*); Lorin Raker (*Rouletabille [Joe-Jo]*); Jean Gauthier (*Jean Sinclair*); W.H. Burton (*Daddy Jacques*); Henry S. Koser (*Bernier*); Jean Ewing (*Mme. Bernier*); William Morrison (*Judge de Marquet*); Louis Grisel (*Monsieur Maleine*); John McQuire (*Mathieu*); Catherine Ashley (*Mme. Mathieu*); Ivan Doubble (*The Green Man*)

CREDITS: *Producer/Director* Emile Chautard; *Scenario* Emile Chautard; based on the novel, *Le Mystère de la chambre jaune*, by Gaston Leroux (Paris, 1908); *Cinematographer* Jacques Bizeul; *Musical Accompaniment Score* Dr. Hugo Reisenfeld

For many (fairly venerable) fans of Universal's classic horror films of the 1930s and 1940s, the company name "Realart Pictures" connotes the Jack Broder/Joseph Harris rerelease/distribution outfit to which William Goetz sold every Universal feature film that hadn't met the lofty standards of his newly-formed Universal-International. Realart bought the rights to promote, distribute, edit, retitle, and/or kill off (Sorry, Sir Arthur) the lion's share of the Universal canon that had almost overnight become embarrassing to the newly settled U-I moguls. (Nonetheless, TV rights weren't included in the deal, so the Shock Theater program-oriented concept won *that* bid on the horror/mystery titles a couple of years later.) *The Mystery of the Yellow Room* was not one of those edited and/or retitled Lugosi, Karloff, or Chaney Jr. thrillers, though; rather, it was the very first picture shopped and shown by Realart Pictures Corporation, the *original* 1919 company, way back when, the first time around.

The then-fledgling organization inked the deal with the Mayflower Photoplay Corporation (see *Unseen Forces, The Miracle Man, Whispering Shadows/The Invisible Foe*), which collaborated with the Emile Chautard Pictures Corporation (back you go to *Whispering Shadows/The Invisible Foe*) to bring Gaston Leroux's popular old, dark house thriller to the screen. Leroux had penned *Le Mystère de la chambre jaune* in 1908 (the same year *Le Fantôme de l'Opera* was published) and the novel — an escape-from-a-locked-room deal — caught on with American readers much faster than did the tale of Erik, Christine, and all that accursed ugliness. In fact, the yellow room's mysteries were presented to the ticket-buying public *thrice* — deux fois dans la France* and the picture presently under discussion, all courtesy of M. Chautard — before Uncle Carl Laemmle, Rupert Julian and Lon Chaney thrust Leroux's baffling chamber-thriller into the Opera Ghost's shadow.

In its 24 October 1919 edition, *Variety* laid out the nuts and bolts of the tale thus:

> Mlle. Stangerson has worked with her father up to midnight in the laboratory. She rose, kissed him good-night, went to her room, and locked the door. Her father continued working for some time, when he heard her scream frantically for help. When the door was finally broken down the young lady, in her night-

dress, was lying on the floor in the midst of great disorder. She was covered with blood and had fingermarks on her throat. Nobody could be found under the bed or elsewhere. The rescuers discovered bloodstained marks of a man's hand on the walls and on the door, a handkerchief red with blood, an old cap, footmarks of a man on the floor. There was no chimney in the room, he could not have escaped via the door as the rescuers entered that way, while the window was secured from the inside.

Put that way, the film's plot certainly hinted at supernatural involvement, *n'est-ce pas? The New York Dramatic Mirror* (26 October 1919) introduced several more dramatis personae into its recap; again, without spilling any beans:

> *The Mystery of the Yellow Room* involves an incomprehensible attempt to murder Mathilde Stangerson, daughter of Professor Stangerson, a scientist, in her apartment, known as the yellow room, adjoining the laboratory where the two worked. The mystery is found in the fact that since it is certain the assassin could not escape from the room except through the door which is bolted inside and has to be broken in by Professor Stangerson, he has apparently disappeared into thin air. Frederic Larsan, a celebrated detective, is put on the case and a cub reporter known as Joe-Jo determines to ferret out the mystery too. Larsan suspects and accuses Robert Darzac, Mlle. Stangerson's fiancé, and the action of the story also directs suspicion to him. Joe-Jo believes him innocent, however, and after spending two nights in the chateau only to have the criminal elude him and kill another suspect, the reporter suddenly announces that he is going to America to get evidence in the case. He returns during the trial of Darzac.

Devoid of all the persiflage about bloodstained handkerchiefs and bloodied marks on the walls and door, the summary now appears to intimate a science-fiction angle: an invisible man, perhaps? It was left to the 1 November 1919 *Exhibitor's Trade Review* to blow the whistle:

> When Mathilde Stangerson is strangely attacked and certain documents taken from her father's safe, the master detective, Frederick [*sic*] Larsan, is called in to solve the crime. The assault takes place on the eve of the announcement of her engagement to Robert Darzac. And no one seems to be able to solve the mystery. The star reporter of "The Globe," Rouletabille, however, is persistent, and he follows down every clue. But even he is completely baffled, for this mystery is followed by another which concerns a murder. The gamekeeper, known as the Green Man, is the victim. Suspicion points so strongly at Darzac that he is arrested and placed on trial. But he remains silent. When events loom up black for him, the reporter bursts into the courtroom with the mysteries solved. He refuses to give the name of the guilty man until the latter has had time to escape. After four hours, he tells the Court that Larsan, the detective, is the criminal. And as he unfolds his evidence the two mysteries are enacted by the characters.

Joe-Jo, then, is Rouletabille; the gamekeeper is the Green Man; the Yellow Room is still pretty much the Yellow Room; but the detective is the murderer (and attempted murderer!), and the reporter feels sufficiently justified to let the bugger off — the court going along with this — and not a single published critical commentary on this picture will tell us why!

Tiptoeing through a translation of Leroux's novel, we can offer the following explication. *Spoiler alert!* (And we're not kid-

---

Rouletabille (Part 1): *Le Mystère de la chamber jaune*—Éclair, 1913; Chautard and Maurice Tourneur. This marked Tourneur's first effort as a full-fledged director. *Rouletabille* (Part 2): *La Derniere incarnation de Larsan*—Éclair, 1914; Chautard. According to Harry Waldman's *Maurice Tourneur: The Life and Films*, Tourneur told Marie Epstein that he, and not Chautard, actually directed Part 2 of *Rouletabille* (pp. 13–14).

ding; they keep remaking this old plum, the last time being a French-Belgian effort released in 2003.)

What had really occurred is that Mathilde had once been married to Larsan in America. Larsan is really Ballmeyer, an infamous criminal. Larsan tried to use his position and true knowledge of the crime to implicate Darzac. This subterfuge only helps to increase the mystery. However, Rouletabille is not convinced. Unraveling what truly happened, he journeys to America and brings back a key witness (Arthur Rance) just as the trial starts. Rance tells of the marriage and further reveals that the couple had a son. Rouletabille makes the case in court that Larsan/Ballmeyer had broken into the room to get Mathilde back. In fact, he had broken in and struck Mathilde well before the actual ruckus was overheard by the group and had already escaped. Mathilde had been hiding everything to avoid scandal. She feigned the later "attack" that everyone witnessed to hide things as best she could … even by firing a pistol shot when nobody was there. Darzac, ever loyal to her even while facing blame for the crime, knew and kept Mathilde's secret.

Anyone still possessed of the slightest interest as to who did what to whom (1) will definitely have noted that there's no Arthur Rance in the cast list; (2) will most likely have recognized that the stolen papers were nothing but a MacGuffin; and (3) will probably have suspected that Rouletabille is Mathilde and Larsan's son and *that's* why he held the court enthralled with card tricks and impressions for four hours. Distressingly, despite our best shot, there still are unresolved bits, but we maintain that old Gaston himself would be hard-pressed to talk his way through that next-to-last-chapter he penned and then left for posterity.

And the Green Man? Damned if we know…

Keeping the audience's ear amused while the audience's eye was being amazed by Rouletabille or Joe-Jo or whomever was the task of Dr. Hugo Reisenfeld (aka Riesenfeld), a classically-trained Viennese violinist and composer who moved to the States in 1907 and hung his hat at Oscar Hammerstein's Manhattan Opera Company for several years thereafter. Commissioned by Raoul Walsh to flesh out Georges Bizet's score for the director's 1915 Theda Bara vehicle, *Carmen*, Reisenfeld soon became one of the most prominent Go-To musical men in 1920s Hollywood. No one may have stopped the presses to thank him for his work under *The Mystery of the Yellow Room*, but among the more prominent genre features that unreeled over his compositions were *The Sorrows of Satan* (1926), *The Cat and the Canary* (1927), and *The Bat Whispers* (1930). Reisenfeld died in Hollywood in mid–September 1939, but much of his work — immortalized among the more popular stock-music themes — has been heard time and again ever since.

Few of the first-cast names in *Yellow Room* will ring bells for us genre folk. Edmund Elton had a featured role in 1916's near-miss *In the Diplomatic Service*; George Cowl popped up in 1923's near-miss *Fashionable Fakers*; Ethel Grey Terry was seen in *The Unknown Purple* (see essay on this latter title) that same year; and Lorin Raker (Rouletabille/Joe-Jo) never made another silent film. Producer/Director/Screenwriter Emile Chautard's name ought to sound a tone or two, though, and a fuller melody-line on the Avignon-born filmmaker may be found in our coverage of *The Haunted House*.   — *SJ/HN/JTS*

The Mystic Hour

The Mystic Hour. Apollo Pictures, Inc./Arts Dramas, Inc., 17 May 1917, 5 reels [LOST]

CAST: Alma Hanlon (*Margaret Buchanan*); Charles Hutchinson (*Guido Ferrari*); John Sainpolis (*Holbrook Clavering*); Florence Short (*Rene*); Helen Strickland (*Mrs. Corland Buchanan*)

CREDITS: *Producer* Harry Raver; *Director* Richard Ridgely; *Scenario* Frederick Rath; based on a story by Agnes Fletcher Bain; *Cinematographer* George W. Lane

If we take the extant body of criticism at face value, this is a picture that belongs on Ko-Ko's list of things that never would be missed. Damnation à la faint praise had seldom been laid on as thick as it was by the run of 1910s critics who had to deal with this particular picture, yet who nonetheless endeavored to come up with counterbalancing blarney in an effort to maintain studio goodwill. The 2 June 1917 *Exhibitor's Trade Review*, for instance, tap danced around and about the film's mediocrity by claiming that "*The Mystic Hour* reverses the general order of things in that its story is really better than the telling of it." Okay. Then, too, the 25 May 1917 *Variety* opined that "The scenario could have been made just as effective with several hundred feet omitted" before jerking the string back a bit with "The principals make much of a plot that has been worked before in filmdom." *Motion Picture News* (9 June 1917) also jumped on the give-and-take bandwagon: "*The Mystic Hour* … never approaches the high-water mark of dramatic action nor does it rise to the heights which its strong title would suggest. The scenario offers strong possibilities by virtue of its originality, but many of these possibilities were apparently overlooked by the director."

The inattentive director was Richard Ridgely, he of *The Magic Skin* (1915) and *The Ghost of Old Morro* (1917), assessments of which may be found elsewhere within this volume. The Long Island native started out as a thespian over at the Edison Studios, and then quickly took on the additional (and, occasionally, simultaneous) duties of scribe and helmsman. Most of his film work there was in the field of short subjects, and many of those shorts involved vintage Edison heroine, Mabel Trunnelle. *The Mystic Hour* was one of the very few productions directed by Ridgely that was *not* produced by the Wizard of Menlo Park; it was one of but eight "Apollo Pictures" made, and our man helmed half of them. But for his last film credit — the aforementioned *The Ghost of Old Morro* — he returned to Edison (and Miss Trunnelle) after *Mystic* was in the can.

What was this "mystic hour," you ask? Well, the following is a patchwork quit of synopses culled from the trade journals of the day:

Guido Ferrari, an artist, is obsessed with the desire for the death of Holbrook Clavering [a drunkard and a libertine], who has married Margaret Buchanan, the girl Guido loves. [Margaret had turned for "sympathy and comfort" to Guido *after* she discovered that Clavering — with all his money — "does not make a good husband." Also: she "married Clavering for his money and earned it when she saw her hubby making love to another woman right after her marriage."] The thought accompanies him in his work, his sleep, and fills his every movement. One night he awakes from a dream in which he has murdered Clavering. In the morning, he goes to Clavering's room ["the artist has been staying in the house, painting Mrs. Clavering's picture"] and finds that he has been murdered and he labors under the uncanny feeling that he is the murderer. That he may rid himself of the thought he paints the picture revealed to him in his dream. [Margaret "advises him to paint the picture of his dream."] The butler at the home of Clavering is ordered to move Guido's belongings from the studio atop Clavering's home. He sees the painting, which is a picture of his master lying on a bed dead [*sic*]. The butler, who has committed the murder for his master's money, is so horror-stricken that he loses control and admits that it was he who killed Clavering [pieces taken from *Variety* (25 May 1917); *The New York Dramatic Mirror* (26 May 1917); *Exhibitor's Trade Review* (2 June 1917); *Motion Picture News* (9 June 1917); and *Moving Picture World* (2 June 1917)].

It's that almost paranormal bit about the painting of the dream that stokes the fire here, even if the resultant flame is more a spark than a conflagration. Once again, the reviewers had their views. *MPN*'s Joseph L. Kelley bypassed the structure of Fred Rath's scenario and hurled another lemon at Ridgely: "Psychology, the basic principle of the story, is the one sustaining 'prop' for the superstructure of its five reels and it is the one point which the director has left until the last reel to bring out and then in a half-hearted manner which fails to register." All smoke, then, and no fire. The anonymous critic at the *Exhibitor's Trade Review* struck a slightly more positive note: "For a long time it looks like *The Mystic Hour* would be nothing more than a trite, conventional domestic melodrama, but the moment events steer their course toward the climax of the play there is a perceptible change for the better in the atmosphere and mood of the picture."

Or, you can't fall off the floor. On the extreme opposite ends of this middling tepidness, the *Dramatic Mirror*'s write-up gives us the only clues we have as to the staging of the pivotal scene ("some excellent double-exposure effects in a weird dream murder scene"), while the 24 May 1917 *Wid's* wastes little ink, finding the Apollo-Arts production an "Ordinary surface action movie that never impresses."

It would take the insight of an exegete to extrude whence came the title, *The Mystic Hour*, from all this painting and killing and stealing and shtupping. It may be that Giorgio spent that hour whipping up that damning painting; or, perhaps, the dream in which he erroneously thought that he had killed Clavering lasted that long; or the butler may either have been entranced/aghast by the painting or was resisted desperately by the drunken libertine for that period of time. We don't know, and no one who saw the film and lived long enough to have his impressions published bothered to share his own theory. Maybe *The Mystic Hour* referred to the running time.

Just so you know, the biggest name in the cast crawl belonged to John Sainpolis, whose best-known genre role was that of Norman Kerry's big brother — le Comte Philip de Chagny — in 1925's *The Phantom of the Opera*. Coming in a distant second was Helen Strickland, who would soon take on the title role in *The Ghost of Old Morro*. The lady may have won this discorporate prize thanks to the observation (made in the *ETR* critique) that "Helen Strickland has a role, that of the mother, which is highly improbable if she is supposed to represent a living person."

Florence Short — Rene, the artist's model with whom Claver-

ing was canoodling — received little press mention for her escapades; she was also to be found in 1924's *The Enchanted Cottage* (see essay), where her contributions were virtually ignored by the Fourth Estate. Mayhaps that's why the young woman thereafter abandoned her cinematic endeavors. Pittsburgh-born Charles Hutchinson had few genre credits to his name, but did get to see his name onscreen for any number of silent chapter-plays (like 1918's *Wolves of Kultur*, with perennial heavy, Sheldon Lewis); he participated in some sound serials, too, but, for the most part, in uncredited bits. For trivia fans, Hutchinson was also a featured player in the 1933 talkie-thriller, *The Mystic Hour*, which — thankfully — failed miserably on its own merits, and not as a misguided remake of the dog that ran this race.

We defer to *Wid's* for our closing thoughts: "As a filler of routine caliber, this has some melodramatic spots that may impress those who accept the old methods. If you belong to the progressive class, I would advise you to forget it."

— *JTS*

The Nation's Peril

The Nation's Peril. Lubin Manufacturing Company/V-L-S-E, Inc., 22 November 1915, 5 reels [LOST]

CAST: Ormi Hawley (*Ruth Lyons*); William H. Turner (*Admiral Lyons*); Earl Metcalfe (*Lieutenant Sawyer*); Eleanor Barry (*Mrs. Sawyer*); Arthur Matthews (*Oswald Dudley*); Herbert Fortier (*Bertold Henchman*); Kempton Greene (*Enlisted man*); with Louise Huff, Mae De Metz, Hazel Hubbard, Edward Luck, Mrs. George Terwilliger, Edgar Jones

AS THEMSELVES: Josephus Daniels (Secretary of the Navy), Admiral Cameron McRae Winslow (U.S. Pacific fleet), Admiral Frank Friday Fletcher (U.S. Atlantic fleet), Captain W. S. Sims and staff (torpedo boat flotilla), Captain Willoughby (naval aerial squadron), Vice-Admiral Mayo

CREDITS: *Director* George Terwilliger; *Writers* Harry Chandlee, George Terwilliger; *Cinematographers* William Cooper, Edward Earle

Our synopsis is taken from a studio-generated promotional herald:

> With the United States covered by spies, and with thousands of foreign mechanics working in our factories, ready to take up arms against us, the leader of the enemy [Oswald Dudley] wins the favor of the daughter [Ruth Lyons] of one of our high naval officials [Admiral Lyons]. At his request, she steals the plans of an aerial torpedo controlled by wireless, which is America's chief refuge of defense. The inventor, a lieutenant [Lieutenant Sawyer] in love with her, is kidnapped and the siege of America begins.
>
> The girl learns of the duplicity of the conspirator, and seizing her father's sword kills him. A destroyer gives chase to the yacht carrying the important plans and shoots it to pieces. Meanwhile the foreign battery opens fire. The lieutenant electrocutes his guard and summons the Atlantic Fleet by wireless. The militia is also called. The fleet annihilates the enemy's artillery. Sunrise finds the lieutenant and the girl united under the stars and stripes.

The Lubin Manufacturing Company's *The Nation's Peril* — one of the "What if?" war-preparedness tales common to the mid–1910s — was released scant weeks after *The Rights of Man: a Story of War's Red Blotch*, another Lubin feature (but one that had promoted the flip-side, pacifist point of view of man's future). Only a couple of months earlier still, *The Battle Cry of Peace* (see entry)—taken from the writings of preparedness-kingpin, Hudson Maxim—had been playing the circuit. What with all that cinematic thought percolating on the Conflict to Come, *Peril* may have fallen somewhere short of *Battle Cry* in terms of impact. Still, as Lubin biographer, Joseph P. Eckhardt, informed us: "The film was one of Lubin's great successes, although it came too late to help the floundering company. The film was still being shown well into 1916, and, in some places, even after Lubin had folded in September 1916."

Like both *Battle Cry* and *The Fall of a Nation* (which was released some eight months after the film at hand), *The Nation's Peril* provided the war-wary country with a dose of cautionary

LUBIN FEATURE
"THE NATION'S PERIL"
THE TOPIC OF THE HOUR

A TERRIFIC SEA BATTLE

WRITTEN AND DIRECTED BY George Terwilliger
Featuring EARL METCALFE
Supported by ORMI HAWLEY *and a Strong Cast*

Thanks largely to Earl Metcalfe, the Nation is 235 years old and still kicking.

formula, which was concocted using all the standard ingredients: the duplicitous Enemy Agent; the naïve, Peace-Loving Heroine; the jilted, Defense-Minded Hero; and the Sneak Attack by an Imaginary Foe.

In addition, this time 'round the plot centered on the aerial torpedo—forerunner of today's cruise missiles—a concept that had been kicking around in the mind of Hiram Maxim (Hudson's brother) back in the early 1890s, before the Wright brothers had even lifted off the ground. With the advent of the Great War, attempts at developing remote-controlled flying bombs accelerated, thanks to the efforts of men like Elmer Sperry and Charles Kettering and to the sponsorship of U.S. Navy Secretary, Josephus Daniels. Airborne explosives weren't perfected prior to the end of the War, though—save for in the fictional realms—but Daniels' influence was felt in those venues as well, inasmuch as he (along with other navy luminaries) appeared in *The Nation's Peril*.

With the navy's full support, director George Terwilliger's camera crew was able to film the bombardment of the battleship Utah and shoot key footage aboard the U.S.S. *Patterson* and the U.S.S. *Yankton*. Thousands of sailors and marines from the Atlantic squadron participated in the picture, and soldiers from Rhode Island and Massachusetts posed as hostile forces. One of the major sequences called for a huge street-mob scene depicting wartime carnage; this was photographed in Lubinville, Pennsylvania. Another, shot in Newport, Rhode Island, depicted the obliteration of a large motor boat, with said destruction accomplished via 40 pounds of dynamite. Adding to overall effect, the 4 December 1915 *Motography* reported that many of the key battle scenes "are all in natural colors, which makes them more effective."

Like most films of the same ilk, *The Nation's Peril* met with favorable political bias in its reviews. Thus, knowing full well the stance of former president and Rough Rider Teddy Roosevelt, Edward Weitzel wove some pointed editorial opinion into his critique of the film in the 27 November 1915 edition of *The Motion Picture World*:

> The sight of marching men, of a great fleet in battle array, of mighty gunsbelching forth flames and the missiles of death—all "the pomp and circumstance" of War—how it quickens the blood and stirs the soul of even less ardent patriots than Col. Roosevelt! When these things are shown on the screen, as part and parcel of a vivid plea for National preparedness, coupled with a well worked out love story and all the concomitants of an engrossing photoplay, the combination must appeal to every good American.
>
> It is hardly necessary to state which side is the winner in this suppostitious [*sic*] war. The naval officer here received the proper reward at the finish of this splendid object lesson to the peace-at-any-price adherents.

Thomas C. Kennedy also endorsed the film's message in his *Motography* review:

> If it lies within the power of the motion picture to sway public opinion in a matter of this kind, *The Nation's Peril* will do so, and in that event it will accomplish immeasurable good. As has been said before, the picture is strongest in its spectacular scenes, which add force to certain statements of fact. Without showing any horrible consequences, the story convincingly depicts the dangers of unpreparedness, and the romance with its elements of intrigue and misguided faith in the "peace at any price" policy, is in this way justified.

Variety (19 November 1915) thought well of the U.S. Navy maneuvers, stating: "These are all interesting making up the best bits in the production." Still, one detail failed to impress: "The ships are seen steaming into the harbor with electric lights showing their outlines. Rather an unusual thing, considering they were coming in to bombard the enemy." *Variety* was more critical of the film than of U.S. Navy policy and enumerated some acting pluses and minuses: "Earl Metcalfe as the lieutenant did some of the saddest work of his career. The part did not warrant any great effort for him. Much of the time he is seen running around in the woods. Miss [Ormi] Hawley did fairly well. William Turner, as the admiral, did satisfactorily what was asked of him."

In spite of *Variety*'s sad opinion of him, Metcalfe received top billing; he gets additional mention in our chapter on 1919's *The Poison Pen*. His co-star, Ormi Hawley, moved from the stage to the screen during the Silent Era, but retired to marriage and farm life in the late 1920s. Along with director Terwilliger, scenarist Harry Chandlee co-wrote *The Nation's Peril*. Stints as a producer and a film editor kept Chandlee fairly busy from the 1910s to late 1940s, but his big love — and chief talent — lay in writing; *The Return of Chandu* (1934) and *Tarzan's Magic Fountain* (1949) mark his talkie genre efforts.

— *SJ*

Ransom

Ransom. Columbia Pictures Corp./Columbia, 30 June 1928, 6 reels/5584 feet [LOST]

CAST: Lois Wilson (*Lois Brewster*); Edmund Burns (*Burton Meredith*); William V. Mong (*Wu Fang*); Blue Washington (*Oliver*); James B. Leong (*Scarface*); Jackie Coombs (*Bobby*)

CREDITS: *Producer* Harry Cohn; *Director* George B. Seitz; *Adaptation* Elmer Harris; *Continuity* Dorothy Howell; based upon the story, "San Francisco," by George B. Seitz (publication details unknown); *Assistant Director* Joe Nadel; *Cinematographer* Joe Walker, A.S.C.; *Art Director* Joe Wright; *Title Cards* Mort Blumenstock

George Brackett Seitz (see *Black Magic*) was indubitably one of the kings of silent chapter-plays, not only directing, but also writing, producing and acting in countless episodes. Serial queen Pearl White, who— beginning with 1914's famed *The Perils of Pauline* — toiled under his tutelage for much of her career, also appeared in the Seitz-led vehicles *The Exploits of Elaine* (also 1914), *The Romance of Elaine* (1915), *The Iron Claw* (1916), *The House of Hate* (1918) and *Plunder* (1923), all chapter-plays that included borderline science-fiction gimmickry. In 1919's *Bound and Gagged*, a ten-chapter serial purposely entitles à la the cliché, Seitz went so far as to parody his own and others' work in the weekly art form. The most purely science-fictional of his silent serials has to be 1921's *The Sky Ranger*, wherein two scientists— one good, one evil, one armed with a prototype laser and the other with a forerunner of a jet rocket — duke it out for 15 installments.

Ransom was adapted from Seitz's story *San Francisco*, and although released as a six-reel feature, it was not far removed from type of entertainment that brought joy to serial fans' hearts. These excerpts from the Library of Congress copyright summary should give the gist of things:

Burton Meredith, head of the western laboratories of the U.S. Government Chemical Research Bureau, creates an explosive which, when released, will strike dead people, animals and all vegetation for miles around. He carefully guards the secret of his formula.

Burton is engaged to marry Lois Brewster, a widow with a small son. Lois meets Burton at the laboratory, and he escorts her home. Upon leaving, Burton instructs Oliver, a giant Negro watchman, to guard the vault containing the sample vial of the deadly gas.

Hardly does Meredith arrive at the Brewster home, when he is summoned to the telephone. A message informs the inventor that a band of Chinese thugs has attacked Oliver and knocked him senseless with clubs. They failed, however, in their attempt to obtain the gas or its formula.

Burton hurries to the laboratory to learn the details of the plot to rob him of his discovery.

Wu Fang, who is at the head of the Chinese underworld gang, is furious when he learns that his men have failed to secure the gas and formula. Knowing that Burton is engaged to Lois, Wu plans to force Meredith into submission by abducting the widow's child. He feels that through this strategy he will be able to force Lois to aid him in his scheme.

The child is thus abducted by a scar-faced Chinaman, and Lois pleads with Burton to meet the kidnappers' demands. Meredith refuses to give up the secret, informing Lois that it is not his to give as it belongs to the United States Government. Lois becomes unreasonable. In her frenzy she accuses Burton of being a selfish, heartless brute. She locks Burton in a vault, grabs a vial of the gas, and delivers it to Wu Fang, who quickly realizes that it is simply water. Meanwhile, Oliver frees Burton, Burton battles and overcomes "Scarface."

Then, in order to discover the headquarters of the gang, Burton, assisted by Oliver, arranges to release Scarface in such a manner that the Chinaman will believe he has escaped. The prisoner falls into the trap and Burton is able to follow him to Wu's hangout. From there, the resourceful inventor rescues Lois and the child. But first he brawls with Wu Fang and his henchmen, one which is ultimately settled when Oliver and the police arrive. Lois and Burton are reunited. They return home with the child and arrange to culminate their adventures in a speedy marriage.

Eagle-eyed readers have no doubt noticed that the above text contradicts itself in the first two paragraphs: does Meredith's formula produce an *explosive* or a *gas*? Inasmuch as other sources consulted agree unanimously on a gas, we find we're not dealing with much above and beyond the dirty tricks used in the trenches of World War I.

Variety (15 August 1928) wasted little space in passing judgment on the film. In an extremely succinct summary and review (two sentences), it declared: "It's a lot of the hoke stuff familiar to every fan, but here is plenty of quick motion that will key up and satisfy grind audiences." *Film Daily* (26 August 1928) labeled the plot "time worn," the direction "okay" and the photography "satisfactory" under a telling headline that read in part, "No Unusual Merit." On the 11 August 1928, *Harrison's* reported that the picture was "Just fair. The acting and directing are conventional although its suspense is mildly tense." As for the cast, "Miss Wilson is good as the heroine and Edmund Burns is good as the hero. Blue Washington is quite good and William V. Mong is acceptable...." For those who may be interested, Miss Wilson appeared in the 1918 production of *The Bells*, Mr. Burns in *Whispering Wires* (19266), and Mr. Mong in a bunch of pertinent titles, including *A Connecticut Yankee in King Arthur's Court* (1921). Most of Shanghai-born James B. Leong's genre appearances came during the Sound Era.

Ransom holds the honor of being one of the few silent films to have its preview trailer copyrighted. Other than that, it seems there wasn't much to distinguish it from a raft of similar programmers.   — *SJ*

Restitution

Restitution. Mena Films Corp./States' Rights, 12 May 1918, 9–12 reels*; The original film is lost, but two reels of *The Conquering Christ*, a reissue title, are held at the Library of Congress.

CAST: Eugene Corry (*Adam*); Lois Gardner (*Eve*); Alfred Garcia (*Lucifer and Satan*); Frank Whitson (*Abraham*); Amy Jerome (*Sarah*); Pomeroy Cannon (*Pharaoh*); Frederick Vroom (*Joseph*); Mabel Harvey (*Mary*); Harold Quintin Driscoll (*Jesus, the boy*); Howard Gaye (*Jesus, the Man*); F.A. Turner (*Herod*); John Steppling (*Nero*); Mary Wise (*Poppoeia*); C. Norman Hammond ("*Modern Ruler*"); Venita Fitzhugh (*Columbia*); Edward Cecil (*Dr. John Boyd*); Virginia Chester (*Claire Boyd*); Jack Cosgrove (*Dr. Thomas*); C.E. Collins (*Blind Man*); Georgia French (*His little daughter*); Yvonne Chappella (*Dancer*).

Per *The AFI Catalog*: "One sources credits Virginia Chester with the role of Columbia."

CREDITS: *Director* Howard Gaye; *Assistant Director* Herbert Sutch; *Supervisor* G.C. Driscoll; *Cinematographer* Delbert L. Davis, Hal Mohr; *Musical accompaniment orchestral music specially prepared by* Harry Alford, John T. Read

Our synopsis is taken from *The AFI Catalog*:

After Adam and Eve are banished from the Garden of Eden, man is reduced to vassalage, and Satan assumes a determining role in human affairs. Man's struggles against Satan are depicted through the biblical stories of Cain and Abel, Abraham and Sarah, and the life, temptation and crucifixion of Christ. In the first century A.D., Nero tortures the Christians. Satan introduces internecine warfare within the Church, culminating in the Inquisition. Napoleon rises and repudiates the theory of kings ruling by divine right. America is established by the providential arrangement of God so people could worship according to the dictates of their own conscience. In the present day Satan seeks to regain his power by recourse to the ancient theory of the divine right of kings and joins forces with a "Modern Ruler" (Kaiser Wilhelm of Germany), but Columbia beats autocracy. Christ conquers Satan, who is condemned to eternal death, and Abraham, reincarnated through Christ, restores the dead to life.

And if you're shaking your head in disbelief after reading this description, rest assured contemporary reviewers did likewise. The film sounds like a combination of the Irwin Alllen fiasco, *The Story of Mankind*, and the *Left Behind* series made by Christian fundamentalists.

Of main interest here are not the Biblical tales or the propagandistic history lessons, but rather the bizarre contemporary story (which the critics found absurd) in which the Modern Ruler becomes the pawn of Satan. The Ruler is certainly meant to be Kaiser Wilhelm but is never identified as such or made to resemble the real Kaiser. Critics found that annoying, and *Variety* speculated (in its 31 May 1918 issue) that it may have been "a weak attempt on the part of the producers to cater to the many foreigners in this country who may see the picture and at the same time have secret and silent leanings toward the Central Powers."

Satan's defeat is given a tongue-in-cheek description by Peter Milne of *Motion Picture News* (8 June 1918): "It remains for Columbia, emblem of democracy and righteousness, to break the Devil's spell and push him through the face of the earth down to his own infernal regions to be consumed by fire. He fell through the surface at a point embracing several of the United States and a number of Canadian territories."

The return of Abraham ("clothed like an elderly Tyrolean yodeler") was likewise received with bemused bafflement by the critics. A spirit calls Abraham from the grave and, "in the form of a Don Quixote," the great Patriarch travels the world saving sinners and curing the sick. He also restores to life a doctor who has been dead and buried, and reunites him with his wife (as well as returning their baby).

One of three (!) MPN reviews mentions that "Lois Gardner has the role of Eve and her reincarnated forms throughout the ages." However, there's no indication of what part these reincarnations played in the story, and the credits only list Gardner as Eve.

Restitution reputedly was two years in the making and cost $100,000. Critics appreciated the size and scope of the film, the many sets and extras, and the sincerity with which it was made, but found parts of it nonsensical and inept. The Biblical sequences received the most praise, though Robert Mc Elravy (in the 8 June 1918 *Moving Picture World*) found the scenes depicting the Slaughter of the Innocents and the later torture of Christians "an overdose of the unpleasant" and called for them to be toned down. The special effects got mixed notices with only the creation of Eve from Adam's rib singled out favorably. Some of the double exposures were adjudged unconvincing and the miniature work was thought clever, if obvious. A special score was created for the film and, according to Peter Milne, "If it had not been for the impressive organ recital that accompanied the private showing at Wurlitzer Hall it is doubtful whether those present could have refrained from laughing."

Restitution (working titles: *God's Tomorrow* and *By Super Strategy)* was made by Mena Film Company, an outfit run by Christians who were so devout they had misgivings about selling stock in the picture to "worldly" people. Pastor Charles T. Russell had started on a film — then entitled *Creation*— but after his death Mena took over the footage and made plans to turn it into a full-scale epic. The company built a studio and, according to one story, planned *Restitution* as the first of a series of Biblical films, parts of which would be shot in Palestine once the war ended. Nonetheless, despite a later announcement of a picture about famous historical Egyptians, *Restitution* proved to be Mena's only production and, in 1919, the studio was sold to Brentwood Film Corporation for $45,000.

The biggest name in *Restitution* was Howard Gaye, who directed and was also cast as Jesus, the man (a role he had played, in an understated and effective manner, in *Intolerance*). Gaye had been active in Labour-Party politics in his native England and had edited their paper *The Daily Mail* before coming to the States and turning to acting; his most notable early role was

---

*Variety's reviewer saw the nine-reel version and said it lasted about two hours. The different *MPN* reviews alternate between nine and 12 reels, and one states the film lasted 75 minutes.

Robert E. Lee in *Birth of a Nation*. The noble characters portrayed by Gaye, the actor, apparently didn't impact Gaye, the man, who—though married—reputedly seduced a star-struck young woman and took her away with him to England. He deserted her when he returned to the States, she filed a complaint, and Gaye found himself charged with violating the Mann Act. In 1924, after finishing his part as Virgil in *Dante's Inferno* (see entry), he was deported to England.

— HN

The Ruling Passion

The Ruling Passion. Fox Film Corp./Fox Film Corp., 30 January 1916, 5 reels [LOST]

CAST: William E. Shay (*Ram Singh, the Rajah of Mawar*); Claire Whitney (*Claire Sherlock*); Harry Burkhardt (*Harvey Walcott*); Edward Boring (*Ramlaal*); Thelma Parker (*Nadia*); Florence Deschon (*Blanche Walcott*); Stephen Gratton (*Gov. of Raj Putana*); with Katherine Gilbert, Violet Rockwell, Augustus Balfour, Milly Liston.

CREDITS: *Supervisor* Herbert Brenon; *Director* James McKay; *Scenario* Herbert Brenon.

In 1915, Fox's star director, Herbert Brenon, accompanied by a large entourage of technicians, actors and press agents, established a beachhead for his studio in Kingston, Jamaica. The focus of all this activity was the new Annette Kellerman vehicle, *A Daughter of the Gods* (see entry), advertised again and again as a million-dollar production. While working on his main project, though, Brenon had time—with the help of film editor and sometimes-director James McKay—to supervise another film using *Daughter's* male lead, William E. Shay, and no doubt utilizing extras and sets meant for his weightier epic. The resulting picture was a mixture of sex and sadism, with a dash of hypnotism thrown in to add to the exotica.

The various synopses don't always agree on the plot details, but we will trust in "Wynn" of *Variety* (4 February 1916) for our rundown:

> *The Ruling Passion* tells the experiences of an orphan girl who, on the death of her mother, journeys to India to become the ward of her aunt. She meets an English officer and their marriage eventually follows. She attracts the attention of the so-called Rajah of Mawar and, failing in his initial overtures, he exercises his unusual hypnotic powers to compel her to do as he wishes. Under this peculiar power, she seemingly shows an affection for the Rajah and later on becomes an inmate of his harem, having been cast off by her husband. His [the Rajah's] extreme brutality results in her escape and she shares the hut of a native dancing girl, where her child, apparently the daughter of her lawful husband, is her only comfort. Learning of the Rajah's plan to sell her child, she takes flight and arrives at the home of her sister-in-law who recognizes and cares for her, the husband having, meanwhile, returned to London to recover from an injury. Events lead up to a revolution, during which the Rajah is assassinated and eventually the complications are pleasantly adjusted.

Ads for the film seldom mention the hypnotism element, but stress that the movie provides "Pictures of an Oriental harem, fatal love and the incense of the East." It's quite possible that the Rajah's hypnotic powers are there simply to provide an excuse for the white heroine to submit to a man of another race and/or experience the fantasy of living in a harem. To audiences of 1916, her survival at the last reel might be hard to justify otherwise (that would change a few years later with Rudolph Valentino and *The Sheik*). The fact that the heroine is able to escape the rajah's influence quite on her own would suggest that he's no Svengali, but the AFI synopsis does add that it takes his death to break the spell, a cliché quite in keeping with the Trilby tradition of mesmerized damsels and followed almost without exception in both the silent and sound eras.

Oscar Cooper of *Motion Picture News* (12 February 1916) seemed to find the film's violence a bit unsettling:

> The prince's bestial nature leads him to poison a harem favorite after he tires of her, and to beat another one when she displeases him. He also orders the eyes of his one of his slaves gouged out with hot irons. The scene is shown in some detail…. In contrast to much of the action, which is necessarily concerned with the prince's brutality and pleasure-seeking performances, a full-screen close-up of a smiling infant is introduced near the end. This is preceded by a pretty scene between the unfortunate Englishwoman and her husband, who apparently never learns of her harrowing experience in the harem.

Reviewers commented on the effective use of Jamaica as a stand-in for India and the impressive sets, particularly the interior of the rajah's palace. William E. Shay's brutal prince came in for the most praise. Shay—more likely, the public relations department—claimed he prepared for his role by spending two months studying with a Hindu mystic: "At the end of that time I had accomplished my purpose. I had dabbled in India's religion, her social life, her customs. Above all, I had learned no little about her seers and far-famed practitioners of legerdemain." (*The Odgen* [Utah] *Standard*, 19 February 1916) It's hard to say how any of this would have helpful in playing a sadistic Oriental tyrant. Shay (see *Neptune's Daughter* and *A Daughter of the Gods*) was directed by Herbert Brenon dozens of times and was also one of Theda Bara's early leading men.

Claire Whitney (see *The Dream Woman* and *The Woman of Mystery*) got her biggest star build-up at Fox, but soon ended up supporting the studio's flashier attractions, Theda Bara and Valeska Suratt. When her film roles dwindled in the 1920s, Whitney went on the road with her husband—vaudeville comic Robert Emmett Keane—before suffering the usual fate of many silent movie stars: bit parts in the talkies and "Where are they now?" articles in the press.

— HN

The Sacred Ruby see *The House of Mystery*

The Satin Girl

The Satin Girl. Ben Wilson/Grand-Asher Distributing Corp., 30 November 1923, 6 reels/5591 feet [LOST]

CAST: Mabel Forrest (*Lenore Vance*); Norman Kerry (*Dr. Richard Taunton*); Marc MacDermott (*Fargo*); Clarence Burton (*Marian*); Florence Lawrence (*Sylvia*); Kate Lester (*Mrs. Brown-Potter*); Reed House (*Norton Pless*); William H. Turner (*Silas Gregg*); Walter Stevens (*Harg*).

CREDITS: *Director* Arthur Rosson; *Adaptation* Arthur Statter, George Plympton; based on a story by Adam Hull Shirk.

More hypnotism, more folks doing things they wouldn't do were it not for more hypnotism, more evil geniuses … but who's keeping count? Appendix-fodder from the get-go, here's the synopsis, in two parts:

From *The AFI Catalog*:

> A girl loses her memory and, falling under the influence of an eccentric master-criminal, is forced to commit robberies. A young doctor falls in love with her and unravels the mystery of her identity. It develops that the whole story is a novel that Lenore has been reading in which she visualizes herself and Dr. Taunton as the leading characters.

From *Harrison's Reports*, 1 December 1923:

> The story concerns the hypnotic influence exerted by a malevolent old man over the daughter (heroine) of a man he had hated. Under this influence, the girl becomes a thief, earning the sobriquet "The Satin Girl" because after each theft she invariably left behind a piece of satin. She is sent to rob the safe of a doctor whom she had repeatedly met at social functions; he catches her and then realizes that she is The Satin Girl who had been baffling the police. After learning of the circumstance of her criminal career, they marry.

Which of the two recaps is the more *b-l-a-a-a-h* is debatable, but it's the hypnotic influence of the malevolent old man (who *may* be an "eccentric master-criminal" but might just be a son of a bitch) that has Lenore and her satin swatches in this book in the first place. It's not a little disturbing, though, to note that neither of those recaps identifies any of the dramatis personae other than Juliet and her Romeo. Thus, we turn to *The New York Times'* online summation of *The Satin Girl*, brought to you by Ovaltine.

> The miserly Silas Gregg is murdered and his daughter mysteriously vanishes. Shortly afterwards, a series of thefts occur and the culprit is known to the police only as "the satin girl." At a fashionable party, Dr. Richard Taunton meets Lenore Vance, and it doesn't take much to figure out that not only is she the satin girl, she is also Gregg's daughter. The twist comes when it turns out that she is committing these robberies while under the strange mental influence of a man named Fargo — the same character who killed Gregg. When his ruby turns up missing, Taunton figures everything out, but when the police arrive to arrest Fargo, they find he has committed suicide.

First off, we're indebted to *The Times'* online movie maven, Janiss Garza (of the website's "All Movie Guide"), for plugging up the gaps. Let's then give a slap to our collective forehead for not realizing *immediately* that there has never been anyone yclept "Silas" in the movies who was not either a skinflinty miser or a miserly skinflint. (Those readers who have been following these essays alphabetically may recall that we noted this back in our essay on *The Black Pearl*. If you'll allow us this redundancy, we'll forgive your being anal.) A bit of a surprise was to be had, though, at the twin revelations that he was not the malevolent old duck that got things going dramatically and that he had been murdered. Thankfully, Ms. Garza's précis is in keeping with *The AFI Catalog's* reporting that Lenore lost her memory and vanished, and *Harrison's Reports'* fleshing out why the ... errr ... lost Lenore ended up under the spell of the mysterious Fargo. No one's telling just *how* all of this came to pass and, to be brutally honest, we couldn't care less. The only question we have left are whether that ruby of Dr. Taunton's had been stolen in his youth from an Oriental idol, and whether Fargo — is his name an anagram for something like "Get away from our ruby!"? — is a member of a cult, sent to do in thieving

infidels while strewing pieces of cloth across the heathen landscape.

Among the more drearily predictable elements of this story is the stuff about the leaving behind of those satin scraps, aka the criminal's trademark. One has to ask: was the piece-of-cloth calling-card the mesmerized Lenore's idea (you know; sort of a somehow-dredged-up-from-her-subconscious plea to be identified and caught?), or the brainstorm of the aforementioned evil genius? In which case, what the hell!? How much more intriguing for him and baffling to the cops would have been his purposefully putting them on the scent of, say, "The Goat Entrails Girl"?

More on the satin scraps.... The 3 April 1924 *Bridgeport* [CT] *Telegram* added spice to the stew when it advised its readers that

> local police circles are considerably mystified and are being harassed to small extent by the depredations of a mysterious young woman, said to be very beautiful, who has been termed the "Satin Girl" because the only time she was almost in the law's clutches, she escaped but left a piece of her black satin dress in the hands of the officers. The most remarkable thing about the matter is that the Satin Girl robs only wealthy people, usually of gems, and then spends much of the result in charity. Baskets of food, etc. are frequently received by the poor people with a black card on which is penned, in white ink: "From the 'Satin Girl.'"

Now, where in blazes did that Robin Hood shtick come from? Please don't ask us to believe that Fargo had purposefully programmed Lenore to rob from the rich and give to the poor as the crux of his vengeful plan to get back at Silas Gregg? Not the old "Gregg's shade will never know eternal rest so long as his daughter continues with these random acts of charitable larceny" ploy? And the dress... Do the cops get another handful each time they show up late at the robbery? What is this? Stop me before I'm naked?

More drearily predictable still — in fact, the most tired of all Silent Era movie conventions — was the inevitable marital union of the juveniles, and it took Buster Keaton (in 1924's *Sherlock, Jr.*) to offer the ultimate take, with his last-reel depiction of his hero-and-heroine's future, in which their lifelong union leads inexorably to a pair of matching headstones. Critics were wowed, audiences were happily satisfied, and studios took no notice whatsoever: the American cinema's closing moments would see the Innocents continuing to process to the altar or to the justice of the peace for quite some time to come. And, again, one must ask: Why was there not — even once — a movie about a fearless young doctor who rushed in to save a damsel in distress only to find that, looks-wise, she ran a dead-heat with the troll who lived under the bridge? Why was there not one solitary instance in which, instead of asking for herself's hand in wedlock following the resolution of the dilemma, he instead delivered to hers a restraining order, keeping her at a distance of some three hundred yards ever thereafter? Alas! Having the Machiavellian chops to choose his hypnotic stooge on the basis of the likelihood of her *never* having some young schmuck run to her rescue might well have bolstered *Satin*'s eccentric master-criminal to the Pantheon of Great Movie Malevolents. Sadly, he did not, and thus the old bastard is left to wander endlessly here in the appendix.

Dr. Taunton, the young schmuck who came running to save that ruby-snatching hottie, was played by Norman Kerry. If you don't know who Norman Kerry is, a) Shame on you, and b) see our essay on *The Hunchback of Notre Dame*. The Satin Girl herself was impersonated by Mabel Forrest, an on-again/off-again actress whose career length (the lady was sporadically active in the movies or on television for *six decades*) is belied somewhat by the relative sparsity of her credits (some 40-odd screen appearances during that time). None of the reviews of *Satin* we consulted mentioned any of the actors' names in conjunction with performance-dedicated adjectives, so we may assume that Miss Forrest's performance was neither as good as a well nor as bad as a churchyard (profound apologies to Mr. Shakespeare). The Ohio-born actress's only other genre credit was her role as Mrs. Ferguson in one of *Twilight Zone*'s most memorable episodes, 1962's "The Last Rites of Jeff Myrtlebank."

Irishman William H. Turner's appearance herein (as the doomed Silas-the-Miser) was preceded by his Admiral Lyons in 1915's *A Nation's Peril* (see entry), and that's about all we can offer Mr. Turner's fans at this point. Fargo the Heavy was enacted by Aussie Marc MacDermott, who counted this appearance as but one in a couple of hundred he turned in before the Silent Era died off — as did he — in 1929. There's more on Mr. MacDermott in our essay on the 1919 *The Thirteenth Chair*. We should also mention that *The Satin Girl* hosted yet another pantomime by the former Biograph Girl *and* the former Imp Girl: both in the person of Florence Lawrence, whose prodigious output dwarfed even that of Mr. MacDermott. (An ad for *Satin* in a local paper gushed that "Old time favorite comes back to the current screen." We know not how Miss Lawrence reacted to that statement.) Please head to the chapter on *Elusive Isabel* for further detail on Miss Lawrence.

The Satin Girl was directed by Arthur Rosson, the brother of Hal Rosson (the Oscar-winning cinematographer of such popular genre-ish pictures as *Tarzan, the Ape Man* [1932], *The Ghost Goes West* [1935], and *The Wizard of Oz* [1939]); of Richard Rosson, a fairly prolific 1910s/1920s actor in short films and the director of 1927's *The Wizard* (see entry); and of actress, Helene Rosson, whose genre highlight was *The Light* (see entry). Other than *The Satin Girl*, Arthur Rosson offered little to such as us.

Harrison's felt that the film "may prove perfectly satisfying to non-exacting picture-goers." It was thought, though, that *exacting* ticket-buyers "may find it mostly 'hokum'." An uncited review at hand adds a bit of fuel to this not-bright fire: "While *The Satin Girl* is a highly improbable tale, it may find favor with those who are willing to swallow their pictures whole and are not concerned too much with the legitimacy or veracity of situations." And, then again, it may not.

— *JTS*

The Sky Skidder

The Sky Skidder. Universal Pictures/Universal, 13 January 1929, 5 reels/4364 feet [LOST]

CAST: Al Wilson (*Al Simpkins*); Helen Foster (*Stella Hearns*); Wilbur McGaugh (*Silas Smythe*); Pee Wee Holmes (*Bert Beatle*)

CREDITS: *Director* Bruce Mitchell; *Story/Continuity* Carl Krusada (as Val Cleveland); *Titles* Gardner Bradford; *Cinematographer* William Adams; *Film Editor* Harry Marker

Al Simpkins invented a new fuel, "Economo," for which he claims great things. During a trial flight, he sees his sweetheart, Stella Hearns, riding with wealthy and dishonest Silas Smythe. The car gets out of control and Al rescues Stella by means of a rope ladder. Just before the "Economo" demonstration flight Silas Smythe steals the last of the mixture and refills the tank with gasoline. When Al makes the exhibition his plane runs out of fuel and he is forced to land by parachute. Centerville loses faith in Al's invention, but when he enters the air derby with a powerful monoplane he has a thankful of "Economo." He entrusts Stella with the formula which Silas' mechanic manages to steal from her. When Stella discovers her loss she and Al go into the air after Silas. After a terrific fight he retrieves the formula, regains his plane and wins the race and Stella [Copyright registration documents].

To the above mélange, *The AFI Catalog* adds the fact that Al's new fuel gets *1000 miles to the pint* (Al, where are you now that we need you?), that Stella finances Al's entry in the Big Air Race, and that Al gets his Economo back from Snidely's … errr … Silas's monoplane via another junket down that trusty rope ladder.

The Sky Skidder was one of those B features that had been planned and shot as a silent and that, *The Jazz Singer* or no, was released as a silent. Retooling and upgrading to deal with the exigencies of sound technology was expensive and was best left to those A pictures that would doubtless render even more to Caesar with the addition of voices and aural effects. Universal had assigned the picture to Bruce Mitchell, a veteran director who had successfully helmed a number of aerial adventure films for them (*Three Miles Up*, *Sky-High Saunders* [both 1927], *The Air Patrol*, *The Cloud Dodger* [both 1928], and the like) and for some indie studios for several years, due both to the man's acuity with the topic, perspicacious timing (this was the Age of Al Wilson! [see below]), and the plethora of available pertinent stock footage. Mitchell — a native of Freeport, Illinois — was another of those resilient movie folk who could (and *did*) do everything competently without doing anything remarkably. *The Sky Skidder* was thus perceived as being another in a disjointed series of pilots-in-action pics and as nothing worthy of extra time, attention, or money. (In all fairness to Mitchell, he made a slew of them thar uncredited screen appearances during the 1930s and 1940s, including bits in Charlie Chan, Philo Vance, Perry Mason and other, popular, character-driven series.) Still, if it weren't for the kind of mileage one can get with a spoonful of Economo, this movie wouldn't even be here in the Appendix.

Al Simpkins was played by Al Wilson, surely *not* an actor who needs no introduction. Wilson, a licensed pilot, had "acted" in all of the Universal/Bruce Mitchell titles we listed above, plus in just about every other mid–1920s cinematic air adventure picture made in the USA. What's more, Wilson also seems to have been involved in crafting the stories (such as they were) for a good number of these films, including those in which he emoted as well as steered and climbed rope ladders. (Note: Al did not write any of *The Sky Skidder*; he merely emoted, steered and climbed rope ladders.) All in all, it might be fair to say that this 1920s sub-genre might not have had the durability it had or made the impact it did without Mr. Wilson. Still, despite heading the cast in most of the movies in which he appeared,

Al's most impressive credit remains his uncredit (as a stunt pilot) Howard Hughes' 1930 *Hell's Angels*. Wilson died with his boots on in early September 1932 as the result of injuries sustained from a crash at the National Air Races.

Helen Foster — a 1929 WAMPAS Baby Star — was Al's leading lady here, and she had been Al's leading lady in 1928's *Won in the Clouds*, another flying feature produced à la the Wilson/Mitchell/Universal formula. Like so many pretty girls in the movies, Helen started out as the ingénue and then moved into featured roles as she grew older; come the Sound Era, she likewise moved from small(er) parts to uncredited bits. The lady's uncredits stretched into the mid–1950s and the lady herself made it to Christmas day, 1982.

The 20 February 1929 *Variety* may have put the film (and the sub-genre) in perspective:

> Couple of minutes of thrilling air stuff and long sequences of straight flying stand out. Otherwise particularly flagrant example of bad writing, worse acting and indifferent direction…. Wilson is a good-looking hero but his acting is not impressive, and the simpering heroine of Miss Foster doesn't help the situation.

— JTS

Smilin' Through

Smilin' Through. Norma Talmadge Productions/Associated First National Pictures, 13 February 1922, 8 reels/8,000 feet, Library of Congress, Nederlands Filmmuseum (part of the Raymond Rohauer Collection). Library of Congress Notes on the print: "Severe decomposition in some places. Preservation seems complete although we are a bit short of AFI's estimated length. Library of Congress titles added. First Nat'l logos on head and tail seem to be in the wrong place — both are printed into the nitrate in that position — so it must be assumed that is the original position."

CAST: Norma Talmadge (*Kathleen/Moonyeen*); Wyndham Standing (*John Cartaret*); Harrison Ford (*Kenneth Wayne/Jeremiah Wayne*); Alec B. Francis (*Dr. Owen*); Glenn Hunter (*Willie Ainsley*); Grace Griswold (*Ellen*); Miriam Battista (*Little Mary, Moonyeen's Sister*); Eugene Lockhart (*Village Rector*)

CREDITS: *Presented by* Joseph M. Schenck; *Supervisor* Joe Aller; *Director* Sidney A. Franklin; *Adaptation* Sidney A. Franklin, James Ashmore Creelman; based on the eponymous play by Allen Langdon Martin (Jane Cowl, Jane Murfin; New York, c. 1924); *Cinematographers* Charles Rosher, Roy Hunt

Copyright title: *Smiling Through*

This Norma Talmadge vehicle is not nearly as cheery as its title would have one believe, although its intermittent supernatural blather and last-reel catharsis work enough schmaltz-cum-emotional-magic that vintage–1922 viewers doubtless made for the exits while smiling through a tear or two. Based on the eponymous comedy-fantasy that had run at New York City's Broadhurst Theatre for about 6 months back in early 1920, the picture borrowed heavily (and fairly faithfully) from the narrative of playwright Allen Langdon Martin.

About that Allen Langdon Martin… In reality, said gentleman was a lady, or, more accurately, two ladies. Sometimes. In greater reality, said gentleman's name was the *nom de plume* of Grace Bailey, a young gal from Beantown who would go on to estimable success on the Broadway stage as the actress, Jane Cowl, and who would find fame in equal measure as the playwright, Jane Cowl. Or as Allen Langdon Martin, either under

her own steam, or when sharing the labors with fellow scribe, Jane Murfin.

Wow!

Under her stage name, Miss Bailey … err … Ms. Cowl received acclaim for interpreting the great Shakespearean heroines — it is reported that, in 1923, she played the Bard's Juliet over 1000 time consecutively, thus breaking Lou Gehrig's record — while still taking time to dip her toe in the Bastard Art in such feature-length fare as 1915's *Garden of Lies* (wherein she essayed a dual role) and 1917's *The Spreading Dawn* (which featured genre favorite, Edmund Lowe, among the dramatis personae). The lady was still going strong in the late 1940s, when she starred (opposite Henry Daniell) in a revival of St. John Ervine's *The First Mrs. Fraser* at Broadway's Shubert Theatre. As Jane Cowl, the playwright, she penned *Lilac Time* and *Daybreak* (both 1917), *Information Please* (1918), and *Smilin' Through* (1919), all either in partnership with Jane Murfin, or under the pseudonym, Allen Langdon Martin, or both. Details are fairly ambiguous. She closed out her literary career in 1928, when — together with Theodore Charles — she co-authored *The Jealous Moon*.

Miss Murfin, a playwright and a screenwriter in her own right, adapted to the screen not only the stage pieces she and Miss Cowl had crafted, but also work that was disseminated solely her own name *and* any number of novels, stories and dramas that had been published over others' names. Genre-wise, Miss Murfin is conjoined with First National's (*The Savage*, 1926; *vid.*); genre-near-miss-wise, the lady's name may also be spotted in the credits of 1929's talkie, *Seven Keys to Baldpate*.

There's a bit of a kerfuffle over the relationship between "Smilin' Through," the ballad composed by Arthur Penn in 1919, and the play by "Allan Langdon Martin" that debuted in December that same year. Just whether the song led to some rewriting of the play or awareness of the theme of the play influenced Mr. Penn's lyrics and music is still the topic of some discussion online, in print, and possibly (albeit not very likely) over coffee someplace. Maudlin is as maudlin does, and the third stanza of the ballad — the most relevant, Kleenex-wise — is as follows:

> And if ever I'm left in this world all alone
> I shall wait for my call patiently
> For if Heaven be kind
> I shall wait there to find
> Those two eyes o' blue
> Come smilin' through at me

Anyhow, the following synopsis is taken from *The AFI Catalog*:

> On the very day that John Carteret is to wed Moonyeen, Jeremiah Wayne, one of Moonyeen's rejected suitors, inadvertently kills her while attempting to shoot John. Twenty years later, John's niece, Kathleen, announces to his shock that she is going to marry Jeremiah Wayne's son, Kenneth. John bitterly opposes the match and orders Kathleen never to see Kenneth again. The World War breaks out, and Kenneth goes to France, where he is badly wounded. Returning to the United States, he allows Kathleen (who has waited patiently for him to return) to believe that he has come to love another. Kathleen is heartbroken, and John, feeling her sorrow keenly, arranges for her to be united with Kenneth. With the young lovers together again, John quietly dies, joining the spirit of Moonyeen in the Great Beyond.

Now, we're all for tales of lifelong hate-fests—like the one that John Carteret has been conducting—but we've seen all that sort of thing before, what with our literary and pop-culture awareness of hate-fests involving everyone from the Montagues and the Capulets to the Hatfields and the McCoys. We're in this for the supernatural stuff—the "spirit of Moonyeen in the Great Beyond" and such. Genre fans counting on the 10 March 1922 *Variety* for the skinny on the supernatural in *this* film, though, might very well have opted to stay home and fold socks. To wit:

> The story centers around the life of John Cartaret. On his wedding day his bride is killed by a rival suitor. Years later his adopted niece falls in love with the son of the man who had committed the crime. Hate had predominated the life of Cartaret for all members of the family of the murderer. That his niece had fallen in love with the culprit's son sends his blood to a boiling point. Only after much persuasion he is made tosee the light, with the story culminating in a happy romance for the young couple.
> Cartaret dies peacefully after having been won over to the other side.

Folks looking for shots of ectoplasm or evidence of Eternal Joy would not, we think, be encouraged by such piddling (and ambiguous) phrases as "to see the light" or "won over to the other side." While the play was still fresh in the public's mind (a *Film Daily* review from the 5 March 1922 maintains that—as of the previous week—Jane Cowl had been appearing in it onstage in Brooklyn!), reviewing the celluloid adaptation without so much as hinting of its otherworldly dimensions seems to have been the wrong road to hoe. Still, this lack of focus may not have been entirely the fault of *Variety*'s "Hart" or his critical colleagues. In an editorial printed in the 15 April 1922 issue of *Moving Picture World*, Arthur James may have been alluding to the fuzzy publicity campaign the studio accorded the picture when he wrote of his "astonishment" that First National "made so little noise" about the movie.

MPW had reviewed the film a month earlier (in its 18 March 1922 number) and did not fail to mention Moonyeen's discorporate presence, if only briefly: "The ghost stuff is unusually well done." Having viewed the print at the Library of Congress, we found most of the ghost stuff to be the usual double exposure, although cinematographers Roy (*A Daughter of the Gods*) Hunt and Charles (*Sparrows, Sunrise*) Rosher brought an unusually high level of expertise and artistry to the picture. Still, there are also some fairly interesting shots of a moonlit John Cartaret (Wyndham Standing) trying to summon back Moonyeen from the Land Beyond with a doll his darling had given him. Some sort of nod to Voodoo? Or just another tug at the heartstrings?

The most pertinent comments on Cartaret's Soul Mate are to be found in the 17 April 1922 issue of *The New York Times*, wherein we read:

> The dead bride is kept personally in the main story and her union with Carteret at the end is actualized by means of spiritualistic manifestations, and it is in presenting these, as may be imagined, that the photoplay becomes most characteristically and expressively a motion picture. The scenes in which the spirits appear are the best, from the cinematographic point of view, and also, it would seem, from the sentimental. They are all effectively done, especially that in which the rejuvenated spirit of Carteret leaves its aged body to join the eternally young spirit of Moonyeen.

The first and fullest entry we've made featuring Norma Talmadge is *De Luxe Annie*, Wyndham Standing gets his due in our essay on *Earthbound*, Harrison Ford garners some attention in *The Crystal Gazer*, and Glenn Hunter's name pops up yet again in *Puritan Passions*. Just FYI, *Smilin' Through* marked the cinematic debut—and, apparently, the only silent film appearance—of character man, Gene Lockhart.

The picture was remade twice (in 1932, also directed by Sidney A. Franklin, and in 1941, helmed by Frank Borzage), although neither sound version was as faithful to the Broadway play as was the 1922 original.

—*JTS*

The Soul of Bronze

The Soul of Bronze. Houdini Picture Corporation, c. 19 November 1921(?), Length undetermined, Existence debated
CAST: Harry Houdini
CREDITS: *Producer* Harry Houdini; *Scenario* Henry Rousell; Based on a story by Georges Le Faure (additional information unavailable)

One of Houdini's most famous stage illusions was "The Vanishing Elephant," wherein a pachyderm of appreciable heft lumbered into a box of sufficient size to accommodate it and then vanished from same to the astonishment of ticket-holders. Eyewitnesses to the effect may have failed to notice that while it took four stagehands to bring the box out onto the stage, it required nearly a dozen to remove it afterwards, but there's no doubt that post-performance pubs and parlors were filled with spirited conversation (and repeated rounds of spirits) after miracles such as this came to pass.

The Soul of Bronze, a bizarre feature supposedly adapted by Henry Roussell from a story by Georges Le Faure, was to have been the first feature of the (in 1921) newly-formed Houdini Picture Corporation. We say *was to have been* as there is some controversy as to whether the film was ever made. William McIlhany—magical film historian, collector and author—responded to our query for help by opining, "It was never made to my knowledge." And he ought to know.

Still, Harry Houdini himself submitted the copyright registration synopsis (quoted in its entirety, below) to the appropriate authorities on the 19 November 1921, along with the notation, "532 prints." In an email to us, Library of Congress librarian, Josie L. Walters-Johnston, cleared up the vagaries of that phrase: "'Prints' does not refer to the number of film prints made, it's the number of still shots from the film sent to the Copyright Office for descriptive purposes; as you might guess, these are nowhere to be found, which is often the case with the early films."

We can easily buy the photos' disappearance, but the fact that Houdini sent a detailed plot summary—accompanied by *five hundred thirty-two movie stills*—seems to indicate that *some* footage was shot on this title.

Was *The Soul of Bronze* Houdini's ultimate illusion, or merely an example of the master showman's letting his imagination get the best of him? The story was (or wasn't) as follows.

> In an interior town in France live Jacques and his fiancée, Nanette. Jacques is an engineer employed in a gun works of great magnitude.

One day they are out on a picnic. On their return home, their wagon breaks down. Captain Duval van Jean, of the French army, comes along in a two-seated automobile and offers to give them a lift. Nanette goes along in the automobile to be taken home while Jacques, the engineer, remains with the wagon.

On the way home Nanette is attracted to Capt. Duval van Jean who, by a coincidence, is working on the invention of a new cannon which is being constructed in the same factory where Jacques is employed.

Many meetings between Capt. Duval van Jean and Nanette follow and, as Jacques is somewhat older than Nanette, she soon breaks with him and announces her engagement to the officer. Jacques has watched the captain woo Nanette on various occasions and when Nanette makes her decision his jealousy toward the officer knows no bounds.

The last day on which the cannon invention of the officer is to be molded, the great traveling crane is carrying along the various ingredients which are to be poured into the fiery molten bronze, the ingredients a secret known only to Capt. Duval van Jean. As it is traveling to the proper place, the crane stops and will not turn over to allow the contents to drop into the cauldron below. Jacques is shouting orders to the man who is at the foot of the crane and who does not seem to be able to make it function. Capt. Duval van Jean grabs a big monkey wrench and starts to climb to the top of the traveling crane. He balances there carefully and manages to loosen the bolt. He starts to descend but the heat below must have affected him for he faints, falls, manages to grasp the cable and dangles there right over the terrible cauldron filled with white-heated bronze.

In that instant Jacques sees a vision of the captain seated under a tree with Nanette. Jealousy causes his brain to reel. He runs to the bottom of the windlass, pulls the lever and precipitates the officer into the cauldron below. It is a terrible scene. He walks out perspiring with fear and horror. He joins the crowd, no one suspecting that he is a murderer.

When the bronze is poured into the mold everyone takes off his hat knowing that the officer is being buried forever.

The cannon is finished and flowers are brought and placed in memory of the captain. The cannon also bears a brass oval plate, inscribed:

> Sacred to the memory of Capt. Duval van Jean,
> Born 1867, died March 16th, 1914.

Nanette is soon dressed in black and is sorrowfully led away. Jacques is shown with clenched fists and with perspiration streaming down his face.

The next day the war starts. Jacques enters the service of his country and emerges from many a bloody battle. The time comes when, after an assault by the Germans, Jacques alone is left alive of the little French group. He is badly wounded. Shells burst about him, and as he is lying on the ground, a vision appears to him and he rises. He staggers to his feet.

The vision points to the cannon. He staggers, manages to reach it and finds a full complement of shells. He starts to load and as he does so he clenches the cannon for support. It has the oval brass plate with Duval's inscription on it which he reads through his misty, stark eyes. The vision is the spirit of Duval.

Again and again he loads the cannon. He has managed to get his range and decisively turns the tide of battle just before he staggers and falls against the cannon wheel. As he expires, the spirit of the man whose life he took takes the French flag and places it over Jacques' body.

The essence/existence of *The Soul of Bronze* pose a particular challenge to the researcher, as the movie was/was to have been the fourth (in a total out put of six) pictures that Houdini either appeared in, and/or produced, and/or wrote, and/or directed. Had it been his earliest film venture — or even his last — doubt

about its production and/or release would be more readily comprehensible. (It was/was to have been the first production of the Houdini Picture Corporation, though, so a hiccup on the financing end for the would-be mogul might have brought things to a speedy halt.)

Whither Harry in the story as posited? We assume that he appeared/was to have appeared in the picture (probably as Capt. Duval van Jean, the guy who gets the gal, has the death scene, and is resurrected as forgiving hero), even if there's no record of any of the dramatis personae bearing the initials H.H. (The King of Handcuffs' only cinematic alter-ego to foreswear the "Double H" was Quentin Locke [*The Master Mystery*, 1920], and Harry was being a real cutie in coming up with *that* one.)

We could probably be forgiven for imagining Houdini's thought processes here: the audience would be on the edge of its seat, waiting for old Harry to somehow escape from what was obviously an inevitable plunge into the cauldron, only to be blown away when they saw him fall to his death, as if he were some sort of mortal man! And then the moviegoers would witness how Capt. Duval van Jean — the biggest man and greatest patriot who ever lived — helped save his country from beyond the grave, even escaping (momentarily) the arms of the Grim Reaper himself to place *les couleurs* over his fallen comrade. And thus stealing away both Jacques' glory *and* the closing fade.

Of course, the vagaries of time and space have stolen away *everything* in this case.

— JTS

The Soul's Cycle

The Soul's Cycle. Centaur Film Co., David Horsley Productions/ Mutual Film Corp., Mutual Masterpictures De Luxe Edition, 12 February 1916, 5 reels [LOST]

CAST: Margaret Gibson (*Nadia/Agnes*); John Oaker (*Lucian/ Arthur*); George Claire, Jr. (*Syrus, Nadia's Father*); George Stanley (*Theron*); Roy Watson (*Henry Kimball*)

CREDITS: *Producer* David Horsley; *Director* Ulysses Davis; *Scenario* Theodosia Harris

We're dealing with the perennially-pissed-off ancient Greek gods here — the Mount Olympus crowd to whom no one (hopefully) still is donating time or money — so this five-reeler has found its foothold on Mount Appendix.

First bit of incense in the fire is the recap, provided by *The AFI Catalog*:

> In ancient Greece, Nadia elopes with Lucian to avoid marrying Theron, a powerful senator who, enraged at being jilted, has the couple captured and thrown into an active volcano. The gods punish Theron, however, turning him into a lion and condemning him to stay that way until he makes amends for killing Nadia and Lucian. In modern times, Agnes is in love with Arthur, who works as a Wall Street broker and hunts big game as a hobby. Rival broker Henry Kimball wants to kill Arthur, and so frees the lion the amateur hunter has captured. Instead of attacking Arthur, however, the lion, who is really Theron, kills Henry, and, by so guaranteeing the happiness of Agnes and Arthur, frees the ancient Greek's soul from the animal's body.

Okay; let's take this one slowly...

(A) Theron is lionized (lionated?) for committing cold-blooded murder and then redeemed for committing coldblooded murder. Sounds fair...

(B) We can either assume that the gods turned Theron into a lion in Greece, which made him not only cursed but absolutely unique, or that his soul was zapped from his body (leaving his cadaver where, exactly?) and sent hurtling into a real-life lion, then hunting or mating or napping somewhere in Africa, India, or maybe even the Rocky Mountains. (The kind of lion Theron has become is left rather vague in the supporting documents.) This theory of the transmigration of souls is supported by the last line of the synopsis, which was taken from contemporary trade coverage.

(C) With that synopsis, but without the film, we can only surmise that Arthur — the big-game-hunter hobbyist — doesn't really *shoot* big game, but rather (as he does here) pens them up, looks at them, maybe pokes them with a stick, and then lets them go. Or maybe he *does* shoot them, once they've been "captured" and are at fairly close range in their cage. If the former, Arthur is a nice guy, but definitely not a "big-game hunter." If the latter, Arthur is a bastard, Agnes is a sap, and Henry Kimball is inadvertently about to dispense justice and not indulge in assault with a deadly mammal.

Where the Greek gods are concerned, though, we know well enough at this point not to bandy words or assign blame: they are a selfish, horny, vengeful lot, and the real reason that Theron got screwed was probably because Zeus wanted Nadia for himself, and only Hera knows who else wanted Lucian. How many demi-gods can you fit on the head of a pin, anyhow?

The framework of *The Soul's Cycle* is a familiar one to silent movie aficionados: parallel tales wherein either the same moral is taught at either end of recorded history, or the sins committed early on are atoned for in our modern age. Here, we're obviously dealing with Door Number Two. Still, if Theron's soul was assigned the body of a lion prowling an African savanna, the upside (for the lion, at any rate) was that the animal immediately became invulnerable; not until Theron did a charitable act (as a lion? Paging Androcles!) would the ex–Senator's soul be freed and the superannuated big cat be free to find rest. No big game hunter (including Arthur) was going take it down by putting a couple into its side from a hundred yards (or five feet) away, and maybe this frees up our Wall Street bwana from the dreaded conundrum of Exhibit C (above): at least he *tried* to shoot down the animal like an animal and failed.

The usual practice for these parallel tale set-ups was to have the same actors play the corresponding roles in both ends of the story, and *The Soul's Cycle* ran true to form. The unfortunate Nadia and the maybe-unfortunate Agnes was played by Margaret Gibson, born Ella Margaret Gibson and later known as Patricia Palmer, one of the slew of folks who made deathbed confessions to shooting William Desmond Taylor way back when. Miss Gibson/Palmer made about 150 films in a career that ended when Silence Was Broken, albeit most of them were shorts and virtually none other than *Cycle* lay within our parameters. Lucian/Arthur were impersonated by John Oaker, a Canadian whose silent film credentials played out at about two dozen appearances within a half-dozen years; he, too, had noth-

ing to offer to fans such as us other than the film under discussion. Theron (the man) was George Stanley, a San Franciscan who moved south to get in the flickers in 1912, showed his face in a hundred of them (again, only *Cycle* was genre-friendly), and then apparently called it quits in 1923. Theron (the lion) received no screen credit, albeit publicity on the film reveals that the King of the Beasts appeared courtesy of the Bostock Animals, a circus that had even then been around for decades.

The big horror "name" in the film was thus Roy Kimball, if only because he had a *second* genre credit (1925's *Wolf Blood*), and a tad more on him may be found in our coverage of that movie.

Intriguingly, *The Soul's Cycle* was produced by The Centaur Film Company, was written by a lady named Theodosia, and was directed by a man named Ulysses. (In all fairness, the picture was co-produced by David Horsley Productions, a firm that obviously had no ties with Greek nomenclature; still, if you play along the centaur-"horse" lines...) Centaur for the most part cranked out shorts which were, for the most part, released between 1914 and 1916 and which, to a large extent, featured the four cast members mentioned above. Many of those were helmed by Ulysses Davis, who— despite his classical moniker — was from South Amboy, New Jersey; like everyone else's (save Kimball's), Davis's resume includes nothing that would get our attention apart from than this tale of lions and rotters.

Theodosia Harris— about which even *less* is known — gets a rather complex sentence on the bounce. Other than *Cycle*, the lady penned the screenplay for *The House of a Thousand Scandals*, a nondescript meller about grandfathers' estates that is memorable only because the film attempted to rip off the title of *The House of a Thousand Candles*, a contemporaneous feature film — based on a then-very-popular novel concerning grandfathers' estates—covered at length in this book (see also, *Haunting Shadows*).

Woof!   — *JTS*

The Speed Spook

The Speed Spook. East Coast Films/East Coast Films, 30 August 1924, 7 reels/6,750 feet, available
CAST: Johnny Hines ("*Blue Streak*" Billings); Faire Binney (*Betty West*); Edmund Breese (*Chuck*); Warner Richmond (*Jud Skerrit*); Frank Losee (*Sheriff West*); Henry West (*Hiram Smith*)
CREDITS: *Director* Charles Hines; *Scenario* Raymond S. Harris; based on a story by William Wallace Cook; *Titles* Ralph Spence; *Cinematographers* Charles E. Gilson, John Geisel

Still another film turning on an invention found somewhere in that imaginative gamut running from the unlikely to the downright impossible, *The Speed Spook* was also still another film centering on the energetic comedy of Johnny Hines (see *Chinatown Charlie*). Directed by Charles Hines (Johnny's brother), the picture was received with neither a hoot nor a Hosanna, and it finds its way herein because (a) who wouldn't want a car that would leave the cops in the dust? and (b) Mordaunt Hall's intriguing observation about the plot's debt to— of all people!— Washington Irving.

The story isn't much, at least, not per *The AFI Catalog*:

"Blue Streak" Billings returns to his hometown to prove the qualities of the Comet brand of automobile sold by his girl, Betty West, whose trade has suffered through the schemings of a wealthier competitor. While exploiting his "driverless" car, he learns that his rival is faking the ballots for the sheriff's election, exposes him, and identifies himself as the mysterious driver of the car.

We sat through a video of the picture and feel the AFI summation is good to go. Mordaunt Hall's take on the picture — as related in the 21 October 1924 edition of *The New York Times* — incorporates as much of the spook factor as it does the speed, and the canny reviewer's spot-on recognizing the source of the pseudo-science fiction plot is the *raison d'être* for this brief essay.

> The story is a species of modernized "Headless Horseman," being concerned with the activities of a mysterious, driverless automobile which periodically plunges through the streets of Westwood with amazing speed, turning corners with uncanny ease and rapidity, and eluding the Sheriff by suddenly disappearing in a country lane....
> The driverless automobile sequences are interestingly pictured, the car having a wavy streak of white on the gray surface. It is seen dashing through the streets, alarming the citizens and annoying the Sheriff, and the way in which it is made to disappear is quite unexpected and original.

The car's so-called super-science is debunked at the denouement, when the skinny on the "ghost driver" is also forthcoming. Still, the unfolding of the plot fabric must have given the audiences their money's worth, as in 1924 ticket-buyers were more or less conditioned to have anything that smacked on the supernatural explained away before the music stopped and the lights were raised.

Faire Binney, *Spook*'s ingénue, was the younger sister of the actress, Constance Binney (see 1921's *The Case of Becky*). Faire made a couple of dozen (more or less) rather nondescript features between 1918 and 1925, and then left the industry for a quarter-century before returning to a brief series of uncredited bits in a handful of decent, early 1950s' movies (like 1952's *Monkey Business* and 1954's *The Eddie Cantor Story*).

Of greater relevance to us was character man, Edmund Breese, who started off in pictures as the lead in1914's *The Master Mind*, reprising the role he had created on Broadway. Breese, a Brooklynite, had trod those Broadway boards in a variety of productions — including a short run as the lead in Percy MacKaye's supernatural thriller, *The Scarecrow*, and a brief turn as Romeo in *You-Know-What* — and he returned to the New York theater scene whenever he could maneuver some stage work into his film schedule. Appearing in such silent genre fare as 1923's *Little Red School House* and 1928's *The Haunted House* (see essays on both), the busy actor played an array of character types and ethnic parts into the Sound Era and up to his death in April 1936. For all that — and despite his association with the popular Torchy Blane series of short films — Breese's name (and accoutered face) is perhaps most strongly linked to his sundry early–1930s, casually racist, Oriental roles: his Le Fong in Stuart Paton's 1931 meller, *Chinatown after Dark*; his Yu Chang (in company with Edward G. Robinson's deadly Wong Low Get) in William Wellman's *The Hatchet Man* (1932); or his Doctor Wong, whose pronouncements keep W.C. Fields' Professor Quail quarantined in Eddie Sutherland's 1933 comic classic, *International House* — all may spring to mind more quickly than the man's more frequent Occidental portrayals.

For the record, the titles for *The Speed Spook* were penned by Ralph (*The Gorilla*, *Sh! The Octopus*) Spence.

— *JTS*

The Star of India

The Star of India. Blaché Features, Inc./Blaché Features, 17 November 1913, 4 reels [LOST]
CAST: Fraunie Fraunholtz (*Captain Kenneth*); Claire Whitney (*Alice*); Andrew Watson (*Hindu servant*); Joseph Levering (*Richard Dare*); Fred English (*Carrick*); with James O'Neill, Theodore Burkart, William Boyd, Herbert Baker
CREDITS: *Director* Herbert Blaché

The "Star of India" was a fabulous blue sapphire from Sri Lanka that was purchased by robber baron, J.P. Morgan, who later donated it to the Museum of Natural History in New York (where it can be found today). In spite of its title, our film has nothing to do with the real Star of India, but is, rather, yet another variation on William Wilkie Collins' *The Moonstone* which seems to have been quite popular in the mid 1910s, at least with scenario writers.

Our synopsis is based on the cutting continuity of the film:

> The Star of India is a diamond with a curse on it; anyone who sees it becomes obsessed with having it for himself. The stone rests in the forehead of a statue of the Buddha in a temple in India. The rajah shows the jewel to British attaché Captain Kenneth and the man immediately falls under its spell. Kenneth tunnels from his room to right underneath the floor of the temple and overpowers the blind priest who is the jewel's caretaker. However, Kenneth is bitten by one of the priest's poisonous snakes. Kenneth makes it back to his room but his wounded arm turns from purple to black and he wanders out into the woods. His cries are heard by Richard Dare and his Hindu guide. Kenneth dies and Dare takes the diamond, but he has to fight his guide for it.
> Dare returns to the United States, but his Hindu guide is not far behind. Dare is in love with Alice, but he has a rival named Carrick who spies on the couple when Dare comes to visit. Dare shows Alice the diamond, and she goes from sweet to covetous in barely in an instant. Dare declines to give her the jewel and the two have a quarrel which ends with Alice returning his engagement ring. Later Carrick tells Alice he will get the diamond for her, and Alice agrees to be his wife if he succeeds.
> Carrick meets with Red Harry and his gang of crooks in a nearby tavern. The Hindu guide has also made contact with the criminals. Dare accidentally injures a newsboy named Willie and brings him to his house to recover. Dare reads a newspaper account of the theft of the Star of India and decides to contact the British consul about returning it. He shows the stone to the newsboy who is not affected by its power. Dare hides the jewel in a flower pot for the night and then gives Willie a dollar and sends him home. Meanwhile, no longer under the power of the stone, Alice regrets her actions.
> Later Red Harry and his gang break into Dare's house and demand the diamond. Dare refuses to give it up so the crooks wrap him in a carpet and carry him to their den. Coincidentally, Willie also lives there but gives no sign of recognition when he sees Dare. The crooks torture Dare with a hot iron to make him reveal the diamond's whereabouts. To spare his friend more suffering, Willie tells Red Harry where the jewel is hidden. Willie also slips Dare a note telling him he will help him escape.
> Disguised as a telephone repairman, Red gains entrance to

Dare's house just as Alice turns up to ask Dare's forgiveness. Red finds the Star of India but Alice, watching from behind a curtain, sees his false moustache come off. Suspicious, she follows Red via taxi. Meanwhile, Willie has freed Dare and gives him a rope so he may escape the thieves' den via the roof. Red returns and tells the gang he was unable to find the jewel. When he sees Alice spying through a window, he has her brought inside and tied up.

Dare returns home to find the jewel gone. His butler tells him about Alice and the two of them head for the gang's hideout. They arrive just in time to see the crooks bundle Alice and Willie off in a van. They follow them to another house where Alice is again tied up. Dare has a shootout with the crooks. Carrick discovers Harry has the jewel, wrests it from him and flees, but the Hindu guide follows him. Dare, Willie and Alice escape but the gang pursues them. Willie goes for the police.

The Hindu catches up with Carrick at the top of a hill and stabs him in the back, but both fall from the precipice to the mud below and are killed. Dare and Alice find them and take the diamond from Carrick's stiff hand. The police arrive and the gang hides in a sewer, but the police flood the sewer and the crooks drown. Later at home Dare gives Alice the engagement ring she had returned. Willie comes in with a newspaper featuring a headline about the Star's return to India. The closing shot shows the blind priest putting the diamond back in its proper place.

It's not clear how the power of the diamond works. One can understand why Willie, a pure-of-heart urchin, would not be affected by the curse, but the spell seems very temporary when it comes to Dare and Alice. Perhaps we are to assume that good people are able to quickly shake off the deadly attraction while corrupt characters are helpless in its grip.

The notion of Captain Kenneth singlehandedly *tunneling* from his room to the temple seems a bit outrageous; surely even Edmond Dantès and the Abbé Faria would have been daunted by such an endeavor. A still shows Captain Kenneth popping his head up through the floor of the temple, looking around like a groundhog in search of its shadow; the priest does appear a tad disconcerted but, in the background, the Buddha is as placid as ever. (One of the trade papers, apparently unfamiliar with the accouterments of Buddhist temples, describes the statue as "an ugly idol!")

The reviewer for *Motion Picture World*, while acknowledging that the story had (by the 6 December 1913) *already* been told many times, still found that "lovers of melodrama can make no complaint for there is no lack of thrills and sensations." The anonymous critic *did* think the story was "overdrawn in spots" with situations that "sometimes seem to be forced," and he *was* disturbed by the torture and the high body count: "we regret to record certain scenes of violence that would better be omitted at this particular time when the question of censorship is being unduly agitated." Nonetheless, he found the photography, acting and sets to be commendable.

The *Motion Picture News* scribe (writing on the same date as his *MPW* competitor) thought the film "an excellent vehicle for several novel and startling features" and went on to elaborate: "There are magnificent palace scenes, the Star of India, a huge diamond in the temple protected by serpents galore, and a blind priest, a race through the air on a slack wire, a den of thieves, a flooded sewer which snuffs out several lives, a fight on a mountain top, elephants and several other unusual elements."

On the other hand, *The New York Dramatic Mirror* (31 De-

cember 1913) dismissed the film as a "melodramatic offering that staggers our credence" and found that so much of the action was devoted to the heroine's predicament that the quest for the jewel was "almost forgotten" though really of little interest in the first place.

The Star of India was the first feature of Blaché Features Inc., whose president, Herbert Blaché, was married to the more celebrated Alice Guy, who had both founded the Solax Film Company in 1910 and ran its studio in Fort Lee, New Jersey. Guy named her husband president of Solax in 1913, but apparently that wasn't enough and Herbert insisted on forming a company bearing his own name. Blaché Features used the Solax studio and its actors and personnel, so it's not clear what real difference there was between the two companies. In fact, *Moving Picture World* described the *The Star of India* as "being produced by Herbert Blaché of the Solax Company." Solax pretty much ceased production the next year, while Blaché Features focused on making four-reelers rather than the shorter films with which Solax was associated. More on Herbert Blaché can be found in the entry on *The Untameable*, while his long-suffering spouse Alice Guy is represented in *The Dream Woman* (another film from Blaché Features).

Stars Fraunie Fraunholtz (Captain Kenneth) and Claire Whitney (Alice) receive their due in the entry on *Woman of Mystery* (another work by Madame Blaché). Joseph Levering was Solax's resident villain, but he's the heroic (and aptly named) "Dare" in *The Star of India*. Levering was a onetime athlete who left behind his success in baseball and track to become leading man to stage star, Maxine Elliott. No doubt his athletic prowess served him well, as he was made to climb up roofs and prance across wires in *India*. We shall meet him again in these pages as the star of *The Temptations of Satan* and the director of *Luring Shadows*.

The *Motion Picture News* review lists "Willie Boyd" among the cast. According to *The AFI Catalog*, this is William "Stage" Boyd, well known for his performance as Sergeant Quirt in *What Price Glory* and most notorious for being a hardcore carouser whose antics almost ruined the career of *another* William Boyd: the De Mille star who later played Hopalong Cassidy. It's not known which part "Stage"—assuming it *was* he—played in *The Star of India*.

The genuine "Star of India" actually *was* stolen in 1964 by a crook named "Murph the Surf" and a couple of his pals. They didn't tunnel through the floor of the Museum of Natural History, but simply came in by way of a bathroom window they'd unlocked earlier in the day. No poisonous snakes awaited them and, thanks to a combination of incredibly lax security and dumb luck, they made away with the "Star of India" and some other treasures. In this instance, however, life did not imitate art, and the gang was ultimately undone, not by a curse, but by the FBI.   — HN

Stark Mad

Stark Mad. Warner Brothers Pictures/Warner Bros., 2 Feb 1929, 7 reels/6,681 feet sound version; 4,917 feet, silent version [LOST]

CAST: H.B. Warner (*Percy Dangerfield**); Louise Fazenda (*Mrs. Fleming*); Jacqueline Logan (*Irene*); Henry B. Walthall (*Captain Rhodes*); Claude Gillingwater (*James Rutherford*); John Miljan (*Dr. Milo*); Andre Beranger (*Simpson, the guide*); Warner Richmond (*First Mate*); Floyd Shackelford (*Sam, the cook*); Lionel Belmore (*Amos Sewald*)

CREDITS: *Director* Lloyd Bacon; *Assistant Director* Frank Shaw; *Scenario* Harvey Gates; *Story* Jerome Kingston; *Titles* Francis Powers; *Cinematographer* Barney McGill; *Music:* Louis Silvers

"Not since *The Terror* has a talking picture so spookily ludicrous come to the screen."

— promo for *Stark Mad*

In 1929, the process whereby theaters converted to sound was marching along inexorably. Billings, the largest city in Montana, boasted four movie theaters, and the switchover to sound in one of them, The Regent, was the subject of an article in *The Billings Gazette*:

In announcing the change to sound pictures Eugene O'Keefe and Max Fregger of the Theater Amusement Company which operates the Babcock, Lyric and Regent theaters pointed out that virtually all the outstanding films of the day are made with sound and there are at the present time more good pictures than the Babcock could show from one season to another and still present all the latest attractions to the Billings theater-going public. [The Babcock was the only sound game in town, having been wired the year before.] For this reason it was decided to install sound picture devices at the Regent and present many of the high class sound pictures which ordinarily might not be brought to the Babcock. The Regent will show this season some of the outstanding successes of last season, including some films which were shown at the Babcock and others which have never been booked here before [12 September 1929].

It took 45 days to convert The Regent into a sound theater. The first film to be shown there was *Stark Mad*, accompanied by some Vitaphone shorts. While the market for silent films was shrinking, the transition to sound wasn't happening overnight and there was still the foreign market to consider so silent versions of talkies continued to be made. *Stark Mad* was Warner Brothers' follow-up to its earlier horror talkie, *The Terror* (see entry in appendix), and was likewise released as a silent. Critics ignored these mute versions as poor cousins to the originals and we are following suit, relegating them to the Appendix in spite of the full-blooded horror content of a film like *Stark Mad*.

Like *The Terror*, the sound *Stark Mad* had no written credits; both cast scrawl and technical list were read aloud. In the case of the latter film, the credits are read by a masked figure who then offers a warning to the audience; we could not discover whether a *written* warning was afforded the viewers of the silent version:

Now the Warner Brothers and the management of this theater offer a cash reward for anyone caught dead or alive who in any way reveals or exposes the secret of this mystery. We all have a past and you can never tell but some day you may to keep a secret from us.

Perhaps fearing murderous bounty hunters, the writer of the press-book synopsis for *Stark Mad* was very vague and confusing. However, having fearlessly ignored the similar threats made by the maniac at the end of *Night of Terror*, we have made bold to supplement the press-book with some information from the dialogue script to come up with a synopsis that is (almost) coherent.

Bob Rutherford and Simpson, his guide, have disappeared while on a hunting trip to a dangerous part of the Central American jungle. Rutherford's father organizes a search party which anchors at the point on the coast where the hunter was last seen. The party includes Mrs. Fleming; his secretary; Irene Hawley, Bob's fiancée; Captain Rhodes, commander of the yacht (called "The Regret"); Amos Sewald, an explorer who has been engaged to head the expedition; Dr. Milo, a naturalist; and, of course the elder Rutherford.

As the film begins one of The Regret's sailors is being buried at sea. The sailor had accompanied Captain Rhodes ashore and, according to Rhodes, had been fatally bitten by a poisonous Batopilas snake. The crew, fearful that the place is jinxed, threatens mutiny. Percy Dangerfield, an authority on Central America, canoes 400 miles to intercept the party, bringing with him Simpson the guide, who has escaped from the jungle. Simpson is a raving maniac constantly talking about an ape. Dangerfield attempts to dissuade the party from landing since Simpson's condition practically proves the death of young Rutherford. Mr. Rutherford, however, insists on continuing the search for his son.

Dangerfield is skeptical of Rhodes' claim as to how the sailor died, stating that there are no Batopilas snakes in the region. Dangerfield also is at odds with Sewald, who seems more interested in exploring the inside of a liquor bottle than the jungle. Dangerfield's credentials are questioned, but they cannot be verified as the ship's radio has been mysteriously destroyed. Irene is strangely attracted to Dangerfield and later admits that however much she hopes to find Bob Rutherford alive, she is not truly in love with him.

Leaving Simpson chained to the deck, the party goes ashore, bringing with them a pack of bloodhounds. Making their way through the perilous jungle, the group discovers the ruins of an ancient Mayan temple and decides to spend the night in its spacious halls. The baying bloodhounds dash off after some unseen foe. Rutherford, Irene and Dangerfield follow the dogs and come upon a huge door leading into more ruins that were apparently the site of human sacrifice. They discover a gigantic ape chained to the floor. Suddenly, Captain Rhodes disappears.

The party regroups and then discovers that the ape has vanished. Later Rhodes is found unconscious. Upon awakening, he claims that he was gripped by the throat by a pair of hairy talons and dragged off. It is assumed the ape was responsible. A note is found warning the group to leave or die. Suspicions and distrust among the group continue to grow. A strange whistling sound is heard and Mr. Rutherford insists it must be from his son since it sounds like their old hunting signal. No one is found.

Later it is discovered that the ape has learned to fasten and unfasten his chain, and does it instinctively when returning from some foray. A poisoned arrow narrowly misses Dangerfield. The lanterns have been going off periodically and ultimately the oil containers are found to be punctured. The lights go out and Sewald becomes hysterical, screaming that he won't tell. He is promptly killed by a poisoned arrow. Except for Irene, the party suspects Dangerfield of the crime. However, Dangerfield has his own theory: "Now this killer stands among us. His body is sound … but his mind is warped. The man is stark mad."

The first mate of The Regret arrives with the news that Simpson the maniac has escaped. Dangerfield throws the poisoned arrow at Rhodes who catches it with his supposedly paralyzed right hand. Realizing that he has been exposed, Rhodes rushes out of the room in which they are all congregated, bolting the door after him. He releases a mechanism causing the floor to slowly disintegrate,

---

*The dialogue script and the preview transcript spell the character's name *Daingerfield*.

gradually dropping the stones into the quagmire below. As Dangerfield lifts Irene up to the window the ape appears and drags her through. Simpson turns up and, with some cajoling from the group, finally unbolts the door just in time to release the party before the fall of the entire floor. Rhodes is killed by the ape.

Simpson, his reason slowly returning, offers an explanation: He and Bob Rutherford ran across a hermit who lived in the temple. Once a big game hunter, the hermit has been driven mad by the jungle but he has discovered a fabulous treasure in the ruins. He also owned the ape who is actually as "tame as a lamb." Fearing that Bob and Simpson meant to steal his treasure, the hermit killed Bob and imprisoned and tortured Simpson. Simpson finally escaped, killed the hermit, and buried him next to Bob. Simpson learned the strange whistling signal from Bob. He also witnessed Rhodes and the sailor discovering the treasure a few days earlier. Rhodes and the sailor quarreled and Rhodes killed his partner and came up with the snake-bite story. Dangerfield reveals that Rhodes was actually a notorious Central American criminal whose real identity Dangerfield suspected from the first.

The press-book synopsis has Rhodes actually carried off by a "strange monster with great hairy talons," but — unless it was the gorilla and the writer was just mixed up — that would seem to be a mistake (and the biggest dangling loose end in a plot full of them) as Rhodes only *claims* to have experienced such an abduction. Nor does the press-book version even *mention* the treasure, a rather significant story point.

According to the mysterious intoner of credits at the beginning of the film, the ape was "played by himself." Publicity claimed the character to be was an actual ape, named Bunawunga (!); however, stills would suggest that Bunawunga hailed from the wilds of Burbank, and not Africa.

There was not a great deal of critical enthusiasm for *Stark Mad*. "Mae Tinee" of *The Chicago Tribune* opined in the 5 March 1929 issue that "nothing believable or convincing" transpires in the film, and that it was full of vain attempts at humor and scares that would only work with the "amateur moviegoer." Between the constantly baying hounds, Louise Fazenda's annoying dialogue delivery, and Louis Silvers' overpowering musical accompaniment, Mae found that she "almost succumbed to a wave of nostalgia for the good old silent movies."

Some fondness for the Silent Era was also expressed by a writer in 9 March 1929 number of *The Harvard Crimson*:

> It seems highly unfortunate that the culmination of twenty years of experience and work in photography, lighting and acting, and all the other component parts of good moving pictures should be subordinated to poor directing and a worse scenario as they are in *Stark Mad* ... in order that we may hear as well as see…. In the whole picture there are really only two changes of scene, which is even less than one has on the stage. All sense of tempo, a quality which has been highly developed lately, is completely lost due to the necessity of close-ups as the characters speak.

Harrison's Reports (11 May 1929) found the film to be "pretty good entertainment" but inferior to *The Terror*. As per usual (see entry on *The Gorilla*), the reviewer was easily spooked by

Louise Fazenda takes on a gorilla; the smart money's on Louise. Fama est the gorilla was enacted by an uncredited Charles Gemora.

marauding apes: "The situations where he [the gorilla] is shown following the unaware characters and stretching his arms to grab them, the unaware victims just escaping by a hair's breadth should make most spectators gasp for breath."

Whatever the quality of the film, it did have a good cast, including Henry B. Walthall (see *The Raven*), Jacqueline Logan (*The Leopard Lady*) and H.B. Warner (*The Ghost Breaker*). The romance between Logan and the much older Warner is an unusual touch; perhaps it was meant to make up for the unrequited love Miss Logan (Mary Magdalene) felt for Warner (Jesus) in *The King of Kings*.   — HN

The Tame Cat

The Tame Cat. Dramafilms/Arrow Film Corp., July 1921, 5 reels/4,943 feet [LOST]

CAST: Ray Irwin, Marion Bradley

CREDITS: *Director* William Bradley; based on the short story, "The Rajah's Diamond," by Robert Louis Stevenson (*London Magazine*, June–October 1878).

This is one of a handful of *really* obscure features we've squinted at critically herein, and — despite our best efforts — our squinting has produced little more than doubt and a collective headache. It's poor consolation that the fact that there aren't many facts out there on this film means that — if our including it in our quest for comprehensiveness is shown to have been a mistake on our part somewhere down the line — we haven't wasted much of your time.

All evidence indicates that the picture marked the only cinematic appearance of both Ray Irwin and Marion Harding, and the second (and last) film by an outfit yclept Dramafilms, a company that had burst (or crept) on the scene with its *first film* (*Bitter Fruit*) a year earlier. Still, just as The Shadow would occasionally intone that "The seeds of crime bear bitter fruit," so did pruning *Bitter Fruit* lead to a small seed or two of information about Will Bradley, the guy who helmed it and *Cat*. We had no luck with respect to his (or Ray's or Marion's) debut or departure, but we did find out that (a) Will was employed in the industry (as a writer and a director) from around 1916 to about 1927; (b) he was associated (saith the IMDB) with a fantasy entitled *Moongold*, which the 12 October 1921 edition of *The Anaconda Standard* called "the outstanding short-subject sensation of the season"; and (c) the gentleman fancified/formalized his professional moniker into the more sonorous "Willard King Bradley" (quite possibly his birth name) around the time that *The Tame Cat* was released.

The AFI Catalog tersely notes "country of origin undetermined" with respect to our picture, so there's a possibility that the epic at hand was shot in foreign climes. No one knows, not even The Shadow. What's more, the catalog provides only the slimmest of details on the plot — "The gem is supposedly a creation of a Hindu magician, with a power of producing in the minds of all those who gaze upon it an overpowering desire to secure it, regardless of price" — and their researchers had to get *that* tidbit from the December 1921 issue of the *Motion Picture News Booking Guide*. That augurs not well at all. About the only thing the AFI did turn up that actually led somewhere is the pronouncement that the film based on "The Rajah's Diamond," a short story by Robert Louis Stevenson.

And that's what we *thought* we knew…

El problema starts out with the fact that Stevenson's original story — a tale of minxes marrying old men for money and of a singularly ineffectual private secretary — is rich in its complete lack of genre elements. Not a hint of a haint anywhere, nor of fakirs or felines. Thus, it must have been the Dramafilms scenarist who jazzed things up to the point that the picture — wherever it got off to shortly after whatever sort of release it had — turned on Hindu magicians rather than fops fearful of becoming freckled in the British sun. There are no cats whatsoever in the story (tame or otherwise), but a recurring term — *bandbox* — had us scurrying to a dictionary, whence we inferred that Mr. Stevenson did not use the term to refer to a small, home-run-happy baseball park, but, rather, to a "light cylindrical box for holding light articles of attire." And maybe — in some alternate universe — cats.

We then came across some information on the film from the records of the New York Board of Censors, but this was but the list of cuts demanded by that august body before the picture could be screened in the Empire State. Thus, if anything, we discovered clues as to what the picture perhaps once *had* been, but (in 1921 New York, at any rate) wasn't any longer:

> Reel 2: Eliminate those words from the subtitle: "The cleric longs for a bit of deviltry"
> Reel 3: Eliminate episode relating to the dagger and the deadly drug
>   Eliminate subtitle: "A minister of the gospel with lurking desire to mix in a bit of deviltry"
>   Eliminate subtitle: "Ah — the drug — I shall use it"
> Reel 4: Eliminate scene of pouring drug in coffee

> Eliminate scene of dragging out and robbing the cleric
> Reel 5: Eliminate scene of wife in old abbey with knife

These bits were excised on the grounds that the censors found them to be "immoral" and felt that they would thus "tend to incite crime." The fact that, on the face of it, *nothing* that was eliminated had anything to do with Stevenson's original story or the terse plot recap offered by the *Motion Picture News Booking Guide* (as quoted above and in *The AFI Catalog*) leads us to question whether the *Booking Guide* might not have cocked up the source of the storyline in the first place. If that is indeed the case, our trying to reconstruct the pictorial content of a motion picture by concentrating on the elements that were removed from same is very much akin to a scientist being asked to prove a negative.

A second fly in the ointment is that it was not Dramafilms that applied for a license to project *The Tame Cat* all over New York State, but, rather, Webster Films — an outfit about which we could find zilch. Webster Films may have been an out-of-somebody's-basement concern looking to purchase the rights to exhibit Dramafilms' latest epic (via a States' Rights arrangement) that submitted a print of *The Tame Cat* as part of the process. This theory, though, flies in the face of another factoid listed in *The AFI Catalog* entry: that Arrow Films (almost ten dozen movies released from 1918 to 1925, including 1920's *The House of Mystery*, covered herein) was the distributor.

The fact that *Harrison's Reports*, *The New York Times*, *Variety*, *MPN*, and *MPW* et al all took a bye on *The Tame Cat* doubtless robbed the AFI researchers of their accustomed sources of information. Dramafilms' not bothering to file for copyright with the Library of Congress means no registration summary on file and no cast/credits details available, either.

Given that we can't even begin to articulate the stuff we don't know about this picture, please allow us escape with a shred of dignity by claiming that while we're not sure whether *The Tame Cat* is a yet-undiscovered masterpiece of fantasy or horror, it sure is one pip of a mystery.

— *JTS/HN*

The Temple of Venus

The Temple of Venus. Fox Film Corp./Fox Film Corp., 29 October 1923, 7 reels/6695 feet [LOST]

CAST: William Walling (*Dennis Dean*); Mary Philbin (*Moria*); Mickey McBan (*Mickey*); Alice Day (*Peggy*); David Butler (*Nat Harper*); William Boyd (*Stanley Dale*); Phyllis Haver (*Constance Lane*); Leon Barry (*Phil Greyson*); Celeste Lee (*Venus*); Señorita Consuela (*Thetis*); Robert Klein (*Neptune*); Marilyn Boyd (*Juno*); Frank Keller (*Jupiter*); Lorraine Eason (*Echo*); Helen Vigil (*Diana*)

CREDITS: *Presented by* William Fox; *Director* Henry Otto; *Story and Scenario* Henry Otto, Catherine Carr; *Cinematographer* Joe August

By the pricking of our thumbs, something iffy this way comes.

By 1923 the Twenties were Roaring and all was well with the world; well, with the USA. Well, with a good part of the USA. Human nature being what it was, is, and always will be, the country was home to as many floppers as flappers, and for every champagne bath taken there was a hot-water shortage somewhere else. Still, the hi-jinks of the Haves could always be experienced by the Have-Nots, if only vicariously, like at the movies. In the movies, the celebration of the beauty of the girl next door meant that the viewer could take a temporary respite from wondering what in hell had happened to the girl who lived next door to *him*. Feminine pulchritude was now available by the metric ton, and many, many films were constructed — as would be the soap operas and nighttime TV serials of the 1970s, 80s and 90s — on the conceit that the average shlub could find happiness and fulfillment by following doggedly the adventures of the moneyed class, all of whom were impossibly beautiful and inevitably unsatisfied.

A giant step for man (meaning *males*) toward this end had been taken in the 1910s, when the aquatic fantasies of Annette Kellerman(n) gave those males artistically-rendered views of the unadorned female form on the big screen. Perfection of this female form was spelled out in exploitation campaigns, and gals like Annette (see *A Daughter of the Gods*) and Ida (*Undine*) Schnall were held up as physical specimens to be emulated by the women and ... ummmm ... enjoyed by the men. Doing so without the proper dramatic grounding would have led to charges of pornography by religious conservatives, so the acres of frolicking, nubile near-nudes had to be set, just so, against a background of classical myth and fantasy. This became art. (For those who might care to see a wry — yet completely accurate — take on catering to prurient interests in a publically prudish society, *Gentlemen's Relish*, a 2001 production of the BBC, is required viewing.)

Come the 1920s and, along with the post-war gratitude and relief and joy and renewed appreciation for life and love, etc., etc., one found that society was more open to ... well ... *openness*, at least where the female form was concerned. Pornography, which had flourished — no matter what — since the days of cave-wall drawings, continued to flourish, prompting some wags to conclude that man's becoming hot and bothered over representations of the unadorned female figure was as inevitable as his dying and more inevitable than his paying his fair share of taxes. But it was now possible for moviegoers to experience the latest flock of Hollywood beauties in various stages of dishabille away from those venues wherein one draped one's raincoat over one's lap. This newfound trend at celebrating the display of peacetime abundance brought with it the display of the fruits of monetary extravagance: women.

While movie vamps became less cartoonish, they were now ubiquitous; no one knew with certainty who the other woman was, as eye makeup laid on with a trowel was no longer in fashion. Gold-diggers and Sugar Daddies proliferated, scantily clad femmes fatales came with money as surely as did compound interest, and owning a mansion or a manor house meant that wild parties were as de rigueur as that elderly butler with the stick up his ass. With very little trouble, then, the average Joe and Josie could find a film that might encourage a bit of wishful thinking and permit a decent enough dose of Schadenfreude. For those who were seeking a tad of titillation without wishing to indulge in yet another "social drama," there was the occasional, cheerfully unrepentant myth/art hybrid.

Have we made ourselves clear?

Beauty, of course, has always been lodged in the beholder's eye, so we offer several disparate views of *The Temple of Venus*. The first comes from the studio's copyright registration summary, which was written to be lodged at the rather staid Library of Congress: "Venus sends Cupid to earth to find if romance still exists there. He finds Moira and Peggy, a fisherman's daughters, who become entangled in the amorous pursuits of an artist and a fisherman. Cupid returns to Venus with his report."

Well, you can't get more dispassionate and straightforward than *that*, can you? Had Moira and Peggy been *farmer's* daughter*s*, of course, there might be cause for alarm. But a couple of Irish colleens, batting their virginal eyelashes at a couple of local boys...? See "wholesome" in your Merriam-Webster's.

One the 1 November 1923, the movie critic for *The New York Times* attempted to explain the onscreen workings of *Temple* to his readership. In part, he revealed...

> According to the story a young artist fed up with jollity and jazz flees to the rugged island and meets the fair Moria. In the opening to a cave on the brink of still, reflective waters, paying little heed to his canvas, he tells Moria about the prattling Echo, whom he is painting from memory of others' works. The film fades into his narrative and Juno, Jupiter, Thetis, Echo and others are introduced. This gives the director another opportunity to show girls, the stellar one being Queen Thetis (Senorita Consuella), the film painter having given her a costume of green gold.... One sees Greek gods and goddesses, life on a rock-ribbed island, a bevy of dancing nymphs, scenes of ultra-modern jazz existence, a love affair between an artist and an unsophisticated maiden, and truly marvelous pictures of seals.... This series of pictures lasts so long that one forgets the artist, who is telling the yarn, and Moria, who is listening.

The more astute reader will have noticed that Moira has become Moria, and that Peggy has disappeared (unless she's the "unsophisticated maiden" in the parade of the characters that aren't seals); so much for a breath of Irish Spring. The more classically educated will recall that, per Greek mythology, Echo was a nymph in love with the sound of her own voice, Thetis was a sea nymph who gave birth to Achilles, and Jupiter and Juno were nowhere to be found, since they came later when the Romans took over and stole every idea that hadn't been nailed down. The artist (and the scenarist) probably meant Zeus and Hera, but as Moria is described as being "fair" and not "bright," we're assuming the artist is handing her a line, anyhow. For those keeping score, then: zero Greek gods and goddesses, a brace of mythological nymphs to supplement the terpsichorean variety, rock-ribbed island jazz (or something), naïve Peggy, and the seals. Just FYI, *The Times* felt that

> undoubtedly the most interesting portion of this film is where the seals are shown. There are old seals, young seals and baby seals being lugged to safety in their mothers' mouths. This is such an extraordinary bit of footage that it inspired more applause than anything else.

Harrison's Reports (10 November 1923) also noticed the old seals. In fact, "The rocky scenes by the sea, some showing cormorants, and some seals, have undoubtedly been taken out of old news-reels — it is noticed that no one scene shows both the seals and the cormorants; but they are interesting."

Harrison's also felt that most of the mythological scenes were old: "It is said that they are remnants of scenes from pictures that have been produced in the past, such as *Queen of the Sea*,

Daughter of the Gods [*sic*], and others." Still, the journal looked past the seals and the gods and saw what was being peddled to the audiences: Hotties. "It seems that this picture has been produced chiefly for the purpose of showing a jazz party with women naked but around the waist...." This image is hard to reconcile with *Harrison's* describing the hand-colored short skirt worn by the alpha female at the jazz-fest: "This causes the attention to be pinned to this character's bodily 'charms'—to her hoochy-koochy motions, and to her hula hula dance, but particularly to her bare legs." Never send a leg man out to do a movie critic's work: nowhere in the review is either Cupid or Venus mentioned.

Then again, neither Mother nor Son made the following PR statistics list, either:

1000 American beauties in a modern magnificent spectacle
22 weeks camerawork on Santa Cruz Island, Paradise of the Pacific
Special town of 1500 inhabitants built
Gowns worth $100,000 worn in the play
200 classic dancers in exotic interpretations
Most perfectly formed woman in America selected from more than 1,000 candidates to portray the modern Venus
Pacific Ocean islands, "uninhabited," used as locations
Dances and allegorical scenes in subterranean grottos staged by use of special artificial lights for the first time in motion picture history
15 world class divers from all classes in startling exhibitions
Deep sea photography by new process perfected to record these features
Milady's coat in living form — the seal in schools of thousands — shown on lonely sea-lashed rocks where man never before intruded
Rookeries alive with baby seals filmed with special permission of the U.S. government
[*Titusville* (Pennsylvania) *Herald*, 29 April 1924]

The cast: Mary Philbin, of course, was still a couple of years away from *The Phantom of the Opera*, and that's where her bona fides are. William Boyd would go on to iconic status as Hopalong Cassidy, we're all Hoppy fans, and — genre-wise — the tall Ohioan had a few other credits: see, for example, 1922's *The Young Rajah* and 1925's *The Road to Yesterday*. Alice Day (*Peggy*) started off as a Mack Sennett bathing beauty, so maybe her bare legs played a crucial part of the plot development here; regardless, there's more on Miss Day in our chapter on *The Gorilla*. (Aficionados of the Mack Sennett bathing beauties will be pleased to learn that the part of Constance Lane — about which we know nothing whatsoever — was played by Phyllis Haver, also a former MSbb.) William Walling, a character man who was 50 years old if he was a day when the picture was released, essayed the artist, and you won't find another mention of his name anywhere else herein. The role of Jupiter (who would have been Zeus if anyone had had any idea as to what was going on) was enacted by Frank Keller; Mr. Keller — doubtless sensing that, once you've played the king of the gods, there's nowhere to go but down — apparently then called it quits, industry-wise. Director Henry Otto was no quitter, and his contributions to the genre are noted hither, thither and yon throughout these

pages (although you'll find the most info on him in our essay about *The Willow Tree*).

Perhaps *The Temple of Venus* was *meant* to be a cut-and-paste affair, what with its incorporating snippets of the Annette Kellerman canon for the with-it crowd, wildlife stock footage for the elderly or sexually inactive, and mythological figures for the kiddies. Our problem is that we can't tell the extent to which said figures — Greek or Roman, who cares? — worked any sort of mythic magic in this movie. Every source we consulted placed a different emphasis on the picture's attractions, and none gave much play to the fantasy dimension. The 30 June 1923 *Moving Picture World*, for example, informed its readership that the company intended to have "Beautiful Women in *The Temple of Venus*," but what in hell else would you expect in a place bearing that name?

Underappreciated mytho-linguistic fact: In Latin, the genitive (possessive) form of the proper noun, *Venus*, is *Veneris* — whence comes the word "venereal." *Hmmmm*... might this film, after all, have been targeted toward those raincoat-heavy venues we wrote of, above?

— *JTS*

The Terror

The Terror. Warner Bros. Pictures, Inc./Warner Bros., 6 September 1928, Sound version (Vitaphone), 80 minutes/9 reels/7,654 feet*; Silent version 5,443 feet, Silent version released 20 October 1928 [LOST], but Sound Discs at UCLA

CAST: May McAvoy (*Olga Redmayne*); Louise Fazenda (*Mrs. Elvery*); Edward Everett Horton (*Ferdinand Mane*); Alec B. Francis (*Dr. Redmayne*); Matthew Betz (*Joe Connors*); Holmes Herbert (*Goodman*); Otto Hoffman (*Soapy Marks*); Joseph W. Girard (*Superintendant Hallick*); Frank Austin (*Cotton*); John Miljan (*Alfred Katman*)

CREDITS: *Director* Roy Del Ruth; Scenario and Dialogue: Harvey Gates; based on the eponymous play by Edgar Wallace (London, 1929); *Titles* Joseph Jackson; *Cinematographer* Chick McGill; *Film Editors* Thomas Pratt, Jack Killifer

"There are spiritualistic séances, sliding panels, glistening knives, groans, mysterious organ music, screams-all the paraphernalia of spookdom, enough to give the willies to the most phlegmatic, even if it were all silent, but Vitaphone makes the effect almost hysterical."

— publicity puff for *The Terror*

Of course there *was* an all-silent version and that's why the film is being briefly considered here. Warner Bros.' *The Terror* was largely sold — and reviewed — on the basis of it being the second all-talkie, and there was no interest whatsoever in the silent edition that was prepared for the many theaters that were not equipped for sound. Earlier in 1928 Warner's had done *The Lights of New York* and promoted it as the first all-talkie, but that hokey gangster melodrama did have a few title cards, so *The Terror* took it one step further and eliminated all titles, including the cast/credits scrawl that was read on screen by a man wearing a mask (and having the voice of Conrad Nagel).

The Terror was based on a play by popular mystery writer, Edgar Wallace; it had been a big hit in London but had failed

---

*These footage/running time statistics from *The AFI Catalog*. *Harrison's* lists the film at 7,754 feet and running 90–110 minutes.

to cross the pond. *Variety* sniffed that it wasn't good enough for Broadway but ideal for the movies.

Our synopsis comes from contemporary reviews and the dialog script:

> The Terror is a maniacal criminal who leaves a black glove by the bodies of his mutilated victims. Police believe he is actually Leonard O'Shea but no one really knows what O'Shea looks like since he's a master of disguise. The Terror's most famous crime was a bank heist which netted him a huge amount of gold. The Terror's confederates in this caper were crooks Joe Connors and Soapy Marks both of whom the Terror betrayed to the police. After serving a ten-year sentence, Marks and Connors are both eager for revenge. Shortly before their release, Superintendant Hallick urges them to come clean but they refuse. Clearly, they know where the Terror is to be found even though they don't know what disguise he has assumed.
>
> The scene shifts to a country inn run by Dr. Redmayne. Guests at the Inn include Mrs. Elvery, a spinster who conducts séances; Alfred, an eccentric who loves talking about murder; and Goodman, a wealthy man with a nervous condition. Goodman is in love with Redmayne's daughter Olga who has agreed to marry the older man because of his generosity to her cash-strapped father. The Inn, which was once a monastery, is the scene of many strange sights and sounds in the night, including the prowling of a sinister cloaked figure and eerie organ music. Olga begs her father for an explanation of these odd happenings but he is evasive.
>
> One dark and stormy night, a drunken golfer named Fane turns up. He annoys the other guests with his incessant rhyming but Olga suspects he's playing a part and is to be trusted. Mrs. Ajax, an elderly woman, arrives insisting she has a reservation though Dr. Redmayne can find no record of it. Mrs. Elvery conducts a séance in the hope of dispelling the Inn's evil spirits but instead Mrs. Ajax is stabbed to death. "She" turns out to be Soapy Marks in disguise. Connors is also found skulking about the grounds. Dr. Redmayne tries to phone for the police but the line has been cut; nevertheless, Superintendent Hallick shows up (Redmayne: "Who notified you?" Hallick: "We won't go into that now.").
>
> Fane turns out to be a policeman working undercover. He is very suspicious of Goodman but then Goodman is found dead in his room. Cotton, the butler, disappears. Later Fane finds him trussed up in a secret passageway and next to him is the stolen gold. Cotton insists it was Goodman who tied him up. Shortly after, Olga is kidnapped by the cloaked figure and brought to a secret chamber. She is rescued and the mystery man turns out to be Goodman; his "corpse" was really just a wax figure. Redmayne admits that he knew Goodman was the Terror but said nothing because he hoped to one day cure him and of course was grateful for all his financial help.
>
> The masked man who read the credits returns to provide some maniacal laughter and offer a warning to the viewer: "Because you know as well as I know, there are no such things [A loud yell].... There are such things! There are terrors everywhere! The man seated next to you may be one of them."

Obviously, someone at Warner's remembered Van Helsing's curtain speech at the end of *Dracula*.

Some reviewers expressed reservations about the film's use of dialogue; the comments from Marquis Busby of the *Los Angeles Times* (20 August 1928) summed up those doubts:

> While the picture has considerable suspense and holds interest from the first clap of thunder to the last scream of Louise Fazenda as the spinster spiritualist, the tempo is slowed down to meet the exigencies of the talking device. There are too many close-ups of people talking and too little action. While sound effects, the thunder, the playing of the organ and rapping on doors undoubtedly heighten the suspense and nervous tension, the picture would have been fully as effective without so much dialogue.

The film was panned in England where one wag thought the players' slow enunciation of their lines was akin to "people dictating important letters." Nor was Edgar Wallace impressed: "Well," he opined, "I have never thought the talkies would be a serious rival to the stage."

In America, though, the film received mostly enthusiastic notices, especially in the trade press: "Through the medium of the talking pictures it is here shown possible to lend greater power to the simplest dialog and the most inconspicuous action, Situations that would fail to hold on the stage are full of tense, eager interest on the screen" ["Mort," *Variety*, 22 August 1928]. "Mort" even felt the film was well worth the outrageous $2.00 admission price.

Laurence Reid of *Motion Picture News* (10 August 1928) was just as bubbly:

> You can put this down in your little notebook as *there*. When a picture has an assorted collection of thrills and chills, and is plentifully supplied with shivery action which is saturated with suspense it can be chalked up as something to be looked over. Add these essentials of a good crook story to sound effects which emphasize all of the highlights and it becomes a work of real celluloid.... It calls for trick photography when ghostly hands play unseen organs and when they reach out of the eerie atmosphere to clutch a throat or two. These shocking bits call for weird sets and atmosphere — as well as weird lighting effects.

The *Harrison's Reports* reviewer, who had dismissed *Lights of New York* as "junk," found *The Terror* to be totally successful, in no small measure because of its use of sound:

> The picture is thrilling in itself; but the sound effects as well as the talking of the characters add greatly to the suspense as well as to the other entertaining qualities. The scenes that show the characters (Louise Fazenda and May McAvoy) screaming, their screams being heard, give the spectator a thrill that the silent action alone could not give him, at least to the same degree.... It should please everywhere; but its value without the talk is, in my opinion, about twenty per cent: of the value with the talk [28 August 1928].

"Mae Tinee," writing in the 22 January 1929 edition of *The Chicago Tribune*, concurred: "Here is a movie thriller as is a movie thriller. Moreover, the production talks. And yells. The things you see with your eyes and hear with your ears will give you summat to think of on dark nights for awhile."

Good or bad, *The Terror* was a hit. While it has the distinction of being the first all-talkie horror film and its use of scary sound effects may have helped pave the way for the horror cycle of the 1930s, its main significance may be its driving another nail into the coffin of the Silent Era. Ironically, all that remains of this genre breakthrough are its sound discs.

— HN

A Thief in the Dark

A Thief in the Dark. Fox Film Corp./Fox Film Corp., 20 May 1928, 6 reels/5937 feet [LOST]

CAST: George Meeker (*Ernest*); Doris Hill (*Elise*); Gwen Lee (*Flo*); Marjorie Beebe (*Jeanne*); Michael Vavitch (*Professor Xeno*); Noah Young (*Monk*); Charles Belcher (*Duke*); Raymond Turner (*Beauregard*); Erville Alderson (*Armstrong*); with James Mason, Yorke Sherwood, Frank Rice, Tom McGuire

CREDITS: *Presented by* William Fox; *Director* Albert Ray; *Scenario*

C. Graham Baker; based on a story by Albert Ray, Kenneth Hawks/ Andrew Bennison; *Titles* William Kernell; *Cinematographer* Arthur Edeson; *Film Editor* Jack Dennis; *Assistant Director* Horace Hough

This Fox six-reeler may have showed up late on the scene, but it brought nothing new and little that is memorable. The derivative story was attributed to either Kenneth Hawks or to the "team" of Andrew Bennison and Albert Ray, and the skinny on the authors is probably worthy of more of our attention than is the plot.

Ray was the cousin of Charles Ray (see *A Midnight Bell*), another of those pioneer-type fellows who started out acting early in the 1910s and then — as the decade(s) passed — produced, directed, wrote, and may have parked cars, as well. The prevailing theory is that Charles got Albert into the movies around 1915 via (What else?) slapstick shorts shot on a shoestring by short-lived studios. It wasn't long before Albert abjured acting in slapstick shorts and began directing them, and not long after that he was helming said shorts for Fox. Features followed soon enough, and his first, full-length genre epic was 1926's *Whispering Wires* (see entry). During the first few years of the Sound Era, Ray's spooky side struck again (twice), with 1932's *The Thirteenth Guest* and 1933's *A Shriek in the Night*, both of which starred Ginger Rogers and Lyle Talbot. As for his literary skills, in addition to co-penning *A Thief in the Dark*, Albert added his two cents' worth to the screenplay of 1939's *Charlie Chan in Reno*, one of the best of the Fox/Toler entries in the series.

We've not much to share on possible *Thief* co-writer, Kenneth Hawks, as the poor guy's day in the cinematic sun was a brief one: films bearing his name in any capacity whatsoever span a mere three-year period (1927–1929). Hawks— more famous for being Howard's brother than for anything he did in his own right — was killed in a plane crash on the 2 January 1930. Andrew Bennison — the *other* possible co-author — had about three dozen more notches in his gun-belt than did Mr. Hawks, including a writer's share (with Harry O. Hoyt) in 1927's *The Wizard* (see entry), and credit (per the IMDb) for "special material" for the 1940 Kay Kyser romp, *You'll Find Out*, with Karloff, Lugosi, and Lorre. We've absolutely no idea what "special material" means, and — to be honest — given all the picture's missed opportunities, we've little desire to find out.

Having put off as long as we can the plot information, let us first off admit that —for a Fox production, late in the 1920s— publicity materials are scant. As we've recounted elsewhere, pictures made on the "Cusp o' Sound"— almost *anything* that demonstrated an iota of creativity, a dash of flair, a hint of better revenue potential, etc. and that was scheduled for production, was wrapping production, was on the verge of release, etc.— were generally held up while older technology was replaced, additional and/or replacement footage was shot, publicity accommodations were made, theaters were wired, etc. (and we're getting awfully tired of typing "etc."). Once the Sound Era came thundering in, said adjustments were made faster and furiouser. Backlogged silents were dumped in cheap(er) theaters in poor(er) neighborhoods. Shot-on-a-shoestring movies were sent out as-was, fingers were crossed, receipts were tallied, and folks grabbed the money and ran like hell. "Better" pictures (*better* being a purely subjective term) were afforded more perks:

more revamped film footage, more publicity coverage, more creative packaging. "A" films (like Universal's Jewels or Super-Jewels) were withheld from release until they could be virtually made over to nail the *audire* in "audience," with the Latin verb (meaning "to hear") lending integrity to the English noun, for seat-holders were no longer merely "viewers."

We can pretty much infer (from the scant critical attention it received) that *A Thief in the Dark* was adjudged a "take the money and run" flick that went into release — as an unadulterated silent — some three months after *The Jazz Singer* sent everybody into a tizzy. The following précis is a sequential recounting of paragraph-long details from *The AFI Catalog* and the 20 May 1928 *Motion Picture News*, respectively:

> A troupe of fake spiritualists traveling with a carnival are crooks on the side. Professor Xeno, a mystic, kills a "rich old bunny" for a case of jewels, while Ernest, the newest recruit, falls for Elise, the granddaughter. Ernest relents after his first job and turns hero by exposing Xeno as the murderer. Xeno meets his end when the jewel case, wired for burglars, blows up in his face when he opens it.

> The story has to do with a band of circus crooks, of which Professor Zeno [*sic*], a mystic, is the master mind [*sic*]. In his séances he gets information from his subjects that reveals to him the hiding place of valuables and then he details one of his crooks to the job of bringing in the loot. The big haul is to be made at the mansion of an eccentric old collector of rare jewels, whose beautiful granddaughter falls in love with the newest recruit in the crook band. The latter relents [*sic*] after his first job and turns hero by exposing Zeno as the murderer of the girl's grandfather. There are mysterious passageways and trick doors in the house of the jewel collector which add to the tenseness of the action as the story progresses.

A casual perusal of the above summary will reveal our predicament: mystics (albeit phony), séances (albeit rigged), and spiritualists (albeit fake) were par for the course in the Silent Era, but we've no clue as to how genre-y was their onscreen presentation. Were there all sorts of SPFX (albeit explained away) that would have made us proud? Or did everything unfold in a matter-of-fact fashion that was about as interesting as folding socks? The brief *MPN* entry gives us no hint, and the 13 June 1928 *Variety* is a step down from there: "Hokey, silly and exaggerated, but possessing enough of the familiar hidden panel and secret passage stuff to have some interest for the non-fastidious audiences." The 19 May 1928 *Harrison's Reports* also mentions that "Trap and revolving doors, sliding panels, and the like help to hold the spectator in suspense," without so much as giving a nod to the ersatz supernatural trappings that underlay all these devices. (More disturbing, though, is the moralistic tone that *Harrison's* affects here. "The situation where Mr. Meeker is shown entering the home of one of the victims of his séance-holding employer and stealing his money, which the victim had hidden under his pillow, is not very edifying; it sets a bad example to young men." Wha-a-a-a?)

Our most notable contributor to the cause was cinematographer Arthur Edeson who, surely, will be remembered for his Sound Era masterpieces, *Frankenstein* (1931), *The Old Dark House* (1932), and *The Invisible Man* (1933), to say nothing of 1926's *The Bat* (see entry) and 1927's *The Gorilla* (see entry). Our hero (aptly named Ernest) was impersonated by Brooklynite, George Meeker, at the very start of his lengthy film career. Meeker would appear in a couple of talkie genre items (like 1933's *Night of Terror*), but the lion's share of his credits were decidedly more mainstream. Our heroine was Doris Hill (born in pre–Area 51 Roswell!), whom you may remember (if you've been reading this tome alphabetically) from *Darkened Rooms*. *Variety*'s "Land" credited neither of them, dismissing the entire slate with "Nobody in the cast except Gwen Lee (in a bit) who seems even halfway familiar." Land obviously failed to spot the hulking Noah Young—foe to Laurel and Hardy in such classic comedy shorts as *Do Detectives Think?* and *Battle of the Century* (both 1927)—who must have achieved at least *halfway* familiarity in the course of some 150+ films before *A Thief in the Dark* was available for caustic commentary.

— *JTS*

The Thirteenth Chair

The Thirteenth Chair. Metro-Goldwyn-Mayer Pictures/M-G-M, 19 October 1929, (Movietone sound) 8 reels/6,571 feet, (silent) 5,543 feet, sound version available

CAST: Conrad Nagel (*Richard Crosby*); Leila Hyams (*Helen O'Neill*); Margaret Wycherly (*Mme. Rosalie La Grange*); Helene Millard (*Mary Eastwood*); Holmes Herbert (*Sir Roscoe Crosby*); Mary Forbes (*Lady Crosby*); Bela Lugosi (*Inspector Delzante*); John Davidson (*Edward Wales*); Charles Quartermaine (*Dr. Philip Mason*); Moon Carroll (*Helen Trent*); Cyril Chadwick (*Brandon Trent*); Bertram Johns (*Howard Standish*); Gretchen Holland (*Grace Standish*); Frank Leigh (*Professor Feringeea*); Clarence Geldert (*Commissioner Grimshaw*); Lal Chand Mehra (*Chotee*)

CREDITS: *Director* Tod Browning; *Scenario and Dialogue* Elliott Clawson; based on the eponymous play by Bayard Veiller (New York, 1922); *Titles* Joe Farnham; *Cinematographer* Merritt B. Gerstad; *Art Director* Cedric Gibbons; *Film Editor* Harry Reynolds; *Recording Engineers* Paul Neal, Douglas Shearer; *Gowns* Adrian

Our screed on the original (1919) version of this thriller began with a moan or two about remakes, and it's fitting, we guess, to open our discussion of this Cusp-o'-Sound in similar fashion.

Lots of films that had hit pay-dirt during the Silent Era were done over once sound arrived, as the logic (pretty much irrefutable, given our gift of hindsight) was that the aural dimension would put more flesh on the skeleton. Hollywood did not turn into Remake City immediately once *The Jazz Singer* hit, though; it was years before some old favorites were dusted off and revamped, and most of the movies that *were* remade fairly close in took a distant second place (or third, or fourth...) to the succession of glitzy musicals that not only concentrated on vocal noise, but celebrated its nuance and its rhythm and rhyme while — more than occasionally — regaling their audiences (a proper term, finally) with overblown mediocrity.

In light of this, it's difficult to understand why Metro-Goldwyn-Mayer would more or less rush to release a talkie remake of a picture that hadn't done all that well in the first place. What's more, Bayard Veiller's eponymous play (that had opened in late 1916 at New York City's 48th Street Theatre) had seen its lights dim nearly a dozen years earlier, so this reworking didn't have the advantage of drawing on potential ticket-buyers who,

not long before, had been Broadway ticket-holders. Given too that Veiller did not have the Q-factor of, say, Shakespeare or George M. Cohan, M-G-M certainly couldn't count on the playwright's many fans tipping the production into the black.

What the studio *could* count on was Tod Browning, the Louisville-born Master of the Macabre who had become known as Lon Chaney's director during the decade that was drawing to a close, just as he had come up through the ranks as Priscilla Dean's director (over at Universal) in the latter half of the 1910s. If anyone could take an inexpensively-acquired, offbeat property and (together with Cedric Gibbons' flair for making a silk purse out a bolt of silk) work his oddball magic for the greater glory of M-G-M, it was he.

What *no one* could count on was this Bela Lugosi, the Hungarian émigré with the impressive (and mildly suspect) theatrical portfolio, an outsized personality, and—given the sexual mores of the Roaring Twenties—animal magnetism, per a decent percentage of the country's distaff population. Lugosi had just impressed the hell out of said females on either coast with his portrayal of undead lounge lizard, Dracula, in the eponymous play crafted by Hamilton Deane and John L. Balderston, and Browning's decision to cast him in the role of Inspector Delzante still gives rise to debates on the director's motivation and his assessment of the actor's potential. Given that the same character had been yclept *Donohue* in both the 1919 six-reeler and Veiller's stage-work, Browning's opting to rename his policeman to jibe with Lugosi's persona may indicate that the director saw something in the actor that might lead to beneficial ties in the future. That part is speculation; what is *fact* is that — in the 1930s — the one movie star with whom Browning's name would be most frequently associated was Bela Lugosi.

The remake's plot, of course, is quite similar to that of its cinematic sire (save for the curious relocating of the action to India, a move that adds not so much as a jot of significance to the mix), and so interested parties may repair to our essay on the 1919 feature for general details. What strikes us as disconcerting about the 1929 version is its staginess, a "quality" that is far more understandable in the earlier production, in that it was based directly on the Broadway show, was compromised somewhat by current technology and contemporary acting styles, and was constrained to an extent by the limited scope of director Léonce Perret's vision. Why such dramatic ennui still, ten years later? Browning was an adept in the melodramatic field — with deserved props in the more bizarrely appointed stretches of that field — and the cinema's visual capability had advanced a decade's worth since the Acme Pictures Corporation's movie was premiered, so we can't turn in those directions for answers.

What most likely tamped down the creative proclivities of the director and his cast was the rudimentary sound technology that bedeviled not only this picture, but also a good number of non-epic, non–"solid A" projects made by M-G-M and others this same year. At this point, microphones were still much more at home inside vases on tables, or behind clocks on mantelpieces, or in strategically-situated shrubbery on patios than they were attached to overhead booms that could be moved in synchronization with the actors' studied blocking. Thus, Bela, or

Margaret Wycherly, or Conrad Nagel—or anyone in the cast, actually—could glide across the floor with the steady assurance provided by years of silent-screen muscle memory, but had to pull up short, focus, and project directly into the philodendrons in order for their lines to be heard.

Lugosi's delivery, of course, was always priceless, regardless of whether the Hungarian was swooping onto the scene, arms akimbo, or was planted at the edge of the screen, lost in profound or tortuous thought. In his published notes on this film, William Everson noted that the static nature of some of the direction could do nothing to affect the dramatic impulses of the man from Lugos: "Lugosi's theatrical bravura is totally unrestrained, as are his facial gestures and body movements; 'nuances' would be a totally alien word to apply to Lugosi's acting tricks here, but it is a sheer joy to watch and listen to them."

Indeed, when Bela's Delzante ponders aloud the fact that the scenario's dramatis personae include two women named Helen, we have, perhaps, the first in a lengthy series of classic "Lugosi lines": otherwise unremarkable bits of movie dialogue that are rendered memorable solely because of the intonation, cadence, and timbre with which they are delivered. Love him or hate him, Bela Lugosi never uttered a throwaway line.

Lines apart, we are concerned with the *silent* prints of *The Thirteenth Chair* that made the rounds; they're the reason for this Appendix entry. At this juncture, the more costly talkies (and, per Arthur Lennig's *The Immortal Count*, this talkie ending up setting M-G-M back a cool $262,000) were usually backed up by silent prints, in case theaters either had not yet installed the fledgling sound technology or something went awry, or because the lesser foreign markets could still be relied upon to take whatever they were given, and title cards were much cheaper than target-language co-productions.

For all that, we were unable to come up with even one (1) published review that dealt solely with the silent version of *The Thirteenth Chair*. Was it because, even at that point, the usual suspects regarded sitting through a silent film as passé? Or because no periodical—trade or otherwise—felt it worth its while to assign reviewers to cover films that were either themselves third-rate, or that were relegated to play only in third-rate venues? Reviews on the "all-talking" version were mixed, with the 21 December 1929 assessment from *Harrison's Reports* ("Mediocre") more charitable than most. More to our point, *Harrison's* was the only one of the trades even to so much as address the drag of silence on the release: "The talk is not always intelligible and at times the voices sound harsh. Silent values as poor as the sound." Projecting into the potted palms is one thing; compounding the felony, intelligibility-wise, by having an Irish medium and a Hungarian policeman cross paths in Calcutta in quite another.

Other than Lugosi, the principal cast gave performances that were, for them, pretty standard. Conway Nagel (see *London after Midnight*) did the juvenile pretty much pro forma (albeit Bill Everson opined that Nagel's hero "has little more to do than murmur a frequent and obedient 'Coming, Mother!'"); Margaret Wycherly did a second take on the character she had essayed on Broadway a decade and a bit earlier; Holmes Herbert

(see *The Charlatan*) felt so much at home in his role as Sir Roscoe Crosby he returned to reprise same in the 1937 re-remake; and Leila Hyams (as the first and lovelier of the two Helens) was undeniably lovely. Contributing to the snail-like pace (Everson: "creaky with a vengeance") was both the ongoing battle to vanquish the sound equipment and Bela's tendency to pregnant pauses that feel like they last every day of nine months.

Not a success—David Skal's *Dark Carnival* reveals that the film "showed only half the profit ($148,000) of Browning's recent pictures with Chaney"—*The Thirteenth Chair* marked the last feature Browning would make for M-G-M under his original contract. His next picture, *Outside the Law*, would find him back at Universal, remaking a Priscilla Dean vehicle (with Lon Chaney!) that Browning had himself directed in 1920; his 1930 co-writer was Garrett Fort. The following year, Browning would be reunited at Universal with Garrett Fort … and Bela Lugosi.

Need we say any more?   — JTS

Those Who Dare

Those Who Dare. Creative Pictures/distribution company unknown, 15 November 1924, 6 reels, print at the Cineteca Italiana (Milan), under the title *Gli Stregoni del Mare* (*The Wizards of the Sea*)

CAST: John Bowers (*Captain Manning*); Marguerite De La Motte (*Marjorie*); Joseph Dowling (*David Rollins*); Claire McDowell (*Mrs. Rollins*); Martha Marshall (*Cecilia Thorne*); Edward Burns (*Harry Rollins*); Spottiswoode Aitken (*Thorne Wetherell*); Sheldon Lewis (*Serpent Smith*); Cesare Gravina (*Panka*)

CREDITS: *Director* John B. O'Brien; *Adaptation* Frank Beresford; *Story* I.W. Irving; *Cinematographer* Devereaux Jenkins

A rather confusing tale of seafaring folk fighting superstition, drug abuse, mutiny, lust, and Sheldon Lewis, *Those Who Dare* also tosses in a hint of voodoo, as it might well have been practiced back then, below-decks, on a millionaire's schooner. As the song posits, "Who could ask for anything more?"

Our synopsis is courtesy of the 11 March 1925 *Variety*:

The story is told in flashback style.

Captain Martin Manning, an old captain, is ordered out of the Mariners' Harbor [*sic*] for mooring his schooner, "The Swallow," in the harbor. The order is based upon the sinister reputation of the ship and the belief a sunken ship belongs to the sea and shouldn't be raised.

Manning, in defense, tells the story of the ill-fated ship. Years ago to affect a drug cure for Harry Rollins, son of David Rollins, wealthy ship builder, Manning took charge of a yachting cruise. In mid-ocean, a signal of distress was flown. Manning investigated and discovered the old captain of the schooner seriously ill. His tomboy daughter and a villainous crew, under the leadership of Serpent Smith, a voodoo believer, were the occupants.

Manning obtained permission from the yacht owner to take charge of the schooner and took Harry with him, thereby cutting off his drug supply by separating him from his valet, who was secretly giving him the drug. The crew immediately became ugly, but the two youths assert themselves and with the aid of a loyal cook start the ship under full sail for Honolulu. Smith, the leader, poisons the old captain, leaving the girl an orphan. The crew, in a drunken orgy, overpower Harry and Manning and draw lots for the girl.

Smith loses and is chagrined. He tries to doublecross [*sic*] the winner, which precipitates a fight between he [*sic*] and his followers…. The three make their escape and the schooner, without direction, flounders [*sic*] upon the rocks with all hands aboard lost…. After hearing the story the inmates of Mariners Harbor [*sic*] vote to allow the "Swallow" a permanent anchorage. In gratitude for the saving of his son Rollins presents the schooner to Manning.

Some clarification (taken from *The AFI Catalog*):

Captain Manning, a seasoned salt, is ordered to remove his battered ship, the *Swallow,* from the town's harbor because of a superstition connected with it. The captain, who lives alone, then goes to the Mariners' Home and there relates the story of how he came into possession of the schooner. *Manning was the first mate on the yacht of a wealthy man when it encountered the* Swallow *at sea. Manning went on board, accompanied by the drug-addicted son of his employer, and discovered a mutinous crew and a disabled captain fighting for control of the ship. Manning took charge and brought the ship safely to port, after successfully putting down the mutineers by humiliating their leader, who had kept them in fear by practicing voodoo in the ship's hold. Manning later married the daughter of the* Swallow's *captain.* Now he controls the ship.

Even with the AFI amendment, that doesn't make a hell of a lot of sense. Why one would lug a spaced-out junkie along on a rescue mission is a question only story-department hacks in desperate search for novelty could answer. Then, too, the presence of a couple of additional (more or less) able-bodied men (okay; *one*) on the scene wouldn't make Serpent Smith's mutinous scheme any easier, would it? If you're sitting below decks—voodoo-ing to beat the band and psyching out the dimwits with whom you're working—why wait until *after* the schooner has been boarded by interlopers to make a move on the moribund captain? Or to sell lottery tickets on the tomboy daughter?

Okay; daffy, illogical plot wrinkles such as these have done little to bolster the low standing in which some people have held movies since stupidity evolved into an art form, but inasmuch as there are folk who doubt even whether Holy Writ is 100 percent inerrant, let's not raise another tempest in a teapot. We'll give whomever all these rather silly story twists if only he/she can explain whether a) the *Swallow* was the schooner owned by David Rollins and on which Manning was first mate; if Rollins was so magnanimous as to *give* the schooner to Manning following his subduing the lustful, voodoo mutiny, the millionaire must have owned it, no?; or b) the Swallow was merely some ship Manning—having left David Rollins' "yacht" accompanied by Junkie-Son, Harry—boarded for the purpose of performing heroics, and which thus was most likely owned by one of the other billion or so guys living on the planet. If this was the case, Rollins' "gift" of the schooner to Manning just about caps Harry's worth, doesn't it?

For a *third* take on what may have happened onscreen, repair to Janiss Garza's recap, in the online All Movie Guide. This is not recommended.

Millionaire David Rollins was played by Joseph Dowling—the *Miracle Man,* himself—and his credentials will be found in our essay on that film. Serpent Smith was, of course, Sheldon Lewis, who gets the full treatment in the chapter on 1920's *Dr. Jekyll and Mr. Hyde* (no; the *other* one). Among the second cast may be found Cesare Gravina (unbilled in both *The Hunchback of Notre Dame* and *The Phantom of the Opera,* but in the pivotal role of Ursus in 1928's *The Man Who Laughs* [see essay]) and

Spottiswoode Aitken (see *The Avenging Conscience*). Tomboy daughter was essayed by Marguerite De La Motte, a Minnesotan who managed, somehow, to *not* be a WAMPAS Baby Star, but who did share the screen with Douglas Fairbanks in a ton of his best-known features, including *The Mark of Zorro* (1920), *The Three Musketeers* (1921), and *The Iron Mask* (1929). *Those Who Dare* was De La Motte's only genre feature, although she gets quality points for appearing opposite Lon Chaney in 1922's *Shadows.*

Harry Rollins—David's drugged-up disappointment—was impersonated by Edmund Burns, a thespian from The City of Brotherly Love who was occasionally billed (as he is here) with the Christian name, Edward. Burns' first film (1915's *The Birth of a Nation*) saw him enter the industry sans screen credit, and—like so many of his Silent Era compatriots—his last picture (1936's *Murder with Pictures*) saw him exit the same way. During the intervening decades, he usually could be found in the second cast—silent genre pictures featuring him thus include *One Hour before Dawn* (1920), *Whispering Wires* (1926), and *Ransom* (1928)—but he did venture up near principal territory in Paul Leni's lost *The Chinese Parrot* (1927). John Bowers—the principled Captain Manning—entered films in the mid–1910s, was a bona fide star within a half-dozen years of his debut, and married Marguerite De La Motte along the way, to top it all off. Despite nearly 100 motion picture credits *and* our occasional willingness to be somewhat casual about parameters for inclusion herein, Bowers never made another genre feature. His popularity waned quickly toward the end of the 1920s (and the coming of the Sound Era), and 1931's *Mounted Fury* marked his last film credit. Ironically, the actor committed suicide by drowning in 1936, and Hollywood lore has his nautical death as the inspiration for Norman Maine's in the movie version(s) of *A Star Is Born.*

Those Who Dare was produced by Creative Pictures, a one-shot company whose quest for creativity may have spelled its doom. (Quick, now! Creative types…. To whom does the title refer?) The story on which the scenario was based was written by I.W. Irving, a hitherto unknown story-teller whose creativity then gave up the ghost with his next (and last) movie credit: 1925's *Sky's the Limit* (which was distributed by the Aywon Film Corp., home to such favorites of ours as *The Evolution of Man* [starring Man-Ape Jack] and *When Dr. Quackel Did Hide*). The adaptation of said original story was handled by Frank Beresford—who, by 1924, had had at least a dozen similar assignments under his belt—and we are at a loss whether to blame him or nouveau-scribe, Irving, for the fuzziness we've encountered. Helming everything was John B. O'Brien, an industry vet who had directed, among *two* dozen earlier efforts, *The Flying Torpedo* (see entry).

We were unable to find any top-shelf critiques of *Those Who Dare,* and—to be totally honest—we couldn't find any local-paper coverage that was easy to understand, either. Typical of the latter is this introduction to the review printed in the18 December 1924 *Lowell* [Massachusetts] *Sun:* "*Those Who Dare* … is a drama, the powerful theme of which hits home to many thousands, who, however, are not keen to admit it." (One wonders whether those potential ticket-buyers who were not keen to admit this powerful theme hitting home bothered to plunk down the price of admission.)

About the only even fairly engaging item we stumbled upon while researching *Those Who Dare* concerned the identity of its cinematographer. Although listed in *The AFI Catalog* (and elsewhere) as Devereaux Jenkins, it's virtually certain that the artisan responsible for photographing junkets to/from the Swallow was Dev Jennings, brother of SPFX photographer, Gordon (*When Worlds Collide*) Jennings. Working on 1925's *The Lost World* as J. Devereaux Jennings, Mr. J's name may be found herein in our coverage of such films as 1916's *The Jungle Child*, 1917's *Her Temptation* (in both, as J.D. Jennings), and 1927's *The Missing Link* and 1928's *Vamping Venus* (in both, as Dev). Would that the storyline for *Those Who Dare* have been as readily figure-outable as its photographer's propensity to establish multiple noms de travail.

— JTS

Three Ages

Three Ages. Buster Keaton Productions/Metro Pictures, 24 September 1923, 6 reels/5251 feet [available]

CAST: Buster Keaton (*The Hero*); Margaret Leahy (*The Girl*); Wallace Beery (*The Villain*); Joe Roberts (*The Father*); Horace Morgan (*The Emperor*); Lillian Lawrence (*The Mother*); with Blanche Payson, Lionel Belmore, Oliver Hardy

CREDITS: *Producer* Joseph M. Schenck; *Director* Buster Keaton, Eddie Cline; *Story and Titles* Clyde Bruckman, Joseph Mitchell, Jean Havez; *Cinematographers* Elgin Lessley, William McGann; *Art Director* Fred Gabourie

Aka *The Three Ages*

We spent some time pondering whether to include this 1923 feature, not so much because it has only a couple of brief sequences that technically fit the category, "science fiction," but rather because there's a question as to whether (theoretically, at least) this is a feature film.

That question didn't arise because we're dealing solely with printed data on a film that has not survived; we're not, and we've more than a few pictures herein that have utterly vanished, yet which we have chosen to discuss (as best we can) despite arguments over footage length, country of origin, relevance (and depiction) of the fantastic matter therein, or even whether they had ever been shot and/or released at all. Rather, we were forced to consider whether *Three Ages*— as is argued by film historian, David Moews, in his *Keaton: the Silent Features Close Up*— indeed "consists of three two-reeler love stories cut in pieces and then pasted together." Other, equally comprehensive looks at Buster Keaton's film career tag the picture as The Great Stone Face's first feature, if only for its running time. Therein lies the rub.

In his autobiography, *My Wonderful World of Slapstick*, Keaton told amanuensis Charles Samuels about the day that Joe Schenck — Keaton's brother-in-law and producer — received a telegram from John D. Williams of First National: "We do not wish to renew Keaton contract. Stop. We cannot be bothered with his short subjects." That was delivered only after eleven of the twelve two-reelers covered by the expiring contract were

either already in the can or had been released. Albeit the brothers-in-law later determined that the telegram was but a ploy to counter any demands for more lucrative terms for future Keaton product, they decided to move to Metro, which was more than willing to release anything whatsoever that starred Buster Keaton.

Three Ages, then, was a first feature *of sorts*: although pretty much correctly described by David Moews, it was not meant to be an exercise in the creative mix of edited shorts, but rather a spoof on *Intolerance* (*Love's Struggle through the Ages*), D.W. Griffith's epic-length study of historical bigotry, which ran *four* parallel, intercut tracks. (The chariot race found in The Roman Age scenes was likewise a spoof sequence, drawn from Lew Wallace's novel, *Ben-Hur*. Metro-Goldwyn-Mayer's grand cinematic version wouldn't be shot until 1925.) Inasmuch as we could not find a solitary instance of a film critic — either 1916 vintage or recently published — who posited the theory that Griffith's masterwork was merely a mélange of cleverly interwoven *three*-reelers, we finally ruled in favor of granting Mr. Keaton's effort feature-length status. Thus is *Three Ages* represented within these pages, Mr. Moews' ratiocination notwithstanding.

Three Ages is back in *these* pages (Appendix Land), though, because the pertinent genre element is to be found only in "The Stone Age" segment, and — therein — for mere moments. Sight gags like the prehistoric Keaton's presenting a "calling card" that is a rectangular chunk of rock on which a simple line drawing of his face has been chiseled are representative of mundane but effective anachronistic humor. (Another instance — wherein Keaton and an elderly female seer consult a "WeeGee" by placing their hands on a tortoise that creeps across a flat-rock table to land on the chiseled image of the sun — is a tad closer to a more relevant anachronism for us.) The sole image that demands the picture's inclusion is a brief-isimo sequence that has Keaton standing on a flat surface that is revealed to be the back of an Apatosaurus (or some such). In a brace of long shots, Keaton and the dinosaur are seen to be rudimentary stop-motion figures. And there you go. (Well, there are also a couple of times in which a mastodon lumbers onto the scene, but we're pretty sure that man and mastodon did indeed cross paths some time back.)

The principal cast — who repeated their roles throughout the film, including The Roman Age and The Modern Age —consists of Keaton, Margaret Leahy (a beauty-contest entrant who had won top prize: female lead in some film or another), and Wallace Beery. We cannot begin to do justice to Buster Keaton, a giant of Silent Era comedy, and recommend that the reader repair to our bibliography for sources of more comprehensive detail on The Great Stone Face. Miss Leahy never appeared in another film as long as she lived, even though she was named a WAMPAS Baby Star in 1923. (As we noted elsewhere, it was pretty difficult *not* to be named a WAMPUS baby star for a while there....) As for Wallace Beery, his bona fides may be found in our essay on *The Lost World*.

We're not at all sure who was responsible for the stop-motion Apatosaurus footage. Still, while cinematographer Elgin Lessley was a longtime Keaton technician — this would have been just one more assignment for him — he was partnered with William

McGann, who did go into special effects photography in the 1940s, and was also in on the fantasy-oriented camera images in 1919's *When the Clouds Roll By*. Our money's on McGann.

— JTS

To Hell with the Kaiser

To Hell with the Kaiser. Screen Classics, Inc./Metro Pictures Corp. (All-Star Series), 30 June 1918, 7 reels [LOST]

CAST: Lawrence Grant (*The Kaiser/Robert Graubel*); Olive Tell (*Alice Monroe*); Betty Howe (*Ruth Monroe*); John Sunderland (*Winslow Dodge*); Frank Currier (*Professor Monroe*); Walter P. Lewis (*Satan*); Earl Schenck (*Crown Prince*); Mabel Wright (*Empress*); Frank Farrington (*General Pershing*); Emil Hoch (*Von Hindenburg*); George Trimble (*Von Tirpitz*); Carl Dane (Von Hollweg); Henry Carvill (*Bismarck*); P. Reybo (*Von Mackensen*); Charles Hartley (*Count Zeppelin*); W.J. Gross (*Councilor*); Maud Hill (*Mother Superior*); May McAvoy (*Wounded Girl*); with Allan Walker, Margaret McWade, Marion Stewart, George Ridell, Bertha Willsea, Maureen Powers

CREDITS: *Supervisor* Maxwell Karger; *Director* George Irving; *Assistant Directors* Albert H. Kelley, Alfred Raboch; *Scenario* June Mathis; *Cinematographer* George K. Hollister; *Art Titles* Ferdinand Earle; *Scenic Artist* Ferdinand Earle

Our synopsis is from *Motion Picture News* (6 April 1918):

The picture opens with the death of the present Kaiser's father and the present German emperor's abuse of his mother immediately thereafter. In these scenes are depicted the opening of the secret archives wherein was contemplated the world conquest by Germany and the carrying on by the current incumbent of the German throne from the moment he assumed rule some twenty years ago. It shows how he proposed to place his sons on the thrones of the respective countries of Europe and even the United States. Wilhelm's allegorical destruction of the now-famous "scrap of paper" and his invasion of Belgium follows. The Crown Prince enters Belgium with his invading army and the natives are shown seeking sanctuary in a church. Nothing is sacred to the invaders and when the Mother Superior protests she is shot dead in the presence of the Crown Prince, who declares he will take first choice among the girls and the others may follow suit.

He selects for his victim the daughter of an American inventor who has perfected a noiseless wireless apparatus whose messages cannot be intercepted. The girl's father arrives the next morning and while upbraiding the Crown Prince is shot down like a dog by one of the German soldiers. Another sister elects to remain in Berlin, bent on revenge. She is loved by a young attaché of the American Embassy who, when war is declared upon Germany by the United States, becomes an aviator. There are a number of surefire titles as "No true American was ever afraid of a German."

With the aid of her father's perfected wireless, the girl is enabled to communicate to her love who is with the Allies that the Kaiser is headed for a small town. The aviator rounds up a fleet of aeroplanes, captures the Kaiser and delivers him into the hands of the American commander. The commander tells the Emperor: "Henceforth you shall be the prisoner of the world," whereupon an American soldier knocks the prisoner down with a wallop on the jaw, the soldier declaring it was well worth being shot for this special privilege.

The picture concludes with a title announcing the whole thing is only a fantasy and the Kaiser is revealed in Hades.

The synopsis in *The AFI Catalog* adds that Satan abdicates as ruler of hell in the Kaiser's favor as the Kaiser's tortures are more fiendish than anything the devil himself could devise. (A variation on this theme can be found one world war later, in the 1942 short, *The Devil with Hitler*, proving that bad ideas

never die.) This sequence, the main reason for the film being included here, was presumably very brief.

The film's title derives from a popular slogan in wartime America, and this may be the first time a bit of patriotic jingoism served as the basis for a film. This bizarre combination of fantasy, wartime horror and slapstick humor is an antecedent of sorts to films like 1967's *How I Won the War*, but it's not likely surrealism was the intention of the filmmakers back in 1918.

The picture, a big production with a large cast of principals and a couple of thousand extras (though not likely the 12,000 boasted of in the ads), was apparently a hit with public and critics alike. Still, the *Motion Picture News* reviewer, in an otherwise favorable write-up, chose to strain out gnats while swallowing camels: "There is never a scene showing the coat of arms of the Prussian dynasty; the automobiles are all left drives when most people know that right hand drives prevail throughout Europe and none of the cars are decorated with the Hohenzollern emblems."

The New York Times, however, considered the film trash and derided it:

It seems to be a sort of composite of the ideas of a number of movie-mad men who cast about in their imaginations for whatever would make a remunerative number of people hiss and ha-ha and try to win the war by cheering, and then dumped all they found into a scenario. Many Americans would like to see the Crown Prince killed so they had the deed done. What's easier-on the screen? More Americans would like to see the Kaiser captured. So they had that done too. It was a cinch. And why not put both achievements to the credit of one wonderful American girl? Splendid. Let Alice do it. And she did [1 July 1918].

Nevertheless, the filmmakers put one over on the *Times* by taking one word from the review, "Splendid," and putting it in ad for the movie, along with favorable blurbs from other critics.

Lawrence Grant, best known to horror fans as the burgomaster from *Son of Frankenstein*, played both the kaiser and an actor hired to be his double. (Shades of another Universal film, *The Strange Death of Adolf Hitler*.)

When the armistice was declared later in 1918, ads for subsequent showings of *To Hell with the Kaiser* stated, "This is not a war movie." The public that had been so thirsty for German blood and humiliation on the screen was no longer interested.

— HN

Unseen Hands

Unseen Hands. Encore Pictures/Associated Exhibitors, 25 May 1924, 6 reels/5382 feet [LOST]

CAST: Wallace Beery (*Jean Scholast*); Joseph J. Dowling (*Georges Le Quintrec*); Fontaine La Rue (*Madame Le Quintrec*); Jack Rollins (*Armand Le Quintrec*); Cleo Madison (*Malooka*); Jim Cory (*Wapita*); Jamie Gray (*Nola*)

CREDITS: *Producer* Walker Coleman Graves, Jr; *Director* Jacques Jaccard; *Story* Walker Coleman Graves, Jr.

They lost this film some while back, and there's a decent chance that the folks at *Variety* ("It's a good one for the average exhibitor to pass up," 27 August 1924) helped them do so.

The AFI Catalog has a four-sentence-long plot capitulation, nowhere in which is mentioned the "unseen hands" motif that snuck this Encore Pictures six-reeler into our book. Luckily, we found a slightly more detailed rendering of the usual plot synopsis (we *believe* it to be the *MPW*, dated 7 September 1924), and we present that herewith, said "unseen hands" phraseology italicized so it won't be overlooked.

> The action opens in the coal mining district of northern France and later shifts to a remote corner in Arizona. In France, there is some dramatic action especially in the scene where Scholast, coveting LeQuintrec's fortune and wife, causes the lights to go out as the operation, which will save Quintrec's [sic] life, is being performed. After the man dies Scholast is unable to sleep, becomes irritable and at last absconds with the money received from selling all the worldly goods of his wife.
> There is quite a jump from France to Arizona, which, by the way, isn't the most convincing thing in this picture. In America, however, the *"unseen hands"* still pursue the villain, as it were, and he takes unto himself a squaw wife hoping to gain comfort thereby. However the son of the murdered man and wronged wife back in France gets on the trail of Scholast and when he finds him after the overseas trip, there is a terrific fistic encounter with the son getting the worst of it until Scholast thinks he sees the surgeon in spirit form and has a heart attack. Then it is all over. The son marries the squaw's daughter and all ends well.

The phrase that intrigues us is that "the *unseen hands* still pursue the villain," with the word "still" being operative. The reviewer obviously intended to convey that said *unseen hands* had started pursuing the villain at some *earlier* point, like back in France, maybe. Just as obviously, the scenarist meant those hands to represent the psychological hell that Scholast was going through, although that screen leaves us not at all certain how the hands (inserted into the frame via double-exposure, wouldn't you think?) would be presented or how they would be arranged. Would they be rubbing each other, in some sort of gesture of diabolical satisfaction? Or would they be reenacting the moment Scholast flipped off the light switch, or tripped the breaker, or shot out the lights? Or perhaps they'd be pointing, accusingly, at him, or getting in his face, somehow? Or maybe they belonged to the spirit form of the otherwise unseen surgeon, before he managed somehow to get the rest of himself onscreen during the final moments of the last reel? All we can tell from the brief *MPW* paragraphs is that the phrase "as it were" helps us not at all.

Look... This book is filled with films in which (generally wicked) folks are haunted (as it were) by the shades of the (generally good/morally neutral) folks they have done in, even if these shades prove to be little more than tricks of the mind. As ought to be apparent by now to the reader who has navigated these titles alphabetically, during the Silent Era a feature-length picture involving the supernatural that *wasn't* explained away as a trick of the mind or some kind of hoax was as rare as old hippies who claimed that they *hadn't* been at Woodstock. We were prepared to climb the pulpit steps and preach this gospel here, too, except that, whilst mid-essay, we came upon welcome print corroboration. Thus, we offer this unimpeachable verification from the 21 July 1924 edition of *The* [Connesville, Pennsylvania] *Daily Courier*: "From time to time Berry as Scholast is haunted by the past with visionary hands always clutching at his throat. It is this fear of unseen hands that gives the picture

its unusual title." The copy in a pictorial ad the paper ran for the film also indicates that the film is "most gripping." Let's face it: for both full disclosure on details of the movies it covers *and* literary wit in its film criticism —*MPW* be damned — you just can't beat Connesville, Pennsylvania's *The Daily Courier*.

As for the man who was gripped by those unseen hands, in the ten years or so that separated his 1913 film debut from his participation in the epic under discussion, Wallace Beery appeared in over 150 motion pictures, most of which were shorts, most of which were comedies. We've mentioned his "Sweedie" series (in which the big fella went full drag) in our coverage of *The Lost World*, but the husky Missourian made his move into features in 1917 (or so), and his sadistic U-boat commander, Lieutenant Brandt, in Thomas Ince's *Behind the Door* (1919; a Great War meller with a dash of near-genre imagery in its closing moments) was but one of several Kaiser-friendly roles that fell Beery's way until the decade changed. Still, the actor was versatile enough to win such disparate parts as Pancho Villa (*Patria*, 1917), King Philip IV (*The Spanish Dancer*, 1923), King Richard, the Lion-Hearted (*Robin Hood*, ditto), to Casey in 1927's *Casey at the Bat*. Despite these (and other) sundry impersonations, it was during the first lustrum or so of the 1930s that Beery came into his own — his own being celebrated as a character actor sans pareil — and was nominated twice for the Oscar for Best Actor (*The Big House*, 1930, and *The Champ*, 1931), and snagging the statue once (for *The Champ*, although he shared the honor with Fredric March, who won for *Dr. Jekyll and Mr. Hyde*).

In and among heavy-hitting titles like these, *Unseen Hands* went, if not unseen, at least mostly unnoticed, and for anyone other than Mr. Beery, the notices the film did garner weren't worth clipping and saving: *Variety* (cited above) moaned that "there is no head or tale to the story," and opined that "Jacques Jaccard, who directed, has dragged the action so that it induces sleep." *MPW* concurred: "Not so good. Fails to hold interest. Situations overdrawn and at times amateurishly staged." As for Mr. Jaccard, the journal concluded, "The direction [is] conspicuous by its absence." (Jaccard, a New Yorker who dabbled mostly in horse operas, will not be mentioned again in these pages.) Among the supporting cast members ("Just fair," *MPW*) were Fontaine La Rue (*The Sins of Rosanne, Beyond*, etc.), Cleo Madison (*Black Orchids*), and Joseph J. Dowling (*The Miracle Man*); thankfully, they'd received better notices elsewhere.

Gauging only by the critical indifference the picture evinced, *Unseen Hands* was worth seeing back then only for being Wallace Beery's latest portrayal. Word games about the titular special effects apart, we've no empirical proof that the recurring image was meant to induce horror or evoke sympathy or connote psychological unraveling. Without a print of *Unseen Hands*, we're just flying blind.

— *JTS*

Vamping Venus

Vamping Venus. First National Pictures/First National, 13 May 1928, 7 reels/6021 feet [LOST]

CAST: Charlie Murray (*Michael Cassidy/King Cassidy of Ireland*); Louise Fazenda (*Maggie Cassidy/Circe*); Thelma Todd (*Madame Vanezlos, the dancer/Venus*); Russ Powell (*Pete Papagolos/Bacchus*); Big Boy Williams (*Mars*); Joe Bonomo (*Simonides, the strongman/Hercules*); Spec O'Donnell (*Western Union boy/Mercury*); Fred O'Beck (*Vulcan*); Gustav von Seyffertitz (*Jupiter*); Gus Partos (*Shopkeeper*); Janet MacLeod (*Juno*); Yola D'Avril (*Stenographer*)

CREDITS: *Presented by* Richard A. Rowland; *Director* Eddie Cline; *Titles* Ralph Spence; *Adaptation* Howard J. Green; *Story* Bernard McConville; based on the eponymous novel by John Erskine (New York, 1925) and the play, *The Road to Rome*, by Robert Emmett Sherwood (New York, 1927); *Cinematographer* Dev Jennings; *Film Editor* Paul Weatherwax

The most awkward (and least believable) fantasy personage in this comedy feature may be Circe, the Enchantress, if only because she was played by Louise Fazenda. Such highly unlikely casting — unthinkable outside of low comedy — gets something of a credibility boost here, though, in that the conceit unfolds only while the main character is in a state of unconsciousness.

Our recap is taken from *The AFI Catalog*:

Irish American Michael Cassidy sneaks out one evening to join his buddies at their annual dinner at the Silver Spoon Night Club. There he is knocked unconscious by Simonides, strongman in a troupe of performers, who resents Cassidy's flirting with Madame Vanezlos, another member of the troupe. Cassidy dreams of himself as king of Ireland, cavorting in ancient Greece among the gods and goddesses: Venus, actually Madame Vanezlos; Circe, in real life his wife; and Hercules, in reality Simonides. In time, he becomes ruler of the country by introducing many marvels of modern machinery. Then a rebellion is started against Cassidy and his buzzers, telephones, tanks, and machine guns. In the midst of the battle, Cassidy sees Hercules abducting Venus, and rescues her.

During the late Silent Era, the average American — whether an inveterate movie-goer or a stay-at-home reader/radio fan — would have immediately recognized that the essence of that scenario was a regurgitation of *A Connecticut Yankee at King Arthur's Court*. (In fact, the 12 May 1928 *Harrison's Reports* flat-out warned citizens who both attended movies and *read* about movies of this casual plagiarism, but a bit late, as the picture was released on the 13 May.) Among the plot wrinkles shared by *Venus* and *Connecticut Yankee* is the venerable "modern-day folk find themselves cavorting among denizens of Days of Yore whilst in the throes of unconsciousness" shtick, which — in itself — does not impart genre-dom onto the storyline. Many are the mundane silent films whose plots unfold while their protagonists (1) dream or daydream, (2) have sunken into a drunken or drug-induced delirium, or (3) have been knocked colder than frozen pork chops. As Cicero might have said, we will not bother iterating all those otherwise genre-potent features — like 1915's *The Magic Skin*, 1916's *The Right to Be Happy*, or 1920's *Dr. Jekyll and Mr. Hyde* (no, the *other* one) — that offered as catharsis to the unwary masses the always-wretched "It's a dream" denouement. The reader has probably waded through them already, anyway.

Venus and *Connecticut* also depict vistas of contemporary (i.e., 1920s) American life alongside representations of the wonderful world of mythic history, but neither does this mean we are in the presence of our beloved genre. As with pictures that showed events that transpired only while their participants were here-and-now-challenged, there were also innumerable movies

(and some, like *Intolerance*, very important movies) made during the Silent Era that were constructed to compare and contrast Life as it is lived Now (Now being the Silent Era) with Life as it was lived Then (a variable — but always readily-identifiable and picturesque — earlier Era) and (occasionally; see *Three Ages*) with Ür-Life as it *may* have been lived back before there were snapshots, oil paintings, or even line drawings. In light of this, we cannot consider scenes of shaggy, pelt-wearing cave dwellers to be the genre "smoking gun" unless, of course, said cave dwellers are carrying smoking guns. And therein lies the distinction.

The science-fiction/fantasy element in *Venus* (and *Connecticut Yankee* and *Three Ages* and…) is found in the use of anachronistic elements in the dramatic narrative: motor cars supplanting horses in a joust, Buster Keaton's cave-self riding the brontosaurus to work, etc. (Nota bene: said anachronistic messing around only holds genre water when the temporally incongruous device/situation is clearly from the future. A scene wherein, for example, a 21st-century author is shown writing a letter to the editor with a quill pen is not an example of science fiction or fantasy, but is, rather, a pretty good sign of his/her eccentricity and/or mental illness.) Thus, points gained for having Hercules (himself!) trade colloquial title cards with someone named Michael Cassidy are lost as said bon-mot swaps occur only in Cassidy's mind. Nevertheless, bonuses could have been awarded if only they had shown that the testosterone-heavy demi-god was packing heat, or that divine messenger boy, Mercury, had abjured his winged sandals for Ma Bell.

The extent to which Mr. Cassidy insinuated 20th-century technology into the timeless Hellenic ether is uncertain, though. Insofar as the critical heavy-hitters *did* go on record about the picture, it was mostly to cluck that this latest mix of mortals and mythic types really hadn't moved the concept much beyond Thespis's first shot, millennia earlier. In the same vein, the 26 June 1928 *Variety*'s reminded its readership of more recent (but equally formulaic) variations:

Some genius on the First National lot thought of doing this one so as to utilize the massive sets and props used in *Helen of Troy*. It was intended to be another wow travesty on Greek mythology, which vaudeville used and discarded when James and Sadie Leonard quit doing such skits as "When Caesar Sees Her" 20 years ago. It has turned out to be one of the dreariest and unfunniest film comedies ever to find its way out of the film colony.

With just about every major critic focused on the predictability of the anachronistic bits that were found onscreen rather than their novelty, none mentioned genre specifics that we would find helpful, à la the copyright synopsis (taken by *The AFI Catalog* from the registration documents). It appears that, after *Connecticut Yankee* had successfully mined the silliness-in-the-space/time-continuum mother lode at the outset of the decade, any thematic last gasps that remained after two-reel comics had their way during the intervening lustrum-and-a-half were exploited by First National's costly feature, *The Private Life of Helen of Troy*, released the year before *Venus*. (*Helen*'s screenplay was derived from an amalgam of John Erskine's 1925 eponymous novel and Robert Emmet Sherwood's 1927 play, *The Road to Rome*, which — despite its receiving onscreen credit —

dealt not at all with Helen of Troy. The picture was a comic take on the epic tale of the "Face that Launched a Thousand Ships" and had none of the anachronistic stuff that would interest us, save that the dramatis personae were portrayed as being appealingly down to Earth and — despite those expensive sets and costumes –*very* 1920s, attitudinally. Still, the film's titles streamed from the fecund imagination of Ralph [*The Gorilla*] Spence, and the role of Hector — the Trojan counterpart to Achilles – was played by George [*The Wizard, While London Sleeps*] Kotsonaros!)

Even if *Venus* did fail in its bid for creativity and innovation, no one could argue that its cast wasn't first rate. Charlie Murray (Garrity in First National's *The Gorilla*; see entry) impersonated Michael Cassidy, and it was the era's casual indifference to ethnic stereotypes that shaped the character: the soon-to-be King of Ireland was seen to be hen-pecked, given to intemperance, and — anticipating Og's personal anthem in *Finian's Rainbow*— prone to love the girl he's near. Said girl and Venus were played by doomed comedienne, Thelma Todd (*The Haunted House*), and the roles of Simonides and Hercules went to Joe Bonomo, a bodybuilder/stuntman/sometimes actor who had done some fairly strenuous (and impressive) gags on the QT for the Man of a Thousand Faces (see *The Hunchback of Notre Dame*). Bonomo, a Brooklynite born on Christmas Day 1901, not only went on to double for cinematic ape-man Charles Gemora in 1932's Lugosifest, *Murders in the Rue Morgue*, but he donned all sorts of hair yet again to portray one of the nameless beast-men in Paramount's *Island of Lost Souls*, released in December that same year. *Lost Souls* was Bonomo's ape … errr … *swan* song, and the young man left the industry to start his own physical culture enterprise.

The skinny on La Fazenda may be had by reading our coverage of *The Bat*, and grand old goblin, Gustav von Seyffertitz, gets what's coming to him in the essay on the 1926 remake of *The Bells*. Spec O'Donnell — the Fresno-born teenager who shared screen-time with von Seyffertitz in Mary Pickford's melodrama of baby farms and swamps, *Sparrows*— spent his youth playing freckled-faced pains in the ass and is probably best remembered for his participation in a handful of late silent/early sound Hal Roach comedies starring (among others) Laurel and Hardy, Charley Chase, and Edgar Kennedy. As O'-Donnell's freckles faded due to the passing of years and inroads made by Max Factor, so did his film credits; although the actor's face was seen on the big and small screens another 150 or so times before he retired, his name seldom made the cast scrawls post 1931.

During the Silent Era, director Eddie Cline was associated for the most part with Buster Keaton, while the Sound Era found his name frequently linked with that of W.C. Fields; heck, for legions of savvy moviegoers in both eras, the name *Eddie Cline* and the phrase *film comedy* were virtually synonymous. The critics, however, did not always agree. *Variety*'s "con"— author of the unflattering remarks printed above—felt that the Cline effort under discussion "wouldn't entertain in a nursery."

Harrison's Reports (12 May 1928) acknowledged *Venus*'s lavish appearance, its debt to Mark Twain (and the Fox Film Corporation), and its helmsman ("The picture has been directed by Eddie Cline"), but still doubted whether the film would play well to the average Joe. The 11 November 1928 number of *Film Daily* was as enthusiastic as it was brief, though, tersely crowing that "the original [*sic*] comedy theme is good for some real laughs." Geographically removed from either coast's entertainment capital, America's midland checked in, and W. Ward Marsh, writing in the 14 May 1928 edition of the *Cleveland Plain Dealer*, addressed any concerns *Harrison's* may have had about the masses. Disposing of the entire "back in time" device as being "done after the manner of Harry Myers' one great film, *The Continental* [*sic*] *Yankee in King Arthur's Court*" (Way to go, Mr. Marsh!), the continued:

> You will probably laugh much at *Vamping Venus*, but I daresay you will agree that it lacks spontaneity and that not half enough has been realized from the possibilities the situations offered. *Vamping Venus* earns this verdict: Pretty funny horse-play, much play and scarcely no [*sic*, again] evidence of plot.

Once again, we must pause to note that the King of the Greek Gods was Zeus (not Jupiter) and his wife was Hera (and not Juno). Our lesson: If you want accuracy and/or plot with your Greek pantheon, check out Homer!

— *JTS*

War and the Woman

War and the Woman. Thanhouser Film Corp./Pathé Film Exchange, Inc., 9 September 1917, 5 reels, Unviewable print at Eastman House

CAST: Florence La Badie (Ruth); Tom Brooke (John Braun); Wayne Arey (John Barker); Grace Henderson (His Mother); Arthur Bower (Commander of the Invading Army); Ernst C. Warde (Lieut. Fredericks)

CREDITS: *Director* Ernest C. Warde; *Scenario* Philip Lonergan: *Cameraman* William M. Zollinger

WORKING TITLE: *My Country*

If anything, this 1917 Thanhouser five-reeler is a lower-shelf knockoff of Vitagraph's earlier *Womanhood, the Glory of the Nation* (and its even earlier *The Battle Cry of Peace*), but features only one sterling example of patriotic American womanhood while stinting on the fantasy element (and the war footage, too). As lower budgets usually lead to lower expectations, there are no smartly-attired Ruritanian forces on the march here; rather, the occupying forces are de facto tagged as being German and accepted as being *here* without much evidence as to how they arrived. This is somewhat surprising for, at that point in time, there was still some hesitancy to call a spade a spade, as it were, yet the "usual suspects" among the trade press used the "G" word freely while reiterating that the idea of any such invasion of the Land of the Free would remain firmly in the realm of the fantastic, or — at the very least — require a *very* vivid imagination.

The following synopsis is taken from the above-cited issue of *Motography*:

> John Braun and his step-daughter, Ruth Norton, are under suspicion as German spies. Ruth at first believes her step-father innocent but later learns he is in Germany's employ. To avoid him and his aides she jumps from the train on which they are traveling and Braun loses track of her. Fate leads her to the place where the airplane of John Baker has been wrecked and her "first aid" methods save the aviator's life. Later Ruth marries Baker.

The German army invades the east coast and the Baker home becomes headquarters of the commanding officer. In the officer's staff, Ruth finds her step-father. The Germans try to force Ruth to become a spy for them, but she refuses. Instead, revolted by the treatment to which the women of the village have been subjected, Ruth carries out a plan to blow up the place by dynamite. Just before this, Baker is able to get a message through the lines to Ruth and he arrives with his airplane in time to rescue her before the dynamite blast destroys the house and the people in it. The closing scenes show the downfall of Germany and the triumph of democracy.

Neither did Germany fall nor democracy prevail quite so easily, of course, but, as delineated in the *Motography* précis, the film seems to have dealt solely with those Huns who had hunkered down on America's Atlantic coast. If only…! Another intriguing bit of business is the placement of the phrase *first aid* in quotation marks; either the concept of on-the-spot, minor medical treatment by non-professionals was only then impinging on the consciousness of the average American, or the reviewer found Ruth's life-saving mechanics either picturesque or unlikely.

The 29 September 1917 *Motography* grumped, "There are no battle scenes."

— JTS

The Warning

The Warning. Triumph Film Corp./Equitable Motion Pictures Corp. (released through World Film Corp.), 6 December 1915, 5 reels, 35mm at BFI/National Film and Television Archive (London)

CAST: Henry Kolker (*Robert Denman*); Lily Leslie (*Anna Denman*); Master Frank Longacre (*Bobbie Denman*); Christine Mayo ("*The Woman Who Smiles*"); Edna Mayo (*Martha*); Mayme Kelso (*Camille*); with Edith Thornton, Cyril Rheinhard, William McKey, Ogden Childe.

CREDITS: *Director* Edmund Lawrence; *Story* Julius Steger

The title page of the copyright registration documents on file at the Library of Congress has the name Harry Bonnell as author of this story, but the name is crossed out. The film was re-edited in 1919 by The Aywon Film Corporation and released as *The Eternal Penalty* via the States Rights distribution system. We have been unable to locate any critiques or publicity materials of much worth on this later version. For more on Edna Mayo, see *The Quest of the Sacred Jewel.*

A lost soul and a possibility of the sort of depiction of the Inferno that might make us sit up and take notice were it only available for viewing somewhere within these contiguous United States. Put them all together and they spell "Appendix." And, Lo!

From the copyright registration materials:

Robert Deman, the likable superintendent of a construction firm, gradually becomes an alcoholic to the consternation of his employer, his wife Anna, his sister Martha, and his friend, Henry Morse. On New Year's Eve, after Robert's boss strongly warns him to stop drinking, he continues and later sees a beautiful woman smile at him on Broadway. At home, after Anna and Martha reproach him, Robert dozes while he watches his son Bobbie sleep. Later he rings in the New Year with the Smiling Woman. She becomes his mistress, until he is caught robbing his employer to satisfy her whims and is discharged. Bobbie later finds Robert drunk and pulls at his sleeve in the street, but Robert shoves him and the boy is struck by an auto. Bobbie becomes crippled and Anna divorces him and marries Henry. Robert, now a derelict, dies in the

gutter. After seeing other alcoholics in Hades, he tries to join Bobbie passing above, but finds himself about to be consumed by fire. Robert then awakens in Bobbie's room. He thanks Heaven for his warning and embraces Anna and Bobbie.

It's a bit sobering to consider that scenarist Julius Steger apparently had allotted one of the rings of hell for men who spent more than an inordinate time bending their elbows, and he did so about midway between Congress's passing the Volstead Act over a Woodrow Wilson veto and the death of the formidable Carrie Nation, who had inflicted a mess of "hatchetations" on some of the country's more vulnerable saloons. Of themselves, these deplorable events might pique our curiosity and merit our sympathy, but it is the nightmare of the alcohol-laced Inferno that brings this Triumph Film Corp. effort to the pages.

We've no print at hand, of course, and we've been unable to locate any stills (even at the BFI) that depicted Henry Kolker at any point during the photoplay, let alone while he was rubbing shoulders with any of his smoldering fellowship who were to spend eternity looking for a stiff one with cold water, back. How elaborate and extensive was the footage of the fiery pit? Contemporary critiques do little but tease. The 4 December 1915 edition of *The Moving Picture World*, for example, spends a heady paragraph saying not much at all:

> Warnings in dreams have an element of mystery and weirdness. Under very clever dramatic handling and with the help of splendid acting this warning of the weak-willed drinker is visualized in the most starling and wonderfully convincing way…. I dare say that there is not one man or woman in the audience who does not believe that the unfortunate weakling had really joined the children of perdition.

The New York Dramatic Mirror— on that same date — became a tad more analytic, claiming the picture "is compounded of about equal parts of T.S. Arthur, Zola, and Brown-Potter, with a dash of Dante's 'Inferno' at the end," while *Motography*— a week later — recounted vaguely that "his soul goes out into the depths which make it recoil in fear." The only hint we have as to the staging of the sequence also came from the *Mirror*, as reviewer, "H," groused that "there is, perhaps, a bit too much of the Devil in the vision scenes…."

"H," of course, was entitled to his opinion, but the prospect of a full-blown sequence featuring His Satanic Majesty giving what-for to a surfeit of smoldering lushes would hardly be dismissed out of hand by such as us. Drinks on us for the first bloke who unspools *The Warning* in Londontown and reports in, no questions asked.

— JTS

Wasted Lives

Wasted Lives. Mission Film Corp./Second National Film Corp., 10 January 1923, 5 reels/4,874 feet [LOST]

CAST: Richard Wayne (*Randolph Adams*); Catherine Murphy (*Dorothy Richards*); Winter Hall (*Dr. Wentworth*); Lillian Leighton (*Mrs. Jonathan Adams*); Margaret Loomis (*Madge Richards*); Arthur Osborne (*Ned Hastings*); Walt Whitman (*Noah Redstone*); Philippe De Lacy (*Bobby Adams*); Fannie Midgely (*Mrs. Hastings*)

CREDITS: *Director* Clarence Geldert; *Titles* William B. Laub

While poking around — looking for pictures that require discussion in these pages — we were surprised to find that the first part of the 1920s saw the release of two (2) films entitled *Wasted Lives*. Before getting embroiled in the feature that earned its spot here in the Appendix, we just *have* to share this brief plot summation of the other one:

> After the death of her brother, "Tommy" Carlton makes the acquaintance of a neighbor, Harold Graypon, who invites her to a party. Tommy, who is a bit of a hoyden, attends the party in overalls and shocks the guests. Tommy is later ejected from her home and takes refuge in a shack in the mountains, where she makes rustic furniture for a living....

As Count Floyd used to ask, "Hey, kids... Isn't that Tommy Carlton *scary*...?"

Our Wasted Lives—in theaters two years prior to Tommy's saga—was the first-ever production of the Mission Film Corporation, which would call it quits in 1925 after its third-ever production. (The picture was then distributed by—Are you ready for this? –the *Second* National Film Corporation, for which this was the one and only release.) The five-reeler was also the first-ever directed by Clarence Geldert, and although Geldert would hang up his megaphone after 1925's *My Neighbor's Wife* (his second-ever), he would take direction from someone else in well over 130 feature films that ranged from the mid–1910s (and titles like *The Fall of a Nation*, see entry) to the mid–1930s (when he played uncredited bits in pictures like *Diamond Jim*).

In between, Mr. Geldart (alternate spelling, you see) was in films with profiles that have qualified them for these pages: *The Sins of Rosanne* (1920), *All Souls' Eve* and *The Witching Hour* (both 1921), *Behind the Curtain* (1924), and the 1929 reincarnation of *The Thirteenth Chair*. (He was also in 1929's *The Unholy Night*, but that early talkie had no all-silent version and is thus missing from our tally.) While not in the principal cast for any of these, the New Brunswick–born actor's face and name—in any of several variegations—were familiar to Silent-Era moviegoers; he died, working up until the very end, in May 1935.

As for Mr. Geldert's handiwork here, we needed consult the copyright registration records at the Library of Congress:

> Rich, idle Randolph Adams leaves his medical studies, but an incident with an injured child causes him to return to medicine and devote his life to a children's hospital. He marries Madge Richards, who is also loved by his friend Ned Hastings, and shortly thereafter he goes to war. Randy is reported killed, and in her bitterness his mother withdraws her support of the hospital. Ned asks Madge to marry him, and she is almost persuaded when Mrs. Adams is seriously injured in an accident. [*Harrison's Reports*: "She is struck by an automobile and dies."] Then, Randy suddenly reappears, saves his mother's life with a "vibrameter," a machine of his own invention, and returns to his family and work.

The above, in a nutshell: Mother love, followed by maternal bitterness (targeted at sick children, because her own child is worse than sick), followed by mom's chance meeting with a Model T, and then followed (finalmente!) by her getting all better because her not-dead son has tinkered together a *wonder-machine* that will not only get the old lady back up on her pins, but will fill her heart with contrition and her eyes with tears of gratitude. And the genius son's got a girl in there, somewhere, too, thank God.

Skip all the rest of the baloney and home in on the phrase *wonder-machine*. Whoever wrote the screenplay that was prob-

ably based on a story by somebody else tagged this mother-saving device a "vibrameter," which—leads us to assume that mom is brought back from the Stygian darkness by being shaken awake. *Orrrrr* ... the gizmo's label is not derived from "vibrate" but, rather, from "vibrant," meaning "full of liveliness or energy." Thus, Randolph's invention has been charged full of liveliness or energy (probably after having been plugged into the wall socket overnight) and this is somehow transferred into mater, and the "meter" part of the tag merely allows everyone to measure how much liveliness and energy is being shot into the erstwhile-bitter and rapidly stiffening Mrs. Adams.

As the Old Philosopher used to ask, "Too many present-day cure-alls seen as miracles back then? Is that your problem, Bunky?" Heck, a vibrameter by any other name would probably be a defibrillator nowadays, but who can say how said machine was brought to the table (and, more importantly, applied to mom *on* the table) back in 1923? Was the whole shebang merely a throwaway, not meant to intrude (much) on this heart-warming story of a mom whose heart—and everything else—had cooled? Or did the Mission Film Corp. folks decide to go for the gold and send flunkies off to Anaconda, Montana to fetch young Ken Strickfaden to build a contraption that would have tickled the heart of Rube Goldberg? (The 16 June 1923 *Harrison's Reports* unhelpfully tagged it "an electrical apparatus.") ¿Quién sabe?

A rather interesting thing about this picture—no, not the maudlin malarkey that took up most of the five reels—was the timing of its release. On the 10 January 1923, viewers caught sight of the forerunner/prototype/possibly-stolen design of a rudimentary defibrillator: a piece of cardiac-manipulation equipment that would ultimately prove so crucial in emergency situations that high-school football trainers made sure they had one in the trunks of their cars when heading off to away games. On the 30 July 1923—barely six months later—ticket-buyers witnessed the near-magical, death-defying properties of injectable adrenaline in Universal's *Legally Dead*. Given that these latest scientific discoveries to thwart The Grim Reaper doubtless reached more people thanks to movie theaters than to the second sections of local newspapers, vintage–1923 audiences must have felt it was a great time to be alive.

Not so fast! That vibrameter may have saved the day (and the parental unit) per the copyright registration screed, but the machine made no impression whatsoever in the recollections of a reviewer who had actually eyeballed the film. Gertrude Chase (the *New York Morning Telegraph*) highlighted her recollections of the goings-on thus:

> A man who goes out to kill animals in the woods [?!] remains to save the life of a sick child. From this time his life is devoted to work in children's hospitals and, with the financial assistance of his mother, he founds one of his own. His death is reported and his mother becomes so embittered she withdraws her support from the hospital.

A trifle odd—especially the animal-killing bit—but fairly kosher per the registration materials. Miss Chase flabbergasts, though, when she reveals how mom's financial support has kept otherwise woeful waifs well: "The children are treated with sunshine and music, and wonderful results are obtained." Damn! The check's come back! To the cellar with the children! As for

Mrs. Indian Giver's recuperative moment: "The timely appearance of the son, whose death has been erroneously reported, saves her life." If Randolph did, indeed, show up with that vibrameter under his arm, it was— per Miss Chase — just another case of bringing coals to Newcastle.

The Mission Film Corporation's first mission didn't resonate enough —vibrameter or no— with the usual suspects to merit a critique, so we have to relegate the erstwhile idle Randolph's possibly-near-science-fictional invention to the dustbin of the Appendix.

Had the damned thing been called a *vibrator*, though, we can guarantee it would have received a lot of press and its own full-length chapter.

— JTS

Wee Lady Betty

Wee Lady Betty. Triangle Films Corp./Triangle Film Distributing Corp., 19 August 1917, 5 reels [LOST]

CAST: Bessie Love (*Wee Lady Betty*); Frank Borzage (*Roger O'Reilly*); Charles K. French (*Fergus Mc Clusky*); Walter Perkins (*Shamus McTeague*); L. Jeffries (*Lanty O'Dea*); Walter Whitman (*Mr. O'Reilly*); Aggie Herring (*Mrs. O'Reilly*); Thornton Edwards (*Connor O'Donovan*); Alfred Hollingsworth (*Father Dan*); J.P. Lockney (*Michael O'Brien*)

CREDITS: *Director* Charles Miller; *Writer* J.G. Hawks; *Art Direction* G. Harold Percival

Studio synopsis as printed in *The* [Chicago] *Suburban Economist*, 11 September 1917:

In the Isle of Kilcroney, the Wee Lady Betty ruled the tenants of the O'Reilly Castle with a stern hand and a big heart. Their fear of the Wee Lady was next to the fear of the ghost of "Slasher" O'Reilly that walked in the castle. Then Sir Daniel O'Reilly, the rightful owner of the castle, died, leaving the castle to Roger O'Reilly who announced he was coming to take possession. The tenants would not have this as the Wee Lady had been good to them, but she told them to receive the new master kindly, and prepared to leave the castle.

Not having the wherewithal to provide for her aged father, the Wee Lady contrived a scheme. Feigning to leave the castle, she had her father return with the two servants after dark the same night and she promptly installed her father in the haunted chamber, keeping the key. The next day when Roger O'Reilly arrived his reception was a chilly one, the villagers believing that he was responsible for the Wee Lady's supposed departure. He arrived at the castle with his mother, and the Wee Lady, in the guise of a maid, together with the two servants, showed them through the place, paying particular stress on the haunted chamber and the ghost of "Slasher" O'Reilly.

When Roger had gone, his mother demanded to see the haunted room so the Wee Lady, going ahead, got into an old suit of armor and said in a deep voice, "Be gone!" Mrs. O'Reilly promptly fainted! The Wee Lady fond that she had developed a strong liking for Roger but was thrown into despair when he, hearing about the ghost, declared that he would nail up the door of the chamber until he found time to investigate.

When she was getting food to her father that night she heard a door open and beheld Roger entering the room. Once more she got behind the armor and said "Be gone!" Her answer was a shot from Roger's pistol, grazing her arm. There was a loud noise outside and Roger rushed from the room, not knowing the work his pistol had done. The angry villagers had stormed the castle and were rushing up the steps when Roger appeared at the top. A

rough and tumble fight ensued between Roger and the mob below, when the Wee Lady appeared and commanded them to leave. They left the castle, leaving the Wee Lady Betty and Roger clasped in each other's arms.

Since we know from the get-go that there are no actual ghosts in the story, the Appendix seems the best place for this Bessie Love vehicle. Regrettably the intriguingly named spook, "Slasher" O'Reilly, does not make an appearance, and his stand-in — an old suit of armor — is there for laughs and not thrills. One could look at the story as a kind of romantic comedy reworking of *The Hound of the Baskervilles* with the "Slasher" legend subbing for the murderous mutt and Lady Betty and Roger taking on the Stapleton and Sir Henry roles. Of course the outcome of the initially antagonistic relationship between the little lady and the new laird would not have surprised any savvy moviegoer with the patience to sit through the five reels of contrivances that preceded the inevitable clinch.

(Columbia Pictures tried its hand at a *Wee Lady Betty*–like, supposedly-haunted-castle/protagonist-marries-the-owner groaner with its 1925 *A Fool and His Money*. That epic, based [swore the onscreen credits crawl] on George Barr McCutcheon's eponymous novel, apparently did little other than change locales [Germany for Ireland], switch the gender of the castle-acquirer, and replace the mob of angry villagers with a squad of soldiers. Still, as McCutcheon's page-turner saw print in 1912, we may never know whether it might have had any sort of subliminal influence on the *Wee* scenarist.)

Frank Borzage's performance as Roger marked one of his last turns as an actor; ahead lay a highly successful career as a director of sad love stories. Though he is not credited in the original film, modern sources claim that Borzage co-directed *Wee Lady Betty* with Charles Miller.

Ads for the film naturally highlighted Bessie Love, but there were frequent nods to the Gallic setting of the tale: "How to keep house in an Irish castle" is one description of the film. One puzzling bit of publicity saw print in *The San Antonio* [Texas] *Light* (26 August 1917): "While war pictures are not distinctly in favor at this time, Bessie Love's new picture *Wee Lady Betty* has just enough war scenes to give it a tang and snap that is distinctly appealing." It's not clear where these "appealing" war scenes would have fit into the movie. Possibly, Roger came to Ireland after a stint in the Great War; that might explain his being so trigger-happy, but the gory tang and snap must have been very minimal indeed and perhaps occurs early in the film.

Variety's Fred liked Bessie Love in the title role and found the film "Cute, with a nice comedy vein running through it. A feature that will get a number of laughs" (31 August 1917). No doubt Bessie's fans agreed. The particulars on Miss Love can be found in the entry *Between Friends*. The scenario to *Wee Lady Betty* was but one — albeit the least — of several genre credits of San Franciscan, J(ohn) G. Hawks. Other of his contributions we note in these pages: *A Blind Bargain* (1922), *The Last Warning*, and *The Charlatan* (1929, the pair; see entries). In addition, Hawks helped with the editing on both *Earthbound* (1920, see entry) and Lon Chaney's *The Penalty* (1922), although he did the latter sans screen credit.

— HN

When the Clouds Roll By

When the Clouds Roll By. Douglas Fairbanks Pictures Corp./United Artists Corp., 29 December 1919, 6 reels [available]

CAST: Douglas Fairbanks (*Daniel Boone Brown*); Kathleen Clifford (*Lucette Bancroft*); Frank Campeau (*Mark Drake*); Ralph Lewis (*Curtis Brown*); Herbert Grimwood (*Dr. Metz*); Albert MacQuarrie (*Hobson*); Daisy Robinson (*Bobbie DeVere*)

CREDITS: *Producer* Douglas Fairbanks; *Director* Victor Fleming; *Assistant Director* J. Theodore Reed; *Manager of Production* Robert Fairbanks; *Scenario* Thomas Geraghty; *Story* Douglas Fairbanks; *Cinematographers* Harry Thorpe, William McGann; *Art Direction* Edward Langley; *Art Titles* Henry Clive

Mental telepathy, scientific experiments, abundant superstitions, horrific sequences … just the buzzwords to indicate the sort of far-fetched photoplay that would be tailor-made for these pages. Alas, in this far-fetched photoplay, not one of them proves to be genuine. Even the mental telepathy angle turns out to be a hoax, easily perpetrated by one character's shadowing another's every move. The film *does* revolve around two highly superstitious characters, but we quickly discover that, by "superstition," the scenarist meant belief in wives' tales (like "don't cross a black cat") rather than in creatures of myth or legend. Those scenes of horror that *do* present themselves spring from the dreams of the main protagonist. And as for those experiments, well, they might be more correctly categorized as *pseudo*-scientific were they not hatched in the mind of an escaped madman.

Even putting all of that aside, *When the Clouds Roll By* gets an endorsement here. It's weird enough, original enough, entertaining enough (and, most importantly, *available and accessible* enough) to appeal to anyone interested enough to bother to read these words. Our synopsis is drawn on notes taken during our viewing of the film:

> Dr. Metz, in addressing a group of interested academic types, describes his "fantastic theory of civic design" with his course of action — "I plan to take a human life in the cause of science, but this must remain a professional secret with us."
>
> Metz selects Daniel Boone Brown [Douglas Fairbanks] as his guinea pig; his goal: to secretly implant "germs of fear, worry, superstitious and kindred annoyances" into the man's psyche. As his recruit, Metz enlists Brown's man servant, Hobson, who in turn injects nothing but confusion into Brown's life. Hobson dispenses bad advice to the gullible Brown in one of the very first sequences by informing him that it's perfectly okay to eat a gastronomic concoction of raw onion, lobster, Welsh rarebit and mince pie for a midnight snack.
>
> Dreaming restlessly, Daniel sees ogres and specters. Then, still in his pajamas, he dream-walks into a public gathering. Inexplicably, he leaps first into a large picture and then into a swimming pool where he meets up the onion, the lobster, etc. Without catching his breath, he jumps onto a horse, rides through a phantom wall, leaps over rooftops, dives into a chimney and drops into a large, metal, tank-like container. Upon hearing metal banging on metal, he awakens and realizes that he's hearing the garbage men.
>
> Unfortunately for him, Daniel is two hours late for work at his Uncle Curtis' firm. The tardiness is caused not only because of his night's sleep. Brown's superstition-laden morning ritual is topped off by not one — but several — broken mirrors. The uncle is understandably not pleased and sends him home. Fretting that his opal [often called the "Bad Luck Stone"] ring has caused his misfortune, he tosses it. It's picked up by a pert Oklahoman [Lucette Bancroft], the two bump into one another, and they immediately hit it off. The mutual attraction is cemented by a common superstitious bent.
>
> Meanwhile, Mark Drake, "a boll weevil mayor of a boom oil town in Oklahoma" arrives on the scene. Not only does Drake want to marry Lucette, but he also partners with Curtis Brown to scam her father out of a rich oil claim. In need of a front man to make the scheme successful, Curtis suggests his unwitting nephew.
>
> As a Lucette Bancroft — Mark Drake — Daniel Boone Brown love triangle shapes up, Dr. Metz leverages it to further unhinge poor Brown. Nonetheless, Bancroft opts for Brown. At the wedding, however, Drake has a trick or two up his sleeve. He informs the bride that Brown planned to double cross her father and then furthers his untruthfulness by telling the elder Brown that his nephew has revealed the secret plan. Daniel is fired and Lucette goes off with Drake.
>
> Images of despair (in the form of demons) shoot through Daniel's head. He intends to shoot himself, but his uncle intervenes. An insane asylum truck passes by … but … it's there to apprehend the shadowing Dr. Metz! Daniel laughs the whole thing off, vows to approach life with humor, tells off his overbearing uncle, and, in chasing after Lucette, sheds all of his unfounded taboos along the way.
>
> Daniel — who has appropriated the asylum guard's badge — uses it to have the Oklahoma mayor hauled off as crazy. But Lucette is still not in a forgiving mood. Suddenly, a dam bursts, the neighboring burg is in peril, and the train that they are all on is jeopardized. In the ensuing flood, Daniel helps to save the day by hanging from a tree branch and rescuing stranded passengers. Sunshine breaks through in the morning and he swims to her. All is finally forgiven, a minister on a church steeple floats by and they're married on the spot.

Cheer Up, the picture's working title, had been jettisoned along the way but the final title card retained the same sunny tone: "Never despair, folks, everything will be Jake — When the Clouds Roll By."

Reviews were favorable, and a great e.g. comes from W. Ward Marsh's critique in the 30 December 1919 *Cleveland Plain Dealer*:

> A brighter bit of comedy, a gloomier bit of near-tragedy and a more wholesome dose of real-honest-to-goodness optimism to cap the climax of six reels of semi-hysteria, caused both by suspense and hearty laughter, would not only be difficult, but well nigh impossible to find…. Nothing more can be said except that the picture is "there" — absolutely "there."

Geographically speaking, "there" meant the foothills of the Cascade Mountains in Northern California. That's where Doug's kin, Robert Fairbanks, supervised the construction of the to-be-deluged city, and where a special reservoir with water from the Sacramento River flooded the set at the proper time. With the hindsight afforded by decades of disaster movies, those efforts don't make quite the … *ummm* … splash they once did; still, this was big doin's circa 1920. In the 10 January 1920 *Exhibitors Trade Review*, George T. Pardy focused on the picture's climax: "The big scene is, of course, the breaking of the dam and consequent flood which floats the lovers to wedded bliss. This is a marvelously realistic spectacle likely to linger one in the minds of all beholders."

Other reviews serve to illustrate the general consensus:

> "The whole picture is full of Fairbank's fun, and will greatly please the legion with whom the acrobatic actor is a favorite" [*The New York Times*, 29 December 1919].

> "Everything considered, I think the average movie fan will quite approve of *When the Clouds Roll By*" [Mae Tinee, *Chicago Tribune*, 30 December 1919].

"The best Fairbanks feature in some months" ["Leed," *Variety*, 2 January 1920].

"For continuous and unalloyed good fun, it is in the front rank of Fairbanks' releases" [Edward Wetzel, *Moving Picture World*, 10 January 1920].

"This can safely be called one of Doug's best" [Tom Hamlin (in syndication), *The Anniston* (Texas) *Star*, 4 January 1920].

"The reviewer boldly proclaims this the best Douglas Fairbanks picture since his debut as a star" [*Wid's Daily*, 4 January 1920].

Douglas Fairbanks approached something close to auteurship in *When the Clouds Roll By* via appearing in, producing, and fashioning the story; his curriculum vitae may be found in The *Thief of Bagdad* (1924). Some of director Victor Fleming's particulars are located in our coverage of *Dark Secrets* (1923) and all will be found in just about any comprehensive volume dealing with the 1939 classics, *The Wizard of Oz* or *Gone with the Wind*. It should be noted that famed celebrity artist, Henry Clive, was specially commissioned by Fairbanks to augment the title cards with his painting.

If this one piqued your interest, might we suggest the quite similar *Laughing at Danger* (1924)?

— *SJ*

The Whispering Chorus

The Whispering Chorus. Famous Players–Lasky; a Cecil B. De Mille Star Series Picture/Famous Players–Lasky and Artcraft Pictures, 25 March 1918, 7 reels/6655 feet [available]

CAST: Raymond Hatton (*John Trimble*); Kathlyn Williams (*Jane Trimble*); Elliott Dexter (*George Coggeswell*); Edythe Chapman (*John's Mother*); John Burton (*Charles Barden*); Parks Jones (*Tom Burns*); Tully Marshall (*H.P. Clumley*); Guy Oliver (*Chief McFarland*); W.H. Brown (*Stauberry*); James Neill (*Channing*); Noah Beery (*Longshoreman*); Gustav von Seyffertitz (*Mocking Face*); Walter Lynch (*Evil Face*); Edna Mae Cooper (*Good Face*)

CREDITS: *Producer* Jesse L. Lasky; *Director* Cecil B. De Mille; *Scenario* Jeanne Macpherson; based on the eponymous story by Perley Poore Sheehan, serialized in *All-Star Weekly* (12–26 January 1918); *Cinematographer* Alvin Wyckoff; *Art Director* Wilfred Buckland

This picture is here for one reason and one reason only: the scene in which the protagonist is "haunted" into coming clean by a series of ghostly visages. (Still, if we stop to consider that one of those visages belonged to Gustav von Seyffertitz, that's *two* reasons and two reasons only.)

Dissatisfied with his position in society, John Trimble heeds the dim image of Evil in his mind and embezzles a sum of money from his firm. When a state investigation of company funds threatens to expose his activities, John leaves his wife and mother and hides out on an island near the city waterfront. Changing clothes with a corpse that has drifted ashore, John mutilates the body and sets it adrift, and later, it is reported that John has been murdered. Under the assumed name of Edgar Smith, John wanders aimlessly around the world, and in Hong Kong he becomes addicted to opium. Meanwhile, his wife Jane, believing him to be dead, marries George Coggeswell, who becomes the governor of the state. John returns home to visit his dying mother, who passes away from shock, but as the fictitious Edgar Smith, he is arrested as his own murderer and sentenced to death. Knowing that a pub-

lic revelation of the truth would ruin Jane's happiness, John finally listens to the whispering chorus of conscience and allows himself to be executed.

The above synopsis was taken from the copyright registration file at the Library of Congress, and the astute reader will have noticed that the summary does not so much as mention the series of ghastly visages we wrote of in our opening. Must therefore have been a quite memorable sequence, no?

We've looked long and hard at that plot summary, trying to figure out how any jury anywhere in the world could have convicted the protagonist of murdering himself, and we came away empty. On the one mano, if John's "position in society" was as dissatisfying as all that, it's doubtful that the newspapers would have given his trial the sort of publicity that would have attracted the governor's attention. On the other, since John — as Edgar — never actually murdered either himself or the guy whose corpse John found on the sand, how in blazes is there any evidence that he murdered anybody? More disturbingly, since he *didn't* kill anyone, is that "whispering chorus of conscience" malicious, or merely incompetent? It augurs very ill when one's conscience starts handing out ludicrously bad advice.

In Gene Ringgold and DeWitt Bodeen's *The Films of Cecil B. De Mille*, there is a second rendering of the film's plot, and that one — doubtless taken from a screening of the film — makes a tad (but not much) more sense. Per those authors, John "arranges to have a mutilated body *buried as his own*" (emphasis ours), and not set adrift, as the studio précis had it. Amazingly, no one present at the trial recognizes old John save for his mum, who expires after telling John that — should he reveal that he is, in fact, he, and *not* the fellow who (presumably) had killed him — John's wife, heavy with child, will be bringing into this world *a bastard* (emphasis ours), and where would that leave everyone? There follows that succession of visages (the cast list has them as "mocking face," "evil face" and "good face") that convinces John that it is better that he go to his grave an innocent victim of circumstances than for him to have to explain anything to anybody. With a mother (and a conscience!) like that, who needs enemies? (For another Silent Era tale of selfless stupidity presented with a dash of genre baloney, please see *The Crystal Gazer*.) Anyhow, having also screened the picture,* we can aver that the Messrs. Ringgold and Bodeen did not under- or overstate any of the particulars.

Responsible for the original story of this thing was Perley Poore Sheehan, who also was culpable for the underlying narrative of *The Man Who Saw Tomorrow* (see entry). We couldn't come up with the pertinent issues of *All-Star Weekly*, but we did read the later novelization of PPS's story (published in 1927 by — Who else? Grosset and Dunlap) and came away ready to confess to anything. More responsible for the onscreen silliness than Sheehan, though, was Jeanne Macpherson (see 1914's *The Ghost Breaker*), a prolific actress-cum-scenarist whose impressive run of really good work, in all honesty, earns her a pass for an occasional misfire like this one. Photographing *Chorus* was Alvin Wyckoff, one of De Mille's regular crew, and the man be-

---

*Available from Netflix!

hind the camera for 1917's *The Devil Stone* (see entry). Wyckoff and De Mille's lighting plan on *Chorus* received some critical mention, as did the montage of faces (more than just the three "top-shelf" kissers listed in the cast scrawl) that drove John Trimble to confess to a capital crime he did not, in fact, commit: "The usual tricks of double exposure are employed … but they are not worked to death" (*The Weekly Variety*, 29 March 1918).

John Trimble was portrayed by Raymond Hatton, a character man of amazing longevity (on the payroll from the 1900s through the 1960s), undoubted versatility (although most of his sound roles—*not* the usual uncredited bits contributed by other Silent Era veterans— were in horse operas), and total compatibility: come the 1950s, the man virtually became Mr. Television. *Not* a big genre name (other than *Chorus*, he graced only *The Devil-Stone*, 1917's *The Crystal Gazer*, and *The Hunchback of Notre Dame* [1923; as Gringoire] during the Silent Era), Hatton was an *enduring* presence: his craggy face could be spotted in over 400 movies during the course of his lengthy career.

In the race to be carried off someplace in the tropics by a homicidal maniac, Gladys Hulette beat *Wild Oranges*' Virginia Valli by a good five months. Miss Hulette paid $3.00 and Miss Valli, $2.10.

Besides the aforementioned Gustav von Seyffertitz, *The Whispering Chorus* also presented Noah Beery (on his way up) and Tully Marshall (likewise fairly new to films for an old timer) in parts too small/unimportant/unimpressive to deserve a sentence or two from vintage–1918 Film Criticism's usual suspects. The part of the pregnant bigamist fell to Kathlyn Williams, a pert actress who— it was said, cattily — won more than her fair share of leading roles at Paramount because she had wed one of the studio's muckety-mucks. Who can say for sure? James Neill — the Georgia-born actor who played Channing, a *Chorus* character of such insignificance as to merit no critical ink whatsoever — showed up 1915's *The Case of Becky* and 1922's *Dusk to Dawn* (see entries). Neill, who was later tapped by De Mille to play Aaron to Theodore Roberts' Moses in *The Ten Commandments*, had (seemingly like everybody else affiliated with *The Whispering Chorus*) also shown up for a turn in *The Devil-Stone*.

So, next time someone advises that you "let your conscience be your guide," toss this title in their face and walk away. And that's damned *good* advice.

— *JTS*

Whispering Palms

Whispering Palms. Charles Granlich Feature Photoplays/Fidelity Pictures and States Rights, 9 August 1923, 5 reels [LOST]
CAST: Val Cleary, Gladys Hulette
CREDITS: *Producer* Charles Granlich

Apart from the sketchiest of information and a couple of lobby cards, there's almost nothing out there on *Whispering*

Palms. (A white lie. As we write this, eBay is offering a vintage postcard [c. 1953] from the Whispering Palms Motel, located in Lake Worth, Florida, *and* an old Edison Record Company 78 of "Whispering Palms"— the anthem, we presume. But there's zilch up for grabs from *our Whispering Palms.*)

From the looks of the title card, it may well be that *Palms* shared themes with that other, more well-documented treatment of madmen-on-the-loose-in-the-Land-of-Orange-Juice, *Wild Oranges* (see entry) which it beat to the box office by a whisper. (All right, all right, by five months— a succession of whispers.) It's doubtful that the later Goldwyn Pictures melodrama was influenced by the earlier Charles Granlich Feature Photoplay, if only because a) Joseph Hergescheimer's source novel, *Wild Oranges*, had been written in 1919, thus antedating *Palms* by several years and *many* whispers, and b) *Palms* probably received only the most sporadic of releases in the first place.

The picture was never submitted for copyright, received no critical coverage at any point, and seemingly was distributed in some locales by Fidelity Pictures and via the States Rights program in others. There were no exaggerated PR promises, no publicity puff pieces, no claims of any kind whatsoever with respect to the picture's production, premiere, or impact on the movie-going population. Nada. The best we could come up with was the following, which appeared, sans illustration — in the 14 July 1924 *Clearfield* [Pennsylvania] *Progress*, some 11 months after its opening somewhere else:

An Admirable Motion Picture
Admirable!
Admirably interpreted by an

Admirable cast of
Admirable screen players
Admirably adapted from an
Admirable story, and
Admirably directed.

The odds are good someone was paid to write that. This ad, we note, ran twice in the *Progress* and neither time was anyone's name — other than Miss Hulette's — mentioned.

This was the only Charles Granlich Feature Photoplay, and there's also no pertinent information anywhere on Charles Granlich. There was a Charles Gra*m*lich (with an "m"), though, and we made a few comments on *his* only movie work — *When Dr. Quackel Did Hide* — elsewhere in this volume. Had *Quackel's* director/scenarist somehow morphed into *Palms'* producer? Not if he had relied on the receipts from *Quackel*, he hadn't.

Two cast names survive: Val Cleary and Gladys Hulette. We know nothing of Mr. Cleary, assuming as we must that Val is short for Valentine and that he portrayed either the picture's hero or its heavy. This was his only feature, apparently, although he (she?) is listed among the dramatis personae in a 1913 Kalem two-reeler, *The Sacrifice at the Spillway*. Miss Hulette, a New Yorker from upstate Arcade (south of Buffalo), was in pictures since the age of 12 or thereabouts, had well over ten dozen films to her credit (with many being shorts from the early 1910s), and was also the heroine in 1925's *The Mystic* and 1926's *Unknown Treasures*, both of which we examine (in greater depth than we do *Palms*) within these pages. Other than a couple of bit parts in the early 1930s, Miss Hulette finished acting onscreen when silence gave way to sound.

— *JTS*

The Witching Eyes

The Witching Eyes. Ernest Stern, c. 26 November 1929, feature length assumed [LOST]
CAST: Salem Tutt Whitney, Sylvia Birdsong, Lorenzo Tucker
CREDITS: *Director* Ernest Stern; *Writer* Ernest Stern

There are a few assumptions to be made with respect to this film. Due to its inclusion in *The AFI Catalog*, we're assuming it was feature-length. (Then again, the *Catalog* admits that it's *also* assuming feature-length, so we might not be on terra firma here.) Pretty much ditto with our guess that the picture was American-made, and pretty much ditto, part two (The Sequel!), with our belief that it was a silent, and not an early talkie. Some comfort is to be had in the fact that *Eyes* is listed (as a silent feature) in Larry Richards' *African American Films through 1959*, but Larry may have made *his* assumption after having first visited the AFI documents. (More tsuris: in a listing entitled "Filmografia Stregonesca," the Italian film history website, http://thrauma.it, has the picture a *British* production.)

No matter. Let us at least note the picture's existence and share whatever information (and there ain't much) we have in the interests of comprehensiveness.

The Witching Eyes was written and produced by a man — presumably African American — named Ernest Stern, about whom virtually nothing (except for his involvement in this film) is known. Stern made no other pictures that we can document,

did no theater (unless under a stage name) and cannot be traced via Six Stages of Separation from Oscar Micheaux. The fruit of his typewriter was filmed and then registered for copyright in late November 1929, and the synopsis below — culled from *The AFI Catalog* — seems to mark the only verbiage on *The Witching Eyes* that ever made it into print anywhere:

> Haitian Val Napolo, possessed of a witching hand and the evil eye, is persuaded by his friend Cortex to go to the United States and pose as a leader of his people. Napolo meets with great success and gets to know Sylvia Smith, the daughter of a recently deceased black leader. Napolo develops a burning desire for Sylvia, but she favors Ralph Irving, a gentle poet. Napolo puts a curse on them and breaks up their love affair. When Sylvia still refuses him, Napolo kidnaps her. Ralph learns of the abduction and rescues Sylvia, discrediting Napolo in the eyes of his people.

It's doubtful that Stern's plot offered any novelty to the late 1920s movie-going public, except, perhaps, for his positing that "Cortex" might be somebody's actual name.

Larry Richards avers that *Eyes'* cast included the colorfully-monikered Salem Tutt Whitney, Lorenzo Tucker, and Sylvia Birdsong. All three actors were reportedly discoveries of Oscar Micheaux's, and together or variously they appeared in a number of his pictures. This information of Richards' did *not* stem from the AFI archives, as the entry for *Eyes* is cast-less both in the in-print catalog and on the website.

Not much, admittedly, but better than nothing.

— *JTS*

Woman

Woman. Maurice Tourneur Productions/States Rights; Hiller and Wilk, Inc., October 1918, 7 reels [available]
CAST: Florence Billings (*The woman*); Warren Cook (*The man*); Ethel Hallor (*Eve*); Henry West (*Adam*); Flore Revallies (*Messalina*); Paul Clerget (*Claudius*); Diane Allen (*Heloise*); Escamillo Fernandez (*Abelard*); Gloria Goodwin (*Cyrene*); Chester Barnett (*The fisherman*); Fair Binney (*The girl*); Warner Richmond (*The officer*); with Lyn Donaldson; Rose Rolanda
CREDITS: *Director* Maurice Tourneur; *Writer:* Charles E. Whittaker; *Cinematographer* John van den Broek, René Guissart; *Art Direction* Ben Carré

The synopsis from *The AFI Catalog*:

> When an angry wife storms out of her house, her bewildered husband decides to consult an encyclopedia on the definition and history of woman. Ignoring stories of faithful and courageous women such as Joan of Arc, the young husband turns to tales of woman's perfidy beginning with the story of Adam and Eve. In Rome the wicked Messalina deceives her husband Emperor Claudius and, centuries later, Abelard, a priest, betrays his vows for the enticing Heloise. In Brittany a young wife named Cyrene leaves her husband and, in the American Civil War, a proffered piece of jewelry persuades a girl to reveal the hiding place of a Union soldier. In the end however the husband learns that because of the contributions she has made toward the winning of World War I, woman has emerged from the slavery that made her treacherous to become man's equal.

We would have completely missed covering this film in these volumes had it not played at Cinefest in 2009 where we discovered that Cyrene is not just a discontented housewife, but a sea nymph in an old legend set in Brittany. According to the tale, one night each year dozens of seals swim to the shore, shed their skins and are transformed into women. A young fisherman observes this rite and steals one of the skins. In the morning the other women don their skins and head out to the ocean but one, Cyrene, is forced to stay in her human form. The fisherman brings her clothes, and she reluctantly becomes his wife. Cyrene (the name is probably a play on "siren") bears him two children but yearns for the sea. Eventually, she finds where her husband has hidden the skin and makes for the water. She thinks sadly of her children but nevertheless gladly puts on the skin and returns to her old life. The husband arrives too late to stop her.

This poignant episode, like all the others in the film, is exquisitely lit and photographed, qualities one has come to expect from the movie's director, Maurice Tourneur. Unfortunately, a tragedy occurred during the filming of this story: Tourneur's ace cameraman, John van den Broek, was standing on a ledge at Bel Harbor and — while trying to get an effective shot of the crashing waves — lost his footing and fell to his death.

The reviewer for *The New York Times* thought that the film's theme — that women were trapped in slavery until the Great War finally led to their emancipation — could be considered either poetry or twaddle, but was irrelevant to Tourneur's stunning visualization of the different episodes. The *Motion Picture News* critic was equally impressed but worried that the film's structure and the portrayal of women in a bad light would dampen its box office appeal. (The latter consideration didn't prevent *MPN* from suggesting this tagline: "Women! See yourselves as others see you. You are weak, wicked, frail, vain. You are exposed in *Woman*."

Whatever else Tourneur's intentions may have been, it is obvious here that his tongue was often in cheek. The framing story (the battling couple, by the way, are middle-aged and not young, as per the AFI) is lighthearted, and the book the husband consults is clearly meant to be a joke. Also, in the Adam and Eve sequence, Eve (attired in the usual Lady Godiva tresses) acts like a spoiled teenager and pouts when told she can't eat the forbidden fruit, while Adam hasn't even evolved yet and is depicted as a befuddled ape man! There's even a little dinosaur — that looks very much like "Dino" from *The Flintstones* — wandering around the Garden of Eden. The subsequent stories though are quite grim, but the Cyrene episode stands out as a sad, wistful fairytale and the most memorable part of the film.

— *HN*

Bibliography

Primary Sources

The Abandoned Room (*Love without Question*); C. Wadsworth Camp. New York: A.L. Burt, 1917.

Amos Judd (*The Young Rajah*); J.A. Mitchell. New York: Charles Scribner's Sons, 1901.

At the Mercy of Tiberius (*The Price of Silence*); Augusta Jane Evans. New York: A.L. Burt, 1887.

At the Sign of the Jack O'Lantern; Myrtle Reed. New York: The Knickerbocker Press, 1905.

Athalie (*Unseen Forces*); Robert W. Chambers. London: D. Appleton, 1915.

Balaoo (*The Wizard*); Gaston Leroux. London: Hurst and Blackett, 1914.

The Bat; Mary Roberts Rinehart and Avery Hopwood. New York: George H. Doran, 1926.

The Battle Cry of Peace: A Call to Arms Against War; J. Stuart Blackton. Brooklyn (NY): The M.P. Publishing Company, 1916.

Behind Red Curtains (*One Hour before Dawn*); Mansfield Scott. New York: National Book Company, 1919.

Black Oxen; Gertrude Franklin Atherton. New York: A.L. Burt, 1923.

The Black Pearl; Mrs. Woodrow Wilson. New York: Appleton, 1912.

Blow Your Own Horn — A Merry Adventure in Three Acts; Owen Davis. New York: Samuel French, 1926.

The Cat and the Canary; John Willard. New York: Grosset & Dunlap, 1927.

The City of Mystery (*The Man of Mystery*); Archibald Gunter Clavering. New York: Hurst, 1902.

Conjure Woman; Charles W. Chestnutt. Ann Arbor (MI): Ann Arbor Paperbacks, 1977.

A Connecticut Yankee in King Arthur's Court; Mark Twain. New York: Harper's and Brothers, 1917.

Cursed (*The Devil Within*); George Allan England. New York: Grosset & Dunlap, 1919.

The Dark Mirror; Louis Joseph Vance. Garden City (NY): Doubleday, Page, 1920.

The Dark Star; Robert W. Chambers. New York: A.L. Burt, 1917.

Darkened Rooms; Philip Hamilton Gibbs. Garden City (NY): Doubleday, Doran, 1929.

The Day of Souls (*The Show*); Charles Tenney Jackson. New York: Grosset & Dunlap, 1910.

Defenseless America (*The Battle Cry of Peace*); Hudson Maxim. New York: Hearst's International Library Co., 1915.

The Devil; Ferenc Molnar. New York: Grosset & Dunlap, 1908.

The Devil to Pay; Francis Nimmo Greene. New York: Grosset & Dunlap, 1918.

Dr. Rameau; Georges Ohnet. New York: Hurst, 1889.

Double Trouble; Herbert Quick. Indianapolis: Bobbs-Merrill, 1906.

The Dream Cheater (see: *The Magic Skin*; Honore de Balzac). *The Dream Woman*; Wilkie Collins. In *Strange Stories of the Supernatural*; Mahwah, NJ: The Watermill Press, 1980.

The Eleventh Hour; Lincoln J. Carter. Uncited manuscript, c. 1901.

Eugenie Grandet (*The Conquering Power*); Honore de Balzac. New York: Charles Scribner's Sons, 1915.

The Fall of a Nation; Thomas Dixon. New York: Appleton, 1916.

Feathertop; Nathaniel Hawthorne. In *The Ghouls*; Peter Haining, ed. New York: Stein and Day, 1971.

Feet of Clay; Margaretta Tuttle. Boston: Little, Brown, 1923.

A Fool and His Money; George Barr McCutcheon. New York: Grosset & Dunlap, 1913.

Frankenstein (*Life without Soul*); Mary W. Shelley. New York: Grosset & Dunlap, 1931.

The Gorilla: A Mystery Comedy in Three Acts; Ralph Spence. London: Samuel French, 1950.

"The Gray Mask"; Charles W. Camp. *Colliers — The National Weekly*, Vol. 55, No. 21. 7 August 1915.

The Hand of Peril; Arthur Stringer. New York: McKinley, Stone & Mackenzie, 1915.

The Haunted Pajamas; Francis Perry Elliott. New York: Grosset & Dunlap, 1911.

The Heart Line; Gelett Burgess. Indianapolis: Bobbs-Merrill, 1907. *The House of a Thousand Candles*; Nicholson, Meredith. Indianapolis, IN: Bobbs-Merrill, 1905.

The House of Whispers; William Johnston. New York: Grosset & Dunlap, 1918.

The Hunchback of Notre Dame; Victor Hugo. New York: A.L. Burt, 1923.

"The Inspirations of Harry Larrabee"; Howard Fielding. *Popular Magazine*, 1 February 1914.

The Isle of Dead Ships (*The Isle of Lost Ships*); Crittenden Marriott. Philadelphia: Lippencott, 1925.

"The Last Man on Earth"; John D. Swain. *Munsey's Magazine*, 9 November 1923.

The Last Warning (*The House of Fear*); C. Wadsworth Camp. Garden City, NY: Doubleday, Page, 1916.

Lola; Owen Davis. New York: Grosset & Dunlap, 1915.

The Lost House; Richard Harding Davis. In *The Man Who Could Not Lose*, New York: Charles Scribner and Son, 1911.

The Lost World; Arthur Conan Doyle. New York: A.L. Burt, 1925.

The Magic Skin; Honore de Balzac. New York: Charles Scribner's Sons, 1915.

The Man Who Laughs; Victor Hugo. New York: Grosset & Dunlap, 1927.

A Message from Mars; Richard Ganthony. London: Samuel French, 1923.

A Message from Mars; Lurgan, Lester and Richard Ganthony. London: Greening, 1913.

The Miracle Man; Frank. L. Packard. New York: Grosset & Dunlap, 1914.

Mortmain; Arthur C. Train. New York: Charles Scribner's Sons, 1929.

The Mysterious Dr. Fu Manchu (*The Insidious Dr. Fu Manchu*); Sax Rohmer; New York: A.L. Burt, 1913.

The Mysterious Island; Jules Verne. New York: Grosset & Dunlap, 1929.

The Mystery of the Yellow Room; Gaston Leroux. New York: Grosset & Dunlap, 1908.

The Octave of Claudius (*A Blind Bargain*); Barry Pain. London: Harper & Brothers, 1897.

One Million Francs (*One Million Dollars*); Arnold Fredericks. New York: W.J. Watt, 1912.

One Way Street; Beale Davis. New York: Brentano's, 1924.

Peter Pan; James M. Barrie. New York: Charles Scribner's Sons, 1911.

The Phantom of the Opera; Gaston Leroux. New York: Grosset & Dunlap, 1912.

Puritan Passions (see: *Feathertop*; Nathaniel

Hawthorne) & *The Scarecrow*; Percy Mackaye; in *Chief Contemporary Dramatists*. Boston: Houghton Mifflin, 1915.

The Return of Peter Grimm; David Belasco. New York: Dodd, Mead, 1912.

The Road to Yesterday; Beulah Marie Dix and Evelyn Greenleaf Sutherland. New York: Samuel French, 1925.

Seven Footprints to Satan; A. Merritt. New York: Grosset & Dunlap, 1928.

The Shadow of the East; Edith Maude Hull. New York: A.L. Burt, 1921.

She; H. Rider Haggard. New York: Grosset & Dunlap, 1926.

A Sleeping Memory; E. Phillips Oppenheim. Boston: Little, Brown, 1907.

The Sorrows of Satan; Marie Corelli. New York: A.L. Burt, 1923.

The Star Rover; Jack London. New York: Grosset & Dunlap, 1915.

The Story without a Name; Arthur Stringer and Russell Holman. New York: Grosset & Dunlap, 1924.

Tarzan and the Golden Lion; Edgar Rice Burroughs. New York: Ballantine Books, 1963 (reprint).

"Terror Island"; D. Burton Howard (adaptor). *Motion Picture Stories*, 16 April 1920.

The Thief of Bagdad; Achmed Abdullah. New York: A.L. Burt, 1924.

Trilby; Georges Du Maurier. New York: Harper and Brothers, 1895.

The Two-Soul Woman (*The White Cat*); Gelett Burgess. New York: Grosset & Dunlap, 1907.

20,000 Leagues Under the Sea; Jules Verne. New York: Grosset & Dunlap, 1917.

"Play of the Month — *The Unknown Purple*"; Unknown. *Hearst's Magazine*, April 1919.

The Untameable (*The White Cat*); Gelett Burgess. New York: Grosset & Dunlap, 1907.

Vendetta! Or, the Story of One Forgotten; Marie Corelli. New York: Wm. L. Allison, 1886.

The Whispering Chorus; Perely Poore Sheehan. New York: G. Howard Watt, 1927.

Wild Oranges; Joseph Hergescheimer. New York: Grosset & Dunlap, 1918.

The Witching Hour; Augustus Thomas. New York: Grosset & Dunlap, 1918.

The Young Diana; Marie Corelli. New York: George H. Doran, 1918.

Secondary Sources

Abel, Richard. *Americanizing the Movies and Movie-Mad Audiences, 1910–1914*. Berkeley: University of California Press, 2006.

Abramson, Ivan. *Mother of Truth, a Story of Romance and Retribution Based on the Events of My Own Life*. New York: Graphic Literary Press, 1929.

Ackerman, Forrest J, ed. *M.A.R.S.: Four Lost Films in One*. Wonderama Annual. New York: Pure Imagination, 1993.

Alpert, Hollis. *The Barrymores*. New York: Dial Press, 1964.

Alvarez, Max Joseph. *Index to Motion Pictures Reviewed by* Variety, *1907–1988*. Metuchen, NJ: Scarecrow, 1982.

The American Film Institute Catalogue: Feature Films 1911–1920; 1921–1930. Berkeley: University of California Press, 1988.

Anderson, Robert G. *Faces, Forms, Films: The Artistry of Lon Chaney*. New York: Castle Books, 1971.

Ankerich, Michael G. *The Sound of Silence: Conversations with 16 Film and Stage Personalities Who Bridged the Gap Between Silents and Talkies*. Jefferson, NC: McFarland, 1998.

Archer, Steve. *Willis O'Brien: Special Effects Genius*. Jefferson, NC: McFarland, 1993.

Arliss, George. *Up the Years from Bloomsbury: The Autobiography of George Arliss*. New York: Blue Ribbon Books, 1927.

Astor, Mary. *A Life on Film*. New York: Delacorte Press, 1969.

Atherton, Gertrude. *Adventures of a Novelist*. New York: Blue Ribbon Books, 1932.

Balshofer, Fred J., and Arthur Miller. *One Reel a Week*. Berkeley: University of California Press, 1967.

Barnes, John H. *Forty Years on the Stage*. Boston: E.P. Dutton, 1915.

Barnouw, Erik. *The Magician and the Cinema*. New York: Oxford University Press, 1981.

Barsacq, Leon. *Caligari's Cabinet and Other Grand Illusions: A History of Film Design*. New York: New American Library, 1978.

Baxter, John. *Stunt: The Story of the Great Movie Stunt Men*. Garden City, NY: Doubleday, 1974.

Bean, Jennifer M., and Diana Negra. *A Feminist Reader in Early Cinema*. Durham, NC: Duke University Press, 2002.

Bean, Shawn C. *The First Hollywood: Florida and the Golden Age of Silent Filmmaking*. Miami: University Press of Florida, 2008.

Beasley, David. *Bibliography: McKee Rankin and the Heyday of the American Theater*. Waterloo, Ontario: Wilfrid Laurier University Press, 2002.

Bellamy, Madge. *A Darling of the Twenties: The Autobiography of Madge Bellamy*. New York: Vestal Press, 1989.

Benham, Charles. "Jetta Goudal: The Exotic," *Classic Images*. September 1999.

Benson, Michael. *Vintage Science Fiction Films, 1896–1949*. Jefferson, NC: McFarland, 2000.

Bernstein, Arnie, ed. *The Movies Are: Carl Sandburg's Film Reviews and Essays, 1920–1928*. Chicago: Lake Claremont Press, 2000.

Birchard, Robert S., and Irvin V. Willat. "Conversations with Irvin V. Willat," *Film History*. vol. 12, no. 1. Bloomington: Indiana University Press, 2000.

_____, and Kevin Thomas. *Cecil B. De Mille's Hollywood*. Lexington: University Press of Kentucky, 2004.

Blake, Michael F. *The Films of Lon Chaney*. Lanham, MD: Vestal Press, 1998.

_____. *Lon Chaney: The Man Behind the Thousand Faces*. Vestal, NY: Vestal Press, 1990.

_____. *A Thousand Faces: Lon Chaney's Unique Artistry in Motion Pictures*. Vestal, NY: Vestal Press, 1995.

Bleiler, Everett F. *Science Fiction, the Early Years*. Kent, OH: Kent State University Press, 1990.

Blesh, Rudi. *Keaton*. New York: Collier Books, 1966.

Boardman, Gerald. *American Theater: A Chronicle of Comedy and Drama from 1914–1930*. New York: Oxford University Press, 1995.

Bogdanovitch, Peter. *Allan Dwan — The Last Pioneer*. New York: Praeger, 1971.

Bohrer, Al. "Claire Windsor: One Fan's Fond Remembrance," *Classic Images*. August 1999.

Bojarski, Richard. *The Films of Bela Lugosi*. Secaucus, NJ: Citadel, 1974.

_____, and Kenneth Beals. *The Films of Boris Karloff*. Secaucus, NJ: Citadel, 1974.

Bowers, Q. David. *Thanhouser Films: An Encyclopedia and History* (CD). Portland, OR: Thanhouser Company Film Preservations, 1997.

Bowser, Pearl, Jane Gaines and Charles Musser. *Oscar Micheaux & His Circle*. Bloomington: Indiana University Press, 2001.

_____, and Louise Spence. *Writing Himself into History: Oscar Micheaux, His Silent Films, and His Audiences*. New Brunswick, NJ: Rutgers University Press, 2000.

Branff, Richard. *The Universal Silents: A Filmography of the Universal Motion Picture Manufacturing Company, 1912–1929*. Jefferson, NC: McFarland, 1999.

Brownlow, Kevin. *Behind the Mask of Innocence*. London: Jonathan Cape, 1990.

_____. *The Parade's Gone By…*. New York: Alfred A. Knopf, 1968.

Burgess, Thomas N. *Take Me Under the Sea — The Dream Merchants of the Deep*. Salem, OR: Ocean Archives, 1993.

Burroughs, Edgar Rice. "Tarzan's Seven Lives," *Screen Play*. May 1934.

Butler, Ivan. *Horror in the Cinema*. New York: Paperback Library, 1971.

_____. *Religion in the Cinema*. New York: A.S. Barnes, 1969.

_____. *Silent Magic: Rediscovering the Silent Film Era*. New York: Ungar, 1988.

Card, James. *Seductive Cinema: The Art of the Silent Film*. Minneapolis: University of Minnesota Press, 1994.

Carroll, David. *The Matinee Idols*. New York: Galahad Books, 1972.

Chierichetti, David. *Hollywood Director: The Career of Mitchell Leisen*. New York: Curtis Books, 1973.

Chesnutt, Helen M. *Charles Waddell Chesnutt: Pioneer of the Color Line*. Chapel Hill: University of North Carolina Press, 1952.

Clarens, Carlos. *An Illustrated History of the Horror Film*. New York: Capricorn Books, 1967.

Coghlan, Frank "Junior." *They Still Call Me Junior*. Jefferson, NC: McFarland, 1993.

Cohn, Jan. *Improbable Fiction: The Life of Mary Roberts Rinehart*. Pittsburgh: University of Pittsburgh Press, 1980.

Conan Doyle, Arthur. *The Edge of the Unknown*. New York: G.P. Putnam's Sons, 1930.

Cook, David A. *A Narrative History of Film*. New York: W.W. Norton, 1981.

Cripps, Thomas. *Slow Fade to Black: The Negro in American Film, 1900–1942*. New York: Oxford University Press, 1977.

Cullen, Frank, Florence Hackman and Donald McNeilly. *Vaudeville, Old and New: An Encyclopedia of Variety Performers in America*. London: Routledge, 2007.

Dardis, Tom. *Keaton: The Man Who Wouldn't Lie Down*. Middlesex (England): Penguin Books, 1980.

Davenport-Hines, Richard. *Gothic: Four Hundred Years of Excess, Horror, Evil and Ruin*. New York: North Point Press, 1998.

Davis, Owen. *I'd Like to Do It Again*. New York: Ferrar and Rinehart, 1931.

_____. *My First Fifty Years in the Theater*. Boston: Walter Baker, 1950.

Day, Donald. *The Autobiography of Will Rogers*. Boston: Houghton Mifflin, 1949.

Dodds, John W. *Paul Fejos: A Hungarian-American Odyssey*. New York: Wenner-Gren Foundation, 1973.

Doyle, Billy. "Lost Players," *Classic Images*. December 1990.

_____. "Rosemary Theby and Victoria Ford," *Classic Images*. August 1989.

Drinkwater, John. *The Life and Times of Carl Laemmle*. New York: G.P. Putnam's Sons, 1931.

Dubois, Aaron. *The House of Van Du: A Vignette Biography of the Stage and Screen Actor, Grant Mitchell*. New York: William-Frederick Press, 1962.

Dumaux, Sally A. *King Baggot*. Jefferson, NC: McFarland, 2002.

Durgnat, Raymond, and Scott Simmon. *King Vidor, American*. Berkeley: University of California Press, 1988.

Eckhardt, Joseph P. *The King of Movies: Film Pioneer, Siegmund Lubin*. Cranbury, NJ: Associated University Presses, 1997.

Edmonds, Andy. *Frame Up! The Untold Story of Roscoe "Fatty" Arbuckle*. New York: William Morrow, 1991.

Edmonds, I.G. *Big U: Universal in the Silent Days*. New York: A.S. Barnes, 1977.

Ehrenstein, David. *Open Secret: Gay Hollywood, 1928–2000*. New York: Perennial, 2000.

Ellenberger, Allan R. *Ramon Navarro*. Jefferson, NC: McFarland, 1999.

Engle, Sherri D. *New Women Dramatists in America: 1890–1920*. New York: Palgrave Macmillan, 2007

Everson, William K. *American Silent Film*. New York: Da Capo Press, 1998.

_____. *Classics of the Horror Film*. Secaucus, NJ: Citadel, 1974.

_____. *The Detective in Film*. Secaucus, NJ: Citadel, 1972.

_____. *More Classics of the Horror Film*. Secaucus, NJ: Citadel, 1986.

Eyman, Scott. *Mary Pickford: From Here to Hollywood*. Toronto: Harper Collins, 1990.

_____. *The Speed of Sound: Hollywood and the Talkie Revolution; 1926–1930*. New York: Simon & Schuster, 1997.

Ferguson, Sally Ann H., editor. *Charles W. Chesnutt: Selected Writings*. Boston: Houghton Mifflin, 2001.

Fernett, Gene. *American Film Studios*. Jefferson, NC: McFarland, 1988.

Fitzgerald, Michael G. *Universal Pictures: A Panoramic History in Words, Pictures, and Filmographies*. New Rochelle, NY: Arlington House, 1977.

Fleming, E.J. *Wallace Reid: The Life and Death of a Hollywood Idol*. Jefferson, NC: McFarland, 2007.

Fleury, J. "Aerial Navigation," *The Chautauquan*. v. 17. September 1893.

Franklin, Joe. *Classics of the Silent Screen*. New York: Citadel, 1959.

Fruttero, Carlo, and Franco Lucentini. *The D. Case, or, the Truth About* The Mystery of Edwin Drood. New York: Harcourt, Brace, Jovanovich, 1989.

Gibson, Emily. *The Original Million Dollar Mermaid: The Annette Kellerman Story*. Sydney: Allen & Unwin, 2005.

Gilpatrick, Kristin. *Famous Wisconsin Stars*. Middletown, WI: Badger Books, 2002.

Gold, Eve. *Golden Images: 41 Essays on Silent Film Stars*. Jefferson, NC: McFarland, 2001.

Griffith, Richard, and Arthur Mayer. *The Movies*. New York: Simon & Schuster, 1957.

Guiles, Fred Lawrence. *Marion Davies: A Biography*. Columbus, OH: McGraw-Hill, 1972.

Guy Blaché, Alice. *The Memoirs of Alice Guy Blaché*. Metuchen, NJ: Scarecrow, 1986.

Haberman, Steve. *Silents Screams: Chronicles of Terror*. Baltimore: Luminary Press, 2003.

Haining, Peter, ed. *The Edgar Allan Poe Scrapbook*. Berlin: Schocken Books, 1978.

Haire, Norman Ch. M., M.B. *Rejuvenation—The Work of Steinach, Voronoff, and Others*. New York: Macmillan, 1925.

Hardy, Phil, ed. *The Encyclopedia of Horror Movies*. New York: Harper & Row, 1986.

_____. *The Encyclopedia of Science Fiction Movies*. Minneapolis, MN: Woodbury Press, 1986.

Harmon, Jim, and Donald F. Glut. *The Great Movie Serials: Their Sound and Fury*. Garden City, NY: Doubleday, 1972.

Harpole, Charles and Eileen Bowser. *History of the American Cinema*. Berkeley: University of California Press, 1994.

Hart, Jerome A. *Sardou and the Sardou Plays*. Philadelphia: J.B. Lippincott Company, 1913.

Hawtrey, Charles. *The Truth at Last*. London: Thornton Butterworth, 1924.

Hayakawa, Sessue. *Zen Showed Me the Way*. New York: Bobbs-Merrill, 1960.

Hayne, Donald, ed. *The Autobiography of Cecil B. De Mille*. Englewood Cliffs, NJ: Prentice-Hall, 1959.

Heinink, Juan B., and Robert Dickson. *Cita en Hollywood*. Bilbao: Ediciones Mensajero, 1990.

Herman, Hal C., ed. *How I Broke into the Movies: Autobiographies by Sixty Famous Screen Stars*. Hollywood, CA: self-published, 1930.

Hernández Girbal, Florentino, and Juan B. Heinink. *Los que pasaron por Hollywood*. Madrid: Verdoux, undated.

Higham, Charles. *The Merchant of Dreams: A Biography of Louis B. Mayer*. New York: D.I. Fine, 1993.

Hirschhorn, Clive. *The Universal Story*. New York: Crown, 1983.

Hoffman, Daniel. *Poe, Poe, Poe, Poe, Poe, Poe, Poe*. New York: Avon/Discus, 1978.

Houdini, Harry. *A Magician Among the Spirits*. New York: Harper & Brothers, 1924.

Irving, Laurence. *Henry Irving: The Actor and His World*. London: Columbia Books, 1989.

Jacobs, Lewis. *The Rise of the American Film: A Critical History*. New York: Teachers College Press, 1975.

Jast, L. Stanley, ed. *The Memoirs of Robert Houdin—Ambassador, Author and Conjurer, by Himself*. London: T. Werner Laurie, 1942.

Jensen, Paul M. *The Men Who Made the Monsters*. New York: Twayne, 1996.

Jura, Jean-Jacques, and Rodney Norman Barden II. *Balboa Films: A History and Filmography of the Silent Film Studio*. Jefferson, NC: McFarland, 1999.

Katchmer, George. "The Four Moore Brothers," *Classic Images*. May 1988.

Keaton, Buster, with Charles Samuels. *Buster Keaton: My Wonderful World of Slapstick*. New York: Da Capo Press, 1982.

Kellock, Harold, ed. *Houdini—His Life-Story from the Recollections and Documents of Beatrice Houdini*. New York: Blue Ribbon Books, 1928.

Kerr, Walter. *The Silent Clowns*. New York: Alfred A. Knopf, 1975.

Kibler, M. Alison. *Rank Ladies: Gender and Cultural Hierarchy in American Vaudeville*. Chapel Hill: University of North Carolina Press, 1999.

Kinnard, Roy. *Horror in Silent Films: A Filmography, 1896–1929*. Jefferson, NC: McFarland, 1995.

_____. *"The Lost World" of Willis O'Brien: The Original Shooting Script of the 1925 Landmark Special Effects Dinosaur Film, with Photographs*. Jefferson, NC: McFarland, 1993.

Kline, Jim. *The Complete Films of Buster Keaton*. New York: Citadel Press, 1993.

Knight, Arthur. *The Liveliest Art: A Panoramic History of the Movies*. New York: Macmillan, 1978.

Knopf, Robert. *The Theater and Cinema of Buster Keaton*. Princeton, NJ: Princeton University Press, 1999.

Knox, Holly. *Sally Rand—From Film to Fans*. Bend, OR: Maverick Publications, 1988.

Koszarski, Richard. *The Man You Love to Hate: Erich von Stroheim and Hollywood*. Oxford: Oxford University Press, 1983.

Kotsilibas-Davis, James. *The Barrymores: The Royal Family in Hollywood*. New York: Crown Publishers, 1981.

Lahue, Kalton C. *Dreams for Sale: The Rise and Fall of the Triangle Film Corporation*. Cranbury, NJ: Barnes, 1971.

_____. *Gentlemen to the Rescue: The Heroes of the Silent Screen*. New York: Castle Books, 1972.

Langman, Larry. *American Film Cycles: The Silent Era*. Westport, CT: Greenwood Press, 1998.

Lebel, J.-P. *Buster Keaton*. London: A. Zwemmer, 1967.

Lee, Walt. *Reference Guide to Fantastic Films, 3 Volumes*. Los Angeles: Chelsea-Lee Books, 1975.

Leider, Emily Wortis. *California's Daughter—Gertrude Atherton and Her Times*. Palo Alto, CA: Stanford University Press, 1991.

Lennig, Arthur. *The Immortal Count: The Life and Films of Bela Lugosi*. Lexington: University Press of Kentucky, 2003.

_____. *The Silent Voice: The Golden Age of the Cinema*. New York: Faculty-Student Association of the State University at Albany, 1966.

_____. *Stroheim*. Lexington: University Press of Kentucky, 2000.

Lindsay, Cynthia. *Dear Boris: The Life of William Henry Pratt a.k.a. Boris Karloff*. New York: Alfred A. Knopf, 1975.

London, Rose. *Cinema of Mystery*. New York: Random House, 1975.

Lottman, Herbert R. *Jules Verne: An Exploratory Biography*. New York: St. Martin's Press, 1996.

Lowrey, Carolyn. *The First One Hundred Noted Men and Women of the Screen*. New York: Moffat, Yard, 1920.

Lupack, Barbara Tepa. *Literary Adaptations in Black American Cinema: From Micheaux to Morrison.* Rochester, NY: University of Rochester Press, 2002.

Lupoff, Richard. *Edgar Rice Burroughs: Master of Adventure.* New York: Ace Books, 1965.

Mabbott, Thomas Ollive. "Edgar Allan Poe: A Biography in Brief," in *The Man Who Called Himself Poe.* Sam Moskowitz, ed. New York: Doubleday, 1969.

Mann, William. *Behind the Screen: How Gays and Lesbians Shaped Hollywood, 1910–1969.* New York: Viking Adult Press, 2001.

MacQueen, Scott. "The Lost World — Merely Misplaced," *American Cinematographer.* v.73 n.6. June 1992.

_____. "Roland West," in *Between Action and Cut: Five American Directors.* Frank Thompson, editor. Metuchen, NJ: Scarecrow, 1985.

Marion, Frances. *Off with Their Heads! A Serio-Comic Tale of Hollywood.* New York: Macmillan, 1972.

Mayer, David, ed. *Henry Irving and The Bells.* Manchester University Press, 1980.

McCarty, John, ed. *The Fearmakers.* New York: St. Martin's Press, 1994.

McKinven, John A. *The Hanlon Brothers: Their Amazing Acrobatics, Pantomimes and Stage Spectaculars.* Glenwood, IL: Meyerbooks, 1998.

Meade, Marion. *Buster Keaton: Cut to the Chase.* New York: HarperCollins, 1995.

Menjou, Adolphe. *It Took Nine Tailors.* NY: Whittelsey House, 1948.

Messent, Peter B. and Louis J. Budd. *A Companion to Mark Twain.* Oxford: Blackwell, 2005.

Miller, Walter James and Frederick Paul Walter. *20,000 Leagues Under the Sea — The Complete, Restored and Annotated Edition.* Annapolis, MD: Naval Institute Press, 1993.

Mitchell, Charles. P. *The Devil on Screen: Feature Films Worldwide, 1913 through 2000.* Jefferson, NC: McFarland, 2002.

Moews, Daniel. *Keaton: The Silent Features Close Up.* Berkeley: University of California Press, 1977.

Morrell, Ed. *The 25th Man: The Strange Story of Ed Morrell, the Hero of Jack London's* The Star Rover. Montclair, NJ: New Era, 1924.

Moskowitz, Sam. *A. Merritt: Reflections in the Moon Pool.* Philadelphia: Oswald Train, 1985.

Napley, Sir David. *Rasputin in Hollywood.* London: George Weidenfeld and Nicholson, Ltd., 1990.

Nathan, George. "The Potboilermakers," *The Smart Set.* v. LIX, no. 3. July 1919.

Norden, Martin F. *The Cinema of Isolation: A History of Physical Disability in the Movies.* New Brunswick, NJ: Rutgers University Press, 1994.

O'Dell, Paul. *Griffith and the Rise of Hollywood.* New York: Castle Books, 1970.

O'Dell, Scott. *Representative Photoplays Analyzed.* Hollywood: Palmer Institute of Authorship, 1924.

Oderman, Stuart. *Talking to the Piano Player: Silent Screen Stars, Writers and Directors Remember.* Boalsburg, PA: Bear Manor Media, 2005.

O'Leary, Liam. *Rex Ingram: Master of the Silent Cinema.* New York: Barnes and Noble, 1980.

Overton, Grant. *Authors of the Day.* New York:

George H. Doran Company on Murray Hill, 1923.

Palmer, Laura Kay. *Osgood and Anthony Perkins: A Comprehensive History of Their Work in Theater, Film, and Other Media with Credits and an Annotated Bibliography.* Jefferson, NC: McFarland, 1991.

Pendle, George. *Strange Angel: The Otherworldly Life of Rocket Scientist John Whiteside Parsons.* Orlando, FL: Harcourt, 2005.

Pensel, Hans. *Seastrom and Stiller in Hollywood: Two Swedish Directors in Silent American Films, 1923–1930.* New York: Vantage Press, 1969.

Peters, Margot. *The House of Barrymore.* New York: Alfred A. Knopf, 1990.

Petrie, Graham. *Hollywood Destinies: European Directors in America, 1922–1931.* London: Routledge & Kegan Paul, 1985.

Pick, Daniel. *Svengali's Web: The Alien Enchanter in Modern Culture.* New Haven, CT: Yale University Press, 2000.

Pitts, Michael R. *Famous Movie Detectives III.* Lanham, MD: Scarecrow, 2004.

Pizzitola, Louis. *Hearst Over Hollywood: Power, Passion and Propaganda in the Movies.* New York: Columbia University Press, 2002.

Popa, Gene. "Five Tarzans — The Silent Apemen," *Classic Images.* June 1997.

Powell, Michael. *A Life in the Movies.* New York: Alfred A. Knopf, 1987.

Pratt, George C. *Spellbound in Darkness: A History of the Silent Film.* Greenwich, CT: New York Graphic Society, 1966.

Putnam, George Haven. *Memoirs of a Publisher: 1865–1915.* New York: G.P. Putnam's Sons, 1915.

Ralston, Esther. *Some Day We'll Laugh.* Metuchen, NJ: Scarecrow, 1985.

Ramseye, Terry. *A Million and One Nights: A History of the Motion Picture through 1925.* New York: Simon & Schuster, 1986.

Ransom, Teresa. *Miss Marie Corelli, Queen of Victorian Bestsellers.* London: Sutton, 1999.

Reginald, R., and Douglas Menville. *Things to Come: An Illustrated Story of the Science Fiction Film.* San Bernardino, CA: Burgo Press, 1977.

Renzi, Thomas C. *Jules Verne on Film.* Jefferson, NC: McFarland, 1998.

Rhodes, Gary Don. *Lugosi: His Life in Films, on Stage, and in the Hearts of Horror Lovers.* Jefferson, NC: McFarland, 1997.

Richards, Larry. *African American Films through 1959: A Comprehensive, Illustrated Filmography.* Jefferson, NC: McFarland, 1998.

Rigby, Jonathan. *American Gothic.* London: Reynolds & Hearn, 2007.

Riley, Philip J. *A Blind Bargain.* Atlantic City, NJ: MagicImage Filmbooks, 1988.

_____. "Jacqueline Logan," *Classic Images,* July 1979.

_____. *London After Midnight.* Atlantic City, NJ: MagicImage Filmbooks, 1985.

_____. *The Making of* The Phantom of the Opera. Atlantic City, NJ: MagicImage Filmbooks, 1999.

Ringgold, Gene, and DeWitt Bodeen. *The Films of Cecil B. DeMille.* New York: Citadel, 1969.

Rivkin, Allen, and Laura Kerr. *Hello, Hollywood.* New York: Doubleday, 1962.

Roach, Mary. *The Curious Coupling of Science and Sex.* New York: W.W. Norton, 2008.

Robertson, James C. *The Casablanca Man: The Cinema of Michael Curtiz.* London: Routledge, 1993.

Robinson, David. *Buster Keaton.* Bloomington: Indiana University Press, 1969.

_____. *Hollywood in the Twenties.* New York: A.S. Barnes, 1970.

Robinson, Kenneth. *Wilkie Collins: A Biography.* New York: MacMillan, 1952.

Robinson, Ray. *American Original — A Life of Will Rogers.* New York: Oxford University Press, 1996.

Rotha, Paul, and Richard Griffith. *The Film til Now: A Survey of World Cinema.* Middlesex (England): Hamlyn Publishing Group, 1967.

Sampson, Henry T. *Blacks in Black and White: A Source Book on Black Films.* Metuchen, NJ: Scarecrow, 1977.

Sandburg, Carl. *The Movies Are.* Chicago: Lake Claremont Press, 2000.

Schatz, Thomas. *The Genius of the System: Hollywood Filmmaking in the Studio Era.* New York: Pantheon Books, 1988.

Schickel, Richard. *D.W. Griffith: An American Life.* New York: Touchstone, 1984.

Schildkraut, Joseph. *My Father and I.* New York: Viking Press, 1959.

Scott, Evelyn F. *Hollywood: When Silents Were Golden.* New York: McGraw-Hill, 1972.

Scott, Wilbur. *Introduction to Edgar Allan Poe: Complete Tales and Poems.* Secaucus, NJ: Castle Books, 2001.

Scully, Frank. *Cross My Heart.* New York: Greenberg, 1955.

Shay, Don, ed. "Photographs and Memories — Ralph Hammeras," *Cinefex.* January 1984.

_____. "Willis O'Brien — Creator of the Impossible," *Focus on Film.* Autumn 1973.

Sherwood, Robert. *The Best Moving Pictures of 1922–1923.* New York: Revisionist Press, 1974.

Silverman, Kenneth. *Houdini!!! The Career of Erich Weiss.* New York: Harper Collins, 1996.

Sinyard, Neil. *Silent Movies.* New York: Gallery Books, 1990.

Skal, David J., and Elias Savada. *Dark Carnival: The Secret World of Tod Browning.* New York: Anchor Books, 1995.

Slide, Anthony. *American Racist: The Life and Films of Thomas Dixon.* Lexington: University Press of Kentucky, 2004.

_____. *The Big V: A History of the Vitagraph Company.* Metuchen, NJ: Scarecrow, 1987.

_____. *Early American Cinema.* New York: A.S. Barnes, 1970.

_____. *Silent Players: A Biographical and Autobiographical of 100 Silent Film Actors and Actresses.* Lexington: University of Kentucky Press, 2002.

Soister, John T. *Conrad Veidt on Screen.* Jefferson, NC: McFarland, 2002.

_____. *Of Gods and Monsters: A Critical Guide to Universal Studios' Science Fiction, Horror and Mystery Films, 1929–1939.* Jefferson, NC: McFarland, 1998.

_____. *Up from the Vault: Rare Thrillers of the 1920s and 1930s.* Jefferson, NC: McFarland, 2004.

Spears, Jack. *Hollywood: The Golden Era.* New York: Castle Books, 1971.

Spehr, Paul C., with Gunnar Lundquist. *Amer-*

ican Film Personnel and Company Credits, 1908–1920. Jefferson, NC: McFarland, 1996.

Stashower, Daniel. *Teller of Tales: The Life of Arthur Conan Doyle.* New York: Henry Holt, 1999.

Strickland, A.W., and Forrest J Ackerman. *A Reference Guide to American Science Fiction Films: Volume One.* Bloomington, IN: T.I.S. Publications, 1981.

Swanson, Gloria. *Swanson on Swanson.* New York: Random House, 1980.

Taves, Brian. "With Williamson Beneath the Sea," *Journal of Film Preservation.* vol. XXV, no. 52. April 1996.

_____ and Stephen Michaluk, Jr. *The Jules Verne Encyclopedia.* Lanham, MD: Scarecrow, 1996.

Taylor, Al and Sue Roy. *Making a Monster: The Creation of Screen Characters by the Great Makeup Artists.* New York: Crown, 1980.

Thompson, Frank, ed. *Between Action and Cut: Five American Directors.* Metuchen, NJ: Scarecrow, 1985.

Thurston, Howard. *My Life of Magic.* Philadelphia: Dorrance, 1929.

Trimble, Marie Blackton. *J. Stuart Blackton: A Personal Biography by His Daughter.* Metuchen, NJ: Scarecrow, 1985.

Tropp, Martin. *Mary Shelley's Monster: The Story of Frankenstein.* Boston: Houghton Mifflin, 1976.

Trottier, James. "Just Jane: or Jane Gail's Story," *Classic Images.* September 1997.

Turner, George, E., ed. *The Cinema of Adventure, Romance & Terror.* Hollywood: ASC Press, 1989.

Tuttle, Frank. *They Started Talking.* Boalsburg, PA: Bear Manor Media, 2005.

Twain, Mark, and David Ketter, ed. *The Science Fiction of Mark Twain.* Hamden, CT: Archon Books, 1984.

Underwood, Peter. *Karloff.* New York: Drake Publishers, 1972.

Usai, Paolo Cherchi. *Burning Passions: An Introduction to the Study of Silent Cinema.* London: BFI Publishing, 1994.

Vance, Jeffrey, with Tony Maietta. *Douglas Fairbanks.* Berkeley: University of California Press, 1970.

Wagenknecht, Edward. *The Movies in the Age of Innocence.* Norman: University of Oklahoma Press, 1962.

Wakeman, John, ed. *World Film Directors 1890–1945.* The Bronx, NY: H.W. Wilson, 1987.

Waldman, Harry. *Hollywood and the Foreign Touch: A Dictionary of Foreign Filmmakers and Their Films from America, 1910–1995.* Lanham, MD: Scarecrow, 1996.

_____. *Maurice Tourneur: The Life and Films.* Jefferson, NC: McFarland, 2001.

Wead, George, and George Lellis. *The Film Career of Buster Keaton.* Pleasantville, NY: Redgrave, 1977.

Whitfield, Eileen. *Pickford: The Woman Who Made Hollywood.* Lexington: University of Kentucky Press, 1997.

Williamson, J.E. *Twenty Years Under the Sea.* New York: Hale, Cushman & Flint, 1936.

Wolfe, Donald H. *The Black Dahlia Files.* Los Angeles: Regan Books, 2006.

Wollstein, Hans J. "The Strange Case of Valda Valkyrien," *Classic Images.* January 1997.

Worthington, Thomas Chew. *Recollections of Howard Thurston: Conjurer, Illusionist and Author.* Baltimore: Baker and Taylor, 1938.

Wottrich, Erika, ed. *Deutsche Universal: Transatlantische Verleih-und Produktionsstrategien eines Hollywood-Studios in den 20er und 30er Jahren.* Hamburg: CineGraph, 2001.

Index

Page numbers in **bold italics** indicate illustrations.

The Abandoned Room (book) 350
Abbe, Charles S. 432
Abbe, Jack 729
Abbott, Anthony 593
Abbott, Lyman 27
Abbott and Costello 240, 400
Die Abenteuer eines Zehenmarks-scheines (The Adventure of a Ten Mark Note) 630
The Aborigine's Devotion 329
Abraham Lincoln 20
Abramson, Ivan 265, 266, 267
The Abysmal Brute 620
An Accident (stage play) 92
Accord, Art 683
Accusee, levez-vouz! 605
The Ace of Hearts 58, 289
Acker, Jean 275, 679
Ackerman, Forrest J 438
Across the Border (book) 497
Across the Border (stage play) 199
Adamas, William S. 283
Adams, Claire ***318***
Adams, Doris Mills 156
Adams, Jane 467
Adams, Maude 389, 448, 662
Adam's Rib 184, 217
Adaptation 141
Adelman, Joseph 634
The Admirable Crichton 217
The Admirable Crichton (book) 449
Adolfi, John G. 475, 476, 726
Adorée, Renée 518
The Adventure Shop 347
An Adventure to Remember 718n
The Adventures of Captain Marvel (serial) 500, 652
The Adventures of Huckleberry Finn (book) 100
The Adventures of Ichabod and Mr. Toad 261
The Adventures of Jim Bowie (television) 68
The Adventures of Robin Hood 86, 439
The Adventures of Robinson Crusoe (serial) 576–577
The Adventures of Ruth (serial) 546

The Adventures of Sherlock Holmes 691
The Adventures of Tarzan (serial) 53, 89, 555, 576
The Adventures of Tom Sawyer (book) 100
The Adventuress 258
The Aerial Anarchists 208
The Aerial Submarine 208
The Aerial Torpedo 208
Aeschylus 636
Aesop 451
The Affairs of Anatol 62, 217, 497
After His Own Heart 5–7
Agnew, Robert 614
Aida (opera) 359, 602
Air Circus 233
The Air Mail Pilot 465
The Air Patrol 749
The Airship Destroyer 208
Aitken, Harry E. 208
Aitken, Spottiswoode 18, 20, 209, 765
Aitken brothers 134
Akin, Mary 695
Al diavolo la celebrità 200
Alabama 327
Aladdin; or, a Lad Out 7
Aladdin and the Wonderful Lamp (1899) 7
Aladdin and the Wonderful Lamp (1917) 3, 7
Aladdin in Pearlies (1912) 7
Aladdin Jones 7
Aladdin Up-to-Date 7
Aladdin's Other Lamp 7–9, 180, 281, 352, 441, 495, 654, 690
The Alaskan 646
Albers, Hans 447
Albert, Edward 306
Albin, Charles 474
The Alchemist's Hallucination 208
Aldrich, Charles T. 362
Alexander (the Magician) 592
Alexander, Ben 264
Alexander, J. Grubb 142
Alexander, John 249
Alfred, Carl 93

The Alfred Hitchcock Hour (television) 422
Alger, Horatio 5
Algeria (musical composition) 93
Algol 340
Ali Baba and the Forty Thieves 8
Alias Jimmy Valentine 220, 321, 548
Alice Adams 296, 524
Alice in Wonderland 20, 23, 562
Alighieri, Dante 113, 114, 115, ***115***, 116, 136
All Quiet on the Western Front 306, 310, 487
All Souls' Eve 9–10, 29, 664, 772
All Souls' Eve (stage play) 10
All That Heaven Allows 336
All the Brothers Were Valiant 79, 286
All the King's Men (stage play) 593
Allen, Alta 380, 381
Allen, Diana 624, 625
Allen, Irwin 746
Allen, Robert 634
Allison, Jean 411
Allison, May 6, 258
Aloha Oe 644
Along the Moonbeam Trail 241
Alonzo the Armless 606
Alraune 367, 576
Alvarado, Don 401, 403, ***403***
Alvarez, Louis 394
Amazing Mr. X 406, 423
The Amazing Transparent Man 275
An Ambassador from the Dead 214
America 306
The American Beauty 433, 447
An American Bride 428
An American Citizen 154
The American Girl (stage play) 222
American Methods 296
The American Venus 69
Amid the Wonders of the Deep 588
Amos Judd (book) 677
Amos Judd: A Play in a Prologue in Four Acts 677
Anastasia (1997) 481
The Ancient Mariner 10–12, 105, 113, 114, 115, 181, 267, 347

And a Still Small Voice 394
And Starring Pancho Villa as Himself (television) 160
And the Law Says 317
Der Andere (stage play) 112
Andersen, Hans Christian 41, 451, 676
Anderson, G.M. ("Bronco Billy") 14, 53, 163, 482, 597, 669
Anderson, Mignon 185–186
Anderson, Pamela 104
Anderson, Sherwood 132
The Andersonville Trial (stage play) 350
Angel, Criss 598
Angel, Heather 418
Angel Child 425
Angel on My Shoulder 614
Anglin, Margaret 92
Ankers, Evelyn 459
Anna and the King of Siam 217
Anna Christie (1923) 75, 92
Anna Karenina 154
Annabel Lee (poem) 19, 739
Anne Pedersdotter (stage play) 658
Annie Laurie 511
Annie Oakley (television) 68
Ansell, Mary 449
Anstey, F. 71
The Answer of the Sea 601
Anthony, De Leon 96
Anthony, Joe 251
The Antique Dealer 242
Antony and Cleopatra (stage play) 424
Aoki, Tsuru 66
The Ape (1928) 12–14, 84, 241, 620
The Ape (1940) 241, 459
The Ape (stage play) 241, 391
Apfel, Oscar 78, 220, 222, 446, 447
Aphrodite (stage play) 118
Arab (movie horse) 274
The Arab 364, 369
The Arabian Nights (book) 63
Arbuckle, Rocoe ("Fatty") 15, 62, 175–176, 223, 257, 439, 478, 559
Archainbaud, George 68, 175, 359, 514
Archibald, F.N. 48

Arden, Edwin 708
Are We Civilized? 696
Arendt, Hannah 136
Arey, Wayne 503
Arizona 190
Arizona (stage play) 190, 659
The Arizona Express 179
Arlen, Richard 223
Arling, Charles 477
Arliss, Florence 137
Arliss, George 43, 132, 136–137, 269, 325, 582, 617
Armstrong, Jack 216
Armstrong, Paul 321
Armstrong, Robert 321
Armstrong, Roxy 426
Arnold, Edward 491
Arnold, Jack 654
Arnold, Lieut. Leslie 596
Around the World in 80 Days (1956) 667, 730
Around the World in 80 Days (stage play) 588
Arsène Lupin 33
Arsenic and Old Lace 249, 385, 448
Arsenic and Old Lace (stage play) 249
Arthur, George K. 338
Arthur, Jean 448, 740
Arthur, Johnny 22, 82, 404, 405, 407, 408, 613
Artificial Intelligence: AI 471
Arvidson, Linda 17
As the Girls Go (stage play) 382
Ash, Gordon 388
Asher, Irving 82
Asher, Max 723
Ashes of Vengeance 248, 270, 290
Ashley, Arthur 480
Asimov, Isaac 100
Assassin of Youth 597
Astaire, Fred 203
Astor, Gertrude 82
Astor, Mary 474
At the Mercy of Tiberius 233, 465
At the Mercy of Tiberius (book) 233, 726
At the Sign of the Jack O'Lantern 14–16, 37, 72, 218
At the Sign of the Jack O'Lantern (book) 14, 218
At the White Horse Inn (stage play) 716
Athalie (book) 615
Atherton, Gertrude 48, 49, 51, 172, 674
Atlas, Leopold 419
Atom Man vs. Superman (serial) 82
Atwill, Lionel 241, 270, 312, 444, 585, 699
Auer, John 307
Die Augen der Mumie Ma (*Eyes of the Mummy*) 168
August, Edwin 159, 465
August, Joseph 114, 212
Austin, Frederick Britten 71, 72
Austin, George 405
Austin, Jere 699
Austin, Leslie 156
Avatar 731
The Avenging Conscience 16–21, *17*, 31, 32, 45, 75, 103, 115, 209, 248, 267, 382, 434, 481, 482, 613, 765
The Avenging Shadow 53
The Awakening of a Man 185
Aylott, David 208

Ayres, Agnes 62, 63, 231, 232, 341, 549, 550, *550*
Ayres, Lew 599
Az Ordog (stage play) 61, 132

Babes in Bagdad 312
Babes in Toyland 362, 400
"Baby" Carmen De Rue 617
Baby Face 224
Baby Marie Osborne 260, 545
Bach, William 656
Bachelor Apartment 289
Bachleda, Alicja 601
Back to God's Country 477
Backstairs 81
Backus, George 276
Baclnova, Olga 376, *378*, 628
Bacon, Kevin 215
Bacon, Lloyd 702
Badet, Regina 604
Badger, Clarence 487
Baggot(t), King 29, 150, 325n, 326, 395, 592, 634, 646, 735, 736
Bainter, Fay 654
Baird, Leah 264
The Bait 639
Baker, Carroll 46
Baker, George D. 72, 169, 170, 295
Baker, Josephine 311
Baker, Robert B. 209
Baker, Robert M. 208, 209
Baker, Sam 399, 400
Balaoo (book) 665, 667
Balaoo, the Demon Baboon (1913) 665
Balcon, Michael 376
The Balcony 79
Balderston, John 337, 419, 763
Ball, Lucille 259
The Ballad of Reading Goal (poem) 216
Le Ballet Mécanique 349
Balshofer, Fred 216, 256, 257, 258
Balzac, Honoré de 138, 160–161, 359, 360, 361, 715
The Bamboo Saucer 407
Bandmann, Daniel E. 42, 74
Bankhead, Tallulah 265, 325
Banks, Leslie 448
Banky, Vilma 199
The Barada 41, 46, 47, 123–124, 125, 126, 212, 218, 249, 273, 332, 336, 515, 574, 582, 605, 650, 657, 681, 682, 697, 742, 747
Barabbas (book) 674
Barbara Frietchie (stage play) 115
Barbara Frietchie (Whittier) 168
Barclay, J. Searle 155
Barcroft, Roy 697
Bare Fists 493
Baree, Son of Kazan 643
Barker, Bradley 14
Barker, Reginald 134–135
The Barker 397
Barlatier, Andre 129, 173
Barnabel, Clementine 598
Barnes, Al G. 255
Barnes, George 251
Barnett, Chester 580
Baron, Henry 290
Baroud 369
Barr, Robert 509
Barras, Charles 40
Barrat, Robert 641
Barrett, Albert 273
Barrett, Edith 444

The Barretts of Wimpole Street (1934) 617
The Barretts of Wimpole Street (1957) 617
Barrie, J.M. 182, 191, 420, 448, 449, 450
Barrie, Nigel 341
The Barrier 336
Barrington, George 206
Barriscale, Bessie 133, 134, *134*, 135
Barrows, George 455, 733
Barrows, Henry A 455, 733
Barry, Wesley 229, 231, 439
Barrymore, Drew 154, 205
Barrymore, Ethel 43, 119, 154, 170, 214 215, 244–245, 410, 444, 484, 568, 650, 659, 736
Barrymore, John (aka The Great Profile) 8, 33, 60, 76, 106, 111, 149, 150, *150*, 151, 152, *152*, 153–154, 155, 156, 157, 162, 175, 190, 202, 214, 223, 244, 259, 272, 307, 322, 336, 377, 542, 550, 579, 580, 583, 587, 636, 643, 646, 702, 734
Barrymore, Lionel 29, 32, 33, *33*, 34, 112, 154, 214, 215, 244, 288, 292, 304, *415*, 416, 417, 418, 491, 518, 550, 569, 608, 630, 646, 656, 662
Barsow, G. 609
Bart, Jean 585
Barthelmess, Richard 182, 183–184, 238, 649, 651
Bartlett, Lanier 468
The Barton Mystery (stage play) 641
The Baseball Bug 43
Baseball, That's All 169
Basevi, James 418
The Bat (1926) 21–24, *22*, 91, 130, 139, 145, 174, 175, 201, 226, 380, 404, 406, 407, 437, 562, 563, 701, 702, 762, 770
The Bat (1959) 406
The Bat (book) 21, 91
The Bat (stage play) 219, 222, 238, 390, 434, 436, 437, 460, 485, 643, 704
The Bat Whispers 34, 131, 500, 742
Bates, Guy Post 581, 582
Bates, Ralph 157
The Battle Cry of Peace 24–28, *26*, *27*, 94, 95, 130, 131, 194, 195, 196, 208, 244, 252, 272, 283, 345, 352, 414, 672, 673, 735, 743, 744, 770
The Battle Cry of War 672
The Battle Hymn of the Republic 169
The Battle in the Clouds 208
Battle of Hearts 222
Battle of the Century 763
Baudelaire, Charles 575
Baum, L. Frank 451, 473, 668
Baur, Harry 481
Baxter, Warner 174, 628, 630, 631, 685, 686
Beard, Daniel C. 100
Beardsley, Aubrey 562
The Beast 632
The Beast of Hollow Mountain 342
The Beast with a Million Eyes 255
The Beast with Five Fingers 411
Beatrice Fairfax (serial) 1922
Beau Geste (1926) 358, 429, 673
Beau Revel 47
Beauchamp, Christine 502

Beaudet, Louise 27
Beaudine, William 279, 681
Beauty and the Barge 242
Beauty and the Beast (1945) 458
The Beauty Contest 163
Beck, Arthur 264
Becky Sharp 82, 329
Bedford, Barbara 256
Beerbohm-Tree, Sir Herbert 76
Beery, Noah 44, *231*, 719, 729, 776
Beery, Wallace 58, 123, 187, 203, 210, 256, 287, 341, *342*, 343, 344, 349, 470, 596, 766, 768
"The Beetle" (story) 252
Before Dawn 193
Before I Hang 711
Beggars in Ermine 681
Behind Red Curtains 440
Behind the Curtain 10, 28–30, 434, 594, 624, 772
Behind the Door 544, 629, 768
Behind the Evidence 14
Behind the Front 664
Behind the Mask 10, 82, 702
Bel Geddes, Norman 539
Belasco, David 59, 75, 78, 79, 99, 190, 218, 235, 236, 384, 385, 413, 488, 520, 552, 595, 599, 656, 657, 727
Belasco, Jay 727
Belasco, Walter 727
Belcher, Charles 559, 564
Belford, Major Wellington 664
Bell, Monta 213
Bell, Rex 52
Bell, Spencer 451
The Bell (stage play) 389
The Bell Boy 478
The Bell of the Fog (book) 51
Bellamy, Madge 354, 739
Bellew, Kyrle 41
The Bells (1918) 30–31, 138, 139, 398, 715, 745
The Bells (1926) 32–34, *33*, 112, 272, 331, 377, 416, 569, 614, 668, 770
The Bells (poem) 32
The Bells (stage play) 30, 31, 244, 295
Belmore, Lionel 332, 341, 488, 491
Belot, Adolphe 552
Beloved Enemy 256
Beloved Infidel 260
The Beloved Rogue 307, 336
Benet, Stephen Vincent 91
Benham, Grace 727
Benham, Harry 43, 149, 234
Ben-Hur (1925) 106, 151, 160, 184, 259, 283, 364, 369, 382, 468, 484, 542, 576, 585, 639, 652, 680, 711
Ben-Hur (book) 275, 766
Ben-Hur (stage play) 227
Benjamin, Harry (Dr.) 48
Bennett, Alma 343
Bennett, Barbara 611
Bennett, Catherine 468
Bennett, Chester 12
Bennett, Constance 611
Bennett, Enid 251, 467, 468
Bennett, Joan 611
Bennett, Mae 648
Bennett, Marjorie 468
Bennett, Richard 485, 611
Bennett, Spencer Gordon 391
Bennett, Wilda 235
Bennison, Andrew 762

Benny, Jack 400, 564
Benoit, Georges 582
Benrimo, J.H. 654
Benton, Curtis 592
Benton, Laura 166–167
Beranger, Clara 150, 151, 155, 156, 202
Beresford, Frank 765
Beresford, Leslie 637
Bergère, Ouida 215, 501–502
Bergman, Ingmar 246, 653
Berkeley, Busby 100, 562, 573, 739
Berlin, Irving 189
Berlioz, Hector 132
Bern, Paul 606, 622, 623
Bernhardt, Sarah 35, 193, 488, 518, 656, 658
Bernstein, Isidore 48, 339
Bernstein, Leonard 448
Berserk 609
Bertelet, Arthur 7
Bertini, Francesca 650
Besserer, Eugenie 91–92, 247
The Best of Enemies 158
Beswick, Martine 157
Betsy's Burglar 175
The Better 'Ole 399
Betty Be Good 425
Between Friends 34–36, 175, 266, 295, 300, 434, 441, 443, 445, 622, 716, 773
Between Friends (book) 36, 122, 202, 616
Between Two Worlds 62
Between Two Worlds (stage play) 212
Bevan, Billy 176
Beverly of Graustark 122
Beynon, George W. 446, 447
Beyond 9, 15, 36–38, 72, 214, 646, 664, 768
Beyond the Rocks 682
Beyond the Time Barrier 275
Beyond the Veil 96
Bickel, George 722
Bierce, Ambrose 51
The Big City 336, 397
The Big House 123, 768
The Big Parade 167, 516, 518, 653
Biggers, Earl Derr 15, 654, 705
Billy the Kid vs. Dracula 2
Bingham, Edfrid 522
Binney, Constance 78, *78*, 79, 754
Binney, Faire 78, 754
Bird of Paradise (stage play) 64, 296, 581, 584, 644
Bird of Paradise 584, 650
Birdsong, Sylvia 777
The Birth of a Flivver 341
The Birth of a Nation 18, 19, 20, 27, 75, 103, 115, 127, 143, 194, 195, 209, 210, 243, 248, 282, 300, 329, 459, 482, 538, 560, 597, 672, 732, 747, 765
The Birth of a Race 660, 696
The Birth of the Blues 490
Birthright 99
Bishop, Washington Irving 659
The Bishop of the Ozarks 38–39, 304, 686, 719
Bits of Life 232, 563
Bitter Fruit 758
Bitzer, G.W. ("Billy") 17, 19, 247, 574
Bitzer, John 301
Bizet, Georges 742

Bizeul, Jacques 641
Blaché, Alice Guy 123, 163, 164–165, 420, 556, 603, 619, 671, 755
Blaché, Herbert 165, 272, 419, 420, 556, 618–619, 671, 692, 755
Black, William J. 106
"Black: The Story of a Dog" (story) 632
The Black Book 562
The Black Camel 460
The Black Cat (1934) 111, 368, 370, 392, 448
"The Black Cat" (story) 15, 17, 18, 599, 609, 699
The Black Circle 120
The Black Coin (serial) 680
The Black Crook (stage play) 40
The Black Crook 39–42, 625
Black Dragons 96, 175, 317, 679
Black Fear 42–43, 711
Black Friday 347, 733
The Black Gate 414
The Black King 382
Black Magic (1929) 20, 43–46, 303, 320, 470, 490, 704, 745
Black Magic (1944) 496, 681
Black Moon 10, 283, 336, 711
Black Orchids 46–48, 363, 364, 454, 492, 493, 494, 573, 592, 604, 648, 662, 768
Black Orchids (working title for *Trifling Women*) 573, 574, 575
Black Oxen 6, 11, 48–52, *50*, *52*, 172, 180, 296, 304, 394, 439, 522, 523, 594, 674
Black Oxen (book) 172
The Black Pearl 52–54, 748
Black Phantoms (stage play) 174
The Black Pirate 138, 190, 350, 433
The Black Room 30, 186, 274, 313, 634, 721
Black Shadows 54–55, 272, 466
Black Sunday 151, 644
The Black Tower 270, 299
The Blackbird 517, 606
Blackmer, Sidney 217
Blackstone, Harry 592
Blackstone, Harry Jr. 593
Blackton, J. Stuart 25, 26–28, 35, 168, 283, 345, 414, 617, 672, 734
Blackwell, Carlyle 75, 516
Blade Runner 471
Blasco-Ibáñez, Vicente 689
The Blasphemer 355
A Blind Bargain 6, 37, 55–58, *57*, 284, 286, 289, 305, 321, 405, 407, 445, 773
Blind Husbands 459
Blind Justice 254
The Blindness of Devotion 604
Blish, James 202, 616
Blonde for a Night 487
Blood, Adele 144, 145
Blood and Sand (1922) 155, 251, 371, 439, 680
Blood and Sand (1941) 679
The Blood of Our Brothers 259
Blood of the Children 462
Blood Ship 45
Bloodbath 270
Bloom, Abraham 703
The Blot 186
Blow Your Own Horn 39, 316, 685–686, 715
Blow Your Own Horn (stage play) 252, 329, 622

The Blue Angel 607
The Blue Bird (1918) 154, 450, 460
The Blue Flame (stage play) 273, 332
The Blue Mouse (stage play) 143
Bluebeard (1909) 451
Bluebeard's Ten Honeymoons 110
Blum, Ralph 259
Blystone, John G. 304
Blystone, William Stanley 304
Blyth(e), Maurice 154
Blyth, E.M. 244
Blythe, Betty 42, 51, 211–212, 516
Boardman, Eleanor 335, 524, *524*
Bob Hampton of Placer 271
Boccaccio, Giovanni 113
Bodu Saved from Drowning (stage play) 400
Body and Soul (1915) 662
Body and Soul (1920) 37, 58–61, 130, 142, 274, 605, 613, 624, 671
Body and Soul (1925) 98, 535
Body and Soul (1927) 608
The Body Disappears 82
Bogart, Humphrey 66, 393, 548
Bogdanavich, Peter 108
La Bohème (opera) 76
The Bohemian Girl 168, 243
Bohn, Jack 549
Boito, Arrigo 132
Bolder, Bobby 163
Boles, John 38, 311, 312, 313, 349
Bolshevism on Trial 243, 293, 395, 594
The Bonded Woman 644
The Bondman (stage play) 73
Bonnie Marie 587
Bonomo, Joe 34, 288, 770
The Boob 108
Booth, Edwin 154, 266, 321, 695
Booth, John Wilkes 736
Booth, Walter R. 208, 384
Borch, Gustav 377
Bordeaux, Joe 240
Borden, Lizzie 656–657
Borden, Olive 233, 401, 402, 403, *403*, 700, 701, *701*
Borderland 61–63, *62*, 214, 320, 497
Borgia, Lucretia 574
Borland, Carroll 335, 336
Borzage, Frank 285, 312, 321, 354, 369, 406, 491, 519, 585, 695, 740, 751, 773
Bosch, Hieronymus 364
Boston Blackie's Little Pal 585
Bosworth, Hobart 148, 341, 548
Boteler, Wade 15
The Bottle Imp 63–66, 75, 87, 92, 131, 141, 232, 299, 644, 654
The Bottle Imp (book) 63
The Bottle Imp: A Melodramatic Romance in Two Acts (stage play) 63
A Bottle of Rye 383
Bottomley, Roland 42, 137
Boucicault, Dion 448
Boucicault, Nina 448
Bought and Paid For (stage play) 28, 468
Bound and Gagged (serial) 745
Bow, Clara 11, 12, 49, 50, 51–52, *52*, 58, 168, 172, 253, 304, 597
Bow, Robert 52
Bow, Sara 52
Bowers, John 765
Bowery at Midnight 606

The Bowery Boys 129
Boyd, William 200, 498–499, *499*, 670, 681, 755, 760
Boyd, William "Stage" 498–499, 755
Boyer, Charles 262, 585
Boyle, Jack 304, 305
Brabin, Charles 20, 281, 482, 484
Brace Up 686
Bracey, Sidney 181, 234
Bracken, Bertram 105
Bradbury, James 321
Bradbury, James Jr. 321
Bradley, Will 758
Brady, Edward J. 546
Brady, Jasper Ewing 611
Brady, William 305, 478
Braham, Horace 594
Brahms, John 314
Braid, James 54
Brain Cinema 686–687
The Brand of Satan 66–68, 78, 145, 176, 414, 514
A Branded Soul 105
Brandon, Dorothy 444
The Brass Bottle 68–71, *69*, 102, 138, 289, 343, 382, 522, 564, 579, 598
The Brass Bottle (book) 71
The Brass Bottle (stage play) 132
Brautigam, Otto 586–587
Brawn of the North 96
Breamer, Sylvia 137, *616*, 617
Brecher, Egon 448
Breen, Joseph 119
Breese, Edmund 471, 725, 754, 971
Brendel, El 315, 407
Brenon, Herbert 127, 128, 129, 395, 428, 429, 430, 449, 450, 475, 476, 478, 585, 631, 747
Brent, Evelyn 474, 512, 513, 514, 564, 692, *692*
Brent, George 289
Bretherton, Howard 636
Brewster's Millions (1914) 455
Brewster's Millions (1921) 15
Brewster's Millions (book) 15, 275
Brewster's Millions (stage play) 480
Bride of Frankenstein 59, 80, 258, 313
Bride of Mystery 463
The Bride of the Beast 301
Bride of the Monster 296
The Bridge of San Luis Rey 20, 484
The Bridge on the River Kwai 66
Brigham, Leslie 394
The Bright Shawl 651
Bringing up Baby 701
Brinkman, Dolores 416
British Intelligence 501, 696
Britton, Barbara 622
Britton, Edna 507
Broadway 290, 310, 317
Broadway Melody 344
Brockwell, Gladys 11, 104–105, 267, 268, 639
Broder, Jack 741
Broken Barriers 614
Broken Blossoms 184, 247, 248, 540, 652, 690, 729
Broken Fetters 46
Bromberg, J. Edward 448
The Bromley Case 713
Bronson, Betty 3, 449, 450, 451
Bronston, Douglas 717
Brooke, Van Dyke 131, 389

Brooks, Clive 69
The Brothers Grimm 451, 676
Brower, Robert 522
Brown, Clarence 568, 673
Brown, Dan 128
Brown, Frank 620
Brown, Helen Gurley 739
Brown, John W. 737–738
Brown, Karl 559
Brown, Walter 387
Brown of Harvard 390
Browne, Earle 348
Browne, Lewis Allen 384
Browning, Tod 19, 20, 33, 82, 86, 110, 117, 119, 130, 160, 161, 169, 174, 230, 271, 279, 284, 285, 286, 289, 308, 321, 333, 335, 336–337, 363, 377, 396, 402, 416, 421, 422, 423, 487, 516, 517, 518, 540, 566, 571, 596, 605–606, 607, 608, 609, 610, 614, 627, 628, 629, 630, 667, 668, 686, 692, 763, 764
Brownlow, Kevin 8, 24
Bruce, Nigel 200, 623, 721
Brulatour, Jules 639, 640
Brunette, Fritzi 139, 161, 715
Brunton, Robert 138, 139
The Brute Man 467
Bryan, Alfred 719
Bryan, William Jennings 506, 672
Brynner, Yul 640
The Buccaneer (stage play) 721
Buchanan's Wife 272
Buck Rogers (serial) 96, 732
A Bucket of Blood 270
Buckland, Wilfred 110
Buckley, Floyd 372
Buckshot John 617
Budd, Ruth 505, 506, 507, 507
Buferd, Marilyn 200
Buffalo Bill, Jr. (television) 68
The Builders (stage play) 69–70
Bulger, Harry 279
Bulldog Drummond 222
Bulldog Drummond (1929) 562, 706
Bulldog Drummond (stage play) 437
Bulldog Drummond Comes Back 290
Bulldog Drummond Escapes 290
Bulldog Drummond in Africa 290
Bulldog Drummond Strikes Back 193
Bulldog Drummond's Revenge 83, 290
Bulldog Drummond's Secret Police 290
Bullin' the Bullsheviki 669
Bulson, Harry 288
Bulwer-Lytton, Edward George 252
The Bump 661
Bunny, George 344, 465
Bunny, John 28, 82, 169, 234, 344, 465, 731
Bunty Pulls the Strings (stage play) 492
Burdell, Elwood ("Woody") 733
The Burden of Race 99
Burgess, Dorothy 283, 336
Burgess, Gelett 263, 264, 265, 502, 595, 596, 618
The Burglar's Daughter (stage play) 620

Buried Treasure (1921) 15, 39, 71–72, 120, 169, 214, 295
Burke, Billie 86, 94
Burke, Thomas 690
Burlesque of Carmen 615
"Burn, Witch, Burn!" (story) 511
Burnett, Carol 618
Burnham, Beatrice 268
Burning Daylight 306, 382, 543
The Burning Question 355
Burning the Candle 107
Burns, Edmund 643–644, 745, 765
Burns, Vinnie 420, 556, 671–672
Burns, William J. 29
Burr, C.C. 89
Burr, Raymond 706
Burroughs, Edgar Rice 222, 554, 555, 596, 597
Burt, Katherine Newlin 520, 522
Burt, Willard 149
Burton, J.W. 220
Burton, Richard 536
Burton, Tim 261
Burton, William A. 174
Bury Me Dead 400
Busch, Mae 738
Bushman, Francis X. 160, 258, 447
Bushman, Francis X. Jr. 391
Busoni, Ferruccio 132
Buster Keaton: A Hard Act to Follow (documentary) 8
Butt, Clara 115
Butt, Lawson 115, 115, 173, 207, 207, 399
Butterfield, Everett 361
By Divine Right 234, 241
By Love Redeemed 350
By Super Strategy 746
"By the Light of the Silvery Moon" (song) 143
By Whose Hand? 82

Cabanne, William ("Christy") 159–160, 437, 597
The Cabinet of Dr. Caligari 149, 375, 405, 412, 464, 676
Cabiria 659
Cable, George W. 98
A Café in Cairo 596
Cagliostro 87
Cagney, James 476
Cahn, Edward L. 377
Cain, James M. 424
Cain, Robert 617
Calamity Anne 123
Caleb Conover, Railroader (book) 201
Calhoun, Alice 35
Calhoun, Harold Gilmore 734
The Call of the Flesh 518
The Call of the North 110
The Call of the Soul 72–73, 105, 594
Calvert, Catherine 354
Camaniti, Tullio 23
The Cameraman 259, 336
Camille (1921) 289, 679
Camille (1926) 132, 289
Camille (stage play) 656
Camp, Wadsworth 314, 315, 350, 353
Campbell, Alan 167, 169, 170
Campbell, Eric 76
Campbell, Mrs. Patrick 42, 137, 169, 567
Campbell, Webster 347

Campeau, Frank 300, 643
The Canadian 279
The Canary Murder Case 445
Cane Fire 186
Cannon, Maurice 583
The Canterville Ghost 154
"The Canterville Ghost" (story) 17
Cape Smoke (stage play) 44
Capek, Karel 549, 559
Capellani, Albert 675
Capra, Frank 14, 20, 33, 240, 296, 440, 737, 740
Caprice 235
Captain America (serial) 95, 597
Captain Blood 301
Captain Blood (1924) 715
Captain Jinks of the Horse Marines (stage play) 244
Captain Kidd 740
Captain of the Guard 310
Captive Wild Woman 669
Captured in Chinatown 597
The Career of Waterloo Peterson 339
The Careless Woman 73–74
Carewe, Arthur Edmund 7, 80, 457, 460, 583
Carewe, Edwin 245, 256, 343, 695–696
Carey, Harry 493
Carillo, Leo 193
Carleton, Henry Guy 244, 453
Carleton, Lloyd B. 206, 207, 696
Carlton, William 197
Carmen 119, 146, 147, 216, 582, 742
Carmen, Jewel 21, 22
Carnarvon, Lord 301
Carnival 24
The Carol Burnett Show (television) 618
Carousel 585
Carousel (stage play) 584
Carpenter, Edward Childs 320
Carpenter, Grant 620
Carr, Trem 53
Carradine, John 599, 669, 271
Carré, Ben 232, 456, 458, 460
Carroll, Leo G. 311
Carter, Harry 6, 7, 519
Carter, Howard 301
Carter, Lin 616
Carter, Lincoln Jared 178, 179, 179
Caruso, Enrico 350, 672
The Case of Becky (1915) 20, 59, 74–77, 74, 76, 776
The Case of Becky (1921) 29, 59, 67, 77–79, 78, 235, 243, 465, 480, 488, 505, 754
The Case of Becky (stage play) 75, 78, 502, 519, 595, 727
Casey at the Bat 524, 768
Cashman, Harry 427
Casino Royale (1967) 433
"The Cask of Amontillado" (story) 17, 18, 454, 546, 604
Cassidy, William F. 383, 384
Castle, Irene 203, 203
Castle, Vernon 203
Castle, William 637
Castle in the Desert 83
The Castle of Otranto (novel) 83
Castles for Two 217, 687–688
The Cat and the Canary 21, 69, 79–84, 80, 83, 174, 175, 219, 222, 253, 277, 311, 312, 313, 314, 315, 375, 377, 380, 404, 405, 433, 437,

458, 460, 487, 511, 560, 567, 621, 702, 742
The Cat and the Canary (stage play) 21, 79–80, 99, 103, 238, 239, 252, 305, 332, 434, 436, 437, 460, 510, 597, 627, 643, 704
The Cat Creeps 59, 407, 458
Cat People 10
The Cat's Paw 234
The Catman of Paris 670
Cavalcade 296
Cavalier's Dream 345
The Cave Man 169
Cecil, Edward 105
Cerdan, Marcel 200
Cervantes, Miguel de 114
The Chalice of Sorrow 46, 47
The Challenge of Chance 646
Chambers, Robert W. 34, 36, 121, 122, 123, 202, 615–616, 625
The Champ 123, 344, 768
The Champion 625
A Chance Deception 159
Chandlee, Harry 745
Chandler, Helen 376
Chandu the Magician 20, 242, 449, 468, 562, 640, 667
Chaney, Hazel 285
Chaney, Lon 5, 8, 20, 53, 56, 57, 57, 58, 86, 87, 103, 117, 119, 123, 153, 172, 181, 183, 211, 221, 230, 240, 254, 255, 272, 284–285, 286, 287, 289, 290, 291, 292, 296, 306, 308, 312, 329, 333, 334, 334, 335, 336, 337, 339, 364, 375, 378, 390, 392, 395, 396, 397, 398, 402, 404, 405, 406, 406, 407, 407, 408, 416, 421, 422, 423, 451, 456, 457, 458, 459, 460, 461, 481, 493, 495, 496, 524, 542, 551, 571, 580, 592, 596, 605, 606–607, 608, 609, 610, 614, 619, 624, 627–628, 629, 630, 630, 637, 638, 638, 640, 681, 741, 763, 764, 770, 773
Chaney, Lon Jr. 46, 391, 496, 607, 741
Changed Lives 462
The Chaperon (stage play) 231
Chaplin, Charlie 7, 20, 69, 100, 108, 241, 245, 255, 256, 312, 347, 348, 399, 400, 406, 433, 442, 482, 513, 560, 605, 607, 625, 664, 688, 734
Chaplin, Sydney 399, 400
Charcuterie Mechanique 707
Charlap, Mark 449
The Charlatan 84–87, 86, 110, 183, 260, 339, 400, 504, 505, 711, 736, 764, 773
Charles, John 72, 276
Charles, Theodore 750
Charley's Aunt (1925) 399
Charlie (movie elephant) 71, 576
Charlie Chan at the Circus 120
Charlie Chan at the Olympics 95
Charlie Chan at the Opera 542
Charlie Chan at the Racetrack 120, 290
Charlie Chan at the Ringside 193
Charlie Chan in Egypt 120, 290
Charlie Chan in Paris 290
Charlie Chan in Reno 312, 762
Charlie Chan in Shanghai 290
Charlie Chan in the Secret Service 681
Charlie Chan on Broadway 82

Charlie Chan's Secret 460
Charters, Spencer 325
Chase, Charley 83, 255, 400, 706, 770
Chase, Colin 105
Chatrian, Alexandre 30, 32
Chatterton, Tom 466
Chaucer, Geoffrey 132
Chautard, Emile 641, 741, 742
The Cheat 65, 66, 218, 598
The Cheaters (television) 184
Cheating Cheaters 614
The Cheerful Fraud 82
Chelsea 7750 712
Chenault, Lawrence 99, 192
Cher 184
Cheseboro, George 669, 670
Chesnutt, Charles Waddell 98, 99
Chesterton. G.K. (Gilbert Keith) 419
Cheyenne Autumn 20
Child, Richard Washburn 708, 709
Child Bride 732
Childers, Naomi 7, *171*, 173, *173*, 735
The Children of Captain Grant 588
Children of Fate 99
Children of the Ritz 166
The Chimes 420, 672
Chin, Chin (stage play) 122
China Clipper 20
Chinatown after Dark 754
Chinatown Charlie 87–89, *88*, 449, 654, 753
Chinatown Charlie, the Opium Fiend (book) 89
Chinatown Charlie, the Opium Fiend (stage play) 89, 252, 329, 622, 685
The Chinese Cat 496, 681
The Chinese Parrot *23*, 82, 87, 142, 228, 312, 563, 564, 654, 765
"The Chink and the Child" (story) 690
Chloe, Love Is Calling You 232–233, 403
The Chorus Lady (stage play) 42
A Chorus Line (stage play) 224
Chris and His Wonderful Lamp 8
Christensen, Benjamin 7, 39, 234, 252, 253, 254–255, 256, 416, 433, 454, 509, 510, 511
The Christian 347
The Christian (stage play) 193
Christie, Al 397, 463
Christine, Virginia 46
A Christmas Carol (1908) 495
A Christmas Carol (1910) 495
"A Christmas Carol" (story) 113, 172, 386, 494, 680
The Chronicles of Cleek 185
Chu Chin Chow (stage play) 106
Chung-Ling-Soo 592
A Cigarette — That's All 184
Cinderella (1914) 450, 451
Cinderella (fairy tale) 7
Circe the Enchantress 688–689, 690
Circles 383
The Circular Staircase (1915) 89–92, 245, 707
The Circular Staircase (book) 21, 89–91
Circumstantial Evidence 713n
The Circus Queen Murders 524
The Circus Queen Murders (book) 593

Circus Rookies 338
Citizen Kane 639
City Lights 102, 467, 607
The City of Mystery (book) 373, 374
Civilization 2, 92–95, 134, 135, 195, 306, 368, 395, 468, 490, 555, 647, 719
The Claim 599
Clair, René 340
The Clairvoyant 490
The Clairvoyant Swindlers 683
Clampett, Bob 228
Clancy, Carl Stearns 261, 263
The Clansman (book/play) 194, 243, 329
Clarendon, Hal 453
Clark, Edward 131, 611
Clark, Edwin 197
Clark(e), Marguerite 100, 258, 329, 451
Clarke, Betty Ross 15
Clarke, Wallace 181, 592
Clary, Charles 103, 644
Clash of the Wolves 96
Classified 51
Claudia 377
Clawson, Elliott 355, 495, 624
Clawson, Lawrence "Dal" 355, 382
Clayton, Ethel 37, *213*, 214, 631
Clayton, Marguerite 163, 199, 669–670, 725
Cleary, Val 777
Clemens, Olivia ("Libby") 100
Clemens, Samuel Langhorne 99–100
Cleopatra (1899) 167
Clifford, William 668
Clifton, Elmer 218, 597, 686
Clifton, Emma Bell 602
Climax (television) 245, 568
The Climax (1944) 79, 82, 407, 456, 734
The Climax (stage play) 79
Cline, Eddie 770
Clinging Vine 358
Clive, E.E. 240
Clive, Henry 775
Clonbough, G. Butler (aka Gustav von Seyffertitz) 122. etc.614
The Cloud Dodger 749
Clovelly, Cecil 152
The Clutching Hand (serial) 558
Clyde, Andy 343
Coates, Grant 166
Cobb, Irving S. 230
Coburn, Gladys 42, 624, 625
Cochrane, William 95
Cock o' the Walk (stage play) 468
Cocteau, Jean 458
Code of the Air 95–97
Cody, Bill 572–573
Cody, Iron Eyes 500
Cody, Lew 271
Coffee, Lenore 348
Coghlan, Frank "Junior" 500
Coghlan, Rose 266
Cohan, George M. 6, 15, 325, 385, 395, 398, 468, 497, 648, 662, 763
Cohen and Kelly 240
Cohen, Bennett 267, 390, 391, 615
Cohen, Max 301
Cohen at Coney Island 234
Cohen's Luck 282
Cohill, William 324–325
Cohn, Alfred 315, 433

Cohn, Harry 232
Cohn, Jack 240
Colbert, Claudette 275
Colbert, Suzanne 568
Colby, A.E. 208
Coleridge, Samuel Taylor 10, 11, 12, 111, 114
College 268
College Days 194
Collier, Constance 214, 217
Collier, William Sr. 411
Collins, John H. 7, 8, 16
Collins, Milt 13
Collins, Richard 619
Collins, Tom 713
Collins, William Wilkie 163, 164, 409, 410, 411, 476, 477, 492, 671, 754
Colman, Ronald 139, 186, 581, 706
Colonel Blood 324
Colonel Sellers (stage play) 100
La Colonne de feu (The Column of Fire) 514
Colorado (stage play) 659
Colton, John 310
Come and Get It 563
El comediante 307
A Comedy of Women (stage play) 428
The Comet 297
The Coming of Amos 310, 359
Coming Through 664
The Commanding Officer (stage play) 646
Common Clay (stage play) 660
Compson, Betty 397, 398, 522, 631, 644, 645–646
Le Comte Kostia 73
Conan Doyle, Sir Arthur 11, 132, 170, 172, 190, 246, 301, 330, 339, 340, 341, 343, 370, 371, 394, 543, 566, 593, 704
Conan the Barbarian 720
Condemned to Live 119
Conjure Woman (The) 97–99, 192
The Conjure Woman (book) 98
Conklin, Chester 240, 252, 253, 255, 381, 416
Conklin, Heinie 240, 644, 706
Conklin, William 546
The Connecticut Yankee (1921) 97
A Connecticut Yankee in King Arthur's Court (1920) 7, 69, 97, 99–104, *101*, *103*, 237, 408, 434, 617, 745, 769, 770
A Connecticut Yankee in King Arthur's Court (1931) 154, 343, 377, 439
A (Connecticut Yankee in King Arthur's Court book) 100
A Connecticut Yankee in King Arthur's Court (stage play) 100
Connelly, Edward J. 133, 134, *134*, 235, 237, *479*, 518, 574, 575, *654*
Connelly, Jane 371
Connelly, Marc 473
Conness, Robert 228
The Conquering Power 20, 133, 312, 364, 385, 594, 681
Conquest 262
Conquest of the North Pole 339
Conrad, Joseph 627, 652
Conrad in Search of His Youth 227
Conscience 11, 104–105, 213, 267, 434, 703, 707, 711, 725
The Conspiracy (1914) 209

The Conspiracy (1930) 209, 210
The Conspiracy (book) 209
The Conspiracy (stage play) 209
Constance, Marian 35
Constant, Max 583, 584
A Continental Girl 633
Converse, F.S. 473
Coogan, Jackie 296
Cook, Clyde 381
Cook, John 496
Cook, Warren 716
Cooke, Alistair 562
Cooley, Hallam 404, 406
Coolidge, Calvin 347
Cooper, Bigelow 228
Cooper, Gary 217
Cooper, George 571
Cooper, Gladys 397, 537
Cooper, Merion C. 45, 321, 342
The Cop 321, 495
The Copperhead 662
The Copperhead (stage play) 662
Coquette 619
Corbin, Virginia Lee 8
Corelli, Marie 47, 134, 301, 454, 492, 536, 537, 538, 604, 674–675, 676
The Corianton 382
Corman, Roger 302, 326
Cornish, Robert 219
The Corpse Vanishes 96, 175, 317, 380
Corrigan, D'Arcy 311, 313
Corsair 22, 24
The Corsican Brothers (1920) 118
The Corsican Brothers (book) 117, 118
Cortez, Ricardo 200, 393, 394, 540, 678, 729
Cortez, Stanley 393, 540, 678
The Cossack Whip 358
The Cossacks 518
Cossar, John 163
Costello, Dolores 211, 240, 580, 636, 646, 702, 734
Costello, Helene 635, 636, 702, 734
Costello, Maurice 46, 549, 636, 702, 734, 735
Cotner, Frank 427
Cotton, Lucy 137, 324, 641
Coulter, Frazer 273
Counsellor-at-Law (stage play) 212
The Count of Monte Cristo (1913) 382
The Count of Monte Cristo (book) 295, 604, 632, 667
The Countess Cathleen (stage play) 48, 50 (note)
The Courtesan 328
Courtleigh, William Jr. 664
Courtney, William 501
Courtot, Marguerite 693, 694, 699, 700
The Courtshop of Myles Standish 389, 503
Cousin Lucy (stage play) 352
The Covered Wagon 439, 559, 659, 715
Coward, Noël 227, 405
The Coward 305, 389
The Cowardly Way 105–106, 617, 699
Cowl, George 641, 742
Cowl, Jane 750, 751
Cowles, Jules 343
Cracked Ice 163

The Cradle Buster 471, 700
The Cradle of Courage 256
Craft, William James 723
Craig Kennedy — Criminologist (television) 558
Craig, Eugene 115
Craig's Wife 382
Crampton, Howard 592
Crane, Frank 410, 411, 548
Crane, Ward 122
Crane, William H. 258
Craven, Frank 648
The Craving 107–108
Crawford, Joan 73, 289, 488, 607, **607**, 608, 609, 664
Crawford, Kathryn 79, 723
Crawford, Marion 252
Crazy to Marry 439
Creation 342
Creation of the Humanoids 231, 407
Creature from the Black Lagoon 168
Creelman, James Ashmore 310, 472
Crime and Punishment (1935) 405
Crime Doctor (series) 631, 686
The Crime Doctor 155
Crimmins, Dan 722
The Crimson Cross 8, 212, 273, 689–690, 706
The Crimson Fog 99
The Crimson Ghost (serial) 573
The Crimson Stain Mystery (serial) 173
Crinoline and Romance 659
The Crinoline Girl (stage play) 42
Crisp, Donald 248
Criswell 423
Crock-King, C.H. 437
Crompton, Charles 248
The Crooked Circle 37, 213, 214, 241
Crosby, Bing 261, 490
Crosland, Alan 8
Cross, Dr. H.A. 148, 149
Crossley, Syd 239
The Crowd 167, 524, 653
Crowdin, J. Cheever 339
Crowell, Josephine 248
Crowley, Aleister 368, 508, 598–599, 688
Cruger, Paul A. 174
Crute, Sally 361
Cruze, James 43, 149, 230, 234, 240, 267, 397, 414, 433, 438, 558–559, 627, 735
The Crystal Gazer 1, 87, 108–111, **109**, **110**, 298, 572, 659, 682, 711, 775, 776
The Cub 231
Cult of the Cobra 619
Cummings, Irving 186, 481
Cunard, Grace 108, 304, 461, 462, 463, 464, 520
Cuneo, Lester 271
Cunningham, Jack 138, 715
The Cure 734
The Curious Case of Judge Legarde 67, 68, 111–112, 130, 295, 442, 592, 671
The Curious Case of Judge Legarde (stage play) 112, 325, 580, 671
"A Curious Pleasure Excursion" (story) 100
"The Curious Republic of Gondour" (story) 100
Curlytop 193, 210, 212, 512, 654, 690–691, 711

Curran, Thomas 53
Currier, Frank 245
Curse of the Cat People 481
Curse of the Undead 2
Curtiz, Michael 79, 542, 584, 646
Curwood, James Oliver 481
Cushing, Bartley 640–641
The Cyclone Rider 179
Cynara 186
Cyrano de Bergerac (stage play) 132, 235n
Cytherea 501, 619, 651
The Czarina (stage play) 243

Daddy Long Legs 231, 603
Dadmun, Leon 453
Dalton, Dorothy 117, 118–119, **118**, 119, 120, 121, 166, 175, 391, 468, 622, 647, 719, 720, 721, 736
Daly, Jane 418
Damaged Lives 336
The Damnation of Faust 392
Dan 243
Dana, Viola 7, 8, 9, 16, 180, 281, 343, 358, 495, 654, **654**, 669
Dancing Days 614
The Dancing Girl of Butte 237
Dancing Mothers 673
Dane, Karl 338, 416, 587, 640
Daniell, Henry 750
Daniels, Bebe 166, 224, 289, 397, 433, 444, 520, **521**, 522, 596
Daniels, Ernest 539
Daniels, Nixola 249
Danny Donovan 397
Dante's Inferno (1911) 419
Dante's Inferno (1924) 12, 20, 61, 113–116, **115**, 120, 173, 207, 210, 399, 654, 686, 747
Dante's Inferno (1935) 20, 82, 366, 367, 460, 681
D'Arcy, Roy 416
Darde, Paul 370
Dark Eyes of London 606
The Dark Mirror (1920) 116–119, **118**, 135, 166, 492, 675, 720, 721, 736
The Dark Mirror (1946) 118
The Dark Mirror (book) 116
The Dark Road 647
Dark Secrets 113, 119–121, 214, 716, 775
The Dark Star 39, 72, 121–123, 202, 214, 571, 592, 614, 675
The Dark Star (book) 616, 639
Dark Streets 167
Darkened Rooms 453, 513, 691–693, **692**, 711, 763
Darkened Rooms (book) 692–693
The Darling of Paris 123–126, 249, 467, 507, 515, 604, 681, 712
The Darling of the Gods (stage play) 217
"The Darling of the Gods" (story) 217
Darmond, Grace 276
Darnton, Charles 211
Darrow, Clarence 132, 165, 506
Darwin, Charles 506, 647, 666, 693
Daudet, Alphonse 537
Daugherty, Jack 426
Daughter of Shanghai 564
Daughter of the Dragon 88, 564, 740
A Daughter of the Gods 60, 126, 126–129, 173, 266, 425, 430, 434,

434, 449, 474, 475, 599, 600, 747, 751, 759, 760
Daughter of the Samurai 66
Daumery, Carrie 312–313
Davenport, Dorothy 217, 223, 697
David Harum 258, 485
Davidson, William B. 245, 649–650
Davies, Arthur Llewelen 449
Davies, Howard 297
Davies, Marion 39, 41, 71, 72, 121, 122, 123, 191, 289, 305, 675–676, **675**
Davis, Beale 443
Davis, Bette 118, 248, 312, 476, 609
Davis, Edward (Rev.) 145
Davis, Forest 193
Davis, Joan 400
Davis, Owen 89, 252, 253, 329, 331, 332, 336, 620, 621, 622, 685, 717
Davis, Ulysses 753
Davis, Will S. 112, 295
Davison, Grace 269
Davy Crockett — In Hearts United 37
Daw, Marjorie 105, 341
Dawley, Herbert M. 341, 450, 451, 452, 495, 551, 712, 725
Dawley, J. Searle 7, 8, 105, 235, 236
Dawn, Hazel 431, 432, **432**
The Dawn of Freedom 59, 129–130, 347, 646
The Dawn Patrol 184, 233
Day, Alice 240, 336, 760
Day, Doris 714
Day, Dorothy 651
Day, Marceline 194, 240, **334**, 336
The Day of the Locust 576
Day of Wrath 658
The Day of Souls (book) 516
Daybreak (stage play) 750
Days of Wine and Roses 107
The Dead Alive 192, 356, 693–694, 700
The Dead Hand see *Mortmain*
Dean, Faxon 10
Dean, Jack 109, **109**, 659
Dean, Julia 481
Dean, Mae Preston 596
Dean, Priscilla 118, 186, 289, 335, 422, 595, 596, 606, 618, 621, 622, 646, 763, 764
Dean, Raye 388
Deane, Hamilton 337, 763
Deane, Hazel 140
Dear Me (stage play) 7
Dearholt, Ashton 328, 596, 597
Death from a Distance 82
Death Takes a Holiday 24, 105
Death Takes a Holiday (1934) 562
Death Takes a Holiday (stage play) 24, 657
de Bothezat, George 349
De Brulier, Nigel 11, 140, 287, 289, 652
The Debtors (stage play) 544
The Debutante 431
Decameron 113
DeCarlton, George 325
DeCicco, Pasquale 255
Déclassée 51
de Cordoba, Pedro 119, 675–676, **675**
De Cordova, Tessie 420
Deep in the Heart of Texas 597

The Deep Purple (stage play) 321
Deep Waters 256, 300, 639
De Felice, Carlotta 442
Defenseless America (book) 25
de Grainville, Jean 302
De Grasse, Sam 375, 617
de Havilland, Olivia 118
De Kay, Loys 161
de la Bigne, Andree (aka Andree Lafayette) 582, **582**, 583–584
de la Bigne, Valtesse 582
De La Motte, Marguerite 765
Delaney, Charles 193–194, **193**, 570
Delgado, Marcel 341, 342, 343
The Delicious Little Devil 267
Delirium 108
Deliverance (1919) 493
DeLorde, Andre 636–637
del Rio, Dolores 256, 695, 696
del Rio, Jaime 695
Del Ruth, Hampton 379, 380, 381, 382
Deluge 592, 723
DeLuise, Dom 328
De Luxe Annie 63, 130–131, 145, 611, 683, 751
De Luxe Annie (stage play) 131, 611
Delva, Yvonne 568
Delys, Gaby 574
Delysia, Alice 514
Demarest, William 702
De Maupassant, Guy 47
De Mille, Beatrice 90, 146, 147, 598, 688
De Mille, Cecil B. 9, 69, 75, 90, 105, 110, 119, 126, 146, 147, 148, 184, 190, 198, 199, 200, 217, 218, 220, 221, 222, 227, 231, 232, 251, 292, 320, 321, 322, 328, 347, 348, 356, 357, 358, 359, 397, 413, 439, 440, 447, 487–488, 496, 497, 498, 499, 500, 515, 537–538, 561, 562, 598, 602, 606, 648, 649, 680, 755, 775, 776
De Mille, William 90, 155, 225, 226, 227, 397, 488, 598, 657
The Demon Shadow (serial) 234
De Mond, Albert 723
Dempsey, Jack 550
Dempster, Carole 245, 435, 436, 437, 540
Deneubourg, Georges **479**
d'Ennery, Adolphe 588
Dennistoun, Lieut. Col. Ian 243
Denny, Reginald 431
Depp, Henry 730
Depp, Johnny 261
de Putti, Lya 539, 540
Derleth, August 202, 616
"Le Dernier Homme" (story) 302
De Roy, Harry 257, 259
De Sagurola, Andres 350
De Savallo, Doña Teresa 280
"Descent into the Maelstrom" (story) 66
Desert Nights 630
The Desert Song 349
Desire 610
Destiny 106
Destiny; or, the Soul of a Woman 245, 442, 694–696
The Destroying Angel 716
Destruction 249
DeVaull, William 267
The Devil (1908) 234, 237

The Devil (1915) 61, 131–135, **134**, 135, 234, 251, 625, 738
The Devil (1921) 42, 113, 120, 135–137, **137**, 138, 269, 325, 331, 582, 617, 641, 667
The Devil (1908; book; Fiske version) 133
The Devil (1908; book; Savage version) 133
The Devil (1928; book) 310
The Devil (stage play) 37, 61, 145, 537
The Devil (stage play; Fiske version) 132, 133
The Devil (stage play; Savage version) 132, 133, 234
The Devil Bat 668
Devil Bat's Daughter 669
The Devil Commands 186, 274, 711
The Devil Doll 20, 33, 119, 481, 511
The Devil in the Studio 495
The Devil Rides Out 368
The Devil to Pay (1912) 139
The Devil to Pay (1920) 137–139, 161, 162, 398, 715
The Devil to Pay! (1930) 139
The Devil to Pay (book) 138
The Devil with Hitler 767
The Devil Within 139–140, 289
The Devil Within (book) 140
The Devil within Her 585
The Devil's Angel 140; see also *The Sleep of Cym(b)a Roget*
The Devil's Bait 147, 546
The Devil's Bondwoman 207, 696–697, 730
The Devil's Circus 254
The Devil's Claim 61, 134, 138, 141–143, 409, 697
The Devil's Confession 697
Devil's Dice 614
The Devil's Hand 82
Devil's Island 262
The Devil's Paradise (stage play) 730
The Devil's Partner 625
The Devil's Passkey 336
The Devil's Riddle 105
The Devil-Stone 69, 75, 146–148, 221, 379, 614, 688, 776
The Devil's Toy 78, 133, 143–145, 243, 343, 627
The Devil's Wheel 105, 267
De Vinna, Clyde 467
De Vonde, Chester 624–625, 627, 628–629
Dewey, George 267
Dexter, Elliott 217, 470, 663, 688
Le Diable en boutelle 66
The Diamond Crown 712
The Diamond from the Sky (serial) 143
Diamond Jim 772
The Diamond Maker (1914) 698
The Diamond Makers (1913) 698
The Diamond Master (book) 181, 698
The Diamond Master (serial; 1929) 698
The Diamond Queen (serial) 698
The Diary of Dr. Hart 81
Dick, Philip K. 268
Dick Tracy, Detective 82
Dick Tracy Meets Gruesome 312
Dick Tracy's G-Men (serial) 96, 680
Dick Whittington and His Cat 619

Dickens, Charles 40, 46, 113, 129, 163, 168, 296, 306, 386, 418, 419, 420, 494, 495, 496, 544, 577
Dickey, Basil 573
Dickey, Paul 43, 220, 222, 315
Dieterle, William 562
Dietrich, Marlene 217, 564
Dietz, Charles 551
Dietz, Howard 651
Dillenback, George P. 347
Dillon, John Webb 207
The Dinosaur and the Missing Link 342
Dinosaurus 342
Dinty 143, 231, 233
Dion, Hector 503
The Disciple 48, 118
Dishonored 365
"The Disintegration Machine" (story) 340
Disraeli (1929) 137
Disraeli (stage play) 137
La Divina Commedia (poem) 113, 114
The Divine Lady 51, 296
Divorce Coupons 51
The Divorcee 520, 627
Dix, Beulah Marie 44, 62, 63, 199, 200, 212, 213, 226, 320, 497, 498, 567, 602, 647
Dix, Richard 540, 646
Dixey, Henry E. 712
Dixon, Thomas 27, 94, 194, 243, 395, 672
Dmytryk, Edward 711
Do Detectives Think? 763
Do the Dead Talk? 148–149
Dr. Belgraff (stage play) 580
Dr. Cyclops 511
Doctor Faustus (book) 392, 536
Dr. Jekyll and Mr. Hyde (1908) 430
Dr. Jekyll and Mr. Hyde (1912) 234, 559
Dr. Jekyll and Mr. Hyde (1913) 326, 429, 592, 634
Dr. Jekyll and Mr. Hyde (1920; Barrymore) 143, 149–155, **150**, **152**, 156, 157, 202, 272, 288, 319 365, 371, 377, 405, 445, 550, 559, 579, 671, 725
Dr. Jekyll and Mr. Hyde (1920; Lewis) 143, 155–158, 273, 697, 702, 725, 765
Dr. Jekyll and Mr. Hyde (1920; Mann) 713
Dr. Jekyll and Mr. Hyde (1931) 86, 153, 768
Dr. Jekyll and Mr. Hyde (1941) 108, 120, 154
Dr. Jekyll and Mr. Hyde (stage play) 42, 549, 595
Dr. Jekyll and Mr. Hyde, Done to a Frazzle 150
Dr. Kildare (television) 548
Dr. Mabuse (1922) 740
Dr. Pyckle and Mr. Pryde 5, 150
Dr. Rameau 61, 434
Doctor Rameau (book) 739
Dr. Renault's Secret 312, 571, 665
Dr. Syn 137
Doctor X 229, 460, 562
Dodsworth 474
A Dog of Mystery 569
A Dog's Life 400
"The Doings of Raffles Haw" (story) 340

The Dollar-a-Year Man 439
The Dollar Mark 145
A Doll's House 70
Domestic Relations 270
Don Giovanni (opera) 676
Don Juan 34, 153, 193, 524, 542
Don Q, Son of Zorro 138
Don Quixote (book) 114
The Donovan Affair 192
Don't Think About It (book) 259
Doomed to Die 459
The Doomswoman (book) 51
Dope over America 730
Doré, Gustave 12, 95, 114, 133
Doro, Marie 217, 688
Dorothy Vernon of Haddon Hall 480, 565
Dorris, Anita 584
Dostoevsky, Fyodor 733
Double Door 105, 269
Double Indemnity 424
The Double Life of Veronique 165
Double Trouble 158–160
Double Trouble (book) 158
Douglas, Kirk 378
Douglas, Michael 510
Dove, Billie 58, 186, 210, 212, 433
The Dove 22
Dovey, Alice 501
Dowlan, William C. 328, 329
Dowling, Constance 622
Dowling, Joseph J. 138, 139, **397**, 398, 610, 765, 768
Down and Out in Beverly Hills 400
Down to Earth 723
Down to the Sea in Ships 58, 597
Dracula 24, 79, 82, 83, 84, 86, 110, 174, 279, 301, 337, 349, 359, 366, 376, 392, 433, 456, 540, 609, 617, 702, 760
Drácula 110, 298, 307, 505, 668, 677
Dracula (book) 252, 265, 305, 409, 577, 706
Dracula (stage play) 335, 337, 501, 611, 763
Dracula's Daughter 14, 176, 203, 359, 524, 702
Draft 258 160
Dragnet (television) 264
The Dragnet 317
A Dragon 383
The Dramatic Life of Abraham Lincoln 194, 681
The Dream Cheater 138, 139, 160–162, 359, 715
The Dream Doll 162–163, 199
The Dream Girl (stage play) 8, 9, 497
Dream Street 436
The Dream Woman 163–165, 671, 747, 755
"The Dream Woman" (story) 163
Dreiser, Theodore 132
Dressler, Marie 494
Drew, Ellen 242
Drew, John 411
Drew, Sidney 205
Dreyer, Carl 20, 537, 658
Drifting 335, 596
Drums of Fate 449
The Drums of Fu Manchu (serial) 739
The Drums of Jeopardy 251
Drumwold, George **626**
Drurer, Albrecht 363

The Duality of Man 149
Du Barry (stage play) 727
Du Brey, Claire 494, 715, 733
Duck Soup 30, 313
Dudley, John 325–326, 327
Dudley, S.H. 191
Duel in the Dark 502
The Duke of West Point 433
Dumas, Alexandre (pere) 604, 632, 667
Du Maurier, Daphne 578
Du Maurier, George 60, 76, 112, 213, 214, 215, 366, 503, 546, 577, 578, 579, 581, 582, 583
Du Maurier, Gerald 169, 578
The Dumb Girl of Portici 186, 289, 455, 738
Dunaew, Nicholas 492, 493, 494
Dunbar, Dorothy 554
Dunbar, Paul Laurence 98
Duncan, Corporal Lee 634, 636
Duncan, Malcolm 643
Dunkinson, Harry 482, 484
Dunn, James 190
Dunn, Josephine 45
Dunn, William R. 282
Dunn, Winifred 251
DuPont, E.A. (Ewald André) 81, 377, 540, 564
Dupree, Minnie 497
Durbin, Deanna 221, 350
Durning, Bernard 140
Dusk to Dawn 75, 165–167, 212, 776
The Dust of Egypt 7, 67, 72, 167–170, **169**, 173, 205, 295, 414, 549, 735
The Dust of Egypt (stage play) 167
Dwan, Allan 58, 122, 123, 232, 639
Dyer, William 492
Dynamite Dan 355

Each to His Kind 64
The Eagle's Eye (serial) 29
Earle Williams in a Liberty Loan Appeal 11
Earthbound 7, 36, 115, 129, 148, 170–174, **171**, **173**, 198, 207, 225, 246, 330, 394, 489, 566, 631, 717, 751, 773
Earthbound (1940) 174, 490
"Earthbound" (story) 170–171
Eastman, George 110
Easy Money (1921) 191
Easy Money (stage play) 7
Easy Pickings 174–176, 514
Easy Pickings (stage play) 174
The Eddie Cantor Story 754
Eddy, Helen Jerome 394, 564
Eden, Barbara 71
Edeson, Arthur 23, 145, 343, 562, 627, 762
Edeson, Robert 200, 412, 413, **413**, **414**
Edgar Allan Poe 16, 354, 481
Edgar Allan Poe (stage play) 224, 354
Edison, Charles 46
Edison, Thomas 28, 46, 58, 74, 196, 258, 347, 681, 685, 712, 742
Edwards, Blake 126
Edwards, Cricket 564
Edwards, Evelyn 564
Edwards, Harry Stillwell 98
Edwards, J. Gordon 126, 248, 249, 604

Edwards, Marian 564
Edwards, Snitz 80, 358, 416, 457, 459–460, 559, *561*, 564
Edwards, Thornton 426, 427
Eisenstein, Sergei 20, 575
Eldridge, Charles 551
Eldridge, Florence 325
Eldridge, John 448
Eleanor's Catch 48
Electrocuting an Elephant 71
Eleven PM 176–178
The Eleventh Hour 8, 88, 140, 178–180, *179*, 439, 481, 495, 682, 691
The Eleventh Hour (book) 178
The Eleventh Virgin (book) 651
Elga (stage play) 321
Elkas, Edward *413*, 414
Ellery Queen's Penthouse Mystery 564
Ellington, Duke 99
Elliott, Maxine 755
Ellis, Robert 120
Elliston, Grace 43
Elmo the Fearless (serial) 88
Elsa (movie lion) 71, 576
Eltinge, Julian 42, 258, 352
Elton, Edmund 742
Elusive Isabel 180–182, 430, 592, 698, 749
Elusive Isabel (book) 180, 181
Elvey, Maurice 210, 212, 690
Elvidge, June 379, *464*, 465, 480, 681, 682
Emerson, John 159–160, 208, 209
Emanuel, Victor Rousseau (H.H. Egbert) 462
The Emperor Jones (stage play) 192, 627
The Emperor Waltz 481
L'Empire du diamant (novel) 698
The Empire of Diamonds 697–698
The Enchanted Cottage (1924) 78, 86, 155, 182–184, 215, 283, 504, 743
The Enchanted Cottage (1945) 184
The Enchanted Cottage (stage play) 182
An Enemy of the People (stage play) 183
Engels, Erich 77
England, George Allan 140
Enlighten Thy Daughter 267
Enoch Arden 18
Enoch Arden (poem) 36, 37
Erckmann, Emile 30, 32
Erckmann-Chatrian 30, 31, 331
Erickson, Knute 405
Erik the Great 306
Erté 423
Erwin, Stuart 231
Escape (radio) 653
Esmeralda (La) 123
Esmeralda (stage play) 580
Esper, Dwayne 680
E.T.: The Extra Terrestrial 290
The Eternal Light 355
The Eternal Mother 106, 295, 698–699
The Eternal Penalty 771
The Eternal Sin 106
The Eternal Three 659
Ethan Frome (stage play) 620
Ethier, Alphonz 388, 514
"Les Etrangleurs de Paris" (story) 552
Eumenides (stage play) 636, 637

Evangeline 42
Evans, Madge 144, 305
Even as Eve 614, 625
Even as You and I 184–186, 707, 738
Evening Primrose 270
Everett, George 690
Everton, Paul 43
Every Woman (stage play) 591
Everywoman (1919) 694, 695
Everywoman (stage play) 145, 185, 243, 468
Eve's Daughter 699
Eve's Leaves 358
The Evil Men Do 46
The Evil Power 430
The Evolution of Man 186–187, 428, 631, 765
Excess Baggage 45
"An Exchange of Souls" (story) 56
Excuse Me Madame 477
Excuse My Dust 459
Execution of Czolgosz with Panorama of Auburn Prison 237
The Exorcist 142
The Exploits of Elaine (serial) 82, 156, 567, 745
The Exquisite Sinner 681
The Eye of Horus 726, 727
The Eyes of Julia Deep 161, 274
The Eyes of Mystery 169
Eyes of Youth (1919) 62, 103, 115, 168, 187–191, *189*, *191*, 300, 306, 331, 347, 348, 349, 350, 379, 507, 580, 581, 648, 667, 699
Eyes of Youth (1920) 191–192
Eyes of Youth (stage play) 188, 501, 507, 519, 648, 649
Eyton, Bessie 39

The Face at the Window 661
The Face Behind the Mask 467, 711
"Face in the Abyss" (story) 508
The Face in the Fog 304, 465
Face Value 183
Fahrney, Milton J. 73, 463
Fairall, Harry K. 707
Fairbanks, Douglas 20, 23, 102, 123, 138, 139, 145, 158–159, 160, 190, 230, 245, 256, 258, 276, 284, 286, 288, 300, 316, 350, 364, 433, 459, 559, *560*, 560–561, *561*, 562, 563, 564, 565, 575, 646, 651, 664, 678, 765, 774, 775
Fairbanks, Douglas Jr. 560
Fairbanks, Flobelle 349, 350
Fairbanks, Robert 562, 774
Faire, Virginia Brown 343, 450
Fairfax, Marion 69–70, 111, 231, 232, 343
The Fairy and the Waif 660
Faith 394
The Faith Healer 394
The Faker 82, 86, 192–194, *193*, 260, 416, 604, 691
The Fall of a Nation 27, 94, 95, 194–196, 208, 395, 497, 672, 744, 772
The Fall of a Nation (book) 194–5
"The Fall of the House of Usher" (story) 604
The Fall of the Romanoffs 133, 478, 479, *479*
Fallon, Thomas 314, 315
The False Faces 117, 396
Fame and the Devil 200

Fanchon, the Cricket 450–451
Fangs of Justice 96
Fanny Elssler 368
Fantasia 652
Fantasma 196–198, 451
Fantasma (stage play) 196, 197
The Fantastic Four (comic book) 467
Fanatastic Voyage 342
Fantastic Voyage (book) 100
Fantomas 310
Fantomas (serial) 96, 259
Le Fantôme de l'opera (book) 213, 454, 456, 462, 463, 508, 667, 741
Farjeon, Joseph Jefferson 243
Farley, Ralph Milne 549
Farmer, Philip José 100
Farnham, Joe 517
Farnum, Dustin 140, 295, 650, 659, 720
Farnum, Franklyn 295
Farnum, Joseph 681
Farnum, William 42, 43, 295, 720, 721
Farrar, Geraldine 614, 677
Farrell, Charles 213, 585, 652
Farrell, Colin 601
Farrington, Adele 696–697
Fashionable Fakers 96, 641, 742
Fast Workers 518
Fate 639
Father Brown, Detective 459
Fatty's Magic Pants 312
Fauchois, Rene 400
Faulkner, Ralph 300–301
Faust (1909) 237, 634
Faust (1915) 544
Faust (1926) 22, 539
Faust (opera) 222 360, 392
Faust (stage play) 145, 392
Faust and Marguerite (1900) 208, 237, 392
Faversham, William 442
Fawcett, George 341, 621
Fawcett, Percy Harrison 340
Faye, Julia 199–200, *199*
Fazenda, Louise 21, 22, 23, 24, 103, 601, 701, 702, 706, 757, *757*, 761, 769, 770
Fazenda. Trixie 499, 520
Feathertop (1912) 471
Feathertop (1913) 471
Feathertop (1916) 471, 694, 699–700
Feathertop (short story) 470, 699
Fedora (stage play) 655, 656
Feeney's Social Experiment 722
Feet First 487
Feet of Clay 83, 163, 198–200, *199*, 413
Feet of Clay (book) 199
Fejos, Paul 84, 306, 307, 308, 309–310, 317, 376
Feld, Fritz 45–46
Felix the Cat 592
Felix the Ghost Breaker 224
Fellowes, Rockliffe 86, *86*
Fenton, Leslie 10–11, 226, 306, 307
Ferguson, Casson 499
Ferguson, Elsie 215, 217
Ferguson, Helen 341
Ferguson, William J. 28
Fernley, Jane 553
Ferrar, Geraldine 35, 119, 146
Ferris, Audrey 636
Fetchit, Stepin 723

Field, Betty 448
Field, Gladys 156
Fielding, Howard 717
Fields, W.C. 2, 69, 138, 212, 213, 272, 313, 325, 661, 754, 770
Fig Leaves 403, 700–701, *701*
Fight That Ghost 99
The Fighter 200–202, 711
The Fighter (book) 201
The Fighting Gringo 272
Fighting Through 160
Figures de cire (1914) 637
Figures de cire (stage play) 637
La Fin du monde (1929) 302, 340
"La Fin du monde" (story) 302
Finch, Flora 80, *80*, 82, 312
Fincher, David 510
Find Your Man 96
Finding Neverland 141
Findlay, Ruth 411
Findlay, Thomas 72
Finger Prints 80, 82, 701–702, *702*
Finlayson, Jimmy 706
The Firing Line 42, 63, 202–204, *203*, 214, 453, 568, 625
The Firing Line (book) 122, 202, 616
The First Men in the Moon (book) 385
The First Mrs. Fraser (stage play) 750
Fischbeck, Harry 269, 539, 540
Fischer, Margarita 716, 738
Fisher, George 95
Fiske, Harrison Grey 132
Fiske, Minnie Maddern (Mrs.) 132, 329, 586
Fitch, Clyde 115, 244, 385
Fitzball, Edward 206
Fitzgerald, F. Scott 259, 260, 651
Fitzgerald, J.A. 687
Fitzmaurice, George 215, 216, 217, 477 478, 500, 501, 502
Fitzroy, Emily 21, 22–23
Five 302, 723
The Five Dollar Plate 29
The Five Pennies 20
Five Star Final 231
Flagg, James Montgomery 352
The Flame (stage play) 581, 597
Flame of the Yukon 468
Flaming Fury 96, 194
The Flaming Signal 336
Flaming Youth 143
Flaming Youth (book) 49
Flammarion, Camille 302
Flash (movie dog) 336
Flash Gordon (serial) 319
Flash Gordon (television) 289–290
Flash Gordon Conquers the Universe (serial) 466
Flebbe, George 497
The Fleet's In 490
Fleming, Victor 120, 775
Flesh and Spirit 394
Flesh and the Devil 568
Flexner, Anne Crawford 10
Der fliegende Holländer (opera) 206
The Flintstones (television) 700, 778
The Flirt 620
The Flirting Princess (stage play) 279
Flood, James 394
Floradora Girl 122
The Florentine Dagger 97, 138

Florey, Robert 183, 275, 309, 365, 424, 564, 573, 652
A Florida Enchantment 169, 204–205
A Florida Enchantment (book) 204, 373
A Florida Re-enchantment 205
Flower of the Night 651
Flower(s) of Doom 47
Flowers of Evil (poetry) 575
Flowing Gold 584
Flugrath, Edna 8, 180
The Flying Deuces 664
The Flying Dutchman 115, 126, 129, 205–207, **207**, 520
The Flying Dutchman (legend) 10, 206, 536
The Flying Dutchman (stage play) 206
The Flying Serpent 20
The Flying Torpedo 20, 115, 207–210, 765
Flynn, Emmett 103
Flynn, Errol 289, 439, 690
Flynn, William J. 29
Fog 716
Fog Bound 120
The Foghorn (book) 51
The Folly of Vanity 210–212, 433
Folsey, George 78, 505
Fontaine, Evan Burrows 733
Fontaine, Joan 582
The Fool 716
A Fool and His Money 201, 773
A Fool and His Money (book) 773
The Fool and the Dancer 702–703
The Fool Killer 306
A Fool There Was (1915) 124, 657, 682
A Fool There Was (stage play) 193, 696
Foolish Wives 279, 286, 289, 459, 575
Fools in the Dark 289, 564, 703–704
A Fool's Paradise 617
The Fool's Revenge 266
Foote, Courtenay 544
Foque, Fredrich de La Motte 599
For the Defense 212–214, **213**, 497
For the Defense (stage play) 212
For the Freedom of the World 586
For the Honor of the Crew 650
Forbidden Planet 79, 240
Ford, Francis 107, 108, 413, 461, 462, 463, 520
Ford, Harrison 110, 711
Ford, Henry 26, 27
Ford, Hugh 431
Ford, John ("Jack") 20, 108, 168, 211, 336, 391, 406, 463, 493, 631, 644
Forde, Eugenie 328, 648
Forde, Victoria 328
Forest, Louis 112
Forever 214–217, 264, 470, 478, 502, 688
Forever After (stage play) 336
Forever My Love 359
The Forged Bride 455
Forgotten Children 295
Forman, Jules 649
Forrest, Allan 274
Forrest, Mabel 749
The Forsythe Saga 661
Fort, Garret 263, 359, 433, 764

Fortune, Peggy 416
The Fortune Hunter (stage play) 154
The Fortune Teller 598
Forty-Five Minutes to Broadway 648
42nd Street (1933) 686
42nd Street (stage play) 601, 631
Foshay, Harold 156, 697
Fossey, Dian 187
Foster, Helen 750
Foster, Morris 186
Foster, Susanna 79
Fouche Miriam 515
Found Alive 271
The Foundling 646
Fountain, Leatrice Gilbert 639
Four Devils 336
The Four Feathers 661, 692
The Four Horsemen of the Apocalypse 48, 275, 289, 363, 367, 493, 573, 575, 585, 677, 679, 680, 681, 689
Four Hours to Kill 184
Four Sons 391
The Fourth Face 14
Fox, Finis 38
Fox, John 438, 439
Fox, John Jr. 686
Fox, Lucy 649
Fox, Sidney 15
Fox, William 114, 115, 123, 126, 127, 128, 129, 179, 281, 381, 401, 475, 476, 515, 604, 666, 672, 690
The Fox Woman 217–218
The Fox Woman (book) 218
Foxe, Earle 45, 303–304, 470
F.P.I. Antwortet 376, 728
France, Hermain (Hermina, etc.) 149
Francesca de Rimini 168
Francis, Alec B. **171**, 489, 490, 491
Frank, Alexander F. 713
Frank, J. Herbert 67, 414, **414**
Franken, Al 614
Frankenheimer, John 644
Frankenstein (1910) 7, 8, 33, 79, 145, 196, 235, 441, 451, 680, 690
Frankenstein (1931) 312, 326, 330, 342, 349, 359, 366, 433, 491, 562, 762
Frankenstein (book) 196, 323, 326, 330, 331, 687
Frankenstein Meets the Wolf Man 292, 721
Frankenstein's Daughter 275
Franklin, Ben 155
Franklin, Chester M. 10, 29, 79, 569, 570
Franklin, Harry L. 7
Franklin, Sidney 10, 29, 119, 616–617, 751
Franz, Arthur 568
Fraser, Brandon 184
Die Frau im Mond 340
Fraunholz, Fraunie 165, 556, **567**, 671, 755
Frazer, Robert 243, 293, 739
Freaks 363, 376, 514, 517, 608, 628, 667
Freckles 439
Fredericks, Arnold (Frederick Arnold Kummer) 441
Freidlander, Lewis (Lew Landers) 377
Der Freischütz (opera) 40

French, Charles 37
Freud, Sigmund 117, 608, 706
Freund, Karl 573
Frick, Ford 58
Friends and Lovers 221
Frohman, Charles 190, 325, 659, 661
Frohman, Daniel 329, 373, 450, 578, 659, 661, 672
Frohman, Gustave 659–660, 661
From Morn to Midnight 599
From the Earth to the Moon (book) 588
From the Earth to the Moon (stage play) 588
From the Manger to the Cross 41
The Front Page 231, 306, 474, 523
Front Page Detective (television) 667
Frost, Walter Archer 44
Frye, Dwight 609, 643
Fryer, Richard 319
Fuller, Dale 279
Fuller, Mary 185
Fulton, Robert 589
Funny Face (stage play) 45
Furber, Douglas 569
Furcht (Fear) 409
Furthman, Charles 317
Furthman, Jules 317
Futrelle, Jacques 180–181, 698

Gable, Clark 516, 664
Gadsdon, Jacqueline (also "Gadsden") 416, 570, 630
Gahagan, Helen 515
Gaillard, Robert 734–735
The Gale Storm Show (television) 213
The Gallery of Madame Liu-Tsong (television) 564
The Galloping Ace 339
The Galloping Fish 601
Gambling 662
The Game 510
"A Game of Chess" (story) 509
Gance, Abel 247, 302, 340
Gant, Harry 98
Ganthoney, Richard 134, 386, 388
Ganz, Harry 186
Garbo, Greta 23, 123, 154, 168, 262, 335, 350, 358, 502, 608, 677
Garcia, Ralph Ernest 115
The Garden of Eden 51
Garden of Lies 750
Gardner, Helen 551
Gardner, Lois 746
Gargan, William 315
Garland, Judy 132
Garrett, Pauline Madden 331
Garrison, Lindley M. 27
Garson, Greer 240
Garson, Harry 143, 188
Garvin, Anita 86
Garwood, William 727
Gaskill, Charles 35, 551
Gaslight (1944) 459
Gasnier, Louis 507, 567, 692
Gasoline Gus 439
Gates, Harvey 316–317, 416, 726
The Gates of Horn (book) 647
The Gaucho 256, 434
Gaudio, Antonio ("Tony") 39, 62, 257
Gaye, Howard 115, **115**, 746–747
Gaynor, Janet 321, 489, 491

Geheimnis des blauen Zimmers 77
Geldart, Clarence 772
Gemier, Firmin 365
Gemora, Charles 15, 239, 321–322, 614, 757, **757**, 770
The General 264, 268
General Crack 643
The Gentleman Cracksman 397
Gentlemen Prefer Blondes (book) 209
Gentlemen's Relish 759
George, John 48, 87, 491, 609
Gerárd, Rosamund 235
Gerasch, Alfred 187
Gerber, Nerva 185
The Germ 219
Gernsback, Hugo 383
Geronimo 359
Gerrard, Douglas 105, 434, 455, 601
Gershwin, George 45, 78, 192
Gerstad, Merritt 608
Gest, Morris 118
Get Rich Quick Wallingford (stage play) 6, 480
Getting Gertie's Garter 487
Gheller, Edward 108
Ghost 207
The Ghost and Mrs. Muir 207
The Ghost Breaker (1914) 219–222, 225, 269, 434, 440, 447, 496, 757, 775
The Ghost Breaker (1922) 75, 83, 146, 147, 217, 222–225, **224**, 434, 437, 459, 461
The Ghost Breaker (book) 220
The Ghost Breaker (stage play) 44, 219–220, 222, 315
The Ghost Breakers 222
The Ghost Goes West 749
The Ghost House 22, 75, 225–227, **226**, 522, 627
The Ghost in the Garret 704–706, **705**
The Ghost of Frankenstein 154, 733
The Ghost of Granleigh 8, 451
The Ghost of Jerry Bundler (stage play) 78
The Ghost of Old Morro 227–228, 360, 710, 715, 742
The Ghost of Rosy Taylor 274
The Ghost of Slumber Mountain 162, 341, 342
The Ghost of the Whispering Oaks 250
The Ghost of Tolston's Manor 228–229, 535
The Ghost Talks 625
The Ghost Walks 256, 405
Ghosts of Yesterday 468
The Ghost's Warning 716
The Ghoul 337, 409
The Giant Claw 343
Gibbons, Cedric 172, 418, 763
Gibbs, Philip Hamilton 692
Giblyn, Charles 117, 118, 119
Gibson, Hoot 259
Gibson, Margaret 753
Gilbert, Florence 596, 597
Gilbert, John 247, 289, 358, 467, 468, 516, 517, 518, 606, 607, 608, 630, 637, 639, 656, 729
Gilbert and Sullivan 655
Giles, Corliss 624, 625
Gill, David 8
Gillette, William 7, 111, 476, 580, 704

Gilligan's Island (television) 439
Gilpin, Charles 191
Girard, Joe 316
Girardot, Etienne 235
Giraudoux, Jean 601
The Girl Friends (series) 255
The Girl from Montmartre 576
A Girl in Every Port 321
The Girl in the Kimono (stage play) 279
Girl of the Golden West 350, 354, 715
Girl of the Sunny South 683
Girl on the Pullman 487
The Girl on the Stairs 212, 289, 646, 689, 706–707
The Girl Who Had Everything (stage play) 106
The Girl Who Stayed Home 247
A Girl's Folly 548
Gish, Dorothy 597, 705, 706
Gish, Lillian 19, 75, 184, 235, 236, 242, 245, 247–248, 289, 540, 651, 652, 705
Glanz und Elend der Kurtisanen 584
Glass, Bonnie 289
Glaum, Louise 306
Gleason, Jackie 51
Gleason, James 321, 668
Gleason, Lilian 668
Gleason, Russell 668
Glen or Glenda? 177, 296
Glidden, Carlton 188
The Glory of Love (book) 637
Gluck, Joe 539
Glyn, Elinor 366, 424, 603
Go and Get It 39, 62, 63, 229–233, **231, 232**, 304, 316, 343, 344, 405, 455, 667, 668, 719
Go Get 'Em Hutch (serial) 670
Go West Young Man (stage play) 361
Goddard, Charles 220, 222
Goddard, Paulette 81, 83
The Goddess 347
The Goddess (serial) 643
The Godless Girl 488
Godowsky, Dagmar 549
God's Tomorrow 746
God's Witness 181, 233–234, 293, 466, 503, 726
Goebel, O.E. 356
Goethe, Johann Wolfgang von 40, 132, 392
Goetz, William 741
Going Up (stage play) 648
Gold and Iron (book) 651
"The Gold Bug" (story) 66, 482
The Gold Rush 312, 664
Goldberg, Rube 249, 772
Goldburg, Jesse J. 112, 323, 324, 325, 326, 327, 339
The Golden Bed 649
The Golden Claw 158
Golden Dawn 44
Goldreyer, Michael 315
Goldstein, Joseph M. 634
Goldwater, Barry 524
Goldwyn, Samuel (also "Goldfish") 13, 139 657, 725
Der Golem (1914) 367
Der Golem: Wie er in die Welt Kam 367
Golem und die Tanzerin 367
Gone with the Wind 95, 298, 499, 516, 561, 775

The Good Earth 564
The Good Earth (stage play) 620
A Good Little Devil 75, 133, 234–237, **236**, 451
A Good Little Devil (stage play) 235, 236
Goodall, Grace 197
The Goose Girl 451
The Goose Hangs High 662
Gorcey, Leo 129
Gordon, Bruce 283
Gordon, Harris 234, 293
Gordon, Huntley **118**, 119
Gordon, James 542, 552–553
Gordon, Kilbourn 627
Gordon, Phyllis 668
Gore, Rose 722
The Gorilla (1927) 39, 69, 145, 174, 237–241, **238, 241**, 336, 404, 433, 437, 505, 562, 570, 571, 704, 754, 760, 762
The Gorilla (1930) 224, 240, 439
The Gorilla (stage play) 21, 238, 272, 460
Gorilla at Large 455
Goudal, Jetta 321, 359, 498, 499
Goulding, Edmund 113, 120
Gounod, Charles 132, 234, 392, 393, 555
The Governor's Ghost 295
Gowland, Gibson 45, 416, 457, 459
The Gracie Allen Murder Case 515
Graf, Max 649
Graft 650
The Grain of Dust 731
A Grand Army Man (stage play) 520
Grand Hotel (stage play) 46
The Grand Passion 396
Granlich, Charles 777
Grant, Lawrence 767
Granville, Fred Leroy 466, 600
Grassby, Bertram 105, 213, 214, 267, 513, 703, 707
Grasso, Al 285, 286, 456
Grauer, Ben 739
Graustark (stage play) 226
Graves, Ralph 240
Gravina, Cesare 374, 376, 765
Gray, John W. 558
Gray, King 391, 392
The Gray Ghost (serial) 596
The Gray Mask 707–708
The Gray Horror 325, 465
The Great Accident (book) 5
The Great Automobile Mystery 162
The Great Diamond Mystery 544
The Great Divide 106, 468
Great Expectations 106, 306
The Great Gabbo 397–398
The Great Gatsby 7, 336, 631
The Great Gatsby (stage play) 620
The Great Image (book) 637
The Great Impersonation (1935) 154
"The Great Keinplatz Experiment" (story) 340
The Great Lie 474
The Great Lover 619
The Great Man Votes 154
The Great Redeemer 639
The Great Reward (serial) 520
The Great Romance 215
The Great Secret (serial) 160
The Great Shadow 243

The Great Train Robbery 16, 208, 237
The Great Universal Mystery (serial) 430
The Great Ziegfeld 520
The Greater Will 78, 144, 241–243, 262, 447, 542
The Greatest Power 244–245, 550, 695
The Greatest Question 20, 92, 245–248, 704
The Greatest Show on Earth 606
The Greatest Story Ever Told (book) 593
Greathouse, Clyde 45
Greed 213, 255, 279, 336, 365, 376, 459, 492, 517, 681
Greeley, Evelyn 67
Green, Alfred 223, 224, 226
Green, Dorothy 122
Green, Howard 194
The Green-Eyed Monster 61, 248–249, 434, 604
The Green Goddess (1923) 673
The Green Goddess (1930) 224, 673
The Green Goddess (stage play) 137
The Green Hornet (serial) 96
The Green Pastures 407
Greene, Frances Nimmo 138, 139
The Greene Murder Case 154
Grey, Ray 705, 706
Grey, Virginia 705
Grey, Zane 296
The Grey Sisterhood 726
Gribbon, Eddie 21, 22, 416
Grieg, Edvard 445
Grieve, Harold 498
Griffith, Corinne 49, 50, 51, **52**, 172, 347, 636
Griffith, D.W. (David Wark) 16–20, 31, 32, 33, 43, 69, 75, 82, 92, 98, 108, 123, 127, 128, 143, 152, 158, 159, 160, 175, 178, 184, 194, 208, 209, 222, 242, 243, 245, 246–247, 248, 254, 256, 258–25, 284, 292, 305, 344, 348, 350, 354, 393, 404, 408, 433, 434, 435, 436, **436**, 437, 481, 482, 498, 536, 538, 539–540, 544, 560, 562, 570, 574, 579, 596, 597, 610, 634, 657, 690, 696, 704, 729, 766
Griffith, Gordon 554–555
Griffith, Raymond 487, **487**
Grifford, Ada 205
The Grim Game 372, 558, 593, 594, 695
Grimm, Brothers 451, 576
Grindell-Matthews, H. 316, 551, 712
Das Grinsende Gesicht (The Smirking Face) 378
The Grip of Iron 552
A Grip of Steel (stage play) 552
Grot, Anton 562
The Grubstake 659
Grumpy 242
Grumpy (stage play) 242, 243
Guernon, Charles 188, 191
Guinan, Texas 669
Guissart, Rene 639
Guitry, Sacha 132
Gunning, Wid 255, 328, 433, 541
Gunter, Archibald Clavering 204, 373
A Guy Named Joe 33, 459
Hackett, Walter 641

Hadley, Bert 218
Hagedorn, Hans 658
Haggard, H. Rider 75, 211, 237, 514, 516, 580, 602
Hagman, Larry 71
Hail the Woman 354
Haines, William 45, 259, 289
Haire, Norman 523
The Hairy Ape (stage play) 305
Haldane, Bert 552
Haldane of the Secret Service 372
Hale, Alan 50, **50**, 180, 321, 439
Hale, Alan Jr. 439
Hale, Creighton 80, 82, 83, 405, 509, **510**, 511, 566, 567–568, 722
Hall, Alex 304
Hall, Charles D. 81, 83
Hall, Ella 207, 520
Hall, Etta 730
Hall, Franklyn 738
Hall, Huntz 129
Hallelujah! 358
Hallgren, Norma 619
Halliday, Jack (John) 145, 274, 501
Hallor, Ray 53
Halperin, Victor 217
Halperin brothers 30, 355
Halsey, Forrest 538
Hamel, Grace 587
Hamilton, Hale 5, 6–7, 706
Hamilton, James Shelley 726
Hamilton, Lloyd 400
Hamilton, Mahlon 173, 341, 602, 603
Hamilton, Neil 692, **692**
Hamlet (stage play) 30, 154, 445, 503, 661, 662, 663
Hammeras, Ralph 342
Hammerstein, Arthur 119, 411
Hammerstein, Elaine 119, 410, 411
Hammerstein, Oscar 119, 411, 584, 585, 742
Hammond, Laurens ("Larry") 383
Hampden, Walter 444
Hamper, Genevieve 248, 249, 604, 605
Hampton, Hope 395, 639
The Hand Invisible 273, 413
The Hand of Fu Manchu (book) 740
The Hand That Rocks the Cradle 186
The Hands of Nara 66, 82, 92, 136, 145, 203, 214, 217, 331, 394, 708–709
The Hands of Nara (book) 708, 709
Hands Up 487
Hands Up (serial) 669
Hanford, Ray 669
Hanlon, Dan 591
Hanlon, George Jr. 196, 197
Hanlon Brothers 196, 197
Hannah, Frank 43
Hansel and Gretel (opera) 676
Hard Cash 166
Harding, Marion 757, 758
Hardwicke, Cedric 173
Hardy, Oliver ("Babe") 53, 69, 76, 136, 292, 451, 706
Hardy, Sam 6
Hardy, Thomas 12
Harlam, Macey 501
Harlan, Kenneth 96, 97, 174, 175
Harlow, Jean 328, 623, 636

Harned, Virginia 373, 501, 548, 578, 579
Harrington, Adele 720
Harris, Elmer 10
Harris, Henry B. 599
Harris, Joel Chandler 98
Harris, Joseph 741
Harris, Mildred 289, 512, 513, *513*
Harris, Theodosia 753
Harris, Wadsworth 730
Harrison, Rex 207, 640
Harron, Charles 21
Harron, John 20–21, 29–30, 636
Harron, Robert 19, 20, 29, 247, 248
Harron, Tessie 21
Hart, Lorenz 100
Hart, William S. 48, 118, 143, 159, 201, 256, 306, 669
Harvey, Harry 542
"Hashashin, the Indifferent" (story) 347
Hastings, Carey 502
The Hatchet Man 754
Hathaway, Henry 217
Hatkin, Phil 681
Hatred's Endless Chain 382
Hatton, Fanny 690
Hatton, Frederic 690
Hatton, Raymond 287, 344, 470, 610, 776
Hatton, Rondo 467
Hauer, Arthur 502
The Haunted Bedroom 135, 249–251, 344, 468, 546
The Haunted Bell 325
The Haunted Castle 208
The Haunted Curiosity Shop 495
Haunted Hearts 462
The Haunted Hotel 345
The Haunted House 24, 39, 78, 82, 89, 97, 105, 234, 252–256, *253*, *254*, 416, 454, 510, 742, 754, 770
The Haunted House (stage play) 252, 253, 329, 622, 685
The Haunted Manor 15, 356
The Haunted Pajamas 62, 256–259, 277, 571, 649
The Haunted Pajamas (book) 256, 258
The Haunted Pajamas (stage play) 258
The Haunted Sentinel Tower 552
The Haunted Ship 53
Haunting Shadows 86, 250, 259–260, 277, 282, 440, 733, 753
Havel, Joseph 426
Haver, Phyllis 760
Hawks, Howard 233, 344, 627, 700, 701, 762
Hawks, J.G. 773
Hawks, Kenneth 762
The Hawk's Nest 39, 183, 255
The Hawk's Trail (serial) 272
Hawley, Ormi 680, 745
Hawley, Wanda 677, 680
Hawthorne, Nathaniel 132, 470, 471, 474, 699, 700
Hawtrey, Charles 386, *386*, 387
Häxan 254, 255, 471
Hay, Will 552
Hayakawa, Sessue 63, 64–66, 87, 141, 142, 213, 218, 260, 598, 707
Haydon, J. Charles 156
Hayes, George ("Gabby") 241
Hayes, Helen 564
Hays, Will 224, 266, 515, 628, 696

Hazelton, George Cochrane 258, 482, 483, 484
Hazzard, Jack 501
He Who Gets Slapped 86, 154, 312, 402, 405, 568
He Who Gets Slapped (stage play) 599
The Headless Horseman (1922) 243, 260–263, *261*, *262*, 439
Hearst, William Randolph 39, 41, 71, 86, 92, 121, 122, 123, 180, 266, 348, 675, 676, 739
Heart of Darkness (book) 627
The Heart of Lincoln 462
The Heart of Rachael 134
Heart o' the Hills 709
The Heart of the Hills 228, 709–710
The Heart Line 263–265
The Heart Line (book) 263
Hearts Adrift 258
"Hearts Aflame" (story) 703
Hearts Are Thumps 363, 368
Hearts in Dixie 358
Hearts of Love 477
Hearts of the World 20
Hecht, Ben 227, 474
Hedman, Martha 274
Heffron, Thomas N. 277
Hegger, Albert 92
Heggie, O.P. 257
Held, Tom 232, 233
Hell Harbor 45
The Hellion 265, 355, 716–717
Hell's Angels 62, 444, 750
Hell's 400 201, 336, 710–711
The Helmet of Navarre (stage play) 325
Help Wanted 243, 477
Help Wanted (stage play) 243
Helton, Percy 488
Hemingway, Ernest 10, 260
Hendricks, Ben Jr. 262
Henley, Hobart 620
Henning, Doug 592, 593
Hepburn, Audrey 601
Hepburn, Katharine 102
Hepburn, T.N. 102
Her Elephant Man 267
Her Escape 329
Her Father's Gold 293
Her First Appearance 228
Her Five-Foot Highness 267
Her Greatest Power 244
Her Indian Lover 73
Her Majesty: The Girl Queen of Nordenmark (stage play) 397
Her Reputation 231
Her Surrender 265–267, 669
Her Temptation 11, 105, 213, 267–268, 391, 513, 707, 766
Herbert, Holmes 85, 86, *86*, 183, 621, 736, 764
Herbert, Hugh 280
Herbert, Victor 93, 195, 306, 441, 497
Here Comes Mr. Jordan 734
Hergesheimer, Joseph 424, 651, 652, 653, 776
Herne, James A. 28, 596
Heroes for Sale 184
Herrmann the Great 592
Hersholt, Jean 45, 79, 193, 488, 524
Herzka, Julius 378
Hesser, Edwin Bower 586
Heyes, Herbert 126

Heyl, Martin J. 726
Heston, Charlton 447, 576
Hetzel, Pierre-Jules 587
Hiatt, Ruth 399, 400
Hiawatha 325n
Hickman, Alfred 657
Hickman, Howard C. 95, 134
Hickock, Rodney 420
Hicks, Sir Seymour 495
The Hidden Code 268–269, 273
The Hidden Corpse 83
The Hidden Hand (serial) 646
The Hidden Menace 269–271, 713
Hidden Pearls 66
Hiers, Walter 223
High Jinks (stage play) 411
High Sierra 306, 404
High Treason 95, 621, 691
Hilburn, Percy 417, 418
Hilde Warren and Death 106
Hill, Arthur 235, *236*
Hill, Doris 692, 763
Hill, Katherine 166
Hilliard, Robert 248
Hillie, Verna 241
Hilliker, Katherine 571
Hillyer, Lambert 14, 176
Himmelskibet 340
Hines, Charles 88, 753
Hines, Johnny 88, *88*, 89, 119, 753
Die Hintertreppe 81
Hired and Fired 705
Hirsh, Nathan 186, 187, 631
His Brother's Keeper 271–273, 465
His Glorious Night 247, 656
His Hour 423–424
His Majesty, Dick Turpin (Behind the Mask) 462
His Majesty, the Scarecrow of Oz 156, 451, 513
His Picture in the Papers 158
His Wife's Double 693
Historia of Dr. Johann Faust (book) 392
Hitchcock, Alfred 155, 168, 243, 251, 314, 490, 494, 537, 691
Hitchcock, Reginald 46; *see also* Ingram, Rex
Hitler, Adolph 368
Hobart, George V. 332
Hobart, Henry 352
Hobart, Rose 585
Hobling, Franz 378
Hodkinson, W.W. 640
Hodkinson System 13, 14n
Hoffman, Dustin 236
Hoffman, Gertrude 610
Hoffman, Hugh 618
Hoffman, M.H. 108
Hogan, James P. 97
Hold Your Husband 353
A Hole in Space 383
The Hole in the Wall (1921) 273–275, 353
The Hole in the Wall (1929) 275
The Hole in the Wall (stage play) 45, 273
Holland, Cecil 39, 230
Holland, Steve 290
Hollingsworth, A. 61
Hollywood 230, 336
Hollywood (documentary) 8, 24
Hollywood Boulevard 652
The Hollywood Handicap 643
Hollywood Hotel 573
The Hollywood Revue of 1929 571

Holmes, Gerda 67
Holmes, Mrs. Susanna B. 145
Holmes, Stuart 60, 605, 613, 623, 624
Holst, Gustav 31
Holt, Jack 10, 117, 341
Holt, Jennifer 10
Holt, Tim 10
Holt, Ula 597
Holt of the Secret Service (serial) 10
Holubar, Allan 591
Home Brew 191
The Homesteader 98, 99
The Homesteader (book) 98
L'Homme (stage play) 309
L'Homme aux figures de cire 637
L'Homme qui rit 378
L'Homme qui rit (book) 374–375, 456
Honesty — The Best Policy 12
The Honeymooners (television) 692
Hoodman Blind 553
Hooke, Charles Witherle 717
Hooper, Tobe 562
Hoover, J. (John) Edgar 29
Hopalong Cassidy (series) 636, 670, 755, 760
Hope, Bob 81, 83, 224, 490
The Hope Diamond Mystery (serial) 669
Hopkins, Miriam 690
Hopper, DeWolf 524
Hopper, Hedda 52, 222, 343, 524
Hopper, William 524
Hopwood, Avery 21, 91
Horkheimer, E.D. 542, 545
Horkheimer, H.M. 541, 542, 545, 546
Horkheimer brothers 87, 545, 717
The Horn Blows at Midnight 564
Horne, James W. 15, 316, 546, 686
Horner, Violet 128
Horrible Hyde 150
The Horror 382, 409
Horror Island 733
"The Horror of the Heights" (story) 340
Horse Feathers 515
Horton, Aida 356
Horton, Edward Everett 69, 468, 485, 664
Hotelratten (Hotel Rats) 187
The Hottentot (stage play) 112
Houdini, Beatrice (Bess) 558, 593
Houdini, Harry 134, 269, 341, 370, 371, *371*, 421, 439, 453, 506, 507, 557, 558, 559, 592, 593, 644, 695, 751, 752
The Hound of the Baskervilles (1922) 691
The Hound of the Baskervilles (book) 634, 773
An Hour before Dawn 221
"The House and the Brain" (story) 252
"The House Behind the Hedge" (story) 613
A House Divided (book) 5
The House of a Thousand Candles (1915) 250, 259, 275–277, 283, 753
The House of a Thousand Candles (book) 259, 275, 277, 283
The House of a Thousand Candles (stage play) 275

The House of a Thousand Scandals 277, 753
House of Dracula 290
House of Fear (book) 314
The House of Fear (1939) 315
The House of Frankenstein 284, 290
The House of Hate (serial) 745
The House of Horror 23, 39, 255, 277–280, 712–714, 758, 701
House of Horrors (1946) 705
House of Mystery (1934) 154, 241, 269, 409
The House of Mystery (stage play) 272
The House of the Lost Court 8, 227, 280–282, 361
The House of the Lost Court (book) 281
The House of Secrets 726
House of the Seven Gables (1910) 451
House of the Seven Gables (book) 470
The House of the Tolling Bell 184, 250, 259, 282–284
The House of the Tolling Bell (book) 283
House of Wax 406
The House of Whispers 138, 161, 162, 359, 714–715
The House of Whispers (book) 138, 714
House Without a Key (serial) 87
Housman, Arthur 201, 644
Houston, Jane 643
How Green Was My Valley 217, 240
How I Won the War 767
How Molly Made Good 231
How They Do Things on the Bowery 237
How to Write a Talkie (book) 174
Howard, John 154
Howard, Leslie 411
Howard, Milford Wriarson 38, 39
Howard, Warda 482, 484
Howe, James Wong 449
Hoxie, Jack 339
Hoyt, Arthur 343
Hoyt, Charles Hale 389
Hoyt, Edward N. 258
Hoyt, Harry O. 341, 343, 668, 683, 762
Hubbard, Lucien 416, 417, 418
Hubert, Harold 28
Hubert, Rene 348
Hud 449
Hudson, Earl 341, 343, 443, 505
Huff, Louise 226–227, **226**
Hughes, Gareth 189, 191, 699
Hughes, Howard 750
Hughes, Lloyd 251, 341, 343, 344, 416, 418
Hugo, Victor 123, 124, 125, 126, 168, 282, 290, 311, 374, 375, 377, 456, 552, 667
Hulette, Gladys 614, **776**, 777
Hull, Edith Maude 512
Hull, Henry 292, 305–306, 436, 437, 481, 740
Hulling, Lorraine 195
Humanity and Sanity (essay) 26–27
Hume(s), Fred 338, 339
Humpty Dumpty and the Baby 648
The Hunchback (television) 284
The Hunchback of Notre Dame

(1923) 11, 35, 58, 69, 72, 79, 80, 81, 84, 140, 154, 181, 199, 284–292, *285*, *288*, *291*, 311, 319, 337, 365, 376, 377, 396, 456, 461, 513, 561, 605, 609, 628, 652, 679, 703, 707, 749, 765, 770, 776
The Hunchback of Notre Dame (1939) 212
The Hunchback of Notre Dame (book) 124
Der Hund von Baskerville 75
The Hunger 210
Hunt, Roy 751
Hunter, Glenn 78, 79, 471, 473, 474, 700, 751
Hunter, T. Hayes 172, 173
Hurlbut, William 59, 60
Hurley, Elizabeth 131
Hurst, Brandon 150, 152, 154, 155, 156, 239, 271, 288, 319, 358, 374, 377, *378*, 559, 653
Hurst, Paul 298
Hush, Hush, Sweet Charlotte 474
Huston, Walter 627, 629–630
Hutch of the USA 271
Hutchinson, Charles ("Hurricane Hutch") 269, 270, 670, 743
Hutchinson, Josephine 448
Hyams, Leila 667, 764
Hyams and McIntyre 667
Hyland, Peggy 466
"The Hypnotist" (story) 333
The Hypnotist at Work 76
Hypocrites 184, 295, 382, 447

I Am a Fugitive from a Chain Gang 194
I Dream of Jeannie (television) 71
I Love Lucy (television) 459
I Walked with a Zombie 573
Ibanez, Vincente Blasco 363
Ibsen, Henrik 183, 445, 447
Icebound (stage play) 620
The Iced Bullet 251
The Iceman Cometh 233
I'd Like to Do It Again (book) 329, 622
The Idol Dancer 245
If You Believe It, It's So 610
Ignorance 687
Illington, Margaret 410
The Illusionist 593
The Image Maker 234, 292–294, 653, 726
The Imp 130
The Imp of the Bottle 64
Impossible Voyage 339
The Imprudent Young Couple (stage play) 244
In a Lonely Place 548
In Again, Out Again 646
In Hollywood with Potash and Perlmutter 211
In Judgment of 35, 169, 294–296
In New York Town (stage play) 634
In Old Arizona 481, 631, 686
In Old Kentucky 233, 643
In Search of the Castaways 588
In the Diplomatic Service 742
In the Hills of Kentucky 636
In the "Movies" Yesterday and Today (book) 325
In the Year 2000 302
In the Year 2014 302
Ince, John 106
Ince, John E. 106

Ince, Ralph 106, 168, 169, 306, 643
Ince, Thomas H. 61, 65, 86, 92–93, 94, 95, 106, 118, 133, 134, 135, 136, 158, 208, 234, 306, 325, 389, 391, 396, 413, 450, 463, 467, 468, 545, 601, 625, 639, 643, 768
The Indestructible Mr. Jenks 297
Indian Summer (stage play) 567
Indiscretion 699
Das Indische Grabmal 376
Infatuation 51
L'Inferno (1911) 114
Infidelity 212, 715–716
Information Please (stage play) 750
The Informer 212, 540
Ingagi 241, 322
Ingleton, E. Magnus 409, 492, 578
Ingomar the Barbarian (stage play) 42
Ingraham, Lloyd 15, 16, 218
Ingram, Rex 46, 132, 166, 232, 275, 312, 336, 363, 364, 365, 367, 368, 369, 370, 411, 491, 492, 493, 494, 540, 573, 574, 575, 576, 604, 609, 619, 681
L'Inhumaine 340
The Inner Shrine 170
The Inner Sight (book) 353
The Innocent Sinner 519
Inokuchi, Makato 546
The Insidious Dr. Fu Manchu (book) 739
Insinuation 159
Inspiration 163
The Inspirations of Harry Larrabee 105, 546, 717
"The Inspirations of Harry Larrabee" (story) 717
Interference 592
Intermezzo 468
International Crime 199
International House 313, 754
The Interpretation of Dreams (book) 117, 608, 766
Intolerance 19, 20, 22, 115, 159, 209, 248, 256, 258, 289, 344, 426, 769
The Intrigue 37, 49, 296–297, 646
The Intruder 644
Invaders from Mars (1953) 562
Invaders from Mars (1986) 562
The Invisible Agent 296
The Invisible Fluid 610
The Invisible Foe 137, 617, 640, 641, 741
The Invisible Foe (stage play) 640, 641
The Invisible Ghost 129, 240, 266, 398, 646
The Invisible Man 80, 86, 313, 562, 762
The Invisible Man Returns 176
The Invisible Man's Revenge 176
The Invisible Menace 406
The Invisible Power 296, 297–298, 686
The Invisible Ray (1920; serial) 112, 234
The Invisible Ray (1936) 14, 286
The Invisible Woman 154, 664
The Irish Gringo 295
The Iron Claw (serial) 156, 567, 745
The Iron Horse 644
The Iron Man (serial) 34
The Iron Mask 765
Irving, George 660, 661, 662

Irving, H.B. 31
Irving, I.W. 765
Irving, Sir Henry 30, 31, 32, 154, 244, 295
Irving, Washington 206, 261, 263, 753
Irwin, Ray 757, 758
Is He Dead? (stage play) 100
Is Zat So? (stage play) 321
Island of Lost Men 564
Island of Lost Souls 263, 298, 609, 610, 667, 770
Islands' Night Entertainment (book) 63
The Isle of Dead Ships (book) 203, 299, 718
The Isle of Lost Ships (1923) 70, 138, 203, 298–301, 306, 318, 343, 382, 440, 718
The Isle of Lost Ships (1929) 93, 95, 304, 399, 443, 585, 603, 718–719, **718**, 729
Isle of Love 258
Isle of Sunken Gold (serial) 643
Isn't Life Wonderful? 540
It 52
It! The Terror from Beyond Space 239
It Couldn't Have Happened — But It Did 681
It Took Nine Tailors (book) 538
It's a Gift 138
It's a Great Life 391
It's a Mad, Mad, Mad, Mad World 213
It's a Wonderful Life 33, 440, 736
It's Great to Be Alive 304
Ivers, Julia Crawford 36–37, 644, 645, 646, 664
Ives, Charlotte 374
Iwerks, Ub 261

Jack and the Beanstalk 20
Jack the Giant Killer 342
The Jack-Knife Man 165
Jackson, Charles Tenney 516
Jackson, Frances E. 602
Jackson, Fred 273, 275
Jackson, H.L. 195
Jacobs, W.W. 65, 78
Jad-Bal-Ja (movie lion) **555**
The Jade Mask 20, 681
Jaffe, Sam 20
James, M.R. 368
James, Walter 405
Jamison, Bud 115
Jane Eyre (1910) 414
Jane Eyre (1921) 23
Jane Eyre (1944) 20, 154
Janice Meredith 305, 485
Jannings, Emil 168, 607
Jans, Herman F. 352
Der Januskopf 149, 153, 157, 376
Jarrett, Henry 40
Java Head 651
The Jazz Singer 12, 84, 92, 178, 184, 193, 253, 283, 407, 437, 549, 551, 668, 749, 763
The Jealous Moon (stage play) 750
Jefferson, Joseph 72, 185, 596
Jefferson, William Winter 72
Jenkins, Allen 241, 280
Jenkins, William 284
Jenks, George Ellwood 263
Jennings, Dewitt 509
Jennings, Gordon 766

Jennings, J. Devereaux 268, 766
Jennings, Jane 79
Jenny, Jerry and the Chimp 732
Jesse James Meets Frankenstein's Daughter 2, 681
Jesus Christ 2, 18, 41, 93, 94, 95, 115, 119, 168–169, 172, 330
The Jewel of the Seven Stars (book) 301
Joan of Arc 691
Joan the Woman 216
Johann, Zita 168
John Barleycorn 107
Johnny Belinda (stage play) 10
Johnny-on-the-Spot 6
Johnson, Adrian 105, 125, 650
Johnson, Arthur 17
Johnson, Ben 643
Johnson, George 98
Johnson, Jack 708
Johnson, Noble 98, 271, 559, 564
Johnson, Orine 177
Johnston, Julanne 559, **560**, 564
Johnston, W. Ray 53
Johnston, William Andrew 138, 714, 715
Jolson, Al 13, 45, 84, 92, 253, 437, 539
The Jolson Story 224
Jones, Charles ("Buck") 179–180, **179**, 670
Jones, Chuck 228
Jones, Edgar 227, 632
Jones, F. Richard 706
Jones, Fred C. 716
Jones, Henry Arthur 36
Jones, Jennifer 260, 617
Jones, Marc 382
Jones, Morgan 502
Jones, Shirley 585
Jordan, Dorothy 45
Joseph and His Brethren (stage play) 191
Joslin, Margaret 15
Le Joueur d'echecs 376
Journey to Mars 310
Joy, Charlie 631–632
Joy, Leatrice 358, 379
Joy and the Dragon 260
Joyce, Alice 672–673, **673**
Joyner, Joyzelle 681
Jubilo 5
Judith of Bethulia 18, 20, 75
Le Juif polonais (stage play) 30, 331
Julian, Rupert 311, 320–321, 337, 339, 458, 461, 495, 496, 571, 741
Julie Bonbon (stage play) 72
The Jungle (book) 659
Jungle Bride 264
The Jungle Child 302, 719–720, 766
The Jungle Princess (serial) 669
The Jungle Trail 720–721
Jungle Trail of the Son of Tarzan 555
The Just and the Unjust (book) 711
Just Imagine 316, 343, 507

Kahanamoku, Duke 643
The Kaiser, the Beast of Berlin 197
The Kaiser's Shadow 385, 721
Kalich, Bertha 658
Karger, Maxwell 274–275, 388, 585, 654
Karloff, Boris 6, 28, 32, 33–34, 53, 79, 96, 168, 173, 194, 241, 271, 272, 289, 292, 306, 313, 324, 337,

338, 347, 355, 376, 406, 448, 455, 501, 554, 581, 597, 599, 607, 619, 650, 696, 702, 711, 734, 738, 739, 741, 762
Kate Kirby (series) 712
Katterjohn, Monte 468
The Katzenjammer Kids (series) 592, 659
Katzman, Sam 106
Kaufman, Albert 357
Kaufman, George S. 473
Keane, Robert Emmett 747
Keaton, Buster (aka The Great Stone Face) 8, 69, 112, 241, 259, 264, 268, 304, 316, 336, 391, 400, 405, 406, 407, 458, 571, 748, 766, 769
Keaton, Joe 92
Keats, Mildred 476
Keeler, Harry Stephen 87
Keenan, Frank 31, 92, 159, 248
Keep Moving 721–722
Keith, Ian 37, 349–350
Kellar, Harry 592, 593
Kellard, Ralph 507, **507**
Keller, Frank 760
Keller, Helen 493
Kellerman(n), Annette 127, 128, 129, 173, 210, 264, 302, 362, 425, 426, 427, 428, 429, 430, 431, 474, 475, 476, 587, 599, 600, 601, 747, 759, 760
Kelly, Anthony Paul 696
Kelly, Patsy 255
Kelly, Paul 620
Kelsey, Fred 39, 238, **238**, 240, 570
Kelso, Maym 213, 214
Kelson, G. 594
Kennedy, Edgar 702, 770, 487
Kenny, Edward 61
Kent, Barbara 310
Kent, Charles 205, 551
Kent, Crauford 86–87, 400
Kenyon, Doris 305, 306, 620
Kern, Jerome 86
Kerrigan, J. Warren 160, 161, 359, 715
Kerry, Norman 35, 72, 122, 289, 337, 338, 339, 457, 459, 513, **513**, 609, 679, 743, 749
Kesson, David 232
Kester, Vaughan 711
Key Largo (stage play) 212
Keys, James Walter 411
Keyes, Evelyn 467
The Keystone Kops 70, 157, 159, 255, 257, 616, 632, 644, 652
The Kid 400, 664
The Kid's Clever 722–723
Kilgour, Joseph 672
Kimball, Edward 189, 331, 582
Kimball, Roy 753
The Kindling 397
King, Bradley 419, 711
King, Burton 371
King, Emmett 271
King, Henry 45, 184, 260, 292, 440, 542, 545, 651
King, Joe 48
King, Mollie 501
King, Stephen 96
King, William Benjamin Basil 170, 172, 173
The King in Yellow 34
The King in Yellow (book) 616

King Kong 45, 75, 131, 187, 284, 306, 310, 321, 338, 339, 471, 599, 659
King Lear 168
King of Chinatown 564
King of Diamonds 548
King of Jazz 82
King of Kings 9, 69, 221, 321, 357, 440, 515, 562, 757
King of Nowhere (stage play) 352
The King of the Wild (serial) 338
King of the Zombies 514
King Tut-Ankh-Amen's Eighth Wife 301, 357
The Kingdom of God (stage play) 244
Kingsley, Pierce 363, 713
Kingston, William Henry Giles 679
Kingston, Winifred 37
Kipling, Rudyard 602
Kiralfy brothers 588
Kirkwood, James 224, 354
Kirkwood, James Jr. 224, 354
Kirsch, Albert 539
Kismet 562
The Kiss 350
A Kiss for Cinderella 449, 451
Kitty's Kisses 349
Klein, Robert 11, 115
Klondike 596
Klopstock, Friedrich Gottlieb 537
Knapp, George L. 408
The Knickerbocker Buckaroo 190
Knight, Charles R. 341
Knight, Damon 707
Knight, Harlan 725
Knoblock, Edward 562
Knoles, Harley 144, 243
Knowles, Mabel Winifred (Lurgan, Lester) 387
Kohler, Fred 88
Kohler, Fred Jr. 88
Kolker, Henry 92, 201, 711
Kongo (1932) 624, 628, 630, 631
Kongo (stage play) 625, 627, 628, 629, 630, 631
Korda, Alexander 81, 376, 559, 561, 562, 566
Korman, Harvey 618
Kosloff, Theodore 198, 200
Kotsonaros, George 53, 635, **635**, 667, 668, 770
Kramer, Stanley 213
Kraus, Werner 34
Krauss, Henri 123
Krellberg, Sherman S. 399
Kremer, Victor 624, 625
Kroh, George W. 352
Kultur 639
Kultur — or The Devil's Tool; Synopsis of a Motion Picture Scenario (book) 639
Kurosawa, Akira 465, 563
Kuter, Leo 574
Kuwa, George 87
Kyser, Kay 762

La Bohème (opera) 76
La, La, Lucille (stage play) 45
LaBadie, Florence 43, 233–234, 502, 503, 600
"The Labyrinth" (story) 508
The Lace of 1000 Trees and Other Lyrics (book) 610

Lachman, Harry 366, 368
Lackeye, Wilton 548, 577–578, 580, 581, 657
Lady Be Good 166
The Lady of the Harem 271
The Lady of the Lake 168
Lady Tsen Mai 729
Lady Windermere's Fan (1925) 382
The Lady with Red Hair 690
The Lady with the Light Colored Gloves 255
Laemmle, Carl 43, 47, 79, 84, 85, 129, 150, 181, 197, 281, 285, 286, 289, 290, 301, 306, 307, 311, 318, 325n, 326, 337, 339, 395, 462, 591, 592, 600, 672, 741
Laemmle, Carl Jr. 286
Laemmle, Ernest 339
Laemmle, Rosalie 286
Lackeye, Wilton 6, 73, 92, 112, 276, 373, 406, 519
The Lafayette Players 99, 191–192
Lake, Alice 8, 60, 274, **611**, 613
La Manna, Marie 197–198
La Marr, Barbara 69, **69**, 574, 575–576, **576**
The Lamb 158
Lamour, Dorothy 490
"The Land of Mist" (story) 340
The Land of the Lost 723–724
The Land Unknown 700
Landowska, Yona 735
Landy, George 391
Lane, Charles 150, 445
Lane, George 228
Lang, Fritz 20, 106, 178, 340, 540, 559, 561, 562, 585, 740
Langdon, Harry 69, 240
Langdon, Lillian 639
Lannon, Frank 608
La Plante, Laura 80, **80**, 82, 240, 311, 312, **312**, 313, 314
La Plante, Violet 82
Lardner, Ring 230
La Reno, Richard 648
Larkin, George 669
La Roque, Rod 96, 163, 199
La Rue, Fontaine 37, 58, 768
Lash of the Penitentes 680, 732
Lassie (movie dog) 96, 569, 634
Lassie (television) 670
Lasky, Jesse 36, 65, 75, 347, 352, 732
The Last Frontier (serial) 391
The Last Hurrah 393
The Last Laugh 91
"The Last Man" (story) 302
The Last Man on Earth 39, 45, 301–304, **303**, 464, 470, 571
"The Last Man on Earth" (story) 302
The Last Moment 304–306, 309, 437, 481
The Last of Mrs. Cheyney 524
The Last of the Mohicans (1911) 414
The Last of the Mohicans (1920) 55, 70, 256, 511
The Last Performance 1, 12, 84, 306–310, **309**, **310**, 376, 407, 459, 617
The Last Rites of Jeff Myrtlebank (television) 749
The Last Trail 650
The Last Warning (1929) 78, 82, 84, 86, 310–315, **312**, **313**, **314**, 353, 407, 433, 571, 773

The Last Warning (1939) 315
The Last Warning (stage play) 21, 273, 314–315
Last Woman on Earth 302, 723
Laugh, Clown, Laugh 86, 429
Laughing at Danger 315–316, 385, 433, 434, 712, 775
Laughter in the Dark 467
Laughton, Charles 213, 292, 740
Laurel, Stan 53, 69, 150, 262, 697
Laurel and Hardy 7, 69, 83, 86, 168, 255, 300, 304, 316, 362, 400, 763, 770
Lavender and Old Lace 16
LaVerne, Lucille 249
Law, Walter 125, 126, 207, 476
Law of Fear 96
Lawrence, Florence 43, 181, 325n, 468, 749
Lazybones 354
The League of the Future 726
Leahy, Margaret 766
Lean, David 106
Leap Year 439
Lease, Rex 175, 488
The Leatherneck 495
"Leave Her to Heaven" (story) 5
Leaves from Satan's Book 20, 537
Lebende Buddhas 367
Lee, Betty 587
Lee, Catherine 362
Lee, Christopher 378, 739
Lee, Donald W. 303, 571
Lee, Etta 619–620
Lee, Gwen 763
Lee, Jane 362
Lee, Lila 53, 54, 223, 224, **224**, 354, 397, 439, 558, 571
Lee, Louise 697
Lee, Robert 444
Lee, Rowland V. 34, 115, 444, 467, 468, 707, 740
Leeds, Andrea 174
LeFanu, J. Sheridan 252
Le Faure, Georges 751
Left Behind (series) 746
Le Gallienne, Eve 448, 498
Legally Dead 138, 316–319, **318**, 377, 416, 717, 726, 772
The Legend of Hell House 368
"The Legend of Sleepy Hollow" (story) 261
Legende Hongroise 310
Legends of King Arthur and His Court (book) 139
Leigh, Carolyn 448
Leigh, Frank 270–271
Leigh, Jason 573
Leigh, Vivian 516
Leighton, Lillian 659
Leisen, Mitchell 498, 562
L'Engle, Madeleine 353
Lengyel, Melchior 243
Leni, Paul 23, 79, 80–81, 82, 83, 84, 86, 228, 252, 310–311, 312, 313, 314, 315, 374, 375, 376, 377, 378, 461, 571, 617, 765
Leonard, Marion 17
Leonard, Robert Z. 406, 520, 730
Leong, James B. 729–730, 745
The Leopard Lady 239, 319–322, 497, 704, 757
The Leopard Lady (stage play) 320
The Leopard Man 154
The Leopard Woman 306
le Picard, Marcel 129, 266, 724

Lerman, Henry 433
Lerner, Jacques 276, 401, 402, **402**, 403, **403**
Leroux, Gaston 213, 454, 456, 457, 460, 461, 552, 665, 666–667, 741
LeRoy, Mervyn 223
LeSaint, Edward 92, 245, 727
Leslie, Lilie 325
Lessley, Elgin 766
Le Strange (Lestrange), Richard 269, 496
Letters from My Mill (book) 537
Leveau, Marie 598
Leverage, Harry 642–643
Levering, James 356, 556, 694, 755
Levering, Joseph 356
LeVino, Albert Shelby 244, 543
Levy, Ralph 191
Lewin, Albert 564, 571
Lewis, Jerry 225
Lewis, Joseph 398
Lewis, Leopold 31
Lewis, Mitchell 382
Lewis, Ralph 18, 20, 115, 189, 209, 267, 364, 686
Lewis, Sheldon 44, 149, 150, 155, 156, 157–158, 269, 271, 273, 274, 329, 373, 509, **509**, 511, 567, 697, 702, 725, 726, 743, 764, 765
Lewton, Val 10, 70, 653
L'Herbier, Marcel 340
The Liberty Belles (stage play) 217
The Lie (stage play) 661
Lieb, Tod und Teufel (Love, Death and the Devil) 66
Liebof, Oscar 703
Lieutenant What's-His-Name (book) 181
Life 462
Life (stage play) 119
The Life and Death of a Hollywood Extra 309–310
The Life of an American Fireman 16, 237
The Life of General Villa (documentary) 160
The Life of Moses 169
Life or Honor? 265, 352, 724
Life Returns 219, 318
Life with Father 213
Life Without Soul 112, 137, 195, 322–327, 346, 465, 587, 641
Lifeboat 306, 490
Life's Greatest Question 732
Life's Whirl 492
The Lifted Veil 170
The Lifted Veil (stage play) 36
The Light 327–329, 648, 749
The Light in the Dark 395
The Light That Failed (stage play) 661
Lightning Hutch (serial) 271
The Lightning Raider (serial) 619
The Lights of London (stage play) 175
Lights of New York 636, 760
L'il Abner 652
Lilac Time (stage play) 750
Liliom (1919) 584
Liliom (1930) 82, 312, 517, 585
Liliom (stage play) 132, 498, 517, 584, 599
Lillian Russell 481
Lillies of the Field 51
The Lily (stage play) 657

Limehouse Nights: Tales of China-town (book) 690
Lincoln, Elmo 3, 7, 29, 88, 542, 554, 555, 576
Lincoln's Gettysburg Address 168
Lindau, Paul 112, 671
Linder, Max 155, 230, 381, 544
Linow, Ivan 45, 550
The Lion's Ward 597
Lipman, Clara 72
Lipton, Lew 571
Liquid Electricity 345
Liszt, Franz 502
Little Dorritt (stage play) 544
The Little Girl Next Door 3
Little Lady Eileen 687, 724–725
Little Lord Fauntleroy 661
Little Man, What Now? 406
The Little Minister 522
The Little Minister (book) 449
Little Miss Marker 524
Little Old New York 122, 290
Little Orphant [sic] *Annie* 143
The Little Red Schoolhouse (aka *The Little Red School House*) 43, 233, 273, 476, 713, 725–726, 754
The Little Terror 363
The Little White Bird (book) 448
The Little White Savage 610
Little Women 305, 336, 594, 661
Littlefield, Lucien 83, 221–222, 437
Liveright, Horace 227
Lives of a Bengal Lancer 610, 661
The Living Death 605
The Living God (radio) 119
Livingston, Margaret 85, 86, 260, 621, 711
Lloyd, Ethel 205
Lloyd, Frank 49, 52, 285, 296, 297
Lloyd, Harold 69, 80, 241, 347, 406, 505, 520, 522, 558, 686, 723
Lloyd Webber, Andrew 462
Locke, Edward 59, 75, 77, 78, 79
Lockhart, Gene 751
Lockwood, Harold 256, 257, 258, 277, 490
Lo Corio, Maria 228
Lodge, Oliver 246
The Lodger 314, 691
Loew, Marcus 84, 369
Logan, Jacqueline 58, 192–193, **193**, 321, 444, 445, 757
Logue, Charles A. 506, 507, 614
Lola 89, 137, 329–332, **330**, **332**, 709, 717
Lola (stage play) 252, 329, 622, 685
Lombard, Carole 45, 599
Lombardi, Ltd. (stage play) 631
London, Jack 304, 382, 543, 544, 620
London After Midnight 20, 240, 311, 332–337, **334**, 518, 522, 524, 571, 608, 617, 764
The Lone Defender (serial) 96
The Lone Wolf (1917) 431, 585
The Lone Wolf (1924) 112, 119
The Lone Wolf (book) 597
The Lonely Villa 437
Lonergan, Phillip 502
Lonesome 307, 310
Lonesome Corners 632
Long, John Luther 218
Long, Walter 230, 300
A Long Day's Journey into Night (stage play) 191

Long Fliv the King 706
The Longest Night 515
Longworth, Alice Roosevelt 92
Looking Forward 302
Loomis, Margaret 66
Loos, Anita 132, 209
Lopez, John S. 697
Lord, Martha 353
Lord Feathertop 471
Lord Jim 597
Lord John in New York 92, 245, 280, 726–727
Lord John's Journal (serial) 726, 727
Lorna Doone 354, 648
Lorna Doone (1911) 414
Lorne, Marion 641
Lorraine, Louise 88–89, 555
Lorraine of the Lions 87, 259, 289, 337–339, 398
Lorre, Peter 292, 388, 411, 447, 454, 467, 762
"The Los Amigos Fiasco" (story) 340
Losch, Tilly 564
Lost and Won 688
The Lost Bridegroom 587
The Lost City (serial) 399, 669, 680, 732
The Lost City of the Jungle (serial) 20
Lost Horizon 20
The Lost Patrol 176
Lost Souls 408
The Lost Squadron 357
The Lost Weekend 107
The Lost Whirl 343
The Lost World (1925) 39, 111, 210, 230, 231, 251, 316, 339–345, 505, 592, 667, 668, 683, 700, 766, 768
The Lost World (book) 339, 340
The Lost Zeppelin (1929) 29, 393, 544, 585, 727–729, **728**
Lotus Blossom 729–730
Love 358
Love, Bessie 66, 175, 209–210, 341, 343, 344, 571, 773
Love, Montagu(e) xxii, 67, 78, 79, 144, 145, 215, 243, **254**, 271, 273, 311, 312, 313, 314, 394, 416, 417, 480, **480**, 509, 691
Love and Kisses 240
The Love Captive 262, 377
Love Comes Along 459
The Love Doctor 11, 51, 345–347
The Love Dream 215
Love 'Em and Leave 'Em 474
The Love Flower 245
Love from a Stranger 447
The Love Girl 212, 730
Love Me Forever 490
The Love of Sunya 37, 72, 190, 312, 347–350, 379, 648
Love Without Question 314, 350–353, 732
The Love Wraith 682
Lovecraft, H.P. 34, 56, 202, 294, 616
The Loves of Edgar Allan Poe 20
Love's Greatest Mistake 664
Love's Whirlpool 669
Lovett, Josephine 182, 183
Lowe, Edmund 137, 189, 321, 401, 501, 507, 581, 644, 646, 667, 696, 732, 750
Lowe, Edward T. Jr. 285, 286, 290

Lowry, Ed 241
Loy, Myrna 68, 82, 563, 702
Lubin, Sigmund 58
Lubitsch, Ernst 46, 79, 168, 243, 271
Lucas, Wilfred 542
Luce, Althea 679
Lucille Love: Woman of Mystery (serial) 463
Lucky Star 321
Lucretia Lombard 382
Ludlowe, Henry **483**
Lugosi, Bela 8, 52, 53, 82, 87, 96, 106, 112, 126, 129, 190, 214, 240, 241, 270, 271, 273, 283, 292, 299, 306, 307, 310, 313, 317, 338, 339, 347, 350, 365, 376, 380, 398, 439, 468, 501, 519, 587, 606, 607, 618, 631, 640, 646, 661, 667, 668, 679, 681, 696, 702, 730, 741, 762, 763, 764, 770
Lulu Belle (stage play) 99
Lumière, Auguste 74, 460
Lumière, Louis 74, 460
Lunatic in Power 481
The Lure of Love 453
The Lure of the White Lights 703
Luring Shadows 355–356, 556, 755
Lusk, Robert 727
The Lust of the Ages 711, 730–732
Lux Theater (radio) 491
Luxford, Nora 207, **207**
The Lying Truth 231
Lyon, Ben 443, **443**, 444, 504, 505, **505**
Lyons, H. Agar 552, 739
The Lyons Mail (stage play) 31
Lytell, Bert 117, 343, 386, 388, 431, 584–585, 695
Lytell, Wilfred 155
Lytton, L. Rogers 27, 272

M 447
Macbeth 20; 144
Macbeth (stage play) 30, 721
MacCullough, Jack 148, 149
MacDermott, Marc (also "McDermott") 36, 495, 568, 716, 749
MacDonald, Donald 389
MacDonald, J. Farrell **638**
MacDonald, Jack 149; *see also* MacCullough, Jack
MacDonald, Wallace 271, 690, 691, 711
MacGregor, Edgar J. 497
Mack, Willard 8, 9
Mackaill, Dorthoty 166
Mackay, Charles 464, 465
MacKay, Charles (poet/writer) 674
MacKay, Mary 47; *see also* Corelli, Marie
Mackaye, Fred **309**
MacKaye, Percy 471, 472, 474
MacLaren, Mary 610
Macpherson, Jeanie 146, 221, 498, 500, 515
Macpherson, Jeanne 775
MacQuarrie, Albert 726–727
MacQuarrie, Murdock 727
MacWilliams, Glen 490
The Mad Doctor 194
The Mad Genius 154, 562
Mad Love 388, 411, 711
The Mad Magician 406
Madame Butterfly 66, 232

"Madame Butterfly" (story) 218, 563, 645, 653
Madame Curie 240
Madame Satan 562, 564
Madame X (stage play) 7
Madden, Edward 143
Made for Love 356–359
Made in France (stage play) 540
Madison, Cleo 47–48, 494, 768
Madonna 104
Madonnas and Men 113, 120, 388, 667, 732–733
Magda (stage play) 137, 656
The Magic Cloak of Oz 451, 513
The Magic Eye 267, 617, 715, 733, 738
Magic Island (book) 599
The Magic Melody (stage play) 259
The Magic Show (stage play) 592
The Magic Skin (1913/1914) 359, 715, 742, 769
The Magic Skin (1915) 160, 228, 359–362
The Magic Skin (book) 138, 160, 161, 162, 359
The Magic Sword (1901) 495
The Magic Toy Maker 162, 362–363, 713
The Magician (1926) 312, 363–370, **364**, **366**, **369**, 386, 518, 540, 609, 677, 681
The Magician (1929) 308; see also *The Last Performance*
The Magician (book) 599
The Magnificent Ambersons (book) 275
Mahamet, Tarah Ben 594
Maid of Salem 20, 154
Maigne, Charles 63, 203, 299
Mailes, Charles H(ill) 260, 733
The Main Event 321
Main Street (stage play) 361
Les Mains d'Orlacs (book) 411, 414, 462
Majeroni, Giorgio 548
A Maker of Diamonds 698
Male and Female 217, 358, 439, 723
Mallinson, Tom 539
Malone, Dorothy 396
The Maltese Falcon (1931) 393
The Maltese Falcon (1941) 474
Mamoulian, Rouben 151
Man-Ape Jack (movie ape) 186, 187, 765
The Man Between 38
The Man Between (book) 44
The Man from Barclay's 224
The Man from Beyond 134, 269, 370–372, **371**, 593
"The Man from Beyond" (story) 340
The Man from Hell's River 481
The Man from the Diner's Club 407
The Man in Half Moon Street 154
The Man in the Iron Mask 571
The Man in the Iron Mask (book) 632
The Man in the Moonlight 272
A Man in the Open 212
Man Made Monster 515
The Man of a Thousand Faces 396
The Man of Mystery 372, 569, 672
The Man They Could Not Hang 6, 711
The Man Who Came Back (stage play) 305

The Man Who Couldn't Beat God 173, 702, 733–735
The Man Who Cried Wolf 82, 95
The Man Who Fights Alone 289, 720, 721
The Man Who Laughs (1928) 13, 61, 82, 84, 96, 103, 142, 154, 248, 307, 311, 313, 319, 365, 374–378, **375**, **376**, **378**, 459, 617, 618, 653, 765
The Man Who Laughs (1966) 378
The Man Who Laughs (book) 374, 467
The Man Who Played God (stage play) 137
The Man Who Reclaimed His Head 134, 680
The Man Who Saw Tomorrow 75, 379, 481, 682, 775
The Man with Nine Lives 711
The Man Without a Soul 8, 395
Man-Woman-Marriage 732
Mandelstamm, Valentin 698
Manhattan (stage play) 305
Maniac 295
Mann, Hank 157, 240
Mannequin 240
Mannering, Mary 548
Manners, David 418, 598, 643–644
Manning, Mildred **638**, 639
Mannix, Eddie 630
A Man's Man 45
A Man's Past 307
Mansfield, Martha 150, 155, 272–273, 725
Mansfield, Richard 31, 42, 43, 74, 132, 151, 154, 185, 202, 373, 385, 445
The Mansion of Aching Hearts 87
Manslaughter 221, 358, 732
Mantell, Robert B. 248–249, 604, 605
Mantell, Robert B. Jr. 248, 249
Mantell, Robert Shand 248
Mantrap 51
Mapes, Victor 112
"The Maracot Deep" (story) 341
Marah the Pytoness 325
Maran, Frances 539
The Marble Heart (1915) 429, 735–736
The Marble Heart (stage play) 735–736
March, Fredric 58, 137, 151, 153, 154, 325, 768
"Marcheta" (song) 490
Marcin, Max 188, 191
Marconi, Guglielmo 384
Mare Nostrum 365, 369, 460, 494, 574, 609, 689
Margaret Fleming (stage play) 28
Marie 310
Mario Rosa 119
Marion, Frances 122–123, 186, 494, 501
Marion, George F. 92
Mark of the Vampire 33, 279, 321, 333, 334, 335, 336, 449
The Mark of Zorro (1920) 139, 433, 459, 542, 561, 765
Market of Souls 86, 176, 389, 736
Markey, Enid 95, 555
Markham, Dewey "Pigmeat" 99
Marks, Maurice E. 143
Marley, Peverell 499
Marlowe, Christopher 40, 132, 392

Marlowe, Julia 373
Marlowe, June 96, 97, 636
Maro (movie dog) 274
The Marriage Chance 355, 379–382
The Marriage Clause 186
The Marriage Game (stage play) 352
The Marriage Maker 614
The Marriage Price 699
The Marriage Whirl 51
Married in Name Only 265, 724
Marriott, Crittenden 203, 299, 718
Marriott, Moore 552
Marryat, Frederick 206
M.A.R.S. (a.k.a. *Radio-Mania*) 78, 383–386, **383**, 549
La Marseille 310
Marsh, Frances 453
Marsh, Mae 19, 20, 147, 300, 453
Marsh, Marguerite 453
Marsh, Mildred 453
Marsh, Richard 252
Marshall, George 51
Marshall, Tully 69–70, 80, 111, 147, 148, 231, 287, 289, 341, 382, 596, 598, 614, 729, 776
Marshall, William 344
Marsten, Lawrence 519
Marston, Theodore 412, 414
"The Martian" (story) 577
Martin, Allen Langdon 750
Martin, Dean 225
Martin, Edwin 695
Martin, Joe 48, 69, 71
Martin, Joe (movie orangutan) 573, 574, **576**, 576–577
Martin, Mary 448
Martindel, Edward 646
Martinelli, Arthur 388, 585
Marvin, Grace 730
Marx Brothers 255, 313
Mary and Gretel 162
Mary of Scotland 406
Mary the Third (stage play) 227
The Mask of Fu Manchu 39, 484, 702, 739
The Mask of Fu Manchu (book) 739
The Masked Marvel (serial) 95, 96, 405
Maskelyne, John Neville 593
Mason, John 660
Mason, Shirley 8, 179, **179**, 180, 237, 343, 495, 690, 691
The Masque of Kings (stage play) 306
"The Masque of the Red Death" (story) 676
The Masquerader (stage play) 581
The Master Key (serial) 520
The Master Mind 754
The Master Mystery (serial) 14, 372, 453, 506, 507, 558, 614, 752
The Master of Ballantrae (book) 130
Master of the World 342
The Master Thief (stage play) 391
Masters of Men 305
Mata Hari 491
Matheson, Richard 368
Mat(h)ieson, Otto 635–636, 643, 644
Mathis, June 168, 275, 364, 365, 573, 585, 651, 654, 677, 679, 680–681

A Matter of Life and Death 584
Matthews, Dorcas 251
Mattox, Martha 80, 82, 702
Maude, Arthur 134, *134*, 371
Maude, Cyril 78, 242, 243, 446, 447
Maughham, Somerset 366, 367, 368, 386, 599
Maupain, Ernest 163, 482, 484
Maurice, Mary 27, 28, 672, 735
Maurice, Richard 176, 177, 178
Maverick (television) 548
May, Joe 81, 315
Mayall, Herschel 95
Mayer, Carl 81
Mayer, Louis 156
Mayer, Louis B. 156, 232, 233, 254, 285, 286, 344, 364, 365, 516, 518
Mayne, Eric 30
Mayo, Edna 47
Mayo, Frank 513, *513*
Maxim, Hiram 744
Maxim, Hudson 25, 26, 27, 94, 744
Maxim, John R. 636
Mayer, Louis B. 643
Mayne, Eric 594
Mayo, Archie 614, 621
Mayo, Edna 771
Mayo, Frank 650, *651*, 652, 682
The Maze 562
McAllister, Paul 546, 547, 548–549, 581
McAlpine, Jane 713
McArthur, Charles 227, 474
McAvoy, May 182, 183, 184, 231, 259, 283, 504, 505, 619, 761
McCormack, Frank 79, 611
McCoy, Alberta Beatrice 559
McCoy, Gertrude 166, 281
McCoy, William 734
McCrae, Gordon 585
McCullough, Philo 87, 174, 175–176, 339, 505, 736
McCutcheon, George Barr 15, 275, 773
McDermott, John 233
McDonald, Donald 648
McDonald, Francis 48
McDonald, Jack 639
McFadden, Elizabeth 138
McFadden's Flats 238
McGann, William 766–767
McGraw, John J. 580
McGreeney, P.S. 219
McGregor, Malcolm 619
McGuire, Dorothy 184, 377
McGuire, Kathryn 391
McHugh, Frank 241
McIntosh, Burr 313
McKay, James 747
McKean, Michael 160
McKee, Raymond 57, 58
McKenzie, Charles 424
McKim, Robert 139
McKinnon, Al 426
McLaglen, Arthur 338
McLaglen, Victor 45, 321, 338
McLaurin, Kate 643
McNeil, Sally 416
McQueen, Steve 183
McTigue 492
McVey, Lucille 205
The Mechanical Man 261
The Medal and the Maid (stage play) 420
Meek, Donald 275

Meeker, George 762, 763
Meighan, Thomas 217, 379, 396, 397, 398, 610, 664
Melfield, Richard 426
Melford, George 110, 298, 307, 397, 668, 677
Méliès, Gaston 169, 179
Méliès, Georges 7, 41, 76, 108, 136, 167, 169, 178, 179, 197, 198, 208, 234, 237, 339, 383, 392, 460, 463, 514, 561, 588, 632, 691, 700, 707
Memories 477
Men Must Fight 524
Menasco, Milton 342, 343
Mencken, H.L. 424, 651
Mendes, Lothar 168
Menjou, Adolph(e) 48, 522, 523, 524, *524*, 538–539, *539*, 540, 618
"Mental Telegraphy" (story) 100
"Mental Telegraphy Again" (story) 100
Menzies, William Cameron 21, 22, 23, 561–562
Mephistopheles (a.k.a. Satan, Lucifer, His Nibs, etc.) 7, 40, 41, 43, 57, 62, 114, 131–132, 133, 134, 135, 136, 144, 146, 147, 154, 185, 196–197, 234, 536, 540, 555–556, 696, 739, 746, 767, 771
The Merchant of Venice (stage play) 249, 266, 444, 738
Meredith, Charles 37
Meredith, Lois 242, 243, 262, 541, 542
Meredyth, Bess 542
Merivale, Philip 641
Merkyl, Wilmuth 266
Merlin, Iva 235, *236*
The Mermaid 127, 425
Merrick, George M. 301
Merrill, Frank 554
Merrill, Walter 636
Merritt, Abraham 218, 433, 508, 509, 510, 511, 616
Merry-Go-Round 38, 279, 289, 320, 376, 458, 459, 517, 577
The Merry Widow 147, 279
Merton of the Movies 15, 473
Mescall, John 320
A Message from Mars (1921) 134, 140, 245, 274, 386–388, *386*, *388*, 514, 585
A Message from Mars (stage play) 134, 162
The Message of the Dead 2, 108
Messenger, Gertie 8
Der Messias (poem) 537
Mestayer, Harry 276
"The Metal Monster" (story) 508
Metcalfe, Earl 465, *744*, 745
Metropolis 311, 340
Metropolis 559, 621
Meyer, George W. 719
Meyer, Louis 156, 157
Meyers, Harvey 22
Michael Strogoff (stage play) 391, 588
Micheaux, Oscar 98, 99, 176, 178, 228–229, 525, 777
Middleton, Charles 7, 271
Middleton, George 275
The Midget's Revenge 131
Mid-Channel (stage play) 410
Midnight 154
Midnight at Maxim's 484

A Midnight Bell 389–390, 762
Midnight Faces 390–392, 564
The Midnight Flower 428
The Midnight Girl 429
Midstream 29, 200, 392–394, 540, 544, 729
A Midsummer Night's Dream 314
Mighty Joe Young 338
Milestone, Lewis 306
Milford, Mary Beth 270
Miljan, John 614
The Mill of the Gods (poem) 143
Mill of the Stone Women 270
The Mill on the Floss 234
Milland, Ray 454, 710
Millarde, Harry 181
Miller, Alice D.G. 485
Miller, Arthur (cinematographer) 215, 216–217
Miller, Ashley 716
Miller, Charles 467–468, 773
Miller, Henry 481
Miller, J. Clarkson 77, 79, 465
Miller, Marilyn 448
Miller, Patsy Ruth 286, 288–289, 292, 337, 339, 703, 707
Miller, Walter 497
Millhauser, Bertram 200, 704
A Million Bid 193
The Million Dollar Collar 87
The Million Dollar Dollies 212
Million Dollar Mermaid (1952) 476
The Million Dollar Mystery (serial) 82, 433, 567
The Million Dollar Robbery 272
Milton, John 104, 105, 114, 132, 537
Milton, Maude 388
The Mind of Man 230
The "Mind the Paint" Girl (stage play) 86
Mindlin, Michael 315
Minnie 233
Minter, Mary Miles 9–10, 37, 161–162, 223, 274, 329, 354, 660, 664
The Miracle (stage play) 46
Miracle Maid 682
The Miracle Man (1919) 2, 115, 120, 139, 172, 182, 207, 241, 284, 379, 394–399, *397*, 445, 641, 646, 681, 708, 709, 737, 741, 768
The Miracle Man (1931) 550
The Miracle Man (book) 395, 610, 709
The Miracle of Life (1915) 716, 737–739
The Miracle of Life (1926) 738
The Mirage (stage play) 664
Les Misérables 296
Les Misérables (Part 1) 168
Les Misérables (stage play) 580
The Miser's Doom 208
The Mishaps of Musty Suffer (series) 722
Miss Ambition 347
Miss Bluebeard 474
Miss Jackie of the Navy (serial) 597
Miss Jekyll and the Madame Hyde 347
Miss Jerry 501
Miss Lulu Bett 227
Miss Nobody 175
Miss Potter 141
Missile to the Moon 275
The Missing Guest 77
The Missing Link 268, 399–400, 505, 766

Mississippi 138
Mr. Barnes of New York (book) 373
Mr. Broadway 96
Mr. Moto's Last Warning 571
Mr. Smith Goes to Washington 264
Mr. Wu (1919) 691
Mr. Wu (1927) 87, 406, 564, 681
Mitchell, Abby 192
Mitchell, Bruce 355, 669, 749, 750
Mitchell, Cameron 455
Mitchell, Grant 384, 385
Mitchell, John Ames 677, 679
Mitchell, John Purroy 27
Mitchell, Langdon 329
Mitchell, Rhea 134, 143
Mitchum, Robert 247
Mix, Tom 102, 116, 142, 259, 316, 328, 650
Mixx, Emmett 294
Moby Dick (1930) 154
Mockery 255, 256, 312
"The Mocking Bird" (song) 116
The Modern Dr. Jekyll 149
A Modern Musketeer 300
The Modern Sphinx 168
Modest Suzanne (stage play) 69
Modjeska, Helena 249
Moffatt, Graham 552
Mohr, Hal 314, 407
Molly and I 237
The Mollycoddle 664
Molnar, Ferenc/Franz 61, 132, 133–134, 136, 145, 234, 517, 584, 585
Moloch (stage play) 567
Mong, William V. 7, 48, 96, 97, 103, 252, 509, *511*, 621, 745
Monkey Business (1931) 515
Monkey Business (1952) 754
The Monkey Talks 187, 400–404, *402*, *403*, 564, 701
The Monkey Talks (stage play) 276, 580, 599
The Monkey's Paw (1933) 289, 306
"The Monkey's Paw" (story) 65, 78
Monsieur Beaucaire 306, 565, 679
The Monster 5, 8, 21, 22, 130, 219, 251, 380, 396, 404, *406*, *407*, 437, 560, 610, 613, 639, 715
The Monster (stage play) 21, 406, 519, 580, 611
The Monster and the Girl 242
The Monster Walks 82, 199, 702
Montalban, Ricardo 427
Montana, Bull 45, 187, 229, 230, *231*, 300, 305, 316, 341, 343, 344, 505, 614, 667
Montgomery, Robert 73
"The Moon Pool" (story) 508
"The Moon Slave" (story) 56
The Moonchild (book) 368
Moonrise 369
The Moonstone (1909) 409
The Moonstone (1911) 409
The Moonstone (1915) 131, 147, 409–411, 492, 548
The Moonstone (1934) 34, 135, 411
The Moonstone (book) 163, 248, 409, 476, 477, 541, 709, 754
Moore, Carlyle 610–611, 612
Moore, Colleen 42, 49, 143, 224, 391, 571, 619, 621
Moore, Demi 207
Moore, Eugene 293
Moore, Joe 464, 518, 592
Moore, Matt 41, 122, 464, 518, 592, 596, 703

Moore, Owen 325n, 464, 518, 592
Moore, Tom 5, 464, 518, 571, 592, 673
Moore, Vin 723
The Moral Fabric 468
Moran, Leo 621, 622
Moran, Polly 570, 609, 706
Moran, Priscilla Dean 621–622
More Limehouse Nights (book) 690
Moreno, Antonio 12, 168, 169, 365, 549, 550
Moreno, Rosita 304
Morey, Harry T. 672, 735
Morgan, J.P. 754
Morgan, Kewpie 400
Morgan, Ralph 190
Morley, Robert 292
Morocco 256
Morosco, Oliver 119, 631, 636
Morosco, Walter 51, 636
Morpheus Mike 342
Morphia (stage play) 352
Morrell, Edward M. 543
Morris, Chester 24, 304, 399, 499–500
Morris, Gouverneur 172, 224
Morrison, Arthur 442
Morrison, James 27, 28, 352, 672
Morse, Harrington 145
Morse, N. Brewster 690
Mortensen, C.N. 61
Mortmain 67, 200, 345, 411–414, **413, 414**
Mortmain (book) 411
Mosjoukine, Ivan 622
Moss, Howard S. 162–163
The Most Dangerous Game 7, 245, 310, 448, 634, 650
The Mother and the Law 20
Mother of Truth: A Story of Romance and Retribution... (book) 266–267
The Mountain Eagle 155
Mounted Fury 765
Mourning Becomes Electra (stage play) 106
A Movie Star 705
Mrs. Miniver 240
Mrs. Warren's Profession (stage play) 361
Mrs. Wiggs of the Cabbage Patch 213
Mrs. Wiggs of the Cabbage Patch (stage play) 10
Der müde Todd 562
Mudie, Leonard 388
Mulhall, Jack 166–167, 212, 240
The Mummy (1911) 168, 481, 727
The Mummy (1932) 358, 366, 481, 541, 573
The Mummy of the King of Ramses [sic] 167
Mummy's Boys 571
The Mummy's Curse 46, 240, 721
The Mummy's Ghost 599, 659
The Mummy's Hand 160, 733
The Mummy's Tomb 311
Muni, Paul 562, 564, 614
Murder at Dawn 45, 167
Murder at Midnight 424, 644
Murder by Television 112
Murder by the Clock 82, 544, 622, 702, 710
Murder in a Private Car 487
Murder in the Blue Room 77
Murder in the Fleet 459

A Murder in the Madhouse (stage play) 42
Murder with Pictures 765
Murdered Alive 270, 299
Murders in the Rue Morgue 15, 116, 154, 301, 312, 313, 319, 322, 365, 402, 482, 571, 697, 770
"Murders in the Rue Morgue" (story) 66, 231, 238, 320, 350
Murders in the Zoo 105, 447, 664
Murfin, Jane 504, 750
Murillo, Mary 249, 515, 604, 605
Murnau, F.W. 22, 79, 86, 149, 157, 178, 336, 337, 374, 491, 539, 540, 621
Murphy, Dudley 349
Murphy, Joe 80
Murphy, Ralph 280, 299
Murray and Mack 240
Murray, Charlie 103, 238, **238**, 240, 768–770
Murray, K. Gordon 561
Murray, Mae 304, 520, 688, 689
Muse, Clarence 192
The Music Master 491
The Music Master (stage play) 489
Mussalli, Hassan 587
The Mutiny of the Elsinore 382, 543
Mutiny on the Bounty 296
My Fair Lady 212
My First Fifty Years in the Theater (book) 622
My Friend, the Devil 738–739
My Golden Girl (stage play) 441
My Little Margie (television) 213
My Neighbor's Wife 772
Myers, Carmel 257, 258–259
Myers, Harry 69, 102, 103, 408
Le Mystère de la chamber jaune (book) 741
Mysteries of Dr. Fu Manchu (series) 208
The Mysteries of Myra (serial) 220
The Mysterious Doctor 82
The Mysterious Dr. Fu Manchu 193, 269, 416, 597, 641, 739–740, **740**
The Mysterious Dr. Fu Manchu (book) 739
Mysterious Dr. Satan (serial) 96
The Mysterious Island (1929) 33, 69, 78, 251, 255, 299, 312, 414–418, **415, 417**, 459, 460, 587, 630
Mysterious Island (1961) 406
The Mysterious Island (book) 415, 587, 591
The Mysterious Mr. Wong 87, 681
Mysterious Mr. X 254
The Mystery Mind (serial) 272, 295
The Mystery of Dr. Fu Manchu (series) 324
The Mystery of Edwin Drood (1909) 418
The Mystery of Edwin Drood (1914) 418–420, 556, 672
The Mystery of Edwin Drood (1935) 313, 418, 419
The Mystery of Edwin Drood (book) 418
The Mystery of Edwin Drood (stage play) 420
The Mystery of Life 244
The Mystery of Marie Roget 681, 733
The Mystery of the Leaping Fish 159, 560

The Mystery of the Mary Celeste 283, 459
The Mystery of the Poison Pool 553
The Mystery of the Silent Death 290
The Mystery of the Wax Museum 81, 86, 229, 245, 270, 460, 562
The Mystery of the Yellow Room 617, 641, 741–742
"Mystery of the Yellow Room" (story) 350, 461–462
The Mystery of the Yellow Room (book) 545, 667
Mystery Ranch 644
The Mystery Ship (serial) 185
The Mystic 50, 86, 133, 192, 201, 271, 382, 420–424, 614, 710, 729, 777
The Mystic Hour 227, 228, 298, 359, 465, 710, 742–743

Nagel, Conrad 336, 416, **521**, 522, 524, 571, 572, **616**, 617, 760, 764
Naldi, Nita 151, 152, 155, 156, 157, 738
Nana (book) 582
Napoleon (movie dog) 96, 194, 569, 570
Narcotic 680
Narcotics—The Menace to Children (book) 730
Nation, Carry 107
National Velvet 643
The Nation's Peril 95, 680, 743–745, **744**, 749
Natteford, J.F. 271
Naughty 382
Naughty Marietta (stage play) 646
Navarro, Ramon 350, 364, 518
The Navigator 264, 391
Nazimova, Alla 183, 193, 679
Neal of the Navy (serial) 664
The Necronomicon (book) 725
Negri, Pola 168, 679
Neilan, Marshall 20, 63, 64, 65, 142, 224, 229, 230, 231, 232–233, 271, 304, 343, 416, 455, 487, 563, 639
Neill, James 75, 776
Neill, Roy William 137, 385, 623, 721
Nelson, Frances 548
Nemesis (stage play) 352
Neptune's Bride 425–427, 428
Neptune's Daughter (1912) 427
Neptune's Daughter (1914) 127, 129, 264, 362, 425, 427–31, 474, 599, 601, 747
Neptune's Daughter (1949) 427
Nero, Curtis 631
The Nervous Wreck 664
Nesbitt, Miriam 716
Nesmith, Miriam 594
Neumann, Alfred 310
Neumann, Kurt 573
Neville, Harry 409
The New Adventures of Tarzan 596, 597
The New Exploits of Elaine (serial) 82, 704
"The New Gulliver" (story) 56
The New Henrietta (stage play) 112
The New Revelation (book) 371
Newfield, Sam 99
Newhall, Bob 621
The Newlyweds and Their Baby 39
Newman, Walter Brown 568

Newmeyer, Fred 505
Die Nibelungen 561, 562
Niblo, Fred 79, 251, 404, 467, 468, 484, 639
Nicholas II (Czar) 45, 478
Nichols, George 542
Nichols, Red 99
Nicholson, Leta Vance 332
Nicholson, Meredith (author) 259, 275, 283
Nicholson, Meredith (cinematographer) 275
Nielsen 445
The Nigger (stage play) 305
Nigh, William 681
A Night at the Opera 460
Night Club Lady 524
The Night Cry 96
Night Life of the Gods 255, 270, 312
Night Monster 599
Night of Terror 8, 756, 763
Night of the Demon 365, 368
Night of the Ghouls 422
The Night of the Hunter 247
Night of Vengeance 254
Night Rose 493
Night World 34
Nightmare Alley 113, 317, 423, 682
Nightmare on Elm Street 404
Nijinsky, Vaslav 678
Nilsson, Anna Q. 28, 35, 174, 175, 265, 266, 289, 295, 300, 343, 440, 443, **443**, 494, 622, 623–624, 716
Nina the Flower Girl 467
1984 (book) 57
Niobe 170, 237, 430–432, **432**
Niobe (stage play) 170, 431
Nixon, Richard M. 516
Noble, John W. 43, 442
Noble, Ruth 66
Nobody's Children 176
Nolan, Mary 628, 630–631
Nomads of the North 20, 211
Norcross, Frank 362
Normand, Mabel 37, 240, 255
Norris, Frank 492
Norris, William 235, **236**
North, Wilfred 28
Northrup, Harry 295
Norton, Barry 668
Norton, Jack 201
Norwood, Eille 691
Nosferatu 83, 149, 337, 538
Notorious 168
The Notorious Colonel Blake (stage play) 664
Notre Dame de Paris (book) 123, 284, 286, 375
Novak, Eve 316
Novak, Jane 12
Novarro, Ramon 574, 575, 576, 606, 679, 680
Novello, Ivor 243
Nowell, Wedgewood 48
Number Seven (stage play) 243
Number Seventeen 243
The Nut 561
Nye, Carroll 636

The Oakdale Affair 222
Oaker, John 753
Oakman, Wheeler 422, 596
Oboler, Arch 549
O'Brian, Hugh 474
O'Brien, Eugene 131, 410–411
O'Brien, George 223, 403, 700, 701

O'Brien, John B. 765
O'Brien, Willis 162, 340, 341, 342, 343, 592
O'Connor, Frank 233
O'Connor, Robert E. 719
O'Connor, Una 80
The Octave of Claudius (book) 56, 57
Odell, Eric 56; *see also* Pain, Barry
O'Dell, Delsie 705
Odell, Maude 431, 432
O'Donnell, Spec 770
Of All People 241
Offenbach, Jacques 588
Officer 444 (serial) 185
Ogle, Charles 166, 324, 495, 551, 677, 680
O'Hara (film series) 131
O. Henry 241, 302
Ohnet, Georges 739
O'Keefe, Dennis 568
Okito 592
Oland, Warner 120, 192, 193, **193**, 203, 304, 416, 690, 691, 739, 740
Olcott, Sidney 41
The Old Dark House 81, 174, 405, 562, 762
Old Dutch (stage play) 501
The Old Fashioned Way 138
Old Lady Mary: A Story of the Seen and Unseen (book) 488–489
Old Loves for New 240
The Old Man and the Sea (book) 10
Old San Francisco 193
Old Wives for New 217
The Old Woman (stage play) 42
Oliphant, Mrs. Margaret 488
Oliver, Edna May 441
Oliver, Guy 66, 92
Oliver Twist (1912) 672
Oliver Twist (1916) 688
Oliver Twist (1922) 53, 296
Oliver Twist (book) 163
Oliver Twist (stage play) 544, 656, 688
Olivier, Laurence 563–564
Olmsted, Gertrude 404, 405, 406, **406**
O'Malley, Pat 231–232
Omar, the Tent-Maker 597
Omar the Tentmaker (stage play) 581
On Borrowed Time 33, 95, 491
"On Moonlight Bay" (song) 143
On the Broad Stairway 712
On the Origin of Species (book) 666
On the Trial of the Conquistadores 39
On Time 212, 316, 432–434
On Trial (stage play) 188, 243
Ondine (2010) 427, 601
Ondine (stage play) 601
One Body Too Many 83
One Exciting Night 20, 175, 219, 222, 305, 390, 408, 434–437, **436**, 481, 539, 704, 706
One Frightened Night 83, 160, 437, 524
One Glorious Day 53, 180, 224, 321, 437–439, 558, 559, 686
"One Head Well Done" (story) 302
One Hour 549
One Hour before Dawn 260, 271, 439–441, 622, 716, 765

One Hour Past Midnight 14
One Hundred Men and a Girl 456
One Hundred Years After 302
One Hysterical Night 138, 564
One Million B.C. 20, 82, 100, 211, 289, 518
The $1,000,000 Reward (serial) 731
One Million Dollars 213, 441–442
One Million Francs 441
One Night in Rome 619
One Romantic Night 247
One Way Street 441, 442–444, **443**, 505, 622
One Week of Love 411
O'Neil, Nance 92, 655, 656–657
O'Neil, Sally 416
O'Neill, Eugene 191, 192, 556
O'Neill, James 191, 556, 661
Only Angels Have Wings 184
Only 38 336
Operator 13 123
The Opium Smugglers of Frisco (stage play) 620
Oppenheim, James 227
Orlacs Hande 376, 411, 462, 499
Ormsby, Albert B. 425, 426, 427
Orphans of the Storm 82, 292, 306, 434, 498, 693
Orwell, George 57
Osmun, Leighton 146, 147, 598, 688
Ost und West 266
"The Ostler" (story) 163
Ostriche, Muriel 413, 414, 471
O'Sullivan, Maureen 491
Oswald, Richard 75, 81, 447
Othello (opera) 676
Othello (stage play) 30, 599
Otto, Henry 12, 114, 115, 116, 210, 211, 212, 600, 601, 654, 655, 760
The Ouija Board (stage play) 273, 274, 406
Our American Cousin (stage play) 28
Our Children (stage play) 352
Our Christianity 176
Our Daily Bread 234
Our Hospitality 291
Our Mrs. Chesney (stage play) 119
Oursler, Charles Fulton 593
Ouspenskaya, Maria 217, 292
Out of Singapore 271
Out of the Storm 172
Outbound Bound (stage play) 106, 199
Outrageous Fortune (stage play) 217
Outside the Law (1920) 20, 285, 416, 422, 596, 605, 630, 764
Outside the Law (1930) 422
The Outsider 444–445
Outward Bound 106, 142, 407, 491
Over There 28
Overbough, Roy 153
Ovey, George 73
Owen, Reginald 313, 697
Owen, Seena 218

Pabst, G.W. 363
Packard, Frank L. 395, 398
Pagan Passions 682
Page, Thomas Nelson 98
Pagliacci (opera) 464
Paige, Robert 242
Pain, Barry 56–57
The Painted Veil 368

Painting the Town 722, 723
A Pair of Sixes 228
Palance, Jack 152
Pallen, Conde 355
Palmer, Harry 40
Pamela's Past 634
Pangborn, Franklin 405, 485, 702
Pantages, Alexander 494
Panthea 131
Panzer, Paul 11, 181, 414
Papa's Delicate Condition (book) 51
Paradise Alley 51
Paradise Lost (poem) 104, 114, 537
Paramount on Parade 740
Paris qui dort 340
Parke, William 319
Parker, Albert 190, 348, 349, 350
Parrish, Maxfield 562
Parsifal (opera) 676
Parsons, Louella 22, 310, 524, 575, 646
Party Time at the Club Roma (television) 264
Pascal, Ernest 85, 504
Pasha, Kalla 628
The Passing of the Third Floor Back (1918) 429
The Passing of the Third Floor Back (1935) 376, 641
Pastrone, Giovanni 659
The Patchwork Girl of Oz 451, 668
The Patent Leather Kid 183, 238
Paths of Glory 524
Paths to Paradise 487
Paton, Stuart 112, 180, 588, 592, 754
Patria (serial) 122, 190, 203, 548, 768
Patrick, Jerome 264
The Patriot 336
Paulton, Edward 170, 431
Paulton, Harry 170, 431
Pawn, Doris 390
Pawns of Mars 414
Pay Day 400
Pay Dirt 541
Pay Me 542
Payton, Lucy 738
Peacock Alley 96, 569
Peale, Norman Vincent 246
The Pearl of Death 704
The Pearl of Love 453
The Pearl of the Antilles 420
Pearl of the Army (serial) 546
Pearson, Virginia 274
Le Peau de chagrin (book) see *The Magic Skin*
Peck, Gregory 653
Pecos Dandy 587
Peel, L. May 180–181
Peer Gynt (1915) 78, 222, 242, 445–447
Peer Gynt (1918) 447
Peer Gynt (1934) 447
Peer Gynt (1941) 447
Peer Gynt (stage play) 193, 445
Peggy 490
Pembroke, Scott 53
The Penalty 58, 103, 131, 172, 286, 289, 292, 390, 606, 627, 773
Pendleton, Edna 12, 591, 592
Penn and Teller 593
Penrod 231, 233
Penton, Curtis 591
Peppy Polly 248
Percy, Eileen 544, 587

The Percylma 544
Percyval, Wigney 514
Perdue, Derelys 39, 304, 686
The Perfect Specimen 690
The Perils of Pauline (serial) 11, 122, 220, 542, 573, 580, 680, 692, 745, 548
Perkins, Osgood 471, 473, 474
Perret, Léonce 568, 698, 763
Perry, Francis Elliot 256, 258
Perry, Howard 62
Perry, Paul 522
Perry, Sam A. 292
Perry Mason (television) 524, 706
Perugini, Frank 697
Pesci, Joe 177
Peter and Wendy (stage play) 449
Peter Gunn (television) 548
Peter Ibbetson (1935) 145, 215, 217; see also *Forever*
Peter Ibbetson (book) 214, 215, 217, 577
Peter Ibbetson (stage play) 162, 214, 215
Peter Pan (1924) 3, 69, 87, 429, 447–451, **450**
Peter Pan (stage play) 448
Peter Pan; or, the Boy Who Wouldn't Grow Up (book) 448
Peter Pan in Kensington Gardens (book) 448
Peter the Great (movie dog) 335
Peters, Frederic 554
Peters, House 712
Peters, House Jr. 712
Peterson, Jerry 305
The Petrified Forest 614
"Petrified Man" (story) 100
Petrova, Olga 602–603
Petrovich, Ivan 367, 368, 370
The Phantom Buccaneer 156
The Phantom Empire (serial) 711
The Phantom Honeymoon 203, 214, 451–453, 495, 712, 725
The Phantom Killer 96, 266
The Phantom Legion 273, 696
The Phantom Melody 105, 434, 453–455, 660
The Phantom of Chinatown 681
The Phantom of Paris 15, 155, 542
The Phantom of the Crestwood 393, 424
The Phantom of the Opera (1925) 56, 58, 79, 81, 84, 105, 181, 259, 284, 285, 286, 289, 309, 311, 320, 337, 339, 355, 365, 375, 376, 392, 396, 405, 406, 407, 455–461, **457**, **459**, 496, 564, 571, 605, 614, 619, 628, 736, 743, 760, 765
Phantom of the Opera (1943) 79, 289, 314, 456, 463
Phantom of the Rue Morgue 82
The Phantom Ship (book) 206
The Phantom Speaks 466
The Phantom Violin 108, 304, 456, 461–464
The Phantom's Secret 61
Philbin, Mary 289, 306, **309**, 309, **310**, 374, **375**, 376, 378, 391, 457, 459, **459**, 460, 461, 760
Phillippi, Erich 77
Phillips, Alexandra 72–73
Phillips, Augustus 8, 441, 551, 690
Phillips, Dorothy 591
Phillips, Edward 32, 34, 271
Phillips-Fahrney, Alexandra 72, 73

Piave, Francesco Maria 227
Picadilly 564
Piccadilly Jim 7
Pichel, Irving 544, 702
Pickford, Jack 21, 22, 224, 226, **226**, 227, 354, 522, 626, **626**, 627, 664
Pickford, Lotte 274
Pickford, Mary 17, 20, 21, 75, 93, 123, 175, 224, 226, 232, 235, 236–237, **236**, 245, 251, 258, 259, 271, 331, 348, 354, 355, 433, 449, 450, 451, 520, 560, 564, 565, 599, 603, 605, 610, 619, 622, 626, 646, 664, 681, 709, 725, 770
Pickles, Art and Sauerkraut 33
Picon, Molly 266
The Picture of Dorian Gray (1913) 223, 738
The Picture of Dorian Gray (1915) 147, 514
The Picture of Dorian Gray (1945) 30, 37, 459, 571
The Picture of Dorian Gray (book) 151
The Picture of Dorian Gray (stage play) 145
Pidgeon, Walter 240–241, 444
Piel, Edward 260
Pierce, Jack P. 86, **313**, 375, 404, 413, 686
Pierce, James 554, **555**
Pierce, Joan Burroughs 554
Pilgrimage 211
The Pilgrimage Play (stage play) 212
Pilgrim's Progress 193
H.M.S. Pinafore (stage play) 503
Pinero, Arthur Wing 86, 182
The Pink Lady (serial) 664
The Pink Lady (stage play) 501
Pinto, Effingham 276
The Pirates of 1920 208
The Pit 190, 581
The Pit (stage play) 6, 329
The Pit and the Pendulum (1913) 163, 481
"The Pit and the Pendulum" (story) 163, 231
Pitts, ZaSu 213, 214, 255, 289, 576
Pivar, Maurice 377
The Place of Honeymoons 453
Plan 9 from Outer Space 177, 296
Planet Outlaws 732
The Planets (musical composition) 31
Player, Wellington 422
Playing the Game (stage play) 72
Playmates 154
Playter, Wellington 596
The Pleasure Garden 155
Plumes in the Dust (stage play) 306
Plunder (serial) 704, 745
The Poacher 43
Poe, Edgar Allan 15, 16, 17, 19, 21, 32, 47, 66, 104, 132, 163, 206, 231, 248, 256, 319, 320, 412, 454, 481, 482, 483, 484, 604, 637, 643, 650, 676, 733
Poe, John Allan 19
Poe, Virginia 17
Poff, Lon 115
"The Poison Belt" (story) 340
The Poison Pen 464–465, **464**, 481, 682, 745

Polito, Sol 39, 255, 510, 719
Pollar, Gene 301, 555
Pollard, Harry A. 736, 737, 738
Pollard, L.J. 149
Polly Ann 209
Polly of the Circus 20
Polo, Eddie 544
Pommer, Erich 254
Pool of Flame 409
Poor Jake's Demise 396
Poppy 664
Porgy and Bess (stage play) 192
The Port of Doom 712
Porter, Edwin S. 16, 208, 234, 235, 237, 258, 431, 451, 634
Porter, Gene Stratton 439
Portrait in Black 564
Portrait of Jennie 212
Possessed 664
Post, Charles A **651**, 652
Postal Inspector 82
The Poster Girls and the Hypnotist 578
The Postman Always Rings Twice 424
Potel, Victor 15
Potter, Paul 577
The Potters 325
Powell, David 203
Powell, Frank 655, 656, 657
Powell, Michael 367, 369, 584
Powell, Paul 62–63, 214
Powell, Robert 420
Powell, William 692
Powell, William (H.) 190, 213
Power, Tyrone 549, 550, 679
Power, Tyrone Sr. 406
The Power God (serial) 185
The Power of Love 707
The Power of Money (stage play) 620
The Power of Silence 289
The Power Within 266
Praskins, Leonard 85
Pratt, William Henry 251; *see also* Karloff, Boris
Preer, Evelyn 99, 192
Prehistoric Poultry 342
Premature Burial 454
The Premature Burial (1962) 710
"The Premature Burial" (story) 604
The Prestige 593
Pretty Ladies 213
Pretty, Arline 645, 646
The Preview Murder Mystery 424
Prevost, Marie 175, 487
Price, Vincent 248, 454
A Price for Folly 347
The Price of Her Soul 105
The Price of Silence 233, 465–466, 600
The Primrose Path 373
The Prince and the Pauper (1909) 100
The Prince and the Pauper (1915) 100
The Prince and the Pauper (book) 100
The Prince and the Pauper (stage play) 411
Prince Karl (stage play) 373
Prince, Morton (Dr.) 502, 503
A Prince of India 147
Prince of Players 20
A Princess of Bagdad 551

Princess of the Dark 235, 251, 467–468
Princess Pat (operetta) 306
Princess Romanoff 655
The Princess' Necklace 147
Pringle, Aileen 423, 424
Pringle, Eunice 494
Prior, Herbert 228, 341, 361, **626**, 710, 715
The Prisoner of Shark Island 631
The Prisoner of Zenda (1922) 364, 436, 573, 574, 575, 619
The Prisoner of Zenda (1937) 301, 474
The Prisoner of Zenda (stage play) 485, 661
The Private Life of Helen of Troy 769
The Private Life of Helen of Troy (book) 769
Probert, George 611
Proctor, George D. 441
The Producer (stage play) 166
Professor Beware 154
Professor Oldboy's Rejuvenator 297
Project Moon Base 433
Proof 467
Prouty, Jed 614
Prunella 299
The Prussian Cur 301
Prussing, Margaret 420
P.S. Your Cat Is Dead 224
"The Public Be Damned" (story) 8
Public Enemy 81, 460
Public Opinion 217, 469–470, 657, 659
Puccini, Giacomo 76
Pudd'nhead Wilson 100, 598
Les Puits de Jacob 211
Pulitzer, Joseph 122
Pulitzer Prize Playhouse (television) 622
Punjola 175
Puritan Passions 78, 310, 336, 470–474, **473**, 599, 700, 751
The Purple Monster Strikes (serial) 573
Putnam, George Haven 16
Putting One Over on Ignatz 425
Pygmalion (stage play) 567
Pythagoras 633

Queen Kelly 147, 627
Queen of Sheba 211
Queen of the Movies (stage play) 501
Queen of the Sea 128, 210, 425, 474–476, 697, 726, 759
The Quest of the Sacred Jewel 409, 476–478, 501, 771
Quick, Herbert 158
Quincy Adams Sawyer 286
Quinn, Anthony 287
Quo Vadis? (1913) 18, 419

The Racket 487
Racketty-Packetty House (stage play) 243
Racomar, Ramon 539
"The Radio Beasts" (story) 549
The Radio Detective (serial) 558
"The Radio Man" (story) 549
Radio Patrol 439
"The Radio Planet" (story) 549
Radio-Mania 549, 721; *see also* M.A.R.S.

Rae, Zoe 733
Raffles, the Amateur Cracksman 712
Ragland, John 622
Rags 232
Rain (stage play) 627, 628
Rainer, Luise 564
Rains, Claude 7, 292, 418, 463, 562, 614, 690, 691, 734
Rains, Fred 7
"The Rajah's Diamond" (story) 758
Raker, Lorin 742
Rambeau, Marjorie 188, 347, 350, 648, 657, 664
Rambova, Natacha 679
Ramona 695
Ramper der Tiermensch 367
Rand, Ayn 508
Rand, Sally 500
Randolf, Anders 71, 350, 732
Ranger (movie dog) 96, 194
The Ranger 327
Rankin, Arthur 97, 624
Rankin, Gladys 205
Rankin, McKee 656
Ransom 97, 745–746, 765
Raphael, John 214
Rappe, Virginia 62, 176, 433
Rappee, Erno 116
Rascals, Hal Roach's (a.k.a. "The Little Rascals"; series) 706
Rashômon 213
Rasputin (Gregori Novik) 478, 479, 480, 481
Rasputin and the Empress 34, 83, 154, 481, 484
Rasputin, Damon der Frauen 481
Rasputin, the Black Monk 78, 105, 243, 248, 267, 305, 394, 478–481, 682, 707
Rath, Fred 743
Rathbone, Basil 200, 215, 243, 447, 501–502, 623, 644, 697, 704, 721, 740
Der Rattenfanger von Hamelin 367
The Raven (1912) 66
The Raven (1915) 20, 258, 281, 481–484, 757
The Raven (1935) 365, 456, 519
The Raven (poem) 17, 66, 114
The Raven: The Love Story of Edgar Allan Poe (stage play) 482, **483**
Raver, Harry R. 327
Rawlinson, Herbert 29, 686
Ray, Albert 389, 644, 762
Ray, Charles 143, 159, 255, 389, 490, 503, 648, 762
Razet(t)o, Stella 92, 727
Read, J. Parker 304, 305, 306
The Rear Car (stage play) 485, **485**
Rebecca 251
Rebecca (stage play) 106
Rebecca of Sunnybrook Farm 232, 599
The Red Badge of Courage (book) 305
Red Berry (serial) 392
The Red Dance 45, 310, 480
The Red Dragon 681
Red Lights 96, 174, 274, 408, 484–488, **487**, 702, 704
The Red Lily 468, 542
The Red Mill 103
Redd, Clarence 631
Redemption 518

Redmond, Fergus 204*n*
Reducing 267
Reed, Dr. R. Ralston 657, 658, 659
Reed, Florence 106, 699
Reed, Luther 674
Reed, Myrtle 15–16, 218
Reed, Tom 81
Reefer Madness 107, 523, 692
Reeve, Arthur B. 558, 708
Regeneration 91, 404, 582
Rehearsal for Murder (television) 311
Reicher, Emanuel 321, 599
Reicher, Ernest 321
Reicher, Frank 75, 110, 169, 321, 397, 401, 470 471, 598, 599, 658, 659, 688, 697
Reicher, Hedwig 321
Reid, Hal 726
Reid, Wallace 62, 147, 215, 216, 217, 222, 223–224, **224**, 225, 678, 697
Reidt, Robert 626
Reifenstahl, Leni 564
Reign of Terror 562
The Reincarnation of Karma 544, 647, 668
Reinhardt, Max 46, 81, 247
Reinhold, Judge 71
Reisner, Charles 399, 400
The Rejected Woman 190, 661
Rejuvenation (book) 423
Remember Last Night? 34, 691
The Remittance Man 619
Remo, Andrew 301
Renaldo, Duncan 643
Renard, Maurice 411, 462
Renegades 631
Renick, Ruth 664
Rescher, Jay 416
Restitution 115, 746–747
The Restless Sex 123
Resurrection (1927) 256, 695
Resurrection (1931) 38, 696
Resurrection (stage play) 634
The Return of Chandu (serial) 331, 468, 680, 745
The Return of Dr. Fu Manchu 597
The Return of Dr. Fu Manchu (book) 739
The Return of Dr. X 82
The Return of Jimmy Valentine 548
The Return of Martin Donnelly 345
The Return of Peter Grimm (1926) 93, 225, 469, 488–491
The Return of Peter Grimm (1935) 33, 491
The Return of Peter Grimm (stage play) 397, 488, 711
The Return of Sherlock Holmes 673
The Return of Tarzan 301, 555
The Return of the Ape Man 271, 681
The Return of the Terror 138, 145, 636, 641
The Return of the Vampire 130
Reubens, Alma 41
Revalles, Flora 173
Revenge of the Zombies 496
Revier, Dorothy 240, 732
Revier, Harry 731–732
Revolt of the Zombies 585
The Reward of the Faithless 47, 363, 454, 491–494, 604, 609, 648, 730
Reynolds, Ben 571
Reynolds, Vera 199, 499, **499**
R.F.D. 10,000 B.C. 342
Rhodes, Harrison 654

Rice, Elmer 212, 213
Rich, Irene 380, 381, 382
Rich, Lillian 37
Richard III (stage play) 30, 154
Richardson, Ralph 173
Richman, Charles 27, 28, 130
Ricketts, Tom 258, 495
Ricksen, Lucille 30, 624
The Riddle 145
Riders of the Purple Sage 296
Ridgely, Cleo 298
Ridgely, Richard 228, 298, 359, 360, 361, 710, 742, 743
Riesenfeld, Dr. Hugo (also "Reisenfeld") 290, 578, 742
Rigby, L.G. 401
The Right to be Happy 7, 494–496, **495**, 769
The Rights of Man: A Story of War's Red Blotch 743
Rigoletto (opera) 227, 228, 266
Riley, Edna 111
Riley, James Whitcomb 275
The Rime of the Ancient Mariner (poem) 10, 11, 12, 111, 114
Rin-Tin-Tin (movie dog) 96, 569, 634, **635**, 635, 636
Rin Tin Tin Unter Verbrechern (*Rin-Tin-Tin among Criminals*) 635
Rinehart, Mary Roberts 21, 89–90, 174, 390, 391
Ring, Frances 397, 603
The Ring 616
Rio Bravo 317
Rio Rita 349
Ripley, Arthur 249
Risdon, Elisabeth 297
Ristori, Adelaide 548
Ritchard, Cyril 448
Ritchie, Franklyn 328–329
Ritter, John 89
Ritz Brothers 241
The Rivals 617
The River's End 231
Riverworld (stories) 100
Rizard, George 390
Roach, Bert 301, 311, 312, 571, 649
Roach, Hal 20, 28, 53, 82, 86, 96, 255, 289, 403, 705, 706, 723, 770
The Road to Arcady (stage play) 283
The Road to Mandalay 20, 355, 563, 606, 609, 630
The Road to Rome (stage play) 769
The Road to Ruin 468
The Road to Yesterday 44, 62, 199, 200, 212, 221, 320, 348, 357, 358, 496–500, **499**, 602, 647, 648, 760
The Roaring Twenties 404
Robards, Jason **718**, 719
Robbins, Clarence Aaron "Tod" 421
Robbins, Marc 60
Robbins, Tod 606
Robert-Houdin, Jean Eugene 558, 592
Roberts, John 209
Roberts, Mr. 374
Roberts, R.R. 363
Roberts, Theodore **74**, 75, **76**, 76, 221, 242, 341, 379, 776
Robertson, Imogene 630
Robertson, John Stuart 152–153, 154–155, 182–183, 184

Robeson, Paul 98, 132
Robin Hood 561, 562, 565, 768
Robin Hood (1922) 286, 400, 433, 436, 439, 468
Robinson, Edward G. 275, 292, 524, 651, 754
Robinson, G.H. 609
Robot Monster 455
Robson, Eleanore 41
Robson, Mary 276–277
Robur el conquistador (*Robur the Conqueror*) (book) 208
Rock, Joe 53
Rocket from Manhattan (radio special) 549
Rocky Jones, Space Ranger (television) 37, 496
Rodin, Auguste 70
Roemheld, Heinz 292
Rogers, Charles 339
Rogers, Ginger 203, 762
Rogers, Marion 641
Rogers, Richard 100, 584, 585
Rogers, Roy 669
Rogers, Will 5, 102, 243, 261–262, **262**, 263, 304, 343, 382, 438, 439
The Rogues of Sherwood Forest 439
The Rogues Tavern 331
Rohmer, Sax 290, 739, 740
Roland, Ruth 542, 545, 546, 669
Rolfe, B.A. 352
Roman Scandals 474
The Romance of Elaine (serial) 82, 704, 745
The Romance of Tarzan 48, 95, 289, 339, 542, 555
The Romance of the Mummy 167
The Romantic Journey 215, 478, 500–502
Romeo and Juliet (1916) 43
Romeo and Juliet (1936) 424
Romeo and Juliet (stage play) 41, 249
Römer, Rev. A.H.C. 206
Romero, George 108, 735
Romola 292
Rooney, Mickey 699
Roop, J.L. 343
Roosevelt, Theodore 27, 672, 744
Root, Elihu 27
Rope 691
Roscoe, Alan 256
Rose, Edward E. 485
Rose, Jackson 29, 544
Rose of the Alley 329
Rose of the Rancho 221, 503
Rose of the Rancho (stage play) 581
The Rose Tattoo 449
Rosell, William 477
Rosemary's Baby 368
Rosen, Phil 126, 193, 194, 249, 604, 605, 679, 681
Rosenberg, Alfred 368
Rosenberg, Sol 481
Rosher, Clarence 751
Rosher, Dorothy 703
Rosita 271
Rosseau, Paul 695
Rossitto, Angelo 510, **510**, 511, **511**
Rosson, Arthur 328, 668, 749
Rosson, Gladys 328
Rosson, Hal 120, 214, 328, 668, 749
Rosson, Helen(e) 328, 329, 647, 648, 749
Rosson, Queenie 328
Rosson, Richard 328, 668

Rostand, Edmund 132, 235*n*
Rostand, Maurice 235
Rothacker, Watterson S. 241
Rothapfel, S.L. 27, 349, 578
Roussell, Henry 751
Rowland, Richard 253, 254, 573
Royster, Sarah Elmira 19
Ruben, José 120–121
Ruggles, Charles 447, 487
Ruggles of Red Gap 69, 213, 659
Rule, B.C. (Beverly) 14
The Ruling Passion 429, 430, 747
Rumplestiltskin 450
Running Wild 212, 272, 661
Rupert of Hentzau 411
R.U.R. 549, 559
R.U.R. (stage play) 231
Russell, John 538
Russell, Lillian 481
Russell, Maria 249
Russell, Martha 427
Russell, Reid 224
Ruth of the Range (serial) 546
Ruth of the Rockies (serial) 546
Rye, Stellan 32

Saboteur 691
The Sacred Ruby 713–714
The Sacred Ruby see *The House of Mystery*
The Sacrifice at the Spillway 777
Sag Harbor (stage play) 329
Sainpolis, John 212, 457, 465, 491, 618, 619, 743
Saint, Devil and Woman 502–503, 519
St. John, Howard 622
Sal of Singapore 495
Salisbury, Monroe 455
Sally in Our Alley 641
Sally of the Sawdust 350, 661
Salmonova, Lyda 367
Salome (1923) 382
Salome (stage play) 99
The Salvation Hunters 108, 643
Salvation Nell (1915) 428
Sampson, Teddy 218
Samuelson, G.B. 465, 537
"San Francisco" (story) 745
Sands of Iwo Jima 123
Sanford, Stanley (Tiny) 7
Santa 168
Santell, Alfred 238, 704
Santschi, Tom 720
The Saphead 112
Sardou, Victorien 46, 488, 655, 656
Satan Junior 8
Satan, or the Drama of Humanity 537
Satan's Pawn 135
Satan's Private Door 156
Satana (1912) 537
The Satin Girl 241, 747–749
Saturday Night 105, 358
Saunders, Mrs. Celestine 641
Savage, Fred 71
Savage, Henry W. 132, 133
The Savage 79, 343, 505–507, **505**, 750
Saved by Wireless 158
Saville, Victor 367
Sawyer, Laura 712
Sawyer, Lucile 545
The Scar of Shame 697
The Scarabaeus 602

Scaramouche 364, 576, 643
Scardon, Paul 211, 347
The Scarecrow (stage play) 599, 754
The Scarecrow, Or The Glass of Truth, a Tragedy of the Ludicrous (stage play) 471, 474
Scared Stiff (1945) 83
Scared Stiff (1953) 82, 222, 225
Scared to Death 160, 724
Scarface (1932) 474, 548, 701
The Scarlet Band 208; see also *The Flying Torpedo*
The Scarlet Car 592
The Scarlet Claw 82
The Scarlet Clue 681
Scarlet Day 92
The Scarlet Empress 564
The Scarlet Letter 42
Scarlet Pages 217
The Scarlet Pimpernel 650
The Scarlet Virgin 620
Schade, Betty 493, 597, 730
Schade, Fritz 493
Schayer, E. Richard 481
Scheherazade 7, 8, 29, 127, 678
Schenck, Earl 15, 37, 71
Schenck, Joseph 22, 131, 406, 611, 766
Schertzinger, Victor 93, 94, 195, 468, 490
Schildkraut, Joseph 310, 498, 499, 517
Schildkraut, Rudolf 498
Schnab, Mirza Ahmed 515
Schnall, Ida 600, 601, 759
Schneiderman, George 644
Scholl, Danny 51
Schraber, Ella 622
Schrader, Genevieve 394
Schreier, Otto K. 391
Schrock, Raymond L. 181
Schüfftan, Eugen 559
Schwarzenegger, Arnold 720
Scott, Agnes 594
Scott, Howard 426
Scott, Mansfield 440
Scott, Sir Walter 168
Scott, William 114–115
The Scoundrel 105, 227
Scrambled Wives 725
The Scrap of Paper 713n
A Scream in the Night (1919) 268, 320, 338, 352, 372, 505–507, 614
A Scream in the Night (1935) 496
The Screaming Shadow (serial) 317
Screen Highlights #1 395
Scrooge (1913) 495
Scrooge (1935) 495
Scrooge; or Marley's Ghost 495
Scully, Frank 47
The Sea Beast 153, 154, 542
The Sea Hawk 301, 468, 568
The Sea Urchin 221
The Sea Wolf (1920) 553
The Sea Wolf (1930) 191, 704
The Sea Wolf (book) 304
Seabrook, William 599
Sealed Lips 501
The Sealed Room 17, 481
Séance on a Wet Afternoon 275
The Searchers 168
Searle, Kamuela 555
Searle, Veta 657
Seay, Charles M. 196
Sebastian, Dorothy 570

Second Fiddle 474
"The Secret History of Edypus, the World Empire" (story) 100
The Secret Kingdom (serial) 597
Secret of the Blue Room 59, 77, 81, 350, 573, 641, 714
Secret of the Chateau 283, 388, 442
The Secret of the Dead 466
Secret of the Loch 459
The Secret of Treasure Island (serial) 680
The Secret Power (book) 674
Secret Sorrow 191
The Secret Window 141
Secrets of the French Police 270, 405, 664
Seddon, Margaret 79
Sedgwick, Edward 96, 257, 259, 337, 339, 458, 459, 571, 572, 649
Sedgwick, Eileen 571
Sedley, Henry 624, 625
Seigman(n), George 19, 20
Seitz, Geroge B. 45, 97, 745
Seitz, John 574
Seizure 141
Selander, Lesley 670
Selbie, Evelyn 140
Selby, Charles 735
Sellers, Peter 739
Selwyn, Arch 401
Selwyn, Edgar 664
Selwynne, Clarissa 304
Selznick, David O. 468, 653
Selznick, Louis J 188
Selznick, Myron 411
Semon, Larry 451, 622
Sennett, Mack 17, 21, 23, 69, 158, 176, 208, 237, 240, 255, 256, 258, 303, 312, 315, 316, 379, 382, 399, 433, 487, 493, 558, 570, 639, 657, 680, 705, 706, 760
Señorita 520, 596
Sensation Seekers 186
Sentimental Tommy 184, 191
Sentimental Tommy (stage play) 191
The Sequel to the Diamond from the Sky (serial) 143
Sequoia 569
The Serpent of Paris 575
Serrano, Vincent 189, 190, *191*
Service, Robert 692
Seven Brides for Seven Brothers 79
Seven Footprints to Satan 7, 39, 82, 97, 255, 432, 433, 434, 485, 507–511, *509, 510, 511*, 563, 567, 703, 722
Seven Keys to Baldpate 3, 142, 238, 276, 354, 389
Seven Keys to Baldpate (1917) 325, 465, 524
Seven Keys to Baldpate (1929) 135
Seven Keys to Baldpate (1929) 750
Seven Keys to Baldpate (book) 701, 705
The Seven Pearls (serial) 567
The Seven Samurai 563
Seven Years Bad Luck 381, 544
Seventh Heaven 491
The Seventh Victim 513
The Severed Hand 97
Sewall, Olivia 99
Sewell, Alma 99
Sex 306
The Sex Lure 265, 724
Seymour, Laura 409

Sh! The Octopus (1937) 280, 283, 299, 448, 507, 754
Sh! The Octopus (stage play) 138, 151, 511
The Shadow (serial) 15
Shadow of a Doubt 691
Shadow of Chinatown (serial) 339
The Shadow of the East 61, 105, 267, 511–514, *513*, 690, 692
The Shadow of the East (book) 512
The Shadow of the Law 289
The Shadow Returns 681
The Shadow Strikes 96, 199, 266
Shadows 765
Shadows (1914) 150
Shadows of Suspicion 425
Shadows of the North 512
Shadows of the Sea 512
Shadows of the West 512
Shakespeare, William 132, 168, 249, 544, 763
Shame 729
The Shanghai Gesture (stage play) 106
Shannon, Alexander 156
Shannon, Norris 267
The Shark God 644
Shattered Dreams 243
Shaw, Brinsley 374
Shaw, George Bernard 536, 567
Shaw, Harold 578
Shaw, Irwin 564
Shay, William E. 128, 747
Shayne, Edith 72
She (1908) 237, 514, 602
She (1911) 388, 414, 514, 559
She (1916) 514
She (1917) 514–516, 605
She (1925) 75, 211, 516
She (1935) 34, 342, 516
She (book) 366, 580, 602, 720
The She-Creature 82
She Demons 275
She Goes to War 45
The She Wolf 669
She-Wolf of London 669
Shearer, Athole 627
Shearer, Norma 119, 254, 617, 619, 627
Shearne, Edith 193
Sheehan, Perley Poore 285, 775
The Sheik 62, 211, 231 364, 434, 468, 512, 523, 677, 747
The Sheik Steps Out 680
Sheldon, E. Lloyd 105
Sheldon, Edward 305
Sheldon, Jean 249
Shelley, Mary Wollstonecraft 196, 302, 323, 324, 735
Sherlock Holmes (1916) 476, 484
Sherlock Holmes (1922) 34, 190, 524
Sherlock Holmes (1932) 69, 154, 704
Sherlock Holmes (2009) 368
Sherlock Holmes (stage play) 7, 111, 688
Sherlock Holmes and the Secret Weapon 290
Sherlock Holmes in the Great Murder Mystery 481
Sherlock Holmes, Jr. (1911) 237, 738
Sherlock, Jr. (1924) 407, 748
Sherman, Evelyn 594
Sherman, Lowell 242

Sherry, J. Barney 134, *134*, 455
Sherwood, George J. 103
Sherwood, Robert 41
Sherwood, Robert Emmett 769
Sherwood, William 587
The Shielding Shadow (serial) 272, 507
Shields, Ernest 493
"Ship of Ishtar" (story) 508
"Ship of My Dreams" (song) 719
Shipman, Nell 477
Shirk, Adam Hull 241, 391
Shirley, Arthur 195
The Shooting of Dan McGrew 692
Shore Acres 364
Short, Dan 140
Short, Florence 743
Short, Josephine 183
Shotwell, Marie 566, 567, 568, 661–662
Should Husbands Work? 668
Should She Obey? 161
Shoulder Arms 400
The Show 33, 39, 335, 377, 421, 516–519
Show Boat 82, 240
The Show of Shows 8
A Shriek in the Night (1915) 715
A Shriek in the Night (1933) 644, 762
Shubert, Lee 329
Shurtleff, C.E. 543
"The Shuttle Soul" (story) 166
The Sideshow 487
Sidney, George 240
Sidney, Sylvia 399
Siegel, Mr. 374
Siegfried and Roy 593
Siegler, Allen 274
Siegmann, George 103, 434
Sierra, Gregorio Martínez 244
The Si-Fan Mysteries (book) 740
The Sign of the Cross 562, 610, 631, 732
Silence 664
The Silent Accuser 335
The Silent Call 96
The Silent Command (1915) 7, 212, 274, 519–520
The Silent Command (1923) 126, 273, 519, 696, 730
Silents Please (television) 500
Sills, Milton 62, 183, 189, 190–191, 255, 265, 300, 306, 317, 319, 380, 382
Silver Threads Among the Gold (stage play) 362
Silverstreak (movie dog) 96, 97
The Simple Case of Susan (book) 181
Sinclair, Upton 659
Sing Sing Nights 87
Le Singe qui parle (stage play) 400, 401, 403
Singed Wings 440, 520–522, *521*, 571
Singin' in the Rain 13, 84
The Singing Fool 45, 646
Single Wives 51
Singleton, Joseph 738
Sinister Hands 167
Sinners in Silk 6, 47, 133, 264, 272, 394, 400, 488, 522–524, *524*, 571, 622
The Sins of Rosanne 10, 37, 768, 772

The Sins of the Children 697
Siodmak, Curt 229, 290, 573
Siodmak, Robert 244
The Siren of Seville 596
The Siren of the Sea (1911) 127, 425
Sirens of the Seas (1917) 259, 587
The Sisters-in-Law (book) 50
A Sister's Silence 268
Six Hours to Live 92, 631
Sjöström, Victor 254, 568
Den Skaebnesvangre Opfindelse 149
Skelton, Red 15, 427
The Sketch Book of Geoffrey Crayon, Gent 261
The Skin of Our Teeth (stage play) 106, 325
Skinner, Cornelia Otis 468
Skinner, Marian (Marion) 484
Skippy 235, 468
Skirts (1921) 381
Skladanowsky, Emil 74
Skladanowsky, Max 74
Sky Eye 713
Sky-High Saunders 749
The Sky Ranger (serial) 745
The Sky Skidder 283, 749–750
The Sky Train (stage play) 174
Sky's the Limit 765
Skyscraper 495
The Slacker 160, 694–695
Slave of Desire 133, 160, 259, 295
Sleep No More (radio) 739
The Sleep of Cym(b)a Roget 273, 551
A Sleeping Memory 131, 169, 244, 295, 695
Sloan, Tod 708
Sloane, Paul 358, 359
Sloman, Edward 543, 544–545, 620, 622
Small, Edward 239
Smalley, Phillips 186, 738
Smiley, Joseph W. 325, 326, 465
Smilin' Through 78, 110, 131, 173, 273, 310, 750–751
"Smilin' Through" (song) 750
Smilin' Through (stage play) 750, 751
The Smiling Ghost 82, 241
Smith, Albert E. 35, 345
Smith, C. Aubrey 566, 660, 661
Smith, Charlotte 22
Smith, Dick 152
Smith, George Albert 7, 198, 208
Smith, Hamilton 683
Smith, Noel Mason 96, 97
Smith, Pete 232
Smith, Richard John (aka "O. Smith") 63, 65
Smuggler's Island 462
Snatched from a Burning Death 493
Snow, Marguerite 29, 234, 414, 514, 559
Snow, Mortimer 145
Snow White (1916) 450
So This Is Marriage? 193, 335
The Social Leper 617
Sojin, Kamiyama 21, 23, **23**, 87, 88, 271, 511, 560, 563, 654, 739
Something Always Happens 564
Something to Think About 217
Somewhere in America 329
The Son-Daughter 564
The Son of Dr. Jekyll 151
Son of Dracula 81, 311, 448, 662

Son of Frankenstein 34, 81, 413, 444, 491, 767
Son of Kong 306
A Son of Satan 99, 228, 535
The Son of Tarzan (serial) 555, 732
Son of the Sheik 231, 679
The Song of Bernadette 217, 260
Song of Hate 46
Song of the West 349
Sonny 649
The Sons of the the Sheik (book) 512
The Sorceress 465
"La Sorcière" (story) 655
Sorrell, William 634
Sorrell and Son 429, 630
The Sorrows of Satan 20, 272, 393, 437, 454, 522
The Sorrows of Satan (1911) 537
The Sorrows of Satan (1917) 537
The Sorrows of Satan (1926) 536–540, **537**, **539**, 674, 729, 742
The Sorrows of Satan (book) 134, 536, 604, 674
The Sorrows of Satan (stage play) 636
Sothern, Ann 248
Sothern, E.H. (Edward Hugh) 372, 373, 374, 672
The Soul of Bronze 593, 751–752
The Soul of Satan 105, 267
The Soul's Cycle 752–753
Souls for Sale 524, 576
Souls Which Pass in the Night 29
Sous le ciel d'Orient (*Under the Eastern Sky*) 466
Sousa, John Philip 490
Southard, John Bennett 106
Southern, E.H. 119
Southern, Eve 105, 254, 256
The Spaniard 498
The Spanish Dancer 768
Sparks, Ned 209, 441
Sparrows 138, 407, 653, 681, 751, 770
"Sparrows" (story) 251
Speare, Edith 36
The Speckled Band (stage play) 132
"The Speckled Band" (story) 132, 320
The Speed Spook 723, 726, 753–754
Speeding Venus 723
Spellbound 540–542, 546
Spellbound (1916) 243
Spence, Ralph 21, 174, 237–238, 240, 241, 433, 434, 505, 571, 754, 770
Spencer, Len 549
The Sphinx 96, 681
The Sphinx Has Spoken 221
The Spider 315, 449, 501, 524, 562
The Spider (stage play) 593
The Spider's Web 99
Spielberg, Steven 290
The Spiral Staircase 244
Spiritisme (stage play) 488
The Spoilers 720
Spooks Run Wild 129, 266, 681
Spoor, George K. 14
The Sport of the Gods 191
The Spreading Dawn 750
The Squall (stage play) 585
The Squaw Man 140, 221, 282, 468, 497, 648, 732
Stahl, Rose 42
Stallings, Charles 416

Standing, Aubrey 295
Standing, Guy 173, 295
Standing, Herbert 173, 295
Standing, Herbert Jr. 295
Standing, Percy 195, 295, 323, 324, 587
Standing, Wyndham *171*, 173, *173*, 295, 324, 751
Stanlaws, Penrhyn 440, 521, 522
Stanley, Arthur 552
Stanley, Forrest 621, 675
Stanley, George 753
Stanton, Richard 268, 650
Stanwood, Rita 221
Stanwyck, Barbara 224, 608
A Star Is Born 765
The Star of India 147, 356, 556, 671, 754–755
The Star Rover 29, 542–545
The Star Rover (book) 543
Star Trek (television) 388
Stark Mad 20, 23, 317, 440, 614, 701, 702, 755–757, **757**
Starke, Pauline 102, 115, 189
Starlight (movie horse) 89
Starr, Frances 78
State of the Union 34
Staulcup, M.P. 654
Steamboat Bill, Jr. 69, 268
Stecher, "Daredevil" Curly Joe 71, 576
Stedman, Marshall 447
Stedman, Myrtle 447
Steel(e), Vernon 203, 213–214, 453
Steele, Frederic Dorr 708
Steger, Julius 771
Stein, Evaleen 275
Steinach, Eugen (Dr.) 48, 49
Steinach Procedure 48, 49, 50, 50*n*, 51, 623
Steinbeck, John 652
Steiner, William 269, 713
Stella Dallas 260, 673
Stella Maris 217, 232, 662
Stephens, Edwin 132, 133
Stepping Out (stage play) 7
Sterling, Ford 70, 255, 258, 652
Sterling, Paul 420
Stern, Ernest 777
Stevens, Edwin 37, 144, 145
Stevens, Emily 695
Stevens, Louis 174
Stevenson, Charles A. 641
Stevenson, Robert Louis 59, 60, 63, 64, 65, 74, 130, 149, 150, 151, 152, 153, 157, 158, 202, 330, 549, 671, 691, 735, 758
Stewart, Anita 11, 232, 347, 643
Stewart, Frederic 8
Stewart, Jimmy 606
Stewart, Roy 138–139
Stillson, George D. 589
The Sting 456
Stingaree 424
Stockdale, Carlton 53
Stoker, Bram 30, 100, 301, 409, 577
Stokowski, Leopold 502
Stolen Orders 594
The Stolen Play 542, 545–546
The Stolen Voice 266, 411, 546–549, 581
Stone, Lewis 241, 341, **342**, 343, 344, 575, 576, 643
Stonehouse, Ruth 14
The Stool Pigeon 572

Storey, Edith 168–169, **169**, 170, 204, 205, 599
Storm, Gale 213
The Story of Alexander Graham Bell 481
The Story of Mankind 746
The Story of Vernon and Irene Castle 203
The Story Without a Name 62, 93, 120, 214, 245, 306, 433, 549–551, **550**
Stowe, Harriet Beecher 100
Stowitts, (Hubert I.) 368, 370
Strait-Jacket 609
Strange, Michael 377
Strange Adventure 382
The Strange Case of Dr. Jekyll and Mr. Hyde (novel) 74, 77, 149, 157, 502
The Strange Case of Mary Page (serial) 477
The Strange Death of Adolf Hitler 767
The Strange Mr. Gregory 667, 681
The Strange Story of Sylvia Gray 35, 345
"The Strange Woman" (story) 5
Stranger Than Fiction 141
Strangers of the Evening 83
Strangler of the Swamp 641
The Stranglers of Paris 552–553
The Stranglers of Paris (stage play) 552
Street Angel 695
Street Scene (stage play) 212
Streets of Laredo 11
The Streets of New York (stage play) 468
Strickfaden, Kenneth 772
Strickland, Helen 227–228, 281, 743
Striker, Joseph 713
Strindberg, August 193
Stripped for a Million 625
Strode, Woody 368
Stromberg, Hunt 416
Strong, Austin 235
Strong, Eugene 716
Strong, Porter 436, 437, 706
The Strong Way 594
The Strongest 518
Strongheart (movie dog) 96
The Struggle 108
The Strugglers (stage play) 545
Struss, Karl 153, 711
Stuart, Alexander 687
Stuart Webbs: Das Panzergewölbe 81
Stubborn Cinderella (stage play) 501
The Student of Prague (1916) 32, 367
The Student of Prague (1926) 376
A Study in Scarlet (1914) 463, 564
A Study in Scarlet (book) 340
Stumar, Charles 573
Sturgess, Preston 548
Submarine 14
Such a Little Queen 258
Such Men Are Dangerous 631
Sugarfoot 548
The Suicide Club 78, 691
Sullivan, C. Gardner 93, 94, 95, 251
Sullivan, E.P 40, 41, 42
Sullivan, Frederick 503

Sullivan, Pat 592
Sullivan, Sir Arthur 503
Sullivan, Thomas Russell 151, 202
Sullivan's Travels 548
Sully, Anna Beth 560
Summers, Mary 161
Summerville, George ("Slim") 312, 381, 706
Sumurun 367
The Sun God 462
The Sun Sets at Dawn 359
Sunrise 79, 81, 86, 206, 491, 621, 711, 751
Sunset Blvd. 35, 256, 316, 350, 440, 524, 622
Super Speed 723
Superman (television) 83
Supernatural 440, 585
Suratt, Valeska 514, 515, 516, 747
Surrender 622
Survival 584
Susan and God (stage play) 474
Susan Lennox, Her Fall and Rise 335, 336
Suspense 186
Sutherland, Edward 210, 664, 754
Sutherland, Evelyn Greenleaf 497
Svengali (stage play) 373
Svengali (1927) 584
Svengali (1931) 142, 152, 154, 259, 366, 562, 579, 583, 614
Svengali (1954) 580
Svengali and the Posters 578
Swain, John D. 302
Swain, Mack 255, 312, 644
The Swamp 65
Swanson, Gloria 119, 147, 168, 190, 336, 347, 348, 349, 350, 358, 379, 397, 449, 614, 622, 648, 680, 682
Swanson, Louise 643
Swayze, Patrick 207
Swedenborg, Emanuel 170
Sweet, Blanche 18, 20, 75, **76**, 76, 232, 470, 657
Sweet Kitty Bellairs (1916) 522
Sweet Little Devil (stage play) 78
Swept Away 723
Swickard, Charles 61, 142
Swickard, Joseph/Josef 61, 114, 115, 513, 677, 680
Sydmoth, Louise 643
Sylvia Gray a.k.a. *The Strange Story of Sylvia Gray* 551–552
Sylvia on a Spree 617
The Symbol of the Unconquered 535
Symonds, Henry Roberts 233
"The System of Dr. Tarr and Professor Feather" (story) 481, 637

Tabler, P. Dempsey 555
Das Tagebuch des Dr. Hart 81
Taggart, Ben 514, 515
Talbot, Haydon 60
Talbot, Lyle 762
A Tale of Two Cities 28, 46, 176, 296, 382, 644
A Tale of Two Worlds (book) 674
The Tales of Hoffman (opera) 676
The Tales of Hoffman (stage play) 477
Tales of Terror 454
Taliaferro, Edith 660
Talk About Girls (stage play) 325
The Talker (stage play) 231
Talmadge, Constance 27, 28, 131, 175, 621

Talmadge, Natalie 28, 131
Talmadge, Norma 27, 28, 131, 240, 468, 605, 611, 750, 751
Talmadge, Peggy 131
Talmadge, Richard 89, 315–316, 432, 433, 434, 563
The Tame Cat 757–758
Tampico 168
Tangerine Dream (band) 114
Tanks a Million 289
The Tarantula 169, 311, 697
Target Earth 705
Tarkington, Booth 275, 620
Tarzan and the Golden Lion 313, 553–555, **555**
Tarzan and the Golden Lion (book) 554, 720
Tarzan at the Earth's Core (book) 555
Tarzan of the Apes (1918) 95, 338, 339, 542, 555, 631, 738
Tarzan the Ape Man (1932) 328, 554, 749
Tarzan the Fearless (serial) 573
Tarzan the Mighty (serial) 554
Tarzan the Tiger (serial) 554
Tarzan's Desert Mystery 290
Tarzan's Magic Fountain 745
Tarzan's New York Adventure 95
Tarzan's Revenge 524
Tashman, Lilyan 87
Taurog, Norman 235
Tavares, Arthur (Arturo) 505
Taylor, E. Forrest 647, 648
Taylor, Eleanor 564
Taylor, Elizabeth 104
Taylor, Estelle 682
Taylor, J.O. 306
Taylor, Laurette 329
Taylor, Robert 45, 524
Taylor, William Desmond 9, 37, 53, 62, 223, 545, 644, 646, 662, 663, 664, 753
Taylor, Wilton 558
The Tea House of the August Moon 730
Tearle, Conway 49–50, **50**, **52**, 172, 201, 411, 424, 710, 729
Tell, Olive 352
Tell It to the Marines 306, 481, 524, 607
"The Tell-Tale Heart" (story) 18, 19, 32, 248, 643
Tellegen, Lou 35, 36, 352, 444, 445
The Tempest (stage play) 164
Temple, Shirley 123, 217, 481, 621, 690
The Temple of Venus 115, 654, 758–760
The Temptations of Satan 356, 555–557, 671, 672, 711, 755
The Ten Commandments (1923) 75, 200, 358
The Ten Commandments (1956) 126, 200, 561, 776
Ten Laps to Go 488
Ten Nights in a Barroom 222, 501
Tender Is the Night 260
Tenderloin 646
Tennant, Barbara 708
Tennyson, Alfred Lord 36
Terhune, Albert Payson 201
"La Terribula" (story) 408
Terriss, Tom 418, 419, 420
The Terror 23, 84, 86, 283, 336, 491, 614, 701, 756, 757, 760–761

The Terror (stage play) 760
Terror Aboard 145, 269, 358, 447
Terror Island 267, 372, 434, 439, 557–559, 593, 627
Terrors of the Deep 589
Terry, Alice 364, **364**, 365, 367, 368, 370, 411, 494, 574
Terry, Ellen 42
Terry, Ethel Grey 742
Terwilliger, George 744, 745
Tess of the D'Urbevilles 75, 451
Tess of the D'Urbevilles (book) 12
Tess of the Storm Country 258, 355, 662
Test Pilot 610
Der Teufel (stage play) 132; see also *The Devil*
Tex, Elucidator of Mysteries (series) 712, 713
The Texas Chainsaw Massacre 652
Thalberg, Irving 285, 286, 289, 416, 564, 680
Theby, Rosemary 102, 617
Thelma (book) 674
Thesiger, Ernest 173
They Knew What They Wanted (stage play) 628
The Thief (stage play) 410
A Thief in the Dark 644, 761–763
The Thief of Bagdad (1924) 23, 87, 154, 159, 319, 364, 377, 399, 404, 459, 559–566, **560**, **561**, 619, 775
The Thief of Bagdad (1940) 376, 559, 561, 566
The Thieving Hand 414
Thilby (stage play) 578
The Thin Man 82, 449, 515
The Thin Man (book) 670
The Thin Man (series) 702
The Thing (from Another World) 701
"The Thing on the Doorstep" (story) 56
The Things Men Do 394
Things to Come 562
Think Fast, Mr. Moto 571
The Thinking Machine (book) 180
The Third Degree 272
Thirteen Women 15, 68, 393, 702
The Thirteenth Chair (1919) 82, 86, 126, 207, 476, 566–568, **567**, 661, 671, 716, 749
The Thirteenth Chair (1929) 271, 336, 355, 566, 667, 763–764, 772
The Thirteenth Chair (1937) 566
The Thirteenth Chair (stage play) 566, 763
The Thirteenth Chair (television) 245, 568
The Thirteenth Guest 34, 245, 644, 762
The Thirteenth Hour 29, 96, 194, 416, 568–570, **570**, 630
Thirty Thousand Leagues Under the Sea 589
This Gun for Hire (1942) 474
This Side of Heaven 119
Thomas, Augustus 15, 37, 294, 315, 327, 519, 567, 659, 660, 661, 662
Thomas, Olive 119, 226, 669
Thomas, Queenie 168
Thompson, Duane 489, 573
Thompson, Frederick A. 264
Thompson, Hugh 476
Thompson, William 295–296
Thornton, Edith 270, 271

Thorpe, Morgan 283
Those Who Dare 376, 764–766
Three Ages 400, 766–767, 769
Three Bad Men 403, 644
The Three Black Pennys (book) 651
Three Faces East 501
Three Faces East (stage play) 696
Three-Fingered Jenny 726
Three Miles Up 749
The Three Musketeers (1916) 61
The Three Musketeers (1921) 523, 561, 565, 575, 652, 765
The Three Musketeers (1935) 652
The Three Musketeers (book) 632
The Three Must-Get-Theres 230
The Three Passions 369
Three Sinners 115
The Three Stooges 129, 197, 692
"3,000 Years among the Microbes" (story) 100
Three Wax Men 79
Three Weeks 336, 603
Three Wise Fools 524
Three Wise Girls 488
Thrillby (stage play) 578
Thriller (television) 184
Through the Dark 621
Through the Impossible (stage play) 588
"Through the Veil" (story) 340
Through the Years (stage play) 217
Thunder 607
Thunderbolt 317
Thundering Fleas 706
Thurber, James 651
Thurston, Howard 460, 592, 593, 594
Tia Juana (stage play) 627
Tichenor, Edna **334**, 335–336, 518
Tierney, Gene 207
Tiger Love 459–460
The Tigress 270
Tillie and Gus 484
Tillie's Punctured Romance (1914) 380, 382
Tillie's Punctured Romance (1928) 23
Tin Gods 7
Tin Hats 259, 570–572
Tinney, Frank 630
The Tip Off 572–573
To Have and Have Not 317
To Hell with the Kaiser 15, 245, 283, 352, 416, 587, 767
Tobacco Road (stage play) 306, 432
Todd, Arthur L. 138, 715
Todd, Lola 32, **33**, 34
The Toddlma 24, 252–252, **254**, 255, 256, 509, **510**, 511, 770
Die Todlichen Wünsche (opera) 162
Tokyo Joe 66
Tol'able David 184, 260, 390, 542, 651, 652
Toler, Sidney 176, 193, 762
The Toll of the Sea 87, 563, 621
Tolstoy, Leo 634
Tom Sawyer 226
Tomorrow at Seven 21, 241
Too Many Cooks (stage play) 42
Too Wise Wives 184
Tooker, William H. 112, 266
Topper Takes a Trip 515
Topsy and Eva 630
Torchy Blane (series) 754
Torrence, David 69

Torrence, Ernest 69, 222, 287, 289, 292, 449, 520, 522
Torn Curtain 314, 456
La Tosca (stage play) 46
Toscanini, Arturo 739
The Toss of a Coin 92
Tourneur, Jacques 70, 354, 368
Tourneur, Maurice 70, 71, 172, 173, 203, 217, 232, 256, 285, 299–300, 336, 416, 450, 460, 519, 546, 547, 549, 578, 579, 590, 602, 603, 605, 637, 638, 639, 640, 648, 682, 718, 778
Tovar, Lupita 110, 168
Tower of Ivory (book) 172
Tower of London (1939) 444, 740
Towers, Harry Alan 739
Tracy, Lee 231
Tracy, Spencer 108, 151, 153, 157
Traffic in Souls 282, 395, 592
La Tragedie imperiale 481
The Tragedies of the Crystal Globe 647
The Tragical History of Doctor Faustus (stage play) 132
The Trail of Robin Hood 669
The Trail of the Cigarette 713n
The Trail of the Octopus (serial) 142
Train, Arthur 411, 412
Transatlantic Tunnel 448, 691, 728
Transgression 347
The Transgressor 355
Travolta, John 236
Treacher, Arthur 239
Treasure Girl (stage play) 45
Treasure of Fear 83
The Treasure of the Sea 169
Tree, Herbert Beerbohm 536, 578, 579
Trenton, Pell **654**
The Trey o' Hearts (serial) 47
Trick for Trick (1933) 194, 562, 592
Trick for Trick (stage play) 276
Trifling Women 47, 48, 69, 71, 133, 344, 402, 573–577, **576**, 604
Trilby (1908) 76
Trilby (1915) 70, 271, 330, 331, 519, 546, 547, 577–580, 618
Trilby (1923) 33, 82, 87, 175, 331, 405–406, 460, 461, 492, 581–584, **582**, 594, 603
Trilby (book) 60, 214, 242, 463, 546, 547, 577, 581, 706
Trilby (stage play) 77, 112, 212, 214, 274, 501, 502, 536, 546, 548, 577–578, 657, 667
Trilby and Little Billee 578
A Trip to Mars 384
A Trip to Paradise 132, 140, 199, 274, 388, 584–585, 654, 719
A Trip to the Moon 339, 588
The Triple Clue 713n
"The Triple Cross" (story) 721
Tritschler, Conrad 583
The Triumph of Venus 324, 389, 586–587
Trog 609
Trotsky, Leon 27
Trouble in Paradise 243
Truex, Ernest 235, **236**, 237
The Trumpet Blows 524
Trunnelle, Mabel 228, 360, 361, 522, 710, 742
Trutz Simplex (book) 63, 65
Tryon, Glenn 722, 723

Tucker, George Loane 172, 395, 397, 398, 639, 709
Tucker, Lorenzo 777
Tully, Richard Watson 296, 581, 582, 583, 584, 597, 644
Tupper, Edith Sessions 283
"The Turn of the Screw" (story) 252
Turn to the Right 166, 494, 501
Turn to the Right (stage play) 573
Turnbull, Margaret 75, 77, 469, 470, 657
Turner, J. Alan 656
Turner, Lana 564
Turner, Otis 430
Turner, Ted 184
Turner, William H. 745, 749
Turpin, Ben 240, 706
Tut-Tut and His Terrible Tomb 168, 301
Tut! Tut! King 301
Tuttle, Frank 310 471, 472, 474
Tuttle, Margaret 199
Twain, Mark 99, **103**, 577, 59, 640, 770; see also Clemens, Samuel Langhorne
"Twelve Golden Curls" (story) 690
Twenty Thousand Feats Under the Sea 592
Twenty Thousand Laughs Under the Sea 592
20,000 Leagues Under the Sea (1905) 588
20,000 Leagues Under the Sea (1916) 112, 180, 300, 415, 430, 557, 559, 587–592, **588**, **590**, **591**, 703
20,000 Leagues Under the Sea (1954) 343
Twenty Thousand Leagues Under the Sea (book) 587, 590
Twenty Thousand Legs Under the Sea 592
Twentieth Century 445
The Twilight Zone (television) 749
Twinkle, Twinkle (stage play) 45
The Twinkler 643
The Twins' Double 463
Twisted Souls 592–594
Two Arabian Knights 306
The Two Diamonds (book) 602
Two-Faced Woman 23
The Two Mrs. Carrolls 82
The Two Natures within Him 68
The Two Orphans 659 594
The Two-Soul Woman 140, 186, 265, 316, 502, 594–597, 618, 686
2001: A Space Odyssey 559
The Typhoon (stage play) 65

Ulivi, Giulio 712
Ulmer, Edgar G. 312, 368, 370
Ulrich, Lenore 296
El último varón sobre la tierra 304
The Unbroken Road 112
"Uncle Silas" (story) 252
Uncle Tom's Cabin (1918) 725
Uncle Tom's Cabin (1927) 311
Uncle Tom's Cabin (stage play) 40, 580
Unconquered 470, 597–599, 659, 688
Under the Red Robe 605
Under the Top 212
Under Two Flags 286, 421, 596
Under Two Flags (stage play) 193
Undersea Kingdom (serial) 619

Underworld 317
Undine (1912) 600
Undine (1916) 210, 434, 466, 599–602, 654, 759
Undine (book) 599–600
Undine (stage play) 601
The Undying Flame 173, 602–603, 716
"The Undying Thing" (story) 56
The Uneasy Three 230
The Unfaithful Wife 193, 248, 603–605
Unger, Gladys 419
Unheimliche Geschichten (1920) 376
Unheimliche Geschichten (1932) 367
Die Unheimlichen Wünsche (*Unholy Wishes*) 162
The Unholy Night 33, 69, 563, 614, 772
The Unholy Three (1925) 133, 312, 421, 517, 605, 606, 639
The Unholy Three (1930) 45, 224, 240, 422, 439, 551, 614
The Unholy Three (book) 60
The Uninvited 225
The Uninvited Guest 592
Union Pacific 200
The Unknown (1921) 433
The Unknown (1927) 289, 517, 605–610, **607**, 619, 639
Unknown Island 700, 705
The Unknown Lover 217
The Unknown Purple 20, 60, 61, 130, 274, 315, 404, 405, 406, 433, 434, 610–613, **611**, 742
The Unknown Purple (stage play) 610–611
Unknown Treasures 613–615, 777
Unseen Forces 10, 34, 122, 137, 202, 336, 615–617, **616**, 741
Unseen Hands 37, 48, 139, 398, 767–768
The Unseen Witness 713
Unsell, Eve 110–111
The Unsuspected 542
The Untameable 4, 212, 265, 272, 491, 502, 556, 596, 618–620, 755
Untamed 73
Untamed Youth 394
Untamed Justice 274
Untamed Youth 39, 139, 398
An Unwilling Cowboy 169
Up the Ladder 29, 97, 620–622, 675, 729
Up the Ladder (stage play) 252, 305, 329, 620, 685
Up the Ladder (television) 622
"The Upper Berth" (story) 252
Urban, Charles 208
Urban, Josef 72
Urban, Joseph 583, 676
Urson, Frank 233
The Userer's Grip 281

Vale, Louise 683
Vale, Travers 682–683
Valentine, Joseph A. 212, 691
Valentino (1951) 368
Valentino, Rudolph 37, 48, 62, 123, 155, 168, 189, 231, 257, 275, 289, 306, 358, 364, 365, 371, 393, 404, 439, 512, 513, 565, 576, 607, 677, 678, **678**, 679–681, 682, 695, 747
Valkyrien, Valda 293–294

Vallee, Rudy 154
The Valley of Lost Souls 697
The Valley of Night 67, 68; see also: *The Curious Case of Judge Legarde*
Valley of the Giants 224, 306
Valley of the Zombies 350
Valli, Alida 585
Valli, Virginia 140, 584–585, 620, 621, 650, **651**, 652, 653, **718**, 719, 729
Vamping Venus 34, 103, 255, 766, 768–770
The Vampire (1913) 41, 173
The Vampire (stage play) 193, 448
The Vampire Bat 97, 290
The Vampire's Ghost 670
The Vampire's Trail 173
Van Auker, Cecil 297
Vance, Louis Joseph 112, 116, 117, 119, 409, 597
Vanderbilt, Cornelius III 27
Vanderbilt, Gloria 255
van den Broek, John 778
van der Vyer, Bertha 675
Van Dyke, W.S. 272, 670
Vane, Sutton 199
Van Enger, Charles 458
The Vanishing American 45
The Vanishing Body 111
The Vanishing Dagger (serial) 544
The Vanishing Lady 345
The Vanishing Shadow (serial) 319, 433, 573
Vanity Fair 586
Vanity's Price 173, 385, 394, 441, 443, 622–624, 721
Van Sloan, Edward 611
Van Trees, James C. 37, 297, 644, 645, 664
Varesi, Vilda 374
Variety (*Variete*) 377, 540
Veidt, Conrad 73, 81, 87, 135, 149, 150, 153, 292, 306, 307, 308, 309, **309**, 310, 337, 365, 374, 375, **375**, 376, **376**, 377, 378, 409, 411, 447, 459, 461, 462, 481, 562, 617
Veiller, Bayard 245, 273, 373, 566, 567, 568, 763
Vélez, Lupe 38, 45, 423
Vendetta (book) 47, 454, 492
Vendetta, a Story of One Forgotten (book) 604, 674
The Vengeance of Egypt 168
Vengeance of the Dead 2, 108, 260, 546
Venturini, Edward 263
Venus of the South Seas 476
Verdi, Giuseppe 227
The Vermilion Pencil 65
Verne, Jules 208, 415, 587, 588, 591
Verne, Michael 588
Vernot, Henry 694, 700
Verwayen, Percy 99
Very Good Eddie (stage play) 501
"Vice Versa" (story) 71
Victor, Henry 514
Victory (1919) 230, 639
Victory (book) 652
The Victory of Virtue 634
Una vida por otra 307
Vidor, Florence 165, 166, 296–297
Vidor, King 165, 167, 234, 251, 254, 296, 524, 650, 651, 652, 653
Viennese Nights 240
Vignola, Robert 41–42, 675–676

Vigus, Mary Spain 613
Villa, Pancho 160
Virgil (Publius Vergilius Maro) 114, 115, *115*
The Virgin of Stamboul 289
The Virgin Spring 246
The Virginian 62, 140, 175, 232
Virtue 633, 634
Visaroff, Michael 279–280
A Visit to a Spiritualist 345
The Vital Question 584
The Vivisectionist 683
Het Vliegend Schip (book) 206
The Voice on the Wire (serial) 185
Voices 624–625, 697
Voices of the City 58
The Volga Boatmen 358
La voluntad del muerto (*The Cat Creeps*) 59, 110, 168, 298, 350; see also *The Cat Creeps*
The Volunteer 305
von Grimmelshausen, Hans Jakob Christoffel 63
von Seyffertitz, Gustav 32, 34, 103, 122, 132, 147–148, 613, 614, 667–668, 732, 770, 775, 776
von Sternberg, Josef 108, 254, 256, 317, 365, 623
von Stroheim, Erich 172, 209, 213, 232, 255, 279, 284, 285, 286, 289, 299, 320, 336, 364–65, 376, 398, 458, 459, 474, 571, 575, 627, 681
von Weber, Paula 490
Voodoo Man 106, 129, 266, 404, 724
Vorins, Henri 123
Voronoff, Serge Abrahamovitch (Dr.) 55–56
Vosburgh, Alfred 468
Voshell, Jack 233
La Voyage dans la lune 707
The Voyage Through the Impossible 588
Voyage to Botany Bay (book) 206
Voyage to the Bottom of the Sea 240
Vroom, Frederick 264

Das Wachsfigurenkabinett 79, 376
Wages of Tin 116
Waggoner, George 691
Wagner, Leon 723
Wagner, Richard 206
Wagon Train (television) 513, 548
Wainwright, J.G. 341
Waite. Arthur Dr. 470
Waipahu, Lehua 64, 66
Waking Up the Town 226, 385, 559, 625–627, *626*
Walk on the Wild Side 608
Walker, Jimmy 347
Walker, Johnnie 96
Walker, Lillian 731
Walker, Robert 36
The Walking Dead 96, 407
The Walking Gentleman (stage play) 593
Wall, David 713
The Wall Street Mystery 713n
Wallace, Edgar 760, 761
Wallace, Inez 573
Wallace, Lew 275, 766
Wallace, Morgan 435
Waller, Fred 539
Waller, J. Wallet 387
Walling, William 760
Wallis, Hal B. 23

Walpole, Horace 36
Walsh, Blanche 657
Walsh, Raoul 78, 251, 285, 402, 403, 404, 498, 562, 564, 631, 742
Walthall, Henry B. 17, *17*, 18, 19, 20, 42, 45, 117, 380, 382, 396, 482, 484, 489, 596, 613, 757
Walton, Gladys 14, 618, 619, 620
The Wandering Jew (1923) 691
The Wandering Jew (1933) 691
War and the Woman 770–771
War Correspondent 439
The War of the Worlds (1953) 251
Ward, Arthur Sarsfield 87
Ward, Fannie 65, 109, *110*, 110, 598, 657, 659
Ward, Frederick 162
Ward, Lillian 697
Ward, Luci 271
Ward, May 633–634
Warde, Ernest C. 31, 138, 161, 714, 715
Warfield, David 488, 489, 490, 491, 520
Warner, H.B. 220, 221, 260, 440
The Warning 185, 213, 711, 771
Warnock, Charles Swinton 219
Warren, E. Alyn 32
The Warrens of Virginia 155
The Warrens of Virginia (stage play) 520
Warrenton, Gilbert 81, 377
The Warrior's Husband 241
Warwick, Robert 145, 411, 537, 547, 548, 549
Washington, Blue 745
Wasted Lives 771–773
Watch Him Step 433
Waterloo Bridge (1930) 468
Watson, Harry Jr. 722
Waxworks 79, 81, 375
Way Down East 82, 152, 184, 242, 247, 371, 696
The Way Men Love 241
"The Way Men Love" (story) 241
The Way of All Flesh 336
The Way of the Cross 168
Wayburn, Ned 166
Waycoff, Leon 301
Wayne, John 123, 168, 524, 720
The Weakling 650
Weary River 184
A Weaver of Dreams 16
The Weavers (stage play) 321
Webb, Jack 264
Webber, George 726
Weber, Carl Maria von 40
Weber, Lois 48, 184, 185, 265, 274, 295, 382, 393, 447, 738
Weber and Fields 656
The Wedding March 213, 279, 336
Wee Lady Betty 427, 773
Wegener, Paul 32, 46, *364*, 365, *366*, 367, 370, 509, 584
Weine, Robert 340, 375, 411, 499, 676
Weissmuller, Johnny 554
Welch, William 430, 431, 591
Welles, Orson 121, 292, 388
Wellman, William 754
Wells, H.G. 263, 667, 693
We're in the Navy Now 664
The Werewolf (1913) 668
The Werewolf (stage play) 190
Werewolf of London 193, 306, 740
West, Mae 151

West, Paul 63, 130, 131, 683
West, Roland 8, 21, 22, 23, 24, 79, 130, 131, 139, 251, 255, 390, 404, 405, 406, 407, 408, 409, 500, 610, 611, 612
West, William H. 298
West of Hot Dog 53
West of Shanghai 406
West of the Water Tower (stage play) 628
West of Zanzibar 33, 335, 336, 355, 624, 627–631, *629*, 630, 639
Western Pluck 683
A Western Welcome 169
Westober, Winifred 201
Weston, Bert 482, 484
Whale, James 34, 80, 174, 312, 326, 330, 468, 562, 571, 691
The Whales of August 248
Wharton, Leopold 29
Wharton, Theodore 29
What a Life (stage play) 45
What a Widow 349
What Actors Eat and When They Eat (book) 175
What Do We Know? (stage play) 603
What Happened to Jones (stage play) 72
What Happened to Mary (serial) 281, 282
What Price Glory? 404, 755
What Shall We Do with Him? 732
What Women Love 476
Whatever Happened to Baby Jane? 609
Wheatley, William 40
Wheeler, Bert 241
Wheeler and Woolsey 520
When a Man Loves 12, 542, 580
When Arizona Won 625
When Caesar Ran a Paper 610
When Claudia Smiles (stage play) 603
When Dr. Quackel Did Hide 631–632, 765, 777
When Knighthood Was in Flower 41, 122, 675–676
When Quackel Did Hyde 186, 227, 428
When Soul Meets Soul 168
When the Bell Tolls (stage play) 683
When the Clouds Roll By 767, 774–775
"When the World Screamed" (story) 340
When the Young Vine Blooms (stage play) 321
When Wendy Grew Up-An After-thought (book) 448–449
When Worlds Collide 82, 766
Where Are My Children? 184, 265, 738
Where East Is East 423, 630
Where Is My Father? 74, 632–634
While London Sleeps 53, 96, 634–636, *635*, 643, 667, 702, 734, 770
While Paris Sleeps 299, 636–640, *638*
While the City Sleeps 607
While the Patient Slept 154
The Whip 549, 637, 682
The Whirl of Life 203
The Whispering Chorus 69, 775–776

The Whispering Chorus (book) 775
Whispering Palms 614, 776–777, *776*
The Whispering Shadow (serial) 37, 214, 587, 619, 640
Whispering Shadows 137, 148, 325, 640–642, 741
Whispering Smith 11
Whispering Wires 11, 103, 201, 213, 241, 300, 312, 636, 642–644, 745, 762, 765
Whispering Wires (book) 642
Whispering Wires (stage play) 352, 643
Whitaker, Charles 504
Whitcomb, D.F. 545
White, Glen(n) 123, 125, 126, 712, 713
White, Pearl 45, 119, 122, 193, 546, 567, 580, 619, 704, 745
The White Brother 650
White Cargo (stage play) 627
The White Cat (working title for *The Two-Soul Woman*) 596
The White Cat (book) 265, 502, 595, 618
The White Circle 639
The White Flower 644–646, 664
White Gold 359
White Heat (1934) 186, 738
White Heat (1949) 34, 404
The White Heather 300, 416
The White Rosette 328, 646–648
White Shadows in the South Seas 467
The White Slave 540
A White Slave Tragedy 295
The White Tiger 487
White Zombie 21, 30, 154, 217, 243, 293, 354, 355, 377, 380, 583, 585, 722, 739
Whiteman, Paul 86
Whiteside, Walker 619
Whitman, Alfred see Vosburgh, Alfred
Whitman, Gayne see Vosburgh, Alfred
Whitney, Claire 165, 671, 747, 755
Whitney, Cornelius Vanderbilt 733
Whitney, Salem Tutt 777
Whittier, John Greenleaf 168
Who Killed Olga Carew? 319
Why Get Married? 584
Why I Would Not Marry 648–650
Why Not Marry? 697
Why the Sphinx Laughed 716
Whytock, Grant 574
The Wicked Darling 20, 82, 284, 285, 396, 422, 605
Wiers-Jenssen, H. 658
Wilbur, Crane 273, 404, 406, 407, 408, 611, 625
Wild Oranges 167, 289, 297, 429, 513, 585, 618, 650–653, *651*, 682, 719, 776
Wild Oranges (book) 651
Wild, Wild, Susan 510, 522
Wilde, Oscar 17, 36, 151, 216, 571
Wilder, Billy 35, 524, 622
Wilder, Gene 474
Wilder, Thornton 325
Wilhelm Tell (1923) 562
Willard, Jess 646
Willard, John 79–80, 252, 332
Willat, Edwin 93
Willat, Irvin 93, 433, 719

Willets, Gilson 275
William Faversham in a Liberty Loan Appeal 442
"William Wilson" (story) 32
Williams, Ben Ames 5
Williams, Earle 11, 12, 346
Williams, Esther 427, 476
Williams, Frank (actor) 697
Williams, Frank D. (cinematographer) 141, 474, 697
Williams, George 736
Williams, J.E. 300
Williams, John D. 766
Williams, Kathlyn 776
Williams, Robin 236
Williamson, A(lice) M(uriel) 280, 726, 727
Williamson, Charles 589
Williamson, C(harles) N(orris) 280, 726, 727
Williamson, George M(aurice) 415, 589–590
Williamson, J.E. 415, 416, 417, 589–590, 592
The Williamson Submarine Expedition 589
Willis, F. McGrew 454
The Willow Tree 8, 12, 162, 212, 601, 653–655, **654**, 760
The Willow Tree (stage play) 564
Wilson 260
Wilson, Al 749, 750
Wilson, Alice 161–162
Wilson, Augusta Jane Evans 233, 466, 726
Wilson, Basil 14
Wilson, Ben 185
Wilson, Carey 485
Wilson, Dooley 192
Wilson, Henry **366**
Wilson, Lois 745
Wilson, Margery 159
Wilson, Tom 704
Wilson, Woodrow 26, 94, 95, 226, 301, 302, 605, 659, 672, 771
Wilson, Woodrow (Mrs.) 53–54
Winchell, Walter 45
The Wind 247
Windrow, Stellan S. 555
Windsor, Claire 51, 289, 343, 393, 394, 571, 695
"Wine for Anubis" (story) 299
Wing, Toby 13
Wings 52, 62, 416
The Winning of Beatrice 6
Winters, Roland 176

The Winter's Tale 64
Winterset 704
The Wishing Ring 579, 580
The Wishing Ring (stage play) 329
The Witch (1922) 254, 464, 501, 655–657
The Witch (stage play) 658
The Witch Woman 37
Witchcraft 109, 657–659
Witchcraft Through the Ages 255
The Witching Eyes 777
The Witching Hour (1916) 228, 271, 294, 327, 566, 659–662, **660**, 696
The Witching Hour (1921) 37, 217, 617, 644, 646, 662–664, 772
The Witching Hour (1934) 662, 663
The Witching Hour (book) 37, 315
The Witching Hour (stage play) 487, 519, 567, 659, 662
Witherspoon, Reese 586
Within Our Gates 525
Within the Law (stage play) 243, 273, 294
Without a Soul 331, 332
Without Benefit of Clergy 597, 619
Without Warning 550; see also *The Story without a Name*
Witness for the Defense 217
Witty, Dame May 566
The Wizard 34, 137, 343, 614, 635, 646, 665–668, **666**, **667**, 683, 749, 770
The Wizard of Oz (1925) 451, 680
The Wizard of Oz (1939) 39, 120, 214, 328, 381, 382, 749, 775
The Wizard's Plot 120
Wolf Blood 163, 355, 391, 668–670, 753
Wolf Fangs 96
The Wolf Man (1915) 214
The Wolf Man (1924) 140, 514
The Wolf Man (1941) 212, 691
Wolf, the Wonder Dog (movie dog) 643
Wolfe, Jane **74**, 598–599, 688
Wolfen 668
Wolfit, Sir Donald 580
Wolf's Clothing 434
Wol(l)heim, Louis 230, 244, 300, 305, 306, 549, 550
Wolkof, Herman 703
Wolves of Kultur (serial) 269, 743
Woman 173, 777–778
The Woman Between Friends 36
A Woman Commands 697
The Woman Hater 651

A Woman in Grey (serial) 646
The Woman in White 82
The Woman in White (book) 163
Woman of Mystery 165, 420, 556, 569, 670–672, 747, 755
A Woman of the Sea 108, 256
Womanhood, the Glory of a Nation 7, 28, 173, 194, 195–196, 244, 672–674, **673**, 735, 770
A Woman's Debt 262
A Woman's Honor 409
Women and Gold 650
Women of All Nations 338
Won in the Clouds 750
The Wonderful Wizard of Oz (1910) 92, 522
Wong, Anna May 66, 87–88, **88**, 89, 449, 560, 563–564, 620, 729
Wood, Cyrus 113, 115
Wood, Edward D. 98, 177, 178, 229, 258, 296, 641
Wood, Leonard 27
Wooden Kimono (stage play) 106
Woodgate, Herbert 536
Woods, A.H. 238, 332, 611
Woods, Walter 558, 600
Woollcott, Alexander 273, 274, 332
The World and the Woman 394
The World Gone Mad 160
The World, the Flesh and the Devil 302, 723
World War I (documentary) 119
Worsley, Wallace 58, 286, 289, 290, 292, 319, 390
Worsely, Wallace Jr. 289–290
Worthington, William 141, 707
The Wrath of the Gods 64, 65, 135
Wray, Fay 691
Wray, John 399
Wray, John Griffith 354
Wright, S. Fowler 592
Wurtzel, Sol 339
Wuthering Heights (book) 629
Wyckoff, Alvin 148, 379, 775–776
Wyler, William 286
Wylie, Philip 263
Wyncherley, Margaret 373, 566, 764
Wynn, Ed 13, 31
Wynn, Keenan 31

The Yankee Clipper 358, 359
The Yearling 569
Yeats, William Butler 48, 50*n*
The Yellow Ticket (stage play) 99

Yes, Yes, Nanette 706
Yesterday's Girl (book) 631
The Yiddische King Lear 96
Der Yoghi 367
Yost, Herbert 17
You Are in Danger 3
You Can't Take It With You 445
You Never Know Your Luck 657
You'll Find Out 762
Young, Brigham 609
Young, Clara Kimball 119, 137, 143, 188, **189**, 189–190, 191, **191**, 192, 330, **330**, 331, 332, 347, 348, 379, 507, 519, 578, 579, 580, 581, 582, 583, 648, 709
Young, Edna 284
Young, James 32–33, 110, 136, 137, 331, 377, 581, 582
Young, Loretta 139
Young, Mahonri 609–610
Young, Noah 763
Young, Rida Johnson 497
Young, Robert 184
Young, Roland 697
Young, Waldemar 333, 517, 608, 609–610, 624, 686
The Young Diana 39, 122, 301, 394, 405, 621, 674–676, **675**
The Young Diana: An Experiment of the Future (book) 674, **676**
The Young Rajah 20, 105, 115, 194, 363, 513, 564, 585, 676–681, **678**, 760
Younger, A.P. 620
Yukon King 96
Yurka, Blanche 349

Zanuck, Darryl F. 184, 400, 646
Zellner, Arthur J. 134, 140
The Zero Hour 131, 192, 343, 465, 513, 681–683
"The Zero Hour" (story) 683
Ziegfeld, Florenz 431, 630
The Ziegfeld Follies (stage play) 237, 293
Ziegfeld Follies of 1916 122
Zimbo (movie dog) 96
Zola, Émile 582
Zoo in Budapest 740
Zorro Rides Again (serial) 680
Zucco, George 312, 681
Zudora — The Twenty Million Dollar Mystery (serial) 234
Zukor, Adolph 75, 156, 157, 236, 478, 537, 538, 680